International Directory of
COMPANY
HISTORIES

International Directory of
COMPANY HISTORIES

VOLUME 42

Editor
Jay P. Pederson

St. James Press

GALE GROUP

THOMSON LEARNING

Detroit • New York • San Diego • San Francisco
Boston • New Haven, Conn. • Waterville, Maine
London • Munich

STAFF

Jay P. Pederson, *Editor*

Miranda H. Ferrara, *Project Manager*

Erin Bealmear, Joann Cerrito, Steve Cusack, Kristin Hart,
Melissa Hill, Margaret Mazurkiewicz, Carol Schwartz,
Christine Tomassini, Michael J. Tyrkus, *St. James Press Editorial Staff*

Peter M. Gareffa, *Managing Editor, St. James Press*

Library of Congress Catalog Number: 89-190943

British Library Cataloguing in Publication Data

International directory of company histories. Vol. 42
I. Jay P. Pederson
338.7409

ISBN 1-55862-447-3

Printed in Canada
Published simultaneously in the United Kingdom

St. James Press is an imprint of The Gale Group

Cover photograph: Russian Trading System
(courtesy: Russian Trading System)

10 9 8 7 6 5 4 3 2 1

CONTENTS _____

Company Histories

PREFACE

The St. James Press series *The International Directory of Company Histories (IDCH)* is intended for reference use by students, business people, librarians, historians, economists, investors, job candidates, and others who seek to learn more about the historical development of the world's most important companies. To date, *IDCH* has covered over 5,200 companies in 42 volumes.

Inclusion Criteria

Most companies chosen for inclusion in *IDCH* have achieved a minimum of US$25 million in annual sales and are leading influences in their industries or geographical locations. Companies may be publicly held, private, or nonprofit. State-owned companies that are important in their industries and that may operate much like public or private companies also are included. Wholly owned subsidiaries and divisions are profiled if they meet the requirements for inclusion. Entries on companies that have had major changes since they were last profiled may be selected for updating.

The *IDCH* series highlights 10% private and nonprofit companies, and features updated entries on approximately 45 companies per volume.

Entry Format

Each entry begins with the company's legal name, the address of its headquarters, its telephone, toll-free, and fax numbers, and its web site. A statement of public, private, state, or parent ownership follows. A company with a legal name in both English and the language of its headquarters country is listed by the English name, with the native-language name in parentheses.

The company's founding or earliest incorporation date, the number of employees, and the most recent available sales figures follow. Sales figures are given in local currencies with equivalents in U.S. dollars. For some private companies, sales figures are estimates and indicated by the abbreviation *est.* The entry lists the exchanges on which a company's stock is traded and its ticker symbol, as well as the company's NAIC codes.

Entries generally contain a *Company Perspectives* box which provides a short summary of the company's mission, goals, and ideals, a *Key Dates* box highlighting milestones in the company's history, lists of *Principal Subsidiaries, Principal Divisions, Principal Operating Units, Principal Competitors,* and articles for *Further Reading.*

American spelling is used throughout *IDCH*, and the word "billion" is used in its U.S. sense of one thousand million.

Sources

Entries have been compiled from publicly accessible sources both in print and on the Internet such as general and academic periodicals, books, annual reports, and material supplied by the companies themselves.

Cumulative Indexes

IDCH contains three indexes: the **Index to Companies**, which provides an alphabetical index to companies discussed in the text as well as to companies profiled, the **Index to Industries**, which allows researchers to locate companies by their principal industry, and the **Geographic Index**, which lists companies alphabetically by the country of their headquarters. The indexes are cumulative and specific instructions for using them are found immediately preceding each index.

Suggestions Welcome

Comments and suggestions from users of *IDCH* on any aspect of the product as well as suggestions for companies to be included or updated are cordially invited. Please write:

The Editor
International Directory of Company Histories
St. James Press
27500 Drake Rd.
Farmington Hills, Michigan 48331-3535

ABBREVIATIONS FOR FORMS OF COMPANY INCORPORATION

A.B.	Aktiebolaget (Sweden)
A.G.	Aktiengesellschaft (Germany, Switzerland)
A.S.	Aksjeselskap (Denmark, Norway)
A.S.	Atieselskab (Denmark)
A.Ş.	Anomin Şirket (Turkey)
B.V.	Besloten Vennootschap met beperkte, Aansprakelijkheid (The Netherlands)
Co.	Company (United Kingdom, United States)
Corp.	Corporation (United States)
G.I.E.	Groupement d'Intérêt Economique (France)
GmbH	Gesellschaft mit beschränkter Haftung (Germany)
H.B.	Handelsbolaget (Sweden)
Inc.	Incorporated (United States)
KGaA	Kommanditgesellschaft auf Aktien (Germany)
K.K.	Kabushiki Kaisha (Japan)
LLC	Limited Liability Company (Middle East)
Ltd.	Limited (Canada, Japan, United Kingdom, United States)
N.V.	Naamloze Vennootschap (The Netherlands)
OY	Osakeyhtiöt (Finland)
PLC	Public Limited Company (United Kingdom)
PTY.	Proprietary (Australia, Hong Kong, South Africa)
S.A.	Société Anonyme (Belgium, France, Switzerland)
SpA	Società per Azioni (Italy)

ABBREVIATIONS FOR CURRENCY

$	United States dollar	KD	Kuwaiti dinar
£	United Kingdom pound	L	Italian lira
¥	Japanese yen	LuxFr	Luxembourgian franc
A$	Australian dollar	M$	Malaysian ringgit
AED	United Arab Emirates dirham	N	Nigerian naira
		Nfl	Netherlands florin
B	Thai baht	NIS	Israeli new shekel
B	Venezuelan bolivar	NKr	Norwegian krone
BFr	Belgian franc	NT$	Taiwanese dollar
C$	Canadian dollar	NZ$	New Zealand dollar
CHF	Switzerland franc	P	Philippine peso
COL	Colombian peso	PLN	Polish zloty
Cr	Brazilian cruzado	Pta	Spanish peseta
CZK	Czech Republic koruny	R	Brazilian real
DA	Algerian dinar	R	South African rand
Dfl	Netherlands florin	RMB	Chinese renminbi
DKr	Danish krone	RO	Omani rial
DM	German mark	Rp	Indonesian rupiah
E£	Egyptian pound	Rs	Indian rupee
Esc	Portuguese escudo	Ru	Russian ruble
EUR	Euro dollars	S$	Singapore dollar
FFr	French franc	Sch	Austrian schilling
Fmk	Finnish markka	SFr	Swiss franc
GRD	Greek drachma	SKr	Swedish krona
HK$	Hong Kong dollar	SRls	Saudi Arabian riyal
HUF	Hungarian forint	W	Korean won
IR£	Irish pound	W	South Korean won
K	Zambian kwacha		

International Directory of
COMPANY HISTORIES

Alterra Healthcare Corporation

1000 Innovation Drive
Milwaukee, Wisconsin 53221
U.S.A.
Telephone: (414) 918-5000
Toll Free: (888) 780-1200
Fax: (414) 918-5050
Web site: http://www.assisted.com

Public Company
Incorporated: 1981 as Alternative Living Services
Employees: 14,400
Sales: $466.5 million (2000)
Stock Exchanges: American
Ticker Symbol: ALI
NAIC: 623312 Homes for the Elderly

Alterra Healthcare Corporation is the largest operator of assisted living residences for frail elderly and memory-impaired elderly in the United States. It is also one of the oldest companies in this specialized field. The company operates over 450 assisted living residences, spread across 28 states, with the capacity to serve up to 22,000 residents. Alterra's residences operate under a variety of names, including Clare Bridge, Wynwood, Sterling House, Wovenhearts, and Crossings. The company's residences are home-like structures, designed to provide an alternative to the more hospital-like model of traditional nursing homes. Alterra's residences are not in fact nursing homes, and are not regulated as such. Some of Alterra's residences are dedicated to the care of people with Alzheimer's disease or other memory-impairing conditions. Others are intended for people typically in their eighties needing some daily assistance from staff for tasks such as bathing or dressing but not the more medically oriented care of a nursing home. Despite a growing elderly population and consistent expansion by the company, Alterra encountered particular financial difficulties in the late 1990s and in mid-2001 made private arrangements with its creditors to restructure and thus avoid bankruptcy.

Filling a Need for Something Different

Alterra Healthcare was started by William Lasky in 1981, under the name Alternative Living Services. Lasky had a bachelor of science degree in psychology and further certification in healthcare administration, and had been in charge of running several nursing homes and a psychiatric treatment center. He then became the regional director for a company called Unicare Health Facilities. Unicare ran homes for the elderly, as well as residential programs for the mentally ill and developmentally disabled. Lasky had seen how the care of the elderly had changed since the federal government's growing involvement in the nursing home industry in the 1960s and 1970s. Through the Medicare program, the federal government had become the biggest customer of the nursing home industry. The industry was highly regulated, and nursing homes had become uniform. Nursing homes were run on a medical model. They were more like hospitals and less like private homes. Lasky realized the need for a different model of elderly care, especially for people who did not require the degree of nursing care that traditional nursing homes provided. Lasky and his business partners opened what they called an assisted living facility, which was meant for people who needed help with some daily activities, possibly around the clock, but did not need constant medical supervision. The residents were often characterized as "frail" elderly. They did not need home healthcare, as someone with a grave illness might, but they had unscheduled needs that could not necessarily be met by helpers showing up by appointment. From a single building, Alternative Living Services soon expanded into a small chain of residences in Wisconsin. They were built as stand-alone houses or groups of townhouses, and residents or their families paid out of pocket for the monthly fees. Because assisted living facilities were technically not nursing homes, they escaped the federal regulations that dictated much of how a nursing home could be designed, built, and run. Lasky saw his company's product as almost totally consumer-driven, answering a need that could not be met by the regulation-entwined traditional nursing home.

In 1985 Alternative Living began building a new kind of facility, designed for people with Alzheimer's or other memory impairment. Such people were often otherwise healthy and

Company Perspectives:

Since our founding in 1981, the Company's mission has remained steadfast: to maximize the quality of life and dignity of older adults.

mobile, but needed constant monitoring because of their mental state. Alternative Living's residence for the memory-impaired was the first such facility in the state of Wisconsin. The company grew slowly, and over the next ten years it expanded to 17 facilities in four states. However, Alternative Living was on the verge of a period of rapid expansion. Providing services to the elderly was a growth industry, largely because of demographic factors. By 1990, U.S. Census figures put the number of people in the nation aged 65 and over at 31 million. That number was expected to more than double over the coming decades, reaching an estimated 65 million by 2030. Census experts predicted an even greater percentage increase in the number of people aged 85 and older. From about 2.5 million in 1990, there were expected to be around eight million people aged 85 and up by 2030, and 15 million by 2050. Because of social factors, including the increase in divorce, many of these elderly people were expected to be living alone. Hence the core population Alternative Living aimed to serve was enlarging year by year.

The company was ready to expand. In 1993 it received a capital infusion from two other healthcare companies, the publicly traded Evergreen Healthcare Inc. and Care Living Centers. Evergreen's parent company eventually owned close to 20 percent of Alternative Living. Fresh with new cash, Alternative Living moved to build new facilities and to buy up others. The company's revenue was still relatively small, estimated at under $5 million for 1994. The company ran less than 20 facilities in 1995, but by the next year it operated 62 residences in nine states. Alternative Living featured four distinct types of residences, offering different levels of service. Clare Bridge was the name of its facilities for people with Alzheimer's, and its other lines were called Wynwood, Crossings, and Wovenhearts. The company also acquired other firms in the assisted living industry. It purchased Heartland Retirement Services Inc. in early 1996, and acquired New Crossings International Corp. a few months later. Alternative Living also had many more facilities under development.

IPO and Merger: Mid-1990s

Other companies had also entered the assisted living field. At least in part because of the incontrovertible math of the demographic picture, these companies were attracting investors. At least six assisted living companies went public over 1995 and 1996. Alternative Living had its initial public offering in August 1996, selling its stock on the American Stock Exchange. The company sold six million shares, including a large stake owned by a previous investor, GranCare Inc. The money raised went to retire debt and to fund further construction of new residences. Alternative Living did not have a particularly rosy financial picture for the short-term. It operated at a loss through 1994 and 1995, and even as it solicited investors for its IPO, it expected to continue in the red for at least another year.

Yet the assisted living niche seemed hot. The industry as a whole served only a small fraction of the elderly, but brought in around $7 billion annually in the mid-1990s, according to an industry trade group. Revenue overall for the industry was growing at between 30 to 40 percent; consequently, Alternative Living forged ahead with expansion plans.

In 1997 Alternative Living agreed to merge with a Kansas-based assisted living company called Sterling House Corp. Sterling House was around the same size as Alternative Living, with 105 facilities. The two merged through a stock swap, and the new company, still for the time being called Alternative Living, found itself the largest assisted living company in the nation. It now had over 200 facilities in 20 states, with nearly 100 more under development and about 75 more already under construction. This was the peak of Wall Street's infatuation with nursing home and assisted living companies. Though Alternative Living was still operating at a loss at the time of the Sterling merger, industry analysts predicted soaring revenue. By 1998, the company's stock was trading at approximately double its 1996 IPO price, reaching a high of $35.25 a share that year.

In 1999, the company changed its name to Alterra Healthcare Corporation. It was running 365 facilities under five separate brand names, and chose Alterra as a unifying banner. The beginning letters stood for "alternative," and "terra" was chosen for its connotation of firm foundation and groundedness. Around this time, the company was building new facilities so quickly that it claimed to be opening a new residence every 56 hours. But this quick pace led to a perception that Alterra, along with the rest of the assisted living industry, was overbuilt. The boom turned to bust as Wall Street retreated from the industry it had poured some $13 billion into in the mid-1990s. Alterra arranged for $230 million in financing in August 1999, finding a consortium of banks to provide credit for continued building and acquisition of residences. A few months later, Alterra engaged Merrill Lynch and another investment firm to help it put together a deal with private investors.

Cutting Back to Keep Going in the 2000s

By February 2000, Alterra's stock had plunged to just $7. The rest of the assisted living and nursing care sector was also doing poorly, and the company struggled to improve its cash flow. Alterra first moved to buy up 19 residences that it had operated through a leasing arrangement with a real estate investment trust. These residences were almost full and were quite profitable, so it was in Alterra's interest to quit the lease arrangement and own them outright. Alterra had also developed some of its new residences through joint ventures with other companies. In early 2000 Alterra announced it would cut back on its development of joint ventures and shut down its construction subsidiary. It took a fourth quarter charge of some $38 million to do so. Next Alterra stated it would halt plans to develop some 100 new residences. It would complete what was already under construction, but concentrate most on running the homes it already had. During this same period, the company was hit by a lawsuit regarding charges of neglect at a home it ran for Alzheimer's patients in Minnesota. Stories of understaffing and neglect circulated in the press, not only about several Alterra homes but about other assisted living residences. These stories often pointed out the lack of federal oversight for

Key Dates:

1981: Company begins business with single building.
1985: Alternative Living Services opens first residence specifically for people with memory impairment.
1996: Company goes public on the American Stock Exchange.
1997: Alternative Living merges with Sterling House to become the largest assisted living company in the nation.
1999: Company adopts the name Alterra Healthcare Corporation.

assisted living facilities. State laws did cover assisted living, but as Alterra had homes in 28 different states, it had to contend with a patchwork of regulations. Labor costs and liability insurance were both particularly high for the company, just as its stock was falling to less than a dollar. The company posted a third quarter loss of $16.7 million in November 2000, its fourth consecutive quarter in the red. Founder Bill Lasky offered to step down as CEO. He had held the job since 1985. He became vice-chairman of the board, and eventually the CEO post was filled by former COO Steven Vick, who had come over to Alterra with the Sterling House merger.

Alterra brought in $466.5 million in revenue in 2000, an increase of almost 25 percent over 1999. But it still showed a loss of $117.8 million. Even as Alterra's financial difficulties deepened, Vick believed that Alterra had a sound strategy and a priceless niche. Assisted living was "something that was grass roots, fundamentally built, stick and bricks, by consumer demand and desire to have an alternative to traditional [nursing home] institutions and privately pay," Vick told the *Business Journal-Milwaukee* in April 2001. Vick admitted Alterra had overbuilt in certain markets, but insisted that the assisted living concept was here to stay. In another interview, with *Contemporary Long Term Care* for March 2001, Vick also said, "The reason no one likes nursing homes is because they're all the same. Assisted living offers '31 flavors'." The business concept was good, and there was no reason to bail out of the industry. The residences Alterra had operated prior to 1998 were profitable, and the company made plans to sell off homes that were not doing well. This meant getting rid of 67 facilities, out of its mid-2001 total of 474. Vick believed that the assisted living industry was in the trough of a business cycle, like the cycles that affected hotels, nursing homes, and commercial office space, and Alterra would find itself on the upswing in another two to two-and-a-half years. In March 2001, Alterra secured a $7.5 million loan from some of its investors. The company

hoped to arrange a private restructuring of its debt to keep it out of bankruptcy court. Even as revenue rose in mid-2001, Alterra reported a first quarter loss, and was in default with several of its creditors. Alterra increased the number of residences it offered for sale from 67 to 84. The company remained firm in its conviction that its core business was sound and improving, and that Alterra would be profitable again soon.

Principal Subsidiaries

Sterling House Corporation.

Principal Competitors

Sunrise Assisted Living, Inc.; ARV Assisted Living, Inc.; Manor Care, Inc.

Further Reading

Adler, Sam, "Alterra Reports $230M in New Financing," *Contemporary Long Term Care*, August 1999, p. 52.
——, "Alterra's Multipronged Strategy," *Contemporary Long Term Care*, February 2000, p. 49.
"Alternative Living Services to Become 'Alterra'," *Contemporary Long Term Care*, April 1999, p. 68.
"Assisted Living: A Brave New World," *Nursing Homes*, July-August 1995, p. 40.
Goldstein, Amy, "Assisted Living: Helping Hand May Not Be Enough," *Washington Post*, February 19, 2001, p. A01.
Joshi, Pradnya, "Wisconsin's Alternative Living Services Inc. Plans IPO," *Knight-Ridder/Tribune Business News*, August 1, 1996, p. 8010353.
Karash, Julius A., "Merger Creates Biggest U.S. Assisted-Living Center Company," *Knight-Ridder/Tribune Business News*, October 25, 1997, p. 1025B0916.
"Loan Is Closed As Work Continues on Restructuring," *Wall Street Journal*, March 8, 2001, p. B15.
Pagan, Joyce, "Alterra COO Is Now President," *Contemporary Long Term Care*, March 2001, p. 74.
Sneider, Julie, "ALS Looks for New Growth with Acquisition of Competitor," *Business Journal-Milwaukee*, October 24, 1997, p. 6.
——, "Buying Binge," *Business Journal-Milwaukee*, October 5, 1996, p. 16.
Trewyn, Phill, "For Alterra, Changes Within Changes," *Business Journal-Milwaukee*, December 8, 2000, p. 3.
——, "On a Mission," *Business Journal-Milwaukee*, April 20, 2001, p. 29.
"Wauwatosa, Wis.-Based Company Sells Elder Care Facilities," *Knight-Ridder/Tribune Business News*, April 3, 2001, p. 01093023.
"Wisconsin-Based Operator of Assisted-Living Residences Posts Bigger Loss," *Knight-Ridder/Tribune Business News*, May 16, 2001, p. 01136001.

—A. Woodward

Altos Hornos de México, S.A. de C.V.

Prolongación Juarez
Monclova, Coahuila 25750
Mexico
Telephone: (528) 649-3400
Fax: (528) 649-2310
Web site: http://www.ahmsa.com

Public Subsidiary of Grupo Acerero del Norte, S.A. de C.V.
Incorporated: 1942
Employees: 16,961
Sales: 12.54 billion pesos ($1.31 billion) (2000)
Stock Exchanges: Mexico City New York
Ticker Symbols: AHMSA; IAM (ADR)
NAIC: 212111 Bituminous Coal and Lignite Surface Mining; 212112 Bituminous Coal Underground Mining; 21221 Iron Ore Mining; 331111 Iron & Steel Mills; 331221 Cold-Rolled Steel Shape Manufacturing; 331222 Steel Wire Drawing

Altos Hornos de México, S.A. de C.V. (often referred to by its acronym, AHMSA) is the largest steel producer in Mexico, converting raw steel into a variety of flat steel products and also into wire rod, wire derivative products, and heavy and light sections. Subsidiaries of the company mine iron ore for conversion into steel, and coal, not only for the steelmaking process, but also for sale to fuel power plants. Grupo Acerero del Norte, S.A. de C.V. (GAN) is its controlling stockholder.

Big Government-Run Enterprise: 1942–90

Altos Hornos (which means ''blast furnaces'') was established in 1942, when Mexico was having difficulty obtaining steel from the United States because of the World War II effort. A group of Mexican businessmen with financial support from Nacional Financiera, S.N.C. (NAFIN)—a Mexican government-owned development bank—formed a joint venture with Armco International Co., an affiliate of American Rolling Mills Co. Armco provided the equipment and technical assistance for the

steel mill, which was located in Monclova, Coahuila, about 125 miles south of the Texas border. Due to war production, only secondhand equipment was available, and the blast furnace—imported from the United States, dating from 1916 and out of production since 1923—was said to be more appropriate for a museum than for an operating factory. Nevertheless, it was modernized and rebuilt and coupled with a rolling mill purchased from Youngstown Sheet & Tube. A subsidiary was established to secure necessary supplies of the coal needed to make coke, and another for exploiting the deposits of iron ore to be converted to steel. AHMSA began turning out flat steel in 1944 and plates and sheets in 1946. It also produced steel tubes from 1944 to 1953.

The ownership of Altos Hornos was mixed. The Mexican government and NAFIN took all the preferred stock. A group of financiers and industrial interests held a majority of the common stock, with NAFIN holding 25 percent. In 1954, however, NAFIN raised its share of the common stock to 75 percent. Administration of the enterprise was dominated by government functionaries.

Steel production at AHMSA averaged 38,000 metric tons a year between 1944 and 1946; 202,000 tons between 1947 and 1958; and one million tons between 1959 and 1970. Production of steel rods began in 1961, commercial bars in 1967, and wire and other heavy structural forms in 1971.

A second open-hearth furnace was installed in 1954 and a third in 1966. (Altos Hornos also began producing steel in more advanced basic-oxygen furnaces in 1971.) A new rolling mill was imported from the United States in 1953. La Perla, Chihuahua, soon became the main source of iron ore. This ore arrived by railroad until 1982, when it was replaced by a ferroduct. Plants were established in 1957 and 1967 to convert the ore into cinder. This was followed by plants at La Perla (1973) and Monclova (1982) to turn the ore into pellets.

By the late 1960s steel production at Altos Hornos had increased to two million metric tons of raw steel a year and, in 1976, an adjoining plant was completed, increasing nominal annual capacity to 3.75 million metric tons a year. The Monclova complex was the largest of its kind in Latin America, and AHMSA was operating 27 subsidiaries. However, overproduction was proving a problem throughout the world, and large complexes with aging equipment were giving way to smaller but more economical, technologically advanced mills. Altos Hornos was barely profitable in the 1970s. Administration was centralized in Mexico City in 1971 and given over to inexperienced personnel. Labor relations deteriorated during the decade and were punctuated by strikes, slowdowns, and sitdowns. Among those who left the company in the early 1970s was Harold R. Pape, the U.S. engineer credited with the critical role in AHMSA's operation since its inception. In the late 1970s Sidermex, S.A. de C.V., a government-owned corporation, took control of management. According to Ted Kuster of *New Steel*, "The succession of mill managers who started out as mere bureaucrats but left the job as unaccountably wealthy men became a national joke."

The collapse of world oil prices in 1982 led to a devaluation of the peso and a severe recession in Mexico; AHMSA's debt reached about $540 million at this time. Product quality suffered from worker discontent and deterioration of equipment. At the same time overstaffing resulted in high labor costs. Little notice was given to the degradation of the surrounding environment, and workers suffered from pollution-related respiratory ailments. The company was not profitable in the 1980s, and it was so inefficient that many policymakers wanted to sell it for scrap, but its lack of competitiveness was masked by access to a protected domestic market. In 1990 AHMSA set a company production record for raw steel of nearly 3.1 million metric tons.

By the end of the decade, however, the Mexican government was seeking to dispose of this economic albatross. To make Altos Hornos more attractive to investors, it slashed the labor force by more than half and closed some of its facilities, including the antiquated Siemens Martin open-hearth furnaces. The company was sold, with certain other properties, to Grupo Acerero del Norte (GAN) in 1991 for $145 million in cash, $535 million in promised investment, and $350 million in assumption of long-term debt.

Private Company in the 1990s

GAN was a holding company established by members of the Ancira family, who had made a fortune in mining, and the Autrey family, owners of Mexico's leading wholesaler and retailer of pharmaceutical products. By 1994 Altos Hornos was spending more than $300 million on a modernization project, including a larger-capacity basic-oxygen furnace, a new continuous caster, and a rebuilt hot-strip mill and coke oven. More than $60 million was earmarked to build water-treatment systems and make other environmental improvements. The investment program enabled AHMSA to become the first Latin American steelmaker to receive ISO 9002 certification—a standard of high quality—for certain manufacturing processes.

The flight from the peso by investors in late 1994 led to a heavy loss by Altos Hornos in 1994 and a recession that resulted in a sharp slump in domestic steel demand. However, the devaluation of the peso also resulted in much lower production costs in dollar terms, allowing the company to sell its steel abroad cheaply. Forty-three percent of AHMSA's output was exported in 1995, compared to only 5 percent the previous year. The company earned a net profit of 886.5 million pesos (about $130 million) that year on a 23 percent increase in sales. It also became Mexico's first and only producer of tin-free steel, a product formerly imported for use in food and beverage packaging.

AHMSA also had signed long-term supply agreements with a number of German, Japanese, and U.S. companies. These included a joint sales agreement with Chaparral Steel Co. for marketing steel beams in 1993 and a joint venture in 1994 with Inland Steel Industries, Inc., supplying such customers as Ford Motor, Chrysler, and Whirlpool. GAN became self-sufficient in both iron-ore and coal supplies by purchasing a number of Mexican properties and reopening the La Perla mine, which had been closed in 1991 because of low ore grades and obsolete equipment. AHMSA began to build a new coal-fired power station for electricity generation and to collect the methane gas that builds up in coal mines as a supplementary fuel in its blast furnaces. A new galvanizing plant began production in 1996.

AHMSA registered new records in 1996 for net sales of 15.31 billion pesos (about $2 billion) and net income of 5.03 billion pesos (about $660 million). Both figures dwindled in 1997, however, and in 1998 the company lost 1.86 billion pesos ($188.2 million) on net sales of 13.5 billion pesos ($1.36 billion). Although sales of finished products reached 2.89 billion metric tons a year, export sales fell to 14 percent of the total, a result that management blamed on financial crises in Asia and Eastern Europe.

In mid-1999, GAN and AHMSA filed for bankruptcy protection, suspending payments on $1.85 billion in debt, including $942 million in loans that were coming due during the year. The business journalists who had been praising GAN's efforts to modernize its subsidiary now reported a different picture entirely. For example, AHMSA, according to Jonathan Friedland and Joel Millman of the *Wall Street Journal*, "underwrote trash collection . . . paid for a nature preserve that featured 400 white-tail deer, and expanded the airstrip at Monclova's airport. The airport became 'international' after Ahmsa bankrolled a daily commercial flight to San Antonio by guaranteeing the purchase of half the seats—although Mr. Ancira commuted to a home in the same city on one of the group's five private aircraft. . . . 'It was bread and circuses for the populace,' sums up Jose Manuel Luna, a Monclova historian. 'The way they spent money was nuts.' " As for the vaunted modernization drive, a former company consultant told Friedland and Millman, "You normally have to go east of the Russian border to see this type of technology."

Altos Hornos subsequently sought mergers with other steelmakers that failed to reach fruition. An agreement was not reached until May 2001, when a consortium of Mexican and U.S. banks received 40 percent of the shares in exchange for excusing $500 million in debt. (GAN retained 50.1 percent of the shares, compared to the 77 percent it held at the end of 1998.) The banks

Key Dates:

1942: Altos Hornos de México (AHMSA) is founded.
1944: Production begins, with output of flat steel and steel tubes.
1976: Altos Hornos is the largest steel mill in Latin America.
1991: Altos Hornos is sold to Grupo Acerero del Norte, a private holding company.
1999: Company files for bankruptcy protection.
2001: Altos Hornos reduces its debt by giving creditor banks 40 percent of its stock.

also agreed to allow AHMSA to retire nearly $200 million in debt at a discount, paying out this sum by selling an oxygen plant, a water-treatment plant, and real estate. The remaining $1.14 billion in debt was to be serviced from current cash flow. Altos Hornos registered a net profit of 1.36 billion pesos ($142.09 million) in 1999 on net sales of 13.08 billion pesos ($1.36 billion) and 1.13 billion pesos ($117.5 million) in 2000 on net sales of 12.54 billion pesos ($1.31 billion).

Altos Hornos in the Late 1990s

AHMSA was the largest steel producer in Mexico in 1998, accounting for 27 percent of the overall domestic steel market. It was manufacturing a variety of flat steel products, such as plate, hot- and cold-rolled coil, and tin plate), as well as certain long products, such as wire rod, heavy and light sections, and wire derivative products. In the domestic market, its products served primarily the manufacturing, construction, petroleum, packaging, and home appliance industries. Exports accounted for only 7 percent of net sales in 2000, of which North America was the destination for 85 percent.

AHMSA also was operating, through subsidiaries, six iron-ore and nine coal mines. Minera del Norte, S.A. de C.V. (MINOSA) was the subsidiary for the extraction, exploitation, and sale of iron ore used by the company in making steel. Minerales Monclova, S.A. de C.V. (MIMOSA) was in charge of the extraction, exploitation, and sale of metallurgical coal used in the company's steelmaking process. Minera Carbonifera Río Escondido, S.A. de C.V. (MICARE) was extracting and selling steam coal used by Mexico's Federal Commission of Energy for the generation of electrical energy in its coal-fired plants. La Perla Minas de Fierro y Carbon, S.A. de C.V. was the proprietor of a pellet plant and ferroduct for transporting iron ore to AHMSA's own pellet plant in Monclova.

Altos Hornos owned 50 percent of Centro de Servicio Placa y Lámina, S.A. de C.V., a joint venture with Ryerson Tull to distribute steel through a marketing network. Linea Coahuila-Durango, S.A. de C.V. was its half-owned joint venture with Industrias Peñoles, S.A. de C.V. dedicated to rail transport in order to haul metallurgical coal to its plant. Immobiliaria Dos Carlos, S.A. de C.V. was a residential real estate venture in the Monterrey area still subject to approval by the government of the state of Nuevo Leon.

Principal Subsidiaries

Cerro de Mercado, S.A. de C.V.; La Perla Minas de Fierro, S.A. de C.V.; Minera Carbonifera Río Escondido, S.A. de C.V. (MICARE); Minera Monclova, S.A. de C.V. (MIMOSA); Minera del Norte, S.A. de C.V. (MINOSA).

Principal Competitors

Hylsamex, S.A. de C.V.; Siderurgica Lázáro Cardenas Las Truchas, S.A. de C.V.

Further Reading

Bennett, Keith W., "Mexico's Growth—Building Solidly but Fast," *Iron Age,* November 23, 1972, pp. 70–71.
Coone, Tim, and Francis Freisinger, "Solid Foundations," *Business Latin America,* September 18, 1995, p. 2.
Friedland, Jonathan, and Joel Millman, "A Mexican Steelmaker Finds How Prosperity Makes Life Tougher," *Wall Street Journal,* June 14, 1999, pp. A1 +.
Haflich, Frank, "Ancira Keeps Firm Grip on Ahmsa Reins," *American Metal Market,* June 20, 2000, p. 2.
Kuster, Ted, "Ahmsa and Hylsa Aim for Exports and Added Value," *New Steel,* November 1997, pp. 98 +.
"Mexico Sells 3 Steel Units," *New York Times,* November 23, 1991, p. 46.
Millman, Joel, "Mexico's Ancira to Retain Control of Ahmsa After All," *Wall Street Journal,* May 31, 2001, p. A13.
Minello, Nelson, et al., *El desarrollo de una industria basica: Altos Hornos de México, 1942–1988.* Monclova, Coahuila: Arte y Cultura Monclova, 1995.
Ritt, Adam, "Ahmsa Aims for World-Class Steelmaking in $800 Million Project," *New Steel,* June 1994, pp. 36–37.
Rueda Peiro, Isabel, *Tras las huellas de la privatización: el caso de Altos Hornos de México.* Mexico City: Siglo Veintiuno Editores, 1994.
Zelade, Richard, "About Face," *International Business,* June 1996, pp. 29–30.

—Robert Halasz

American Retirement Corporation

111 Westwood Place, Suite 402
Brentwood, Tennessee 37027
U.S.A.
Telephone: (615) 221-2250
Fax: (615) 221-2269
Web site: http://www.arclp.com

Public Company
Incorporated: 1997
Employees: 7,600
Sales: $206.1 million (2000)
Stock Exchanges: New York
Ticker Symbol: ACR
NAIC: 623311 Continuing Care Retirement Communities

American Retirement Corporation (ARC) owns, leases, and manages more than 60 luxury and upscale senior living communities in 15 states. With resident capacity at more than 14,000 units, ARC provides independent living, assisted-living, skilled nursing, and memory-enhanced (Alzheimer's care) services at its retirement centers and freestanding assisted-living centers. Approximately 95 percent of ARC's revenues originate from private pay sources.

Focusing on the Dignity of Residents: 1978

Jack C. Massey, Dr. Thomas F. Frist, Sr., and a group of Nashville businessmen began what would become American Retirement Corporation in 1978 to provide consulting and management services to retirement communities. Frist and Massey, also cofounders of Hospital Corporation of America, wanted to create environments for senior citizens that offered quality of life by preserving personal freedom, independence, privacy, and dignity in years of declining abilities and health. They emphasized wellness care, such as basic health screening services, exercise classes, and social activities, for emotional and physical well-being.

The company offered marketing, management, and development assistance, and direct management of retirement community properties, seeking customers nationwide. Property management involved administration; human resources; marketing; and resident care, including nursing and nutritional services. The property owner paid for the expense of operations and ARC received a monthly fee for managing the property, either as a percentage of revenues or as a fixed sum, under a three- to five-year contract. Among the properties ARC managed during this period were Burcham Hills in East Lansing, Michigan, begun in 1978; and Williamsburg Landing in Williamsburg, Virginia, begun in 1985.

In the 1990s, ARC began to purchase or lease properties, bearing the full expense of operating and managing the facilities. ARC leased Trinity Towers in Corpus Christi, Texas, in 1990, and Holley Court Terrace in Oak Park, Illinois, in 1993. In 1992 the company purchased the Broadway Plaza in Cityview, near Fort Worth, and Summit at Westlake Hills in Austin, paying $37 million for the two retirement communities. In 1994 the company acquired Santa Catalina Villas in Tucson; Parkplace in Denver; Westlake Village in Cleveland; and The Hampton at Post Oak in Houston. In addition, in 1992 ARC merged with National Retirement Corporation, a senior living management firm.

ARC focused on upmarket and luxury retirement housing, with more than 90 percent of its resident care revenues originating from private pay sources, rather than Medicare or Medicaid. These life care communities incorporated interesting architectural elements and elegant surroundings in traditional or contemporary interior designs. Although each independent living unit included a kitchen for home cooking, residents had the option of taking meals in the dining room amidst the ambiance of a fine restaurant, replete with tablecloths and cloth napkins. Intimate social spaces at many properties included a lobby, lounge, card room, and billiard room, and were designed to encourage interaction among residents, preventing the isolation that had formerly plagued the elderly. Interior design of these properties accounted for the effects of aging, for example, with handrails disguised as moldings along the hallways and dining room chairs with arms that patrons used to steady themselves when sitting or rising. The homelike atmosphere of the independent living facilities extended to assisted-living and special care facilities. ARC marketing was directed to seniors 75 years of age and older.

Company Perspectives:

American Retirement Corporation is committed to the principle that well-planned and well-managed senior living communities offer the best settings within which to meet the physical, mental and social needs of our residents and their families. As the senior living industry evolves, ARC is committed to playing a significant and socially responsible role in its development grounded in providing family values and involvement.

Until 1995 ARC actually operated as several independent companies. That year the American Retirement Communities Limited Partnership (ARCLP) formed in preparation for further development of the company, including an initial public offering of stock. Revenues of the combined entities reached $61 million in 1995, garnering a net income of $2.1 million. Revenues represented an aggregate annual growth rate of 43 percent since 1992, when the companies recorded combined revenues of $17.8 million and a combined loss of $500,000. Revenues derived primarily from operations at leased and owned properties, with management fees and revenues from seven home healthcare agencies contributing to the balance.

Plans for future growth involved development of freestanding, assisted-living facilities and expansion of existing properties into continuing care communities, providing appropriate care for aging residents, such as assisted-living units, memory-enhanced units, and skilled nursing units. New property acquisitions at this time included the Heritage Club in Denver and Richmond Place in Lexington, Kentucky in 1995 and the Carriage Clubs of Charlotte and Jacksonville in 1996. In May 1997 ARCLP purchased the Remington in Corpus Christi and leased the Remington in nearby Victoria. The company changed the name of the Remington properties to its new brand, Homewood Residence.

By the time of the initial public offering of stock, the company owned ten properties, managed seven, and leased two, spread across 12 states, maintaining an aggregate resident capacity of 5,500 units. Development projects involved 19 freestanding, assisted-living facilities with 55 to 110 units, serving a total of 1,684 residents, and eight expansion facilities serving 702 residents.

Funding Ambitious Development Plans: Late 1990s

In preparation for the public offering American Retirement Corporation was formed to purchase the assets of ARCLP in a stock transaction. The June offering of 3.1 million shares of stock at $14 per share raised $43.4 million to fund the purchase of healthcare agencies, expansion projects, and development of assisted-living facilities. ARC completed two acquisitions shortly after the IPO, that of an assisted-living center in Tarpon Springs, Florida, renamed Homewood at Tarpon Springs, and a retirement center in Charlotte, Wilora Lake Lodge. The latter included adjacent land and zoning rights to build a 40-unit assisted-living center.

A new strategy ARC employed in its growth involved leasehold agreements. The agreements gave ARC an operating lease, from four to 20 years in duration, with an option to renew the lease or to purchase the property when the lease expired. In some cases ARC obtained the right of first refusal to purchase a property or to purchase a property at a predetermined formula based on occupancy and revenues. Special-purpose entities were formed to purchase a property, which ARC then managed. John Morris, a director of the company, and others formed these companies. The company initiated its first leasehold agreement in October with the lease of the Imperial Plaza, a 1,000-resident facility in Richmond, Virginia. In the spring of 1998 ARC began leasing operations at the Rossmoor Regency, a retirement community in Laguna Hills, California, and the Bahia Oaks Lodge, an assisted-living center in Sarasota, Florida, both under five-year leasehold agreements. An operating lease for the Park Regency in Chandler, Arizona, which commenced in September, included rights to expand on land adjacent to the facility. ARC opened two company-owned properties in 1998, Village at Homewood in Lady Lake, Florida, a joint venture, and Homewood at Deanne Hill in Knoxville.

In July 1998 ARC acquired Freedom Group Inc., which owned and managed large, luxury senior housing properties. The transaction involved $23.2 million in cash, $9.4 million in assumed debt, $14.9 million in stock, and $5.5 million for two property management agreements with purchase options. ARC obtained three new communities with a total resident capacity of 1,590 at Freedom Plaza Sun City Center in Florida, Freedom Village Holland in Michigan, and Lake Seminole Square in Florida. Three managed communities served a total of 2,100 resident units at Freedom Plaza Arizona in Phoenix, Freedom Square in Seminole Florida, and Glenview at Pelican Bay in Naples, Florida.

A secondary offering of stock, 4.5 million shares at $16 per share, net $64.9 million in July 1998, provided funds for continued development. At the end of 1998 ARC development projects involved 35 freestanding, assisted-living facilities to serve 3,200 residents and six expansion projects to serve 500 residents. In November ARC became an equity partner in LifeMed LLC, a joint venture with Omnicare, a geriatric pharmaceuticals firm, and LifeTrust America, a well-care services provider. LifeMed attended to the special needs for pharmaceuticals at assisted-living residences. The company offered consultation on medication management and distribution and provided health and wellness services at senior life care communities. ARC discontinued its poorly performing home healthcare agencies in 1998.

In February 1999 ARC announced its intention to develop Senior Living Networks offering continuing care facilities in a metropolitan region. The networks included facilities with independent living units, various levels of assisted-living care, and skilled nursing care. The services were to be available at one site or through nearby locations, preferably within a 30-minute to 45-minute driving radius. Potentially, continuing care increased a resident's stay with ARC and improved occupancy rates, yet it eased the transition of relocation during times of declining abilities and health. ARC hoped to attain economies of scale and market penetration while providing excellent service to the elderly and their families.

Key Dates:

1978: Jack Massey, Thomas Frist, Sr., and a group of Nashville businessmen launch a consulting and management service for retirement communities.

1990: Company begins to lease and manage existing retirement communities.

1992: Company purchases first property.

1995: Separate operating entities are combined into American Retirement Communities Limited Partnership.

1997: American Retirement Corporation (ARC) is formed prior to first public offering of stock.

1999: ARC begins to develop Senior Living Networks as regional continuing care services.

2000: ARC adds almost 800 resident units at freestanding assisted-living centers.

Facilities already existed for network development in Denver, Houston, Tampa/St. Petersburg, Cleveland, and Phoenix. In February 1999 ARC commenced operations through a leasehold agreement with the Oakhurst Towers in Denver, adding 171 independent living apartments to that region's Senior Living Network. ARC acquired the leasehold for a continuing care facility in St. Petersburg, operated as Homewood at Bay Pines, and completed an assisted-living facility project in Safety Harbor, managed as Homewood at Countryside. The two facilities brought the Tampa/St. Petersburg network capacity to more than 2,200 residents at seven communities.

Four ARC-developed properties opened in the Houston area, assisted-living centers that operated under the brand name The Hampton. ARC operated The Hampton at Cypress Station and The Hampton at Spring Shadows under lease/purchase option agreements. The Hampton properties at Shadowlake and at Willowbrook were managed communities, from which ARC received a percentage of gross revenues, but took responsibility for losses of more than a certain amount. Other new facilities included the Freedom Plaza Health Center, a skilled nursing center adjacent to a managed property in Phoenix, and an assisted-living facility, Homewood at Sun City Center, a joint venture in Florida. The company also began to develop the Heritage Club brand in Denver, adding two managed assisted-living centers in the area's Senior Living Network, for a total of more than 1,100 resident units at six communities.

Two retirement centers developed by ARC in Alabama initiated a new network in urban markets there. Somerby at Jones Farm in Hunstville and Somerby at University Park in Birmingham provided 258 independent living units, 153 assisted-living units, and 15 memory-enhanced units. The management agreement provided ARC with the option to purchase the properties when occupancy had stabilized.

Cautious New Development amid Changing Market: Late 1990s to Early 2000s

In late 1999 ARC decided to postpone certain development projects, as existing spaces remained open in an overbuilt industry. Higher staffing, insurance, and other expenses influenced the decision. By December ARC made definite arrangements to halt certain projects as high construction costs made acquisition a more attractive growth strategy. ARC halted work on all freestanding, assisted-living projects in the pre-construction or early development stage and delayed development of two expansion projects. The company also sought to focus on existing Senior Living Networks by divesting properties where a significant network had not been established already.

The termination of these projects resulted in a $12.5 million write-down in the last quarter of fiscal 1999. The company reported revenues of $175.3 million in 1999, a 23 percent increase over 1998. Operating income, at $15.1 million compared with $29 million in 1998, declined due to lower management fees, slower new unit sales, and vacancies at Freedom Square and Freedom Plaza in Peoria, Arizona. ARC finished 1999 with net income of $2.1 million, compared with $6.9 million in 1998.

Several construction projects came to completion in 2000. ARC completed two joint venture projects, Homewood at Flint in Michigan, and Homewood at Brookmont Terrace in Nashville, the latter being the first property that the company had ever operated in its home city (Brentwood being a suburb of Nashville). Leasehold properties opened under the Homewood brand name in Boca Raton and Naples, Florida, and in Fort Worth, Austin, and San Antonio, Texas. Two Hampton properties opened in Houston, bringing the total capacity for that Senior Living Network to 766 residents, including 451 assisted-living units. New managed properties provided assisted-living and memory-enhanced services under the Homewood brand in Greenville, South Carolina; Cleveland; Austin; and in Boynton Beach, Delray Beach, and Coconut Creek, Florida. Pursuant to its acquisition agreement with the Freedom Group, ARC purchased Freedom Village Brandywine in Glenmore, Pennsylvania. ARC did start a new development project with the March acquisition of 12.8 acres of land in Belmont, Massachusetts, adjacent to McLean Hospital. ARC planned to construct a continuing care retirement center with 350 independent living units and 136 assisted-living, skilled nursing, and memory-enhanced units.

At the end of 2000 ARC counted 62 properties, which it owned, leased, or managed, with total capacity for 14,506 residents. ARC maintained a stabilized occupancy at owned and leased properties open for at least a year at 92 percent, while total occupancy declined to 83 percent, compared with 86 percent the previous year. Market overcapacity in assisted living facilities resulted in longer time to lease new space; ARC nonetheless added nearly 800 new assisted-living resident units in 2000. While revenues increased to $206.1 million, operating and interest expenses increased as well, leaving ARC with a net loss of $5.9 million.

ARC sought to counter losses by halting operations in areas that did not fit with a Senior Living Network. In 2000 the company leased certain properties, including an assisted-living facility in Marietta, Georgia, to third parties. ARC also sold a retirement center, Westlake Village in Cleveland, and leased the property back from the buyer, for $26 million in deferred income. In June 2001 ARC sold its leasehold for the Rossmoor Regency in California for $21.5 million as projects related to developing a Senior Living Network in the area had been terminated.

Principal Subsidiaries

ARC Capital Corporation; ARC Management Corporation; Freedom Group Management Corporation.

Principal Operating Units

Retirement Centers; Freestanding Assisted-Living Centers.

Principal Competitors

Beverly Enterprises, Inc.; Kindred Healthcare, Inc.; Sun Healthcare Group, Inc.

Further Reading

Gibbs, Melanie L., "ARC Works to Link Country Through Senior Living Networks," *National Real Estate Investor,* April 1999, p. 2S6.

Goodman, Raymond J., and Douglas G. Smith, *Retirement Facilities: Planning, Design, and Marketing,* New York: Whitney Library of Design, 1992.

"Homewood Residence at Rockefeller Gardens," *Nursing Homes,* April 2000, p. S1.

"Imperial Plaza to Get New Owner: Tenn. Company Buying Retirement Community," *Richmond Times-Dispatch,* September 13, 1997.

Walker, Rob, "Retirement Centers Sold by Forum," *Fort Worth Star-Telegram,* April 6, 1992.

—Mary Tradii

Appliance Recycling Centers of America, Inc.

7400 Excelsior Blvd.
St. Louis Park, Minnesota 55426
U.S.A.
Telephone: (952) 930-9000
Toll Free: (800) 654-2722
Fax: (313) 782-3333
Web site: http://www.arcainc.com

Public Company
Incorporated: 1987
Employees: 179
Sales: $21.48 million (2000)
Stock Exchanges: OTC Bulletin Board
Ticker Symbol: ARCI
NAIC: 42193 Recyclable Material Wholesaling; 443111
   Household Appliance Stores

Appliance Recycling Centers of America, Inc. (ARCA) provides appliance recycling services for customers in Minnesota, Ohio, and California. The company has developed large-scale systems for the proper disposal of appliances such as refrigerators, freezers, room air conditioners, dehumidifiers, and vending machines. These appliances contain refrigerants and other materials that are subject to environmental regulation. ARCA removes and reclaims the harmful substances in accordance with federal law and sells the remaining material to scrap metal companies.

ARCA's customers include major appliance retailers, appliance manufacturers, property managers, waste management companies, and the general public. Contracts with electric utilities, primarily in California, are another major source of appliances for ARCA's recycling centers. In addition to recycling old appliances, ARCA operates a chain of retail stores, under the ApplianceSmart name, that sell new special-buy household appliances. The ApplianceSmart stores are an outlet for the reverse logistics services that ARCA offers to appliance manufacturers and retailers. Reverse logistics relates to the handling of products that do

not fit into a company's normal distribution channels, including manufacturer closeouts, factory over-runs, returned items, and scratch and dent appliances. ARCA purchases and resells these virtually new appliances at a discount at eight ApplianceSmart stores in three states. The stores carry Whirlpool, Kitchenaid, and Roper brands and offer customers a 100 percent money back guarantee and warranties on parts and labor.

Developing Responsible Disposal Methods: 1976–92

ARCA was founded by Edward "Jack" Cameron in 1976 and was initially known simply as Major Appliances Pick-up Service. The company contracted with major retailers such as Sears, Montgomery Ward, Dayton's, and J.C. Penney to remove old appliances from the homes of customers. The appliances were either reconditioned for sale at stores in the Minneapolis-St. Paul area or were sold to scrap metal companies for recycling. In the absence of environmental regulations, processing old appliances was a fairly simple matter in the early days of the company's operation.

In the 1980s, increasing concern about the environment led state and federal governments to adopt regulations related to appliance disposal. The Environmental Protection Agency banned the production of polychlorinated biphenyls (PCBs) in 1979 because of their suspected role as carcinogens, and landfills subsequently refused to accept PCB capacitors. Publicity about the potentially thinning ozone layer led some states to enact more stringent regulations relating to chlorofluorocarbons (CFCs) and hydrochlorofluorocarbons (HCFCs), chemicals found in refrigerants. Other sources of concern were mercury, lubricating oils, and sulfur dioxide, all of which were found in appliances.

In response, the Major Appliances Pick-up Service began to refine its disposal systems. In 1987 the company developed a reliable method for separating PCBs from old appliances. The new focus on large-scale processing methods was marked in 1988 with a name change to Appliance Recycling Centers of America, Inc. By 1989 systems were in place to recover CFCs, which could be recycled and sold to the appliance and automo-

Company Perspectives:

As the leader of the appliance recycling industry, ARCA pioneered the development of environmentally-sound appliance recycling systems. Today, ARCA provides a complete range of large-scale collection, processing and recycling services that will help you comply with federal, state and local appliance disposal regulations.

tive repair markets. In 1991 ARCA was able to recover sulfur dioxide refrigerant as well. The company was also responsible for ensuring that mercury components were delivered to a proper facility. Only after all harmful substances were removed was the metal shredded and sold.

Positive publicity for ARCA's environmentally responsible activities helped the company win contracts with the utility industry. Utilities hoped to reduce energy consumption through demand-side management programs, in which consumers were offered incentives to trade old appliances for more energy-efficient models. In 1989 ARCA established an appliance processing center in Milwaukee to support a contract with a Wisconsin utility. That year also brought a structural change, when the company merged with a public shell that had existed since 1983. Energy-efficiency programs for utilities were to be the focus of ARCA's business efforts through the early 1990s. In November 1991 the company made its first public stock offering, hoping to generate funds for opening more recycling centers. The offering through the NASDAQ small-cap market earned $2.3 million. By 1994, ARCA had opened nine recycling centers in the United States and Canada, largely in support of its partnerships with utilities.

Continuing environmental legislation provided an impetus to ARCA's activities. In 1990, amendments to the Clean Air Act called for a phasing out of the production of CFCs. In July 1992, a prohibition on the venting of CFCs during the maintenance, repair, or disposal of an appliance went into effect. The Federal Energy Policy Act of 1992 had a mixed impact on ARCA. The act encouraged energy efficiency and set mandatory energy performance standards for major household appliances. However, the act also provided for the deregulation of utilities, a step that ARCA feared would lead to fewer contracts with electricity providers.

Restructuring During Difficult Times: 1993–97

Concerned about a possible reduction in demand-side energy efficiency programs, ARCA began to seek a new focus. Contracts with appliance retailers, waste management companies, and property management companies could make up for some of the potential loss of business with utilities. Another possibility was to increase the sale of reconditioned appliances in company stores. But ARCA went through some painful years of experimentation and restructuring as it looked for a profitable mix of services.

In 1993 the company moved into a new facility in Excelsior, Minnesota, with 24,000 square feet of office space and 100,000

square feet of warehouse space. The expanded headquarters helped bring geographically scattered departments under one roof. A new facility in Los Angeles, however, was less successful. A recycling center was being built there to support a contract with Southern California Edison (SCE). Unfortunately, the center opened several months late, contributing to a drop in revenue for the year and a loss of 13 cents per share.

The next year brought more trouble from California. An earthquake disrupted appliance recycling programs, and processing volumes were lower than expected. The company took a loss in the first quarter. However, contracts with some customers guaranteed minimum recycling volumes, and the company was able to post a net income of $868,000 for the year.

The next year saw a continued decline in demand-side recycling programs through utilities. Reduced business led to a loss of $943,000 for 1995. In response, ARCA made a move to promote its retail business. The company introduced Encore Recycled Appliances, an outlet for ARCA's reconditioned refrigerators and freezers. ARCA purchased Gateway Appliance Center Inc., a used appliance retailer and recycler in St. Louis, Missouri, planning to convert the facility to an Encore store and open two more stores in St. Louis. ARCA began extensive restructuring to focus resources on the Encore used appliance concept. In addition, the company broke new ground by signing a recycling contract with GE Plastics of Pittsfield, Massachusetts. ARCA agreed to use its fleet of trucks to pick up scrap industrial plastics and discarded auto bumpers in the Rochester, New York area.

The aggressive expansion of the Encore chain continued into 1996. Unfortunately, the used appliance concept proved to be unsuccessful and ARCA retreated late in the year. In the fourth quarter, 12 retail stores and three recycling centers were closed. The combination of early expansion and later reconsolidation led to a $7.26 million loss for the year. One positive development was the extension of a contract with Southern California Edison, whose recycling program was now on solid footing after the initial delay in completing the recycling center. The contract increased from 22,500 to 30,000 the number of refrigerators and freezers that SCE was expected to provide.

The after effects of a consolidation of the Encore stores and the closing down of several recycling centers caused another loss, of $748,000, in 1997. By the end of the year, ARCA had greatly reduced its sphere of operation, with only 13 stores and four recycling centers, down from 30 stores and seven recycling centers a year earlier. As the Encore chain was faltering, a new style of retail offered hope for better years ahead. A pilot program with Whirlpool began in 1997, in which ARCA agreed to handle the manufacturer's returned, discontinued, and scratch and dent appliances. This new approach, of dealing in new appliances acquired through reverse logistics services, would prove to be more profitable than selling used appliances.

A New Focus and New Contracts: 1998–2001

The pilot program with Whirlpool proved successful, and in 1998 ARCA entered into a contract to provide reverse logistics services for the company, agreeing to purchase the appliances that Whirlpool was unable to sell through its normal channels.

Whirlpool initially supplied appliances from distribution centers in the Midwest and western states. In late 1998, ARCA found it had a more than ample supply of like-new appliances and scaled back the contract to acquire appliances primarily from Whirlpool's Ohio distribution center. ARCA decided not to expand its used appliance retail business.

ARCA's strategy for the ApplianceSmart venture was to have fewer but larger stores in selected markets. Accordingly, the company closed the entire St. Louis operation, consisting of two stores and a recycling center. One store in the Minneapolis/St. Paul area was also closed. The company was now operating eight stores in Minnesota, Ohio, and southern California. The store closings led to a loss of $3.06 million for 1998, but perseverance with the ApplianceSmart concept was to pay off in the long run.

The company continued to trim and focus its retail operations in 1999, closing one store in Minneapolis and another in California. Another small Minneapolis store was converted to a superstore. ARCA's efforts finally began to show results. Despite having fewer stores in operation, sales rose 2 percent in 1999 from the previous year and the company reported a net income of $505,000. ApplianceSmart was on solid footing and ready for expansion in 2000.

A new store in Dayton, Ohio, set the standard for future ApplianceSmart stores. The store, opened in May 2000, was larger than ever, had less of a warehouse atmosphere and was located in the middle of a retail area. Meanwhile, a smaller Minneapolis/St. Paul area store was closed. Larger stores and improved advertising contributed to a net income of $927,000 in 2000. More new stores followed in 2001. In January a large store opened in the eastern Minneapolis/St. Paul metro area, and in March a second large store opened in Dayton. Concentration on already established markets allowed ARCA to leverage existing support systems and advertising for the new stores. In May a small Columbus store was replaced with a larger store. As of August 2001, ARCA was operating eight ApplianceSmart

stores: three in Minneapolis/St. Paul, two in Dayton, two in Columbus, and one in Los Angeles. Sales generated by the ApplianceSmart operation accounted for over half of ARCA's revenue. The company stated its intention to open more stores, possibly in new markets, without being so aggressive as to damage overall profitability.

Meanwhile, the energy crisis in California generated new contracts with electric utilities. After a slowdown due to utility deregulation, residential energy efficiency programs once again gained support. In October 2000, Southern California Edison more than doubled its contract with ARCA by arranging to recycle refrigerators and freezers in the service territories of Pacific Gas & Electric and San Diego Gas & Electric. This contract, dubbed the "Summer Initiative," was expected to generate about 36,000 appliances annually for ARCA's recycling centers.

In June 2001 a new one-year contract with the California Public Utilities Commission was announced. The program was modeled on the Summer Initiative but would accept room air conditioners, as well as refrigerators and freezers, from San Diego and surrounding areas. The California legislature, looking for a way to deal with energy blackouts, agreed to fund the program. It was expected to reduce peak residential summer electricity demand by about 21 megawatts, equal to the output of a small power plant.

In 2001, ARCA appeared to have found a profitable mix of business ventures. Founder Jack Cameron, who continued to lead the company as president, chairman, and chief executive officer, had kept ARCA intact through 25 years of changes, first capitalizing on environmental regulations, then persevering as utility deregulation and a faltering used appliance retail business threatened the company's bottom line. In the end, the ApplianceSmart operation filled a profitable niche with its reverse logistics services for appliance manufacturers. Moreover, the company's two decades of experience in appliance recycling made it a sound choice for any organization seeking to dispose of old appliances.

Principal Competitors

Best Buy Co., Inc.; GE Appliances; Philip Services.

Further Reading

"Arca Ices Refrigerator Recycling Deal," *American Metal Market,* September 17, 1996, p. 10.

"Arca Purchases Appliance Outlet with Stock Trade," *American Metal Market,* August 28, 1995, p. 11.

"Arca Shifts Gears After $1M Loss," *American Metal Market,* March 13, 1996, p. 10.

"California Power Crisis Helps Arca Boost 1st-Qtr. Earnings," *American Metal Market,* April 27, 2001, p. 7.

"GE Plastic, Arca in Partnership," *American Metal Market,* January 25, 1995, p. 7.

Kurschner, Dale, "Appliance Recycling Launches Stock Offering to Expand," *Minneapolis-St. Paul City Business,* November 11, 1991, p. 12.

Marley, Michael, "Recycling Helps Push Arca to Record Earnings," *American Metal Market,* April 26, 2000, p. 6.

McCann, Joseph, "Appliance Buyback Program Doubles in Size in California," *American Metal Market,* September 6, 2000.

Reichard, Kevin, "Minneapolis Company Recycles '93 Growth Plans," *Corporate Report Minnesota,* April 1994, pp. 79–81.

"Soaked in Red, Arca Gets Cash," *American Metal Market,* February 25, 1999, p. 7.

Tellijohn, Andrew, "ARCA Expanding," *Minneapolis-St. Paul City-Business,* August 4, 2000, p. 11.

Worden, Edward, "Arca Avoids Red Ink Despite Business Cut," *American Metal Market,* February 16, 1995, p. 6.

——, "Arca Makes Progress but Remains in the Red," *American Metal Market,* March 5, 1998, p. 7.

——, "Arca Posts Bigger Loss for '96," *American Metal Market,* March 5, 1997, p. 9.

—Sarah Ruth Lorenz

BAKER & MᶜKENZIE

Baker & McKenzie

130 East Randolph Drive
Chicago, Illinois 60601
U.S.A.
Telephone: (312) 861-8800
Fax: (312) 861-8823
Web site: http://www.bakerinfo.com

Partnership
Founded: 1949
Employees: 8,000
Sales: $940 million (2000 est.)
NAIC: 54111 Offices of Lawyers

Baker & McKenzie with over 3,000 lawyers ranks as the world's second largest law firm, behind London's Clifford Chance. Its rapid growth from a small partnership started in 1949 is quite remarkable. Baker & McKenzie's practice covers every major field of domestic and international law. Like most large law firms, it plays a major role in globalization, privatization, and other world economic trends. However, Baker & McKenzie is much different from the other so-called "megafirms." It has by far the largest number of offices: 61 in the United States, Canada, Mexico, Central and South America, Europe, Asia, Australia, and the Middle East, and also the largest percentage of lawyers based overseas. The firm stresses the importance of understanding the culture and customs of the areas in which it operates as well the laws. Thus Baker & McKenzie tends to staff its overseas offices with local lawyers, rather than sending U.S. lawyers abroad. In addition, about 75 percent of the revenue generated by a foreign office remains in that country, a much higher share than most firms allow. Because of these practices, many competitors have criticized Baker & McKenzie as a kind of franchise operation akin to a fast-food chain. The firm's strategy has its pros and cons, but no one can argue with the record of success that it has yielded.

Origins

Although Baker & McKenzie was created in 1949, its roots can be traced to founder Russell Baker's initial law practice, established shortly after his 1925 graduation from the University of Chicago Law School. Baker, who had traveled to Chicago from his native New Mexico by hopping freight trains, began his legal career while still in law school. Working for the Chicago Motor Club, Baker was allowed to try minor traffic cases for Club members before a justice of the peace. After graduation, Baker set up a practice with Dana Simpson, a friend and University of Chicago classmate. The firm, Simpson & Baker, specialized in providing services for Chicago's growing Mexican-American community.

Baker's early experience working with Mexican lawyers sparked his interest in international law. Recognizing Chicago's important and expanding role in international trade, Baker conceived the idea of establishing a law firm that would be truly international in scope. After handling the worldwide legal matters for Abbott Laboratories in 1934, Baker built a reputation as an expert in international law. By that time, Simpson had left the practice, and Baker was a partner in Hubbard, Baker & Rice. He was still engaged by Abbott to handle contract negotiations, acquisitions, and patent and trademark litigation, and had the opportunity to travel throughout Latin America and Europe. His notion of creating an international law firm became progressively more concrete.

Since his current partners were not as interested in developing an international practice, Baker began to search for a new partnership. In 1949, he teamed up with John McKenzie, a trial lawyer he had met in a taxi a few years earlier, to form Baker & McKenzie. The firm also included Dwight Hightower and Andrew Brainerd. Since McKenzie had already established a reputation as a skilled litigator, Baker was free to travel in search of international contacts while McKenzie handled the firm's domestic matters.

Baker & McKenzie's list of clients grew impressively in the early 1950s. The list included such major companies as Eli Lilly, G.D. Searle, Wrigley, and Honeywell. As the firm's domestic client list grew so did its international list. In 1955, a Venezuelan lawyer contacted Baker to explore the possibility of setting up a joint venture to handle U.S. business interests in Caracas, prompting the establishment of Baker & McKenzie's first foreign office. By the end of the 1950s, the firm had

Company Perspectives:

Baker & McKenzie was the first law firm to recognize the importance of a global perspective. While competitors focused on domestic markets, we chose to look further afield, with a foresight that enabled us to service our clients wherever their businesses took them.

The Firm was established in 1949, decades before the concept of "globablization" emerged. Founder Russell Baker foresaw an opportunity the legal profession is just now embracing: creating a full-service global law firm servicing clients' needs from every major commercial and financial center in the world.

established six other foreign offices, and its staff of lawyers had grown from four to 30. In 1957, offices were opened in Washington, Brussels, and Amsterdam. Zurich, New York, and Sao Paulo were added over the next two years. International expansion continued throughout the 1960s.

During this period of incredibly rapid international development, the firm hired lawyers trained locally to man the new offices. Once recruited, a lawyer usually spent time working out of the firm's home base in Chicago, learning the finer points of its operations, before being reassigned to the company office in his or her native country. Lawyers working out of these foreign offices were treated as equal partners in the firm, not as affiliates or minor leaguers. They had as much say in firm decisions as their U.S. counterparts, and as much opportunity to share in the firm's profits. Because the lawyers were trained where they worked, the foreign offices were capable of taking on work from local clients as well as from international concerns.

Baker & McKenzie tried to make timely moves into areas where the flow of new business activity was about to create a greater need for available legal services. Thus much of Baker & McKenzie's expansion during the 1970s focused on the Far East. A Hong Kong office was established in 1974, and among others, offices were opened in Bangkok and Taipei three years later. By 1978 Baker & McKenzie had 26 offices in 20 countries.

In nearly every case, Baker & McKenzie would launch its foreign offices from scratch, sending attorneys abroad to open an outpost, or recruiting local lawyers and bringing them to Chicago for a few years of orientation before returning them home to set up shop. The office that opened in 1979 in Bogota, Colombia, was a rare exception, since it was created through a merger with an 11-lawyer Bogota firm already in existence.

Founder Russell Baker died on the last day of the firm's annual partnership meeting in 1979. Under Chairman Wulf Doser, from the company's Frankfurt office, Baker & McKenzie entered a consolidation phase. During this period, in which the Tokyo office was reorganized and the young Minneapolis office was closed, the firm's approach became more businesslike, something of a contrast from Baker's "lawyer's manage thyselves" philosophy.

Doser was succeeded as chairman in 1981 by Thomas Bridgman, a litigator from the firm's Chicago home base. When Bridgman's three-year term expired in 1983, Robert Cox was elected to a five-year term as chairman, and the role of that position in the firm was expanded. Unlike his immediate predecessors, Cox gave up his regular law practice to concentrate on managing the firm full time. By 1985, Baker & McKenzie's lawyer count was at 752 and growing. The firm was operating 30 offices in 22 countries. Its annual revenue was in excess of $125 million, second highest among law firms to Skadden, Arps.

The second half of the 1980s was an extremely prolific period in Baker & McKenzie's spread across the globe. Not only did it open offices along the U.S.-Mexican border in 1986 to take advantage of the industrial boom there, it also was one of the first U.S. law firms to anticipate the opening of Eastern European markets, establishing offices in Budapest (1987), Moscow (1989), and Berlin (1990). Like many other law firms, Baker & McKenzie also launched a full-scale assault on California during the late 1980s, expecting a huge rush of investment there by companies from Japan and elsewhere in Asia. The firm opened offices in Palo Alto, Los Angeles, and San Diego. This California expansion included the assimilation of MacDonald, Halsted, and Laybourne, a 68-partner firm with offices in Los Angeles and San Diego. Western Europe was not ignored either, and an office was established in Barcelona in 1988. In 1989 Baker & McKenzie entered into associations with law firms in Seoul, Korea, and Jakarta, Indonesia.

The firm's revenue and lawyer rolls were growing as quickly as its geographical range. Between 1987 and 1990, annual revenue more than doubled, from $196 million to $404 million. Baker & McKenzie cracked the 1,000-lawyer mark in 1988 (1,179), and it took only two more years to pass 1,500. By 1990, the company was operating a total of 49 offices on six continents. In addition to the company growth, prestige came to the Baker & McKenzie name as well, when David Ruder, the recently retired chairman of the Securities and Exchange Commission, joined the firm's domestic corporate and securities practice.

Three major controversies, however, brought unwanted publicity to Baker & McKenzie. In 1991, Ingrid Beall, who had become the firm's first woman partner in 1961, filed a discrimination suit against the firm. The suit revolved around Ms. Beall's claim that she was systematically deprived of the opportunity to advance within the firm on the basis of her age and gender. In a second well-publicized episode, the firm dropped the Church of Scientology as a client, turning its back on $2 million of revenue in the process. Some observers hinted that the move may have resulted from pressure applied to the firm by Eli Lilly, one of its oldest and best customers. The Church of Scientology had been a vocal critic of the antidepressant drug Prozac, which was manufactured by Lilly. Finally, at the end of 1993, Baker & McKenzie was ordered by the New York State Division of Human Rights to pay $500,000 in compensatory damages and back wages to the estate of Geoffrey Bowers. In one of the earliest AIDS discrimination cases in the United States, Bowers had argued that his firing by the company in 1986 was due to his illness rather than his performance, as was claimed by the firm. The decision was contested by Baker & McKenzie.

Many of the firm's foreign offices were generating a substantial share of their own business by 1992. At the company's Latin American outposts, as much as 35 percent of the client

Key Dates:

1949: Baker & McKenzie is started in Chicago.
1955: Firm opens its first overseas office in Caracas, Venezuela.
1957: New offices in Amsterdam, Brussels, and Washington, D.C., are opened.
1963: Manila, Tokyo, and Paris offices are started.
1982: Melbourne becomes the firm's 30th office.
1989: Moscow office is established.
1997: Houston and Munich offices are started.
1999: Christine Lagarde becomes first woman to lead Baker & McKenzie and one of the few women to lead any major American law firm.
2001: Firm purchases Madrid-based Briones Alonso y Martin.

base was not U.S.-based. The Paris office's clientele was 40 percent French, and a significant portion of the remainder was Japanese or German, as well as American. For 1992, Baker & McKenzie reported revenue of $503.5 million, moving the firm past Skadden, Arps into first place among law firms. The company's foreign offices accounted for 60 percent of that revenue, a figure far higher than that of most other top international firms.

As the 1990s continued, competition among international law firms intensified. Additional competition came from large accounting firms, such as Arthur Andersen, that diversified into legal services by forging alliances with established law firms in foreign countries. Baker & McKenzie prepared for the increased competition under the guidance of the chairman of the executive committee John McGuigan, an Australian, who joined Baker & McKenzie in 1973 and had served most recently as managing partner at the firm's Hong Kong office. In 1993, new offices were established in Prague and Beijing, reflecting the firm's ongoing emphasis on Asia and Eastern Europe.

For much of its history, Baker & McKenzie was derided by its competitors for its approach to global expansion. Critics argued that the firm was a loose alliance of local satellites rather than a unified international entity. By employing lawyers in their native regions, however, Baker & McKenzie succeeded in developing relationships with major companies in those areas more quickly than might otherwise have been possible. Moreover, many of the firm's critics reluctantly admitted that what they called ''McLaw'' had positioned itself remarkably well in the growing markets of Asia and Eastern Europe.

Baker & McKenzie continued to grow in the 1990s as the U.S. economy boomed, international trade increased from the North American Free Trade Agreement (NAFTA), and privatization of government entities occurred in many nations. The *American Lawyer* in July/August 1998 ranked Baker & McKenzie as the second largest U.S. law firm, based on its 1997 gross revenues of $696.5 million. It still had the most lawyers with 2,094, but Skadden, Arps with 1,074 lawyers had far more revenue ($826 million).

In November 1998 the *American Lawyer* in cooperation with London's *Legal Times* published its first survey of the

world's largest law firms. Baker & McKenzie had the most lawyers (2,300), 80 percent being based outside the United States. Thirty of the top 50 firms had less than 10 percent of their lawyers outside their home country, which was good evidence of the unusual way that Baker & McKenzie was structured. Based on revenue, Baker & McKenzie was ranked second, again outpaced by Skadden, Arps.

Although Baker & McKenzie claimed to have balanced local autonomy of its many offices with the centralized authority of the Chicago headquarters, some outsiders were skeptical. Debora Spar in the spring 1997 *California Management Review* concluded that ''the firm appears to suffer a serious lack of consistency, one that keeps Baker & McKenzie, despite its enviable global reach, from being considered among the top tier of international firms.

In the 1990s law firms grew via mergers and internal growth. This consolidation reflected the fact that many of their corporate clients were consolidating into even larger multinational firms. The growth of the megalaw firms was reflected in the intense competition for the top lawyers graduating from law school. Salaries for new associates who just graduated reached well over $150,000. These high salaries also resulted from the opportunities for lawyers to make huge incomes working for computer and Internet-based companies.

In 1999 Christine Lagarde became the first woman to lead Baker & McKenzie and one of the first women, for that matter, to lead any major U.S. law firm. The election of Chairman Lagarde, a resident of Paris, illustrated Baker & McKenzie's international orientation and its openness to diversity.

At the end of its fiscal year ending June 30, 2000, Baker & McKenzie reported global revenue of $940 million, a 15 percent increase over 1999. The firm's revenue came from the following areas: Europe and the Middle East (33 percent); Asia and Pacific (27 percent); and North America and Latin America (40 percent). That distribution illustrated the nature of the firm's international operation.

According to its web site, Baker & McKenzie represented major corporate clients and was involved in many aspects of the world's economy. For example, in 2000 it represented Alcoa Inc. in its acquisition of British Aluminum. On December 21, 2000, Privatisation International named the firm the Privatisation Legal Team of the Year. It served clients such as Allianz Capital Partners GmbH, Canada 3000 Inc., Spherion Corporation, and a subsidiary of Authentos GmbH in a variety of transactions. In March 2001 the firm announced it was to be the exclusive legal sponsor of MainEvent 2001, the world's largest global satellite telecast for businessmen and women.

In the new millennium Baker & McKenzie continued to grow. In early 2001 it acquired the Spanish law firm of Briones Alonso y Martin. Thus the firm's offices in Madrid and Barcelona went by the name Baker & McKenzie Briones Alonso y Martin. The Chicago firm favored the Briones firm's strong reputation in taxation, for 25 of the 40 lawyers joining Baker & McKenzie were tax lawyers. That was particularly important for the firm's work in Latin America, where Spain was one of the largest outside sources of foreign investment. Baker & Mc-

Kenzie was Mexico's largest law firm, with 120 lawyers practicing in five offices in 2000.

At the start of the new millennium, Baker & McKenzie faced tough competition from other large law firms, such as London's Clifford Chance, which merged in 2000 with two other law firms to become the world's largest firm based on the number of its lawyers. Some large firms competed very effectively with far fewer lawyers or offices. With such rivals and the world's rapidly changing social and economic systems, Baker & McKenzie has plenty of challenges to deal with in the years ahead.

Principal Competitors

Clifford Chance LLP; Sidley Austin Brown & Wood; Jones, Day, Reavis & Pogue; Skadden, Arps, Slate, Meagher & Flom.

Further Reading

Abramowitz, Michael, "One Woman v. Her Law Firm," *Washington Post,* October 14, 1991, p. D1.

Baker & McKenzie, Chicago: Baker & McKenzie, 1988.

Baker, Russell, *History of Baker & McKenzie,* Chicago: Baker & McKenzie, 1978.

Baker, Wallace R., *What Is Baker & McKenzie?,* Chicago: Baker & McKenzie, 1991.

Bauman, Jon R., *Pioneering a Global Vision: The Story of Baker & McKenzie,* Chicago: Harcourt Brace Legal & Professional Publishers, 1999.

"Cover Profile: Baker & McKenzie's John McGuigan," *Asia Today,* February 1994, pp. 5–6.

Elstrom, Peter J.W., "Law Firm Gets a Plum As Ruder Joins Practice," *Crain's Chicago Business,* February 26, 1990, p. 47.

Feder, Barnaby J., "The Unorthodox Behemoth of Law Firms," *New York Times,* March 14, 1993, sec. 3, p. 1.

"Firm Drops L.A. Office," *Wall Street Journal,* October 18, 1993, p. B8.

Gill, Donna, "Baker's Unique Niche," *Chicago Lawyer,* January 1992, p. 1.

Goldberg, Stephanie, "Law Firm Blankets Globe," *Crain's Chicago Business,* October 26, 1992, p. 17.

"Lawyers Go Global: The Battle of the Atlantic," *Economist,* February 26, 2000, pp. 79–81.

Lyons, James, "Baker & McKenzie: The Belittled Giant," *American Lawyer,* October 1985, pp. 115–22.

"McLaw Acquitted," *Economist,* July 3, 1993, pp. 61–2.

Navarro, Mireya, "Vindicating a Lawyer with AIDS, Years Too Late," *New York Times,* January 21, 1994, p. B18.

"On the Way to Becoming the Dominant Provider of Legal Services," *Frankfurter Allgemeine Zeitung,* October 15, 1993.

Petersen, Melody, "Baker & McKenzie Takes a Small Step for a Law Firm, Giant Leap for Womankind," *New York Times*, October 9, 1999, p. 1.

Rice, Robert, "Going Global," *Financial Times,* May 18, 1993.

"Spanish Merger Packs Heavy Tax Clout," *International Tax Review,* February 2001, p. 10.

Spar, Debora L., "Lawyers Abroad: The Internationalization of Legal Practice," *California Management Review,* Spring 1997, pp. 8–28.

Stevens, Mark, *Power of Attorney: The Rise of the Giant Law Firms,* New York: McGraw-Hill, 1986.

White, Jeremy, and Jo Witt, "The World's Fastest Growers Revealed," *International Tax Review,* 2000, pp. 12–16.

—Robert R. Jacobson
—update: David M. Walden

Balchem Corporation

2007 Route 284, P.O. Box 175
Slate Hill, New York 10973
U.S.A.
Telephone: (845) 355-5300
Toll Free: (800) 431-5641
Fax: (845) 355-6314
Web site: http://www.balchem.com

Public Company
Incorporated: 1967
Employees: 133
Sales: $33.2 million (2000)
Stock Exchanges: American
Ticker Symbol: BCP
NAIC: 325199 All Other Basic Organic Chemical
　　Manufacturing

Balchem Corporation of Slate Hill, New York, is a chemical company engaged in two primary niche businesses: specialty gases and encapsulated products. Balchem's Specialty Products group produces three gases: ethylene oxide, propylene oxide, and methyl chloride. Ethylene oxide is used as a sterilizing agent by hospitals, medical device manufacturers, and contract sterilizers. Because it can treat either hard or soft surfaces, the gas is used to sterilize a wide range of products—from syringes, catheters, and scalpels to gauze, bandages, and surgical kits. Propylene oxide is sold to the chemical synthesis market and used for bacteria reduction in spice treatment. It is also used in the manufacturing process to coat textiles, treat specialty starches, and enhance the strength of paint. Balchem's third gas product is methyl chloride, which is used as a raw material in herbicides, fertilizers, and pharmaceuticals. It is also added to malt and wine preservers. Balchem's Encapsulated Products group is the company's signature business line, one in which it is a world leader. Encapsulation allows nutrients and additives to be protected and controlled in their delivery to both humans and animals. The most commonly recognized form of the encapsulation technique is the time-release cold medicine capsule; the protective shell dissolves at a rate that allows the ingredients

to be slowly released into the blood system. Balchem applies its patented encapsulation techniques in a wide range of applications. The food industry is a major customer. Encapsulation fortifies processed foods with vitamins and nutrients, improves flavor, and extends shelf life. It is used in baked goods, refrigerated and frozen dough, processed meats, seasoning blends, and candies. In recent years the company has made great strides in flavor enhancement through encapsulation. Animal feed has also greatly benefited from Balchem's encapsulation methods. Vitamin C can be delivered as pellets to fish farms, where fish are deprived of natural sources of the vitamin. Animals such as horses, guinea pigs, and primates also take advantage of encapsulated Vitamin C. Microencapsulated choline chloride is used by the animal feed industry for ruminant animals: protected nutrients are able to pass through an animal's first stomach to the second, where delivery is needed. In addition, Balchem's Encapsulated Products group works with a marketing partner to sell chemical agents to makers of foamed plastics.

Establishment of Balchem: 1967

According to *Forbes,* the impetus behind the creation of Balchem came from chemist Dr. Herbert Weiss. In 1967 he noticed an advertisement in the *Wall Street Journal* that touted an invention that could individually coat particles that would allow the measured delivery of nutrients. Weiss tracked down the inventor, Dr. Leslie L. Balassa, who had earned his doctorate in chemistry at the University of Vienna in 1926, after which he worked for E.I. du Pont de Nemours & Company for a number of years. Today he is primarily remembered for his contributions in pain relief. He developed treatments to alleviate pain in molar extractions, as well as an arthritis treatment to ease long-term pain. His patented microencapsulation process would become the basis for time-release medicine. Weiss and Balassa joined forces with three ex-officers of Baltimore's Alcolac, Inc. and some other Baltimore investors to create Balchem, which acquired the rights to Balassa's inventions, processes, and technologies. The company was incorporated in Maryland in 1967, with Balassa initially serving as president.

Balchem underwent a long development phase before it was ready to begin actual operations, which commenced in 1970. At

---

Company Perspectives:

Mission Statement: To provide the benefits of Balchem's advanced technology to customers throughout the world, while enhancing stockholder value. This will be done by continuing to furnish value-added microencapsulated ingredients for a multiplicity of expanding applications in the human and animal food industries; and by maintaining a leadership position in supplying essential hazardous specialty chemicals in environmentally sound returnable containers.

This mission will be accomplished by providing superior quality products and service to customers; by having highly skilled and motivated employees and according equitable treatment to all; by continuing to develop new products and new markets and by continuing to conduct business in an environmentally and socially responsible manner.

---

first the company worked out of laboratory facilities on the top floor of the Chemists Club located in midtown Manhattan. The company would relocate to Slate Hill, establishing its operations on the site of a former dairy. In addition, it purchased a nearby parcel of land to serve as an industrial waste site. Despite Balchem's long gestation period, it soon became apparent that the company would need even more time to build its encapsulation business. In order to generate cash, the company decided to produce and sell what it called known products for known markets. It had the expertise and its equipment was easily adapted to the manufacture of synthetic organic chemicals without interfering with future encapsulation production. In October 1970 Balchem created a subsidiary, Arc Chemical Corporation, to take on this secondary business, which in the early years would provide the bulk of company revenues.

In 1971 Arc Chemical went into production and Balchem began commercial work encapsulating solids for the food industry, including flavor enhancers fumaric acid and adipic acid, preservative sodium nitrate, leavening agent sodium bicarbonate, and nutrient ferrous sulfate. Balchem's encapsulation efforts received a major break when the company landed a contract with General Foods, which was looking to simplify a lemon pudding mix. Balchem reduced the three-step process to just one step by using encapsulation to combine lemon oil, powdered starch, and citric acid. Not only did General Foods become a major customer for the next 20 years, its cachet as a client helped bring other food manufacturers into the fold, including Nestlé, Nabisco, and Unilever. For the year the company would generate almost $350,000, resulting in an operating loss of nearly $180,000.

Early Growth Despite Chemical Fires: 1970s–80s

Balchem's momentum would be halted on February 2, 1972, when a fire in one of its chemical producing facilities damaged both a building and its contents. Enough temporary repairs were completed by the end of the month to allow the company to continue manufacture on a limited basis. On April 20, 1972, a $300,000 settlement was reached with the company's insurer that would allow for the proper repair of the building as well as

replacement of damaged equipment. Balchem took advantage of the accident to rebuild its facility with anti-pollution devices that were becoming mandatory in the chemical industry during the early 1970s. Not only did Arc Chemical return to production, it expanded its product line to include monomers used in plastics and specialty ethoxylates needed in textiles, plastics, and cosmetics. Revenues for 1972 were approximately $850,000. The company's operating loss was reduced to $36,500. Moreover, in 1972 Balassa retired and was replaced by Weiss.

Balchem and Arc Chemical made considerable progress toward profitability in 1973, generating almost $1.2 million in revenues, but on January 21, 1974, another fire caused by the manufacture of specialty chemicals once again set back the company's efforts. Balchem sold whatever equipment could be salvaged, but in the end the fire produced a loss of more than $222,000. For the year the company lost $524,000, with revenues falling to $706,000. Management decided to cease the direct production of specialty chemicals, electing to have an outside company produce the items that it would market on a commission basis.

Balchem finally produced a profit in 1975, netting $236,000 on revenues of $967,285. The benefits of encapsulation were becoming widely understood, which boded well for the company's future. Revenues rose steadily through the rest of the 1970s, reaching $5.15 million by 1980, resulting in profits for each year. In 1976 Balchem employed 12 people, but by the end of the decade its staff had increased to 50. In late 1976 the company also returned to the direct sale of specialty chemicals after a three-year hiatus. This time, however, it hoped to protect its encapsulation business by establishing a separate South Carolina facility to produce the volatile substances. In January 1977 the Arc Chemical subsidiary merged with Balchem to form the Arc Chemical Division, and the corporation was dissolved. The South Carolina plant was completed and operational by May 1979.

Generally Balchem enjoyed steady growth through the 1980s, reaching almost $10 million in revenues by the end of the decade. The company's prospects in the 1990s would be bolstered by new uses for encapsulation. In 1990 Weiss was approached by a New York trade delegation looking for local products to promote during a trip to Thailand. Aware that Far East shrimp farmers threw raw vitamin C into ponds, he suggested that encapsulating the vitamin would not only last longer but would provide more effective delivery, and save the farmers money. In short order, Balchem had a representative in Thailand generating an entirely new revenue stream for the company.

Food Labeling Laws and Expansion of the Business: 1990s

Revised food-labeling laws would also have a major impact on Balchem. In 1990 Congress passed a new food labeling law, requiring that food packages list complete nutritional information, which previously had been provided on a voluntary basis by manufacturers. The format for the label was not completed until 1994, and was required on 90 percent of all processed food. To avoid a fallout with consumers, who were becoming increasingly more health conscious, food manufacturers were motivated to list more than just trace levels of nutrients on their

Key Dates:

1967: Balchem Corporation is incorporated.
1970: Balchem Corporation begins operations.
1971: Arc Chemical subsidiary begins to produce special-ity chemicals.
1974: Fire leads to company suspending direct manufac-ture of chemicals.
1977: Balchem Corporation merges with Arc Chemical in preparation for return to chemical production.
1994: Balchem Corporation acquires sterilant gas business of Allied Signal.
1996: Balchem Corporation is listed on American Stock Exchange.

labels. Encapsulation that extended the shelf life of nutrients was the ready answer, and Balchem was a major beneficiary.

In June 1994 Balchem also bolstered its specialty chemical business by acquiring the ethylene oxide (sterilant) business of Allied Signal Inc. It also took over Allied's current accounts. In 1995 Balchem moved from the NASDAQ to the American Stock Exchange. Overall the company was making great strides in the mid-1990s, reaching $25 million in revenues in 1995 and record net income of $1.6 million.

After 30 years with Balchem, Weiss stepped down as the company's chief executive at the end of 1996. He was replaced by Dino Rossi, who had joined the company early in the year as its chief financial officer. He had previous management experi-ence with chemical companies Norit Americas Inc. and Oakite Products Inc. He was eager to find new niches for Balchem's encapsulation technology. He increased the company's annual research and development budget to the $1 million level. By way of comparison, 20 years earlier the company devoted ap-proximately $50,000 a year to R&D. Rossi was especially keen on expanding its animal nutrition business.

In 1999 Balchem introduced an encapsulated choline prod-uct it called Reashure, intended to deliver essential nutrients to dairy cows during transition periods, resulting in increased milk production. Encapsulation allowed the choline to pass through the animal's first stomach in order to be absorbed in the small intestine and provide the maximum benefit. The concept of rumen bypass had been around for some 20 years, but not until Balchem's encapsulation solution did it become viable. In 2000 the company received a patent for its Reashure technology. It also took a significant step towards expanding into the global dairy marketplace when it signed an agreement with NYC Co., Ltd., a major importer of agricultural products to Japan, to distribute Reashure Choline to feed companies and farms in Japan. Balchem created a subsidiary to run its animal nutrient

fortification business, which it further bolstered in 2001 by acquiring the DCV Inc. and its affiliate DuCoa LP in a deal valued at nearly $15 million. The two companies were involved in the choline animal feed, human choline nutrient, and encap-sulated products business, with most of its annual sales of $17 million generated in North America.

Balchem's R&D efforts also created new food products for people. It introduced Flavorshure Cinnamon, an encapsulated product that promised radical use of cinnamon in baking. Cin-namon naturally inhibits the ability of yeast to rise, resulting in smaller loaves of cinnamon bread. Encapsulated cinnamon did not interfere with leavening while retaining the spice's aroma and flavor. Balchem also improved the delivery of preserva-tives, as well as flavor enhancements. It introduced Confecshure Burst pop rocks, encapsulated sodium bicarbonate that brought what the company called an ''interactive'' taste sensation to candy products. Balchem also introduced Vitashure nutrients, including flaxseed (highly regarded for its health benefits, in-cluding its ability to fight cancer and lower blood pressure and cholesterol levels) and guarana (a natural stimulant that pur-portedly not only suppresses appetite but helps reduce smoking and pain). Encapsulation was employed to mask the bitter aftertaste of guarana, allowing it to be used in such products as yogurt, cereals, candy, and ice cream.

To continue its growth in encapsulation, Balchem increased its 2001 R&D budget by 80 percent. With revenues of $33.2 million in 2000 and net income of $3.7 million, the company appeared ready to reach an entirely new level of financial success.

Principal Operating Units

Encapsulated Products; Specialty Gases.

Principal Competitors

Clariant; Hercules Inc.; Nutrition 21; Opta Food Ingredients; Pharmacia & Upjohn Inc.; Praxair, Inc.

Further Reading

Gellene, Denise, ''FDA Gets Strict with 'Healthy' Definition Food,'' *Los Angeles Times,* May 5, 1994, p 2.
Ingersoll, Bruce, ''FDA Plans to Propose New Rules for Nutritional Labeling on Food,'' *Wall Street Journal,* June 27, 1990, p. B1.
Krivyakina, Marina, ''Balchem Expands Its Animal Nutrition Encapsu-lation,'' *Chemical Marketing Reporter,* March 25, 1996, p. 28.
Setton, Dolly, ''A Tale of Two Stomachs,'' *Forbes,* November 3, 1997, p. 181.
Sugarman, Carole, ''The FDA Tries Some New Math; Which Nutri-tional Label Adds Up?,'' *Washington Post,* July 22, 1992, p. 1.

—Ed Dinger

Baltimore Technologies Plc

39/41 Parkgate Street
Dublin 8
Ireland
Telephone: +353-1-8816405
Fax: +353-1-8817400
Web site: http://www.baltimore.com

Public Company
Incorporated: 1976
Employees: 1,185
Sales: £74.2 million ($110 million) (2000)
Stock Exchanges: London NASDAQ
Ticker Symbols: BLM; BALT (ADR)
NAIC: 511210 Software Publishers; 541511 Custom
    Computer Programming Services

Baltimore Technologies Plc is one of the world's leading ''e-security'' companies and has built up a strong portfolio of primarily software-based security systems protecting data transmission, communication, access, and financial and other transactions over intranets and the Internet. With operations headquarters in Ireland (and financial headquarters in Reading, England), Baltimore Technologies has grown quickly from its original focus on public key infrastructure (PKI) applications to include content security (Baltimore MIMEsweeper); third-party server hosting facilities; access management and access authorization (Baltimore SelectAccess); and wireless transmissions security (Baltimore Telepathy). Nearly all of the company's product range has been added through a series of acquisitions made in 2000 and 2001, including the purchases of CyberTrust Solutions Inc., formerly of GTE; Content Technologies; more than 72 percent of NSJ Corporation, renamed as Baltimore Technologies Japan; Nevex Software Technologies, based in Toronto; and others. The company's revenues have skyrocketed from less than £10 million in 1998 to more than £74 million in 2000. With the market for e-security solutions expected to be worth more than $21 billion by 2005, Baltimore Technologies is well placed, with the leadership position in North America and Europe and the number two position in Japan. Yet the company,

battered by the plunge in technology stocks in the year 2000, remained a candidate for takeover, a possibility brought still closer with the July 2001 resignation of CEO Francis (''Fran'') J. Rooney. The company trades on the London and NASDAQ stock exchanges.

E-Security Pioneer in the 1990s

Baltimore Technologies resulted from a reverse takeover by Zergo Holdings made in 1999. Zergo had been founded by Henry Beker in 1988 and had developed itself as one of England's leading data security consulting firms. The company went public in 1995, listing its shares on the London Stock Exchange's tech stock AIM board before transferring to the main index. Zergo's original concentration had been on developing and implementing third-party hardware and software systems, and in providing consulting and servicing for customers' systems.

By the mid-1990s, Zergo had shifted into software development, targeting especially the market for anti-hacking and anti-piracy software. The company introduced its well-received Firewall system of credit-card encryption software at the end of 1995. By then, the company was posting £4 million in sales. The company's primary customer base was among government offices and banks.

In 1998, Zergo strengthened its software development activity with the acquisition of Security Domain, based in Australia, which not only afforded the company access to the Asian-Pacific region, but also gave Zergo its first range of software. This rapidly became the company's focus, and in 1999, Zergo began looking for a new acquisition with which to develop this potentially huge market.

By then, the world had seen the coinage of new terms such as ''e-commerce'' and ''e-security'' as the Internet and Internet-based financial and commercial transactions were set to become commonplace. A number of primary concerns governed the expansion of these sectors, however. Among these were concerns about security especially, not only for the transmission of financial data, but also the protection of privacy, the control of access and authorization, the setting up of firewalls,

Company Perspectives:

Our aim is to be the leader in e-security. We will continue to broaden our product and service portfolio by a combination of organic and acquisitive growth, and will continue to deliver leading edge e-security solutions to our customers to enable the adoption of e-business on a global basis. We enter 2001 with confidence, and the Board remains committed to its programme of investment, a strategy which it believes will provide the platform for long-term growth and profitability for Baltimore Technologies.

and so on. One of the technologies then being developed was application of so-called public key infrastructure, or PKI, which offered a means of authenticating senders and receivers of data and other transmissions, in order to ensure security.

Baltimore Technologies, based in Dublin, Ireland, had quickly set itself up as one of the leaders of PKI software implementation. That company, too, had originally been formed as a technology consulting firm, in 1976. In 1996, however, the privately owned company came to the attention of Fran Rooney and Dermot Desmond. A former professional soccer player-turned accountant, Rooney had held various positions with the Irish government before joining the National Irish Bank. In the early 1990s, Rooney worked for payments processing company Meridian International, serving as managing director until 1994. At that time, Rooney joined financier Dermot Desmond at Quay Financial Software, serving as corporate manager and successfully restructuring the troubled company. In 1996, Rooney saw the opportunity represented by security systems for the rapidly growing Internet-based transmissions sector. Backed by Desmond and joined by other investors, Rooney acquired Baltimore Technologies for £500,000. Desmond's share of the company neared 60 percent.

Rooney, named CEO, promptly refocused Baltimore to the market for PKI software systems. Starting with a staff of just six, the company became one of the symbols for the sudden late 1990s high-technology boom. The company opened offices in a number of countries; it also entered Japan in 1997, with a distribution agreement with that country's NSJ Corp. In this Baltimore Technologies was aided by a worldwide marketing coup in 1998, when U.S. President Bill Clinton and Irish Prime Minister Bertie Ahern used Baltimore's system to place digital signatures to an agreement between the two leaders. The digital signing made e-security history—and established the Baltimore Technologies brand name worldwide.

The company, which had posted less than £2 million in sales in 1997, was now attracting customers worldwide, and signed a number of new contracts with such major organizations as Deutsche Bank, the British Post Office, and the Irish government. Baltimore's growing success also attracted the attention of Henry Beker and Zergo Holdings. In December 1998, Baltimore agreed to be acquired by Zergo Holdings, with Desmond selling out most of his stake in the company. Rooney and Beker shared responsibility for the company's direction, with Rooney taking the COO spot, while the company itself took on the

stronger Baltimore Technologies brand name. The merger created one of Europe's leading PKI-focused e-security companies; yet Baltimore remained a minor player in the North American market dominated by such companies as Entrust and Verisign.

Gorilla in the 21st Century E-Security Market

The takeover quickly turned out to be a reverse takeover, as disagreements between Rooney and Beker soon led to the latter's resignation. Rooney was named to the CEO spot in Beker's stead. Baltimore now began an aggressive expansion, boosting its number of sales and service offices to more than 20 worldwide. The company was boosted in July 1999 when it announced that it had been awarded the security systems contract for banking consortium Identrus, whose members included such banking heavyweights as ABN AMRO, Citigroup, Deutsche Bank, Chase Manhattan, Barclay's, and Bank of America.

Soon after, the company raised a war chest with a new listing on the prestigious NASDAQ, raising some $170 million. Baltimore Technologies then hit the acquisition highway. As Rooney told *Reuters:* "We want to be the gorilla in the marketplace. We're going to need a several billion dollar company with a thousand plus employees or more. What we want to do is position ourselves so that we can grow into whatever infrastructure we need."

Baltimore Technologies soon revealed its ambition to build an across-the-board e-security business. In January 2000, the company acquired CyberTrust Solutions, formerly a subsidiary of GTE. CyberTrust, which held a 15 percent share of the North American encryption market, gave Baltimore Technologies a vigorous new entry into that market, boosting its share to 20 percent and a solid third-place position. The deal, worth some $150 million in stock, also catapulted Baltimore Technologies' stock into the big leagues—where it became a symbol of the high-flying tech stocks of the period. Indeed, at one point the company was valued at more than £4.5 billion ($7.5 billion)—at a time when its revenues barely surpassed £23 million, and it continued operating at a loss. The company's soaring stock price gave it a brief run in the London exchange's prestigious FTSE-100 index.

The CyberTrust acquisition was followed quickly by several more as Baltimore branched out beyond its PKI core to transform itself into a full-service e-security group. In March 2000, the company acquired 72.5 percent of the sales agency that had been handling its products in Japan, NSJ Corp., in a deal worth ¥2.67 billion (£20 million). The purchase made Baltimore Technologies the number two e-security company in Japan and gave it a strong position in other Asian markets as well. The company changed the name of its new subsidiary to Baltimore Technologies Japan.

In September 2000, Baltimore Technologies struck again, now acquiring Content Technologies, of the United Kingdom, in a deal worth more than £700 million in Baltimore stock. The acquisition of Content—which posted just £16 million in 1999—gave Baltimore that company's suite of MIMEsweeper software, extending its operations into such lucrative areas as

Key Dates:

1976: Baltimore Technologies is formed as a technology consulting firm.
1988: Zergo Holdings is founded.
1995: Zergo lists on the London Stock Exchange AIM board.
1996: Fran Rooney and investor group acquire Baltimore Technologies.
1999: Zergo acquires and renames itself Baltimore Technologies.
2001: Rooney resigns as company CEO.

antivirus protection and data and database protection. The new software was promptly renamed Baltimore MIMEsweeper.

Baltimore Technologies' next big move came in October 2000 when it announced that it had acquired Toronto, Canada's Nevex Software Technologies, a developer of Internet-based secure access and authorization management software. That company had been founded only in 1999, by the same group of developers who had been behind the launch of one of the earliest firewall systems, produced by Border Network Technologies. The deal, for £29 million in stock, helped complete Baltimore Technologies' e-security software offerings in its core IT and corporate servers market. More importantly, it helped Baltimore Technologies capture the leading e-security spot in the United States.

Baltimore Technologies paused to catch its breath at the beginning of 2001. The collapse of the high-tech stock boom, starting in March 2000, had decimated the company's share price. By April 2001, the company was valued at just £400 million. Rooney, who had been vaunted as one of the great success stories of the ''new'' economy, now found himself under pressure. The company also was forced to issue profit warnings, as its losses for the first quarter of the year topped £100 million, compared with just £10 million in the year before. The company attempted to slow its mounting losses with the announcement of a restructuring resulting in the elimination of some 250 jobs in May of that year. Meantime, the slump in the Internet-based economy continued to cut into Baltimore Technologies' order books.

By July 2001, the company found itself denying persistent rumors that it had become the target for takeovers or that it was putting itself up for sale. At that time, Rooney resigned from his position as CEO. A temporary CEO, Paul Sanders, was installed while the company continued to shop for a new leader. Yet many in the industry forecast that Baltimore Technologies now presented a strong potential for acquisition—possibly by a giant company, such as Microsoft, desiring to take control of the

company's strong e-security portfolio. Baltimore Technologies refused to close out any options. As Sanders told the *Guardian:* ''We haven't had any formal approaches but, given our profile as a plc and our product, I'm sure people will be interested.'' Among those known to be interested was Chantilley Corporation Ltd., of the United Kingdom, which already had made two overtures to the beleaguered Irish company—most likely as an easy means to gain its own public listing.

Principal Subsidiaries

Baltimore Technologies Limited; Baltimore Technologies (U.K.) Limited; Baltimore Technologies Holdings Limited (U.K.); Data Innovation Benelux BV (Netherlands); Baltimore Technologies BV (Netherlands); Baltimore Technologies Pty Limited (Australia); Certificates Australia Pty Limited (Australia); Baltimore Technologies Inc. (U.S.A.); Baltimore Technologies KK (Japan); Baltimore Limited (Hong Kong); Baltimore Technologies AB (Sweden); Baltimore Technologies EURL (France); Content Technologies Holdings Limited (U.K.); Content Technologies Limited (U.K.); Content Technologies SAS (France); Content Technologies GmbH (Germany); Baltimore Technologies Japan KK; Content Technologies KK (Japan); Baltimore Technologies PTE (Singapore); Content Technologies (Asia/Pacific) Pty; Limited (Australia); Baltimore Technologies Inc. (Canada); CyberTrust Solutions Inc. (U.S.A.); Content Technologies Inc. (U.S.A.).

Principal Competitors

Certicom Corp.; Crypto AG; enCommerce; Entrust Inc.; International Business Machines Corporation; iD2; IAIK; nCipher; Network Associates, Inc.; Phaos; RSA Data Security, Inc.; Sonera SmartTrust; Sun Microsystems, Inc.; Symantec Inc.; Verisign, Inc.

Further Reading

Casey, John, ''Rooney Balks at Challenge,'' *Guardian,* July 11, 2001.
Dandy, Emma, ''Baltimore Needs Radical Surgery—Rooney,'' *Independent,* July 6, 2001, p. 14.
Kane, Frank, ''Rooney Reads the Runes,'' *Observer,* April 15, 2001.
Lyons, Madeleine, ''Baltimore U.S. Deal Makes Firm a Major Player,'' *Irish Times,* January 18, 2000.
McGrath, ''Brendan, Baltimore Set to Return to FTSE,'' *Irish Times,* September 6, 2000.
Monaghan, Elain, ''Baltimore Aims to Be Acquisitive 'Gorilla,' '' *Reuters Business Report,* September 29, 1999.
Parkin, Chris, ''BALTIMORE Takeover Rumours Dismissed,'' *Mirror,* July 17, 2001, p. 41.
Roe, David, ''Baltimore Technologies Founder Rooney Resigns,'' *Irish Times,* July 10, 2001.

—M. L. Cohen

Bass Pro Shops, Inc.

<table>
<tr><td>

2500 E. Kearney
Springfield, Missouri 65898
U.S.A.
Telephone: (417) 873-5000
Toll Free: (800) 227-7776
Fax: (417) 831-2802
Web site: http://www.basspro.com

Private Company
Incorporated: 1971
Employees: 7,900
Sales: $950 million (2000 est.)
NAIC: 451111 Sporting Goods Stores; 454110 Mail-
   Order Houses

</td></tr>
</table>

Bass Pro Shops, Inc. is a multifaceted sporting equipment retailer, with a special emphasis on fishing, hunting, and camping. Operating out of Springfield, Missouri, the company is best known for its Outdoor World stores, massive facilities that combine a large selection of goods with amusement features, such as target ranges, fish tanks, restaurants, and video arcades. The original Outdoor World is located in Springfield and has become the single most popular tourist destination in the state of Missouri, attracting approximately four million visitors each year. Nearby Branson, Missouri, a mini-Nashville with two dozen country music theaters, draws more tourists overall, many of whom make the pilgrimage to Springfield to visit what has become the Mecca of fishing and hunting. Bass Pro Shops also runs a major mail-order business, which originally provided the platform for the company's entry into megastores. Its private label sporting goods are also distributed to other sporting goods stores through its American Rod & Gun wholesale operation. In addition, Bass Pro Shops owns Tracker Marine, one of the largest U.S. boat manufacturers. In recent years Tracker has extended its brand to a line of recreational land vehicles to serve the fishing and hunting market. Moreover, the company runs an upscale, 850-acre resort, Big Cedar Lodge, in Missouri's Ozark Mountains. Through one of its corporate partners, Gaylord Entertainment, Bass Pro Shops is able to expand its brand awareness through radio and television programs, as well as a nationally available magazine.

Formation of Bass Pro Shops: 1971

The founder of Bass Pro Shops, John L. Morris, grew up in Springfield, and as a boy fished with his father and uncles in the Ozark area lakes, which featured some of the best bass fishing in the world. While earning a business degree from local Drury College he competed in one of the early tournaments of the fledgling pro bass fishing tour. He learned that the specialized lures used by the top pros, as well as high-tech tackle, were not available in the stores. He asked a local retailer, Gibsons Discount Store, which boasted the area's largest fishing department, to stock some of these items, but the manager refused. In addition to a love for fishing, Morris also gained an entrepreneurial spirit from his father. The elder Morris had started out running a service station and restaurant in Springfield, and later operated a number of Brown Derby Liquor stores and some dry cleaning shops. Rebuffed by Gibsons, Morris turned to his father and asked if he could have space in one of the Brown Derby liquor stores in order to sell fishing merchandise. Despite the fact that his father had already tried selling bait out of the stores, and still had boxes of lures stored in the basement to remind him of the failed attempt, Morris finally received permission. His father also co-signed a $10,000 inventory loan. After graduating from college in 1971 Morris took to the road with a trailer, buying up regional fishing lures until he ran out of cash. With eight feet of shelf space in one of his father's Brown Derby liquor stores, he then began to sell his lures to local fishermen. Because his focus was providing gear for bass fishermen, he named his business Bass Pro Shops. Morris knew his market because he was an avid Bass fisherman himself and had talked to his customers about what they wanted. He also traveled the tournament fishing circuit to keep tabs on the kinds of lures the winners were using.

Although selling beer and spirits remained the primary business of the liquor store, Morris continued to add to his supply of baits and fish. Business expanded by word of mouth, and soon customers were calling to buy over the telephone, asking if he could send his products to them by United Parcel Service. This development prompted Morris to enter the mail-order business.

He bought mailing lists of potential customers and then compiled a catalog that featured some 1,500 items in 180 pages. In 1971 he mailed his catalog to 10,000 names in 20 states. Using the basement of his father's warehouse as a distribution center, Morris's mail-order business took off. The catalog grew in size and increased in distribution, soon gaining a reputation as the bass fisherman's Bible. It would one day exceed 400 pages in length and be mailed to some four million people throughout the world. In later years a hunting catalog, RedHead hunting, would be added. More than 500 customer service representatives would eventually be hired to accept orders 24 hours a day, 365 days a year.

Morris was fortunate that bass fishing was surging in popularity, but he was also smart enough to let his business evolve naturally. Because he had a catalog business, he could arrange to have a large number of products manufactured as exclusives. To meet the demand for these products, in 1975 Morris set up the American Rod & Gun wholesale operation to distribute Bass Pro brand merchandise to independent sporting goods stores. Against all advice, Morris also began to sell boats through his catalog, which led to his entry into the boat building business. He found a niche in boats because, again, he knew what his customer wanted. From personal experience he understood how difficult it was to buy a complete fishing rig. After buying the boat the customer had to then pick out an appropriate motor and trailer. Anything beyond that, like a trolling motor or electronic fish finder, had to be purchased separately. Morris had a simple but elegant insight: sell an entire boat package that included the boat, motor, and trailer, as well as extras such as trolling motor, fish finders, built-in coolers, and padded seats. Overall the package offered the kind of value the customers were looking for. The marketing concept was simple but effective: "Just add water."

Introduction of Fishing Boat Packages: 1978

Morris named his new business Tracker Marine. The first aluminum boats he offered in 1978 were made by a Louisiana company. Meanwhile, his Trailstar Trailers were constructed in Springfield until a trailer plant opened in Nixa, Missouri, in 1980. As business picked up he opened his own boat manufacturing plant in Lebanon, Missouri, in 1982. Tracker rapidly added to its product mix. The first pontoon boat package was introduced in 1983, the first fiberglass boat package in 1985. Tracker expanded beyond fresh water vessels in 1987 when it acquired the SeaCraft saltwater boat line. In 1988 it acquired the Nitro performance bass boat line, then two years later offered Nitro boat packages on a nationwide basis. In the 1990s Tracker would also become involved in the houseboat business, acquiring Myacht Houseboats. Although precise sales figures were not available from the privately held company, in the early 1990s analysts ranked Tracker among the top ten boat builders in the United States.

Morris involved two of his sisters in the Bass Pro Shops business. Carol did advertising work for the company through an agency she headed, while Susie became an executive vice-president. Suzie, in fact, was with Morris when he received a major dose of the inspiration that would lead to the creation of Outdoor World. Although the catalog business was thriving in the late 1970s, Morris still felt the need for a showroom where customers could actually handle the merchandise. He and several employees began to scout retail operations in preparation of building a Bass Pro Shops store. He and Suzie were especially impressed by their visit to the hugely popular L.L. Bean store in Freeport, Maine. "I said, heck, if they can draw all those people to the middle of nowhere," Morris told the press, "we can do that in Springfield."

Adjacent to the Bass Pro Shops catalog operations in Springfield, Outdoor World opened in 1981. Although the focus of the superstore in the beginning was its breadth of selection and ability to service a range of needs, Outdoor World began to offer more and more entertainment features (as it also continued to expand in size), eventually taking up nearly 300,000 square feet. Again, it was a matter of paying attention to what the customers wanted. Morris used an old storage tank to create a fishing pond that could also be used for fish-feeding shows, something he first witnessed at Chicago's Shedd Aquarium. He added a pistol and rifle range, which he knew were features in German and Swedish sporting goods stores. Outdoor World became an extension of Morris's desire for his customers to have fun, as well as to sell them the equipment they wanted. In addition to fishing gear, Outdoor World offered hunting equipment, camping supplies, boats, and golf and general sporting equipment. It also featured service departments, book and gift stores, a cutlery shop, and a wildlife art gallery. Outdoor World essentially grew into a sportsman's version of Disneyland, featuring a four-story high waterfall, a two-story indoor cabin, a 100-yard-long indoor rifle range, 25-yard ranges for handguns and archery, a taxidermy shop, countless stuffed animals and mounted fish adorning the interior, a trout stream that meandered through the store, a barber shop, and a 250-seat auditorium and conference room. Promoted in the Bass Pro Shops catalog, Outdoor World began to attract visitors from around the world, eclipsing even St. Louis's better known Gateway Arch as a tourist destination.

Opening of Big Cedar Lodge Resort: 1988

The megastore concept was clearly a winner, but it would also be an expensive gamble to open other units, so Morris was cautious about expansion. First, he became involved in the resort business. In 1988 Bass Pro Shops opened Big Cedar Lodge Resort located by Table Rock Lake in the Ozark Mountains. The property had originally been the vacation retreat in the early 1920s of two wealthy Missouri businessmen who were both friends and sportsmen: Jude Simmons, who made his money in real estate and manufacturing, and Harry Worman, one-time president of Frisco Railroad. On 300 acres of land they both built log mansions that would now be put to other uses. Simmons's home became the Devil's Pool restaurant, while Worman's home became the resort's registration building and gift shop. Simmons's garage was large enough to be converted into the Truman Smokehouse, a casual eatery. Big Cedar Lodge

Key Dates:

1971: John L. Morris establishes Bass Pro Shops.
1974: First catalog is mailed.
1975: American Rod & Gun wholesale operation is launched.
1977: Company starts selling boats through Tracker Marine.
1981: Original Outdoor World opens.
1982: Tracker Marine opens its own manufacturing plant.
1988: Big Cedar Lodge Resort, located in the Ozarks near Branson, Missouri, opens.
1995: First retail store outside of Missouri is opened.
1998: Tracker Marine begins to sell RV vehicles.
2001: New Outdoor World opens in Nashville, Tennessee.

World opened in the Dallas/Ft. Worth area, located across from a Mills mall and connected to an Embassy Suites hotel. At 200,000 square feet, the Texas store was still significantly smaller than the Springfield Outdoor World, yet it stocked almost the same number of items. Also in 1999 a Detroit-area Outdoor World opened, again serving as a mall anchor. Late in 1999 Bass Pro Shops decided to sell the land across from its Duluth, Georgia, Sportsman's Warehouse, electing to build a new and larger Outdoor World as part of a Mills mall under development in the area. From Mills's point of view, a Bass Pro Shop was a desired part of every new mall project. Although rollout of the concept was gathering momentum, Morris remained careful about not extending Bass Pro Shop too far, too quickly. Essentially he was expanding to prime fishing areas. In 2001 Bass Pro Shops opened an Outdoor World in Nashville, Tennessee, in conjunction with both of its partners, Mills and Gaylord. It also expanded to Charlotte, North Carolina; Cincinnati, Ohio; and the Maryland/Washington, D.C. area. In addition, a second Missouri store was added, located in the Mark Twain Center in St. Charles, Missouri.

With 15 showrooms, Bass Pro Shops was still looking to pursue judicious expansion. Many of the locations had become local tourist attractions, although not to the extent of the Springfield original, which remained by far the company's largest showroom. Morris seemed intent on maintaining the allure of the original site. He bolstered its appeal by opening a nearby Wildlife Museum in 1993. The museum was also a reflection of his personal commitment to the conservation of the outdoors. He created Dogwood Canyon, a 10,000-acre wilderness area located near Big Cedar Lodge. Bass Pro Shops also contributed millions of dollars to a number of nonprofit wildlife conservation organizations, earning Morris a number of honors. At the same time, Bass Pro Shops continued to grow its varied business interests. In 1998 Tracker Marine introduce a full line of RVs, travel trailers, slide-in pickup truck campers, and minimotorhomes. In 2000 it signed an agreement with Bluegreen Corp., which planned to build a timeshare resort adjacent to Big Cedar Lodge, amounting to some 300 vacation homes. Bass Pro Shops also looked to become a major Internet retailer, leveraging its brand to sell merchandise online. The only area of true concern for the company was the decline in the number of hunters in recent years. Studies also showed, however, that people who did hunt now hunted more often. Although Bass Pro Shops catered to hunters, the focus of the company had always been on fishing, and its efforts to pursue the full range of outdoor activities and sports in general appeared to bode well for its future. The more open question was whether Morris would take his company public in order to raise capital for even greater growth, or remain private and continue to pursue his own path without the close scrutiny of shareholders.

would encompass almost three times as much property as the original site and feature three lodges, as well as 81 private cabins. In addition to fishing, the resort offered water skiing, hiking, trail rides, cave explorations, and miniature golf. Big Cedar was expensive, with some cabins approaching $1,000 a night during the peak summer season, and attracted many celebrity guests, especially the country music stars that performed at nearby Branson.

To spread some of the risk in growing Bass Pro Shops, Morris began to form strategic partnerships, raising cash while keeping the company private. In 1992 Brunswick Corporation paid $25 million for a minority interest in Tracker Marine and thereby became the exclusive provider of engines, trolling motors, and other equipment for Tracker boats. In 1993 Morris sold a minority stake in Bass Pro Shops to Gaylord Entertainment Company for $60 million. A country music giant, Gaylord owned Country Music Television and The Nashville Network (TNN, which was later renamed The National Network to broaden its appeal). Through Gaylord, the company would be able to produce a syndicated radio show called ''Bass Pro Shops Outdoor World,'' which was not only heard in the United States, but throughout the world over more than 400 radio stations on the Armed Forces Radio Network. Through Gaylord, Bass Pro Shops was able to produce hunting and fishing television shows. Morris also aligned his company with the Mills Corporation, a Virginia mall developer, in anticipation of spreading the Outdoor World concept. In a similar vein, he also began to work with a Springfield-based hotel operator, John Q. Hammons, to combine Outdoor World outlets with Embassy Suite hotels.

The first retail venture outside of Springfield came in 1995 when Bass Pro Shops opened the 90,000-square-foot Sportsman's Warehouse in Duluth, Georgia. Morris also purchased an adjacent property with plans to open an Outdoor World should the initial property prove to be successful. That same year Bass Pro Shops purchased the 27,000-square-foot World Wide Sportsman store in Islamorada in the Florida Keys. The second true Outdoor World megastore, a 125,000-square-foot mall anchor, opened in the fall of 1997 outside of Chicago in Gurnee, Illinois. It was followed by a 160,000-square-foot Outdoor World located near Ft. Lauderdale, Florida. In 1999 an Outdoor

Principal Subsidiaries

American Rod & Gun; Big Cedar Lodge Resort; Dogwood Canyon; Tracker Marine.

Principal Competitors

Cabela's Inc.; The Orvis Company, Inc.; L.L. Bean, Inc.; MarineMax; Oshman's Sporting Goods; The Sports Authority; Travis Boats & Motors.

Further Reading

Backover, Andrew, ''Bass Pro Shops Ready to Open Huge Outdoor World Store in Grapevine, Texas,'' *Fort Worth Star-Telegram,* March 23, 1999.

Bridges, Toby, ''Bass Pro: A Transcendental Marketer,'' *Direct Marketing,* October 1992, p. 20.

Childress, William, ''Bass Pro Shops Reeling in the Customers,'' *St. Louis Post-Dispatch,* February 20, 1993, p. 3D.

Fass, Allison, ''A Joint Venture Hope to Tie the Product to the Entertainment and Create a Shopping Experience,'' *New York Times,* June 1, 2001, p. C7.

Kempner, Matt, ''Sporting Goods Entrepreneur Turned Hobby into a Business,'' *Atlanta Constitution,* September 25, 1994, p. G9.

McDowell, Edwin, ''A Successful Outfitter Ranges Beyond Its Territory,'' *New York Times,* March 20, 1999, p. 1.

Mitchell, Rick, ''A Showroom As Big As the Great Outdoors,'' *Houston Chronicle,* June 14, 1992, p. 1.

—Ed Dinger

BERKSHIRE HATHAWAY INC.

Berkshire Hathaway Inc.

1440 Kiewit Plaza
Omaha, Nebraska 68131
U.S.A.
Telephone: (402) 346-1400
Toll Free: (800) 800-3481
Fax: (402) 346-3375
Web site: http://www.berkshirehathaway.com

Public Company
Incorporated: 1889 as Berkshire Cotton Manufacturing
  Company
Employees: 45,000
Total Assets: $135.79 billion (2000)
Stock Exchanges: New York
Ticker Symbols: BRK.A; BRK.B
NAIC: 51111 Newspaper Publishers; 51113 Book
  Publishers; 524113 Direct Life Insurance Carriers;
  524126 Direct Property and Casualty Insurance
  Carriers (pt); 524130 Reinsurance Carriers; 551112
  Offices of Other Holding Companies

Berkshire Hathaway Inc. is a holding company with an ever increasing number of subsidiaries engaged in a myriad of business activities. Originally in textiles, Berkshire's reach has extended to insurance, retailing, manufacturing, publishing, and banking. Run by the dynamic Warren Buffett and his partner Charles Munger, Berkshire has become synonymous with its legendary investment portfolio, which historically has garnered results far in excess of advances in the S&P 500 and other benchmark indices. Berkshire Hathaway Inc. and its subsidiaries are involved in several different businesses, the most significant of which is property, casualty, and auto insurance, both directly (GEICO) and through reinsurance (General Reinsurance Corporation). Noninsurance subsidiaries include the furniture retailers Nebraska Furniture Mart, R.C. Willey Home Furnishings, Star Furniture, and Jordon's Furniture; the fine jewelry retailers Borsheim's, Helzberg Diamond Shops, and Ben Bridge Jeweler; and footwear retailers H.H. Brown, Dexter, and Justin Brands. Berkshire's other businesses include publishing (the *Buffalo News, World Book, Childcraft*); manufacturing (See's Candies, Campbell Hausfeld, Kirby, Fechheimer Brothers Company); and interior decorating supplies (paint and stain manufacturer Benjamin Moore, carpet manufacturer Shaw Industries). Investing through its insurance subsidiaries, Berkshire often buys major shares of other publicly traded companies (American Express, Capital Cities/ABC, Coca-Cola, Gillette, The Washington Post Company, and Wells Fargo). Its chairman, Warren Buffett, is renowned for his expertise in selecting stocks with hidden appeal and staying power.

Humble Beginnings: 1889 Through the 1940s

Berkshire Hathaway Inc. began as a textile company, incorporated as Berkshire Cotton Manufacturing Company in Massachusetts in 1889. In 1929 several other New England textile manufacturers with much common ownership—Valley Falls Company, Coventry Company, Greylock Mills, and Fort Dummer Mills—merged into the company, which was then renamed Berkshire Fine Spinning Associates. This operation accounted for about 25 percent of the fine cotton textile production in the United States.

The glory years of the New England textile industry were numbered. The Great Depression of the 1930s contributed to its decline, as did competition from the South and overseas. Wages were lower in the South, and Southern workers had fewer alternatives than New Englanders for working in the textile mills. Further, market factors favored the coarser types of goods produced in the South, while wage differentials between the United States and foreign competition were often significant.

The New England textile business recovered somewhat during World War II, thanks to military demand for its products, and had a similar brief recovery during the Korean conflict. Still, the industry declined again after each of these upswings.

Diversification: 1950s–60s

In 1955 Berkshire Fine Spinning merged with Hathaway Manufacturing Company, a New Bedford, Massachusetts textile maker dating back to 1888. The resulting company, Berkshire Hathaway Inc., had more than 10,000 employees and

Company Perspectives:

Although our form is corporate, our attitude is partnership. Charlie Munger and I think of our shareholders as owner-partners, and of ourselves as managing partners. (Because of the size of our shareholdings we are also, for better or worse, controlling partners.) We do not view the company itself as the ultimate owner of our business assets but instead view the company as a conduit through which our shareholders own the assets.

Charlie and I hope that you do not think of yourself as merely owning a piece of paper whose price wiggles around daily and that is a candidate for sale when some economic or political event makes you nervous. We hope you instead visualize yourself as a part owner of a business that you expect to stay with indefinitely, much as you might if you owned a farm or apartment house in partnership with members of your family. For our part, we do not view Berkshire shareholders as faceless members of an ever-shifting crowd, but rather as co-venturers who have entrusted their funds to us for what may well turn out to be the remainder of their lives.

The evidence suggests that most Berkshire shareholders have indeed embraced this long-term partnership concept.
   —Warren Buffett, chairman and CEO

nearly six million square feet of plant space, but its financial performance was dismal. Berkshire Hathaway closed its extensive operations in Adams, Massachusetts, in 1958, and the same year sold its curtain plant in Warren, Rhode Island, to Pilgrim Curtain Company. The company recovered a bit the following year; a contract negotiated between Berkshire and its unionized employees in 1959 marked the first wage increase for New England textile workers since 1956.

By late 1959 and into 1960, the company was operating profitably and had a backlog of unfilled orders. Depressed conditions returned quickly, however, and in 1961 Berkshire cut its work week to four days at several plants and showed a loss for the year. In 1962 the company closed three plants in Rhode Island and showed even greater losses, due to depressed prices for its products. The financial hemorrhaging continued into the mid-1960s, despite cuts in Berkshire's workforce and an extensive plant modernization. In 1965 came a major change in the company's management: a partnership led by investor Warren Buffett had purchased enough stock to control the company, and in a resulting dispute Seabury Stanton, a 50-year Berkshire employee, resigned as president. Kenneth V. Chace, a vice-president who had been with the company 18 years, replaced Stanton. After Buffett gained control of Berkshire, its operations were gradually moved from New Bedford to Omaha, Nebraska, where Buffett was based.

Berkshire Hathaway was profitable in 1965 and 1966, but profits fell sharply as it began its 1967 fiscal year. The company was actively shopping for acquisitions to help it diversify, and in 1967 it entered the insurance business, buying National Indemnity Company and National Fire & Marine Insurance Company for a total of $8.5 million. Acquisition of the two Omaha-based companies, which primarily handled automobile

insurance, was expected to help Berkshire overcome the cyclical nature of the textile business. In 1968 the company made another significant acquisition, of Sun Newspapers, a group of Omaha-area weeklies. In 1969 it bought Illinois National Bank & Trust Company of Rockford. Buffett, who became Berkshire's chairman in 1969, tended to acquire companies whose management and products he liked, rather than buying companies with the intention of making major changes. Both Buffett's company and his reputation as an expert investor continued to grow for decades to come.

From Medium to Large: 1970–79

Berkshire Hathaway's expansion and diversification continued at a steady pace. During 1969 and 1970 it bought controlling interests in Blue Chip Stamps (which owned See's Candies, a chocolate maker and retailer) and Wesco Financial Corporation, a savings and loan operator. Berkshire's insurance operations grew with the formation of Cornhusker Casualty Company as part of the National Indemnity group in 1970 and Lakeland Fire and Casualty Company (later National Indemnity Company of Minnesota) also as part of that group, in 1971. In addition, in 1971, Berkshire acquired Home & Automobile Insurance Company (later National Liability and Fire Insurance Company) and in 1972 formed Texas United Insurance Company, which it eventually merged into National Indemnity. Four years later, in 1976, the National Fire & Marine subsidiary acquired its only wholly owned subsidiary, Redwood Fire & Casualty Insurance Company, and Berkshire began buying shares in GEICO (Government Employees Insurance Company).

In 1977 Berkshire continued to acquire related businesses, with the acquisition of Cypress Insurance Company and the formation of the Kansas Fire & Casualty Company. The same year, it made another move into the newspaper business by purchasing, through Blue Chip Stamps, the *Buffalo Evening News,* a six-day afternoon paper. The *News* competed against a morning paper with a Sunday edition, at a time when morning papers were outstripping evening papers in popularity. After the acquisition by Berkshire, the *News* increased competition by publishing a Sunday edition and within five years had bested its rival, the *Courier-Express,* which then went out of business.

Berkshire formed another insurance company, Continental Divide Insurance Company, in 1978. Through a merger with Diversified Retailing Company, Berkshire acquired two more insurers, Columbia Insurance Company and Southern Casualty Insurance Company, in 1978; Southern Casualty was later merged into National Indemnity. Even with Warren Buffett's growing reputation, not every company was eager to become part of Berkshire; CSE Corporation, the holding company for Civil Service Employees Insurance Company, turned down an informal takeover offer in 1979. Because Berkshire did not execute hostile takeovers, the acquisition was not pursued.

From Large to Gargantuan: 1980s

In 1980 Berkshire spun off Illinois National Bank & Trust, a move required by the Bank Holding Company Act of 1969. A year later the company sold Sun Newspapers to Chicago publisher Bruce Sagan and began work on a rather unheard of practice. The next year, 1982, Berkshire instituted an unusual corporate philanthropy program that won praise from shareholders by allowing them to direct a portion of the company's charitable contributions. With this policy, Buffett said he hoped to foster an "owner mentality" among shareholders. Shareholders responded enthusiastically, with more than 95 percent of eligible shareholders participating in each year since the program's inception. The amount directed to charities of their choice was $2 a share in 1981 (the figure rose to $6 a share by 1989). Buffett's own favorite causes included population control and nuclear disarmament.

During the early 1980s the textile business continued to languish and the insurance industry was hit by poor sales and price cutting. Berkshire's performance, however, was buoyed by the performance of its investment portfolio. Buying significant but noncontrolling blocks of stock in such companies as The Washington Post Company, Media General, and additional shares of GEICO Corporation, Berkshire's holdings grew in value by 21 percent in 1981—a year in which the Dow Jones Industrial Average declined by 9.2 percent—and earnings grew 23 percent per share.

In 1983 the 60 percent-owned Blue Chip Stamps merged with Berkshire Hathaway, the same year the company acquired 90 percent of the Nebraska Furniture Mart, a high-volume Omaha discount retailer and the largest U.S. home furnishings store founded by a Russian immigrant, Rose Blumkin. The Blumkin family retained management and the remaining ownership of the store. Buffett had been known to promote it during annual shareholder meetings, often running buses to the store (a practice continued to this day). Also in 1983, another insurance company, National Indemnity Company of Florida, was formed and added to the National Indemnity group.

The mid-1980s proved a heady time for Berkshire with several monumental agreements and the sad denouement of its textiles business. Early in 1985 the company participated in Capital Cities Communications' acquisition of the American Broadcasting Company (ABC). Buffett agreed to put up $517.5 million in financing for the deal and came out with an 18 percent share of the merged company, Capital Cities/ABC. The investment community saw the move as unusual for Buffett, who tended to hunt for undervalued companies and stay away from high-priced deals. Buffett, however, said he saw the investment climate changing, with good prospects for companies like television networks that had intangible assets rather than heavy investments in plants and equipment.

Then came the end of Berkshire Hathaway's money-losing textiles operation, which the company had tried to sell. After finding no buyer, Berkshire liquidated the conglomerate's originating business due to increasing lower-cost foreign competition. Buffett lauded the efforts of Kenneth Chace—who remained a Berkshire director—and of Garry Morrison, who had succeeded him as president of textiles. Buffett had kind words for the unionized textile workers as well, who had made only reasonable demands in view of the company's financial position.

Later the same year Berkshire agreed to acquire Scott & Fetzer Company, a Cleveland, Ohio-based diversified manufacturing and marketing company, for about $320 million. Scott & Fetzer's products included *World Book* and *Childcraft* encyclopedias and Kirby vacuum cleaners. At the same time Berkshire's insurance business underwent several changes. In a tight market for insurance, many commercial insurance buyers needed a financially stable company to underwrite large risks, so National Indemnity, Berkshire Hathaway's largest insurance company, advertised in an insurance trade publication its willingness to write property and casualty policies with a premium of $1 million or more. The advertisement produced an explosion in large-premium business for Berkshire; the company wrote $184.5 million in net premiums for large accounts from August 1985 through December 1986, compared with virtually no such business previously.

Also during 1985, Berkshire reached an agreement with Fireman's Fund Insurance Company, which allowed it a 7 percent participation in Fireman's business. John J. Byrne, an executive of GEICO—an insurer partly owned by Berkshire and that shared a long history with Buffett—left to become chairman of Fireman's Fund earlier in the year, and had arranged the deal. Another insurance move during 1985 was the establishment of Wesco-Financial Insurance Company by Berkshire's Wesco Financial Corporation subsidiary.

In 1986 Berkshire finalized its Scott & Fetzer deal and went on to acquire 84 percent of Fechheimer Bros. Company, a uniform manufacturer and distributor based in Cincinnati, Ohio. The next year, as the stock market continued the upward rise begun earlier in the decade, Buffett's policy of buying under-valued stocks and holding them for the long term paid off well. In August 1987 the *Wall Street Journal* reported that in the five years since the market's surge began, Berkshire's stock portfolio had grown in value by 748 percent, far surpassing the Dow Jones average (which increased 233.6 percent) and Standard & Poor's (S&P) 500 stock index (which gained 215.4 percent).

When the stock market crashed in October and wiped out the year's gains, Berkshire's portfolio weathered the storm and was up 2.8 percent—while the S&P 500 experienced a 2.5 percent decline. Just before the crash, Berkshire had bought $700 million worth of preferred stock (convertible to a 12 percent common stake) in Salomon Inc., the Wall Street investment firm whose fortunes were closely tied to the market. Even after the crash, however, Buffett expressed his confidence in Salomon's management and the investment's inherent value. Another major event of 1988 was the listing of Berkshire's stock on the New York Stock Exchange (NYSE). Although the stock had previously traded in the over-the-counter market, the move was designed to reduce transaction costs for shareholders.

Berkshire Hathaway became the highest-priced stock on the exchange, at about $4,300 a share, up from $12 a share when Buffett first bought the company. The price hit a high for the decade of more than $8,000 a share, but Buffett always encouraged buyers to be in the market for the long haul. He was not of the do-as-I-say-not-as-I-do school, for both he and Berkshire had proven themselves to be long-term shareholders in other companies, leading some to view Buffett as a protector against hostile takeovers. During 1989 the company bought significant shares of the Gillette Company, USAir Group, and Champion International Corporation, with each purchase widely interpreted as a defense against takeovers. Another major purchase was 6.3 percent or $1 billion worth of the Coca-Cola Company (making Berkshire Coke's second largest shareholder) and an 80 percent interest in Borsheim's, an Omaha jewelry store run by the Friedman family, relatives of the Nebraska Furniture Mart's Blumkins.

As Berkshire grew, so did Buffett's recognition and reputation as a no-nonsense businessman. To many, part of Buffett's charm was speaking his mind, even if his opinions were not always fashionable. Buffett's frank assessment of situations brought him both fans and foes, including when he pulled the Wesco Financial-owned Mutual Savings & Loan Association of Pasadena, California, out of the U.S. League of Savings Institutions in 1989. Buffett's move was in response to the League's lobby for more leniency during the federal bailout of the S & L industry, which Buffett likened to a ''mugging'' of taxpayers. Another of Buffett's business stratagems, to the chagrin of many corporate honchos, was his belief that executive compensation be tied to a company's performance, not its size.

The Mega-Conglomerate with a Down-Home Feel: 1990s

In the early 1990s Berkshire continued its trend of buying complementary companies and large blocks of stock, with the acquisition of H.H. Brown Shoe Company, 31.2 million shares of Guinness PLC, and 82 percent of Central States Indemnity in 1991, and Lowell Shoe Company and 14.1 percent of General Dynamics Corp. in 1992. In a related though somewhat surprising move in 1991, Buffett was appointed interim chairman of Salomon Inc. (in which the company still owned stock). After serving ten months and effecting a turnaround, Buffett was happily back at the helm of Berkshire Hathaway full-time, although both Buffett and Munger joined the board of the ailing USAir in 1992.

The following year, H.H. Brown added Dexter Shoe to its holdings, Buffett sold ten million shares of Capital Cities/ABC, and net earnings posted a spectacular surge from 1992's $407.3 million (down from 1991's $439.9 million) to $688.1 million. In 1994, Berkshire added major stock holdings of two companies to its portfolio (4.9 percent of Gannett Co., Inc. and 8.3 percent of PNC Bank Corp.) and Buffett admitted to two expensive gaffes: a $222.5 million faux pas from unloading ten million Cap Cities shares for $64 each when prices topped $85, and taking a $268.5 million writedown for its questionable USAir stock (both Buffett and Munger stepped down from the airline's board after a year). Though Buffett was perhaps too optimistic with USAir and a bit pessimistic about Cap Cities, neither setback made more than a tiny ripple in Berkshire's bottom line.

During the mid-1990s Berkshire Hathaway imperceptibly changed course from a strategic long-term investment conglomerate to one still very much interested in investing but leaning more heavily toward acquiring and actually operating these investment opportunities. As early as 1993 in its annual solicitation for attractive acquisitions, Berkshire had raised the stakes by including the statement, ''We would be likely to make an acquisition in the $2–3 billion range.'' By 1995, after the company acquired Helzberg's Diamond Shops and R.C. Willey Home Furnishings through stock swaps, the stakes had risen further—up to the $5 billion range. Meanwhile, as Berkshire's ''permanent four'' (Capital Cities/ABC, Coca-Cola, GEICO, and The Washington Post) lost a hint of their luster in 1995, the retailing segment more than offset this slip with Borsheim's, Kirby, Nebraska Furniture Mart, and Scott Fetzer (which posted exceptional numbers for the entire decade) exceeding expectations.

Late in 1995 Berkshire began the process of taking GEICO, the seventh largest auto insurer in the nation, private. Buffett's long history (45 years) with GEICO came full circle—after years of mentoring from Ben Graham and Lorimer Davidson, 43 years after selling his original 350 shares, and 15 years since Berkshire paid $45.7 million for a 33.3 percent stake of GEICO (which grew to 50 percent in the ensuing years)—the company spent $2.3 billion to make GEICO its own. With the GEICO deal completed in January 1996, Berkshire Hathaway's insurance segment mushroomed in both float and potential earnings, becoming more stalwart as the company's core segment. Number-wise, Berkshire finished 1995 with $29.9 billion in assets, a good-sized leap from the previous year's $21.3 billion, while Berkshire stock traded at $36,000 per share, more than three-and-a-half times higher than 1992's mere $10,000 a share.

News in 1996 was the planned issuance of $100 million in new Class ''B'' stock (the company's original shares were now designated Class "A" stock), valued at one-30th the price of its predecessor. The recapitalization was done in part, Buffett explained in the 1995 annual report, to discourage brokers from marketing unit trusts and seducing clients with the Berkshire name. Since most small investors found Berkshire's per share cost prohibitive, Buffett was attempting to make the company's stock available at a lower price without going through "expense-laden unit trusts" pretending to be Berkshire "clones." Yet what folks needed to remember, according to Buffett, was not *book* value, but *intrinsic* value. By measuring intrinsic value, an economic indicator rather than an accounting concept, investors had a better handle on worth and whether or not something was a good long-term risk. In these terms, Buffett hoped to double Berkshire's per-share intrinsic value (of Class A stock) every five years, which was still a rather daunting task.

The Late 1990s: No Dot Coms for Buffett

Buffett's interest in companies as acquisitions rather than investments increased in the late 1990s. Berkshire Hathaway upped its investment in the ice cream retailer International Dairy Queen in 1998 and Allied Domecq, owner of Dunkin' Donuts, in 1999. In 1998, however, the company made the uncharacteristic purchase of Executive Jet, an aviation company that initiated time-share purchases of private jets by businesses. The $725 million purchase brought Berkshire Hathaway into an emerging market, something Buffett had always avoided. In a more predictable move that year, Buffett added to Berkshire Hathaway's insurance group with the acquisition of General Reinsurance Corporation for $22 billion. One of the top three global property and casualty reinsurance companies, General Re had a reputation as one of the best-managed U.S. insurers.

The General Re purchase, however, contributed greatly to Berkshire Hathaway's poor performance in 1999. The transition to Berkshire Hathaway ownership was rocky: Ronald E. Ferguson, General Re's CEO, had kept the negotiations secret. Once the deal was signed, James Gustafson, General Re's president and COO, immediately resigned. Ferguson still had not replaced him by early 2000. In the leadership void, the company's underwriters seemed to be operating aimlessly. In addition, General Re was struck with a series of underwriting losses, combining to a total loss in 1999 of $1.6 billion. Buffett's hands-off management style left the subsidiary to find its own way through the muddle.

In part as a result of General Re's losses, net income for Berkshire Hathaway dropped from $2.8 billion to $1.6 billion in 1999. Earnings per share were cut in half. Criticism of Buffett and his investment philosophy became more common. His insistence on holding a stock for the long term was seen by some as stubborn and misguided when Coca-Cola stock hit a high of $87 a share in 1998. A sale at that point would have meant a $15.7 billion gain for Berkshire Hathaway; however, Buffett held the stock as it fell to $50 a share. Some questioned his continued resistance to high-tech and Internet stocks, which were driving a boom in the stock market. While the S&P 500 rose approximately 20 points in 1999, Berkshire Hathaway's per-share book value rose only 0.5 percent.

Buffett was, in large part, vindicated in 2000 as the high-tech bubble burst. The S&P 500 ended the year down approximately 9 percent, while Berkshire Hathaway's book value rose 6.5 percent. Buffett continued his strategy of acquiring low-tech companies in mundane, though proven, markets. In 2000 Berkshire Hathaway completed its acquisitions of the power company MidAmerican Energy and the "rent-to-rent" furniture company CORT Business Services. Berkshire also added to its insurance group with the purchase of U.S. Liability, to its jewelry retailers with Ben Bridge Jewelers, and to its manufacturers with boot and brick maker Justin Industries. Just before the end of the year, Berkshire purchased Benjamin Moore Paint for $1 billion cash and building products manufacturer Johns Manville Corporation for about $1.8 billion, although both deals were not completed until early 2001.

Back in 1973 Buffett warned that Bershire Hathaway's sheer bulk would prohibit it from continuing to grow at rates of 15 to 20 percent a year. That warning was premature. For the next decade, the company expanded at that rate, sometimes significantly more. As the century changed, however, the prediction was perhaps being realized. With sales of $34 billion, could Berkshire Hathaway keep up its phenomenal growth rate? Perhaps more important, how much longer would its 71-year-old mastermind, Warren Buffett, be around to lead the company?

Principal Subsidiaries

Acme Building Brands; Ben Bridge Jeweler; Benjamin Moore & Co.; Berkshire Hathaway Group; Berkshire Hathaway Homestates Companies; Borsheim's Fine Jewelry; Buffalo News; Central States Indemnity Company; CORT Business Services; Dexter Shoe Company; Executive Jet, Inc.; Fechheimer Brothers Company; FlightSafety International, Inc.; GEICO Corporation; General & Cologne Re Group; H.H. Brown Shoe Company, Inc.; Helzberg's Diamonds; International Dairy Queen, Inc.; Johns Manville Corporation; Jordan's Furniture; Justin Brands; Lowell Shoe Company; MidAmerican Energy Holdings Company; MiTek Inc.; National Indemnity Company; Nebraska Furniture Mart; Precision Steel Warehouse; RC Willey Home Furnishings; Scott Fetzer Company; See's Candies, Inc.; Shaw Industries; Star Furniture; United States Liability Insurance Group.

Principal Competitors

AIG; The Allstate Corporation; Andersen Group; AXA Financial; CIGNA Corporation; Citigroup Inc.; CNA Financial Corporation; GE Capital; The Hartford Insurance Group; Lincoln National Corporation; Loews Corporation; Munich Reinsurance; Prudential Insurance Company of America; State Farm Insurance Companies; Swiss Reinsurance Company; Washington Mutual, Inc.

Further Reading

Collins, Linda, J., "Berkshire's Buffett Sees More Competition Ahead," *Business Insurance,* May 7, 1990, p. 67.
Grant, Linda, "The $4 Billion Regular Guy," *Los Angeles Times,* April 7, 1991, p. 36.
Hagstrom, Robert G., Jr., *The Warren Buffett Way: Investment Strategies of the World's Greatest Investor,* New York: John Wiley & Sons, 1994.
Kilpatrick, Andrew, *Of Permanent Value: The Story of Warren Buffett,* Birmingham, Ala.: Andy Kilpatrick Publishing Empire, 1994.

——, *Warren Buffett: The Good Guy of Wall Street,* New York: Donald I. Fine, 1992.

Laing, Jonathan R., "The Collector: Investor Who Piled Up $100 Million in the '60s Piles Up Firms Today," *Wall Street Journal,* March 31, 1977.

Loomis, Carol J., "The Inside Story of Warren Buffett," *Fortune,* April 11, 1988.

Lowenstein, Roger, *Warren Buffett: The Making of an American Capitalist,* New York: Random House, 1995.

"The Sage Has Some Explaining to Do," *Business Week,* March 20, 2000, p. 100.

Sosnoff, Martin, "Larry the Tortoise, Warren the Hare," *Forbes,* January 27, 1997.

"Warren the Buffett You Don't Know," *Business Week,* July 5, 1999, p. 54.

—Trudy Ring
—updates: Taryn Benbow-Pfalzgraf,
Susan Windisch Brown

BIRKENSTOCK®

Birkenstock Footprint Sandals, Inc.

8171 Redwood Boulevard
Novato, California 94945
U.S.A.
Telephone: (415) 892-4200
Toll Free: (800) 487-9255
Fax: (415) 899-1324
Web site: http://www.birkenstock.com

Private Company
Incorporated: 1972
Employees: 230
Sales: $95 million (2000 est.)
NAIC: 42234 Footwear Wholesalers; 44821 Shoe Stores
   (Retail)

Birkenstock Footprint Sandals, Inc. is the primary U.S. distributor for Birkenstock Original Contoured Footbed products made by Germany's Birkenstock Orthopädie GmbH. The Birkenstock family of Germany has a long history in the shoe-making trade. Throughout the first half of the 20th century, the company marketed orthopedic shoe inserts. In the 1960s, Birkenstock used the principles behind these products to create a homey-looking sandal, designed with comfort foremost in mind. After these shoes were introduced to the United States in the late 1960s, they gained popularity with hippies and academics and were sold mainly in health food stores before reaching a mass market in the late 1980s. In 2001 Birkenstock was selling sandals, clogs, shoes, and boots in over 400 styles, colors, or materials to men, women, and children. Top fashion designers in the United States and Europe use Birkenstocks in their shows emphasizing the latest trends. Specialized Birkenstocks are sold to podiatrists, other health professionals, sports enthusiasts, computer workers, and others in niche markets. Birkenstock Footprint Sandals, also known as Birkenstock USA, sells its products in company-owned stores in San Francisco and Berkeley, California; company-owned mall outlet stores in Gilroy, California, Wrentham, Massachusetts, and Orlando, Florida; over 160 licensed stores; and over 3,500 retail shoe stores and department stores, including Nordstrom, REI, Parisian, and Macy's.

German Roots of Birkenstock Products

Birkenstock traces its roots to the late 18th century, when a German cobbler named Johann Adam Birkenstock, who was born in 1754, was first registered as a "subject and shoemaker" in the church archives of Langenbergheim, a town in the duchy of Hesse, Germany. By the end of the 19th century, Konrad Birkenstock, a descendant, owned two shoe stores in Frankfort, the capital of Hesse. These stores would become the foundation of the modern Birkenstock businesses.

Konrad Birkenstock had the inspiration that would form the basis for his family's business for the next hundred years. At the time, shoes were made with flat soles, despite the fact that the bottom of the human foot is curved. Birkenstock realized that a sole curved to complement the shape of the foot would be more comfortable than a flat surface. In 1897, he designed the first Birkenstock contoured shoe last, a tool used in shoe-making, to help his cobblers make customized footwear for patrons.

On the strength of this innovation, Konrad Birkenstock began to spread the word of his new kind of shoe. He gave frequent talks to other leading members of the shoemaker's guild, explaining his fully contoured footbed. Birkenstock traveled throughout Germany promoting his new idea, and licensed other cobblers to produce shoes made with his technique. By the start of the 20th century, he had moved beyond the borders of his native country, traveling to Austria and Switzerland as well.

By 1902, however, the popularity of custom-made shoes had begun to wane, as factory-manufactured footwear began to be more widely distributed. Adapting the essence of his idea for this new and growing market, Konrad Birkenstock developed flexible, contoured arch supports, which could be inserted into mass-produced shoes to make them more comfortable. Birkenstock's arch supports, which bent to accommodate the foot, differed from the other supports on the market, which were made of unyielding metal. With the rise of mass-produced shoes, the Birkenstock family business moved away from the crafting of custom-designed shoes to concentrate on the production of shoe inserts.

In 1908, Birkenstock pushed forward with the foot support when he developed his own substance and built molding presses to manufacture the flexible orthopedic insert. Four years later,

---

Company Perspectives:

Our purpose is to share our heartfelt belief that comfortable, healthy footwear contributes to happiness and well-being. Through our distribution of high quality footwear, we strive to create positive, harmonious relationships with employees, customers, vendors and the environment, emphasizing honesty and integrity in all we do. Within our company, our goals are to provide an atmosphere that stimulates growth and creativity among employees and to reward and encourage contributions.

---

the firm continued its technological innovation when it created a new method for using rubber, a material just beginning to be developed, in shoe inserts. In 1913, Konrad Birkenstock's son Carl joined the family firm, insuring that continuity in the company's activities would be possible. In the wake of Carl's arrival, Konrad Birkenstock committed the bulk of his family's considerable assets to the research and development of rubber as a material for foot supports.

In the same year that Birkenstock undertook these efforts, Germany entered World War I. The company's contribution to the war was the design and manufacture of orthopedic shoes to be worn by wounded soldiers in a large military hospital in Frankfort. As a result of these activities, Birkenstock's products came to the attention of the doctor in charge of the hospital, who praised his efforts and encouraged him to market his orthopedic inserts more widely. In 1915, Carl Birkenstock began to travel throughout Germany, introducing the family's products to new buyers.

Two years after the end of World War I, a second Birkenstock brother, Heinrich, entered the family business. Though Germany's economy suffered following the war, the Birkenstock business thrived. The family opened a branch in Vienna, the capital of Austria, in 1923, and soon expanded its distribution to countries across Europe, selling orthopedic inserts in Austria, Switzerland, France, Italy, Belgium, Czechoslovakia, Holland, Luxembourg, Denmark, Sweden, and Norway. To accommodate this expanded customer base, Birkenstock opened a larger factory in the town of Friedberg, in Hesse. When demand for the Birkenstock product necessitated even greater manufacturing capacity, the company added night shifts at the factory.

The late 1920s and early 1930s saw the company make many changes and additions to its product line. In 1926 and again in 1935, Birkenstock expanded its line of footbeds, adding different widths to better fit the foot and to accommodate fashionable shoes. In 1937, Birkenstock further altered the footbed, adding a "ring," which it patented, that allowed the insert to be easily adjusted to fit each foot. By 1928, Birkenstock's success had attracted the notice of its competitors, and other companies began to market non-metallic arch supports. For the first time, the company had competition for its products.

With the start of the 1930s, Birkenstock expanded its education and promotion efforts beyond people who made shoes to the public itself. The company published 70,000 copies of "The

Foot and its Treatment," a heavily illustrated pamphlet of 50 pages, in an effort to inform customers about the company's theories of orthopedics. Two years later, in 1932, Birkenstock stepped up its education efforts when it began to offer training seminars and lectures to orthotic appliance sellers in most European countries. These sessions lasted a week, and included more than 5,000 people in the mid-1930s.

Germany's defeat in World War II changed but did not seriously disrupt Birkenstock's development. With the coming of peace in 1945, the company transferred its operations from the Frankfort area in Hesse, to the town of Bad Honnef on the Rhine. Innovation and education continued apace; in 1946 the company introduced a toe-free insert and in 1947 it began to distribute a pamphlet for shoe sellers titled "Footorthotics System Birkenstock," with 112 pages and 55 illustrations. In 1950, Konrad Birkenstock, the creator of the flexible footbed and the company's driving force for half a century, died at the age of 77.

The decade following Konrad Birkenstock's death saw a number of changes in the venerable company. In 1956, Birkenstock introduced an insole made of shaped foam that was created through thermoplastic compression. Two years earlier, in 1954, a new generation of Birkenstocks had joined the family firm, when Karl Birkenstock, Carl Birkenstock's son, came aboard. Although his father envisioned the company's future exclusively in terms of orthopedic shoe inserts, the younger Birkenstock had more ambitious plans. He hoped to create a shoe that provided all of the benefits of walking barefoot. To do this, he experimented, combining his grandfather Konrad's techniques of flexible, contoured arch support, with his own understanding of how the foot works and moves.

Within a decade of Karl Birkenstock's arrival at the family firm, the company had re-entered the shoe business. In 1964, it began to manufacture a shoe whose design was based on the shape and function of the human foot. The new Birkenstock shoe was built from the inside out, starting with an orthopedically-based footbed, which gave firm support to the bottom of the foot. The company's goal was to make the wearer feel that he or she was walking on a surface that would yield, such as wet sand. In order to accomplish this, Birkenstock designed a footbed made of cork, latex, and jute, which absorbed shocks to the foot. The company also added a raised toe bar, to facilitate the instinctive gripping motion of the toes, and a heel cup, to cradle the heel and better distribute the body's weight. In 1965, Karl Birkenstock attached this sole to two simple leather straps to create a clunky, but comfortable, orthopedic sandal.

Margot Fraser and the Origins of Birkenstock Footprint Sandals

One year after Birkenstock began to market its new sandals, the shoes came to the attention of Margot Fraser, a German-born dress designer who had immigrated to the United States. While she was vacationing at a spa in Bavaria, workers suggested that she try Birkenstock sandals to ease her chronic foot problems. Several months later, her foot pain greatly improved. Fraser was hooked, and she believed that other American women would also want an alternative to the uncomfortable high-fashion shoes typically marketed to women. She spread the word about Birkenstock sandals to her friends, bringing them shoes from Germany. Finally, along with her husband, a cookware importer, Fraser arranged with Karl Birkenstock to market his sandals in the United States.

When Fraser approached the owners of shoe stores about selling Birkenstock sandals in their stores, she was universally rebuffed. Repeatedly, shoe sellers assured her that no American woman would ever wear shoes that ugly, regardless of how comfortable they might be. Seeking alternate marketing channels, Fraser turned to the health food industry. "We had to sell to people with a different vision," Fraser later recounted to *People* magazine. "It was very tough at first," she told the *New York Times*. "But it was when I went to a health fair, and people there wanted them that I got a start. They were interested in fitness." At a trade show, Fraser sold her first pair of sandals to a woman who was limping among the booths, holding her high-heeled shoes in her hands. After trying the Birkenstock sandals, this woman began wearing them constantly and also bought several pairs to sell in her health food store.

Fraser set up business in her home in Santa Cruz, California, using her garage as a warehouse. Sales of the sandals through health food stores increased, and the shoes gained a reputation for their comfort. In addition, Fraser sold the shoes through the mail. She bought shoes directly from the factory, often in lots of 20 pairs, and had them shipped parcel post to her house.

In 1971, Fraser moved her business out of her house, leasing a small office on top of a San Rafael, California, health food store for $25 a month. In 1972 she incorporated her company under the name Birkenstock Footprint Sandals, Inc., and formally became the sole U.S. distributor of Birkenstock products. Fraser hired a part-time bookkeeper and packer. "We made enough money to survive," she later told the *Sacramento Bee*. "We were pinching our pennies, but we managed." By the end of that year, the company had sold 10,000 pairs of shoes to the U.S. market, promoting the product through homemade fliers, small ads in health food publications, and booths at trade fairs and shoe shows. Often, the shoes were first bought by the owners of health food stores, who had to stand behind a cash register all day. With their recommendation, the popularity of the shoes spread through word of mouth.

While Fraser was working to sell Birkenstock products in the United States, the German parent firm was furthering its efforts to develop its line. In 1966, the company introduced a special paper, on which a customer's footprint could be marked, for a better fitting shoe. In the following year, Birkenstock developed and began to use "Birko-Cork," a natural thermopliable product for use in footbeds. Two years later, the company also began to sell insoles that massaged the feet in its "noppy-fit" sandals.

During the 1970s the popularity of Birkenstock footwear exploded, as the shoes became associated with the Bohemian lifestyle popular with young people. In the United States, sales of Birkenstock sandals grew dramatically, and the company introduced a number of new styles. In 1970, a sandal called "Roma," with a strap that encircled the heel, was sent to stores. In the following year, "Arizona," designed with two classic wide straps, was introduced. Overall, there were 12 different varieties of the basic Birkenstock shoe, all sold in natural earth tones.

In Germany, the Birkenstock company expanded its production facilities in order to meet the new demand. The company leased a factory in the town of St. Katharinen that housed punching presses to cut out the leather pieces for its shoes in 1974. Two years later, Birkenstock introduced "Birko Foam," yet another new material for use in its shoes, and in 1978, the company began to use superelastic light material to make new specially contoured soles.

At the start of the 1980s, Birkenstock modernized its production processes further, installing computerized last-making machinery to make the molds for shoes. Two years later, Birkenstock introduced its first significant variation on the basic sandal, the thong-sandal, which it began to sell in five different styles. In the next two years, the company received nearly 40 different design protection rights from the German Patent Office for its products, including two developed for the thong sandal. In 1984 Birkenstock opened a larger warehouse for its products.

Despite the innovation of the thong sandal, sales of Birkenstock shoes began to wane in the early 1980s, as fashions shifted away from the functional and down-to-earth. We were struggling with the image . . . that we were a hippie shoe," Fraser later told *Forbes*. "We wanted to change that." In 1989, her company ditched its old, chunky logo, replacing it with something sleeker. In addition, the company joined with Birkenstock's German designers to increase the number of styles and colors offered to customers. Gradually, the number of Birkenstock sandal styles available grew to 125, with colors such as mango, moss, fuchsia, and cognac. In addition, Birkenstock sandals for children were introduced under the name Birkikids.

Developments in the 1990s and Beyond

In 1990, Birkenstock began to sell its shoes through a glossy mail-order catalogue, which it updated every six months. Soon other catalog merchants, such as L.L. Bean and the Sharper Image, were marketing the company's wares. By the early 1990s, popularity of Birkenstock sandals was once again soaring, as baby boomers aged and comfort became chic. In 1992, Birkenstock purchased a large warehouse to distribute its products, which were shipped from Germany to Houston in containers, and then moved by rail to Novato, California. This facility used a mile of conveyor belts and a computerized barcode inventory system to control stock after a $1 million renovation. From this warehouse, shoes were sent to more than 90 Birkenstock specialty stores, large department stores, and other vendors.

Meanwhile, Birkenstock Footprint Sandal's financial performance kept improving. Sales increased 30 percent annually from 1988 to 1990, then jumped another 44 percent from 1990 to 1991, aided by an increased selection of footwear and celebrities including Madonna and Harrison Ford buying Birkenstocks.

In 1992 Mary Scott and Howard Rothman wrote a chapter about Birkenstock in their book *Companies with a Conscience*. They emphasized that founder Margot Fraser's open communication style and caring about her employees, vendors, and customers had been the key from the beginning. For example, Melanie Grimes, Birkenstock Footprint's first licensed retailer, said, ''I started selling Birkenstocks from the closet of my college dorm in 1972. When I eventually opened a store of my own . . . the shipment arrived with a letter from Margot saying 'If the shoes are not for you and your customers, please send them back for a full refund.' '' Keeping the letter as a reminder of how Fraser had built their business relationship, Grimes in 1992 had three Birkenstock licensed stores in or near Seattle.

Birkenstock worked with M.J. Feet, the name of Melanie Grimes' retail stores, when the store decided in 1996 to use the Internet to sell Birkenstocks. The retailer made sure corporate headquarters approved the items sold online and how they would be marketed.

In the late 1990s, Birkenstock Footprint Sandals received several awards or honors. *Footwear News* in 1997 inducted founder Margot Fraser into the Footwear Hall of Fame. *Working Woman Magazine* in May 1998 rated the company by revenue as number 140 in its list of the Top 500 Women-Owned Businesses. Margaret and Phyllis A. Katz in their 1997 book *The Feminist Dollar: The Wise Woman's Buying Guide* included Birkenstock as the sixth most female friendly company out of 386 total companies. The *Business Journal* published for Sonoma, Marin, and Napa counties concluded that Birkenstock was the largest minority or women-owned business in that area.

Unlike their earlier history of rejection, Birkenstock products, especially the Boston clog, were quite popular with many international clothes designers. For example, Stephen DiGeronimo used Birkenstock products in his November 4, 1997 fashion show. After Narciso Rodriguez used cashmere flannel-covered Bostons in his fashion show in Milan, Italy, several other clothing designers followed his lead. For example, Charles Chang-Lima, Perry Ellis, John Scher, Paco Rabanne, Gene Meyer, and Ron Chereskin also featured Birkenstocks in their fashion shows.

Trish Donnally, fashion editor for the *San Francisco Chronicle* said on August 20, 1998 that ''the crunchy granola of shoe styles is in'' and that they indeed were ''trendy.'' Although some said the company's clogs were ugly, they enjoyed the footwear comfort. ''Everything in a Birkenstock is reparable,'' pointed out Laurie Davenport, the Birkenstock San Francisco store manager. ''You can replace foot beds, hammer out the cork edge to cradle bunions, and you can remove the toe bar [in sandals] if people find them uncomfortable.''

Birkenstock in the 1990s set a good example of combining the profit motive with environmental protection. In 1991 a group of employees organized themselves as the Green Team to promote environmentally sound practices by both employees and the corporation. It attempted to reduce paper consumption and trim office waste, and it offered several commuting options. In 2001 Birkenstock continued to decrease its energy consumption through facility improvements and new technology.

With strict vegetarians or vegans unwilling to eat or use any animal products, Birkenstock found alternatives to its leather products. Its catalog listed footwear made from wool, polyurethane, and acrylic. It said these nonleather products used ''breathable, durable materials which hold their 'new' look longer than most real leathers.'' People for the Ethical Treatment of Animals (PETA) included Birkenstocks in its free Shopping Guide to Nonleather Products.

In 2001 Birkenstock Footprint Sandals remained under the leadership of its founder and President Margot Fraser, while Mary Jones, the firm's first employee, was its vice-president and manager of human resources. However, employees owned about 40 percent of the company. Based in Novato, California, in Marin County, Birkenstock Footprint's headquarters included 157,000 square feet for its offices and warehouses. It annually sold about two million pairs of its footwear to men, women, and children and looked forward to serving others in the future.

Principal Competitors

NIKE, Inc.; Ecco; The Timberland Company; SAS; Mephisto; Naot.

Further Reading

Chan, Gilbert, ''Step By Step,'' *Sacramento Bee*, May 2, 1994, p. C1.

''Deja Vu Shoe,'' *People*, August 26, 1991.

Donnally, Trish, ''Don't Smirk at Birks,'' *San Francisco Chronicle*, August 20, 1998, pp. E6–E7.

Magiera, Marcy, ''Woodstock's Kids Slip into Birkenstocks,'' *Advertising Age*, August 24, 1992, p. 12.

Mikutel, Sarah, ''Live and Let Live: For Vegans, Respect for Others Includes Animals, and the Things They Eat, Wear and Buy Reflect That,'' *Morning Star* (Wilmington, N.C.), August 22, 2000, pp. 1D, 5D.

Montalbano, Elizabeth, ''A Seattle Shoe Seller Who Got It,'' *Computer Reseller News*, August 21, 2000, p. 74.

Patterson, Cecily, ''From Woodstock to Wall Street,'' *Forbes*, November 11, 1991, p. 214.

''PETA Offers Alternative Shopping Guide,'' *Houston Chronicle*, October 26, 2000, p. 3.

Scott, Mary, and Howard Rothman, ''One Step Ahead,'' in *Companies with a Conscience: Intimate Portraits of Twelve Firms That Make a Difference*, New York: Carol Publishing Group, 1992, pp. 35–45.

Stengel, Richard, ''Be It Ever So Birkenstock,'' *New York Times*, August 30, 1992.

—Elizabeth Rourke
—update: David M. Walden

Bombardier Inc.

800 René-Lévesque Blvd. West
Montreal, Quebec H3B 1Y8
Canada
Telephone: (514) 861-9481
Fax: (514) 861-7053
Web site: http://www.bombardier.com

Public Company
Incorporated: 1942 as L'Auto-Neige Bombardier Limitée
Employees: 79,000
Sales: C$16.1 billion ($10.71 billion) (2001)
Stock Exchanges: Toronto Brussels Frankfurt
Ticker Symbol: BBD
NAIC: 336411 Aircraft Manufacturing; 336510 Railroad
  Rolling Stock Manufacturing; 336999 Other
  Transportation Equipment Manufacturing; 532411
  Commercial Air, Rail, and Water Transportation
  Equipment Rental and Leasing

A diversified manufacturer of transportation equipment, Bombardier Inc. is best known as the world's leading maker of regional aircraft and business jets. The company is also the world's leading manufacturer of passenger rail equipment and produces recreational vehicles, including snowmobiles (the Ski-Doo and Lynx brands), personal watercraft (Sea-Doo), and all-terrain vehicles. About 92 percent of its revenues in 2001 came from sales outside of Canada, and the company's main production facilities were located in Canada, the United States, and the United Kingdom. The company boasts a rich legacy of innovation in the motorized transportation industry and is among the most successful manufacturing companies in Canada. After stumbling in the 1970s, Bombardier (pronounced bohn-BAR-dee-ay) reemerged as a force, particularly in the aircraft and rail equipment industries, in the final decades of the 20th century, enjoying healthy sales and profit gains into the new millennium.

Early History: Focusing on Snowmobiles

Bombardier Inc. is the progeny of inventor and entrepreneur Joseph-Armand Bombardier, who was born near the eastern Quebec village of Valcourt in 1902. An inveterate tinkerer, Bombardier took it upon himself early in life to devise a solution to the difficulty of traveling during the winter when snow-covered roads in his native Quebec kept people isolated. At the age of 19, Bombardier started his own garage and worked as a mechanic, while he labored diligently in his spare time to create a vehicle that would allow easy winter travel, eventually building several prototypes that could travel on snow. Over a ten-year period, in fact, he crafted motorized test vehicles ranging from one-seat units to multipassenger carriers.

Bombardier finally came up with what he believed was a suitable solution to winter travel. In 1936 he submitted his patent application for the B7, a seven-passenger snowmobile that sported a revolutionary rear-wheel drive and suspension system (patent approval came in 1937). Bombardier soon found himself besieged with 20 orders for the innovative vehicle, and he quickly assembled a work crew—comprised largely of relatives and friends—in order to begin manufacturing B7s for country doctors, veterinarians, telephone companies, foresters, and others who benefited from easy winter travel. In 1940 he built a modern factory with an annual production capacity of 200 vehicles, and in 1941 he introduced a bigger version of the B7 named the B12. The B12, used for cargo and mail transport as well as ambulance and rescue services, resembled a small blue school bus with round passenger windows, tanklike treads on the rear, and skis on the front.

Despite strong demand, wartime material and fuel restrictions reduced Bombardier's output during the early 1940s. Nevertheless, the optimistic Joseph-Armand incorporated the company in 1942 as L'Auto-Neige Bombardier Limitée, or Bombardier Snowmobile Limited. The war eventually turned out to be a boon for the company—in 1942 the government ordered 130 B1s, which were a specially tailored version of the original B12. Moreover, in 1943 Bombardier was asked to design and produce a special armored all-track snowmobile—the Khaki—which led to the development of the armored Mark

Company Perspectives:

Bombardier's mission is to be the leader in all the markets in which it operates. This objective will be achieved through excellence in the fields of aerospace, rail transportation equipment, recreational products and financial services.

All Bombardier units must meet the needs of their customers and markets as well as reach and maintain world-class performance. They must also create added value in order to sustain their own growth and achieve a superior level of economic return to shareholders.

I. Between 1942 and 1946 Bombardier produced more than 1,900 tracked vehicles for the armed forces. Unfortunately, the company reaped few profits from the sales, and Joseph-Armand was even forced to give up the royalties for the use of his patents in all military vehicles.

The massive production boom did help Bombardier to hone his manufacturing and design skills, experience that proved useful after the war, when civilian orders for the company's snow vehicles ballooned. Between 1945 and 1952 the company shipped 1,600 B12s. It also began producing the C18, which was a larger version of the B12 that could carry 25 school children. By 1947 the company was generating annual sales of C$2.3 million and realizing profits of more than C$300,000. Unfortunately, sales plummeted to less than C$1 million in 1949 after the Quebec government implemented a snow-removal program for rural roads. Joseph-Armand scrambled to compensate for the setback, relying on his inventiveness to come up with new products that could utilize his patented technologies.

Among several new products the company tested during the late 1940s was the Tractor Tracking Attachment, a patented tread mechanism that could be attached to a tractor, thus improving performance in muddy terrain. Between 1949 and 1954 Bombardier sold thousands of the devices throughout North America, and cash from that successful product was dumped into research and development of a variety of all-terrain vehicles for the mining, oil, agriculture, and forest industries. Two of the most successful innovations introduced during that period were the Muskeg and the J5. The Muskeg was a breakthrough tractor-type machine that could perform multiple functions in difficult terrain. Joseph-Armand considered it one of his greatest inventions, and modern versions of the vehicle were still being produced in the early 1990s. The J5 was the first tracked vehicle designed specifically for logging.

By the end of the 1950s Bombardier's sales were approaching C$4 million annually as profits soared toward the C$1 million mark. It was during that time that Joseph-Armand, who was still managing the business, renewed his childhood dream of building a small snowmobile that could whisk a person over snow-covered terrain. With the advent of lighter engines, high-performance synthetic rubbers, and an improved tracking technology patented by his son Germain, Joseph-Armand believed that he could accomplish his goal. By 1959 the Bombardier team had developed a working prototype that lived up to Joseph-Armand's

dream, and that year the company began mass production of the acclaimed Ski-Doo snowmobile. The first model sported five-foot wooden skis, a coil-spring suspension system, and could travel at speeds of 25 miles per hour.

The vehicles, which originally sold at a price of C$900 each, launched an entirely new industry that would explode during the next two decades. Although demand for the new snowmobile was slow in the first two years after its introduction—production rose from just 225 in 1959 to about 250 in 1960—in 1961 unit sales lurched to 1,200 before rocketing to more than 2,500 in 1962. Besides capturing the interest of trappers, foresters, prospectors, and other workers, the Ski-Doo became popular as a sport vehicle.

Bombardier continued to improve the vehicle and began introducing new lines. By 1964 the company was shipping more than 8,000 Ski-Doos annually, and Joseph-Armand died knowing he had realized his original dream of providing safe, practical, and economical transportation in isolated, snow-covered regions. During his career, Bombardier secured more than 40 patents, and he left his sons in charge of a financially sound company with more than C$10 million in annual sales and profits of more than C$2 million annually. Germain, Joseph-Armand's eldest son, assumed the presidency, but passed the torch to his brother-in-law, Laurent Beaudoin, in 1966.

Beaudoin (pronounced bow-DWAN) was only 27 years old when he assumed the presidency at Bombardier Limited, as it was named in 1967. Also, he was joined by an aggressive young group of top managers that averaged 30 years in age. That group of executives successfully guided the company through its headiest growth stage—North American snowmobile shipments vaulted from 60,000 units in 1966 to a peak of 495,000 units annually in 1972, and Bombardier produced more than one-third of that number. During that period the company's sales and profits surged from C$20 million and C$3 million, respectively, to C$183 million and C$12 million, an impressive growth that was achieved by attacking the giant U.S. market, unveiling a broad line of new snowmobiles, and pursuing an aggressive marketing initiative.

1970s: Snowmobile Downturn, Diversification

In 1969 Beaudoin took Bombardier public, planning to use the resulting cash to vertically integrate the company and profit from related economies of scale. In fact, during the 1960s and early 1970s Bombardier acquired several new companies, the largest of which was the Austrian firm Lohnerwerke GmbH. The two companies were merged to form Bombardier-Rotax in 1970—Lohnerwerke's subsidiary, Rotax, had previously supplied engines for Bombardier's Ski-Doos. Lohnerwerke, a tramway manufacturer founded in 1823, gave Bombardier an entry into the tram and rail transit industry. A year later, Bombardier also purchased its largest competitor, Bouchard Inc., which produced the third best-selling snowmobile on the market. As it turned out, Bouchard exited the snowmobile industry at an opportune time, as demand for the vehicles began tumbling shortly after the buyout.

Indeed, the energy crises of the early 1970s left the snowmobile industry gasping. Of 100 North American manufacturers,

Key Dates:

1937: Joseph-Armand Bombardier receives approval of his patent for the B7, a seven-passenger snowmobile.

1942: Bombardier incorporates his company as L'Auto-Neige Bombardier Limitée, or Bombardier Snowmobile Limited.

1959: The Ski-Doo snowmobile makes its debut.

1967: Company is renamed Bombardier Limited.

1969: Company goes public.

1974: Contract with Montreal to supply 423 subway cars marks first major move into rail equipment.

1976: Bombardier enters the aviation industry through purchase of controlling interest in Herous Limited.

1986: Air carrier Canadair is purchased from the Canadian government.

1988: The Sea-Doo personal watercraft is introduced.

1989: Company buys Short Brother PLC, a Northern Ireland aircraft producer.

1990: Learjet Corporation, famed builder of business jets, is acquired.

1992: Company assumes a controlling stake in de Havilland, a maker of turboprop aircraft (five years later the remaining interest is acquired); the first Canadair Regional Jet (CRJ) is delivered.

1998: Deutsche Waggonbau AG, a Berlin-based maker of train and subway cars, is acquired.

1999: The first Global Express business jet is delivered.

2001: Adtranz is acquired for $725 million, making Bombardier the world's largest producer of passenger-rail equipment; company begins delivery of the CRJ 700.

only six survived the ugly industry shakeout of the mid-1970s. The ever resilient Bombardier was one of those left standing. Confident that the industry would one day recover, Bombardier management remained committed to sustaining its leadership position and capturing as much market share as possible. Still, Bombardier suffered serious sales and earnings declines. Just as it had done following the creation of the Quebec snow-clearing program of 1949, Bombardier scrambled during the early and mid-1970s to develop new products to bolster sagging snowmobile sales. The Can-Am off-road motorcycle, which used parts supplied by manufacturers of Ski-Doo components, was introduced in 1972, and two years later the company began manufacturing a fiberglass sailboat. Bombardier also landed a big contract to produce stadium seats for the 1976 Montreal Olympic Games. In addition, the company entered the aviation industry in 1976 when it purchased a controlling interest in Herous Limited, a manufacturer of aircraft maintenance and landing gear.

In 1974 Bombardier had won a C$118 million contract with the city of Montreal to supply 423 subway cars by 1978. At the time, snowmobiles still accounted for about 90 percent of the struggling company's sales, so the subway car contract represented a major new push for Bombardier. Some analysts, however, frowned upon the move because most of North America's rail equipment manufacturers had already exited the business in the 1960s in light of foreign competition and stagnant demand. In contrast, Bombardier worked to acquire and master related

technologies during the 1970s as part of an effort to position itself as a major player in the global rolling stock industry. In addition to the Montreal contract, Bombardier supplied 36 self-propelled commuter cars to Chicago in 1977, 21 locomotives and 50 rail cars to VIA Rail Canada in 1978, and 117 commuter cars to the New Jersey Transit Corporation in 1980. In 1981, moreover, Bombardier received an order for 180 subway cars to be used in Mexico City.

Acquisitive 1980s

After slogging through the snowmobile industry downturn of the 1970s, Bombardier was beginning to reshape itself into a successful manufacturer of transit equipment by the early 1980s. Importantly, Bombardier landed a huge contract in 1982 to supply New York City with 825 subway cars. Also during the early 1980s, Bombardier diversified into military equipment, believing that it could implement the same strategy it was using to dominate the North American rail transit market. In 1977 the company had purchased the marketing rights, at a discount, to a truck developed by Am General Corporation of the United States, a deal that turned out to be a boon for the company. In 1981 the Canadian government awarded Bombardier a contract to supply 2,767 trucks. Bombardier delivered the last truck ahead of schedule in 1983, leading to a second order for 1,900 of the vehicles. The company also received a contract in 1985 to supply 2,500 trucks to the Belgian Army.

By the mid-1980s Bombardier was again generating hefty profits, despite turbulence in the North American transit market and ongoing sluggishness in snowmobile sales. Beaudoin, who was known as a savvy dealmaker, capitalized on the downturn in the transit industry to increase market share and bolster its competitive position. In 1987, for example, Bombardier acquired Pullman Technology, a division of Pullman-Peabody, followed the next year by the purchase of the Transit America division of The Budd Company. The company also acquired major interests in transit companies in Belgium and France. In the early 1990s Bombardier acquired UTDC, a major Canadian competitor, and Concarril, Mexico's top manufacturer of railway rolling stock. Those purchases cemented Bombardier's role as a leading global supplier of transit cars. That status was confirmed when Bombardier was awarded the contract to build specialized rail cars for the massive Eurotunnel, a transit system linking England and France beneath the English Channel.

At the same time Bombardier was expanding in the transit industry, the company was also launching an aggressive diversification drive into the aerospace market. That drive began with the 1986 purchase of the troubled air carrier Canadair from the Canadian government. The government had dumped $2 billion into the development of the Challenger corporate jet, a nine-seat craft that was to be the foundation of Canadair. Bombardier paid just $121 million for the company and was quickly able to turn the operation around through cost-cutting and aggressive marketing of the project's sophisticated technology. The acquisition effectively doubled Bombardier's size and represented its intent to become a player in the aerospace industry. To that end, in 1989 Bombardier purchased Short Brother PLC, a Northern Ireland aircraft producer, and the following year bought Learjet Corporation, builder of the well-known business jets.

1990s and Beyond: Becoming a Global Leader in Aircraft and Rail

Meanwhile, Bombardier continued to firm up its position in the sporadic snowmobile market. Although the business represented less than 10 percent of sales by the early 1990s, Beaudoin refused to exit the market, citing Bombardier's historic expertise in the industry. Throughout the mid-1980s, in fact, Bombardier continued to beef up its snowmobile division with new technology and products. By the early 1990s Bombardier was still controlling about 50 percent of the Canadian snowmobile market and more than 25 percent of the entire North American market. In addition, Bombardier introduced the Sea-Doo watercraft in 1988 to compete in the growing market for individual sit-down jet-boats—the design was actually the offspring of a 1968 effort by Bombardier's research staff, and it was chosen as the number one watercraft of its type by *Popular Mechanics* in 1988. By the early 1990s Bombardier was serving about 40 percent of that emerging North American segment. Bombardier was also branching out globally with its motorized consumer products division, as evidenced by its 1993 buyout of the leading Finnish snowmobile maker.

Throughout the 1980s and early 1990s Bombardier grew and prospered by purchasing undervalued operations and turning them around with sound management, but not all of its efforts proved profitable. For example, several of its transit deals, including the giant Eurotunnel contract, actually lost money for the company. In general, though, Beaudoin's deals were successful and most of the company's operations thrived. As a result, Bombardier's sales mushroomed from C$1.4 billion in 1987 to an impressive C$4.4 billion in 1992. Profits rose at a rate of 15 percent annually during the period to C$133 million in 1992. Bombardier had become one of Canada's largest and most successful manufacturing companies, and it was steadily expanding throughout Europe and North America.

Further expansion of Bombardier's aerospace operations came in 1992 when the company gained a controlling 51 percent stake in Ontario-based de Havilland, a manufacturer of turboprop aircraft, such as the Dash 8 regional airplane. The Province of Ontario took the remaining 49 percent interest in de Havilland, which had been a division of Boeing, retaining the stake until January 1997, when Bombardier gained full control. Another key development in aircraft also occurred in 1992: the delivery of the first Canadair Regional Jet (CRJ), an aircraft that helped revolutionize the airline industry in the 1990s. The CRJ 100 was a redesigned version of Canadair's Challenger business jet, having been fitted with 50 seats and designed to fly routes of 650 to 1,500 kilometers (400 to 950 miles) in length. For consumers, it had the advantage over traditional turboprop regional planes, such as the Dash 8, of being a jet—and a particularly quiet one at that—while for airliners the plane's flight range made it ideal for routes longer than those that had been served by regional turboprops and shorter than those covered by conventional jets. Orders poured in for the CRJ during the mid-1990s as regional airliners proliferated and conventional airliners began setting up ''spoke-to-spoke'' routes in the ''hub-and-spoke'' system that had recently overtaken the industry. After delivery of the first CRJ 100 to Germany's Lufthansa CityLine in November 1992, Bombardier went on to deliver another 168 planes to 16 airlines in 11 countries by mid-1997.

At that time the company had firm orders for another 86 CRJs and options from customers to purchase 198 more.

Bombardier continued to expand its operations and acquire new companies in the mid-1990s. In April 1995, for example, it purchased German transportation equipment manufacturer Waggonfabrik Talbot, which employed a workforce of about 1,200. Importantly, the wisdom of Bombardier's decision to retain its motorized consumer craft business became evident when that market rebounded in 1994. Buoyed by new product introductions, sales by that division surged 39 percent in 1994 to account for roughly 17 percent of company revenues. More importantly, profits from Ski-Doo and Sea-Doo products represented 37 percent of total company profits, making that division central to Bombardier's gains in that year. As a result of new acquisitions and improving markets, Bombardier's revenues sailed from C$4.77 billion in 1993 to C$5.94 billion in 1994, as net income climbed from C$177.3 million to C$247.3 million. Revenues increased still further in 1995, to C$7.12 billion, but net income dropped to C$158 million because of a C$155 million writedown of the company's 3 percent stake in Eurotunnel.

In April 1996 Bombardier was reorganized into five groups: Bombardier Aerospace, Bombardier Transportation (the rail operations), Bombardier Recreational Products, Bombardier Services (later Bombardier International), and Bombardier Capital. It was the first of these groups, Bombardier Aerospace, that led the company to new heights of prosperity in the final years of the 20th century. In addition to the continued success of the CRJ 100 regional jet, Bombardier successfully rolled out more aircraft models, including two new business jets. In 1998 came the first delivery of the Learjet 45 business jet, which had been jointly developed by Learjet, de Havilland, and Shorts. This super-light jet had a maximum range of 2,120 nautical miles and a cruising speed of 534 miles per hour. Within two years, Bombardier had delivered more than 100 of the new jets. During 1999, Bombardier completed another key introduction, the Global Express business jet, an ultra-long-range, high-speed corporate jet capable of circling the globe with just two stopovers. Bombardier invested C$400 million in the project, which began in the early 1990s and was codeveloped by Canadair, Learjet, de Havilland, and Shorts, with the assistance of 11 outside partners, who ponied up another C$400 million. The addition of Global Express gave Bombardier a full range of business jets, ranging from the lower end Learjet through the middle-market Challenger to the high-end Global Express, which sold for a cool $34 million.

With sales of regional jets booming and the red-hot U.S. economy driving sales of corporate jets to record levels (the U.S. market accounted for more than half of Bombardier's overall revenues), Bombardier Aerospace's revenues skyrocketed, jumping from C$4.28 billion in 1996 to C$6.44 billion in 1998 to C$10.56 billion in 2000. By the latter year, aerospace operations accounted for two-thirds of overall revenues and more than 85 percent of the company's profits. The head of Bombardier Aerospace, Robert E. Brown, was rewarded for this stellar performance in February 1999 with a promotion to president and CEO of Bombardier Inc., with Beaudoin remaining chairman of the board.

It should be noted that a number of observers were critical of what they perceived as too-close ties between Bombardier and the government of Canada and pointed out that Bombardier's rapid ascension in the aerospace industry was aided by government subsidies—particularly in regard to the development of the CRJ. In fact, Bombardier's chief competitor in the area of regional aircraft, Empresa Brasileira de Aeronáutica S.A. (Embraer) of Brazil, took its case of unfair trade practices to the World Trade Organization (WTO). Bombardier did likewise, accusing Embraer of gaining market advantages from its ties to the Brazilian government. At times the competitive battle between the world's two main regional jet makers threatened to escalate into an all-out trade war between their respective home nations. The conflict continued unresolved into the early 21st century, although a number of WTO rulings in the matter supported the Canadian position.

In the late 1990s and early years of the 21st century, Bombardier Transportation began playing a more prominent role within the company. In February 1998 Bombardier acquired Deutsche Waggonbau AG, a Berlin-based maker of train and subway cars, thereby doubling the size of its European rail equipment operations. In December of that same year, Bombardier signed its biggest rail contract ever, a $1.8 billion deal with Virgin Rail Group of Britain to build 78 high-speed diesel-electric locomotives and train coaches. The company entered the burgeoning Chinese market in November 1999 by establishing a joint venture that would construct a manufacturing facility in China to build 300 intercity mass transit railcars for the Ministry of Railways. In August 2000 Bombardier agreed to acquire Berlin-based DaimlerChrysler Rail Systems GmbH (known as Adtranz) from DaimlerChrysler AG for $725 million. Adtranz was a major maker of rail equipment with 1999 revenues of $3.4 billion and 22,000 employees. In addition to production of electric locomotives, Adtranz specialized in propulsion and train controls, services, and signaling, providing Bombardier Transportation with a broader range of activities and making Bombardier the world's largest producer of passenger-rail equipment. The acquisition of Adtranz, which was completed in May 2001 and was the largest in company history, meant that 40 percent of Bombardier's revenues would be generated by the rail transportation unit.

In addition to creating a more powerful rail unit, Bombardier also worked hard to remain at the forefront of the regional aircraft and business jet sectors. Having concluded that there was still room in the market for regional turboprops, Bombardier in late 1999 made its first deliveries of the Dash 8-Q400, a 70-passenger twin-turboprop designed for regional airliners' high-density, short-haul routes. By early 2001, Bombardier had delivered 29 of the new models and had firm orders for an additional 33 and options on 32. In January 2001 deliveries started for the CRJ 700 model regional jet, a stretched, 70-seat version of the CRJ 100/200. Bombardier already had firm orders for 173 additional CRJ 700s and options had been taken on 313 more. Moreover, the company was already developing the next-generation CRJ, the 900, an 86-passenger model scheduled to enter airline service in early 2003. For all of its models of regional aircraft, Bombardier entered 2001 with firm orders for 574 units and 1,047 options, a backlog that represented potential sales of tens of billions of dollars (the jets, for example, sold for between C$33 billion and C$45 billion each).

Also under development was the Bombardier Continental business jet, an all-new super midsize corporate jet designed for transcontinental flights. The company hoped to received certification of the Continental by early 2003.

Meanwhile, in March 2001, Bombardier bolstered its recreational vehicles operations with the purchase of the engine assets of Outboard Marine Corporation, including the Evinrude and Johnson outboard marine engine brands. Despite this acquisition, recreational products, the founding business of Bombardier, had been left in the exhaust of the rapidly expanding aircraft and rail units. Only 11 percent of the revenues and 6 percent of the profits for the fiscal year ending in January 2001 came from recreational products. These percentages were certain to fall even further with the addition of Adtranz and the continuing rollout of new aircraft models. Bombardier's order backlog totaled C$31.71 billion as of January 2001, boding well for the future of a company that had within the span of decade or so become one of the world's major transportation equipment companies. The one cloud on the horizon was the impact that a prolonged economic slowdown might have on the company's operations, with business jet sales being particularly vulnerable during economic downturns. Furthermore, the regional jet industry that Bombardier had pioneered had never been through an economic downturn, providing an air of uncertainty surrounding the company.

Principal Subsidiaries

AEROSPACE: Bombardier Inc.; Learjet Inc. (U.S.A.); Short Brothers plc (U.K.). TRANSPORTATION: Bombardier Inc.; Bombardier Transit Corporation (U.S.A.); Bombardier-Concarril, S.A. de C.V. (Mexico); DWA Deutsche Waggonbau GmbH (Germany); Talbot GmbH & Co. KG (Germany); Bombardier-Wien Schienenfahzeuge AG (Austria); BN S.A. (Belgium); Société ANF-Industrie S.A. (France); Vagónka _eská Lípa a.s. (Czech Republic); Prorail Limited (U.K.); Vevey Technologies S.A. (Switzerland). RECREATIONAL PRODUCTS: Bombardier Inc.; Bombardier Motor Corporation of America (U.S.A.); Bombardier-Rotax GmbH (Austria); Bombardier-Nordtrac Oy (Finland). CAPITAL: Bombardier Capital Inc. (U.S.A.); Bombardier Credit Receivables Corporation (U.S.A.); BCI Finance Inc. (U.S.A.); Bombardier Capital Rail Inc. (U.S.A.); Bombardier Capital Ltd.; Bombardier Capital Leasing Ltd.; Bombardier Finance Inc.; Bombardier Capital Mortgage Securitization Corporation (U.S.A.); Bombardier Capital CF II Inc. (U.S.A.); Bombardier Capital Insurance Agency Inc. (U.S.A.); RJ Finance Corp. Two (U.S.A.); Bombardier Capital International B.V. (Finland); Bombardier Capital International S.A. (France); Bombardier Inc. INTERNATIONAL: Bombardier Inc.

Principal Operating Units

Bombardier Aerospace; Bombardier Transportation; Bombardier Recreational Products; Bombardier Capital; Bombardier International.

Principal Competitors

Empresa Brasileira de Aeronáutica S.A.; Fairchild Dornier Corporation; Gulfstream Aerospace Corporation; The Boeing

Company; Airbus S.A.S.; Textron Inc.; Raytheon Company; BAE Systems; Dassault Aviation SA.

Further Reading

Bertin, Oliver, "Bombardier Targets New Niche," *Globe and Mail,* November 24, 1997, p. B8.

——, "A Global Gamble: Bombardier, the Montreal Maker of Snowmobiles, Jet Skis and Regional Airliners, Is Betting $400-Million That Its New Executive Jet Will Solidify a World-Class Reputation and Give It More Respect at Home," *Globe and Mail,* August 24, 1996, p. B1.

Bombardier: A Dream With an International Reach, Montreal: Bombardier Inc., 1992.

Bombeau, Bernard, "Regional Manufacturers Carve Up the Market," *Interavia,* May 1997, pp. 33, 36–38.

Bourette, Susan, "Bombardier Reward Brown by Promoting Him to Top Job," *Globe and Mail,* December 9, 1998, p. B1.

Came, Barry, "Sky King: Bombardier's New Regional Jet Is Revolutionizing the Way People Fly," *Maclean's,* August 11, 1997, pp. 30–36.

Chipello, Christopher J., "Bombardier, Going Outside Family, Names Brown CEO," *Wall Street Journal,* December 9, 1998, p. B13.

——, "Jet Maker Looks to the Old Economy: Bombardier of Canada Seeks a Smoother Ride with Railroad Deal," *Wall Street Journal,* September 12, 2000, p. A21.

Crowe, Nancy, "Bombardier Gears Up," *Vermont Business,* December 1986, p. 89.

DePalma, Anthony, "The Transportation Giant up North: Bombardier Rises, with Some Help from Friends in Ottawa," *New York Times,* December 25, 1998, p. C1.

Ferrabee, James, "Bombardier Stock on a Magic Carpet Ride," *Gazette,* December 19, 1994, p. C2.

——, "Confident Chunnel Man," *Gazette,* February 1995, p. D7.

Ford, Royal, "Red Line Cars Are Born in Vermont," *Boston Globe,* November 7, 1993, p. 69.

Gibbens, Robert, "Bombardier Buys German Railcar Firm," *Financial Post,* February 25, 1995, p. 19.

——, "Bombardier Is Aiming High," *Financial Post,* April 11, 1991, p. 21.

Goldsmith, Charles, "Gulfstream and Bombardier Stage Business-Jet Dogfight," *Wall Street Journal,* June 20, 1997, p. B4.

Hadekel, Peter, "Bombardier's Ski-Doo Division Is Profiting from Borrowed Techniques," *Gazette,* April 16, 1993, p. F1.

Koselka, Rita, "Let's Make a Deal," *Forbes,* April 27, 1992, p. 62.

Lang, Amanda, "Dynasties," *Globe and Mail,* Report on Business Magazine, June 1, 1995, p. 60.

Leger, Kathryn, "Tough Guy on the Tarmac: Laurent Beaudoin Keeps Bombardier on Top of Global Markets with a Combination of High Technology and Hardball," *Financial Post,* August 1, 1998, p. 8.

Livesay, Bruce, "Ceiling Unlimited: Bombardier's Global Ambition and Constant Innovation Have Propelled It to No. 1 in Our CEO Survey," *Globe and Mail,* March 28, 1997, p. 36.

McArthur, Keith, "Bombardier Endures Jet Controversy," *Globe and Mail,* June 25, 2001, p. B3.

McGovern, Sheila, "On the Move: The Snowmobiles Bombardier Built for Rural Quebec Are the Still-Thriving Roots of a World Transportation Empire That Includes Planes, Trains, and Sea-Doos," *Gazette,* November 1, 1993, p. C8.

Moorman, Robert W., "Bigger and Better," *Air Transport World,* May 1999, pp. 32–34 +.

——, "Booming with Bombardier," *Air Transport World,* August 1998, pp. 102 +.

——, "The Deal Maker: From Selling Snowmobiles to Saving Aircraft Companies, Laurent Beaudoin Has Made Bombardier a World-Class Player," *Air Transport World,* July 1992, p. 44.

Newman, Peter C., "A Lesson in How to Choose the Right Stuff," *Maclean's,* December 21, 1998, p. 50.

Pasztor, Andy, and Daniel Michaels, "Regional-Jet Makers, Flying High, See Clouds Looming: Economic Slowdown, Labor Disputes and Large-Plane Rivals Could Stall Demand," *Wall Street Journal,* July 12, 2001, p. B4.

Shalom, Francois, "Firefighting: Canadair Says Bomber's Problems Are Merely Glitches, and Promises to Fix Them for Unhappy French," *Gazette,* March 18, 1995, p. C3.

Sheppard, Robert, "The Nimble and the Bulky: Small Regional Jets and Giant Airliners Appear to Be the Way of the Future for the International Aviation Industry," *Maclean's,* August 7, 2000, pp. 24–25.

Shifrin, Carole A., "Bombardier Bets on New Regional Turboprop," *Aviation Week and Space Technology,* December 15, 1997, pp. 38–42.

Tremblay, Miville, *Le sang jaune de Bombardier: La gestion de Laurent Beaudoin,* Sainte-Foy, Québec: Presses de l'Université du Québec, 1994, 131 p.

Velocci, Anthony L., Jr., "Claims, Counterclaims Intensify Gulfstream, Bombardier Rivalry," *Aviation Week and Space Technology,* June 28, 1999, p. 66.

Walmsley, Ann, "Meet the New Boss Same As the Old Boss?: Bombardier's Robert Brown Has a Tough Act to Follow As He Steps into Laurent Beaudoin's Shoes," *Globe and Mail,* March 26, 1999, p. 85.

Wells, Jennifer, "Bombardier's Big Gamble," *Maclean's,* September 2, 1996, pp. 36–38.

Yakabuski, Konrad, "Bob Brown in Command: Who Would Have Guessed That Plain Robert Brown—Spit-and-Polish Soldier, Career Civil Servant—Could Match Laurent Beaudoin's Fabled Record As CEO of Bombardier," *Globe and Mail,* Report on Business Magazine, October 27, 2000, p. 74.

——, "Bombardier Sets Out on a European Odyssey: Canadian Firm Establishes New Trade Beachhead on Old Continent," *Toronto Star,* December 19, 1993, p. D1.

—Dave Mote
—update: David E. Salamie

Brambles Industries Limited

Level 40, Gateway
One Macquarie Place
Sydney 2000
Australia
Telephone: (+61) 2-9256-5222
Fax: (+61)-2-9256-5299
Web site: http://www.brambles.com

Public Company
Incorporated: 1877 as Bramble's Butchering
　　Establishment
Employees: 14,546
Sales: A$4.92 billion ($2.46 billion) (2000)
Stock Exchanges: Australia
Ticker Symbol: BIL
NAIC: 421840 Industrial Supplies Wholesalers; 532490
　　Other Commercial and Industrial Machinery and
　　Equipment Rental and Leasing; 483111 Deep Sea
　　Freight Transportation; 562112 Hazardous Waste
　　Collection; 562111 Solid Waste Collection; 562211
　　Hazardous Waste Treatment and Disposal

Australian conglomerate Brambles Industries Limited has taken its motto of "dig, lift, load and haul" literally, constructing one of the world's most successful business-to-business industrial services company. From its roots as a materials handling company, Brambles has established globally operating equipment rental—particularly its CHEP pallets leasing subsidiary and its CAIB wagon leasing arm—and waste management services. The company operates through nearly 200 subsidiaries affiliated with CHEP, Cleanaway (waste management), Recall (records management), and various equipment rental service firms, including CAIB. In Australia, Brambles also operates a number of regionally focused companies, offering a wide range of logistics services such as marine services, heavy hauling, and others. Since the mid-1990s, Brambles has oriented its focus to its Northern Hemisphere business, to the extent that two-thirds of its operating profits now come from its United States and European operations. These two markets also account for more

than half of Brambles' annual sales, which neared A$5 billion in 2000. The company is moving to consolidate its CHEP and other industrial services businesses, particularly the European branches that have historically been operated in joint ventures with the United Kingdom's GKN plc. In 2001, the two companies began negotiating a merger of their industrial services branches. Brambles, which celebrated its 125th anniversary in 2000, continued to be led by CEO John Fletcher, who, while scheduled to retire in March 2001, expected to remain in his post until the GKN merger had been resolved. At that point, GKN chief executive C.K. Chow would likely become Fletcher's successor.

Establishing a Global Conglomerate in the 19th Century

Walter Bramble's family moved to Australia from England at the middle of the 19th century. Bramble, who grew up in the region north of Sydney, began his professional life in 1875, when he opened a butcher's shop near the town of Newcastle. Two years later, the then 20-year-old Bramble incorporated his company as Bramble's Butchering Establishment, moving his business to Newcastle itself. Among Bramble's customers were the ships docked and anchored in the ports and harbors around the Sydney region, and from the start Bramble began supplying ships—transporting meats and vegetables at first by rowboat.

From these beginnings, Bramble moved into full-fledged distribution operations, now using horse-drawn wagons and the railroad link to Sydney. Starting in 1890, the distribution activity became the company's major focus. At the turn of the century, Bramble had expanded to become one of the Newcastle region's major haulers, dealing in goods ranging from meats and produce to construction materials. The company's reputation for heavy hauling was boosted by a contract to handle the transport and other ancillary services of the new steel mill set up in Newcastle by Australian mining company BHP (Broken Hill Proprietary) in 1915.

The following year, Bramble brought his three sons into the family business, renaming the company W.E. Bramble & Sons. The company continued to modernize its operations, adding

---

Company Perspectives:

Our goal is to ensure that you, our customers, are satisfied with every aspect of our service. We want you to feel that the services we provide are the best in the market, that our prices represent value, and that it is easy to do business with us. This means we are constantly looking outwards. We want to know about your business. What further services can we supply? How can we grow with you? We have the commitment, and the capacity, to respond positively. Our industrial services are diverse and increasingly international in scale. But no matter how different our services, cultures and geographic locations, our employees all share the same Brambles values. This allows us to provide extensive services that meet your global needs, while understanding and responding to regional and local imperatives.

---

motor vehicles and especially modernized mobile and fixed cranes and other heavy lifting equipment. In 1920, Bramble expanded beyond Newcastle for the first time, when it was contracted to transport rabbits to the railroad in Nimmitabel.

Walter Bramble retired in 1925 and died in 1930. Eldest son Walter, Jr., aided by his brothers, took over the company's leadership and began expanding its operations still further, especially toward the region around the fast-growing city of Sydney. The new generation of Brambles was quick to adopt the latest in motor vehicle transport and lifting equipment, enabling the company to gain a strong reputation for its hauling and lifting services. In the mid-1930s, Bramble interests in heavy equipment brought it further afield, when it joined with longtime client BHP on a contract to excavate the Port Kembla mine in the Sydney area.

Postwar Expansion

The firm's biggest expansion was to come after World War II. By then the Bramble brothers had left the company—Walter, Jr., and brother Alan had died, while the third brother, Milton, had retired—and the company's leadership was now taken over by Tom Price, Alan Bramble's son-in-law. Price was to guide the company through a number of significant expansion moves.

Australia's postwar production boom greatly helped Bramble's own expansion. In order to fund the investment needed to fuel its growth, Bramble went public in 1954, changing its name to W.E. Brambles & Sons Transport Co. Ltd. Still a relatively small, regional company, Brambles was preparing its drive to become a national and then international company. The company moved its headquarters to Sydney in time to take part in that city's own expansion. Under the motto "dig, lift, load and haul," Brambles became one of the area's largest operators of transport and industrial services—such as excavation and hauling—to the city's building boom.

An important event in Brambles' history came in 1958, when the company purchased the Commonwealth Handling Equipment Pool, later to be known as CHEP and to provide the backbone to Brambles' international expansion. CHEP, originally known as

the Australian Materials Handling Standing Committee, had been set up during World War II as an umbrella organization for the storage, allocation, and maintenance of the large fleet of materials handling equipment—such as forklift trucks, pallet equipment, and the like—brought to that country by the United States to support its Pacific war effort. After the war, the CHEP, controlled by the Australian government, grew with the acquisition of much of the materials handling fleet left by the United States in the Pacific region. During the 1950s, however, a growing number of voices were suggesting the government's operation of CHEP placed it in direct competition with private enterprise—with the unfair advantages of being a government agency and thus tax-exempt. The Australian government sold off much of CHEP's holding to the relative local institutions, including the country's state and local port authorities.

In 1958, however, the equipment pool for a number of cities, including the important industrial centers of Brisbane, Sydney, and Townsville, remained unsold. In that year, Brambles, led by director J.H.D. Marks, tendered a bid to take over the remaining CHEP operations. The company's bid was accepted, and Brambles was granted the right to continue operations under the Commonwealth Handling Equipment Pool name until the beginning of the new decade (the new operations would eventually form CHEP Pty Ltd.).

CHEP was to provide the platform for the company's national and then international platform. The acquisition had brought the company a large fleet of forklifts, cranes, and pallets—the latter an innovation that was still relatively new to the Australian continent. The company quickly focused CHEP on its pallet operations, building up a complete pallet and pallet transport system, and establishing a leasing pool of pallets that was to reach more than 100 million pallets worldwide by the end of the century.

The 1970s were to represent two new important developments for the company. The first was the company's diversification into a new area of operations, the waste management market. Then in its infancy, waste management was to take on a greater importance as the corporate and political worlds were confronted with the growing urgency of a number of environmental concerns. Brambles' establishment of its Cleanaway subsidiary operations in 1970 placed the company at the forefront of Australia's new waste management industry. Cleanaway was also part of another important development for the company in that decade: starting in 1975, Brambles, which had by then extended its operations to become a nationally operating Australian company, was turning to the international market.

International Industrial Services Leader for the 21st Century

Still a relatively small company by international standards, Brambles looked for a partner in order to help it establish its first foreign operations. That partnership came with a joint-venture agreement with British company GKN plc and the creation of GKN UK in 1975. The two companies soon agreed to extend CHEP's operations into continental Europe, where CHEP became one of Europe's leading pallet leasing concerns. By then CHEP had already begun to play a significant part in Brambles' rising revenues—and profits.

Key Dates:

1875: Walter Bramble opens a butcher shop near Newcastle.

1877: Bramble incorporates his business as Bramble's Butchering Establishment.

1890: Company begins distribution and transportation operations.

1915: Company becomes transport services provider for BHP Newcastle steelworks.

1916: Business is renamed W.E. Bramble & Sons.

1920: Company undertakes its first expansion beyond Newcastle.

1925: Walter Bramble retires.

1937: Company begins mining excavation activities.

1954: Business goes public on the Australian exchange as W.E. Brambles & Sons Transport Co. Ltd.

1958: Company acquires Commonwealth Handling Equipment Pool (CHEP).

1959: Brambles moves headquarters to Sydney.

1984: Company acquires Swedish firm CAIB, launches Bass Strait shipping service.

1992: Brambles purchases U.S.-based Environmental Systems Company (ENSCO) for A$360 million; the unsuccessful acquisition is put up for sale in 2001.

1998: CHEP expands into Hong Kong and other international markets.

2000: Company begins disposal of non-core operations.

2001: Brambles acquires Serviceteam Holdings and begins merger talks with GKN plc.

The CHEP joint-venture provided the model for the company's extension of its Cleanaway subsidiary to Europe. In 1981, the two companies formed a new joint venture to bring Cleanaway to the United Kingdom and then to the rest of Europe. Cleanaway's expertise had by then extended to such activities as recycling and resources management, treatment and disposal, hazardous waste disposal, landfill operations, and emergency environmental response services.

During the 1980s, Brambles continued to expand its materials handling and other operations, now looking to enter new territories. The United States was becoming an increasingly important part of Brambles' operations, particularly through CHEP, which led the company's entry into that market during the late 1970s and early 1980s. Brambles was meanwhile targeting new potential markets as it began to take on its future status as a global conglomerate. In 1984, the company extended its expertise in leasing to a new area when it acquired Sweden's CAIB—and that company's strong wagon leasing business, with operations across western Europe. Back at home, Brambles continued to expand, now launching a shipping service across the Bass Strait. The company also expanded into document handling, establishing the subsidiary Recall.

The 1990s saw the company flesh out its global operations, setting up footholds in the nearby Asia Pacific markets. After a three-year takeover battle, Brambles acquired the United States Environmental Systems Company (ENSCO), forming the core of its new North American waste management effort. The A$360 million ENSCO acquisition proved an unsuccessful one for the company. Losing money, ENSCO would be put up for sale at the beginning of 2001. ENSCO was expected to bring in only about half of what the company had originally paid for it.

Elsewhere, however, the company continued to record steady growth, despite the prevailing economic downturn of the early 1990s. From revenues of A$2.3 billion in 1991, the company's sales were to top A$3 billion by mid-decade. Yet the recession, and losses from ENSCO, had already begun to hurt the company's bottom line, and by 1994, Brambles was recording losses of more than A$233 million.

By then, however, John Fletcher had been appointed as the company's CEO and, together with the company's management, had put into effect a new business strategy to take the company into the next century. Greater emphasis was placed on the company's European waste management operations. In 1994 the company acquired Leto Recycling, of the Netherlands, then, two years later, Germany's Mabeg, deepening its waste management capacity on the European continent. Both companies were acquired through the CHEP joint venture.

The company then turned its attention to its stronger performer, CHEP, bringing that company into such new markets as Hong Kong, Brazil, Switzerland, the Scandinavian countries, and Austria through the end of the decade. At the same time, it began exporting its Recall document handling subsidiary's operations, entering Europe and North America, starting in 1994.

As the largest share of the company's operating profits now shifted from Australia to the company's North American and European operations—representing more than 60 percent in 2000—the possibility was raised that Brambles might one day choose to move its headquarters to be closer to these markets. The company meanwhile began to refocus its operations around its higher-margin businesses, targeting new acquisitions—such as the A$489 million purchase of Short Bros. Europe-based industrial services operations in 2000—and a number of divestitures, including its Australian forklift operations, its Italian railcar leasing business, the CAIB Germany subsidiary, and ENSCO, starting in 2000.

In January 2001 the company announced its acquisition of Serviceteam Holdings, a waste management firm present in some 80 local U.K. markets. The acquisition, which cost Brambles A$350 million, was quickly overshadowed by a new development: the proposed merger of the industrial services operations of GKN and Brambles. The merger, which would group 100 percent control of the CHEP and Cleanaway operations under a single owner, was expected to create a new entity worth some A$17 billion. The merger talks which extended through the first quarter of 2001 spelled a new opportunity for Brambles to take a place as one of the global industrial services leaders. As the two sides waded through the many tax questions and other issues involved in a particularly complicated merger process, CEO John Fletcher, who had announced his retirement for April 2001, agreed to stay on to see the company through this new historic moment in its 125-year record of growth.

Principal Subsidiaries

CHEP Pty Ltd.; Cleanaway; Recall; Brambles Italia Srl (Italy); CAIB Benelux SA (Belgium); CAIB UK Limited; CITRANS GmbH (Germany); ETRA AG (Switzerland); OEVA GmbH (Austria); Saltra SA (Spain); Simotra SA (France); EVA GmbH (Germany).

Principal Competitors

ABB Ltd.; Algeco SA; Allied Waste Industries, Inc.; Anacomp, Inc.; Atlas Copco AB; Bechtel Group , Inc.; Caterpillar Inc.; Iron Mountain Incorporated; Kelda Group plc; Lason, Inc.; NACCO Industries, Inc.; PalEx, Inc.; Pennon Group Plc; Suez Lyonnaise des Eaux SA; United Rentals, Inc.; Vivendi SA; Waste Management, Inc.

Further Reading

Crew, Edna, *Brambles: Working Its Way Around the World*, Sydney: Brambles Industries Limited, 2000.

Huntley, Ian, "Brambles: Blue Ribbon Vanilla," *Australia's Shares Magazine*, December 1999.

Knight, Elizabeth, "Brambles Deal Loses Its Glow," *Sydney Morning Herald*, March 9, 2001.

Manuel, D.L., *Men and Machines: The Brambles Story*, North Sydney: Brambles Industries Limited, 1970.

Marsh, Peter, "GKN Chief Facing the Prickly Question of Brambles Move," *Financial Times*, January 30, 2001.

Tait, Victoria, "Brambles Steers Rough Profit Road," *Reuters*, February 22, 2001.

Todd, Mark, "Brambles, GKN Merger Talks Struggle Through Tax Maze," *Sydney Morning Herald*, March 22, 2001.

—M. L. Cohen

BUCKEYE

Buckeye Technologies, Inc.

1001 Tillman Street
Memphis, Tennessee 38108-0407
U.S.A.
Telephone: (901) 320-8100
Fax: (901) 320-8216
Web site: http://www.bkitech.com

Public Company
Incorporated: 1993
Employees: 2,200
Sales: $731.52 million (2000)
Stock Exchanges: New York
Ticker Symbol: BKI
NAIC: 322110 Pulp Mills

Buckeye Technologies, Inc. manufactures and processes cotton linter pulp and wood pulp used by other manufacturers for a variety of consumer products. With Procter & Gamble as its largest customer, Buckeye produces and processes absorbent materials for use in the manufacturing of diapers, feminine hygiene products, and other absorbent products. Chemical cellulose products are used to make a variety of plastics as well as rayon fabric and acetate films. Buckeye also produces specialty pulp for fine paper products.

Supplying Raw Materials for Procter & Gamble: 1901

Buckeye Technologies originated as Buckeye Cotton Oil Company, a behind-the-scenes subsidiary of Procter & Gamble (P&G) which provided raw materials for certain products. P&G started Buckeye in 1901, leasing a cottonseed crushing mill in Greenwood, Mississippi, to maintain a steady supply of cottonseed oil for the manufacture of Ivory soap and the then new White Naphtha laundry soap. Competition for cottonseed oil had increased with demand for consumer products which used the oil, including lard and soaps. By 1905, Buckeye owned and operated eight mills throughout the cotton-producing South, having bought three mills and built five.

P&G also sold cottonseed oil as a salad oil to hotels, restaurants, hospitals, and other bulk users. By removing the stearine from cottonseed oil, P&G had refined a "winter oil" that maintained its liquid consistency at cool temperatures. P&G did not distribute the oil to the consumer market because of costly implementation and insufficient testing for appropriate use, the latter of which P&G assumed its institutional buyers had conducted.

In 1907 P&G began to work on developing a shortening made from vegetable oil to compete with lard, butter, and other cooking fats. By chance a German chemist, E.C. Kayser, wrote to P&G about a process he developed to transform liquid oil into a solid. He visited P&G's research facilities in Ivorydale, Ohio, and showed the research staff his new hydrogenation process. P&G bought the rights to the process and P&G's research staff applied that knowledge to create Crisco shortening, a blend of liquid cottonseed oil and solid, partially hydrogenated cottonseed oil. P&G introduced Crisco, the first all vegetable shortening, in 1910, becoming the largest consumer of cottonseed oil worldwide.

With P&G as a parent company, Buckeye Cotton Oil Company operated with a plentiful outlet for its products. An infestation of boll weevils nearly destroyed cotton crops in 1911, leading to a temporary shortage just as Crisco shortening was becoming known among consumers. But the company generally operated successfully, supplying raw material for P&G's popular soap brands, including Lava bar soap, and Oxydol and Duz laundry soaps, as well as for Crisco shortening. Also, Buckeye found practical and profitable uses for its cottonseed waste. The cotton lint removed from cotton seeds before milling was transformed into sheets of pulp and sold to paper manufacturers under the brand Tuff-Fluff. In 1921 Buckeye constructed the largest cotton linter plant in the world in Memphis at a cost of $1 million. By 1930 the company operated 14 cottonseed crushing mills, supplying raw materials for P&G products and paper pulp.

During the Great Depression, the well-being of Buckeye depended on the success of P&G product sales. Despite the economic difficulties of the 1930s, P&G maintained public visibility with consistent advertising. Buckeye benefited from increased sales of the products which required cottonseed oil to be produced. Sales of Crisco tripled between 1933 and 1939,

---

Company Perspectives:

Buckeye Technologies has been a leading manufacturer and worldwide marketer of value-added cellulose products for more than 80 years. The company uses its expertise in polymer chemistry and its state-of-the-art manufacturing facilities to develop and produce innovative and proprietary products for customers in a broad range of technically demanding niche markets. These proprietary products combined with the company's commitment to customer technical service give it a distinct competitive advantage.

---

while sales of Ivory soap and flakes doubled; sales of other soaps increased as much as 50 percent. With so much demand for its products, Buckeye acquired the Cotton Oil Refining Company in Portsmouth, Virginia, in 1937. That company produced shortening, cooking, and salad oils from soybean and cottonseed oil for bulk use.

During World War II, Buckeye converted the Memphis cotton linter plant to the production of cellulose for smokeless powder. Buckeye treated the cellulose with nitric and sulfuric acid to produce gun cotton. One bale of lint produced enough smokeless powder for 100,000 bullets.

Growth amid Changing Consumer Markets: Post-World War II Era

After World War II P&G considered discontinuing the cellulose pulp operations in order to focus on its consumer products. Yet dissolving pulps such as cellulose ethers, acetates, nitrate, and viscose were in demand for the production of rayon fibers for clothing, and for tire cords, photographic film, and many plastics. P&G and Buckeye researchers found that cellulose of similar qualities could be made from pine pulp, providing strength, transparency, viscosity, and purity, but to continue in that business would require a large investment. P&G had begun construction of a large plant for manufacturing consumer products, and did not have the resources to sustain and update the infrastructure needed at Buckeye.

The start of the Korean War created a new opportunity for Buckeye. The federal government needed cellulose for munitions manufacturing and offered tax incentives for construction of new manufacturing facilities. P&G took advantage of the opportunity. In 1951 P&G purchased two 550,000-acre tracts of land in northern Florida, together almost half the size of Rhode Island, to supply wood for a mill built in Perry, Florida, the largest mill of its kind at the time. Mill construction and land acquisition cost $40 million; P&G funded the project with $30 million in long-term notes.

When the mill opened in 1954, P&G renamed the subsidiary Buckeye Cellulose to reflect its new emphasis on providing a variety of cellulose products. The company opened new research facilities to find new uses for the cellulose it produced, often tailoring cellulose products to the needs of its customers. New products included synthetic sponges, cellophane, floor rugs, and battery components. Customers included Eastman Chemical, which used cellulose acetate for cigarette filter fibers;

Hercules, Inc., which used cellulose ethers for sausage casing and other food applications; and Akzo Nobel NV, which purchased rayon filament and cellulose ethers.

Foresters at Buckeye's Florida facilities determined ways to obtain the optimum yield from the company's pine forests based on the annual number of cords per acre. They developed a system of rotating land use for raw material, as well as reseeding and replanting trees for future supply, treating pine trees as a crop for maximum harvest, including application of pest control. Foresters increased tree production by grafting cuttings from trees with a genetic disposition for rapid growth onto mature roots. The seeds produced from the graft carried the trait to new generations of trees.

In addition to providing cellulose to a variety of industries, Buckeye continued to provide substantial raw materials to P&G. P&G wanted to make paper and paper products compatible with its existing consumer products which sold through grocery stores and required regular replenishment. The company needed a softer, more flexible pulp for paper products, however. In 1957 P&G purchased the Charmin Paper Mill in order to learn the business. Also, P&G wanted to produce a softer, more absorbent paper tissue for toilet paper, facial tissues, and paper towels. After five years of research by combined Charmin and Buckeye staff, the company achieved this goal. New products that resulted from the research included White Cloud toilet tissue, Puffs facial tissue, an improved version of Charmin toilet tissue, and Bounty paper towels, the last introduced in 1965.

A significant new product that assured the long-term well-being of the company was Pampers disposable diapers, introduced by P&G in 1962. Although the high price of the diapers dissuaded customers from purchasing Pampers, P&G worked on the product to reduce the price and slowly gained a significant market. By the mid-1970s Pampers sold in more than 70 countries.

Demand for disposable paper products required the company to build several pulp mills, and to search for a supply of long fiber pulp. Buckeye found seven million acres of virgin forest land in Alberta, Canada, which the company leased from the province to supply pulp for disposable diapers. The company constructed a pulp mill in Grande Prairie with a capacity to produce 295,000 metric tons of air-dried pulp per year. Also, by the late 1970s the company's tree farm in Florida produced ten million trees annually through reseeding and replanting of rapidly growing hybrids.

Buckeye relied on new product development from researchers at both P&G and Buckeye to generate new uses for cellulose pulp. In 1972 P&G introduced Bounce, a fabric softener applied to cellulose sheets for use in the dryer. In 1974 P&G introduced Rely tampons, a superabsorbent feminine hygiene product which used polyester and carboxymethycellulose, a wood pulp derivative, instead of cotton. The wood derivative induced toxic shock syndrome in women who used Rely tampons, and P&G discontinued the product in 1980. Later, P&G created the Always brand of sanitary napkins. Research led to the development of surgical drapes and hospital gowns, sold under the Boundary brand. The fabric-like material provided a protective

Key Dates:

1901: Procter & Gamble (P&G) creates subsidiary Buckeye Cotton Oil Company to provide cottonseed oil needed to make soap products.
1910: P&G introduces Crisco shortening, made with cottonseed oil.
1954: Buckeye begins to produce wood pulp for rayon, film, plastics, and other uses.
1962: Introduction of Pampers disposable diapers increases demand for pulp cellulose.
1993: Buckeye becomes an independent company as P&G restructures.
1995: An initial public offering of stock raises $132 million.
1997: Buckeye enters airlaid nonwovens business with acquisition of Merfin International.
1999: The acquisition of Walkisoft includes North Carolina plant where Buckeye plans to build largest ever airlaid nonwovens machine.

barrier to prevent the spread of infection from germ migration and moisture. Buckeye opened a manufacturing plant in Huntsville, Alabama, in 1980 to produce the material.

With widespread use of Pampers, Luvs disposable diapers (introduced by P&G in 1976), and other brand name pulp products, Buckeye became the largest worldwide producer of cotton linter pulp and the largest manufacturer of wood pulp. P&G renamed the company Procter & Gamble Cellulose Company.

Spinoff of P&G's Cellulose Division: 1993

In an early 1990s restructuring, P&G decided to focus its resources on consumer products and dismantled its Cellulose and Specialties Division, divesting $1.2 billion in pulp mills and timber interests. Madison Dearborn Partners, a group of investors led by former P&G executives Robert Cannon and D.B. Ferraro, acquired the two largest segments of the division, the cotton linter pulp business and mill operations in Florida. In March 1993 the group acquired the cotton linter pulp business, including the 75-acre property in Memphis, the site of company headquarters, research facilities, and the cotton linter pulp plant, which produced more than 85,000 metric tons per year (mtpy). The new owners entered into joint ownership of the Foley plant in Perry, Florida, with P&G, under Buckeye Florida LP, with the intention of obtaining full ownership in the near future. The new company took its former name, Buckeye Cellulose, appointing Cannon as CEO and Ferraro as president.

At this time Buckeye was in transition as emphasis shifted from production of dissolving pulps to specialty paper pulps for use in high quality technical and writing paper, absorbents, and industrial filter paper. In 1991 dissolving pulps accounted for 82.2 percent of revenues; by 1993 they accounted for 69.8 percent of revenues, with the balance in the more expensive specialty paper pulps. The company invested heavily in upgrading for processing specialty paper pulp, spending over $75 million from 1994 to 1996.

In November 1995 Buckeye went public with an initial offering of 7.2 million shares at $18.50 per share. The $132 million in funds raised from the IPO allowed Buckeye to acquire the remaining interest of Buckeye Florida LP for $68.9 million. Buckeye paid a total of $425 million for all of the assets it acquired from P&G. Assets in Florida included 13 acres of real estate and a pulp mill with the capacity to produce 165,000 mtpy of fluff pulp, 180,000 mtpy of dissolving pulp, and 85,000 mtpy of specialty paper pulp and cotton linter pulp.

Full ownership of Buckeye Florida made a significant difference in annual revenues. At the end of fiscal 1994, Buckeye recorded revenues of $79.8 million and net income of $7.9 million; in 1995 the company recorded revenues of $371.5 million and net income of $13 million. P&G remained Buckeye's largest customer, accounting for 39 percent of revenues, with nearly all absorbent pulps being sold to P&G, in accordance with a long term contract. Longtime customers Eastman Chemical, Hercules, and Akzo Nobel accounted for a significant portion of revenues, as well.

Expecting demand for specialty pulp to continue to grow, Buckeye sought to expand its capacity for producing specialty pulps through acquisitions. In May 1996, Buckeye purchased a linter factory, with a capacity for 30,000 mtpy, in Gluckstadt, Germany, near Hamburg, from Peter Demming AG. The acquisition included four paper machines which produced 40,000 mtpy of printing and writing grade pulp. The following September Buckeye purchased Alpha Cellulose Corporation in Lumberton, North Carolina, a manufacturer of high quality specialty pulps.

Buckeye expanded into airlaid nonwoven fabrics with the acquisition of Merfin International of Vancouver in July 1997. The airlaid nonwoven process involved using air to form natural and manmade fibers flexible enough to be shaped as desired. Merfin manufactured airlaid material for use in feminine hygiene and adult incontinence products, obtaining much of its business from P&G. The company operated two manufacturing lines at its Vancouver plant, with a capacity of 30,000 mtpy. Buckeye's $200 million acquisition included a new, $60 million manufacturing facility in Cork, Ireland, generating annual output of 15,000 metric tons on ten lines. A plant in King, North Carolina, produced 12,000 mtpy of airlaid fabric, as well as wet-laid paper for wipes, towels, and tissues for industrial and commercial uses.

Buckeye planned to combine its knowledge of pulp fiber with airlaid technology to create products with greater absorbency than others on the market. In August 1998 Buckeye Technologies—the name it had adopted the previous year to better reflect a more diversified set of products and services—announced its plans to build a pilot plant to speed the development of new airlaid nonwoven products. Located at Buckeye's Research and Development Center in Memphis, the plant utilized advanced technologies to process a combination of speciality fibers, superabsorbent polymers, and other material to create a compact yet highly absorbent material for multiple uses.

By 1999 Buckeye was ready to construct the largest airlaid nonwovens machine in the world, with a capacity to produce 50,000 mtpy of airlaid products. The company began to scout a location for the facility in Memphis and the mid-South region.

This led to the September 2000 acquisition of Walkisoft from UPM-Kymmene Corporation, a Finnish forestry group, for $120 million. Walkisoft operated a 380,000-square-foot plant in Mt. Holly, North Carolina, with a 40,000 mtpy capacity. Buckeye began to upgrade the facility with new manufacturing technology, a $100 million investment. The acquisition of Walkisoft included a plant in Steinfurt, Germany, a research and engineering operation in Kotka, Finland, and a dismantled airlaid machine in Denmark. Also, Buckeye purchased a proprietary packaging technology for efficient, compact shipping of airlaid materials from Stac-Pac Technologies, Inc. for $25 million.

To insure a supply of slash pine, Buckeye signed a long-term agreement with Foley Timber & Lumber, which owned 553,000 acres of forest land formerly owned by P&G and which was adjacent to Buckeye's Florida property. The contract increased the existing supply agreement by 50 percent through 2010.

As the company already obtained a significant portion of revenue from foreign companies, international expansion continued to be a priority. Of $712.8 million in revenues in fiscal 2000, 37 percent originated in Europe; 36 percent in North America; 15 percent in Asia; 7 percent in South America; and 5 percent in other regions. In June 2000 Buckeye invested an additional $12 million to build another airlaid nonwoven machine in Cork, bringing annual plant capacity to 30,000 metric tons. The company acquired the cotton cellulose operations from Brazil Fibria AS for $35 million in August. The operation continued to provide textile fibers for Fibria's rayon producing business.

In December Buckeye introduced a new airlaid absorbent product called ''Unicore.'' The single-ply nonwoven material provided better absorption, distribution, and storage for feminine hygiene products. The company also introduced ''Duocore,'' a two-layer product which used Unicore for the top layer and Bizorb for the bottom.

While Buckeye had remained profitable through fluctuations in pulp prices in the 1990s, the company began to cut costs in the spring of 2001 as pulp prices declined. While strong sales in 2000 had yielded an impressive $59.1 million in net income, the decrease in pulp prices in 2001 meant lower revenues and lower profits. Buckeye began to reduce expenses by eliminating tasks in administration and in research and development, doing some tasks in-house rather than outsourcing, and by cutting executive bonuses.

The good news for 2001 involved a non-detect rating for dioxin effluence at the Perry pulp mill. Buckeye and the Environmental Protection Agency had been working to eliminate dioxin since 1993 when Buckeye was bought from P&G; Buckeye spent $60 million on the project.

Principal Subsidiaries

Buckeye Florida Corporation; Buckeye Foley Corporation; Buckeye Lumberton, Inc.; Buckeye Canada, Inc.; Buckeye Technologies Ireland Ltd.; Merfin Systems, Inc.; BKI International, Inc.; Buckeye Finland OY; Buckeye Holdings GmbH (Germany).

Principal Divisions

Absorbent Products; Specialty Cellulose.

Principal Competitors

BBA Nonwovens; E.I. du Pont de Nemours & Company; Honshu Paper Co., Ltd.; International Paper Company; Polymer Group, Inc.; Rayonier Inc.; Southern Cellulose Products, Inc.; Western Pulp LP; Weyerhaeuser Company.

Further Reading

Bailey, Jeff, ''Investors Who Bought P&G Mills Stand to Reap Big Returns on IPO,'' *Wall Street Journal*, November 3, 1995.

Breskin, Ira, ''Pulp & P&G,'' *Investor's Business Daily*, June 28, 1996, p. A3.

''Buckeye Cellulose Makes Buyout Offer,'' *Tennessean*, March 26, 1997, p. E3.

''Buckeye Technologies Acquires Brazilian plant,'' *Memphis Business Journal*, August 4, 2000, p. 10.

''Buckeye Ties Down Purchase from P&G,'' *Memphis Commercial Appeal*, March 18, 1993, p. B5.

''Buckeye to Acquire Airlaid Pulp Business,'' *Pulp & Paper*, September 1999, p. 19.

''Buckeye to Buy German Business,'' *Pulp & Paper*, November 1995, p. 27.

''Buckeye to Repurchase Shares from Venture Firm,'' *Memphis Commercial Appeal*, June 5, 1996, p. B4.

Ducey, Michael, J. ''Golden Age Ahead for Tree-Free Papers,'' *Graphic Arts Monthly*, July 1996, p. 76.

Editors of *Advertising Age, Procter and Gamble: The House That Ivory Built*, Lincolnwood, Ill.: NTC Business Books, 1988.

''Investor Group Buys, Renames P&G Cellulose,'' *Memphis Commercial Appeal*, December 1992, p. B4.

Melnbardis, Robert, ''Procter & Gamble Unit Plans to Expand Pulp and Sawmill Operations in Alberta, *Wall Street Journal*, December 19, 1988, p. 1.

''Memphis, Tenn.-Based Cellulose-Products Firm Trims Costs,'' *Knight-Ridder/Tribune Business News*, April 20, 2001, p. ITEM01110001.

Merfin Accepts Buckeye Offer,'' *Pulp & Paper*, June 1997, p. 27.

Paulk, Michael, ''Buckeye Acquires Proprietary Packaging Technology,'' *Memphis Business Journal*, March 17, 2000, p. 16.

——, ''Buckeye Banks Future on Nonwoven Investments,'' *Memphis Business Journal*, June 30, 2000, p. 1.

Schisgall, Oscar, *Eyes on Tomorrow: The Evolution of Procter & Gamble*, Chicago: J.G. Ferguson Publishing Company, 1981.

Scott, Jonathan, ''Buckeye Seeks Mid-South Site for Expansion,'' *Memphis Business Journal*, July 16, 1999, p. 1.

Swasy, Alecia, *Soap Opera: The Inside Story of Procter & Gamble*, New York: Times Books, 1993.

—Mary Tradii

C.F. Martin & Co., Inc.

510 Sycamore St.
Nazareth, Pennsylvania 18064-1046
U.S.A.
Telephone: (610) 759-2837
Toll Free: (800) 633-2060
Fax: (610) 759-5757
Web site: http://www.martinguitar.com

Private Company
Incorporated: 1833
Employees: 700
Sales: $60 million (2000 est.)
NAIC: 339992 Musical Instrument Manufacturing

C.F. Martin & Co., Inc., also referred to as The Martin Guitar Company (the name of its chief subsidiary), makes what are generally considered to be the finest acoustic guitars in the world. Prized by musicians for their durability and tonal quality, Martin guitars have been used by legendary performers such as Jimmie Rodgers, Willie Nelson, Eric Clapton, Joan Baez, Johnny Cash, and many, many more. The company's offerings range from budget-priced composite material instruments to custom-built models that can cost $20,000 or more. Martin also makes ukuleles, guitar strings, and other accessories. Located in Nazareth, Pennsylvania, since 1839, the company has been run by the same family for six generations.

Roots

Martin traces its beginnings to Mark Neukirchen, Saxony (later a part of Germany), where in 1796 Christian Frederick Martin was born. Martin's father was a furniture and guitar maker, and the young man was sent to Vienna at 15 to learn instrument making from Johann Stauffer, a master guitar builder. After working his way up to foreman in Stauffer's guitar shop, Martin returned to Mark Neukirchen to build guitars on his own and raise a family. He soon found himself caught up in a battle between the area's furniture makers and the Violin Makers' Guild, which sought to bar those who were not members from building guitars. Though the Guild ultimately lost its case in local courts, Martin felt his opportunities would be limited by the Guild system, and he decided to immigrate with his wife and two young children to the United States.

Soon after their arrival in New York in the fall of 1833, Martin opened a shop on the lower east side of Manhattan where he built and repaired guitars and sold sheet music and other instruments. In the early days Martin accepted bartered items such as clothing and wine for his wares, as well as money. He soon found several parties who were willing to distribute his guitars outside of the city, which helped boost sales.

Unhappy with the overcrowded living conditions in New York, Martin and his wife decided to move to Pennsylvania, where they purchased eight acres of land near Nazareth in 1839. The small town was in an area that reminded them of the rolling hills back home in Germany, and in fact many of the town's predominantly Moravian inhabitants spoke German.

Although Martin initially made all of the guitars himself, the popularity of his finely crafted instruments soon brought greater demand than he could handle alone. In 1859 a factory was built at the corner of Main and North Streets in Nazareth to house the company's now dozen-plus employees. Guitars made during these early years were shipped to eastern cities such as New York, Boston, and Philadelphia, and as far away as Nashville, St. Louis, and New Orleans.

The early Martin guitars were entirely handcrafted, and no two were exactly alike. Models built until the mid-1840s had their six tuning keys all on one side of the guitar's headstock, as well as an adjustable neck which allowed the tension of the strings to be changed to suit individual users. Both of these features were discontinued after a time. A major innovation came around 1850 with the introduction of the "X" bracing system behind the face of the guitar. This feature strengthened the instrument and also enriched the tonal quality of Martin's guitars. At this time the firm's instruments were typically built from imported Brazilian rosewood, with a birch or maple neck, a spruce top, and an ebony fingerboard. They had an understated, elegant appearance, with a minimum of ornamentation, although this varied with customer preference. Retail prices ranged from $36 to $90.

Company Perspectives:

Our Vision: Be the best fretted instrument and string manu-facturer in the world, providing the highest quality products and services for our customers while preserving and en-hancing our unique heritage. Our Mission:
Concentrate on the profitable manufacture, distribution and service of the highest quality fretted instruments, strings and related accessories. We will investigate and develop new and improved products, methods, markets and channels of distribution.

In 1867 C.F. Martin retired, leaving the company in the hands of his son, Christian Frederick Martin, Jr., and a cousin, fellow Mark Neukirchen immigrant C.F. Hartmann. C.F. Martin, Jr., then in his 40s and himself a master guitar maker, saw the company through the post-Civil War years, where for a time sales were hurt by a national currency crisis. Martin weathered the storm, however, and the company built an addition to its factory in 1887, where steam-powered woodworking machinery was installed. When C.F. Martin, Jr., died unexpectedly in 1888 (the company's founder had passed away in 1873), the firm was left to his widow and his son, Frank Henry Martin, then only 22 years old. Partner C.F. Hartmann had by this time given up his stake, though he remained with the firm as an employee.

Taking Control of Distribution; Success with Mandolins

Frank Martin faced serious challenges almost immediately, as he took control at a time when Martin's output was hampered by a sluggish distribution system. The firm's principal sales agent, C.A. Zoebisch & Sons, was not pushing Martin products as strongly as the company wished, and was also not interested in distributing mandolins, which Martin felt would find favor with the growing number of Italian immigrants entering the United States. Ultimately Frank Martin decided to terminate the company's longstanding relationship with Zoebisch to handle sales on its own.

After taking on this major new responsibility, Frank Martin became the company's primary salesperson, visiting music dealers throughout New York State and New England on lengthy annual trips. The company was still small, with annual production of less than 300 guitars. Martin soon introduced a line of mandolins, and sales of these instruments jumped to 150 per year and even came to surpass guitar production between 1906 and 1909.

During the early years of the 20th century the company also experimented with other instrument styles, along with produc-tion of guitar strings, though the latter were discontinued after a time. Martin's success with the mandolin led to the manufacture of such related instruments as the mandola and mando-cello, and in 1915 the firm began making guitars for sale under the labels of other companies, which led to a contract with the Oliver Ditson Company of Boston. At Ditson's request, in 1916 Martin began producing a new oversized guitar that was named after the largest class of British warship, the Dreadnought.

Though relatively few of these were made, this guitar design would later figure heavily in the Martin legend. Around the close of World War I, Frank Martin's Princeton-educated sons Christian Frederick III and Herbert Keller Martin also became involved with the business, with Herbert handling sales and Christian in charge of manufacturing.

In addition to mandolins, the growing company capitalized on crazes for Hawaiian guitars and ukuleles, becoming one of the leading makers of the latter, after retooling an early design that sounded dull. A Martin ukulele became the first musical instrument to cross the North Pole, when a plane bearing one flew above it. In 1922 the company also introduced its first standard guitar model designed for use with steel, rather than gut, strings, which required additional internal bracing. The steel-strung guitars, which were louder than gut models, were a hit, and their sales grew steadily. Martin also dabbled in banjos, though these were only produced from 1923 to 1926 before being abandoned.

The company's reputation for quality was now well known, and its instruments were purchased by celebrities including author Mark Twain, silent film comedian Buster Keaton, and country music pioneer Jimmie Rodgers, whose custom Martin guitar had his name inlaid in pearl on the fingerboard. By 1928 annual production of guitars had reached 5,215, up from 1,361 just eight years earlier. Ukulele production was more than dou-ble this figure. To keep up with the growth, the company's factory was enlarged in 1925 and again in 1927.

Surviving the Depression

From the time it hit in October 1929, the Great Depression had a dramatic effect on makers of leisure goods. At Martin, guitar production dropped by nearly half between 1929 and 1931. Struggling to stay afloat, the company cut wages and even adopted a three-day work week for a time. Martin also began producing other wooden products to keep its craftsmen busy, including violin parts and wooden bracelets. Efforts to stimulate guitar sales with new designs were made as well, which led to production of a number of different styles, including what would turn out to be some of Martin's most famous instruments.

One new design was the 14-fret neck (frets being the bars on the guitar's neck which determine musical tones when a string is pressed against one and plucked). Prior to 1929 most guitars were built with only 12 frets extending away from the guitar's body, but when banjo player Perry Bechtel requested a new guitar design with more frets and a better-braced flat top for steel strings, Martin created the "Orchestra Model" (OM). The new 14-fret design proved immensely popular, and soon was taken up as the standard format for almost all U.S. guitars.

Another major Martin success of the 1930s was actually an update of a design from 1916. In 1931, after the Ditson Com-pany went out of business, Martin started producing Dreadnought guitars under its own nameplate with bracing added for steel strings. The improved guitar found favor with solo performers, who could more easily reach the ears of a large audience with the boomier sound produced by the instrument. A special top-of-the-line Dreadnought, the D-45 model, was also custom-made for well-heeled artists such as Gene Autry. It

Key Dates:

1833: C. F. Martin arrives in New York City from Germany, opens a guitar shop.

1839: Martin moves his business to Nazareth, Pennsylvania.

1850: "X-braced" guitar design, which improves strength and tone, is introduced.

1859: Martin opens a new factory on North Street in Nazareth.

1867: Martin's son C.F. Martin, Jr., takes control of the company from his father.

1888: Frank Henry Martin takes reins upon death of C.F. Martin, Jr.

1890s: Firm begins handling its own distribution, starts building mandolins.

1929: Fourteen-fret Orchestra Model guitar is introduced; format is soon adopted as industry norm.

1931: Production of Dreadnought guitar style begins under Martin nameplate.

1948: Frank Henry Martin dies; C.F. Martin III assumes control of company.

1964: New factory opens on Sycamore St. in Nazareth.

1970: Frank Herbert Martin is named CEO, begins round of unsuccessful acquisitions.

1977: Martin employees begin a nine-month strike.

1982: Frank Herbert Martin is forced out; C.F. Martin III reassumes control of failing company.

1986: C. F. Martin IV is named chairman and CEO upon his grandfather's death.

1995: First Martin signature-series guitar debuts; low-cost Backpacker model is introduced.

1999: Company spends $6.5 million to expand factory by more than 85,000 square feet.

featured a generous amount of mother-of-pearl inlay and often had the musician's name inlaid on the fingerboard. In contrast to standard industry practice, Martin did not provide guitars to celebrities free of charge to help promote the company's name, but nonetheless received many paid orders for them from stars who were impressed by their quality. The 91 D-45s made before World War II later became something of a "holy grail" to guitar collectors, with the 70-plus surviving examples typically valued at more than $125,000 by the late 1990s.

Martin's efforts to remain afloat during the Depression were successful, and the company began to prosper once again following the war as the United States entered a period of economic growth. In 1948 Frank Henry Martin passed away, leaving the firm in the hands of Christian Frederick Martin III (his brother Herbert had died in 1927). Frederick Martin, as he was known, took as one of his first tasks a pruning of the catalog, which had seen a profusion of different instrument styles added during the 1930s. In 1955 his son Frank Herbert Martin also joined the firm.

The year 1958 saw C.F. Martin & Co. introduce its first electric guitar, an acoustic model with added electrical pickups.

The instrument did not find favor among musicians, however, and later attempts to make solid-body electric guitars and amplifiers were also unsuccessful.

The 1960s Folk Boom

The folk music revival of the early 1960s, exemplified by Martin-playing artists The Kingston Trio, Joan Baez, and Johnny Cash, gave a tremendous boost to the company's sales. For a time customers faced a wait of up to three years for certain models. A new factory on Sycamore Street just north of Nazareth was completed in 1964, and its single-story design (compared with the 1859 plant's four stories) increased efficiency and production, which reached 10,000 for the first time in 1965. In 1968 Martin hired Mike Longworth, a Tennessee guitar customizer, to resume the practice of putting pearl inlay on the company's top-of-the-line instruments at its factory. Longworth, also a guitar historian, later published the first book-length history of the firm in 1975.

In 1970 C.F. Martin III's son Frank Herbert began to take increasing control of the company from his father (he was named president the following year), and for the first time Martin began to make acquisitions. During 1970 Vega Banjo Works, Fibes Drum Company, and Darco String Company were all purchased. Several years later a drumstick manufacturer and the A.B. Herman Carlson Levin Company of Sweden, a guitar maker, were also acquired. By the early 1980s all save Darco were sold off or folded, however. Martin also began importing inexpensive Japanese Sigma guitars to compete with the tide of Martin knockoffs that were flooding the market, and built a new sawmill behind the company's plant in 1974.

Many of these changes did not sit well on the factory floor, where some employees had worked for decades, and their parents and grandparents before them. In 1977, after a series of new management directives caused increasing friction, newly unionized Martin workers went on strike. Nine months later they returned to their jobs, but an air of distrust lingered for some time to come.

Hitting a Sour Note

Frank Herbert Martin's management of the company was turning out to be a disaster. In addition to the failed acquisitions and the worker strike, Martin's reputation and quality were in decline, with the company even briefly rescinding the lifetime warranty it had always offered on its guitars. Frank Herbert had also sold some of his shares in the company to help pay for his four divorces, and management of the firm was now overseen by a board of directors.

By 1982, a general decline in sales for acoustic guitars brought the company's instrument production to less than 4,000, down from 22,637 in 1971. Unwilling to allow the 150-year-old family business to perish, octogenarian C.F. Martin III returned from retirement to try to pull the company back from the brink. In May 1982 the firm's board voted to fire Frank Martin and replace him with his father. The company continued to struggle, however, and by 1985 the directors began to contemplate liquidating Martin's assets.

An impassioned appeal from a new, young member of the board helped stave off this fate, however. It came from Frank Herbert Martin's son Christian Frederick Martin IV, known as Chris. Following his parents' divorce, Chris had spent a great deal of time with his grandfather C.F. III, from whom he began to learn about the family business. After studying economics and business at UCLA and Boston University, Chris began working at Martin in a variety of departments to learn the company from the ground up. In 1985 he was named vice-president of marketing, in addition to serving on the board, and he became CEO and chairman the following year when C.F. Martin III passed away.

Chris Martin quickly began to put his own stamp on the company. He was particularly interested in reaching a new generation of guitar players, and oversaw introduction of several less-expensive models including the scaled-down Backpacker travel guitar and the "1 Series" model built with computer-aided tools. Martin Backpackers later became the first guitars to ascend Mt. Everest and to travel into outer space, with a Backpacker played in orbit aboard the space shuttle Columbia in March 1994. The Backpacker, along with the Darco string line, was produced at a factory in Mexico that employed 50. A number of reissued versions of classic Martins were also being built, including a reproduction of the famed D-45 Dreadnought that sold for $18,000.

Martin also began to make limited-edition "signature" model guitars named after such luminary performers as Eric Clapton, Johnny Cash, and Gene Autry. Part of the price of the instruments, which sold for between $3,000 and $10,000 depending on the design, went to a charity designated by the performer. While some sold quickly (including an extra-special $22,000 Clapton model), others proved difficult for dealers to move.

By 1996 sales topped 23,000, a new company record. Martin's renewed focus on its core values coincided with a revived interest in acoustic guitars, partially due to the "unplugged" phenomenon introduced by MTV (which featured rock performers performing on acoustic instruments). Another development which helped sales was a new generation of microphones that gave a clean, distortion-free sound in amplified rock band settings which had largely been off-limits to acoustic guitars.

In 1998 construction began on a new $6.5 million, 85,000-square-foot addition to the Sycamore St. factory, which had seen a $2.2 million addition less than a decade earlier. Completed in 1999, the space also included room for a Martin museum. The company was now more aware of its history than ever, and had begun buying up prime examples of its older guitars as well as offering daily factory tours to visitors. Martin's customers now included nostalgic baby boomers flush with cash from the strong economy of the late 1990s, as well as young guitarists interested in a quality instrument with a long tradition behind it. At the turn of the century the company courted the latter with its least expensive guitar ever, the composite-material DXM model which sold for less than $600. Annual production by the year 2000 was over 40,000, nearly double the record-setting figure of just four years earlier.

Revitalized under the guiding hand of Chris Martin IV, C.F. Martin & Co. was in its healthiest shape ever as it entered the 21st century. Its reputation for quality was once again high, its annual output of instruments was growing rapidly, and, perhaps most importantly, Martin guitars continued to be favored by a wide range of musicians, from beginners purchasing a DXM model to top stars who could afford the very best the company had to offer.

Principal Subsidiaries

The Martin Guitar Company; Darco Strings.

Principal Competitors

Taylor Guitars; Gibson Guitar Corp.; Jean Larrivee Guitars Ltd.; Takamine Company; Alvarez Guitars.

Further Reading

Boak, Dick, "Why Acoustic Guitar Sales Are Booming," *Music Trades*, January 1, 1994, p. 88.

Carter, Walter, *The Martin Book,* London: Balafon Books, 1995.

Jordan, Tracy, "Martin Guitar's Special Is Stephen Stills This Year—Investment Value of $19,000 Signed Guitar Is Debatable," *Allentown Morning Call*, July 23, 1999, p. B8.

Leming, John, "Martin Guitar Strums Its Way to Higher Profit," *Eastern Pennsylvania Business Journal*, January 1, 1994, p. 1.

Longworth, Mike, *Martin Guitars: A History,* Cedar Knolls, N.J.: Colonial Press, 1975.

"Martin Bets Big on Guitar's Future," *Music Trades*, July 1, 1999, p. 162.

Mercer, Timothy A., "Then and NOW: Industry 'Savior' Continues to Craft Sought-After Guitars," *Eastern Pennsylvania Business Journal*, May 15, 2000, p. 49.

Schuch, Beverly, "Guitar to the Stars" (television transcript), *CNNfn: Business Unusual*, July 31, 2000.

Washburn, Jim, and Richard Johnston, *Martin Guitars: An Illustrated Celebration of America's Premier Guitarmaker,* Emmaus, Pa.: Rodale Press, 1997.

—Frank Uhle

Canfor Corporation

3000-Four Bentall Centre
1055 Dunsmuir Street
Vancouver, British Columbia V7X 1B5
Canada
Telephone: (604) 661-5241
Fax: (604) 661-5235
Web site: http://www.canfor.com

Public Company
Incorporated: 1938 as Pacific Veneer
Employees: 6,574
Sales: C$2.26 billion (2000)
Stock Exchanges: Toronto
Ticker Symbol: CFP
NAIC: 11531 Support Activities for Forestry

Canfor Corporation is the largest producer of lumber in Canada and one of the country's leading producers of pulp. The company's mills, facilities, and timber resources are located principally in British Columbia and, to a lesser extent, in Alberta. Wood products account for the majority of the company's sales, including products such as dimension lumber, studs, plywood, and trim board. Roughly 75 percent of the company's overall sales are made in North America.

Origins

A Canadian company with Austrian heritage, Canfor was founded by John G. Prentice and his brother-in-law, Leopold Bentley. Prentice and Bentley fled their native Austria on the eve of World War II, seeking refuge from the threat of subjugation by Nazi Germany. *Anschluss*, the incorporation of Austria into the German Reich, occurred in 1938, the same year Prentice and Bentley moved with their families to Vancouver, British Columbia. Before the end of the year, the two men started their own company, Pacific Veneer, a small furniture veneer company that ultimately evolved into Canada's largest softwood lumber producer, Canfor Corporation.

Pacific Veneer began as a small company, but its growth was quickly fanned by the outbreak of hostilities overseas. Prentice and Bentley built a small mill along the Fraser River in New Westminster, British Columbia, not long after starting their entrepreneurial careers in Canada. Initially, the mill employed 28 workers, but after Great Britain was severed from its European wood supplies in 1939, employment at the mill mushroomed. Pacific Veneer began supplying plywood for wartime aviation and marine purposes, which delivered explosive growth, soon raising the mill's employment rolls to 1,000. With their profits, Prentice and Bentley were quick to expand, acquiring Eburne Saw Mills Limited in 1940. Situated near the mouth of the Fraser River, the Eburne mill was improved and converted to cut hemlock and balsam. The acquisition also made Pacific Veneer a shareholder in a Vancouver-based wood products marketing and shipping consortium named Seaboard Lumber Sales Ltd. Through its interest in Seaboard, Pacific Veneer gained advantages it could immediately put to use, such as better access to overseas markets and lower freight rates.

Prentice and Bentley continued to develop Pacific Veneer into a timber concern during the war years. The two partners were intent on obtaining control over a stable log supply to feed into their mills, and in 1943 they began to vertically integrate their operations by purchasing a handful of small logging operations in the Fraser Valley. The following year they bolstered their timber supply by acquiring logging rights in the Nimpkish Valley on Vancouver Island, a purchase that served as the foundation of their company's Englewood Logging division. By the end of the war, Prentice and Bentley controlled far more than a furniture veneer company, the realization of which prompted the two founders to search for a new name for their company. Pacific Veneer no longer accurately reflected the logging and mill operations that composed the company. In 1947, they renamed their company Canadian Forest Products Limited, adopting the name of a small timber operation included in the acquisition of timber rights in the Nimpkish Valley.

Post-World War II: Diversification and Growth

Canadian Forest entered the 1950s primed for growth and ready to diversify its operations. The company continued to add to its portfolio of mills and timber resources, but the most significant move of the decade pushed Canadian Forest in a new direction. In 1951, the company acquired a small, unbleached kraft pulp mill, marking its entry into the pulp business. Named Howe Sound Pulp Company Limited, the mill was closed when Canadian Forest completed the acquisition, but the shuttered mill was soon expanded and converted to produce bleached pulp.

A series of acquisitions charted Canadian Forest's growth during the postwar years. The company expanded geographically and it broadened its business scope, developing a spectrum of operations that were organized into several divisions. In 1955, shortly after diversifying into the pulp business for the first time, Canadian Forest purchased a 50 percent interest in Northern Plywood Ltd., located in Grande Prairie, Alberta. The company later acquired the rest of Northern Plywood, which formed the foundation for Canadian Forest's Grande Prairie Logging division, comprising Northern Plywood and nearby mills that were acquired later. In 1963, the basis of Canadian Forest's Chetwynd division was established when a handful of sawmills and planer mills were purchased in the Peace River District. The acquisitions marked Canadian Forest's march into the northern British Columbia interior, where the company also secured timber rights and mills owned by the Fort St. John Lumber Company. A year after the acquisitions were completed, the assets were consolidated to form the company's Chetwynd division.

Diversification and expansion continued into the 1970s and 1980s. After establishing a mill in Alberta—the Hines Creek mill—in 1970, Canadian Forest acquired a majority interest in Westcoast Cellufibre Industries Ltd. Completed in 1973, the investment provided Canadian Forest with a supplier of chips for its Howe Sound Pulp mill. Two years after taking control of Westcoast Cellufibre, Canadian Forest gained a new leader. Peter Bentley, the son of cofounder Leopold Bentley, was named president and chief executive officer, assuming day-to-day control over the company in 1975.

1975: The Peter Bentley Era Begins

Before his penultimate promotion (he was later named chairman), Bentley accumulated a wealth of working experience, both at Canfor and at other timber-related companies. As a teen, the Vienna-born Bentley worked as a sparkchaser in a firefighting crew, then worked as a truck driver and a surveyor. As a salesman for a lumber wholesaler in Chicago, Bentley secured prized contracts with Caterpillar, Pontiac, and Ford, winning over the Midwest's influential industrial executives at prestigious golf clubs.

After leaving Chicago at age 23, Bentley returned to his family's business. ''I was put where they put me,'' Bentley remembered in an October 1995 interview with *BC Business*. ''I was more or less ordered to take forestry at UBC (University of British Columbia).'' He worked his way up through the organization, earning his promotions by taking on responsibilities related to nearly every facet of the company's activities, from stints at the

Eburne sawmill in Vancouver to working at Canadian Forest's sales offices in Europe. In 1970, when the company's annual sales reached C$144 million, Bentley was named executive vice-president of operations, awarded the post as he entered his early 40s.

When Bentley was named executive vice-president, Canadian Forest was in the midst of a significant transformation. For years, Bentley's father and uncle had been developing Canadian Forest beyond its roots as a coastal wood-products manufacturer and into an integrated forest company operating throughout western Canada. When Bentley assumed control over the company in 1975, he continued to chase the strategic objective of the previous generation, but his structural changes went deeper. In the early 1970s, before he accepted the posts of president and chief executive officer, Bentley was approached by a large U.S.-based forest products company. Bentley considered accepting the job offer, but his father and uncle were intent on retaining their experienced protégé. Bentley offered to stay, provided, he stipulated, they allow him to manage the company the way he saw fit. The co-founders agreed, ushering in a new management style that helped fuel robust growth.

Before Bentley began making his changes, Canadian Forest had conducted business in the traditional style of a family-owned business. Decisions were made at the top, with all department managers reporting directly to the cofounders, who then issued their instructions. Bentley insisted on a less hierarchical, less centralized mode of management, instead promoting communication among department managers and the dissemination of all pertinent information throughout the company. Access to information and interdepartmental interaction made for a more successful corporate organization, one better equipped to contend with the challenges that lay ahead. Canadian Forest was in the midst of shaking off the last vestiges of its entrepreneurial beginnings and set to become a full-fledged corporation.

Under the leadership of a new generation, Canadian Forest continued its steady expansion. In 1981, the company purchased Swanson Lumber Co. Ltd., which owned and operated valuable sawmills and woodlands operations. Two years later, the company converted to public ownership. Concurrently, the company changed its name for the second time in its history, becoming Canfor Corporation. The company's former name, Canadian Forest Products, became the new name for a wholly owned subsidiary. The achievements of Bentley's first years in control also included continuing the process of transforming Canfor into an integrated forest products company. Bentley sold Canfor's shingle and plywood mills, divested non-forest assets, such as a trust company and several shipyards, and focused the company's efforts on three business areas: lumber, pulp and paper, and fiber products.

1990s: The Search for Strategic Focus

Despite a narrowed focus on its operating activities, Canfor entered the 1990s struggling to turn a profit. The company had grown tremendously since Bentley's ascension to leadership, increasing its annual sales to more than C$1 billion and swelling its stature to become Canada's largest lumber producer, but profitability, once a strong suit, had become an issue forcing a response. In 1991, a companywide reorganization was implemented as a solution to Canfor's problems. The company's business was structured into three groups: pulp and paper, coastal wood

Key Dates:

1938: Canfor's predecessor, Pacific Veneer, is founded.
1947: Company is renamed Canadian Forest Products Limited.
1951: Company enters the pulp business through the acquisition of Howe Sound Pulp Company Ltd.
1975: Peter Bentley is named president and chief executive officer.
1983: Now rechristened as Canfor Corporation, the company begins trading on the Toronto Stock Exchange.
1999: Northwood Inc. is acquired, doubling Canfor's lumber and pulp capacity.

products, and northern wood products. To aid Bentley in executing the new structure, Arild Nielssen was appointed president and chief operating officer, assuming the posts in 1991.

Canfor's efforts to restore the luster of profitability were not helped by the onset of anemic economic conditions. The early 1990s were years of severe economic downturn, hobbling the efforts of Canfor, along with a litany of other companies, to demonstrate financial vitality. Once the economic climate began to improve, Canfor moved boldly forward, hoping to join the industry-wide trend toward consolidation and to realize the expected financial benefits. In December 1994, the company announced its intention to take over Vancouver-based Slocan Forest Products Ltd. Canfor offered C$650 million for Slocan, which ranked as Canada's fourth largest lumber producer. Provided the deal was accepted by Slocan shareholders and approved by provincial authorities, Canfor would gain control over nearly 40 percent of the provincial timber in the Prince George area and, of strategic importance, the company would benefit from Slocan's valuable wood chip output. The deal collapsed, however, in early 1995, meeting stiff resistance from Slocan, its shareholders, and the B.C. Forest Minister.

Following the disappointment of the scuttled Slocan takeover, more distressing news cast a pall over Canfor's Vancouver headquarters. The company's financial results were miserable, despite an increase in revenues to more than C$1.5 billion. In 1996, the company's before-tax losses totaled C$56.9 million, followed by a C$32.9 million loss in 1997. Arild Nielssen left the company in July 1997, offering no public explanation, which marked the return of Peter Bentley to the offices of president and chief executive officer. Bentley's tenure was brief, however, ending once a replacement for Nielssen was found. David Emerson, the former deputy finance minister and deputy minister to British Columbia's Premier, was selected as Canfor's new steward. Before joining Canfor in 1998, Emerson served as president and chief executive officer of the Vancouver International Airport Authority, the identical posts he would occupy at Canfor.

The partnership of Bentley and Emerson combined to revitalize a beleaguered company. A restructuring program was begun in 1998, its aim to focus on efficiencies and to reduce costs. The reorganization marked the first major initiative of Emerson's tenure, and it began with the reduction of the company's workforce by 20 percent, which represented the loss of 250 jobs. Structurally, Canfor was divided into three divisions:

pulp and paper products, northern wood products, and coastal wood products. Each business group was organized as an autonomous business, responsible for its financial performance and management in much the same way as a stand-alone business. Growth in pulp and paper products, a key facet of the company's business scope, was expected to be realized by turning the division into a specialty kraft operation. Although capital spending was cut back drastically during the reorganization, C$8 million was set aside to upgrade Canfor's paper machines at its Prince George pulp and paper mill. Longer-range plans called for production to be tripled.

With Emerson spearheading the efforts toward recovery, Canfor demonstrated a newfound strength. In 1998, the company reported another devastating loss of more than C$200 million, but its bottom line improved dramatically the following year. In 1999, the company's net income surged to C$102.6 million in a year highlighted by a mammoth acquisition. In August, the company entered into an agreement to purchase Northwood Inc. for C$635 million. The acquisition agreement closed in November, giving Canfor a wealth of new assets located principally in the Prince George area of British Columbia. From the acquisition, Canfor gained four sawmills, one plywood mill, one pulp mill, one wood treatment plant, two log-chipping facilities, and timber-cutting rights, nearly doubling the company's pulp and lumber capacity.

Much of 2000 was devoted to integrating Northwood's assets into the Canfor fold, a process that was expected to continue into 2001. Revenue in 2000 surged past the C$2 billion mark, reaching C$2.26 billion, while net income swelled to C$125.6 million. With the company's efforts sharply focused on wood products and pulp and specialty kraft paper, Canfor entered the 21st century rejuvenated, exhibiting the type of strength that had proved elusive in the 1990s. The tandem of Bentley and Emerson appeared to be a partnership well equipped to shepherd Canfor into the future.

Principal Subsidiaries

Canadian Forest Products Ltd.; Genus Resource Management Technologies Inc.; Howe Sound Pulp and Paper (50%).

Principal Competitors

Abitibi-Consolidated Inc.; West Fraser Timber Co. Ltd.; Nexfor Inc.

Further Reading

"Arild Nielssen," *Pulp & Paper,* December 1991, p. 129.
"Canfor Bid for Slocan Falls Short," *Pulp & Paper,* March 1995, p. 21.
"Canfor Corp.," *Pulp & Paper,* January 1998, p. 37.
"Canfor Corp.," *Pulp & Paper,* June 1995, p. 33.
"Canfor Restructures for Profitability," *Pulp & Paper,* August 1998, p. 19.
"David Emerson," *Wood Technology,* March 1998, p. 74.
McCullough, Michael, "Peter Bentley," *BC Business,* October 1995, p. 37.
"Slocan Fends Off Canfor; Buyout Bid Stirs B.C. Issue," *Wood Technology,* March–April 1995, p. 11.

—Jeffrey L. Covell

Canterbury Park Holding Corporation

1100 Canterbury Road
Shakopee, Minnesota 55379
U.S.A.
Telephone: (952) 445-7223
Toll Free: (800) 340-6361
Fax: (952) 496-6400
Web site: http://www.canterburypark.com

Public Company
Incorporated: 1994
Employees: 700
Sales: $32.5 million (2000)
Stock Exchanges: NASDAQ
Ticker Symbol: TRAK
NAIC: 711212 Race Tracks

Canterbury Park Holding Corporation owns and operates the Canterbury Park Racetrack and Card Club in Shakopee, Minnesota, a short drive south from both Minneapolis and St. Paul. The company's primary business operations are parimutuel horse racing and unbanked card games (in which patrons play against one another, rather than the house). Canterbury Park conducts live thoroughbred, quarterhorse, and harness racing with approximately 60 live-race days annually from May to September. It is the state's only parimutuel horseracing facility. Canterbury Park also offers patrons daily simulcast races from around the country for wagering. Simulcast race proceeds are used to subsidize onsite racing purses. In 2000, the Canterbury Card Club began offering unbanked card games 24 hours a day, seven days a week. Since 1998, the track has hosted the Annual Claiming Crown meet, giving Canterbury Park national exposure. The company also rents its facilities for special events and hosts community-oriented celebrations.

Early 1980s: An Idea Becomes Reality

The idea of creating a horse-racing industry in Minnesota began to take shape in 1982 when State Representative Dick Kostohryz pushed Minnesota voters to approve a constitutional amendment allowing parimutuel betting in the state. As soon as the amendment passed, Kostohryz introduced a parimutuel bill in the legislature and Minnesota's horseracing industry was out of the starting gate. Two years later ground was broken for Minnesota's first track, Canterbury Downs.

Brooks Fields and his nephew Brooks Hauser, of Minnesota Racetrack, Inc., were granted the first license by the Minnesota Racing Commission. They planned to build in Shakopee. The initial investors included, among others, owners of the Santa Anita track in southern California and the City of Shakopee, which granted $6 million in tax-increment bond financing. The facility was built for a controversial $67 million, making it one of the most expensive tracks in a decade.

In addition to authorizing parimutuel betting, the Minnesota legislature created the Racing Commission to oversee licensing of tracks and help advance the industry in Minnesota. To help strengthen Minnesota's struggling breeding enterprises, the legislature added a breeders' incentive provision to the parimutuel law, which allocated a portion of funds raised to go toward a breeders' fund. The state would reap the benefits of the additional tax revenues.

The owners of the new track were concerned early on about how Minnesotans would embrace horseracing when few had knowledge of the parimutuel industry. Prior to the track's opening, therefore, racetrack officials worked to educate potential customers about horseracing and parimutuel wagering. Minnesota Racetrack hired Stan Bowker, an experienced track manager in Omaha, to serve as general manager of the new track. Bowker spent months visiting other tracks to persuade respected trainers to race their horses at Canterbury Downs during its inaugural season.

Success of Canterbury Downs hinged on attendance numbers and how much visitors were willing to wager. Owners speculated that they would see daily attendance figures of 10,500. Projected handle amounts—the total amount wagered on the race—were based on each patron betting an average of $120. By Minnesota law, the purses, or the prize monies, were set at 5 percent of the total handle.

The track opened in 1985 with a great deal of excitement and fanfare. Attendance figures after two weeks showed an impres-

Company Perspectives:

Canterbury Park strives to provide a premier, diverse entertainment center, where guests and employees are treated with respect and experience a unique, enjoyable place to work and play.

sive average of 13,661 visitors, but wagering was well below projections, amounting to just $57 per patron. The track also suffered from a smaller than expected number of horses competing, which limited the number and sizes of races. In its first season Canterbury Downs attracted average daily attendance of 13,163 but posted a loss of $1.4 million.

In the track's second year the numbers surpassed those of the inaugural year, but they were still below projections. A total of $135 million was wagered, but average attendance slipped slightly to 9,104 visitors. Minnesota gained more than $7 million for the state's general fund, but Canterbury Downs lost $11 million.

The following year Stan Bowker left to start a racetrack consulting business. Mike Manning, from the Santa Anita Track in California, replaced Bowker as general manager. The track set an attendance record of 27,439 on June 28, 1987, but the operation still fell short of its revenue goals. The per capita average wager was up to $108, but attendance continued to slip to 8,570 per race day. Discouraged by the shrinking purses, horse owners were looking elsewhere to race.

1990: New Ownership

Despite Canterbury's losses, the impact of the track on the state's horse breeding industry was growing. Breeding farms were sprouting up all over the state, and there was talk of opening a second track in the Little Falls area northwest of the Twin Cities. In an effort to increase wagering revenues and ultimately purse amounts, horse breeders and Canterbury Downs owners asked the legislature to allow Canterbury Downs races to be televised at off-track locations simulcast around the state.

Canterbury Downs' finances were still shaky at the close of the 1989 season. Average attendance dipped to 7,239, just over half of the 1985 attendance. Purse amounts were decreased to combat financial problems. Several prospective buyers for Canterbury Downs began to make headlines as speculation about the track being sold ebbed and flowed throughout the 1989 live-racing season. Finally, in 1990 the track was purchased by Ladbroke Racing Corporation, the U.S. subsidiary of British hotel and racing giant Ladbroke Group PLC, for about $21 million.

In the previous legislative season, track officials had been lobbying legislators for permission to simulcast races for wagering from other tracks, which would draw patrons to Canterbury Downs year round. In 1990, regular simulcast race wagering began at Canterbury. Patrons were able to watch and bet on simulcast races from other parts of the country via television at Canterbury Downs. With simulcasting races, the track received a portion of the money bet on each race. The simul-

casting revenues helped generate additional revenue for the company, but live racing attendance dipped to a low of 6,054 daily visitors.

Adding to the track's woes, competition for gaming dollars in the state was increasing. The Minnesota State Lottery was launched in 1990. A year later Native American casinos began to open up on reservations around the state. Racetrack gambling fell to only 1–2 percent of gambling revenues in the state.

Canterbury Downs' annual losses continued to be in the millions, while attendance continued to slide, so much so that in 1992 a live-race card was cancelled because small purses did not attract enough competitors.

Ladbroke and the previous owners had been lobbying for the off-track provision in the state for several years to increase statewide exposure for Canterbury Downs and increase wagering on live races. After a nod of approval of off-track betting by the Minnesota Legislature, the Minnesota State Supreme Court ruled unanimously in July 1992 that off-track betting on horse races at Canterbury Downs was unconstitutional. As the *Star Tribune* reported on July 31, "the court said it was compelled to abide by the 'literal and unambiguous meaning' of a 1982 constitutional amendment approved by voters. That ballot question specifically authorized 'on-track' parimutuel betting."

With losses mounting and little hope for off-track betting, Ladbroke would not guarantee the Minnesota Racing Commission a live meet the following season. The Racing Commission responded by outlawing simulcasting of horse races. Ladbroke Group closed the track and decided to sell.

Prospective buyers began to surface in 1993, and in early 1994 Minnesota businessman Irwin Jacobs bought Canterbury Downs for $9 million from Ladbroke. His purchase came after a drawn out court battle with a North Dakota woman who claimed previous rights to buy the track. Jacobs commented to *CityBusiness* in January 1994 that he bought the property because he felt it was undervalued. Jacobs considered other options for the Canterbury site, such as a car racetrack, amphitheater, convention center, or a casino to supplement track finances.

1994: Resale and Public Offering

After having done their financial homework on the viability of operating the track, Curt Sampson and Dale Schenian bought Canterbury Downs from Jacobs for $9 million in March 1994, establishing Canterbury Park Holding Corporation. In August the new owners took the company public to generate working capital and help offset debt, raising $4.8 million through the initial offering.

Sampson had a background in the industry as the son of a horse breeder and former president of the Minnesota Thoroughbred Association. The new owners' commitment to and involvement in the Minnesota horse industry helped them win community and political support. To make live racing more financially feasible in Minnesota, Sampson proposed shortening the live racing season and offering simulcast racing year-round. He planned to offer less than 60 days of live racing each year, with 365 days of simulcast racing, compared to 283 offered in 1992.

<table>
<tr><td colspan="2">Key Dates:</td></tr>
</table>

Key Dates:

1982: Minnesota voters approve parimutuel betting.

1984: Minnesota Racetrack, Inc. breaks ground for Canterbury Downs.

1985: Live horse racing begins at Canterbury Downs.

1990: Ladbroke Group PLC buys Canterbury Downs business.

1991: Minnesota legislature approves off-track betting, but Minnesota Supreme Court declares it unconstitutional.

1992: Canterbury Downs closes.

1994: Curtis Sampson and Dale Schenian purchase Canterbury Downs; Canterbury Park Holding Corporation goes public.

1995: Live racing returns to Minnesota; name of track officially changes to Canterbury Park.

1996: Minnesota legislature passes legislation exempting some parimutuel revenues from tax.

1999: Inaugural Claiming Crown race is held at Canterbury Park.

2000: Canterbury Park Card Club begins operations.

In April 1994 the new owners hired Stan Bowker back as general manager of the track. Bowker was committed to returning Canterbury to the level of racing it had in 1985 and 1986. Randy Sampson, Curt's son, became president.

That first year back in business, Canterbury Downs offered only simulcast racing, giving the new owners an opportunity to raise revenue to invest in purses the next season. Under the new ownership, the early numbers were promising. In the first four days, the 10,000 people who visited the track wagered more than $1.5 million. The new owners were hoping the earnings from the simulcast races would ensure a minimum daily purse of $40,000 for the 1995 live-race season.

The new owners also worked the political angle of the business. The legislature had approved a statewide public referendum to add a constitutional amendment to legalize off-track betting in Minnesota. Proponents of the amendment worked hard to educate Minnesotans about the referendum, especially since each blank ballot was considered a no vote. The referendum was narrowly defeated. It would have allowed the company to expand the number of live racing days, increase horseracing revenues, and ultimately would have benefited breeders in the state.

The return to live racing in 1995 began with the owners officially unveiling the new Canterbury Park logo and name. The new name for the racetrack was intended to symbolize a more family-friendly atmosphere and help bolster attendance. Canterbury Park developed more of an entertainment focus, with frequent music, pony rides, a paddock, and a large playground.

The track's 55 days of live racing drew nearly 4,000 bettors per day, but overall handle was low. Owners offered patrons year-round simulcast races, and for the first time, Canterbury Park races were simulcast to out of state tracks as well. Samp-

son pushed hard to attract more special events to the facility, such as craft shows, snowmobile races, boat shows, food festivals, rodeos—all drawing additional revenue and people to Canterbury Park.

1996: Turning the Corner

Canterbury Park's finances improved in 1996 because of tax relief legislation signed by Governor Arne Carlson. The new state law exempted Canterbury's first $12 million of parimutuel revenue from the 6 percent Minnesota parimutuel tax and allowed the company to keep all uncashed winning tickets (which were previously turned over to the racing commission). The law, which was set to expire in three years, became effective during the last half of the 1996 fiscal year, reducing the company's expenses by approximately $435,000 and providing an additional $122,000 contribution to the purse fund.

Thanks to the tax break, Canterbury Park Holding Corporation reported its first profitable year in 1996, earning $71,149, compared with a loss of more than $800,000 in 1995. The owners continued lobbying for additional revenue sources such as slot machines or poker.

In 1997 Canterbury gained the full benefit of the tax law changes, reducing expenses by $841,000 and providing $240,000 in additional revenue to the purse fund. Attendance was on the rise, and Canterbury Park reported a net profit for the 1997 fiscal year of $135,788 on revenues of $18.2 million. The company was unsuccessful, however, at gaining legislative approval for casino-style slots at Canterbury Park. The proceeds would have helped fund a Minnesota Twins baseball stadium.

Owners continued to build on the Park's off-season usage. Beginning in 1997 Canterbury Park hosted a highly successful Holiday in Lights for families, which featured holiday light displays, a sliding hill, ice skating, and sled dog racing. During the warmer seasons Canterbury hosted motorcycle races and motocross events.

In 1998 Canterbury Park was helped by an omnibus tax bill which allowed the tax relief legislation from 1996 to become permanent. This significantly added to the company's outlook for long-term stability. Track executives continued to increase the number of live racing days, and purses grew to $70,000 per day in 1999, up from a low of $20,000 in 1992.

The highlight of 1999 was Canterbury's hosting of a new national event—the first annual Claiming Crown—a championship for claiming horses, or the best of the horses competing at the lower levels. Canterbury Park received nationwide revenue as well as nationwide exposure for hosting. The track saw a record handle and attendance for Canterbury Park that day. The Claiming Crown was so well received at Canterbury that it was scheduled to be held at the site through 2007. The company reported a profit that year of $386,619, the company's third consecutive year of profit.

Canterbury officials soon found some success in the political arena when the Minnesota legislature gave approval for implementation of a 24-hour-a-day Unbanked Card Club. In April 2000 the Canterbury Card Club started dealing, and the impact was even greater than owners anticipated. With "unbanked games'' Canterbury Park collected a small amount from each hand for operating the Card Club, but patrons played against one another rather than the house. The legislation governing the Card Club stipulated that Canterbury Park was the only location in Minnesota allowed to have a card club. A portion of the proceeds from the Card Club were earmarked for purse increases and the state breeders' fund. The Card Club made available 42 tables where guests could play poker variations such as Texas Hold'em, Omaha, and 7-card Stud, as well as Pai Gow Poker, Super Nine, Let it Ride, Caribbean Stud, and Minnesota 21, a version of Blackjack.

The Card Club was popular immediately, and allowed the track to subsidize purses twice by 10 percent during the 2000 season. The track experienced promising growth that season in both attendance and handle size. Since 1996 live racing days increased from 51 to 60 days. Total purses paid grew from $4.1 million to $6.5 million. On-track wagering on live races increased 12.8 percent from the previous year. The track's success was obvious. In August 2000, *Minneapolis-St. Paul CityBusiness* magazine reported that ''industry insiders say Canterbury Park, which not long ago nearly became an amphitheater, is on the verge of becoming an elite second-tier racecourse.''

At the end of 2000, Canterbury Park reported its most successful racing season in company history. Attendance rose 11 percent, and on-track handle increased 5 percent. The second Claiming Crown set another attendance record of 15,000. It was the fifth consecutive year of record operating results, due in part to the addition of the Card Club.

For the 2001 season, track officials increased the Card Club to the allowed maximum of 50 tables, added more card games, and improved food and beverage service. Live racing days were increased to 63, with the third annual Claiming Crown highlighting the summer season. Canterbury Park was becoming a preferred track of owners and trainers as well. For the 2001 season, track executives received a record number of stall applications—2,200 for 1,600 stalls. They planned to offer average daily purses of more than $120,000.

Canterbury Park continued to explore new possibilities for hosting events. It also purchased a new, moveable structure, the ''Paddock Pavilion,'' to expand the indoor available space in the grandstand area, thus increasing possibilities for hosting events in the unpredictable Minnesota climate.

Although the Minnesota legislature was not eager to expand gambling in the state, Canterbury Park officials and horse breeders continued to pursue legislative avenues for off-track betting, slot machines, and more, all in an effort to support the state's growing horse breeding and racing industry.

Principal Subsidiaries

Canterbury Park Concessions, Inc.

Principal Divisions

Canterbury Park Racetrack; Canterbury Park Card Club.

Principal Competitors

Argosy Gaming Company; Minnesota State Lottery; Mystic Lake Casino; Racing Association; Youbet.com.

Further Reading

Beulke, Diane, ''As Purses Shrink, Horsemen Leave Canterbury Downs,'' *Minneapolis-St. Paul CityBusiness,* September 23, 1987, p. 1.

——, ''Attendance Down, Betting Up for 1988 Canterbury Downs Season,'' *Minneapolis-St. Paul CityBusiness,* October 17, 1988, p. 9.

Blahnik, Mike, ''Canterbury Park at Last May Be Able to Bet on Success,'' *Minneapolis Star Tribune,* March 19, 1997, p. 1D.

Blount, Rachel, ''Ahead at the Turn; Canterbury Park Operators Are Betting Shakopee Facility Has a Winning Future,'' *Minneapolis Star Tribune,* June 16, 1996, p. 1D.

''Canterbury Downs Has Slow Start Out of the Revenue Gate,'' *Minneapolis-St. Paul CityBusiness,* July 17, 1985, p. 9.

''Godfather of Horse Racing—His Finest Legislative Year,'' *Suburban Business,* July/August 1983, p. 9.

Gelfand, Mike, ''High Stakes Are Involved in Keeping Track Open,'' *Minneapolis-St. Paul CityBusiness,* February 8, 1988, p. 4.

Huber, Tim, ''Canterbury Park's Temp Tax Break Is Permanent,'' *Minneapolis-St. Paul CityBusiness,* May 1, 1998, pp. 1, 48.

Kaeter, Margaret, ''Betting on the Future,'' *Twin Cities Business Monthly,* April 1999, pp. 29–33.

Maler, Kevin, ''Jacobs Has No Plans, or Does He?'' *Minneapolis-St. Paul CityBusiness,* January 21, 1994, pp. 1, 8.

Marcotty, Josephine, ''Canterbury Park Holdings Stock Marks 1st Trading Day with 37 ½ Cent Increase,'' *Star Tribune,* August 20, 1994, p.1D.

——, ''Canterbury Shifts Focus, Alters Name,'' *Minneapolis Star Tribune,* January 15, 1995, p. 3D.

——, ''Horse-Racing Industry Dismayed After Defeat at Polls,'' *Star Tribune,* November 10, 1994, p. 1D.

Nelson, Wayne, ''The Real Gamblers at Canterbury: $67 Million Track Is Most Expensive in Decade,'' *Minneapolis-St. Paul CityBusiness,* May, 22, 1985, pp. 1, 20–21.

——, ''Shakopee Runs Off with RaceTrack Site,'' *Minneapolis-St. Paul CityBusiness,* April 11, 1984, p. 8.

Price, Dave, ''Do Canterbury Owners Have Winning Hand?'' *Minneapolis-St. Paul CityBusiness,* May 13, 1994, p. 5.

Schafer, Lee, and Eric Wieffring, ''Coming Out of the Starting Gate—Again,'' *Corporate Report Minnesota,* July 1994, p. 116.

Smith, Dane, ''State Supreme Court Says Off-Track Bets Are Unconstitutional,'' *Star Tribune,* July 31, 1992, pp. 1A, 12A.

''Special Events Beat Horses at the Track,'' *Ventures,* April, 1999, pp. 66–67.

Tellijohn, Andrew, ''Canterbury Hitting the Home Stretch,'' *Minneapolis-St. Paul CityBusiness,* August 18, 2000, p. 5.

—Mary Heer-Forsberg

Charles River Laboratories International, Inc.

251 Ballardvale St.
Wilmington, Massachusetts 01887-1000
U.S.A.
Telephone: (978) 658-6000
Toll Free: (800) 522-7287
Fax: (978) 658-7132
Web site: http://www.criver.com

Public Company
Incorporated: 1947 as Charles River Breeding
    Laboratories
Employees: 3,500
Sales: $306.6 million (2000)
Stock Exchanges: New York
Ticker Symbol: CRL
NAIC: 325414 Biological Product (Except Diagnostic)
    Manufacturing

Charles River Laboratories International, Inc. is the holding company for Charles River Laboratories, Inc., which is a leading provider of laboratory animals used in preclinical experiments by the pharmaceutical and biotech industries. Animal sales still account for approximately 62 percent of revenues, although the company, in operation for more than 50 years, has made significant strides in diversifying its business. It offers such biomedical products as hamster ova and mouse embryos, pathogen-free chicken eggs, and an antibody test kit. Services now include drug safety assessment and testing, biotech safety testing, and medical device testing. The company also supports researchers by developing and maintaining laboratory animal colonies, as well as providing staffing services on a contract basis. With its headquarters located in Wilmington, Massachusetts, Charles River Laboratories operates more than 50 facilities in 15 countries, selling to a customer base in 50 countries. After operating as a subsidiary of Bausch & Lomb for 15 years, the company is now independently run, the result of a 1999 management buyout arranged by the investment firm of Donaldson, Lufkin & Jenrette (now Credit Suisse First Boston), which owns more than 45 percent of the company's stock.

Birth of Charles River Breeding: 1947

The ancestor of today's holding company was Charles River Breeding Laboratories. Its founder, Dr. Henry L. Foster, was the son of a Boston garment manufacturer. He studied piano as a child and almost attended the Juilliard School of Music. Instead he opted for a more practical education and attended Middlesex Veterinary College. After graduating in 1946, he saved up money to start his own business by working as a vet on ships transporting horses to Poland. While searching for a place to establish a practice he visited the Sunny Hill Rat Farm in Clinton, Maryland, whose owner convinced him to buy out the business. Foster paid $12,000 for the cages and animals, which he then moved to Boston. After some difficulty in finding a landlord willing to rent to an aspiring rat breeder, he was able to secure a second-story loft in the West End of Boston, a seedy part of the city at the time.

In 1947 when he began Charles River Breeding, Foster was the only employee of the company. He cared for the animals, called on customers, and completed his own paperwork. He did not have a secretary until he married Lois Bronstein, who not only had to overcome her family's doubts about her husband's profession, she also had to overcome her own aversion to rats in order to reach her desk. Over the next few years, as Foster expanded his rat colonies, the criticism of his neighbors also grew. They especially disliked the smells that his exhaust fans, particularly in the summer, blew into their apartments.

In 1952 Foster moved his business to the country, setting up his cages in Wilmington, some 20 miles north of Boston. That was also when he established himself as a pioneer in the breeding of laboratory animals. At the time, researchers were severely handicapped by a lack of control over the microorganisms that each rat might carry. They simply could not be certain that a subject was reacting to a test substance or that the symptoms were actually caused by an infection acquired at the rat farm. The obvious need was for a germfree rat, one that provided researchers with a reasonable chance to control their experiments. A technique had already been developed, but it was confined to university laboratories. Mother rats were "sacrificed" by breaking their necks just before they were to give birth. The pups were then delivered by caesarean section and

Company Perspectives:

We have a strong commitment to quality. Our vision is to be the premier company Contributing to the Search for Healthier Lives.

immediately placed in a sterile, germfree environment. It was Foster who turned the technique into a commercial venture. Once produced on a large scale, Foster's disease-free rats would be kept in barrier rooms, the integrity of which were maintained by a number of precautions. Workers fastidiously showered and wore sterile coveralls, plastic gloves, surgical masks, and caps. Violating rules against bringing in unsterilized items was grounds for immediate dismissal. Moreover, as employees entered a barrier room, the air would be automatically sprayed to kill any flying insects that might happen in. Over the years, the company would also build a fleet of climate-controlled trucks to deliver the animals and eventually build facilities within trucking distance of all the major pharmaceutical houses. Expansion overseas would then follow.

Germfree laboratory animals proved to be a good business for Foster. He could charge more for them because the models were worth the extra expense to researchers. The cost of laboratory animals accounted for just 15 percent of an experiment's cost. Therefore, it made little sense to risk the reliability of the resulting data by pinching pennies on rats and mice. Foster was able to charge a sliding scale, depending on weight. The top of the line animal, in effect, cost several hundred dollars per pound.

In 1959 Foster's younger brother, Sumner, joined the company and took over marketing. Charles River was well regarded by its customers and became the market leader. Testing that required the use of laboratory animals picked up significantly after the 1960 passage of the Federal Hazardous Substances Act and other legislation that followed. Seeing how lucrative was the business, a number of major companies tried to enter the field, but they enjoyed little success. Becton Dickson, makers of medical supplies, set up operations in 1964, but ten years later would sell its animal business to Charles River. Giant corporation Ralston Purina bought out a small breeder in 1966 to jump start operations and also failed to dislodge Charles River from its dominant position.

Going Public: 1968

In 1968 Foster made an initial public offering of stock for Charles River Breeding Laboratories, selling 80,000 shares at $16 each. Another 110,000 shares were sold by stockholders. Proceeds were earmarked for the purchase of real estate and equipment to fuel company growth. By 1970, Charles River generated $5.5 million in revenues, resulting in net income of $564,100. In January 1971 the company sold another 55,000 shares of stock to finance further construction of facilities. Foster and his brother sold an additional 55,000 shares for their own benefit, although between them they still retained 58 percent of the common stock. By now, the company had subsidiaries in Canada, Britain, France, and Italy. In addition to laboratory rats and mice, Charles River was also offering disease-free

hamsters and guinea pigs, and working on rabbits. It would not be until 1977, after much expense, that the company would be able to ship rabbits in large quantities. Revenues continued their steady growth, approaching $10 million in 1973, with a net profit exceeding $1 million for the first time. By 1980 the company would be selling 18 million animals a year, its revenues would top $35 million, and net income would reach $3.85 million.

In 1972 Charles River became involved in breeding germfree Rhesus monkeys. Foster took part in the trapping expedition in the foothills of the Himalayas that procured the first animals, from which the company was then able to create a disease-free stock of 800 that were transported to two isolated islands in the Florida Keys that Foster bought and named Key Lois and Key Raccoon. The monkey population quickly grew to 3,000. The animals received monkey chow each day from workers who visited the islands and periodically trapped young subjects, some 400 to 500 each year, that were then sold to laboratories at premium prices, ranging from $1,500 to $4,500 each. The demand for the monkeys increased after India banned the export of Rhesus monkeys in 1978, following the revelation that the U.S. military was testing the effects of neutron radiation on the animals. The Indian prime minister considered that research to violate a 1955 agreement, which restricted the use of Indian monkeys to medical purposes only. By 1981, however, Florida conservationists were beginning efforts to force Charles River to remove its monkey colonies, an issue that would heat up considerably 15 years later.

Breeders such as Charles River and the researchers that used their animals as test subjects were coming under increased scrutiny. Critics maintained that many experiments were so poorly conceived that animals were subjected to painful procedures in exchange for little useful data. In actuality, use of laboratory animals declined sharply between 1968 and 1978, dipping from 33 million to 20 million, according to a study conducted by the National Academy of Sciences. Charles River, however, actually benefited from this change in climate. Researchers turned to the company and its uniform animal stock to ensure they got the most from each test subject. Charles River was a consistent money maker in the early 1980s and soon found a large corporate suitor, Bausch & Lomb, who was in the market for an acquisition that could provide steady cash flow as it transformed itself from a troubled optical company to a diversified healthcare and medical services company.

Acquisition by Bausch & Lomb: 1984

In 1980 Bausch & Lomb was highly dependent on the sale of contact lenses and, to a lesser degree, sunglasses, but management had failed to keep up with changes in eye care. As a result, profits fell and Daniel Gill was named the chief executive and charged with reversing the company's fortunes. He originally came to Bausch & Lomb in 1978 to run the contact lens division, after gaining 23 years of experience in the medical field at Abbott Laboratories, where he rose to become the president of the hospital products division. Once in charge at Bausch & Lomb in 1981, Gill reorganized the company, in the process selling off the industrial instruments and eyeglass units. He then added new businesses, such as German drug manufacturer Dr. Mann Pharma and Dental Research Corp., which sold

```
┌─────────────────────────────────────────────────┐
│                  Key Dates:                      │
│                                                  │
│  1947:  Dr. Henry L. Foster establishes Charles  │
│         River Breeding Laboratories.             │
│  1952:  Foster begins breeding germfree ani-     │
│         mals for laboratory research.            │
│  1968:  Charles River Breeding goes public.      │
│  1984:  Bausch & Lomb acquires company.          │
│  1992:  James C. Foster takes over as CEO.       │
│  1999:  Bausch & Lomb sells business in man-     │
│         agement-led leveraged buyout.            │
│  2000:  Charles River Laboratories Interna-      │
│         tional goes public on the New York       │
│         Stock Exchange.                          │
└─────────────────────────────────────────────────┘
```

the Interplak electric toothbrush. In a move that surprised a number of observers, Gill also acquired Charles River Laboratories in 1984 in an exchange of stock worth approximately $130 million. For Bausch & Lomb, Charles River served as a stabilizing effect on the bottom line during a period of volatility. It could be counted on to generate consistent cash flow and grow at a steady rate. By 1992 it was estimated that Charles River added $200 million to the annual revenues of Bausch & Lomb.

Charles River now had a corporate parent, but little changed in the day-to-day operations, although the company began to diversify into other areas: offering cell culture products and testing services. Generally Gill believed in delegating a great deal of responsibility to his managers, allowing Foster to essentially continue to run the business as he saw fit. In 1992 Foster would step down as chief operating officer in favor of his son, James C. Foster, although he would continue to serve as chairman of the board. James had joined the company in 1976 as counsel and held a number of management positions as he prepared to succeed his father, who at the age of 67 had other interests to occupy his time. He and his wife had become contemporary art collectors, and in 1991 he was named as chairman of the board for Boston's Museum of Fine Arts, which was gearing up for a major funding campaign.

In the 1990s breeders and users of laboratory animals received even more criticism from animal rights activists. For Charles River much of that bad publicity emanated from the company's monkey colonies in the Florida Keys, where community leaders and conservationists combined their voices. The monkeys ravaged state-protected red mangrove trees, the leaves of which had proven to be irresistibly tasty. Environmentalists claimed that the water surrounding the keys were tainted by untreated fecal matter. Several monkeys managed to escape the colonies, mostly wandering off during low tide, which prompted residents of nearby islands to join the protests, fearful that a hurricane could spread monkeys in all directions. Even though the monkeys were well monitored to ensure they were disease free, locals worried about marauding monkeys with rabies. The rhetoric became even more heated from animal rights activists. When the company attempted to move some monkeys to a Houston facility, the director of the Houston Animal Rights Team maintained that "Charles River is nothing more than an animal slave trader." After several more years of

court hearings, the company's monkey colonies would be evicted from the Florida Keys.

The ethical questions underlying his business were not lost on Dr. Foster, a man with artistic leanings who had been trained as a veterinarian. Not only were his animals sold to be subjected to experimentation, the nature of running a commercial enterprise reduced living creatures to the status of inventory. To make sure researchers had animals available with the necessary features, the company had to overproduce, and in the case of rats, researchers required 70 percent males. The result was an excess of animals, ones that ate up resources, both in terms of food and labor. They had to be humanely destroyed, which in truth meant they were suffocated by carbon dioxide. As Dr. Foster explained to an interviewer, "Every animal we raise will ultimately die. It's being raised for the benefit of mankind. If you don't use animals, you don't do research. People see a cat or a dog exposed to experimentation and they become emotionally involved. I become more emotionally involved if I have a loved one in a hospital and there is no medical cure." Critics, on the other hand, questioned the benefit to mankind of testing cosmetics by dropping them in the eyes of rabbits to see how much they burn. Many researchers began to turn to computer simulation techniques, in other words virtual lab animals. In 1999 Charles River began to offer CaseTox software to mimic animal research.

In the mid-1990s Bausch & Lomb suffered a downturn in business, which eventually forced Gill to step down as CEO. The company underwent a restructuring effort and by 1999 decided to focus on its core eye-care business. In conjunction with Charles River management, the Global Health Care Partners unit of Donaldson, Lufkin & Jenrette paid Bausch & Lomb $400 million in cash and a $43 million promissory note for an 87.5 percent stake in Charles River. According to the last numbers made available by Bausch & Lomb, Charles River was generating some $230 million a year in revenues. Global Health announced that it hoped to grow the business to $500 million a year and then take it public. Because of the success of the initial public offerings of biotechnology companies, Global Health decided to take Charles River public before meeting that sales threshold. Although not a bio-tech firm itself, it serviced the segment and in many ways was a safer bet. No one could be sure which of the bio-techs would emerge as major players, but investors could be relatively certain they would be customers of Charles River. Despite the earlier belief that lab animals would be replaced by computer software, the need of bio-techs for animal subjects served to boost the prospects of Charles River.

The holding company for Charles River was renamed Charles River Laboratories International in late 1999. In June 2000 the company raised $224 million in an initial public offering of stock. The company continued the diversification efforts that began under Bausch & Lomb. In 1999 it acquired Sierra Biomedical, a drug testing business, for $23.3 million. In 2001 Charles River paid $51.9 million for Primedica Corp., a preclinical research subsidiary. Nevertheless, over 60 percent of the company's revenues were derived from its traditional business of selling laboratory animals. It was the mouse—given that animal's physiological and genetic similarities to humans—that was becoming a major source of income. So important were mice to new genetic research that they were scheduled as the only other mammal for complete genetic sequencing. Because of Charles River's predominant position in its field and the broadening of its business, despite taking on some debt, it appeared well positioned to maintain steady growth for many years to come.

Principal Subsidiaries

Charles River Laboratories, Inc.; Primedica Corporation.

Principal Competitors

ClinTrials Research Inc.; Harlan Sprague Dawley; Huntingdon Life Sciences Group plc; The Jackson Laboratory; MDS; Taconic Farms.

Further Reading

Bulkeley, William M., ''Bausch & Lomb Says It Agrees to Sell Research-Animal Unit for $443 Million,'' *Wall Street Journal,* July 27, 1999, p. B6.

Demaree, Allan T., ''Henry Foster's Primately-for-Profit Business,'' *Fortune,* April 10, 1978, pp. 70.

DeWitt, Karen, ''A Company That Thrives on Regulation,'' *New York Times,* December 7, 1980, p. 9.

Feder, Barnaby J., ''Breeding Animals for the Lab,'' *New York Times,* February 17, 1982, p. D1.

Malakoff, David, ''The Rise of the Mouse, Biomedicine's Model Mammal,'' *Science,* April 14, 2000, p. 248.

Richey, Warren, '' 'Monkey Business' to Come to an End in Florida Keys,'' *Christian Science Monitor,* September 24, 1997, p. 3.

—Ed Dinger

Children's Comprehensive Services, Inc.

3401 West End Ave., Ste. 400
Nashville, Tennessee 37203
U.S.A.
Telephone: (615) 250-0000
Fax: (615) 250-1000
Web site: http://www.ccskids.com

Public Company
Incorporated: 1985
Employees: 3,000
Sales: $126.77 million (2000)
Stock Exchanges: NASDAQ
Ticker Symbol: KIDS
NAIC: 623990 Other Residential Care Facilities; 624110
   Child and Youth Services; 611110 Private Schools
   Elementary or Secondary; 922140 Correctional
   Institutions

Children's Comprehensive Services, Inc. (CCS) based in Nashville, Tennessee, is one of the nation's leading providers of educational services, psychiatric treatment, and juvenile corrections for at-risk children and juveniles in the United States. Operating in 14 states and serving over 3,700 children and their families, CCS staffs both residential and day treatment facilities that provide services ranging from special education for autistic and developmentally delayed children to more intensive boot-camp programs set up to rehabilitate juvenile offenders. CCS has contracts with both governmental and non-governmental nonprofit agencies in Alabama, Arkansas, California, Florida, Hawaii, Kentucky, Louisiana, Michigan, Montana, North Carolina, Ohio, Pennsylvania, Tennessee, and Utah.

Early History

The contemporary privatization of government correctional facilities seemed to have been born out of the inspiration of several groups of investors from Nashville, Tennessee. Nashville was the birthplace of two of the three earliest and largest pioneering companies in the business—Corrections Corporation of America and Pricor Inc.

Pricor was founded in 1985 in response to a need for more and better run prisons in the United States and the belief that there was money to be made offering smaller municipalities private assistance. Prisons were overcrowded and significant amounts of money were being spent on building and maintaining correctional institutions. Pricor and its investors believed that through privatizing the industry it could successfully manage and correct the flawed system of both adult and juvenile corrections, and turn a profit at the same time.

Originally most of the available contracts for private prison operation were with women's detention centers, immigration holding centers, and juvenile justice placements, but Pricor succeeded in obtaining a contract for staffing and managing a maximum security jail in Greene County, Tennessee, in the late 1980s.

Pricor expanded operations into Alabama and Virginia in 1986, opening minimum security detention centers for a total of 170 inmates. In 1987, Pricor leased two facilities from a hospital system in California, and began its California operation. The state of California and its various municipalities remained one of CCS's largest client populations.

While still hoping to make significant strides with adult corrections, Pricor took what contracts it could get and ended up working closely with juvenile offender populations throughout the 1980s. In 1988 the company acquired Advocate Schools, a company dedicated to the care, education, and treatment of at-risk youth in California. Advocate Schools contracted with school districts based on referrals. Offering both community-based programs in which students attended an Advocate School on a day-to-day basis, and residential schools for students with more intensive needs, the school maintained nine community based sites throughout California. The original site in San Bernardino was established in 1982 with other sites opening throughout the 1990s. Nine residential schools made up the remainder of the Advocate Schools campus, making it the largest nonpublic alternative school system in California.

Advocate Schools was cofounded by Amy Harrison and Martha Petrey, who were retained by Pricor as vice-chairman/president and executive vice-president, respectively. Harrison was also cofounder and executive director of Helicon, a non-

Company Perspectives:

CCS, created in 1985, is not just a corporation . . . or a leader of educational and treatment services in the country . . . or thousands of employees dedicated to making a difference in the life of a child . . . CCS is all of these things and more.

CCS is about providing services to thousands of children and adolescents who are not succeeding in their traditional educational, family or everyday life setting. CCS is more than just a business, and it's more than a job. It's about getting up every day and imagining and working on an idea to add to a lesson plan, or finding a special computer software program that will excite and inspire a student who has never succeeded in school. It's about praising a child or youth for all the right things they do. It's about operating a detention center knowing that the CCS exceptional and specialized training will ensure a safe and secure setting for the youth, staff and the community.

profit group that contracted with CCS in a number of joint ventures.

It was during the Reagan Era, with its tougher prison sentences and stiffer drug conviction penalties, that Pricor made its most ambitious attempt to deal with overcrowded prison conditions in metropolitan counties. Pricor convinced rural county jails to contract with the company and offer their largely empty jails to prisoners from more populous regions for a fee. Pricor teamed up with Houston-based N-Group and first pitched the "jails for hire" plan in west Texas in 1990. The companies convinced municipalities to build new facilities with millions in government bonds and Pricor experienced tremendous initial success, with revenues of over $30 million in fiscal 1991. However, the lucrative payoff to Pricor was mainly in short term up-front fees. Eventually the deal turned sour, with the private prisons remaining empty and therefore unprofitable; for its alleged corporate misdeeds, Pricor was named by a Texas grand jury as an "unindicted co-conspirator" with N-Group. N-Group's penalties were far greater, however, as it was indicted on criminal antitrust charges.

A Change of Identity: 1994

With the Texas dealings now a nightmare, the company found itself losing money in 1992. Facing a tenuous financial future in adult corrections, Pricor exited the business in 1993. Instead, Pricor was increasingly moving forward with its juvenile facilities, and in 1994 the company's board of directors approved a re-direction of the company and an accompanying name change. Pricor was now to be known as Children's Comprehensive Services Inc. (CCS). The company was traded under the symbol KIDS on the NASDAQ. By the end of fiscal 1994, CCS was serving over 1,500 children and their families in Alabama, California, Louisiana, and Tennessee.

Pricor benefited greatly with the passage of The Individuals with Disabilities Education Act (I.D.E.A.). The new federal law mandated that states provide every school-age child with a free

and appropriate public education. If a public school was unable to accomplish the mandate through its normal operations, a school district was enabled to refer a student to a nonpublic school able to provide the services required. Pricor and Advocate Schools functioned to provide special needs services to school districts all over the state of California.

In addition to redirecting the company in 1994, CCS also undertook a financial restructuring in an attempt to keep the company solvent. In 1993, Pricor had solicited help from T. Rowe Price Strategic Partners Fund II, L.P. in the form of a one-year $1.5 million term loan. The company was also granted a renewal of a $10 million revolving credit facility through its banks. Pricor was in default on the credit and T. Rowe Price and Pricor settled on approximately one-third of Pricor's outstanding common stock shares at a purchase price of $1.8 million for its having cured its default status and for re-securing the loan.

The second part of the financial restructuring involved converting the company's short-term loans from both its banks and T. Rowe Price into long-term obligations. Pricor, now CCS, had commitments to National Health Investors, Inc. for $6.5 million and T. Rowe Price for $1 million. The local First American Bank of Nashville completed the financial overhaul when it extended a line of credit to CCS for the purposes of supplying working capital to keep CCS afloat. All told, the company was dangerously close to bankruptcy and had it not been for the aid of the financial institutions CCS would have more than likely folded.

CCS provided services in a variety of areas for children and adolescents. Treatment facilities were devoted to rehabilitating youth who were sexually abusive, had substance abuse issues, or needed crisis intervention for all sorts of emotional needs. The special education service centers, including Advocate Schools, concentrated their care on students suffering from a diverse range of special needs, including autism and attention deficit disorders.

Children's Comprehensive Services relied on reimbursement from medicaid, managed care, and private insurance companies. Day treatment programs provided the greatest financial return to the company, but rates varied according to the contracting parties. Some states cut reimbursement costs, greatly affecting CCS's profit margin and sometimes leading to discontinued services, as in the case of CCS of Montana and the Helicon Youth Center in California.

The Programs: 1990s–2000s

CCS offered programs to deal with a wide variety of problem areas for the child and juvenile patient. The company tailored its operations to very individualized treatment plans and had centers throughout its 14-state region that met the diverse needs of its target population.

In September 1998, CCS acquired Ameris Health Systems, Inc. Ameris' wholly owned subsidiary American Clinical Schools, Inc. operated treatment facilities for juvenile sex offenders in several states. The following December the company acquired Somerset Inc., a California company that provided educational day treatment to children and their families. The company merged with Ventures Healthcare of Gainesville, Inc.

Key Dates:

1985: Pricor Inc. is founded by a group of Nashville investors.

1986: Pricor enters the adult private prison business.

1987: Pricor leases two facilities in California.

1988: Pricor acquires Advocate Schools, a business dedicated to the care and education of at-risk youth in California.

1989: Pricor enters deal in the United Kingdom to staff private prison facility.

1990: Pricor pitches "prisons for hire" in rural west Texas.

1991: Pricor posts earnings of $30 million.

1992: Texas project fails.

1993: Pricor exits adult corrections business and focuses on children's education and treatment.

1994: Pricor changes its name to Children's Comprehensive Services, Inc. (CCS).

1999: CCS closes its Helicon Youth Center in Riverside County, California.

2001: Possible buyout of CCS by undisclosed competitor is reported.

---

in June 1998, making the year an important one for company growth.

In August 2000 CCS opened the Dallas alternative education program as well as Bristol Youth Academy in Liberty County, Florida. The company also expanded the hospital facility it operated in Ohio.

In October 2000 the company retained McDonald Investments Inc. to assist the company with its financial resources. The company was looking at a possible sale to a competitor. It was undetermined at the time whether the company would be divided up or sold in its entirety. Company leadership was looking to McDonald Investments as well to assist them in their decision making.

In November 2000, CCS closed its long established Helicon Youth Center (HYC) and its related school. Helicon Youth Center had undergone a licensing investigation by Community Care Licensing (CCL), a division of California's Department of Social Services, and CCL had some concerns with the center. A two-year probationary agreement was established between CCL and HYC but in the meantime referrals were no longer made by Riverside County and there was a significant drop-off in the number of clients. The company also experienced a decline in students to its non-residential day treatment programs.

As the company entered the new millennium the outlook for Children's Comprehensive Services was mixed. William Ballard, chairman and CEO, optimistically stated, "We believe CCS's prospects for additional profitable growth are supported by the market's continued strong demand for services for at-risk youth. Our pipeline of potential contracts has expanded because of our reputation for quality, the wide variety of services we

offer, and increased interest in our specialty programs such as the gender specific treatment programs." Yet the company appeared unprepared to forge ahead on its own. Indeed, CCS ended fiscal 2001 with an offer of a buyout. The details remained undisclosed, but the potential buyer was described as one of CCS's major competitors.

There was no disputing that mental health issues among youth were now at crisis proportions in the United States and that the juvenile justice system was overcrowded and in need of assistance.

With the rising demand for specialty services among youth, CCS, or whomever was involved in its takeover, appeared to be well positioned to help in the education and treatment of some of the nation's highest at-risk youth. A larger public policy question was whether the country and its municipal governments would be willing to pay the high cost of such services to private companies over the long haul. If government entities believed that CCS could provide quality care at a reasonable cost to the taxpayer the contracts would continue to be signed and CCS and its investors would reap the benefits.

Principal Subsidiaries

Children's Comprehensive Services of California, Inc. d/b/a/ Advocate Schools; CCS/ Altacare of Arkansas, Inc.; CCS/ Bay County, Inc.; CCS/ Gulf Pines, Inc.; CCS/ Lansing, Inc. d/b/a/ Rivendell Center for Behavioral Health; CCS of Montana, Inc.; CCS/ Rivendell of Arkansas, Inc.; CCS/ Rivendell of Kentucky, Inc.; CCS/ Salt Lake City, Inc., d/b/a/ Copper Hills Youth Center; Ventures Healthcare of Gainesville, Inc.; Chad Youth Enhancement Center; CCS/Meadow Pines, Inc.; American Clinical Schools, Inc.; Tennessee Clinical Schools, Inc., d/b/a Hermitage Hall; Alabama Clinical Schools, Inc.; Pennsylvania Clinical Schools, Inc.; Somerset, Inc.; CCS of Hawaii, Inc.

Principal Competitors

Cornell Corrections Inc.; Ramsay Youth Services, Inc.; Res-Care, Inc.

Further Reading

"Children's Comp Could Shop Itself," *Mergers & Acquisitions Report,* October 16, 2000.

"Children's Comprehensive Services Inc. First Quarter Financial Results, *Managed Behavioral Health News,* November 23, 2000.

"Children's Comprehensive Services Inc. (in Talks to Sell Firm)," *New York Times,* June 16, 2001, p. B3.

"County Hears Sales Pitch by Jail Firms," *St. Petersburg Times,* November 13, 1987, p. 1.

"Education Microcap Chalks Up Possible Buyer ... Perhaps," *Mergers & Acquisitions Report,* June 25, 2001.

Hodges, Lucy, "Removing the Bars to Private Jails," *Daily Telegraph,* March 1, 1989, p. 17.

"Hospital to Be Used to House Juveniles," *Los Angeles Times,* Metro Section, November 25, 1987, p. 11.

McCartney, Leslie, "BU-School-Funds," *Montana Standard,* April 1, 2001.

—Susan B. Culligan

Christopher & Banks Corporation

2400 Xenium Lane North
Plymouth, Minnesota 55441
U.S.A.
Telephone: (763) 551-5000
Fax: (763) 551-5198
Web site: http://www.christopherandbanks.com

Public Company
Incorporated: 1986 as Brauns Acquisition Holding
  Company
Employees: 2,900
Sales: $209.2 million (2001)
Stock Exchanges: NASDAQ
Ticker Symbol: CHBS
NAIC: 448120 Women's Clothing Stores

Christopher & Banks Corporation operates through its wholly owned subsidiary Christopher & Banks, Inc., which is a publicly owned specialty retailer of women's apparel headquartered in Minneapolis, Minnesota. Christopher & Banks has 320 stores in 27 states. The stores operate under the names Christopher & Banks, CJ Banks, and Brauns, and are located primarily in shopping malls in the northern half of the United States. In July 2000, the 44-year-old company changed its name from Brauns Fashions to Christopher & Banks Corporation. The company's primary customers are working women from 35 to 55 who are looking for clothing with style, high quality, moderate price, and versatility. The company hit its stride in 2000, making national business headlines rare for a small company and winning kudos for its financial turnaround and market success.

Minneapolis Roots and Beyond: 1956–86

Gil Braun opened the first Brauns women's clothing store in 1956. He had 20 years of retail experience with J.C. Penney and Buttreys. The store was located in the Miracle Mile Shopping center near his home in St. Louis Park, a suburb of Minneapolis. At the time, shopping centers were just beginning to sprout up in the growing suburbs of the Twin Cities of Minneapolis and St. Paul. Brauns Fashions served middle-income women. In 1960 Braun opened his second store, which tripled in size soon after.

Brauns' merchandise included coats, suits, dresses, sportswear, accessories, and lingerie. Gil Braun believed in providing quality apparel at a reasonable price. In addition, he believed strongly in giving a personal touch and running a friendly business similar to those he frequented in the small South Dakota town where he grew up. He encouraged his store employees to get acquainted with customers, learn their names, and find out their clothing preferences.

By the late 1960s, Brauns had grown to 20 stores in the Twin Cities. During the 1970s and early 1980s Brauns expanded to ten other midwestern states, continuing to focus on quality, value, and attention to the needs of its customers. In 1974 the company opened the first Gigi store targeted to teenage girls and younger women looking for more contemporary styles. The Gigi stores grew in number as well, but were always a much smaller part of the overall operation. Over nearly three decades, Gil Braun saw the demand for suits and dresses decrease, while his customers' appetite for sportswear and casual wear continued to grow. To meet the merchandise needs of the growing chain, the company moved to a larger distribution facility in nearby Eden Prairie in 1981.

By 1986 Brauns Fashions had grown to 110 stores in 11 midwestern states, with revenues of approximately $50 million. At that time Braun and his wife were spending the winters in warmer climates to escape the Minnesota cold. But that interfered with his ability to stick to his hands-on approach to managing the company. He was ready for a change. That year he sold the company for $25 million to Marc Ostrow and James Fuld in a leveraged buyout. The company was incorporated by Pennwood Capital Corporation as Brauns Acquisition Holding Company (later changed to Brauns Fashions Corporation).

New Ownership, a Shaky Market: 1986

The new ownership, with Larry Kelly as company president and chief operating officer, made changes right away. They altered the merchandise mix from primarily casual wear to more distinctive career wear. The focus shifted away from the traditional Brauns customer—a middle-income, value-conscious woman looking for a versatile wardrobe—to a more upscale career woman. The new owners planned to further expand the chain nationally.

Company Perspectives:

Christopher & Banks serves the clothing needs of today's busy, fashion conscious woman offering quality, everyday fashion options suitable for your work and leisure activities.

The new Brauns charged full speed ahead, opening more than 30 new stores from 1987 to 1990, but not always in the company's traditional locations. Some stores were opened in areas with much different demographics, including larger cities such as Chicago. The addition of new stores and the change in marketing focus coincided with a nationwide drop in retail sales, which hurt the company. Company losses increased from $21.6 million in early 1987 to $27 million in early 1989. Over the next three years, same store sales fell considerably. (Same store sales is the retail measure of a company's performance considered most accurate because it examines sales from stores open at least one year and ignores sales fluctuations due to new store openings.)

The new owners responded to the downturn by implementing a management turnover and strategic restructuring plan. Nicholas Cook was appointed president in May 1989. Cook had valuable experience in the industry and company as a 15-year veteran of Brauns. Cook updated stores and altered the merchandise mix back to more casual apparel that was interchangeable between a woman's work, home, and outside activities. During the next two years, new stores performed well, but same store sales did not improve. The company saw overall improvement, however, and reported its first full year of profit in five years in December 1991.

Public Offering

To solve debt problems it had been battling with since the 1986 takeover, and to finance renovation and expansion plans, Brauns Fashions decided to go public in 1992. The company made an initial offering of 1.25 million shares at $7 per share. Shareholders offered another 625,000 shares. At the time the company had grown to 143 stores in 16 midwestern states. In addition, Brauns had a $10 million public debt offering in the fall of 1993, which helped restructure mounting corporate debt. New stores that were opening during this time were positioned in smaller markets such as mid-sized cities with cultures similar to those in communities where Brauns stores were successful.

In 1994 Brauns had a growing number of stores to keep supplied and needed larger facilities. The company doubled its warehouse space by moving from Eden Prairie to a 210,000-square-foot facility in Plymouth, in suburban Minneapolis. Despite the company's store expansion, Brauns had sales of $94 million and a net loss of $245,000 that year. Same store sales were still sluggish.

In 1995 Nicholas Cook became chairman and chief executive officer and Herbert Froemming became president and chief operating officer. Recognizing that the fastest growing demographic group in the market was women from age 35 to 54, the leadership took steps to further define its primary customer and weave her character into the fabric of the company. The typical Brauns customer was determined to be Mary, age 39, who worked full time and had a family income of $55,000 or more.

She preferred a more business casual look that she could wear to both work and to community meetings, or to her children's events later in the day. Discussions about Mary's needs pervaded all aspects of the company.

To highlight unique products that Mary could not get elsewhere, Brauns focused on selling more private label casual merchandise under the names Christopher & Banks, Chelsea Studio, Eurosport, and Exparte. Executives increased imports from manufacturers in Asia from 14 percent in 1993 to 45 percent in 1995. The high percentage of imports allowed the company to offer customers higher quality apparel at a lower cost.

By 1995, Brauns had 225 stores in 22 states. The company had losses of more than $2 million during the first six months of 1995 on sales of $43.5 million. In June 1996 Brauns extended the terms of its credit agreement to avoid possible technical default.

1996: Chapter 11 and Recovery

After experiencing the effects of a three-year retail slowdown and consecutive annual losses, Brauns Fashions filed for chapter 11 bankruptcy protection in July 1996. As part of the strategic restructuring plan, it closed nearly 50 marginal or unprofitable stores. The company outlined a plan to fully pay all creditors and become profitable by 1997. Restructuring was, at the time, a growing trend in the retail community.

Brauns scaled back its store operations to 172 stores in 20 states. All Gigi stores were closed in the transition. Management instituted a store credit card and focused the merchandise mix more on sweaters and sportswear, and less on dresses and coats. In addition, Brauns reorganized its distribution center and freed up an additional 33,000 square feet of space to sublease. By March 1997 the company had satisfied claims of the reorganization plan.

New leadership took over the company in 1998 when William Prange became president and chief executive officer. Prange had been head of merchandising operations since 1994. Nicholas Cook continued on as chairman of the board. The company redesigned its stores, enhanced customer service in subtle but effective ways, and focused the marketing lens more closely on "Mary" and her needs. Prange initiated a store makeover that he thought customers would respond to. Store changes included adding all wooden hangers, handled paper bags, tissue paper wrapping, and envelopes for receipts, all of which communicated a classier store environment. Store managers also worked harder to hire women who reflected their target customers, often hiring teachers who were enticed by a 50 percent off corporate benefit.

Prange also increased imports, primarily importing directly from factories in Asia. He worked closely with factory owners without the expense of a middleman, thus passing on savings to Brauns' customers with lower-priced apparel. Brauns thus offered customers inexpensive, but original clothing. Prange and other company executives visited factories regularly and established relationships to ensure that the apparel was not being manufactured in sweatshops.

Customers responded, and Brauns started growing again. Sales revenues increased, primarily from new store openings. Store growth continued with 179 stores in 1998 and 195 in 1999. Brauns' financials began showing increasing profitability.

2000: New Name and National Recognition

By the second quarter of 2000, company sales were up 42.3 percent from the previous year and same store sales had risen 21 percent. The company was gaining attention on Wall Street for its impressive growth. *Forbes* magazine ranked it 27th on its 200 Best Small Companies in America list for 2000.

In July Brauns shareholders approved a company name change from Brauns Fashions Corporation to Christopher & Banks Corporation. The new name identified the company more closely with the successful Christopher & Banks brand, which had gained recognition and loyalty among the customer base over several years. The company's new ticker symbol became CHBS.

Soon after, Christopher & Banks launched a new division of stores called CJ Banks for size 14–24 women. The company targeted the same geographic areas and identified the CJ Banks customer as "Tracy," Mary's younger sister, who had the same lifestyle and tastes. Retailers estimated that the women's plus-size market was the fastest growing, with 35–40 percent of women in that category. Christopher & Banks opened 20 CJ Banks stores in the fall of 2000 and continued with steady expansion.

In fiscal 2000 Christopher & Banks reported a 46 percent growth in sales to $209.2 million, resulting in earnings doubling to $1.50 per share. Management continued to expand both store formats, and transition several Brauns stores to Christopher & Banks. They expected complete name changes at all Brauns stores by the end of 2002. Management continued to focus on customer service, high quality products, original merchandise, and the visual presentation in stores. Marketing remained secondary, with the company's storefront windows still considered the best form of advertising. By 2001 the company directly imported 80 percent of merchandise from Asia under the Christopher & Banks label.

In June 2001 *Money* magazine declared Christopher & Banks "the best performing stock in America." This was based on the fact that over five years the company's stock had grown from a split-adjusted 44 cents to around $39, a staggering 8,800 percent increase that far exceeded advances during the same period by tech heavyweights EMC, Microsoft, and Cisco, among others. *Money* noted that even in the slump of early 2001, Christopher & Banks increased earnings 62 percent and thus continued to attract huge investor interest.

By July 2001 Christopher & Banks operated 320 stores in 27 states. The company was ranked 70th in *Business Week* magazine's 100 Hot Growth Companies in 2000, and in 2001 moved up to 16th. With increasing national recognition, stable financial resources, and a commitment to its mission, Christopher & Banks was poised to meet the apparel needs of "Mary" and "Tracy" for many years to come.

Principal Subsidiaries

Christopher & Banks, Incorporated.

Principal Divisions

Christopher & Banks; CJ Banks.

Principal Competitors

Marshall Field's; Bloomingdales Inc.; R.H. Macy & Co., Inc.; AnnTaylor Stores Corporation; The Talbots, Inc.; Bernard Chaus, Inc.

Further Reading

Apgar, Sally, "Marketing to Mary: Brauns Targeting 'Profile Customer,' Taking Other Steps to End Recent Slide," *Star Tribune*, September 25, 1995, p. 1D.
——, "Survival Strategy: Troubled Retailers Are Using Bankruptcy As a Business Tool," *Star Tribune*, August 12, 1996, p. 1D.
Birger, Jon, "The Best Stock You've Never Heard Of," *Money*, June 1, 2001, pp. 27+.
Braun, Gil, Interview by Mary Heer-Forsberg, July 23, 2001.
Groeneveld, Benno, "A Whole New Look," *Minneapolis-St. Paul CityBusiness*, October 6, 2000, p. S28.
"Hot Growth Companies," *Business Week*, June 11, 2001, p. 106.
"Huge Increase for C&B," *Women's Wear Daily*, September 18, 2000, p. 44.
Linecker, Adelia Cellini, "Retailer Puts Big Emphasis on Plus-Sized Clothes," *Investor's Business Daily*, April 30, 2001.
Moore, Janet, "Old-Time Merchandising, Display Make Christopher & Banks a Winner," *Star Tribune*, April 8, 2001, p. 1D.
Much, Marilyn, "Sticking to Casual Clothes with Midwest Flair," *Investor's Business Daily*, July 6, 1999, pp. 1, 13.
Rich, Andrew, "Brauns Plans to Show Its Muscles," *Minneapolis-St. Paul CityBusiness*, June 3, 1987, p. 6.
Waters, Jennifer, "Brauns Fashions to Try on Bigger HQ," *Minneapolis-St. Paul CityBusiness*, May 13, 1994, p. 2.
Weinburger, Betsy, "Brauns Bucks a Retail Trend, Plans an IPO," *Minneapolis-St. Paul CityBusiness*, March 2, 1992, pp. 1, 27.
Weitzman, Jennifer, C&B Profits Continue to Soar," *WWD*, June 22, 2001, p. 11.
Youngblood, Dick, "Brauns' Stock Offering Is an Attempt to Undo Damage from Buyout," *Star Tribune*, April 1, 1992, p. 2D.

—Mary Heer-Forsberg

Citizens Financial Group, Inc.

One Citizens Plaza
Providence, Rhode Island 02903-1339
U.S.A.
Telephone: (401) 456-7000
Fax: (401) 456-7819
Web site: http://www.citizensbank.com

Wholly Owned Subsidiary of The Royal Bank of Scotland Group plc
Incorporated: 1871 as Citizens Savings Bank
Employees: 12,000
Total Assets: $32.4 billion (2001)
NAIC: 551111 Offices of Bank Holding Companies; 522110 Commercial Banking; 522120 Savings Institutions

Citizens Financial Group, Inc. is the second largest commercial bank holding company in New England, behind only the much larger FleetBoston Financial Corporation, and was one of the top 30 commercial banks in the United States as of mid-2001. Wholly owned by The Royal Bank of Scotland Group plc, Citizens Financial owned retail banks in four states as of mid-2001: Rhode Island, where it had 66 branches and $7.4 billion in assets; Massachusetts, 140 branches and $16.8 billion in assets; Connecticut, 43 branches and $2.4 billion in assets; and New Hampshire, 80 branches and $5.7 billion in assets. In July 2001 Citizens reached an agreement to acquire the regional banking business of Mellon Financial Corporation, a deal that, if completed, would add to Citizens' holdings 345 branches in Pennsylvania, Delaware, and New Jersey, along with $16.4 billion in assets. This deal would catapult Citizens into a position as one of the top 20 banks in the United States, with nearly $50 billion in assets.

The group, which traces its origins back to the founding of High Street Bank in 1828, had assets of only about $1.5 billion when it went public in 1985. After being acquired by the Royal Bank of Scotland in 1988, Citizens began a period of spectacularly rapid growth through acquisition following the appointment of Lawrence K. Fish as chairman and CEO in 1992.

19th-Century Beginnings As High Street Bank and Citizens Savings Bank

High Street Bank, which was chartered as a commercial bank, was founded in 1828 in Providence, Rhode Island's Hoyle Square, at the time one of the city's busiest intersections for travelers from the nearby manufacturing towns and from the countryside. Hoyle Square was named after the Hoyle Tavern, a very popular locale in the city, while the bank took its name from its offices, which were located in two rooms of a residence on High Street.

With Rhode Island serving as one of the main industrial areas of New England in the mid-19th century, competition was fierce in the commercial banking sector. Eventually, as the need for banks serving ordinary citizens increased, the directors of High Street Bank decided to branch out. In 1871 they obtained a second charter from the Rhode Island legislature that established Citizens Savings Bank, a mutual savings bank. Jessie Grant, the daughter of the bank's vice-president, made the first deposit into the bank on April 19 of that year, and by the end of the year the new bank had deposits of $52,000. The next 50 years consisted of a period of slow growth for both Citizens Savings and the Hoyle Square neighborhood as Providence's position as an industrial center and seaport deteriorated. By the early 1920s, the bank's future seemed more promising, so the bank built a new headquarters on the site of Hoyle Tavern, which had been torn down in 1890.

The Great Depression of the 1930s hit New England hard, with Rhode Island suffering particularly from the ongoing decline of its important textile industries. Citizens Savings saw its deposits decline and had to contend with increased numbers of defaulted mortgages, but because the bank's lending practices were fairly prudent, its travails were not as severe as those of many other financial institutions.

Recovery and change came during the 1940s. In 1943 Citizens Savings gained the ability to acquire stock in High Street Bank because of a change in Rhode Island investment law. Citizens quickly gained full control of its former parent, foiling an attempt by a High Street stockholder to take control of High Street Bank. In 1947 High Street Bank relocated its offices to

Company Perspectives:

We will build a great company where every employee shares a deep commitment to our customers. We will provide exceptional service to and earn the long-term loyalty of those customers who choose Citizens as their primary bank. We will be the absolute leader in commitment to our employees, communities, and to the highest ethical standards. We will remain the leading New England super-community bank, and be one of the best financial performers nationally in banking.

those of Citizens Savings. One year later, High Street Bank was renamed Citizens Trust Company.

Citizens began developing a branch network in 1947, when it opened an office in Cranston. Three years later the bank became a member of the Federal Deposit Insurance Corporation (FDIC). It was the first mutual savings bank to do so. Expansion continued in 1954 with the acquisition of Greenville Trust Company. This added two more branches as well as assets of more than $8 million. Growth continued throughout the 1960s and 1970s. By 1971 Citizens Savings was the 80th largest mutual savings bank in the United States. Ten years later, the bank was operating 29 branches throughout Rhode Island, and assets totaled $971 million.

1981–92: Emergence of Citizens As Unit of Royal Bank

Also in 1981, George Graboys was named CEO of the bank. Graboys had practiced law before joining his family's asset-based lending company, U.S. Finance Corp., in the mid-1960s. After Citizens acquired U.S. Finance in 1969, Graboys began working within the commercial bank unit, then was elected president of Citizens Savings in 1975. It was during Graboys' tenure as CEO of Citizens that the bank would be transformed into a more modern financial institution as well as trade its independence for the security of a deep-pocketed parent.

Citizens avoided the fate of other savings and loan institutions during the disastrous and criminal savings and loan crisis of the 1980s by sticking to its conservative business and lending practices. Graboys did, however, respond surely to the key events of the decade for financial institutions: the deregulation of interest rates, the removal of interstate barriers, and increased competition. He sought to expand his bank's loan and retail banking businesses outside of Rhode Island and to engage in all aspects of retail banking and middle-market corporate lending. In 1983 the bank opened its first commercial loan office outside of Rhode Island, locating it in Boston. To prepare to convert from a mutual savings bank to a stock savings bank, Citizens Bank became a federal savings bank in October 1984. Then in mid-1985, Citizens Financial Group, Inc. was created as a bank holding company for both Citizens Bank and Citizens Trust. Citizens Financial then sold 4.3 million shares of common stock at $23 per share in an initial public offering. The new holding company began its existence with assets of $1.6 billion. The holding company structure enabled the group to move into other financial services businesses and into other geographic markets.

Graboys began using the proceeds from the stock offering to fund acquisitions. In 1986 the group acquired Gulf States Mortgage Company, an Atlanta-based residential mortgage origination and service firm with a loan portfolio of just over $1 billion. The new subsidiary was later renamed Citizens Mortgage Corporation. In July 1988 Citizens Financial completed its first acquisition of a retail bank located outside Rhode Island by spending $39 million for Fairhaven Savings Bank, which was based in Fairhaven, Massachusetts, and had five branches in the southeastern portion of that state and $266 million in assets. Fairhaven Savings became the initial building block for Citizens Bank of Massachusetts, which would eventually become the group's largest retail banking unit.

By 1988 Citizens Financial was the fifth largest bank in New England but was far smaller than the top four at the time: Bank of Boston, Fleet Financial Group, Bank of New England, and Shawmut National. Graboys believed that Citizens needed to ally itself with a larger company if it were to have any chance of competing against its much larger rivals. At the same time, however, Graboys wished to keep his bank at least semi-independent. The solution to this dilemma was for Citizens to be acquired by a foreign bank that would allow it to operate as a separate U.S. bank. That bank turned out to be the Edinburgh-based Royal Bank of Scotland Group plc, which at the time was the sixth largest U.K. bank with assets of more than $36 billion. Royal Bank paid about $440 million for Citizens in a transaction that was completed in December 1988. Citizens would now be able to tap into the deep pockets of its new parent to fund further growth, while Royal Bank gained a platform for U.S. expansion.

The well-run Royal Bank also helped Citizens survive a turbulent period for New England banking in the late 1980s and early 1990s, following the collapse of the New England real estate market and the resulting wave of loan defaults. Both Bank of New England and Bank of Boston fell into serious financial difficulties in the early 1990s; the former failed and was taken over by Fleet in 1991.

Citizens Financial began the 1990s by moving into a new 13-story headquarters called One Citizens Plaza. The building was located in downtown Providence at the confluence of the Moshassuck and Woonasquatucket Rivers. Citizens' desire for growth through acquisition was initially stymied by the crisis in New England banking. A number of acquisition targets were dropped from consideration because of the level of nonperforming loans in their portfolios. In fact, Citizens reached an agreement to acquire BankWorcester Corporation of Worcester, Massachusetts, for $149 million in early 1990, only to pull out of the deal later in the year because of the growing size of BankWorcester's nonperforming assets. Graboys nevertheless completed one acquisition in late 1990, that of Old Colony, the Rhode Island subsidiary of the troubled Bank of New England. Citizens thereby added 22 branches to its Rhode Island network of 30 branches, giving it the largest branch network in the state. Adding Old Colony's $1.2 billion in assets moved Citizens from fourth to second place in size among the state's banks. Old Colony was founded in 1803 as Newport Bank, which was the 12th bank founded in the United States.

Key Dates:

1828: High Street Bank is chartered as a commercial bank based in Providence, Rhode Island.

1871: Directors of High Street Bank obtain a second charter for Citizens Savings Bank, a mutual savings bank.

1943: Citizens Savings gains control of High Street Bank, its former parent.

1947: Citizens begins developing a branch network.

1948: High Street Bank is renamed Citizens Trust Company.

1950: Citizens joins the Federal Deposit Insurance Corporation (FDIC), becoming the first mutual savings bank to do so.

1954: Acquisition of Greenville Trust Company adds two more branches.

1981: Citizens is operating 29 branches throughout Rhode Island and has assets of $971 million; George Graboys takes over as CEO.

1985: Citizens Financial Group, Inc. is created as a bank holding company for both Citizens Bank and Citizens Trust; Citizens Financial is then taken public.

1988: Fairhaven Savings Bank is acquired and becomes base for Citizens Bank of Massachusetts; Royal Bank of Scotland Group plc acquires Citizens Financial, which begins operating as a wholly owned subsidiary.

1990: Citizens acquires Old Colony, the Rhode Island subsidiary of Bank of New England.

1992: Lawrence K. Fish is named chairman and CEO.

1993: Citizens enters the Connecticut market with the purchase of New England Savings, which becomes the base for Citizens Bank of Connecticut; Boston Five Bancorp, operating in the Boston area, is acquired.

1994: Neworld Bancorp, Coastal Federal Savings Bank, and Old Stone Federal Savings Bank are all acquired.

1995: Quincy Savings Bank is acquired.

1996: Citizens Financial merges with First NH Bank (owned by Bank of Ireland), which is renamed Citizens Bank of New Hampshire; Bank of Ireland now holds 23.5 percent stake in Citizens Financial, Royal Bank holds 76.5 percent stake; Farmers & Mechanics Bank (CT) is acquired.

1997: Grove Bank and Bank of New Haven are acquired.

1998: Royal Bank of Scotland pays Bank of Ireland $750 million to regain full control of Citizens Financial.

1999: Citizens acquires the retail banking unit of Boston-based State Street Corporation.

2000: Boston-based UST Corporation is acquired.

2001: Citizens reaches an agreement to acquire the regional banking business of Mellon Financial Corporation, including 345 branches in Pennsylvania, Delaware, and New Jersey, for $2.1 billion.

Doubling in Size Under Lawrence K. Fish: 1992–95

By 1992 Graboys had accomplished a quadrupling of the bank's assets during little more than a decade of leadership, to $4 billion. That year, Lawrence K. Fish succeeded Graboys as chairman and CEO. A banking veteran, Fish was a former executive at Bank of Boston who received accolades for his efforts to revive the failing Bank of New England during his brief tenure from 1990 to 1991 as chairman and CEO of the Boston-based bank. The Royal Bank of Scotland handed Fish the mission of taking a more aggressive approach to expanding its U.S. subsidiary.

Fish quickly delivered for his new bosses, completing seven acquisitions from September 1992 through January 1995, in the process increasing Citizen's assets to more than $10 billion. A number of the deals were for failed banks and savings and loans that were being liquidated by the FDIC or the Resolution Trust Corporation (RTC), a U.S. government agency set up to sell insolvent financial institutions. This was the case with the bank acquired in September 1992, Plymouth Five Cents Savings Bank, which was acquired from the FDIC and whose eight branches doubled the size of Citizens Bank of Massachusetts. Also bought from the FDIC was New England Savings Bank, acquired in May 1993. Citizens gained its first presence in Connecticut through the purchase of New London, Connecticut-based New England Savings, which became the base for Citizens Bank of Connecticut. New England Savings had 21 branches and $695 million in assets. Later in 1993, Citizens Financial completed its largest acquisition to date, the purchase

of The Boston Five Bancorp and its 22 metropolitan Boston branches for $95 million. Boston Five, which boasted assets of $1.63 billion, also had an extensive New England mortgage operation, which was added to Citizens Mortgage, doubling that subsidiary's mortgage portfolio to more than $8 billion.

During 1994 Citizens Financial completed three more acquisitions: Neworld Bancorp, Coastal Federal Savings Bank, and Old Stone Federal Savings Bank. Boston-based Neworld had 14 branches in Boston and another eight on Cape Cod, bringing Citizens Bank of Massachusetts' branch total to 55. Purchased for $144.3 million, Neworld had assets of $1.1 billion. Coastal was another failed thrift and was purchased from the RTC for $10.7 million. This added nine branches and $100 million in assets to Citizens Bank of Connecticut. Also acquired from the RTC for $133.6 million was Old Stone, which was the fourth largest bank in Rhode Island with 28 branches and assets totaling $501 million. Citizens now held 29 percent of the bank deposits in its home state, second only to Fleet's 34 percent. Also in 1994, Citizens Financial became one of the last large banks to begin selling mutual funds through its branches. It formed alliances with two major Boston-based fund managers, Fidelity Investments and Putnam Cos., to sell 30 of their stock and bond funds.

In early 1995 Citizens further entrenched itself in the Massachusetts market by acquiring Quincy Savings Bank for $141 million. Quincy operated 14 branches in Boston's suburban South Shore and had assets of $813 million. This latest acquisition increased the assets of Citizens Financial to $10.3 billion, more than double the figure when Fish took over. During the same period earnings tripled to $52.7 million as Fish found success with a strategy of positioning Citizens as a service-oriented, ''supercommunity'' banking franchise catering to the needs of working-class customers. This approach involved more of the old-fashioned human contact than the high-tech electronic services, such as ATMs and online banking, that rivals were rapidly adopting as the wave of the future. This focus on community banking also led Citizens to open its first supermarket banking branches in 1995 through a deal with Shaw's Supermarkets. Later deals placed Citizens branches within such supermarkets as Stop & Shop, Star, Victory, Shop'n'Save, and Wal-Mart.

1996 and Beyond: Accelerating the Pace of Growth

In April 1996 Citizens Financial merged with First NH Bank, which was based in Manchester, New Hampshire, was the largest financial services firm in the state, and was owned by Bank of Ireland. Royal Bank of Scotland paid $245 million in cash and notes to Bank of Ireland, which also gained a 23.5 percent stake in Citizens. Royal Bank retained 76.5 percent ownership of Citizens. First NH was recast as Citizens Bank of New Hampshire, bringing to Citizens Financial 73 bank branches, 12 supermarket banks, and 153 ATMs. The addition of $4 billion in assets made Citizens the third largest bank in New England, trailing Fleet (which had acquired Shawmut in 1995) and Bank of Boston. Citizens also leaped into the top 50 among U.S. banks.

The newly enlarged bank completed two more significant acquisitions within the next 12 months. In November 1996 Farmers & Mechanics Bank, based in Middletown, Connecticut, was acquired for $53.2 million in cash. The purchase expanded Citizens Bank of Connecticut by 12 branches and $569 million in assets. Citizens Bank of Massachusetts grew through the March 1997 buyout of Grove Bank, which was headquartered in Chestnut Hill, Massachusetts, and had ten branches in the lucrative suburban markets west of Boston. Purchased for $87 million, Grove Bank had assets of $747 million. Also in late 1996 and early 1997, Citizens Financial exited from the mortgage servicing market, believing that its Atlanta-based mortgage servicing unit was too small to compete with large national mortgage servicers. Citizens Mortgage continued to originate and process mortgages from the bank's New England branches. In late 1996 Citizens Capital, Inc. was formed as a Boston-based subsidiary specializing in making loans to small and medium-sized businesses. In keeping with the bank's traditional conservative lending practices, the loans would range from $1 million to $50 million, with the vast majority consisting of loans of less than $10 million. In yet another development around this same time, Citizens in January 1997 launched a four-state marketing campaign featuring the slogan ''Not Your Typical Bank.'' The campaign was designed to emphasize the bank's strategy of being a supercommunity bank offering the personal service of a smaller, neighborhood bank in contrast to the impersonal reputations of its much larger rivals.

Continuing to fill in geographic gaps in its New England base, Citizens spent $57.2 million for Bank of New Haven in August 1997. The $350 million in assets bank operated 11 branches in Connecticut, bringing Citizens' network in that state to 41. In August 1998 Citizens Bank of Massachusetts expanded into Boston's northern suburbs with the purchase of Woburn National

Bank and its five branches and $165 million in assets. One month later, Royal Bank of Scotland regained full control of Citizens Financial by paying Bank of Ireland $750 million for its 23.5 percent stake. In October 1998 Citizens Bank of Connecticut added four branches of Branford Savings Bank, expanding its presence in the greater New Haven area. Later that same year, Citizens sold its Visa credit-card portfolio to Bankcard Services of MBNA, one of the giants of the credit card industry. Citizens continued to offer credit cards to its customers, but the cards would now be serviced by MBNA instead of the bank.

While continuing to emphasize personal, branch-based banking, Citizens in 1999 also launched Citizens Bank Online, a full-service electronic banking and bill payment service. The year was also significant because of the merger of Fleet and BankBoston that created FleetBoston Financial Corporation, a $190 billion financial giant that ranked as the eighth largest bank in the United States. Citizens Financial thereby gained the number two spot among New England banks but with just $18 billion in assets was now dwarfed by its much larger rival. This increased the pressure on Citizens to complete more acquisitions, and it did just that. In October 1999 the bank paid $350 million to acquire State Street Corp.'s retail bank, which included four branches in Boston and Quincy, Massachusetts, and a commercial loan portfolio totaling $2.2 billion. The deal was particularly significant for its bulking up of Citizens' commercial portfolio by nearly 50 percent, to $7 billion, or one-third of its total assets of $21 billion. Citizens was now well-positioned to be a major player in New England in middle-market loans to corporations, small businesses, and nonprofits.

In January 2000 Citizens Financial completed its largest acquisition yet, the $1.4 billion purchase of Boston-based UST Corporation. This deal doubled the size of Citizens Bank of Massachusetts to $14 billion in assets, adding 87 more branches to that unit. It also increased Citizens Financial's commercial loan portfolio by another $4.4 billion. Citizens also gained United States Trust Company of Boston, UST's asset management unit, which had more than $3.5 billion under management for individual and institutional investors; and Brewer & Lord, a full-service insurance agency. Overall, the State Street and UST deals helped increase Citizens Financial's assets to nearly $31 billion by the end of 2000, making the bank one of the 30 largest banks in the nation. Meanwhile, Citizens' parent had also bulked itself up during 2000, acquiring National Westminster Bank Plc for $33 billion and becoming one of the top three banks in the United Kingdom, with total assets of nearly $500 billion. For Citizens, having a larger Royal Bank of Scotland as a parent appeared likely to open up even more avenues for growth because the U.S. unit would now generate a much smaller proportion of Royal Bank's operating earnings.

This soon proved to be the case as Citizens Financial announced in July 2001 that it would purchase the retail banking operations of Pittsburgh-based Mellon Financial Corporation for about $2.1 billion. If completed, the deal would be not only Citizens' largest in history but also its first foray outside its New

England base. Included in the purchase would be 345 branches in Pennsylvania, Delaware, and southern New Jersey and $13.4 billion in consumer and commercial deposits, as well as $6.1 billion in loans, mainly to small and middle-market banking customers. Citizens would instantly become the third largest bank in Pennsylvania and with nearly $50 billion in total assets become one of the 20 largest commercial banks in the United States. It appeared quite likely that additional acquisitions would follow the Mellon deal, with speculation centering on gaps in Citizens' geographic coverage, such as in northern New Jersey and New York state, and on further expansion of Citizens' territorial extent, such as moving west into Ohio. Regardless of future deals, however, Citizens seemed certain to maintain its winning formula of a focus on customer service coupled with a local, conservative approach to lending.

Principal Subsidiaries

Citizens Bank of Rhode Island; Citizens Bank of Connecticut; Citizens Bank of Massachusetts; Citizens Bank of New Hampshire; Citizens Business Credit; Citizens Capital, Inc.; Citizens Ventures, Inc.; Citizens eBusiness; Citizens Financial Services, Inc.; Citizens Leasing Corporation; Citizens Mortgage Corporation; Brewer & Lord; Firestone Financial; United States Trust Company of Boston.

Principal Competitors

FleetBoston Financial Corporation; Sovereign Bancorp, Inc.

Further Reading

Arditi, Lynn, "Citizens Completes $350-Million Deal for State Street," *Providence Journal*, May 7, 1999, p. F1.

——, "Citizens to Buy Grove," *Providence Journal-Bulletin*, November 5, 1996, p. E1.

Bailey, Douglas M., "Scot Bank to Buy Citizens Financial," *Boston Globe*, April 29, 1988, p. 25.

Barry, David G., "Citizens Bank Buys into the Bay State," *Boston Business Journal*, March 10, 1995, pp. 26+.

Beckett, Paul, "Mellon Financial Sells Retail Bank for $2.1 Billion," *Wall Street Journal*, July 18, 2001, p. C11.

Blanton, Kimberly, "A Bigger Pond Still: Larry Fish Buys Another Boston Bank," *Boston Globe*, October 26, 1993, p. 37.

Browning, Lynnley, "Citizens Struggles to Keep That 'Local Bank' Image," *Boston Globe*, June 27, 1999, p. G1.

——, "Citizens to Buy State Street's Retail Bank," *Boston Globe*, May 7, 1999, p. C1.

——, "$1.4b Citizens-UST Deal Recasts Financial Scene," *Boston Globe*, June 22, 1999, p. A1.

Christie, Claudia M., "Businessperson of the Year," *New England Business*, December 1, 1988, p. 36.

"Citizens Plans to Buy Another Connecticut Bank," *Providence Journal-Bulletin*, June 14, 1996, p. G1.

Collins, William E., "Graboys of Citizens: Our Businessperson of the Year for 1989," *Ocean State Business*, January 15, 1990, p. 10.

Davis, Paul, "Citizens Acquires Bank in Mass.," *Providence Journal-Bulletin*, September 19, 1992.

——, "Citizens Acquires Connecticut Bank Chain," *Providence Journal-Bulletin*, May 22, 1993.

——, "Citizens to Buy Boston Five," *Providence Journal-Bulletin*, April 14, 1993.

Fasig, Lisa Biank, "With Mellon Deal, Citizens Financial's Business Model Branches Out," *Providence Journal*, July 18, 2001.

Forrest, Wayne, "Citizens Hooks Fish: Ex-BNE Chief to Lead Era of Expansion," *Providence Business News*, February 10, 1992, p. 1.

Graham, George, and Victoria Griffith, "Bank Shuffles Cards in Boston's High Stakes Poker Game," *Financial Times*, June 22, 1999, p. 29.

Healy, Beth, "Larry Fish Prepares Citizens to Swim with the Big Banks," *Boston Business Journal*, December 3, 1993.

Hiday, Jeffrey L., "Citizens Financial Agrees to Acquire UST of Boston in a $1.4 Billion Deal," *Wall Street Journal*, June 22, 1999, p. A6.

——, "Citizens' NH Bank Purchase Puts It Among the Top 50 in Size," *Providence Journal-Bulletin*, December 19, 1995, p. E1.

Hirsch, Michelle, "Lawrence K. Fish: Citizen's New President Looks Forward to Next, 'Exciting,' Five Years," *Providence Business News*, April 26, 1993, p. 2.

Holtzman, Robert, "Thanks to Royal, Citizens Is Tops in New England," *Ocean State Business*, January 30, 1989, p. 1.

Hooper, Molly, "Rhode Island Thrift Plans to Go Public with Stock Offer," *American Banker*, May 8, 1985, p. 3.

Kapiloff, Howard, "Larry Fish Has Finally Made It Big—with Little R.I.'s Citizens Financial," *American Banker*, October 6, 1994, p. 4.

Kostrzewa, John, "Citizens Confirms Plans to Acquire BNE-Old Colony for $75 Million," *Providence Journal-Bulletin*, September 5, 1990, p. 5.

——, "Interest in Bank Expected to Soar," *Providence Journal-Bulletin*, March 22, 1988, p. 1.

——, "Royal Bank Agrees to Buy Citizens for $440 Million," *Providence Journal-Bulletin*, April 29, 1988, p. 1.

Kraus, James R., "Bank of Ireland Selling Its Stake in R.I. Regional," *American Banker*, August 20, 1998.

——, "Citizens Races Clock, New England Rivals for Size," *American Banker*, January 7, 1997, pp. 1+.

——, "Scottish, Irish Banks Merging Their Units in New England," *American Banker*, December 19, 1995.

Kutler, Jeffrey, and Mark Basch, "Which Is No. 1 Thrift?: Here's a Vote for Citizens Savings," *American Banker*, September 26, 1985, p. 3.

Moyer, Liz, "Bulking Up in Its Region, R.I.'s Citizens to Buy UST," *American Banker*, June 22, 1999, pp. 1+.

——, "Citizens Looks to Wider Horizons," *American Banker*, July 18, 2001, p. 1.

"Now There Are Two: Citizens Buys in As Fleet's Top Rival in R.I.," *Providence Journal-Bulletin*, July 10, 1994.

Plasencia, William, "Citizens Bank of R.I. Taking the Plunge in Funds," *American Banker*, May 5, 1994, p. 12.

Rebello, Joseph, "Radical Ways of Its CEO Are a Boon to Bank," *Wall Street Journal*, March 20, 1995, p. B1.

Sabatini, Patricia, "Mellon Financial to Exit Retail Banking," *Pittsburgh Post-Gazette*, July 18, 2001.

Stein, Charles, "Citizens Financial Group: Backed by Scottish Parent, Institution No Longer Content to Sit on the Sidelines," *Boston Globe*, November 9, 1997, p. E1.

Syre, Steven, and Charles Stein, "Banks Driven to Get Deal Done: Citizens and UST Chiefs Pushed into Action by Fleet-BankBoston Merger," *Boston Globe*, June 22, 1999, p. D1.

Vogelstein, Fred, "Larry Fish on New England Acquisition Trail," *American Banker*, June 7, 1993.

Wyss, Bob, "Citizens to Purchase USTrust for $1.4 Billion," *Providence Journal*, June 22, 1999, p. A1.

—David E. Salamie

Commercial Metals Company

7800 Stemmons Freeway
Dallas, Texas 75247
U.S.A.
Telephone: (214) 689-4300
Fax: (214) 689-5886
Web site: http://www.commercialmetals.com

Public Company
Incorporated: 1946
Employees: 8,379
Sales: $2.66 billion (2000)
Stock Exchanges: New York
Ticker Symbol: CMC
NAIC: 331111 Iron and Steel Mills; 331492 Secondary
  Smelting, Refining, and Alloying of Nonferrous
  Metals; 331421 Copper Rolling, Drawing, and
  Extruding; 332312 Fabricated Structural Metal
  Manufacturing; 42151 Metals Service Centers and
  Offices; 42193 Recyclable Material Wholesalers

Commercial Metals Company (CMC) is a major vertically integrated player in the metals industry. The manufacturing division is the company's dominant and most rapidly expanding business. This segment consists of two entities, the CMC Steel Group and Howell Metal Company. The CMC Steel Group is vertically integrated and includes four steel minimills with a capacity of 2.3 million tons and over 70 manufacturing plants located from California through the Southeast. The products produced include reinforcing bars, beams, angles, rounds, channels, flats, steel joists, castellated and cellular beams, metal fence post stock, sign posts, and squares. The products are sold to the construction, service center, energy, petrochemical, transportation, steel warehousing, fabrication, and original equipment manufacturing industries. Howell Metal Company manufactures primarily copper water tubing and air conditioning and refrigeration tubing, for use in commercial, industrial, and residential construction. CMC's recycling division is one of the largest processors of scrap ferrous and nonferrous metals in the United States. It operates 34 metal recycling plants, excluding

eight recycling plants in the CMC Steel Group. The recycled metals are sold to steel mills, specialty steel producers, high temperature alloy manufacturers, foundries, aluminum refineries and mills, copper and brass mills, and other consumers. The marketing and trading division is involved in marketing steel, nonferrous metals, and other industrial products through a network of 17 offices located around the world.

Origins and Early Post-World War II Years

The resurgence of the U.S. economy following the conclusion of World War II obliterated any lingering effects of the country's decade-long, financial free-fall during the 1930s, invigorating businesses and industries across the nation. For the decades to follow, a general and wide-sweeping era of prosperity reigned, increasing the magnitude of the country's major industries and engendering the rise of subsidiary, or minor, industries to levels of importance and worth substantially higher than during the first half of the 20th century.

Among other major industries in the United States, the metals industry achieved robust growth during the postwar era, strengthened by an increasing demand for metals as manufacturers labored to produce larger quantities of consumer and industrial products. As the country's metals needs mounted, the metals industry was propelled forward, recording growth that closely paralleled the growth of the U.S. population following the war, but as the need for metals increased, the primary reserves of metallic ores dwindled, a natural effect of ravenous demand that dramatically altered the stature of the country's scrap metals industry. For decades, scrap metals companies had represented a largely insignificant segment of the broad-based metals industry, earning little compared to the manufacturers of virgin metal and suffering from the opprobrious image that they were junkyard peddlers. All this changed when soaring metals demand threatened to deplete ore reserves and technological advancements lowered the processing costs associated with converting scrap metals into "new" metals. Long the shunned stepchildren of the metals industry, scrap metals companies underwent a significant transformation, becoming integral contributors to annual production volume and, along the way, garnering a greater share of the revenues generated by the

---

Company Perspectives:

CMC's history goes back more than 85 years. By all key internal measures we are an extremely successful company. But there still is much more for us to achieve. We are committed to creating long-term growth and building earnings power through continuous internal improvements, a focus on cash flows, strong regional positions and outstanding people. In the past several years we have taken major steps to increase our output, expand our product lines, add value downstream and build our talent pool.

---

metals industry as a whole. By purchasing scrap metals from small individual dealers, salvage firms, manufacturing facilities, refineries, automobile wreckers, and other sources, and then processing the materials through giant presses, power shears, or shredders, scrap metal companies became essential suppliers of recycled metals to primary metals processors, carving a lasting position for themselves within the metals industry.

Such was the case for Commercial Metals, a scrap metals company that struggled to survive during its early years, then blossomed into one of the largest companies of its kind during the halcyon years following World War II. The company's historical roots stretch back to 1915, when Moses Feldman started a scrap metals company named American Iron & Metal Company. Feldman, who emigrated from Russia and settled in Houston ten years before he founded American Iron & Metal, superintended his company's growth during its early years, then was joined by son Jacob Feldman, who eventually would take control of the company. The younger Feldman joined the family business after he graduated from Southern Methodist University and in 1932, with the help of family members, formed a brokerage house in Dallas named Commercial Metals Company to buttress the family's scrap operations. In 1946, the two family-owned operations were incorporated, just as the scrap metals industry as a whole began to burgeon, with the combined company's first acquisition occurring seven years later, when Jacob Feldman negotiated the purchase of the Charles Harley Company, a California-based scrap metals processor founded in 1856.

The 1960s

By the beginning of the 1960s, nearly five decades of operation had built a roughly $50 million company, one that was ready to take on the trappings characterizing Commercial Metals during the 1990s. In 1960, ownership of Commercial Metals changed from private to public hands when the company became the first independent metals firm to be listed on the American Stock Exchange (the company would eventually move to the New York Stock Exchange). The switch to public ownership ushered in a period of diversification and expansion, touching off the first definitive surge of growth recorded by the company.

Entering the decade, Commercial Metals' scrap business was thriving, prompting Jacob Feldman to diversify the company's interests and branch into manufacturing. During the 1960s, Feldman orchestrated the acquisition of a small steel manufacturer, a copper fabricator, and then later he started another steel minimill, making Commercial Metals one of the few scrap metals compa-

nies to operate its own steel mills. The broadening of the company's interests began in 1963, when Commercial Metals acquired a 74 percent interest in Structural Metals, Inc. Located in Seguin, Texas, near San Antonio, Structural Metals operated an electric furnace steel mill that provided Commercial Metals with a new source of sales and increased the company's market for its own processed raw materials. The remaining percentage of Structural Metals, which constituted Commercial Metals' largest operating division during the 1990s, was purchased between 1963 and 1969, pushing the company's sales upward as more and more of the electric furnace steel mill came under Commercial Metals' ownership. Annual sales swelled from slightly less than $60 million in 1963 to nearly $150 million four years later, while the company's net income leaped from just under $600,000 to $1.85 million during the four-year period.

The acquisition of Structural Metals provided a significant boost to Commercial Metals' standing in the scrap metals industry, distinguishing it as a model for other scrap metals companies to emulate as they too diversified into the manufacturing side of the business, but the financial growth recorded during the 1960s was also fueled by the company's accomplishments overseas. During the years bridging the conclusion of World War II and the completion of the Structural Metals acquisition, Commercial Metals had extended its corporate reach overseas, establishing metals trading offices in key foreign markets. By the late 1960s, Commercial Metals ranked as the largest single exporter of ferrous scrap metals in the United States and one of the largest competitors in the metals industry in the world, deriving nearly half of its annual sales from abroad, particularly from Japan and Mexico, the company's two largest export markets. Its sixth international office was opened at the end of 1967 in Zug, Switzerland, complementing the company's other trading offices in Amsterdam, Tokyo, Taipei, Montreal, and Mexico City. In total, the growing Commercial Metals empire comprised 32 plants and offices in the United States and abroad by the late 1960s, positioning it as a major competitor in what was becoming an increasingly important and lucrative global industry.

The 1970s and 1980s

The company continued to expand its international network as it entered the 1970s, recording financial growth as its foreign offices solidified their position in respective overseas markets. In 1970, three years into its program to foster trade in Central and Latin American countries, Commercial Metals generated nearly $290 million in sales and earned nearly $6.5 million in net income, the product of the company's resolute expansion during the 1960s. As the decade began, Commercial Metals was obtaining half of its annual sales and 40 percent of its profits from direct trading operations, while, comparatively, the company was deriving a third of its sales volume from the processing of secondary metals, 9 percent from manufacturing operations, and the balance from the production of semi-finished products and other metals-related businesses.

By virtue of its success as a broker, manufacturer, and processor of scrap metals, Commercial Metals soared to the top of its industry, ranking as one of the largest independent companies in the country, but after the encouraging results of 1970, Jacob Feldman suffered a heart attack a year later and the company's financial health likewise deteriorated. Though Feldman remained titular head of the company, Charlie Merritt, who joined Commercial Metals in 1937 as a stenographer, essentially assumed control of the company's day-to-day operations. Under Merritt's stewardship, Commercial Metals' financial growth came to an abrupt halt, but the blame did not rest on Merritt's shoulders. A nationwide recession and laggard demand overseas combined to hamper Commercial Metals' growth, curtailing production volume at its 22 scrap processing plants and diminishing its scrap metals trading activities. Annual sales declined as a result, plunging from $287 million in 1970 to $207 million in 1971, then slipped again the following year, falling to $200 million.

Despite the retrogressive financial slide, Commercial Metals continued to be regarded as one of the largest independent worldwide processors and brokers of secondary metals, so when national economic conditions rallied and ferrous scrap prices rose to as high as $100 a ton, the company benefited commensurately. Annual sales eclipsed $320 million in 1973, then nearly doubled the following year, reaching $643 million, while earnings nearly quadrupled, soaring to more than $19 million.

Once the company's financial health was restored, it diversified into new areas and into new metals. Commercial Metals expanded its vital trading business into commodities such as coal, then bolstered its core businesses when it acquired part interest in two companies in 1976, Corpus Christi, Texas-based General Export Iron and Metals Company and Mobile, Alabama-based Pinto Island Metals Company.

Entering the 1980s, the company was once again subjected to recessionary economic conditions, its financial health drained by the pernicious effects of an anemic economy. Like a decade earlier, however, the passing of time healed all wounds. When the economy recovered, Commercial Metals resumed its strategy of controlled growth and strengthening of its core businesses. In 1984, the company acquired Connors Steel Co.'s mini-mill in Birmingham, Alabama. Next, the company acquired Galveston, Texas-based Island City Iron & Supply Inc. in January 1984, then purchased two additional companies, Newell Recycling Co. and Richelson Iron and Metal, later in 1984.

The following year, 1985, marked Commercial Metals' 70th year of business, a milestone that marked the passing of two world wars and numerous economic hills and valleys since Moses Feldman had arrived in Galveston and founded American Iron & Metals Company. Over the course of seven decades, Commercial Metals had evolved into an internationally recognized firm, involved in three main metals-related businesses through the manufacturing and fabrication of steel products and copper tubing, the recycling of ferrous and nonferrous scrap metals, and the marketing and trading of metals products and raw materials. As the company moved past its anniversary year, it endeavored to augment its core businesses, acquiring Industrial Salvage in Corpus Christi in 1988, two scrap metal yards in Victoria, Texas, in 1989, and the processing operations of four companies, three based in Florida and one in Tennessee, in 1990.

The 1990s and Beyond

The new decade brought the familiar refrain of economic malaise in the United States, but Commercial Metals emerged from the recessive early 1990s with dynamic vigor, its recovery engendered by the gradual recovery of the economy and the strides gained by steel minimills. Minimills such as Nucor Corporation and Birmingham Steel Corporation relied heavily on scrap steel to feed their manufacturing facilities, a dependence that buoyed the price of scrap and fueled Commercial Metals' resurgence. During the 1980s, minimills began to wrest away market share from large steel corporations, increasing their share of total steel production in the country from 25 percent to 35 percent. As minimills grew in stature, producing increasingly greater amounts of the nation's steel output, the price of scrap rose as demand increased, providing Commercial Metals with a much needed boost to its business. Once economic conditions regained their prerecessionary vitality, Commercial Metals began to realize the financial benefits accrued from the burgeoning minimill industry. During the first nine months of 1993, the company's revenues increased 44 percent, while its profits exploded exponentially, jumping a prodigious 135 percent.

With scrap prices remaining at enviable levels, Commercial Metals moved to expand its operations in 1994. In August, the company acquired Jacksonville, Florida-based Tri-State Recycling Corporation, then at the end of the year completed its acquisition of Columbia, South Carolina-based Owen Steel Co. Inc. for $50 million. The addition of Owen Steel, which was renamed SMI-Owen Steel Co. Inc. and absorbed by Commercial Metals' largest manufacturing division, the CMC Steel Group, increased annual steel production capacity to more than 1.7 million tons and raised steel fabrication capacity to more than 500,000 tons.

As Commercial Metals entered the mid-1990s and prepared for the remainder of the 1990s, its expectations for future growth were optimistic, predicated on the anticipated increasing demand for scrap metals and its own stalwart position within the industry as a diversified secondary metals processor, broker, and manufacturer. Lending credence to the company's confidence in achieving sustained growth, sales increased strongly in 1995, climbing from $1.65 billion to $2.1 billion. More encouraging, the company's earnings ballooned between 1994 and 1995, soaring 44 percent to $38.2 million. As these financial records were being achieved, the company strengthened its processing capabilities further, acquiring the assets of three Texas scrap processing facilities, Atlas Iron & Metal, Federal Iron & Metal, and Laredo Scrap Metals, in September 1995.

In 1998 CMC purchased A-1 Iron & Metal Company, one of Houston's major nonferrous metals processors and recyclers. The new acquisition was used to expand the operations of CMC's Houston plant on Quitman Street.

A CMC press release on May 2, 2000 announced the company's acquisitions of two southern California rebar fabrication companies. Operating in Rancho Cucamonga and San Marcos, Fontana Steel, Inc. had been started in 1946 by Paul Ware. It employed over 400 persons. C&M Steel, Inc. was a 40-employee, Fontana company that had been founded in 1983.

Commercial Metals Company reported sales of $2.7 billion and net earnings of $46.3 million for its fiscal year ending August 31, 2000. That compared to sales of $2.3 billion and net earnings of $47.1 million the previous year. CMC Chairman, President, and CEO Stanley A. Rabin also stated in a company press release that CMC's four minimills shipped 1.85 million tons of steel, up from 1.68 million tons the year before.

In 2001 the company continued to grow, partly through acquisitions. Effective February 13, 2001, it acquired Allform Inc. based in Tampa, Florida, with another operation in Orlando. Started in 1984, Allform provided concrete forms and supplies and related accessories for the central Florida area. It became part of CMC Concrete Accessories, Inc.

Strengthened by vertical integration in which its scrap metals production was used in its minimills, Commercial Metals Company seemed well prepared for the challenges of the new millennium. It was diversified to the point where downturns in one part of its business could be offset by good performance in another segment. A still growing U.S. economy in mid-2001 also helped. Of course, with stiff competition from other U.S. steel and metals companies and also foreign steel producers, Commercial Metals Company faced plenty of challenges in the days ahead.

Principal Subsidiaries

AHT, Inc., CMC (Australia) Pty. Ltd.; CMC Commercio de Metias, Ltda. (Brazil); CMC Concrete Accessories, Inc. (90%); CMC Fareast Ltd. (Hong Kong); CMC International (S.E. Asia) Pte. Ltd. (Singapore); CMC Oil Co.; CMC Steel Holding Co.; CMC Steel Fabricators, Inc.; CMC Steel IPH Company; CMC Trading AG (Switzerland); CMC Trinec GmbH (Germany); CMC (UK) Limited; Cometals China, Inc.; Cometals Far East, Inc.; Cometals, Inc.; Commercial Metals - Austin Inc.; Commercial Metals Deutschland GmbH (Germany); Commercial Metals (International) A.G. (Switzerland); Commercial Metals Overseas Export Co.; Commercial Metals Overseas Export (FSC) Corp.; Commercial Metals Railroad Salvage Co.; Commercial Metals SF/JV Co.; Commonwealth Metal Corp.; Construction Materials, Inc.; Daltrading Ltd. (South Korea); Howell Metal Co.; Owen Electric Steel Company of South Carolina; Owen Industrial Products, Inc.; Owen Joist Corporation; Owen Joist of Florida, Inc.; Owen of Georgia, Inc.; Owen Steel Company of Florida; Owen Steel Company of N.C., Inc.; Owen Supply Company, Inc.; Pyrosteel Limited, Sydney (Australia); Regency Advertising Agency, Inc.; SMI-Owen Steel Company, Inc.; SMSI Rebar Coating JV, Inc.; SMI Steel Inc.; Structural Metals, Inc.; Zenith Finance & Construction Co.

Principal Divisions

Manufacturing; Recycling; Marketing and Trading.

Principal Competitors

Nucor Corporation; Birmingham Steel Corporation; Oregon Steel Mills, Inc.; Schnitzer Steel Industries, Inc.

Further Reading

"CMC Acquires A-1 Iron & Metal Company in Houston," *PR Newswire*, October 26, 1998, p. 1.

"Commercial Metals Sees Sales Increase As Economy Improves," *American Metal Market*, June 30, 1993, p. 3.

"Commercial, Owen Deal Complete," *American Metal Market*, December 2, 1994, p. 3.

Goodfriend, Martin I., "Commercial Metals Co.," *Wall Street Transcript*, December 18, 1972, p. 31,190.

Goodwin, Morgan E., "CMC Acquires Three Scrap Yards in Texas," *American Metal Market*, September 4, 1995, p. 8.

Haflich, Frank, "CMC Expands Global Market," *American Metal Market*, August 30, 1990, p. 2.

Lawton, Clark, "Commercial Metals Expands and Diversifies to Process Scrap Metals for World Markets," *Investment Dealers' Digest*, August 5, 1968, p. 51.

Lubove, Seth, "Golden Grunge," *Forbes*, August 2, 1993, p. 103.

Rabin, Stanley, "Commercial Metals Looks Ahead," *American Metal Market*, May 18, 1988, p. 19.

"Scrap Is Beautiful," *Forbes*, May 1, 1975, p. 26.

Sherman, Joseph V., "Sophisticated Scrap," *Barron's*, December 4, 1967, p. 3.

Willat, Norris, "More Than Warehouses," *Barron's*, April 27, 1964, p. 5.

Worden, Edward, "CMC Zeroing in on Steel Market," *American Metal Market*, April 15, 1988, p. 4.

—Jeffrey L. Covell
—update: David M. Walden

Compagnie Générale des Établissements Michelin

12, cours Sablon
63000 Clermont-Ferrand
France
Telephone: (+33) 4-73-98-59-00
Fax: (+33) 4-73-98-59-04
Web site: http://www.michelin.com

Public Company
Incorporated: 1889 as Michelin et Compagnie
Employees: 128,122
Sales: ($14.88 billion) (2000)
Stock Exchanges: Euronext Paris
Ticker Symbol: ML
NAIC: 326211 Tire Manufacturing (Except Retreading)

Compagnie Générale des Établissements Michelin (Michelin) is the world's largest tire company, and one of the largest auto wheel manufacturers. Still controlled by the founding Michelin family from French headquarters, it is an international operation with outlets in 170 countries. It owns about 80 manufacturing plants located in 19 countries across four continents; rubber plantations in Brazil and Nigeria provide part of the company's raw materials requirements. The company produces tires and other products under the Michelin, BF Goodrich, Kleber, Taurus, Uniroyal, and other brand names, and also operates tire service centers under the Tyre Master and Euromaster brand names. The company's related products include wheels and wheel assemblies and suspension systems for automobiles, trucks, tramways, airplanes—including the Concorde—and other vehicles. Michelin is also a notable publisher of maps and guides, of which it sells 18 million per year. Although accounting for only a small proportion of its revenue, these items have immense promotional value. The stars awarded to restaurants by Michelin Guide Rouge inspectors are among the most coveted accolades of European haute cuisine. The company is led by Edouard Michelin, taking over from his father, François Michelin, and by René Zingraff.

Rubber Tire Pioneer in the 19th Century

As a tire company, Michelin dates back to the 1880s, when the original Michelin brothers, André and Edouard, took over a rubber products business created by their grandfather, Aristide Barbier, and his cousin, Edouard Daubrée. This firm's premises were in Clermont-Ferrand, in the Auvergne. Set up in 1830 to manufacture sugar, the Daubrée-Barbier enterprise had diversified into rubber a couple of years later at the instigation of Daubrée's Scottish wife, Elizabeth. As a child, Elizabeth had played with rubber balls made by her uncle, Charles Macintosh, an inventor who pioneered the use of rubber in waterproofing clothes, and gave his name to rubberized raincoats. A rubber workshop was opened at Clermont-Ferrand, and was soon making not only these balls, but also other rubber products, including hoses and drive belts.

After the death of the original partners, the firm, then also manufacturing agricultural equipment, was run for a few years by a manager. Business had declined by 1886, when the 33-year-old André Michelin stepped in. He was already an entrepreneur in his own right, making picture frames and locks in Paris, and under his management the Clermont-Ferrand enterprise took a turn for the better. However, André sometimes had to attend to his Paris shops at the expense of Clermont-Ferrand. In 1888, André's brother Edouard, six years his junior, was prevailed upon by the family to abandon his fine arts studies and come to Clermont-Ferrand. The following year, the firm, whose most successful line was then rubber brake pads for horse-drawn vehicles, was incorporated as Michelin et Compagnie.

It was in this same year, 1889, that a cyclist arrived at the workshop asking to have a punctured Dunlop tire repaired. Pneumatic tires, first patented in 1845 but not commercially exploited at the time, had been reintroduced in 1888 by Scotsman John Boyd Dunlop, but were still rare enough to be a curiosity as solid ones were the norm. Edouard Michelin found the repair a major undertaking, involving three hours' worth of work followed by an all night drying session. The repair did not hold, but Edouard, struck by the comfortable ride that the troublesome tires gave, set to work on a design that would retain the comfort without the trouble. In 1891 the workshop patented

Key Dates:

1886: André and Edouard Michelin take over rubber manufacturing business.
1891: Company launches its first detachable pneumatic tire design.
1895: Company launches first pneumatic automobile tire.
1898: The Michelin man, or Monsieur Bibendum, logo debuts.
1910: Company begins publishing road maps.
1935: Michelin rescues bankrupt automaker Citroën, running the company for the next 40 years.
1946: Company launches its radial tire.
1955: François Michelin takes over company leadership.
1975: Company opens a manufacturing plant in South Carolina.
1990: Michelin acquires Uniroyal Goodrich and becomes the market leader in the tire industry.
1999: Company acquires Tire Centers LLC.
2001: Company unveils new tire design for Concorde airplane.

a detachable tire, repairable in minutes rather than hours. That fall the brothers persuaded a cyclist to demonstrate their tires in a 1,200-kilometer race. Michelin's rider sustained five punctures on the first day. Even so, he won the race, with an eight-hour lead over the favorite. The earliest Michelin tire took 15 minutes to change, but by June 1892 the time was down to two minutes. Michelin organized another race. Nails surreptitiously planted in the road caused 244 punctures, affording ample opportunity to prove how easy repairs were. By 1893, 10,000 cyclists had fitted with Michelin tires.

The following year, Michelin launched a pneumatic tire for horse-drawn hackney carriages. The fleet of five Paris cabs that test drove the tires gained such an advantage in terms of quietness and comfort that the other cabbies were driven to sabotage. Soon even the saboteurs were converted and by 1903, 600 Paris cabs were running on Michelin tires. In 1895 Michelin announced the world's first pneumatic tire for automobiles. Three cars, specially built to test the tire, were entered for a race in June 1895. One, the Eclair, meaning forked lightning, was driven by the Michelin brothers themselves. Despite frequent punctures, engine fires, and gearbox failures, the Eclair was a success. Only nine out of 19 competitors finished within the time allowed of 100 hours for 1,209 kilometers. The Eclair was the ninth. This was the first of many races in which Michelin tires distinguished themselves.

Around the turn of the century, pneumatic tires were becoming the norm for the automobile industry, as well as for bicycles, carriages, and cabs. Competition was intense, with 150 tire companies in France alone by 1903. Elsewhere, Pirelli, Dunlop, Goodyear, Goodrich, and Firestone were all coming along fast. A strong brand image was crucial in this climate, and Michelin had come up with a brilliant one. The Michelin man, a rotund figure composed of tires, was born around 1898. His nickname of Monsieur Bibendum came from the caption of an early poster that read *Nunc est bibendum,* a phrase from Horace meaning

something like "Time for a drink." The glass flourished by the convivial Michelin man contained not alcohol but nails and sharp pebbles. Michelin tires, it was implied, would gobble up such objects with no lasting ill effects. Today, Monsieur Bibendum has become one of the most widely recognized logos in the world. Apart from promoting tires, Monsieur Bibendum embellishes Michelin guides and maps. The first such publication, the Guide Rouge to France, appeared in 1900. Initially distributed free, it contained tire information together with journey planning advice, including hotel listings. Guides to Europe, North Africa, and Egypt followed as, in 1909, did an English-language edition of the guide to France. Michelin also furnished motorists with itineraries, via an information bureau.

About the same time as its foreign guides appeared, the company was opening its first foreign subsidiaries. The U.K. operation was launched in 1905, the Italian, the following year. In 1905 came the acquisition of rubber plantations in Indo-China. Meanwhile, tire technology was advancing rapidly. In 1903 Michelin introduced a tire with a sole of leather and studs of steel. Three years later came the detachable wheel rim, allowing a car to carry spare Michelin tires, as did the victor of the first ever Grand Prix, at the La Sarthe circuit. By 1913 Michelin had simplified the way wheels were attached to the vehicle, giving a neater solution to the problem of punctures. Motorists could then carry a spare wheel.

Expansion in the 1920s

Michelin was on the lookout for new applications for its tires. Around 1908 they were starting to be fitted to trucks, using twin wheels to take the heavy weight, a system tested on Clermont-Ferrand buses. Michelin linked its name to the aeronautical industry by instituting a flying competition, offering FFr 100,000 for the first pilot to complete a difficult course culminating in a landing on the peak of the Puy de Dôme mountain, near Clermont-Ferrand. Cynics said the brothers were getting free publicity by setting an impossible task, but in fact the prize was won in 1911, on the third anniversary of its creation.

When World War I came in 1914, Michelin showed a more serious side of its commitment to aeronautics by adapting its workshops to the production of bombers for the French air force. It supplied 100 bombers free and the remaining 1,800 at cost. After the war Michelin's technological developments continued apace. In 1917 it had introduced the Roulement Universel, or all-purpose, tire with molded treads. Two years later the woven canvas infrastructure of previous tires was replaced by parallel cord plies. During the interwar period, advances in low-pressure tires dramatically extended tire life expectancy. The first hackney carriage tire had been capable of about 129 kilometers, with pressure of 4.3 kilograms per square centimeter. Thirty years later, in 1923, there was a car tire with pressure of 2.5 kilograms per square centimeter, able to cover 15,000 kilometers. The 1932 figures were 1.5 kilograms and 24,195 kilometers or more. Improvements to durability and road holding continued throughout the 1930s.

By 1930 Michelin was the 17th largest tire vendor in the world. Throughout the 1920s and 1930s it continued to expand overseas, with tire plants at Karlsruhe, Germany, and in Belgium, Spain, and Holland. The opening of a wire factory in

Trento, Italy, illustrated that Michelin was aware of the advantages of controlling the manufacture of components of the tire making process, as well as that process itself.

To all parts of the developed world, the interwar years brought a surge in the amount of motorized traffic. Michelin eased the motorist's lot not only by its reliable tires but also through its guides and maps. As early as 1910 the company had started to publish road maps, the first maps of France especially designed for motorists. Now Michelin extended coverage to more European countries, and to Africa and the United States. It published a series of detailed regional guides, the forerunners of today's Guides Verts. Michelin's Information Bureau continued to offer free advice and itineraries, and Michelin campaigned for road numbering and signposting.

The technical advances of the 1930s included the Pilote, a car tire giving superior road holding by increasing the ratio of width to depth. In 1937 the Metallic, an innovative design reinforcing rubber with steel cords to support heavier truckloads, appeared. U.S. competitors were experimenting with synthetic rubber. Michelin, too, was researching this technology in the late 1930s, although it was not until after the war that the company began to manufacture butyl for making inner tubes.

In 1935 Michelin, initially in the person of Edouard's son Pierre, went to the rescue of automobile manufacturer Citroën, then bankrupt. For almost 40 years, until Peugeot took it over in 1974, Michelin effectively ran Citroën and together the two companies made up the largest industrial group in France. Assisted by other family members, André and Edouard Michelin remained at Michelin's helm until they died, André in 1931 and Edouard in 1940. On Edouard's death his son-in-law Robert Puiseux took charge. Puiseux led the company through the war and on to a fertile period of expansion and innovation. The family was closely involved with the resistance movement during World War II, and several Michelins were interned in concentration camps. André's son Marcel died in Buchenwald, and Marcel's son Jean-Pierre was shot in action in Corsica. Despite these tragedies, Michelin kept going, although its German, Italian, and Czech plants were confiscated, and the factory at Cataroux, France, was crippled by Allied bombardments in 1944. Michelin had a long established policy of admitting only employees to its factories. Remarkably, although its French factories were obliged to produce tires for the Nazis, it managed to keep even the Germans off the premises. Inside, the patriotic Michelin workers were ''customizing'' their products for the occupying forces. Encountering the subzero temperatures of the Russian front, Michelin tires mysteriously disintegrated—but only the ones that were fitted to German vehicles.

Michelin maps were an invaluable weapon in the Allied armory. Michelin provided official maps for the French army at the outbreak of war, and more than two million were distributed to the liberating forces in 1944. The U.S. War Department reprinted the Guide Rouge for use during the Normandy landings. After the war Michelin, unlike some French companies, was free of any suggestion of Nazi collaboration. It swiftly regained its Italian and German property and reconstructed its bombed-out Cataroux plant. It declared a policy of expansion in both the industrialized and the developing world, which would be energetically pursued in the following decades. In France, many new factories would open, making not only tires but also wire, wheels, and tooling. In Italy, Germany, the United Kingdom, and other parts of Europe, existing plants would be modernized and new ones added.

Revolutionizing Driving in the 1940s

In 1946 came what is arguably Michelin's most important single contribution to tire technology, the radial tire. Instead of a crisscross or cross-ply casing of fabric or steel cords, the radial tire casing was a single ply of cords placed across the tire, perpendicular to the direction of travel. This technology vastly improved road holding, flexibility, and durability. The radial tire, developed in secret during the German occupation, was commercially launched in 1949 as the X-tire, and Michelin had to expand its capacity rapidly to keep pace with the public demand for these tires. By 1969, 30 million X-tires per year were racing off the production lines. Michelin built on its early lead by quickly making radial tires available for more and more vehicle types. During the 1950s X-tires for trucks and earthmovers were launched. In common with other manufacturers, Michelin also began to make tubeless tires. It had patented such a tire in 1930, but had encountered some practical problems. During the middle to late 1950s, however, tubeless tires caught on, and by the early 1960s, there were tubeless X-tires.

Meanwhile, there were changes at the top of the company. In 1955 François Michelin, the 29-year-old grandson of Edouard the cofounder, became gérant, or joint managing partner, alongside head partner Robert Puiseux. On Puiseux's retirement in 1960, François became head partner, and over the next 30 years, led Michelin to the number-one position in the world tire market. Unlike many of its European competitors, which set up agreements with U.S. manufacturers, Michelin had continued to undertake the vast majority of its research and development activities itself. François maintained this policy, and 1963 marked the opening of a new Michelin test center at Ladoux, not far from Clermont-Ferrand.

The company had been expanding steadily in Europe. Now it was time to look further afield. During the 1960s factories opened in Nigeria, Algeria, and Vietnam. Michelin also had an eye on the United States, where it had started a sales office in 1948, targeting owners of foreign cars. In 1965, however, Michelin entered into a contract with Sears, Roebuck to supply replacement tires for U.S. cars. So successful did this venture prove that by 1970 Michelin was selling 2.5 million tires per year through its own U.S. outlets. Overcapacity was felt in the European tire market during the 1970s, but Michelin pursued its expansion elsewhere. In the United States it constructed its first manufacturing plants in South Carolina and also built plants in Canada and Brazil. Much research continued to go toward perfecting radial technology. During the mid-1960s the XAS tire made the radial concept available to the fastest cars. Radial tires would achieve the ultimate cachet in 1979 when they helped Jody Scheckter drive his Ferrari to victory as the Formula 1 World Champion. In the 1970s, Michelin targeted several new product lines at the long distance road haulage market. With the introduction of radial tires for aircraft in 1981, and motorcycles in 1987, Michelin could offer radial technology for virtually all types of vehicles. The basic technology continued to improve, with new ranges being launched almost every year. The M series, which appeared in 1985, offered a completely new range of state-of-the-art radial tires. Among these, the MXL became Europe's best selling tire by 1990, when its replacement, the MXT, was introduced.

Market Leader for the New Century

In 1960 Michelin had been the 10th largest tire manufacturer in the world, but by 1980, it was second only to Goodyear. In 1990 came a major acquisition, that of the U.S. tire company Uniroyal Goodrich, which made Michelin indisputably the market leader. Unfortunately, the Uniroyal deal was concluded just as a major recession hit the automobile and tire market. Faced with a FFr 5.27 billion loss for 1990, Michelin in April 1991 had to cut costs by laying off 15 percent of its workforce. This, not the first but the largest round of job cuts during that period, was an especially painful step for an employer that had encouraged its workers to see themselves as participants in the enterprise. François Michelin told the press that the main problem was not the acquisition of Uniroyal, but pressure from the automobile industry which in the past decade had forced tire prices down by 50% in real terms. In 1991, despite the pessimism expressed by some analysts about Michelin's prospects, the company itself was looking forward to reaping the benefits of the Uniroyal acquisition when the economy emerged from recession. The strengths of the two companies in the U.S. replacement tire market were complementary, and North America represented more than one-third of the total tire market. Michelin also planned to build on its footholds in Japan, Thailand, and South America.

Michelin continued to innovate and expand during the 1990s. The company targeted the booming Asian markets for expansion—going head-to-head with Japan's Bridgestone and other major tire makers. After the opening of its first joint-venture factory with Thailand's Siam Cement in 1988, Michelin's presence in that country increased, adding new factories in 1992 and 1993. The two companies opened a fourth factory in the Philippines in 1995. A year later, Michelin entered China with a joint venture with Shen Yang Tire Factory, opening a new plant in Shen Yang.

In Europe, Michelin established its Euromaster service center chain, acquiring a number of existing chains across Europe and converting them to the Euromaster format, launched in 1991. Michelin moved deeper into Eastern Europe, buying the largest tire manufacturer in Poland, Stomil-Olsztyn, in 1995, followed by leading Hungarian rubber producer Taurus, in 1996. One year later, Michelin enhanced its wheel production with the acquisition of Germany's Kronprinz GA. In the United States, meanwhile, Michelin recovered from the recession and, with its Michelin, Goodrich, and Uniroyal brands, captured one of the leading shares of the U.S. tire market.

On the consumer front, Michelin introduced the "green tire" in 1992, capable of reducing pollution and increasing fuel efficiency. Later in the decade, the company unveiled its revolutionary new PAX tire and wheel "run-flat" system, capable of rolling for as much as 80 miles after a puncture. In 1999, the company debuted a tubeless tire for mountain bicycles. The company boosted not only its automobile tires, but also its

heavy vehicle tires—in 1998, Michelin opened a new facility in South Carolina to produce "Earthmover" tires, such as the 3.92 meter tall low-pressure tire capable of supporting loads up to 600 tons. The following year, Michelin boosted its U.S. presence and extended its service operations with the acquisition of Tire Centers LLC, the leading independent tire distributor in the United States. In 2001, Michelin's tire expertise triumphed again when the company unveiled a new tire design for the Concorde jet, which had been grounded after an accident two years earlier.

François Michelin formally appointed youngest son Edouard to take over leadership of the company, in 1999; the elder Michelin, who had by then reached the retirement age of 72, nonetheless extended his own contract to remain with the company for another three years. The following year, the massive recall of more than 4.5 million Firestone tires in the United States opened a new opportunity for the French company. Michelin ramped up production to help fill the gap left by its U.S. rival, and along the way managed to win contracts to outfit a number of new car designs. Yet the boost proved short-lived—by the middle of 2001, the dip in the U.S. economy, responsible for a dramatic dropoff in new car purchases, sent Michelin's U.S. revenues plunging.

In its first century, Michelin had grown with, and often ahead of, the tire industry, by a process of unrelenting innovation and improvement. Meanwhile its Bibendum figurehead ranked as one of the most important and most widely recognized logos of the 20th century. At the beginning of the 21st century, Michelin tires were to be found on motor vehicles of all kinds, on the trains of the Paris and other metro systems, and on aircraft. Worldwide, one in five tires was made by Michelin. The firm knew better than any the tough and fast changing nature of its chosen market. Having long enjoyed one of the top spots, Michelin, second only to Goodyear, showed every intention of staying there.

Principal Subsidiaries

Compagnie Financière Michelin (Switzerland; 93%); Manufacture Française des Pneumatiques Michelin (96%); Michelin Aircraft Tire Corporation (U.S.A.; 93%); Michelin Americas Research & Development Corporation (U.S.A.; 93%); Michelin Asia (Hong Kong) Ltd. (93%); Michelin Ceská republika sro (Czech Republic; 93%); Michelin Corporation (U.S.A.; 93%); Michelin Investment Holding Company Limited (Bermuda; 93%); Michelin Korea Co., Ltd. (93%); Michelin North America, Inc. (U.S.A.; 93%); Norsk Michelin Gummi A/S (Norway; 93%); Société d'Exportation Michelin; Société Michelin de Transformation des Gravanches (96%); Spika SA; Taurus Rubber Company Ltd (Hungary; 93%); Transityre France SA (93%).

Principal Competitors

Bandag Inc.; Bridgestone Corporation; Continental AG; Cooper Tire & Rubber Company; The Goodyear Tire & Rubber Company; Sime Darby Berhad; Sumitomo Group; Toyo Tire & Rubber Co., Ltd; Vredestein; The Yokohama Rubber Co., Ltd.

Further Reading

Les Brevets Michelin ont Cent Ans, Clermont-Ferrand: Compagnie Générale des Établissements Michelin, 1991.
Dawkins, Will, "Michelin's Man Aims to Ride out the Bumps," *Financial Times,* April 15, 1991.
Il y a 100 Ans . . ., Clermont-Ferrand: Compagnie Générale des Établissements Michelin, 1991.
Jemain, Alain, *Michelin, Un Siécle de Secrets,* Paris: Calmann-Lévy, 1982.

The Michelin Magic, Blue Ridge Summit, Penn.: Tab Books Inc., Modern Automotive Series, 1982.
Les Services de Tourisme Michelin, Une Histoire Passionnante, Clermont-Ferrand: Compagnie Générale des Établissements Michelin, [n.d.].

—Alison Classe
—update: M.L. Cohen

ConAgra Foods

ConAgra Foods, Inc.

One ConAgra Drive
Omaha, Nebraska 68102-5001
U.S.A.
Telephone: (402) 595-4000
Fax: (402) 595-4665
Web site: http://www.conagrafoods.com

Public Company
Incorporated: 1919 as Nebraska Consolidated Mills
    Company
Employees: 80,000
Sales: $27.19 billion (2001)
Stock Exchanges: New York
Ticker Symbol: CAG
NAIC: 112112 Cattle Feedlots; 112511 Finfish Farming
    and Fish Hatcheries; 311111 Dog and Cat Food Manu-
    facturing; 311211 Flour Milling; 311223 Other Oilseed
    Processing; 311340 Nonchocolate Confectionery Manu-
    facturing; 311411 Frozen Fruit, Juice, and Vegetable
    Processing; 311412 Frozen Specialty Food Manufactur-
    ing; 311421 Fruit and Vegetable Canning; 311423
    Dried and Dehydrated Food Manufacturing; 311513
    Cheese Manufacturing; 311514 Dry, Condensed, and
    Evaporated Dairy Product Manufacturing; 311611 Ani-
    mal (Except Poultry) Slaughtering; 311612 Meat Pro-
    cessed from Carcasses; 311615 Poultry Processing;
    311711 Seafood Canning; 311712 Fresh and Frozen
    Seafood Processing; 311830 Tortilla Manufacturing;
    311911 Roasted Nuts and Peanut Butter Manufactur-
    ing; 311941 Mayonnaise, Dressing, and Other Prepared
    Sauce Manufacturing; 311999 All Other Miscellaneous
    Food Manufacturing; 422510 Grain and Field Bean
    Wholesalers

In 1919 Alva Kinney brought four grain milling companies in
south central Nebraska together to take advantage of increasing
grain production in the Midwest, and the Nebraska Consolidated
Mills Company was born. More than 80 years and two name

changes later, ConAgra Foods, Inc. stands as one of the world's
largest food companies, holding the number one position in North
America in foodservice manufacturing and the number two spot
(behind Kraft Foods, Inc.) in retail food sales. The company's
numerous consumer brands include Hunt's tomato products,
Healthy Choice, Banquet, Armour, Bumble Bee, Louis Kemp, La
Choy, Wesson, Country Pride, Blue Bonnet, Parkay, Marie Callender's, Cook's, Swift Premium, Butterball, Slim Jim, Chef
Boyardee, Orville Redenbacher's, PAM Cooking Spray, Van
Camp's, Peter Pan, and Swiss Miss. Approximately 80 percent of
ConAgra's revenues are derived from its retail and foodservice
businesses. Responsible for the remaining 20 percent of sales are
the company's agricultural products businesses, which are involved in the manufacturing and distribution of food ingredients,
seeds, crop protection chemicals, and fertilizers, as well as in
worldwide trading of bulk agricultural commodities.

Early History: From Milling to Animal Feed to Poultry Processing

Officially formed on September 29, 1919, the Nebraska Consolidated Mills Company (NCM) was headquartered in Grand
Island, Nebraska. At first Kinney concentrated on milling the
bumper postwar wheat crops at his four Nebraska locations. But
soon, to accommodate his growing business, Kinney added a mill
in Omaha, in 1922, and moved the headquarters of the company
there. He continued to run a profitable and relatively quiet company solely in Nebraska until he retired as president in 1936.

Kinney was succeeded by R.S. Dickinson. Initially, Dickinson followed his predecessor's simple but successful policy
of milling grain in Nebraska. World War II and the postwar
boom kept the demand for grain high and the milling business
profitable.

During the early 1940s Dickinson began to use the company's profits to expand. Other successful milling operations,
such as General Mills and Pillsbury, were expanding both the
number of plants and the number of products they offered, and
NCM followed the same trend. In 1942 Dickinson opened a
flour mill and animal feed mill in Alabama. He also promoted
research into new types of prepared foods that used flour, which

Company Perspectives:

ConAgra is one of the world's largest and most successful food companies. As North America's largest foodservice manufacturer and second largest retail food supplier, ConAgra is a leader in multiple segments of the food business and focuses on adding value for customers in retail food, foodservice, and agricultural product channels.

led to the development of Duncan Hines cake mixes, introduced in the early 1950s.

The Alabama expansion was profitable, but Dickinson found that it was more difficult to gain a foothold in the prepared-foods market. Cake mixes, though only a small proportion of the total flour market, accounted for as much as $140 million a year in retail sales by 1947. But the market was dominated by General Mills's Betty Crocker brand and by Pillsbury, each with one-third of the market share, while Duncan Hines controlled only 10 to 12 percent. Unable to increase its share of the highly competitive cake mix market, NCM eventually decided to get out of prepared foods and use the money it raised to expand in basic commodities: grains and feeds. So, in 1956 the company sold its Duncan Hines brand to Procter & Gamble.

The new president of Nebraska Consolidated Mills, J. Allan Mactier, used the proceeds from the sale to expand aggressively. In 1957, NCM built the first major grain processing plant in Puerto Rico through its subsidiary Caribe Company. The $3 million plant processed flour, corn meal, and animal feeds at Catano in San Juan harbor. Production at the plant did not compete with the parent company's already existing concerns; none of the flours and feeds produced there were exported to the mainland.

Caribe's foothold on the island led to further Puerto Rican expansion in new areas. A second subsidiary, Molinos de Puerto Rico, took over Caribe's animal feed business on the island while also developing Puerto Rico's virtually nonexistent beef industry as a market for its products. In Molinos' first five years of operation, consumption of animal feeds in Puerto Rico increased from 136,516 tons, of which 100,314 were imported, to 249,267 tons, of which only 46,723 were imported. The company also profited from an increased demand for meat and milk on the island.

Elsewhere, however, flour millers faced shrinking profits as demand leveled off in both domestic and foreign markets. European grain production had recovered from the disruption of World War II, and prosperity at home in the 1950s and 1960s allowed consumers to buy more expensive food items, leading to lower flour consumption.

Large millers turned to diversification to offset declining profitability. Industry leaders General Mills and Pillsbury developed their consumer foods lines and introduced new types of convenience foods, while the third of the "Big Three" in flour milling, International Milling Company, Inc., diversified primarily into animal feeds. Nebraska Consolidated Mills, perhaps unwilling to compete again in packaged foods after its experi-

ence with Duncan Hines, also developed the animal feed end of its business. Throughout the 1960s and into the 1970s, the company established mills and distribution centers for feed and flour in the Southeast and Northwest.

NCM also turned to another basic commodity: chicken. It developed poultry growing and processing complexes in Georgia, Louisiana, and Alabama during the 1960s. In 1965 the company also began to expand into the European market by going into partnership with Bioter-Biona, S.A., a Spanish producer of animal feed and animal health products and breeder of pigs, chickens, and trout.

Emerging As ConAgra in the 1970s

By 1971 Nebraska Consolidated Mills had outgrown its early base in Nebraska as well as its name. It chose a new name to reflect its new concerns: ConAgra, meaning "in partnership with the land." ConAgra, Inc. was listed on the New York Stock Exchange in 1973.

The new name, however, did not necessarily mean continuing success. The early 1970s, in fact, brought the company to a low point. Many of its acquisitions during the expansion of the 1960s and early 1970s were only marginally profitable at best. In 1974 the company posted net losses and suspended dividends. Heavy losses in commodity speculations brought ConAgra to the brink of bankruptcy in 1975.

ConAgra's first high-profile leader, former Pillsbury executive Charles "Mike" Harper, was named president and CEO in 1976 with a mandate to turn the ailing company around. Essential to Harper's turnaround plan were strict financial goals combined with a series of acquisitions that served to broaden ConAgra's sales base. To reduce debt, Harper first sold nonessential operations. He then began to buy agricultural businesses at the low end of their profit cycles and turn them around. Harper originally intended to stick with ConAgra's emphasis on basic commodities rather than compete with the packaged-food giants. When he purchased Banquet Foods Company in 1980, he said that the acquisition was a way to increase ConAgra's chicken capacity. ConAgra's chicken production did increase by a third, bringing the company from eighth to fifth place among chicken producers. ConAgra expanded into fish as well as poultry in the 1970s with investments in catfish aquaculture.

Creating a Diversified Food Company in the 1980s

Another of Harper's acquisitions put ConAgra back in the forefront of the flour market. In 1982 ConAgra bought the Peavey Company, a Minneapolis-based flour miller and grain trader, giving it 16.3 percent of the nation's wheat-milling capacity and a system of grain exporting terminals. Political barriers to U.S. grain exports had depressed Peavey's profits, and the acquisition was not the early success story that Banquet was for ConAgra. By 1986, however, Peavey was posting a $16.4 million profit on sales of $1.2 billion, a promising upward trend.

Harper also kept to a commodity-oriented approach by diversifying into agricultural chemicals. ConAgra expanded into fertilizers, and in 1978 acquired United Agri Products, a distrib-

Key Dates:

1919: Four grain milling companies are merged as Nebraska Consolidated Mills Company.

1950s: Company embarks on short-lived foray into prepared foods via Duncan Hines cake mixes.

1960s: Company enters the poultry processing market.

1965: Expansion into Europe begins through joint venture with Bioter-Biona, S.A. of Spain.

1971: Company changes its name to ConAgra, Inc.

1976: Charles "Mike" Harper is named president and CEO.

1978: United Agri Products, agricultural chemicals distributor, is acquired.

1980: Banquet Foods Company is acquired.

1981: Company enters prepared seafood market through purchases of Singleton Seafood and Sea-Alaska Products.

1982: Country Poultry, Inc. is formed and soon becomes the top poultry producer in the country.

1983: Red meats processor Armour Food Company is acquired.

1987: Three more red meat acquisitions are completed: E.A. Miller, Inc.; Monfort of Colorado, Inc.; and Swift Independent Packing Company.

1990: ConAgra acquires Beatrice Company.

1992: Phil Fletcher becomes president and CEO.

1996: Major restructuring cuts 6,300 jobs and shutters more than 50 plants; Bruce C. Rohde is named president, having been the company's chief outside counsel since 1984 (he later assumes the titles of CEO and chairman).

1998: Margarine and egg substitute business of Nabisco, Inc. is acquired.

1999: Company announces major restructuring that involves 8,450 job cuts, the closure of 137 facilities, and the divestment of 18 noncore businesses.

2000: International Home Foods, Inc. is acquired; company changes its name to ConAgra Foods, Inc.

utor of herbicides and pesticides. Higher grain prices, Harper reasoned, would mean increased demand for such chemicals.

But, in an attempt to counter the cyclical profit pattern of basic agricultural commodities, Harper also entered areas that did not mesh well with the company's traditional orientation: pet accessories, a Mexican restaurant chain, and a fabrics and crafts chain, among others.

In a dramatic change of direction during the 1980s, ConAgra decided on prepared foods as a better way to balance cyclical profits in the food industry. The company's stringent financial goals were being met: return on equity averaged 20 percent, annual growth in trend-line earnings were over 14 percent, and long-term debt was held to below 35 percent of total capitalization. With the company on firmer financial ground, ConAgra began a series of acquisitions that would ultimately make it the nation's second largest food company.

ConAgra moved into the prepared seafood market in 1981 with the purchase of Singleton Seafood, the largest shrimp

processor in the country, and Sea-Alaska Products. In 1987 ConAgra bought Trident Seafoods and O'Donnell-Usen Fisheries, the producer of Taste O' Sea frozen seafood products, thus positioning the company to compete against the leading frozen seafood brands, Mrs. Paul's Kitchens, Gorton's, and Van de Kamp's.

In 1982, during a low in the poultry cycle, ConAgra moved to take first place in the chicken industry by forming Country Poultry, Inc. By the next year, Country Poultry was delivering more than a billion pounds of brand-name broilers to markets, making it the biggest poultry producer in the country. In 1986, the company formed ConAgra Turkey Company and in 1987 it acquired another poultry company, Longmont Foods, further strengthening its position in the field. But ConAgra's poultry concerns no longer focused on the basic bird Harper purchased Banquet for: Country Poultry introduced a number of higher-profit convenience poultry products, such as marinated chicken breasts, chicken hot dogs, and processed chicken for fast-food restaurants.

ConAgra moved into another area of processed foods in 1983 when the company purchased Armour Food Company, a processor of red meats such as hot dogs, sausage, bacon, ham, and luncheon meats. The acquisition also included Armour's line of frozen gourmet entrees, Dinner Classics, which complemented Banquet's line of frozen foods. As with many of his other acquisitions, Harper bought Armour in a down cycle for book value ($182 million). By waiting to complete the deal until Armour closed several plants, Harper painlessly eliminated about 40 percent of Armour's major union's members. Some Armour plants still have unions, but without a master contract labor costs were slashed. Harper then reorganized the company, emphasizing new marketing strategies (reintroducing the familiar Armour jingle to take advantage of consumer recognition) and refocusing product lines. The Dinner Classics line was hurt by price competition and the introduction of new brands of premium frozen dinners. Armour as a whole was still unprofitable through the early 1990s, but profits for the Classics line increased.

In 1986, Harper increased ConAgra's presence in frozen foods by purchasing the Morton, Patio, and Chun King brands. The following year, the company expanded in red meats with its purchase of E.A. Miller, Inc., a western producer of beef products, and Monfort of Colorado, Inc. Almost a decade earlier, ConAgra had tried to purchase MBPXL Corp., the number two beef packer in the country, only to be blocked at the last minute by the privately owned Cargill Inc. The Monfort deal, for $365 million in stock, made ConAgra the third largest U.S. beef producer. Health-conscious consumers began eating less beef in the late 1980s and ConAgra responded by working to create new, leaner beef products as it developed new poultry products. Another 1987 acquisition, 50 percent of Swift Independent Packing Company, a processor of beef, pork, and lamb, made ConAgra a leading meat processor as well. Harper rounded out his changes at ConAgra by developing the company's international trading position and by forming its own financial services subsidiary.

By the late 1980s, ConAgra had grown into a well diversified food company, better able to absorb the ups and downs of the industry. The year 1987 was a banner one for ConAgra's poultry division, which posted $130 million in operating profits due to a tremendous (and ultimately unsustainable) upswing in the poultry market. The poultry division's operating profits plummeted the following year to $20 million, but by then ConAgra's other divisions were strong enough to make up the difference. The company posted net earnings of $155 million, about 5 percent higher than the previous year. The late 1980s also saw ConAgra lose a prolonged takeover battle to poultry rival Tyson Foods, Inc. over Holly Farms Corporation; had ConAgra acquired Holly Farms it would have gained the top position in the U.S. chicken market.

Restructurings and More Acquisitions in the 1990s and Beyond

In 1988 Harper boasted that ConAgra was probably the only food products company to "participate across the entire food chain." In the grocery store, however, the majority of its packaged food products were found in the frozen foods section, where it held the top market share in the country. In 1990, sensing that even greater diversification was necessary to ensure steady earnings growth, Harper led the purchase of Beatrice Company, which produced top brands such as Hunt's Tomato Paste and Butterball Turkey and had annual sales of more than $4 billion. The Beatrice purchase gave ConAgra a broader portfolio of products and provided a strong sales and distribution system in the "dry goods" segment. ConAgra paid $2.35 billion for the company and assumed a debt of about $1 billion in the process.

In the early 1990s ConAgra expanded at a rate of about 35 acquisitions and joint ventures a year. The company's international presence grew as it formed joint ventures in Japan, Thailand, France, Canada, Chile, and Australia. Key acquisitions included the malt and wool businesses of Elders IXL Ltd. and 50 percent of its beef business, known as Australia Meat Holdings. On the home front, ConAgra made its first foray into the kosher foods business with the purchase of National Foods and also entered the private label consumer products market with the acquisition of Arrow Industries, a clothing manufacturer.

Around this same time the company enlarged its frozen foods market share further with the introduction of Healthy Choice, a low fat, low sodium, and low cholesterol line of frozen dinner entrees. By 1993, the Healthy Choice line numbered 300-plus products. By 1993 Healthy Choice posted sales of over $1 billion and was lauded as the "most successful new food brand introduction in two decades" by *Advertising Age*.

The company also reorganized some of its divisions in the early 1990s, creating ConAgra Grocery Products Companies to unite its Hunt-Wesson companies with its frozen food businesses and ConAgra Meat Products Companies to bring together its branded package meat business and its fresh red meat businesses. Sales for 1992 surpassed $20 billion for the first time, as the company posted its 12th consecutive year of record earnings.

In 1993 Harper resigned his post at ConAgra to become chairman and CEO at RJR Nabisco Holdings Corp. Phil Fletcher, ConAgra's longtime president and chief operating officer, assumed Harper's post. In his first two years at the helm, Fletcher cut operating costs by enforcing stricter cost-control measures and fostering greater communication and cooperation between the company's six dozen individual units. Continuing Harper's acquisition strategy, ConAgra began expanding globally, with new ventures in China, Australia, Denmark, and Mexico. Earnings for 1994 reached $437 million on sales of $23.5 billion. That year also marked ConAgra's 75th anniversary, and, as part of the company's celebration, $200,000 was donated to a museum in Grand Island, Nebraska, for the erection of a replica of the original Glade Mill, one of the four mills merged to create the company in 1919.

During the mid-1990s, ConAgra was involved in two separate lawsuits. In 1995 the company agreed to pay $13.6 million to settle a class-action suit brought by fish distributors and processors who claimed that ConAgra's Country Skillet Catfish Co. and six other catfish wholesalers conspired to fix prices for nearly a decade. While some of the smaller defendants had admitted guilt in the case, neither ConAgra nor the other major defendants—Hormel Foods Corporation and Delta Pride Catfish Inc.—admitted responsibility. Two years later ConAgra agreed to plea guilty to a felony charge of wire fraud as well as misdemeanor charges of misgrading crops and adding water to grain in a federal case involving ConAgra's Peavey grain elevators in Indiana. ConAgra employees at the elevators had been accused of cheating farmers who sold crops to ConAgra and of spraying water on grain before selling it in order to increase its value (since it was sold by weight). Four former ConAgra employees pled guilty to criminal charges, and ConAgra agreed to pay $8.3 million in criminal penalties. ConAgra said that top executives at the company were unaware of the alleged activities of the elevator employees.

Meanwhile, moving to improve profitability, ConAgra launched a major restructuring in mid-1996. Approximately 6,300 employees were cut from the workforce, representing a 7 percent reduction, and more than 50 production facilities were closed or sold. A pretax restructuring charge of $507.8 million was taken, leading to a reduced net income figure for fiscal 1996 of $211.8 million (on sales of $24.32 billion). The company hoped to eventually realize more than $100 million in annual cost savings from the job cuts and plant closings.

In August 1996 Bruce C. Rohde was named president and vice-chairman of ConAgra, having been the company's chief outside counsel since 1984. In September 1997 Rohde was named CEO, and he then added the chairmanship the following year. Acquisitions continued during this period of management transition, with Gilroy Foods, a California-based processor of dehydrated garlic and onion products and other spices, purchased in 1996, and GoodMark Foods Inc., maker of the Slim Jim brand of meat snacks, bought in 1998. Also acquired in 1998, for $400 million, was the margarine and egg substitute business of Nabisco, Inc. Among the brands gained through this deal were Parkay, Blue Bonnet, Fleischmann's, and Chiffon margarines and the Egg Beaters egg substitute product.

ConAgra announced another major restructuring in May 1999, which resulted in 8,450 employees losing their jobs. By the end of the 2000 fiscal year, 31 production plants and 106 nonproduction facilities had been shut down and 18 noncore businesses had been divested. The restructuring resulted in pretax charges of $440.8 million and $621.4 million in 1999 and 2000, respectively. This latest restructuring was part of a larger program called "Operation Overdrive," which aimed at generating $600 million in annual cost savings. In addition to the cost cutting, Operation Overdrive also involved a reorganization of the company by customer channel—an abandonment of the decentralized structure installed by Harper in 1980s in favor of a more centralized approach—and an increase in marketing expenditures, including a new emphasis on cross-selling among the various company brands.

Acquisitions continued in 2000. In January 2000 ConAgra acquired Seaboard Farms, the poultry division of Seaboard Corporation, for about $360 million. Seaboard Farms, which had annual sales of $480 million, was a producer and marketer of value-added poultry products primarily to foodservice customers. ConAgra in July 2000 acquired Lightlife Foods, Inc., a leading producer of premium vegetarian and soy products. Lightlife's product line was a good fit with ConAgra's blockbuster Healthy Choice brand. Then one month later, ConAgra completed one of its largest acquisitions in history, a $2 billion deal for International Home Foods, Inc. ConAgra gained a number of well-known consumer brands, including Chef Boyardee pasta products, PAM cooking spray, Gulden's mustard, Bumble Bee seafood, and Jiffy Pop popcorn. International Home Foods had posted 1999 revenues of $2.1 billion. With the company continuing its transformation from its agricultural origins to its position as primarily a producer of packaged foods, the decision was made to add "Foods" to the company name, resulting in the introduction of the ConAgra Foods, Inc. name in September 2000. Plans were also laid to elevate the company's profile with the public as most consumers recognized the company's brands but not the company itself. The new name was slated to be placed on more than 100 brand name products produced by ConAgra.

In its 75-plus-year history, ConAgra had evolved from a low-profile flour miller into an international food company with sales of more than $27 billion. It gained its stature through a remarkable mix of conservative fiscal management and aggressive expansion through acquisitions and joint ventures. Building on the work of his predecessors, Rohde was transforming ConAgra into a leaner, more efficient company, and was likely to seek additional acquisitions in a food industry that was rapidly consolidating at the turn of the millennium.

Principal Operating Units

ConAgra Foodservice Company; ConAgra Grocery Products Companies; ConAgra Frozen Prepared Foods; ConAgra Dairy Case Companies; ConAgra Refrigerated Prepared Foods; ConAgra Meat Companies; ConAgra Poultry Company; ConAgra Food Ingredients; United Agri Products Companies; ConAgra Trade Group.

Principal Competitors

Archer Daniels Midland Company; Campbell Soup Company; Cargill, Incorporated; Cenex Harvest States Cooperative; Groupe Danone; Dean Foods Company; Del Monte Foods Company; Farmland Industries, Inc.; Frito-Lay, Inc.; General Mills, Inc.; Gold Kist Inc.; H.J. Heinz Company; Hormel Foods Corporation; IBP, Inc.; Kraft Foods, Inc.; Land O'Lakes, Inc.; McCain Foods Limited; Nestlé S.A.; Perdue Farms Incorporated; The Pillsbury Company; The Quaker Oats Company; Sara Lee Corporation; Schwan's Sales Enterprises, Inc.; Smithfield Foods, Inc.; Suiza Foods Corporation; Tyson Foods, Inc.; Unilever.

Further Reading

Andreas, Carol, *Meatpackers and Beef Barons*, Niwot, Colo.: University Press of Colorado, 1994, 225 p.

Bailey, Jeff, and Richard Gibson, "ConAgra to Cut 6,500 Jobs, Close Plants," *Wall Street Journal,* May 15, 1996, p. A3.

Blyskal, Jeff, " 'The Best Damn Food Company in the United States,' " *Forbes,* October 24, 1983, pp. 48 + .

Brandon, Copple, "Synergy in Ketchup?," *Forbes,* February 7, 2000, pp. 68–69.

Burns, Greg, "How a New Boss Got ConAgra Cooking Again," *Business Week,* July 25, 1994, p. 72.

Byrne, Harlan S., "A Growing Presence: From Farm to Table, ConAgra Is on the Move," *Barron's,* June 20, 1988, pp. 13 + .

Cahill, William R., "Cultivating Profits: ConAgra Is on a Seven-Year Winning Streak," *Barron's,* March 2, 1987, pp. 49 + .

Campanella, Frank W., "Fish and Fowl and Flour, Too, Prove Profitable Mix for ConAgra Inc.," *Barron's,* May 4, 1981, pp. 52 + .

"ConAgra: Buying a Frozen-Food Maker to Get at Its Chickens," *Business Week,* December 1, 1980, p. 124.

"ConAgra's Quantum Leap in Buying Beatrice Co.," *Mergers and Acquisitions,* September/October 1990, p. 54.

"ConAgra: The Payoff Could Be Huge from Its Risky Bet on Armour," *Business Week,* December 19, 1983, pp. 85 + .

Epstein, Victor, "A Game of Chicken: ConAgra Beating the Drumstick for Poultry Sales," *Omaha World-Herald,* September 3, 2000, p. 1M.

Gibson, Richard, "ConAgra, Hormel Pay a Pretty Penny in an Ugly Catfish Price-Fixing Case," *Wall Street Journal,* December 29, 1995, p. A3.

Henkoff, Ronald, "A Giant That Keeps Innovating," *Fortune,* December 16, 1991, p. 101.

Ivey, Mike, "How ConAgra Grew Big—and Now, Beefy," *Business Week,* May 18, 1987, pp. 87–88.

Kilman, Scott, "ConAgra, International Home Foods Join Food Sector's Consolidation Bandwagon," *Wall Street Journal,* June 26, 2000, p. B14.

——, "ConAgra to Pay $8.3 Million to Settle Fraud Charges in Grain-Handling Case," *Wall Street Journal,* March 20, 1997, p. B12.

Miller, James P., "ConAgra to Cut 7,000 from Work Force," *Wall Street Journal,* May 13, 1999, p. A3.

Neiman, Janet, "ConAgra Fertilizes Plans for Branded Foods Growth," *Advertising Age,* September 6, 1982, pp. 4 + .

Rasmussen, Jim, "Rohde Ready to Lead ConAgra," *Omaha World-Herald,* July 12, 1997.

Sachar, Laura, "An Eye on Your Stomach," *Financial World,* April 21, 1987, pp. 26 + .

Saporito, Bill, and Cynthia Hutton, "ConAgra's Profits Aren't Chicken Feed," *Fortune,* October 27, 1986, pp. 70 + .

Taylor, John, "ConAgra Adds Big Brands to Larder," *Omaha World-Herald,* June 24, 2000.

——, "ConAgra Aims to Widen 'Sea of Green,' " *Omaha World-Herald,* December 8, 1996, p. 1M.

——, "Foreign Flavor: ConAgra Adapts Products for International Tastes," *Omaha World-Herald,* March 30, 1998.

—Maura Troester
—update: David E. Salamie

Croscill, Inc.

261 5th Avenue
New York, New York 10016
U.S.A.
Telephone: (212) 689-7222
Fax: (212) 481-8656
Web site: http://www.croscill.com

Private Company
Incorporated: 1946 as Croscill Curtain Company
Employees: 1,500
Sales: $300 million (2000 est.)
NAIC: 31321 Broadwoven Fabric Mills (pt); 313210
   Textile Products (Except Apparel) Made in
   Broadwoven Fabric Mills; 44229 Other Home
   Furnishings Stores

Family-owned and managed, Croscill, Inc. is the Fifth Avenue corporate parent for Croscill Home, known for its high quality home furnishing products. In addition, the company owns five textile mills in North Carolina, a small number of outlet stores, a distribution system, and a licensing operation. Its Royal Home Fashions unit sells a complete list of Croscill products in its specialty stores as well as through the Internet. Primarily a drapery and curtain designer and manufacturer until the mid-1980s, Croscill was in the vanguard of companies that challenged the supremacy of mills in such areas as bedding and bath products. In the process, it has evolved into one of the top ten textile producers in the United States.

For most of its history, Croscill sold to major department stores, in particular J.C. Penney, which still accounts for 10 percent of annual sales, but in recent years the home furnishings environment has changed dramatically, so that today Croscill sells a great deal of its merchandise through such retailers as Linens 'n Things and Bed, Bath & Beyond. Croscill is a pioneer in the total room concept, offering consumers a fully coordinated ensemble of products for the bedroom and bathroom, including non-textile products such as furniture, lamps, and hardware, much of which is provided by licensees. Despite never spending money on a national consumer advertising campaign, Croscill has established an enviable cachet among consumers, who may not be able to pronounce the name of the company but recognize and appreciate its distinctive style. The goal for Croscill is to expand its offering of coordinated home furnishing products one room at a time.

Post-World War II Era Roots

The history of Croscill is very much the story of the Kahn family, who in the years before World War II ran a small curtain manufacturing shop on Ellery Street in the Williamsburg section of Brooklyn, New York. The three children—George, Max, and Sophie—all went on to establish their own businesses: Croscill Curtain Company, Max Kahn Curtains, and Ellery Curtains. George Kahn, trained as a machine mechanic but also possessing strong organizational skills, started Croscill in 1946, deriving the name for his company from a product he called "Croscilla," which was a reference to the popular Priscilla curtain style. Known as a valance, Croscilla was a separate section of curtain that masked the curtain rod and mounting hardware. The company grew up along with the children of the Baby Boom, as multitudes of Americans moved to the suburbs and indulged in a passion to decorate their new homes. Croscill introduced other innovations, including mix and match kitchen curtains, the Blouson Valance, and an Antique Satin drapery. It also developed a recognizable Croscill look: embellished floral patterns, or what one of the company's longtime designers called "sweet cottage-type patterns." In the late 1960s, Croscill applied those patterns to decorative comforters, which allowed coordination with the bed skirt as well as Croscill window treatments. This approach was to evolve many years later into the total room approach.

In the 1970s Croscill was still very much a curtain company, now run by George Kahn's sons, Mike and Stanley. Window products accounted for 80 percent of annual revenues. A change in the retail environment in the early 1980s forced Croscill to change its approach. Department stores began to eliminate separate curtain and drapery (C&D) departments, opting instead for a general domestics department. Because most of its products had been carried in the old C&D departments, Croscill experienced a decline in sales. Clearly, the company had to find a way

Company Perspectives:

Our customers repeatedly tell us, "It's like getting a decorator's custom look." That is why at Croscill we say, "It's in the Details!"

to position its window products in the domestics department. It decided to apply its patterns to sheets, a product that was dominated by the major domestic mills. In 1985 Croscill signed a year-long agreement with mill J.P. Stevens to produce and market sheets that coordinated with the company's best-selling Chestnut Hill pattern. The sheets and Croscill's other products created a synergistic effect, the sale of one prompting the sale of the others. In effect, sheets became the wedge that helped Croscill gain a position in the new domestic department. After the J.P. Stevens agreement lapsed, Croscill contracted with Canadian mill Dominion Textile but by 1988 the company was introducing bedroom ensembles with sheets produced in its own North Carolina mills. Croscill was selling a lot of sheets, but more importantly it was selling a lot of ensembles.

Total Room Concept Developed in the Late 1980s

Selling ensembles led to Croscill adopting a total room concept. No longer did the company feel limited to just making curtains or bedding; anything in the room now became fair game. By licensing its patterns, Croscill was soon offering table linens, lamps, hat boxes, picture frames, padded hangers, wall coverings, cosmetics trays, and even potpourri. It also made an entry into the bathroom through coordinated shower curtains and towels. The ultimate purpose of the total room strategy was to increase the retailers' Average Transaction Value, or ATV. Instead of consumers buying a single item, they bought an entire look. Rather than spending $50 they might now spend $500. Croscill also knew the consumer it wanted to target: a married career woman with a home and children, for whom money was less an issue than time. If she liked the look, she was likely to buy the entire room. In effect, Croscill was serving as an interior decorator. To help retailers increase their sales, thereby increasing sales for Croscill, the company began to focus on in-store shops that could present its merchandise in the best light and generate more dollars per square-foot for the retailers. By early 1989 Croscill had almost 100 shops in J.C. Penney stores and was quickly expanding to other department and specialty stores. To showcase its accessories, Croscill provided freestanding wooden fixtures. Already its management was talking about becoming a total home company, branching out one room at a time.

The Croscill look was also evolving, due in large part to the influence of design director Terry Dikomeit. She started out in the 1950s as a colorist for United Merchants, then became familiar with numerous designs and trends through her work at Ex-Cell Home Fashions, Hollander Home Fashions, and CHF. After joining Croscill in the mid-1980s, Dikomeit moved the company beyond its traditional floral styling to more contemporary looks, including some masculine designs. Croscill also added some designer collections to its base of patterns. Moreover, to reinforce the company's new direction, Croscill changed the look of its

packaging and created a new logo to go with a new name, Croscill Home Fashions, after a brief spell as Croscill Home Furnishings. To help preserve the association of the Croscill name with quality, the company's wares sold through mass merchants were packaged under a new label, Ambiance.

Although the vast majority of Croscill's marketing effort was devoted to its point of purchase presentations and brochures, it also spent some money in 1989 on consumer advertising, mostly with regional magazines. More importantly, Croscill had a sterling reputation with retailers who were more than happy to support the company's product expansion. Annual sales grew from $48 million in 1985 to $90 million in 1989. To ensure continuity in the running of the business, an executive committee of 16 individuals was formed, and Mike Kahn's son, David, was being groomed to one day take over the business. The only persistent problem Croscill had was in large part a result of its success. Warehousing and delivery systems had difficulty keeping pace with manufacturing. The company bought a new computer system and created a Quick-Ship program, as well as adding 200,000 square feet of warehouse space.

In 1993 the management of Croscill began to shift to a third generation of the Kahn family. David took over as president, while Mike Kahn assumed the chief executive officer role, while remaining as co-chairman of the board with his brother, Stanley Kahn. In his new role, David oversaw sales and product development. He had joined Croscill in 1982, becoming vice-president of marketing in 1987. His brother, Douglas, also began working for the family business in 1993 after ten years working as an investment banker. He would be based in North Carolina, taking over Royal Home Fashions, the company's manufacturing subsidiary. The brothers worked well together, their abilities complementing one another, and Croscill continued its steady growth.

Growing the Bath Business: Early 1990s

In the early 1990s Croscill stepped up its bath business in an effort to create the total room synergy that the company already enjoyed in the bedroom. It added such products as bath ceramics, benches, shower curtain hooks and fabric-covered rings, and benches, as well as adding to its towel offerings. Because accessories were becoming a major portion of sales, Croscill continued to expand its offerings, especially in non-textile products, including waste baskets, decorative drapery hardware, lamps, framed mirrors, wall art, and wallpaper. Rather than depend on licensees, the company increasingly looked to either manufacture accessories or subcontract them. In order to capture more of the high-end portion of the mass market business, while again preserving Croscill as a brand name associated with quality merchandise, the company created the Chapel Hill line. Essentially it offered the total room concept to the value-oriented customer. Croscill also opened its first factory outlet store in 1995, although it was not a business that management was especially keen on growing. It simply allowed the company to cut some of the losses it might incur from overruns and irregulars, which were minimal because of the attention Croscill paid to quality manufacturing.

Some retailers expressed concern that the company's expansion into so many different products had resulted in Croscill

Key Dates:

1946: George Kahn starts Croscill Curtain Company.
1976: Operating company changes name to Croscill Home Fashions Inc. to reflect changing business.
1985: Company begins producing sheets for J.P. Stevens.
1990: Annual sales exceed $100 million.
1993: David and Douglas Kahn, third generation family members, gain top management positions.
2000: Operating company changes name to Croscill Home Inc.
2001: David Kahn and Douglas Kahn are named CEO and COO, respectively.

neglecting its original curtain and drapery business. In 1996 the company offered a comprehensive selection of curtains and drapes, as well as decorative window hardware, which was enjoying explosive growth. The other criticism Croscill faced was a perennial one: delivery capabilities catching up with manufacturing growth. In 1999 the company added its first distribution center in the West, located in Reno, Nevada. It also added a new facility in North Carolina, but just a year later Croscill was again playing catch-up. It purchased land in order to build yet another distribution center.

Delivery problems, however, were in many ways a testament to Croscill's continued pattern of growth. Revenues reached $218 million in 1998, $250 million in 1999, and over $300 million in 2000. With the gross sales of licensed products included, the Croscill name and its mass market labels were generating well in excess of $500 million in business each year. To maintain the momentum, management focused on building the company into a lifestyle brand, supported by three major segments: bedding, window, and bath products. It shortened its operating name to Croscill Home. It spent $4 million in 1999 alone in fixtures for its in-store shops, which now numbered more than 500. It also developed a brochure to promote the Croscill lifestyle image, to be inserted in most product packages. Coordination between bed and bath products continued to grow, with bath becoming increasingly more important to the bottom line. In 2001 Croscill Window Fashions debuted its most impressive line in 15 years, its range of fabrics greatly improved through new relationships with vendors in China, India, and Korea. Not only could Croscill customers purchase curtains for the bedroom and bathroom, they could also buy them for the living room, as the company continued to pursue its goal of selling products for each room in the house. The one area in which Croscill did not budge was on price. It kept adding value to products with the Croscill name, believing that its core customers were willing to pay for quality.

The company continue to evolve in 2001. David Kahn was named CEO of Croscill Home and brother Doug became chief operating officer while remaining CEO of Royal Home Fashions. In truth, the title changes were just a confirmation of the roles the two men had already assumed in the company. Mike and Stanley Kahn continued as co-chairmen, but the torch was all but passed to the third generation. In April 2001 Dikomeit retired, after 15 years at Croscill and more than four decades working in the home textile industry. She had served as mentor for numerous designers, leaving the company well stocked with talent to develop the new patterns that would serve to keep the Croscill brand in good stead with consumers. Even as the company adapted to a changing retail environment, it continued to work with longtime partners. In May 2001 it rolled out a new sheet program, Croscill Classics, with J.C. Penney. It also struck up deals with new partners, such as licensing Croscill designs to Portmeirion, an upscale European tabletop supplier, as the company expanded into the dining room. Products for the living room were also enhanced by a licensing agreement with California's Classic Slipcovers Inc. to provide furniture slipcovers with the Croscill name. Overall, the textile industry was changing, as more and more companies outsourced manufacturing to less expensive overseas facilities. Roughly a third of Croscill's sales involved outsourced materials. The value-added, cut and sew part of the manufacturing process continued to be done in-house, but whether it would ever turn to overseas facilities to provide finished products remained an open question. Given Croscill's history of adapting to new conditions, it was safe to say that it would not only find a way to survive, but very likely thrive in its chosen niche.

Principal Subsidiaries

Croscill Home Inc.; Royal Home Fashions Inc.

Principal Competitors

Pillowtex Corporation; Springs Industries, Inc.; WestPoint Stevens Inc.

Further Reading

Adler, Sam, ''Croscill Delivers,'' *HFD,* June 27, 1994, p. 28.
Johnson, Sarah, ''New Directions: Croscill's Rolling Out a Drive on All Fronts,'' *HFN,* April 1, 1996, p. 21.
Page, Melinda, ''For Croscill, Building Brand Awareness Is in the Details,'' *HFN,* May 29, 2000, p. 74S.
Parker, Madeline, ''From Curtains to Croscill,'' *HFN,* June 14, 1999, p. 12.
Schwartz, Donna Boyle, ''Croscill Home Fashions: A Rising Star in Sheets,'' *HFD,* July 18, 1988, p. 1.
——, ''Croscill Home Fashions Takes Aim with Accessories,'' *HFD,* April 17, 1989, pp. 48–49.
——, ''Croscill Stays Hot,'' *HFD,* December 25, 1989, p. 30.

—Ed Dinger

The Daimaru, Inc.

1-7-1, Shinsaibashi-Suji
Chuo-ku, Osaka 542-8501
Japan
Telephone: 6-6271-1231
Fax: 6-6245-1343
Web site: http://www.daimaru.co.jp

Public Company
Incorporated: 1920 as The Daimaru Drapery Store, Inc.
Employees: 6,800
Sales: ¥822.6 billion (US$6.8 billion) (2000)
Stock Exchanges: Tokyo
Ticker Symbol: 8234
NAIC: 452110 Department Stores

At the center of the vast international marketing complex known as The Daimaru, Inc. (Daimaru) is a network of department stores that ranks among the five largest department store companies in Japan. In addition to its department stores, located in Japan and overseas, and its closely associated credit card, data center, and mail-order businesses, Daimaru encompasses chains of supermarkets, restaurants, and specialty stores that help make it one of the top retailers in the world. Daimaru operations extend to advertising and printing; freight shipment; fitness and sports; and the manufacture, import, and export of a variety of merchandise. The company also operates its own research center, where it develops and tests merchandise.

Early Days: Three Drapery Shops

From the opening of Daimaru's first store, a drapery shop in Kyoto, in 1717, the company has been known for the close ties it cultivates with the communities in which its stores are situated, and for its upscale, high-quality goods and services. These characteristics evoke comparison with another pioneering retailer, the top-ranking Mitsukoshi department store company.

Aside from the few stores opened by Mitsukoshi's predecessor in other areas in the 30-some years preceding 1717, the purchasing process in most of Japan was inconvenient and costly for both consumer and merchant. Only wealthy persons could afford to patronize the drapery purveyors, who, as traveling salesmen, had to haul their samples over rough terrain in all kinds of weather in order to show the fabric to customers in their homes. The costs involved in this time-consuming process ran up the prices of the goods. Earnings were meager, for few sales could be made relative to the number of hours worked.

Locating the business in a shop increased the pace of sales, lowered overhead, and provided customers with a greater selection of samples than could be carried in a salesman's backpack. The stores also became meeting places where customers could relax with a cup of tea and exchange ideas.

Hikoemon Shimomura chose a propitious place to open his drapery business. Kyoto in 1717 was the home of the imperial family and the nobles of the court. Although long bereft of political power, they were supported in style by Japan's ruler, the Tokugawa shogun. Far removed though they were from the new capital, Edo(later to be known as Tokyo), they had an ardent desire for traditional garments and fine fabrics. This provided a willing and able customer base at a time when purchasing power was largely held in a few widely scattered clusters of wealthy families.

Service before profit was a principle Hikoemon Shimomura announced to his customers. Daimaru's president, Shotaro Shimomura, in the early 1990s explained that it is still the stores' guiding principle to consider service to the customer first, in the belief that profits will follow. In 1726 Daimaru's founder opened a shop in Osaka, a busy trade center. Purchasing power was beginning to spread into the hands of a rising merchant class. This meant that the new business, given its start among titled and wealthy patrons, could continue to grow. The shogun's political power and isolationist policies had created a kind of stability that allowed Japan's economy time to recover from the drain imposed on it by centuries of civil strife. The country's stability and unity under the shogun also made it possible to establish a standard currency that helped accelerate the pace at which transactions could be made.

By 1728 Hikoemon Shimomura was able to open a third shop, locating it in Nagoya, another busy trade center. The name Daimaru-ya came into use for the first time.

Key Dates:

1717: Hikoemon Shimomura opens a drapery shop in Kyoto.
1726: Shimomura opens a second shop, in Osaka.
1728: Shimomura opens a third shop, in Nagoya; the name Daimaru-ya is used for the first time.
1907: Daimaru becomes a partnership, named The Partnership Daimaru Drapery Store.
1920: Daimaru becomes a corporation, named The Daimaru Drapery Store, Inc.
1933: Company forms an affiliate to handle wholesale importation and exportation.
1949: Daimaru adds a unit for the leasing of real estate and vehicles.
1950: Company forms a furniture manufacturing and construction contracting business.
1960: Daimaru opens the first of a chain of supermarkets; opens stores in Hong Kong.
1964: Daimaru opens a store in Bangkok.
1983: Company forms a mail-order division; opens store in Singapore.
1991: Daimaru opens a store in Australia.
1997: Daimaru closes its operations in France and Hong Kong; sells its stake in Thai joint venture.
2001: Company joins with three other Japanese department store operators to form a common distribution network.

During Daimaru stores' first 150 years, the shogunate's intricate web of restrictions held Japanese lifestyles in a fairly rigid pattern, but below the change-resistant surface of life in a feudal state, the nation's commercial economy was racing toward modernization. That became apparent in the mid-19th century, when the weakened shogunate government had to yield to foreign pressures to open its ports to international trade. By 1868, when the progressive Meiji emperor replaced the shogun, Japan had a number of commercial entities that were ready to compete in international markets.

Early 1900s: A Transformation

Western nations' styles at first repelled some segments of the Japanese populace, but increasingly the majority of purchasers of goods were attracted to imports. At the same time, just before and after the turn of the century, brief wars with China and Russia had brought increasing numbers of workers from rural Japan to urban centers for the manufacture of essential materials. Responding to their needs and to a new demand for variety in consumer goods, Daimaru transformed its shops.

Little by little, the transformation was reflected in Daimaru's organizational structure and, eventually, in its official name and written policies. In 1907, with ¥500,000 in capital, Daimaru became a partnership, and took the name The Partnership Daimaru Drapery Store. The store management took some steps forward, hiring women as sales clerks for the first time in 1913 and accelerating the pace of business as Japan's victorious participation in World War I expanded the economy. By 1920 Daimaru was ready for another reorganization, this time as a corporation, with ¥12 million in capital.

The new corporation also had a new name: Daimaru Drapery Store, Inc. Although the name did not hint at the widened variety of goods and services Daimaru offered, it conveyed continuity with the company's centuries of service.

The Great Kanto Earthquake of 1923 destroyed the Tokyo store. In 1925, when the rebuilding process was completed, the modernized premises, constructed to accommodate Daimaru's many types of merchandise, were obviously those of a department store. Three years later, the name was officially changed to The Daimaru, Inc.

Expansion and Diversification: 1930s–70s

Japan's rapid military-based expansion in the 1930s brought an influx of workers into urban and manufacturing centers, creating new customer bases. The company formed an affiliate, Daimaru Kogyo Co., Ltd. which started wholesale import and export operations in 1933. Japan's devastation and defeat in World War II, however, brought the nation's economy to a virtual standstill.

The nation's new constitution provided for the dissolution of the monopolistic *zaibatsu* and supported the development of individual enterprises. During the seven years of occupation by the Allied forces under U.S. General Douglas MacArthur, Daimaru reorganized, starting several new businesses and acquiring affiliates. In July 1947 Daimaru Creation Co., Ltd., was established as a subsidiary, to plan marketing strategies and provide printing and advertising services. A facility for leasing real estate and vehicles was added to Daimaru in October 1949. The following year, Daimaru began a furniture manufacturing and construction contracting business under the name of Daimaru Mokko Co., Ltd.

All the new businesses were centered in Osaka and began to expand their operations as the nation's economy recovered from the ravages of war. Postwar construction and repair of highways and the building of shopping malls through the countryside helped make a greater variety of merchandise accessible.

Interest in foreign fashions and accessories reached a new height in Japan's post-World War II period. With the economy's rapid recovery came expanded buying power. In 1953 Daimaru, with stores in Osaka, Kyoto, Tottori, Shimonoseki, Hakata, and Nihama, became the first retailer in Japan to sign an exclusive agreement with Christian Dior. The following year, a new multistory Tokyo store was opened. Daimaru began selling its own ready-made men's wear in 1959.

At the requests of local business communities, Daimaru opened stores in Hong Kong in 1960 and Bangkok four years later. In 1960, in Japan, Daimaru opened the first of a chain of supermarkets. In 1974 the Peacock Sangyo, with 24 shops, became Daimaru Peacock Co., Ltd., a subsidiary of Daimaru. By 1991 this company had 50 outlets. Daimaru formed an exclusive agreement with the fashion designer Givenchy and also began manufacturing its own line of women's fashions. With the opening of stores in Paris and Lyon and the addition of specialty stores and restaurants, Daimaru was well established by 1975 as one of Japan's top five department store companies. The company sustained its position through the ensuing years, despite such woes as the late 1980s stock market crash and some fluctuations in the value of the yen. Daimaru began the 1990s in third place.

New Markets and New Challenges: 1980s–90s

Close attention to changes in consumers' buying habits led to the remodeling and expansion of some of the stores and to the creation of new businesses. The increase in dual-career families with little time to visit department stores, for example, led to the organization of the Home Shopping Division, a mail-order facility, in 1983. In a sense, for these shoppers, the purchasing process had come full circle since Hikoemon Shimomura had set up his first drapery store in 1717. The popularity of the mail-order service soon exceeded the volume a division could handle, and the service became Daimaru Home-Shopping Co., Ltd., in 1988.

In 1987 Daimaru transformed its store in Machida, a depressed area in Tokyo, from a fiscally ailing outlet to a profit-making venture by reorganizing it and creating a separate corporation, Machida Daimaru Co. Ltd., to operate it. The reduced costs to Daimaru, resulting from its separation from the Machida store, have also to some degree offset the company's huge investment in the 1983 opening of its highrise, ultramodern Osaka Umeda store.

During the 1980s, Daimaru stepped up its activities in Southeast Asia. The company opened its second store in Bangkok in 1980 and a store in Singapore in 1983. The same year, it added an annex to the Hong Kong Daimaru, doubling its space.

In October 1991 Daimaru Australia was opened in Melbourne. Unfortunately, Australia's economic climate had changed considerably since Daimaru officials first decided, four years earlier, to move into that market. In the intervening years, the country had slid into one of its worst recessions of the century. The store got off to a slow start. Australian consumers perceived Daimaru as high-end and expensive—an image that frightened off recession-stricken shoppers. Within a year of opening in Melbourne, management began restructuring the store—laying off 15 percent of the total workforce, adding lower-priced merchandise to its product mix, and modifying the interior of the store to make it look less posh.

Meanwhile, Daimaru's domestic operations were undergoing their own trials. Japan's bubble economy had burst, driving consumer spending to damagingly low levels. For the fiscal year ended in 1993, Daimaru posted a 51 percent decline in net profit. The company began reducing expenses, announcing that it would cut 1,000 head office staff over the coming 18 months. It also partnered with Tokyo-based competitor Mitsukoshi Ltd. The partnership—which was to include the development of private-label merchandise, the importation of foreign goods, and the stocking of certain products—was designed to reduce development and procurement costs for the two chains. The joint venture was groundbreaking; up until that point, such cooperative arrangements had not existed in Japan's department store industry.

Daimaru suffered still another blow in early 1995, when an earthquake caused major damage to its store in Kobe. The resulting shutdown and lost sales only compounded the company's already depressed financial condition, and it had to trim costs further, eliminating another 300 jobs. The Kobe store was not fully rebuilt and operational until March 1997.

By that time, Daimaru had a new president. Tsutomo Okuda, previously the company's managing director, became its president on March 1, 1997. The change in leadership portended operational changes ahead. At a press conference, outgoing president Shotaro Shimomura explained that the move was designed to rejuvenate Daimaru's management.

Okuda wasted no time in his quest to turn Daimaru around. Just three months into his presidency, the company announced that it was closing down its operations in both Hong Kong and France—three stores, in total. The company also made plans to sell its stake in its Thai joint venture. These moves substantially reduced the company's overseas operations, leaving stores in only Singapore and Australia. Domestically, Daimaru moved to cut costs by closing down a nonperforming store in Wakayama, and again reducing its workforce—this time by almost 750 employees, or 11 percent of its total workforce.

Even as it withdrew from France, Hong Kong, and Thailand, Daimaru made deeper commitments to its Australian and Singapore operations. The company opened a second Australian outlet in 1998, on the country's Gold Coast. It also opened a third store in Singapore.

A New Century

As Daimaru entered the 21st century, it was still struggling against Japan's sluggish economy. The company continued to explore cost-reduction measures—some traditional, some innovative. In February 2001, it shut down still another unprofitable store, in Niihama. In a more unusual move, it entered into an alliance with three other Japanese department store operators to develop a joint distribution network. The network was designed to substantially reduce the partners' distribution costs, allowing them to close down redundant distribution centers and consolidate operations.

Principal Subsidiaries

Daimaru Home-Shopping Co., Ltd.; Daimaru Credit Service Co., Ltd.; Daimaru Information Center Co., Ltd.; Daimaru Peacock Co., Ltd.; Restaurant Peacock Co., Ltd.; Daimaru Mariepaul Co., Ltd.; Daimaru Kogyo Co., Ltd.; Daimaru Sports Co., Ltd.; Daimaru Creation Co., Ltd.; Daimaru Mode Atelier Co., Ltd.; Alembic Co., Ltd.; Mich International Co., Ltd.; Daimaru Mokko Co., Ltd.; Consumer Product End-Use Research Institute Co., Ltd.; Daimaru Transportation Co., Ltd.; Rakuto Transportation Co., Ltd.; Chuo Kogyo Co., Ltd.; Daimaru Plan & Development Co., Ltd.; Daimaru Realty Co., Ltd.; Daito Realty Co., Ltd.; Roots Japan Inc.

Principal Competitors

Mycal Corporation; The Seiyu, LTD.; Takashimaya Company, Limited.

Further Reading

Daimaru Now: 1989, Osaka: The Daimaru, Inc., 1989.

—Betty T. Moore
—update: Shawna Brynildssen

JOHN DEERE

Deere & Company

1 John Deere Place
Moline, Illinois 61265-8098
U.S.A.
Telephone: (309) 765-8000
Fax: (309) 765-5671
Web site: http://www.deere.com

Public Company
Incorporated: 1868
Employees: 43,700
Sales: $13.14 billion (2000)
Stock Exchanges: New York
Ticker Symbol: DE
NAIC: 333618 Other Engine Equipment Manufacturing;
333111 Farm Machinery and Equipment
Manufacturing; 333112 Lawn and Garden Tractor and
Home Lawn and Garden Equipment; 33312
Construction Machinery Manufacturing; 332997
Industrial Pattern Manufacturing; 42183 Industrial
Machinery and Equipment Wholesalers; 52221 Credit
Card Issuing; 52222 Sales Financing; 541512
Computer Systems Design Services

One of the five oldest companies in the United States, Deere & Company is the world's largest manufacturer of agricultural equipment and a major U.S. producer of construction, forestry, and lawn and grounds care equipment. The company has factories throughout the world and distributes its products in more than 160 countries through independent retail dealers—nearly 5,000 worldwide. It is also active in financial services. Deere has been an industry innovator since John Deere introduced the first successful self-cleaning steel plow in 1837. At that time, most Americans lived on farms; now many of Deere's customers belong to the upper 5 percent of the nation's farmers, who take in 80 percent of the net farm income; these farmers run big farms that need sophisticated equipment.

Early History

Born in 1804 in Vermont, John Deere was a blacksmith renowned for his craftsmanship and inventiveness. After a business depression in the 1830s, Deere, like many young Easterners, migrated west. He settled in Grand Detour, Illinois, where his blacksmith business thrived. He soon saw that the cast-iron hand plow that pioneers had brought from the East did not work well in midwestern soil, which clung to the plow's bottom and made it necessary for the farmer to scrape off the soil every few feet. Deere developed a plow with a polished and specially shaped moldboard and share, which scoured itself after lifting the soil.

This first plow was made from a broken sawblade, but the tool quickly became so popular with Deere's customers that he began to make plows before he got orders for them—a revolutionary practice in those days. In 1843 Deere ordered a shipment of rolled steel from England. This move enabled him to expand his business, and three years later, he was able to get steel made to his specifications from Pittsburgh, Pennsylvania mills. In 1847 Deere moved his business to Moline, Illinois, near the Mississippi River, which provided water power and convenient transportation. By 1850 he was producing 1,600 plows a year.

Known to say, "I will never put my name on a plow that does not have in it the best that is in me," Deere continued to improve his plows and to tailor them for different soil conditions. In 1868 the business was incorporated as Deere & Company. In 1869 Deere named his son, Charles Deere, vice-president and treasurer of the company. When John Deere died in 1886, Charles succeeded him as president.

Charles Deere focused on the company's distribution system, establishing wholesale branches to market and distribute Deere equipment to the independent dealers who sold it. The product line was also expanded. The Gilpin Sulky Plow, launched in 1874, had the capacity to plow three acres in 12 hours, and in 1898 the new Deere Gang Plow, which used four horses instead of three and could plow six acres in 12 hours, was introduced. In the early 1900s, Deere plows were powered by steam engines. By the time Charles Deere died in 1907, the

Company Perspectives:

Deere's businesses are working to fulfill the company's mission of doubling and doubling again the John Deere Experience of genuine value. Specifically, we aim to double and double again our market value, largely through growth in sales and improvements in profitability. The John Deere Experience is increasingly a global one, taking root wherever in the world crops are grown, grounds are tended, or construction activity is under way.

company was manufacturing a range of cultivators, steel plows, corn and cotton planters, and other tools.

Growing Through Acquisitions in the Early 20th Century

William Butterworth, a son-in-law of Charles Deere who was responsible for bringing together under the John Deere name other farm equipment companies with whom Deere had done business, became the next president, in 1907. As president, Butterworth engineered the 1911 acquisition of the Van Brunt Manufacturing Company of Horicon, Wisconsin, which produced the first working broadcast seeder and grain drill. Also in 1911, Deere & Mansur Works, which had been established in 1877 by the company to make corn planters, was merged with Deere, as was Joseph Dain's hay-making tool company. In 1918, Deere bought Waterloo Gasoline Engine Company in Waterloo, Iowa, one of the first makers of tractors.

During World War I, the demand for food motivated many more farmers to begin to use tractors, and agriculture gradually lost its dependence on animal power. Deere sold 8,000 Waterloo Boy tractors in 1918. In 1823 Deere introduced its own tractor, called the Model D.

In 1928, Charles Deere Wiman, John Deere's great-grandson, became president of the company. Wiman concentrated on engineering and product development, and the company grew rapidly. In the 1930s, when the John Deere Combination Unit was introduced, the farmer could bed, plant, and fertilize cotton ten times faster than four men with four mules. The four-row tractor corn planter allowed one man to plant and fertilize between 40 and 50 acres a day. In 1937, despite the Great Depression, Deere reached $100 million in gross sales.

During World War II Burton F. Peek was president. Peek served during the two years that Wiman held the post of colonel of ordinance, in Washington, D.C. Peek and Wiman, when the latter returned to Deere, focused on innovation in product design, and by the end of the war Deere was a leader. In 1952 Deere was the first farm equipment manufacturer to modify the self-propelled combine for picking and shelling corn. Three years later, Deere was one of the 100 largest manufacturing companies in the United States.

Major Period of Growth Following World War II

After Wiman died in 1955, his son-in-law, William A. Hewitt, became president and CEO. He led the company into a major growth period. Seeing that Deere's decentralized operations needed to be coordinated, Hewitt accomplished this by increasing communication between different branches of the company. He also promoted Elwood Curtis, Deere's controller, to vice-president.

During the mid-1950s, while Deere's competitors were expanding abroad, Hewitt seized the opportunity to manufacture overseas. In 1956 he sent one of Deere's factory leaders, Harry Pence, to look for possible acquisitions overseas. The first was a small German tractor company called Heinrich Lanz, which was in financial trouble and could be bought cheaply. Other acquisitions or plant constructions followed in France, Spain, Argentina, Mexico, and South Africa. For 15 years, overseas operations suffered huge losses due to managerial mistakes and unforeseen problems in start-up activities and in foreign exchange, but Hewitt believed the company had to expand internationally or risk being forced out of the market. Deere continued to expand in Canada, Western Europe, and Latin America.

In 1957, Hewitt hired Finnish architect Eero Saarinen, the designer of the Gateway Arch in St. Louis, Missouri, to design a new headquarters building that would belie Deere's provincial, rather conservative image. The new building was completed seven years later in the same Moline location, and it became a tourist site, particularly attractive to farmers.

In the late 1950s, Vice-President Elwood Curtis convinced Hewitt to diversify into finance. In 1958 Deere donated its capital stock in Moline National Bank to the John Deere Foundation, and, freed of antitrust constraints, the John Deere Credit Company was established to help finance farm equipment dealerships. Ten years later, Deere acquired Fulton Insurance Company in New York. Insurance and finance were to become important Deere operations when equipment sales slumped.

Hewitt diversified and expanded Deere to help balance the company's farm equipment operations. Since tractor sales were dependent on the income of farmers, sales fluctuated according to weather, agricultural prices, and government policy. Although agricultural machinery still accounted for most of Deere's sales, in the late 1950s, Deere began to make machinery for construction, along with equipment for street and road maintenance and logging. In 1963, the company began to manufacture and market lawn care and garden equipment. This branch of the company grew rapidly. By 1969, there were 3,700 independent John Deere dealers in the United States and Canada. In 1969, through the dealers, Deere began to operate a network of John Deere parts and service centers.

Late 1960s and 1970s Marked by Series of Strikes

Although the 1960s were a decade of growth and diversification for Deere, it was also a turbulent time. Earnings decreased markedly in 1966 and 1967, mainly because of overseas operations. In 1968, the company suffered losses due to unfavorable weather, low crop prices, and a six-week strike. The United Auto Workers (UAW) demanded a contract from Deere similar to that won from Caterpillar Tractor Company, one of Deere's competitors. Deere refused, and the strike finally ended when the UAW proposed an inverse seniority plan, which gave senior workers up to 95 percent of their pay if they volunteered to be

Key Dates:

1837: Working in Grand Detour, Illinois, John Deere fashions his famous "self-polishing" plow for prairie soil.

1847: Deere moves his business to Moline, Illinois, near the Mississippi River, which provided water power and convenient transportation.

1911: The purchase of six companies gives Deere & Co. a full line of farm equipment.

1918: After another acquisition, Deere begins making its first tractors.

1937: Sales reach $100 million.

1956: Manufacturing and marketing expand internationally, into Mexico and Germany.

1958: John Deere Credit Company is created.

1969: John Deere Insurance Group is formed.

1978: Sales reach $4 billion.

1991: Lawn & Grounds Care becomes a separate division.

1996: The Ukraine buys $187 million worth of combines, Deere's largest single sale to date.

1998: Earnings reach $1 billion.

laid off for one year. This allowed older workers, who were closer to retirement, to take time off while collecting UAW supplemental unemployment benefits. The plan went into effect in late 1967, and in three years Deere laid off 1,698 people, about 70 percent of them with high seniority.

Throughout the 1960s, Deere expanded its lawn and garden product line to include snowmobiles, hand tools, portable heaters, lanterns, chain saws, and other products. In 1972 Deere introduced the John Deere bicycle in an effort to take advantage of a rapidly expanding market. This was also the first year Deere made a profit overseas, as the demand for farm machinery increased both within the United States and abroad.

In 1975, overseas plants accounted for $681 million in sales and the company expected to grow more in foreign operations than domestically. That year, Deere also began a seven-year, $1.8 billion capital program to increase the capacity of its factories and plants by 30 percent.

During the 1970s, Deere repeatedly had conflicts with the UAW, as the firm began to mechanize further its manufacturing operations, cut back costs, and lay off workers. In 1976 a six-week strike reduced inventory at a time when the demand for equipment remained strong, and Deere lost a significant amount. In October 1979 UAW members went on strike again, demanding more paid time off and cost-of-living wage increases. Deere argued that its workers already had more paid time off than employees at similar companies and changes would be too costly. Consequently, Deere factories were shut down for three weeks, until a new contract was agreed upon.

In 1978 Hewitt committed $350 million to overseas expansion. Nonetheless, that year overseas operations took serious losses due to foreign-exchange fluctuation and high start-up costs for its new line of German tractors.

In the late 1970s Deere added 20 products to its construction equipment sector and doubled the size of its Davenport, Iowa plant, with the expectation that the construction industry would grow twice as fast as the farm equipment industry. By 1982, however, because of high interest rates, the construction equipment business was in a slump.

Difficulty During Farm Recession: 1980s

In 1982 Deere also experienced the first effects of the farm recession. Hewitt retired as head of the company and later became the U.S. ambassador to Jamaica. Robert Hanson, a longtime Deere employee and Moline native, became president and CEO (he was the first chief executive to be unrelated to the Deere family). He took up the post at a challenging time. The country was in the midst of a recession and farm equipment sales were low. The company's dealers were overstocked and its plants were running at about 50 percent capacity. To help its dealers survive, Deere incurred a large amount of short-term debt. Hanson cut capital spending by 30 percent, much of it in labor costs, and Deere began its dramatic reduction of salaried employees. Between 1980 and 1983, the company laid off about 40 percent of its employees.

In 1982 the newly robotized Waterloo tractor plant lost money, only a year after it began production. Although the plant required fewer workers, the demand for tractors was so low that the plant had to run at a fraction of its capacity and overhead was high. In fact, manufacturing operations lost money continually until 1986.

To recoup some of the losses, Deere continued to develop its financial sector. In 1982 the company acquired Central National Life Insurance Company and expanded its John Deere Credit Company to include leasing operations. During the early and mid-1980s, Deere was active in helping farmers to finance tractor purchases, offering credit incentives. Deere won the loyalty of many farmers this way. This helped sales at a time when many farmers were tightening their budgets. Farmers' net incomes had decreased about 75 percent in the past decade, basically because of overproduction, which, in turn, cost the government a great deal in surplus storage. In 1983 President Ronald Reagan introduced a payment-in-kind program, which paid farmers not to plant a certain number of acres, to alleviate the overproduction problem.

Deere's investment in overseas expansion had not paid off, and in 1983 the company still held a small share of the European market. In an effort to strengthen its links with Japan, Deere began to import Hitachi construction equipment.

Despite Deere's financial troubles, the recession hit Deere much less severely than it did its competitors, and Hanson found ways for the company to make money in sectors other than farm implements. In 1984 Deere acquired a rotating-combustion-engine business from the Curtiss-Wright Corporation, and Deere also bought all rights to Farm Plan, an agricultural financing service.

Sales in farm equipment continued to decrease markedly. The company survived mainly from its sale of lawn tractors, European sales, and its financial operations. In 1985 Deere continued to cut back on labor costs when it simplified the design of its basic engine and reorganized its factory system, laying off 480 workers. "When you're on the way to the gallows, your attention is clearly focused," Hanson told *Financial World,* May 2, 1989.

In 1985, a $100,000 John Deere tractor sold for about $70,000. About 20 percent of the dealers in the Midwest closed. This attrition helped the stronger dealers to survive. With sales at $4 billion, Deere lost money before taxes. Despite the dire times, Deere began a health maintenance organization for small cities and rural communities in 1985, called Heritage National Health Plan.

In 1986 Deere won an $11 million military contract to develop an implement for repairing bomb-damaged runways. Also in 1986, 12,000 UAW members struck four key plants, seeking a new contract that would protect employees against cutbacks and maintain a cost-of-living adjustment. Deere shut down its remaining UAW plants and the UAW accused the company of a lockout. Deere's dealers had enough inventory to last several months at the rate they were selling them and the strike allowed Deere to reduce inventory and overhead. Deere said it could not afford the proposed labor contract and the strike lasted five-and-a-half months before Deere and the UAW could come to an agreement.

Deere lost $99 million in 1987, mainly due to depressed sales and the effect of the strike. Hanson continued to push Deere into manufacturing parts such as hydraulic cylinders for other companies, and he also expanded credit operations. Although the lawn care business continued to do well, the company still depended on the farm implements sector for 60 percent of its sales.

In 1987 Hans W. Becherer was named president of Deere and Hanson remained CEO. In 1988 the farm economy began to recover from its slump because of the lower dollar and the improvement of the North American agricultural economy. As the main survivor in the industry, Deere had increased its market share during the recession from 45 to 55 percent. In 1988 sales increased 30 percent to $5.4 billion and net income reached a record $315 million, a one-year turnaround of $414 million. Sales of tractors rose 90 percent and sales of harvesting machinery tripled. As the recession lifted, many farmers were ready to buy new equipment.

Deere offered its largest selection of new agricultural products ever in 1988 and 1989, spending about $16 million to display its 44 new combines, tractors, and balers in Denver and Palm Springs, Colorado. In 1988 Deere formed a joint venture with Hitachi called Deere-Hitachi Construction Machinery, which would produce and market earth excavators.

In March 1989, Deere settled a court dispute with the Equal Employment Opportunity Commission (EEOC), which was acting on behalf of 116 former employees who were laid off as part of the labor reductions in 1984. The EEOC alleged that age discrimination was involved, and although Deere denied the allegation, it agreed to pay $4.3 million to settle the dispute rather than go through further litigation. In October 1989, a one-month strike slowed production at Deere's Wisconsin lawn care products plant. Also in 1989, Deere paid $87 million for Funk Manufacturing, a maker of powertrain components.

Improving Conditions: Early to Mid-1990s

In August 1989 Becherer became CEO of Deere, then became chairman as well in June 1990 when Hanson retired. Although Deere enjoyed profits of $411.1 million in 1990, it then lost $20.2 million in 1991 and made only $37.4 million in 1992. Sales fell in both 1991 and 1992. The difficulties stemmed in part from the early 1990s recession, which hit Deere's $1 billion construction equipment business particularly hard, and in part from farmers' reluctance to buy new equipment despite an improved farm sector economy.

In response, Deere poured money into a $120 million 1991 restructuring program and into research and development— $280 million in 1992 alone. The result was the company's 1992 introduction of the 6000/7000 series of tractors, touted as Deere's most significant new products since 1960. The line consisted of six new tractors with horsepower ranging from 66 to 145, and featuring the largest cabs in the industry—cabs that included comfortable seats, stereo cassettes, air conditioning, and better visibility thanks to 29 percent more glass. Deere's revitalized new product development efforts did not let up, however. Just two years later, the company introduced the 8000 series tractors, including the 8400 model, which was the world's first 225-horsepower row-crop tractor.

Meanwhile, Deere continued to seek ways to bolster its nonfarming sectors. In 1990 the company had established a Worldwide Lawn & Grounds Care Division, separating this product group from the agricultural equipment business. Deere then made a series of moves to strengthen its new division. In 1991 the company purchased a majority stake in SABO Maschinenfabrik AG, a maker of high-quality walk-behind mowers and commercial lawn mowers based in Germany. Three years later, Deere acquired the Homelite division of the conglomerate Textron, Inc. Homelite, based in Charlotte, North Carolina, was a leading manufacturer of handheld and walk-behind power products for the consumer and commercial markets. With this acquisition, Deere's lawn and ground care equipment business generated almost as much revenue as the industrial equipment division. The company in 1995 introduced the new "Sabre by John Deere" line of mid-priced lawn tractors and walk-behind mowers. The following year the name of this division was changed to Worldwide Commercial & Consumer Equipment Division.

Although Deere had long been active manufacturing its farm product overseas, the company had not been as aggressive as its competitors in selling tractors and other farm equipment outside the United States and Canada. The mid-1990s saw Deere become much more active in this area. In 1993 the company entered into a marketing agreement with Zetor s.p., a tractor manufacturer in the Czech Republic, whereby Zetor would provide Deere with a lower-priced line of 43 to 93 horsepower tractors, which Deere would sell into developing markets worldwide, particularly in Latin America and Asia. In 1996 Deere concluded its largest single agricultural sale ever when it sold $187 million in combines to Ukraine. The following year, the company established a joint venture with the Jiamusi Combine Harvester Factory based in China. The venture, called John Deere Jiamusi Harvester Company Ltd., of which Deere held a 60 percent interest, would produce smaller combines for export in the Asia-Pacific region.

Following the middling success of 1993 (in which Deere would have posted profits of $184.4 million were it not forced to take a noncash charge of $1.11 billion as the result of new accounting standards in relation to retiree healthcare and life insurance benefits), Deere enjoyed three consecutive years of record sales and profits. Farmers, whose coffers were overflowing as a result of high commodity prices, were finally replacing their old equipment with the innovative new models Deere introduced earlier in the decade. Sales outside the United States and Canada were becoming increasingly important to the company's success, increasing more than 75 percent from 1993 to 1996, going from $1.55 billion to $2.75 billion.

Despite the impressive results of the mid-1990s, Deere remained vulnerable to the inevitable economic downturn. The Deere of the mid-1990s, however, was somewhat more diversified than the Deere of the late 1980s. In 1989 agricultural equipment was responsible for 66 percent of net sales, industrial equipment 21 percent, and commercial/consumer equipment 13 percent, while in 1996 the figures were 63 percent, 20 percent, and 17 percent, respectively. Likewise, the company was becoming more geographically diverse, as sales from outside the United States and Canada increased from 22.8 percent of overall sales in 1989 to 28.6 percent in 1996. It seemed certain that into the 21st century Deere & Company would maintain its leading position in agricultural equipment through innovative new product development and would continue its history of careful diversification.

Ukraine bought 1,049 of Deere's combines in April 1996 at a price of $187 million, the company's largest single agricultural equipment sale to date. Sales were also booming in Argentina and Australia. China, which harvested seven-eighths of its acreage by hand, seemed to provide the greatest room for growth.

At home, Deere had to contend with new competition from Peoria-based Caterpillar Inc., which had launched its own line of agricultural equipment in the late 1980s. Cat was teaming with German farm equipment maker Claas KGaA to develop a combine intended for large commercial farms. Caterpillar, used to dealing with large construction companies, had fewer dealers than Deere but promised onsite service. In the construction sector, both Cat and Deere were introducing their own skid-steer loaders to compete with the Bobcat made by Ingersoll-Rand subsidiary Melroe Co.

Deere's revenues grew by $1 billion a year between 1993 and 1997, with profits growing by $100 million annually. *Crain's Chicago Business* credited a six-year labor agreement signed with the United Auto Workers in 1997 that lowered starting pay. A growing economy, new product lines, and new joint ventures in China, Brazil, and India also contributed to the company's improved outlook, though the healthcare subsidiary lost money in 1997. (Sentry Insurance would buy the John Deere Insurance Group in 1999.)

By the fall of 1998, some of the lowest grain prices in 20 years ended the company's recovery, and unsold machinery began to pile up on dealers' lots. Deere responded with temporary layoffs and placed its hopes on its new lawn care business. Diversification was also an important survival strategy for rivals Case Corp. and Caterpillar Inc., which extended their financing and distribution capabilities, respectively, into other fields. (Case merged with New Holland to form CNH Global in November 1999.)

New Challenges in the New Millennium

Robert Lane, a banking and construction industry executive named president and chief operating officer in January 2000, succeeded Hans Becherer as Deere CEO in June. The company announced a subtle change to its well-known logo the next month, making the deer silhouette appear to be leaping forward rather than landing.

In June 2000, the company's new $30 million, highly automated plant near Williamsburg, Virginia, began turning out lightweight, versatile Gator utility vehicles, which were also produced in Ontario. There were ten variants, including a military version designed to be dropped by parachute, priced between $6,000 and $12,500. In July, Deere's finance arm received approval to charter its own federal savings bank, which would take over the existing credit card program.

In the fall of 2000, Arizona State University (ASU) launched a unique, two-year M.B.A. program specifically tailored for John Deere executives. The company paid $2 million, or $25,000 per employee per year, for the program, representing a $9,000 premium. ASU's reputation in supply management made it especially attractive to John Deere. Since the school's facilities were entirely filled, distance learning and customized corporate material were used to deliver the curriculum.

Later in the year, RDO Equipment Co., a John Deere dealership, sued the manufacturer, alleging the company had unfairly prevented it from acquiring other dealers of Deere's construction equipment. Deere had been buying up dealers itself, trying to strengthen them to better compete with the network of huge independent companies that sold Caterpillar's construction equipment.

In spite of weaknesses in certain markets, Deere posted worldwide net income of $485.5 million for the 2000 fiscal year on sales of $13.1 billion. *Fortune* magazine picked Deere as the United States' most admired company in the industrial and farm equipment category. Although it continued to pick up market share in farm equipment, by March 2001 falling grain prices and slowness in Deere's lawn care and construction businesses made its immediate outlook ''hazy,'' according to *Investor's Business Daily*. The company soon announced new production cutbacks, as well as an early retirement program for 2,500 office workers.

Seeking to expand into related businesses, Deere announced the purchase of irrigation products manufacturer Richton International for $170 million in May 2001. Part of the new acquisition was to be combined with another new purchase, McGinnis Farms, to create a landscaping and irrigation supply division.

Principal Subsidiaries

John Deere Construction Equipment Company; John Deere Agricultural Holdings, Inc.; John Deere Construction Holdings, Inc.; John Deere Lawn and Grounds Care Holdings, Inc.; John Deere Turf Care, Inc.; John Deere Commercial Worksite Products, Inc.; John Deere Limited (Canada); John Deere - Lanz Verwaltungs A.G. (Germany; 99.9%); John Deere S.A. (France); John Deere Iberica S.A. (Spain); John Deere Intercontinental GmbH (Germany); John Deere International GmbH (Germany); Chamberlain Holdings Limited (Australia); John Deere Limited (Australia); Industrias John Deere Argentina S.A.; John Deere Foreign Sales Corporation Limited (Jamaica); John Deere Credit Company; John Deere Capital Corporation; John Deere Credit Inc. (Canada); John Deere Receivables, Inc.; John Deere Funding Corporation; Deere Receivables Corporation; Deere Credit, Inc.; Deere Credit Services, Inc.; Farm Plan Corporation; Arrendadora John Deere S.A. de C.V. (Mexico; 99.9%); John Deere Credit Limited (Australia); John Deere Jiamusi Harvester Company Ltd. (China; 60%); John Deere Credit Group, PLC (U.K.); Senstar Capital Corporation; John Deere Health Care, Inc.; John Deere Health Plan, Inc.; Funk Manufacturing Company; Cameco Industries, Inc.; Cameco Marine, Inc.; Cameco International, Inc.; Sprayfab, LLC; John Deere Brasil Participacoes LTDA; SLC Distribuidora De Titulos e Valores (Brazil); John Deere Ltd. Scotland (E. Kilbride) (U.K.); John Deere Consumer Products, Inc.; John Deere S.A. de C.V.(Mexico); Industrias John Deere, S.A. de C.V.(Mexico); Componentes John Deere S.A. de C.V.(Mexico); Motores John Deere S.A. de C.V.(Mexico); John Deere Torreon S.A. de C.V. (Mexico); John Deere Mexico S.A. de C.V.

Principal Divisions

Agricultural Equipment; Construction Equipment; Commercial & Consumer Equipment; Credit; Parts; Power Systems; Special Technologies; Health Care.

Principal Operating Units

Equipment Operations; Credit Operations; Support Operations.

Principal Competitors

Agco Corp.; Caterpillar Inc.; CNH Global N.V.; Kubota Corporation.

Further Reading

Arndorfer, James B., "Deere Hunts Construction Equipment Dealerships, But Buyout Push Sparks Legal Shootout," *Crain's Chicago Business,* November 20, 2000, p. 1.

Banham, Russ, "Cultivating New Markets," *Journal of Commerce,* July 15, 1996, p. 1C.

Bankston, John, "John Deere Announces Plans to Scale Back Production," *Augusta Chronicle,* March 22, 2001.

Barboza, David, "Aiming for Greener Pastures; Farm-Equipment Makers Step Up Efforts to Diversify," *New York Times,* April 14, 1999, p. C1.

Blackwell, John Reid, "John Deere Turns Out Tractors in James City County, Va.," *Richmond Times-Dispatch,* August 6, 2000.

Broehl, Wayne G., Jr., *John Deere's Company: A History of Deere & Company and Its Times,* New York: Doubleday, 1984.

——, "The Plow That Broke the Prairies," *American History Illustrated,* January 1985, p. 16.

Christie, Jim, "Inventor John Deere—Relied on Skill, Determination to Provide the World with Farming Solutions," *Investor's Business Daily,* December 3, 1999, p. A4.

Crown, Judith, "Cat Stalking Deere in New Market: Bobcat Territory," *Crain's Chicago Business,* October 20, 1997, p. 3.

"Deere to Cut 1,250 Jobs, Offers Early Retirement to 2,500," *Associated Press State & Local Wire,* June 28, 2001.

Deveny, Kathleen, "As John Deere Sowed, So Shall It Reap," *Business Week,* June 6, 1988, p. 84.

Eaton, Leslie, "William Hewitt, 83, Responsible for Overseas Expansion of Deere," *New York Times,* May 22, 1998, p. A23.

Fehr-Snyder, Kerry, "Arizona University Launches Online MBA Program Tailored for Deere Executives," *Arizona Republic,* September 12, 2000.

Flint, Jerry, "Root, Hog! Or Die," *Forbes,* November 4, 1985, p. 170.

Gose, Joe, "John Deere to Put Facility in Lenexa," *Kansas City Star,* May 27, 1998, p. B1.

Gross, Lisa, and Jill Bettner, "Planting Deep and Wide at John Deere," *Forbes,* March 14, 1983, p. 119.

Historical Highlights: 150 Years of John Deere Contributions to Agriculture, Moline, Ill.: Deere & Company, 1990.

Hughes, Jay, "Deere Logo's Change from Land to Leap Symbolic," *Associated Press State & Local Wire,* July 30, 2000.

Kelly, Kevin, "Deere's Surprising Harvest in Health Care," *Business Week,* July 11, 1994, pp. 107, 111.

——, "The New Soul of John Deere," *Business Week,* January 31, 1994, pp. 64–66.

"Lean Future for Farm Equipment Makers; John Deere's Ready for Troubled Times," *St. Louis Post-Dispatch,* September 22, 1998, p. D8.

Murphy, H. Lee, "Farm Crisis Ruins Deere's Sales Harvest: Heavy Equipment Revenues Tumble As Cat Sharpens Claws," *Crain's Chicago Business,* March 8, 1999, p. 4.

——, "New Markets Help Boost Deere Harvest: Company Taps into Emerging Areas," *Crain's Chicago Business,* March 23, 1998, p. 26.

Slutsker, Gary, "Plowing Ahead," *Forbes,* October 26, 1992, pp. 186–88.

The Story of John Deere, Moline, Ill.: Deere & Company, 1989.

Symonds, William C., "Off-Road, On-Target," *Business Week,* June 2, 1997, p. 108.

Tait, Nikki, "John Deere Plans New Production Cutbacks," *Financial Times,* March 22, 2001, p. 32.

——, "Profits Rise at Farm Equipment Makers," *Financial Times,* February 14, 2001, p. 21.

Watkins, Steve, "Bad Weather, Economy Have Deere Running Toward Hazy Sales Future," *Investor's Business Daily,* March 22, 2001, p. A1.

Weiner, Steve, "Staying on Top in a Tough Business in a Tough Year," *Forbes,* May 27, 1991, pp. 46, 48.

—René Steinke
—updates: David E. Salamie, Frederick C. Ingram

Deutsch

Deutsch, Inc.

111 Eighth Avenue
New York, New York 10011
U.S.A.
Telephone (212) 981-7600
Fax: (212) 981-7525
Web site: http://www.deutschinc.com

Wholly Owned Subsidiary of Interpublic Group
Incorporated: 1969 as David Deutsch Associates
Employees: 880
Gross Billings: $1.8 billion (2001 est.)
NAIC: 541810 Advertising Agencies

Deutsch, Inc. is a New York-based boutique advertising agency that was bought in December 2000 by Interpublic Group, one of the world's largest advertising conglomerates. After taking over a small shop that his father founded, CEO Donny Deutsch has transformed the reputation of the agency from conservative and staid to hip and edgy, in the process building up a client list with approximately $1.8 billion worth of billings. Outspoken and irreverent, Donny Deutsch has gained a mixed reputation in Madison Avenue circles. All too often he has been characterized as brash, a term which Deutsch openly dislikes, as well as egomaniacal and grandstanding. Critics also dismiss his reputation for producing cutting edge work as overstated. Deutsch has mellowed with age and made attempts to dispel the notion that Deutsch, Inc. is a one-man shop by granting equity stakes to several top executives and making a concerted effort to couch comments in terms of "we" rather than "I." Recognition by major trade publications has provided some vindication of his style, and the generous deal with Interpublic has brought respect, however begrudging, from his industry critics, who recognize that he has achieved what few others have, establishing his own agency as a formidable brand. Imbued with the personality of Donny Deutsch, Deutsch, Inc. has name value that rivals can only envy.

David Deutsch Associates: 1969

Donny Deutsch's father, David, was a longtime New York adman, working at established agencies such as Ogilvy & Mather and McCann-Erickson. In 1969 he struck out on his own, establishing David Deutsch Associates. The company specialized in print advertising and became known for distinctive photography. Clients included Oneida, Louis Vuitton, and Crouch & Fitzgerald. By the time Donny joined the firm, billings totaled a modest $12 million.

Donny Deutsch graduated cum laude from the University of Pennsylvania's well-regarded Wharton School of Business. He took his first job in advertising at Ogilvy & Mather in 1979, but was quickly bored with his role as an assistant account executive on the Maxwell House Coffee account. He made an impromptu trip to Los Angeles, became a contestant on *The Match Game,* and won $5,000. He then quit his job and traveled on his winnings, which according to lore was supplemented by selling blue jeans at flea markets. He returned to New York in 1983, applied to law schools, and in the meantime took a job at his father's firm as an account executive. After six months David Deutsch fired his son because, as he would later say, Donny "was slacking off."

Donny Deutsch convinced his father to take him back, but this time in a different role: a rainmaker. He soon landed the agency's largest account, the $3 million Tri-State Pontiac Dealers business, and expanded the agency into television advertising. Law school was forgotten, Donny continued to drum up new business, and he became increasingly more involved in the creative side of the agency. In 1986 he was named creative director. By 1989 billings increased to $75 million, then his father stepped aside, selling out to him in 1990. Donny changed the company name to Deutsch, Inc. and quickly moved to reinvent the agency's reputation and culture.

Deutsch developed a notable style for its television commercials. Its in-your-face, sometimes insulting edge was not new, but Deutsch was relentless in its application. One of its Tri-State Pontiac commercials gained a bit of notoriety, not unwanted, when it engaged in what was perceived as Japan bashing by

> ## Company Perspectives:
>
> *Deutsch is a different kind of agency—we think of ourselves as* leaner, meaner, smarter, and faster *than others. We have a passion for the business that you don't find at many shops: a way of working that cuts through the minutiae and gets to the essence of a brand and to the heart of the consumer more effectively than most. This approach has led to our creative philosophy "Human Spoken Here," where we aim to engage the consumer in a dialogue that speaks directly to them about what matters most. Ultimately, this process produces a "natural conversation with the consumer."*

referring to Rockefeller Center as "Mitsubishi Center" at a time when the Japanese economy was soaring and many Japanese companies were buying up Manhattan real estate. Deutsch commercials also tried to be non-commercials by casting real people over actors. In addition, the agency became known for its wacky office culture, one that anticipated the environments of the Internet start-ups several years later. A 1992 *New York Times* profile of the shop describes the atmosphere: "Everyday is a circus at Deutsch Advertising. The office is more like a set of *Saturday Night Live* than a New York advertising agency.... Rock music blares from an office at one end of the hall. In another, several executives are singing theme songs from vintage television programs like *The Patty Duke Show*. People are running down the hall, shouting. One young man seems to be practicing a stand-up comedy routine, to which no one pays the slightest attention." Employees essentially dressed any way they liked. Deutsch himself was known for his jeans and cowboy boots and rarely wore a tie. The office layout was open, designed to foster creative exchange, another feature that predated Internet companies. Deutsch also hired a lot of young people who traveled the local club scene in order to keep abreast of rising trends. Taken altogether, Deutsch was perceived as a hot, creative ad agency and Donny Deutsch, despite reaching his mid-30s, remained something of an enfant terrible.

Dworin and Deutsch: 1991

Although a reputation for being particularly creative was generally a plus for Deutsch, which resulted in the agency landing the highly coveted business of Ikea (and earning the *Advertising Age* Retail Marketing Campaign of the year), most corporate executives who decided on what agency to contract were wary about its reliability. Donny Deutsch wanted to take his agency to another level; already he was talking about opening an office in Los Angeles. To alleviate concerns about the business, Deutsch in 1991 hired a seasoned executive, Steve Dworin, formerly a senior vice-president and director of account management at J. Walter Thompson, as its new president. Although little known in the advertising world, Dworin was a solid veteran of the business. Deutsch met Dworin during his brief stint at Ogilvy & Mather, where Dworin was earning a reputation as an up-and-coming executive at the same time Deutsch was getting ready to appear on *The Match Game*. At the age of 24 Dworin became the youngest account supervisor Ogilvy ever produced. He went to work at J. Walter Thompson in 1980 and by the age of 31 was responsible for a major share

of the agency's business. He was regarded as an odds-on favorite to be named president of the New York office of the London-based agency, but the appointment never came. As early as 1987 Deutsch tried to hire Dworin, but it was not until 1991, when Deutsch Inc. was clearly an agency on the uptick and Dworin had grown weary of waiting for his promotion, that he came aboard.

Quickly the team of Deutsch and Dworin displayed what both men described as "magic." Writing for the *New York Times,* Stuart Elliott explained that "their partnership worked so well because the two men had complementary skills to offer each other. As Katharine Hepburn once said on the secret of the pairing of Fred Astaire and Ginger Rodgers, he gave her class and she gave him sex. The affable, buttoned-down Mr. Dworin gave Mr. Deutsch a solid grounding in account management and the care and feeding of clients. And Mr. Deutsch, a voluble, loquacious man who is occasionally accused of over-enthusiastic self-promotion, gave Mr. Dworin the creative spark to fire up his efforts to attract clients." Over the next two years the combination of Deutsch and Dworin added a dozen new clients with $200 million in billings, including the Hardees fast food chain, Prudential Securities, Lens Crafters, and Tanqueray Gin. To acknowledge the importance of Dworin, who held a 25 percent stake, the agency changed its name to Deutsch/Dworin in November 1992.

In 1992 Donny Deutsch gained even more attention when Bill Clinton's presidential campaign selected him as one of a handful of advertising executives to help guide its advertising strategy. After Clinton won, Donny Deutsch was accused of attempting to reap an undue share of the credit, a charge that fed into his reputation as brash and self-centered. Nevertheless, the association with a winner was good for the agency, which continued to gain momentum in 1993. Early in 1994, however, Dworin announced he was leaving the agency, following two months of confidential talks with Deutsch. Likening their partnership to a marriage, the two men explained that they had grown apart and rather than let their strained relationship hurt the agency they agreed to a separation in which Deutsch would repurchase Dworin's 25 percent of the business. Dworin also agreed not to take any clients with him or talk further about his reasons for leaving. As one unnamed individual who knew both men told the *Wall Street Journal,* "Steve probably wanted more in terms of money, power and recognition than Donny was willing to give. It is, in the end, the Deutsch candy store."

Deutsch took on the title of chief executive officer and changed the agency's name back to Deutsch, Inc. He expressed confidence that the business would continue to grow. He even talked about the possibility of using his in-house production facilities to produce television programming, including a real-life *Seinfeld* set in a diner located in the neighborhood. Although nothing came of these plans, Deutsch's predilection for reality-based television proved to be well ahead of the curve. Deutsch did break new ground in 1994 when one of its Ikea ads featured two gay men, the first time a major television commercial broached the subject of homosexuality.

As Deutsch predicted, the business continued to grow despite the loss of Dworin. In 1995 Deutsch Inc. became the first midsized ad agency to help clients take advantage of new media

Key Dates:

1969: David Deutsch Associates is established.
1983: Donny Deutsch joins father's firm.
1986: Donny Deutsch is named creative director.
1989: Donny Deutsch succeeds father, renames company Deutsch, Inc.
1991: Steve Dworin, a senior vice-president at J. Walter Thompson, joins company.
1992: Agency name is changed to Deutsch/Dworin.
1994: Dworin leaves agency and name reverts to Deutsch, Inc.
1998: Agency lands $250 million Mitsubishi account.
2000: Deutsch, Inc. is sold to Interpublic Group.

by setting up Interactive Deutsch, later renamed iDeutsch. The company also opened a southern California office in Santa Monica, territory that many New York agencies had tried to crack but failed. What Deutsch did not have was an automotive client, which in many respects was the ultimate proof than an ad agency had become a major player. Car makers spent hundreds of millions of dollars on advertising each year; in the case of General Motors annual billings were in the $2 billion range. Deutsch spent considerable time and money, some $400,000, trying to land the Volkswagen $110 million North American account in 1994. Deutsch was one of a handful of agencies included in the final review process for VW, which had suffered through 15 lackluster years. Deutsch was confident about its presentation but in the end was not hired. The decision was a bitter pill to swallow for both Donny Deutsch and his team.

In the next couple of years the agency would pitch but fail to win the accounts for Mazda and Acura. Deutsch even created a direct marketing unit in order to bolster its chances. Despite being frustrated with landing an automaker, Deutsch continued to grow rapidly. Its billings increased in 1997 by 32 percent over the previous year, reaching $500 million. The West Coast office was well established, signing accounts worth almost $100 million, including Bank of America and retailer Old Navy. To reward his seven top executives, Deutsch gave out equity stakes in the agency, although he still retained approximately 85 percent. In 1998 the agency opened a Chicago office to service area clients. It also moved into new Manhattan offices in order to accommodate its growing staff.

Winning the Mitsubishi Account: 1998

In December 1998 Deutsch finally secured a major auto client, the $250 million Mitsubishi Motor Sales of America account. Deutsch's earlier, unfavorable reference to Mitsubishi in one of its ads was now all but forgotten. First the agency won the contract to represent the 41 regional dealer associations, followed by the campaign to introduce the redesigned Galant sedan. Finally, it consolidated the entire account. It was a special moment for Donny Deutsch, one he compared to a sports team that finally won a championship. Nevertheless, he still had his share of critics, whose motives he was more willing than ever to attribute to simple envy. What was not open to debate were the major accounts that the agency was winning,

now totaling well over $800 million in billings. Because Deutsch was privately held, financial details on the company were slight, but it was reported that the agency generated some $86 million in profits for 1998. To cap the run of success, Deutsch was honored as the agency of the year by both *Adweek* and *Advertising Age*.

In 1999 Deutsch reached $1 billion in clients' billables, while income topped $133 million. The agency pitched and won a host of new clients, including Domino's, Pfizer, Tommy Hilfiger, Brinks Home Security, and SunAmerica. Mitsubishi, in the meantime, enjoyed a 37 percent surge in sales, a large part of which its management attributed to Deutsch's ad campaign. The agency opened a Boston office, headed by two area executives it lured away from New England's largest ad agency, Arnold Communications. Deutsch also formed a joint venture agency with Rush Communications, controlled by Russell Simmons who ran a number of businesses that catered to urban youth, including Def Jam Recordings and Phat Farm Fashions. The new agency, called dRush, looked to design campaigns for young consumers between the ages of eight and 17. Donny Deutsch was also traveling to London to actively pursue the possibility of opening an office there. In addition, he was talking about opening other branches in Asia and South America.

Deutsch was now the largest U.S. independent ad agency. Clearly Donny Deutsch was looking to expand globally to keep pace with major clients such as Mitsubishi, but the resources required were massive. For some time he had been approached by suitors, and according to press accounts had been offered as much as $175 million for the business. Finally in December 2000 he agreed to sell the agency to the Interpublic Group in a stock deal worth in the neighborhood of $250 million, in what most knowledgeable observers considered an excellent deal for Donny Deutsch who stood to become the largest single Interpublic stockholder in the years to come. Although he did not gain a seat on Interpublic's board, he remained CEO at Deutsch and was essentially granted autonomy. "It's the right time with the right partners," he told the *New York Times*, "This was a deeply thought-out decision because we've been independent our whole life. But it's the natural next step, next challenge, next level for us." For Interpublic the deal made it the world's largest advertising company. As Deutsch began its new existence in 2001, only time would tell how the agency that prided itself on being a maverick would react to a corporate parent looking over its shoulder. Moreover, would it continue to grow and reach new levels of success, or might it actually lose the spark that made it such a desirable acquisition in the first place?

Principal Competitors

Bcom3 Group, Inc.; Chisholm-Mingo Group; Grey Global; Omnicom Group; Publicis S.A.; UniWorld Group; WPP Group plc.

Further Reading

David, Wendy, and Laura Q. Hughes, "Deutsch Now Part of Interpublic Empire," *Advertising Age,* December 4, 2000, p. 1.

Elliott, Stuart, "A Long Courtship Ends As Deutsch, the Last of the Big Independents, Says Yes to Interpublic," *New York Times,* December 4, 2000, p. C5.

——, "Deutsch, the Hot Midsized Shop, Lands a Trophy National Assignment That Has Competitors Talking," *New York Times,* December 4, 1998, p. C2.

——, "Portrait of an Adman on a Hot Streak," *New York Times,* October 14, 1992, p. C1.

——, "With Spirit Gone, Ad Partners Split" *New York Times,* February 17, 1994, p. D1.

Foltz, Kim, "At This Ad Agency, Creative Lunacy Reigns," *New York Times Current Events Edition,* February 16, 1992, p. 332.

Miller, Annetta, and Seema Nayyar, "Captain Outrageous," *Newsweek,* October 31, 1994, p. 41.

O'Connell, Vanessa, "Interpublic Agrees to Buy Deutsch in Stock Deal," *Wall Street Journal,* December 1, 2000, p. B6.

Petrecca, Laura, "Deutsch Raises the Bar to Earn Agency of the Year Honor," *Advertising Age,* January 25, 1999, p. S1.

Wells, Melanie, "Bad Boy Makes Good," *Forbes,* November 29, 1999, p. 100.

—Ed Dinger

Dexia Group

7 à 11 quai Andre Citroën
BP 1002
F-75901 Paris Cedex 15
France
Telephone: (+33) 143-92-77-77
Fax: (+33) 143-92-70-00
Web site: http://www.dexia.com

Public Company
Incorporated: 1996
Employees: 17,112
Total Assets: EUR 257 billion (2000)
Stock Exchanges: Euronext Paris Brussels Luxembourg
Ticker Symbol: DX
NAIC: 551111 Offices of Bank Holding Companies;
523110 Investment Banking and Securities Dealing;
522120 Savings Institutions; 522210 Credit Card
Issuing; 522110 Commercial Banking; 522293
International Trade Financing

Dexia Group is one of the first and largest pan-European banks and a fast-growing bank with global ambitions. With headquarters in Brussels, Dexia is the product of a 1996 merger between that country's Crédit Communal de Belgique (CCB, also known as Gemeentebank) and Crédit Local de France; and includes Banque Internationale de Luxembourg (BIL), the operations of Dutch investment banks Kemper and Labouchere, Belgium's Artesia, and, since August 2000, the United States' Financial Security Assurance (FSA). Dexia is also reportedly negotiating a merger agreement with a major Japanese bank in order to expand its presence in the Asian market. One of Europe's 20 largest banks, Dexia has made a particular specialty of municipal lending, holding 90 percent of the Belgium market and 42 percent of the French market—along with a leading share of the U.S. market through FSA—to become the largest municipal lender in Europe. The company also offers retail financial services in the Benelux market, notably through CCB's 1,000-strong branch network, and investment management services, such as private banking, asset management and investment fund administration. This latter division also includes Dexia's shareholding in online banking venture Zebank. Dexia, quoted on the Euronext Paris, Brussels, and Luxembourg stock exchanges, is led by CEO Pierre Richard and Chairman François Narmon. The company's assets totaled more than EUR 257 billion in 2000, generating a net banking income of EUR 3.76 billion.

Funding European Infrastructure in the 19th Century

Dexia traces its history back to the early 19th century through founding banks Crédit Communal de Belgique (CCB) and especially Crédit Local de France (CLF). The French municipal lending institution had been created as part of the Caisse des Dépôts et Consignations (CDC). The CDC had been formed in 1816, with the restoration of the French monarchy and the need to provide funding and financial management assistance for institutions and government bodies. Part of the CDC's mandate was to manage retirement funds for France's body of civil servants. The CDC also acted as holder of escrow accounts.

The CDC began its municipal lending activity in 1822, when it provided an equity loan to the Port of Dunkerque. In 1837, the CDC was given a new national stature when France's parliament decided to join the Caisse d'Epargne (savings bank), which had been created in 1818, to the CDC. By then, the Caisse d'Epargne had grown to a network of more than 100 branches across France. With access to these funds, the CDC's role as funding agency for France's infrastructure projects began in earnest. The CDC was to play an important part in financing many of the country's large-scale projects, such as the construction of the Midi, Orléans, Somme, and Loing canals, the building of the country's dense system of roadways, as well as its railway, public utility, telephone, and water systems.

Starting in the 1850s, the CDC was given charge of the country's first retirement pension fund. In 1878, the CDC was mandated to provide funding for the expansion of the French national public school system, particularly in financing the construction of primary schools, and later junior high and high schools, throughout the country's smaller towns and villages.

By the end of the century, the CDC was also playing an active
role in addressing France's chronically inadequate housing supply, participating in the creation of the Société Française
d'Habitation à Bon Marché (SFHBM, or French Low-Priced
Housing Society). Laws promulgated in 1912, which created
the first French low-cost housing projects, called HLMs, mandated the CDC as the lending authority for all HLM developments. The CDC's municipal lending wing finished the 19th
century under the title of Caisse d'Equipement des Collectivités
Locales, before becoming Crédit Local de France.

In Belgium, a banking body similar to CDC had been
founded in 1860. That bank, called Crédit Communal de
Belgique (CCB, and known as Gemeentebank in the Flemish-
speaking areas of Beligum) came into being as an interest-
paying savings bank that used its customers' savings in order to
provide loans to local governments for their infrastructure and
other projects. The CCB gained still more prominence after
World War I, as communities turned to the bank to help in the
rebuilding effort. Similar assistance was needed following
World War II. Soon after the end of that war, the CCB began
opening branch offices, expanding beyond public works funding into private and corporate banking activities. By the end of
the 20th century, the CCB operated more than 1,000 branch
offices. Like the CDC, the CCB remained government-owned
before being privatized in the mid-1990s.

Another important member of the future Dexia family was
formed in 1856, with the creation of the Banque International à
Luxembourg (BIL). One of the first of the young duchy's banks,
and given the right to issue banknotes, the BIL initially turned
its investment activities to Germany—the two countries had
long been united in the Zollverein custom union, while Luxembourg shared the German mark as its own currency. Yet the
collapse of the German economy following World War I left
BIL reeling as well. In 1918, Luxembourg left the Zollverein in
favor of a new customs treaty with Belgium—and later formed
the Benelux economic unit with the Netherlands. BIL played a
prominent role in the development of Luxembourg as a financial capital, and helped in establishing the Luxembourg stock
exchange in 1929.

Nazi occupation of Luxembourg ended BIL's activity for the
duration. Following the war, BIL became one of the engines for
the development of Luxembourg's high-powered economy,
backing the formation of a number of notable Luxembourg
businesses, such as Luxair in 1948, Société Electrique de l'Our
in 1951, and the CLT in 1955. In 1977, BIL grew with the
acquisition of Banque Lambert Luxembourg; BIL now had a

market capitalization of more than LuxFr 1 billion. By the early
1980s, BIL acquired new majority owners, in the form of Belgium's Banque Lambert and Pargesa.

Creating a European Superbank for the 21st Century

The approach of full European economic union—beginning
with the Maastricht treaty of 1992 and culminating with the
launch of the euro at the end of the decade—signaled the start of
a new era of European banking. The CCB's own international
expansion began in 1990, when the company set up the Cregem
International Bank in Luxembourg, specializing in assets management. A year later, CCB began buying up a position in BIL,
taking full control in 1999.

In France, meanwhile, the CDC had split into two parts,
spinning off its municipal lending body as Crédit Local de
France (CLF) in 1987. CLF started independent activity as a
small bank, with just 200 employees and revenues of just FFr
3.5 billion per year (then worth less than $500 million). Placed
at the head of the CLF, however, was Pierre Richard, who led
the government-owned bank into the private arena in 1993, and
then became the architect of the bank's growth.

Already in 1993, Pierre Richard and his counterpart at CCB,
François Narmon, had begun discussing the possibility of cross-
border banking mergers in the new Europe. As yet no legislation had been provided to create such mergers, however, and
any possible unions were fraught with difficulties, ranging from
distinct domestic cultures to differing tax and accounting laws.
The CCB began looking for a partner within Belgium.

Nonetheless, Pierre Richard continued to press discussions
linking the CLF and the CCB. A merger was seen as particularly
attractive given that CCB had captured 90 percent of Belgium's
municipal lending market, while CLF accounted for more than
40 percent of that market in France. As Richard told *Time
International:* ''We were convinced that with the creation of the
euro zone, European business conditions would be turned upside down and that it would be necessary for a company to have
a European vision and identity.''

Narmon came to agree with Richard's assessment of the
European banking industry's future. In 1996, the two companies announced the formation of a new company as an umbrella
for their merger. Yet because of the difficulties in creating a
''European'' company, the two banks maintained their domestic operations, linking through a complex shareholding exchange. The bridging name became Dexia, while the company
continued to operate under two holding companies, Dexia Belgium and Dexia France—with each company maintaining its
former headquarters, management, and staff. Richard was
named Dexia's CEO, while Narmon became chairman.

Starting out, the new company showed its intention of becoming one of Europe's superbanks, while continuing to focus
on its specialty areas of municipal lending, private banking, and
assets management, the latter led especially through BIL, which
shortly became a full subsidiary, changing its name to Dexia
Banque de Luxembourg. Following a quickly aborted plan to
take over French bank CIL, Dexia began a series of acquisitions
to boost its position in other EC member countries.

<table>
<tr><td colspan="2">Key Dates:</td></tr>
<tr><td>1816:</td><td>Caisse des Dépôts et Consignations (CDC) is formed.</td></tr>
<tr><td>1818:</td><td>Caisse d'Epargne is created.</td></tr>
<tr><td>1837:</td><td>CDC takes over Caisse d'Epargne and assumes role as funding agency for France's major infrastructure projects.</td></tr>
<tr><td>1856:</td><td>Banque Internationale de Luxembourg (BIL) is launched.</td></tr>
<tr><td>1860:</td><td>Crédit Communal de Belgique (CCB, or Gemeentebank) is formed.</td></tr>
<tr><td>1987:</td><td>CDC spins off its municipal lending body, Crédit Local de France (CLF).</td></tr>
<tr><td>1990:</td><td>CCB creates Cregem International Bank.</td></tr>
<tr><td>1991:</td><td>CCB acquires stake in BIL.</td></tr>
<tr><td>1993:</td><td>CLF becomes private company.</td></tr>
<tr><td>1996:</td><td>CCB and CLF announce merger to form dual Dexia companies.</td></tr>
<tr><td>1997:</td><td>Dexia acquires 40 percent of Crediop (Italy).</td></tr>
<tr><td>1998:</td><td>Company raises Crediop stake to 60 percent.</td></tr>
<tr><td>1999:</td><td>Dexia becomes a single company, acquires full control of BIL.</td></tr>
</table>

The first of these was the acquisition of 40 percent of Italy's Crediop, a municipal lending and public project financing specialist, made in 1997. A year later, Dexia took majority control of that bank when it acquired 20 percent more from San Paolo-IMI, paying more than $1 billion. At the same time, Dexia acquired 55 percent of France's Ifax, a insurance provider to local governments. In 1999, the bank increased its insurance activity again, acquiring Elvia Assurances, based in Belgium.

The year 1999 marked the turning point for Dexia. In October, the bank announced a unification plan by which Dexia Belgium would acquire Dexia France's shares. Two months later, the bank announced the formation of a single holding company for all of the bank's operations, called Dexia, with headquarters in Brussels and listings on the Brussels, Luxembourg, and Paris stock exchanges. By the end of that year, Dexia's revenues had topped the FFr 20 billion mark.

Dexia continued to show an aggressive appetite for acquisitions. In March 2000 the company announced two new purchases. Paying nearly EUR 900 million, Dexia acquired Labouchere, a private banking and assets management specialist based in the Netherlands and formerly owned by Aegon NV. At the same time, Dexia implanted itself in the United States, paying $2.6 billion to acquire Financial Security Assurance (FSA), the leading municipal lending and public projects financing specialist to that market.

A capital increase in June 2000, raising EUR 2.3 billion, enabled Dexia to continue its acquisition drive into the new century. In March 2001, the company paid EUR 3.2 billion for Belgian banker Artesia Banking Corp. At the same time, the company launched a EUR 1.05 billion cash offer for the Netherlands' merchant bank Kempen, which was then grouped under Dexia's Labouchere subsidiary. The company also bought a stake—including control of two-thirds of voting rights—in Tel Aviv bank Otzar Hashilton Hamekomi, and then prepared to make a new acquisition in the Czech Republic.

By mid-2001, Dexia was prepared to take a breather, having by then spent more than EUR 9 billion acquiring a major position in the European banking industry—and a leading spot in its municipal lending niche. Yet Dexia was far from finished with its expansion, setting its sights on further development throughout Europe, particularly in the United Kingdom. Dexia also acknowledged that it was in talks with a Japanese bank in order to establish its operations in that important financial market. Meanwhile, the bank had launched itself onto the Internet, acquiring a strong interest in online bank Zebank. In just a few years, Dexia had raised itself to the status of superbank—and one of a few truly European companies.

Principal Subsidiaries

Assureco; AUSBIL Partners (Australia); Banque Internationale a Luxembourg; CLF Lease Services; Crédit Associatif; Crédit Communal de Belgique; Crédit Local de France; Dexia Asset Management Luxembourg; Dexia Banco Local (Spain); Dexia Banque Privee France; Dexia Hypothekenbank Berlin; Dexia Kommunbank (Sweden); Dexia Municipal Bank (U.K.); Dexia Project & Public Finance International Bank; Dexia Belgium; Dexia France; Editions Local de France; Experta-BIL (Switzerland); Financial Security Assurance Holdings (U.S.A.); Flobail; Floral; Labouchere (Netherlands); Mega (Belgium); Mega Life (Belgium); Mega Life Lux (Luxembourg); Quadra Invest (Belgium); Rekord (Germany); Societé Monegasque de Banque Privee (Monaco).

Principal Competitors

ABN AMRO Holding N.V.; AXA; Banca Nazionale del Lavoro S.p.A.; BNP Paribas Group; Crédit Commercial de France SA; Crédit Lyonnais; Credit Suisse Group; Caisse Nationale de Crédit Agricole; DePfa Deutsche Pfandbrief Bank AG; Deutsche Bank AG; IntesaBci S.p.A.; KBC Bank and Insurance Holding Company NV; Natexis Banques Populaires; UniCredito Italiano S.p.A.

Further Reading

Adler, Leslie, "Dexia to Merge Parent Companies," *Reuters*, September 19, 1999.

Brafman, Nathalie, "Pierre Richard: le banquier de choc qu'on n'attendait pas," *L'Expansion*, April 27, 2000.

Mallet, Victor, and Raphael Minder, "Dexia Looks to Expand Outside Europe," *Financial Times*, June 20, 2001.

Patton, Susannah, "Making the Euro Work: Banking on Change, Dexia Forges a New Identity As a Truly European Company," *Time International*, December 10, 1998, p. 154.

—M. L. Cohen

Discovery Communications, Inc.

7700 Wisconsin Avenue
Bethesda, Maryland 20814
U.S.A.
Telephone: (301) 986-0444
Toll Free: (877) 394-0266
Fax: (301) 771-4064
Web site: http://www.discovery.com

Private Company
Incorporated: 1982 as Cable Educational Network, Inc.
Employees: 3,500
Sales: $1.73 billion (2000)
NAIC: 51321 Cable Networks; 45112 Hobby, Toy, and
    Game Stores; 511210 Software Publishers; 51212
    Motion Picture and Video Distribution; 511130 Book
    Publishers

Discovery Communications, Inc. (DCI) is a leading player in the global cable television market. The company operates 33 channels worldwide including the Discovery Channel, Animal Planet, The Learning Channel, Discovery Health, and the Travel Channel. Discovery Communications also sells videos, CD-ROMs, magazines, and books; runs web sites; and operates 165 retail stores. The privately held company is owned by a group consisting of Liberty Media Corporation (formerly a unit of Tele-Communications, Inc.), Advance/Newhouse Communications, Cox Cable Communications, Inc., and company founder and CEO John Hendricks.

Beginnings

The company known as Discovery Communications, Inc. traces its roots to 1982, when a University of Alabama history graduate named John Hendricks founded the Cable Educational Network, Inc. in Maryland. The new company's goal was to help present informational and documentary programming on television. Hendricks, a West Virginia native, had earlier founded a consulting firm that assisted producers of educational videos with marketing. In 1985, after raising $5 million,

Hendricks's small company launched a new cable television network, which was dubbed the Discovery Channel. Discovery, which initially broadcast a variety of licensed documentaries but no original programming, was available in only 156,000 households.

The new channel's revenues were small, and within six months Hendricks owed $1 million to the British Broadcasting Corporation (BBC) but had only $5,000 in the bank. Desperate for funding, he sought out new investors. Although he was turned down by the large entertainment companies he approached, he was able to convince a group of cable operators led by Tele-Communications, Inc. (TCI), Cox Cable Communications, Inc., and Newhouse Broadcasting Corp. to take a flyer on the network, retaining ownership of 1.4 percent for himself. TCI (whose stake later was transferred to Liberty Media) owned 49 percent, with Newhouse (later known as Advance/Newhouse) and Cox holding a quarter each. The company now was able to pay its creditors, and the new investors also boosted Discovery's audience base when they added the channel to their systems.

By its first anniversary in June 1986, Discovery counted seven million subscribers. Over the next several years the company broadened its range of programming, with events such as the February 1987 broadcast of 66 hours of live Russian television, gaining the company wider media interest. Discovery also lengthened its schedule to 18 hours per day from 12 during the year.

By 1988 Discovery's growing subscriber base had hit 32 million. The following year saw the company offer its first overseas cable service, with some 200,000 subscribers in the United Kingdom and Scandinavia receiving Discovery Channel Europe. In addition, 1989 was the year Discovery commissioned its first original programming, having heretofore relied exclusively on material from outside sources, among them the BBC. One new show, "Assignment Discovery," was a daily, one-hour program designed to be used in school classrooms. In 1990 Discovery expanded its overseas operations to Israel and began to sell videos through the newly created Discovery Interactive Library unit. The company, which had employed only 19 when the channel first went on the air, now had a staff of more than 250.

1991 Acquisition of The Learning Channel

In June 1991 the company purchased The Learning Channel (TLC) for $30 million. TLC had 15.2 million subscribers at the time of the acquisition, but was struggling financially. In October a new programming schedule for TLC was announced, replacing its lineup of business and career information, self-help, and hobby programs with 18 hours of educational and entertainment programming aimed at an upscale adult audience. The following spring a six-hour block of children's programming was added. October 1991 also saw the company renamed Discovery Communications, Inc. (DCI).

The future of cable was expected to encompass as many as 500 channels, and John Hendricks began giving thought to ways to deal with so many options. Announced in late 1992, Your Choice TV, Inc. was a new subsidiary that offered a prototype cable remote control device that could organize the hundreds of choices into 11 thematic categories for ease of use. Over the next several years the Your Choice efforts also began to focus on creating a time-shifting service through which unused channels would broadcast paid repeats of selected programs for individual viewers. Experiments were carried out on eight cable systems with some success, but the concept faced great logistical hurdles, primarily the problem of reaching agreements with the numerous content providers.

In the fall of 1993 DCI released its first CD-ROM, ''In the Company of Whales,'' which was based on the hugely popular documentary of the same name shown on the Discovery Channel. Discovery now was producing more original programming than ever before, though the company did not have its own production company, but rather contracted with outside firms for all of its shows. Popular offerings around this time included specials marking the 50th anniversary of the Normandy D-Day invasion and the 25th anniversary of the resignation of Richard Nixon. The network was available in 62 million homes by 1994, or 98 percent of U.S. households with cable TV. The Learning Channel also had doubled its own subscriber base to 30 million homes.

During 1994 the Federal Communications Commission relaxed its regulations for cable broadcasters, allowing them to add more channels and charge more for their services. DCI responded by announcing that it would form four new channels in 1995, including ones on nature, science, history, and a home improvement/cooking combination. The barrier to new cable channels was high, however, and a successful launch could require an investment of $200 million or more in cable system fees to get enough subscribers to make the service pay off.

Expansion into Retail in the Mid-1990s

In 1995 DCI spent $10 million to buy the coincidentally named Discovery Store Inc. chain of 11 Texas and southeastern U.S. educational and learning product stores. DCI already had begun selling its own licensed items through such stores as PetsMart and The Nature Company, and the deal was seen as a good fit with its expansion into marketing. Plans soon were laid to add more locations to the chain. DCI also was increasing its advertising, which featured the tag line, ''Explore Your World.'' By 1995 $20 million was being budgeted annually. In some cases DCI used highly targeted campaigns, such as one for a special on submarines that was promoted through U.S. military publications. When the program aired, it received the highest prime-time ratings to date for the Discovery Channel.

The company's brand-building strategy was working well, as was shown in a 1995 study by Total Research Corp., which ranked Discovery second only to the National Geographic Society in consumer perception of brand quality. The company finished ahead of such major names as AT&T, IBM, and the *Wall Street Journal* in the process. DCI also launched a web site during 1995, earmarking $10 million for the project. The result was an award-winning combination of original articles, video and sound clips, and more. Earlier, DCI had begun publishing a magazine that also complemented its programming.

During the mid-1990s DCI began to focus increasingly on overseas expansion. In 1994 the company launched spinoff channels in Asia, Latin America, and the Middle East, followed in 1995 by others in Canada, India, and Australia/New Zealand. More were added later in Italy, Africa, Brazil, Germany, Japan, and Turkey. Channels ultimately would be available in 150 countries. Dubbing the company's documentary and informational programs into foreign languages was typically much less expensive, and less complicated, than creating foreign versions of dramatic material, and much of the subject matter was universal, appealing equally well to viewers throughout the world. During this period DCI also announced a move into feature film production, forming a new subsidiary for this purpose that was expected to issue one or two titles per year, including some shot in the large-format Imax process.

In February 1996 DCI announced a joint venture with one of its investors, Tele-Communications, Inc. The new company, ETC w/TCI, would offer seven hours of commercial-free cable programming directly to schools, including some material taken from the Discovery and Learning Channels. Former U.S. Congressman Tony Coelho was named chairman and CEO. The new company, which initially targeted some 700 large schools nationwide, planned to charge $265 a year per student for the service. The fee also would cover installation of the necessary hardware and software, as well as training on its use.

A short time after this, DCI broadened its retail presence with the $40 million acquisition of The Nature Company's chain of 110 stores in 34 states. Over time the stores were to be rebranded as Discovery Channel Stores. The move was in line with what other large media companies such as Disney and Warner Brothers were attempting—operating chains of stores that served to bolster brand identity while also trading on public familiarity with the name. A new 25,000-square-foot flagship superstore was soon announced for the Washington, D.C., area, near DCI's Bethesda, Maryland headquarters. Typical stores in the chain were smaller, falling in the range of 3,000 to 5,000 square feet.

Key Dates:

1982: John Hendricks founds Cable Educational Network, Inc.

1985: Discovery Channel debuts on cable television with 156,000 subscribers.

1986: Cable system operators buy into the company; subscribers top seven million.

1989: Discovery Channel Europe is launched.

1990: Line of home videos is introduced.

1991: Learning Channel is purchased; company name is changed to Discovery Communications.

1993: Company begins marketing CD-ROMs based on its television programs.

1994: International expansion widens to Asia, Africa, Latin America, and the Middle East.

1995: A $10 million web site is launched featuring original news content and more.

1996: Two retail chains, Discovery Stores and Nature Company, are purchased.

1997: Company buys 70 percent of the Travel Channel, later acquiring the remainder.

1998: Animal Planet is launched as part of a deal with the BBC; Eye on People channel is bought.

1999: Discovery Health Channel is launched as part of new Health Media division.

2000: Internet operations are folded into Discovery.com; People channel is shuttered.

In October 1996 two other major steps were taken by DCI. One was a new partnership with the British Broadcasting Corporation to produce a BBC-branded cable channel in the United States. BBC America would feature the respected dramatic and performing arts programming for which the British company was known, with DCI handling the logistics and also contributing some of the content. DCI anticipated spending more than $500 million over a five-year period on the deal, which would possibly include other cable channels and the programming necessary to flesh them out. DCI also was given ''first look'' options on new BBC programming, putting the company ahead of such competitors as the Arts & Entertainment and Public Broadcasting networks.

Creation of Animal Planet in the Mid-1990s

At the same time the company launched Animal Planet, a new cable channel focusing on both domestic and wild animals, which was 20 percent owned by the BBC. After its launch the channel's audience grew quickly, its appeal cutting across age and ethnic lines. Part of the growth also was due to fees DCI paid cable companies to add Animal Planet to their lineups. DCI simultaneously announced the creation of four digital broadcast channels, which were available to only a limited number of viewers. The channels, Discovery Home & Leisure, Discovery Kids, Discovery Science, and Discovery Civilization, were expected to become more widely seen when digital broadcasting took hold as a popular medium. In the meantime the new channels, produced with smaller budgets than the company's primary ones, served as useful trial balloons to test the viability of new concepts.

In September 1997 Discovery announced that it would buy 70 percent of the Travel Channel from Paxson Communications for $20 million. The Travel Channel had 20.8 million subscribers and presented a mix of travel tips and vacation site profiles. Discovery soon began providing programming and logistical support for the channel. Later, in February 1999, DCI purchased the remaining 30 percent of the operation.

The company's flagship store opened in February 1998, six months late and $10 million over budget. The now 30,000-square-foot store featured a television studio, an 82-seat theater, a T-Rex skeleton, and the nose of a World War II era B-25 bomber that customers could climb into. Products offered for sale ranged from DCI's full line of videos to games, telescopes, fossils, and even an ice-age bear skeleton priced at $75,000.

During early 1998 DCI also attempted to purchase the low-rated Court TV cable channel from its owners, a consortium led by Time Warner. The $350 million deal was nixed by Time Warner shareholder and Vice-Chairman Ted Turner, however, reportedly because he feared DCI might convert Court TV into a concept that would compete with one of his own channels. In December DCI completed another acquisition attempt and bought CBS's struggling Eye on People channel, after initially planning to purchase only 50 percent of it. Eye on People (later changed to Discovery People) had only 11 million subscribers and was losing money for its parent company. DCI planned to continue to air the channel's mix of celebrity news and profiles, which included some content provided by CBS. During the year DCI also added two channels to its digital broadcasting lineup, Discovery Wings and the Discovery Health Channel. A Spanish-language digital channel was being offered by this time as well.

Entering the Field of Health in the Late 1990s

At year's end DCI formed a new subsidiary, Discovery Health Media, Inc., a multimedia venture that was intended to make the company a leader in the field of health and medical information. More than $300 million was allocated for the start-up, which was to include a web site that offered health news and information. The following summer digital channel Discovery Health was upgraded to regular cable status as part of the initiative.

The late 1990s also saw DCI lay plans to move its operations from Bethesda to Silver Spring, Maryland, by 2003. The company would occupy three buildings, two of which were to be newly constructed. Several other high-profile organizations soon followed suit and prepared to move to the once blighted Silver Spring. One was the American Film Institute, which would open a facility there and also co-produce a documentary film festival with DCI.

In November 1999 the company shut down its themed entertainment unit as a cost-cutting measure. The closing would mean the end of Discovery Channel Pictures, which had made Imax films including *Africa's Elephant Kingdom,* as well as the ''Eco Challenge'' made-for-TV sports event. At the same time DCI invested in Petstore.com, an online pet supply and information site that was expected to be used to cross-promote Animal Planet. DCI subsequently reshuffled its online operations and placed its web companies in a new subsidiary, Discovery.com, Inc., which was reportedly on the verge of being spun off to investors. DCI head John Hendricks also announced that he was helping to launch a new women's soccer league, which would field eight newly formed teams in 2001.

The summer of 2000 saw Discovery.com's IPO plans shelved, with $500 million in new financing sought through private investors. The move followed a downturn in investor confidence in the potential of the Web as a profit-making entity. In November the company laid off 40 percent of Discovery.com's staff, as profitability for the venture appeared more and more elusive. DCI's web site was redesigned to focus on the core television properties, with news stories and other original content reduced. Later in the year DCI also scaled back its plans for the Silver Spring facilities, canceling construction of one of the new buildings. The company had by this time quietly abandoned its Eye on People and Your Choice TV ventures, as well.

In early 2001 a potential challenge to DCI's dominance of the cable documentary market was launched by the National Geographic Society with the backing of Fox Cable Networks. DCI's Hendricks dismissed the start-up as too little, too late, noting that it would cost at least $250 million to get a comparable subscriber base to meet Discovery on its own turf. An Equitrend consumer survey recently had ranked Discovery as the number one most trusted brand name, eclipsing National Geographic's hold on the top spot. National Geographic went on the air with ten million subscribers, with plans over the next several years to reach 28 million—a figure still far below Discovery Channel's 81.2 million, The Learning Channel's 77.3 million, or Animal Planet's 66.9 million. Meanwhile, Discovery specials *Raising the Mammoth* and *Walking with Dinosaurs* set back-to-back records for cable documentaries with 10.1 million and 10.7 million viewers, respectively.

Nearing its 20th year in business, Discovery Communications, Inc. had assembled a formidable multimedia empire that was still growing. Firmly established on cable television, the company's well-regarded brand name was helping drive its moves into digital cable, cyberspace, and retail sales. Although not yet profitable, these operations positioned DCI well for future developments in the rapidly evolving media world of the 21st century.

Principal Subsidiaries

Discovery Networks U.S.; Discovery Networks International; Discovery Enterprises Worldwide; Discovery Health Media.

Principal Competitors

AOL Time Warner, Inc.; Walt Disney Company; The Corporation for Public Broadcasting; Viacom, Inc.; A&E Television Networks; Fox Entertainment Group, Inc.; National Geographic Society.

Further Reading

Breznick, Alan, "Discovery Readies New Health Net," *Cable World*, December 21, 1998, p. 1.

Chandrasekaran, Rajiv, "A Top-Dollar Web Service Awaits Returns," *Washington Post*, November 4, 1996, p. F19.

Dawtrey, Adam, "BBC, Discovery in Fact Pact," *Variety*, March 23, 1998, p. 38.

Farhi, Paul, "Big Game Hunting: Geographic Takes on Discovery in the Nonfiction-TV Market," *Washington Post*, December 14, 1998, p. F13.

——, "For the Shows You Wish You Hadn't Missed ... Discovery Communications Explores a Personalized Service in Your Choice TV," *Washington Post*, June 19, 1995, p. F8.

Fry, Andy, "Discovery at 15: When the Beeb Lends a Hand," *Variety*, June 5, 2000, p. 36.

Gately, Gary, "Putting Discovery Channel on Map," *Baltimore Sun*, September 29, 1995, p. 1C.

Grove, Christopher, "Hendricks Leads Global Discovery Mission," *Variety*, November 20, 2000, p. 33.

Grove, Christopher, and Stephanie Argy, "Discovery at 15: Fight for Online Shelf Space, Specialty Focus High on Broadband Priorities," *Variety*, June 5, 2000, p. 36.

Guider, Elizabeth, "Spotlight—Mipcom '97 John Hendricks," *Variety*, September 22, 1997, p. M29.

Johnson, Carrie, and John Irwin, "Discovery.com Lays Off 40% of Its Staff: Company to Focus on TV Operations," *Washington Post*, November 14, 2000, p. E1.

Kaplan, Peter, "John Hendricks: Cable Pioneer Discovers Value of Putting Substance over Style," *Washington Times*, December 23, 1996, p. 2.

——, "New TV Behemoth BBC, Discovery to Co-create a Cable Channel," *Washington Times*, September 28, 1996, p. C11.

Lee, Melissa, "Discovery Communications Looks to New Lands, Interactive Media," *Washington Post*, September 5, 1994, p. F9.

Marriott, Anne, "A Store to Explore—Discovery Channels into the World of Retail," *Washington Times*, February 26, 1998, p. B7.

Moss, Linda, "Not So Fast, Mel," *Cable World*, April 9, 2001, p. 6.

Noguchi, Yuki, "Discovery.com Drops IPO Plan; Unit to Finance Expansion Privately," *Washington Post*, July 22, 2000, p. E1.

Robichaux, Mark, "Discovery Communications Is Jumping into Jungle of Nationwide Retailing," *Wall Street Journal*, May 16, 1995, p. B9.

Sentementes, Gus G., "500 Million Subscribers Bursting: Discovery Communications, the Cable Programmer, Is Moving to Silver Spring to Accommodate Its Growth," *Baltimore Sun*, February 25, 2001, p. 1D.

Swibel, Matthew, "Curtain Falls on Discovery Unit," *Washington Business Journal*, November 19, 1999, p. 1.

Twomey, Steve, "Network's Roots May Help Town Bloom," *Washington Post*, February 14, 2000, p. A1.

—Frank Uhle

Duck Head Apparel Company, Inc.

1020 Barrow Industrial Parkway
P.O. Box 688
Winder, Georgia 30680
U.S.A.
Telephone: (770) 867-3111
Toll Free: (800) 933-0680
Fax: (770) 307-1800
Web site: http://www.duckhead.com

Wholly Owned Subsidiary of Tropical Sportswear Int'l
  Corporation
Incorporated: 2000
Employees: 550
Sales: $53.3 million (2000)
NAIC: 315211 Men's and Boys' Cut and Sew Apparel

Duck Head Apparel Company, Inc. is a very young company with a very old label that dates back to the 1800s. After a dozen years of operating as a subsidiary of textile firm Delta Woodside, Duck Head began flying solo, the result of a 2000 spinoff, but in 2001 was again purchased by a larger corporation. The company has very strong name recognition in the South, where Duck Heads are all but synonymous with khaki pants. Recent efforts, however, to spread the Duck Head name to the rest of the country, as well as forays overseas, have met with limited success. Duck Head products, which expanded greatly in the 1990s through licensing deals, are sold in special shops located within select department stores, as well as company-owned retail and factory outlet stores that specialize in discontinued and imperfect items. The company's headquarters are located in Winder, Georgia, but most manufacturing is now done overseas.

Duck Pants in the Post-Civil War Era

The Duck Head name can be traced back to 1865 and two brothers in Nashville, Tennessee. George and Joe O'Bryan, according to lore, bought surplus Army tents made out of a heavy, canvas-like material known as duck. Although it was not intended as a clothing material, duck proved to make durable work pants and overalls. These early khakis also made a success of the O'Bryan Brothers Manufacturing Company and created a Southern clothing staple. In 1892 the brothers tried to trademark the name "duck," but were turned down by the Trademark and Registration Office in Washington because the term was in general usage. Told that "duck head" was available, the O'Bryan brothers registered the term, which naturally led to the head of a mallard duck becoming the lasting symbol of their products.

Duck Heads continued to be manufactured in the 20th century by O'Bryan Brothers, although during World War II the business turned its exclusive attention to making military uniforms. Following the war the company latched onto the popularity of country music, a natural connection given its Nashville location, and with such stars as Hank Williams sporting Duck Heads, the product line gained even greater regional appeal. During the 1980s, Duck Heads were all but the official uniform of the Southern college fraternity brother. By 1989 Delta Woodside decided to buy the Duck Head brand and attempt to roll it out on a national basis.

Delta Woodside was created by two Southern businessmen, Bettis Rainsford and Erwin Maddrey. Rainsford grew up on a South Carolina dairy farm before earning an undergraduate degree from Harvard University. After law school at the University of South Carolina, he then tried his hand at a number of businesses: operating a nursing home, running a newspaper, and setting up an alternative energy project in New Hampshire. He drifted into the textile business in 1982 when he decided to buy Edgefield Cotton Yarns, a troubled mill in his hometown of Edgefield, South Carolina. Knowing nothing about the industry, he turned to Erwin Maddrey, whom he had learned about from a *Wall Street Journal* article. It was reported that Maddrey had resigned as president of a South Carolina textile company because he wanted to strike out on his own. Rainsford telephoned Maddrey, and the two met and agreed to become partners. After buying Edgefield Cotton in 1983, they formed a corporation called Alchem Capital Corp., the name alluding to the medieval

Company Perspectives:

Today, Duck Head is still America's brand. The 100 year tradition lives. ''Khakis'' still mean Duck Head. Relaxed times still mean Duck Head. Value still means Duck Head.

science of alchemy, which espoused that base metals could be transformed into gold.

Purchase of Duck Head Label by Delta Woodside: 1989

The base metals for Alchem Capital were distressed U.S. mills that could be bought cheaply due to increasingly stiff competition with foreign mills, which had the advantage of extremely cheap labor. The company changed its name to Delta Woodside, a combination of the names of two major acquisitions, and went public in 1987. By 1988 Delta Woodside operated 37 plants, generating revenues of $488 million and earning a profit of $28 million. Not only was Delta Woodside producing fabrics, it was also interested in making apparel and began to buy up businesses to bolster that segment. In 1989 it acquired O'Bryan Brothers and its Duck Head brand for approximately $14.1 million. It then created Duck Head Apparel Company by merging O'Bryan Brothers with Carwood Manufacturing Co., which was already doing some contract work for Duck Head products, along with the knitting operations of Royal Manufacturing, Standard Knitting, and Maiden Knitting Mills. The result was a manufacturing subsidiary that employed more than 3,100 people in both the United States and Costa Rica, working in four knit plants, five woven manufacturing plants, a textile facility, plus three distribution centers.

Duck Head grew rapidly, especially after a national expansion program that was launched in the summer of 1990 and supported by advertising that targeted 20- to 40-year-old men. The company also made efforts to sell its products overseas, conducting market research to learn the connotations of ''duck'' in other countries. It concluded that there was a European niche for mid-priced khakis, as well as the company's knit products. Overall the company was quite hopeful about the growth of European sales. In the fall of 1991 the company introduced two new businesses to create an activewear division to be run out of Scottsdale, Arizona: the Duck Head Sport Line—comprised of the Athletic Club, Mountain Club, and Country Club individual lines—and Delta Gold. The company also created Baby Duck Head, which emphasized cloth baby diapers, designed with velcro tabs and elastic in the legs and waists, and marketed to appeal to contemporary parents sensitive to environmental issue. As a result of all these efforts, Duck Head grew revenues from $20 million in fiscal 1989 to $130.4 million in 1992.

Duck Head encountered some problems in 1991 when it switched from independent sales reps, who earned a 5 percent commission, to inhouse reps, who were paid just 0.5 percent plus salary. Three independents were given a chance to join the staff and declined. They then sued Duck Head when a large number of their contracts were cancelled, representing $1 mil-

lion in commissions. Customers informed them that the orders had simply been rewritten by staff salespeople. The matter would finally be aired in a 1993 trial, in which the jury awarded the reps $29 million, including $7 million for mental anguish. The judge would subsequently reduce the award to $22.9 million, an amount that the company still called unjust and unsupported by the facts.

Duck Head management predicted that revenues would reach $180 million for fiscal 1992. Instead, the company generated just $137.3 million, a number that would turn out to be a high water mark for the decade. Duck Head hired a New York advertising firm and bumped its ad budget from $1 million to $5 million. Again, the goal was to expand Duck Head beyond its core Southern market, which accounted for 70 percent of sales. The company appeared ready to take a step to a new level, eschewing such discounters as Kmart and Wal-Mart in favor of more upscale department stores. The company also looked to extend its reach by establishing a women's division. Nevertheless, the results that management anticipated simply did not materialize, and 1994 saw the company take a few steps backwards. Even before the final numbers came in, a sharp drop to $95.4 million in sales and a net loss of $17 million for fiscal 1994, the company's president, Phil Brader, resigned. He was replaced on an interim basis by Maddrey, who continued to serve as CEO of Delta Woodside. Maddrey predicted that the company would rebound, portraying Duck Head as a victim of its own success and blaming much of the sales shortfall on a poor distribution system that resulted in extremely slow delivery times and cancelled orders.

Aside from improving the company's infrastructure and regaining the trust of its customers, Maddrey continued an aggressive effort to grow Duck Head, especially through licensing deals for apparel and accessories. It licensed Pine State Knitwear to produce a line of sweaters; Mayo Knitting Mills for hosiery; ROLFS for leather goods and belts for both men and women; International Travel Brands for small luggage, backpacks, and duffle bags; IMA Fashions for women's handbags; Lifeguard Apparel for men's and boys' underwear; Quinmax for young men's and boys' swimwear; Liberty Childrenswear for children's sportswear; McGee Eye Fashion for men's and women's prescription eyewear; Water's Edge for outerwear and rainwear; and Schertz Umbrellas for Duck Head umbrellas. Duck Head became a licensee of the NASCAR stock car racing association, authorized to produce garments using NASCAR graphics. In the fall of 1994, the company also opened its first regular-price retail store, augmenting the 37 outlet stores the company already operated. Duck Head hoped to eventually open a flagship store in Manhattan.

After a year-and-a-half search for a new president, Duck Head named Paul A. Robb to the post in November 1995. Robb had considerable experience in the women's apparel business, working at Haggar, Levi Strauss, and Nygard International. He quickly closed down Duck Head's women's apparel business, opting to rely on licensing the label to others in order to focus on Duck Head's core menswear business. He also closed the company's Monroe, Georgia, clothing factory, shifting production to less expensive plants in Turkey, Pakistan, and Costa Rica. Nevertheless, revenues continued to fall, dipping to $81 million in 1995 and $79 million in 1996. The company then appeared to be on the road to recovery in 1997. Licensing sales increased significantly, and Robb reestablished the women's business. In April 1997 Duck Head opened its first Duck Head Shops, totaling some 200 menswear shops and 175 boys' shops located in such department stores as Parisian, Dillard's, and J.C. Penney.

Major Ad Campaign: 1998

For fiscal 1997 Duck Head posted a $2 million profit on sales of $90 million, and the company's prospects appeared promising, especially in light of the sudden popularity of khakis. In 1998 Duck Head launched a nine month, $10 million regional marketing campaign, its first consumer-based effort in six years. Management was also optimistic about realizing its long cherished goal of becoming a nationally recognized brand, hopefully building its Duck Head Shops as a moderately priced alternative to Hilfiger, Nautica, and Polo in department stores across the country. Once again, however, Duck Head fell short of its hype. Sales for fiscal 1998 grew to $92 million, just $2 million over the previous year. At the same time, parent company Delta Woodside was reporting disastrous results: revenues dropped from $651.8 million in 1997 to $535.5 million in 1998. Moreover, the company posted a net loss of $43.8 million. Textile manufacturing and the apparel business were simply not providing the synergistic opportunities that Rainsford and Maddrey had banked on in the 1980s.

In October 1998 Maddrey announced that Duck Head was up for sale, prompting rumors of a number of suitors ready to bid for the company. Maddrey insisted that Delta Woodside was not in need of cash, but that Duck Head was ideally positioned to be sold and that a bigger apparel company would have a better chance of making Duck Head a national brand. Robb was part of a management buyout effort, but when that failed he was fired in January 1999. Although he quickly surfaced as president and CEO of Block Sportswear, taking several Duck Head executives with him, Robb sued Delta Woodside, claiming he had been denied stock options and other benefits. Again Maddrey stepped in to run Duck Head on an interim basis, vowing to keep the business going until he found a suitable buyer, but within weeks he announced that Delta Woodside would spin off Duck Head and the Delta Apparel divisions into two separate companies. Delta Woodside shareholders would

receive stock in the new businesses. Rainsford, on the other hand, was not in favor of the spinoff strategy and resigned as Delta Woodside's chief financial officer, indicating that he planned to make an offer to buy the company himself. That effort failed and the spinoffs went forward, with a new Duck Head CEO and president hired to prepare for a separate corporate existence. The former president of Levi Strauss North America, Rob Rockey, was hired in March 1999. In early 2000 registration papers were filed with the Securities and Exchange Commission and in June the spinoff was completed, resulting in the creation of Duck Head Apparel Company, Inc.

While Rockey made efforts to grow Duck Head by cutting costs, the company was far from free of its parent corporation, the founders of which were still at odds over the fate of Duck Head. Both Maddrey, who retired, and Rainsford, who also left the company, remained major shareholders of the parent company and spinoffs. The Duck Head board instituted a "poison pill" shareholders rights plan to make it difficult for a party to acquire a majority interest in the company. Rainsford believed the plan was designed to thwart his efforts to take over the company. In the fall of 2000 he announced plans to nominate his own slate of directors in order to force a sale to Knight Textile Corp. One of his nominees was Talmadge Knight, owner of Knight Textile. Rainsford dropped his hostile takeover bid when the Duck Head board agreed to rescind the shareholders rights plan and hire an investment banking firm to consider a possible merger or sale. When Rockey warned of poor second quarter results in December 2000, Rainsford was quick to call for the immediate sale of the company.

In 2001 Duck Head looked at ways to generate cash, including the sell-off of its headquarters and distribution center in Winder. William Roberti, a former Brooks Brothers executive who had been brought in several months earlier as president and chief operating officer, now took over as CEO. Rockey became chairman of the board, but within a few weeks he retired and Roberti assumed that role as well. Aside from the distinct possibility of a change in ownership, Duck Head faced an uncertain future. No doubt it retained a high degree of name recognition, as well as consumer loyalty, in Southern states, but dreams of national popularity seemed unlikely. Management decided to focus on younger males, with the hope that older males would follow them. The likelihood of that strategy working was also open to debate. As a November 2000 *Forbes* article analyzed the situation: "Youngsters' fashion trends today often start with an inner-city crowd and end up on affluent college kids. That doesn't describe Duck Head at all." In June 2001 the company was sold to Tropical Sportswear Int'l Corporation, makers of Savane and Farah pants, in a stock and assumed debt transaction worth almost $21 million. Duck Head's new corporate parent expressed hope that the business would become profitable as early as fiscal 2002.

Principal Competitors

Abercrombie & Fitch Co.; The Gap, Inc.; Levi Strauss & Co.

Further Reading

Abend, Jules, "How to Boost a Brand," *Bobbin,* April 1999, pp. 58–62.

Addis, Ronit, "Iconoclasts," *Forbes,* April 17, 1989, p. 49.

Black, Susan S., "Duck Head Flying High," *Bobbin,* March 1991, p. 36.

Bond, Patti, "Duck Head Board Avoids Bid for Hostile Takeover," *Atlanta Constitution,* November 7, 2000, p. D1.

Gellers, Stan, "Duck Head Brand Ready to Fly Nationally," *Daily News Record,* April 1, 1998, p. 4.

Glanton, Eileen, "Duck Soup," *Forbes,* November 13, 2000, p. 256.

Lamm, Marcy, "New CEO Shakes up Duck Head, Inside and Out," *Atlanta Business Chronicle,* September 19, 1997. p. 10A.

Malone, Scott, "Delta Woodside to Spin Off Apparel, Mill," *Women's Wear Daily,* February 9, 1999, p. 12.

Scott, Jeffry, "Wings Spread, Duck Head Hoping to Fly," *Atlanta Constitution,* November 20, 1992, p. F1.

—Ed Dinger

ECC International Corp.

2001 West Oak Ridge Road
Orlando, Florida 32809-3803
U.S.A.
Telephone: (407) 859-7410
Toll Free: (800) 327-1020
Fax: (407) 855-4840
Web site: http://www.eccic.com

Public Company
Incorporated: 1969 as EDP Technology Inc.
Employees: 210
Sales: $40.88 million (2000)
Stock Exchanges: American
Ticker Symbol: ECC
NAIC: 333319 Other Commercial and Service Industry
    Machinery Manufacturing

ECC International Corp. produces specialized computer simulators used to train military personnel how to operate and fix military weapons systems, including ships, planes, armored vehicles, and small arms. Its clients include all branches of the U.S. military as well as the armed forces of two dozen other nations. Nearly 90 percent of its sales are to primary contractors for ultimate use by the U.S. Department of Defense. The company also applies its technology to industrial and vocational training.

Origins

Engineers from Martin-Marietta created what would become ECC International Corp. in 1969. First called EDP Technology Inc., the company was renamed Ed Tech Corp. in October 1973, then Educational Computer Corp. in August 1976, and finally ECC International Corp. in February 1988.

The company constructed simulators to train military personnel on how to operate or repair a variety of equipment, including aircraft, ships, armored vehicles, and weapons. It was an obscure specialty in 1988, wrote *Barron's*, yet it saved armed forces in two dozen countries money by protecting the expensive real equipment from beginner's mishaps and by diverting fewer experienced crew from their duties in the field. *Barron's* predicted the market would grow as military equipment grew more complex.

ECC's revenues were $38 million in 1988, twice those of 1984, as profits approached $4 million. The company had a backlog of nearly $75 million. Foreign armies accounted for just 10 percent of business, although the company was building a new facility in Great Britain to gain better access to the European market. In fact, ECC (UK) Limited soon won a $7 million contract from Switzerland for tank gunnery and maintenance training simulators. ECC was also upping its employment at its main Florida plant by 20 percent.

In spite of its relatively small size, ECC had some advantages over other defense contractors. For example, it did not have to invest the same exorbitant sums to win orders.

Orders and Losses in 1989

By May 1989 the backlog had grown to $165 million, largely on the strength of the company's biggest order ever: a $133 million contract to build maintenance simulators for the new C-17 transport aircraft. A couple of months later, ECC was subcontracted to provide simulators for the U.S. Army's Advanced Anti-Armor Weapons System-Medium (AAWS-M), an order initially worth $23 million. Unfortunately, problems with both prime contractors and suppliers were delaying completion of other contracts, and forcing the company to post a loss in fiscal 1989, its first in 15 years.

Fortunately, the contracts kept coming, including a $6 million award from McDonnell Aircraft Corp. to produce maintenance simulators for F-18 attack jets sold to Kuwait. For the fiscal year ended June 30, 1990, ECC reported net income of $3.1 million on record sales of $55.9 million.

ECC announced higher than anticipated costs on its C-17 project in the spring of 1992, but these were not enough to make the contract unprofitable. The company did have to restructure its debt after violating certain loan covenants; it was paying more than $3 million a year on interest—a quarter of its total expenses.

Company Perspectives:

ECC International Corp. is a world leader in the design, development and production of simulators and related training for all branches of the U.S. Department of Defense and 25 other countries.

A contract awarded in 1989 to supply weapons-training simulators for the Javelin antitank missile system would become ECC's largest program. The company's workforce numbered more than 800 in the early 1990s.

In December 1992, IBM subcontracted ECC to produce simulated weapons systems modules for its Close Combat Tactical Trainer (CCTT) project. The deal was initially worth $58 million, with a potential value of $88 million. Saudi Arabia awarded ECC another lucrative contract six months later, a $31 million agreement to design and manufacture maintenance training simulators for the M1A2 Abrams tank.

Vending Machines in 1992

Seeking some relief from the cyclical nature of defense contracting, ECC entered a more civil business in 1992: vending machines. The company first built frozen food vending machines under license from a German manufacturer, Deutsche Wurlitzer GmbH.

ECC designed a custom glass-front unit for Snapple Beverages Corporation that was unveiled in 1994. About 10,000 units worth $28 million were to be shipped the first year, beginning in April. (The order helped push ECC's backlog past $200 million.) The cases were designed to display up to 54 of Snapple's signature glass bottles. Patrons were treated to the sight of the bottles falling up to 3.5 feet without breaking during the vending. A space age piece of foam cushioned the fall. A subsidiary, ECC Vending Corp., was formed in July 1996 to manage these operations; however, it was to be short-lived.

ECC reported income of $7.3 million on sales of $107.6 million for fiscal 1995, both figures up about 70 percent from the previous year. The next year, sales were up to $117.1 million but profits fell to $2.9 million, the beginning of a long, painful slide.

By the end of 1996, the company was looking for a buyer. In March 1997, at the request of an unidentified major shareholder, ECC canceled a recently adopted provision to raise the level of stock ownership at which shareholder rights were triggered from 22.5 percent to 30 percent. This had been intended as a defense against hostile takeovers. In August 1997, ECC said it was no longer looking for a buyer, although the next month it announced a tentative agreement to sell certain vending machine-related assets to Maytag Corporation, which eventually paid $7.9 million for the money-losing ECC Vending Corp. subsidiary, which had failed to live up to its original parent's expectations after losing its two main clients, Snapple and Häagen Dazs. ECC earmarked the proceeds from the sale to pay down debt.

Layoffs were another part of the formula to restore elusive profits in the face of falling revenues. The company terminated 300 employees and contract laborers between July 1996 and May 1997.

In spite of a new $6.6 million Lockheed Martin contract, ECC continued to lose money in the spring of 1998. Delays among its suppliers were again cited. Sales were also down slightly. As losses continued into the fall, ECC was forced to renegotiate for more time to pay an $8.7 million loan from First Union National Bank.

Florida-Bound in 1998

Dr. James C. Garrett, formerly with Raytheon and Rockwell International, was named president and CEO in June 1998. He immediately set out to cut costs while increasing revenues at successful programs through such means as aggressively vying for follow-up orders.

In July 1998, ECC announced plans to relocate its headquarters from Wayne, Pennsylvania, to Orlando, where it already employed 500 people. The concentration of defense contractors in Florida was one factor making the move attractive. It was also a means to cut administrative expenses. In fiscal 1999, ECC discontinued its U.K. subsidiary, ECC Simulation Limited. It had lost more than $10 million in the preceding two years, contributing inordinately to the parent company's losses.

The late 1990s were not ECC's best years. The company lost $20 million from 1997 to 1999. It laid off half its workforce. As its stock price fell 80 percent (it had peaked at $15 in 1994), ECC was nearly delisted from the New York Stock Exchange, according to the *Orlando Sentinel*. This delisting ultimately did happen in November 2000, and ECC began trading on the American Stock Exchange (AMEX).

Other indicators were already looking up, however. Gross margins increased from 25 percent to 33 percent in fiscal 2000. The company reported income of $3.4 million on sales of $40.9 million—welcome results after years of agony. Among its newest programs was the small arms Engagement Skills Trainer (EST), which the company was pitching at military conferences. In September, the U.S. Army approved EST for delivery.

ECC laid off one-fifth of its 250 employees in July 2000 after its role in the Javelin antitank field trainer program was reduced. Javelin was headed by a joint venture of Lockheed Martin Corp. and Raytheon Co.; ECC had been involved in the program, its largest, since 1989. ECC officials claimed Lockheed gave most of the upcoming business to the Dutch aerospace firm Fokker N.V. because it wanted the Netherlands to buy the missile system for its military. Lockheed countered that Fokker simply offered a lower bid.

In September 2000, CEO Garrett told the *Orlando Sentinel* he felt the company had become the right size for the work it expected to be doing. After years of cuts, employment was at 275 and rising (for the moment). The company was especially seeking engineers, programmers, and "systems integration people." The company's simulation work over the years had shifted from hardware manufacturing to systems integration, Garrett stated. At the same time, the increasing capabilities of

---

Key Dates:

1969: Former Martin-Marietta engineers create EDP Technology.
1989: Under the new name ECC International, company begins the Javelin simulator program.
1992: ECC begins making vending machines.
1994: Share price peaks at $15.
1997: Vending unit is sold to Maytag.
1999: U.K. operations are discontinued.
2000: A slimmer ECC announces profits, layoffs.

---

the PC threatened to reduce the need for high fidelity, dedicated simulators.

In spite of the company's improved fortunes, investors were not snapping up ECC shares. An investment expert interviewed by the *Orlando Sentinel* blamed the unpredictable nature of the custom simulation business.

In October 2000, ECC won a four-year, $17 million contract to build 392 Javelin basic-skills trainers for Lockheed Martin and Texas Instruments Inc., which had bought Raytheon's defense business. (The contract for Javelin's tactical skills trainer that ECC had earlier lost to Fokker was probably worth twice as much. However, the U.S. Army ordered 21 field tactical trainers worth $1.7 million from ECC in April 2001.)

In November 2000, ECC unleashed its second round of layoffs in a year, dismissing 70 employees. General restructuring and a short-term decline in business were the reasons given. The pattern was all too familiar, yet ECC continued to win contracts, particularly with the U.S. Army and ECC's biggest client, the Navy.

Principal Subsidiaries

Educational Computer International, Inc.; ECC International Inc. (Virgin Islands).

Principal Divisions

Instructional Systems Development Group; Simulation Design and Production Center; Systems Design and Production Center.

Principal Competitors

Groupe Dassault Aviation SA; Evans & Sutherland Computer Corporation; Reflectone Inc.

Further Reading

Burnett, Richard, "Orlando, Fla.-Based Defense Contractor ECC Lays Off Almost 50 Workers," *Orlando Sentinel,* July 14, 2000.
——, "Orlando, Fla.-Based Defense Contractor ECC Lays Off Nearly 24 Percent of Staff," *Orlando Sentinel,* November 3, 2000.
——, "Painful Cost-Cutting Puts Orlando, Fla. Defense Simulator Back on Its Feet," *Orlando Sentinel,* September 4, 2000.
Dillon, Paul, "ECC Makes Dramatic Cuts in Orlando Work Force," *Orlando Business Journal,* May 16, 1997.
——, "ECC to Shop for Buyer; Sale Could Boost Local Operations," *Orlando Business Journal,* December 6, 1996.
"ECC International: Simulation Draws a Real Profit Picture," *Barron's,* August 15, 1988, pp. 39–40.
Jabbonsky, Larry, "Snapple Tends to Vending with 54-Selection Glass Bottle Unit," *Beverage World,* February 28, 1994, p. 4.

—Frederick C. Ingram

Edw. C. Levy Co.

9300 Dix Avenue
Detroit, Michigan 48120
U.S.A.
Telephone: (313) 843-7200
Fax: (313) 849-9447
Web site: http://www.edwclevy.com

Private Company
Incorporated: 1946
Employees: 3,000
Sales: $350 million (2000 est.)
NAIC: 327992 Ground or Treated Mineral and Earth
    Manufacturing; 32732 Ready-Mix Concrete
    Manufacturing; 42132 Brick, Stone, and Related
    Construction Material Wholesalers; 324121 Asphalt
    Paving Mixture and Block Manufacturing; 23411
    Highway and Street Construction

Edw. C. Levy Co. is a Detroit, Michigan-based firm that hauls, processes, and resells slag (an iron- and steel-production waste product); manufactures and ships concrete and asphalt; and performs other related tasks including limestone, sand, and gravel production and metal recovery. Levy operates in the United States, Australia, and Thailand through a number of subsidiaries and joint ventures. The privately held firm is owned by the heirs of its founder and run by his son, Ed Levy, Jr.

Beginnings

The Edw. C. Levy Company was founded in 1918 by its namesake near Detroit, Michigan, as a trucking company. Over the next decade the company began to haul slag from the Ford Motor Company's Rouge plant and the Hanna Furnace Co. on Zug Island, later crushing and selling it for use as a road base material. Slag, a byproduct of iron and steel production, was also used as an ingredient in concrete, as landfill, and for other applications. Slag forms on the surface of molten metal during the manufacturing process, and is separated as waste. The com-

position and usable qualities of slag vary depending upon whether steel or iron production is its source.

During the 1930s Levy expanded its capabilities, building a plant to crush slag and mix it with calcium chloride for use as a road base. In the late 1940s the company enlarged its slag operation by constructing a plant on Dix Avenue in Detroit to handle Ford-generated slag. Edw. C. Levy Co. was formally incorporated in 1946.

A new contract was won in 1950 from Great Lakes Steel to remove slag from that company's Zug Island steel mill; a similar contract with McLouth Steel Corp. followed in 1954. That same year the company built two more slag processing plants in Trenton, Michigan, just south of Detroit. During the 1950s the company also began to perform additional metal handling and processing services for other companies, and developed new processes for reclaiming metal from steel slag.

The 1960s was a period of rapid growth for Edw. C. Levy. In 1961 the company formed a subsidiary, Delta Trucking Co., to haul aggregate products to customers. Aggregate was a main ingredient of cement, and consisted of a mixture of materials such as sand, gravel, and slag. Levy also overhauled its Dix Avenue plant during the year, making it one of the most efficient facilities of its type in the United States. The year 1962 saw the acquisition of three asphalt plants from Cadillac Asphalt Paving Co., and the formation of another subsidiary, Asphalt Products. The company patented a transportable liquid slag carrier for use in trucks during the year as well. In 1963 another subsidiary, Lyon Sand & Gravel Co., was formed in Lyon Township, Michigan, to produce sand and gravel. Its first plant was put into operation the following year.

Manufacturing Concrete

The year 1964 was the company's busiest to date. During the year Levy purchased three concrete plants from Clawson Transit Mix, built three new ones of its own in the Detroit area, and formed a ready-mix concrete business in Redford Township, Michigan. Levy also formed two new subsidiaries, Eagle Trucking Company in Wixom, which hauled sand and gravel aggregate to areas outside of Detroit, and Detroit Lime Co.,

---

Company Perspectives:

Our Mission: Supply our employees with a safe and secure work environment and equip them with the tools to enable them to meet their individual objectives.

Provide our internal and external customers with the highest quality products and services through a complete understanding of their needs and a total commitment to their success.

Enrich our culture through trust, teamwork, individual initiative, high expectations, active involvement and open communications. Promote innovations and harvest ideas at all levels of the organization to foster personal growth and continuous corporate improvement. Repay the communities that support us by operating safe and environmentally sound businesses while sharing our success with worthy charitable causes. Grow our business through marketing, research, and technical advances, while recycling and using the earth's natural resources in a manner which enhances the quality of life. Observe standards of moral and ethical conduct which will easily withstand any public or private scrutiny. Always treat others as we would wish to be treated and work hard to gain the same treatment from others.

---

which sold burnt lime to steelmakers and other companies from a newly built plant. The company also licensed Kress Corp. of Illinois to manufacture the liquid slag carrier it had patented.

Another trucking concern was formed in 1966. Falcon Trucking Co. would haul aggregate and cement to customers in Michigan. The same year Levy built a central-mix concrete plant in the Detroit suburb of Southfield. In 1967 two inactive Detroit-area concrete plants were purchased and reopened, and a limestone quarrying and processing operation was acquired from Medusa Cement Company. The Kelleys Island, Ohio-based plant was Levy's first foray outside of Michigan.

The company continued to expand its concrete operations at the end of the 1960s, building new central-mix plants in Romulus, Michigan, and at Lyon Sand & Gravel, and purchasing Breckling Concrete Co. of Cleveland, Ohio, most of whose facilities were subsequently leased to Collingwood Shale. Killins Gravel of Ann Arbor, Michigan, was also bought, and a central-mix concrete plant opened at its facility there, while a subsidiary called Concrete Components Co. was formed to make hollow-core building members at a new plant in Novi, Michigan. The company also built an asphalt mixing plant in Sterling Heights, and a slag processing facility at Burns Harbor, Indiana, to service Bethlehem Steel, and began marketing a mix of slag, lime, and fly ash under the trade name Slagcrete for use as a road base.

The early 1970s saw Levy's growth continue. In 1972 the company purchased the ready mix and sand and gravel businesses of South Bend, Indiana-based South Lake Service Co., which then began operating under the name St. Joseph Materials Co. Levy also purchased a cement plant in Detroit which it christened Jefferson Marine Terminal and began using it for receiving, grinding, and shipping cement, and bought Cadillac

Asphalt Paving Co. Another patent was received during this period for a chemical treatment of slag cooling water that eliminated odors. In 1973 and 1974 Levy formed three additional subsidiaries: Hatchet, Inc., which operated portable facilities for recovering foundry waste scrap; Gravel Trucking Co., which hauled hot asphalt mixtures and construction and steel mill wastes; and Indian Trucking Co., which transported aggregates in northern Indiana.

In the early 1980s Levy bought dock and ready-mix, pre-stressed concrete facilities on the Saginaw River in Michigan, as well as the ready-mix cement assets of Genesee Cement Products Co. of Flint, which was renamed Clawson Flint. In 1983 Levy bought Ace Asphalt & Paving Co. of Flint and Medusa Cement Co. of Oakland County, Michigan, renaming the latter Milford Sand & Gravel Co. New service contracts were signed during this period with U.S. Steel, LTV, and Timken and the company also formed more trucking subsidiaries, including Stacy Trucking and Triple E Trucking, the latter located in Colorado Springs, Colorado. At the same time Levy purchased the asphalt making and paving equipment of Colorado Springs-based Schmidt Construction Co., and also acquired sand, gravel, and crushed stone operations from Blount Materials in Michigan, which it renamed Burroughs Material Co.

The company expanded into Florida in 1986 with acquisitions of trucking company Advantage Transportation, limestone quarry operator Coral Rock, Inc., concrete maker West Coast Industries, and builder SEU Construction. In 1987 Levy's Colorado-based asphalt operations were expanded, and Colorado quarrying and sand/gravel businesses were bought. That year Levy also purchased an asphalt production and aggregate mining operation from Mesa Material Co. of Phoenix, Arizona. Closer to home, in 1988 portions of Levy's Dix Avenue slag plant and Jefferson Marine Terminal facilities were rebuilt and upgraded, making the former more environmentally friendly. The year 1988 also saw another trucking business created, State Trucking, which hauled and paved asphalt.

Launch of Foreign Operations: 1989

With Levy now expanding into select areas around the United States, it was only logical that a foreign move would be made. This took place in 1989, when a joint venture in Port Kembla, Australia, was formed with trucking company Cleary Bros. and Queensland Cement Ltd. The new entity was named Australian Steel Mill Services Pty Ltd. (ASMS), and was expected to process up to 1.5 million tons of slag per year for removal of metal content, with 200,000 tons to be shipped to Queensland Cement for use as an ingredient in concrete. Some 50 people were to be employed by ASMS, which would spend A$60 million to build a private road system for transporting the heavy loads of slag. An Australian scrap detinning facility was added in 1992 under the name Australian Metal Recovery (AMR).

Stateside, Levy continued to form new subsidiaries in the early 1990s, including Centennial Materials Co., which acquired aggregate, mining, and sand and gravel businesses in Colorado; Exact Express, a Michigan-based trucking company; and Mercier Analytical Laboratory Co. Levy also leased its Detroit Lime Co. operation to Global Stone Co., and expanded the Mesa Materials Co. operation in Arizona.

Key Dates:

1918: Edward C. Levy forms a trucking company in Detroit, Michigan.
1920s: First slag-hauling contracts are received from Ford Motor Co. and Hanna Furnace Co.
1930s: Levy builds a plant to crush slag and manufacture calcium chloride.
1946: Company is incorporated in Michigan.
1948: Facility built in Detroit to process slag for Ford.
1954: Two new slag processing plants built in Trenton, Michigan.
1962: Company patents a mobile carrier for molten slag.
1964: Levy Co. purchases, constructs a total of six concrete plants.
1969: Trade name ''Slagcrete'' is registered for mix of slag, lime, and fly ash.
1972: Levy patents a chemical spray that neutralizes slag odors.
1986: Levy acquires trucking, quarrying, concrete, and construction firms in Florida.
1989: Australian slag processing joint venture is formed.
1996: Two joint ventures are formed in Thailand to process slag.
1998: Levy subsidiary in Ohio receives ISO 9002 certification, others follow.

In 1996 Levy formed several companies to perform services for Steel Minimills (steel mills that melted scrap metal to make new steel), including Fulton Mill Services in Ohio, Charleston Mill Services in South Carolina, and Midwest Mill Services in Illinois. The company also formed two other international joint ventures in Thailand. Siam Steel Mill Services (SSMS) and Chonburi Steel Mill Services (CSMS) would perform slag removal at six steel mills.

The following year, Levy acquired the sand & gravel operations of Vulcan Materials of Indiana and American Aggregates of Michigan. The company also sold concrete plants in Florida and Flint, Michigan, and formed an aggregate trucking subsidiary in Oxford, Michigan, called Norse Trucking. A new aggregate shipping dock was opened on the Rouge River in Dearborn, Michigan as well.

The late 1990s saw Edw. C. Levy Co. in pursuit of ISO 9002 certification, which was won for its Canton and Delta, Ohio steel mill service facilities, Australian Metal Recovery, and its two Thai joint ventures. In 2000, Levy also formed a slag

service company in Ashland, Kentucky, to operate as A-K Steel Corporation's Ashland plant.

After more than 80 years in operation, Edw. C. Levy Co. had assembled an extensive portfolio of companies. Best known for processing and selling over ten million tons of slag per year, Levy's metal recovery operations returned more than 1.5 million tons of steel to its clients, which included the largest U.S. steelmaking companies. The firm also operated a number of aggregate making, cement, asphalt, and trucking operations in the United States and abroad. Levy was responsible for several technical innovations, including the molten slag carrier and slag-odor neutralizing chemical sprays, as well.

Principal Subsidiaries

Delta Trucking Co.; Asphalt Products; Lyon Sand & Gravel Co.; Eagle Trucking Co.; Detroit Lime Co.; Falcon Trucking Co.; Killins Gravel Co.; Breckling Concrete Co.; Concrete Components Co.; St. Joseph Materials Co.; Jefferson Marine Terminal; Cadillac Asphalt Paving Co.; Hatchet, Inc.; Gravel Trucking Co.; Indian Trucking Co.; Stacy Trucking; Milford Sand & Gravel Co.; Clawson Concrete Co.; Ace Asphalt & Paving; Triple E Trucking Co.; Burroughs Materials Co.; Advantage Transportation; Coral Rock, Inc.; West Coast Industries; SEU Construction; Schmidt Construction Co.; State Trucking; Centennial Materials Co.; Australian Metal Recovery Pty Ltd. (Australia); Exact Express; Mercier Analytical Laboratory Co.; Fulton Mill Services; Charleston Mill Services; Midwest Mill Services; Norse Trucking; Ashland Slag Co.; Australian Steel Mill Services Pty Ltd. (Australia; 50%); SSMS (Siam Steel Mill Services) (Thailand; 50%); CSMS (Chonburi Steel Mill Services) (Thailand; 50%.

Principal Competitors

Envirosource, Inc.; Harsco Corporation; Holnam Cement Co.; LaFarge Corporation; U.S. Aggregates, Inc.

Further Reading

Deans, Alan, ''Competition—A Concrete Case,'' *Australian Financial Review,* August 9, 1993, p. 56.
——, ''Spin-Off for Kembla Slag,'' *Sydney Morning Herald,* March 4, 1989, p. 45.
''Levy Gets Slag Pacts,'' *American Metal Market,* November 22, 1995, p. 13.
''Rich Sand Born of Slag, Effluent,'' *Sydney Morning Herald,* March 26, 1992, p. 4.

—Frank Uhle

Elmer's Restaurants, Inc.

11802 SE Stark Street
Portland, Oregon 97216
U.S.A.
Telephone: (503) 252-1485
Fax: (503) 257-7448
Web site: http://www.elmers-restaurants.com

Public Company
Incorporated: 1983
Employees: 532
Sales: $25.85 million (2001)
Stock Exchanges: NASDAQ
Ticker Symbol: ELMS
NAIC: 72211 Full-Service Restaurants, 53311 Owners
   and Lessors of Other Non-Financial Assets

Founded in 1960, Elmer's Restaurants, Inc. is a franchiser and operator of full-service, family oriented restaurants under the names ''Elmer's Pancake & Steak House'' and ''Elmer's Breakfast • Lunch • Dinner'' and an operator of delicatessen restaurants under the names ''Ashley's Café'' and ''Richard's Deli and Pub.'' The company considers itself the Cadillac of coffeehouses and is noted in the industry for its customer loyalty.

From Family Business to Regional Chain: 1960s–70s

In 1939, at the end of the Great Depression, Walter Elmer borrowed $2,000 on his house and bought what was to become Elmer's Milky Way in Portland. There, he worked 16 hours a day, selling malts and hamburgers and turning a profit. His wife, Dorothy, baked the restaurant's pies and cakes. Elmer, whose father had been born in Elm, Switzerland, had grown up in Troutlake, Washington, where he worked for the U.S. Forest Service for five years before moving to Portland and working there for the Roseway Dairy. Seven years after starting Elmer's Milky Way, Elmer sold his malt shop and bought the coffee shop in the city's Medical Arts Building in 1946. The coffee shop did so well that Elmer was able to acquire a second coffee shop, called the Polly Ann Grill, in the Terminal Sales Building.

Finally, in 1960, against the advice of several restaurateurs, Elmer started Elmer's Colonial Pancake House on Portland's northeast side. The restaurant's menu was devoted almost entirely to pancakes, including nearly 30 different varieties of the favorite breakfast food, which it served all day. The original recipe for pancake batter came from ''a fellow in Seattle,'' according to Walter Elmer in a 1971 *Oregon Journal* article. He paid $1,000 to acquire it.

Elmer's Pancake & Steak House employed Elmer's wife, brothers, sons, and daughters-in-law. It grew slowly, adding a second restaurant in neighboring Vancouver, Washington, in 1962. Eventually, it became Elmer's Pancake & Steak House. In 1966, it expanded its menu, adding more lunch and dinner items, and granted its first franchise. Between 1968 and 1979, it expanded rapidly, adding additional franchises throughout Oregon and in Idaho, California, Montana, and Washington. Elmer attributed his company's success above all to atmosphere and personnel. Throughout the early 1980s, expansion continued with more franchises, including several in Arizona, until the company totaled 29 establishments, two in Portland and 27 others in six Western states. In 1980, the Elmers sold the original Elmer's Pancake & Steak House in Portland to a local team of two brothers named Danna Bros.

New Ownership: 1980s

In 1984, Elmer's earned $92,000 on revenues of almost $3 million. Early that same year, a group of private investors led by Herman Goldberg, a 60-year-old business consultant and investment manager, purchased the company. Members of the Elmer family participated in the purchase and planned to remain active in the company, though Goldberg would become the new chairman and CEO. The Elmers, who owned and operated two of the company's 29 restaurants at that time, had approached Goldberg in 1983 to see whether he would buy their restaurant chain. At first Goldberg, who was familiar with the chain because his secretary's husband owned three franchises, bought just one unit in order to gain industry experience. By 1985, however, Goldberg had paved the way for an initial public offering of the chain, now 30 units strong. At the same time, the company's name was changed to Elmer's Restaurant, Inc., with Elmer's Pancake and Steak House, Inc. operating as a subsidiary.

The second half of the 1980s was a time of updating for Elmer's. While retaining touches of its traditional décor, such as stone fireplaces, flowers on every table, and decorative plates on the walls, Elmer's began to leave behind its colonial image. It expanded its menu of made-from-scratch food to include a ''Seniors Pleasers'' section of smaller portions and a ''Home Town Favorites'' section of local market specialties. It also adopted a new slogan: ''Come home to Elmer's, Homestyle Cooking Since 1960.'' The company that boasted ''breakfast—morning, noon, and night'' began to sell its own line of syrups, jams, preserves, and coffee in its establishments under the label ''Elmer's Gourmet Choice.''

The company launched a new franchise program, which it called The Elmer's Connection, in 1987. The plan offered investors the chance to put their money to work while leaving the day-to-day management of the franchise to the parent company. Under the agreement, investors put up a minimum of $250,000 for start-up expenses and another $300,000 for land and building costs. They then paid Elmer's an annual management fee of 2 percent of gross revenues for running the restaurant. According to Goldberg in a 1987 *Restaurants and Institutions* article, the plan was a response to the fact that ''[t]he mom-and-pop phase of the restaurant business is over.... It's become very capital intensive.''

Goldberg was nothing if not an innovator. In 1990, in an unconventional move, Goldberg diverted $180,000—80 percent—of Elmer's annual advertising budget for a hard-hitting multimedia campaign against drug use, directed at children and their parents, and purchased anti-drug spots for local radio and television. A 30-minute videotape of stories of drug abuse by kids was distributed to school counselors, the news media, and interested companies. The campaign brought Elmer's tremendous positive publicity: glowing features in the *Wall Street Journal*, the *Seattle Post-Intelligencer*, and a mention in *Nation's Business*.

Six years later, the campaign still drew attention. When Goldberg died at age 71 in 1996, the Oregon Liquor Commis-sion, the Congressional Record, and President Bush all recognized Goldberg's work in dissuading school-age children from using drugs. Walter Elmer died the following year at age 91. Following Goldberg's death, his wife, Anita, succeeded him as president, CEO, and principal shareholder of the 30-restaurant chain. Two years later, Anita Goldberg sold her 53.8 percent of the company's common stock to an investor group led by restaurant industry veterans for more than $4.5 million, a nearly 60 percent premium over what Elmer's shares then traded for. Elmer's then had sales of $16 million a year, although its ''colonial'' breakfast still cost only $5.75.

New Growth Phase Under New Management: Late 1990s

CBW Inc., the Oregon-based entity that acquired Elmer's, was led by Cordy Jensen, along with William Service and Bruce Davis, partners and operators of 14 delicatessen-style restaurants in Oregon, and Tom Connor and Donald Woolley, local real estate investors. Jensen was president and owner of several restaurants in Oregon and California and a founder, major shareholder, and director of Centennial Bancorp, Oregon's largest independent bank.

William Service became Elmer's chief executive officer and Bruce Davis its president. The two had been friends since sixth grade and still lived in their native Eugene, Oregon. Service had attended Stanford University's graduate school of business and Davis, the Yale School of Management. In 1993, the two had formed Jasper's Food Management, which ran Jasper's Delis where patrons could play video poker and the Oregon Lottery. In 1995, Davis and Service teamed up with Jensen to form CBW Inc. Almost immediately upon assuming control of Elmer's, the two introduced video poker to the 38-year-old pancake chain that still featured endless coffee refills. The significance of this move extended beyond Elmer's: bringing video poker to the mainstream chain moved some of Portland's gambling scene away from the small taverns and delicatessens that had dominated this niche since its legalization in Oregon in 1991. To lure the morning crowd back in the evening, the new management expanded a seafood and steak menu and added alcohol service.

There had been little growth at Elmer's since the early 1980s. The company had added only four new restaurants since 1985, the most recent ones in 1994. It had continued, however, to be profitable, with an average increase in revenue of 5.5 percent each year between 1991 and 1998 and profits that more than tripled to $530,000. However, franchisees had begun to grumble that the management did little to help them grow. Profits were used to buy back and retire shares. According to one Portland-based franchisee, quoted in the *Register Guard* in 1999, Elmer's had become ''almost like a collection agency.... They didn't have much to do operationally—they left the franchises pretty much alone.''

To address this problem and reposition itself as a three-meal, family-style eatery, Elmer's began phasing out the ''Elmer's Pancake & Steak House'' signs in 1999, replacing them with ''Elmer's Breakfast • Lunch • Dinner'' when a survey showed that many customers did not even know that Elmer's was open for dinner. The company also dropped a third of its least popular

---

Key Dates:

1960: Walker and Dorothy Elmer open Elmer's Colonial Pancake House.
1966: The Elmer family grants its first franchise.
1980: Danna Bros. purchases franchise of the original Elmer's.
1984: Herman Goldberg buys the Elmer's franchise rights.
1985: Goldberg takes the company public as Elmer's Restaurants, Inc. and becomes president and chief executive officer.
1996: Herman Goldberg dies and is succeeded by his wife, Anita Goldberg.
1997: Walter Elmer dies.
1998: CBW Inc., comprised of a group of professional restaurant managers, purchases a controlling interest in Elmer's; Bruce Davis becomes president and William Service becomes chief executive.
2000: The company acquires Mitzel's American Kitchen.

---

items and introduced a redesigned menu. For the first time, all franchisees began to use the same menu.

In 1999, Elmer's acquired CBW Inc. and combined the management teams of the two firms, assuming $4 million of the debt the latter had assumed to finance the 1998 purchase of Elmer's. With the transaction, Davis and Service became the two largest Elmer's shareholders.

By 2000, the company was experiencing steady growth under its new management. In addition to the almost 29 Elmer's in six states, the company owned ten delis operating in Oregon as Ashley's or Richard's. In August 2000, it purchased its first new restaurant in six years, reducing real estate costs by converting an existing restaurant to its concept rather than building a new one. In December, it purchased the Mitzel's American Kitchen chain of seven Puget Sound family restaurants.

For fiscal 2001, the company reported record revenues and net income of $25.85 million and $956,000, respectively. In 2000, the company had earned $939,000 on revenues of $22.2 million. The *Business Journal* named it the second fastest growing company in Oregon for the second year in a row. The company, eager to pick up investors, doled out its second dividend, having paid out the first in its history in 1999. Although recognizing that competition for new locations would be costly in the years to come, Elmer's nonetheless had plans for continued growth.

Principal Subsidiaries

Elmer's Pancake & Steak House, Inc.; CBW Food Company, LLC; Grass Valley Ltd., Inc.

Principal Competitors

IHOP Corp.; Vip's; Denny's Restaurants Inc.; Shari's; VICORP Restaurants, Inc.

Further Reading

Baker, Doug, "Pancakes to Gschetzlets," *Oregon Journal*, December 1971, p. 3C.

DeSilver, Drew, "Eugene, Oregon Group Pays Higher Price for Restaurant Company's Takeover," *Knight-Ridder/Tribune Business News*, August, 11, 1998.

——, "Local Entrepreneur Hopes to Put Sizzle Back in Elmer's Chain," *Register Guard*, September, 5, 1999, p. 1C.

"Elmer's Planning to Go Public," *Nation's Restaurant News*, July 1, 1985, p. 62.

Jones, Steven D., "Video Poker Is Coming to Elmer's," *Wall Street Journal/Northwest*, October 7, 1998, p. NW1.

Paglin, Catherine, "Goldberg Capitalizes on Elmer's Standard Menu," *Business Journal-Portland*, June 9, 1986, p. 12.

Tripp, Julie, "Pancake Chain Wins Applause for Campaign Against Drug Use," *Oregonian*, November 18, 1990, p. C5.

Troseth, Erica, "Elmer's Bulge Begins," *Business Journal-Portland*, April 4, 2000, p.12.

——, "Elmer's Execs Eager to Pitch Growth to Wall Street," *Business Journal-Portland*, December 1, 2000, p. 7.

—Carrie Rothburd

FarmJournal

Farm Journal Corporation

1500 Market Street, Centre Sq. West
Philadelphia, Pennsylvania 19102
U.S.A.
Telephone: (215) 557-8900
Fax: (215) 568-4436

Private Company
Founded: 1877
Employees: 400
Sales: $25 million (2000 est.)
NAIC: 511120 Periodical Publishers

Farm Journal Corporation is the holding company for a number of media interests that have grown out of *Farm Journal,* the influential Philadelphia-based magazine that was established in 1877. Throughout its history, its owners have embraced new technologies and publishing concepts. Creating a brand out of the Farm Journal name is in many ways a continuation of that forward thinking, in large part borne out of necessity because of the ever-shrinking numbers of U.S. farmers. In addition to its flagship magazine, Farm Journal also publishes *Top Producer, Beef Today, and Dairy Today,* as well as several newsletters. The company also holds broadcast interests: the Farm Journal Radio Network and two nationally syndicated television programs, AgDay and WeekEnd MarketPlace. Involved in the Internet since 1995, Farm Journal has merged its operations with other partners to launch AgWeb.com, for which it provides much of the content. Farm Journal is controlled by a limited partnership, which includes top management of the company.

Influence of Farming Publications in the 19th Century

Agricultural journalism has a deep, although somewhat overlooked, history in the United States. Not only did early farm publications connect and entertain isolated farm families and help disseminate information on new machinery, techniques, and business practices, their editorial pages championed causes that were important to their readers. Although almanacs, such as those published by Benjamin Franklin, included agricultural content, the beginning of the farm press is generally traced to the 1819 foundation of the *American Farmer,* published in Baltimore by John Stuart Skinner. According to its title page, the publication contained "Original Essays and Selections on Rural Economy and Internal Improvements With Illustrative Engravings and the Prices Current of Country Produce." Skinner would join forces with the legendary Horace Greeley in the mid-1840s to publish the *Monthly Journal of Agriculture.* William Dempster Hoard, future governor of Wisconsin, was also a pioneer of farm journalism, and was especially influenced by Greeley's use of editorials. Hoard's papers became known for their strong editorial pages that weighed in on a range of issues in addition to agriculture. Emerging from this tradition was the founder of *Farm Journal,* Wilmer Atkinson.

Atkinson was born in 1840 in Bucks County, Pennsylvania, the son of Quaker parents. After spending a year in a seminary he taught school while helping his father on the family farm. His first experience running a publication came in 1862 when he and a partner purchased the *Norristown Republican.* Two years later he sold his interest in the paper and moved to Wilmington, Delaware, where he established the state's first daily newspaper, the *Wilmington Daily Commercial,* which he sold in 1876. He then moved to Philadelphia to start a monthly agricultural paper, the *Farm Journal,* which he said was intended for farmers within a day's ride of Philadelphia and dedicated to "practical, not fancy farming." The first issue, priced at 25 cents, was published in March 1877 with an initial press run of 25,000 copies.

Atkinson also established a sense of integrity by announcing in the first issue that *Farm Journal* would refuse to print "quack medical advertisements." At the time, patent medicines and medical devices of dubious value were a mainstay of the popular press. In 1880 Atkinson was the first publisher to issue a personal guarantee, the "Fair Play" code, against the claims made by his magazine's advertisers, anticipating "the *Good Housekeeping* seal of approval." In 1913 *Farm Journal* became the first magazine to issued a money-back guarantee that allowed its subscribers to cancel "at any time, for any reason or for no reason."

Like Hoard, Atkinson used the power of his magazine to champion causes: rural free delivery of mail, postal savings banks, and the preservation of birds. Atkinson wrote in one of the early issues: "We do not publish the *Farm Journal* for the money there is in it, but for the good we can do." This belief became an enduring legacy, as succeeding editors were encouraged to have a cause and to use *Farm Journal* to promote it. One example, of many, was the campaign to abolish the "Widow's Tax," which had forced many farms to be put on the block to pay off the taxes incurred when the husband had died. Laws were changed to recognize the full partnership of women in running family farms. In his day, Atkinson also championed women's rights, heading the Pennsylvania Men's League for Women's Suffrage that operated out of the *Farm Journal* offices in 1915. Atkinson even led a march through the streets of Philadelphia that began at the front steps of *Farm Journal.*

Reaching a Million Subscribers with Farm Journal: 1915

During the 40 years that Atkinson ran *Farm Journal,* the magazine extended its reach well beyond a day's ride of Philadelphia. By 1915 it boasted a national circulation of one million. Although there was a major migration from the country to the cities in the early 20th century, the overall increase in population meant that the number of rural Americans grew from 44 million in 1900 to almost 50 million in 1910, when for the first time, according to the census, the number of farms surpassed six million. The need for farm publications was greater than ever. With the Depression of the 1930s, however, the farm economy suffered greatly. In 1935 *Farm Journal* was sold to the Pew family, owners of Sun Oil Co. (ownership was later transferred to The Pew Charitable Trusts). Subsequently, publisher Graham Patterson sold the magazine's printing press, electing to have R.R. Donnelley & Son do the printing. It was the start of a relationship that would eventually lead to publishing breakthroughs. The magazine also broadened its content in the 1930s. In 1939 it purchased *The Farmer's Wife,* a national women's magazine, which was then included as a magazine within *Farm Journal.* As wives became more instrumental in running farms, the magazine changed with the times. The women's section was eventually replaced by *Farm Family Living,* which catered to all members of the family.

Although circulation of *Farm Journal* continued to rise, reaching a peak of almost 3.7 million in 1953, the dynamics of publishing were changing. Farm magazines simply could not compete with mass market consumer magazines, not to mention television, for consumer product advertising. National farm magazines, which also faced stiff competition from regional farm publications, had to find a way to help farm product advertisers to target specific audiences. A company selling corn seed, for instance, did not want to pay to reach a hog farmer or a wheat farmer. In an effort to address this concern, *Farm Journal* became the first national magazine to publish regional editions. It set up satellite offices to provide content that would appeal to different groups of readers: the wheat farmers in the Midwest, the cotton farmers in the South, and so on. The parent company of the magazine, Farm Journal, Inc., also tried to expand beyond agriculture with the introduction of *Town Journal,* a general interest family monthly, which grew out of a news weekly named *Pathfinder* that had been acquired ten years earlier. Although *Town Journal* built its circulation to more than two million and gross ad revenues surpassed $3 million, the publication was too expensive to produce and was discontinued in December 1956. *Farm Journal,* with $13.6 million in gross ad revenues, was doing well, but faced an uncertain future.

Early in 1958 *Farm Journal* announced that it would voluntarily reduce circulation and advertising rates. Because the magazine had no newsstand sales, it could reduce circulation by removing subscribers, targeting people with non-rural addresses, who were offered their money back or subscriptions to other magazines. Intentionally cutting circulation seemed counterintuitive, but to management the move would "purify" the magazine. According to the president of the company, Richard J. Babcock, "The non-farm readers don't appeal to our advertisers and since it costs more to send a subscription than we make on subscription rates, we save money dropping them. . . . Why not give the advertiser what he wants and make a better profit?" The immediate goal was to drop from a circulation of 3.4 million to 3.1 million.

The next step for *Farm Journal* was to determined who among the rural readers were actually active farmers. In 1962 it began creating a database on its readers, which it soon took advantage of in a rudimentary way. It inserted a "Hog Extra" in the magazines that were mailed to the five leading hog-producing counties in the country. The subscriber received the insert whether he raised hogs or not, but this early effort at targeted publishing led to other inserts in 1964, "Beef Extra" and "Dairy Extra," followed later by a "Cotton Extra." The magazine then began to employ computers in 1965 and gathered specific livestock and crop production information from its subscribers.

Purchase of Company by Management Team: 1973

After a group of seven employees led by Dale E. Smith bought Farm Journal Inc. from The Pew Charitable Trusts in 1973, the magazine became even more aggressive in gathering information, by the use of phone interviews, to further purge its subscription lists. Subscribers had to be preapproved in order to receive the magazine. It was estimated that 95 percent of the people contacted cooperated with the surveys. Although expensive to create and maintain, Farm Journal's database would prove to be a valuable asset. It formed the basis for Rockwood Research, a company that would generate information and lists for commercial clients. In addition to lowering its subscription base to around 800,000, the magazine was then able to take

Key Dates:

1877: Wilmer Atkinson founds *Farm Journal.*
1915: Circulation reaches one million.
1935: Pew Family purchases company.
1952: *Farm Family* begins printing regional editions.
1973: Management group buys company.
1984: *Farm Family* becomes first magazine to use se-lectronic binding, a method of micro-targeting its readership.
1994: Tribune Company buys Farm Journal Corporation.
1997: Investors and management buy back the company.

targeted publishing to an unprecedented level when Donnelley achieved a breakthrough in printing technology.

What Donnelley called selectronic binding was the ability to incorporate the computerized information that *Farm Journal* had gathered on its readers to select specific sections that would be of interest to a particular subscriber. No longer would an insert like "Hog Extra" be sent to every subscriber in a particular county. The method, which came into use in 1982, required that *Farm Journal* supply more content to satisfy both regional and demographic needs, resulting in the hiring of a large number of freelance writers around the country. Selectronic binding gained a great deal of notice with the May 1984 edition of *Farm Journal*, which was printed in more than 8,000 different versions. Because the database also made it feasible to launch magazines that were targeted for specific readers, some of the inserts were then spun off, creating *Hog Extra, Dairy Extra,* and *Beef Extra.* Another insert, devoted to farmers with more than 250 acres, would later be launched as *Top Producer.* The upscale magazine was modeled after *Fortune.*

Although no other magazine could rival *Farm Journal* in technical innovations, the magazine was far from thriving financially. More than half of *Farm Journal* subscribers received the magazine for free, the result of the early 1980s when increasing postal rates made it more costly to mail renewal notices than to send free copies. Management began talking to Chicago media giant Tribune Company in 1993 about a possible sale. After reviewing the books, Tribune management urged Farm Journal to cut costs before further discussions could take place. Farm Journal then trimmed its staff by about 10 percent, and in June 1994 Tribune purchased the company for a reported $20 million. The Farm Journal magazines and database were expected to create synergy with Tribune's nationally syndicated television program, "U.S. Farm Report," but the combination was short-lived. In 1997 a group of investors, including some employees of the magazine, bought back Farm Journal Inc. from Tribune for $17 million. It then created the holding company Farm Journal Corporation.

New management initiated efforts to make Farm Journal into a multimedia company, following the lead of other publishing companies that extended the brand name of a magazine in any number of directions. While still under Tribune ownership, an Internet site, Farmjournal.com, was created. To provide more content for it, *Pro Farmer*, the largest circulation agricultural newsletter in the United States, was acquired. In 1997 Farm Journal began organizing policy conferences in Washington, D.C. More than just admission fees, the events added to the company's prestige. In January 1998 Farm Journal purchased AgDay, the longest running nationally syndicated agribusiness news television program. In 1999 Farm Journal purchased a syndicated radio program to augment its broadcast interests. It also acquired Globalink and the AgCast Network to provide agricultural news and market data to farmers via satellite and the internet.

Farm Journal filed with the SEC in June 1998 in preparation for going public. The hope was to raise some $30 million to fuel acquisitions as well as to pay off long-term debt, which stood at $19.6 million. The offering was shelved, however, when the IPO market soured. By November 1999, management decided to scrap the plan altogether, after concluding that an offering would fail to sufficiently excite investors. Nevertheless, the company continued its efforts at becoming a multimedia company. In January 2000 it teamed with Internet holding company Safeguard Scientifics Inc. and private equity fund Madison Dearborn Partners to start a new Internet business, AgWeb.com. Again it was the database, with information on 90 percent of the nation's farmers and ranchers, that was a major selling point, along with its existing Farmjournal.com operation and the AgCast and Globalink data services. Madison Dearborn, which reviewed hundreds of Internet-based e-commerce companies, decided to invest in AgWeb.com because of Farm Journal's information and editorial content, as well as the ability to promote the site in Farm Journal publications. Furthermore, the numbers of farmers and ranchers gaining access to the Internet were reaching critical mass. The goal of AgWeb.com was to become a portal where clients could set up online storefronts so that commodities as well as farm-related products could be sold. The site would then collect a commission on each sale. The company also hoped to sell banner ads and provide information technology services for farming-related companies.

The president and CEO of Farm Journal, Roger D. Randall, stepped down in order to run AgWeb.com, which set up offices outside of Philadelphia in King of Prussia. He was replaced by Andy Weber in May 2000. Weber was previously an executive at Cahners Business Information, where he was involved in the running of 41 magazine titles in the United States and Europe. He also worked at Chilton, where he was not only responsible for magazines but also five trade shows and 13 web sites. As the number of farmers continued to decline, while competition over revenues increased, Weber faced formidable challenges in leading Farm Journal into its third century. Maintaining the data that the company had so assiduously gathered over the previous 40 years would remain key. According to Weber, "That database and our field presence tells us what shifts are taking place and allows us to understand farming trends first. It allows us to reflect those trends in our magazines, television, radio, over the Internet and everywhere else." Given the historic willingness of Farm Journal to change with the times, there was no reason to doubt that the company, like the practical farmers it served, would find a way to successfully adapt.

Principal Operating Units

Broadcasting; Internet (33% of AgWeb.com); Magazines; Newsletters.

Principal Competitors

Dairylea; Meredith Corporation; Primedia Inc.; Vance Publishing; eMerge Interactive.

Further Reading

Anderson, Barb Baylor, "Celebrating 125 Years: Practical Platform Still Serves *Farm Journal Well, Agri-Marketing Magazine,* July/August 2001.

Barr, Stephen, "In a Selective Bind," *Folio,* September 1, 1992, p. 64.

Callahan, Sean, " 'Farm Journal' Leverages Database to Sow Seeds for Brand Extension," *Business Marketing,* January 1, 1999, p. 9.

Covaleski, John, "Society Hill Address, Farmland Readership," *Philadelphia Business Journal,* September 25, 1989, p. 1.

Fritz, Michael, "Tribune Co. Near Deal to Bring Farm Magazines into Its Fold," *Crain's Chicago Business,* April 25, 1994.

Hamilton, Patricia W., "Farm Journal Feels Its Oats," *D&B Reports,* July/August, pp. 23–25.

Joyce, Marilyn, "Tribune Co. Will Buy Phila.-Based Farm Journal," *Philadelphia Business Journal,* June 10, 1994, p. 3.

Shulman, Stuart, "The Progressive Era Farm Press," *Journalism History,* Spring 1999, pp. 23–35.

—Ed Dinger

FASTENAL COMPANY

INDUSTRIAL & CONSTRUCTION SUPPLIES

Fastenal Company

2001 Theurer Boulevard
Winona, Minnesota 55987-1500
U.S.A.
Telephone: (507) 454-5374
Fax: (507) 453-8049
Web site: http://www.fastenal.com

Public Company
Incorporated: 1968
Employees: 6,477
Sales: $745.7 million (2000)
Stock Exchanges: NASDAQ
Ticker Symbol: FAST
NAIC: 421710 Hardware Wholesalers; 332722 Bolt, Nut,
   Screw, Rivet, and Washer Manufacturing

Fastenal Company sells nuts, bolts, screws, and other fasteners and related supplies (the company's original product line); power tools; cutting tools; hydraulics and pneumatics products; material handling products; janitorial supplies; electrical supplies; welding supplies; and safety supplies. Going into 2001 it offered as many as 195,000 different parts at its 897 company-operated stores throughout the continental United States, Puerto Rico, and Canada. The stores are stocked via 11 distribution centers. Famous for the frugality of the company founder, Fastenal is also distinguished by its record of rapid, highly successful growth since going public in 1987.

Rocky Beginnings

The idea for Fastenal was conceived by 11-year-old Robert (Bob) A. Kierlin. When Kierlin assisted his father at the family's auto supply shop in Winona, Minnesota, he noticed that customers typically drove from store to store looking for fasteners that they needed for particular jobs. If a hardware store did not have the right nut or bolt, the owner would often send the customer to the Kierlins' store, and vice-versa. In many instances, Bob noted, the fastener simply could not be found and the buyer would have to place a special order and wait. "I

wondered if you could put together a store with all the parts," Kierlin recalled in the November 9, 1992 issue of *Forbes*.

The idea stuck with Kierlin. After graduating from high school in 1957 he went on to major in mechanical engineering at the University of Minnesota, where he later earned his M.B.A. After college Kierlin accepted a job with IBM in nearby Rochester. He worked as a financial analyst for about ten years, but was itching to start his own business. According to Kierlin, the opportunity came when he missed an interview for an international position because of a late plane. Instead of getting the job, he ended up starting the company he had envisioned as a boy.

With some effort, he was able to persuade an IBM coworker, Jack Remick, to help him pursue his goal of selling nuts and bolts. Also joining Kierlin were former high school buddies Michael Gostomski, Dan McConnon, and Steve Slaggie. Slaggie, Kierlin, and McConnon had graduated from Winona Cotter High School in 1957, and Gostomski had followed in 1958. The five partners ponied up $30,000 and rented a 20-foot-wide storefront in Winona. The group's first dispute was over what to name the store. Someone suggested "Lightning Bolts," but two of the founders were so opposed to the name that they threatened to take their money and leave. The men finally settled on Fastenal, as in "Fasten All." Remick hand-painted the store sign, which one day would be framed and hung in the company's headquarters offices.

The founders' goal with Fastenal was to devise a means of making all kinds of nuts and bolts readily available to the general consumer. The group tinkered with various solutions, including an idea for a nuts and bolts vending machine. They finally settled on a retail strategy to stock a store with thousands of fasteners that would serve as a dependable one-stop shop. Most of the initial planning was done during the weekends and other times when the group could get time off from work. "It was almost like a hobby," Remick reminisced in the November 1994 *Corporate Report Minnesota*.

The first Fastenal shop opened its doors in 1967 on Winona's Lafayette Street. Despite sluggish sales, the group opened a second outlet in Rochester a few years later, thinking that the larger city might provide the customers that the Fastenal concept needed. It soon became clear to the partners, however, that the venture was a flop. The partners were delivering nuts and bolts in a 1949 Cadillac and having to periodically chip in $1,000 from their savings just to keep the company afloat. "The ship almost went under," Slaggie recalled. "We'd look at the income statement and say, 'We lost how much money?' and then order a round of Budweisers. There was so much red ink."

1970s and 1980s: Finding the Right Formula and Expanding It

The group finally determined that their retail strategy was flawed. Rather than targeting the general consumer, they decided to focus on the commercial market. It turned out that price was much less of a factor than timeliness for that market segment, because contractors and companies often lost money searching or waiting for a particular part. Kierlin and his partners discovered that there was a great need for a service that could quickly provide the fastener or part that a buyer needed. The change turned out to be exactly what the stores needed to become profitable, and Kierlin left IBM in 1973 to run Fastenal full time.

Kierlin continued to improve Fastenal's strategy during the 1970s and gradually began expanding with new stores. The concept became relatively simple: the partners would open outlets in small to medium-sized towns like Winona and Rochester, where price competition tended to be lower than in large cities, which had special fasteners and parts more readily available. As a result, Fastenal was able to generate profits on the basis of reliability and quick service. The company also targeted towns that had healthy manufacturing and construction industries, seeking to become those customers' one-stop shop for fasteners and related parts. The stores stocked a large selection and promised prompt delivery of any item that was not on the shelf. Later, Fastenal even began manufacturing custom parts that could not be found on the market, at a manufacturing and distribution plant established in Winona.

Fastenal branched out during the early 1980s. Importantly, in 1981 Fastenal purchased the inventory and customer list of the fastener lines of Briese Steel in Rochester. That move spurred growth, first into La Crosse, Wisconsin, and then throughout the upper Midwest. By the early 1980s Fastenal was operating more than 30 company-owned stores. Although all of the original founders contributed to the venture's growth, Kierlin was always the driving force; in fact, the other founders, with the exception of Slaggie, went on to start their own small companies while remaining part-owners in Fastenal. Kierlin focused aggressively on customer service and used his financial background to keep tight control on the company's finances.

Kierlin was a singular personality. His cluttered office in Winona housed a telescope that he used to birdwatch (Winona is perched along a scenic stretch of the Mississippi River about 100 miles south of Minneapolis). He rarely wore a tie to work and was known for his informal style, as well as a unique salary plan. Even when his company became a publicly traded, multimillion-dollar corporation, he paid himself only $120,000 annually, which was less than he paid several of his employees. In addition, unlike other chief executives who received low salaries, he paid himself no incentive bonus of any kind. Instead, he was content to watch his ownership interest in Fastenal grow along with the company. Also unusual was the fact that no employees had their own parking spaces and everyone, including Kierlin, received the same vacation benefits.

Beneath his casual exterior, Kierlin was an aggressive capitalist and ideologue with little patience for the methods of government or organized labor. He also held a fierce commitment to education. In a book that he self-published in the early 1990s, *The Unified Theory of Life,* Kierlin condemned the state of public education. "Increasingly," he wrote, "ownership of what goes on at the public schools resides not with the parents, nor even with local voters, but rather with state legislatures and state departments of education. . . . 'Experts' impose their beliefs on what schools should teach and how the schools should teach them. The sense of omniscience leads the 'experts' to get into the minutiae of school schedules, start-times, extra-curriculars and hot-lunch programs."

Kierlin backed his rhetoric financially. In 1987 he and the other Fastenal cofounders set up the Hiawatha Education Foundation to help Cotter, their alma mater, and other area Catholic schools. Within six years the foundation had contributed $25 million. Much of that was used to transform Cotter into a world-class, technology-rich institution that was ultimately attracting hundreds of boarding students from around the country and even the world. The Cotter campus was moved to the closed College of St. Teresa, where ceilings were lowered to house computer networking infrastructure. In addition, a $2 million sports complex was built that incorporated six indoor tennis courts. Because of the foundation's endowment, tuition to the school was a relatively low $1,225 by the mid-1990s, and each graduate was entitled to a college scholarship ranging from $500 to $7,000.

Kierlin continued to expand Fastenal at a rapid rate. By 1985 the chain had grown to a total of 35 company-owned stores. That number grew to 45 in 1986 and 58 in 1987. To generate cash for more expansion, Fastenal's founders took the company public in 1987. The stock jumped from $9 to $15 by year-end, making the Fastenal initial public offering the most successful of the 627 conducted during the year of the October 1987 crash. Fastenal tapped the proceeds of the sale to add new outlets to its burgeoning chain. Seventeen shops were added in 1988, 28 in 1990, and 32 in 1991. By 1992 Fastenal was operating 200 stores throughout the industrial heartland of Pennsylvania, Ohio, Michigan, and Minnesota, but also as far away as Texas, New York, the Dakotas, and West Virginia.

Rapid Growth in the Early 1990s

Fastenal's gains were the result of Kierlin's profitable strategy and constant adaptation to markets. By the early 1990s each Fastenal store was offering a huge 30,000 items. Four thousand of those were stocked, while the rest could be delivered within

24 hours from regional distribution facilities in Winona, Indianapolis, and Scranton (Pennsylvania). Store operators were trained to find the answer to any question posed to them by a customer, as service was the centerpiece of the Fastenal strategy, and any parts that Fastenal employees could not track down could be custom manufactured in the Winona plant. The stores were typically able to garner profit margins of between 50 percent and 80 percent, which was far above the industry average of about 37 percent. Costs were kept low by locating shops in low-rent districts and minimizing other overhead.

As Fastenal carried its successful strategy into small and medium-sized towns throughout the United States and into Canada, sales and profits surged. Even per-store sales continued to climb, despite economic recession in the early 1990s. Fastenal's revenues grew from $11.6 million in 1985 to $20.3 million and $41.2 million in 1987 and 1989, respectively, while net earnings climbed from $818,000 to $4.3 million. Between 1989 and 1992, sales doubled to $81.3 million as net income climbed to $8.83 million. In 1992 Fastenal opened a fourth distribution center in Dallas and agreed to purchase a fifth in Atlanta. It also entered its 29th state. Kierlin and the other cofounders, who still owned a combined 45 percent of the company, had become millionaires.

The reason for Fastenal's proliferating base of customers was readily apparent: customers were willing to pay a premium for a dependable service that could save them a lot of money. About 50 percent of Fastenal's sales during the early 1990s came from manufacturing companies, while another 30 percent came from the construction industry. As an example, a contractor paying employees $30 per hour in wages and benefits could not afford to have a project held up by the lack of a special fastener for a piece of equipment—and he knew he could find it at Fastenal. In one instance, a Ford plant's assembly line was shut down by a breakdown that required a few dozen special bolts. Ford's regular supplier told the company it would have to wait until Monday—three days later. "Meanwhile, it's costing them something like $50,000 an hour to have this line not operating," Slaggie said in the March 11, 1992, *Successful Business.* "They called us and the part is an oddball, something we don't have in stock. We had them fax us the blueprint for the machine and we determined we could make it. . . . We had them finished Sunday afternoon."

Amazingly, Fastenal moved through the early 1990s with virtually no long-term debt, while expanding at a rampant pace.

New stores were added from the East Coast to the West Coast, and the company opened up a sixth distribution center. The total number of Fastenal outlets grew to 256 in 1993 and 324 by the end of 1994. With solid gains in existing store sales, company revenues increased to $110 million in 1993 and $161 million in 1994. After posting record net earnings of $11.9 million in 1993, Fastenal's net income surged to $18.7 million in 1994.

Fastenal entered 1995 with 330 stores in 44 states, each of which offered 37,000 different items, and the company was planning to add 150 outlets to the chain within the next few years. Some of the stores were called FastTool, which debuted in 1993. Positioned next to Fastenal shops, FastTool carried the same concept to the tool market by offering about 3,000 different power and hand tools and safety products. The company was also experimenting in 1995 with a small Fastenal/FastTool combination store for small towns with 5,000 to 8,000 residents.

Expanding the Product Line, Entering the 21st Century

The final years of the 20th century saw Fastenal expand both its product lines and the number of stores it operated. Product introductions during 1996 included the SharpCut line of metal cutting tools, the PowerFlow line of fluid transfer parts and accessories for hydraulic and pneumatic power, the EquipRite line of material handling and storage products, and the CleanChoice line of janitorial and paper products. Two more product lines were added the following year: the PowerPhase line of electrical supplies and the FastArc line of welding supplies. By this time, the company had nine distribution centers; it then opened two more in early 1998, in Winston-Salem, North Carolina, and Kansas City, Missouri. Expansions of the distribution centers in Scranton and Dallas were begun in 1998 and completed in 1999. Meanwhile, by year-end 1997, Fastenal was operating 644 stores, which were located in all 48 of the contiguous United States, as well as in Puerto Rico and Canada. Another 122 stores were opened in 1998, a year in which net sales reached $503.1 million, a 26.4 percent increase over the preceding year.

Another development in 1998 was the establishment of a subsidiary in Mexico, which employed a sales force dedicated to marketing within that country. Also that year came the distribution of the company's first all-inclusive catalog, an 824-page color-coded behemoth. The following year Fastenal began accepting orders via the company web site; as of mid-2001, however, only 1 percent of overall sales came in over the Internet. Sales and earnings growth slowed in 1998 and 1999 due in part to the aftereffects of the Asian financial crisis, which began in late 1997 and dampened demand for North American manufacturing exports. The opening of new stores was consequently slowed down, with only 43 stores opening in 1999 and 88 in 2000. One area of increased growth was in so-called in-plant stores, which were supply depots set up and run by Fastenal within the plants of large customers. There were eight such locations at the beginning of 1999 and 21 at the end of that year. Another method that Fastenal employed to make up for the revenues that would have accrued from the previous faster pace of store openings was to place increased emphasis on sales of the newer product lines. Older Fastenal stores were seeing much of their growth coming from the sale of products outside the original fastener line. By 2000, 35.5 percent of overall sales were being generated by the newer, nonfastener product lines.

In 2000 Fastenal began operating a second manufacturing facility at its Fresno, California, distribution center. Sales for 2000 increased 22.4 percent over the previous year, reaching $745.7 million, while net earnings totaled $80.7 million, an increase of 23.3 percent. Toward the end of the year, the slowdown of the U.S. economy began affecting Fastenal's sales, a trend that continued into 2001. This left some doubt about whether Fastenal could sustain its remarkable record of continuous and fast growth. Nevertheless, the company continued to carry no long-term debt and had plans to open between 100 and 150 stores in 2001, depending on the strength of the economy. Giving credence to the optimistic view of the company's future was Fastenal's proven ability to select the right sites for its stores; only four locations had been closed in the entire history of the company. Another cause for optimism was the continued leadership of the thrifty Kierlin, who remained firmly in charge as chairman, president, and CEO, and who continued to hold a 10.6 percent stake in the firm he cofounded, a stake worth more than $250 million as of mid-2001.

Principal Subsidiaries

Fastenal Canada Company; Fastenal Company Services; Fastenal Company Purchasing; Fastenal Company Leasing; Fastenal Mexico Services S. de R.L. de C.V.; Fastenal Mexico S. de R.L. de C.V.

Principal Competitors

W.W. Grainger, Inc.; Primus, Inc.; Applied Industrial Technologies, Inc.; Lawson Products, Inc.; MSC Industrial Direct Co., Inc.; Park-Ohio Holdings Corp.; Noland Corporation; Pentacon, Inc.; PennEngineering; Production Tool Supply.

Further Reading

Ballon, Marc, "The Cheapest CEO in America," *Inc.,* October 1997, pp. 52–54+.

Barrett, William P., "Bob Kierlin Versus the Shorts," *Forbes,* November 9, 1992, p. 204.

Burcum, Jill P., "Winona's Fastenal Bolts Past $100-Million Mark," *Corporate Report Minnesota,* November 1994, p. 22.

Buttweiler, Joe, "Fastenal Was Best IPO Performer," *Minneapolis-St. Paul CityBusiness,* February 8, 1988, p. 16.

Ciccantelli, Meg, "Corporate Capsule: Fastenal Co.," *Minneapolis-St. Paul CityBusiness,* November 26, 1993, p. 21.

Croghan, Lore, "The Wal-Mart of Nuts and Bolts," *Financial World,* July 18, 1995, p. 51.

Forster, Julie, "Nuts-and-Bolts Style Suits Fastenal's Kierlin," *Corporate Report Minnesota,* July 1999, p. 22.

Manthey, David J., "Fastenal Accelerates Growth," *Industrial Distribution,* November 2000, p. 16.

McLeod, Reggie, "Fastenal's Success Boon to Schools: Winona Firm's Founders Aid Private Education," *Successful Business,* August 29, 1989, p. 30.

Metzler, Melissa, " 'Renaissance Man' Still Underpaid, Despite Raise," *Minneapolis-St. Paul CityBusiness,* July 7, 2000, p. S28.

Morse, Dan, "Hardware Distributor Sticks to Nuts-and-Bolts Strategy," *Wall Street Journal,* July 3, 2001, p. B2.

Parker, Walter, "Fastenal Corp. Founders Remake a Tiny World-Class High School," *Knight-Ridder/Tribune Business News,* December 12, 1993.

Storm, Sheila, "Fastenal to Add New Stores," *Successful Business,* December 9, 1991, p. 1.

Swalboski, Gran, "Booming Fastenal Driven by Service," *Successful Business,* March 11, 1991, p. 22.

Teitelbaum, Richard, "Who Is Bob Kierlin—and Why Is He So Successful?," *Fortune,* December 8, 1997, pp. 245–46, 248.

Youngblood, Dick, "Fastenal Co. Doing Well by Sticking to Nuts and Bolts," *Minneapolis Star Tribune,* September 27, 1993.

——, "Fastenal Keeps on Growing, Making Life Tough for Short Sellers," *Minneapolis Star Tribune,* November 3, 1997, p. 1D.

—Dave Mote
—update: David E. Salamie

FedEx Corporation

942 South Shady Grove Road
Memphis, Tennessee 38120
U.S.A.
Telephone: (901) 818-7500
Toll Free: (800) 463-3339
Fax: (901) 395-2000
Web site: http://www.fedex.com

Public Company
Incorporated: 1971 as Federal Express Corporation
Employees: 215,000
Sales: $19.62 billion (2001)
Stock Exchanges: New York Toronto Boston Midwest
   Pacific
Ticker Symbol: FDX
NAIC: 48411 General Freight Trucking, Local; 484122
   General Freight Trucking, Long-Distance, Less Than
   Truckload (LTL); 49221 Local Messengers and Local
   Delivery; 483111 Deep Sea Freight Transportation;
   481112 Scheduled Freight Air Transportation; 49211
   Couriers; 481212 Nonscheduled Chartered Freight Air
   Transportation

FedEx Corporation is synonymous with overnight delivery, an industry the company developed during the 1970s and one which, nearly three decades later, it continues to dominate. The market leader has restructured for the 21st century and is now composed of five major operating companies: FedEx Express, FedEx Ground, FedEx Freight, FedEx Custom Critical, and FedEx Trade Networks. Operating in 211 countries, FedEx Express is the world's largest express shipping company. FedEx Ground ships small packages by ground and is the second largest provider of such services in North America. FedEx Freight provides regional freight deliveries on a less-than-truckload basis. FedEx Custom Critical serves customers who need very critically timed shipments. Finally, FedEx Trade Networks furnishes a variety of consulting, customs brokerage, and information technology services. Every business day FedEx makes almost five million physical shipments and processes over 100 million electronic transactions. FedEx thus uses its planes, ground vehicles, and electronic technologies to speed up transportation so that companies and individuals can transfer time-sensitive material across vast distances in virtually seamless fashion.

From Term Paper Topic to Reality: 1970s

FedEx was founded as Federal Express Corporation in 1971, by 28-year-old Memphis, Tennessee, native Frederick W. Smith. Smith, a former Marine pilot in Vietnam, originally outlined his idea for an overnight delivery service in a term paper he wrote for a Yale University economics class. He felt that air freight had different requirements than air passenger service and that a company specializing in air freight rather than making it an add-on to passenger service would find a lucrative business niche. Speed was more important than cost, in Smith's view, and access to smaller cities was essential. His strategies included shipping all packages through a single hub and building a private fleet of aircraft. Company-owned planes would free the service from commercial airline schedules and shipping regulations, while a single hub would permit the tight control that got packages to their destinations overnight. In making his dream a reality, Smith selected Memphis as his hub: it was centrally located and despite inclement weather its modern airport rarely closed.

Smith supplemented a $4 million inheritance from his father with $91 million in venture capital to get his idea off the ground. In 1973 FedEx began service in 25 cities with a fleet of 14 Dassault Falcon aircraft and 389 employees. The planes, which were relatively small in size, collected packages from airports every night and brought them to Memphis, where they were immediately sorted. They were then flown to airports close to their destination and delivered by FedEx trucks the following morning.

Smith's idea was costly indeed; it required creating an entire system before the company's first day of business. FedEx added to these start-up costs by beginning expensive advertising and direct-mail campaigns in 1975. The company lost $29 million in its first 26 months of operation: in 1975 alone it gained $43.5

million in sales against an $11.5 million loss. Smith's investors considered removing him from the helm of the fledgling company, but company President Arthur Bass backed the young founder. Bass improved delivery schedules and FedEx's volume climbed to the point where it was profitable: By late 1976 the company was carrying an average of 19,000 packages a night, and by year's end it was $3.6 million in the black.

In 1977 company profits hit $8 million on sales of $110 million. The company had 31,000 regular customers, including such giants as IBM and the U.S. Air Force, which used it to ship spare parts. It also shipped blood, organs for transplant, drugs, and other items requiring swift transport. FedEx serviced 75 airports and 130 cities. While the major airlines gave the company stiff competition on heavily traveled passenger routes, there was virtually no competition on routes between smaller cities. Its principal competitor, Emery Air Freight, used commercial airlines to ship packages, giving FedEx an important time advantage.

Airline Deregulation Fueling Growth: 1977

Deregulation of the airline industry in 1977 gave the still-struggling company an important boost. At the time of FedEx's startup, the U.S. airline industry had been subject to tight federal regulation. In fact, the company had only managed to get into business through an exemption that allowed any company to enter the common carrier business if its payloads were under 7,500 pounds. These self-same regulations, written in 1938 to protect passenger airlines, would ultimately hold back FedEx's growth. The company was forced to fly up to eight small Falcon jets side-by-side to bigger markets when use of one larger jet would have saved money. Smith led a legislative fight to end regulation, and a bill doing so was passed in 1977. Deregulation meant the company could fly anywhere in the United States anytime, and use larger aircraft including 727s, and later, DC-10s. FedEx bought a fleet of used 727-1OOCs, using its Falcons to expand into small- and medium-sized markets.

In 1978, with its prospects looking solid, FedEx went public, selling its first shares on the New York Stock Exchange. The move raised needed capital and gave the company's backers a chance to regain a portion of their initial investment. Profits for 1979 were $21.4 million on sales of $258.5 million. By late 1980 FedEx was well established and growing at about 40 percent a year. It had 6,700 employees and flew 65,000 packages a night to 89 cities across the United States. Its fleet included 32 Falcons, 15 727s, and five 737s.

Explosive growth continued as a tidal wave of businesses switched to overnight service. Miniaturization of consumer electronics and scientific instruments translated into increasing numbers of small, valuable packages needing express shipment. In addition, many U.S. companies were shifting to just-in-time

inventories as a way to keep prices down, lessen quality-control problems, and cut costs. Consequently, these companies often needed emergency shipment of goods and parts, and FedEx was there to provide that much needed service. It soon began billing itself as a ''500-mile-an-hour warehouse.''

Competition and Price Wars During the 1980s

A decline in the reliability of the U.S. Postal Service caused even more companies to switch to FedEx for important packages. Courier-Paks became the fastest growing part of the company's business, accounting for about 40 percent of revenue. In 1980 Courier-Paks—envelopes, boxes, or tubes used for important documents, photographs, blueprints, and other items—cost the consumer $17 but guaranteed overnight delivery. By mid-1980 the company had eight DC-10s on order or option from Continental Airlines, each capable of carrying 100,000 pounds of small packages. It had also acquired 23 additional used 727s, and operated 2,000 delivery vans.

In mid-1981 FedEx announced a new product that would bring it into direct competition with the United States Postal Service (USPS) for the first time: the overnight letter. The document-size cardboard envelope, which could contain up to two ounces, would be delivered overnight for $9.50 at that time.

By 1981 Federal Express had the largest sales of any U.S. air freight company, unseating competitors such as Emery, Airborne Freight, and Purolator Courier, which had gone into business about two decades earlier. Unlike FedEx, competitors shipped packages of all sizes using regularly scheduled airlines, and did not stress speed; FedEx's narrowly focused, speed-oriented service won over many of its competitor's customers. To compete, Emery copied FedEx's strategy, buying its own planes, opening a small-package sorting center, and pushing overnight delivery. Airborne also entered the small-package air express business. United Parcel Service (UPS), the leading package-shipper by truck, moved into the air-express business in 1981. The USPS began heavily marketing its own overnight-mail service after FedEx's Courier-Pak began eating into its revenues. The Postal Service's overnight mail was about half the price of FedEx's, but was not as accessible in many locations.

While FedEx was the leader in the U.S. overnight package-delivery industry, DHL Worldwide Courier Express Network built a similar service overseas; the two would become major competitors when FedEx started building its own overseas network. Such increased competition put pressure on FedEx's niche, but its lead was large and its reputation excellent. In 1983 the company reached $1 billion in annual revenues, the first company in the United States to do so within ten years of its start-up without mergers or acquisitions.

Aggressively Pursuing International Market Dominance: 1980s

In 1984 FedEx made its first acquisition, Gelco Express, a Minneapolis-based package courier that served 84 countries. Hoping to recreate its U.S. market dominance overseas, the company made further acquisitions in Britain, the Netherlands, and the United Arab Emirates. Meanwhile, UPS also began building a competing overseas system.

Key Dates:

1971: Federal Express Corporation is founded.
1973: Company begins its operations with overnight shipping to 25 cities in the United States.
1977: Federal deregulation of the airlines leads to growth for company.
1978: Federal Express is first listed on the New York Stock Exchange.
1981: Company introduces its overnight letter.
1984: Purchase of Gelco Express International leads to service in Europe and the Pacific Rim; company begins its ZapMail system of electronic mail but ends it two years later.
1985: Federal Express opens its European hub at Brussels.
1986: Sorting centers in Oakland, California, and Newark, New Jersey, are opened.
1989: Company buys Tiger International, Inc. to greatly expand its international business.
1994: Federal Express Corporation shortens its name to FedEx.
1995: Latin American and Caribbean division is started; company begins its AsiaOne program through a new hub at Subic Bay, Philippines.
1998: FedEx becomes FDX Corporation and acquires Caliber System, Inc.
1999: opens first European hub at Paris' Charles de Gaulle Airport and a Miami office to serve Latin America.
2000: FDX Corporation reverts to the name FedEx Corporation.
2001: American Freightways Corporation is acquired and FedEx is reorganized; FedEx and the U.S. Postal Service begin a seven-year cooperative venture.

By the late 1970s Smith had realized that up to 15 percent of the company's Courier-Pak business was information that would eventually be digitally transmitted as telephone and computer technology improved. He spent $100 million to develop his own electronic-mail system, which was launched in 1984 as ZapMail. A system for sending letters by fax machine and couriers, ZapMail was plagued by technology problems from the beginning: fax machines broke down frequently; light-toned originals would not transmit; minor telephone-line disturbances interrupted transmissions. ZapMail cost $35 for documents up to five pages, plus $1.00 for each additional page, and high-volume customers soon discovered it was less expensive to install their own fax machines. The program also faced competition from MCI Communications' electronic-mail system. ZapMail was still losing money in 1986 when FedEx abandoned the system, taking a $340 million charge against earnings. In line with the company's policy of limiting layoffs, the 1,300 employees working on the ZapMail system were absorbed into other FedEx operations.

In 1985 FedEx took a major step in its attempt to expand its services to Europe by opening a European hub at the Brussels airport. Revenue reached $2 billion in 1985. In 1986 the company opened sorting centers in Oakland, California, and Newark, New Jersey, to more quickly handle shipments to nearby high-volume destinations. In addition, FedEx's hubs were being transformed into warehouses for its clients, as parts were stored there until customers needed them, then shipped overnight. For example, IBM used FedEx to store mainframe parts and get them quickly to malfunctioning computer systems. This trend coincided with a decline in FedEx's overnight mail volume, which was hurt by the spread of fax machines and the lower rates charged by competitors. Revenue for 1987 was $3.2 billion, while rival UPS collected about $1.7 billion from overnight delivery.

By 1988 FedEx, with 54,000 employees, was providing service to about 90 countries and claimed to ship about 50 percent of U.S. overnight packages. Mounting competition, however, had led to a price war that eroded company profits from 16.9 percent of revenue in 1981 to 11 percent in 1987. Profits in 1988 were $188 million on revenue of $3.9 billion.

Expanding overseas proved tougher than FedEx had anticipated, and the company's international business lost $74 million between 1985 and 1989. In February 1989, hoping to quickly develop a global delivery system, FedEx bought Tiger International, Inc., for $883 million, thereby acquiring its heavy cargo airline, Flying Tiger Line. Before the acquisition, FedEx had landing rights in five airports outside the United States: Montreal, Toronto, Brussels, London, and limited rights in Tokyo. The company hoped to supplement these with the delivery routes Tiger had built over its 40-year history, which included landing rights in Paris and Frankfurt, three Japanese airports, and cities throughout east Asia and South America. FedEx could use its own planes on these routes instead of subcontract to other carriers, which the company had been doing in many countries. Tiger's large fleet of long-range aircraft also gave FedEx an important foothold in the heavy-freight business. In 1988 Tiger had 22 747s, 11 727s, and six DC-8s; 6,500 employees; and revenue of $1.4 billion. Unfortunately, many of Tiger's planes needed quick repairs to meet U.S. government safety deadlines, which led to lower than anticipated profits.

The purchase price paid by the company, which several analysts claimed was too much, also increased FedEx's debt by nearly 250 percent to $2.1 billion, and put the company into a market that was more capital-intensive and cyclical than the domestic small-package market. Owning Tiger also put FedEx in an awkward position, since many of Tiger's best customers were FedEx's competitors, and the company feared it might lose many of them. Such fears proved unfounded, although Tiger's on-time record temporarily fell to 80 percent after the takeover, climbing to 96 percent by early 1990.

At the same time price wars continued with competitors, some of which made inroads into the overnight market. Earnings from UPS's overnight service rose 63 percent between 1984 and 1988, and its revenues tripled. FedEx had a 55 percent share of the U.S. overnight letter market and shipped 33 percent of U.S. overnight packages. It was clearly the leader in the express delivery business, but its growth was slowing. FedEx's U.S. shipment volume grew 58 percent in 1984 but declined to 25 percent in 1988. The company compensated by pushing its higher-margin package service, which grew 53 percent from 1987 to 1989. Analysts estimated that packages provided 80 percent of FedEx's revenues and about 90 percent of its profits.

In April 1990 FedEx raised its domestic prices, ending the seven-year price war. The U.S. air-freight industry was consolidating, and rival UPS had heavy capital expenses from its own overnight air service, giving its competitor room to raise its prices. FedEx needed the extra profits, estimated at between $50 million and $75 million a year, to help pay for losses in its international business. Its foreign operations lost $194 million in 1989 as it struggled to integrate Tiger and build a delivery system in Europe. Tiger was unionized but unstructured; FedEx was non-union but bureaucratic. Several uneasy months passed while the two systems were unified and a pilot seniority list was drawn up. To help increase overseas tonnage, the company introduced one-, two-, and three-day service to large shippers between 25 cities worldwide and 85 cities in the United States.

Business in the Early 1990s

FedEx entered the 1990s with increasing competition in the U.S. market, but was able to maintain its leading market share. UPS, now its main competitor, continued to slowly woo away some customers by introducing volume discounts, a policy which it had resisted for years. FedEx responded by instituting a customer-by-customer review of its own pricing strategy that resulted in a consolidation of subcontractor trucking routes, the streamlining of pickup and delivery routes, and an increased profitability of certain freight runs; in some cases prices were also adjusted upward. Enhancements were offered to express-service customers, including earlier-in-the day service options, computer software that allowed FedEx clients to electronically prepare all shipping documentation, and Internet tracking of shipments via FedEx's new homepage. The company's network of retail affiliates was also expanded, with new FedEx drop-boxes installed in more than 870 office supply superstores nationwide. The results: Despite erosion from aggressive competitors, FedEx's domestic package volume rallied in mid-1992, with revenues growing from $7.6 billion to $7.8 billion over the previous year.

Internally, FedEx began companywide cost-containment policies to reduce waste and overhead, as well as gain increased efficiency in meeting the needs of its customers. The company's Station Review Process allowed the most effective local policies to be shared by the entire FedEx station network. Despite cost-cutting measures, however, employee-related expenses rose when FedEx became mired in over two years of contract negotiations with the Air Line Pilots Association (ALPA). Despite what Smith had considered generous enough salaries and benefit packages to keep the threat of unionization at bay, heated labor negotiations ultimately resulted in the 1996 unionization of FedEx's 3,100 pilots. However, only a few weeks after the pro-union vote, an organization of company pilots was petitioning the National Labor Mediation Board to call a second vote to oust the union, leading analysts to doubt ALPA's continued influence over FedEx budgetary policy. On the plus side, the expiration of a federal cargo tax during the federal budget impasse of January 1996 would provide FedEx with a fiscal boost as the company maintained prices despite a temporary hiatus in federally directed excise payments.

In the early 1990s FedEx's foreign operations were troubled, and their losses dragged down company earnings. While overall sales rose from $5.2 billion in 1989 to $7.69 billion in fiscal 1991, operating income fell from $424 million to $279 million over the same period, much of it resulting from the costly development of overseas markets. Industry analysts were divided over whether or how soon the company would be able to make its foreign operations profitable. Some analysts questioned how long FedEx could accept international losses while carrying $2.15 billion in long-term debt.

Smith countered such concerns by arguing that when the company's international volume increased, international service would become profitable. In an effort to boost that volume, FedEx traded in its 727s for larger capacity Airbus Industrie jet aircraft for their three daily European-destination flights, filling extra cargo space with non-express packages to increase per-flight profitability. In 1994 the company became the first international express cargo carrier to receive systemwide ISO 9001 certification; by mid-decade international service accounted for 12 percent of the company's business: FedEx linked over 200 countries and territories worldwide, representing the bulk of global economic transactions. By 1996 the company could boast sales of $10.27 billion against operating income of $624 million.

Expansion in the Late 1990s and the New Century

Aggressive international route expansion included creating divisions in several hemispheres. A Latin America and Caribbean division was created in 1995 to integrate services within the world's second-fastest growing economic region. In September of that year the company introduced FedEx AsiaOne: a next-business-day service between Asian countries and the United States. Via a hub established at Subic Bay, Philippines, FedEx planned to duplicate its successful hub-and-spoke delivery service within 11 of that continent's commercial and financial centers. Unfortunately, the company's plans were confounded by the Japanese government, which limited FedEx's flying rights from Japan to other Asian countries in mid-1996, after a series of talks between the United States and Japan failed to yield a compromise. While the U.S. government contemplated appropriate sanctions against the Japanese government for its failure to honor existing flight privileges with FedEx, Japan viewed the company's growing success in Asia as a threat to its own overseas cargo industry. Despite difficulties with Japan, the extension of its world renowned service to the Pacific Rim area placed FedEx in a strategic position within one of the fastest-growing economic centers in the world, particularly with regard to China, where the company was the sole U.S.-based cargo service then authorized to do business.

In 2001 FedEx worked to gain approval to create a new hub at the Piedmont Triad International (PTI) Airport near Greensboro, North Carolina. PTI planned to build a new runway to accommodate FedEx. Critics included the Cardinal West and Prestwich homeowners associations that opposed the noise, air, and water pollution, and decreased land values that they felt would result from the new hub. Meanwhile, FedEx and the U.S. Postal Service in January 2001 announced a $6.3 billion, seven-year cooperative agreement in which FedEx would use its planes to carry first-class, Express, and Priority mail. In June 2001 FedEx began putting its collection boxes at post offices, and the system became operational a few months later. Responding to these developments, Emery Worldwide Airlines filed a lawsuit against the USPS deal for lack of competition. Ryan International Airlines and Evergreen International Aviation also protested the alliance in U.S. House of Representatives committee meetings. The U.S. Justice Department considered starting an antitrust investigation into the USPS/FedEx arrangement.

In 2001 FedEx Corporation was a holding company with five main subsidiaries. FedEx Express served customers in 211 countries. Every business day it delivered 3.3 million packages using a fleet of 662 aircraft, including large planes such as the Airbus A300, McDonnell DC10, and Boeing 727, and also smaller planes such as the Cessna 208. With over 45,500 ground vehicles, FedEx Express remained the leader in the overnight express delivery business. Based in Pittsburgh, FedEx Ground (formerly RPS) handled small-package delivery with over 9,000 vehicles. It delivered about 1.6 million packages every business day, according to the company web site. With services in the United States, Canada, Puerto Rico, and Mexico, FedEx Ground was North America's second largest ground carrier and delivered small packages business to business. Its FedEx Home Delivery was added in March 2000. FedEx Ground reported annual revenue of $2 billion in fiscal 2000. According to a *Morning Call* article on February 8, 2001, FedEx Ground delivered items in 70 percent of the United States, compared to its competitors United Parcel Service (UPS) and the U.S. Postal Service, which had full coverage.

FedEx Freight, the third subsidiary, provided next-day and second-day regional freight services on a less than truckload (LTL) basis. With $1.9 billion in annual sales, FedEx Freight included two formerly independent trucking companies. Viking Freight, Inc. was founded in 1966 in San Jose, California. It shipped goods in Arizona, California, Colorado, Idaho, Nevada, New Mexico, Oregon, Utah, Washington, parts of Texas near El Paso, and also Alaska and Hawaii via ocean shipping. It also transported goods into Mexico and Canada. FedEx Freight's second trucking firm was American Freightways Corporation, based in Harrison, Arkansas. Founded in 1982, it served most states and also the Caribbean islands, Guam, and Central and South America through partnerships with other companies. This LTL carrier's history was included on its web site at www.arfw.com. In 2000 its 17,000 employees brought in annual sales of $1.43 billion. FedEx acquired American Freightways in February 2001. Subsidiary FedEx Custom Critical picked up and delivered whatever its customers needed around the clock and every day of the year. Based in Akron, Ohio, FedEx Custom Critical delivered about 1,000 shipments daily to customers in the United States, Canada, and Europe. The FedEx web site described this subsidiary as "North America's largest time-specific, critical shipment carrier." FedEx Trade Networks served customers worldwide by providing customs brokerage, consulting, and electronic services. Founded in February 2000, this fifth subsidiary employed about 1,600 persons. Its operating companies included Tower Group International, Inc., which had 63 North American offices and also Asian offices through agent partners; Worldtariff, Limited, which published customs duty and tax data for 101 nations; and Caribbean Transportation Services, the "leading provider of airfreight forwarding services between the United States and Puerto

Rico," according to the FedEx Web site. FedEx customers placed 60,000 daily telephone calls to company representatives to keep track of their shipments. The Internet and electronic technology were used for 1.2 million daily delivery trackings through the fedex.com web site. This combination of high-touch and high-tech methods of tracking millions of daily shipments proved crucial to the success of FedEx.

FedEx in 2001 used 94,800 ground vehicles, including its long-haul trucks, to deliver letters, small packages, and larger freight items to international destinations. That was combined with its air fleet of small and large planes, electronic message system, and strategic alliances, including that with La Poste in Europe. "FedEx has built what is the most seamless global air and ground network in its industry, connecting more than 90 percent of the world's economic activity," said William G. Margaritis, FedEx Corporation's vice president for world communications and investor relations. With the rapid rise of virtually instantaneous electronic mail, some wondered if FedEx overnight mail delivery was as important as it was in the past. Margaritis pointed out that the company received only 9.3 percent of its revenue from overnight express mail, and that much of that mail could not be delivered electronically, such as gifts, electronic components, and medical equipment.

FedEx completed its fiscal year ending May 31, 2001 with mixed financial results. The good news was an 8 percent increase in company revenue to $19.6 billion from $18.3 billion the year before. However, operating income fell 12 percent from $1.22 billion to $1.07 billion, and net income decreased 15 percent from $688 million to $584 million. In 2001 FedEx faced tough competition, especially from United Parcel Service, the industry leader in ground deliveries. It still competed with the U.S. Postal Service, but its cooperative venture with the latter was a major step for both entities. In any case, FedEx had expanded far beyond what Frederick W. Smith started back in 1971. Thirty years later, CEO Smith remained as the head of FedEx, providing leadership continuity during the company's rapid expansion and change.

Principal Subsidiaries

FedEx Ground; FedEx Express; FedEx Freight, comprised of Viking Freight, Inc. and American Freightways, Inc.; FedEx Custom Critical; FedEx Trade Networks; Federal Express Aviation Services; Federal Express International; Flying Tiger Line Inc.; Tiger Inter Modal Inc.; Tiger Trucking Subsidiary Inc.; Warren Transport Inc.

Principal Competitors

DHL Worldwide Express; United Parcel Service, Inc.; United States Postal Service.

Further Reading

"Cargo Airlines Escalate Opposition to New Pact Between U.S. Postal Service and Federal Express," *PR Newswire*, April 3, 2001, p. 1.

"FedEx Drop Boxes Now at Post Offices," *Salt Lake Tribune*, June 20, 2001, p. B4.

"FedEx's Rob Carter Charts the Course for the Future of Business," *PR Newswire*, June 11, 2001.

Flaherty, Robert J., "Breathing Under Water," *Forbes*, March 1, 1977.

——, "Transportation," *Business Week,* March 31, 1980.

Foust, Dean, et al., "Mr. Smith Goes Global: He's Putting Federal Express' Future on the Line to Expand Overseas," *Business Week,* February 13, 1989.

Greising, David, "Watch Out for Flying Packages," *Business Week,* November 14, 1994. "Ground Wars," *Business Week,* May 21, 2001.

Magaritis, William G., "The Ascent of Federal Express," *Business Week,* June 11, 2001, p. 24.

Levering, Robert, and Milton Moskowitz, "Viking Freight System," *The 100 Best Companies to Work for in America,* New York: Currency Doubleday, 1993, pp. 471–74.

Moorman, Robert W., "Postal Service/FedEx Alliance Challenged by Rivals," *Aviation Week & Space Technology,* January 22, 2001, pp. 42–43.

Nomani, Asra Q., "Sparks Fly over Air-Cargo Agreement," *Wall Street Journal,* March 1, 1996.

Savidge, Mariella, "FedEx Opens Allentown Office; Company Has Increased Its Package Delivery to Compete with UPS and Postal Service," *Morning Call* [Allentown, Pennsylvania], February 8, 2001, p. A15.

Sigafoos, Robert A., with Roger R. Easson, *Absolutely, Positively Overnight!,* Memphis: St. Luke's Press, 1988.

Trimble, Vance H., *Overnight Success: Federal Express and Frederick Smith, Its Renegade Creator,* New York: Crown Publishers, Inc., 1993.

Wetherbe, James C., *The World on Time: The 11 Management Principles That Made FedEx an Overnight Sensation,* Santa Monica, Calif.: Knowledge Exchange, 1996.

Wireback, Taft, "Subdivisions Join to Oppose FedEx Hub; Airport-Area Neighborhoods Are Going on Record Against the Planned Air Cargo Hub," *Greensboro News Record,* June 8, 2001, p. B1.

—Scott M. Lewis
—updates: Pamela L. Shelton, David M. Walden

Fujitsu Limited

6-1, Marunouchi 1-chome
Chiyoda-ku
Tokyo 100-8211
Japan
Telephone: (03) 3216-3211
Fax: (03) 3216-9365
Web site: http://www.fujitsu.co.jp

Public Company
Incorporated: 1935
Employees: 187,399
Sales: ¥5.26 trillion ($44.23 billion) (2001)
Stock Exchanges: Tokyo Osaka Nagoya Frankfurt
London Swiss
Ticker Symbol: FJTSY (OTC)
NAIC: 334111 Electronic Computer Manufacturing;
334112 Computer Storage Device Manufacturing;
334119 Other Computer Peripheral Equipment Manufacturing; 334210 Telephone Apparatus Manufacturing;
334220 Radio and Television Broadcasting and Wireless Communications Equipment Manufacturing;
334290 Other Communications Equipment Manufacturing; 334413 Semiconductor and Related Device Manufacturing; 514191 On-Line Information Services;
541511 Custom Computer Programming Services;
541512 Computer Systems Design Services; 541513
Computer Facilities Management Services; 541519
Other Computer Related Services; 541610 Management
Consulting Services; 511210 Software Publishers

Fujitsu Limited is one of the world's leading makers of computers, semiconductors, and telecommunications equipment and is considered one of Japan's *sogo denki,* or general electric companies, a group that is typically said to also include Hitachi, Ltd.; Mitsubishi Electric Corporation; NEC Corporation; and Toshiba Corporation. Historically, Fujitsu was best known as the world's number two maker of mainframe computers, behind IBM, but Fujitsu exited from that market at the turn of the millennium to focus its hardware efforts on Unix-based servers, personal computers (vying with NEC for the top spot in Japan), and peripherals. The Fujitsu of the early 21st century, however, was deemphasizing its hardware roots, billing itself as an Internet-centered company, and generating increasing amounts of revenues from services and software. The latter, which included such areas as system integration services, network services, Internet service (including Japan's leading ISP, Nifty Serve), and system maintenance and monitoring, accounted for 37 percent of overall revenue in fiscal 2001. Hardware generated 27 percent of sales, telecommunications equipment, 15 percent, semiconductors, 14 percent, and other operations, 7 percent.

Early History

Fujitsu was created on June 20, 1935, as the manufacturing subsidiary of Fuji Electric Limited and charged with continuing the parent company's production of telephones and automatic exchange equipment. Fuji Electric, itself a joint venture of Japan's Furukawa Electric and the German industrial conglomerate Siemens, was part of Japan's attempt to overcome its late start in modern telecommunications. Spurred by Japan's expanding military economy, Fujitsu quickly branched off into the production of carrier transmission equipment in 1937 and radio communication two years later. Yet the country's telephone system remained archaic and incomplete, with German and British systems in use that were not fully compatible. World War II ruined a large part of this primitive system, destroying some 500,000 connections out of a total of 1.1 million, and leaving the country in a state of what might be called communication chaos. At the insistence of the occupying U.S. forces, Japan's Ministry of Communications was reorganized and nearly became a privately owned corporation that would have simply adopted existing U.S. technology to rebuild the country's telephone grid. A coalition led by Eisaku Sato, however, persuaded the government to instead form a new public utility, Nippon Telephone and Telegraph (NTT). Created in 1952, NTT soon became a leading sponsor and purchaser of advanced electronic research, and it continued to be one of Fujitsu's key customers.

The link with NTT may well have been Fujitsu's greatest asset, but Fujitsu was only one of a series of increasingly

---

Company Perspectives:

The rapid expansion of the Internet is dramatically changing individual lifestyles and the conduct of business throughout the world, presenting tremendous new challenges and opportunities. We are determined to help our customers succeed in this dynamic new era by focusing squarely on their needs, and by leveraging our technological strengths, highly reliable products and services, and global expertise in systems and services to deliver solutions that unleash the infinite possibilities of the Internet.

---

determined government partners for the country's young computer industry. Fujitsu first became interested in computers in the early 1950s, when Western governments and large corporations began making extensive use of them for time-consuming calculations. After a number of years of experimentation Fujitsu succeeded in marketing Japan's first commercial computer, the FACOM 100, in 1954.

This was a start, but the Japanese computer business was still in its infancy when IBM brought out the first transistorized computer in 1959. So great was the shock of this quantum leap in design that the Japanese government realized it would have to play a far more vigorous role if the country was not to fall permanently behind the United States. The government formulated a comprehensive plan that included restrictions on the number and kind of foreign computers imported, low-cost loans and other subsidies to native manufacturers, and the overall management of national production to avoid needless competition while encouraging technological innovation. Of equal importance, in 1961 the Japanese government negotiated with IBM for the right to license critical patents, in exchange allowing the U.S. giant to form IBM Japan and begin local production.

Computer Developments: 1960s

Patents in hand, seven Japanese companies entered the computer race. All of them except Fujitsu quickly formed alliances with U.S. companies to further their research; Fujitsu, refused by IBM in a similar offer, remained the only ''pure,'' or *junketsu,* Japanese computer firm, committed to the development of its own technological expertise. The other Japanese companies were all much larger than Fujitsu and devoted only a fraction of their energy to computers, while Fujitsu soon devoted itself to communications and computers.

Able to build on its already substantial electronics experience Fujitsu was directed by the government to concentrate on the development of mainframes and integrated circuitry, and in late 1962 it was given the specific goal of developing a competitor to IBM's new 1401 transistorized computer. The government stalled IBM's plans for local production and enlisted Hitachi, NEC, and Fujitsu in what it called project FONTAC, the first in what would become a series of government-industry drives. From the perspective of the marketplace, FONTAC was a complete failure—before it got off the ground IBM had launched its revolutionary 360 series, pushing the Japanese further behind than when they started—but as a first try at a coordinated national

computer program, FONTAC proved to be extremely important. Fujitsu and the other Japanese manufacturers could afford poor initial performance, knowing that funds were available for further research and development. In particular, the Japanese government had by this time formed the Japanese Electronic Computer Company (JECC), a quasi-private corporation owned by the seven computer makers but given unlimited low-interest government loans with which to buy and then rent out newly produced computers. In effect, this allowed Fujitsu and the others to receive full payment for their wares immediately, thus greatly increasing corporate cash flow and making possible the huge outlays for research and development.

The result of JECC's largesse was immediate: in the space of a single year—1961 to 1962—Japanese computer sales increased by 203 percent. In 1965 Fujitsu, relying largely on technology developed as part of the FONTAC project, brought out the most advanced domestic computer yet built, the FACOM 230. The company had quickly become JECC's leading manufacturer, supplying approximately 25 percent of all computers purchased by the firm during the 1960s. In addition, Fujitsu had continued its substantial work for NTT, with over half of its telecommunication products going to the phone company by the end of the decade. NTT remained a critically important governmental agency for Fujitsu and the computer industry, routinely shouldering research-and-development costs and paying high prices to ensure that its suppliers remained profitable. NTT also sponsored a super-high-performance computer project in 1968, similar in design and scope to one begun the previous year by the Ministry for Trade and Industry (MITI), to develop a new computer for its complex telecommunications needs. Both of these ambitious programs were paid for by rival government ministries.

Development of the M Series in the 1970s

Despite this concerted effort, however, by 1970 the Japanese were suffering from IBM's recent introduction of its 370 line. Worse yet, under international pressure the Japanese government had agreed to liberalize its import policy by 1975, giving the local computer industry a scant five years in which to become truly competitive. MITI responded by making computer prowess a national goal, greatly increasing subsidies, and reorganizing the six remaining companies into three groups of cooperative pairs. Fujitsu, as the leading mainframe maker, was paired with its arch-rival Hitachi and given the task of matching IBM's 370 line with a quartet of its own heavy-duty computers, to be called the M series.

The need to build IBM-compatible machines led Fujitsu to an important decision. In 1972 the company invested a small but vital sum of money in a new venture started by Gene Amdahl, a former IBM engineer who had been largely responsible for the design of its 360 series computers. Amdahl Corporation had been formed with the express intent of building a cheaper, more efficient version of IBM's 370 line, which made a joint venture with Fujitsu highly advantageous for both partners. With its strong government support, Fujitsu had access to the capital Amdahl badly needed, while the U.S. engineer was a valuable source of information about IBM operating systems. Fujitsu and Amdahl persevered in what became a most profitable sharing of technology and capital.

Key Dates:

1935: Fujitsu is created as a telecommunications manufacturing subsidiary of Fuji Electric.

1954: Fujitsu successfully markets Japan's first commercial computer, the FACOM 100.

1965: Company introduces the FACOM 230.

1972: Fujitsu invests in Amdahl Corporation, a new venture formed to build IBM-compatible mainframes.

Late 1970s: The M series of high-speed computers is introduced through a joint effort of Fujitsu and Hitachi.

1982: Fujitsu introduces the first Japanese supercomputer.

1990: Company purchases an 80 percent stake in International Computers Ltd. (ICL), the U.K.'s leading mainframe maker.

1997: Fujitsu spends $878 million to take full control of Amdahl.

1998: Naoyuki Akikusa becomes company president and places increasing emphasis on software and services, adopting "Everything on the Internet" as the company slogan.

2000: Amdahl announces that it will exit from the mainframe market to focus on software, services, and consulting.

2001: Major restructuring involving a ¥300 billion ($2.43 billion) charge and job cuts totaling 16,400 jobs is announced.

A key factor in the Fujitsu-Amdahl deal was the Japanese company's confidence that it could rely on NTT to pay top dollar for whatever computer evolved from the new venture. In this, as in many other situations, NTT served as a kind of guaranteed market for Fujitsu, which in turn was well on its way to becoming a world leader in telecommunication technology and hence a more valuable supplier to NTT. The Fujitsu-Hitachi M series of high-speed computers emerged in the late 1970s. With the M series, the Japanese had achieved a rough parity with the IBM systems. Fujitsu had become one of IBM's very few real competitors in the area of general purpose mainframe computers; in 1979 Fujitsu took a narrow lead over IBM in Japanese computer sales that held through the mid-1990s.

New Initiatives of the 1980s

After the watershed events of the 1970s, Fujitsu in the 1980s pushed ahead with an impressive array of projects in each of its three main marketing areas. In computers, which generated 60 to 70 percent of overall corporate revenue, Fujitsu continued the success of its M series while branching out into minicomputers, workstations, and personal computers. The company spent much of the 1980s in a legal dispute with IBM over the latter's charge that Fujitsu had improperly copied IBM's software. An arbitrator decided in 1988 that, after $833 million in payments to IBM, Fujitsu could continue to buy access to IBM software for ten years at a cost of at least $25 million a year. The agreement was meant as a spur to further mainframe competition. After introducing the first Japanese supercomputer in 1982, Fujitsu became a leading manufacturer of supercomputers, with some 80 such units installed by the end of the 1980s. Though easily the leading mainframe maker in Japan, Fujitsu had little success exporting its products—with only 22 percent of corporate sales made overseas, Fujitsu remained overly dependent on its Japanese business. In particular, the company was unable to break into the U.S. market, where, in addition to the obvious presence of IBM, its mainframe bias was seen as somewhat outdated. The trend in large computer systems at the time was toward greater distribution of processing power, aided by individually tailored software applications—two areas in which Fujitsu was notably weak.

Fujitsu remained strong in telecommunications, however, continuing its close relationship with NTT as well as with the newly emerging New Common Carriers. In light of its origin in the telecommunication field, it was not surprising that Fujitsu became a world leader in the development of Integrated Services Digital Network (ISDN), a convergence of data processing and telecommunications aiming to carry voice, image, data, and text all on one system. Fujitsu was also active in other improvements in telecommunications such as COINS (corporate information network systems), PBXs (private branch exchanges), and digital switching systems. The company also provided important terminal and branching equipment for the Trans-Pacific Cable #3, the Pacific Ocean's first optical submarine cable.

Fujitsu maintained a strong presence in its third product area as well, electronic devices. In 1987 the firm was prevented by the U.S. government from acquiring Fairchild Camera, a leading U.S. manufacturer of memory chips, but it still managed to sell about $2.5 billion worth of chips annually. The very fact that Fujitsu was barred from purchasing Fairchild was a testament to the company's strength in semiconductors as well as computers. In conjunction with the Japanese government and other Japanese computer firms, Fujitsu continued to refine its chip technology in anticipation of the arrival of the fifth generation of computers, proposed machines that would be able to write their own software and in some meaningful sense "think."

Partnering and Restructuring in the Early 1990s

In the end, however, Fujitsu's 1980s activities proved unable to carry a healthy firm into the 1990s. Observers noted (in hindsight) that the company had played a mainly follow-the-leader (IBM) strategy which emphasized mainframe computers—this began to catch up with Fujitsu in the early 1990s as the shift to networked systems and client-server systems accelerated, cutting the market for mainframes dramatically. Other initiatives undertaken in the 1980s to great fanfare proved less important long-term than little noticed projects; in telecommunications, for example, ISDN was still being touted as the system of the future as late as 1996, while Fujitsu's Nifty Serve online service, which debuted in 1986, was seen as the centerpiece of the company's telecommunications operation in the mid-1990s because of the emergence of the Internet (Nifty-Serve had about 1.6 million subscribers in Japan in 1996).

The year 1990, then, became a year of transition for Fujitsu upon the appointment of Tadashi Sekizawa, a telecommunications engineer, as president. Sekizawa wanted Fujitsu to be more aggressive in its pursuit of foreign markets (80 percent of revenue in 1989 came from Japan), to become more market-driven in general, and to lessen the stifling bureaucracy that impeded product development.

To bolster the firm internationally, Sekizawa continued to seek non-Japanese partners for growth, wishing to utilize local experts knowledgeable about local markets. Already having a partner in the United States through its 43 percent stake in Amdahl, Fujitsu gained a major European partner in July 1990 when it spent £700 million ($1.3 billion) for an 80 percent stake in International Computers Ltd. (ICL), Britain's largest and most important mainframe maker. Fujitsu and ICL—which had become a subsidiary of STC in 1984—had already collaborated on several projects, beginning in 1981. Fujitsu's European operations were further bolstered in 1991 when ICL acquired Nokia's data systems group, which was the largest computer company in Scandinavia. The U.S. market was further targeted as well with a $40 million investment in HaL Computer Systems, Inc., a start-up firm aiming to develop UNIX systems, UNIX being an increasingly popular operating system.

Unfortunately for Fujitsu, the Japanese economic bubble burst in 1991 just as the company was beginning to implement Sekizawa's program. As a result, profits fell 85.2 percent from ¥82.67 billion in fiscal 1990 to ¥12.21 billion in fiscal 1991; the following two years, Fujitsu posted losses—¥32.6 billion in fiscal 1992 and ¥37.67 billion in fiscal 1993. Looming over these figures was the downside of the company's huge investments of the 1980s—a $12.4 billion debt by 1992.

The recession precluded Fujitsu from making further international moves in 1991, and capital spending was slashed one-third that year. Strategically, however, research and development spending was not cut. Since the Japanese culture prevented companies in Fujitsu's position from making large workforce reductions to cut costs, Sekizawa dramatically cut the number of new hires. Meanwhile, to lessen its dependence on mainframe sales and strengthen its PC area, Sekizawa in 1992 established a cross-functional Personal Systems Business Group with the aim of speeding up product development. Also intended to improve product development speed was a restructuring that created a flatter organizational structure and lessened corporate bureaucracy.

Fujitsu's huge debt ruled out any major investments to create new products, so the company turned to partnerships to an even greater degree as the decade continued. The deals included: developing a next generation of less expensive mainframes with Siemens; establishing a joint venture with Advanced Micro Devices, Inc. called Fujitsu AMD Semiconductor Limited to produce flash memory; creating multimedia technology with Sharp Corp.; developing microprocessors for Sun workstations with Sun Microsystems; and relying on Computer Associates to market Jasmine software in the United States.

Mid-1990s into the 21st Century: Moving Toward an Emphasis on Software and Services

Clearly, Fujitsu in the mid-1990s was juggling a number of initiatives as well as dealing with weakening mainframe sales and a difficult, highly competitive semiconductor market. Encouragingly, revenues rose sharply in fiscal 1994 (¥3.26 trillion)

and 1995 (¥3.76 trillion), while the company also returned to profitability, posting net income of ¥45.02 billion in 1994 and ¥63.11 billion in 1995. Part of the sales increase in 1995 was attributable to a huge increase in sales of Fujitsu personal computers. During the year, by offering its models at extremely low prices—possibly at a loss—the company more than doubled its share of the Japanese PC market to 18.4 percent, placing it second to NEC; overall sales of PCs in Japan increased an astounding 70 percent that year as Japanese companies began making the transition from mainframes to networked PCs. Fujitsu also made a strong push to expand its share of the overseas PC market, aiming to become the number five computer maker by 2000. According to Sekizawa, the renewed PC drive had an ancillary benefit of providing Fujitsu with opportunities to develop a much stronger position in software and services connected with computer networks and with the broader—and emerging—Internet.

The heightened activity in the area of software and services became increasingly important in the late 1990s and into the 21st century as all of the Japanese electronics firms saw their profit margins on computers, semiconductors, and telecommunications gear decline steadily. Nowhere was the shift from hardware to software and services more apparent than in Fujitsu's floundering mainframe affiliate Amdahl. By mid-1997, Amdahl had posted six consecutive quarters in the red and appeared on the verge of bankruptcy. In September of that year, Fujitsu stepped in and purchased the 57 percent of Amdahl it did not already own for $878 million. The cash infusion saved Amdahl from bankruptcy, and the company began to place increasing emphasis on its software, services, and consulting operations. Similarly, ICL had also been transformed into a leading U.K. information technology services company by the time Fujitsu took full control of it in 1998. Under Fujitsu's new president, Naoyuki Akikusa, who took over during 1998, the transformation of Amdahl reached its logical conclusion when the firm announced in late 2000 that it would exit from the mainframe business altogether, reducing its hardware business to servers and storage systems.

Under Akikusa, Fujitsu adopted the slogan "Everything on the Internet," and these words were put into action in 1999 when the company gained full control of Nifty Serve, merged it with another online service, and thereby created the leading Internet service provider in Japan. Akikusa also took decisive action within the company's semiconductor operations, which were losing money because of falling computer chip prices. He shut down Fujitsu's chip operations in England, taking a $480 million writeoff (which contributed to a net loss for the 1999 fiscal year), closed older chip operations at home, and began buying more of the chips it needed for its own products from Taiwanese firms. Of its remaining chip operations, Fujitsu planned to scale back production of dynamic random-access memory chips (DRAMs), which were used in personal computers, in favor of an increased focus on advanced semiconductors used in such products as cellular phones. Alliances played a role in this shift as Fujitsu in May 2000 entered into an agreement with Advanced Micro Devices Inc. of the United States to manufacture flash memory used in cellular phones, computer-network devices, digital cameras, car navigation systems, and other increasingly popular high-tech gear. Fujitsu was also involved in other semiconductor collaborations, including tie-ups with Sony to develop system large-scale integrated circuits (LSIs), which combined memory and processing in a single chip that could be used in digital audio-video devices and in mobile communications products; and with Toshiba to develop a next-generation, one-gigabit memory chip.

Another key alliance was launched in June 1999 with Siemens AG. A jointly owned company called Fujitsu Siemens Computers was created to combine the European computer operations of the two firms. After a troubled beginning marked by squabbling by the two partners over the direction of the joint venture, which initially focused on desktop PCs, Fujitsu Siemens shifted ground in late 2000, announcing plans to focus on selling servers and mobile computers to businesses and to enter the hand-held computer segment. Back on the Internet front, Fujitsu and Sakura Bank Ltd. announced in July 1999 that they had formed a joint venture to establish the first Internet/online bank in Japan.

Fujitsu's shift of emphasis to the Internet, software, and services failed to buffet the firm from the effects of the severe downturn in the tech sector that began in the later months of 2000. The company faced a simultaneous slowdown in the U.S. telecommunications industry, weakening demand in the mobile phone market worldwide, a deep falloff in demand for computers from consumers and small businesses, and corporate belt-tightening that hit the tech sector particularly hard. Consequently, Fujitsu barely eked out a profit for the 2001 fiscal year. The company then announced in July 2001 that it would take a ¥300 billion ($2.43 billion) charge in the year ending in March 2002 for a major restructuring. The company planned to merge business units, divest noncore operations, and combine several plants into one. One month later, Akikusa announced plans to cut 16,400 jobs, or about 9 percent of the company workforce as part of the restructuring. About 5,000 of the cuts would come in Japan but they would not involve any layoffs of full-time employees but would rather come through attrition and the elimination of temporary positions. This was one of the most dramatic restructurings undertaken by a major Japanese electronics firm, and its success or failure would go a long way toward determining the future direction of Fujitsu in the initial years of the 21st century.

Principal Subsidiaries

Fujitsu Laboratories Ltd.; Fujitsu Denso Ltd. (50%); FDK Corporation (61%); Shinko Electric Industries Co., Ltd. (50%); Fujitsu Systems Construction Ltd. (67%); Fujitsu Support and Service Inc. (56%); Takamisawa Electric Co., Ltd. (53%); Fujitsu Kiden Ltd. (54%); Fujitsu Devices Inc. (67%); Fujitsu Business Systems Ltd. (53%); Fujitsu AMD Semiconductor Ltd. (50%); Fujitsu Hitachi Plasma Display Ltd. (50%); Fujitsu TEN Ltd. (55%); PFU Ltd. (61%); Fujitsu Quantum Devices Ltd.; Fujitsu Media Devices Ltd.; Fujitsu FIP Corporation; NIFTY Corporation; Fujitsu Leasing Co., Ltd. (50%); Fujitsu Basic Software Corporation (70%); ICL PLC (U.K.); Amdahl Corporation (U.S.A.); DMR Consulting Group, Inc. (U.S.A.); Fujitsu Network Communications, Inc. (U.S.A.).

Principal Competitors

NEC Corporation; Hitachi, Ltd.; Toshiba Corporation; Mitsubishi Electric Corporation; Sony Corporation; Hewlett-Packard Company; International Business Machines Corporation; Compaq Computer Corporation; Matsushita Electric Industrial Co., Ltd.; Samsung Group; Intel Corporation; Dell Computer Corporation; Gateway, Inc.; Sun Microsystems, Inc.; Sharp Corporation; SANYO Electric Co., Ltd.; Electronic Data Systems Corporation; Unisys Corporation.

Further Reading

Anchordoguy, Marie, *Computers Inc.: Japan's Challenge to IBM,* Cambridge: Harvard University Press, 1989, 273 p.

Brull, Steven V., and Gary McWilliams, " 'Fujitsu *Shokku*' Is Jolting American PC Makers," *Business Week,* February 19, 1996, p. 50.

Brull, Steven V., et al., "Fujitsu Gets Wired: The Company Is Staking Its Future on the Still Elusive Frontiers of Cyberspace," *Business Week,* March 18, 1996, pp. 110–12.

Clark, Don, "Fujitsu's Amdahl Plans to Stop Making IBM Compatibles, Seeing Little to Gain," *Wall Street Journal,* October 19, 2000.

Creative Partners in Technology, Santa Clara, Calif.: Amdahl Corporation, 1989.

Eisenstodt, Gale, "Race Against Time," *Forbes,* December 21, 1992, pp. 292–96.

"Fujitsu's Sekizawa: Dealing with Changing User Requirements," *Datamation,* September 1, 1992, pp. 87–89.

Gomes, Lee, "Amdahl's Autonomy Fades As Fujitsu Offers $850 Million for Remaining Stake," *Wall Street Journal,* July 31, 1997, p. A3.

Gross, Neil, and Robert D. Hof, "Fujitsu Gets a Helping Hand from an American Buddy," *Business Week,* June 28, 1993, p. 46.

Hamilton, David P., "Harder Drive: Decade After Failing, Japan Firms Try Anew to Sell PCs in U.S.," *Wall Street Journal,* June 5, 1996, pp. A1+.

Hills, Jill, *Deregulating Telecoms,* Westport, Conn.: Quorum Books, 1986, 220 p.

"Japanese Semiconductors: Flat As a Pancake," *Economist,* May 4, 1996, p. 66.

"Japan's Less-Than-Invincible Computer Makers," *Economist,* January 11, 1992, pp. 59–60.

"Japan's Lou Gerstner," *Economist,* November 23, 1996, p. 80.

Johnston, Marsha W., "ICL Builds a Software House," *Datamation,* May 1, 1991, pp. 80–87.

Keenan, Faith, and Peter Landers, "Staggering Giants," *Far Eastern Economic Review,* April 1, 1999, pp. 10–13.

Kirkpatrick, David, "Your Next PC May Be Japanese," *Fortune,* October 28, 1996, pp. 141+.

Kunii, Irene M., et al., "Fujitsu: Beyond Big Iron," *Business Week,* March 29, 1999, pp. 76, 78.

Landers, Peter, "Fujitsu Plans to Cut 9 Percent of Work Force, Citing Effects of Tech Slowdown in U.S.," *Wall Street Journal,* August 21, 2001, p. A16.

——, "Fujitsu Plans $2.43 Billion Charge Due to Slump," *Wall Street Journal,* July 30, 2001, p. A16.

——, "Japan's Fujitsu Looks to America Online As Model in Attempt to Become a Leader in E-Commerce," *Wall Street Journal,* August 10, 1999, p. A18.

McWilliams, Gary, Emily Thornton, and Paul M. Eng, "If at First You Falter, Reboot," *Business Week,* June 30, 1997, pp. 81–82.

Meyer, Richard, "Japan's Brave New World: The Industry Fears the Commodity Computer. Fujitsu Prepares for It," *Financial World,* January 21, 1992, pp. 48–49.

Meyer, Richard, and Sana Siwolop, ''The Samurai Have Landed: How the Japanese Computer Makers Slipped into Europe Almost Unnoticed,'' *Financial World,* September 18, 1990, pp. 46–50.

Mood, Jeff, ''Next Stop, World Markets,'' *Datamation,* August 1, 1989, p. 28.

Morris, Kathleen, ''What IBM Could Have Done: IBM Almost Halved Its Staff, and It Still Has Problems. Fujitsu Thinks It Can Grow Its Way Out of Mainframe Dependence,'' *Financial World,* March 15, 1994, pp. 32–34.

Nusbaum, Alexandra, ''Japan Inc.'s Internet Crusader: The President of Fujitsu Has Launched a Bold Mission to Put His Company at the Forefront of the Online Revolution,'' *Financial Times,* March 23, 2000, p. 24.

Schlender, Brenton R., ''How Fujitsu Will Tackle the Giants,'' *Fortune,* July 1, 1991, pp. 78–82.

Sender, Henny, ''Fujitsu Seeks to Become a Global Software Maker,'' *Asian Wall Street Journal,* September 26, 2000, p. 17.

—Jonathan Martin
—update: David E. Salamie

Gecina SA

2 ter, boulevard Saint-Martin
75473 Paris Cedex 10
France
Telephone: (+33) 140-40-50-50
Fax: (+33) 140-40-52-41
Web site: http://www.gecina.fr

Public Company
Incorporated: 1959 as Groupement pour le Financement
    de la Construction
Employees: 605
Sales: EUR 263 million (FFr 1.72 billion) ($358.1
    million) (2000)
Stock Exchanges: Euronext Paris
Ticker Symbol: GFC
NAIC: 531110 Real Estate Rental or Leasing of
    Residential Building; 531311 Residential Property
    Managers; 531312 Nonresidential Property Managers

Gecina SA is the leading real estate management company in France and one of the largest in Europe. The result of a series of mergers in the late 1990s, Gecina's portfolio includes nearly two million square meters of office and residential space. More than 93 percent of the company's properties are located in the Paris region; 70 percent of properties are residential, including a strong portfolio of prime Haussmann-era buildings. The company also owns the Carré Saint-Germain office and commercial complex, the renovation of which is expected to be completed in 2002 and feature 10,000 square meters of retail space for clients including The Nature Company, H&M, and Gap, and a 4,7000-square-meter single client office complex. The company's portfolio, valued at EUR 4.7 billion, generated EUR 263 million in rental revenues, for net profits of EUR 107 million in 2000. Much of the company's growth during the 1990s was guided by Eliane Sermondadaz, chairman and managing director, who stepped down at the end of June 2001. She has been succeeded by Antoine Jeancourt-Galignani. The company trades on the Euronext Paris stock exchange, but most of its stock is owned by just a few institutional shareholders, including its largest shareholder, Assurances Générales de France.

Real Estate Investments in the 1950s

The Groupement pour le Financement de la Construction (GFC) was established in 1959 in answer to a need for new rental housing in the Parisian area. The company assumed the status of a Société d'Investissement Immobilier, or SII, a category set up by the French government providing tax incentives in order to encourage the development of residential property in the French capital. The end of World War II and the economic boom years beginning in the 1950s as the French completed their postwar reconstruction found Paris with a steadily growing population—the capital was to become home to approximately one-quarter of the French population—and an extreme housing shortage. Exacerbating the housing shortage was legislation passed shortly after the war meant to protect renters from exploitation during the housing shortage. The new rent control laws, however, had the immediate effect of ending new housing construction.

The Parisian housing shortage, particularly among lower income properties, reached crisis proportions during the mid-1950s, especially during the severe winter of 1954, and the resulting outcry stimulated legislators to offer new incentives to stimulate housing construction. The late 1950s saw the creation of new classes of real estate companies, the Société Immobilières Conventionnée or SIC, directed especially to encourage construction of middle-income grade housing, and the Société d'Investissement Immobilier, or SII, which, in addition to offering tax advantages to offset losses incurred since the institution of rent control, allowed companies to go public and raise capital on the stock exchange. SIIs were, however, limited to the residential housing market.

GFC itself went public in 1963, and participated in a new building boom that was to transform much of the French capital, creating a huge new suburban ring, while, especially in the late 1960s after building codes were eased, adding large numbers of new—and modern—residential properties within Paris itself. These new buildings reached ten stories in height—doubling previous height restrictions—and often contained hundreds of apartments. The new class of building became highly sought after by the city's rental customers. The tightening of building codes in 1977, coupled with a recession, brought a new lull to construction in the capital.

Parisian Real Estate Leader in the New Century

The late 1980s saw an intense yet brief construction boom that collapsed with a new recession at the beginning of the 1990s. The result was a glut of office space that continued to depress the real estate market throughout the decade and helped spark a consolidation of the Parisian real estate sector. GFC was to prove itself one of the strongest survivors of the period.

By the end of the 1980s, GFC had built up a strong portfolio of properties, valued at more than FFr 3.5 billion. The company nonetheless trailed behind its major SII competitors, including leaders Sefimeg, Simco, and UIF. The beginning of the new decade, however, proved a turning point in GFC's growth. With the downturn in the real estate market and the perspective of changes to the SII legislation expected in 1993, GFC went looking for a new partner. In 1991, the company announced it had agreed to merge with another SII, Groupement Français pour l'Investissement Immobilier (GFII). This group had been seeking to restructure its own portfolio, then valued at FFr 3 billion. In the early 1990s, GFII had taken steps to build up its assets in Paris and the surrounding area, which then represented 50 percent of its portfolio, while reducing its holdings in Lyon, which accounted for 30 percent of its portfolio, and in the north of France, which had represented the remaining 20 percent of its assets. Both GFC and GFII already shared a principal investor, Assurances Générales de France (AGF), which became the combined group's largest shareholder with some 25 percent of GFC's shares.

The merger with GFII launched GFC into the top five of France's publicly quoted SIIs. The company's newly enlarged portfolio gave it the financial clout to begin acquiring new properties. GFC now adopted a policy of restructuring its portfolio to emphasis high-quality properties in Paris, selling off its provincial holdings and reducing its stake in the Lyon market. The company also began to look at shifting the balance of commercial and rental properties in its holdings.

The company shed its SII status in 1993, as it brought on a new chairman, Eliane Sermondadaz, who came to GFC from AGF and who was to guide the company's growth throughout the decade, transforming it into one of the top real estate companies in Europe. The continuing depression in the building market enabled the company to build up its portfolio, particularly as a number of banks, insurance companies, and other financial institutions, which previously had invested in real estate, began selling off their property portfolios at discount rates. By 1996, the company's portfolio neared a value of FFr 5 billion, generating revenues of more than FFr 363 million.

The late 1990s, however, provided still greater opportunities for growth. The bottoming out of the property market cycle, coupled with dropping interest rates, enabled GFC to seek to expand its real estate empire. Part of GFC's new growth drive came from a need to gain size in order to compete against the growing numbers of foreign investors entering the Parisian market. At the same time, GFC was beginning to seek international investors to balance out its major shareholders, including longtime leading shareholder AGF.

In 1997, the company made the first of a series of acquisitions that propelled it into the top rank among Paris's real estate companies, acquiring Foncina, an SII, which added another FFr 1.4 billion in property value to GFC. As Sermondadaz told *La Tribune:* "At the end of 1996, we were at the cycle's low point. The company was tempting, with very beautiful buildings, very well maintained." The Foncina acquisition was in keeping with the company's determination not only to gain size, but also to balance its portfolio of properties among the high-end Haussmann-style buildings, dating from the 19th century, 1970s-era apartment complexes, and modern residential space. The company also began to eye reducing its reliance on residential properties. Following the Foncina acquisition, the company established Fongicef, a new sales and marketing subsidiary for its commercial and residential properties.

Now with assets topping EUR 1 billion, GFC looked for new acquisition targets. The company struck hard in 1998, doubling its size after acquiring UIF (Union Immobilier de France) and La Foncière Vendôme. These purchases boosted the worth of GFC's portfolio to more than FFr 12 billion, and reinforced the share of Parisian properties, which now accounted for 71 percent of its properties and 84 percent of its rental revenues. The two acquisitions added nearly 400,000 square meters of prime Parisian real estate, and especially a strong group of Haussmann-style buildings. The purchases also enabled GFC to increase its position in the commercial sector, reducing its proportion of residential properties to just 75 percent of its total assets. The company's new stature—it now placed second in the Parisian market, behind Simco—led it to change its name to Gecina at the end of 1998.

"After the merger with UIF, Sefimeg's portfolio corresponded exactly with the strategy that we had fixed for ourselves," Sermondadaz told *Les Echos* when describing Gecina's reasons for acquiring longtime rival Sefimeg in 1999, "It's principally situated in Paris. It has high quality. Finally, it will enable us to maintain a balanced ratio of residential and office space. When the operation is completed, 70 percent of Gecina's portfolio will be composed of apartments, and 30 percent of offices, in terms of surface area. But in terms of rent, the ratio will be more like 60–40." The company completed its acquisition of Sefimeg, which had been part of French financier François Pinault's Atresia, in July 1999, boosting its total floor space to more than 1.8 million square meters.

One month later, it announced its intention to acquire Immobilier Batibail, a move completed in December 1999. The acquisition of Batibail, coupled with that of Sefimeg, helped Gecina close the year with double the assets over the year before. The group now boasted a portfolio valued at more than FFr 26.5 billion (EUR 4.1 billion), while continuing to reinforce the company's strategy of focusing on the Parisian market. More than 87 percent of the company's properties were now

Key Dates:

1959: Groupement pour le Financement de la Construction (GFC) is created.

1963: GFC goes public.

1991: Company acquires Groupement Français pour l'Investissement Immobilier (GFII).

1993: GFC converts from a Société d'Investissement Immobilier (SII) structure, which had restricted it to residential property investments.

1997: Company purchases Foncina, heightening its stature among Paris real estate companies; company establishes Fongicef, a new sales and marketing subsidiary for its commercial and residential properties.

1998: Company, now second in the Paris real estate market, renames itself Gecina SA.

1999: Gecina acquires Immobilier Batibail and Sefimeg, doubling its assets of the previous year and propelling it into the leadership position in the Parisian real estate market.

2001: Eliane Sermondadaz, responsible for much of the company's growth during the 1990s, steps down as chairman and managing director, replaced by Antoine Jeancourt-Galignani.

located within the Paris area. The Batibail acquisition had also boosted the proportion of Haussmann buildings, accounting for 23 percent of floor space, while commercial property topped 36 percent of the company's portfolio. At the same time, Gecina had captured the leadership position in the Parisian real estate market.

In 2000, Gecina acquired a new prime property, the Carré Saint-Germain complex in Paris's prestigious sixth arrondissement. The company immediately launched a massive conversion program on the property, creating 10,000 square meters of retail space and a 4,700-square-meter single-client office complex, to be completed by 2002.

Yet the rise of interest rates and the upswing in the property cycle spelled a temporary end to the company's acquisition spree. Instead, Gecina concentrated on absorbing its new properties and operations, including instituting a vast restructuring program. The company's acquisitions had swelled the ranks of its subsidiaries to more than 50 companies, many of which controlled only single properties. Gecina therefore began trimming the ranks of subsidiaries, merging the various entities into a more manageable—and less costly—handful of primary subsidiaries. Meanwhile, the company launched a restructuring of

its portfolio as well, planning to sell off as much as EUR 1 billion in assets, including a complete sell-off of all of its remaining provincial properties other than in Lyon.

By mid-2001, Gecina was able to begin looking for clients for its Carré Saint Germain project, quickly finding such notable retail tenants as H&M, Fnac, The Nature Company, and Gap. The company was also looking forward to turning over the project's office spaces to its new tenant—who was expected to pay as much as FFr 5,000 per square meter per year. On a total investment of FFr 750 million, Gecina hoped to make a profit of some 7.5 percent.

After leading the company's expansion, Eliane Sermondadaz stepped down from her position as chairman at the end of June 2001. The company appointed in her place Antoine Jeancourt-Galignani, who in turn named former Banque Worms chief Serge Gryzbowski as the new Gecina CEO. As the company completed its restructuring, and began enjoying the fruits of its new heavyweight status, it looked forward to capturing a still larger share of the Parisian real estate market.

Principal Subsidiaries

SAS Fc Transactions; SAS Foncière De La Cité; SAS Geciter; Investibail; La Foncière Vendôme; La Fourmi Immobilier.

Principal Competitors

Assurances Générales de France; American International Group, Inc.; Bail Investissement S.A.; British Land Plc; Capital Shopping Centres Plc; CB Richard Ellis Services, Inc.; Credit Suisse First Boston; Foncière Euris S.A.; La Fourmi Immobilière SA; La Fourmi Immobilière SA; Interbail SA; Klépierre S.A.; Société Foncière Lyonnaise S.A.; Peel Holdings Plc; Société Immobilier de Location pour l'Industrie et le Commerce (SILIC); Simco SA; U.I.S. Percier Group; Unibail SA; Wates City of London Properties.

Further Reading

Besses-Boumard, Pascale, "Cinq questions 'a . . . Eliane Sermondadaz," *Les Echos,* May 20, 1999, p. 53.

——, "Rebaptisée Gecina, la société GFC se hisse au deuxième rang français des foncières," *Les Echos,* November 6, 1998 p. 20.

Cohen-Chabaud, Michèle, "Les habits neufs des foncières françaises," *La Tribune,* January 25, 2000.

de Vaublanc, Aude, "Gecina lance la commercialisation du Carré Saint-Germain," *La Tribune,* March 15, 2001.

Rowe, Michael, "Investors Flock to Paris," *European,* March 13, 1997, p. 26.

—M. L. Cohen

PERFECTION

Glock Ges.m.b.H.

PO Box 9
2232 Deutsch-Wagram
Austria
Telephone: 43-2247-90300-0
Fax: 43-2247-90300-312
Web site: http://www.glock.com

Private Company
Incorporated: 1963
Employees: 450
Sales: $150 million (1995 est.)
NAIC: 332994 Small Arms Manufacturing; 332211
    Cutlery and Flatware (Except Precious)
    Manufacturing; 332212 Hand and Edge Tool
    Manufacturing

Glock Ges.m.b.H. is virtually synonymous with the lightweight Glock pistol designed by its founder in the early 1980s. Since that time, the pistol has equipped numerous armies and won a leading market share in the law enforcement market. The firm also makes other military items, and got its start fabricating plastic and metal products for a variety of markets.

Origins

Gaston Glock, an Austrian engineer, formed Glock Ges.m.b.H. in 1963. At first the company, based in the quiet town of Deutsch-Wagram, Austria, produced steel and plastic products, doorknobs and hinges, and commercial appliances. In the 1970s, Glock began making knives, grenades, machine gun belts, and entrenching tools for the Austrian Army.

In the early 1980s, Gaston Glock, who had never before designed a gun, developed a 9mm semi-automatic pistol to meet an Austrian Army requirement. The first prototypes were created in 1981 after six months of development. (The company continued to develop other military products during this time, such as its combination field knife, saw, and spade.)

The next year, the Glock 17 beat out all competitors to win the Austrian Army contract. An initial order of 30,000 guns was placed in 1983. In 1984, Norway became the first NATO country to adopt the weapon for its army. (As part of NATO acceptance tests, the test pistols each fired 10,000 rounds within five hours while showing no measurable wear.)

Heavy use of polymer made Glock's gun lightweight (up to 40 percent lighter than conventional pistols) and relatively inexpensive to produce. Glock claimed to be the first company to incorporate polymer into the design of a pistol from the beginning stages. Other advantages to synthetic materials included ease of maintenance as well as climate and corrosion resistance. Further, the "tenifer" hardening coating applied to the metal surfaces allowed the pistols to be carried by scuba divers. Molding a synthetic frame required the fashioning of fewer parts, resulting in lower assembly costs and fewer individual spares to stock.

International in 1985

A U.S. subsidiary, Glock, Inc., was established in late 1985, headquartered in the Atlanta suburb of Smyrna, Georgia. In addition to sales, the unit assembled guns from imported components. The popularity of shooting sports in the South likely helped make the region an attractive location—the area purportedly was home to nearly half the country's firearms. The Glock Shooting Sports Foundation hosted an annual contest near Atlanta that attracted 400 competitors from all over the country and a diverse array of lifestyles, from cops to church organists.

The expansion to the United States came just as legions of policemen across the country were trading in their trusty service revolvers for semiautomatic pistols. As the company founder told *Advertising Age,* Glock aimed its initial marketing efforts at law enforcement, hoping to later gain sales in the commercial market. In fact, the company sometimes gave the guns away to police departments.

However, political conditions seemed less than favorable for Glock in the U.S. Congress, which was debating a ban on the pistol. Some perceived it as a terrorist threat, believing the use of plastic parts in it made it less visible to airport X-ray machines—a charge countered by the Federal Aviation Administration. Ironically, in 1988 Congress funded the gun for the Washington, D.C., police department.

154

Georgia's lax gun laws came under national scrutiny in 1996 after a New York City police officer was killed with a Glock pistol that had been bought in Atlanta. New York drug gangs were buying them through "straw buyers." Glocks were worth up to three times their $500 retail price on the black market.

The U.S. Bureau of Alcohol, Tobacco, and Firearms reported that more than half of the 2,560 guns stolen from interstate carriers were stolen in Georgia, home to United Parcel Service as well as Glock. Glock responded by making its packaging less distinguishable and more secure, noted the *Atlanta Journal and Constitution*. It also enclosed exploding ink packs with its shipments.

Critics of the Glock 17 complained that its trigger-pulling requirement was too light, making it susceptible to accidental discharges. Glock faced several lawsuits alleging this in the mid-1990s. Supporters countered that with proper training, the Glock pistols were as safe as any weapon.

A second plant was opened in Ferlach, Austria, in 1987. At the same time, the company was developing its Glock 18 "Selective Fire" machine pistol, which would be the smallest weapon of its type in the world.

Glock (H.K.) Ltd. was established in Hong Kong in 1988 to market the company's wares in Asia, Australia, and Oceania. The same year, production started for the Glock 19 "Compact" and Glock 17L "Competition" pistols.

By the end of 1990, there were more than 300,000 Glock pistols in use in North America. Glocks were also being exported to 45 other countries. Approximately 2,000 police departments in the United States had adopted Glock pistols, accounting for approximately 150,000 units.

Rapid Growth in the 1990s

Another international sales facility, Glock America N.V., was set up in Uruguay in 1990. With its new Glock 22 and Glock 23 pistols, the firm claimed to become the first to supply law enforcement agencies with .40 caliber handguns in quantity. The larger rounds of these weapons carried more stopping power; they were seen as an alternative to bulkier .45 caliber pistols which could only carry half the rounds of a 9mm.

Glock's original plant in Deutsche Wagram was expanded in 1990. The next year, production began on the Glock 20 (10mm) and Glock 21 (.45) Automatic pistols. A fourth subsidiary, Glock France S.A., was created in 1992 to handle sales to France and Francophone Africa.

Another .40 caliber weapon, the Glock 24, began production in 1994. The .380 caliber Auto Glock 25, and two "subcompact" models, the 9mm Glock 26 and .40 caliber Glock 27, were launched the next year. In 1996, Glock began production of the .380 caliber Glock 28 as well as a training version of its original pistol, known as the Glock 17T. This weapon could fire either low-velocity color marking cartridges or rubber bullets.

In 1995, a company spokesperson said Glock was selling 20,000 pistols a month at an average price of $600 each, producing estimated revenues of nearly $150 million a year. The company curtailed its trade magazine advertising due to the high amount of back orders at its plants. The relaxation of concealed weapons laws in several states contributed to demand.

New federal laws, were limiting handgun magazines to ten rounds. However, Glock introduced an 11-shot model, the 9mm G26, in September 1995 that held one round in the chamber. Gun control proponents were critical of this and Glock's police trade-in program, which brought into the company (for resale) larger capacity magazines that predated the ten-round limit. For its part, Glock said the palm-sized G26 and .40 caliber G27 were "the perfect choice for women."

By 1996, Glock had sold two million pistols to police, military, and commercial buyers in 60 countries. Its original Glock 17 pistol was then accompanied by 32 other models in eight calibers. No one in Europe, company literature stated, was making more guns per day.

Two new models began production in 1997: the 10mm Auto Glock 29 and .45 caliber Auto Glock 30. Also in 1997, the company completed an extension of the plant in Ferlach, Austria, and began building a new headquarters building in Deutsch-Wagram.

Glock began producing its own .357 caliber weapons—the Glock 31, Glock 32, and Glock 33—in 1998. The 9mm Glock 34 and .40 caliber Glock 35 also began production. A "slimline" .45 Auto pistol, the Glock 36, entered production the next year, and other training models were unveiled.

Big Easy Showdown in the Late 1990s

Glock entered a stormy chapter in its dealings with the city of New Orleans in 1997. Glock, Inc. and a distributor, Kiesler's Police Supply Co., arranged for the New Orleans police to trade in 8,000 old weapons for 1,700 new Glock .40 caliber handguns. It later emerged that 230 of the guns traded in were semiautomatic assault weapons. Another of the guns was evidence in a murder case. Officials also questioned whether Kiesler's paid a fair price for the trades, which were then advertised for sale out of state. New Orleans subsequently instituted a policy of destroying confiscated guns.

In late 1998, the city of New Orleans launched a tobacco industry-style lawsuit against Glock and many other gun manufacturers. The suit alleged that since technology existed that could prevent non-owners from firing handguns, any designed without these safety features were therefore defective by nature. Other municipalities—even Atlanta—soon filed similar suits seeking to recover the costs related to handgun violence and accidental firings. A Glock spokesperson accused mayors of

<table>
</table>

Key Dates:

1963: Austrian engineer Gaston Glock forms his namesake company.
1981: Glock creates the Glock 17 pistol in response to a military requirement.
1984: Norway becomes the first NATO country to adopt the Glock pistol.
1985: U.S. subsidiary Glock, Inc. is established in order to take the company international.
1999: Glock produces its two millionth pistol, completes new headquarters.

trying to shift the blame for gun-related crimes from perpetrators to legitimate manufacturers.

The stormy relationship between Glock and New Orleans reached its peak on January 26, 1999, when Glock Vice-President Paul Jannuzzo and Mayor Marc Morial both appeared on NBC's *Today* show. Jannuzzo called the city's negligence lawsuit "the height of hypocrisy."

In January 2001, Glock responded to the New Orleans suit by giving the city locking devices for the 1,700 .40 caliber handguns the New Orleans Police Department had just purchased. The devices were similar to bicycle cable locks and required the removal of the magazine and the round in the chamber.

Eventually, the federal government launched its own suit against the handgun industry. Although Glock did not initially join Smith & Wesson (a unit of Britain's Tomkins PLC) and others in the settlement, it ultimately agreed to catalog its new guns in the Integrated Ballistic Identification System, an existing national database. Critics countered that criminals could easily and quickly change the unique markings guns were supposed to make on bullets and casings.

Glock officials were opposed to the mandate to develop a "smart gun" in Smith & Wesson's settlement. They felt the technology was unproven and would ruin the mechanical simplicity of Glock's pistols. The company did consider joining S&W in requiring its dealers to submit to sales restrictions that went far beyond existing federal law. Apart from their lawsuits, several large cities, including Atlanta, joined a Clinton administration-backed initiative to boycott gunmakers that refused to curb certain business practices. In June 2000, Glock announced that the sale of 2,000 pistols to five municipal police departments had been placed on hold for this reason. By early 2001, 32 cities had filed suit against various gunmakers; New York was the first state government to sue them.

Glock produced 2.5 million pistols between 1985 and 1999. It had a more than 50 percent market share in the law enforcement market and a 5 to 7 percent share of the consumer market.

Principal Subsidiaries

Glock America N.V. (Uruguay); Glock France S.A.; Glock, Inc. (U.S.A.); Glock (H.K.) Ltd. (Hong Kong).

Principal Competitors

Colt Manufacturing Co.; Fabbrica D'Armi Pietro Beretta S.p.A.; Forjas Taurus SA; Sigarms Inc. (Sig/Sauer); Sturm, Ruger & Co.; Tomkins PLC.

Further Reading

Anderson, Will, "Gun Maker Takes Aim at Cities' Lawsuit," *Atlanta Journal and Constitution,* February 14, 1999, p. D5.
Armstrong, David, and Andrea Estes, "Gun Deal Raises Questions," *Boston Herald,* November 29, 1992, p. 1.
Barrett, Paul M., "Glock Feels Pinch of Push to Limit Gun-Sale Practices," *Wall Street Journal,* June 15, 2000, p. B16.
Barrett, Paul M., Vanessa O'Connell, and Joe Matthews, "Glock May Accept Handgun Restrictions," *Wall Street Journal,* March 20, 2000, p. A3.
Brice, Arthur, and Alfred Charles, "Smyrna-Based Gun Maker Rejects Settlement on Guns," *Atlanta Constitution,* March 22, 2000, p. A3.
Brogan, Joe, "Studies, Advertising Entice Local Agencies to Get Bigger Barrels," *Palm Beach Post,* June 2, 1996, p. 4B.
Estes, Andrea, and David Armstrong, "Competitor Raps No-Bid Gun Contract," *Boston Herald,* December 1, 1992, p. 18.
"Introduction to Glock, Inc.," Smyrna, Ga.: Glock, Inc., 1990.
Jannuzzo, Paul F., "Glock Critical of Morial on Gun Transaction," *Times-Picayune* (Letters to the Editor), February 2, 1999, p. B4.
Long, Duncan, *Glock's Handguns,* El Dorado, Ariz.: Desert Publications, 1996.
Mitchell, Kent, "Shooting for a Good Time; Glock Shoot Brings All Types Together," *Atlanta Journal and Constitution,* October 13, 1996, p. 16E.
"New Orleans Is Suing Gun Makers, Two in State," *Hartford Courant,* October 31, 1998, p. D1.
O'Connell, Vanessa, "Glock Plans Change in How It Sells Guns," *Wall Street Journal,* March 21, 2000, p. A3.
Perlstein, Michael, "Guns Destined for the Deep; Seized Weapons to Become Anchor," *Times-Picayune,* March 13, 2001, p. 1.
Persica, Dennis, "Sued by City, Glock Fires Back with Gift," *Times-Picayune,* January 27, 1999, p. B1.
Philbin, Walt, "Gun Swap Broke No Laws, ATF Says," *Times-Picayune,* December 11, 1999, p. 1B.
Schrade, Brad, "Glock Will Mark Pistols to Aid Tracing in Crimes," *Atlanta Journal and Constitution,* March 24, 2000, p. F1.
Scruggs, Kathy, "Deliveries Under Fire," *Atlanta Journal and Constitution,* October 12, 1997, p. C4.
——, "Glock, UPS Working to Thwart Gun Thieves," *Atlanta Journal and Constitution,* October 12, 1997, p. A1.
Skiba, Katherine M., "As Laws Relax, Little Guns Are Big Business," *Milwaukee Journal Sentinel,* December 24, 1995, p. 1.
Spain, William, "The Marketing 100: Gaston Glock," *Advertising Age,* June 26, 1995, p. S30.
"Suits Miss Mark; Don't Blame the Manufacturer for the Customer's Recklessness," *Colorado Springs Gazette-Telegraph,* August 12, 2000, p. 11.
Thorpy, Bill, "Booming Business," *Atlanta Constitution,* August 30, 1990, p. D1.
——, "Small Handguns Are Giant Sellers," *Commercial Appeal* (Memphis), December 17, 1995, p. 14A.
Vaishnav, Anand, and Walt Philbin, "Report Blames Police Brass in Gun Swap," *Times-Picayune,* November 25, 1999, p. 1B.
Williams, Monte, "Gun Makers Seek Dismissal of New York State's Suit Against Them," *New York Times,* February 1, 2001, p. B4.

—Frederick C. Ingram

Goodman Holding Company

1501 Seamist
Houston, Texas 77008
U.S.A.
Telephone: (713) 861-2500
Fax: (713) 861-2176
Web site: http://www.goodmanmfg.com

Private Company
Founded: 1975 as Goodman Manufacturing Company, L.P.
Employees: 7,750
Sales: $2.16 billion (2000 est.)
NAIC: 333415 Air-Conditioning and Warm Air Heating
 Equipment and Commercial and Industrial Refrigera-
 tion Equipment Manufacturing; 335224 Household
 Laundry Equipment Manufacturing; 335221 House-
 hold Cooking Appliance Manufacturing; 421620
 Other Major Household Appliance Manufacturing

Goodman Holding Company is the world's largest privately held manufacturer in the heating, ventilation, and air conditioning (HVAC) industry and ranks second in HVAC market share. It makes a broad array of products, from small room air conditioners to central air and heating systems sold under the names Goodman, Janitrol, Caloric, GMC, and Modern Maid. Until the sale of its Amana appliance division to Maytag, scheduled for completion before the end of 2001, it was also making name brand home appliances, such as washers, dryers, refrigerators, dishwashers, ranges, and microwave ovens. As an industry leader, Goodman has received several honors from The Air-Conditioning and Refrigeration Institute and other organizations. It operates seven plants with a total of over four million square feet of space in Houston; Dayton, Tennessee; Amana, Iowa; Fayetteville, Tennessee; Florence, South Carolina; and Searcy, Arkansas. Independent distributors maintain over 800 stock locations in the United States and Canada as a way of getting Goodman products quickly to contractors. *Forbes* has listed Goodman as one of the top 100 privately held companies in the United States.

Origins and Early Years

Starting in 1954, Harold V. Goodman gained years of experience as a contractor who installed home air conditioners. He owned American Airco, once the "largest residential installer in the U.S. (15,000 systems a year in Houston)," according to writer Mark Skaer. That background led Goodman to start a company to make equipment for air conditioner contractors. "He was looking for two things: 1) better price and 2) not having to go back to work on what was just installed," said Jim Plant, who worked with Goodman from the time he founded the company.

Harold V. Goodman in September 1975 began Goodman Manufacturing Company, L.P. Initially the company made flexible air ducts and plastic blade registers. By buying certain assets of Smith Jones, Inc. in 1982, Goodman acquired the Janitrol brand of air conditioning and heat pump devices. The company then moved Janitrol production machinery and inventory from Ohio to its Houston plant. That year Goodman began manufacturing split system air conditioners (external condenser and internal fixtures, allowing for central air), and in 1983 it started making split system heat pumps.

From its beginning, Goodman Manufacturing emphasized quality manufactured items available at the lowest possible price. Around 1982 Harold V. Goodman said, "We will revolutionize the heating and air conditioning industry with the highest quality equipment manufactured by the best producing work force in the business and sold at the lowest prices in the market." That quote was used in the years ahead to guide the company.

In the mid-1980s Goodman Manufacturing began making gas furnaces and later started producing packaged units that the company designed.

Business in the 1990s and Beyond

In 1990 Goodman Manufacturing began offering a five-year warranty on its parts, which started a trend for competitors to also offer longer warranties. By the mid-1990s heating and air conditioning manufacturers offered a standard ten-year warranty, which was opposed by some wholesalers and contractors in that industry. According to the August 1996 *Supply House Times*, at a meeting of the North American Heating, Refrigeration and Air Conditioning Wholesalers Association, David Shaw of Shaw Curtis Company said he was "deeply opposed to the trend [started by Goodman] for longer and longer warranties in our industry. I believe it is harming the dealer and the distributor, and I can't believe that something that harms both those parties can be good for the homeowner."

Like any business, Goodman lost some contracts to its competitors. In 1992 it lost a bid for a contract with the Texas state government to Trane, a part of American Standard. Since Goodman's bid appeared to be lower than Trane's, President Harold V. Goodman lodged a protest in writing to the Texas Department of Commerce. Critics maintained that the bidding procedure was improper and that the state government may have broken the rules when it gave Trane $5 million to expand in Texas. In any case, Trane retained the state contract.

The company in August 1996 began replacing high-temperature plastic vent (HTPV) pipe used on about 8,000 Goodman gas furnaces. Defective vent pipes could release deadly carbon monoxide into the air. HTPV pipes were made by another company, but Goodman in cooperation with the U.S. Consumer Product Safety Commission set up a program where the vent pipes would be replaced free of charge. Consumers also could choose to buy a new furnace and new venting for just the company's manufacturing price of the furnace, while not paying for any labor, associated materials, or dealer markup costs.

Since distributors sold Goodman products, the company kept close track of its franchise holders. When a Memphis distributor ended his business, that franchise to sell Goodman's GMC products was taken over by Valley Supply Inc., a newly formed subsidiary of ACR Group Inc. Valley Supply's franchise territory covered western Tennessee, eastern Arkansas, and northern Mississippi. Another ACR subsidiary called Total Supply distributed GMC items in the Atlanta area, while ACR subsidiary Heating and Cooling Supply distributed Goodman's Janitrol line in the Las Vegas area. Goodman President Harold Goodman said in the May 11, 1994 *Business Wire* that the ACR subsidiaries "certainly impressed us with their ability to implement our marketing strategy and programs. We include them among our most valued distributors. . . .''

The 1994 *Manufacturing USA* reference guide listed Goodman Manufacturing with annual sales of $400 million. According to *Forbes* magazine, Goodman Manufacturing in 1995 brought in $500 million in revenues and also $58 million in operating profits.

Goodman increased its sales in the 1990s and gained market share in its industry through both internal expansion and a major acquisition. In 1994 it opened a new plant in Dayton, Tennessee to produce room air conditioners. In 1995 the company opened its 11th Street plant in Houston to increase its production of gas furnaces and also electric and gas packaged units. The following year it again expanded in Houston with a new 350,000-square-foot plant designed to make insulation and flexible duct items.

In 1997 Goodman purchased the Amana line of commercial and household appliances from Raytheon Appliance Group, which sold Amana to concentrate on its military products. Maytag had considered but decided not to buy Amana. In this deal Goodman spent $550 million for a plant in Amana, Iowa, that made refrigerators and microwave ovens; a Fayetteville, Tennessee plant that manufactured heating and air-conditioning equipment; a cooking equipment plant in Florence, South Carolina; and a Searcy, Arkansas factory that made home dryers. About 5,500 individuals worked at those four plants.

George Foerstner of Amana, Iowa, had founded Amana Refrigeration in 1934. By the time Amana was purchased by Raytheon Company in 1965, it was making refrigerators, freezers, and air conditioners. In 1967 Amana began selling the "world's first successful 115-volt countertop microwave oven for the home," according to its web site at www.amana.com. It also sold a variety of stoves, dishwashers, and laundry machines.

Amana became in 1995 the first company to quit using chlorofluorocarbons (CFCs) in its refrigerators as a way to protect the atmosphere's ozone layer. The CFC scientific and public policy controversy began in the 1970s when two scientists published their theory that CFCs could hurt the ozone layer that protects humans against ultraviolet light that can cause skin cancer. In 1987, 24 nations signed the Montreal Protocol as a promise to limit CFCs. The main villain was freon, a CFC commonly used in air conditioning and refrigeration equipment. In 1992 President George Bush set December 31, 1995 as the deadline for American manufacturers to cease producing almost all ozone-damaging chemicals. Although some prominent scientists disputed the ozone scare, the government's move against CFCs caused a major change in the HVAC and refrigeration industries. This latest issue was hardly the first for the air-conditioning industry, for even in the early 20th century critics had attacked efforts to use technology to make indoor environments cooler and more comfortable.

When a heat wave hit Texas in the summer of 1998, both government and corporations stepped up to help. The federal government provided a $2.9 million subsidy to help the poor buy air conditioners and pay their electrical bills. In cooperation with a local contractor named John Moore Services and the Gallery Furniture Company, Goodman Manufacturing Corporation increased its number of donated window air conditioners to a total of 1,040 units, while its rival Carrier Corporation donated 200 units. Another time, Goodman helped Houston residents by donating 100 Janitrol central air conditioning and heating units to the city's Habitat for Humanity program.

In 2000 the Goodman Holding Company was reorganized into four divisions. Garland I. Winningham served as the presi-

Key Dates:

1975: Harold V. Goodman starts the Goodman Manufacturing Company.
1982: Goodman purchases the Janitrol brand of air conditioning and heat pump items.
1986: Company's first gas furnaces are introduced.
1987: Firm begins making its Goodman-designed Packaged Units.
1990: Company begins offering a five-year warranty on all parts.
1994: New air conditioner plant in Dayton, Tennessee, is opened.
1995: Goodman opens gas/electric packaged unit plant in Houston.
1996: Company builds a new factory to make flexible duct items and insulation.
1997: Goodman purchases the Amana home appliance line from Raytheon.
1999: John B. Goodman becomes Goodman Holding Company's chairman, president, and CEO.
2000: Goodman acquires Pioneer Metals, Inc. a large air conditioner distributor based in Miami.
2001: Goodman in the summer announces sale of Amana to Maytag.

dent and chief executive of the Goodman Manufacturing Division and also as the interim head of the Amana Heating and Air Conditioning Division. The other two divisions were the Quietflex Division and the Amana Home Appliances Division.

The four divisions reported to John B. Goodman, the chairman, president, and CEO of Goodman Holding Company since 1999. Goodman was the son of the company's deceased founder Harold V. Goodman.

Although the Goodman family retained ownership of the firm, outside investors also played a role. For example, as of January 31, 1997 international mutual fund company GT Global, Inc. owned 2.85 percent of Goodman Manufacturing's net asset value through its GT Global Floating Rate Fund.

According to Goodman's web site, in 1998 it had 13.7 percent of the market for core comfort conditioning, which included room air conditioners, unitary air conditioners/heat pumps, and gas furnaces. That ranked it second to Carrier with 15 percent of that industry's market share. In 2000 Goodman continued as the second-ranked company in the core comfort conditioning market behind United Technologies, the market leader and owner of Carrier.

Forbes ranked Goodman Manufacturing as number 73 in its list of the largest private companies in the United States. That was based on its estimated revenues of $2.16 billion for 2000. Goodman Manufacturing's brand names at the time included Amana, Caloric, Glenwood, Goodman, GMC, Janitrol, Sunray, RadarLine, Speed, Queen, Radarange, Menumaster, and Convection Express.

In 2000 Goodman acquired Miami-based Pioneer Metals, Inc. (PMI), a former independent distributor of Goodman products. PMI with its 380 employees continued to operate under its own name.

Frost & Sullivan, a consulting, marketing, and training company that served the heating and air-conditioning industry, in 2000 produced a report on industry developments and also honored the leaders in the residential HVAC industry. Goodman Manufacturing received the Sales Strategy Award for its 1999 accomplishments, while its competitors Lennox Industries Incorporated and Carrier Corporation also won awards. Frost & Sullivan reported that the U.S. residential HVAC industry was led by a few large corporations acquiring smaller firms and increasingly focusing on global strategies. Such consolidation occurred in many other industries as well.

In the summer of 2001 Goodman Holding Company announced it was selling Amana to Maytag Corporation for a total of $325 million in stock and cash. Maytag was buying the Amana line of home appliances but not its air conditioning and heating products. The deal, expected to close later in the year, would increase Maytag's annual sales by $900 million and thus decrease Goodman's sales by the same amount.

As the new millennium started, the residential HVAC industry in the United States was slowly growing, mainly due to new construction and replacing older models. Frost & Sullivan indicated that the industry's expansion was limited by little new technology, high costs of HVAC equipment, and a saturated market. Two general trends impacting the industry were the increased use of the Internet to provide information for both consumers and contractors and also higher equipment and refrigerant costs due to replacing freon with more environmentally friendly substitutes. Goodman thus faced many challenges to its position near the top of the heating, ventilation, and air conditioning industry.

Principal Subsidiaries

Goodman Manufacturing Company, L.P.; Goodman Company, L.P.; Pioneer Metals, Inc.; NITEK.

Principal Competitors

Carrier Corporation; Fedders Corp.; Rheem/Paloma Industries; American Standard Companies Inc.; Frigidaire Home Products; Whirlpool Corporation; International Comfort Products; Lennox International Inc.; York International Corporation; Nortek, Inc.; Electrolux Group; LG Electronics Inc.; GE Appliances; Maytag Corporation.

Further Reading

Allen, Michael, "Inside an Economic-Development Deal—Trane Got $5 Million from Texas, but Some Say Rules Were Bent," *Wall Street Journal*, October 12, 1994, p. T1.
Byrne, Harlan S., "Whither Maytag?" *Barron's*, August 4, 1997, pp. 12–13.
Cooper, Gail, *Air-Conditioning America: Engineers and the Controlled Environment, 1900–1960,* Baltimore: Johns Hopkins University Press, 1998.

Faloon, Kelly, "Carrier Adds Purafil to IAQ Product Line," *Supply House Times*, May 2000, p. 30.

——, "HVAC Residential Market Growth Is Slow But Steady," *Contractor*, April 2000, p. 26.

"Goodman, Amana Realign," *Contractor*, April 2000, p. 26.

"John B. Goodman Named Chairman, President, CEO," *Air Conditioning, Heating & Refrigeration News*, July 12, 1999, pp. 1, 5.

"Lennox Ready to Offer IPO to Pay Debt, Buy Dealerships," *Air Conditioning, Heating & Refrigeration News*, April 19, 1999, pp. 1, 4.

Linden, Eugene, "Who Lost the Ozone," *Time*, May 10, 1993, pp. 56–58.

Mahoney, Thomas A., "Is This a Maturing Industry or What?" *Air Conditioning, Heating & Refrigeration News*, July 12, 1999, p. 14.

Martin, Mary Jo, "NHRAW Convention Will Focus on Warranty Trends," *Supply House Times*, August 1996, p. 13.

"Maytag to Buy Rival Amana Appliances," *Salt Lake Tribune*, June 6, 2001, p. B7.

"Raytheon Sells Amana As Part of $750 Million Deal," *Fort Worth Star-Telegram*, July 15, 1997, p. 1.

Roberts, Paul Craig, "Quietly, Now, Let's Rethink the Ozone Apocalypse," *Business Week*, June 19, 1995, p. 26.

Sallee, Rad, "Lending a Cooling Hand: Private Sources Jump in After Federal Relief Dries Up," *Houston Chronicle*, August 11, 1998, p. 15.

Schneider, Keith, "Bush Orders End to Making of Ozone-Depleting Agents," *New York Times*, February 13, 1992, p. A13.

Sixel, L.M., "EEOC Sues to Get Quietflex Papers," *Houston Chronicle*, April 1, 2000, p. C1.

Skaer, Mark, "At Goodman, 'Contractors Are Our Customers,'" *Air Conditioning, Heating & Refrigeration News*, October 16, 2000, p. 47.

"Texas Firm Buys Amana," *Omaha World-Herald*, September 11, 1997.

—David M. Walden

Granite Broadcasting Corporation

767 Third Avenue, 34th Floor
New York, New York 10017
U.S.A.
Telephone: (212) 826-2530
Fax: (212) 826-2858
Web site: http://www.granitetv.com

Public Company
Incorporated: 1988
Employees: 900
Sales: $140.1 million (2000)
Stock Exchanges: NASDAQ
Ticker Symbol: GBTVK
NAIC: 513120 Television Broadcasting Stations

Granite Broadcasting Corporation, based in New York City, owns and operates nine television stations in the states of California, Illinois, Indiana, Michigan, Minnesota, New York, and Wisconsin. It is one of the most important minority-controlled media companies in the United States, named by *Black Enterprise* magazine as its 1995 company of the year. In Granite's brief history it has displayed a willingness to be innovative. Well ahead of the curve, it teamed up with Yahoo! to provide local newscasts via the Internet as well as to develop other online features. A controversial deal with NBC in 2000, however, in which Granite agreed to pay the network for the right of one of its stations to be an affiliate, not only sent shock waves throughout the industry, it has had a detrimental effect on the company's stock price and profitability. Although publicly traded, Granite is controlled by founders W. Don Cornwell, chairman and CEO, and Stuart Beck, president, who hold all of the company's voting stock.

Establishing Granite Broadcasting: 1988

Cornwell is the driving force behind Granite. One of five children, he was born in Cushing, Oklahoma, in 1948 and was raised in Tacoma, Washington. His mother was a schoolteacher who instilled in him a love for academics. While an undergraduate at Occidental College in Los Angeles he studied pre-law,

more interested in politics than business. In addition to applying for law school, however, he decided to apply for business school, resulting in the rare option of choosing between Harvard Law School and Harvard Business School. He chose the business school and soon discovered a penchant for finance. After earning his Harvard M.B.A. in 1971 he went to work on Wall Street with investment bank Goldman Sachs, where he would be employed for the next 17 years. He gained valuable experience that would prove helpful when he finally was able to pursue a dream of owning television stations. In a 1994 press interview, well after Granite was established, he explained, ''I spent the last seven years at Goldman as chief operating officer of corporate finance. I dealt with 150 professionals and 90 support staffers, handling everything from compensation to technology. That prepared me a lot better for this job than people might think.'' Moreover, at Goldman he learned the perspective of advertisers by working with a number of consumer products companies, including American Greetings, Bristol-Myers, Gerber, Hershey Foods, and Rubbermaid.

In 1982 Cornwell was introduced to his business partner Beck by a mutual friend. A graduate of Harvard College and Yale Law School, Beck was a trial lawyer with practices in both New York and Washington, D.C. He also had contacts to the broadcast industry through his father, Martin Beck, chairman of Beck-Ross Communications. Cornwell and Beck's first media venture together was an unsuccessful application for a New Jersey radio station. Then in 1987 they decided to form a company. Beck's father and James Greenwald, chairman of Katz Communications, were instrumental in helping them attract investors. On February 8, 1988, Granite was incorporated in Delaware. For Cornwell, ''granite'' had significance because it was a black rock that served as a ready symbol for both himself and his company. The new venture raised initial funds of $45 million from investors that included Goldman Sachs, influential Washington attorney Vernon Jordan, and talk show host Oprah Winfrey.

Cornwell shopped for his first acquisitions in 1988, with a five-year goal of Granite owning at least six and perhaps as many as eight television stations. A major advantage Granite possessed, in addition to its solid backing, was a Federal Com-

Company Perspectives:

In every market where it produces news, Granite is determined to be the leading provider of local news, weather and sports information. Granite takes a highly aggressive approach to station management and consistently achieves some of the best operating results in the industry.

munications Commission (FCC) tax break intended to encourage minority media ownership that would be bestowed upon sellers. The program began in 1978 at a time when less than 1 percent of all broadcast television stations was owned by minorities. What Cornwell was looking for in an acquisition candidate was a station in a medium-sized market that had the potential to be the area's leading news outlet and was not realizing its potential revenues. News was local television's unquestioned moneymaker. Cornwell told *Black Enterprise* in 1995, "If you can buy the news leader [in a market] that underperforms and is fat, it's like dying and going to heaven." Granite closed on its first two television stations in October 1988, buying WEEK-TV in Peoria, Illinois, for $30 million in cash, and KBJR-TV in Duluth, Minnesota, for approximately $10.8 million in cash and stock. Cornwell then began to apply the principles that would become the hallmark of Granite ownership. He believed that the most important corporate decision was the hiring of the station manager, who would be granted considerable latitude after agreeing to a strict business plan. Granite emphasized the strict control of operating expenses, but more important was its emphasis on expanding local news coverage, to not only increase the number of broadcast hours devoted to news, but to find additional outlets for the station's news franchise through local radio and cable TV systems. Granite also wanted its station managers to develop what it called value-added advertising opportunities by producing local programming, as well as sponsoring community events that targeted specific audiences for the station. In general, Granite hoped to attract advertisers who had never before turned to television.

First Major-Market Acquisition in 1990

Granite bought its third television station in late 1989 when it paid $26.5 million for WPTA-TV in Fort Wayne, Indiana. Three months later it made its first major-market buy, acquiring KNTV, located in San Jose, California, for $58.7 million with the help of a $38 million loan. Servicing that loan, however, would prove difficult during the country's ailing economic climate of the early 1990s. Although ad revenues were down industrywide, Granite stations performed fairly well. In 1990 KNTV posted the highest revenues in station history, but interest payments on the $38 million loan resulted in a net loss. Overall, Granite's debt was close to $110 million, and the company looked to go deeper in debt as it added to its roster of stations. Moreover, the company had lost some $30 million during this start-up phase.

To reduce its debt load, Granite made an initial public offering of stock in 1992. It was hardly a good time for an offering, with many broadcast stocks suffering in the market, but Cornwell's Wall Street experience proved to be decisive. He was able to convince analysts that as the economy improved Granite would be poised to grow. Almost $3.5 million nonvoting shares were sold, netting $24 million. Granite stock was listed on the NASDAQ where it initially traded in the $7 range. Later in 1992 Granite initiated a $100 million junk bond sale to refinance the rest of the company's debt, but high-yield market conditions soured, and Cornwell was forced to cancel the offering.

By December 1993 Granite's balance sheet was strong enough to allow renewed expansion. The company paid Meredith Corp. $30 million for two stations, WTVH-TV in Syracuse, New York, and KSEE-TV in Fresno, California. It also paid Prudential Securities $7.5 million for a 45 percent interest in WNBW of Buffalo, New York, and acquired a $29 million note that Prudential held from the station's majority owner, Queen City Broadcasting. Queen City appeared to be on the verge of defaulting on the note, which would allow Granite to pick up WKBW-TV at a fraction of its $110 million value. The transaction was not without controversy, however, because Queen City was owned by one of America's leading black businessmen, J. Bruce Llewellyn, who portrayed Cornwell's deal as an act of betrayal. To Cornwell, on the other hand, not only was he practicing good business, he was guaranteeing that the Buffalo television station remained minority-owned. It would eventually become part of the Granite fold in June 1995 and be renamed WNBW-TV.

With the addition of the Syracuse and Fresno stations, Granite saw its net revenues soar by 75 percent in 1994, totaling almost $63 million, after posting just $37.5 million in 1993. The price of Granite stock, which had languished since its IPO, also increased in value by 70 percent, making it the top performing media stock in the country. As a whole the television industry rebounded, the economy improved, and advertising revenues were aided by election year political ads. In addition, Granite benefited from increased competition between the major networks, as an aggressive Fox precipitated a number of affiliation changes that resulted in higher network compensation to broadcast stations.

Granite was now well positioned to add new television stations in 1995. In February it paid $54 million for KEYE-TV of Austin, Texas, and then in June it paid $98.9 million for WWMT-TV, which served Grand Rapids, Kalamazoo, and Battle Creek. With nine stations under its control, Granite was content to consolidate its gains before taking on any new acquisitions, which in any case would have to be accomplished with the aid of the FCC minority-ownership tax break. Congress repealed the program in 1995 after a number of media conglomerates used minority fronts to gain massive capital-gains tax breaks. A prime example was the $2.3 billion sale of Viacom's cable television operations to black businessman Frank Washington, who owned only 21 percent of the purchasing company. The major player was actually Tele-Communications Inc., holder of the nation's largest cable television system. While Granite was established and was expected to maintain its growth, other minority owners would now find it much more difficult to emulate Cornwell's success.

Granite displayed its innovative spirit in 1996 by backing Datacast, a business that planned to transmit data over the analog spectrum to customers. The venture would lose money but lead to a digital business a few years later. More important in 1996 was Granite's affiliation with Yahoo! before the Internet portal went public and became a major success story. Granite was the first to feature its local news content on Yahoo!, with both parties sharing advertising revenues. Granite also looked to expansion in the established medium of radio. In May 1996 it paid $1 million to acquire WIVR-FM in Eureka, Illinois. The call letters were changed to WEEK-FM, and then reformatted to augment Granite's WEEK-TV station. Not only did the radio station use the television station's news content, it featured local TV personalities as call-in show hosts, and also simulcast local programming, such as area minor league baseball and hockey games. Cornwell considered radio to be "a fairly low-cost way of expanding our franchise."

First Top-Ten Acquisition in 1997

Granite added to its roster of television stations in 1997 by buying its first top-ten market property, paying $175 million for WXON-TV in Detroit, Michigan. Granite television stations now reached 7.75 percent of the total U.S. audience. A family-run business for many years, WXON-TV was the number six station in Detroit and did not even subscribe to the Nielsen ratings, a decision that kept ad rates low because advertisers had no verification of viewership. It was a classic example of an underperforming station that Granite had proven it could turn around. Coupled with its other Michigan station, Granite was now in a position to deliver 80 percent of all Michigan households to advertisers. Nevertheless, WXON-TV, soon renamed WDWB-TV, was the company's first major-market project. Investors took a wait-and-see attitude and did not bid up Granite's stock, which had been languishing in recent months. Moreover, Granite's reported debt load had reached $376.5 million.

To restore Wall Street confidence and perhaps float a new stock offering, Granite looked to clean up its balance sheet. In July 1998 it sold its first Michigan acquisition, WWMT-TV, to Freedom Communications for $150.5 million. The company then exercised a right to purchase WLAJ-TV of Lansing, Michigan, and immediately resold it to Freedom. The proceeds from these transactions were then used to fund another purchase of a major market television station, San Francisco's KBWB-TV, for which Granite paid more than $170 million in total compensation. Granite unloaded other properties in 1999, selling its

Austin television station for $160 million in cash and WEEK-FM for $1.15 million (thereby putting at least a temporary end to Cornwell's plan of creating synergy between local television and radio stations).

Wall Street approved of Granite's moves and its stock price improved significantly, but the company's next step would prompt immediate and harsh negative response from investors in 2000. Granite's San Jose station, KNTV, was set to lose its affiliation with ABC, after accepting a $14 million payment from the network to give up that affiliation five years early. At the same time in San Francisco, NBC failed in an attempt to purchase its longtime affiliate KRON-TV, losing out to Young Broadcasting. The network demanded that the station now pay it $10 million a year to keep its affiliation, a reversal of the traditional arrangement in which networks paid stations to be affiliates. Young refused to comply. The industry, as well as Wall Street, was then stunned when NBC and Granite announced that Granite had agreed to pay NBC $362 million to make KNTV the NBC affiliate that would serve San Francisco beginning in 2002. In addition, three Granite stations located in Duluth, Fresno, and Peoria would receive ten-year deals at no extra cost. The signal of KNTV reached only portions of San Francisco and was not represented on all the city's cable systems, but Granite expected to work out those problems by 2002. From Cornwell's point of view, the deal was a masterstroke. Young had just paid $823 million for what it expected was the NBC affiliate for San Francisco, and now for less than half the price Cornwell was able to transform KNTV into that level of franchise. He also was looking to team with NBC to create a Bay Area cable news channel that would compete with Young's Bay TV.

Other broadcast stations as well as Wall Street did not share Cornwell's vision. They were horrified and angry, believing that in a single stroke Granite had changed the dynamics of television economics. Whereas most believed that the amount networks paid to affiliates needed to be lowered to reflect current realities, the thought of reverse compensation in which stations would pay the networks was nothing short of heresy. Network compensation provided between 5 percent and 10 percent of station revenues. The elimination or reversal of compensation would have significant adverse effect on the value of stations. Wall Street showed its displeasure with Granite by punishing its stock, which had only just rebounded. Famed money manager Mario Gabelli, one of whose funds was Granite's third largest institutional investor, even called for Cornwell to resign. By the end of 2000 Granite stock was trading as low as $1 and in danger of being delisted. Although the company's market capitalization was now just $20 million, Granite's television stations were clearly worth far more than if sold off. Nevertheless, going into 2001 Granite was in serious financial difficulty. Soft ad revenues had hurt the company's recent earnings, which only fueled the company's plummeting stock price. To make matters worse, Granite faced large initial payments due on the NBC deal. The network, however, wished to see Granite succeed (even though it retained the right to cancel the affiliation deal should it find an unlikely means to pry KRON-TV away from Young). In addition, NBC agreed to provide KNTV with some program content to help it survive during the two years it would have to operate as an independent. It was Cornwell's old firm, Goldman Sachs, however, that provided an even more important boost to Granite's sagging fortunes when it arranged $205 million in financing. The company's stock finally appeared to stabilize. Nevertheless, the true test of Cornwell's gamble would come only when KNTV became an operational NBC affiliate. Should the station turn into a cash cow, the NBC deal would seem like an act of genius that would overshadow any temporary controversy over reverse compensation.

Principal Operating Units

KBWB-TV, San Francisco; WDWB-TV, Detroit; WNBW-TV, Buffalo; KNTV, San Jose; KSEE-TV, Fresno; WTVH-TV, Syracuse; WPTA-TV, Fort Wayne; WEEK-TV, Peoria; KBJR-TV, Duluth.

Principal Competitors

Sinclair Broadcast Group, Inc.; Young Broadcasting Inc.

Further Reading

Block, Valerie, "Granite Tries to Steady Its Shaky Picture," *Crain's New York Business,* December 18, 2000, p. 3.

Flint, Joe, "NBC Affiliate Agrees to Pay for Programs," *Wall Street Journal,* February 15, 2000, p. A3.

Foisie, Geoffrey, "W. Don Cornwell," *Broadcasting & Cable,* May 30, 1994, p. 69.

Lowery, Mark, "Solid As a Rock," *Black Enterprise,* June 1995, p. 122.

McClellan, Steve, "Granite Stock in a Tailspin," *Broadcasting & Cable,* December 18, 2000.

——, "Reversal of Fortune," *Broadcasting & Cable,* February 21, 2000, p. 10.

Mermigas, Diane, "Granite Gets Time to Pay the Peacock," *Electronic Media,* March 12, 2001, p. 5.

——, "Granite Scrambles to Avoid Hitting Rock Bottom," *Electronic Media,* December 11, 2000, p. 2.

——, "Testing Granite's Mettle," *Electronic Media,* April 17, 2000, p. 1A.

—Ed Dinger

Group 4 Falck A/S

Polititorvet
DK-1780
Copenhagen V
Denmark
Telephone: (+45) 70-13-43-43
Fax: (+45) 33-91-00-26
Web site: http://www.group4falck.com

Public Company
Incorporated: 1901 as Kjobenhavn Frederiksberg
Nattevagt
Employees: 125,000
Sales: DKr 18.21 billion ($2.31 billion) (2000)
Stock Exchanges: Copenhagen
Ticker Symbol: FALCK
NAIC: 561612 Security Guards and Patrol Services;
561621 Security Systems Services (Except
Locksmiths)

Group 4 Falck A/S is gunning for the top spot among the world's leading security services companies. The Copenhagen-based firm, formed from the 2000 merger of Falck and Group 4 Securitas, is the number two security services company, behind Sweden's Securitas. Unlike that company, which has extensive operations in the United States through its Pinkerton's subsidiary, Group 4 Falck has staked out Europe for its strongest growth. The company is already the leading security services firm in the United Kingdom, Belgium, The Netherlands, Denmark, and Austria in Western Europe, and has captured leading shares in a number of former Eastern Bloc countries, including Latvia, Estonia, Poland, Hungary, and the Czech Republic. The company is also strongly represented in France and Germany. Since 2001, Group 4 Falck has redefined itself for the opening years of the new century, streamlining its focus to three core divisions: Security, including guard services, alarm, and cash and other transport services; Safety, including ambulance, rescue (including crisis counseling), and fire services; and Global Solutions, including prison and court services and meter reading

services through its AccuRead joint venture. The company plans to dispose of operations not involved in these three areas. Traded on the Copenhagen stock exchange, Group 4 Falck posted combined revenues of more than DKr 18 billion ($2.3 billion) in 2000. Former Group 4 Chairman Jorgen Philip-Sorensen is chairman of the company; former Falck CEO and Chairman Lars Norby Johansen has become the enlarged company's president and CEO.

Scandinavian Security Pioneers: 1900s–20s

Both Group 4 and Falck trace their origins to the beginnings of the security services industry in Scandinavia. The older of the two, Group 4, originated with the founding of Kjobenhavn Frederiksberg Nattevagt by Philip-Sorensen and Marius Hogrefe in 1901. That company also formed the basis of what became Securitas AB, based in Sweden, which captured the world leadership in the security services industry at the end of the 20th century.

Philip-Sorensen soon became the driving force behind the company, which provided guard and other security services in Denmark, and the Philip-Sorensen family remained an active force in the security services industry throughout the century. In 1918, the company merged with another company to form De Forenede Vagtselskaber, which in turn lay the foundation for Danish services provider ISS (which later shed security services to focus on cleaning services).

Meanwhile, Denmark, and Copenhagen in particular, saw the appearance of a number of other firms providing a variety of security, guard, and even fire and rescue services. One of these companies was Redningskorpset for Kobenhavn og Frederiksberg A/S, set up by Sophus Falck in 1906. That company initially began operating as an ambulance and rescue service; in 1908, it became the first company in Denmark to offer ambulance services using automobiles. Redningskorpset later expanded into fire and other rescue services after the Danish government authorized private companies to provide fire-fighting services in 1926. By the end of that decade, Sophus Falck had expanded his business to cover all of Denmark.

Focus on Sweden, Then Other Parts of Europe: 1930s–70s

The 1930s saw the expansion of Philip-Sorensen's interests as well. In 1934, Erik Philip-Sorensen brought his father's company to Sweden, acquiring that country's Hälsingbords Nattvakt, in Helsingborg. This acquisition formed the basis for Securitas AB, which continued to operate as a subsidiary of De Forenede Vagtselskaber. The family bought out the larger company in 1938, taking full control of the Swedish Securitas (ISS maintained the Securitas name elsewhere). Sweden now became the family's primary activity.

The Philip-Sorensen family's move into Sweden gave it protection under that country's neutral status during World War II. After the war, both the Philip-Sorensens and the Falcks continued to build their businesses in their respective markets and targeted areas of operations. The Falck company grew in the early 1960s when it acquired another rescue services company, Zonen Redningskorps, in 1963.

The Philip-Sorensens, meanwhile, had begun expanding throughout Sweden, acquiring a number of other small security services firms, including that of AB Svensk Nattvakt, based in Stockholm. In 1950, the company looked beyond Scandinavia for the first time, opening a subsidiary operation in England. A second U.K. branch was opened by the end of the decade, as the company turned toward other European markets. At that time, the family renamed all of its operations under the single Securitas International name.

Erik Philip-Sorensen's sons, Jorgen and Sven, joined the company and began taking an active role in its expansion—after first serving as security guards themselves and working their way up the company's ranks. Jorgen was involved particularly in the company's international growth, while Sven concentrated on its Swedish operations. Securitas's U.K. business soon took on greater weight when, in 1963, the company launched two new British security services companies, Store Detectives Ltd. and Securitas Alarms Ltd.

Two years later, Jorgen Philip-Sorensen was placed in charge of Securitas's U.K. business and given the title of managing director. In 1968, these operations were joined with the company's other U.K. businesses to form a new independent subsidiary, Group 4 (Total Security).

Falck maintained its focus on fire and rescue services throughout the 1970s, becoming one of the largest in the Danish market. The company continued to be led by the Falck family into the 1980s. Meanwhile, across the Kattegat, the Philip-Sorensen family was preparing a changing of the guard. In 1974, the company was turned over to Sven and Jorgen Philip-Sorensen. In 1981, however, the brothers agreed to split the company into two, with Sven taking charge of the Sweden-based Securitas operations, and Jorgen taking control of the company's U.K.-centered European activities. This company was then renamed Group 4 Securitas.

Gunning for World Leadership in the 21st Century

If Sven Philip-Sorensen quickly exited the business, selling his company in 1983, Jorgen Philip-Sorensen continued to build up Group 4 throughout the 1980s. Expanding beyond Europe, the company established a business in India, starting with 1,400 employees, in 1989. That move was a prelude into other far-flung areas, such as Bangladesh, in the late 1990s. Throughout the decade, Group 4 built up a major share in the Indian subcontinent's security services market.

In 1990, the company turned to the United States, acquiring American Magnetics Corporation and its specialty in access control systems. Group 4 also moved into Eastern Europe, with an agreement with the Hungarian government to provide services in that country. The following year, Group 4 captured a leading share of the Belgian market with its acquisition of that country's IMS; Group 4 also had strengthened its position in the United Kingdom, being the first private company there to be awarded a prison management contract.

By then, the Falck family had sold its company, which had branched out into the larger security services field with the formation of Falck Sikring, to insurance company Baltica, in 1988. At that time, Lars Norby Johansen, the first non-Falck family member, took over as president and CEO of the group. Under Johansen, Falck was to see accelerated growth catapulting it into the top ranks of Europe's security services market. Baltica soon sold off a majority of its shares to a consortium of investors.

Falck began its expansion in earnest in 1993 when it acquired ISS's Securitas operations. Falck merged these with its own Falck Sikring business to form Falck Securitas. Two years later, Falck took a listing on the Copenhagen stock exchange, and then acquired Norway's Trygghetssentralen. The following year, Falck grew larger with the purchases of Partena Security, based in Sweden, and Norway's Falken, a safety services business.

Group 4 also was expanding rapidly during this time. The company had moved into Turkey in 1991, and then Austria and Canada with the 1993 acquisition of EWWS Group. A year later, the company established operations in the United Arab Emirates and in Ukraine. Meanwhile Group 4 exited the Spanish market by swapping its Spanish holdings for shares in former sister company Securitas AB. Group 4 also began to

Key Dates:

1901: Kjobenhavn Frederiksberg Nattevagt is formed.

1906: Redningskorpset for Kobenhavn og Frederiksberg is launched.

1908: Redningskorpset introduces first automobile ambulances in Scandinavia.

1918: Kjobenhavn Frederiksberg Nattevagt merges into De Forenede Vagtselskaber.

1934: Securitas AB (Sweden) is formed.

1950: Securitas establishes U.K. subsidiary.

1963: Falck acquires Zonen Redningskorps; Securitas launches Store Detectives Ltd. and Securitas Alarms Ltd. in the United Kingdom.

1968: Securitas renames U.K. operations as Group 4 Securitas.

1981: Securitas splits in two; Jorgen Philip-Sorensen is given control of Group 4 Securitas.

1988: Baltica acquires Falck.

1989: Group 4 enters India.

1991: Group 4 acquires Belgium-based IMS.

1993: Falck acquires ISS Securitas and forms Falck Securitas; Group 4 enters the Austrian and Canadian markets through the purchase of EWWS.

1995: Falck lists on the Copenhagen stock exchange.

1998: Falck acquires Germany's Simis, Poland's Sezam, and Estonia's AS ESS.

1999: Falck acquires Nederlandse Veiligheidsdienst.

2000: Falck and Group 4 merge and form Group 4 Falck A/S.

2001: Company acquires Germany's Top Control; company sells its Belgian cleaning services arm.

diversify a bit during this period, notably through the formation of AccuRead, a joint venture with British Gas to provide meter-reading services throughout the United Kingdom.

Both Falck and Group 4 expanded steadily throughout the second half of the 1990s before joining together to confront the growing strength of Securitas AB on the world's security services scene. The companies targeted rather different markets, however, which heightened the interest of their eventual merger—at that time, the companies had overlapping business in just four domestic markets. Falck continued to expand throughout Scandinavia, acquiring two small security businesses in Finland in 1997; the company remained close to home in its expansion moves in 1998, when it picked up Germany's Simis, Poland's Sezam, and Estonia's AS ESS. The following year, Falck took the leadership position in The Netherlands, with the purchase of Nederlandse Veiligsheidsdienst. The company also acquired Lithuania's UAB Gelvora that year, giving it the lead in that market.

Falck's public status had given it the backing for an aggressive acquisition campaign at the end of the decade. In 1999, the company became the largest security company in Latvia with its acquisition of SIA Apsargs. The company had by then strengthened its position in Poland with the acquisition of Erminus. In 2000, Falck added Germany's ADS Sicherheit

Group, and then gained a plum contract when it took over the newly privatized guard and security services operations of Denmark's government.

The two companies announced their decision to merge and form Group 4 Falck in May 2000. The new company became the world's second largest security services firm in the world. As part of the merger agreement, Jorgen Philip-Sorensen was named company chairman, while Johansen became president and CEO; the company retained Falck's listing on the Copenhagen stock exchange. Group 4 Falck also quickly showed its intention to become number one, as the acquisition drive mounted by Falck continued into the new century.

Among the company's acquisitions after the merger were those of Austria's SOS; Finland's SPAC; Hungary's Banktech Security Rt; Unikey, of Norway; and, in July 2001, Top Control Group, of Germany. At the same time, Group 4 Falck stepped up its position in France, where it acquired OGS, adding another DKr 125 million in sales and, especially, the number two firm in that country, Euroguard, which added another DKr 650 million.

Group 4 Falck's expansion at the dawn of the 21st century had more than doubled the group's pro forma consolidated sales—which had reached a combined DKr 8 billion in 1996, before topping DKr 18 billion in the newly enlarged group's first annual report in 2000. At that time, Group 4 Falck announced a new strategic vision to lead it though 2003. The company announced its intention to step up the consolidation of the highly fragmented security services industry, with a goal of topping rival Securitas for the number one position. Group 4 Falck also announced its intention to streamline its own operations in order to tighten its focus on three core divisions: Security, Safety, and Global Solutions. As such, the company began to sell off operations outside of this core, such as its Belgian cleaning services arm, sold to ISS at the beginning of 2001.

Principal Subsidiaries

AccuRead Limited (U.K.; 51%); ADS Holding GmbH (Germany); Erste Wiener Wach- und Schliessg. AG (Austria); Euroguard SA/NV (Belgium; 55%); Falck Denmark; Falken Gruppen AS (Norway); Falck Estonia (ESS); Falck Germany; Falck Norway; Falck Poland; Falck Räddningskår AB (Sweden); Falck Security Oy (Finland); Falck Sweden; First Select (India); GCS Securiton (Austria); Group 4 Austria; Group 4 Belgium; Group 4 Canada; Group 4 Correction Services Pty Ltd (Australia); Group 4 Czech Republic; Group 4 Falck Managed Services; Group 4 Falck Security Support Services; Group 4 Falck Slovakia; Group 4 India; Group 4 Ireland; Group 4 Monitoring Services; Group 4 Prison Services (U.K.); Group 4 Poland; Group 4 Technology UK; Group 4 Total Security UK; Nederlandse Veiligheidsdienst Holding BV (Netherlands); Ratownictwo Falck Sp.z.o.o. (Poland); Seceurop Receptieservices BV BA (Belgium).

Principal Divisions

Security; Safety; Global Solutions.

Principal Competitors

AHLS/Argenbright; Allied; Chubb plc; Command Security Corporation; Guardsmark; Home Security International, Inc.; Initial; The Pittston Company; Prosegur; Compañía de Seguridad, S.A; Protection One, Inc.; Rentokil Initial plc; Secom Co., Ltd.; Securicor plc; Transnational Security Group; Tyco International Ltd.; The Wackenhut Corporation.

Further Reading

George, Nicolas, "Falck to Acquire Group 4 Securitas," *Financial Times,* May 3, 2000.

"Group 4 Falck Aims High," *Financial Times,* November 29, 2000.

"Group 4, Falck Merger to Open up Security Services Market," *Economic Times,* May 14, 2000.

—M. L. Cohen

Guilbert S.A.

126 Avenue du Poteau
F-60451 Senlis Cedex
France
Telephone: (+33) 3 44-54-54-45
Fax: (+33) 3-44-54-55-99
Web site: http://www.guilbert.fr

Wholly Owned Subsidiary of Pinault-Printemps-Redoute S.A.
Incorporated: 1959 as Entreprises Marcel Guilbert S.A.
Employees: 7,128
Sales: EUR 1.5 billion (US $1.41 billion) (2000)
Stock Exchanges: Euronext Paris
Ticker Symbol: GUI
NAIC: 4221 Paper and Paper Product Wholesalers; 422110 Printing and Writing Paper Wholesalers; 422130 Industrial and Personal Service Paper Wholesalers; 322299 All Other Converted Paper Product Manufacturing

Guilbert S.A. is Europe's leading office supplies provider. Fully owned by retailing and distribution giant Pinault-Printemps-Redoute (PPR) S.A., led by François Pinault, Guilbert has pursued an international expansion strategy focused on its European base. The company offers more than 9,500 products, nearly 2,500 of which are marketed under its own Niceday brand launched in 2001. The company's products span the entire range of office supply goods, from paper to furniture and fixtures, targeted at the corporate, rather than consumer, market. With more of its clients seeking global solutions for their office supply needs, Guilbert has entered into an agreement with the United States' Boise Cascade—one of the world's largest office supply products distributors—to acquire that company's European operations, which include mail-order group JPG, Neat Ideas in the United Kingdom, and Kalamazoo in Spain. The agreement also called for the establishment of a joint venture to provide global capabilities for the two companies' largest customers. Guilbert, whose shares were withdrawn from the Euronext Paris stock exchange after PPR completed its holding in the company in 2000, posted EUR 1.5 billion in sales that year. The company is led by CEO Jean-Charles Pauze and President and PPR Chief Executive Serge Weinberg.

Retail Beginnings in the 1950s

André Guilbert opened up a stationer's shop in the town of Roubaix, France, in 1955. By 1959, however, the Guilbert family had begun to expand beyond retail into office supply distribution. In that year, the family incorporated its growing operations as Entreprises Marcel Guilbert S.A. The company continued to develop its distribution activities through the next decade, abandoning its retail operation to focus on direct sales. The company hired a highly motivated direct sales force, without base salaries, company vehicles, or expense accounts. Instead, its salespeople were paid on commission only. The commission, however, was on gross orders and thus the prospect for high earnings was strong. By the 1990s, some of Guilbert's salespeople were earning the equivalent of $12,000 per month and more.

Joining the company in 1965 was André Guilbert's son-in-law, Philippe Cuvelier. Together, the Guilbert family built the company into a major force in the French, and then European, office supply market. Cuvelier was to take the position of president of the company in 1992, and to lead its international expansion, before stepping down in 1998.

Guilbert moved its office supply distribution business to new headquarters in the town of Senlis in 1970. The following year, the company made the first of a long series of external expansion moves, merging with the paper firm Papeteries Esnor, based in Reims. This company, as with other acquisitions to follow, was to remain a separately operating subsidiary, supplying the parent company, until a restructuring in the late 1980s.

The absorption of the Esnor company was followed with that of carbon-paper producer Compagnie Française des Carbonnes, based in Bayonne, in 1973. Paper wholesaler Comptoir de la Papeterie was added three years later, giving the company a base in Grenoble as well. In 1978, Guilbert expanded again when it acquired office supply distributor Diffusion Européenne de Papeterie, in Reuil-Malmaison.

Company Perspectives:

Guilbert's strategy is to strengthen its European leadership and develop multi-channel distribution.

Guilbert was also pursuing organic expansion in the 1970s. The company began opening regional sales agency offices in 1977, with the first in the city of Lyon. Other offices were to follow as the company sought to build a national presence. After opening an agency in Rennes in 1980, the company turned to Strasbourg in 1984, then to Bordeaux and Aix in 1987. Many other offices and distribution platforms were added through the rest of the decade, giving Guilbert a presence throughout France in cities including Reims, Poitiers, Caen, Toulouse, Orléans, Nice, and Besançon. The company also established a new subsidiary in 1981, Papeteries du Midi, based in Marseille, giving it a strong base from which to supply France's Mediterranean market.

European Leader in the 21st Century

Guilbert gained steadily in the highly fragmented office supplies market in France during the 1980s. A series of new acquisitions helped it to grow into the domestic leader. The company started the decade with the purchase of Romainville-based Novel-Carbel, a specialist in office automation products, acquired in 1981. In this way, Guilbert responded to the growing demand for computer supplies and equipment. After buying new warehouse and distribution facilities near its Senlis home base in 1982, Guilbert turned toward Paris, acquiring office furniture, fittings, and interiors supplier Excelsior in 1983. In order to help finance its growth, Guilbert took a listing on the Paris stock exchange's secondary board in 1984, transferring to the main board only in 1994.

Guilbert restructured much of its French organization in 1989, consolidating its subsidiaries Diffusion Européenne de Papeterie, Compagnie Française des Carbonnes, Comptoir de la Papeterie, and Papeteries Guilbert Esnor into the parent company. By now the leader of the French office supplies market, the company began to prepare its international expansion. One of its first moves towards becoming the European leader was the purchase of a 20 percent stake in Spanish stationery and office supplies distributor Kanguros, a stake the company sold off again just three years later.

Nonetheless, Guilbert, which received a new president when Philippe Cuvelier took over the company's leadership, began to build its foreign position in earnest at the beginning of the 1990s. In 1991, the company acquired the Belgium company Robal; the following year, Guilbert moved into the larger U.K. market, with the purchase of office supplies distributor Ofrex, founded in 1936 and based in Stockport. Ofrex was to become the vehicle for Guilbert's further expansion into the U.K. market, which found itself in disarray with the deep recession of the early part of the decade.

Guilbert's transfer to the Parisian exchange's main board in 1994 was to help the company's expansion drive in the mid-1990s. The company, which posted sales of more than FFr

2.5 billion in 1995 quickly doubled in size—topping FFr 5.6 billion by 1997. Much of this growth came from its international development, particularly with the acquisitions of British office supplies and commercial printing businesses Esse and Arkle, both in 1995, and of Germany's Schacht & Westerich that same year.

The year 1996 was to prove a turning point for Guilbert. In that year the company formed the 3G joint venture with mail-order giant 3 Suisses to acquire JM Bruneau, a mail-order supplier of office supplies and equipment, posting approximately FFr 1 billion in revenues per year. The company added to its operations in Germany with the acquisition of Walther & Sohn. But Guilbert's biggest coup came in April 1996 when it paid more than FFr 1 billion to acquire the struggling Business Supplies Ltd., a subsidiary focused on supplying the corporate market built up by bookseller WH Smith through a series of acquisitions during the 1990s. The addition of this unit added nearly FFr 1.3 billion to Guilbert's sales, and also gave it a new brand name, Niceday, which had gained success in the United Kingdom with its Snoopy-like cartoon dog mascot.

The newly enlarged Guilbert was now able to claim leadership in the European office supplies market, with the number one spot in both France and the United Kingdom, and a place among the leaders in the German market as well. Yet the arrival of new competition—notably the U.S. giants Office Depot and Staples—on the European continent forced Guilbert to turn to deeper pockets in order to help it secure its leading position. In 1998, the company—and the Guilbert family—agreed to sell a 56.5 percent majority stake to the Pinault-Printemps-Redoute S.A. (PPR) retail empire led by François Pinault and Serge Weinberg.

PPR already held such retailing and mail-order giants as Fnac, La Redoute, and furniture and appliance seller Conforama. With the highly fragmented European office supplies network worth an estimated FFr 150 billion (more than $20 billion), the acquisition of Guilbert instantly gave PPR the European leadership in this market as well. Guilbert, meanwhile, gained access not only to PPR's deeper pockets, but also to the expertise of its other units, such as in computer supplies, through Fnac, and office furniture, through Conforama, and particularly in the mail-order field, through La Redoute.

Until then Guilbert had focused primarily on its higher-cost direct sales organization, continuing to open sales agencies throughout France during the decade. The rising popularity of Internet-based marketing and the ending of many trade restrictions among the European Community's member countries were combining to challenge traditional sales methods. Guilbert stood to gain from its new majority shareholder; the Guilbert family members, however, were less fortunate. Soon after their company's acquisition, Philippe Cuvelier, who had tripled the company's sales in just five years, was replaced by a new CEO and president, Jean-Charles Pauze, who came to the company from Strafor-Steelcase.

Guilbert, which had been building its presence in Spain, Italy, and Belgium during the decade, now turned to the Dutch and Portuguese markets. In 1999, the company acquired the Netherlands Kantic, and Portugal's Sete. With these acquisi-

Key Dates:

1955: André Guilbert opens an office supplies store in Roubaix, France.
1959: Company incorporates as Entreprises Marcel Guilbert S.A. and enters office supply distribution.
1970: Headquarters are transferred to Senlis.
1971: Guilbert acquires Reims-based Papeteries Esnor and enters the stationery market.
1983: Company moves into office furniture market with purchase of Excelsior, based in Paris.
1984: Guilbert takes a listing on secondary market of the Paris stock exchange, opens sales agency in Strasbourg.
1989: Company reorganizes holdings with absorption of Diffusion Européenne de Papeterie, Compagnie Française des Carbonnes, Comptoir de la Papeterie, and Papeteries Guilbert Esnor; acquires 20 percent of Spanish office supplies and stationery firm Kanguros.
1992: Guilbert acquires Ofrex Supplies and enters the U.K. market, sells Kanguros stake.
1996: Company steps up international expansion with acquisitions of Niceday, the office supply division of WH Smith, Germany's Walther & Sohn, and mail-order office supplies specialist JM Bruneau.
1998: Pinault-Printemps-Redoute acquires 56.5 percent of Guilbert's shares.
1999: Guilbert boosts European presence with purchases of Kantic and Sete.
2000: Acquires German office supplies provider Hutter Group to capture second position in that market; Pinault-Printemps-Redoute acquires 100 percent of Guilbert; acquires European office supply operations from Boise Cascade, adding JPG, Europa, Kalamazoo, and Neat Ideas brands, and signs international cooperation agreement.

tions, the company's international sales now accounted for 60 percent of its total revenues. That figure was boosted still higher in 2000, when Guilbert gained control of Germany's Hutter. This acquisition gave Guilbert the number two position in the German office supplies market.

By then, PPR had increased its position in the company, to more than 91 percent in 1999 and to full control in 2000. Guilbert was delisted from the Paris stock exchange and structured as a wholly owned subsidiary of PPR. Soon after, Guilbert made a new move to reaffirm its European dominance—and to give it a foothold in the increasingly global market for office supplies. In September 2000, the company reached an agreement to acquire Boise Cascade Office Products (BCOP)'s European operations, which included the mail-order specialist JPG, active in France and Belgium and via the Internet, and the office

suppliers and distributors Europa, Kalamazoo, and Neat Ideas, strengthening Guilbert in a number of European markets, including Spain, Germany, Italy, Belgium, and the United Kingdom.

The terms of the BCOP acquisition also featured a cooperation agreement between the two companies to create a global product range available to the two companies' globally operating customers. Boise Cascade was to become responsible for customers' needs in the North and South American markets, while Guilbert was to handle those same customers' orders in Europe.

Guilbert moved into the new century with a secure position as Europe's leading office supplies specialist. It had also gained a place at the table with the largely U.S.-based leaders of the global market. That market was set to grow still further as e-commerce activities were expected to increase in the early years of the century. Guilbert took steps to position itself to capture a share of that market, too, grouping its small and home office e-commerce business around its JPG web site, while launching, in July 2001, its Guilweb e-commerce site for mid- to large-sized corporations. The company revealed ambitious goals for these projects, forecasting that as much as 25 percent of its sales were to come from its electronic ordering facilities by the year 2004.

Principal Subsidiaries

Guilbert Allemagne (Germany); Guilbert Belgique (Belgium); Guilbert Espagne (Spain); Guilbert France; Guilbert Irlande (Ireland); Guilbert Italie (Titanedi) (Italy); Guilbert Pays-Bas; Guilbert Portugal; Guilbert UK; JPG; JPG Belgique (Belgium); Kalamazoo (Spain); Mondoffice (Italy); Neat Ideas (U.K.).

Principal Competitors

Arjo Wiggins Appleton p.l.c.; Boise Cascade Office Products Corporation; Buhrmann NV; David S. Smith (Holdings) PLC; IKON Office Solutions, Inc.; International Paper Company; Manutan International SA; Moore Corporation Limited; Office Depot, Inc.; OfficeMax, Inc.; Online Office Supplies Company; Grupo Picking Pack, S.A.; Quill Corp.; United Stationers Inc.

Further Reading

"Accord stratégique entre Guilbert et Boise Cascade," *Les Echos,* September 29, 2000, p. 31.
Besses-Boumard, Pascale, "François Pinault installe un nouveau président à la tête de Guilbert," *Les Echos,* October 12, 1998, p. 24.
Chauveau, Julie, "Guilbert se renforce dans la vente par correspondence," *La Tribune,* September 29, 2000.
Santrot, Florence, "Patrick Lasfargues: Directeur Général Adjoint, Guilbert," *Journal du Net,* June 15, 2001.
Triouleyre, Nicole, "Guilbert s'adosse à un groupe international pour se développer," *La Tribune,* January 23, 1998.

—M. L. Cohen

Hakuhodo, Inc.

4-1 Shibaura 3-chome
Minato-ku Tokyo 108-8088
Japan
Telephone: (81) 3 5446 6161
Fax: (81) 3 5446 6166
Web site: http://www.hakuhodo.co.jp

Private Company
Incorporated: 1924
Employees: 3,405
Sales: ¥101.9 billion ($849.2 million)
NAIC: 54181 Advertising Agencies

Hakuhodo, Inc., is Japan's second largest advertising agency, after Dentsu, Ltd. The agency has extensive relationships with all aspects of Japanese media, and offers its clients a wide range of services including marketing research, media planning, advertising production, brand management, interactive marketing, and public relations. The agency is known for its Institute of Life and Living, which was established in 1981 to study consumer and sociological trends. Hakuhodo has extensive overseas operations—39 offices in 16 countries—and in this respect is a pioneer among Japanese agencies. Also notable is Hakuhodo's ability to rapidly respond to changing trends within the industry and its use of technology in its approach to producing advertising.

Late 1800s to Early 1900s: Inception of an Ad Agency

The roots of Hakuhodo can be traced back to 1895, when a young businessman, Hironao Seki, established himself as an agent for a publisher of educational magazines and books. The word ''hakuhodo'' translates literally as ''news release firm,'' which reflected the emphasis of Seki's business: to impart information about educational services and announce the opening of new schools. Japan was in a period of great change during the late 19th century, having rapidly developed from an economy based on agriculture to a major industrial power by 1900. This transformation required a large-scale effort on the part of Ja-

pan's rulers to educate the population in Western methods and technology, and was accompanied by a huge growth in the publishing and printing industries. Although newspapers and books had been available in Japan for some centuries, the vast amount of new information being absorbed by the nation resulted in a surge of new books, magazines, and newspapers. Seki saw this as a prime opportunity to begin his agency business. At first he acted only as an agent on behalf of publishers, selling the advertising space, and was not involved in creating the advertisements themselves, but this began to change as clients requested more and more from him. The official name of his business was changed to Hakuhodo Newspaper and Magazine Advertising in 1900, reflecting the nature of Seki's work. To take advantage of the market for newspapers, Seki started a daily named *Naigai Tsushin* in 1910, which soon became an integral part of his business. The paper published general news, and Seki sold its advertising space.

Advertising in Japan at the time consisted largely of notice boards on public display. Newspapers and magazines were slowly emerging as popular means of promotion. Japan's new and expanding trading companies found this to be a lucrative and successful means of selling goods. Seki's business grew steadily, and he began to produce advertisements for clients as part of his services. To raise additional funds for expansion, Seki officially formed Hakuhodo as a joint stock company in 1924, with headquarters in central Tokyo. The company was capitalized at ¥500,000; Hironao Seki was the firm's first president. At the time, Hakuhodo represented one of the largest advertising agencies in Tokyo, but it was still far smaller than its rival, Dentsu, Ltd. In 1926 Hakuhodo donated funds for the establishment of the Meiji Newspaper and Magazine Library at Tokyo University, the most prestigious university in Japan. It was a first step in establishing Hakuhodo's reputation as a specialist in research and the gathering of information.

By 1930 a substantial middle class had developed in Japan, with the business world dominated by a small number of huge conglomerates or ''zaibatsu'' centered around large trading companies. It was common for smaller companies to form links with a particular conglomerate resulting in cartel-like behavior among Japanese companies. Hakuhodo, being one of Japan's first advertising agencies, was well connected with all of the major zaibatsu and commanded a good deal of influence when purchasing advertising space for its clients, who by now consisted largely of consumer goods companies.

World War II: Starting Over

Between 1930 and 1945 Japan was effectively at war, and the economy was geared toward the production of armaments. Consumer goods exported from the West became scarcer and the Japanese military government instituted rationing for a number of goods during the height of the war in 1944. This was not a prosperous time for the Japanese advertising industry, with many companies going out of business. Hakuhodo's advertising revenues declined during this period, but the company's publishing operations remained steady. The bombing of Tokyo in 1945 was a disaster for Hakuhodo; its building in Kanda in downtown Tokyo was severely damaged, and much of its advertising business disappeared. Overall, Japan's industry was decimated, and what remained was reorganized by the U.S. occupation forces into smaller units.

With its client base lacking money to spend on advertising, Seki attempted to rebuild his company from the bottom up. He formed a planning and research department to try to help his clients plan their marketing campaigns and in 1948 started a magazine entitled *Hakuhodo Monthly News*, in addition to the daily *Naigai Tsushin* newspaper. In fact, he briefly changed the name of his company in 1950 to Naigai Tsushin Hakuhodo to reflect the importance of the publications to the business.

1950s–60s: New Approaches

By the early 1950s Japan was rapidly recovering. One of the first products to be mass-produced by the new Japanese industry was the transistor radio by Sony and other companies. This spawned a new media and advertising industry. Seki saw this as a huge growth market and formed a radio department within his company to prepare for the introduction of commercial radio. This soon became a major source of information and entertainment for the average Japanese and engendered a new way of selling products, from city gas to household appliances. The company opened its first office outside Tokyo in 1952 with the establishment of a branch in Osaka. The company's name was changed back to Hakuhodo in 1955 as the agency celebrated its 60th anniversary and two additional offices were opened in Nagoya and Fukuoka. The advent of radio was largely responsi-

ble for Hakuhodo's rapid growth; also, the capitalization of the company had increased eightfold from 1951 to 1956. To service Hakuhodo's range of clients, which included most of Japan's largest companies at the time, a network of offices was set up nationwide to enable effective planning of advertising campaigns. The number of offices reached 12 by 1959.

The year 1960 marked a turning point in the history of Hakuhodo. A group of the agency's senior managers visited the United States, studied advertising techniques used by large American agencies, and realized how much they had to learn. As a result of this experience, the "Hakuhodo Declaration" was formulated, trumpeting Hakuhodo's desire to modernize its methods and create an agency based on scientific market research methods and artistic ability. The account executive system was adopted to create a continuous contact point for clients and enable better servicing of the accounts. Hakuhodo also began its now extensive overseas network in 1960 with the establishment of a representative office in New York. The function of the office was largely to gather information about U.S. advertising techniques and new products. Like most Japanese businesses at the time, Hakuhodo regarded the United States as an economic superpower from which much knowledge could be gained.

Also in 1960 Hakuhodo formed a joint venture with U.S. advertising giant McCann-Erickson, named McCann-Erickson Hakuhodo, Ltd. The joint venture drew upon the creative and market research expertise of one of the most prestigious agencies in the United States as well as Hakuhodo's established network in Japan. The new venture's clients were initially McCann-Erickson's client companies in the United States, and an early success was the penetration of the Japanese market by Coca-Cola. The early success of this internationalization gave Hakuhodo the resources and confidence to expand into Asia, setting up an office in Bangkok in 1963 and in Jakarta in 1971, largely to promote its Japanese clients' products in these countries.

Hakuhodo entered the computer age in 1964 with the establishment of a data processing center in its head office in Kanda, Tokyo. Almost a decade later, an online marketing database was installed to provide instant information on almost any aspect of any market in Japan. In 1966 the company was restructured to cope with its growing size. Three separate accounts divisions were set up, all based in Tokyo, with client accounts split between the three. One reason for the split was to protect the confidentiality of clients within the same industry.

1970s–80s: Growth, New Initiatives, and Reorganization

In 1970 the Hakuhodo Foundation was established on the 75th anniversary of the agency to provide monetary awards for students. That same year *Ad Age* magazine ranked Hakuhodo as the 15th largest agency in the world. Hakuhodo's overseas expansion continued, with the opening of an office in Malaysia in 1973 and the Jakarta office closing in the same year due to lack of business. An international planning department was set up in Tokyo, and Hakuhodo Advertising America was formed as an independent subsidiary based in Los Angeles. The New York representative office was closed.

Key Dates:

1895: Hironao Seki becomes an advertising agent for an educational publisher.
1910: Seki begins publishing the daily newspaper *Naigai Tsushin*.
1924: Seki establishes Hakuhodo as a joint stock company.
1945: Hakuhodo's offices are badly damaged when Tokyo is bombed.
1948: Hakuhodo begins publishing *Hakuhodo Monthly News*.
1951: Hakuhodo establishes a Radio Department for the purpose of radio advertising.
1952: Hakuhodo opens its first office outside Tokyo, in Osaka.
1960: Hakuhodo Declaration is announced; company opens first overseas office, in New York City; company forms joint venture with U.S. ad agency McCann-Erickson.
1981: Hakuhodo Institute of Life and Living is established.
1983: Ritsuo Isobe becomes president of Hakuhodo.
1992: Nissan Motor increases its business with Hakuhodo by $76.5 million, making the company its primary ad agency.
1994: Hakuhodo sells its 49 percent stake in McCann-Erickson Hakuhodo, Ltd.; Takashi Shoji becomes the company's new president.
2000: Company partners with TBWA to form H & T Worldwide, a partnership dedicated to serving Nissan's advertising needs around the world.

By 1975 Hakuhodo had reached a stage of technological advancement on par with almost any advertising agency in the world. What some industry analysts felt the firm lacked was the creative power to conceive radical new advertising campaigns effectively. Concerned about this situation, Hakuhodo bolstered its creative department in 1976 by forming a creative center. Creative staff from abroad were hired in an attempt to increase the center's output. A communications center was added in 1977, located in Tokyo and combining Hakuhodo's public relations, sales promotion, and marketing divisions. In 1981 all of Hakuhodo's Tokyo offices were combined under one roof within the busy Marunouchi district of Tokyo. Also in 1981, the Hakuhodo Institute of Life and Living was set up as an independent organization. It was designed to be Hakuhodo's research center, conducting research into the behavior of Japanese society. The institute was based in Tokyo and served Hakuhodo and its affiliated organizations.

In 1982 Hakuhodo again underwent a major reorganization. Under President Mitchitaka Kondo, who succeeded Hiromasa Seki (the founder's son) in 1975, a new approach to client service was conceived. Hakuhodo was reborn as a "marketing engineering" company. The company now regarded its staff as marketing engineers who assembled teams of specialists to design a successful marketing campaign for clients. The new approach proved confusing at first to both clients and staff, but was soon accepted as a novel and efficient approach to the

business. Following this reorganization, Hakuhodo scored some impressive successes. In June 1982 it won the Grand Prize at the Cannes International Ad Film Festival and in July it was decorated with the Order of St. Sylvester by Pope John Paul II for its handling of the Pope's successful tour of Japan. An affiliation with the huge U.S. agency Lintas Worldwide effectively created the world's largest international advertising network. Similar agreements were formed with advertising agencies in South Korea and Taiwan in 1983. President Kondo retired in 1983 to become chairman, making way for new president Ritsuo Isobe. In 1984 Hakuhodo again walked away with a disproportionate share of the world's advertising awards, showing itself as a major creative force in world advertising. Hakuhodo's expansion had been roughly parallel with the explosion of consumer spending in Japan in the 1980s. Fierce competition in all markets, but especially consumer products, ensured that the services of Hakuhodo's extensive agency would be required.

Recession and Turnaround: 1990s

The 1990s ushered in a serious downturn in Japan's economy. As consumer spending dropped off, consumer-goods companies suffered declines in revenues, and their advertising budgets tightened accordingly. In 1991, Hakuhodo experienced its first decrease in revenue since 1967.

The company's dip in income was soon brightened by good news, however. In early 1992, Nissan Motor Co. moved $76.5 million of its advertising dollars away from Hakuhodo's biggest competitor, Dentsu, and gave it to Hakuhodo. Hakuhodo already had a relationship with Nissan; it had previously been handling approximately 30 percent of the automaker's advertising budget. With Nissan's firing of Dentsu, however, Hakuhodo's share of Nissan's advertising grew to 60 percent. More good news came in 1993, when Hakuhodo again took high honors at the Cannes International Advertising Festival. The company won the Grand Prize for an ad spot created for Nissin Food Products' Cup Noodles.

In 1994, Hakuhodo sold its 49 percent stake in its joint venture, McCann-Erickson Hakuhodo, Ltd., to its U.S. partner McCann-Erickson. McCann-Erickson Hakuhodo had grown to become the sixth largest ad agency in Japan since its establishment in 1960. But as the company grew, it found itself more and more often competing directly against Hakuhodo for clients, leading the partners to dissolve the alliance.

The year 1994 also saw a change in leadership at Hakuhodo. The company's president, Ritsuo Isobe, stepped down from his post, and was succeeded by Takashi Shoji. Shoji's appointment was unusual in that it marked the first time since 1975 that Hakuhodo had been led by an advertising professional. The previous two presidents had been retired public servants from the Ministry of Finance.

In early 1995, Hakuhodo's downturn reversed. The company announced that 1994 sales had increased by 3 percent over the previous year, the first such increase in four years. The increases continued through the year; in the spring of 1996, Hakuhodo posted a 10.3 percent growth in billings for fiscal 1995.

With the turnaround in revenues, Hakuhodo began to again focus on growth. During the latter part of the decade, the company kept busy forging new relationships, opening new offices, and pursuing new avenues of opportunity. Among other initiatives, it allied with a number of other ad agencies to establish Digital Advertising Consortium, an Internet advertising venture; teamed up with Toyota Tsusho Co. and e-Parcel, LLC to sell digital content over the Internet; and established Percept-Hakuhodo, a 50–50 joint venture with an Indian advertising agency. The company also opened its third office in China, and began implementing plans to further its Asian presence through affiliates in the Philippines, Indonesia, India, and South Korea.

In early 2000, the company also strengthened ties to major client Nissan Motors when Nissan decided it wanted to consolidate all its global advertising with a single agency. To win the account, Hakuhodo teamed up with the American agency TBWA Worldwide, forming H & T Worldwide, a partnership exclusively dedicated to Nissan, with branches in Japan, the United States, and Europe. Together the two agencies became responsible for Nissan's $1 billion advertising account.

Hakuhodo's goals for the future focused heavily on overseas expansion, particularly in Asia. Priorities after Asia included the United Kingdom, followed by continental Europe. To fuel expansion, the company was planning a public offering for 2003.

Principal Subsidiaries

Hakuhodo Australia; Shanghai Hakuhodo Advertising; Morioka Hakuhodo; Aomori Hakuhodo; Fukushima Hakuhodo; Hakuhodo Hong Kong; Hakuhodo Creative Vox; Hakuhodo Tokyo; AD-DAM; Incentive Promotions, Inc.; HANA; Hakuhodo in Progress; Hakuhodo Creative & Development; Hakuhodo Lintas Co.; Hakuhodo i-studio; Hakuhodo Erg; Hakuhodo Malaysia; Adformatix; Hakuhodo Singapore; Hakuhodo Cheil (Korea); HY Marketing (China); Hakuhodo Bangkok Co.; Hakuhodo Advertising America (U.S.A.); Hakuhodo Percept (India); Hakuhodo Deutschland; Hakuhodo France; Group Nexus/H (U.K.); Hakuhodo UK; Hakuhodo Netherlands; Thai Hakuhodo.

Principal Competitors

Asatsu-DK, Inc.; Dentsu Inc.; WPP Group plc.

Further Reading

Garrett, Jade, "CAM's Advertising Giants: Takashi Shoji," *Campaign*, February 18, 2000, p. 36.
Guide to Hakuhodo (company publication in Japanese), Tokyo: Hakuhodo, Inc., 1986.
Hakuhodo's History, Tokyo: Hakuhodo, Inc., 1992.
Russell, Jack, "Agency Has Grown to Become Among the World's Largest," *Advertising Age*, June 19, 1995, p. H3.

—Dylan Tanner
—update: Shawna Brynildssen

Holt's Cigar Holdings, Inc.

12270 Townsend Road
Philadelphia, Pennsylvania 19154
U.S.A.
Telephone: (215) 676-8778
Toll Free: (800) 523-1641; (877) 464-6587
Fax: (215) 676-0438
Web site: http://www.holts.com

Private Company
Founded: 1911 as Holt's Cigar Co.
Employees: 70
Sales: $32.92 million (2000)
NAIC: 42294 Tobacco & Tobacco Product Wholesalers;
   453991 Tobacco Stores; 551112 Offices of Other
   Holding Companies

Holt's Cigar Holdings, Inc. is a holding company that, through its operating subsidiaries, is a leading wholesaler and retailer of brand-name premium cigars and smokers' accessories. Holt's owns the Ashton brand of premium cigars and is its exclusive wholesale distributor. The company maintains three retail stores and its distribution center in Philadelphia, from where it sends out a mail-order catalog twice a year. The company handles over 170 brands of premium cigars.

Philadelphia Institution: 1911–97

Holt's Cigar Co. was founded in 1911 and operated a small store across from Philadelphia's City Hall, selling cheap "seconds" or "closeouts" to bargain hunters. In 1957 Albert Levin, a Philadelphia manufacturer of women's blouses who had closed this operation, purchased Holt's Cigar Co. for about $40,000. The company's annual revenues came to between $100,000 and $200,000 at the time. A mail-order division was added by the early 1960s for select retail customers. Albert's son Robert began working in the store while still in grade school, sweeping floors, packing shipments, and taking inventory. He joined the company full-time in the early 1970s. Although he planned to stay only briefly, he found he enjoyed the

business and succeeded his father as chairman, president, and chief executive officer in the late 1970s.

The focus of the business changed in 1980, when Levin purchased H.A. Tint & Sons. Founded in 1898, Tint & Sons was Philadelphia's store for quality cigars—especially Cuban cigars before the embargo—but its business had declined to about $250,000 in annual revenue, and it had lost its lease. The Tint purchase, for between $50,000 and $100,000, marked Holt's Cigar's entry into the premium cigar market. Premium cigars are defined by the company as generally imported, hand-made or hand-rolled, with long filler and all-natural tobacco leaf, selling for more than $1 each retail. In the mid-1980s Holt's sales volume passed $1 million a year. Most of the revenue was in cigars, but the company also sold pipes and had started to sell pens as well.

One area of the Holt's business not proving lucrative was importing/distributing. When the company bought Tint, it was importing Consolidated Cigar Co. products from the Canary Islands. At this point Consolidated moved the operation to the Dominican Republic. When it experienced major quality problems, Consolidated designated Holt's and about 15 other retailers to be its U.S. distributors. Competition between these retailers became so intense that Levin dropped out. However, the experience convinced him that he could market his own proprietary brand. A friend who was the importer and distributor of Ashton Pipes, an English manufacturer, suggested that he use the Ashton name for the product, thereby building up brand recognition for the pipes as well. Holt's introduced Ashton in 1985 and later purchased the name from the pipe manufacturer. This top-of-the-line cigar was originally made by a firm named Tabadom, with production reaching 300,000 a year by 1988, when Levin turned to a cigar manufacturer in the Dominican Republic named Carlos Fuente, Jr., for the filler and binder, with a Connecticut shade wrapper added to the product. The company subsequently added its own Holt's brand of premium cigars, sold—unlike Ashton—exclusively through its retail stores and catalogs.

Holt's Cigar's sales of its proprietary brands were slow at first but increased with the cigar boom of the 1990s, which in some ways paralleled the growing penchant of affluent Americans for gourmet coffee, fine wines, single-malt scotch, and microbrewed beers. By quantity, U.S. cigar consumption peaked in 1973, but cigar smoking increased measurably in the early 1990s, and premium cigars led the way. The number of premium hand-rolled cigars sold in the United States rose from about 100 million in 1992 to about 280 million in 1996. Holt's own cigar sales reached about 2.8 million in the latter year. The company's revenues increased from $3.04 million in fiscal 1993 (the year ended March 31, 1993) to $5.67 million in 1995 and $9.47 million in 1996.

In May 1995 Holt's moved its downtown retail store to Walnut Street, spending $800,000 to renovate the building. This store was an instant hit, soon selling over 2,000 cigars a day at prices between 30 cents and $30. It included a 1,200-square-foot walk-in humidor, a smoking lounge, and display space for cigar accessories, some of them valued at $6,000 or more. A climate-controlled room with 56 storage lockers for cigars was fully leased, at $400 a year each. "The new store is beyond my wildest expectations and dreams," Levin told Marvin R. Shanken of *Cigar Aficionado* in 1996. He added that the smoking lounge had been "mobbed ever since we opened the store up. From lunch time on until we close, there are people in there."

The 8,000-square-foot distribution center in northeast Philadelphia was also the site of Holt's executive offices and its mail-order operation, which was sending out 70,000 catalogs three times a year. The company also maintained a small retail space and cigar club at the First Union Center, home of professional basketball's Philadelphia 76ers and hockey's Philadelphia Flyers. It also sponsored cigar dinners in the Philadelphia area. Nearly three million Ashtons were being sold a year by the company and also by 1,000 retail tobacco stores across the United States. The Walnut Street store represented about one-third of Holt's revenues, the catalog operation another third, and the Ashton brand the remaining third.

So sudden and overwhelming was the cigar boom that Levin and other cigar merchants were having trouble finding enough quality product to sell. "You have to use tobacco that's been properly aged," Levin explained to Shanken. "Therefore, there can only be so much increased production every year because you still have to use tobacco from the 1991 and 1992 crops, which was before the boom started." Holt's had a back order of about three million cigars in late 1996 and was hoping to receive 4.5 million cigars in 1997. "I think if I had 10 million cigars now, I could sell 10 million cigars," Levin told Shanken.

In April 1997 Holt's Cigar entered a manufacturing agreement with Fuente Cigar Ltd. The Fuente family agreed to sell Holt's a minimum of five million premium cigars per year for

an initial term of ten years, including the Ashton and Holt's brands and others made by Fuente under its trademarks. By 1997 Fuente Cigar employed more than 1,900 workers in four factories and, during Holt's fiscal year, supplied the company with 47 percent of the premium cigars it purchased. The Fuente Investment Partnership took a 24 percent stake in Holt's, and two members of the Fuente family became directors of Holt's.

Public Company: 1997–2000

After rising by 30 percent in 1995, sales of premium cigars soared 68 percent in 1996. Wall Street had already hearkened to the call of profit, and in November 1997 Holt's Cigar took advantage of the boom in its business by issuing its initial public offering, selling 1.75 million shares—about one-fourth of the total—to the public at $11 each and collecting net proceeds of $17.1 million. Holt's net sales had nearly doubled again in fiscal 1997, to $17.28 million. Of this total, wholesale and mail-order operations accounted for 38 percent each and retail for the remaining 24 percent. Holt's net income increased more than fourfold in fiscal 1997, reaching $2.28 million.

Sales of Ashton accounted for about 45 percent of Holt's Cigar's revenues in fiscal 1998, and it ranked in a survey as one of the top three U.S. best-selling cigar brands. Holt's established its own sales force for Ashton to replace its prior reliance through brokers and subcontractors and introduced an advertising campaign featuring an illustration of a cherub and the slogan, "Good for the soul." The company also became exclusive U.S. distributor for three more brands: the Savoy, from Ecuador, aimed at the price-conscious smoker; the full-flavored Castano, made in Honduras; and the Premium Dominicana, produced by Fuente Cigar. These brands were to be combined with Ashton as "Ashton Brands" in the ad campaign. Holt's also introduced its first cooperative campaign, sharing the cost of Ashton advertisements with retailers who, in return, were allowed to publicize their stores.

Holt's Cigar's revenues increased 70 percent in fiscal 1998—three-quarters of it in calendar 1997—to $29.07 million, while net income doubled to $5.04 million, and the company extinguished its small long-term debt. Some of the money raised from its earlier sale of stock was to be used to establish retail stores in other cities, according to the company's prospectus. But the cigar boom was over by 1998. This was reflected in Holt's fiscal 1999 performance. Net sales barely increased from the previous year, to $30.53 million, and net income fell to $3.64 million. Levin continued to establish new supply relationships, however. In June 1999 the company signed an agreement with Antillian Cigar Corp. to become the exclusive U.S. distributor for Sosa, Sosa Family, and Imperio Cubano premium cigars. The Sosa and Sosa Family brands each came in nine different sizes and shapes, while the Imperio Cubano brand consisted of 15 different sizes and shapes. (The Sosa brands were also being produced at a Fuente factory.) Holt's also entered a five-year agreement with Kapp and Peterson Ltd. to serve as the exclusive distributor in the United States for Peterson of Dublin Pipes, a full line of premium, hand-crafted pipes imported from Ireland.

Holt's Cigar's net sales rose modestly in fiscal 2000, to $32.92 million, but net income decreased slightly, to $3.24

Key Dates:

1911: Holt's Cigar Co. is founded as a small Philadelphia retail store.
1957: Albert Levin purchases the business.
1980: Albert's son Robert, now CEO, purchases H.A. Tint & Sons, a Philadelphia store for quality cigars.
1986: Holt's introduces its first proprietary cigar brand, Ashton.
1995: The company moves its downtown retail store to Walnut Street.
1997: Holt's completes its initial public offering of stock.
2000: With Holt's sales stagnant and its stock price lagging, the company is privatized again.

million, due to major investments in co-op advertising programs and promotion expenses, customer-service staff additions, and the hiring of staff to monitor and maintain the company's e-commerce debut. Ashton Virgin Sungrown (VSG) cigars—dubbed "robust and potent" by the company—were among the cigar market's hottest items. Ashton VSG was said to be the fourth most requested brand in the United States and enabled the Holt's wholesale division to outperform the market substantially, according to Levin.

Shares of Holt's Cigar common stock were trading at about $3 each in November 2000, when the company announced it would go private again. Shareholders other than Levin (who owned about 45 percent of the company) and Fuente Investment Partnership (which owned about 29 percent) received $5.50 a share for their stock, or half what investors paid for the stock when the company went public in 1997. "I think going private is the right thing to do," a financial analyst told Harold Brubaker of the *Philadelphia Inquirer.* "When Holt's came public, cigar companies were hot," he said, adding that the reason for the stock's fall in price was not so much a function of disappointing earnings but a loss of investor interest in the industry. A sufficient number of shares had been tendered for the privatization of the company to be accomplished by the end of the year.

Holt's Cigar in 2000

Premium cigars accounted for 98 percent of Holt's net sales in fiscal 2000. The company was marketing more than 170 brands, ranging in price from $1 to $28 per cigar. Foremost of these was the Ashton brand, composed of 30 different sizes and shapes, with retail prices between $4.50 and $17 each. Targeted at the upper end of the premium-cigar market, Ashtons were normally aged after the manufacturing process from three months to one year in specially constructed climate-controlled

aging rooms. The Holt's brand consisted of 18 different sizes and shapes, with retail prices generally between $2.75 and $4.50. These cigars were at the middle of the premium-cigar market. The Sosa brand was selling at retail prices generally between $3.50 and $6.75 per cigar; the Sosa Family brand for between $3 and $7; and the Imperio Cubano brand generally between $4 and $9. Holt's also was selling a broad range of cigar accessories, such as humidors, cigar cutters, cigar cases, lighters, and ashtrays. In addition, the company offered a limited selection of other tobacco products, including mass-market cigars, smokeless tobacco, pipes, pipe tobacco, and pipe accessories. A limited number of imported cigarettes were sold only through the retail stores.

Wholesale operations accounted for 53 percent of Holt's Cigar's net sales in fiscal 2000. The company's distribution center in northeastern Philadelphia had grown to 21,360 square feet by this time, including a humidified and climate-controlled cigar-storage warehouse of about 5,000 square feet. It was also the site of mail-order operations. Holt's Cigar's glossy four-color catalogs were being distributed in production runs of about 100,000 each. In addition, the company was producing other mailings sent to prospective customers several times a year. Its interactive e-commerce site was introduced in February 2000.

Holt's Cigar was maintaining long-term relationships with more than 50 suppliers. Fuente Cigar supplied about 58 percent of all premium cigars purchased, on a dollar basis, by Holt's during fiscal 2000. General Cigar Co. supplied another 7 percent in the form of Castanos produced by Villazon & Co., Inc.

Principal Subsidiaries

Ashton Distributors, Inc.; Ashton Pipe Company, Inc.; Holt's Cigar Company, Inc.; Holt's Mail Order, Inc.

Principal Competitors

Altadis; General Cigar Co.; JR Cigar Inc.

Further Reading

Brubaker, Harold, "Burnout of Cigar Boom Sends Holt's Private Again," *Philadelphia Inquirer,* November 11, 2000, pp. D1, D6.
"Holt's Cigar Holdings Agrees to Be Acquired by HCH Associates," *Wall Street Journal,* November 13, 2000, p. B19A.
Kasrel, Deni, "As Trend Slows, Holt's Stokes Its Cigar Brands," *Philadelphia Business Journal,* September 4, 1998, p. 6.
McCalla, John, "Holt's Cigar Lights Up Post-Trend Growth Plans," *Philadelphia Business Journal,* August 18, 2000, p. 7.
Shanken, Marvin R., "An Interview with Robert Levin," *Cigar Aficionado,* Winter 1996.
"This Merchant's Sales Are Up—and Smokin'," *Philadelphia Inquirer,* February 24, 1997, pp. C1, C3.

—Robert Halasz

Home Properties of New York, Inc.

850 Clinton Square
Rochester, New York 14604
U.S.A.
Telephone: (716) 546-4900
Toll Free: (866) 808-2787
Fax: (716) 546-5433
Web site: http://www.homeproperties.com

Public Company
Incorporated: 1967 as Home Leasing Corp.
Employees: 2,100
Sales: $319.05 million (2000)
Stock Exchanges: New York
Ticker Symbol: HME
NAIC: 52593 Real Estate Investment Trusts; 531311
    Residential Property Managers; 531312 Nonresidential
    Property Managers

Home Properties of New York, Inc. is a real estate investment trust (REIT) that owns, manages, acquires, rehabilitates, and develops apartment complexes (which the company describes as "communities") in the northeastern, mid-Atlantic, and midwestern United States. Through a limited partnership and two management companies, it owns and operates many apartment complexes and also manages complexes and units for other owners. Home Properties also fee-manages office and retail properties. Home Properties targets older renters who are less likely to move for its apartments and, in so doing, enjoys a turnover rate far below the average for the industry.

Privately Owned Developer and Manager: 1967–93

Twin brothers Nelson and Norman Leenhouts developed an early work ethic after their father died, serving as teenage soda jerks in the ice cream bar of their mother's dairy. Interviewed by Frank Bilovksy for the *Rochester Democrat and Chronicle* in 1998, Nelson recalled, "My mom would tell us when someone came in and asked how you were doing or how was your day, always come back with a smile and try to do something to uplift

that customer." After graduating from the University of Rochester, they founded a company named Home Leasing Corp. They began by purchasing houses to rent out and later switched to apartments. Even during recessions, Home Leasing increased its income from apartments each year. The company developed the Piano Works Mall in East Rochester, the White Spruce office complex in Brighton, and the Blue Heron Hills community in Gananda. It also secured a number of management contracts. By 1994 half of the 12-person management team were family members, consisting of Norman's two daughters and the husband of one of the daughters, plus the husband of Nelson's daughter, as well as the Leenhoutses themselves.

When the Leenhouts brothers decided to become the first real estate investment trust in upstate New York, they decided to specialize in apartments. Such trusts, usually publicly traded, are exempt from federal corporate taxes if 75 percent of their income comes from real property and 95 percent of the taxable income is distributed to shareholders. They also can use operating partnership units instead of cash to make acquisitions, and these units can be converted to stock after a year without payment of capital gains tax until sold. Home Properties of New York was established in 1993 as a corporation conducting its business through Home Properties of New York, L.P., a limited partnership in which the company held a 90 percent partnership interest at the time. The company completed its initial public offering of 5.4 million shares in 1994 at $19 a share, netting $95.56 million.

Predecessor Home Leasing had revenues of $21.42 million and net income of $1.8 million in 1993. Its holdings at that time included 11 apartment complexes and a mobile home park in the Rochester area, six commercial properties in Rochester, including the Clinton Square office building downtown, the Piano Works Mall in East Rochester, and an apartment complex and shopping center in Columbus, Ohio. Its portfolio was valued at about $140 million. The new company acquired four upstate New York apartment complexes in Baldwinsville, Buffalo, Greece, and Penfield. These acquisitions maintained Home Leasing's focus on renting to middle-income persons 55 or older.

The real estate investment trust did not include Home Leasing's commercial properties or several multifamily residential properties that it was running under management contracts. These came under a subsidiary.

Expanding West and South: 1994–99

Home Properties' revenues rose modestly in 1994, a little faster in 1995, and significantly higher in 1996, when they reached $45.7 million. Its pace of acquisitions, financed by money from the stock offering and a $45 million credit line, was also modest at first, with about $23 million spent in 1994 for three complexes, about $21 million in 1995 for three more, and about $52 million in 1996. Effective on the first day of 1996, the company acquired Rochester-based Conifer Realty, Inc. and Conifer Development, Inc. for $13.4 million. The transaction gave Home Properties two more apartment complexes, with 260 units. It also gave the firm management contracts for 4,867 Conifer apartment units and a general partner interest in 3,777 units. The acquisitions increased Home Properties' business to ownership or management of 10,957 apartment units and 1.8 million square feet of commercial space.

In 1997 Home Properties spent $266 million to purchase 7,496 apartments in four states—New Jersey, Pennsylvania, Indiana, and Michigan—by means of 11 acquisitions. Revenues rose to $69.7 million that year. A secondary stock offering of one million shares was sold to BancAmerica Robertson Stephens for $25.8 million. Home Properties' acquisitions in 1997 included a $63 million purchase in the Philadelphia area and a $105 million acquisition of 3,108 apartment units in the Detroit metropolitan area. To hold down debt, the company sought to pay for its acquisitions in partnership units rather than cash or stock. Sellers, too, could benefit in tax-deferral strategies, and the units were redeemable in cash or stock at the option of the company.

Home Properties was seeking apartment complexes with affordable units in urban areas of the Northeast where new construction was unlikely and there were few other REITs to offer competition. The goal was to achieve operating income yield of 10 percent by purchasing and upgrading complexes at about 60 percent of new construction. Typically, the company was focusing on purchasing middle-income, brick-construction apartment complexes in relatively tight markets that needed some repair but were not badly deteriorated. Norman Leenhouts was in charge of acquisitions at this time, while Nelson was directing management. "We like to keep the predominant number of our acquisitions in major metropolitan areas," Norman told Bilovsky. "If you go into an area where there is just one industry and it falls dead, we're in trouble. But let's say a major industry leaves Philadelphia. We think we can manage better

and the slack would end up being taken by the people who don't manage as well."

Home Properties was claiming an annual turnover rate of 40 percent in its complexes, compared to the industry standard of 60 to 70 percent, and an average stay of 30 months, compared to the standard of 18 months. About 40 percent of the people living in the 14,000 units the company owned outright were age 55 or older, a group less likely than younger people to move because of job changes or changes in family size. But Home Properties also was focusing on customer satisfaction to hold tenants. To keep residents happy, it sometimes built a pool and clubhouse, arranged for church services, circulated a newsletter, or started a bridge club. Tenants also were offered the option to buy stock in the company at a discount for as little as $50 a month, through a dividend reinvestment program.

Another tenant-friendly initiative, adopted in 1995, offered to release dissatisfied tenants from their leases during the first 30 days of the contract and to let them break a lease, for reasons beyond their control, on 60 days' notice. In addition, Home Properties guaranteed quick response to maintenance problems and promised to treat its tenants "fairly, honestly and courteously by caring and qualified people." The seven-point pledge, featured in radio, newspaper, and direct-mail advertising, stated that tenants not fully satisfied could receive rent rebates. Writing in the *Rochester Business Journal,* Will Astor called it "a marked departure from the industry norm for tenant guarantees."

Picking up the acquisition pace, Home Properties acquired properties in Indiana, Maryland, New Jersey, Virginia, and Washington, D.C., in the first three months of 1998 alone. By now fully 86 percent of its properties were in states other than New York. Acquisitions made later in the year included three apartment complexes in Baldwin, Pennsylvania, a suburb of Pittsburgh. The neighboring properties, purchased for $20 million, comprised more than 150 buildings with 1,079 units, covering at least 50 acres. Another $11 million was earmarked to upgrade the facilities, utilizing federal tax breaks intended to encourage private investment to keep rents affordable. "The tax credits are a significant motivation," Amy Tait—one of Norman Leenhouts's daughters—told Murray Coleman of the *Pittsburgh Business Times & Journal.* "Without the tax credits, making these improvements probably couldn't be justified without raising rents." Home Properties also promised to build a $600,000 community center with computer access for senior citizens and programs for children to enhance their reading skills.

The action continued hot and heavy in 1999. At midyear, Home Properties bought seven apartment complexes from Community Realty Co. of Gaithersburg, Maryland, for $180.6 million. Two weeks later it spent $157.5 million to purchase a dozen rental complexes in the Baltimore and Wilmington, Delaware, metropolitan areas from Macks & Macks Inc. These transactions made Home Properties the 26th largest apartment owner in the United States, with 43,473 units. Company revenues rose from $149 million in 1998 to $234.46 million in 1999, while net income increased from $18.69 million to $25.13 million.

Home Properties in 2000 and 2001

Home Properties' revenues increased to $319.05 million in 2000, and its net income to $29.28 million. At the end of the

Key Dates:

1967: Twin brothers Norman and Nelson Leenhouts found Home Leasing Corp.
1994: As Home Properties of New York, Inc., the firm becomes a public real estate investment trust (REIT).
1997: Home Properties spends $266 million to acquire properties in four additional states, New Jersey, Pennsylvania, Indiana, and Michigan.
1998: Eighty-six percent of the company's properties are now outside New York.
2000: Home Properties is the nation's 11th largest apartment owner.

year it owned outright 39,041 units in 147 communities and another 8,325 units in 136 communities through its participation in the limited partnership as general partner. It also managed for other owners 3,546 units in 36 complexes. By this time the company had staked out a presence in Chicago, where it owned 2,018 apartments, and in Connecticut and Maine, bringing the extent of its operations to 11 states and the District of Columbia and making it the nation's 11th largest apartment company. The company's long-term debt was $832.8 million at the end of the year.

Home Properties was planning to sell some of its holdings in 2001, having identified about two dozen complexes with over 5,000 units in all for sale at an estimated $200 million. The majority were in the Buffalo, Rochester, and Syracuse areas. Some of these sales, it anticipated, would be matched with suitable acquisitions, using tax-deferred exchanges. Effective on the last day of 2000, the parent company sold its affordable-housing development operations to Conifer, LLC, having concluded that these government-subsidized activities required a disproportionate allocation of financial and management resources. Its property-management activities, by contrast, were seen as providing a pipeline for future acquisitions and positioning the company to build market-rate or affordable complexes when and if market factors warranted doing so.

Home Properties Management, Inc. and Conifer Realty Corp. were created in 1994 and 1995, respectively, as Home Properties of New York management companies. Formed to comply with the technical requirements of federal income tax laws, both were Maryland corporations that, effective in 2001, elected to convert to taxable REIT subsidiaries. Conifer Realty was renamed Home Properties Resident Services, Inc. Both managed, for a fee, certain of the residential, commercial, and development activities of the parent company and provided construction, development, and redevelopment services for the company. In 1997 Home Properties Trust was formed as a Maryland real estate trust and REIT subsidiary. It became a limited partner of the operating partnership, Home Properties of New York, L.P., which at the end of 2000 was 62.5 percent owned by Home Properties of New York, Inc.

Norman and Nelson Leenhouts were co-chief executive officers of the corporation, with Norman chairman of the board and Nelson president. Each owned about 2 percent of the stock in early 2001. All 18 executives and directors owned in total about 14 percent. In February 2001 Rochester banker Edward Pettinella was hired as executive vice-president and likely successor to the brothers, succeeding Amy Tait, who resigned to spend more time with her children and husband as well as to open her own real estate consulting business. (Her husband, Robert Tait, remained the firm's vice-president of commercial property management.)

Principal Subsidiaries

Home Properties Management, Inc.; Home Properties of New York, L.P; Home Properties Resident Services, Inc.; Home Properties Trust.

Principal Competitors

Associated Estates Realty Co.; Duke-Weeks Realty Corp.; Glimcher Realty Trust; HRPT Properties Trust; Kranzoo Realty Trust.

Further Reading

Astor, Will, "Home Properties Gets Wall Street's Attention," *Rochester Business Journal,* October 10, 1997, p. 1.
——, "Home Properties Plans Guarantees for Tenants," *Rochester Business Journal,* March 31, 1995, p. 1.
——, "Mutual-Fund Manager Sees Potential in REIT," *Rochester Business Journal,* June 24, 1994, p. 1.
——, "REIT Analysts Welcome Home Properties Move," *Rochester Business Journal,* September 29, 1995, p. 4.
——, "REIT Intends to Rev Up Rate of Expansion," *Rochester Business Journal,* May 8, 1998, p. 1.
Bilovsky, Frank, "Location Location Location," *Rochester Democrat and Chronicle,* March 9, 1998, pp. 1F, 9F.
Coleman, Murray, "Local Apartment Acquisition Utilizes Tax Credits to Pursue Renovations," *Pittsburgh Business Times & Journal,* August 21, 1998, p. 26.
Haaland, Lynette, "Home Properties Hires Heir Apparent," *Rochester Business Journal,* February 2, 2001, p. 1.
Halls, Bill, "New York Firm Buys 3,108 Metro Detroit Apartments," *Detroit News,* October 31, 1997, p. 3B.
McQuaid, Kevin L., "N.Y. REIT Buys 12 Rental Complexes from Area Developer," *Baltimore Sun,* July 17, 1999, p. 9C.

—Robert Halasz

Huntingdon Life Sciences Group plc

Wooley Road, Alconbury
Huntingdon, Cambridgeshire PE17 5HS
United Kingdom
Telephone: +44-1480-892-000
Fax: +44-1480-892-205
Web site: http://www.huntingdon.com

Public Company
Incorporated: 1951 as Nutrition Research Co. Ltd.
Employees: 1,303
Sales: $94.5 million (2000)
Stock Exchanges: London
Ticker Symbol: HTD
NAIC: 541380 Testing Laboratories

Based in the United Kingdom, Huntingdon Life Sciences Group plc is a contract research organization (CRO) involved in safety evaluation of products for the pharmaceutical and biopharmaceutical, agricultural, and industrial chemical industries. After conducting business for 45 years in relative obscurity, Huntingdon has since become the focus of animal rights activists concerned about the company's treatment of its laboratory animals. While facilities have been picketed in both the United States and Britain, activists in the latter have vowed to drive Huntingdon out of business and have resorted to intimidation tactics and, in some cases, violence. Shareholders, brokers, and banks have all been scared away from Huntingdon, driving down the price of the company's stock so low that it was delisted from the New York Stock Exchange. A backlash against the activists in 2001, however, has led the British government, the pharmaceutical industry, and the banks to rally behind the beleaguered company.

Formation of Huntingdon in 1951

Huntingdon was originally incorporated in the United Kingdom in 1951 as Nutrition Research Co. Ltd., a CRO that initially focused on nutrition, veterinary, and biochemical research. It then became involved with pharmaceuticals, food additives, and industrial and consumer chemicals. In 1959 it changed its name

to Nutritional Research Unit Ltd. The company benefited in the early 1960s from increased government testing requirements, especially in the pharmaceutical industry. In 1964 it was acquired by the U.S. medical supply firm of Becton Dickinson.

Becton Dickinson, originally founded in 1897, was one of the first U.S. companies to manufacture hypodermic needles. Over the years, it developed disposable syringes and manufactured other medical products, such as stethoscopes and the Vacutainer used in laboratories to collect blood. In 1963 Becton Dickinson made a public stock offering to raise capital for expansion. In addition to its purchase of Nutritional Research Unit, it bought up dozens of medical supply, testing, and lab companies over the next several years, as well as delving into businesses unrelated to medicine. Nutritional Research Unit would operate as a subsidiary of its American corporate parent for the next 20 years, at which point Becton Dickinson decided to change course. After fending off a takeover bid by Sun Company in 1978, management began to shed non-essential businesses. Because Becton Dickinson was looking to manufacture medical products that would compete with customers of Nutritional Research Unit, it decided to sell off the testing business.

In April 1983 Becton Dickinson created Huntingdon Research Centre PLC. It then offered four million American depositary receipts (ADRs) for sale at $15 each, representing the company's entire interest in Huntingdon. In 1985, as it began to expand its operations, the company changed its name to Huntingdon International Holdings plc. In that year it established Huntingdon Analytical Services Inc. to do business in the United States, gaining a toehold in upstate New York after being courted by the New York Department of Economic Development, which helped Huntingdon comply with U.S. regulations. Even though Huntingdon ADRs were traded on the NASDAQ, securing a U.S. presence helped the company gain the attention of U.S. investors, which in turn was instrumental in the company achieving a U.K. quotation in 1988.

To augment its CRO business, Huntingdon acquired Minnesota's Twin City Testing Laboratory Inc. and affiliated companies in 1985, followed by the acquisition of Nebraska Testing Corporation in 1986; Travis Laboratories and Kansas City Test Laboratory Inc. in 1989; and Southwestern Laboratories, Inc. in

Company Perspectives:

Huntingdon Life Sciences is one of the world's foremost product development companies. We work with a wide variety of products, including Pharmaceuticals, Industrial Chemicals, Veterinary Products, Foods & Flavourings, to help their manufacturers develop safer products for the market.

1990. Huntingdon also decided to diversify its operations, primarily in the United States, by becoming involved in engineering and environmental services. In 1987 it purchased Northern Engineering and Testing, Inc., and then in 1988 bought Empire Soils Investigations Inc., Chen Associates Inc., and Asteco Inc. In 1990 Huntingdon acquired the St. Louis branch of Envirodyne Engineers Inc. and Whiteley Holdings Ltd. In 1991 it acquired Austin Research Engineers, Inc., followed by Travers Morgan Ltd., Huntingdon's most expensive deal.

By the early 1990s Huntingdon was organized into three business groups: the Life Sciences Group, the Engineering/Environmental Group, and the Travers Morgan Group, which offered engineering and environmental consulting services outside of the United States. The mix of business, however, did not prove successful, in large part because of a downturn in the U.S. economy and a retreat from strict enforcement of environmental regulations. Only the Life Sciences Group showed long-term promise. Travers Morgan was a drain from the outset. By 1995 it was allowed to lapse into insolvency, control passed into other hands, and Huntingdon wrote off the investment. In 1995 the engineering and environmental businesses, which had lost $3 million in the previous fiscal year, were sold to Maxim Engineers Inc. of Dallas, Texas, for $14 million and the assumption of $6.7 million in debt.

Focus on Life Sciences: Mid-1990s

To bolster its CRO business and reinforce its U.S. presence, Huntingdon in 1995 acquired the toxicology business of Applied Biosciences International for $32.5 million in cash, plus Huntingdon's Leicester Clinical Research Centre. The deal not only included a U.S. laboratory located near Princeton, New Jersey, it brought with it two British facilities as well. In 1997 Huntingdon International Holdings changed its name to Huntingdon Life Sciences Group. The U.K. subsidiary, Huntingdon Research Centre, changed its name to Huntingdon Life Sciences Ltd., while the U.S. business operated as Huntingdon Life Sciences Inc.

After almost 15 years since Becton Dickinson floated the company, Huntingdon appeared to have finally found its feet. It was now committed to the CRO business, in which it had become one of the leading companies in the world, boasting scores of major customers, and benefiting from a presence on both sides of the Atlantic. The company appeared poised for a bright future when it found itself caught up in controversy and the target of animal rights groups in both the United States and Britain.

In the United States, the Huntingdon laboratory in New Jersey was infiltrated by an investigator of the People for the Ethical Treatment of Animals. PETA, formed in 1980, relied on undercover work to produce what they considered evidence of animal abuse, which in turn sparked protests that resulted in government investigations, as well as attracting new recruits to the organization. PETA estimated that its membership exceeded 600,000. One of its undercover agents was Michele Rokke, a former Minnesota hairdresser.

In September 1996 Rokke was hired as a lab technician at Huntingdon's New Jersey lab. Wearing glasses with a pinpoint video camera in the bridge, she taped some 50 hours of laboratory activities during the eight months she was employed. In addition, she made some six hours of audiotapes and photocopied 8,000 pages of documents, including a client list. Huntingdon, at the time, was using dogs to test an antibacterial agent that Colgate-Palmolive wanted to add to toothpaste. Using Rokke's material as support, PETA accused Huntingdon of mistreating the dogs. Moreover, PETA revealed that beagles were to have their legs broken in order to test a new drug, intended to combat osteoporosis, for a Japanese company, Yamanouchi Pharmaceuticals. PETA also accused Huntingdon technicians of not properly anesthetizing monkeys before removing organs in a Procter & Gamble study. PETA urged consumers to boycott Colgate-Palmolive and pressured Procter & Gamble to sever its ties with Huntingdon. The group garnered a great deal of publicity when actress Kim Basinger showed up at the lab in an orchestrated attempt to adopt some 40 beagles. Although she was turned away, Yamanouchi soon canceled its contract and the dogs were eventually put up for adoption.

Huntingdon believed that its laboratory methods complied with the standards laid out in the Animal Welfare Act, and that PETA employed tactics worthy of extortionists. The company filed a civil lawsuit against PETA under the Racketeering Influenced Corrupt Organization Act, better known as RICO, which was generally reserved for criminal organizations. Huntingdon contended that PETA had engaged in a practice of making baseless charges that ruined scientific careers and devastated legitimate businesses. In December 1997 the two parties settled the suit out of court, and both claimed victory. The charges were dropped and PETA did not have to pay damages, but it did agree to return documents, videotapes, and audiotapes, as well as not to further interfere with Huntingdon's customer relationships or investigate the company for five years. Several months later, as a result of the PETA investigation, Huntingdon was fined $50,000 by the Department of Agriculture for violating laws regulating the care and treatment of laboratory animals, although most of the violations related to record keeping and the failure to maintain a proper committee to oversee the laboratory's use of animals.

1997 Documentary a Threat to Huntingdon's Existence

Around the same time that Rokke was working at the New Jersey facility, the U.K. operation also was infiltrated. England had a long history of opposing animal experimentation and championing animal rights in general. It was British activists in 1980 who were instrumental in the movement to oppose the use of animal furs in apparel. Huntingdon also had been the frequent site of protesters since the 1970s and already had been infiltrated in 1989 when an investigator for the British Union for the Abolition of Vivisection (BUAV) documented and photographed laboratory practices. Then, in March 1997, undercover videotape

---

Key Dates:

1951: Company is established as Nutrition Research Co. Ltd.
1959: Company's name is changed to Nutritional Research Unit Ltd.
1964: Company is acquired by Becton Dickinson.
1983: Company is renamed Huntingdon Research Centre plc and is floated as a separate company.
1985: Company's name is changed to Huntingdon International Holdings plc and business is expanded to include engineering and environmental consulting services.
1995: Huntingdon sells off engineering and environmental businesses.
1997: Company changes its name to Huntingdon Life Sciences Group plc; major protests by animal rights groups begin.

---

would be broadcast on Britain's Channel 4, in its "Countryside Undercover" series. Scenes of workers mistreating animals caused a public uproar and led to the company firing a worker who had been filmed punching a dog. Huntingdon, contending that the incident was an aberration, did not apologize, a failure that resulted in even more bad publicity. Although the government imposed a number of conditions on Huntingdon, the company was soon permitted to resume its business. Animal rights activists, led by a group called the Coalition to Ruin Huntingdon Life Sciences, regularly picketed the company. Customers abandoned the company, and its finances soured as did the price of its stock. Huntingdon was on the brink of receivership in August 1998 when a major loan was due. The company, however, received an infusion of cash from American investors headed by Andrew Baker, who had experience running Corning's clinical laboratory business. The new group gained a 43.4 percent stake in Huntingdon and installed a fresh management team. The company appeared to have weathered the storm and over the next year began to make strides at resurrecting its business when it was targeted by a new group of animal rights supporters, SHAC (Stop Huntingdon Animal Cruelty), who vowed to drive Huntingdon out of business within three years.

In January 2000 SHAC began its campaign, initially focusing on major Huntingdon shareholders, such as investment firm Phillips & Drew. Demonstrations were conducted outside the homes of the firm's directors, a hoax bomb threat was called into the office, and within a month Phillips & Drew dumped its Huntingdon shares. Huntingdon's bank, Natwest, then experienced a spate of vandalism, as ATM machines were disabled by cards dipped in glue. Following months of staff intimidation, the Royal Bank of Scotland, which acquired NatWest, eventually cut off Huntingdon's overdraft facility, which allowed the company to borrow sufficient operational funds. Directors of Huntingdon's corporate broker, WestLB Panmure, also were targeted. After a number of late-night phone calls, demonstrations, and death threats, WestLB dropped Huntingdon as a client. Individual investors, including a 70-year-old pensioner, also were targeted by demonstrators who picketed random shareholders' homes for 24 straight hours.

Meanwhile, activities directed at Huntingdon facilities were conducted on a daily basis, with protesters reportedly spitting on workers' cars and shouting, "We know where your children go to school." SHAC then published the names and addresses of Huntingdon employees—clerks and secretaries in addition to lab technicians. One night in August 2000 several Huntingdon employees had their cars firebombed. Over the subsequent months, more cars would be torched, a senior manager would have a chemical agent splashed into his eyes as he was about to enter his home, and Huntingdon's chief operating officer was beaten by masked men wielding ax handles. Police also linked a series of mail bombs containing nails to animal activists. SHAC disavowed these acts of violence, attributing them to frustrated fringe elements.

In January 2001 Citibank severed ties with Huntingdon. Under pressure from the Royal Bank of Scotland to repay a $33 million loan, the company was again on the brink of collapse. Only a last-minute deal with a backer, whose name was to remain secret, kept the company in business. Within a week, however, the backer was identified as the Stephens Group of Little Rock, Arkansas, an investment bank headed by Warren Stephens. SHAC then drew on American counterparts to provide pressure on Stephens, which was now Huntingdon's largest shareholder, with a 15 percent stake. In addition to demonstrations outside of Huntingdon's New Jersey lab, protesters picketed the Augusta National Golf Club where Mr. Stephens was a member, as well as disrupted a Las Vegas junket for clients of his firm. In England, Winterflood Securities, one of Huntingdon's marketmakers (or brokers), succumbed to SHAC and dropped Huntingdon after the police denied its request for staff protection. Dresdner Kleinwort Wasserstein also withdrew, citing its policy not to serve as sole broker. Moreover, TD Waterhouse and Charles Schwab Europe ceased trading Huntingdon stock, citing concern for the safety of staff.

The tactics of SHAC and other activists began to produce a backlash. The British government passed legislation to prevent the violent intimidation of staff at research laboratories, as well as providing funds for the local police in dealing with the protests. In May 2001 several leading pharmaceutical companies, no doubt fearing that they might be future targets, threatened to boycott banks and other financial institutions if they failed to stand up to animal activists. After the government and police assured banks of protection, the British Bankers' Association announced "a renewed determination to maintain a service to customers regardless of intimidation." Despite receiving support after months of virtual isolation, Huntingdon continued to face a coalition of groups who were determined to drive the company out of business. Whether it would manage to survive, let alone rebuild its business, remained open to question.

Principal Subsidiaries

Huntingdon Life Sciences Limited; Huntingdon Life Sciences Inc.; HIH Capital Ltd.

Principal Competitors

Covance Inc.; Inveresk Research; Quintiles Transnational Corporation.

Further Reading

Carlson, Peter, ''Spy in the Henhouse,'' *Washington Post,* January 3, 1998, p. C1.

Cullen, Kevin, ''British Animal-Rights Group Targets Drug-Test Laboratory,'' *Boston Globe,* January 28, 2001, p. A8.

Kolata, Gina, ''Tough Tactics in One Battle Over Animals in the Lab,'' *New York Times,* March 24, 1998, p. E1.

Moukheiber, Zina, ''Of Mice and Mischief,'' *Forbes,* April 2, 2001, p. 56.

Naik, Gautam, ''Tooth and Nail: A U.K. Lab Company Is Besieged by Protests Against Animal Testing,'' *Wall Street Journal,* April 27, 2001, p. A1.

Underhill, William, ''War on Science,'' *Newsweek,* May 7, 2001, p. 60.

—Ed Dinger

IEC Electronics Corp.

105 Norton Street
P.O. Box 271
Newark, New York 14513
U.S.A.
Telephone: (315) 331-7742
Fax: (315) 331-3547
Web site: http://www.iec-electronics.com

Public Company
Incorporated: 1966 as Intercontinental Electronics Corp.
Employees: 1,509
Sales: $204.16 million (2000)
Stock Exchanges: NASDAQ
Ticker Symbol: IEC
NAIC: 334412 Bare Printed Circuit Board Manufacturing

IEC Electronics Corp. is a contract electronics manufacturer of complex printed circuit-board assemblies and electronic products and systems. Its wide spectrum of services includes product design, material procurement and control, manufacturing and test engineering support, statistical quality assurance, complete resource management, final packaging, and distribution. IEC's customer list of original equipment manufacturers is international and includes *Fortune* 500 companies.

Concentrating on Printed Circuit Boards: 1966–93

The company was founded in 1966 as Intercontinental Electronics Corp. by Roger E. Main and two other executives of General Dynamics Corporation's electronics division. Originally located in Fairport, a suburb of Rochester, New York, it moved to East Rochester in 1970 and the rural community of Newark, about equidistant from Rochester and Syracuse, three years later. It became a public company as IEC Electronics in 1967 and was making handheld radios on contract in fiscal 1972 (the year ended September 30, 1972), when it earned net income of $165,160 on sales of $1.9 million.

IEC revenues reached $3.3 million in fiscal 1974, but the following year its sales dropped by one-third and it incurred a loss. Accordingly, the company entered the consumer products field, chiefly by the manufacture of TV games. It enjoyed a profitable fiscal 1976 on sales of $4.06 million but lost money the following two years in spite of annual revenues that reached close to $5 million. IEC's largest contract customers in the late 1970s were Coleco Industries, IBM, and Xerox. Its consumer line consisted of radio communications products, especially VHF and UHF portable radio transceivers and mobile handheld adapter systems, VHF and UHF paging receivers, and a base-station encoding control system. In 1980 IEC sold its consumer-products operations to Sab Harmon Industries Inc. for an estimated $1.3 million in cash, plus royalty payments on future sales of the acquired products.

IEC Electronics lost money in fiscal 1980 and 1981 but became profitable again the next year, when it doubled its sales. By fiscal 1985 it had again doubled its revenues, and its net income passed $1 million for the first time, on net sales of $14.42 million. At this time IEC was producing electronic assemblies for a range of products, such as computers and computer peripherals, office copies and high-speed duplicators, industrial photography and video imaging systems, communications systems, and medical electronics. These customers included Control Data, Digital Equipment, Eastman Kodak, and Polaroid, as well as IBM and Xerox. The company faced severe competition from low-balling Asian firms, but IEC contended that its own costs were actually lower because of a superior level of quality control.

In order to limit its expenses, IEC was concentrating its efforts on labor-only sales where the material was supplied by the customer. However, in a 1986 talk to security analysts, Main, who was president and chief executive of IEC, indicated the company now was in a position to seek contracts whereby it purchased materials as well. Specifically, Main saw a growing opportunity in surface mount technology (SMT), a relatively new process of making electronic circuit boards with devices mounted directly on the printed circuit rather than the older method of inserting wire leads into holes drilled in a printed board. IEC eventually would become one of the largest independent SMT contract manufacturers in the United States.

IEC Electronics was purchased by four of its own executives and the New York City investment firm of DeMuth, Folger & Terhune in 1988 for $30.4 million. IEC officers and employees retained 20 percent of the shares, with the investment firm

Company Perspectives:

IEC's customer focus is on emerging and established high-technology manufacturers of telecommunication and industrial and instrumentation equipment. IEC's customer list is international, and includes Fortune *500 companies. An important element of IEC's strategy is the establishment of partnerships with major and emerging leaders in the electronics industry. The company's goal is to provide its customers with total manufacturing solutions for both new and present products, and to meet customer needs as they evolve.*

holding the rest. In 1989, some 400 different products were in production or on order at the Newark factory for the company's 125 customers. Sales reached $55.06 million in fiscal 1990. In 1992 IEC purchased Calidad Electronics Inc., a manufacturer of printed circuit boards based in Edinburg, Texas. The purchase was enabled or enhanced by $29.74 million in funds raised from a 1993 offering of shares that took IEC public again. The money also allowed IEC to reduce its long-term debt to $3.92 million, compared to $21.82 million in 1989.

IEC's Best Years: 1993–97

During 1993 IEC Electronics' net sales reached $102.96 million—nearly double the 1990 total—and its net income climbed to $8.44 million. CEO Main and General Manager Russell Stingel attributed the increase to growth in the markets for security devices, certain types of computers, medical instrumentation, and machine control. IEC was now serving 64 different customers, but Compaq Computer accounted for 60 percent of sales. To keep up with its increased orders, IEC more than doubled its workforce. IEC's sales reached $130.3 million in fiscal 1994 and its net income $10.95 million. That year the company acquired a southern firm, Accutek Inc. of Arab, Alabama, for $4 million. Sales dipped a little the following year, and net income fell by more than 50 percent.

Main died in 1996 and was succeeded as chief executive by Stingel, an original stockholder who had worked with Main at General Dynamics and had joined IEC in 1977. By this time supply shortages had cost the company at least $30 million in sales in 1994 and 1995, according to Stingel, leading to a reduction—albeit temporary—of the workforce to 1,000 from a peak of 1,700. In order to meet its needs faster, IEC arranged partnerships in 1997 with two large electronics-supply companies, Arrow Electronics Inc. and Pioneer-Standard Electronics Inc., that allowed personnel from these companies entry into IEC's factories. The partnerships were credited with enabling IEC to obtain supplies three days ahead of production, instead of the two weeks it needed before. The company also designed and installed computer databases allowing it to cut its price-quotation time to its customers from several days to 24 hours. That year IEC received an award for the highest overall customer rating given to a large contract electronics manufacturer.

Another important IEC decision was to focus on turnkey manufacturing, in which the company directed every stage in the process, starting with obtaining the materials and extending, in some cases, to distribution. By contrast, as late as 1994 about 90 percent of the company's work was dependent on materials provided by its own customers. IEC also upgraded its management, hiring senior level managers with a broader level of experience. In addition, the company reduced its dependence on Compaq and the personal computer market, adding networking, telecommunications, and communications customers. In place of the standard weekday eight-hour shifts at its factories, IEC converted to 12-hour shifts every day. Besides putting the company's expensive equipment to work around the clock, the conversion gave employees more free time, resulting, Stingel said, in higher productivity and lower absenteeism. Net sales soared to $260.69 million in fiscal 1997—more than double the 1995 level—and net income was nearly three times greater than the previous year.

Immersed in Red Ink: 1998–2000

Interviewed by Mike Dickinson of the *Rochester Business Journal*, Stingel was not shy about accepting the credit. While crediting Main, whom he described as "a good partner and a good friend" with the "sheer guts" needed to create IEC, Stingel said that Main "was trying to do everything himself and that does not work." Stingel, by contrast, called himself "a team player. I believe in team management, team motivation." IEC's chief executive did not have much time to bask in the good news, however. By mid 1998 the company was losing money, and its stock, which peaked at $22.25 a share in September 1997, was trading at only about a third of that level. With the price now below book value, the board of directors adopted a "poison pill" plan to forestall a possible takeover bid. Heartland Advisers, Inc., a mutual fund manager, controlled about 26 percent of the company's stock while the top 13 officers and directors owned only 7.6 percent combined.

IEC's net sales dropped by more than $12 million in 1998, and it lost $6.16 million, which included a $4.7 million restructuring charge to close the Alabama plant, which had been operating in the red after several key customers canceled or reduced their contracts. The company shed 38 percent of its workforce. IEC's sudden fall from grace resulted from the loss of its two leading customers, Compaq and Matrox Graphics, Inc. Both were personal computer manufacturers that shifted their work to low-cost, foreign producers. Their departure left IEC with no choice but to accelerate its transition to low-volume production runs and an emphasis on rapid changes, targeting the communications and industrial sectors. During fiscal 1999 industrial accounts made up 65 percent of IEC's revenues and telecommunications comprised 30 percent. (IEC's industrial market consisted of making the bar-code scanners used in retail stores.)

Stingel now also sought more international business by acquiring a plant in Langford, Ireland, from Ohshima Electronics Manufacturing Ltd. for $1.2 million. In addition, he also leased a newly constructed factory in Reynosa, Mexico, only 32 miles from the Edinburg facility. "The close proximity of our new Mexican facility will allow IEC to leverage the excellent purchasing, program-management, engineering, quality, and transportation infrastructure in Edinburg, thus offering our customers a low-risk transition into low-cost manufacturing in Mexico," a company executive told Darrell Dunn of *Electronic Buyers'*

News. The company's new ''TexMex'' strategy bore fruit almost immediately, when it won a major contract to produce a variety of industrial electronics products for General Electric.

Nevertheless, fiscal 1999 was by far the worst year ever experienced by IEC Electronics. Net sales sank to $157.49 million from $248.16 million the previous year, and the net loss widened to a record $20.57 million. Company stock dropped to as low as $1 a share. Before the year was out, Stingel's hand-picked successor, David Fradin, died suddenly, forcing the retired chief executive to resume his job on an interim basis. As part of a restructuring plan, IEC sold the manufacturing assets of its Irish plant in late 1999 and leased the facility to the buyer.

Thomas W. Lovelock, a specialist in repairing ailing companies, became chief executive officer of IEC Electronics in August 2000, shortly before the company reported net sales of $204.16 million and a net loss of $8.03 million in the fiscal year. He said that he wanted to broaden IEC's customer base to reduce its dependence on a few large orders from a small number of industries. By the end of the year, however, IEC was reported to be planning to reduce its client list from 65 to 25 in an effort to recast itself as a niche service provider. The company canceled, for example, its contract with struggling communications equipment manufacturer Lucent Technologies Inc. and looked instead to grow by signing contracts with telecommunications companies such as JDS Uniphase. ''We've made a number of changes [but] the challenge is taking this company that has been floundering for the last three years, with a turnover in leadership, and [to] refocus it and pull it up by its bootstraps,'' Lovelock told Claire Serant of *Electronics Buyers' News.* ''The company has been operating in a high-mix, medium-volume environment as opposed to a low-mix, high-volume environment, which is a big change.''

During fiscal 2000 IEC Electronics provided contract manufacturing services to about 75 customers. These were primarily for telecommunications equipment, measuring devices, medical instrumentation, imaging equipment, office equipment, micro, mini, and mainframe computers, and computer peripheral equipment. The company's long-term debt was $15.27 million at the end of 2000. Fifteen directors and officers collectively owned a total of 21 percent of the common stock. Heartland Advisers remained the largest institutional investor, with 11 percent.

IEC Electronics announced in 2001 that it would downsize its Edinburg plant, moving some of the production lines to the Mexican facility. It also signed a contract for a variety of services with RiverDelta Network Inc., a provider of broadband routing and switching communications products. As a long-term goal, the company was seeking to enter the upper end of a group of about 250 midsized U.S. contract electronics manufacturers—those with annual revenues ranging between $100 million and $1 billion. To further this goal, the company in 1998 opened a state-of-the-art technology center at its Newark manufacturing facility. During 2000 the center added prototype assembly to its services and an advanced materials technology laboratory.

Principal Subsidiaries

IEC Electronics-Edinburg, Texas, Inc.; IEC Electronics Foreign Sales Corporation (Barbados).

Principal Competitors

Flextronics International Ltd.; Hadco Corporation; Sanmina Corp.; Solectron Corp.

Further Reading

Breskin, Ira, ''Winning Back the Work That Got Away,'' *Business Week,* June 16, 1989, p. 140.

Conklin, Jason, ''IEC CEO Aims to Get Firm Back on Profit Track,'' *Rochester Business Journal,* September 8, 2000, pp. 1+.

——, ''IEC Still Losing Money but Expects Profits This Year,'' *Rochester Business Journal,* February 9, 2001, p. 3.

Dickinson, Mike, ''IEC Partnerships a Boost for Future,'' *Rochester Business Journal,* April 11, 1997, pp. 1+.

——, ''IEC Starts Fourth Decade in Wake of Difficult Year,'' *Rochester Business Journal,* November 15, 1996, p. 4.

——, ''Mexican-Plant Opening Key Step in IEC Strategy,'' *Rochester Business Journal,* March 5, 1999, p. 4.

——, ''Russell Stingel Makes His Mark on IEC,'' *Rochester Business Journal,* July 25, 1997, p. 10.

Dunn, Darrell, ''IEC Building International Base,'' *Electronic Buyers' News,* September 7, 1998, p. 48.

——, ''IEC Sets Up Shop in Mexico,'' *Electronic Buyers' News,* January 18, 1999, p. 54.

Ebersole, Phil, ''IEC Board Adopts Poison Pill,'' *Rochester Democrat and Chronicle,* June 15, 1998, p. 12D.

Hovis, Kathy, ''Surge Expected to Double IEC Electronics' Sales,'' *Rochester Business Journal,* October 2, 1992, pp. 1+.

''IEC Electronics Corporation,'' *Wall Street Transcript,* March 17, 1986, pp. 81,222–81,223.

Post, Tom, ''Working Smarter,'' *Forbes,* December 29, 1997, p. 64.

Serant, Claire, ''IEC Electronics Preparing for Comeback,'' *Electronic Buyers' News,* January 24, 2000, p. 68.

——, ''IEC to Reposition As Niche Provider,'' *Electronic Buyers' News,* January 1, 2001, p. 18.

——, ''Shifting from PCs to Telecom—IEC Signs with Riverdelta,'' *Electronic Buyers' News,* February 12, 2001, p. 86.

—Robert Halasz

Ito-Yokado Co., Ltd.

4-1-4 Shibakoen
Minato-ku
Tokyo 105-8571
Japan
Telephone: (03) 3459-2111
Fax: (03) 3459-6873
Web site: http://www.itoyokado.iyg.co.jp

Public Company
Incorporated: 1958 as Yokado Co., Ltd.
Employees: 53,020
Sales: ¥3.10 trillion ($26.76 billion) (2001)
Stock Exchanges: Tokyo Luxembourg Paris NASDAQ
Ticker Symbol: IYCOY (ADR)
NAIC: 452910 Warehouse Clubs and Superstores;
445120 Convenience Stores; 447110 Gasoline
Stations with Convenience Stores; 722110 Full-
Service Restaurants; 445110 Supermarkets and Other
Grocery (Except Convenience) Stores; 452110
Department Stores; 452990 All Other General
Merchandise Stores; 454110 Electronic Shopping and
Mail-Order Houses; 551112 Offices of Other Holding
Companies

Ito-Yokado Co., Ltd. and its 58 subsidiaries and affiliated companies—known collectively as the Ito-Yokado Group (or IY Group)—represent the largest retailing group in Japan and one of the 15 largest in the world, in terms of sales. It is also one of the most diversified. The group is one of the top supermarket companies in Japan, with nearly 190 superstores (which feature both food and nonfood merchandise) mostly operating under the Ito-Yokado name, more than 90 York Benimaru supermarkets, and another 60 supermarkets doing business as York Mart or Sanei. The group also includes 30 Daikuma discount stores, four Robinson's Japan department stores, and more than 60 specialty stores under the names Mary Ann (women's clothing), Oshman's Japan (sporting goods), and Steps (menswear). Another key group sector is convenience stores, in which Ito-Yokado holds majority stakes in Seven-Eleven Japan, Japan's largest convenience store

chain with more than 8,650 outlets, and 7-Eleven, Inc., the largest such chain in the United States with in excess of 5,750 units. In restaurants, Ito-Yokado has majority ownership of Denny's Japan, the Japanese version of the U.S. chain, which operates more than 530 outlets, and some 460 additional restaurants under the names Famil and York Bussan. Other operations include the manufacturing and processing of food products, the operating of superstores in China through a joint venture, and ownership of a publishing firm. In 2001 Ito-Yokado established IYBank, a branch-free bank that within months of its creation had more than 1,550 automatic teller machines (ATMs) located within Seven-Eleven stores in Japan.

Early History

Ito-Yokado developed from a subsidiary of Yokado Clothing Store—Yokado Yohin-ten in Japanese—established by Binyu Yoshikawa in 1920. The store was located in the Asakusa area of Tokyo and its main customers were prosperous members of the emerging Japanese middle class. Japan was in a period of high economic growth following its military defeat of China and Russia in conflicts in 1897 and 1904. Western goods such as home appliances and business suits were in high demand, and stores specializing in such goods flourished. By 1930, Yoshikawa's business had expanded to include four stores in the Asakusa area, but sales suffered in the late stages of World War II, as rationing of basic goods was introduced by Japan's military government. The public had very little money to spend on nonessential goods and the stores were forced to close because of bombing raids by the U.S. Air Force in the first half of 1945. The original store in Asakusa was destroyed in the air raids, and the other stores were badly damaged. Yoshikawa's situation was similar to that of numerous small retailers in postwar Tokyo and, like them, he began the painful task of rebuilding his business. He chose to relocate to the Kitasenju part of Tokyo, not far from Asakusa. Like his old stores, the new store sold goods imported from the West, such as clothes and cosmetics, but it also stocked household goods.

During the 1950s the Japanese economy was growing rapidly, fueled by exports and growing consumer demand. Yoshikawa gave his nephew Masatoshi Ito's parents control of the Yokado store in 1958, and they established Yokado Co., Ltd. It was here that the history of Ito-Yokado really began. Ito was determined to make his mark on the company. In 1961, at the age of 39, Ito traveled to the United States and Europe to gather information on Western retailing methods. This flow of information from the West to Japan was occurring in most sectors of the Japanese business world at the time. Ito studied the major U.S. retailing chains and was convinced that the future of consumer goods retailing in Japan lay in the establishment of such chains. Following his return to Japan, Ito began to take an active role in the family business. In October 1961 a second Yokado store was opened in the Tokyo region of Akabane, and this came about largely as a result of Ito's efforts. He succeeded in raising the capital to open another store in 1963 and two more in 1964. The stores were based on large U.S. retail outlets, and stocked food as well as clothes and household goods. In 1965, to avoid confusion with the original Yokado stores, the name was changed from Yokado Co., Ltd. to Ito-Yokado Co., Ltd., with Ito as president. He continued his policy of making the company a major supermarket chain by opening nine new Ito-Yokado stores between 1965 and 1970. They included a supermarket in Noda, Chiba prefecture, the first store outside Tokyo.

1970s to Mid-1980s: Diversification through Establishment of Several Chains

By the early 1970s Ito-Yokado was a medium-sized but fast-growing supermarket chain in Tokyo, and in 1972 it obtained a listing on the Second Section of the Tokyo Stock Exchange. Also in this year the corporate logo, which became a familiar sight all over Japan, was conceived. It consists of a white dove on a background of red and blue. Japan's economy, led by consumer spending, was booming, and Ito wished to expand his company's business into other areas. In 1972 the restaurant chain Famil was established with the opening of a family diner in Tokyo. Like the Ito-Yokado supermarkets, the Famil chain was aimed at the middle-class family market. The company's diversification into the restaurant business continued in the following year when, under license from the U.S. chain Denny's, Denny's Japan Co. Ltd. was formed. The plan was to open restaurants with a visible Western brand name in the Tokyo suburbs by the side of major roads. The first store, in Tokyo, was highly successful, and Denny's restaurants were soon open-

ing up all over Japan. In 1973 Ito-Yokado was listed on the First Section of the Tokyo Stock Exchange, and the company acquired a stake in the Fukushima-based supermarket chain Benimaru Co. Ltd. A joint-venture company, York-Benimaru, was established. Ito-Yokado contributed its knowledge of chain retailing as well as the familiar Ito-Yokado company logo. Established in 1948, the Benimaru chain of supermarkets thus became an affiliate of Ito-Yokado, and aided in the latter company's plans for nationwide expansion.

In 1973 under license from the Dallas-based Southland Corporation, Ito-Yokado established York Seven Inc. (renamed Seven-Eleven Japan in 1978), with a majority shareholding retained by Ito-Yokado. At the time 7-Eleven was the leading convenience-store franchise in the United States, and Ito was determined to establish his company's dominance in the Japanese market with the aid of the 7-Eleven brand name (rendered as ''Seven-Eleven'' in Japan). The stores were extremely successful and were opened at the rate of about 100 a year, initially in the Kanto region and subsequently all over Japan. Like the Denny's restaurants, Ito-Yokado's Seven-Eleven stores were mainly located in suburban regions near major roads.

In the middle to late 1970s Japanese consumers were becoming increasingly concerned about the quality of the goods they bought, as well as the cost. Young Japanese consumers, notably women, were displaying a growing fashion-consciousness and discernment in their shopping. In 1978 Ito-Yokado established Mary Ann Co. Ltd., a chain store specializing in fashionable women's clothing, and the stores became boutiques within shopping centers. The expansion of the Ito-Yokado stores continued. The stores became known as ''superstores'' because of their large size and abundant floor space. They began to stock such goods as electrical appliances and furniture, and many of them were multilevel. In the 1970s Ito-Yokado opened more than 70 new flagship (Ito-Yokado) stores, with the expansion mainly occurring in the prefectures of Tokyo, Kanagawa, and Chiba. In 1975, meantime, Ito-Yokado launched a new supermarket chain called York Mart; the new supermarkets were located in markets not large enough to support an Ito-Yokado superstore.

In 1978 Ito-Yokado increased its penetration of the retail sector in Kanagawa by its purchase of Daikuma Co. Ltd., a Kanagawa-based chain specializing in discount retailing. The stores sold everything from clothes to television sets in warehouse-like buildings. The Ito-Yokado logo was not incorporated into these stores. In 1978 Ito-Yokado joined forces with Japan's most prestigious department store chain, Matsuzakaya Co. Ltd., to establish a department store in Hokkaido, Japan's northernmost island. The store was 90 percent owned by Ito-Yokado and was called York-Matsuzakaya. This venture highlighted the company's aim to expand into every sector of retailing in Japan. In 1981 Steps Co. Ltd., a chain of menswear stores, was established to complement the existing Mary Ann chain. That same year, Seven-Eleven Japan was listed on the First Section of the Tokyo Stock Exchange. By 1982 a computerized point-of-sale (POS) stock monitoring system was introduced throughout the chain. The system speeded up the checkout process and also enabled information such as the time of purchase and type of customer to be recorded. The information was sent to the mainframe computer at Seven-Eleven Japan's headquarters, which then returned information to the individual

Key Dates:

1958: Yokado Co., Ltd. is established, originally to operate department stores.

1961: Led by Masatoshi Ito, Yokado opens a new store, which is essentially a superstore—a supermarket also selling nonfood items.

1965: Company name is changed to Ito-Yokado Co., Ltd.; superstores are renamed Ito-Yokado.

1972: Ito-Yokado goes public, with a listing on the Tokyo Stock Exchange; company expands into restaurants, with the establishment of the Famil chain.

1973: Denny's Japan is established to open Denny's restaurants in Japan; company acquires stake in Benimaru supermarket chain, establishing joint venture York-Benimaru; through license deal with Southland Corporation, Ito-Yokado establishes Seven-Eleven Japan to open Seven-Eleven convenience stores throughout Japan.

1975: York Mart supermarket chain is established.

1978: Company launches Mary Ann, a chain store specializing in fashionable women's clothing; company purchases the Daikuma discount store chain.

1981: Steps, a chain of menswear stores, is established.

1984: Company establishes the Robinson's Japan department store business and the Oshman's Japan sporting goods business.

1991: Ito-Yokado acquires a 70 percent stake in Southland Corporation, owner of the 7-Eleven chain.

1992: A scandal involving payoffs to local gangsters leads to the resignation of Ito as president.

1995: Shiba Park Publishing is formed as a magazine publisher.

1997: Company expands into China for the first time with the opening of a superstore in Cheng Du, Sichuan.

2001: IYBank begins operations as a branch-free, ATM-only bank.

---

store to aid in ordering decisions. The presence of a bar code on all products sold and a scanner capable of identifying the code made the system possible. With the high rate of stock turnover and slim profit margins on sales, this became a vital ingredient in the chain's success. POS systems were introduced into all Ito-Yokado stores by 1985.

In 1984 Ito-Yokado made further inroads into the department store business in Japan with the establishment of Robinson's Japan Co. Ltd., a wholly owned subsidiary of Ito-Yokado. Although the name suggested foreign influence, the concept was conceived by Ito-Yokado. The first store opened in 1985 in Kasukabe, Saitama prefecture, near Tokyo, and sold a range of luxury goods in a relaxed atmosphere, contrasting with the more frantic pace of the Ito-Yokado superstores. In 1990 a second Robinson's store was opened in Utsunomiya, Tochigi prefecture. Ito-Yokado entered the sporting goods market with the establishment of Oshman's Japan Co. Ltd., also in 1984. By 1986 the Ito-Yokado chain was well established in the Kanto region as one of the leading retail chains. This was also true in the northern Japanese island of Hokkaido, and northern

Honshu. However, the company had yet to open a store in Japan's second largest metropolitan area, the Kansai plain. In 1986 Ito-Yokado's first store in Kansai opened in Osaka.

Late 1980s and Beyond: Expanding Overseas

The company, with Masatoshi Ito still at the helm, began expansion overseas in 1989 with the opening of a liaison office in Seattle, Washington. In the same year Seven-Eleven Japan acquired the 58 branches of 7-Eleven in Hawaii, at the request of parent company Southland Corporation. It was apparent that Southland was in financial difficulty, and—according to Seven-Eleven Japan's president, Toshifumi Suzuki—was not responding to the changing U.S. retail market. In reorganizing the stores in Hawaii, Suzuki noticed that the amount of inventory present at a given time was three times the average for his stores in Japan. In addition the stores in Japan had an average floor space of 100 square meters and daily sales of ¥650,000. The equivalent figures for the stores in Hawaii were 170 square meters and ¥400,000. Suzuki realized that tight inventory control was the key to success, and in 1991 Ito-Yokado acquired a 70 percent stake in Southland Corporation, with the full cooperation of the latter firm's management, for $430 million. One of the prerequisites put forward by Ito-Yokado before the purchase was that Southland's management would have to be prepared to listen and learn from Seven-Eleven Japan. This represented a major purchase for Ito-Yokado and pushed the group's annual sales past the ¥4 trillion mark, the largest for a Japanese-owned retail group.

In 1992 Ito-Yokado became the latest Japanese company that investigators found had made payoffs to local gangsters, known as *sokaiya,* in order to prevent the mobsters from disrupting annual meetings. In the wake of the scandal, Ito resigned as president but remained on the company board with the title of honorary chairman. Toshifumi Suzuki, a company vice-president in charge of Seven-Eleven Japan, was promoted to president.

One of Suzuki's first major undertakings was to turn around the fortunes of the 7-Eleven chain. Among the key initial moves were the shuttering of 1,180 loss-making U.S. stores by 1994, a massive store remodeling effort, an overhaul of the merchandise mix, and the replacement of "insult pricing"—the huge markups that customers were forced to pay for convenience—with an "everyday fair pricing" policy featuring lower prices on much of the inventory. Southland also replaced its in-house distribution system with a third-party arrangement with McLane Co., Inc., a subsidiary of Wal-Mart Stores, Inc., the U.S. retail giant. McLane was the country's largest convenience store distributor and began providing coast-to-coast distribution service to the 7-Eleven chain. Another key strategy that Southland adopted to revitalize the chain was to improve the quality and value of the convenience items offered by the stores. This included moving toward daily deliveries of fresh perishables and the introduction of new ready-to-eat fresh foods, such as sandwiches and pastries, and eventually dinner entrees.

Perhaps the most important initiative, however, was the implementation of a chainwide proprietary retail information system, similar to the system already in use at Seven-Eleven Japan. Development of the system began in 1994 and was rolled out nationwide over the remainder of the decade. The system was designed to enable each store to improve its inventory management, reduce the incidence of out-of-stock items, and tailor its product mix to better match the needs of its customers. Southland returned to the black by 1994, then posted steadily rising profits into the 21st century. During the late 1990s Southland began adding more stores than it was closing, as growth was put back on the agenda. During 1998, 299 stores were either opened or acquired while 96 were closed. Another 165 were opened in 1999 and 120 more in 2000. In April 1999, meantime, the nearly fully recovered Southland Corporation changed its name to 7-Eleven, Inc. in a move reflecting the fact that the corporation was involved in only one business.

Back in Japan, Ito-Yokado struggled throughout the 1990s with the stagnant Japanese economy but remained profitable by retaining its keen cost-control strategy and its cautious approach to expansion. Seeking to increase the percentage of imported goods that it sold in Japan from 15 percent to 30 percent, Ito-Yokado reached agreements in 1993 and 1994 with the world's two largest retailers, Wal-Mart and Germany's Metro, to import and sell some of the retail giants' goods. In the early and mid-1990s, Ito-Yokado opened only about five stores per year in Japan, with most of them concentrated in eastern Japan, near the group's distribution centers. The group also entered the rapidly expanding Chinese market for the first time in the late 1990s through joint ventures. In November 1997 a superstore was opened in Cheng Du, Sichuan, then another one was opened in Beijing in April 1998. Although initially unprofitable, the two stores showed steadily improving performance, laying the groundwork for further expansion in that nation.

Despite the group's slow pace of retail growth, Suzuki continued to seek new growth opportunities. Ito-Yokado branched out into magazine publishing in 1995 with the establishment of Shiba Park Publishing, which launched a new women's magazine called *saita* that year. In the late 1990s and early 21st century, the group became increasingly involved in the e-commerce sector, particularly through Seven-Eleven Japan. In February 2000, for example, 7dream.com made its debut. Through this web site, Seven-Eleven customers in Japan could order products at any time over the Internet and then pick up and pay for their order at a prearranged time at a nearby store. The group also entered banking in May 2001, when IYBank began operations. IYBank was a branch-free, ATM-only bank offering lower ATM fees than other banks. The new bank aimed to install 3,650 automatic teller machines at Seven-Eleven convenience stores in its first year of operation, all of which would operate 24 hours a day, year-round. This would far eclipse the four largest banking groups in Japan combined, which together had only about 1,000 24-hour ATMs.

The retail environment in Japan around the turn of the millennium was a particularly troubled one, with some prominent Japanese retailers declaring bankruptcy. Supermarkets and department stores, including those operated by Ito-Yokado, were hit the hardest, but Ito-Yokado remained safely profitable due almost entirely to its highly successful convenience store operations in both Japan and the United States. The group did, however, see its net income tumble 28.5 percent in fiscal 2000 and then increase just 2.6 percent the following year. Ito-Yokado's continued profitability in such difficult economic times proved the wisdom of Ito's strategy of diversification and seemed likely to keep secure the group's position at the top of Japanese retailing.

Principal Subsidiaries

Seven-Eleven Japan Co., Ltd. (50.7%); Denny's Japan Co., Ltd. (51.6%); Daikuma Co., Ltd. (85.7%); York Mart Co., Ltd. (89.9%); IYBank Co., Ltd.; 7-Eleven, Inc. (72.7%).

Principal Competitors

The Daiei, Inc.; AEON Co., Ltd.; Mycal Corporation; The Seiyu, Ltd.; Uny Co., Ltd.; Ultramar Diamond Shamrock Corporation; Tosco Corporation; FamilyMart Company Ltd.; Wal-Mart Stores, Inc.; Carrefour SA.

Further Reading

Barr, Vilma, "Masatoshi Ito," *Stores,* January 1998, pp. 104, 106.

Dvorak, Phred, "Japanese Banks Face New Competitors: Changes in Rule Would Open Door to Sony, 7-Eleven," *Wall Street Journal,* May 17, 2000, p. A21.

"Ito-Yokado Rolls a 7-Eleven," *Chain Store Age,* January 1992, pp. 33+.

Jameson, Sam, "Steady Does It," *Asian Business,* July 1999, pp. 11+.

"Japanese Retailing: The Emporia Strike Back," *Economist,* October 29, 1994, p. 83.

"Japan's Ito Yokado Driven by a Successful Blend of Seasoned Operating Philosophies," *Discount Store News,* May 6, 1991, pp. 81+.

Ono, Yumiko, and Quentin Hardy, "President's Exit in a Scandal Fails to Shake Backers of 'Safe' Ito-Yokado," *Wall Street Journal,* October 30, 1992, p. A6.

Sakamaki, Sachiko, "We're Listening: Ito-Yokado Is Shaking Up Japan's Staid Retailing World," *Far Eastern Economic Review,* April 4, 1996, pp. 54–55.

Suzuki, Toshifumi, "The Quest to Rebuild Seven-Eleven Founder Southland," *Tokyo Business Today,* September 1991, pp. 44+.

Tanzer, Andrew, "A Form of Flattery," *Forbes,* June 2, 1986, pp. 110+.

—Dylan Tanner
—update: David E. Salamie

John Hancock Financial Services, Inc.

John Hancock Place
Boston, Massachusetts 02117
U.S.A.
Telephone: (617) 572-6000
Toll Free: (877) 416-0280
Fax: (617) 572-6451
Web site: http://www.johnhancock.com

Public Company
Incorporated: 1862 as John Hancock Mutual Life
    Insurance Company
Employees: 9,700
Total Assets: $87.35 billion (2000)
Stock Exchanges: New York
Ticker Symbol: JHF
NAIC: 524113 Direct Life Insurance Carriers

John Hancock Financial Services, Inc. provides a wide range of insurance and investment products and services. Its historic mainstay, the issuance of insurance policies, remains an important part of the company. Its variable, universal, and term life insurance account for almost 40 percent of revenues. Annuities and mutual funds make up the bulk of its investment products. In recent years Hancock has been expanding into institutional asset management and alternate sales channels, including the Internet.

Civil War Beginnings

John Hancock Mutual Life Insurance Company was founded in 1862. Of six life insurance companies founded that year in the United States, it alone survives. A total of 28 such companies were founded between 1860 and 1865; only seven survived to the 1950s. In the two years following the Civil War, 24 more were started. It was a boom time for life insurance, and hard selling by the new companies reaped a rich harvest. Life insurance in force rose to an estimated $2 billion in the 1860s.

Hancock was chartered on April 21, 1862, in Massachusetts, where a Department of Insurance had been established in 1855, the first of its kind in the United States. It was the first company to

be formed under two recently signed laws that helped to regularize a previously uncertain and at times dishonest business. As if to emphasize the point, the new company took for its namesake the Massachusetts native John Hancock—first to sign the Declaration of Independence and later governor of the state—whose signature became synonymous with a pledge of fidelity.

The more important of the two laws dealt with nonforfeiture. The practice in the industry had been to confiscate policies after one payment was missed. Nonforfeiture, paying surrender value of a life policy after the fifth year, became the U.S. norm after passage of this 1861 law in Massachusetts. The other law, passed in 1858, required each insurance company to demonstrate its worth yearly.

Hancock's first president was George P. Sanger. At 43 years of age, Sanger was district attorney for Suffolk County, in which Boston is located, and a former judge. Indeed, he continued as district attorney for seven years. Only then, in 1869, did he quit public office to be a full-time insurance executive.

By November 1863 Hancock had 176 policies in force, for a total value of $332,700. In the next two months, the company wrote 111 more policies. The company continued to experience success and, in 1869, moved from a small office, where the company medical examiner screened applicants in a crowded corner, to roomier quarters in the Sears Building. In 1872 the company redeemed its guarantee capital and became a mutual company.

Sanger returned to public life as U.S. attorney for Massachusetts in 1874; his successor was George Thornton. During the economic depression of that time, Hancock suffered financially, but it remained solvent and honored its obligations.

1880s: Pioneer in Industrial Life Insurance

Prudential Insurance Company had at the same time introduced industrial life insurance for the less affluent. Premiums were paid weekly rather than annually or semiannually. Its premiums and benefits were lower than those of ordinary life insurance. Policies were started for as little as five cents. For many years it was the only insurance available on the lives of

Company Perspectives:

The mission of John Hancock is to be the highest quality financial services company. We offer a broad range of insurance and financial products and services nationally and internationally to meet the needs of our customers and provide our customers with the highest quality service. We maintain superior financial strength, offering those products and services that provide attractive rates of return, competitive product value and expectations for growth. We offer challenging career opportunities and personal development for all associates, enable all associates to contribute to their fullest potential and promote open cooperative relationships among all associates, customers and the public. In all that we do, we exemplify the highest standards of business ethics and personal integrity, and recognize our corporate obligation to the social and economic well-being of our community.

children—a feature that was to envelop it in controversy. Industrial life was new, and no one knew how closely U.S. mortality would mirror English mortality rates, on which this insurance was based. In addition, U.S. companies had to keep fixed reserves, while the English did not.

Industrial agents' work was part social work. The agent was expected to know everyone on his route. His territory required up to 1,000 calls a week for collection of premiums. If the total collections for which the agent was responsible held steady, he was rewarded; if they fell, he was penalized. Agents were to make calls three or four days a week and solicit new business on the other days. They were welcome to sell other kinds of insurance as well.

Prudential had the field to itself for four years. Then, in March 1879, Hancock got a new president, no less a figure than the Massachusetts insurance commissioner, Stephen H. Rhodes, who by midsummer was selling industrial insurance in Boston. By year's end, Hancock had 9,327 industrial policies totaling $951,000, after only six months of selling the coverage. It was a welcome addition to the line. Metropolitan Life Insurance Company entered the industrial field the same year. These three—Prudential, Metropolitan, and Hancock—were to dominate that business, with Boston-based Hancock trailing a distant third behind the other two, both based around New York.

By 1881 Hancock had 36,012 industrial policies in force, and by 1889 it had issued 256,000 industrial policies worth $30 million. Hancock's burgeoning prosperity was demonstrated in part by its move in February 1891 to its own richly ornamented home office building in Boston, with "monumental figures in colored mosaic" in the staircase hall, against a background of "nearly thirty thousand cubes or 'tessera' of enamel overlaid with gold and covered with a thin film of glass . . . made by a process known alone to the Venetians," as described by R. Carlyle Buley in *The American Life Convention, 1906–1952: A Study in the History of Life Insurance.* Such grandeur was and for some time remained typical of insurance companies, whose home offices and other downtown buildings provided almost as much commentary for architects as their policies did for insurance writers.

During 1891 Hancock's insurance in force reached $54.5 million, up from $17.8 million in 1886. Hancock had managed to find its way in the uncharted waters of the early industrial insurance years.

Prudential and Metropolitan still were the leaders by far. Other companies had dropped from the race. Industrial insurance had a high lapse rate, with most lapses occurring in the first six months of the policy. In this period lapses were costly to the companies, who tried hard to prevent them.

The problems of insuring children came to a head in 1895, when Massachusetts considered the prohibition against insuring children under ten. The practice was denounced for five days in a Boston hearing room as encouraging cruelty and even murder. The tide turned when Haley Fiske, the Metropolitan vice-president and a lobbyist, testified, and the bill was soundly defeated. Other states considered such a bill, but only Colorado passed one; it lasted into 1921.

Early 20th-Century Changes and Reforms

In 1902 Hancock's industrial agents were urged to push ordinary life insurance. The name of the company newsletter for agents, "Our Industrial Field," was changed to "The John Hancock Field." Hancock was diversifying, and growing; by 1905 it had 1.5 million policies. Its insurance in force came to $245 million, up from $115 million. This was small compared with Metropolitan and Prudential, who with Hancock together held some 15.5 million industrial policies, of the total of 16.8 million such policies in the United States, worth $2.3 billion.

In 1905 the Armstrong Committee's investigation of the New York State insurance industry achieved a general overhaul of the life insurance industry, and it led to needed reforms. At Hancock, however, 1905 was remembered for its exposure of "the mistakes and misdeeds of a few individuals prominent in the business, followed by an investigation of Draconian severity," according to *Historical Sketch of the John Hancock Mutual Life Insurance Company of Boston, Massachusetts: A Half Century Completed, 1862–1912.*

The investigation produced "tremendous shock" but did "not for a second impair or suspend" operations and "furnished moreover an example of the inherent soundness . . . of the old line insurance plan," according to *The Satchel,* the company magazine, in 1907.

In 1906 Stephen Rhodes died at 83, after more than 30 years at the Hancock helm. He was succeeded by Roland O. Lamb, 58, who had been with the company since 1872. Lamb was no sooner installed than another home office building was completed. It was fire-resistant with an exterior of pink granite; its interior displayed several kinds of marble. Modern for its day, it boasted eight elevators and a drinking fountain offering refrigerated water on each floor.

In 1924 Hancock helped launch the group insurance business in the United States by offering such insurance to employers. By 1990 the company would have 1,000 group clients. Group policies, with life and industrial policies, were to form the core of business through Hancock's first 100 years.

Key Dates:

1862: John Hancock Mutual Life Insurance Company is founded.
1872: Company redeems its guarantee capital and becomes a mutual company owned by its policyholders.
1879: Hancock offers industrial life insurance.
1891: Hancock's insurance in force reaches $54.5 million.
1924: Hancock helps launch the group insurance business in the United States by offering such insurance to employers.
1954: Company is fifth largest U.S. insurance company, with assets of $3.8 billion.
1968: Hancock forms a real estate subsidiary and enters the mutual fund business the next year.
1971: Company enters the property and casualty insurance markets.
1986: Company ranks eighth among U.S. life insurance firms, with assets of $27.3 billion.
1999: Following a class-action lawsuit on behalf of policyholders, Hancock denies any wrongdoing related to "policy churning" but agrees to a settlement approaching $471 million.
2000: Hancock converts from a mutual company to a publicly owned company.

The Great Depression shook up the world; Hancock, however, saw business rise 7.3 percent in 1930, the Depression's first full calendar year. New business began declining by 1932, and Hancock cut its dividend.

Guy W. Cox became Hancock president in 1936. In 1937, its agents picketed the company's New York office on Christmas Eve. Six months later, the National Labor Relations Board considered filing a complaint against Hancock in connection with the petition for union election by the United Office and Professional Workers of America. In November of that year, Hancock's industrial agents sought a union election among Hancock employees.

The company purchased an aircraft carrier, the *Hancock,* in 1944, for use by the U.S. Navy in World War II. It was the result of a joint financing effort by agents, other employees, and policyholders. Agents carried patriotism a step further with their pledge to bring the appeal for a wastepaper-salvage drive to homes they visited in the course of business.

In 1944 Guy Cox became chairman, and Paul F. Clark, a former agent, became president at age 51. Clark would become chairman three years later. In the spirit of postwar recovery, Hancock began on-the-job training for returning veterans in 1946. In the same year, the company advertised on radio for the first time, sponsoring Boston Symphony Orchestra performances.

Conservative Investing Mid-Century

In 1948, Hancock had assets of more than $2 billion. New investments in 1947 had topped $300 million. At that time, Hancock was earning 3 percent, down from 5 percent in the prior years. With a surplus of $166 million, its portfolio was unspectacular; fewer than $15 million was in common stock, though by law the insurance firm was allowed to carry ten times that amount. In addition, Hancock was lending on real estate to only 50 percent to 55 percent of market value rather than the 66.7 percent allowed. Yet Hancock, the largest life insurance company in the United States outside the New York metropolitan area, had the third highest growth rate at that time of all insurance companies. The company's finance committee, by Massachusetts law, made final decisions in investments. Guy Cox chaired the committee, and caution ruled its deliberations. Before investing in the stock of a paper company, analysts were sent to view the whole paper industry. Hancock was willing to take three months to decide on a given issue.

More than 30 percent of Hancock investments lay in U.S. government bonds, with almost as much in public utility bonds and notes. Average net interest for 1947 was 2.91 percent, but the new investments averaged 3.14 percent. Things were looking up, after more than a decade of having to buy low-interest-bearing securities.

During this period, Hancock was experimenting with financing of rental housing. Two "Hancock villages" went up, one in Boston, another in Dearborn, Michigan. The latter encountered labor and other problems. Meanwhile, in Boston a new 26-story home office was constructed, making it the highest building in town. It also had the longest escalator in the United States. As high as the new building was, it was "dwarfed by the life insurance idea," said President Clark at its opening. It replaced a ten-story building that in 1922 had won the Boston Society of Architects award for its designer, J. Harleston Parker.

The 1940s wrought a marked change in the life insurance industry. Government investment rose sharply during the war, to an all-time high of 46 percent of the total. By 1951 it had dropped to 17 percent. The nation looked to the industry for capital, with its net yearly rise in assets of $4 billion to $5 billion. The industry responded, looking beyond the bond market to private, or individual, placements.

The 1950s was a time of political nervousness. Senator Joseph McCarthy of Wisconsin held the stage on Capitol Hill, and the Cold War was a fact of life. Hancock succumbed at least temporarily, refusing a lease renewal in 1953 to the Community Church of Boston, which had rented its home office auditorium for 30 years for its liberal lecturers.

What to do with the money was the main life insurance issue, however. By 1954 Hancock ranked fifth among U.S. insurance companies, with $3.8 billion in assets, and was investing as much as $4.6 million a week. Investments had earned 3.07 percent in 1953, up from the all-time low of 2.9 percent in 1947. Hancock moved to higher yields, looking increasingly to mortgage loans, which had risen to 20 percent of its portfolio, from not quite 12 percent in 1949. High return, however, had to be joined with safety, which made the task difficult.

By the mid-1960s another story was unfolding. Hancock was showing a new aggressiveness. According to the January 15, 1966 issue of *Business Week,* it was "second to none of the old-line mutuals in selling itself," as it did in building its skyscraping monument in Chicago, the John Hancock Center, then second in height only to the Empire State Building. Hancock had just elected its youngest-ever chief executive officer, 49-year-old Robert E. Slater, an actuary and a firm believer in the use of the computer. Slater was busy reshaping the company, looking ahead to a time in which baby boomers, born in the post-World War II decade, would be buying much of the country's life insurance.

In the 1960s ordinary life insurance was the company's biggest moneymaker, followed by group accident and health, group annuities, and group life. The old industrial insurance was no longer a consideration.

New Markets and Strategies: 1970s–80s

With 32 percent of its portfolio in mortgages (compared with 42 percent for Prudential), 63 percent in bonds, and only 5 percent in stocks, Hancock was unquestionably a conservative investor. Changes were coming, however. Hancock formed a real estate subsidiary in 1968 and entered the mutual fund business the next year. An international group program was begun. It was the start of broad diversification.

Hancock entered the Canadian market in 1969, and in 1971 entered the property and casualty insurance markets. Its 1972 income topped $2 billion for the first time. The company was in the securities business by then, with its John Hancock Income Securities Group. Slater resigned in December 1969 and was replaced by Gerhard Bleicken as chairman and CEO. In May 1972 the first black director, who was also the first woman director, Mary Ella Robertson, was elected.

Hancock was again making architectural history with the John Hancock Tower, its new home office building in Boston. The Chicago John Hancock Center, a $95 million investment, had been hailed as innovative and workable. The Hancock Tower, built five years later, was another issue. In 1974, the tower's windows, some 60 stories high, began to blow out and fall to the ground. The cause was a flaw in the design of the windows. The double-pane windows were replaced for $47 million, and the cost of the whole structure rose from an original $52 million to $144 million. The initial construction of the building had created other problems, including a weakening of the foundation of nearby Trinity Church, which sued Hancock for $4 million. Hancock in turn sued the architects, I.M. Pei & Associates; the general contractor; and the window glass manufacturer, who in turn countersued Hancock.

The late 1970s were bringing what Hancock called winds of change into the life insurance industry. Rising inflation and interest rates and deregulation offered circumstances in which policyholders borrowed on life policies at 5 percent or 6 percent to reinvest in money-market securities paying twice that. The prime rate shot up, and in 1980 many life insurance companies found themselves faced with a negative cash flow, for the first time in memory. The prime rate dropped later in the year, from an astronomical 20 percent, and the crisis eased. Insurers knew things would never be the same, however. From this realization came substantial changes in the company that would outdo any changes of the 1970s.

One of the first things to change was the investment strategy. There would be no more fixed-interest, long-term loans. The company would build a liquidity reserve of short-term securities. The fixed-income portfolio would be examined constantly by means of thorough computerized programs.

During the 1980s, Hancock entered most segments of the financial services industry and become a vocal proponent, alone among life insurance companies, of deregulation. The "level playing field" became a byword: all financial institutions—banks, brokerages, insurers—should have equal access to all financial services. By 1985 Hancock was in money management, stock brokerage, venture-capital management, equipment leasing, and real estate syndication. Hancock wanted to be a financial supermarket, but it was an old conservative company in a still more conservative industry. As a mutual company, it had no shareholders and had never been run with profit in mind. It was the sixth largest insurer, down from fifth, with assets of $25 billion. Its old ways had sent it into sharp decline. Its policyholder base had shrunk 30 percent in the previous ten years. New business bookings had peaked in 1981, as consumers moved from whole-life policies to cheaper term coverage.

Hancock had to change. To stay with traditional life insurance would have meant to "shrink the company," said Chairman and CEO John G. McElwee. Instead, it would offer banking, investment, and insurance products. It already had gone into credit cards and a half-dozen other non-insurance products and had bought a regional brokerage house and banks in Ohio and New Hampshire. There was, however, the question of whether its predominantly middle- and lower-income policyholders would buy such services.

McElwee was succeeded by E. James Morton in March 1986. Stephen L. Brown became president and chief operating officer. In 1986 Hancock helped found the Financial Services Council, a coalition of 18 manufacturers, retailers, and financial firms who lobbied for "pro-competitive" reform of laws affecting financial services. Normally rivals, these firms coauthored a draft bill for reform that was unveiled in October 1987.

The United States lagged behind England and Canada in rallying government, business, and consumers around the idea of integration of financial services. Hancock was prevented from buying a savings-and-loan institution, for example, because the savings and loan owned a brokerage that underwrote corporate equities and debt. Instead, Hancock bought a consumer bank, First Signature Bank and Trust Company, in New Hampshire, a limited-purpose bank with a 7 percent growth cap as required by the 1987 banking law. It was the most Hancock could do. Forbidden to become a holding company because it was mutually held, it was unable to demutualize for lack of enabling legislation in Massachusetts.

President Brown offered a goal of "reciprocal access" to financial services, whether for banks or insurance companies, and a vision of financial services as one competitive industry controlled by appropriate legislation. By 1986 Hancock had slipped to number eight among life insurance companies, with assets of $27.3 billion. Manufacturers, retailers, and foreign competitors already had entered the insurance and other financial markets, while bank holding companies and mutual life insurers operated under restraint.

Hancock's group insurance unit, which provided health and life insurance to employees of more than 1,000 companies, contributed to companies' problems. Operating at a loss of $40 million in 1987, the unit was handed over to David D'Alessandro for fixing. He promptly laid off 400 employees and sold unprofitable businesses, including some HMOs. Within a year, the unit was profitable and D'Alessandro was on his way up Hancock's corporate ladder.

Troubles in the 1990s

By 1990, however, John Hancock had fallen to the nation's ninth largest life insurer, with $198 billion of life insurance in force covering 17 million lives. A weakened real estate market fueled concerns about the company. Hancock held 40 percent of its assets in real estate and mortgage loan holdings, for a total of $9.7 billion. To cover any losses, Hancock established a mortgage real estate valuation reserve of $137 million in 1990. Earnings fell, and the company sold its credit card, property/casualty, and banking businesses. In 1992, Hancock passed on its $40 million disability insurance business to Provident Life and Accident Insurance Co. through a reinsurance agreement.

In the mid-1990s, John Hancock struggled with accusations of market misconduct. Along with several other prominent insurance companies, Hancock was fined for misleading advertising and policy churning (persuading customers to use the cash value of their whole life policies to pay for new policies with the mistaken assumption this would eliminate any premium payments). After New York fined Hancock $1 million in 1995, Hancock faced a class-action lawsuit from policyholders. Although Hancock denied any wrongdoing, it agreed to a $350 million settlement in 1997. By 1999 the number of aggrieved policyholders had risen to almost four million, and the settlement cost, to $471 million.

The company expanded overseas in the mid-1990s, primarily in the Pacific Rim. It acquired interests in insurers in Thailand and Singapore and set up a life insurance joint venture in the Philippines in 1997. The same year, Hancock sold its group health and life business for $86.7 million. In 1998, that unit's former head, David D'Alessandro, was named president of John Hancock.

IPO in 2000

The company began preparations in 1999 to demutualize, with plans for an initial public offering (IPO) of stock early in 2000. D'Alessandro, now CEO, hoped the conversion to a public company would make Hancock more results-oriented and would provide cash for more timely acquisitions. First, however, the company had to devise an acceptable plan for compensating policyholders, who owned the mutual company. The proposed plan to distribute a combination of cash, stock, and enhanced benefits hit a snag when Hancock had to spend several months searching for approximately 750,000 policyholders it had lost track of.

The company also had to resolve its share of disability insurance liability in a reinsurance fiasco. Sandwiched in the middle of several layers of reinsurance agreements, Hancock was liable for an uncertain amount of money, although one PaineWebber analyst claimed Hancock was vulnerable to as much as $1 billion in losses. In January 2000, Hancock laid to rest these fears when it announced it would take a non-operating after-tax charge of $134 million to cover its worker's compensation liabilities.

The company continued to prepare for its demutualization, changing its name to John Hancock Financial Services, Inc., and converting its agents into brokers. On January 26, John Hancock completed its IPO of 102 million shares. At $17 a share, the IPO raised $1.7 billion for the company. Policyholders received 230 million shares and some received cash from the IPO.

By mid-2001, the company's conversion to a public company seemed a success. The stock price had more than doubled, to $40 a share. In addition, Hancock continued to diversify its distribution and expand its product line. Internet sales were booming, with 60 percent of its term life policies being sold online in 2000. The company planned to expand its online offerings to include variable annuities, variable life, and long-term care policies. Under the leadership of D'Alessandro, who had been named chairman in May, John Hancock seemed poised for a revitalization of its almost 140-year-old business.

Principal Subsidiaries

John Hancock Life Assurance Company Ltd. (Singapore); John Hancock Subsidiaries; John Hancock Variable Life Insurance Company of Boston; The Maritime Life Assurance Company (Canada); First Signature Bank & Trust Company; Hancock Natural Resource Group, Inc.; Independence Investment LLC; Investors Guaranty Life Insurance Company; John Hancock Advisors, Inc.; John Hancock Advisors International Ltd. (U.K.); John Hancock Funds; John Hancock Realty Advisors; Signator Financial Network; John Hancock Real Estate Finance, Inc.

Principal Competitors

AIG; The Charles Schwab Corporation; Hartford Insurance Group; MassMutual; Merrill Lynch & Co., Inc.; Metropolitan Life Insurance Co.; Morgan Stanley Dean Witter & Company; Mutual of Omaha; New York Life Insurance Company; Principal Financial; Prudential Insurance Company of America; Transamerica Corporation.

Further Reading

Bell, Allison, "Hancock Accord Gets California's OK," *National Underwriter Life & Health,* November 24, 1997, p. 1.

Buley, R. Carlyle, *The American Life Convention, 1906–1952: A Study in the History of Life Insurance,* New York: Appleton-Century-Crofts, 1953.

Concon, Bernard, "The Skeleton in the Closet," *Forbes,* January 24, 2000, p. 60.

Davenport, Carol, "David F. D'Alessandro," *Fortune,* May 22, 1989, p. 154.

Grun, Bernard, *The Timetables of History: A Horizontal Linkage of People and Events,* New York: Simon & Schuster, 1979.

Helman, Christopher, "Stand-Up Brand," *Forbes,* July 9, 2001, p. 127.

Intindola, Brendan, "Provident L&A Will Assume Hancock's DI Book," *National Underwriter Life & Health,* May 25, 1992, p. 12.

James, Marquis, *The Metropolitan Life: A Study in Business Growth,* New York: Viking Press, 1947.

Keller, Morton, *The Life Insurance Enterprise, 1885–1910: A Study in the Limits of Corporate Power,* Cambridge, Mass.: Belknap Press, 1963.

O'Donnell, Terence, *History of Life Insurance in Its Formative Years,* Chicago: American Conservation Company, 1936.

Panko, Ron, "Culture Clash," *Best's Review,* December 2000, p. 101.

Schwab, Emil, ed., *Historical Sketch of the John Hancock Mutual Life Insurance Company of Boston, Massachusetts: A Half Century Completed, 1862–1912,* Boston: John Hancock Printing Shop, 1912.

Thomas, Trevor, "Hancock's IPO Raises $1.7 Billion," *National Underwriter,* January 31, 2000.

—Jim Bowman
—update: Susan Windisch Brown

John Lewis Partnership plc

171 Victoria Street
London SW1E 5NN
United Kingdom
Telephone: (020) 7828 1000
Fax: (020) 7592 6301
Web site: http://www.john-lewis-partnership.co.uk

Partnership
Incorporated: 1929 as John Lewis Partnership Ltd.
Employees: 54,000
Sales: £4.09 billion ($6.04 billion) (2001)
NAIC: 452110 Department Stores; 445110 Supermarkets
and Other Grocery (Except Convenience) Stores;
454110 Electronic Shopping and Mail-Order Houses

John Lewis Partnership plc is unique among large companies in Britain in that it is run for the benefit of its employees, as the majority of its profits are shared among them. Because of the independence this affords, it is perhaps less hungry for publicity than most companies of its size, and outsiders are often surprised to realize how large and successful it is. The company has two main arms, of almost equal size in turnover. The original business was department stores, of which it has 26, a little more than half named John Lewis and the rest under a variety of local monikers (most of which were, at the beginning of the 21st century, in the process of being converted to the John Lewis name). The other arm is supermarkets, of which it has 136, all trading as Waitrose. That these 162 outlets can generate total sales of more than £4 billion ($6 billion) is an indication of the size and efficiency of each unit. The group also includes some factories, which supply the stores with textiles and furniture. John Lewis is also involved in mail-order and e-commerce businesses. It has no overseas operations, and within the United Kingdom its business is mainly concentrated in the south of England.

The business is essentially the creation of two men, John Lewis and his son John Spedan Lewis. The former created the first store and laid down its trading policy; the latter expanded it into a group of stores and gave the company its unique constitu-

tion. Since then the business has continued to thrive under non-family management, but a grandson of the first John Lewis, Peter Lewis, served as chairman from 1972 to 1993, and the ideas of John Spedan Lewis still permeate the whole enterprise.

19th-Century Origins: The Development of the First John Lewis Department Store

The company's first small shop opened in 1864, on part of the site that its main store occupied more than a century later in Oxford Street, London. This street was already well known for its shops, especially those supplying dresses and dress fabrics to the more prosperous classes. Other shops of this kind which were to become very successful included the already well-established Debenham and Freebody (later Debenhams) and Marshall & Snelgrove.

John Lewis was 28 years old when he opened his first shop. He had come to London from Somerset eight years earlier, having served an apprenticeship in the drapery trade. In London he took a job with another Oxford Street drapery shop, Peter Robinson, and became its silk buyer.

The early days were hard and dreary, as John Lewis told his son, but the shop gradually became a success. At first his store specialized in dress fabrics, sewing threads, ribbons, and other trimmings, but then diversified into ready-made clothes, hats, and shoes. He did not advertise, but had a policy of displaying prices clearly, which was not common at that time. He offered a wide assortment, fair dealing, and retained low margins.

By 1875 Lewis was doing well enough to need more space, and he began to take over neighboring properties. With the extra space, he was able to stock more merchandise. From clothing, the store's range broadened to include furniture, carpets, china, and most household goods. During the 1870s Lewis's turnover almost tripled, and it continued growing throughout the 1880s.

By 1895 he was able to rebuild the whole store, which by then had a large corner site with fronts on Oxford Street and Holles Street. The new building occupied six floors, with impressive facades in Renaissance style, and the staff by this time numbered about 150.

In slightly more than 30 years Lewis had created a major department store in one of London's best shopping streets. Even more remarkably, he had done so entirely out of retained profits. In the early years he lived frugally and saved enough of the profits to finance each new step without the need to bring in partners or to turn the business into a joint stock company. The whole store belonged to him alone, and he ran it in a totally autocratic way.

Not until he was 48 did Lewis marry and start to raise a family. His wife was a teacher, 18 years younger than himself, and one of the first women to go to university. She bore him two sons and had a strong influence on them. They received an excellent education and grew up with very different attitudes from those of their father. John Lewis had little education but had strongly individual views; he was an atheist and a liberal and once went to prison for defying a court order in a dispute with his landlord. He was considered a harsh employer, not prone to generosity. Both sons reacted against this hardness in different ways.

Lewis's sons both entered the business on leaving school and were given a quarter share in it upon reaching the age of 21. The younger son, Oswald, soon left the business to study law, provoking a long quarrel with his father, while Spedan became very interested in the business but increasingly critical of his father's methods.

The main issue of contention was staff wages. Spedan was shocked to find that the entire wage bill for 300 employees was a good deal less than the three partners were receiving in interest and profit. To him this was plainly unjust and probably bad for business too. He also discovered inefficiencies in the operation of the store; some departments were trading at a loss, and much of the upper floor space was being wasted. His father, however, angrily rejected all suggestions for change.

John Lewis was over 70 when his sons became partners, but was still full of vigor. Satisfied with the profits the rebuilt store was making, he turned his attention to other things, becoming a member of the London County Council and investing some of his growing fortune in buying a second department store.

Early 20th Century: Adding Peter Jones, Creating the Partnership

The opportunity to do this arose in 1905, when one of his business rivals, Peter Jones, died. Jones had founded another successful store in Sloane Square. Some two miles away from John Lewis's store, it served a different clientele. The business, started in 1877, had grown rapidly and was by this time a limited company. Lewis bought Jones's controlling shareholding and became chairman, but seems not to have taken a close interest in the management of the business.

It proved to be an unrewarding investment. Without the flair of its founder, the store quickly went downhill. Sales dropped by a third, and for six years the company paid no dividends. Eventually, in 1914, Lewis decided to see what his son could do with it. He transferred his shares in the store to Spedan and made him chairman on the condition that he continue working at the Oxford Street store until 5 p.m. each day. Spedan jumped at the chance to try out his ideas, even though it meant giving up most of his evenings to the job.

Following a riding accident a few years earlier, Spedan had spent much time either in hospital or at home, using this time to work out his ideas in detail. At Peter Jones he immediately began to implement them. Pay and working conditions were improved, and sales incentives were introduced. In addition committees were set up to encourage new ideas, management functions were redefined, and new managers were hired. John Lewis became alarmed and demanded his shares back, but Spedan refused to relinquish them. As punishment, his father canceled Spedan's share in the partnership, banished him from Oxford Street, and reinstated Oswald there.

This at least enabled Spedan to give all his time to Peter Jones, and business there improved rapidly under his management. By 1919 the company was making a handsome profit, and John Lewis paid a visit of inspection. He said little to his son, relations between them still being cool, but afterwards told his wife, "That place is a great credit to the boy—a very great credit."

Spedan took his reforms a stage further by introducing a profit-sharing scheme in 1920. Employees became known as partners and received weekly reports on sales and profits through a new house magazine, which also provided a forum for ideas and complaints. At the time, these practices were revolutionary and contrasted sharply with events at Oxford Street, where the employees went on strike for five weeks in 1920, earning the store much bad publicity. Over the next few years, however, there was a general slump in trade, which John Lewis withstood better than Peter Jones. This change in fortunes at last healed the rift between Spedan and his father, who advanced some much needed money to Peter Jones and restored Spedan's share in the Oxford Street business. Around this same time, in 1925 Spedan Lewis introduced the slogan "Never Knowingly Undersold" as the pricing policy for Peter Jones; this well-known motto was eventually adopted by the John Lewis Partnership.

By this time John Lewis was 88 and more or less content to let his sons manage the business. Oswald, however, did not agree with Spedan's radical views, and after two years Spedan persuaded him to give up his share in return for a cash settlement. Oswald was more interested in politics and soon afterwards became a Conservative member of Parliament. From 1926, therefore, Spedan was effectively in control of both businesses and could begin to reorganize the Oxford Street store on the principles established at Peter Jones. All these were swiftly applied except that the transfer of profits had to be delayed until after John Lewis's death, which occurred in 1928. Spedan was left sole owner of the Oxford Street store as well as

Key Dates:

1864: John Lewis opens a draper's shop in Oxford Street, London, and eventually develops it into a full-scale department store.

1905: Peter Jones department store in London is acquired.

1914: John Spedan Lewis, son of the founder, assumes control of Peter Jones and begins making radical changes.

1920: Spedan Lewis introduces a profit-sharing scheme at Peter Jones.

1925: Spedan Lewis introduces the slogan ''Never Knowingly Undersold'' as the pricing policy for Peter Jones.

1928: John Lewis dies; Spedan Lewis assumes full control of the Oxford Street store and of Peter Jones.

1929: Lewis transfers ownership of the company to a new firm called John Lewis Partnership Ltd., which holds the shares in trust for all employees, who in turn become full partners in the business and begin sharing in the profits.

1933: Company acquires its first provincial stores.

1937: Expansion into the food trade occurs with the acquisition of the Waitrose chain of ten grocery shops.

1940: Company pays the Selfridge group £30,000 for 15 provincial department stores operating under various local names, which are retained.

1950s: Waitrose introduces self-service to its shops and begins converting the shops to the supermarket format.

1992: The 100th Waitrose supermarket opens.

1994: First Waitrose food & home store opens in London, marketing a full range of supermarket items along with a selection of household goods from John Lewis department stores.

2000: £300 million, three-year makeover of the department store unit is launched, with local brands being abandoned in favor of creating a nationwide John Lewis chain.

2001: The U.K. arm of Buy.com, an online retailer of electronic goods and computers, is acquired.

majority shareholder in Peter Jones. He immediately converted the former into a public company, John Lewis and Company Ltd. To raise capital for expansion he offered preferred shares to the public, but kept all the ordinary shares in his hands. Then he transferred these and his shares in Peter Jones to another company, John Lewis Partnership Ltd., which was to hold them in trust for the employees. The transfer was not a gift, but was made on very generous terms and was irrevocable. Spedan retained control of the trust for an experimental period.

From then on all employees were considered partners in the business. Spedan worked out an elaborate constitution for the partnership to ensure that all partners were represented in the decision-making process, while at the same time giving the board full powers to manage the business on their behalf. It was a unique structure for a business, devised by a very practical idealist. Having laid these foundations, Spedan and his colleagues turned their energies to building up the business. They proved to

be a very able team. In the 1920s Spedan had begun to recruit men and women from the universities, the best of whom were given quick promotions to important jobs.

The capital raised by the public offer of 1928—and another in 1935—was used to enlarge and modernize the stores. John Lewis acquired two new buildings in seven years, one on the other side of Holles Street, followed by another part of the island site, which the John Lewis store now fills. At the same time Peter Jones was completely rebuilt in stages so that trading could continue. The new building was ultramodern in style, the first in Britain to make full use of curtain walling of steel and glass.

1930s and 1940s: Expanding into the Provinces, Acquiring Waitrose

The company next began to broaden its base by acquiring some provincial stores: two in 1933 and two more the following year. All were in a rundown state, but were gradually made profitable. With six stores in the group there was opportunity for more centralized buying, and a single warehouse was set up in London to service them all.

Most significantly for the future, although the move was not seen that way at the time, the company entered the food trade by buying a chain of ten grocery shops. The business traded as Waitrose, because its first partners were called Waite and Rose, and grew from a single shop in Acton in 1904 to ten in various parts of London by 1937. Like Sainsbury's, Waitrose was at the quality end of the grocery trade and was a well-run business, albeit a small one. As a result of this expansion, the turnover of the John Lewis Partnership grew from £1.25 million in 1928 to £3 million in 1939, and by then the company had some 6,000 partners. In 1940 the business again doubled in size by acquiring 15 more department stores and 4,000 more staff at one stroke.

Encouraged by its success in reviving the four provincial stores it already had, the John Lewis Partnership seized an opportunity to buy all the provincial stores in the Selfridge group. They had never been successful under Selfridge's ownership and were still losing money. Consequently, the John Lewis Partnership was able to buy control of these 15 stores, which had a combined turnover of £3.3 million, for a mere £30,000.

The stores had never traded under Selfridge's name, but had kept their various founders' names and continued to do so when they joined the John Lewis Partnership. Examples were Cole Brothers of Sheffield, Trewin Brothers of Watford, and Caleys of Windsor, all still members of the group.

Their purchase, and the extensions to the Oxford Street store, were to prove a lifesaver over the next few years. By this time Britain was at war, and later in 1940 the main John Lewis building was almost completely destroyed by fire bombs. Four of the John Lewis Partnership's other stores were also destroyed. Had the business not been as widely scattered as it was, this would have been a calamity; as it was, it was just a bad setback. The loss of selling space was matched by shortages of staff and merchandise, which continued for some years after World War II. These shortages, and tight controls on building supplies, delayed further expansion of the John Lewis Partnership until the 1950s.

1950s Through 1970s: Rapid Expansion of Waitrose

Spedan was by then approaching retirement age, and management had largely passed into the hands of the people he had brought into the business. Unlike his father, who never formally retired, Spedan decided to do so at the age of 70, which he reached in 1955. Before retiring he signed over the last of his rights in the business to a corporate trustee. He also wrote two books about the John Lewis Partnership in the hope that its principles would be copied in other businesses. In fact, this did not happen. By 1955 the John Lewis Partnership had acquired the whole of its island site in Oxford Street and began to rebuild its store there. The work had to be done in stages and was not finished until 1960. The new building, still in use, gave the group a bigger selling area in central London than it had ever had before. The other war-damaged stores were also rebuilt at this time, and several more stores were acquired.

The biggest development in the business in the 1950s and 1960s, however, was the rapid expansion of the Waitrose chain. It had more shops than in 1937, but they were all small shops operated on the prewar pattern. In the United States self-service had largely superseded counter service in the 1940s, but retailers in Britain had been unable to experiment with this because of food rationing.

When rationing ended in the early 1950s, Waitrose was among the first British chains to try out self-service. It was also among the first to realize that self-service called for much larger shops. By 1959 it had built seven new-style supermarkets and owned 20 smaller shops. In the 1960s all the smaller shops were replaced by supermarkets. The total reached 50 in 1974 and 70 five years later. The John Lewis Partnership was quicker to embrace the new concept than many traditional food retailers and was rewarded with an increasing share of the retail food trade.

Waitrose became a far more important constituent of the John Lewis Partnership than it had been previously. Its contribution to group turnover jumped from under 15 percent in the early 1960s to over 40 percent by 1979. It developed its own trading style and own label products as well as its own distribution network and management hierarchy within the group.

Continued Expansion into the 21st Century

Department stores, however, remained by far the more profitable part of the business, and investment in these continued. In the 1970s three new stores were started under the John Lewis name (in Edinburgh, Milton Keynes, and Brent Cross, London), and during the 1980s another seven were built or acquired from other owners. These new stores were much bigger than was the norm outside London. Some of the older stores were closed and others rebuilt or enlarged. As a result, the combined turnover of department stores rose almost as fast in the 1980s as that of the Waitrose food shops. Meanwhile, in 1988, the company expanded its manufacturing operations through the purchase of J.H. Birtwistle and Company, a textile supplier based in Lancashire. This brought to three the number of textile suppliers owned by John Lewis Partnership, the company having decades earlier acquired two leading makers of household textiles, Herbert Parkinson, also based in Lancashire, and Stead McAlpin and Company, based in Cumbria.

By the end of the 1980s, almost 40,000 people shared the fruits of this business. Profits reached a peak in 1988 and 1989 of £131 million before taxes, of which £47 million was distributed among the employees.

During the recessionary period of the early 1990s, profits and the profit-sharing payout fell, totaling, for example, £93.2 million and £34.5 million, respectively, in 1993. By this time there were more than 100 Waitrose supermarkets and the partnership ran 22 department stores. The company expanded into the mail-order sector in 1993 with the purchase of Findlater Mackie Todd & Co., which sold wine through the mail and was the basis for Waitrose Wine Direct. Flowers Direct and Beer Direct were added later. Also in 1993 Stuart Hampson succeeded Peter Lewis to become the fourth chairman of the partnership. Hampson joined John Lewis in 1982, switching from a career as a high-ranking civil servant. During 1994, the first Waitrose food & home store opened in London's south end, marketing a full range of supermarket items along with a selection of household goods from John Lewis department stores.

Waitrose lost some ground during the early 1990s as its main rivals began opening on Sundays, in advance of a change in the law, and moved more rapidly to implement high-tech supply and distribution systems. It was not until 1995 that Waitrose began gaining additional revenues from opening its stores on Sundays and also completed the installation of electronic point-of-sale and ordering systems, which gave it better control over inventory and the ability to automatically reorder stock. The new initiatives had an almost immediate effect on sales, with Waitrose posting a 13 percent increase for the year ending in January 1996. This helped lift pretax profits to a record £150 million, an increase of 28 percent. The profit-sharing payout for that year amounted to £57 million, which translated into a bonus of 15 percent of salary.

From fiscal 1994 through fiscal 1998, the modernizing Waitrose chain saw its sales increase by 50 percent and its profits triple. Although continuing to rely on word-of-mouth advertising over the huge television ad expenditures of its larger rivals Tesco, Sainsbury's, and Safeway, Waitrose did step up its print advertising budget during 1998 in a campaign aimed at encouraging its customers to spend more money. By 1999 the number of Waitrose outlets had been increased to more than 130. The John Lewis department store operation was also continuing its slow but steady expansion, with two stores opened in 1999—in Bluewater, Kent, and in Glasgow—bringing the total to 25. Also during 1999, a number of John Lewis partners began pushing for a breakup of the partnership through the sale or stock market flotation of the firm, a move that might have garnered each partner as much as £100,000. Hampson, however, strongly opposed the dissolution of the partnership and also noted that, according to the legal documents put together by John Spedan Lewis, the John Lewis trust could not be dissolved without a full Act of Parliament. In any event, at a meeting of representatives of John Lewis and Waitrose stores held in September 1999, little support for an end to the partnership was voiced, bringing at least a temporary end to talk of a sale.

Pressure for a breakup had arisen at least in part from a dropoff in sales during the first half of fiscal 2000. The group had a stronger second half, but pretax profits for the full year did fall 21 percent from the record level of the previous year. Profit-sharing bonuses totaled £78 million, compared to £98 million for fiscal 1999. During 2000 the company acquired 11 shops from Somerfield plc, which were then converted to Waitrose outlets. That year also saw the partnership enter the burgeoning e-commerce sector with the launch of the John Lewis Now online shopping service and the purchase of a 40 percent interest in Last Mile Solutions, an Internet food retailer later renamed Ocado. This was accompanied by the launch of Waitrose online shopping services for both home and workplaces, as well as the 2001 acquisition of the U.K. arm of Buy.com, an online retailer of electronic goods and computers.

Meanwhile, the profits of John Lewis Partnership were continuing to decline in large measure because of heightened competition for the John Lewis department stores that was coming from discounters, who were forcing prices down. In late 2000 the company announced that it would begin a £300 million, three-year makeover of its 25-unit department store unit. In a perhaps belated modernizing of the operations, all of the stores not using the John Lewis name, with the exception of the flagship Peter Jones store (which was itself in the midst of an £80 million, three-year redesign), would begin doing so by the end of the restructuring/remodeling period. This would create a unified, nationwide chain under the John Lewis name.

While sales surpassed the £4 billion mark for the first time for the year ending in January 2001, pretax profits fell once again, dropping 23 percent to £149.6 million. Profits were affected by the tough retailing environment, which was being hit by price deflation, as well as by the increased investments being made to restructure the department store operations and for the Internet initiatives. The profit-sharing payout for the 53,000 partners amounted to £58.1 million, equivalent to a 10 percent bonus, compared to the 15 percent of the preceding year. It appeared likely that some of the partners might once again press for the dissolving of the partnership. Hampson, however, continued to emphasize that the increased investments that were being made would pay off more handsomely for the partners in the long run than would a one-time payout generated by the sale or flotation of the partnership.

Principal Subsidiaries

John Lewis Partnership Trust Ltd.; John Lewis plc; Bainbridge & Co. Ltd.; Bonds (Norwich) Ltd.; Cavendish Textiles Ltd.; Cole Brothers Ltd.; Herbert Parkinson Ltd.; J.H. Birtwistle and Company Ltd.; John Lewis Building Ltd.; John Lewis Construction Ltd.; John Lewis Overseas Ltd.; John Lewis Properties plc; John Lewis Transport Ltd.; Leckford Mushrooms Ltd.; Odney Estate Ltd.; Peter Jones Ltd.; Stead McAlpin and Company Ltd.; Suburban & Provincial Contracts Ltd.; Suburban & Provincial Stores Ltd.; The Leckford Estate Ltd.; Waitrose Ltd.

Principal Competitors

Marks & Spencer p.l.c.; Tesco PLC; J Sainsbury plc; ASDA Group Limited; Arcadia Group plc; NEXT plc; Safeway plc; Debenhams plc; Mothercare plc; House of Fraser PLC; Somerfield plc; Wm. Morrison Supermarkets PLC.

Further Reading

Bidlake, Suzanne, "A Shopping Partner Is for Life," *Marketing,* June 27, 1991, p. 22.

Bradley, Keith, and Simon Taylor, *Business Performance in the Retail Sector: The Experience of the John Lewis Partnership,* Oxford: Clarendon Press, 1992, 194 p.

Brown, Malcolm, "Stuart Hampson," *Management Today,* August 1994, pp. 44, 46.

Brown-Humes, Christopher, "Goodwill Store," *Financial Times,* November 6, 1996, p. 19.

Day, Julia, "Waitrose Wises Up to Nineties Values," *Marketing Week,* June 4, 1998, pp. 21–22.

"The John Lewis Partnership," *Retail and Consumer Products,* September 1994, pp. 77+.

"John Lewis Profits Slump As Shoppers Demand Price Cuts," *Independent* (U.K.), September 15, 2000, p. 18.

Kennedy, Carol, *The Merchant Princes: Family, Fortune, and Philanthropy,* London: Hutchinson, 2000, 309 p.

Lewis, John Spedan, *Fairer Shares,* London: Staples Press, 1954.

——, *Partnership for All,* London: John Lewis Partnership, 1948.

Macpherson, Hugh, ed., *John Spedan Lewis, 1885–1963, Remembered by Some of His Contemporaries in the Centenary Year of His Birth,* London: John Lewis Partnership, 1985.

Morrison, Dianne See, "Will a Bargain Boost John Lewis's Online Prospects?," *New Media Age,* March 22, 2001, p. 38.

Rigby, Rhymer, "Never Knowingly Under-Generous," *Management Today,* October 1998, p. 126.

Spivey, Nigel, "The Dinosaur That Is Never Knowingly Undersold," *Financial Times,* March 22, 1997, p. 20.

"A Stake in the Store," *Economist,* June 11, 1994, p. 60.

—John Swan
—update: David E. Salamie

KAMAN

Kaman Corporation

1332 Blue Hills Avenue
Bloomfield, Connecticut 06002
U.S.A.
Telephone: (860) 243-7100
Fax: (203) 243-6365
Web site: http://www.kaman.com

Public Company
Incorporated: 1945 as Kaman Aircraft
Employees: 4,200
Sales: $1.03 billion (2000)
Stock Exchanges: NASDAQ
Ticker Symbol: KAMNA
NAIC: 336412 Aircraft Engine and Engine Parts
   Manufacturing; 336413 Other Aircraft Parts and
   Auxiliary Equipment Manufacturing; 334511 Search,
   Detection, Navigation, Guidance, Aeronautical, and
   Nautical System and Instrument Manufacturing;
   42183 Industrial Machinery and Equipment Whole-
   salers; 339992 Musical Instrument Manufacturing

Kaman Corporation develops and manufactures high-tech products and provides technical services for government, industrial, and commercial markets. Its operations are broken into three primary segments: Aerospace, Industrial Distribution, and Music Distribution. The company's Aerospace division, which serves U.S. defense, foreign government, and commercial markets, produces helicopters and niche-market products for aircraft applications. Kaman's Industrial Distribution division produces parts and equipment for virtually every sector of U.S. industry. The company's Music Distribution division is one of the world's largest distributors of guitars and other musical instruments and accessories. Kaman has a rich history that parallels the classic American success story of its namesake founder.

An Early Love of Aviation in the 1930s

Kaman is the progeny of American paragon Charles H. Kaman, an inventor, entrepreneur, musician, humanitarian, and visionary. He was born in 1919 and raised in Washington, D.C. His father, a German immigrant, was a construction supervisor who managed work on the Supreme Court building and Union Station. Charles Kaman demonstrated an early interest in aviation design. During the 1930s, he competed in the city's model airplane design contests held at the local playground. He also showed an enthusiasm for music. Kaman became an accomplished guitar player as a teenager and even turned down an offer to play with the Tommy Dorsey band for an alluring $75 per week.

Kaman continued to pursue his interest in aviation during college. For a contest held in Washington, D.C., he made a model plane, which took more than 100 hours to build, was made of balsa wood, covered with an ultra-thin film, and driven by a rubber band. Kaman wound the propeller 1,500 times and asked the judge to clock his warm-up flight. After setting an unofficial record for time aloft, Kaman became determined to surpass his own record. He decided to wind the propeller 3,500 times, using an eggbeater. At about 3,000 turns the band snapped and the plane imploded. Nevertheless, the episode cemented his desire to become an innovator in the burgeoning aviation field.

Kaman graduated magna cum laude with a Bachelor of Aeronautical Engineering degree in 1940 from Washington's Catholic University. Although he had dreamed since childhood of becoming a professional pilot, a severe infection following a tonsillectomy that left him deaf in one ear made that an impossibility. Instead of piloting flying machines, Kaman decided to build them. After college, he accepted a position with aviation pioneer United Aircraft (the forerunner of United Technologies Corporation). He went to work in the company's helicopter division, Hamilton Standard, which was marshaled by renowned inventor Igor Sikorsky. Kaman was told to help design propellers.

The chief dilemma facing helicopter engineers during the industry's inception was stability and control. Engineers were challenged to figure out how to devise a machine that could be easily maneuvered and landed, particularly in high winds. Aside from stability and control, helicopters in the early 1940s suffered from several problems. Vibration was a major obstacle. Because of the way in which the rotor was controlled from its

204

hub, the entire aircraft would vibrate, putting stress on the machine that reduced its durability and dependability.

Kaman's contributions were quickly recognized at United, and by 1943 he had become head of aerodynamics. Despite his success at United, Kaman became frustrated by the company's lack of attention to his ideas. Specifically, Kaman had suggested an improvement that might increase the stability of United's helicopters. He wanted to put flaps on the main rotor and scrap the tail rotor altogether to improve control. On his own time, Kaman built a homemade rig to test his theories. He fashioned the contraption in his mother's garage using junk parts, including an engine from a 1933 Pontiac, the rear end of an old Dodge, and a bathroom scale.

Kaman's initial designs failed. But after several weeks of experimenting he was able to build a device that incorporated his revolutionary servo-flap rotor control system. The new design significantly reduced vibration. It also required much less force by the pilot to maneuver the aircraft, thus improving stability and control. Excited by his discovery, Kaman approached the manager of engineering at United and even demonstrated his rotor blade test rig. "Charlie, we have our inventor at United Aircraft," explained his supervisor. "His name is Igor Sikorsky. We don't need another one."

Going It Alone: 1940s–50s

Because United was not interested in his ideas, Kaman decided to go to work for an employer who would put his theories into practice—himself. With $2,000 and some rudimentary laboratory equipment, Kaman started a company that would become a multimillion-dollar corporation, a leader in aviation technology, and, among other accomplishments, a guitar supplier to rock stars. Kaman shaped his new enterprise around the contraption he made in his mother's garage. He raised development funds by holding weekend flying shows with his homemade aircraft, the K-125, at Bradley Field, where he solicited observers to invest in his idea.

Kaman was able to generate enough capital to build a new helicopter, the K-190, by 1948. It incorporated a dual-rotor system (but no tail rotor) and was touted as the most stable, easy-to-fly helicopter ever built. To reinforce his claim of stability, Kaman conducted a public relations coup in November 1948 at Bradley Field. Ann Griffin, a young housewife with virtually no flying experience, jumped into the cockpit of the exotic contraption and flew it for ten minutes before an astonished audience. The stunt was widely publicized and resulted in an infusion of capital into Kaman's company. Most important, it helped Kaman to get his first helicopter orders.

Kaman, like many of his helicopter industry contemporaries, had grand visions for his flying machines. Many engineers believed that the helicopter would eventually replace the automobile as the vehicle of choice for families. Each family would have a helicopter in its back yard or on its roof. People would zip to work, to the grocery store, or even to vacation destinations in a matter of minutes or hours. Unfortunately, physical realities emerged that made the concept infeasible given 20th-century technology. Thus Kaman determined that the immediate future of his company was in the commercial and defense markets.

Kaman achieved important technical breakthroughs during the late 1940s and 1950s. In 1951, for instance, he designed the world's first gas-turbine powered helicopter. The innovation became a major industry influence on the design of helicopter power systems through the mid-1990s. Despite technical advances, though, Kaman Aircraft realized spotty financial success. Kaman was unsuccessful at marketing his K-225 (successor to the K-125) as a crop duster. In addition, although descendants of the K-190 and K-225 models were purchased for use in search and rescue missions in the 1950s, his servo-flap design never found a mass market.

Kaman's helicopters, which became known as synchropters, had many advantages over other machines. Their chief drawback, however, was slowness. As the military increased its emphasis on speed during the 1950s and 1960s, synchropters lost favor to speedier designs that were more appropriate for battle. Kaman's machines still found demand in a variety of military applications, however, that required improved control and stability (search and rescue operations and heavy lifting jobs, for example), particularly during the Korean War.

One of Kaman Aircraft's crowning achievements in the helicopter industry was its creation of the UH-2 utility helicopter. Kaman won the contract to design the machine in a contest. The project posed a formidable challenge because of the extremely demanding requirements set forth by the Navy. It wanted a vehicle that could fly at night for several hundred miles with no external navigation. It also had to be able to pick up downed pilots at sea under icy conditions and then return to a different location. Because of the complexity of the instrumentation, Kaman found that the machine also had to have less than one-tenth of a G of vibration to make the display panel readable for the pilot. Kaman's UH-2 met the requirements and was introduced into service in 1963.

In addition to the UH-2, other successful Kaman helicopter designs included the H-43 Husky and the SH-2. The former was used during Vietnam to rescue downed pilots, and was the first helicopter to perform with no loss of life or accidents attributable to the aircraft. The SH-2, an antisubmarine aircraft, still was being used by the Navy in the early 1990s. Throughout the 1950s and early 1960s, Kaman Aircraft's inventions relating to airplanes, rotors, drones, and other technologies made pivotal contributions to the field of aviation. Among its most notable contributions were the first servo-controlled rotor, gas-turbine helicopter, twin-turbine helicopter, all-composite rotor blade, and remotely controlled helicopter. Kaman also set numerous records related to time-to-climb, altitude, as well as other factors.

Key Dates:

1945: Kaman Aircraft is established.
1948: Kaman introduces the K-190 helicopter.
1951: Kaman designs the world's first gas-turbine powered helicopter.
1963: Kaman's UH-2 utility helicopter is introduced into the U.S. Navy.
1966: Ovation Instruments is founded.
1968: Kaman Sciences is formed.
1971: Broad campaign of expansion and diversification, through a series of mergers and acquisitions, is begun.
1994: Kaman's new K-MAX "aerial truck" helicopter is certified by the FAA.
1999: Paul Kuhn becomes Kaman's president and CEO, when founder Charles Kaman retires.

Although Kaman managed to show a profit every year during the 1950s and early 1960s, its sales fluctuated because of its dependence on military contracts. In the early 1960s, President John F. Kennedy's administration ordered 220 Seasprite helicopters from Kaman. Five days later, however, Kennedy was assassinated. President Johnson rescinded the order and Kaman's helicopter division was devastated.

Diversification and Expansion: 1960s–80s

The detrimental impact of the loss of the large Pentagon contract was diminished by Kaman's other operations. Since the late 1950s, Kaman had been trying to reduce its dependence on defense contracts, particularly related to helicopters. The board of directors determined that Kaman should have three basic elements to its business: defense, industrial, and commercial. Over time, they decided, each division would be built to approximately one-third of company sales. In the 1950s, Kaman began expanding into aerospace parts manufacturing, aerodynamics subcontracting, and advanced nuclear research, among other defense and industry-related activities. As a result of its diversification, Kaman continued to post profits throughout the 1960s and 1970s.

One of Kaman's most intriguing ventures away from the helicopter business involved musical instruments. In part because of his own interest in playing the guitar, Kaman had long been interested in the music business. In the early 1960s, he set out to develop his own guitar. He sought help from Martin, a Pennsylvania-based manufacturer of acoustic guitars. Kaman was surprised at the primitive methods that Martin and other companies were still using to produce the instruments. He believed that he could improve both the guitars and the production process by incorporating modern manufacturing techniques and aerospace technology.

The owners of Martin refused to sell their company, so Kaman started his own operation. He drew on his knowledge of harmonics, which he gleaned from building helicopter rotors, to build a guitar with composites that still had a natural sound. "In a helicopter, you take vibration out," Kaman explained in the July

26, 1993 *Business Week.* "In a guitar you put it in." The end result of Kaman's early efforts was the Ovation guitar, a top industry seller distinguished by its round-back design. Kaman Music Corporation met with success during the late 1960s and particularly beginning in the 1970s by developing new products and acquiring other manufacturers. In 1974, Kaman's son, C. William Kaman II, started his career making guitars at Kaman Music Corporation. He became president of that division in 1986.

Kaman continued to build its consumer and defense-related businesses throughout the 1960s and 1970s. In addition, it expanded into several industrial segments through merger and acquisition beginning in 1971. In that year, Kaman purchased three industrial distribution businesses, launching a buying spree that would propel Kaman Corporation into the *Fortune* 500 by the 1980s. Kaman purchased more than 30 industrial companies during the 1970s and 1980s, making its Kaman Bearing and Supply subsidiary the third largest U.S. industrial distributor. By 1989, that division accounted for roughly half of Kaman Corporation's revenues. Kaman Bearing and Supply had 156 offices in the United States and Canada and supplied more than 750,000 different parts to every major industry.

Charles Kaman had success integrating the companies that he acquired into a cohesive whole. When appraising buyout candidates, Kaman looked for situations in which both companies stood to gain from each other's competencies. A musical instrument manufacturer, for example, might benefit from Kaman's marketing and distribution channels while Kaman would get access to new production facilities or patented processes or products. In addition, he applied years of experience in determining the integrity and substance of the candidate. "After 45 years I just walk through and I've got it in about 10 minutes, maybe half-an-hour," Kaman told *Enterprise.* "You can read it. . . . When we visit a military base I can tell you what the base commander is like by the attitude of the sentry at the guard house—are we greeted with smiles, does he know what's going on?"

At his home office Kaman set the leadership example that permeated his organization. Kaman was his company's major stockholder, but unlike most executives he had purchased all of his stock on the open market rather than receiving it as compensation, reflecting his faith in the company. In addition, he paid himself a relatively low salary compared with other chief executive officers of companies of similar size, and much of it was tied to the company's performance. Kaman believed in direct communication and candor and advocated empowering workers and recognizing their contributions. "There's no politicking, no vying for power around here," stated Kaman in *Enterprise.* "It's just straight-arrow stuff." Kaman Corporation was recognized for its acute management team and fruitful working environment.

Kaman continued to diversify into new markets and expand its defense, industrial, and consumer divisions during the 1970s and 1980s. Significantly, Kaman reopened its helicopter production line in 1981. It began manufacturing an updated version of its old Seasprite helicopter called the SH-2F, or LAMPS (Light Airborne Multi-purpose System) for the Navy, which wanted to use it as a submarine hunter and utility craft. The SH-2F had Kaman's original servo-flap system as well as a tail rotor. Renewed interest in the servo-flap design was partially a result of new technology and materials that made it more feasible for integration into new helicopters.

As Kaman expanded into new markets and revived old ones, its revenues continued to swell during the 1980s. Sales topped $380 million in 1983, about $6.4 million of which was net income. Receipts increased to $556 million by 1985 and then past $760 million in 1988 as net earnings rose past the $25 million mark. Likewise, Kaman's workforce increased from 4,800 in the early 1980s to nearly 6,500 by 1989. Although sales of musical instruments languished, defense-related work boomed. Kaman continued to be a powerful influence in the high-tech defense arena. One of the company's projects in 1986 was an $8.5 million contract to build an electromagnetic coil gun, a high-tech cannon that used synchronized magnetic waves to fire projectiles at a velocity of 2.5 miles per second.

Ongoing Humanitarian Initiatives and a New Kaman President by 1990

Besides his lauded achievements in aviation and technology, Kaman was also well known for another of his passions, breeding guide dogs for the blind. When a blind boyhood friend had his life improved by a guide dog, Kaman became interested in guide dogs. To improve blind people's access to the dogs, Kaman and his wife launched the Fieldco Guide Dog Foundation, a nonprofit foundation that bred and trained dogs for the blind, in 1960.

Kaman handled his dog breeding operation in the same way he managed his business affairs. He applied rigorous breeding standards and was able to gradually weed out genetic defects, particularly susceptibility to certain disease strains that traditionally plagued guide dogs. The Kamans opened their own school in 1981 to match dogs with owners. The school provided dogs to recipients for $150 in the early 1990s, a mere fraction of the $17,500 training cost. In 1990, Fieldco launched an initiative to begin matching 100 owner and dog teams annually over the next decade.

Charles Kaman stepped aside as president of Kaman Corporation in 1990 at the age of 71, but remained chief executive and chairman of the board. He was succeeded by Harvey S. Levenson. Levenson took the reins just as the company was slipping into a downturn. After doubling its sales between 1980 and 1989, Kaman suffered setbacks primarily attributable to defense industry cutbacks. Several of its contracts ran out and new federal defense spending programs were capped in the wake of the post-Cold War military transition. Net earnings dropped to $8.7 million in 1989 and the rampant revenue growth achieved during much of the 1980s waned.

Adapting to Defense Spending Cutbacks in the 1990s

As defense dollars ebbed, Kaman adjusted to the new environment by restructuring and cutting its workforce to about 5,300 employees by 1993. The company posted a disappointing loss in 1993, mostly as a result of restructuring costs, and total revenues remained below $800 million. Nevertheless, Kaman's strong performance in its industrial technologies, distribution, and music businesses had allowed it to remain profitable between 1990 and 1992. Furthermore, the company held a strong technological edge in its core markets and was solidly posi-

tioned for future growth. Virtually every mass-produced aircraft in the world already utilized Kaman parts, which secured its dominant market presence.

Kaman Music became the largest independent distributor of musical instruments in the United States with more than 13,000 products when it acquired Hamer Guitars, a $100 million guitar manufacturer, in the early 1990s. Boosting that segment's credibility was a long list of star performers who were using Kaman's guitars (and other equipment), including Glen Campbell, Richie Sambora of Bon Jovi, and Phil Collins. By 1993, in fact, music and consumer products comprised about 20 percent of Kaman's total sales. Industrial products and distribution activities represented about 43 percent and defense-related goods and services comprised the remainder of sales.

Kaman offset its defense-related losses by repositioning its helicopter products for use in commercial markets. In 1994, the company's breakthrough K-MAX helicopter was certified by the Federal Aviation Administration. The K-MAX was touted as an "aerial truck" and was designed specifically for repetitive heavy lifting. The K-MAX could lift three tons, more than its weight, and was particularly suited to logging in environmentally sensitive areas, fire fighting, construction, heavy equipment transportation, and a variety of specialty and industrial uses. The helicopter sold for $3.5 million or could be leased for $1 million per thousand hours of use. Kaman's latest helicopter represented the culmination of a lifetime of industry experience. By the end of 1995, the K-MAX was operating in the U.S., Canadian, European, and South American markets.

At the end of 1995, the company's president and COO, Harvey Levenson, retired. Charles Kaman, who still held the positions of CEO and chairman, reassumed the office of president that he had vacated just five years earlier. The second half of the 1990s was marked by a series of honors and awards for the company leader. In 1995, the Department of Defense awarded him its Distinguished Public Service Medal, and in 1996, he was both inducted into the Naval Aviation Hall of Honor and awarded the National Medal of Technology. During the following two years, Kaman received the National Aeronautic Association's Wright Brothers Memorial Trophy and was awarded the Spirit of St. Louis Medal by the American Society of Mechanical Engineers.

As the 1990s progressed, Kaman Corporation continued to focus on building smaller, lightweight aircraft that could nonetheless carry heavy loads. One of its most notable successes was the decision to refurbish its SH-2 Seasprite helicopters and market them to overseas navies. The company took the original SH-2s, which the U.S. Navy has ceased to purchase, and retrofitted them with new avionics, engines, and cockpits. In 1996 and 1997, Kaman won $1 billion in orders for the refurbished Seasprites from Egypt, Australia, and New Zealand. The contracts helped boost Kaman's income substantially, allowing it in 1997 to top $1 billion in annual revenue for the first time in company history.

Another major source of the record revenue for fiscal 1997 was the company's sale of its 40-year-old Kaman Sciences subsidiary. Kaman sold the subsidiary, which provided software support and research to government agencies, to ITT Industries for $135 million.

Changing of the Guard at the End of the 20th Century

By 1998, Charles Kaman was nearing 80. Speculation about who would replace him was pervasive, but the company was offering no information on its succession plan. In August 1998, one possible successor—Kaman's son C. William Kaman II—retired from his position as head of the company's music division, announcing that he would no longer be involved in the day-to-day operations of the business. That same month, the elder Kaman suffered a mild stroke and spent the remainder of the year convalescing. In December 1998, the company announced that it would begin searching for a new CEO. Kaman continued to serve as CEO while the search was conducted.

In July 1999, the company announced that Paul Kuhn would become Kaman Corporation's new CEO. Kuhn had served previously as senior vice-president of operations for the aerospace engine businesses of Coltec Industries.

Kaman relinquished his seat as CEO, but kept his position as chairman of the board. Charles Kaman's health soon became an issue for the company again. In June 2000, the 81-year-old was hospitalized with pneumonia. In August, his condition led the company to transfer his majority voting power to two committees, which included Kaman family members. In March 2001, the company announced that its founder and leader for more than half a century would not be seeking reelection to its board of directors. Kuhn was elected chairman of the board.

Looking Ahead to the 21st Century

At the beginning of the new century, some industry analysts and Kaman shareholders believed that the company had become a melting pot of businesses that did not belong together, and anticipated a breakup and sale. In Kaman's annual meeting held in April 2001, however, Kuhn told shareholders that he did not plan to sell off any of the company's businesses. Rather, he announced, he intended to seek acquisitions, especially in the aerospace sector. Kuhn also said that he planned to expand Kaman's industrial and music distribution operations in geographic areas where its presence was weak.

Principal Subsidiaries

Kaman Aerospace Corporation; Kamatics Corporation; Kaman Industrial Technologies Corporation; Kaman Music Corporation.

Principal Divisions

Aerospace; Industrial Distribution; Music Distribution.

Principal Competitors

United Technologies Corporation; General Dynamics Corporation; Raytheon Company; Lockheed Martin Corporation; Bell Helicopter; Yamaha Corporation; Gibson Musical Instruments; Fender Musical Instruments Corporation; C.F. Martin & Co., Inc.

Further Reading

Birchard, Bill, "The Art of Acquisition," *Enterprise*, Fall 1989, p. 9.

Gertzen, Ian, "Kaman Tightening Workforce," *Norwich Bulletin*, September 10, 1993, p. 1.

Kaman, Charles, in *Rotor Wing International*, May 1991.

Lehrer, Linda, "Charles Kaman, Who Founded His Own *Fortune* 500 Company, Now Takes Time Out to Raise and Train Dogs That Help the Blind," *Trump's Guiding Light*, September 1990.

Nagy, Barbara, "Inventor, Musician, Businessman, Samaritan: A Half Century After He Founded It, Where Will Charlie Kaman Lead His Company Next?," *Hartford Courant*, November 17, 1997, p. D10.

North, Sterling, "A Defensive Move: Kaman Corp. Turns from Whirlybirds to Star Wars," *New England Business*, November 17, 1986, p. 53.

Rose, Peter, "Kaman Industries Goes High-Tech," *Idaho Business Review*, May 2, 1994, p. A10.

Smart, Tim, "What Do Dogs, Guitars, and Choppers Have in Common?," *Business Week*, July 26, 1993.

Stuller, Jay, "The Taming of the Copter," *Air & Space*, December 1990, p. 92.

Valvo, Vincent Michael, "Kaman: Innovation and Ovation," *Intercorp*, May 29, 1987, p. 1.

—Dave Mote
—update: Shawna Brynildssen

Kaplan, Inc.

888 7th Avenue, 23rd Floor
New York, New York 10106
U.S.A.
Telephone: (212) 492-5800
Toll Free: (800) 527-8378
Fax: (212) 492-5933
Web site: http://www.kaplan.com

*Wholly Owned Subsidiary of The Washington Post
    Company*
Incorporated: 1938
Employees: 16,198
Sales: $538.5 million (2000)
NAIC: 611691 Exam Preparation and Tutoring; 61163
    Language Schools; 611710 Educational Support
    Services; 51121 Software Publishers; 511130 Book
    Publishers; 61131 Colleges, Universities, and
    Professional Schools; 61141 Business and Secretarial
    Schools; 61143 Professional and Management
    Development Training; 56131 Employment Placement
    Agencies

Kaplan, Inc. is the leading provider of test preparation services in the United States. The company offers preparatory classes for a wide range of standardized examinations including the Scholastic Assessment Test (SAT) and the Graduate Record Exam (GRE), as well as a number of professional licensing examinations. Kaplan also publishes books and software to assist with test preparation, and it offers many services online. Other areas of activity include after-school learning programs for kindergarten through 12th grade students, college admissions counseling, corporate recruitment services, and college-level education offered through a system of more than 30 bricks-and-mortar schools and several Internet sites. A subsidiary of The Washington Post Company since 1984, Kaplan, Inc. has been growing rapidly since the mid-1990s under CEO Jonathan Grayer.

Early Years

The corporation known as Kaplan, Inc. traces its roots to a Brooklyn, New York basement in 1938, where company founder Stanley Kaplan first began tutoring students for a living. Kaplan, born in 1919 to Jewish immigrant parents, got his first experience as a tutor while in elementary school, where he paid friends a nickel apiece to let him help them with their math. Later, in high school, he earned 25 cents an hour preparing his classmates for the New York State Regents exam. After graduating from New York's City College, Kaplan expected to attend medical school, but he was not accepted. Returning to his love of teaching, he started a business in his basement tutoring elementary and high school students, as well as new immigrants seeking to learn English.

Kaplan was first introduced to the Scholastic Aptitude Test, as it was then known, by a high school student he was tutoring in algebra, and he quickly saw its potential to boost his business. In 1946 he began to offer a 16-session preparatory class, charging $135. Kaplan reportedly would hold a party for each one of his classes after the test was taken, where he would ask every student to tell him one question from it. These were then used to assemble a rough version of the exam for future classes to study. This practice helped earn him the enmity of the Educational Testing Service (ETS), administrators of the exam, who considered having the New York state legislature make Kaplan's tutoring illegal. Although it ultimately did not go that far, the ETS took a public stance that the SAT was uncoachable, and tried to discourage test-takers from using preparatory courses.

The creation of Kaplan's SAT prep course was fortuitously timed, as it coincided with the return from World War II of large numbers of college-bound ex-servicemen. Business was soon booming, and Kaplan later moved from his basement into a larger office space. During the 1950s and 1960s courses for other tests such as the Medical College Admissions Test (MCAT), Law School Admissions Test (LSAT), and Graduate Record Exam (GRE) were added to the growing company's offerings. Word of the preparatory courses spread, and students began coming from around the country to take Kaplan's classes.

In 1970, still operating solely in the New York metropolitan area, Kaplan opened his first branch out of town, in Philadelphia, and the company soon added other locations around the country. By 1975 Kaplan was operating a total of 75 educational centers and reaching 70,000 students per year. During the decade the firm (now known as Stanley H. Kaplan Educational Centers) also broadened its scope, adding courses for the Test of English as a Foreign Language (TOEFL) and English as a Second Language (ESL), among others.

Despite their popularity, test preparation courses continued to be looked at by some as offering little of value, and in the late 1970s the Federal Trade Commission (FTC) investigated Kaplan and several of its competitors. The published report confirmed Kaplan's contention that the courses worked, however, stating that those who took them scored an average of 50 points higher on the 1,600-point SAT than those who did not. Kaplan claimed vindication, while at the same time insisting that the number of points each student's score was raised was actually higher than what the FTC had found.

1984 Sale to The Washington Post Company

In 1984, with nearly half a century of teaching under his belt, Stanley Kaplan sold his business for a reported $33 million to The Washington Post Company, staying on as chief executive. Much of the proceeds from the sale went to the Rita J. and Stanley H. Kaplan Family Foundation, a charitable organization that supported cultural, educational, and health programs, which Stanley Kaplan also ran.

The company's business had grown a great deal during its first half-century, but in many respects the methods for tutoring students had not significantly changed. Having a virtual monopoly on the field of test preparation, Kaplan's firm was reportedly becoming complacent in its middle age. Sensing an opportunity, a competitor emerged in 1981 that directly targeted the company's weaknesses. The Princeton Review, founded by John Katzman in a New York apartment (and having no connection to Princeton University, though Katzman was a graduate of that institution), grew quickly and offered an irreverent, offbeat image compared with the more studious Kaplan. Princeton Review's classes reportedly were smaller and more dynamic than the industry leader's, and the company charged a premium price for its services. In the mid-1980s Princeton began to publish study materials for tests, something that Kaplan had never done and continued to avoid, fearing they might take people away from its courses. By the early 1990s Princeton had grown into a strong contender for Kaplan's position as industry leader, and in fact claimed more SAT prep course students than Kaplan, which still had larger revenues due to its wider range of activities. Princeton's advertising campaigns took direct aim at Kaplan, using such sarcastic tag lines as, "First he lost his

students . . . then he lost his mind." With the upstart now gaining on it, Kaplan was forced to respond, and it issued its first test preparation books in 1993. The company also began to expand its services abroad, opening centers in Europe, Asia, and South America.

The competition continued to heat up, however, with the decidedly irreverent Princeton tweaking Kaplan's nose in 1994 when it registered the Internet domain name of Kaplan.com. Computer users who reached the deceptively named site were immediately informed that they were at the Princeton Review and were asked to add to a list of negative comments about Kaplan. Kaplan sued within four days of the site's launch. The case was later resolved through arbitration, though the legal fees cost Kaplan a reported $30,000. The two antagonists had some months earlier signed a 23-page agreement in which they pledged not to misrepresent themselves or each other in their ads, with rules provided for resolving any disputes that might arise.

Turnaround: 1994–95

Since the early 1990s Kaplan had been operating in the red, with annual losses reportedly reaching the millions. Princeton was continuing to gain ground, and Kaplan needed a strong leader to get it back on track. In June 1994 the company promoted a relative newcomer, 29-year-old Jonathan Grayer, to the posts of president and CEO. Grayer, a Harvard graduate, had worked for Post unit *Newsweek* magazine's marketing department before starting at Kaplan in 1991 as a regional operations director. He quickly drew notice for his creativity and business savvy, and his rise through the ranks was swift. After being placed in charge, Grayer began to hire executives from a wide range of different corporations, and they soon began investing millions to improve the firm's courses and launch lines of books, software, and instructional videos. By this time Kaplan had 155 permanent test preparation centers and 600 satellite sites and was earning an estimated $80 million in annual revenues.

In early 1995 Kaplan was again the focus of controversy when the Educational Testing Service accused the firm of sending trained test-takers to the new computerized version of the GRE for purposes of helping its students cheat. Kaplan had in fact sparked the furor by sending a list of 150 questions its staffers had memorized from the test to the ETS, claiming it wanted to make the testing service aware that it was frequently repeating the same ones. The embarrassed ETS immediately filed suit on grounds of copyright infringement, breach of contract, and fraud. Kaplan agreed to stop sending its staffers to memorize the questions, and later settled the suit out of court for $150,000, though it admitted no guilt. The ETS, for its part, had suspended the test a week after Kaplan made its claim and later reissued it with a larger pool of questions.

The year 1995 also saw the launch of Kaplan's first web site, www.kaplan.com. The company had initiated its online presence the preceding summer on America Online, but waited until its case against Princeton Review was settled to go forward with its own independent site. The web site and the company's increasing array of software offerings were the work of a new division, Kaplan Interactive.

In the spring of 1995 the company also introduced a student loan information program, which was offered in conjunction with UBL Educational Loan Center. Kaplan would offer counseling, seminars, printed and online materials, and a toll-free telephone number to assist students in finding loans, and UBL would gain access to Kaplan's extensive database of loan prospects. In the fall of 1995 Kaplan also acquired Crimson & Brown Associates, a career counseling firm that helped companies find minority recruits and published *Career Access* magazine and the Minority Resume Book.

Launching Kaplan Books Imprint and Moving into K–12 Education: 1996–97

Mid-1996 saw Kaplan's publishing arm link with Simon & Schuster to publish its test preparation guides under the Kaplan Books imprint. Kaplan Books planned to issue 20 titles per year, including such items as "You Can Afford College" and a series of "All in One" test prep guides to the SAT and ACT (American College Test). The year also saw Kaplan acquire Score! Learning, Inc. of San Francisco. Score! provided after-school tutoring programs for K-12 students in a variety of locations.

In 1997 Kaplan and Princeton skirmished again, this time after Kaplan sued the latter over misleading claims on the covers of some of its software boxes. Princeton settled out of court, agreeing to send corrective stickers to stores to cover the incorrect information and to amend future printings. Also during the year, Kaplan acquired the Lendman Group, a 33-year-old Virginia firm that produced job fairs for technology, sales, and marketing companies. Lendman had developed software that could manage large numbers of resumes, as well. Kaplan created a new unit, Kaplan Career Services, to organize the combined operations of Lendman and Crimson & Brown.

The next year Kaplan broadened its ESL offerings by purchasing LCP International Institute, which provided intensive English language training services in California and Washington. Expansion to the East Coast was soon planned. A few

months later Kaplan acquired Perfect Access, Inc., a computer consulting firm, and Dearborn Publishing Group of Chicago. Dearborn's offerings included titles on real estate, business, and finance. Kaplan also opened its largest branch office to date in Greenwich Village, New York. The 34,500-square-foot site offered preparation courses for the New York high school admissions test, as well as various college and graduate school admissions tests and professional licensing examinations. The facility included an auditorium that seated 155 and a computer training room that could handle 100 students. Kaplan's headquarters remained uptown on 56th Street, at which location English language classes, admissions counseling, and a range of test preparation services were offered. The company now had more than 160 permanent centers and 1,200 satellite sites in the United States and abroad.

Founding Concord University School of Law in 1998

The fall of 1998 saw Kaplan take one of its boldest steps ever when it created the first online law school, Concord University School of Law. Concord, initially accredited only in California, operated out of Kaplan's Los Angeles office and offered a four-year degree program at a substantial cost savings over traditional schools. Tuition was estimated at a total of $17,000 for four years. A total of 80 students enrolled for the first class, which started in December. Several months later Kaplan acquired the National Institute for Paralegal Arts and Sciences, which also offered legal training online.

Late in 1998 the company found itself under attack by the College Board, co-administrators of the SAT, when the Board released the results of yet another study that found only minimal gains on test scores for those taking prep courses. The Board claimed that the expensive courses yielded an average increase of about 50 points, which it contended was statistically insignificant. Kaplan responded by pointing out that the College Board published its own line of test preparation guides, and questioned the organization's motives in trying to stifle its competition.

The company continued to broaden its offerings in 1999, adding counseling services to help college-bound students get into the school of their choice. Kaplan counselors would help them fill out their college applications and assist with other strategic necessities. The cost was $700 for four to six sessions. Kaplan also was becoming increasingly focused on assisting students in grades kindergarten through 12, where the widespread adoption of standardized tests that were required for advancement in school offered the firm, and its competitors, a new opportunity for growth. Kaplan soon created specialized, age-appropriate study guides for the tests, which differed for each state.

In early 2000 Kaplan made another acquisition, that of Schweser Study Program of LaCrosse, Wisconsin, which provided test preparation services for the Chartered Financial Analyst examination. Schweser claimed that a third of the 60,000 who took the CFA exam used its products or services. Kaplan subsequently acquired the Career Services subsidiary of Central Newspapers, Inc., which was merged into the recently created Brass Ring subsidiary. Brass Ring offered recruiting and hiring-management services. Kaplan also formed Kaplan Ventures to make investments in education and career services companies. In the first round of spending, stakes were purchased in Apex Learning, Apollo International, Jobscience, and Blackboard, Inc.

Growing Presence on the Web into the 21st Century

As the world became more and more wired, Kaplan was ramping up its online offerings, introducing a number of new services, including a $300 SAT prep course, which was less than half the price of the standard $800 12-session class. The company also was operating several different web sites, including kaptest.com, from which it sold online courses, books, and other materials; eScore.com, which offered parental guidance for child development and learning; kaplanprofessional.com; kaplan.com; and others. In April 2000 Kaplancollege.com was launched, which offered online courses in nursing, real estate, business, and other subjects.

In the summer of 2000 Kaplan acquired Quest Education Corp. in a stock purchase worth $165 million. Quest, based in Georgia, offered associate and bachelor's degrees in business, healthcare, and information technology at 30 small schools in 11 states. Kaplan subsequently changed the Davenport, Iowa-based Quest College's name to Kaplan College. Soon afterward Quest acquired Denver Paralegal Institute, Ltd., which ran five schools for paralegals. In June Kaplan also reached a pact with Encore Software, Inc. to market Kaplan's test prep products around the United States. By the fall, Kaplan's top SAT and GRE computer programs were ranked first, second, and third in their sales category by research firm PC Data.

More acquisitions took place in the winter of 2000 and the spring of 2001. In December Kaplan purchased Speer Software Training, Inc. of New York, which provided training and consultation services for law firms. The company was combined with Kaplan unit Perfect Access, which was renamed Perfect Access Speer. In March 2001, Kaplan's Canadian division acquired The Study Seminar for Financial Analysts of Windsor, Ontario, which offered test preparation for the CFA exam. Several months later, Kaplan acquired Prosource Educational Services, Inc. of Minnesota, which was a provider of professional education for real estate, insurance, and securities professionals.

Under the guidance of CEO Jonathan Grayer, Kaplan was experiencing explosive growth, as well as diversifying to offer K-12 tutoring, college admissions counseling, professional licensing exam preparation, software and book products, college-level instruction, and more, much of it online. The once moribund company had been transformed into a dynamic, aggressive organization that looked for new opportunities wherever they could be found. It remained the leader in the field that Stanley Kaplan had created in his Brooklyn basement more than 60 years before.

Principal Subsidiaries

Quest Education Corporation; Score! Learning, Inc.; Kaplan (Canada) Ltd.; Dearborn Publishing Group, Inc.; Self Test Software, Inc.

Principal Divisions

Kaplan Test Preparation and Admissions; SCORE! Learning, Inc.; The Kaplan Colleges; Kaplan Professional; Quest Education Corporation.

Principal Competitors

Sylvan Learning Systems, Inc.; The Princeton Review, Inc.; Achieva College Prep Centers; Peterson's; The College Board.

Further Reading

Bongiorno, Lori, "The Test Tutors Try to Settle a Score," *Business Week,* November 21, 1994, p. 62.

Bredemeier, Kenneth, "Kaplan to Buy Quest Education, Operator of Specialty Schools," *Washington Post,* June 28, 2000, p. E2.

Bulkeley, William M., "Education: Kaplan Plans a Law School Via the Web," *Wall Street Journal,* September 16, 1998, p. B1.

"CB & Test Prep Companies at Odds Over Legitimacy of SAT Study," *Electronic Education Report,* December 23, 1998.

Cohn, Edward, "Selling Higher Test Scores," *American Prospect,* October 23, 2000, pp. 29–31.

Coleman, Sandy, "Test-Coaching Company Hopes to Ease MCAS Worries—Kaplan Books Point to Growing Role of Tests," *Boston Globe,* January 7, 2000, p. B1.

Dockser Marcus, Amy, "SAT Coaches to Offer Counseling Services to College-Bound Students," *Dow Jones Business News,* June 28, 1999.

FieldsMeyer, Thomas, and Jennifer Frey, "Testmaster—Builder of an International Empire That Improves Kids' SAT Scores, Stanley Kaplan Used to Pay to Give Tutoring," *People Magazine,* December 20, 1999, p. 135.

George, Mary, "Testing Guru Gets 'A' in High Standards," *Denver Post,* March 1, 1990.

"Kaplan Aggressively Courts Internet Alliances, Launches Sites," *Educational Marketer,* April 10, 2000.

Karvetski, Kerstin, "Kaplan to Test Digital Exam-Prep Market with Floppy Launch; CD-ROMs to Follow," *Computer Retail Week,* September 19, 1994, p. 22.

Larini, Rudy, "Test-Coaching Firm Settles Lawsuit over Computerized GRE," *Star-Ledger* (Newark, N.J.), January 28, 1998, p. 21.

Putka, Gary, "Test-Cramming Schools Sign Cease-Fire," *Wall Street Journal,* June 24, 1993, p. B9.

Schwartzman, Paul, "Admission Tests Spell Big Business—Tutor Has National Market," *Record, Northern New Jersey,* June 5, 1987, p. B1.

Scott-Blair, Michael, "Test Coach Says U.S. Students Get Bad Rap," *San Diego Union-Tribune,* March 11, 1984, p. B3.

Sherman, Ted, "College Testing Service Sues Exam Prep Firm in Rift over Computer Quiz," *Star-Ledger* (Newark, N.J.), January 1, 1995.

"Testing Time—As Debate Rages, It's Learning That's the Key," *Intelligencer Journal* (Lancaster, Penn.), December 28, 1999, p. A14.

Thanh Dang, Dan, "Kaplan Illegally Obtained Test Questions, Suit Says," *Baltimore Sun,* January 1, 1995, p. 1C.

—Frank Uhle

La Quinta®
Inns · Inn & Suites

The La Quinta Companies

909 Hidden Ridge, Ste. 600
Irving, Texas 75038
U.S.A.
Telephone: (214) 492-6600
Toll Free: (800) 531-5900
Fax: (214) 492-6971
Web site: http://www.laquinta.com

Public Company
Incorporated: 1968 as La Quinta Motor Inns, Inc.
Employees: 7,500
Sales: $822.8 million (2000)
Stock Exchanges: New York
Ticker Symbol: LQI
NAIC: 52593 Real Estate Investment Trusts; 53311
   Lessors of Nonfinancial Intangible Assets (Except
   Copyrighted Works); 72111 Hotels (Except Casino
   Hotels) and Motels

With more than 300 inns concentrated in the Sun Belt, The La Quinta Companies (formerly The Meditrust Companies) controls one of the largest owner-operated hotel chains in the United States. Its properties, which are located primarily in Florida, California, and particularly Texas, are targeted toward cost-conscious business travelers. La Quinta traditionally has focused on those things a salesperson wants while traveling, such as big beds and ample workspace. Swimming pools, restaurants, and other family-oriented items are cut to keep costs down. Butch Cash, upon becoming CEO in 2000, aimed to take the southwestern-styled chain national.

Origins

La Quinta, which means "the country place" in Spanish, got its start in 1968 during HemisFair, the San Antonio, Texas world's fair. Across from the fairgrounds, entrepreneur Sam Barshop and his brother, Phil, built the first in what would become a successful chain of La Quinta Inns. After the fair, the Barshops used the hotel, as they would later describe the venture, to invent a new lodging industry niche: moderately priced accommodations that catered to the commercial business traveler.

By the time the Barshops built the first La Quinta Inn, they had racked up an impressive resume of experience in the real estate and lodging industries. Their family's successful real estate business had provided them with an adept understanding of finance and property transactions. That knowledge would later surface in a variety of innovative financing strategies, which they would use to fund the La Quinta chain. Moreover, during the early 1960s, the brothers started building and leasing hotels that were licensed by the Ramada Inn chain. Through their company, Barshop Motel Enterprises, they also obtained exclusive franchise rights for Rodeway Inns of America in Texas, Oklahoma, Arkansas, and Kansas. In the mid-1960s, in fact, Sam and Phil Barshop made an unsuccessful bid to purchase the Rodeway chain.

Following their failed attempt to buy Rodeway, the Barshops opened La Quinta Inn. Recognizing the untapped potential of their new market niche, they began duplicating the La Quinta concept in neighboring areas. The Barshops used a variety of financing tools to pay for the construction of new hotels, including various partnership and joint-venture arrangements. They also expanded the chain by selectively licensing, or franchising, the La Quinta name and concept to unrelated third parties. By the late 1970s, La Quinta Inns were springing up primarily across Texas, but also in a few other states. Phil Barshop left the company in 1977 to devote his attention to the family's real estate business, although he remained on the board of directors until 1994.

Aside from the Barshops' creative financing tactics, La Quinta's unique recipe for attracting travelers to its hotels allowed the chain to prosper during the 1970s and 1980s. La Quinta Inns were designed for male business travelers, especially those employed in sales jobs. Rather than striving to entertain guests, as Sam Barshop believed many of his competitors were trying to do, La Quinta simply provided its patrons with clean, comfortable rooms at low prices. Visitors typically enjoyed comparatively large rooms with large beds and ample space to work. The Barshops were able to undercut competing hoteliers, such as Holiday Inn and Rodeway, by eschewing such amenities as swimming pools, elaborate lounges, and restaurants that were of negligible interest to bustling businessmen. By focusing on its core market, La Quinta was able to accrue a large base of repeat customers that sought out La Quinta Inns during their travels.

The Barshops augmented the unique features associated with their individual hotels with a savvy marketing and organizational strategy. La Quinta's expansion came to be guided by the concepts of "clustering, adjacency, and filling in." In other words, the Barshops tried to build name recognition and secure regional market share by locating numerous inns in the same metropolitan areas, putting the hotels within no more than 300 miles of existing properties and then opening inns in smaller cities near established La Quinta markets. The proximity of the La Quintas in each market allowed the hotels to achieve economies of scale by sharing maintenance and purchasing expenses. In addition, Sam Barshop cultivated a reliable group of managers for his properties, hiring mostly ex-military or retired couples to run the hotels.

During this time, franchising had become a popular method of financing the growth of hotel chains because there was often little or no capital investment required by the parent organization. Rather, the parent earned various license and management fees from its franchise in lieu of direct operating profits. However, Barshop was wary of franchising. "You can't control a franchise...," he remarked in the May 14, 1990 issue of *Hotel and Motel Management,* noting that franchises were "not maintaining control; they're not maintaining consistency." Reflecting his commitment to the stratagem of consistency through ownership of La Quinta properties, Barshop ended the company's franchising program in 1977. Barshop focused on building and operating hotels that were owned entirely, or mostly, by La Quinta Motor Inns, Inc.

To fund expansion of the La Quinta chain during the late 1970s and early 1980s, Barshop drew on his real estate and finance background to establish innovative deals that brought investment capital into the organization. In addition to selling stock, he formed joint ventures with well-established financial institutions, particularly insurance companies. For hotels that it did not own completely, La Quinta would earn fees for developing and managing the properties. The company would also keep a portion of the profits reflective of its ownership share in the projects, with the remainder of the income going to its partner. La Quinta typically maintained 40 to 80 percent ownership in the projects, although it retained as little as 1 percent of some hotels.

Integral to Barshop's financial strategy during the early 1980s was his use of a joint venture to fund the development of a new La Quinta headquarters. Built in 1982 to house the hotelier's burgeoning operations, La Quinta Plaza in San Antonio resulted from a joint venture between La Quinta and Israel Fogiel, a local developer. La Quinta eventually purchased Fogiel's share of the complex during the mid-1980s, by which time it was involved in several deals with other investors. By 1986 La Quinta had erected 40, or about one-quarter, of the hotels in its chain with the help of its most active partner, Prudential Insurance Company.

New Structures in 1986

By 1986, La Quinta was operating 170 hotels, generating revenues of nearly $180 million and netting income of about $6 million. While most of its hotels were in Texas and Florida, the company had extended its reach into other regions of the South and Southwest as well. That year, however, Congress passed the Tax Reform Act (TRA), which essentially destroyed many of the valuable tax incentives apportioned to investors in commercial real estate projects and served to eventually diminish the liquidity and value of La Quinta's existing properties. Despite the apparent setback, Barshop characteristically tried to turn the new law into an opportunity.

Observers viewed the TRA of 1986 as a death knell for the formerly red-hot limited partnership market, in which limited partnerships allowed numerous smaller investors to invest in large development projects through publicly traded shares. However, Barshop became one of the first developers to establish a master limited partnership (MLP) under the new law. He created a company called La Quinta Motor Inns Limited Partnership, placed 31 of his properties into the MLP, and then sold shares in the partnership to investors. La Quinta continued to operate the properties to garner management fees from the MLP. The deal resulted in about $75 million in cash that Barshop could use to build new hotels.

Barshop continued to expand the La Quinta chain during 1986 and 1987, using capital raised through various means. In 1987, for example, he formed two joint ventures with investment partnerships managed by CIGNA Investments, Inc. Those two endeavors produced nine hotels and six restaurants. La Quinta owned only 1 percent of the properties but secured long-term contracts to manage the inns on a fee basis. Between 1986 and 1990, La Quinta added a total of about 30 new properties to its holdings, including the properties held by the limited partnership. Steady growth, however, belied serious problems that beset the lodging industry in the Southwest during the late 1980s and early 1990s.

By the end of the 1980s the U.S. economy had tailspinned into a recession, gutting market growth in the lodging industry. Hoteliers in the Southwest, in fact, had started suffering as early as 1988, and hotel and real estate industries across the United States were enduring the delayed effects of the TRA of 1986.

Development of new hotels had virtually halted by the end of the decade as overbuilt markets kept investors away. While the average occupancy rate for hotels plummeted, many of La Quinta's peers struggled to avoid bankruptcy. The downturn signaled an end of the rapid expansion achieved by Barshop during the 1980s. Development of new La Quinta Inns slowed dramatically in 1990 and even into the mid-1990s.

Nevertheless, La Quinta managed to weather the storm with relatively minor difficulties. Importantly, the recession boosted corporate interest in lower-priced hotels. In fact, in 1991, La Quinta posted the highest occupancy rate, 75.7 percent, of any Texas hotel chain in the business-traveler category. Furthermore, La Quinta managed to get a jump on many of its competitors during the slump by updating and renovating its properties. Using the cash he had generated at the start of the recession, originally earmarked for new developments, Barshop refurbished his hotels and boosted La Quinta's share of a stagnating market. With characteristic optimism, Barshop used the recession as an opportunity to position La Quinta for growth in the 1990s. "I think the golden years of this company will be the 1990s," he commented in *Hotel and Motel Management* magazine.

La Quinta bucked industry financial trends again in 1991 when it formed a new MLP, La Quinta Development Partners, L.P. The partnership, entered into with a Boston-based real estate firm, generated about $150 million in new working capital for the La Quinta organization. In addition, restructuring efforts initiated in the early 1990s were cutting La Quinta's overhead and increasing its operating margins. However, during this time, problems surfaced that would soon result in the resignation of many of La Quinta's executives and would later persuade Barshop to abandon the company he and his brother had founded.

In 1991, a group of shareholders based in Fort Worth, led by the Bass and Taylor families, attempted to gain control of the company. Rather than file for bankruptcy to avert the takeover, Barshop came to terms with the group. During the same period,

a group of Connecticut investors filed suit against La Quinta Motor Inns Limited Partnership, alleging violations of securities law and mismanagement. Although Barshop denied the charges and fought the hostile takeover, the struggle resulted in the flight of several of his top managers, who were replaced by appointees of the Bass/Taylor Group. Barshop himself was forced out of his position as chief executive, although he retained his title of chairperson.

New Direction in 1991

Gary L. Mead, a lodging industry veteran (Motel 6), assumed the presidency of La Quinta Motor Inns, Inc. in 1991. Although La Quinta's new management team sustained the chain's legacy of marketing toward business travelers, Mead instigated a reorganization of the company. Restructuring efforts were designed to transform La Quinta from an entrepreneurial style organization, which had served the company well during the 1970s and 1980s, into a more management intensive, efficient corporate enterprise.

Under Mead's direction, La Quinta consolidated most of the holdings under its diverse partnerships and joint ventures into a unified chain of inns operated and owned, in full or in part, by the renamed La Quinta Inns, Inc. Mead also implemented vast staff cuts and slashed La Quinta's operating overhead—the company's workforce dropped from 6,800 in 1991 to about 6,100 by the end of 1993. In addition, during 1993 and 1994, La Quinta conducted a $50 million image-enhancement program to give its hotels a fresher, more contemporary appearance. The company also adopted a more progressive logo. A marketing campaign, featuring Zig Ziglar and other real-life salespeople, encouraged younger sales reps to try the chain.

Although La Quinta quelled development of new hotels during the early 1990s, it managed to increase the number of rooms owned and operated by La Quinta Motor Inns by about 40 percent, to more than 23,000. That feat was accomplished by purchasing La Quinta hotels from the limited partnerships and by acquiring and converting nearly 15 new properties between 1991 and 1994. As lodging markets began to recover and La Quinta's cost-cutting efforts began to pay off, the company started to prosper; after shouldering a net loss in 1992, La Quinta's earnings increased by $20.3 million from record sales of $272 million in 1993. Sales early in 1994, moreover, suggested improved performance. As evidenced by its move to a new corporate headquarters building in 1993, La Quinta was poised for a new era of expansion during the remainder of the decade.

By the end of 1994, the results of the image program were apparent. Occupancy, room rates, and profits were all up. This was true for the United States only, however. In Mexico, a financial crisis and the process of dealing with partners prevented the kind of whirlwind makeover the company had executed north of the border.

La Quinta turned its sights on Colorado, investing $45 million to nearly double its offerings in that state to 15 hotels, or 2,000 rooms, by the end of 1998. The Denver economy and the new Denver International Airport attracted a number of competitors in the same price range to the area, yet occupancy rates remained high.

Two years after revamping its exteriors and signage, the La Quinta chain set out on a $200 million project to redecorate its 30,000 hotel rooms with brighter colors and updated décor. Bigger, 25-inch televisions, dataport phones, video games, and larger desks were also installed. To promote the changes, the company constructed a fully equipped hotel room on top of a trailer bed that was hauled around the country and featured in television ads beginning in the spring of 1997. In January, the company had unveiled its first higher-end La Quinta Inn & Suites concept in Raleigh, North Carolina. The original La Quinta Inns themselves had been moving from the economy to the mid-priced segment.

The large capital commitments, when added to the $310 million already spent buying out franchisees, left La Quinta, formerly nearly debt-free, owing $660 million, reported *Forbes*. Unfortunately, the first telltale signs of overcapacity soon caused investors to dump La Quinta's stock, which lost a quarter of its value in October 1997.

New Owners in 1998

In January 1998, Meditrust, the country's largest healthcare real estate investment trust (REIT), agreed to buy La Quinta Inns for $3 billion in cash and stock, including the assumption of $850 million of debt. Meditrust, led by founder and CEO Abraham D. Gosman, had recently acquired the Santa Anita Companies in California, whose unique paired-share structure allowed it to operate businesses through an affiliate while avoiding corporate taxes as a REIT. (In 1984, Congress outlawed the paired-share structure, which allowed businesses to combine REIT and operating company shares on the stock exchange, though a grandfather clause allowed four existing paired-share companies to remain. Before the Meditrust/La Quinta deal, another paired-share company, Starwood Lodging, had bought ITT, owner of the Sheraton chain, prompting protest against the paired-share structure from rival bidder Hilton Hotels.)

Congress soon removed the paired-share tax loophole, though. As the REIT market softened, Meditrust's shares fell more than 40 percent through the first eight months of 1998, about the time Gosman announced he was leaving the firm.

Francis "Butch" Cash, who had ten years earlier been benchmarking La Quinta for Marriott's developing Courtyard brand (and who also developed a national presence for Red Roof Inn), became CEO in April 2000. He planned to take La Quinta nationwide, again employing franchising as a growth tool.

Heavily overextended, the Meditrust holding company sold healthcare properties and mortgage repayments for $500 million by September 2000. In 1998 and 1999, the company had unloaded its Santa Anita racetrack and Cobblestone golf course. Even so, the company was left with $600 million in debt.

No longer focused on healthcare, Meditrust assumed the name The La Quinta Companies, the holding company for both La Quinta Properties (the REIT portion of the business) and La Quinta Corporation. After decentralizing management of the

hotels and other refinements, the chain was showing signs of recovery.

Principal Subsidiaries

La Quinta Properties, Inc.; La Quinta Corporation.

Principal Competitors

Accor SA; Cendant Corporation; Choice Hotels International, Inc.; Hampton Inns.

Further Reading

Aguayo, Jose, "Control Freak," *Forbes,* May 19, 1997, p. 128.

Bailey, Steve, and Steven Syre, "Gosman Leaving Meditrust; Stock Has Tumbled Since Real Estate Firm Expanded," *Boston Globe,* August 4, 1998, p. C1.

Bissaillon, Francis P., "Strategy 1: 'Always Use Other People's Money'," *Financial Executive,* May/June 1991, pp. 26+.

Honeycutt, T.D., "La Quinta Head Replaced," *San Antonio Light,* March 4, 1992.

Jusko, Jill, "La Quinta Positioned for Future," *Hotel and Motel Management,* May 14, 1990.

Kevles, Barbara, "Irving, Texas-Based Real Estate Firm Buoyed by Purchase of Hotel Chain," *Fort Worth Star-Telegram,* June 20, 2001.

Koss, Laura, "Prognosis Good for La Quinta," *Hotel and Motel Management,* July 26, 1993, pp. 4+.

"Looking Up with La Quinta," *Lodging Hospitality,* May 1995, p. 12.

McCann, Nita Chilton, "With Eye on 'Curb Appeal,' La Quinta Renovates Jackson Hotels," *Mississippi Business Journal,* November 22, 1993, p. 7.

Moore, Paula, "FDIC Sues Barshop; La Quinta Battles Ronin in Court," *San Antonio Business Journal,* March 27, 1992, p. 3.

——, "La Quinta Soars Despite Inner Upheaval," *San Antonio Business Journal,* October 25, 1991, p. 1.

——, "Sources: La Quinta Moving Downtown," *San Antonio Business Journal,* May 21, 1993, p. 1.

Porter, Michael E., "Know Your Place," *Inc.,* September 1991, pp. 90ff.

Rebchook, John, "La Quinta Entrenches in Colorado; Hotel Chain to Have 2,000 Rooms Across State by End of '98," *Denver Rocky Mountain News,* February 21, 1997, p. 4B.

Rowe, Megan, "Out with the Old at La Quinta," *Lodging Hospitality,* December 1994, p. 50.

Schmutz, John, "La Quinta Inns, Inc., Initiates Negotiations to Acquire La Quinta Motor Inns Limited Partnership," *PR Newswire,* October 18, 1993.

Stableford, Joan, "Stamford Group Mounts Hostile Bid for Inn Chain," *Fairfield County Business Journal,* October 21, 1991, p. 1.

Vinocur, Barry, "Betting with a 'Pair'," *Barron's,* January 12, 1998, p. 26.

Vrana, Debora, "Meditrust to Buy La Quinta Inns for $3 Billion," *Los Angeles Times,* January 5, 1998, p. D1.

Wolff, Carlo, "Brightening the Big Picture," *Lodging Hospitality,* April 1997, pp. 55–56.

——, "Growing the La Quinta Brand," *Lodging Hospitality,* October 2000, pp. 22–26.

—Dave Mote
—update: Frederick C. Ingram

Laboratory Corporation of America Holdings

358 S. Main St.
Burlington, North Carolina 27215
U.S.A.
Telephone: (336) 229-1127
Fax: (336) 513-4806
Web site: http://www.labcorp.com

Public Company
Incorporated: 1982
Employees: 18,850
Sales: $1.92 billion (2000)
Stock Exchanges: New York
Ticker Symbol: LH
NAIC: 621511 Medical Laboratories

Laboratory Corporation of America Holdings (LabCorp) owns one of the largest medical testing labs in the United States. It performs 4,000 different tests at 24 testing facilities and 900 service centers across the country. One of the company's predecessors, National Health Laboratories Incorporated, profited wildly until it was busted for Medicare fraud in 1992. After the 1995 merger that joined National Health with Roche Biomedical to create LabCorp, profits and share price plummeted until an aggressive cost competitor was removed, managed care restrictions were loosened, and new molecular diagnostic testing capabilities revived investor interest in the company.

Origins

Roche Biomedical was created by Hoffman-La Roche, the American arm of Roche Holding, Limited, an international biomedical conglomerate based in Switzerland. In 1905 Hoffman-LaRoche began operations in the United States, with headquarters in Nutley, New Jersey. It was not until 1969, however, that the company entered the clinical laboratory business. At that time, it purchased Kings County Research Laboratories, which was based in Brooklyn, New York. Throughout the 1970s, Hoffman-La Roche added to its research laboratory holdings. In 1982 the company made one of its most significant acquisitions in this area, buying a major independent clinical

laboratory business, Biomedical Reference Laboratories of North Carolina. In the following year, Hoffman-La Roche merged all of its laboratory properties into one company, which it called Roche Biomedical Laboratories.

Biomedical Reference Laboratories, Formation of Roche Biomedical: 1960s–80s

The headquarters for the newly formed Roche Biomedical were established in Burlington. This site was chosen because it was the home of Biomedical Reference Laboratories, the largest of the laboratories that Hoffman-La Roche had combined into Roche Biomedical. Biomedical got its start in the late 1960s, when three brothers founded a clinical laboratory in the town of Elon College, North Carolina. In doing so, the brothers were joining a family tradition. Their father, Thomas Edward Powell, Jr., had taught biology at Elon College for 15 years early in the century. Unable to obtain suitable supplies for his students to perform their experiments, he founded Carolina Biological Supply in 1927 to provide dissection specimens. During the Great Depression of the 1930s, when Elon College was unable to pay its faculty's salaries, Powell left the college and entered business full time. As the New Deal increased federal funding for education programs, Carolina Biological Supply prospered. In the 1960s, Powell handed down the family business to his son, Thomas Edward Powell III.

In 1969, Thomas Powell joined with his twin brothers, James B. Powell, a doctor, and John, to form Biomedical Reference Laboratories. With 16 employees, the lab performed testing for physicians, hospitals, researchers, and small companies in the nearby North Carolina Research Triangle. In 1970, the lab moved from its location at Elon College to an old empty hospital in Burlington. James Powell was in the army, stationed in Washington, D.C., and he came down on the weekends to work. During the 1970s, the lab grew quickly, as scientific research in the area surrounding it intensified.

In 1979 Biomedical sold stock to the public for the first time. The company offered $7.2 million worth of stock, which made the lab itself worth about $50 million. With this infusion of funds, Biomedical moved from its old quarters to a nearby office and

Company Perspectives:

LabCorp is at the forefront of providing crucial information for disease management. Applications include sophisticated HIV/AIDS and hepatitis C diagnosis and monitoring, oncology, and genetics. It also offers the most up-to-date techniques for clinical trials testing, where it assists pharmaceutical, biotechnology, and contract research organizations working on new drug development.

laboratory complex called York Court. Three years after Biomedical went public, Hoffman-La Roche purchased the lab for $163.5 million. The company's original owners, the Powell brothers, became multimillionaires. Only one, James, was still involved with the company at that time, and he stayed on as its head.

By the early 1980s, the town where Roche Biomedical was located had suffered a dramatic decline, as businesses fled to the suburbs. This exodus had left a large number of vacant buildings available, and Roche Biomedical seized this opportunity to expand rapidly in Burlington. Although Roche Biomedical comprised labs located all over the country, the North Carolina operations became the company's fastest growing. In 1984, the U.S. Congress approved more stringent Medicare regulations, which forced testing laboratories to provide greater billing information. Because this change required more space for office work, Roche Biomedical moved into larger quarters in Burlington, taking over an 80,000-square-foot building rented from a hosiery company.

In addition to its clinical testing operations, Roche Biomedical also conducted extensive research to develop quicker and more sensitive diagnostic assays. The company focused its efforts on products for which society seemed to have a growing need. "We follow the demands of the health-care system," Powell told *Business North Carolina* in 1993. "But we like to think that we are innovators also. We want to be more than just a service lab." To promote development of new products and procedures, Roche Biomedical established a Center for Molecular Biology, which conducted research on promising ideas in Research Triangle, North Carolina.

In February 1987, Roche Biomedical joined with Pragma Bio-Tech, Inc., a New Jersey-based company, to provide workplace drug and alcohol testing. Under the agreement, Pragma employees would take samples from employees at their jobs and then convey them to Roche Biomedical, which would conduct sensitive gas chromatography/mass spectrometry tests to detect the presence of controlled substances. Results would be available within 48 hours. With this joint venture, Roche Biomedical hoped to tap into the growing concern among employers about drug abuse.

With the help of such corporate programs as employee drug and alcohol testing, Roche Biomedical's business continued to grow throughout the 1980s. In 1989, the company established a new division, the Roche Insurance Laboratory. This enterprise was set up to perform the tests required by insurance companies in determining whether to extend coverage or pay a claim.

At the start of the 1990s, Roche Biomedical consolidated geographically, selling its western regional operations in Au-

gust 1990. Labs in Sacramento, California, and Denver, Colorado, were sold to the Unilab Corporation for $41 million. These facilities included clinical, anatomical, and cytology testing businesses. Under the terms of the sale, Roche Biomedical retained its esoteric and specialty testing operations in those areas. Overall, however, it had withdrawn from participation in the West Coast market.

In 1991, Roche Biomedical used its newly developed DNA technology to help identify the remains of American soldiers killed in the Persian Gulf War. By examining the so-called genetic fingerprint of tissues, the lab was able to help the Armed Forces Institute of Pathology identify all of the missing combatants. Because of this work, Desert Storm was the first war in which no American fighter was buried at the Tomb of the Unknown Soldier. Bodies were also able to be returned to families as intact as possible.

In that same year, Roche expanded its operations by establishing its Consulting Physicians Network in May 1991. This service was established by a subsidiary of Roche Biomedical, the Roche Insurance Laboratory. With this service, the company sought to provide access to a medical insurance board-certified physician to underwriting companies without a full-time physician on their staff. The doctors provided by Roche Biomedical would rate patients according to risk, read EKGs, and review files within one to two days. "The Consulting Physicians Network complements our existing businesses and allows us to respond to the changing needs of the insurance industry," a Roche Biomedical executive told *Business Wire.*

Number Two in Medical Testing: 1991

By the end of 1991, Roche Biomedical had become the second largest medical testing company in the United States, with revenues of more than $600 million. The company had more than 8,000 employees in 400 locations across the country. In February 1992, Hoffman La Roche purchased the Compu-Chem Corporation, based in North Carolina, for $75 million. When this company's operations were combined with those of Roche Biomedical, the Roche laboratory became the second largest drug-screening provider in the United States. Roche Biomedical had previously attained the position of the second largest paternity tester, as well. In May 1992, Roche Biomedical dedicated a new 94,000-square-foot extension of the company's laboratory facilities in Burlington. With this addition, the Roche Biomedical space became one of the world's largest clinical laboratories. More than 850 people worked at this location.

Also in May 1992, Roche Biomedical announced that it would sell off CompuChem's environmental division. Despite the fact that CompuChem had spent several million dollars developing its environmental testing products, the company had discovered that the market for these expensive processes was small, as confusion about state and local regulations left companies in doubt about whether they were necessary. "The environmental operation does not fit with our business," Powell told *Triangle Business* in explaining Roche Biomedical's decision to seek a buyer for the unit.

In July 1992, Roche Biomedical announced that its Raritan, New Jersey, and its North Carolina operations had been li-

+---+
| **Key Dates:** |
| |
| **1969:** Hoffman-La Roche enters the clinical lab |
| business. |
| **1979:** Biomedical Reference Laboratories goes public.|
| **1982:** Biomedical is acquired by Hoffman-LaRoche. |
| **1983:** Hoffman-LaRoche's lab businesses are consoli- |
| dated at Roche Biomedical Laboratories. |
| **1992:** National Health Laboratories pays largest ever|
| Medicare fraud settlement. |
| **1995:** Roche Biomedical merges with National Health, |
| forming LabCorp. |
+---+

censed by the New York City Department of Health to perform tests for the Human Immunodeficiency Virus (HIV). Roche Biomedical was the first laboratory to receive this approval, of 59 that applied. Earlier, Roche Biomedical had also been licensed by the State of New York to perform these tests. With this move, Roche Biomedical stepped up its participation in the rapidly growing field of HIV testing. The company offered all of the available technologies for testing, including antibody tests and a sophisticated DNA test. The latter test involved the use of polymerase chain reaction technology, which duplicated one strand of DNA millions of times to reveal the presence of the virus. This test was particularly useful for detecting the presence of HIV in newborn babies, since their bodies often had not yet formed antibodies to the virus.

In September 1992, Roche Biomedical made a breakthrough when it introduced the first automated allergy test that used histamine levels to determine sensitivities. The company planned to make this test commercially available and sell it to allergy clinics and allergists through 200 sales representatives. In addition, Roche Biomedical planned to make presentations at professional meetings and send out brochures advertising the test. Roche Biomedical's new product employed leukocyte histamines. Before, this test had been labor intensive and expensive, costing from $300 to $400 per antigen and requiring a large blood sample. With the new technology, however, physicians would be able to run 23 tests for $115, using only 2.5 milliliters of blood. During the test, allergens were mixed with the blood to see if a histamine reaction was provoked.

In October 1992, Roche Biomedical made another technological advance that allowed it to fulfill a need in a rapidly growing market. At that time, the lab introduced a new test to detect the tuberculosis bacterium in just 48 hours—a vast improvement over the old test, which took three to six weeks. Because the advent of AIDS and antibiotic-resistant strains of tuberculosis had caused a resurgence of the disease, this product responded to a growing demand, as state and federal health officials struggled to control the outbreak of the disease. The new test was particularly helpful because it permitted treatment to begin earlier, thus shortening the period in which an infectious person might contaminate others while waiting for test results.

The new test achieved its rapid results by applying polymerase chain reaction technology in another context. Technicians duplicated DNA found in sputum and other samples of respiratory matter to detect the presence of tuberculosis. In announcing

the test, Powell said that he expected it ''to become a major weapon in the war against tuberculosis, which has increased in incidence by 15.5 percent in the U.S. since 1984,'' as *Business Wire* reported.

In addition to the tuberculosis test and the HIV test based on polymerase chain reaction technology, Roche Biomedical also offered a variety of other assays using this technology. These included tests for HTLV-1 and HTLV-2, viruses thought to cause certain leukemias and lymphomas; a screen for the Lyme disease agent, Borelia bungdorferi; and diagnostic procedures for the human papilloma virus and chlamydia trachomatis. In addition, this technology could be used to identify people, as had been done in the wake of the Gulf War.

At the end of 1992, Roche Biomedical dedicated a new laboratory and patient service center in Greenville, North Carolina. This facility consolidated operations that had previously been conducted in two locations. By that time, Roche Biomedical also ran facilities in 11 different office buildings in downtown Burlington.

Throughout 1993, Roche Biomedical worked to enhance its testing procedures for HIV, cancer, heart disease, and other illnesses. At the company's Roche Image Analysis Systems center, located in the town of Elon College, the company refined a new approach to cancer screening that used computers to standardize interpretation of pap smear results. In addition, the company further developed its forensic uses of DNA testing and enhanced its already large share of the growing market for paternity testing. In the spring of 1994, Roche Biomedical updated its data management mechanisms to better manage reporting of laboratory results. With a leading position in a rapidly growing field and the backing of a multinational parent, Roche Biomedical appeared assured of continuing success in the years to come.

Formation of LabCorp Through 1995 Merger

It was handsomely profitable, but before merging with Roche Biomedical, National Health Laboratories Incorporated had been the star villain in a highly public Medicare fraud case. In 1992, it agreed to refund $100 million to the federal government and $10 million to state-funded insurance programs, and pay a $1 million fine for billing for unnecessary blood tests. Even after the hefty settlement, the company posted a net income of $40 million. The episode earned company president Robert E. Draper a brief stint in jail and a $500,000 fine.

Ron Perelman, whose MacAndrews & Forbes group owned 20 percent of National Health, then hired investment banker James Maher to head the company and look for strategic acquisitions. National Health had 16 labs in 1993, each of them turning out an impressive five million tests a year, reported *Forbes*.

The merger between National Health and Roche Biomedical was announced in December 1994. It combined the third and fourth largest medical testing companies in the United States. The new entity, Laboratory Corporation of America, would have annual revenues of about $1.7 billion and 39 labs across the country. It was expected that the merger would generate about $90 million in savings within two years, making the new company more competitive in landing managed care contracts, according to the *Los Angeles Times*.

Forbes later reported that the deal was less of a merger between equals than a takeover of National Health by Roche Biomedical. Even though National Health shareholders were to initially receive a 50.1 percent interest in the new company, many took advantage of lucrative payout options. National Health's managers, feeling a clash in corporate culture, were the next to abandon ship, said *Forbes*. Further, the new headquarters were in Burlington, North Carolina, not National Health's La Jolla, California locale, and the CEO of the new entity was Roche Biomedical's former head, Dr. James Powell. Unfortunately, said *Forbes*, Roche Biomedical sorely lacked National Health's management expertise, which kept annual returns in the range of 25 percent or better.

Ultimately, the projected savings from the merger simply did not come through. National Health already had $600 million in debt before the merger; the new company was saddled with twice as much. The freewheeling era that had profited Perelman so greatly ($1.6 billion from taking National Health public and from the merger) was also coming to an end. By 1996, LabCorp was losing money, and its share price was in the dumps, losing three-fourths of its value in a year.

Quest Diagnostic Incorporated, LabCorp's largest rival, had acquired SmithKline Beecham Clinical Laboratories in 1999, removing an aggressive price competitor. Profits eventually did return to LabCorp, which earned $65 million in 1999 and $112 million in 2000.

To combat image problems associated with a low stock price, LabCorp executed a one-for-ten reverse stock split in 2000. However by the next year, the company wanted to increase stock liquidity to gain cash for acquisitions, and initiated a two-for-one stock split.

Investors' latest interest in the company was spurred by revolutionary molecular diagnostic tests—among the first practical applications of new knowledge of the human genetic code. In fact, LabCorp described itself as the first company to fully embrace genetic testing, noted the *New York Times*.

LabCorp bought Los Angeles-based National Genetics Institute Inc. in July 2000 to gain NGI's ultra-sensitive hepatitis C testing capability. Specialty testing was a growing, high-value market, noted a LabCorp spokesperson. By this time, LabCorp already had one molecular testing lab in North Carolina.

Another lab, based in New Hampshire, was acquired several months later. Path Lab Holdings Inc., based in New Hampshire, allowed LabCorp to both strengthen its presence in the Northeast and to expand to a new type of client base—hospitals (the company had previously specialized in serving doctors). LabCorp, seeking national accounts with managed care compa-

nies, had also recently inked deals with insurance companies including Aetna and US Healthcare.

Principal Subsidiaries

Executive Tower Travel, Inc.; Lab Delivery Service of New York City, Inc.; LabCorp Delaware, Inc.; LabCorp Limited (U.K.); LabCorp Virco, b.v.b.a. (Belgium); Laboratory Corporation of America; Tower Collection Center, Inc.; National Genetics Institute, Inc.; POISONLAB, Inc.

Principal Operating Units

Center for Molecular Biology and Pathology; National Genetics Institute; Center for Occupational Testing; Center for Esoteric Testing.

Principal Competitors

Kroll Laboratory Specialists, Inc.; Quest Diagnostics Incorporated; Specialty Laboratories; Unilab Corporation.

Further Reading

Bouchey, Lisa M., "A Clinical Approach," *Business Life*, January 1993.

Chapman, Dan, "From Textiles to Test Tubes," *Business North Carolina*, February 1993, p. 32.

Hall, Kerry, "LabCorp. Acquires N.H. Company," *Greensboro News Record*, March 27, 2001.

——, "LabCorp Says It Will Acquire West Coast Laboratory," *Greensboro News Record*, June 21, 2000, p. B8.

Hayes, John R., "Great Timing," *Forbes*, October 21, 1996, p. 176.

Moukheiber, Zina, "Dealing with Hillarynomics," *Forbes*, July 5, 1993, p. 52.

Mukherjee, Sougata, "Roche May Sell RTP Unit," *Triangle Business*, May 4, 1992.

"National Health Labs' Former CEO Gets Prison Sentence, Fine," *Wall Street Journal*, April 6, 1993, p. A6.

Olmos, David R., "Two Big Diagnostic Firms Plan to Merge," *Los Angeles Times*, December 15, 1994, p. D2.

Perry, Tony, "U.S. Settles Huge Fraud Case with Medical Lab," *Los Angeles Times*, December 19, 1992, p. D1.

Pollack, Andrew, "A Positive Culture for Making Profits; Buoyed by Mergers, Medical Labs Await Era of Gene Testing," *New York Times*, June 14, 2001, p. C1.

"Rapid Detection Test for TB Now Available," *Business Wire*, October 8, 1992.

Robinson, Russ, "One Cell Spawns a Business Empire," *Business North Carolina*, March 1985, p. 47.

"Roche Insurance Laboratory Establishes Consulting Physicians Network," *Business Wire*, May 7, 1991.

Stobbe, Mike, "Interest Grows in Burlington, N.C. Medical Testing Firm," *Charlotte Observer*, May 25, 2001.

Wells, Ken R., "NHL Merger Threatening Many Jobs, Analyst Says," *San Diego Business Journal*, December 19, 1994, p. 1.

—Elizabeth Rourke
—update: Frederick C. Ingram

Laurent·Perrier

Laurent-Perrier SA

32 avenue de Champagne
51150 Tours-sur-Marne
France
Telephone: (+33) 3-26-58-91-22
Fax: (+33) 3-26-58-77-29
Web site: http://www.finance.laurent-perrier.fr

Public Company
Incorporated: 1881
Employees: 378
Sales: EUR 146.9 million ($162.2 million) (2000)
Stock Exchanges: Euronext Paris
Ticker Symbol: 923069
NAIC: 312130 Wineries

Laurent-Perrier SA is one of the top five champagne producers and distributors in the world, and one of the leading—and last—independent champagne houses. Located in the heart of the Marne valley champagne district, Laurent-Perrier governs four primary champagne brands ranging from mid-high to high to very high ranges, for a total production of 8.3 million bottles sold in the 2000–2001 year, and sales of EUR 146.9 million. The company produces a range of champagne styles under the Laurent-Perrier name, including the company's own invention, the champagne rosé; and the prestigious Salon brand, one of the rarest of champagnes, produced from a single grape variety (Chardonnay) and fetching up to $150 and more per bottle. Targeting the mid-high range, the company has two brands, Vicomte de Castellane, sold principally through the large retail network; and Delamotte, with sales primarily handled through the company's own international distribution network. This network operates subsidiaries in Belgium, the United Kingdom, Switzerland, Germany, and the United States. These countries accounted for 32 percent of all of the company sales in 2000; France itself accounted for more than 45 percent of sales. Altogether, Laurent-Perrier's brands are distributed to more than 100 countries. The chief architect of Laurent-Perrier's growth has been Bernard de Nonancourt, who continues to serve as company chairman. Joining him is President Yves Jean Marie Paul Dumont. Once ranked only 100th among cham-

pagne producers, Laurent-Perrier has set its sights on becoming the number two champagne company, behind leader LVMH, in the early part of the 21st century.

Founding a Champagne Dynasty in the 19th Century

Champagne was only developed in the late 17th century, when a Benedictine monk, Dom Perignon, attempted to harness the "mad wine" of France's Champagne region, near Reims. Wines produced there had long been subject to an extreme volatility—the region's cool climate and short growing season tended to produce a bubbly wine subject to fermentation in the bottle. This fermentation—and resulting build-up of carbon dioxide—would often cause bottles to explode. Attempting to do away with this problem, Perignon invented the concept of blending grape varieties—and then went on to develop the modern concept of champagne itself, using thicker bottles and better corking techniques to end the explosive bottle problem.

Champagne soon caught on among the drinking public, and was especially brought to prominence during the reign of Louis XV in the 18th century. The difficult process of creating champagne, which required years of aging and a great deal of capital investment, led the Champagne region's aristocratic landowners to turn over production to specialized merchants. By mid-century, a number of houses had been dedicated to the production of champagne, all located in the Champagne region. This region remained extremely small—representing less than 3 percent of total grape production in France. Among the earliest houses were those of Ruinart, Moët, and Cliquot. Another of the earliest houses was Delamotte, located at Mesnil-sur-Oger, which was founded in 1760 and was later to play a key role in the development of Laurent-Perrier. These merchants continued to refine the production process, and by the early 19th century had succeeded in taming the "mad wine" of Champagne.

Laurent-Perrier's own origins stemmed from 1812, when Alphonse Pierlot founded a champagne firm in Tours-sur-Marne. This location gave the new house a prime position at the heart of the Champagne region, and particularly close to three of the more prominent parcels—Montagne de Reims, Vallée de la Marne, and Côte des Blancs. In the mid-19th century, Pierlot was succeeded at the company by Eugene Laurent and his wife,

---

Mathilde Perrier. The pair gave their combined name to the company in 1881.

After Laurent's death in 1887, Mathilde Laurent-Perrier took over operation of the champagne house, and created a new champagne, Veuve Laurent-Perrier, in the tradition of other so-called champagne widows (veuve means widow in French). Laurent-Perrier successfully expanded the company's operations, boosting production to some 600,000 bottles by the end of the century.

World War I, however, devastated Laurent-Perrier as well as the whole of the Champagne region. Some of the war's most bitter battles were fought in the Marne Valley itself, with much of the countryside, as well as towns and cities, being all but destroyed. Laurent-Perrier suffered on a more personal level as well, as many of Mathilde Laurent-Perrier's family were killed, leaving the family company with no heirs. When Mathilde Laurent-Perrier died in 1925, the company entered a slow decline.

The years between the world wars brought new difficulties to the champagne industry. The Russian Revolution had cut off a primary market for champagne sales, while Prohibition coupled with the Great Depression eliminated sales in the United States. Laurent-Perrier was among the champagne houses to see its fortunes dwindle steadily during this period. By the outbreak of World War II, the company was left with a stock of only some 12,000 already mortgaged bottles.

In 1939, Laurent-Perrier was acquired by Marie-Louise de Nonancourt, another champagne widow. De Nonancourt herself came from the family behind one of the most noted of Champagne houses, the Lanson Pere et Fils, by then operated by her brothers Victor and Henri, and later part of the Marne & Champagne empire. De Nonancourt had long been involved herself in the champagne trade, having acquired the Delamotte house from Lanson Pere et Fils shortly after World War I. This company she turned over to son Charles de Nonancourt.

Another son, Maurice de Nonancourt, was initially tapped to run Laurent-Perrier. Yet Maurice de Nonancourt was killed by the Gestapo during the war. Instead, another son, Bernard de Nonancourt, was placed in charge of the prestigious yet ailing champagne house in 1949.

Building a Postwar Champagne Dynasty

The Marne Valley once again found itself at the center of the war, now occupied by the Nazi forces. During this period, the Champagne region's industry, which had been granted AOC

(Appelations d'Origin Controlé) status in the 1920s, had succeeded in establishing the Comité Interprofessional du Vin de Champagne - C.I.C.C. This organization helped set minimum purchasing prices for grapes, ensuring that the Champagne region's growers were able to remain in business.

Laurent-Perrier, meanwhile, was slowly regaining its own momentum. When Bernard de Nonancourt took over the company's leadership, production had returned to 65,000 bottles per year, placing it near the bottom of the region's industry with a ranking, by number of bottles produced, of 100th. Yet de Nonancourt was to prove an inspirational leader, building the company into one of the region's top players over the next 50 years.

In 1958, de Nonancourt launched a new champagne, the Cuvée Grand Siècle. Yet the company's fortunes took off especially after the introduction of another type of champagne, the Cuvée Rosé Brut, launched in 1968. The first of the so-called rosé champagnes, the new champagne was somewhat fruitier than traditional champagnes and soon became somewhat of a company specialty. Another Laurent-Perrier brand was launched at the beginning of the 1980s, when the Grand Siècle Cuvée Alexandra debuted at the wedding celebration of de Nonancourt's daughter in 1982.

During the 1970s, Laurent-Perrier, which remained steadfastly independent, became interested in developing an international distribution network, bringing it closer to its retail customers. The company's first move in this direction came in 1978, when it established a distribution subsidiary in the United Kingdom. The company expanded its distribution activities to include its primary market countries outside of France, that is, Belgium, Switzerland, the United States, and Germany.

In the 1980s, Laurent-Perrier sought a different kind of expansion, now seeking to diversify its holdings to accommodate different brand names. With a larger brand portfolio, Laurent-Perrier sought to position itself through the different quality levels—from mid-high end to very high-end—with the Laurent-Perrier brand remaining its flagship range. The company's first purchase came in 1983, when it acquired shares in Société Champagne de Castellane, a champagne house founded by the Viscount Florens de Castellane in 1895. De Castellane turned over the company to Fernand Merand soon after the turn of the century, and the house remained in the Merand family's control until its acquisition by Laurent-Perrier.

A Pure Play Champagne Stock in the 21st Century

Laurent-Perrier soon filled out its champagne offering. In 1987, the company bought up the famed champagne house Salon de Mesnil. Founded by Eugene-Aimé Salon at the dawn of the 20th century, the house's champagne had initially been reserved for the Salon's private stock. Salon, a prominent figure in Paris's Belle Epoque, sought to create the perfect champagne from a single of grape. Salon settled on the Chardonnay variety, and particularly grapes from the vineyards at Mesnil-sur-Oger, in the Côtes des Blancs region.

The resulting champagne was the first so-called "blanc des blancs" and was so popular among Salon's acquaintances that in 1921, Salon established the House of Salon. His champagne was to remain among the most rare and prestigious, and was

Key Dates:

1812: Pierlot champagne business is founded in Tours-sur-Marne.
1881: Eugene Laurent and his wife Mathilde Perrier assume control of the newly named Laurent-Perrier.
1939: Marie-Louise de Nonancourt acquires company.
1949: Bernard de Nonancourt becomes president of company.
1983: Laurent-Perrier acquires 34 percent of Société Champagne de Castellane, founded in 1895.
1987: Company buys another prestigious champagne house, Delamotte, founded in 1760 and under the control of the de Nonancourts for much of the 20th century.
1988: Laurent-Perrier purchases Salon de Mesnil, producer of the first ''blanc des blancs'' champagnes.
1993: Grand Metropolitan plc (later Diageo) buys 20 percent of company through its United Distillers and Vintners subsidiary.
1998: Company buys back Grand Metropolitan's shares.
1999: Laurent-Perrier acquires full control of Delamotte, becomes publicly listed on Paris bourse.

only produced in the best vintages. As such, over the next 75 years, only 32 Salon vintages had been produced.

A year after acquiring Salon, Laurent-Perrier acquired another prestigious champagne house—and next-door neighbor to the Salon House—Delamotte, purchased from Bernard de Nonancourt's brother Charles. De Nonancourt now sought to expand Laurent-Perrier still further, seeking to diversify beyond champagnes. Beginning in the late 1980s, the company made a number of acquisitions, including that of Malartic Lagravière, a producer of Bordeaux wines; HPPH, a Cahors region wine producer; and Antonin Rodet, a Burgundy region producer. In 1992, the company added a new distribution subsidiary in Switzerland.

By the early 1990s, some 20 percent of Laurent-Perrier's sales came from its diversification drive. However, the company had taken on a heavy debt load, and, with the added burden of a worldwide recession, the company slipped into losses. At the end of 1993, Laurent-Perrier had turned to a larger partner, allowing distribution giant Grand Metropolitan plc (later Diageo) to acquire 20 percent of its capital through its United Distillers and Vintners subsidiary. This relationship also gave Laurent-Perrier access to Grand Met's worldwide distribution network.

Laurent-Perrier's diversification proved, however, too ambitious and, by the mid-1990s, the company was heavily in debt and facing losses. De Nonancourt brought in a new president, Jean-François Bauer, who was given the task of cleaning up the company's financial problems. Laurent-Perrier began selling off most of its diversified holdings by 1997. In 1998, the company completed its restructuring, selling Joseph-Perrier to champagne group Alain Thiénot. By then under president Yves Dumont, the company was once again in the black.

Grand Met meanwhile had acquired joint-ownership of rival champagne house Moët with champagne leader LVMH. Yet the agreement between the two giants included a non-competition clause. LVMH therefore placed pressure on Grand Metropolitan to sell off its stake in Laurent-Perrier. The resolution to this conflict came in 1998 when Laurent-Perrier itself bought back Grand Met's shares. The company was once again a fully independent champagne producer, one of the few remaining after a broader industry consolidation in the late 1990s.

The end of its relationship with Grand Metropolitan encouraged Laurent-Perrier to reinforce its own distribution operations. In 1998 the company opened two new foreign distribution subsidiaries, in Belgium and the United States. The following year, Laurent-Perrier acquired full control of the Castellane champagne operation. Riding high on the wave of orders leading up to the year 2000 celebration, Laurent-Perrier went public in 1999, with a listing on the Paris stock exchange. The de Nonancourt family nonetheless retained control of the company.

Champagne purchases for the year 2000 celebration helped swell the company's sales to a record high of nearly EUR 170 million in 1999. Yet champagne houses had nonetheless proven too optimistic, and a massive overproduction resulted in a severe hangover for the industry. Paradoxically, widespread concerns of champagne shortages had caused many people to stock up on champagne in 1999, with the result that total industry sales dropped by nearly a third in 2000. Laurent-Perrier too was hit by the sharp drop in sales. However, its concentration on the relatively high-end segments helped to cushion its profits.

The company's fortunes, along with the rest of the industry, were on the road to improvement in 2001. Laurent-Perrier turned optimistically toward its third century as one of the oldest and most prestigious—and last remaining independent—champagne houses with forecasts of a rise in sales on the order of 15 percent for 2001 alone, and plans to build the company into the number two champagne house, at least in terms of profitability, by 2002. The company also celebrated the new millennium with another event, the June 2001 release of a new Salon champagne vintage.

Principal Subsidiaries

Champagne Laurent-Perrier; Champagne de Castellane; Champagne Lemoine.

Principal Competitors

Allied Domecq PLC; LVMH Möet Hennessy Louis Vuitton SA; Marne et Champagne SA; Rémy Cointreau S.A.; Vranken Monopole SA.

Further Reading

''Le champagne tient Salon,'' *La Tribune*, September 20, 2000.
Gervais, Louis, ''Laurent-Perrier: Le champagne petille a nouveau en Europe,'' *Newsbourse*, June 3, 2001.
''Laurent Perrier affiche ses ambitions,'' *La Tribune*, January 3, 1995.
Nivelle, Catherine, ''Les bulles petilleront a nouveau en 2001,'' *Nouvel Economiste*, May 18, 2001.
Oliveau, Daniele, ''La Champagne doit digerer la 'bulle' de l'an 2000,'' *Expansion*, July 12, 2000.

—M. L. Cohen

Liberty Livewire Corporation

520 Broadway
Santa Monica, California 90401
U.S.A.
Telephone: (310) 434-7000
Fax: (310) 434-7001
Web site: http://www.libertylivewire.com

Public Company
Incorporated: 1952 as Todd-AO Corporation
Employees: 3,500
Sales: $253.13 million (2000)
Stock Exchanges: NASDAQ
Ticker Symbol: LWIRA
NAIC: 51211 Motion Picture and Video Production;
    512191 Teleproduction and Other Postproduction
    Services; 51322 Cable and Other Program
    Distribution

Liberty Livewire Corporation is the umbrella organization for a number of audio and video post-production companies operating in the United States and overseas. The company's major operating subsidiaries include Todd-AO Corporation, Soundelux, Four Media Company, and Video Services Corporation, each of which owns its own stable of post-production firms. Together, the major operating subsidiaries and a variety of smaller subsidiaries serve clients in the advertising, feature film, and television industries. On the audio side, Liberty Livewire's services include sound editing, soundtrack recording, and the mixing of dialogue, music, and sound effects. Video post-production services include visual effects and graphics, videotape editing, film-to-video transfer, and the mastering and duplication of videotape and DVD format. Liberty Livewire owns facilities in Los Angeles, New York, New Jersey, Atlanta, San Francisco, and Florida. Internationally, the company operates in Singapore, Madrid, Barcelona, and London. Liberty Media Group owns a controlling interest in Liberty Livewire. Liberty Media Group is in turn owned by AT&T Corp.

Origins

Liberty Livewire was formed in June 2000 by the combination of three prominent post-production companies. The mergers created what *Variety*, in an April 3, 2000 article, termed an "instant oligopoly" in the post-production business, a formidable new force comprising several of the most trusted and vaunted names in the industry. The corporate entity responsible for conducting the negotiations and orchestrating the transactions that ultimately led to the creation of Liberty Livewire was Liberty Media Corporation.

A wholly owned subsidiary of AT&T Corp., Liberty Media possessed financial stakes in a broad range of businesses, including cable, communications, technology, and Internet concerns. Its portfolio of cable channels included BET, Discovery Channel, Encore, QVC, E!, and USA Networks. Prior to its existence as an AT&T subsidiary, Liberty Media operated as a subsidiary of Tele-Communications Inc. (TCI), but when AT&T acquired TCI in 1999, ownership of Liberty Media passed to AT&T. As part of the AT&T and TCI merger, Liberty Media gained $5 billion in cash, the capital the company would use to develop a new, powerful post-production company named Liberty Livewire. Although there were three companies that formed the foundation of Liberty Livewire, the genesis of the company could be traced to one company in particular. Before the end of 1999, an agreement was reached to acquire Todd-AO Corporation, a celebrated audio and video post-production house whose formation in 1952 represented the origins of the Liberty Livewire organization.

In 1952, partners Mike Todd, George Skouras, and Dr. Brian O'Brien formed Todd-AO Corporation with the intent of revolutionizing the motion picture industry. Specifically, they planned to develop a new process in motion picture projection, a technology that resulted in a 70mm film format projected on a curved, wide screen with six-track stereo sound. *Oklahoma!* was the first feature film to use the new system, earning the 1955 Academy Award for Best Sound. The initial success of Todd-AO's six-channel theatrical sound induced the company to concentrate on recording sound services, which led to a string of awards for its efforts in audio innovation. Academy Awards were won by Todd-AO artists for Best Sound in a number of films during the 1950s and 1960s, including *South Pacific*, *The Alamo*, *West Side Story*, and *The Sound of Music*. The legacy of success established during the company's first two decades of innovation continued into the 1970s and 1980s, with Best Sound distinction awarded for Todd-AO's contributions to the making of *Cabaret*, *The Exorcist*, *E.T.-The Extra-Terrestrial*, and *Out of Africa*.

Todd-AO's efforts in the film industry were complemented by the company's involvement in the television industry. Todd-AO entered the business during television's early years, providing sound services for programs such as *Burns and Allen* and *Mr. Ed.* As the company's involvement in motion pictures intensified during the 1960s, so too did its participation in prime-time television programming. Todd-AO supplied sound services for programs such as *The Beverly Hillbillies, Petticoat Junction,* and *Green Acres.* Although the company figured as one of the pioneers in television sound on its own, its reputation in the industry was bolstered substantially after the 1986 acquisition of Glen Glenn Sound. Glen Glenn provided sound services for *I Love Lucy* beginning in 1951, a contract that cemented its reputation as a leader in sound post-production. Following the signal success with *I Love Lucy,* Glen Glenn provided sound services to a host of television programs, including *The Dick Van Dyke Show, Gunsmoke, Bonanza, Mayberry RFD, Gomer Pyle, My Three Sons, Mission Impossible, Get Smart,* and *Wild, Wild West.*

Further expansion through acquisition soon followed the purchase of Glen Glenn. In 1987, Todd-AO acquired New York-based TransAudio and renamed the asset Todd-AO Studios East, its addition marking the company's first move outside Hollywood. The following year Todd-AO added sound stages in Studio City, California, on property owned by CBS, and constructed a scoring stage in 1992. Annual revenue, which totaled $14 million the year Glen Glenn was acquired, grew substantially during the expansion period. By 1994, Todd-AO was generating more than $32 million in revenue, and set to record more robust growth in the coming years.

Salah M. Hassanein, a Todd-AO director since 1962, was named president in 1994 and began implementing an ambitious expansion program. Hassanein intended to diversify the company's post-production services and to greatly extend its geographic reach, hoping to lessen Todd-AO's vulnerability to film production cycles. As a result, the company entered the video services business in 1994 via acquisition, renaming the acquired property Todd-AO Video Services. The following year, the company completed its first move overseas, acquiring the production unit of London-based Chrysalis. In 1996, Todd-AO acquired another London-based post-production company named Filmatic. Together, the two acquisitions extended Todd-AO's video services capabilities into the European market. Also in 1996, the company acquired Editworks, which established a video services presence in Atlanta and moved the company into the commercial and advertising market.

The Union of Todd-AO, Soundelux, and 4MC in 2000

In the years leading up to the merger between TCI and AT&T, Hassanein spearheaded robust growth. By 1999, when AT&T acquired TCI, Todd-AO was generating more than $118 million in sales, nearly twice the amount recorded three years earlier and roughly four times the sales volume registered when Hassanein took command in 1994. It was at this juncture in Todd-AO's development that Liberty Media began cobbling together the companies that would lead the cable and communications conglomerate into the post-production business. At the heart of the new company created by Liberty Media were Todd-AO and two other post-production concerns, Four Media Company (4MC) and Soundelux. Created in June 2000, the new company, named Liberty Livewire, represented a $420 million investment, yielding a corporate entity with a broad reach into the spectrum of post-production services, including sound editing and mixing, film editing, film transfers, special effects, and DVD authoring.

The addition of 4MC and Soundelux to the capabilities possessed by Todd-AO created a well-rounded foundation for the newly formed Liberty Livewire. Established in 1993, 4MC devoted itself to investment in new digital systems and equipment during the seven-year period leading up to its inclusion underneath the Liberty Livewire fold. The company provided feature film and commercial post-production services, serving the motion picture, television production, and multimedia industries. Its facilities were located in Los Angeles, San Francisco, Singapore, and London. Soundelux was founded in 1982 by Wylie Stateman and Lon Bender, two veteran sound editors with numerous awards to their names. As a supervising sound editor, Stateman earned Academy Award nominations for *True Lies, Born on the Fourth of July,* and *Cliffhanger,* as well as a British Academy Award for *JFK,* among other nominations and awards. Bender established his name in sound design with his contributions to the film *Coal Miner's Daughter,* which was nominated for an Academy Award for Best Sound. Bender earned a host of nominations and awards for his work in sound design following *Coal Miner's Daughter,* including the 1995 Academy Award, British Academy Award, and Golden Reel Award for his work in *Braveheart.*

Todd-AO, 4MC, and Soundelux, each operating under the auspices of Liberty Livewire, fell under the control of two TCI veterans. David P. Beddow was selected as Liberty Livewire's

```
┌─────────────────────────────────────────────┐
│                 Key Dates:                    │
│                                               │
│ 1952:  Todd-AO Corporation is formed.         │
│ 1955:  Oklahoma! is the first feature film to │
│        use the com-pany's new sound           │
│        technology, earning that year's        │
│        Academy Award for Best Sound.          │
│ 1986:  Company acquires Glen Glenn Sound.     │
│ 1987:  Todd-AO moves beyond Hollywood by      │
│        acquiring New York-based TransAudio.   │
│ 2000:  Liberty Livewire is formed in June;    │
│        Soundelux and Triumph Communications   │
│        are acquired in July; Soho Group       │
│        Limited is acquired in August; Liberty │
│        Livewire gains control of Video        │
│        Services Corpora-tion in December.     │
│ 2001:  Group W Network Services is acquired.  │
└─────────────────────────────────────────────┘
```

chief executive officer upon the company's formation in June 2000. Formerly an executive vice-president of TCI Communications, Inc.—the U.S. cable subsidiary of TCI—Beddow was joined by another TCI executive, William R. Fitzgerald, who was elected Liberty Livewire's chairman of the board in August 2000. Fitzgerald was a former executive vice-president and chief operating officer of TCI. In day-to-day command over Liberty Livewire, Beddow presided over three former rivals whose union under the Liberty Livewire umbrella presumed less competition among Todd-AO, 4MC, and Soundelux, and consequently more clients and increased revenues for the three companies. Beddow, in an April 3, 2000 interview with *Variety*, remarked, "When you put all of these companies together, you can get a much better utilization of personnel and facilities, enabling you to improve [profit] margins in that respect."

Expansion in 2000 Creates Post-Production Conglomerate

The three companies that formed Liberty Livewire's core were soon joined by other post-production firms. Fitzgerald and Beddow had only taken their first steps down what promised to be a lengthy acquisition trail. On June 21, 2000, the company announced it had agreed to acquire privately held Triumph Communications Group from its founder, Paul Dujardin, in a $29.4 million deal. The acquisition gave Liberty Livewire a toehold in the area of broadcast transmission services. Triumph Communications designed and implemented video transmission services for a variety of clients, including broadcasters, cable networks, news, sports, infomercials, and corporate organizations.

The Triumph Communications acquisition was followed by two separate acquisitions that added substantially to Liberty Livewire's post-production capabilities, both domestically and abroad. The smaller of the two acquisitions was completed under the aegis of 4MC, which paid an estimated $25 million for U.K.-based Soho Group Ltd. The deal included the purchase of real estate in London's Soho area and control over three London-based companies that primarily served the advertising industry. Specifically, the acquisition gave Liberty Livewire ownership of a film lab named Soho Images, a commercial editing shop named Soho 601, and a 50 percent stake in Soho

Computamatch, which provided negative cutting services employing proprietary computerized technology. At roughly the same time, Liberty Livewire acquired Northvale, New Jersey-based Video Services Corporation (VSC), the parent company for eight operating subsidiaries in New York, New Jersey, Florida, and California. The $125 million acquisition represented a significant addition to Liberty Livewire's ever growing portfolio of post-production assets. In an August 2000 article in *SHOOT*, Beddow explained that VSC's "fiber and satellite transmission network in the New York and Washington areas is particularly noteworthy." He continued, "Along with the recent acquisition of Triumph Communications, and 4MC's Burbank and Singapore facilities and Todd-AO's London Broadcast Operations Center, VSC's addition will put Livewire in the forefront in the delivery of broadcast transmission services."

By the time Liberty Livewire celebrated the end of its first year of business, the company had acquired ten media companies. The company had attracted considerable attention within the entertainment industry for its aggressive, acquisitive activities, but the reaction from Wall Street was less than positive. Liberty Livewire's stock began trading at $48 per share and within several weeks rose to a record high of $74.69 per share. By the time the company was celebrating the completion of its first year of business, however, its share price had plummeted, dropping 91 percent in value. Two senior executives left the company during the downward spiral, including Beddow, whose departure in April 2001 left Liberty Livewire without a chief executive officer. Fitzgerald offered his explanation for the tepid response among analysts and investors. In a June 4, 2001 interview with the *Los Angeles Business Journal*, he said, "It's probably because Liberty Livewire is not well understood. We haven't gone a huge distance in telling the story. We decided to walk before we run with our assets and get our ducks in a row on the operating side before getting out and publicly telling the story." Robert T. Walston, chairman and chief executive officer of 4MC before its acquisition by Liberty Livewire, was selected to replace Beddow. To Walston fell the task of continuing Liberty Livewire's development into a post-production conglomerate without parallel.

Principal Subsidiaries

A.F. Associates Inc.; Asia Broadcast Centre; Atlantic Satellite Communication Inc.; Audio Plus Video International Inc.; Audio Plus Video West; Company 3; Digital Image; Editworks; Encore Video; Filmcore; 525 Studios; Four Media Company; Four Media U.K.; Group W Network Services; Hollywood Digital; Level 3 Post; Manhattan Transfer/Edit Inc.; Manhattan Transfer Miami; Method; POP Cinrama DVD; POP Sound; POP Studios; Riot; Rushes; Soho Group; Soundelux; Sound One; SVC; Tele-Cine Ltd.; Todd-AO Corporation; Triumph Communications; Video Services Corporation; Virgin TV; Waterfront Comm. Corp.; West 1 Television.

Principal Competitors

Laser-Pacific Media Corporation; Point.360; Digital Generation Systems, Inc.; Lucas Digital Ltd. LLC.

Further Reading

Berger, Robin, "Livewire Powers Up Interactive Television," *Electronic Media,* December 4, 2000, p. 10.

Diorio, Carl, "Livewire Turns Up Volume with Soundelux," *Variety,* July 24, 2000, p. 63.

Graser, Marc, "Malone Can't Leave Biz Alone," *Variety,* April 3, 2000, p. 1.

Ibold, Hans, "Liberty Media's Post-Production Foray Proves Costly," *Los Angeles Business Journal,* June 4, 2001, p. 7.

Mermigas, Diane, "Profile: David Beddow," *Electronic Media,* September 11, 2000, p. 34.

Takaki, Millie, "Liberty Media Buys Todd-AO, Soundelux," *SHOOT,* August 13, 1999, p. 1.

——, "Liberty Spreads Stateside, Overseas," *SHOOT,* August 25, 2000, p. 1.

—Jeffrey L. Covell

Littlewoods plc

Sir John Moores Building
100 Old Hall Street
Liverpool, Merseyside L70 1DX
United Kingdom
Telephone: (0151) 235 2222
Fax: (0151) 235 2319
Web site: http://www.littlewoods.co.uk

Private Company
Incorporated: 1923 as Littlewoods Pools
Employees: 25,000
Sales: £1.89 billion ($3.45 billion) (2001)
NAIC: 452110 Department Stores; 452990 All Other General Merchandise Stores; 454110 Electronic Shopping and Mail-Order Houses

Littlewoods plc, formerly known as Littlewoods Organisation PLC, is the largest privately owned family company in the United Kingdom, with shareholders' investment valued at £998.3 million. It was started in Liverpool in 1923 as a football (soccer) pool business by John Moores and two partners, all of them then full-time employees of a telegraph company in that city. The name Littlewoods Pools was chosen to conceal their involvement from their employers. After a loss-making first season the other two withdrew, but Moores held on, assisted by other members of his family and, in particular, by his brother Cecil, who joined the business. John Moores entered retailing in 1932 with a mail-order business and in 1937 opened the first Littlewoods chain store. The three businesses prospered. Two more were started in 1985 after Sir John Moores (he was knighted in 1972) had called in non-family executives to take over the day-to-day management of the firm.

By 2001, the company operated 118 Littlewoods stores offering a wide variety of clothing and household products; 181 Littlewoods Index catalog shops, 99 of which were located within Littlewoods stores; and 24 Littlewoods Discount stores featuring a wide range of quality merchandise at discount prices. In addition to being the fourth largest clothing retailer in the United Kingdom and the fifth largest nonfood retailer, Lit-

tlewoods was also the second largest home shopping company in the country through its operation of such catalogs as Littlewoods, Janet Fraser, Burlington, Peter Craig, John Moores, and Littlewoods Extra. The company was also involved in Internet retailing through e-commerce sites. The company participates in two joint ventures: in partnership with Granada Media Group, Littlewoods operates Shop!, a television home shopping channel; while Littlewoods Personal Finance, a venture with Woolwich plc, offers a wide range of financial services to Littlewoods' customer base. By late 2001, the concern was still wholly owned by members of the Moores family, though Sir John Moores had died in September 1993 at age 97.

Football Pools Kickoff

In and after the 1920s, with large corporations already starting to dominate the British economy, promising niches offering opportunities for rapid growth from ploughed-back profit were relatively rare for those lacking capital. That John Moores hit upon football pools at the beginning of the 1923–24 playing season was a most timely stroke of good fortune. The Cup Final, held at Wembley for the first time earlier that year, had drawn much attention to Association Football, which soon developed into a well-supported working-class spectator sport on Saturdays and a topic of conversation for the rest of the week. Wage earners' disposable incomes, though still small, grew rapidly in those years, and a business that gave them an opportunity to place small bets did not have difficulty in attracting some of this surplus. Sales of betting coupons in the form of postal orders reached unprecedented heights as a normally weekend sport became an even more popular weekday pastime offering the chance of winning more than even the most thrifty wage earner could ever hope to save in a lifetime: £13,000 was laid out on a penny bet in one instance during the 1930s.

John Moores was born at Eccles near Manchester in January 1896, the eldest of four sons in a family eventually to number eight children. He left school at 14 to work as a messenger boy at the Manchester Post Office but was soon accepted in a course at the Post Office School of Telegraphy. This enabled him, in 1912, at 16 years of age, to join the Commercial Cable Company as a junior operator. After World War I, in which he served as a wireless operator in the Royal Navy, he rejoined Commercial Cable and in 1921 was transferred from Liverpool to Waterville, the company's base near the southwest tip of Ireland, where he started a private business on the side supplying goods to company colleagues and to the local golf club. Transferred back to Liverpool, he tried again to start his own business, this time with two partners and the idea of a football pool.

Moores and his two partners, Colin Askham and Bill Hughes, entered the business when there was only one small, struggling competitor and little capital was needed—each partner put in £50 originally and later another £50. Having weathered unprofitable beginnings, Littlewoods Pools emerged as a clear market leader because of its organizational skill and attention to detail in the regular dispatch of coupons early each week, careful checking of the results after the Saturday matches, and the handling of an increasing number of small payments. Growth needed to be at a pace to fund the all-important promotional expenditure required, but overhead was relatively cheap: no prestigious high-street premises were required for a postal business.

Expanding into Home Shopping and Retailing in the 1930s

Football pools appealed mainly to men. To appeal to women, Littlewoods Mail Order Stores were begun in January 1932 when Great Universal Stores (GUS), an established mail-order business in nearby Manchester, was in trouble. Britain was soon to start climbing out of the deepest trough of depression—again the timing was right—and Moores offered an element of chance in a venture aimed mainly at working-class women who were prepared to invest a small cash sum each week to buy goods for themselves or their families. This was a logical diversification of the existing business. Besides taking advantage of Littlewoods' already familiar household name, it also built upon the organization and experience gained in postal pools and on John Moores's earlier experience of direct selling in Ireland. Again, nothing was spent on retail outlets, for the business, like GUS, operated on the club principle whereby the many local organizers, working from their own homes, recruited others nearby who paid a small weekly installment in cash for goods shown in a catalog. A £1 club, for instance, consisted of 20 members who each paid a shilling a week. A weekly draw provided the element of luck, the first winner securing her purchases at once and the others in their turn. There were also £2 and £3 clubs on the same principle. The first catalog ran to 167 pages. The initial cost of launching what was to become an extremely successful enterprise was £20,000.

Moores's venture into chain-store retailing in the mid-1930s was well-timed, too, for the British economy was moving up to a prosperous peak in 1937. Real earnings were growing fast and unemployment was falling. Entering chain-store retailing was a

further logical step that took advantage of buying experience and contacts gained in the mail-order business; but this time it did involve costly high-street premises and competition with well-established chain stores, notably Woolworth and Marks & Spencer, which also offered competitively priced goods. The new stores, however, could depend not only upon the familiar Littlewoods name but also on providing basic and serviceable goods at fair prices without undue regard for passing fashion. The first store was opened in Blackpool, Britain's most popular working-class holiday resort, in 1937. By 1939, 24 stores had been opened in various parts of the country.

By then the Moores family had already amassed considerable financial strength. A new building, situated on the outskirts of Liverpool as its Pools headquarters, became the postal censorship center during World War II. Other premises—there were 16 by 1944—produced barrage balloons, parachutes, rubber dinghies, and Wellington bomber fuselages, as well as 12 million shells and six million fuses.

Steady Growth from the 1950s Through the Early 1990s

Immediately after the war the renovation of the stores and the building of new ones were made difficult by building controls. Soon, however, shoppers' habits and tastes were changed by what came to be called the retailing revolution, in which vastly increased purchasing power necessitated a leap in demand for consumer durables, including automobiles. There were nevertheless 52 Littlewoods stores in operation by 1952, more than twice as many as there had been in 1939, 70 by the mid-1960s, 108 in 1984, and 122 in 1990. They were located throughout the United Kingdom, from Belfast to Norwich and from Inverness to Truro, and sold clothing, household goods, food, wines, and spirits; most also had restaurants. Over a third of mothers with young children were said to shop there at least once a month.

In 1953 John Moores, quick to recognize the advent of the credit-buying society, launched Brian Mills, a company based in Sunderland, which supplied goods to customers before any payment was made. Not surprisingly, this made the older club method of mail-order less popular. A second credit mail-order firm, Burlington, also based in Sunderland, was added in 1958 and a third, Littlewoods Warehouses, Liverpool, in 1960, the year after the original business had been renamed the John Moores Home Shopping Service. A fifth credit company, Janet Frazer, was opened in Sunderland in 1964 and a sixth, Peter Craig, followed in 1968.

When he retired from the chairmanship in 1982, Sir John Moores brought in as his successor the first non-family chairman, John Clement, from the dairy business Unigate. Clement, in his turn, recruited as group chief executive Desmond Pitcher, a Liverpudlian and high-tech communications expert, a former employee of Plessey. The corporate board in 1990 was comprised of Sir John, his four children, and other non-family members. Some of Sir John Moores's and Cecil Moores's grandchildren sat on the divisional boards. The new regime reorganized Littlewoods' finances and in 1985 started Index, a catalog shop operation that later became a separate division. By 1990 there were already 50 of these shops within existing

Key Dates:

1923: John Moores and two partners form Littlewoods Pools as a football (soccer) pool business.
1932: Company enters home shopping sector with launch of Littlewoods Mail Order Stores.
1937: Company enters chain-store retailing with the opening of the first Littlewoods store.
1953: Club method of mail-order operation begins to be replaced with credit-based mail order.
1985: Index, a catalog shop operation, is launched.
1993: Company founder dies, leaving some 32 members of the Moores family with full ownership of the firm.
1995: Family feuding leads to takeover bids, which are rejected.
1997: Littlewoods sells 19 of its largest high street stores to Marks & Spencer for £193 million; a £370 million takeover of Freemans is blocked by antitrust authorities.
1998: Company joins with Granada Media Group to launch Shop!, a television home shopping channel.
1999: Littlewoods Personal Finance is formed through a joint venture with Woolwich plc.
2000: Company's pools and betting business, Littlewoods Leisure, is sold for £161 million.

Littlewoods chain stores and a further 46 on their own sites. The second new venture, also started in 1985, was Credit and Data Marketing Services (CDMS), a credit and information business that operated in retail finance, financial services—mainly general insurance—and marketing. A property company, Centreville Estates, formed jointly with P&O Property Holdings, was added in 1990, to which each concern transferred a small number of its premises of equivalent value.

By opening two shops in St. Petersburg's main shopping street in October 1991, Littlewoods became the first major Western retailer to operate in the Soviet Union. These shops were Anglo-Russian ventures, the first selling (for Russian currency) men's and women's clothing, and the second a hard-currency business dealing in electrical and photographic goods, beauty products, clothing, wines and spirits, and food.

The relative importance of the different parts of Littlewoods' extensive business—still located in Liverpool and more dominant there not only because of its own development but also because of the disappearance of most of the city's port activity—could best be seen from a glance at its trading results for 1990. The Home Shopping Division, no longer a club enterprise but a sophisticated and highly automated credit system depending increasingly on telephone orders, produced the largest turnover, £933 million, and profit, £53.5 million. Only GUS, with 40 percent of the U.K. market, was ahead of it. Next came the chain stores, with £623 million turnover and £29.4 million profit. Of the new ventures, Index had the larger turnover, £153 million, but was not yet profitable. CDMS, on an income of £18.6 million, had a profit of £1.8 million. The combined retail sales for all divisions was £1.7 billion, with profits of £83.6 million. Much less financial information was

known about Littlewoods Pools, the foundation upon which the whole Littlewoods Organisation had been built. It could still claim 77 percent of the U.K. pools business. The largest prize—or dividend as the company preferred to call it—that had been paid out at the beginning, in 1923, was £2 and 12 shillings. In 1991 Littlewoods paid out over £2 million for a prize, far more than its other U.K. competitors. It distributed £170 million in prize money altogether in the season ended July 1990.

Littlewoods' football pools operations were threatened at the beginning of the 1990s by a campaign to introduce a national lottery. With over three-quarters of the British pools market, the company responded by proposing an arts and sports foundation to which it would contribute, alongside two other U.K. pools companies, Vernons and Zetters. The foundation was launched at the end of July 1991 for the start of the football season in August. The Chancellor of the Exchequer reduced pools betting duty from 40 percent to 37.5 percent for an initial period of four years with the 2.5 percent difference being made available to the foundation and expected to be worth around £20 million a year. In addition, the pools companies began contributing roughly £40 million annually.

In the recession that marked the beginning of the 1990s, Littlewoods proved the resilience of its retailing methods by producing a 46 percent increase in pretax profits in 1990, in contrast to the downward trend of most of the major U.K. retailers. Profits the following year reached a record level of nearly £100 million. Littlewoods' emphasis on budget shopping and value for money paid off handsomely during the downturn.

Mid-1990s and Beyond: Family Feuding, Restructuring, Fending off Takeover Bids

In April 1993 Pitcher handed over the reins at Littlewoods to Barry Dale, with Pitcher becoming nonexecutive vice-chairman. In September of that same year, Sir John Moores died, leaving ownership of the firm in the hands of some 32 members of the Moores family. The leadership change and the death of the company founder came at an inopportune time as the mid-1990s saw a dramatic reversal of fortune for Littlewoods. Revenues of the pools operations were significantly affected by the launch in November 1994 of the National Lottery, which proved highly popular. Both the Littlewoods and Index chains were being hurt by increasing competition and poor management. In the wake of the death of the dominant founder, under whose watch the company had limited dividend payouts in order to plow money back into the business, the Moores family owners of Littlewoods began demanding and receiving much higher dividends.

Family feuding and interference in the management of Littlewoods were soon more than evident. Pressure from the family led to the ouster of the deputy chief executive in October 1994 and then the sacking of Dale in March 1995. Two months later, Pitcher departed as well via resignation, leaving the company with a dearth of top managers. It appeared that members of the Moores family were jousting for control, with some members pushing for the selloff or flotation of the company in order to cash in their ownership stakes. The company founder, however, had set up a rule whereby a shareholder could sell her stake to an outsider only with a 75 percent vote in favor of the sale.

Takeover bids were soon launched, including a £1.1 billion proposal from Dale, who had also in the meantime sued Littlewoods for wrongful termination. The other bid that surfaced in 1995 was another £1.1 billion offer, this one a combined bid from Iceland Group, a food retailer proposing to take over the high street stores, and N Brown, a mail-order company eager to snatch up Littlewoods' mail-order operations. In December 1995, however, members of the Moores family voted four to one against opening the company's books to either of these parties or any other party, thereby rejecting the idea of a company sale.

Initially Bill Huntley was installed as chief executive following the firing of Dale. Huntley had been director of customer and marketing services at Sperry Computer Systems. In January 1996 Littlewoods announced that it planned a partial flotation of the company within three years, but the plan was never implemented. Just a few months later, more management changes occurred, with James Ross taking over as chairman from the departing Leonard van Geest, who had served in that capacity since 1990. Ross had been chief executive of Cable and Wireless until November 1995, when a serious boardroom battle led to his departure. Assurances were given to Ross that he would have greater power than his predecessors to manage Littlewoods as well as a more clearly defined role, and that the members of the Moores family had agreed to "a clear separation between ownership and management issues." It appeared that the family feuding had come to at least a temporary halt and that Ross could concentrate on turning Littlewoods around.

During an event-filled 1997, the new management team at Littlewoods began the year with a new strategy of shifting the firm's focus from retail to mail order. One move toward this goal had already occurred in 1996, namely the launch of Index Extra, Littlewoods' first direct-mail home shopping catalog. After scrapping a planned £135 million store expansion program in January 1997, Littlewoods reached a preliminary agreement to sell all 135 of its high street stores to Kingfisher; the deal fell through mid-year, however, when the two parties were unable to agree on the final terms. Instead, Littlewoods sold just 19 of its largest stores to Marks & Spencer for £200 million. At the same time, Littlewoods was attempting to expand its mail-order operations. It reached an agreement in March to buy Freemans, Sears PLC's mail-order operation, for £395 million. But this deal was soon trumped by a better offer from N Brown. When that deal fell apart, Littlewoods tried anew with a £370 million bid, only to be rebuffed by the Monopolies and Mergers Commission, which blocked the takeover in November 1997 on antitrust grounds. In the midst of all of this tumult, Barry Gibson was appointed as group chief executive in September 1997. With a strong background in marketing, Gibson had most recently served as group retail director of British Airports Authority (BAA), responsible for developing and implementing the retail strategy at BAA's seven U.K. airports.

Under Gibson, Littlewoods restructured its operations, including the removal of layers of management. The retail and catalog operations were also integrated into a division called Littlewoods Retail, and the company began to emphasize the Littlewoods name. The Index catalog stores were renamed Littlewoods Index, and the Index Extra catalog was redubbed Littlewoods Extra. To further develop the retail operations, Littlewoods in 1998 entered into a joint venture with Granada Media Group to launch Shop!, a television home shopping channel that by 2001 could be viewed by more than eight million U.K. households. Littlewoods held a 65 percent stake in the venture. In July 1999 the company joined forces with Woolwich plc to form Littlewoods Personal Finance. The new venture aimed to use Littlewoods' customer base and Woolwich's telephone-based personal banking system to offer such financial services as personal loans, credit cards, savings accounts, and homeowner's insurance policies. Littlewoods also began moving into e-commerce around the turn of the millennium.

During 1999 a separate board of directors began running the company's pools and betting business, Littlewoods Leisure. This move was a prelude to the sale during 2000 of Littlewoods Leisure to Rodime plc, a firm involved in digital technologies, for £161 million. The divestment of the firm's founding business would enable it to focus exclusively on high street, catalog, and Internet retailing (it also changed its name from Littlewoods Organisation plc to Littlewoods plc in the wake of the divestment). Littlewoods' retail operations were struggling, however, posting a 23 percent drop in profits for the year ending in April 2000. The high street stores were being hard hit by competition from such upstart discount chains as New Look, Matalan, and Peacocks. Gibson announced later in 2000 that Littlewoods would adopt a "better value retailing" strategy, with the prices of some clothing lines reduced by more than 40 percent, in an attempt to better compete with the upstarts. The catalog operations, with the exception of the Littlewoods Extra direct-mail catalog, were in serious decline. During 2001 talks were initiated with N Brown about a possible sale of the company for £500 million ($713 million) but they soon collapsed. The struggling Littlewoods faced an uncertain future as it posted an operating loss of £8.1 million for the 2001 fiscal year. Company management pointed out, however, that the second half of that year had been much stronger than the first half, a sign of a possible recovery.

Principal Subsidiaries

Business Express Couriers Ltd.; Centreville Estates (Holdings) Ltd.; H Littlewood (Scotland) Ltd.; H Littlewood Ltd.; Harrogate Hotels Ltd.; Inside Story Ltd.; J & C Moores (Direct) Ltd.; Littlewoods Chain Stores Holdings Ltd.; Littlewoods Property Developments Ltd.; Littlewoods Property Ltd.; Littlewoods Hampers Ltd.; Littlewoods International (Far East) Limited (Hong Kong); Littlewoods International Ltd.; Littlewoods Mail Order Stores Ltd.; Littlewoods of England Ltd.; Littlewoods Retail Ltd.; Brian Mills Ltd.; Burlington Warehouses Ltd.; C D M S Ltd.; Home Shopping Network (U K) Ltd.; Imagination Homeshop Ltd.; Index Ltd.; Janet Frazer Ltd.; John Moores Home Shopping Service Ltd.; Littlewoods Home Shopping Finance Ltd.; Littlewoods Stores Ltd.; Littlewoods Warehouses Ltd.; M.C. Hitchen & Sons Ltd.; Nationwide Debt Recovery Ltd.; Peter Craig Ltd.; Shopping Mail Ltd.; The Home Shopping Channel Ltd.; Littlewoods Secretarial Services Ltd.; Littlewoods 2000 Ltd.; Liverpool Mail Order Stores Ltd.; Liverpool Stadium Ltd.; Shopping Post Ltd.; The Catalogue Shop Ltd.

Principal Competitors

The Great Universal Stores P.L.C.; ASDA Group Limited; NEXT plc; Otto Versand GmbH & Co.; Matalan Plc; New Look

Group plc; N Brown Group plc; Marks & Spencer p.l.c.; Mothercare plc.

Further Reading

Bagnall, Sarah, "Dynasty Returns As a Real-Life 'Soap,'" *Times* (London), December 8, 1995.

——, "Family at War over Ailing Littlewoods," *Times* (London), May 29, 1995.

Bernoth, Ardyn, "Leaderless Littlewoods in Disarray," *Times* (London), April 2, 1995.

Beyaztas, Binnur, "Overdue Retail Shake-up Puts Littlewoods on a New Track," *Marketing,* June 25, 1998, pp. 14–15.

Blackhurst, Chris, "Sir Desmond Pitcher," *Management Today,* December 1992, pp. 58–60.

Clegg, Barbara, *The Man Who Made Littlewoods: The Story of John Moores,* London: Hodder & Stoughton, 1993, 239 p.

Edgecliffe-Johnson, Andrew, "Littlewoods Empire Strikes Back After Store Wars," *Financial Times,* December 13, 1997, p. 16.

Fazey, Ian Hamilton, "Moores Get-Together Promises Fireworks," *Financial Times,* November 27, 1995, p. 11.

Killgren, Lucy, "Littlewoods Under Scrutiny," *Financial Times,* September 17, 2000.

Marsh, Harriet, "Littlewoods' Double Trouble," *Marketing,* March 13, 1997, pp. 22–23.

Oram, Roderick, "Travails of a Family at War," *Financial Times,* March 25, 1995, p. 9.

Oram, Roderick, and Christopher Brown-Humes, "Littlewood's Game New Chairman," *Financial Times,* June 11, 1996, p. 26.

Patten, Sally, "Littlewoods Adopts Whatever, Wherever, Whenever Mantra," *Times* (London), June 28, 2000, p. 29.

Ramesh, Randeep, "Assault Mounted on Fortress Littlewoods," *Times* (London), October 29, 1995.

Syedain, Hashi, "A Change in Store," *Management Today,* March 1991, pp. 82–85.

Voyle, Susanna, "Catalogue Empire Searching for a Way Out of the Woods," *Financial Times,* February 10, 2001, p. 19.

——, "Littlewoods Takes Down the 'For Sale' Sign," *Financial Times,* June 27, 2001.

—T. C. Barker
—update: David E. Salamie

Luby's, Inc.

2211 Northeast Loop 410
Post Office Box 33069
San Antonio, Texas 78265-3069
U.S.A.
Telephone: (210) 654-9000
Fax: (210) 599-8407
Web site: http://www.lubys.com

Public Company
Incorporated: 1959 as Cafeterias, Inc.
Employees: 14,000
Sales: $493.4 million (2000)
Stock Exchanges: New York
Ticker Symbol: LUB
NAIC: 722212 Cafeterias

Luby's, Inc. is a leading cafeteria-style restaurant chain. From one small cafeteria in 1948 located in downtown San Antonio, Luby's steadily expanded, first in Texas and then in other southern states, to become a cafeteria chain with more than 200 units. In 2000, the company operated 173 units in Texas, 11 in Arizona, eight each in Oklahoma and Tennessee, five each in Arkansas and Florida, three in New Mexico, and two each in Louisiana, Mississippi, and Missouri. Unlike many restaurant chains, Luby's does not franchise its units, but it does compensate each unit manager with a generous portion of the profits from the unit the manager runs.

Luby's cafeterias offer freshly prepared, family-style food at reasonable prices served in attractive settings. The cafeterias cater primarily to shoppers and to store and office personnel at lunchtime, and to families for the dinner meal. The cafeterias do not serve breakfast. They are located in shopping and business developments as well as in residential areas. Prior to the company's financial difficulties that began in the late 1990s, individual units were typically 10,000 to 11,000 square feet in area and could accommodate up to 300 people. As part of an attempted turnaround, a new prototype unit was developed, which was 6,000 to 8,600 square feet in size, seated 170 to 214 guests, and had a more contemporary design. Takeout service is a growing part of the chain's business, and drive-throughs are being added to more and more units.

Luby's Origins

Luby's roots run through America's political, social, and economic history, beginning with the first unit and extending through every successive decade of the 20th century. Although Luby's was incorporated in 1959, the company's history was planted in 1909 when clothes merchant Harry Luby made a business trip from his home in Springfield, Missouri, to Chicago, Illinois. Luby was captivated by a new type of restaurant where patrons picked the food items they wanted from a counter and carried their own trays to dining tables.

Luby immediately saw that the Chicago restaurant was employing the then emerging concepts of mass production and assembly lines in the restaurant business. Two years later, Luby opened a similar operation in Springfield, Missouri. From a 12-foot counter he built himself, Luby dished out freshly prepared food at reasonable prices. One year later in 1912, Luby opened a second cafeteria in Springfield. From Missouri to Oklahoma to Texas, Luby opened one cafeteria after another over the next ten years. In stepping-stone fashion, Luby would sell outright or retain a partial interest in a unit before moving southward to establish his next eatery. In 1927, the 39-year-old Harry Luby had made enough money to retire in San Antonio where he oversaw his investments in seven cafeterias in Texas and one in Kansas.

Amiable and generous, Harry Luby had operated his restaurants on some very simple concepts: good food at reasonable prices for the customers and a generous portion of profits for the managers. "Share the work, share the risks, share the profits" was a guiding principle for Luby. Thus, as an investor in eight cafeterias, Luby gave 40 percent of profits to the unit managers, an unusually large percentage at the time as well as in the years that followed.

A New Generation of Leadership: 1930s to World War II

Harry's son Robert (Bob) M. Luby grew up in the restaurant business, playing after school in cafeteria basements as a young

---

Company Perspectives:

The Company's product strategy is to provide its customers with a wide variety of freshly cooked foods served cafeteria-style at reasonable prices in an attractive and informal environment. These products appeal to a broad range of consumers, including families with children, seniors, shoppers, and business people who want quick, healthy meals. Generally located in close proximity to retail centers, business developments, and residential areas, the restaurants are open seven days a week, year-round, for lunch and dinner. The restaurants also offer take-out service.

---

child and working in cafeterias cleaning grease traps as a teenager. After graduating from college, Bob Luby and his cousin Earl Luby set their entrepreneurial sights on San Francisco, where they opened a cafeteria that failed to produce the Texas-sized profits his father's restaurants generated. Bob returned to Texas undeterred in his goal to establish and run a successful cafeteria. That goal was reached with a cafeteria in Dallas on Live Oak Street. Luby next enlisted his aunt, uncle, and brother-in-law George H. Wenglein to invest in, establish, and operate a cafeteria in El Paso, Texas.

While Bob Luby's cafeterias prospered during the 1930s, business was bleak for others. Homeless, hungry people often visited Luby's for sustenance. During the Great Depression, the cafeterias associated with Harry and Bob Luby served needy people from the food left over at closing time.

World War II and its wake profoundly altered the United States, sparking social changes and robust economic growth. Forced to sell his Dallas cafeteria when he enlisted in the Army Air Corps, Luby nonetheless continued to think about the food business, even while serving as an intelligence officer. The contacts he made while serving his country constituted the foundation of a management team for the cafeteria chain to come.

Postwar Expansion

In 1946, Bob Luby hung up his military uniform and began plans with his cousin, Charles R. Johnston, to establish a cafeteria for the postwar era. In the decade following the war, household incomes would rise, families would move from cities to suburbs, and lifestyles calling for convenient products and services would reshape the fabric of American life. Amid such change, Americans also would seek the threads of the past.

In 1948, Luby and Johnston recognized the promise of these postwar stirrings and opened a cafeteria with capacity to seat 180 people. Located in downtown San Antonio, the restaurant was an immediate success thanks to returning servicemen in the area and to the postwar housing shortage which had forced many people to live in downtown hotels. Nearby movie theaters provided brisk business in the evening. The cafeteria was managed by Norwood W. Jones, a fellow officer of Luby's while stationed at Santa Ana Army Air Base.

Luby and Johnston's next restaurant was located in the growing and affluent San Antonio suburb of Alamo Heights.

Brother-in-law Wenglein was persuaded to co-manage the cafeteria with John Lee, a prewar Luby's associate. The Alamo Heights cafeteria served as a model for future Luby's units.

From the front seat of a sporty Studebaker serving as their office, the two entrepreneurs traveled the Lone Star state in search of new locations. Luby and Johnston were careful to open new cafeterias only when they had managers to operate the units according to the standards Harry Luby had pioneered.

By 1958, Luby and Johnston had opened 11 cafeterias, each of which had a different configuration of investors. In order to build and operate new Luby's cafeterias, the investors formed Cafeterias, Inc. on February 4, 1959. The preexisting cafeterias were not affected by the move, although those units provided the cash to help the investors finance the new corporation.

Cafeterias, Inc. launched its first cafeteria in March 1960 in a strip shopping center in Corpus Christi and two others followed within 60 days. Although in the black, the three units were not generating the profits normally associated with Luby's cafeterias. Downtown locations proved to be a problem while an experiment to serve breakfast was a mild failure.

Luby's hit pay dirt with its fourth cafeteria located in a far north San Antonio suburb in a retail development called North Star Mall. Bob Luby recalled, "Some people thought we had lost our minds because it was so far out that the city buses didn't serve the mall adequately. We actually had to subsidize the bus service in order to get our employees to work." But the fast-growing affluent suburbs surrounding the mall would fill the fourth corporate Luby's restaurant with patrons and provide profits to build more cafeterias.

With Bob Luby as president and Charles Johnston as executive vice-president, Luby's entered the Houston market in 1965 with an upscale cafeteria that offered an expanded menu and more expensive food items. Operating under the Romano name, the cafeteria quickly became a huge money-maker. The modern structure with its rich decor served as a model for revamping efforts at existing Luby's and proved a market existed for cafeterias with a very modern style and design.

Luby's growth in the Houston market was propelled in part by the nation's space program, initiated in the early 1960s, with its mission control headquarters in the area. In subsequent years, the oil industry and its attendant financiers would fuel the economy further. Meanwhile, the first Luby's located outside of Texas opened in Las Cruces, New Mexico, in 1966.

Consolidating Operations and Going Public: 1970s

The corporation forged a link with the original Luby's cafeterias in 1969 when it agreed to manage those units for the next 15 years, bringing the number of corporate-managed units to 26, of which 17 were company-owned. Luby and Johnston passed their executive management reins to George Wenglein and Norwood Jones, respectively, in 1971. Luby, who remained chairman of the board, recalled the reason for stepping aside at age 61: "I had run the company with Charles since the beginning. . . . Before we started selling stock to the public, I wanted to be darn sure the company could operate without me as president. So Charles and I stepped down earlier than we had to."

In January 1973, the company's stock was offered to the public in the over-the-counter market. The company continued to expand into new areas such as Dallas and to strengthen its internal operations, creating the new corporate position of area manager to oversee existing units and to launch new ones in a specific market.

The Yom Kippur War in October 1973 ushered in an era in which the Texas economy would be inexorably tied to Middle Eastern oil and the volatile political situation in that part of the world. The war created gasoline shortages in the United States but no shortages of customers at Luby's, which offered a reasonably priced, convenient suburban alternative to consumers whose pocketbooks were pinched by higher gas prices and whose auto travel was circumscribed by scarce fuel.

High oil prices soon began to work to Luby's advantage as energy exploration and development in Texas, Oklahoma, and Louisiana injected billions of dollars into the region's economy. With more cafeterias opening to meet the demand, Luby's created a formal training program to ensure that each new cafeteria would have adequate managerial staffers who were service-oriented to customers, sensitive to employees, and cost-conscious to the bottom line.

Establishing a School of Management

The Luby's Story, a history of the company published in 1988, explained that trainees were schooled in the theory and practice of running a cafeteria. The boot-camp style training taught the recruits "the intricacies of butchering a side of beef, baking a lemon meringue pie, and mopping the floor," as well as how to clean the restaurant equipment and replenish the cafeteria serving line.

Trainees also learned to show respect to all Luby's employees. "In the kitchen, the young recruit is taught to show deference to his instructors—the fry cook, the baker, the butcher, and the salad maker. Clearly the young college graduate is the disciple and the veteran cook his master," the corporate history stated.

The deference and respect resulted in a stable workforce at the individual Luby's cafeterias. Luby's recorded one of the lowest turnovers of support staff in the restaurant industry. That low turnover translated into experienced and consistent service for the customers and minimal training costs for the individual units. After graduation, the prospective managers spent seven to ten years of additional training in individual cafeterias, moving from assistant manager to associate manager to manager, and from manager of a small unit to manager of larger and larger units.

Luby's cafeteria managers were given a high degree of autonomy. This enabled them to cater to customer tastes in their local markets with specialized menu offerings. The majority of the food ingredients were purchased locally by the individual cafeteria management team. This permitted managers to take advantage of price bargains in the local wholesale markets and to quickly respond to local product shortages.

A few items such as fried haddock were carried by every cafeteria in the Luby's network. Ingredients for these signature items were centrally sourced by the company. The management team of the individual cafeterias received their compensation based on the financial performance of each cafeteria. The management team consisted of a manager, an associate manager, and two to three assistant managers. Each team received 40 percent of the unit's operating profits. After the salaries of the assistant managers were deducted, the remainder in profits was divided in a 65/35 percent split between the manager and associate manager, respectively.

The opportunity for autonomy and for attractive financial compensation gave Luby's managers a strong incentive to operate profitably for the long-term. Approximately 85 percent of the company's unit managers remained with Luby's for ten years or more.

Growth in the 1980s and Early 1990s

The year 1980 saw corporate revenues surpass the $100 million mark, and the company adopted a new name, Luby's Cafeterias, Inc., in 1981. On February 22, 1982, Luby's entered the financial big league when its stock began trading on the New York Stock Exchange under the LUB symbol.

The 1980s represented a period of expansion outside Texas which was suffering from slumping oil prices. Luby's Texas cafeterias weathered the economic downturn by avoiding waste and cutting labor costs. While others in the restaurant industry expended millions of dollars on advertising and borrowed heavily, Luby's relied on word-of-mouth recommendations to build its customer base and internally generated profits to build new cafeterias. The chain expanded into Oklahoma in 1980 and into Arizona, Arkansas, and Florida in 1988.

In a much publicized incident, random and bizarre violence hit a Luby's restaurant in Killeen, Texas, on October 16, 1991. A lone gunman entered the restaurant filled with patrons and employees, shot and killed 23 people, wounded 25 more, and then turned the gun upon himself. When the killing ended, Luby's had acquired the unwanted distinction of being the site of the worst mass shooting in the history of the nation. The killer took his motive for the murders with him to the grave.

When word of the massacre reached company headquarters in San Antonio, Luby's chairman and several senior executives immediately flew to Killeen to provide aid and comfort to the victims' families, the survivors, and to the community. In fact, Luby's management was praised for its sensitive handling of the crisis surrounding the shooting. When the Killeen Luby's reopened on March 12, 1992, hundreds of people, including some of the survivors, came to the cafeteria to eat freshly prepared jalapeno corn bread, pan-grilled catfish, and Jefferson Davis pie.

The 1990s brought a more vibrant economy to the markets Luby's served and some new directions in its operations. In 1991, the company began developing a new marketing program using television and radio advertising in order to build repeat business and to position itself for youthful customers. "Luby's TV ads cut the mustard, go heavy on the wry" was the double entendre headline over an article appearing in the December 5, 1994 issue of *Nation's Restaurant News*. The article noted Luby's ads used humor to convey the message that its restaurants catered to patrons of every age. Unlike the ads for other chains, Luby's did not merely feature glittery shots of the food and the cafeteria.

During fiscal 1994, Luby's conducted its first cooperative promotion, joining forces with Southwest Airlines, Sea World of Texas, and Karena Hotels of Texas to target families with children. Favorable results from the advertising and promotional campaigns led Luby's to earmark 2 percent of sales for marketing efforts in fiscal 1996.

At its January 1996 annual meeting, Luby's unveiled joint venture plans with Waterstreet Inc. for five to seven seafood restaurants over the next five years. Waterstreet's five restaurants in three cities served moderately priced, Gulf-of-Mexico-style seafood.

With a possible hint of a major new direction for the company as it moved toward the 21st century, Luby's Chairman Ralph "Pete" Erben told shareholders, "We will actively explore other potential concepts for diversification and enhancement of shareholder values." He said the company expected the joint venture to furnish Luby's with "restaurant concepts that provide growth and profitability into the future."

Luby's successful strategy was widely recognized by the press. "Why They're Lining Up at Luby's" was the headline for an article by the *New York Times* in the August 18, 1985, issue describing the company's recipe for success. *Kiplinger's Personal Finance Magazine* included Luby's in its list of "39 Stocks for Your Portfolio" which appeared in the August 1994 issue. An October 19, 1990 article in the *Wall Street Journal* examined how the company maintained its profitability during an economic recession. And *Forbes* magazine named Luby's among the top 200 Best Small Companies for eight of the first ten years the publication conducted the survey.

Restaurant management publications also awarded Luby's top honors. *Restaurant Business* profiled Luby's in a May 1989 article entitled "Slow and Steady Wins." In 1996, for the sixth time in seven annual surveys conducted nationally by *Restaurant and Institutions* magazine, consumers voted Luby's as their favorite in the cafeteria/buffet category.

With firm roots in the local communities it served, Luby's cafeterias were closely involved in local community events and philanthropic endeavors. When Hurricane Carla crashed into the Texas Gulf Coast in September 1961, the Corpus Christi Luby's served as an outpost for the National Guard and scores of emergency workers. Using gas-fired stoves, Luby's dispensed food and hot drinks to police, guardsmen, and neighbors. "We didn't charge a thing, but we made a lot of friends," cafeteria manager Bill Lowe recalled. When the cafeteria reopened for normal business, Lowe remembered, "We were swamped with customers."

In addition to such ad hoc measures, unit managers were given a budget to spend on public service in their areas. The company's largest civic program was the Community Drug Education System. Initiated in 1987, the program received a Presidential Citation for educating students, parents, and teachers in 11 states about the dangers of substance abuse. By the end of fiscal 1996, Luby's had spent more than $1.3 million on the program.

Late 1990s and Beyond: Declining Fortunes

The final years of the 20th century saw Luby's falter. Although the results for fiscal 1997 showed another increase in sales, they also brought an end to a streak of 28 consecutive years of increased earnings per share, as net income fell from $39.2 million to $28.4 million. Luby's was finally being affected by the overall decline of the restaurant industry's cafeteria segment, which was now squeezed by the increasing popularity of both lower priced fast-food outlets and higher priced casual dining chains. Long known for its solid leadership, Luby's at the same time faced a sudden management crisis when, within the space of four days in March 1997, CEO and President John E. Curtis, Jr., committed suicide, apparently triggered in part over concern about potential store closings, and the company's chairman, Ralph Erben, resigned unexpectedly. John B. Lahourcade, who had previously served as both CEO and chairman, was named interim chairman and David Daviss became acting CEO. The interim executive team announced in August 1997 that the company would close four stores and take a pretax charge of about $12 million in connection with the closures. Two months later, Barry J.C. Parker was hired as the company's new president and CEO. Parker was a former CEO of County Seat Stores, a nationwide clothing store chain. At the same time, Daviss replaced Lahourcade as chairman.

In 1998, the year that founder Bob Luby died, the new Luby's management team took steps aimed at sparking a turnaround. More than a dozen additional underperforming units were slated for closure with a $36.9 million charge taken in connection with asset impairments and store closings. Luby's began expanding its takeout service and opened its first unit with a drive-through window at a new restaurant in Tulsa, Oklahoma. These initiatives proved successful, leading to the rollout of food-to-go and drive-throughs at additional Luby's outlets. In January 1999 the company changed its name to Luby's, Inc., dropping the word "cafeteria." This move was in line with the company's new store prototype, which imparted a warmer, more casual dining feel by jettisoning the traditional stainless steel tray lines. The new units, which were smaller than usual at 9,600 square feet, also featured a hearth oven where a customer could pick out a steak to be cooked to order and ready by the time the customer reached the cash register. Luby's also introduced a "community restaurant" format in 1999, which was even smaller at about 7,000 square feet, and was specifically designed for markets that were previously considered not large enough to support a traditional Luby's. In a further retrenchment, Luby's sold its joint-venture interest in Water Street Seafood, having determined that the casual dining chain was not a good fit with the company's expertise in limited-service restaurateuring.

Despite price increases, both overall and same-store sales continued to decline through the fiscal year ending in August 2000. Net income that year totaled only $9.1 million, compared to $39.2 million just four years earlier. Another 15 stores were marked for closure during fiscal 2000, leading to a further charge of $14.5 million. With the company's stock price plummeting and a number of Luby's managers unhappy with a new compensation system Parker instituted that tied pay to specific sales targets, Parker resigned suddenly in October 2000. Daviss again assumed the positions of president and CEO on an interim basis. The company announced that it would suspend payment of its quarterly dividend for the first time in its history. It also reinstituted the old profit-sharing compensation plan for managers and launched new marketing campaigns.

The news grew bleaker by December 2000. Luby's reported a net loss of $2 million for the first quarter of fiscal 2001, a dissident group of shareholders began organizing a proxy fight for the annual meeting to be held in January 2001, and the company said it was nearing the end of its credit line, placing it on the verge of bankruptcy. Late that month, however, Christopher J. Pappas and Harris J. Pappas purchased about 6 percent of Luby's outstanding shares for about $6.6 million. The Pappas brothers were the principal owners of Pappas Restaurants Inc., which ran a number of successful casual dining chains, including Cajun, Mexican, and barbecue concepts. After Luby's survived the proxy battle in which the dissidents, angry over the depressed stock price as well as executive pay issues, aimed to gain three seats on the company board, the company gained some financial breathing room in March 2001 when the Pappas brothers agreed to purchase as much as $10 million of the company's debt. At the same time, Chris Pappas was named president and CEO of Luby's while Harris Pappas became chief operating officer. The Pappases also gained seats on the board of directors. Robert T. Herres replaced Daviss as chairman of the company, although Daviss remained on the board. The Pappas brothers were determined to engineer a turnaround at Luby's, which they felt had failed to adapt to changing times, and they appeared eager to take a hands-on approach to doing so. According to the *Dallas Morning News,* Chris Pappas told a group of stock analysts, soon after taking over the reins, "Everything starts and stops at the store level. If it doesn't work at the store level, it won't work at the corporate level. . . . We're great listeners to the market because we get out into the market. We're in the retail business." Industry observers were confident that the Pappases would reinvigorate the Luby's chain, but they also felt that the turnaround would be a difficult one.

Principal Subsidiaries

Luby's Holdings, Inc.; Luby's Limited Partner, Inc.; Luby's Management, Inc.; LUBCO, Inc.; Luby's Restaurants Limited Partnership; Luby's Bevco, Inc.

Principal Competitors

Piccadilly Cafeterias, Inc.; Buffets, Inc.; Furr's Restaurant Group, Inc.; Pancho's Mexican Buffet, Inc.; Boston Market Corporation.

Further Reading

Allen, Robin Lee, "Luby's Eyes Updated Image with Two New Campaigns," *Nation's Restaurant News,* June 6, 1994, p. 12.

Bajaj, Vikas, "Pappas' Stake Infuses Luby's with Optimism," *Dallas Morning News,* December 28, 2000, p. 1D.

Barnhill, Steve, *The Luby's Story,* San Antonio: The Watercress Press, 1988.

Barrett, William P., "The Best Little Hash House in Texas," *Forbes,* November 12, 1990, pp. 220–21.

Barrier, Michael, "First in Line at the Cafeteria," *Nation's Business,* February 1991, pp. 29–31.

Dorfman, John R., "Luby's Cafeterias' Steadiness Seems Suited to Withstand a Forced Diet for the Economy," *Wall Street Journal,* October 19, 1991, p. C2.

Krajewski, Steve, "Luby's: Dining Humor," *Adweek,* August 22, 1994, p. 4.

Lee, Steven H., "Dishing Up Service: Pace-Setting Luby's Not Discouraged by Decline in Cafeterias," *Dallas Morning News,* December 22, 1996, p. 1H.

——, "Luby's Shareholders Angry, but Vote Re-elects Directors," *Dallas Morning News,* January 13, 2001, p. 2F.

——, "Luby's to Take Bottom-Up Approach: Menu Items and Prices May Need Tweaking, New CEO Pappas Says," *Dallas Morning News,* March 29, 2001, p. 3D.

——, "Luby's Will Suspend Dividend: Cafeteria Company Unveils Plan to Turn Eateries Around," *Dallas Morning News,* October 28, 2000, p. 1F.

——, "Nouvells Luby's: Cafeteria Chain Slims Down, Tries to Revive Profits with Scaled-Down Restaurants, New Features," *Dallas Morning News,* September 14, 1999, p. 1D.

——, "Plateful of Trouble: Conflicts over Leadership Loom at Luby's Meeting," *Dallas Morning News,* January 12, 2001, p. 1D.

McDowell, Bill, "The People's Choice," *Restaurants and Institutions,* February 1, 1996, pp. 43–65.

Reinhold, Robert, "Why They're Lining Up at Luby's," *New York Times,* August 18, 1985, p. F11.

Ruggless, Ron, "Luby's Cafeterias Appoints New Chief," *Nation's Restaurant News,* September 29, 1997, pp. 3, 75.

——, "Luby's CEO Parker Quits After Warning About Lowered Profits, Unit Closures," *Nation's Restaurant News,* October 9, 2000, pp. 4, 145.

——, "Luby's Ongoing Slump Results in First Dividend Halt, Resignations," *Nation's Restaurant News,* November 6, 2000, p. 4.

——, "Luby's Seeks New Leaders," *Nation's Restaurant News,* March 31, 1997, p. 3.

——, "Luby's Sells Joint-Venture Interest in Water Street Seafood," *Nation's Restaurant News,* December 20, 1999, p. 11.

——, "Luby's Storms Texas Market with Wyatt's Buy," *Nation's Restaurant News,* July 29, 1996, p. 3.

——, "Luby's TV Ads Cut the Mustard, Go Heavy on the Wry," *Nation's Restaurant News,* December 5, 1994, p. 12.

——, "Pappas Brothers Take Two Top Luby's Posts," *Dallas Morning News,* March 10, 2001, p. 1F.

——, "Pappas Purchases a Piece of Luby's," *Nation's Restaurant News,* January 8, 2001, pp. 1, 62.

——, "Struggling Cafeteria Chains Draft Casual-Dining Vets in Recovery Bids," *Nation's Restaurant News,* May 28, 2001, pp. 4, 73.

Strauss, Gary, "Luby's Proxy Fight Illustrates Investors' Readiness to Act," *USA Today,* January 15, 2001, p. B1.

Tejada, Carlos, "Luby's CEO Takes Own Life, Police Say," *Wall Street Journal,* March 14, 1997, p. A4.

Waters, C. Dickinson, "Luby's Banking on Food-to-Go to Satisfy Wall Street Numbers Hunger," *Nation's Restaurant News,* June 26, 2000, p. 12.

Weil, Jonathan, "After Some Stale Years, Luby's May Have a Recipe for Success," *Wall Street Journal,* April 7, 1999, p. T2.

Weiss, Sebastian, "Luby's Sales Backslide Despite Major Upgrades, Ad Campaign," *San Antonio Business Journal,* February 25, 2000, p. 4.

—Lynn W. Adkins
—update: David E. Salamie

Mack-Cali Realty Corporation

11 Commerce Drive
Cranford, New Jersey 07016-3599
U.S.A.
Telephone: (908) 272-8000
Fax: (908) 272-6755
Web site: http://www.mack-cali.com

Public Company
Incorporated: 1994
Employees: 400
Sales: $661.5 million (2000)
Stock Exchanges: New York
Ticker Symbol: CLI
NAIC: 525930 Real Estate Investment Trusts

Mack-Cali Realty Corporation is one of the largest Real Estate Investment Trusts (REIT) in the United States, with the bulk of its properties located in the Northeast in a corridor that runs from Connecticut through the District of Columbia. The trust is based on the holdings accumulated by the Mack and Cali families, which both have longstanding ties to the real estate business in northern New Jersey. Mack-Cali has a market capitalization of $3.6 billion (as of March 31, 2001). Concentrating on office buildings, it owns or holds an interest in 273 properties totaling some 29 million square feet. Mack-Cali's major tenants include AT&T; AT&T Wireless; Donaldson, Lufkin & Jenrette; IBM; Prentice-Hall; Toys 'R' Us; Waterhouse Securities; and Nabisco.

Creation of REITs: 1960

REITs were created by Congress in 1960 as a way for small investors to become involved in real estate in much the same way a mutual fund allowed them to pool resources in order to buy stock. REITs could be taken public and their shares traded like any other stock; likewise, REITs were also regulated and monitored by the Securities and Exchange Commission. Unlike stocks, however, REITs were required by law to pay out at least 95 percent of their taxable income to shareholders each year, thus severely limiting the ability of REITs to raise funds internally. During the first 30 years of existence, REITs were hindered in their growth because they were only allowed to own

real estate. Third parties had to be engaged to operate or manage the properties. Moreover, the tax code made direct real estate investments an attractive tax shelter for many individuals, thereby absorbing funds that might have been invested in REITs. It was the Tax Reform Act of 1986 that began to change the nature of real estate investment. Interest and depreciation deductions were greatly reduced so that taxpayers could not generate paper losses in order to lower their tax liabilities. The Act also permitted REITs to provide customary services for property, in effect allowing the trusts to operate and manage the properties they owned. Despite these major changes in law, REITs were still not embraced as investment options in the late 1980s, as banks, insurance companies, pension funds, and foreign investors (in particular, the Japanese) provided the lion's share of real estate investment funds. That period also witnessed overbuilding and a glutted marketplace. Commercial property values fell dramatically in the early 1990s, and lending institutions, following the savings and loan debacle, were forced by regulators to be more circumspect about their investments. Capital essentially dried up and REITs finally became an attractive way for many private real estate companies to raise funds.

Of the two families that combined to form Mack-Cali, it was the Cali family that formed a REIT. In 1949 Cali Associates was created by brothers John J. Cali and Angelo R. Cali and boyhood friend Edward Leshowitz. The three men had originally pooled money to invest in a residential development company, but they were disappointed with the quality of the resulting homes and decided to form Cali Associates in order to be in charge of the building process. To help ensure quality, they required the project managers they hired to invest in the project. The company would build some 5,500 housing units in northern and central New Jersey. In 1969 Cali began constructing office properties, which at the time were in great demand in the area. The residential and commercial building programs would soon begin to feed off one another. Office buildings were constructed for self-employed professionals that lived in Cali homes but were forced to commute. Cali also built housing in areas where the company had put up office buildings, again freeing workers from long commutes. Cali associates gained a reputation among their commercial tenants as conscientious landlords who constructed excellent buildings and provided top-notch service. As a result, the company boasted an extremely high renewal rate.

Converting to a REIT, Cali Associates in 1994

After more than 40 years of housing development, Cali had built 2,000 one-family homes, 1,800 rental apartments, and 1,000 condominium townhouses. In addition, after 20 years of commercial construction, Cali had created almost four million square feet of commercial and industrial space, including 2.2 million square feet of class A office space. In the early 1990s, however, the rules of real estate had changed. Unlike those post-World War II years when Cali could secure a bank loan by using a proposed building as collateral, now access to capital was much tighter. Cali began to divest more than it built. Cali, despite a 1993 loss of $1 million, had typically strong cash flow and was not about to lose any of its properties. But a changing of the guard was imminent. The company's founders were turning over the reins to a new generation: John J. Cali's son Brant, Angelo Cali's son John R. Cali, and Brant's friend Thomas Rizk. In August 1994 it was this new management team that was instrumental in taking Cali Associates public, becoming a REIT named Cali Realty Corporation, which consisted of 12 office buildings and one apartment complex. Although Cali had hoped to sell 9.179 million shares at $18 to $20, it actually sold 10.5 million shares at $17.25. Nevertheless, the offering, along with additional financing from Prudential Securities, allowed Cali Realty to pay down a significant amount of debt.

Cali Realty initiated an aggressive acquisition campaign. One of the few REITs in the country to focus on suburban office buildings, the trust spent $200 million buying properties over an 18-month span beginning in 1995. Although concentrating on its home territory of New Jersey, Cali Realty expanded its scope in 1996 by also buying property in Pennsylvania. Already the trust boasted one of the highest returns of any REIT in the country, and investors quickly took note. Cali Realty raised an additional $545 million through two additional equity offerings in 1996. Fortified with cash, the trust was then able to complete its first major deal. In February 1997 Cali Realty bought Westchester-based Robert Martin Company and its portfolio of 65 properties, totaling 4.1 million square feet, for $440 million.

Robert Martin was not the name of a person, rather it was the combination of the first names of the company's founders, Robert F. Weinberg and Martin S. Berger, who created their partnership in 1957. With $15,000 in financing they began their business by constructing five houses, three colonials and two ranches, which they sold for $25,000 each. They became involved in larger projects and also displayed a pioneering spirit. Robert Martin was the first to build condominiums in Westchester. In the mid-1960s the company began to develop office parks and introduced "flex" buildings, which could serve as offices, a warehouse, or industrial space. Over 40 years, Robert Martin constructed more than 2,000 apartments and houses, as well as eight million square feet of commercial, hotel, recreation, medical, and retail space. Like other developers, Robert Martin was adversely affected by sour economic conditions in the early

1990s and began to consider the possibility of becoming a REIT or merging with one. For Cali Realty, Robert Martin was an excellent fit in terms of property mix and location. In one stroke it gained a major presence in the suburbs north of New York City, prompting management to describe itself as a "super regional" REIT. It also retained the Robert Martin name, which was a valuable brand in the Westchester market.

The size of the Robert Martin acquisition, however, would soon pale in comparison to the $1.1 billion merger with the office assets of The Mack Company in August 1997, the largest public to private deal in REIT history. (Mack's 11 million square feet of industrial and retail space were not included.) Also part of the deal was Dallas-based Patriot American Office Group, majority owned by the Mack family. Because the Mack portfolio contained twice as much property as Cali Realty, many observers viewed the transaction as Mack swallowing up Cali Realty. The connection of the Mack family to real estate dated back to 1896 when members became involved in New York demolition as well as residential and industrial construction. The Mack Company was established in New Jersey in 1962 and engaged in a wide range of commercial real estate activities: from developing and acquiring properties to management. By the mid-1990s Mack controlled properties with a total of 20 million square feet, of which 5.9 million square feet was Class A office space. In addition to considerable holdings in New Jersey, the company also owned property in New York, Arizona, Florida, and Pennsylvania. William L. Mack and partners founded Patriot American Office Group in 1992. Most of its 3.6 million square feet of office space was located in Texas.

Despite being a large and successful company, Mack also needed to attract outside capital in order to grow to the next level. Turning to a REIT structure made sense, and joining forces with Cali Realty, another New Jersey family-run business, seemed like a natural combination. Cali Realty's CEO, Thomas Rizk, and Mack's chief operating officer, Mitchell Hersh, had been friends and neighbors for more than ten years. One night in mid-1997 they met for dinner to discuss the possibility of a merger. The result, two months later, was Mack-Cali Realty, which would own 8 percent of all office space in New Jersey. For Cali Realty the deal meant increased size that could attract further investment. For Mack it was an opportunity to convert illiquid real estate into liquid assets. Mack-Cali also looked to gain considerable prestige with Wall Street because of the perception of William Mack as a brilliant investor, a reputation earned by heading the real estate arm of the highly successful Apollo Fund. Mack and his brothers would own 18 percent of Mack-Cali, and the board of the REIT would be restructured to reflect this reality. The board was expanded to accommodate Mack board members, Rizk was named CEO, and Hersh was named president and chief operating officer. Despite the titles, however, the two men were tabbed to co-run the trust.

Over the next year, Mack-Cali went on an acquisition spree, spending $147 million on office buildings in New Jersey, Connecticut, and Texas. In March 1998 it announced a spate of deals totaling $450 million, including the $188 million acquisition of property held by Pacifica Holding Co. in Denver, as well as buildings in Washington, D.C., and Maryland. In its home territory, Mack-Cali now controlled 20 percent of northern New Jersey's Class A office space. REITs in general were buying properties at low prices and bumping rents to grow revenues and

---

Key Dates:

1896: The Mack family becomes involved in various construction and real estate-related projects.
1949: Cali Associates is formed.
1957: Robert Martin Company is established.
1962: The Mack Company is incorporated in New Jersey.
1994: Cali Associates becomes a REIT and is renamed Cali Realty Corporation.
1997: Cali Realty and The Mack Company merge to form Mack-Cali Realty Corporation.

---

stimulate stock prices, but they were unable to maintain that pace and REITs saw the price of their stocks begin to fall. In turn, financing began to dry up. REITs now teamed up with developers to build properties in order to maintain growth. In March 1999 Mack-Cali formed a joint venture with SJP Properties of Parsippany, New Jersey, to construct two office buildings. The trust had not acquired any new properties since September 1998, when a Connecticut deal had increased its portfolio to 253 properties totaling 28 million square feet in 12 states.

Management Changes: 1999

Mack-Cali underwent a significant structural change in April 1999 when Rizk suddenly resigned and Hersch became CEO and the lone leader of the company. According to Hersh, Mack-Cali's shared power arrangement had proved inefficient. Nevertheless, the local press speculated that the ouster of Rizk was the result of a power play by the executive board that favored a Mack executive over a longtime Cali man. Hersh had been a partner with Mack since 1982. Rizk publicly supported the move, and was certainly well compensated as he left, paid $14.5 million immediately and $500,000 annually for the next three years. He was also not bound by any non-competition agreements, so that he was free to continue in the real estate business. Because of Hersch's experience in development, industry observers anticipated that Mack-Cali might pursue more joint ventures with builders, such as the one with SJP Properties.

A year later, in June 2000, Mack-Cali surprised the real estate industry when it announced that it had reached an agreement to acquire Dallas-based office building owner Prentiss Properties Trust for $975.8 million in stock plus the assumption of $1.25 billion in debt and preferred securities. The deal would make Mack-Cali the fourth largest REIT in the country, with a total capitalization of $5.9 billion. Clearly the move was intended to spread risk: by having a national footprint, Mack-Cali would be better situated to weather difficult times in any one particular market. In conjunction with the Prentiss deal, the Calis would also exit the stage, as William Mack became chairman and John J. Cali was named chairman emeritus, while Brent Cali and John R. Cali resigned. The Calis' presence on the 13-member board was also reduced to two seats.

Wall Street's reaction to the $2.3 billion acquisition, however, was decidedly chilly. Analysts at a number of investment firms downgraded Mack-Cali stock, and the price of its shares began to

fall. Essentially the belief was that Mack-Cali was overpaying for Prentiss and had failed to offer a persuasive argument for wanting to become a national REIT, most of which were faring poorly in comparison to well-run regional REITs. Moreover, William Mack's reputation as a dealmaker was being questioned, with one analyst telling the *Wall Street Journal* that "his talents were oversold." By September 2000, Mack-Cali decided to pull out of the deal, a decision which forced it to pay Prentiss $25 million in breakup fees, but at least investors were placated and the company stock began to recover.

The Wall Street message to Mack-Cali in a nutshell was that all real estate is local. If investors wanted diversification, they could do it themselves by spreading their money around the country, while REITs like Mack-Cali should stick to their knitting and service the regions where they had developed relationships with local businesses, leasing brokers, and government officials. Mack-Cali indicated that it would refocus on a regional strategy, announcing in November 2000 that it intended to sell $600 million of its Southwestern portfolio within the next two years. In March 2001 it announced it would sell the 20 office buildings it owned in Colorado. Back in the Northeast, Mack-Cali renewed its efforts to grow its regional assets, announcing plans to build two office towers in Jersey City. The trust also discussed a major merger with Westchester's Reckson Associates Realty Corp., a deal that would make it the largest owner of commercial properties in the New York metropolitan area. Although the deal would ultimately fall apart, it was indicative of Mack-Cali's commitment to achieving growth while sticking close to its home base.

Principal Subsidiaries

Cali Property Holdings; Mack-Cali Realty L.P.; Mack-Cali Services, Inc.; White Plains Realty Associates L.L.C.

Principal Competitors

Boston Properties, Inc.; Equity Office Properties Trust; Liberty Property Trust.

Further Reading

Coolidge, Carrie, "Stay Home," *Forbes,* October 16, 2000, p. 224.
Deutsch, Claudia H., "A Veteran Realty Company Takes the Market Plunge," *New York Times Current Events Edition,* September 18, 1994, p. 915.
Garbarine, Rachelle, "From Two Family Firms, a 'Super-Regional REIT,'" *New York Times,* January 4, 1998, p. 7.
Pacelle, Mitchell, "Cali Realty Agrees to Pay $900 Million to Acquire 55 Mack Co. Office Buildings," *Wall Street Journal,* August 14, 1997, p. A3.
Pandya, Mukul, "Mack and Cali Merge to Form a Mega REIT," *Business News New Jersey,* August 25, 1997, p. 6.
Ruth, Joao-Pierre S., "Mack-Cali Makes Big Management Changes," *Business News New Jersey,* April 26, 1999, p. 6.
Smith, Ray A., "REIT Interest: Bigger Is Always Better—or Maybe Not," *Wall Street Journal,* July 12, 2000, p. B8.
Vizard, Mary McAleer, "Sale of Office Developer to REIT Marks End of Era," *New York Times,* February 16, 1997, p. 9.

—Ed Dinger

Malcolm Pirnie, Inc.

104 Corporate Park Drive, Box 751
White Plains, New York 10602
U.S.A.
Telephone: (914) 694-2100
Fax: (914) 694-9286
Web site: http://www.pirnie.com

Private Company
Incorporated: 1970
Employees: 1,302
Sales: $203 million (2000 est.)
NAIC: 541330 Engineering Services

Malcolm Pirnie, Inc. has been in the business of cleaning water and wastewater for more than 100 years. Named after one of its pioneering sanitary engineers, the company is management-owned, with its corporate headquarters located north of New York City in White Plains, New York. Over the years, Malcolm Pirnie has moved beyond water services to offer a wide range of solutions to environmental problems, working for both the public and private sectors, in the United States and around the world. The company's staff of more than 1,300 engineers, scientists, architects, and consultants service at least 3,000 clients.

19th-Century Roots

The forefather of Malcolm Pirnie was one of the country's first sanitary engineers, Allen Hazen. He was born on a Vermont farm in 1869 and earned a B.S. from the New Hampshire College of Agriculture and the Mechanic Arts before studying sanitary chemistry at Massachusetts Institute of Technology (MIT). At the time, there were very few students interested in the field of sanitary engineering and little recognition for the importance of the field. It was only in the 1870s that Dr. Robert Koch and Dr. Joseph Lister proved that microorganisms in water supplies could cause disease. In 1886 the Massachusetts legislature voted to protect the purity of the state's inland water, and as a result the Board of Health established an experiment station in Lawrence to conduct research on water purification

and sewage treatment. This move represented a major step in the growth of the sanitary field. Although he was not yet 20 years old, Hazen was named the facility's first director. The group conducted research on the effect of sand filters on treating sewage and improving municipal water supplies, which in addition to being troubled by poor taste and a disagreeable odor often spread deadly diseases such as typhoid and cholera. These filters were essentially large patches of land, an acre or two in size, where water or sewage would seep through layers of sand to remove impurities. Europe led the way in this technology. By the end of the 1800s, some 11 million people in England would be supplied by filtered water, 4.6 million in Germany, 1.4 million in Holland, and more than three million in other European countries.

Hazen gained further recognition for his work on sewage disposal at the World's Columbian Exhibition at Chicago in 1893. He then traveled around Europe and studied at the Dresden Polytechnic Institute, accumulating experiences that contributed greatly to the writing of his first book, *The Filtration of Public Water-Supplies,* published in 1895. In that same year, he returned to the United States and teamed up with another sanitary engineer, Alfred F. Noyes, to open a private consulting practice in Boston, specializing in the design of large municipal filtered water systems. When Noyes died the following year, Hazen continued the business alone. He moved his offices to New York City in 1897 to work on the first modern filtration system in the United States, a slow-sand water-filter plant in Albany that treated the highly polluted Hudson River. Within a year, deaths in Albany caused by typhoid fever fell by 80 percent. It was a time of considerable advances in the field. Sanitary engineers would then introduce coagulating agents and settling basins to eliminate some solid matter before water reached the new rapid sand filters, which could process much higher volumes than previous systems. Chlorine also was introduced in the early 1900s to fight disease.

As a leading figure in sanitary engineering, Hazen was in great demand throughout the world. In 1904 he formed a partnership with a fellow student from MIT, George C. Whipple, who also became a professor of sanitary engineering at Harvard. In 1911 a young Harvard graduate student joined Hazen and

Whipple. His name was Malcolm Pirnie. Five years later he was made a partner of the firm, which was now known as Hazen, Whipple & Fuller. In time it would become known as Hazen, Everett & Pirnie. By 1929 Pirnie and Hazen disagreed on methodology and Pirnie struck out on his own, establishing the business Malcolm Pirnie Civil Engineer. While traveling with his daughter in 1930, Hazen died suddenly, and Pirnie essentially inherited the old partnership, receiving the company's books and records, as well as its slate of projects. Pirnie persevered through the Depression years, building up a staff of sanitary engineers, supported by a lone designer/draftsman. His son, Malcolm Pirnie, Jr., also began working for the company, which by 1940 had a staff of 25 working in offices located in Richmond, Virginia, and Miami Beach, Florida, in addition to the New York headquarters. After World War II, when Pirnie focused on military projects, the firm became a partnership known as Malcolm Pirnie Engineers.

Pollution Becoming a Concern in Post-World War II Era

The company was narrowly focused on water supply and treatment facilities, but a growing national concern about the environment would begin to open up new areas of activity. The Water Pollution Control Act of 1948 was the first piece of federal law to address the subject, followed by additional legislation in 1956. In response, Pirnie turned more of its attention to the treatment of wastewater and sewage. Not only did it build municipal systems, Pirnie worked for the private sector, in particular heavy-polluting paper mills. The company eventually would design water treatment facilities for more than a hundred U.S. paper mills.

It was the publication of Rachel Carson's 1962 book *Silent Spring* that would cause a public outcry and lead to the rise of the environmental movement. It was Carson, in fact, who added profound new dimensions to the word "environment," which would never be the same after she wrote: "The most alarming of all man's assaults upon the environment is the contamination of air, earth, rivers and sea with dangerous chemicals, from the moment of conception until death." The book was so explosive at the time, that even before it was officially published, President Kennedy promised an investigation and Congress established a score of committees to study "environmental problems." The first Clean Air Act was passed in 1963, followed in 1965 by the first Clean Water Act. In 1969, when an oil platform spewed 235,000 gallons of black crude oil over 30 miles of pristine beaches in the affluent community of Santa Barbara, California, the environmental movement gained rich, politically connected converts. The following year marked the first celebration of Earth Day. Although viewed skeptically by both the political left and right, Earth Day, at the very least, brought together a number of diverse groups. The organization that was

created to coordinate Earth Day, Environmental Action, would become a major Washington lobby. Also in 1970 President Nixon signed the law that created the Environmental Protection Agency (EPA). Finally, the country would have a single entity charged with monitoring and enforcing environmental protection laws.

Malcolm Pirnie, Sr., who passed away in 1967, was not alive to see the rise of the EPA. His son assumed the chairman's role in 1970, the same year that the company incorporated. Named as president was John H. Foster, who would later become CEO. By now, sanitary engineering was evolving into environmental engineering, and the firm's services were never more in demand. A 1977 study estimated that 95 percent of the country's river basins was polluted. Pirnie expanded staff to cover the many disciplines required in modern project teams, and in 1976 moved into larger quarters in White Plains, New York. It was also during the 1970s that the nation became aware of a small Niagara Falls-area bedroom community called Love Canal, which was plagued by an unusually high number of birth defects, miscarriages, cancer, epilepsy, and other diseases. The situation went from tragedy to scandal when it was revealed that city officials had concealed the fact that the community had been built on land that served as a chemical waste dump for the area's largest employer, Hooker Chemical Company. The environmental movement gained a new political force in the so-called "angry mom" constituency, which applied even more pressure on lawmakers. The result would be legislation commonly known as the "Superfund," an appropriation earmarked for the cleanup of toxic waste sites and oil spills. Pirnie's work at Love Canal would lead to an increasing number of contracts to clean up hazardous waste.

During the early 1980s the environmental movement was slowed somewhat by the Reagan administration. The EPA, in fact, operated a year without a new administrator being named. According to Hal K. Rothman in his book, *Saving the Planet,* "The Reagan administration also worked to curtail EPA's reach. ... Enforcement standards were set so that the $1.6 billion Superfund would not be spent. This meant that the agency generally did not pursue law enforcement, instead resorting to sometimes fruitless negotiation with polluters. ... Later, in 1986, Reagan signed Executive Order 12580, which gave the Department of Justice the right to disapprove any EPA enforcement action against a federal facility. The Justice Department held that the executive branch entities could not sue each other, effectively ending EPA's ability to enforce its mandate on federal lands."

Congressional hearings then revealed that the Pentagon itself recognized 4,611 contaminated sites at 761 military bases, many of which posed grave threats to local communities. In October 1986 Congress re-authorized the Superfund cleanup program, allocating $9 billion for the next five years. As a large number of military bases were closed at the end of the Cold War, there was even more need for the services of companies such as Pirnie to clean up the hazardous wastes left by munitions and military fuels. In 1992 the U.S. Army Corps of Engineers contracted Pirnie to help in cleaning military bases for four years in five EPA regions. In fiscal 1993 alone, the military planned to spend $537 million on active military bases, as well as an additional $120 million on closed bases.

Malcolm Pirnie, Jr., retired in 1987 but the company was not at a loss for leadership. It was staffed by a number of executives with many years of service. John Foster became chairman, and Dr. Paul L. Busch took over as president in 1988 and was named CEO in 1990. After earning undergraduate and master's degrees from MIT and a doctorate from Harvard, Busch would spend his entire 38-year career at Pirnie. When he died in 1999, he was succeeded as chair and CEO by Garret P. Westerhoff, who had been with Pirnie for 34 years. Foster, who served 25 years in top management positions at the company, became chairman emeritus. Westerhoff had been instrumental in an effort to reorganize the business on a regional basis to stimulate growth and provide a geographic balance.

Offering Expanded Services in the 1990s

To meet future environmental problems, Pirnie broadened its capabilities in the final years of the 20th century to deal with such areas as wetland restoration, watershed impacts, energy management, information technology systems, telecommunications installations, and regulation compliance. Because of the complexity of modern mergers and business alliances, which can potentially give consultants an interest in the projects on which they work, Pirnie made efforts to maintain its independence and thereby ensure the integrity of its work. To reassure its municipal clients, for instance, Pirnie pledged not to interact, directly or indirectly, with any clients involved in privatizing utilities.

Because Pirnie was privately held, owned by senior management, it did not face shareholder pressure, nor did it have to release financial information (although the *Westchester County Business Journal* estimated the company generated approximately $190 million in 2000 and had been growing at an annual clip of 10 percent). The company was essentially free to expand at its own pace, mostly through internal efforts, adding offices and staff as its business increased. With more than 100 years in business and a sterling record, Pirnie had no reason to go into debt to acquire other companies and boost its revenues. The company estimated that 85 percent of its clients were repeat customers. In September 2000, Pirnie made a rare stab at external growth when it acquired Red Oak Consulting for an undisclosed sum. Red Oak offered services that would help Pirnie assist utilities to improve organizational efficiency and effectiveness. Operating as a division of Pirnie, Red Oak also would continue to serve its other clients, including *Fortune* 500 companies. The business was established in 1995 by clinical psychologist Stuart Kantor, who had gained experience helping corporate executives with leadership skills. He elected to merge with Pirnie because of a personal commitment to the environment and the opportunity to work in that field. For Pirnie, Red Oak was a way to achieve a goal: Introducing new technologies was not enough, if the people in charge were not changed as well. The company was founded by engineers and primarily owned by engineers, for whom the bottom line involved far more than just making money.

Principal Subsidiaries

Red Oak Consulting.

Principal Competitors

Ecology and Environment, Inc.; CH2M Hill Ltd.; Montgomery Watson.

Further Reading

Jordan, John, "Hazardous Waste Cleanup Contract Opens Door for Malcolm Pirnie," *Westchester County Business Journal,* December 21, 1992, p. 21.
Khaasru, B.Z., "Malcolm Pirnie Acquires Red Oak Consulting," *Westchester County Business Journal,* September 4, 2000, p. 3.
"Malcolm Pirnie Jr. Dies at Age 79," *ENR,* February 3, 1997, p. 26.
Rothman, Hal K., *Saving the Planet,* Chicago: Ivan R. Dee, 2000.
Silverstein, Ken, and Carol L. Bowers, "Water: Watering a Growing Nation," *Utility Business,* June 2000, pp. 62–69.

—Ed Dinger

Marchesi Antinori SRL

Piazza Antinori, 3
50123 Florence
Italy
Telephone: (+39) 055-235-95
Fax: (+39) 055-235-9884
Web site: http://www.antinori.it

Private Company
Incorporated: 1893 as Marchesi L&P Antinori
Sales: EUR 80 million ($74.2 million) (2000 est.)
NAIC: 312130 Wineries

Italy's Marchesi Antinori SRL is one of that country's top wineries. The Florence-based company produces more than 12 million bottles per year, most of which is pressed from the company's own grape production. Antinori owns vineyards across much of Italy's Tuscany region—home of the country's Chianti wine variety—with holdings throughout the Umbria region as well. The company also has begun to invest further south, in Puglia. Outside of Italy, Antinori has acquired vineyards in Hungary; the company also owns the Atlas Peak vineyard in California's Napa Valley, although the company will not control production there until 2005 at the earliest. Antinori also has a production partnership with Chateau Ste. Michelle Winery in Washington state to produce the Col Solare label. Owned entirely by the Antinori family, the company can claim a winemaking history dating back more than 600 years and spanning 26 generations. It is, however, the 25th generation—in the person of Piero Antinori—that is credited with transforming the company into an internationally known and respected winemaker. Piero Antinori is widely viewed as a worldwide ambassador of Italian wine who has helped rebuild the reputation of Italian wines with a renewed commitment to quality and a willingness to experiment with grape varieties and growing and production methods. As such, the company launched the so-called "super Tuscan" wine class and a new wine type, Tignanello. In addition to wine production, the company owns restaurants in Italy, Austria, and Switzerland. Joining Piero Antinori are his three daughters, Albiera, Allegra, and Alessia.

Spanning Centuries of Italian Winemaking

The Antinori family traces its involvement in Tuscan-region winemaking to 1385, although most likely the company's involvement in winemaking was already more than two centuries old. In that year, however, Giovanni di Piero Antinori, a member of a wealthy Florentine merchant family, was accepted into that city's Vintner's Guild. The Antinori family went on to play an important role in the economic and political development of Florence, with primary activities in the silk trade and in banking. Like many aristocratic families, the Antinoris' wine production was maintained for the most part for the family's own table.

By the beginning of the 16th century, the Antinori family had established international activities in such major cities of the period as Bruges, Belgium, and Lyons, France, where the company was known both for its banking operations and for its silks. In 1506, Niccolo Antinori bought a palace in the center of Florence—that palace, later known as the Antinori Palace and one of the most famous in Florence—remained the site of the family's home and headquarters into the 21st century.

By the 18th century, the Antinori family's wine was well known among the Italian royal families, and even at the Vatican, where an uncle of the Antinoris, Clement XII, reigned as pope. Another direct family member became part of the royal court of King Ferdinand I of Austria; this Antinori, named Niccolo, acquired an estate outside Florence, renamed Villa Antinori, during the middle of the 18th century. By then, Tuscan wine production had moved to a more serious level with the inauguration of the Accademia dei Georgofili, the world's first wine academy, in 1753. The growing reputation of Tuscan wines helped build the Antinori family's reputation as well. By the end of the century, the family's wines were being shipped internationally, with special popularity in England.

The Antinoris' role in the battle for independence and the subsequent unification of Italy in the mid-19th century led to the family being given the title of "marquesi" (marquis). In 1861, the new Marquesi Niccolo Antinori adopted a new motto, "Te Duce Proficio" (the pursuit of excellence). By then the family owned four wine estates in Tuscany; in 1873, the family's wine was awarded a diploma of distinction at the Vienna World Exhibition.

Modern Tuscany Wine Production in the 20th Century

The modern era of Antinori wine production began with the next generation of Antinoris, Piero and his brother Ludovico, along with their brother-in-law Guglielmo Guerrini. Together the three partners formed a new company, Marchesi L&P Antinori, with the mission of ''establishing a bit of order among the various viti-vinicultural activities developed by preceding generations of Antinoris since the 14th century.'' The new company modernized the family's four vineyards, and introduced a new label for their wines, featuring a drawing of the Villa Antinori.

In 1898, the company constructed a new cellar, called San Casciano, in Val di Pesa. The company also stepped up its wine exports, now shipping to New York, Buenos Aires, and Sao Paulo, Brazil, as well as London. Antinori began buying new estates as the new century began, including vineyards in Paterno, Santa Maria, and Poggio Niccolino, all of which produced grapes for the Chianti Classico wine variety. The Antinoris also bought another estate, called Tignanello, adding 116 acres to the company's growing land estate.

In 1905, Antinori brought in the noted champagne maker, Lucien Charlemagne, to lead development of the company's own sparkling wine. This activity gained further momentum in 1908 when Charlemagne was succeeded by Georges Grandvalet, who came to the company from famed French champagne house Mumm. Although the Antinoris' champagne was greeted warmly, wine remained the company's primary product.

In 1922, the company leased vineyards in Italy's Umbria region to produce its first Orvieto white wine. By then, the company had been joined by the next generation of Antinoris— Piero's son Niccolo, born in 1891. The latest Niccolo Antinori brought a new spirit to the family's winemaking activities, which remained, nonetheless, only a side business to the family's main fortune. In 1924, Niccolo Antinori created a scandal in the closed world of Chianti wine growers when he introduced Bordeaux grape varieties into his own Chianti blend. The next year, Niccolo took over as head of the family's wine operations.

By 1928, Niccolo had succeeded in producing a wine that could be considered worthy of aging, the Villa Antinori Chianti Classico. Niccolo was to continue experimenting with different varieties of grapes, particularly those of the Bordeaux region, such as Cabernet Sauvignon and Medoc, blending them with the traditional varieties of the Tuscany region. In the 1930s, Antinori also began adopting more modern production and marketing techniques.

The company introduced a new white wine in 1931, called the Villa Antinori Blanco and featuring grapes from Tuscany. That region, however, remained firmly focused on its traditional red Chianti wines. In 1940, therefore, Antinori returned to the Orvieto region, buying up the Castello della Sala estate and its nearly 1,400 acres. Antinori quickly replanted the estate's vineyard, while restoring its 14th-century castle.

Post-World War II Development

The Villa Antinori estate and other Antinori family holdings were destroyed by bombs during World War II. With Italy's capitulation and liberation, the Antinori wine operations returned to business, and by 1946 the family had rebuilt its cellars and introduced a new label, Santa Cristina, a Chianti Classico. In the 1950s and 1960s, Niccolo Antinori's attention was turned more and more toward politics, particularly in his position as mayor of a Florence suburb. The Antinori wine operation remained small, selling no more than 100,000 cases of wine per year.

A new generation, however, was prepared to lead the tiny wine producer. Niccolo's son Piero was born in 1938 and took over the company's operations in 1966. Aiding him was famed Italian oenologist Giacomo Tachis, who had joined the company in 1960, and who was to play a prominent role in rebuilding the Tuscany region's international wine reputation.

Piero immediately distinguished himself from his forebears by taking an active role in the company, devoting his whole attention to building its operations. Antinori had his work cut out for him. Disastrous postwar policies had encouraged Tuscany's growers to adopt a series of poor planting practices—using inferior quality grape varieties, turning toward mass production on densely planted plains and alternating with other crops, further diminishing the quality of the grapes. The DOC classification of Chianti, which set standards for production, also hurt the wine, allowing for aging in huge casks, and blends featuring high concentrations of white grape. These factors and others conspired to give Chianti wines a reputation as a quintessentially inferior wine. Businesses such as Antinori, seeking to produce wines on an international quality level, suffered from industry disdain for Chianti wines.

Piero Antinori and chief winemaker Tachis began experiments toward producing a first-class wine from the Tuscany region. The company replanted with higher quality vines in dedicated vineyards. The company also added new production methods, such as temperature control, small casks made from various wood types, including the famed French white oak, new blends of grape varieties, and bottle aging. The company also turned to malolactic fermentation for its red wines, producing a less acidic wine than the region's traditional governo technique.

By the end of the 1960s, Antinori had succeeded in raising sales to more than 500,000 cases.

By 1971, the company released its first new wine. For this wine, the company adopted a new name—Tignanello—turning its back on the now disreputable Chianti Classico. At any rate, Tignanello's use of nontraditional grape varieties, near absence of white grapes, and aging in small casks, made it ineligible for the Chianti Classico appellation, according to former DOC specifications. The Tignanello proved a highly successful wine, sparking the rise of a new, informal wine type, the "Super Tuscan," while Antinori himself became more and more of an ambassador for the Tuscany region's wine producers, promoting his company's wine not only through Europe but in the United States as well.

By 1984, Antinori had won a new battle, when the Italian government agreed to revise the Chianti Classico's DOC specifications and added the even more stringent DOCG specification, moves that were formalized in 1992. For the white grapes now no longer used in Chianti production, Antinori and four other producers introduced a new wine type, Galestro, a lighter wine with lower alcohol content than Chianti, using the now leftover white Trebbiano grapes.

Celebrating its 600th anniversary in winemaking, Antinori bought the Peppoli wine estate, releasing a limited special blend dubbed Secentenario ("600th anniversary") in 1985. In that year, also, Antinori joined wine and spirits distributor Whitbread Plc in acquiring the Atlas Peak vineyard and winery in California's Napa Valley. Other acquisitions during this period included that of the Badia, a Passignano monastery and its 64 acres of vineyards (the company donated the monastery back to its monks) in 1987; the purchase of wine producer Prunotto, bringing the company into the Piedmont region in 1990; the signing of a long-term lease of another 235 acres in Monteloro, near Florence; and the lease of the La Craccesca estate in DOCG-rated Montepulciano.

New Generation for a New Century

By then, Piero Antinori was faced with a difficult decision. In 1988, Antinori had sold 49 percent of the company to Whitbread Plc. Part of Antinori's motivation for the sale had been to ensure the future of the Antinori wine name—with three daughters and no sons, Antinori had thought that he would have no successors in a wine industry traditionally operated only by men. In 1991, however, Whitbread was negotiating the sale of many of its holdings to liquor distributor Allied Lyons (later Allied Domecq). At the same time, Whitbread began to look into selling the Italian producer—which, by then, had established an international reputation for the high quality of its wines, while also becoming one of Italy's largest wine producers—to another company with more direct interests in fine wines.

To sell Antinori, however, Whitbread sought full control of the company. Yet Antinori refused to sell out; instead, he surprised Whitbread by insisting on buying back his family's company. As Antinori explained to *Wine Spectator:* "I came to the conclusion that I wanted to buy back the company. I realized that my daughters were interested in the wine business, but I also realised that I had to be more emotionally involved in the company." To finance the purchase (estimated to have cost around $40 million), Antinori secured a loan from Italy's Mediabanco, using his personal assets—including the Antinori Palace—as backing. "[Whitbread] didn't think that I had the courage to buy all the shares back," Antinori continued. "In such circumstances, you have to take your decision and never diverge from it. It gave me the chance to start again. It was a gamble, a calculated risk."

Antinori's risk paid off, as the company's sales rose to $60 million per year by the mid-1990s, before nearing an estimated EUR 80 million by the end of the century. Celebrating the arrival of all three of his daughters into the family company, Antinori introduced a new element to its coat of arms, the notation "26 generazioni." Albiera took charge of marketing, Allegra turned to the handling of public relations, and the youngest daughter, Alessia, entered the technical side, studying viticulture and joining the company's production arm.

In the late 1990s and early 2000s, the company continued to expand its operations, developing holdings of more than 3,000 acres of vineyards. New estates included the purchase of Pian delle Vigne in Montalcino, adding 449 acres in 1995, and the Fattoria Aldobrandesca estate in Sovana, adding 235 acres that same year. Outside of Italy, Antinori was building new interests. The collapse of communism had opened entry into the Eastern European market, which had seen its wine industries ruined by years of Soviet domination. In 1993, Antinori took a stake in Hungary's Bátaapáti, strengthening its position later in the decade.

At the close of the 20th century, Antinori's role in revolutionizing—some would say rescuing—Italy's wine industry was recognized as he received the 1999 Distinguished Service Award from *Wine Spectator*. Even as Antinori prepared to turn over the reigns of the company to his family's 26th generation, the company continued to seek new growth opportunities. In 1998, the company entered a production agreement with Chateau Ste. Michelle, based in Washington state in the United States, to produce a new wine, called Col Solare, with the first vintage released in 1999. At the beginning of 2001, the company reached a distribution agreement with Hawesko Holding to distribute its wines in Germany. Meanwhile, the company continued to seek new areas in which to ply its gift for creating fine wines. In January 2001, the company entered the Puglia region in the south of Italy, acquiring some 300 hectares there.

Principal Competitors

Banfi Vintners; Cantine Giorgio Lungarotti S.r.l.; Diageo plc; E. & J. Gallo Winery; Industrie Zignago Santa Margherita S.p.A.; Robert Mondavi Corporation; Viña Concha y Toro S.A.

Further Reading

Campbell-Drake, Melanie, and Michele Banbling, ''The Epicures,'' *Yomiuri Shimbun,* January 13, 2000.
Suckling, James, ''Marchese Piero Antinori,'' *Wine Spectator,* September 1999.
——, ''The Renaissance of Piero Antinori,'' *Wine Spectator,* October 3, 1994.

—M. L. Cohen

MDU Resources Group, Inc.

918 East Divide Avenue
Bismarck, North Dakota 58506-5650
U.S.A.
Telephone: (701) 222-7900
Toll Free: (877) 346-2373
Fax: (701) 222-7606
Web site: http://www.mdu.com

Public Company
Incorporated: 1924 as Minnesota Northern Power
   Company
Employees: 4,087
Sales: $1.9 billion (2000)
Stock Exchanges: New York
Ticker Symbol: MU
NAIC: 211111 Crude Petroleum and Natural Gas
   Extraction; 212319 Other Crushed and Broken Stone
   Mining and Quarrying; 221112 Fossil Fuel Electric
   Power Generation; 221122 Electric Power
   Distribution; 22121 Natural Gas Distribution; 48621
   Pipeline Transportation of Natural Gas

MDU Resources Group, Inc. (MDU) mines coal and aggregates, participates in oil exploration, generates and distributes electricity, and transports and delivers natural gas. The company's subsidiary Montana-Dakota Utilities Co. distributes natural gas and generates, transmits, and distributes electricity in Montana, North Dakota, South Dakota, and Wyoming, as well as holds energy leases in Canada and on the Gulf Coast. Among its other subsidiaries, the Fidelity Exploration & Production Company takes part in oil and natural gas ventures; Knife River Corporation mines aggregate and sells construction materials in the West, primarily for road building; Utility Services, Inc. is a national construction company that specializes in electric, natural gas, and telecommunication utility construction; and WBI Holdings, Inc. gathers, stores, and transports natural gas through pipeline systems.

Early History

R.M. Heskett founded Minnesota Northern Power Company, the progenitor of MDU, in 1924. Heskett was an engineer who began his career building electric streetcar systems in Wisconsin. After the automobile caused the decline of the streetcar industry, he entered the electric utility business with the financial backing of Wausau, Wisconsin investors Cyrus C. Yawkey, Aytch Woodson, and the Alexander brothers. Heskett undertook his first venture during the 1910s and early 1920s, when he built and then sold the Minnesota Utilities Company. He then retired briefly, but at the age of 53 he began the company that would become MDU Resources Group, Inc.

On March 14, 1924, he and his Wausau backers incorporated Minnesota Northern Power Company. Heskett ran the company from Minneapolis and served as vice-president and general manager. Cyrus C. Yawkey and Walter Alexander served as president and secretary, respectively, but had no operational responsibilities. Minnesota Northern began its operational life by purchasing three utilities: Minnesota Electric Light and Power Company in Bemidji, Minnesota; the Glendive Heat, Light and Power Company in Glendive, Montana; and the municipal electric utility at Sidney, Montana.

In 1926, Heskett bought 80 acres of land near Cabin Creek, in eastern Montana, and drilled for natural gas. Drillers found enough gas for Heskett to commission a site report from Hope Engineering. Hope claimed the acreage held enormous reserves, so Heskett quickly bought up the surrounding property. In 1927 Heskett hired Montana gas wildcatter Harry V. Mathews to run Gas Development Company, a subsidiary that would explore for and develop gas, and build pipelines. Gas Development set up four wells in 1927 and 18 wells in 1928. It acquired development interests in the Bowdoin Dome in northeastern Montana and the Pondera Field outside of Conrad, Montana.

Minnesota Northern sold this gas to an increasing territory of homeowners and businesses in the upper Midwest. It built pipelines to Marmarth, North Dakota, and Miles City, Montana, and it laid pipe southeast into the Black Hills of South Dakota. In 1929 the company committed $8 million for a 90-mile line to connect Glendive, Montana, with Williston, North Dakota, and

> ## Company Perspectives:
>
> *Guiding Principles: Provide high-quality, cost-effective products and services. Produce a superior total return to our stockholders. Conduct business with integrity and respect for all. Minimize waste and maximize resources. Recognize our responsibility to be an effective corporate citizen. Develop individual potential and teamwork to maintain employees as our ongoing source of competitive advantage.*

a 220-mile line from the Baker Field site to Bismarck, North Dakota. In addition to this geographic expansion, the company pursued acquisitions as another method of increasing business. In January 1929 Heskett acquired the Havre Natural Gas Company, and in 1930 he bought Montana Cities Gas Company, Northern Natural Gas Development Company, and the manufactured gas properties at Sheridan, Wyoming.

Through the late 1920s, Heskett's electric business followed a similar path of acquisition and extension. In 1925 alone Minnesota Northern acquired electric plants in seven North Dakota towns and seven Montana communities. In most cases, Heskett built long transmission lines, closed inefficient isolated plants, and dropped rates. In 1926, he acquired the Terry, Montana, power plant, installed a 600-kilowatt generator at Fairview, Montana, and hung several transmission lines between Montana and North Dakota, including a line from Bainville, Montana, to Williston, North Dakota.

Such acquisitions and line extensions continued, but the most significant activity of the late 1920s was a successful battle with Montana Power Company for the Miles City, Montana, electric franchise. Both companies organized publicity campaigns that urged Miles City residents to vote for their interests. Minnesota Northern also worked to expand per-customer electrical usage by selling refrigeration equipment to businesses and appliances to homeowners. Consumers could buy an automatic washer through their electric bill for one dollar down and a dollar a month. According to the official company history, *The Mondakonians—Energizers of the Prairies,* Minnesota Northern promoted the offer as "a copper washer for a silver dollar."

Difficulties During the Great Depression

The Depression struck Minnesota Northern's territory in the late 1920s, when drought and depressed farm prices affected the Dakotas and eastern Montana. Following the stock market crash in 1929, conditions became even worse. Heskett committed $5 million to capital projects at the urging of President Herbert Hoover for American utility executives to continue major construction projects in an attempt to aid the ailing U.S. economy. It soon became apparent, however, that business could not spend its way out of the Depression. Credit tightened and Minnesota Northern's income fell from $4 million in 1930 to $3.2 million in 1934. Longtime employee H.N. Elvig noted in *The Mondakonians* that the company's financial structure "was held together by such slender financial threads as to require the founders of the company to guarantee its debts with their own assets." Heskett refinanced troublesome short-term debt, cut

wages across the board, inaugurated a sales campaign led by merchandise manager W.L. "Bill" Hayes, and, perhaps most important, relied on the essential financial soundness of Minnesota Northern's Wausau-based backers.

In 1935, Minnesota Northern was faced with another type of threat when Congress passed the Public Utility Holding Company Act (PUHC), which limited utility holding companies to one operating subsidiary. The law was a reaction to the abuses of several giant electric utility holding companies who then dominated the industry, but it applied to all utility companies. Heskett opposed the bill. Nevertheless, he consolidated all Minnesota Northern's subsidiaries into one operating utility called the Montana-Dakota Utilities Co. Montana-Dakota conformed to the PUHC and was able to continue operations without interruption.

Growth returned in the later half of the 1930s. The needs of natural gas and electric customers expanded, especially around Fort Peck, where the U.S. Army Corps of Engineers was damming the Missouri River. Between 1935 and 1939 revenues fluctuated between $4.4 million and $4.6 million, finally breaking the $5 million mark in 1940. Economic conditions improved further as Europe went to war. In the spring of 1941, Heskett told shareholders that "the year 1940 was one of the most satisfactory in the history of the company. . . . For the first time in its history, total operating revenues of the company exceeded $5 million and net income after all deductions exceeded $1 million," according to *The Mondakonians.*

Also in 1940, the company acquired the gas franchise of Crookston, Minnesota, and completed a 117-mile pipeline from Fort Peck to Glendive, which added six communities to its customer base and connected the Bowdoin Field reserves to its growing pipeline system. By year's end sales of equipment and appliances were up 25 percent and MDU had 23,757 gas customers and 18,052 electric customers.

As the nation geared up for war, many Mondakonians, as Montana-Dakota employees called themselves, joined up, were drafted, or left the region. By June 1942, close to 10 percent of the company's prewar workforce was in the service. During the war itself, labor and materials shortages made repairs difficult and expansion nearly impossible. After the war, Montana-Dakota expanded and took its modern-day shape.

Postwar Boom

On the electric side, MDU made two key acquisitions. In October 1945, it paid $7 million for the Dakota Public Service Company, an electric and mining firm whose subsidiaries provided electricity to 91 communities, including Bismarck, North Dakota, and had yearly revenues close to $2 million. Two years later, Montana-Dakota paid $1.8 million for the Sheridan County Electric Company, its first electric utility in Wyoming.

The company took a variety of steps to secure electricity for its new customers. It bought power from the federal government's Fort Peck dam and agreed to transport power to area electric cooperatives in exchange for 5,000 kilowatts of firm power from the Bureau of Reclamation's Fort Peck dam along the Missouri River. In terms of generating capacity, Montana-Dakota constructed several small diesel and coal-fired genera-

Key Dates:

1924: R.M. Heskett founds Minnesota Northern Power Company.

1925: Minnesota Northern acquires electric plants in seven North Dakota towns and seven Montana communities.

1927: Heskett hires Montana gas wildcatter Harry V. Mathews to run Gas Development Company, a subsidiary that would build pipelines and explore for and develop gas.

1929: Company commits $8 million for a 90-mile line to connect Glendive, Montana, with Williston, North Dakota, and a 220-mile line from the Baker Field site to Bismarck, North Dakota.

1930: Company buys Montana Cities Gas Company, Northern Natural Gas Development Company, and the manufactured gas properties at Sheridan, Wyoming.

1935: Minnesota Northern consolidates its subsidiaries into one operating utility and changes its name to Montana-Dakota Utilities Co.

1940: Total operating revenues of the company exceed $5 million and net income exceeds $1 million.

1945: Company pays $7 million for Dakota Public Service Company.

1947: Montana-Dakota buys Sheridan County Electric Company, its first electric utility in Wyoming, for $1.8 million.

1951: Montana-Dakota acquires Billings Gas and Rocky Mountain Gas Company.

1966: Company headquarters moves from Minneapolis, Minnesota, to Bismarck, North Dakota.

1971: Company joins Minnesota's Otter Tail Power Company and South Dakota's Northwestern Public Service Company to construct a 400,000-kilowatt, lignite-powered generating station near Big Stone Lake in eastern South Dakota.

1977: Montana-Dakota and four regional partners begin building a 410,000-kilowatt, lignite-powered generating station at Beulah, North Dakota.

1985: Individual lines of business are grouped under the new MDU Resources Group, Inc., which is structured as a holding company.

1997: Knife River Coal Mining Company changes its name to Knife River Corporation to reflect its new focus on aggregate mining; MDU creates Utility Services, Inc.

1999: MDU consolidates all its oil and natural gas production and reserve assets under WBI Holdings, Inc.

tors in the 3,400–8,500 kilowatt range and completed its first large steam generator, the 25,000-kilowatt, coal-fired R.M. Heskett Station. Overall generating capacity increased from 14,837 kilowatts to 68,270 kilowatts between 1945 and 1951. Transmission mileage was up from 973 to 2,616. Kilowatt-hour sales grew from 40.5 million to 221.6 million, and electric revenues skyrocketed from $1.5 million to $6.88 million.

In the gas business, Montana-Dakota's primary postwar aim was to firm up supplies, which had begun to run short in 1944 and 1945. In the summer of 1947, Montana-Dakota began storing gas for winter usage in Carter Oil Company's Billy Creek Field south of Buffalo, Wyoming. In 1948 it started buying gas from Pure Oil Company's Worland, Wyoming field, and in 1950 it built a 334-mile, 12-inch gas transmission pipeline from the Worland field to the gas storage field at Cabin Creek.

With established supplies, the gas business again began expanding. In May 1951, Montana-Dakota acquired Billings Gas and the Rocky Mountain Gas Company. Billings Gas owned natural gas properties in Billings, Montana, and eight other Montana towns, and Rocky Mountain owned the Big Horn Pipeline and held the gas franchises in four Wyoming communities. Billings and Rocky Mountain increased Montana-Dakota's natural gas customers by 16,000 and helped push its 1951 gas revenues to $9.1 million. Montana-Dakota's total revenues for 1951 were $16.8 million.

Montana-Dakota also explored new business areas after the war. It acquired the Knife River Coal Mining Company—which switched from underground to surface mining—in the 1945 deal for Dakota Public Service. Then in the 1950s, oil reserves in eastern Montana were tapped. Rather than exploit

the oil themselves, Montana-Dakota executives signed a net proceeds agreement with Shell Western E & P. Shell Western operated the company's 90,000-acre leased properties, which by 1958 were producing more than 860,000 barrels and paying $300,000 to Montana-Dakota.

By the mid-1950s, growth in electrical usage demanded further generating capacity. On June 6, 1956, the company broke ground for the Lewis & Clark Station, a 44,000-kilowatt, lignite-fired unit on the Yellowstone River outside Sidney, Montana. Completed in 1959 for $12 million, Lewis & Clark was succeeded a scant two years later by groundbreaking on a $10.5 million, 66,000-kilowatt addition to Heskett Station.

Continued Expansion: 1960s–70s

As electrical demand continued to increase (kilowatt-hour sales would more than double in the 1960s), Montana-Dakota looked for innovative ways to increase capacity. In 1962, it proposed a seasonal swap of electricity with the Bureau of Reclamation's Pick-Sloan dams but was turned down. In January 1963 it joined the 20-member Mid-Continent Area Power Planners, an organization that worked to strengthen transmission ties in the upper Midwest. In 1965, Mid-Continent members agreed to build a 5,400-mile grid of high-voltage transmission lines across a state region, enabling members and others to buy and sell excess capacity.

In 1964, R.M. Heskett, then in his nineties, stepped down after 30 years at the head of the company. Cecil Smith was named chairman of the board, and his nephew and R.M. Heskett's son, David Heskett, was named Montana-Dakota president and CEO. David Heskett reorganized the company according to modern management practices. He delegated authority to department heads, installed a conventional chain of command, and brought in new outside directors. Two years after R.M. Heskett's death in 1966, David Heskett moved the company headquarters from Minneapolis, Minnesota, to Bismarck, North Dakota.

In the late 1960s, Montana-Dakota experienced continued customer and usage growth. To satisfy electric demand, in 1969 David Heskett and officials of Minnesota's Otter Tail Power Company and South Dakota's Northwestern Public Service Company announced a joint venture to construct a 400,000-kilowatt, lignite-powered generating station near Big Stone Lake in eastern South Dakota. Montana-Dakota would contribute $20 million to the $100 million project, which would break ground in 1971 and be completed in 1975. The plant, the construction of which marked the end of a long rivalry between Montana-Dakota and Northwestern Public Service, would be fueled by coal mined at Knife River Coal Mining Company's Gascoyne Mine in Bowman County in southwestern North Dakota.

In the early 1970s, the company expanded its natural gas distribution system in two ''Progress'' projects. ''Progress '70'' extended gas pipelines 227 miles eastward across North Dakota, bringing service to 12 new communities at a cost of $18.5 million. ''Progress '72'' extended the gas system north to the U.S. Army's Perimeter Acquisition Radar (PAR) site near Cavalier, North Dakota, and led the way to gas service for five North Dakota communities. To supply these new customers, Montana-Dakota explored for gas in the five sedimentary basins of the Rocky Mountain High Plains Region, and in 1974 acquired gas from the Rapelje Lake Basin northwest of Billings.

The major event of 1972 was the Rapid City, South Dakota flood. On June 9, Rapid Creek overflowed, killing 238 people and damaging or destroying more than 2,000 dwellings. Montana-Dakota crews worked through the night for the next two weeks restoring service to the Black Hills and rebuilding much of the devastated gas transmission system.

The Big Stone Plant was finished on time in 1975, but at a higher cost than anticipated. A major component in its $160 million price tag was $30 million for pollution abatement. Pollution control was becoming a major cost throughout the Montana-Dakota system. Between 1973 and 1975, the company spent $8.7 million on electrostatic precipitators, scrubbers, and new smokestacks at existing generators. At Knife River, surface mining was subject to increasingly stringent North Dakota reclamation laws. Pollution control was not the only area where costs rose in the middle and late 1970s. Inflation, high interest rates, and increasingly expensive natural gas squeezed finances and forced the company to repeatedly seek rate relief.

Despite these pressures, Montana-Dakota again needed new generating capacity by the mid-1970s. In 1977, Montana-Dakota and four regional partners announced that they would build a 410,000-kilowatt, lignite-powered generating station at Beulah, North Dakota. Situated adjacent to the Beulah Mine of the Knife River Coal Mining Company, Coyote Station would be a mine-mouth plant, cooled by piped-in Missouri River water.

Montana-Dakota also needed new gas. In the late 1970s, a nationwide natural gas shortage exacerbated the problems the company faced in the cold winter of 1977–78. Because it stored gas in underground formations, Montana-Dakota survived the winter without any major mishaps. It did, however, interrupt service to industrial customers.

On January 1, 1978, David Heskett retired, and Montana-Dakota's chief financial officer, John A. Schuchart, became president. Schuchart aimed to reorganize Montana-Dakota in ways that would exploit its technical knowhow. In the early 1980s, however, the company faced natural gas supply problems brought about by changing policies. To meet a growing demand for gas, Montana-Dakota contracted for supplies of deregulated gas. Deregulated gas proved too pricey for customers, however. Consumers conserved and industrial customers switched to cheaper alternate fuels, leaving Montana-Dakota with multimillion-dollar contracts for gas it could not use.

Reorganization in the 1980s

On the electric side, Schuchart spent the 1980s rearranging Montana-Dakota's supply structure. He retired several older plants and in 1985 acquired further shares of the Big Stone and Coyote generating stations. In June 1986 he bought capacity at Basin Electric Power Cooperative's Antelope Valley II plant.

By the mid-1980s, Schuchart was able to institute his reorganization plan. In 1985, he created MDU Resources Group, Inc., structured as a holding company under which he grouped the individual lines of business, though still operating within the bounds of the PUHC. Schuchart explained in *The Mondakonians* that the reason for the restructuring, begun in 1985, ''was to better enable us to develop the individual assets which prior to that time had really been embedded and lost in the Montana-Dakota Utilities Co. structure.''

Among the new subsidiaries, Williston Basin Interstate Pipeline Company faced a difficult time in the gas supply, production, and transmission business. Under deregulation, the role of the pipeline company changed from merchant to transporter. Rates fell, which was good news for the consumer but bad news for MDU, whose overall gas business suffered as deregulation and warmer than normal winters caused a downward spiral in prices.

The Fidelity Oil Group took proceeds from the Shell-run Cedar Creek Anticline property and invested them in oil and gas operations in the western half of the United States and Canada. From the beginning of the program in 1986, when reserves totaled 12 million barrels, Fidelity increased reserves to 17 million barrels by the end of 1991.

Shifting Focus in the 1990s

At Knife River Coal Mining Company, the late 1980s saw business suffer for two reasons: coal was in oversupply, and sales volume dropped sharply in 1987 after a crack in the rotor shaft caused a shutdown of the Big Stone Plant. After the reorganization, Knife River executives began looking at mineral and aggregate mining and clean coal technology as new ways to exploit their expertise. This effort intensified during the early 1990s, when clean air legislation put the future of the lignite coal business in doubt. In June 1992 it acquired KRC Aggregate, Inc., a sand and gravel mining company based in Lodi, California.

The last element in Schuchart's reorganization was Prairielands Energy Marketing, which expanded markets for the corporation's energy products. In 1991, Prairielands signed a 17-year capacity agreement with the Northern Border Pipeline system. The agreement provided a link between regional natural gas reserves and major national markets. In 1992, Prairielands began using the natural gas futures market.

Through a series of acquisitions in the 1990s, the Knife River Coal Mining Company changed its focus from lignite coal mining to aggregate mining and sales of construction materials. In 1993 the company acquired three aggregate operations in California and Oregon and the assets of an aggregate and construction materials company in Alaska. In 1995 it gained a 50 percent ownership in Hawaiian Cement, one of the largest construction suppliers in Hawaii, then acquired the remaining 50 percent two years later. To better express its broadened business concerns, the subsidiary dropped the reference to coal mining in its name in 1997, becoming Knife River Corporation.

Knife River continued its expansion in aggregate mining and construction materials sales, a lucrative area given the boom in road building in the Pacific Northwest. The Transportation Equity Act of 1998 dedicated some $150 billion to road building, mainly in the West, between 1998 and 2004, and Knife River had more business than it could keep up with. Its backlog in early 2001 hit $126 million. The company stepped up its acquisitions. By the end of 1999, it had acquired four more construction materials businesses, including Oregon-based Morse Bros. and JTL Group, which expanded Knife River's operations into Montana and Wyoming. In 2000, it purchased nine additional companies in California, Oregon, Montana, and Alaska. By mid-2000, the company's aggregate reserves had grown to 880 million tons, giving the company supplies for the next 40 years at current consumption levels.

More important, the growth of Knife River's aggregate business offset the decline of its coal mining operations. In May 2001 the company made the transformation complete by selling its coal mining operations to Westmoreland Coal Company. "Knife River's coal mining operations have been a part of MDU Resources since 1945, so making the decision to exit the coal mining business was not easy," said Terry D. Hildestad, president and CEO of Knife River, in a company press release. "However, with Knife River's growing construction materials operations providing over 90 percent of Knife River's revenues, it is prudent to concentrate on that business and take advantage of Westmoreland's interest in our coal operations."

MDU created Utility Services, Inc., in 1997, contributing to its increasing diversity. As a full-service engineering, design, and build company, the new subsidiary specialized in the con-struction and maintenance of electric lines and natural gas distribution and transmission systems. By 2000, the company had $169 million in annual sales and was expected to bring in almost $300 million in 2001. Its rate of growth looked promising as utility companies struggled to replace aging lines.

MDU continued its program of expansion for Fidelity Oil with great success in the 1990s. Reserves reached 22 million barrels in 1994, and production passed three million barrels. In 1996 the subsidiary acquired two new companies, with properties in Texas, New Mexico, and Alabama. The next year, its operating revenues exceeded $68 million. A significant purchase, the Willow Springs gas field in east Texas was completed in 1998.

Williston Basin Interstate Pipeline Company changed its name to WBI Holdings, Inc., in 1998 to acknowledge its growing lines of business in energy marketing and to prepare for the consolidation of all the corporation's oil and natural gas production and reserve assets. The following year Fidelity Oil Group was renamed Fidelity Exploration & Production Company and became a subsidiary of WBI Holdings. WBI made further acquisitions in the next few years, including a Wyoming pipeline, a gas storage field in western Kentucky, a large coalbed natural gas producer, and an energy technology firm specializing in pipeline and cable location and tracking.

Early in the new millennium, MDU had reduced its emphasis on its utility business. Utility services accounted for less than 10 percent of sales in 2000. Its growth in other areas, fueled in large part by acquisitions (70 between 1993 and 2001), was disciplined rather than haphazard: It only purchased in areas of expertise or closely related enterprises, and the strategy seemed very effective. The company's revenues, which were $464 million in 1995, reached $1.9 billion in 2000.

Principal Subsidiaries

Fidelity Exploration and Production Company; Fidelity Oil Co.; Fidelity Oil Holdings, Inc.; Knife River Corporation; Montana-Dakota Utilities Co.; Prairielands Energy Marketing, Inc.; Utility Services, Inc.; WBI Holdings, Inc.

Principal Competitors

Black Hills Power, Inc.; NorthWestern Corporation; Vulcan Materials Company.

Further Reading

Beck, Bill, *The Mondakonians: Energizers of the Prairie,* Duluth, Minn.: MDU Resources Group, Inc., 1992.
"MDU Resources Group, Inc.," *On Wall Street,* October 2000, p. 6.
Shinkle, Kirk, "Erstwhile Utility Player Eyes Growth Elsewhere," *Investor's Business Daily,* April 17, 2001.

—Jordan Wankoff
—update: Susan Windisch Brown

Media Arts Group, Inc.

900 Lightpost Way
Morgan Hill, California 95037
U.S.A.
Telephone: (408) 201-5000
Toll Free: (800) 366-3733
Fax: (408) 201- 5192
Web site: http://www.mediaarts.com

Public Company
Incorporated: 1990
Employees: 524
Sales: $132.09 million (2001)
Stock Exchanges: New York
Ticker Symbol: MDA
NAIC: 453920 Art Dealers; 511199 All Other Publishers;
    453220 Gift, Novelty, and Souvenir Stores

Open practically any home decorating magazine, page through its contents, and one would be hard-pressed not to find a reference to artist Thomas Kinkade or the company he founded, Media Arts Group, Inc. Based in Morgan Hill, California, just south of San Jose, Media Arts is one of the country's most visible and successful designers, manufacturers, and publishers of art, home decor, gifts, and collectibles. Media Arts oversees licensing agreements for all of artist Thomas Kinkade's prints and the decorative accessories inspired by his art. A host of other "life affirming" artists have signed on with Media Arts as well. Marketing its products through companies such as The Bradford Exchange, Hallmark, QVC, and Avon, Media Arts Group and its premier artist Thomas Kinkade have built a small art-based empire in a few short years. What Martha Stewart has done for entertaining and home and garden enthusiasts, Media Arts aspires to do for art lovers through its "visual content managing."

An Art Partnership: 1990s

In 1990 two friends, artist Thomas Kinkade and business-man Kenneth Raasch, joined together to found Media Arts Group. Kinkade, a graduate of Art Center College of Design in Pasadena, California, was determined to make a living doing what he loved—painting. Kinkade, the self-proclaimed Painter of Light, and Raasch settled on a company based on a lifestyle brand of art production and distribution using Kinkade's and other prominent artist's names and works.

Media Arts opened the first of many Thomas Kinkade Galleries in 1992. The galleries sold good quality reproductions on canvas, prints, and gifts and collectibles based exclusively on Kinkade's work. Kinkade never sold his original artwork but offered signed prints and high-end canvas lithographs with original highlighting.

In 1994 the company acquired John Hines Studios Limited and established licensing agreements with other well-known artists including humorist/illustrator Gary Patterson. In a move to continue company expansion, Media Arts Group went public in 1995. On the heels of its initial public offering Media Arts experienced tremendous growth. The company opened galleries in 26 locations and formed its first wholly owned subsidiary, MAGI. MAGI's business was directed towards the production of gifts and collectibles for the entertainment industry.

The year 1995 proved to be a banner one for Media Arts Group. *Business Week*'s May 22 issue ranked the company third on its list of 100 hot growth companies. Additionally, the company posted record sales that had increased 217 percent over those of the previous year. Much of the jump in sales was initially attributed to the company's acquisition of John Hine Ltd. but its subsidiary, Thomas Kinkade Stores, was also expanding and growing.

In fiscal 1996, Media Arts Group experienced a slight downturn and reported losses of $673,000 on revenues of $54 million. The previous year's profit was recorded as $3.8 million. A marked decline in sales of its miniature cottage and small collectible figures resulted in the downturn, according to company officials, and management took measures to cut costs by $3.6 million to offset the losses and bring the company back on track.

Throughout 1996 and 1997 Media Arts spent a significant amount of its resources launching a line of independently owned galleries in addition to its corporately owned Thomas

Company Perspectives:

The mission of Media Arts Group, Inc. is to create the preeminent visual content management company in the world and to change the way people look at art through the development of life-affirming, emotionally uplifting images, and message driven products, rooted in traditional family values. With our successful business model, Media Arts Group, Inc. is positioned to be the dominant force in art publishing, home decor, and gift products in the coming century.

Kinkade Galleries. The efforts paid off with revenues climbing by 57 percent.

The push of retail storefronts served the dual purpose of bringing the Thomas Kinkade name into the mainstream of American art and art-related collecting and fostering licensing agreements with other retailers, including furniture giant La-Z-boy, Crown Craft, and Avon. La-Z-Boy devoted a whole line of its upholstered furniture to the Kinkade name.

Kinkade's name brand was increasingly associated with an image of nostalgia and old-time family values, an opportunity many home stores recognized as a significant market share to tap. Companies took notice and responded to the large group of consumers looking to create the Kinkade-look or atmosphere through their home furnishings.

In 1998 Media Arts Group opened 11 new galleries and saw its licensed distribution outlets reach 103. Many of these stores were independently owned and operated Thomas Kinkade Galleries and exclusively sold Kinkade merchandise. The independent stores were an unexpected bonus to the company. Through licensing Kinkade outlets, the cost of operating the stores was left to the independent owner and the company made a good profit on the merchandise the store sold at retail.

By the summer of 1998 the company opened eight additional Thomas Kinkade Signature Galleries and two company owned stores. Although in a move that seemed to run counter to what had worked in the past, Media Arts bought back several galleries at this time, including the Signature Gallery on Catalina Island off the California coast.

A 1998 *Forbes* article summed up Media Arts Group's appeal, "Media Arts sells not so much products as image, and sentimentality. ... Thomas Kinkade's luminescent pastoral scenes, reproduced by the thousands every year, have captured the hearts of middle America and turned San Jose, California-based Media Arts Group into one of the fastest growing companies on the 200 list." Kinkade's commercial appeal was illustrated by the reaction he received while guest appearing on QVC shopping network. Kinkade's television appearance in January 1998 helped sell more than $2.2 million worth of items during an hour of air time.

Although Kinkade's original artwork was the inspiration for many gift and collectible pieces, much of what sold under the Kinkade name as a brand was not directly associated with his art. This lifestyle licensing was so successful that Warner Books published a book based on the inspiring artist's thoughts and devotions, entitled *Lightposts for Living,* in 1998.

As if books, art, furniture, gifts, collectibles, and home decor were not enough, in 2000, US Home, a national builder, was licensed to build the first Thomas Kinkade home. The model was based on a house featured in one of Kinkade's most collected prints.

Media Arts took its first steps to join thousands of other companies and retailers on the Internet when in April 1999 the company created another subsidiary to focus on computer-generated sales. Exclaim Technologies Inc. was developed as an ASP (Application Service Provider) and produced the software known as "Marketplace." Exclaim and US Web/CKS and IBM developed web sites for Media Arts, including the www.ThomasKinkade.com site.

The company had hoped to use Exclaim for its own use but also anticipated that its software would become popular among other gifts and collectible merchants who wanted to enhance their Internet business. Exclaim was a comparatively costly start-up but, like many Internet content providers, Exclaim's value to the company would only be determined over time.

Media Arts had grown to a sizable 400 employees by June 2000 and had made plans to build a new corporate headquarters in Morgan Hill, just south of San Jose, California. Four buildings were planned with two of the four to be completed within the year, a 61,000-square-foot corporate office building and a 155,000-square-foot production facility.

In addition, during the same period the greeting card company Hallmark announced its plan to produce an everyday collection based on the art of Thomas Kinkade. Hallmark had contracted with Media Arts since 1995 for seasonal Kinkade merchandise, but the new contract for a 40-unit product line was welcomed by the company.

Diversifying Its Product Offerings

In an effort to "diversify its product offerings," Media Arts Chairman Craig Fleming announced that the company had successfully signed British artist Simon Bull to a five-year licensing agreement. Bull had been recognized by the U.K.'s Fine Arts Trade Guild as a Best Selling Original Print Artist and brought an international reputation and following that was highly appealing to the company's plans to expand worldwide. Artist Howard Behrens also joined the ranks of Kinkade and Bull. The commercial success of Media Arts' featured artists helped attract other artists to its management offers. Thomas Kinkade was now recognized at "the most commercially successful living artist," but it was apparent that Media Arts wanted to ensure that, should things break off in the future with Kinkade, the company had other prominent artists to merchandise.

Media Arts' newest retail chain, the Masters of Light Galleries, were multi-artist galleries and reflected the latest company trend towards diversification. Company Chairman and CEO Craig Fleming explained the marketing strategy of the Masters of Light Galleries in a press release stating, "the Masters of Light Galleries will be very event driven, with approximately two to four artist appearances per year. We know

---

Key Dates:

1990: Company is incorporated when Thomas Kinkade partners with friend Kenneth Raasch.
1992: Media Arts opens first Thomas Kinkade Gallery in Carmel, California.
1995: Media Arts signs distribution agreement with Hallmark.
1998: Company signs licensing agreements with retail giants Crown Craft, Avon, and La-Z-Boy.
1999: Media Arts receives $20 million line of credit from Bank of America; launches new private satellite network and its Impressionist Masterworks Collection.
2000: New corporate office and production facility is built; Craig Fleming is named chairman.
2001: Buyout attempt by Thomas Kinkade is unsuccessful.

---

from our experience with Thomas Kinkade that one of the keys to building a strong customer base is to develop relationships between the artist, the gallery owner and the collector.''

At the same time that Media Arts was enrolling artists and completing its Morgan Hill construction project, the company made plans to retain the New York public relations firm Porter, LeVay & Rose. Fleming issued a statement reflecting the company's strategy in contracting with Porter, LeVay by saying, ''We are pleased that Porter, LeVay & Rose will be helping us communicate with the investment community, our shareholders and business news media. Our goal is to heighten the company's visibility and shareholder value as we diversify our product offerings, pursue the potential for new licensing and distribution opportunities and broaden our Internet exposure.''

Soon after signing the public relations firm, Fleming resigned from his post at Media Arts, and the company named one of its board members as acting chairman. The economy in 2001 was experiencing a downturn and Media Arts took several steps to keep corporate earnings up. Thomas Kinkade himself completed a tour of all the company's U.S.-based Signature Galleries, drawing crowds of collectors. The company now had 5,000 distribution centers and galleries worldwide, but despite its efforts Media Arts reported a decline in revenue in fiscal 2001.

In February 2001 Media Arts signed a five-year contract with renowned artist Robert Lyn Nelson. Nelson, known for his marine life art, joined Kinkade, Howard Behrens, and Simon Bull in selling reproductions of his work at the company's Masters of Light Galleries.

A month later an unveiling at New York's Art Expo revealed original artwork by Kinkade, Behrens, and Bull in their role as official artists for the 2002 Salt Lake City Winter Olympic Games.

Media Arts not only gained international appeal by its Olympics' release, but the company continued its advances into the international marketplace by opening Thomas Kinkade Signature Galleries in Toronto, Canada, and Glasgow, Scotland. Signature Galleries were already established in two of England's upscale shopping districts.

In April 2001 Media Arts announced the opening of the first Howard Behrens Studio Gallery, in Monterey, California. Proclaiming Behrens as ''the world's foremost palette knife artist,'' the company hoped to parlay the artist's name into a mini-industry, just as it had done with the Thomas Kinkade name. Media Arts planned to open three additional Behrens galleries by March 2002.

The new Media Arts world headquarters was completed in the summer of 2001. A new chairman and CEO, Anthony Thomopoulos, brought more changes to the company. Thomopoulos had served on the board of directors since July 2000, and had previously held leadership posts at ABC Entertainment, ABC Broadcasting, Amblin Entertainment, and was formerly chairman of United Artists. Thomopoulos announced that the corporate move to the outskirts of San Jose would mean a significant savings to the company. The company estimated that its relocation saved the company $1 million annually.

An interesting corporate development occurred when in 2001, Thomas Kinkade, Media Arts' second largest shareholder and its Art Director, led an attempt to take control of the company by purchasing all of the outstanding shares of common stock. Kinkade's offer of $6.25 a share was considered by the company's board of directors. The offer was determined to be insufficient and shortly thereafter Kinkade withdrew his offer. Kinkade explained his change of heart saying that his decision was based on ''current economic uncertainties and the difficult lending environment.''

While it was clear that Media Arts Group had aspirations to become one of the corporate retail giants in its art branding distribution, whether or not it could continue to grow exponentially in the softened economy remained to be seen. Specialized retail industries had often suffered during recessionary times or strained economic conditions. The company's attempts to hire seasoned veterans with entertainment connections, and the diversification in product and artists that Media Arts Group was exploring boded well for broadening the company's appeal beyond the collectors interested in Thomas Kinkade.

Principal Subsidiaries

Lightpost Publishing, Inc.; Thomas Kinkade Stores, Inc.; Thomas Kinkade Media, Inc.; MAGI Sales, Inc.; Exclaim Technologies, Inc.

Principal Competitors

Interiors, Inc.; National Picture & Frame Company; Martin Lawrence Limited Editions.

Further Reading

''Construction Imminent on Media Arts' New Home,'' *Business Journal,* June 9, 2000, p. 20.
''First Howard Behrens Studio Gallery Opens,'' *Art Business News,* June 2001, p. 10.
''Home Decor Briefs,'' *HFN,* October 4, 1999, p. 56.
Kehoe, Anne-Margaret, ''Collectibles, Gifts from the MAGI,'' *HFN,* April 17, 1995.
Keller, Julie, ''Spotlight on Media Arts,'' *Art Business News,* August 2000, p. 10.

"Kinkade Art the Focal Point in New 'Music of Light' Label," *Art Business News,* December 2000, p. 18.

"La-Z-Boy Bringing Artist's Designs to Upholstered Line," *HFN,* June 29, 1998, p. 29.

McCormack, Scott, "Making People Feel Good About Themselves," *Forbes,* November 2, 1998, p. 222.

"Media Arts Co-Founder Offers to Buy Rest of Company," *New York Times,* October 19, 2000, p. C4.

"Media Arts Group Adds 11 Galleries," *HFN,* July 6, 1998, p. 47.

"Media Arts Group Expands Licensing for Thomas Kinkade's Inspiring Images," *Gifts & Decorative Accessories,* September 1999, p. S3.

"Media Arts Group Inc.," *Business Journal,* November 26, 1999, p. 42.

"Media Arts Group, Inc. Wins License to Use Gary Patterson Designs," *HFN,* February 20, 1995.

"Media Arts Group Sales Soar but Net Dips in the Third Quarter," *HFN,* February 20, 1995.

"Media Arts Launches Satellite Network," *Gifts & Decorative Accessories,* November 1999, p. 212.

"Media Arts Posts Loss for Year," *HFN,* July 8, 1996, p. 57.

"Media Arts Rejects Kinkade Offer," *Furniture Briefs,* February 26, 2001, p. 46.

"Media Arts Signs New Artist, Plans Charity Event," *Art Business News,* March 2001, p. 12.

Roberts, Ricardo, "Arts Bidder May Learn: You Can't Paint $: He Paints Light, but Can He Conjure up $63 Million?," *Mergers and Acquisitions Report,* November 27, 2000.

——, "At Media Arts, Has Kinkade Painted Himself into a Corner?," *Mergers and Acquisitions Report,* February 26, 2001.

—Susan B. Culligan

NCO Group, Inc.

515 Pennsylvania Avenue
Fort Washington, Pennsylvania 19034-3313
U.S.A.
Telephone: (215) 793-9300
Toll Free: (800) 220-2274
Fax: (215) 793-2939
Web site: http://www.ncogroup.com

Public Company
Incorporated: 1926 as National Collection Office
Employees: 9,200
Sales: $605.9 million (2000)
Stock Exchanges: NASDAQ
Ticker Symbol: NCOG
NAIC: 56144 Collection Agencies

With more than 80 call centers in the United States, NCO Group, Inc., is the largest provider of accounts receivable collection in the world. The company offers accounts receivable and delinquency management; customer and billing service; and market research and telemarketing. In addition to its U.S. operations, the company provides international services in Canada, the United Kingdom, Australia, and throughout Europe.

Small Beginnings: 1926–86

NCO Group, Inc., began its life in 1926, when it was founded as National Collection Office by Louis Barrist. The company was located upstairs from the Schubert Theater on South Broad Street in Philadelphia. For its first 60 years, National Collection Office remained a small company, employing only a few people and basing its futures on small-time collecting of department store bills and rent collection.

By 1986, the company was being operated by Louis's son and daughter-in-law in a small garage at their home in Havertown, Pennsylvania. They had three employees. The company had 60 clients and only $40,000 in profits in 1986. "It was never more than a mom-and-pop operation," said Michael Barrist, grandson of the founder, in a 1992 interview with the *Philadelphia Inquirer*.

1980s and Early 1990s: Third Generation Taking the Reins

Michael J. Barrist took the reins of the company from his retiring parents in 1986. At the time, revenues were only $70,000. He paid $25,000 for the company and renamed it NCO Financial Systems Inc. His experience until that time had not been at the family company but rather at U.S. Healthcare as a certified public accountant. He took leadership of the company immediately, however, and began aggressive plans for growth. His first step was to hire Charles C. Piola, Jr., as the company's executive vice-president. Piola focused on sales and Barrist on operations and service. Together, they grew the company more than 400 percent in the first year alone.

By 1992, the company had more than 800,000 debts to collect and was operating in all 50 states. Many of the company's new clients were in the medical field, but the customer list was diverse, including AT&T, Mellon Bank, Sun Co., National Freight Inc., the Philadelphia 76ers, and the Pennsylvania Higher Education Assistance Agency.

In the eight-year period ending in 1994, the company grew to $5 million in sales and 125 employees. Once sales figures climbed, acquisitions were the next strategy to grow the company. Armed with a revolving loan from Mellon Bank, NCO purchased three companies before 1996: B. Richard Miller Inc., Eastern Business Services, and the collection division of Trans Union Corp. In 1996, the company purchased Management Adjustment Bureau Inc., and Michael Barrist's dream of going public was much closer to reality.

1996: Going Public

In November 1996, the newly renamed NCO Group, Inc. joined the ranks of publicly traded companies when it completed its initial public offering (IPO) of 2,875,000 shares on the NASDAQ exchange. The shares were priced at $13.00 per share, and the company raised $30 million. In slightly more than six months, NCO's stock shot to $35 per share. The capital raised in the IPO helped bring more acquisitions under the NCO Group umbrella, including TeleResearch Center Inc. of Phila-

Company Perspectives:

NCO Group, Inc. (NCO) delivers accounts receivable management and outsourcing solutions that are customized to meet the unique requirements of every major market segment. Creditors in all market segments—from healthcare, financial services, retail, and commercial, to education, telecommunications, utilities, and government—look to NCO as their business partner. Whether the need is to improve customer care and retention, reduce delinquency rates, or improve debt recovery, NCO's integrated solutions provide improved financial performance and customer satisfaction across the revenue cycle.

Behind every NCO solution are our powerful resources—people, technology, facilities, and expertise. Together these resources deliver solutions that present a seamless link between our clients and their customers.

delphia; Goodyear & Associates Inc. of Charlotte, North Carolina; and CMS A/R Services of Jackson, Michigan.

"We run a very aggressive company and are focused on profitability," said Michael Barrist after the acquisitions. "Some of the companies we've bought have been a little slower and [more] methodical than we were and we needed to teach them our culture." What was the NCO culture? Under Barrist it developed as fast-paced and aggressive with a strong dedication to client service.

Late 1990s: Continued Growth As Public Company

By 1998, NCO had acquired 11 companies and was posting $118 million in revenues. Growing the company had been a top priority and the climate for expansion in the collections business could not have been better. Consumer debt rose from $914.4 billion in 1977 to $5.28 trillion in 1997, according to the Federal Reserve. This setting gave NCO Group ideal growth opportunities in addition to the company's continuing acquisitions. Bank expansion and consolidation was another factor in the debt collection industry because bigger banks tended to rely more heavily on debt collection agencies.

The company's client list continued to rise in the late 1990s to more than 7,800 active clients. To serve them, NCO grew in size to 2,200 employees at its 23 processing centers. In 1997, the company had posted $85 million in revenues. The next year, the company experienced a 50 percent increase in revenues, to $125 million. NCO Group was identified in 1998 by Janney Montgomery Scott Inc. as the fastest growing company in the debt collection industry. In May 1999, NCO Group became the largest debt collection company in the United States with the purchase of Compass International Services Corp. and Milliken & Michaels.

Although the acquisitions pushed NCO Group to the top of its industry, stock investors did not respond favorably. The trading price for the stock fell to $25.75 from $34. It regained its price by the end of the month, but the reaction was enough to cause NCO to slow down its acquisition strategy.

2000 and Beyond: New Challenges and Growth

The year 2000 began, not with Y2K problems for NCO, but with departures of two top managers within the company. Charles Piola, Jr., and Bernard R. Miller both announced they were leaving the company. The resignations were tied to contract delays with some healthcare contracts that would create revenue shortfalls. The shortfall warning, issued by the company, also caused NCO's stock to dive to the mid-20s. The decline continued through 2000, with a 25.9 percent drop in August alone. "This is not an NCO production problem," said CEO Michael J. Barrist, who blamed changing consumer payment patterns for the drop in performance.

In October 2000, the company announced the formation of a separate debt-purchasing business in conjunction with the announcement of the purchase of Creditrust Corp. The new subsidiary, NCO Portfolio Management Inc., operated separately and could more aggressively grow while allowing Barrist to keep his promise to stockholders to temporarily halt acquisitions for NCO Group. NCO Portfolio Management, Inc. was designed as a debt-buying company and would use NCO Group's resources for its debt collecting. Therefore, NCO Portfolio Management was a built-in customer for its parent company.

For fiscal 2000, revenue rose to more than $605 million. "While 2000 presented NCO Group's most successful year to date, it also represented one of the most challenging," said CEO Barrist in the annual report. During the turbulent year, the company achieved record revenues and profits.

In February 2001, NCO Portfolio Management completed the purchase of Creditrust Corp. "We are extremely excited about this transaction," stated CEO Michael Barrist in a company press release. "NCO Portfolio Management will be able to leverage the client relationships and the scale of the NCO Group Infrastructure as well as the portfolios, historical data and highly skilled workforce of both Creditrust and NCO Group." Barrist believed that NCO Portfolio would be "the premier player in the purchased debt marketplace" and would achieve the same "best in class brand recognition that NCO Group has already achieved in the accounts receivable marketplace."

NCO Group moved into the age of the Internet in February 2001 with an announcement that it would partner with CyberStarts, Inc. and Collections X to develop e-collection products and services. NCO planned investment in both companies to develop programs and vehicles for online debt collection services.

NCO Group's stock was on the rise when it was identified as a "recession proof" business in 2001. The stock's value jumped from $11 in the third quarter of 2000 to $33 in the first quarter of 2001. But the first quarter brought another surprise for the company—a visit from the Federal Bureau of Investigations (FBI). The FBI visited NCO's Baltimore Call Center with search warrants to view pre-bankruptcy activities of Creditrust prior to its purchase by NCO. To compound the situation, the *Wall Street Journal* mistakenly reported that the FBI search was into NCO's own accounting records. NCO's stock dropped by $4 briefly but recovered quickly as information regarding the reporting gaffe, as well as NCO's immunity from any liability concerning Creditrust's pre-acquisition activities, was made available to stock-

```
┌─────────────────────────────────────────────────┐
│                                                   │
│                  Key Dates:                       │
│                                                   │
│  1926:  The company is founded by Louis Barrist   │
│         and oper- ates for decades as a small     │
│         family-run collection agency.             │
│  1986:  National Collection Office is purchased   │
│         by Michael Barrist, grandson of the       │
│         founder; business is re- named NCO        │
│         Financial Systems Inc.                    │
│  1995:  NCO purchases other collection firms to   │
│         fuel growth.                              │
│  1996:  Management Adjustment Bureau Inc. is      │
│         purchased; company goes public on the     │
│         NASDAQ as NCO Group, Inc.                 │
│  1999:  NCO declares halt in aggressive           │
│         acquisitions.                             │
│  2000:  Subsidiary NCO Portfolio Management is    │
│         formed.                                   │
│  2001:  Purchase of Creditrust is finalized.      │
│                                                   │
└─────────────────────────────────────────────────┘
```

holders. "Our position has always been that it's better to tell investors," said CEO and President Michael Barrist in a follow-up article in the *Philadelphia Business Journal*.

While the stock rose, so did flood waters in June 2001. Tropical storm Allison caused the first-floor personnel at Fort Washington, Pennsylvania headquarters to relocate to other parts of the building. Business was not impacted greatly and resumed a few days later. The first floor, however, was described by the company as a total loss.

Despite the tropical storm and the FBI visit, NCO Group finished the second quarter of 2001 with a 19 percent increase in revenue. Income dropped, however, as one-time charges were levied and payroll expenses increased.

Growing in 15 years from three employees to 9,200, and $40,000 to $21.9 million in net income, NCO Group clearly had exceeded all but the most visionary dreams of its first two generations of management. Third generation leader Michael Barrist had proven himself a master of the expansion game, in an industry that still held much promise for the future.

Principal Subsidiaries

NCO Portfolio Management, Inc.; NCO Financial Systems Inc.; FCA International Ltd. (Canada); Financial Collection Agencies (UK) Ltd. (U.K.); International Account Systems d/b/a MCA International; NCO Benefit Systems, Inc.

Principal Competitors

GC Services; MCM Capital Group, Inc.; Outsourcing Solutions.

Further Reading

Ahles, Andrea, "Collection Agency Finds Profits in Others' Debt," *Knight-Ridder/Tribune Business News,* December 20, 1998.

——, "PA-Based Firm Tops Debt-Collection Field with Buy," *Knight-Ridder/Tribune Business News,* May 13, 1999.

Brickley, Peg, "NCO Group Decides to Hold Off on Buys," *Philadelphia Business Journal,* May 28, 1999, p. 4.

——, "Once a Darling, NCO Struggles with Stock Dip," *Philadelphia Business Journal,* January 21, 2000, p. 6.

"FBI Launches Search of NCO Group Office's Accounting Records," *Wall Street Journal,* March 16, 2001, p. B2.

Fernandez, Bob, "Philadelphia Debt Collector Succeeds Due to Management, Technology," *Knight-Ridder/Tribune Business News,* August 10, 1999.

Gotlieb, Andy, "Collection Firm Hit Hard by Allison," *Philadelphia Business Journal,* June 22, 2001, p. 5.

——, "NCO Sets Record Straight on FBI Search Warrants," *Philadelphia Business Journal,* March 23, 2001, p. 6.

"Industry Debates NCO's Move into Debt-Buying," *Credit & Collections News,* October 20, 2000.

Lewis, Larry, "Big Collections from Little Debts Have a Montco Firm Growing," *Philadelphia Inquirer,* January 16, 1992, p. B7.

"NCO Group Execs Resign," *Philadelphia Business Journal,* January 14, 2000, p. 42.

"NCO Group Is All Set to Collect," *Business Week,* March 19, 2001, p. 113.

"NCO Group 2Q Down 61%," *Philadelphia Business Journal,* August 1, 2001.

"NCO Rescues Busted Buyer," *Credit & Collections News,* October 13, 2000.

"NCO Revenues Gain Ground," *Credit & Collections News,* November 3, 2000.

"NCO Sees Trouble Ahead," *Collections & Credit Risk,* September 2000, p. 8.

"No Good Deed Unpunished," *Philadelphia Business Journal,* August 4, 2000, p. 2.

Patton, Carol, "NCO on the Go," *Philadelphia Business Journal,* May 1, 1998, p. 19.

Waggoner, Darren J., "Commercial Agencies Thrive As Economy Dives," *Collections & Credit Risk,* July 2001, p. 48.

"Wall St. Likes Collectors," *Bloomberg News,* July 29, 1997, p. 4C.

—Melissa Rigney Baxter

OAO Gazprom

Nametkina 16
Moscow 117884
Russia
Telephone: +7-095-719-3001
Fax: +7-095-719-8333
Web site: http://www.gazprom.ru

Public Company
Incorporated: 1993
Employees: 300,000
Sales: Ru 375.1 billion (2000)
Stock Exchanges: Russian
NAIC: 211111 Crude Petroleum and Natural Gas
    Extraction; 211112 Natural Gas Liquid Extraction;
    213111 Drilling Oil and Gas Wells; 213112 Support
    Activities for Oil and Gas Field Operations; 22121
    Natural Gas Distribution; 48621 Pipeline Transporta-
    tion of Natural Gas; 54171 Research and Develop-
    ment in the Physical, Engineering and Life Sciences

OAO Gazprom is the largest natural gas company in the world and the largest company in Russia. It controls one quarter of the world's known natural gas reserves and accounts for 8 percent of Russia's gross domestic product. The company and its numerous subsidiaries are active in all areas of the gas industry, including exploration, extraction, processing, transportation, and marketing. Gazprom was privatized in 1993, although the state still holds a 38 percent stake in the company and controls a majority of the seats on the board of directors. This fact has contributed to an unusually high degree of political involvement at Gazprom. The company is alleged to have received special treatment from the Kremlin, and, in return, to have used its considerable influence and assets for the government's benefit. Not only does Gazprom have tremendous importance for the economy of the Russian Federation, but foreign dependence on Russian gas, especially in countries of the former Soviet Union, allows Gazprom to be used externally as a diplomatic tool. The company's history is peppered with incidents of apparent cooperation with the Kremlin as well as power struggles when inter-

ests clashed. Like most companies in Russia, Gazprom is trying to navigate the economic instability of the country, the insolvency of many of its customers, and the pressure to do business according to Western standards. The company controls 149,000 kilometers of gas pipelines, 22 underground storage facilities, six gas processing plants, 69 producing gas-condensate fields, and 253 compressor stations. Gazprom's holdings also include assets unrelated to the gas industry, from shoe factories to stakes in media companies, some of which the company has received in lieu of cash to settle debts.

Natural Gas in the Soviet Era

Many of the pipelines and facilities controlled by Gazprom were developed in the Soviet era under a succession of state gas ministries. Russia's natural gas reserves were first exploited on a large scale shortly after World War II, when an 843-kilometer (km) pipeline was constructed from Saratov, on the lower Volga River, to Moscow. The success of the Saratov-Moscow project led to more pipeline construction in the 1950s, with the development of a localized network around Leningrad and Moscow as well as pipelines stretching into the Ukraine and Central Asia. Soon the majority of homes in the U.S.S.R.'s largest cities were connected to the natural gas network, decreasing the country's reliance on wood and coal for energy and lessening the burden on the railroad system.

In the late 1960s the gas industry made a major advance by beginning to tap the huge natural gas reserves in western Siberia. Despite the challenges of working in arctic conditions, a pipeline was successfully constructed from the Urengoi gas field to Moscow. By 1983, western Siberia was producing more than half of the U.S.S.R.'s natural gas, and in 2000 Siberian gas fields accounted for more than 70 percent of natural gas production in Russia.

Exports to Western Europe got their start in 1970, when a Soviet export agency signed a contract to supply natural gas to the West German company Ruhrgas. The first Russian gas reached Germany in 1973. The second Western firm to buy Russian gas was Fortum of Finland, which initiated contracts in the 1970s. Exports, especially to Germany, increased through the succeeding decades. In 1982 Soyuzgasexport, the exporting arm of the gas ministry, signed a contract to construct a 5,000 km pipeline from the Urengoi gas field to the West German border. The pipeline was projected to carry 40 billion cubic meters of gas a year to Western Europe.

In the 1980s the development of west Siberian gas fields continued with the opening of the extensive Yamburg reserve. Explorations showed many large untapped gas reserves in the area. As experimental projects relating to crude oil and nuclear power faltered, the U.S.S.R.'s massive natural gas resources took on increased importance. By the time of the breakup of the U.S.S.R. in 1991, it was clear that natural gas would be critical in fulfilling Russia's future energy needs, as well as in supporting the nation's new capitalist economy.

Post-U.S.S.R. Privatization

In 1989 the Ministry of the Gas Industry was transformed into the state gas concern "Gazprom." The name "Gazprom" comes from a contraction of the Russian words for "gas industry." Minister Viktor Chernomyrdin, who had risen from a position as a machinist, became chairman and CEO of the state concern.

After the breakup of the Soviet Union in 1991, government decrees effected the privatization of Gazprom. A November 5, 1992 presidential edict called for the formation of a company to explore and produce gas and to build pipelines. Articles of association for the company were approved by the Council of Ministers on February 17, 1993, and the Russian joint stock company (RAO) Gazprom was formed. A condition of privatization was that the government retain a 40 percent share in the company. Gazprom workers received 15 percent of shares and 28 percent went to people living in Russia's gas-producing regions.

Meanwhile, Chernomyrdin became President Boris Yeltsin's prime minister in 1992 and picked Rem Vyakhirev to succeed him as Gazprom CEO. Chernomyrdin was rumored to have used his political position to grant Gazprom certain tax breaks and unusual privileges during the privatization process. For example, Gazprom retained the right of first refusal, meaning it had the first opportunity to purchase any of its shares that

came on the market. In addition, all sales of shares were to be approved by Gazprom management. *U.S. News & World Report* suggested that Chernomyrdin may have received large amounts of stock in exchange for these concessions, although both Vyakhirev and Chernomyrdin denied the allegation. In any case, the privatization process set a precedent for close ties between the state and the gas industry.

The newly formed RAO Gazprom inherited all the assets of the former gas ministry. Various subsidiary production, transportation, and service amalgamations became Gazprom daughter enterprises. The mammoth company produced 578 billion cubic meters of gas in 1993, more than twice the combined output that year of Royal Dutch/Shell, Exxon, Mobil, Amoco, British Petroleum, Chevron, and Texaco. But because of secrecy surrounding the company's financial situation, financial analysts were unable to pinpoint the value of the company. Gazprom clearly had extensive assets, but its market capitalization was low.

Another blight on Gazprom's financial standing was difficulty receiving payments. Many customers inside Russia and in the former Soviet republics were insolvent, leading to large amounts of outstanding debt. Gazprom, while still a state concern in 1992, had attempted to address this problem by cutting off gas to the Ukraine. The plan backfired, since Russia's major pipeline to Europe ran through the Ukraine, so Ukrainians took for themselves gas that was meant for German customers. Customers inside the Russian Federation, such as electrical utilities, were also unable to pay debts. Gazprom often took in-kind payments in return for gas, accepting anything from vacations and healthcare services for its employees to meat packaging plants and textile factories.

Without hard cash payments, it was difficult to finance new projects. For example, Gazprom had completed a feasibility study for the development of gas fields on the Yamal Peninsula, in western Siberia, in 1988. The company hoped to build a Yamal-Europe pipeline along a northern route, running 4,107 km from Yamal through Belarus and Poland to Germany. The pipeline would bypass the Ukraine and reduce that country's control over exports to Europe. In an attempt to raise funds, the government in 1994 granted Gazprom permission to sell one quarter of state-owned shares, or 9 percent of total shares, to foreign investors. The venture failed, however, because investors found Gazprom to be overvalued under the terms of the offering. Gazprom did make some profitable international connections in 1994. In a partnership with Gaz de France, the French company agreed to assist in the modernization of Russia's natural gas technology and transportation systems. In addition, a contract with Fortum confirmed the supply of Russian gas to Finland for 20 years.

In May 1995 Gazprom held its first shareholders meeting. The board of directors was elected and PricewaterhouseCoopers was chosen to be the firm's auditor. In some respects, Gazprom occupied an enviable position as it developed into a privatized company. The company had an estimated 1.5 trillion cubic feet of gas reserves, a natural monopoly in Russia, and control of much of Europe's export market. Despite these advantages, Gazprom's revenues in 1994 were only $13 billion, compared to $100 billion for the smaller Exxon. Another cause for concern was a deteriorating infrastructure. A November 1995

Key Dates:

1946: Saratov-Moscow pipeline begins era of "big gas."
1966: Opening of Urengoi field marks the start of west Siberian exploitation.
1973: First Russian gas reaches Germany.
1989: The Ministry of the Gas Industry becomes state concern "Gazprom."
1993: The state concern is privatized as RAO Gazprom; Rem Vyakhirev is CEO.
1995: First shareholders meeting is held.
1998: Gazprom opens its doors to international investors after voting to change its name and status from a Russian joint stock company (RAO) to an open joint stock company (OAO).
1999: Major sections of the Yamal-Europe pipeline are inaugurated.
2000: First junction of the Blue Stream pipeline is welded.
2001: Alexei Miller replaces Vyakhirev as CEO.

study, reported in *Oil and Gas Journal,* cited the need for more than $3 billion to improve inefficient compressor stations, leaking valves, corroding pipes, and inadequate environmental protections. Vigilant development was needed to keep Gazprom on a stable course.

The Late 1990s: Increasing International Partnerships

As Gazprom entered 1996 it still faced the tough problem of financing maintenance and construction while having difficulty collecting payments from customers. About 85 percent of the payments from customers in the Ukraine and Russia were more than 90 days in arrears. Foreign investors and customers abroad once again seemed to be the most promising source of capital. In October Gazprom offered 1.15 percent of its shares for sale as American Depository Receipts (ADRs). The offering was oversubscribed by five times. The company also signed contracts with the Italian firm Eni and with Warsaw to bring Siberian gas to Italy and Poland. The proceeds from these deals helped finance the much desired Yamal-Europe pipeline, the first sections of which were opened in Poland and Germany in November. Some of Gazprom's funds, however, were spent to further political ends—the company generously supported Yeltsin's successful 1996 reelection campaign.

The following year brought conflicts with both the Russian and the U.S. governments. Gazprom owed the Russian government $2.6 billion in back taxes, and the International Monetary Fund had been pressuring Yeltsin to reduce Gazprom's monopoly status as a condition for receiving loans. The two sides reached a compromise in April, when Gazprom agreed to pay a portion of the back taxes, yield its monopoly on gas fields, and divest nonessential operations to independent companies. Separate divisions were created within the company for such activities as production, transportation, and investment, in the hopes that it would encourage competition. In return for those concessions, Gazprom was allowed to continue voting the government's stake in the company.

The conflict with Washington related to a contract between Total S.A. in France, Petronas of Malaysia, and Gazprom to develop parts of the South Pars oil field in the Persian Gulf. Washington claimed that the contract violated U.S. sanctions against European firms that helped Iran develop energy projects. The conflict was resolved when the United States waived the sanctions in May 1998 with the understanding that no companies would assist Iran in developing weapons.

International partnerships in 1997 included the formation of North Transgas Oy, a 50–50 venture with Fortum of Finland to build a northern European pipeline that would take gas to central Europe under the Baltic Sea. After exploratory work, a definite route for the pipeline was chosen by the end of 1999. Gazprom also signed its first formal agreement with Royal Dutch/Shell to jointly develop the Zapolyarnoe field in western Siberia. Finally, in December 1997, the groundwork was laid for the momentous "Blue Stream" project, which would bring gas to Turkey via a pipeline under the Black Sea. An agreement was signed between the Russian and Turkish governments to supply Turkey with $25 billion worth of Russian gas between 2001 and 2005.

Gazprom found its first Norwegian partners in 1998, when in May it signed a protocol to work together with Statoil and Norsk Hydro to look for hydrocarbon deposits in the Pechora Sea. That summer the Russian economy crashed and the ruble collapsed. Despite $16.1 billion in sales, Gazprom lost $7 billion in 1998. Nevertheless, the company's size and its extensive assets helped it survive the crash in much better shape than many other Russian companies. Gas production for the year was 554 billion cubic meters, slightly higher than the previous year. Gazprom also further opened its doors to international investors in 1998, when at the annual shareholders meeting it voted to change its name and status from a Russian joint stock company (RAO) to an open joint stock company (OAO). Ruhrgas AG, a longtime customer in Germany, bought 2.5 percent of Gazprom's shares. The following year Ruhrgas increased its stake to almost 4 percent.

As Gazprom entered 1999 it was still having trouble collecting payments and finding the funds to develop new gas fields and construct new pipelines. The depletion of the mainstay Yamburg and Urengoi fields in western Siberia, as well as the continued disappearance of gas from the Ukraine pipeline, put pressure on the company to pursue new projects. Although Gazprom lost $2.8 billion in 1999, several positive steps were taken in the course of the year. In February loans were secured for the Blue Stream pipeline to Turkey, and the Italian firm Eni became Gazprom's partner in the project. The pipeline was planned to extend 373 km over land from Izobilnoye to a Russian port on the Black Sea, then continue for 396 km under the Black Sea.

In September the Polish and Belorussian sections of the crucial Yamal-Europe pipeline were inaugurated. By bypassing the Ukraine and giving Gazprom an alternate route to the German pipeline grid, the project was expected to make gas deliveries to Western Europe more flexible and easier to direct. In 2000, 14 billion cubic meters of gas were exported along the route, bringing valuable hard currency into Russia's economy.

New Management for the 21st Century

The transition into the new millennium at Gazprom was marked by political involvement, struggles with the government, and allegations of mismanagement. In 1999 the Kremlin made a move to increase its control over Gazprom. At the annual shareholders' meeting in June, former Prime Minister Chernomyrdin was chosen to resume his post as chairman of the board, replacing Vyakhirev, who would remain CEO. Chernomyrdin then demanded that the board of directors be reelected, since the state, despite holding a 38 percent stake in Gazprom, was represented by only four out of 11 directors. A new election, which followed in August, gave the government five seats.

More scandals and political involvement clouded Gazprom's business dealings in 2000. Articles in *Business Week* and the *Economist* reported that minority shareholders were concerned that their investments were being depleted by mismanagement and asset stripping. Many of the allegations centered around dealings with Itera, a Florida-based company that acted as a broker for gas export sales. Leaders at Gazprom were suspected of holding large shares in Itera and therefore giving the firm sweetheart deals. In one case, Gazprom paid taxes to a Siberian regional administration in the form of gas valued at a low price. The local administration sold the gas to Itera at the same low price. Itera then made $1.8 billion by selling the gas abroad for up to 30 times the original price. President Yeltsin initiated investigations into these activities, but Itera denied that it was receiving any free assets from Gazprom. Minority shareholders were also concerned that investment at Gazprom was poorly planned, that upper management was transferring assets to relatives, and that money was spent on unnecessary luxury items. At a recent board meeting, for example, management agreed to buy a yacht club in the port of Astrakhan.

In January 2000 Yeltsin abdicated his post to Vladimir Putin, who was then reelected in March. Many of Putin's actions appeared targeted at reducing the power of Yeltsin-era business oligarchies. In May 2000 Gazprom Chairman Chernomyrdin was replaced by Dmitri Medvedev, an official with fairly close ties to the new government. A more radical change followed in the summer of 2001. At the June shareholders meeting, longtime CEO Vyakhirev was replaced with the relatively unknown Alexei Miller. Miller had worked loyally with Putin in the St. Petersburg administration and also served two years as deputy energy minister. He promised to raise the market capitalization of Gazprom and guarantee the full disclosure of investments.

Vyakhirev retained some influence at Gazprom, as he was elected chairman of the board. However, stockholders apparently believed that reform had a much better chance now that the state had more control through Miller. Gazprom's shares rose 10 percent on the London Stock Exchange following news of the switch in leadership.

Also under Putin, Gazprom was mixed up in the struggle between the government and NTV, the only independent television network in Russia. NTV was known for its open criticism of Putin and candid reporting of such events as the war in Chechnya and the Kursk submarine accident. Gazprom owned a 46 percent stake in NTV's parent company, Media Most, and was suspected of acting as an agent of the Kremlin when, in the summer of 2000, it demanded that the media company sell shares to settle millions of dollars in debt to Gazprom. There was some talk of foreign investors helping settle Media Most's debt, but no deals were realized. In April 2001 Gazprom seized control of NTV in a boardroom coup, tossing out the station director. NTV journalists launched a strike, fearing that the era of independent reporting was over. At the July 2001 annual meeting of NTV, Gazprom representatives made no appearance. A decision was still pending on the ownership of a frozen 19 percent share in Media Most, which Gazprom claimed was collateral on a loan to NTV.

Against the backdrop of these shake-ups and scandals, Gazprom projects advanced. The first junction of the Blue Stream pipeline was welded in February 2000. Then CEO Vyakhirev announced that two more parallel pipelines would be built starting in 2003 to increase export capacity to Turkey. The Blue Stream project thwarted U.S. companies, who had hoped to bypass Russia with a pipeline from Turkmenistan to Turkey.

In other international partnerships, Gazprom signed a memorandum in June to work together with Wintershall AG of Germany on the Prirazlomnyi deposit in the Barents Sea. Wintershall had worked with Gazprom on projects in Germany since 1990. In September Wintershall and Gazprom joined in a consortium with Ruhrgas, Gaz de France, and the Italian gas transportation firm Snam to build a pipeline across Poland to Slovakia. In the spring of 2001 work began on the Zapolyarnoe deposit near Yamal, a joint venture with Royal Dutch/Shell. The field was expected to be producing by September 2001. Finally, in August Gazprom and Royal Dutch/Shell agreed to pool their resources to try to win a contract to build a pipeline linking the western Xinjiang region in China to Shanghai on the east coast. Despite concerns over management style at Gazprom, foreign investors could not ignore the tremendous potential of Russia's natural gas reserves. Gazprom forged ahead with the projects necessary to ensure its continued place as a leader in the world gas industry.

Principal Subsidiaries

OOO Astrakhangazprom; OOO Ecological and Analytical Center of the Gas Industry; OOO Gazexport; OOO Gazflot; OOO Gazbezopasnost; OOO Gazprominvestholding; OOO Gazpromokhrana; OOO Gazpromrazvitiye; OOO Informgaz; OOO Mezhregiongaz; OOO Mostransgaz; OOO Nadymgazprom; OOO Novourengoi GCC; OOO Orenburggazprom; OOO Podzemgazprom; OOO Severgazprom; OOO Uraltransgaz; OOO Urengoygazprom; OOO Yamburggazdobycha.

Principal Competitors

BP Amoco p.l.c.; Sidanco Oil; Gasunie; Statoil Energy; OAO LUKOIL; Tatneft; Sibneft; Yukos.

Further Reading

"Bad Vibes: Russian Media," *Economist*, February 3, 2001, p. 3.
"Big Outlays Seen Required for Gas Pipelines in Russia," *Oil and Gas Journal*, November 27, 1995, p. 31.

Birchenough, Tom, "Gazprom Exec No-Shows As NTV Row Brews, *Variety,* July 9, 2001, p. 16.

"Blue Stream Contracts Signed," *Pipeline & Gas Journal,* January 2000, p. 14.

Caryl, Christian, "Putin's Gas-Patch Putsch, *Newsweek International,* June 11, 2001, p. 21.

Dettmer, Jamie, "European Dependence on Russia's Gazprom," *Insight on the News,* August 6, 2001, p. 13.

"The Eighth Sister: Emerging Multinationals," *Economist,* October 15, 1994, p. 93.

"Firms Plan Black Sea Pipe," *Oil Daily,* February 5, 1999.

Fuhrman, Peter, "Robber Baron," *Forbes,* September 11, 1995, pp. 208–12.

"Gassing Away at Gazprom: Gazprom's Shoddy Governance," *Economist,* December 23, 2000, p. 6.

"Gazprom Frets over Gas Prices amid Expansion," *Oil and Gas Journal,* November 8, 1999, pp. 28–32.

"Gazprom on the Grill," *Business Week,* December 4, 2000, p. 62.

"Gazprom Re-Elects Chernomyrdin," *Oil Daily,* August 27, 1999.

"Gazprom Resurgent," *Oil and Gas Journal,* April 21, 1997, p. 32.

"Gazprom, Shell Close to Deal," *Oil Daily,* May 18, 2000.

"Gazprom, Shell to Team Up," *Oil Daily,* August 2, 2001.

"German Gas Concern to Buy More Gazprom Shares," *ITAR/TASS News Agency,* May 19, 1999.

"Giving an Inch: Russia's Energy Monopolies," *Economist,* February 1, 1997, p. 66.

Heath, Michael, "Investors Jubilant at Vyakhirev Ouster," *Russia Journal,* June 1–7, 2001.

Klebnikov, Paul, "Sorcerer's Apprentice," *Forbes,* September 22, 1997, pp. 52–55.

Korchemkin, Mikhail, "Russia's Huge Gazprom Struggles to Adjust to New Realities, *Oil and Gas Journal,* October 18, 1993.

Larina, Ekaterina, "Putin Topples Gazprom's Vyakhirev," *Russia Journal,* June 1–7, 2001.

LeVine, Steve, and Owen Matthews, "The Presidential Pipeline," *Newsweek International,* September 13, 1999, p. 31.

"Norwegian: Agreement to Explore Offshore Field in Pechora Sea," *Oil and Gas Journal,* October 20, 1997, p. 44.

"Reporting Russia's Gas Industry," *Petroleum Economist,* May 1996, pp. 64–72.

Surovtsev, Dmitry, "Gazprom Follows Unique Course to Privatization," *Oil and Gas Journal,* March 25, 1996, pp. 62–65.

Thoenes, Sander, and Alan Cooperman, "What Are Comrades For?" *U.S. News and World Report,* December 11, 1995, pp. 58–61.

"Turkey—Blue Stream," *APS Review Gas Market Trends,* May 1, 2000.

"U.S. Waives Sanctions on South Pars Field," *Oil and Gas Journal,* May 25, 1998, p. 18.

Wilson, David Cameron, "Russian Gas in 1993," *Petroleum Economist,* September 1994, pp. 58–60.

"Wintershall, Gazprom Create JV," *Oil Daily,* June 9, 2000.

—Sarah Ruth Lorenz

OshKosh B'Gosh, Inc.

112 Otter Avenue
Oshkosh, Wisconsin 54901
U.S.A.
Telephone: (920) 231-8800
Toll Free: (800) 282-4674
Fax: (920) 231-8621
Web site: http://www.oshkoshbgosh.com

Public Company
Incorporated: 1895 as Grove Manufacturing Company
Employees: 5,100
Sales: $453.1 million (2000)
Stock Exchanges: NASDAQ
Ticker Symbol: GOSHA
NAIC: 315221 Men's and Boys' Cut and Sew Apparel Contractors; 315212 Women's, Girls', and Infants' Cut and Sew Apparel Contractors; 315220 Men's and Boys' Cut and Sew Apparel Manufacturing; 315230 Women's and Girls' Cut and Sew Apparel Manufacturing; 315291 Infants' Cut and Sew Apparel Manufacturing; 448130 Children's and Infants' Clothing Stores; 454110 Electronic Shopping and Mail-Order Houses

OshKosh B'Gosh, Inc. is a major marketer and manufacturer of children's wear and youth wear, best known for its trademark bib overalls. Most of the manufacturing of OshKosh goods is conducted overseas at company-owned facilities and through third-party contractors, although the company continues to operate two plants in Kentucky. The company's products are marketed through about 5,800 retail stores in the United States (mainly middle-market and upper-market department stores and specialty stores) and through overseas retailers as well. OshKosh B'Gosh also operates more than 130 domestic retail stores, most of which are factory outlets, and sells its products online through the company web site.

Formative Years: From Workwear to Children's Wear

OshKosh B'Gosh was founded in 1895 as Grove Manufacturing Company, a maker of "hickory-striped" bib overalls worn by railroad workers and farmers. Based in Oshkosh, Wisconsin, a town of 50,000 on the Fox River, the company went through several name changes before assuming its unlikely current name in 1937. Its name was changed in 1897 to Oshkosh Clothing Manufacturing Company, and to Oshkosh Overall Company in 1911, the same year that William L. Pollock took over as general manager. Company legend attributes the current name to Pollock, who heard the phrase in a vaudeville skit while he was on a New York buying trip. The company started labeling its bibs "OshKosh B'Gosh" as early as 1911.

The company has been run by one family since Pollock retired in 1934. That year, Earl W. Wyman bought the company with partner Samuel Pickard and over the next few years they rounded out the company's line with painter's pants, work shirts, and denim jackets. By that time, the company had garnered a reputation for manufacturing durable, dependable products. During World War II and the Korean War, OshKosh B'Gosh produced garments for the military, including pants, jungle suits, and underwear. Wyman remained chairman of the board until he died in 1978. Wyman's son-in law, Charles F. Hyde, ran the company as the CEO from 1966 until 1992, when his son, Douglas W. Hyde, took over as CEO. As of 2001, members of the Wyman and Hyde families controlled more than 85 percent of the company's voting shares.

In the early 1960s, after decades of producing heavy-duty utility clothing sold in men's and boys' clothing outlets around the Midwest, the company stumbled on a discovery. Although it had always made pint-sized bibs as a novelty item for boys to wear in order to look like their working fathers, they were not viewed as a serious commodity. That feeling changed in 1962 when Miles Kimball Co., an OshKosh mail-order house, included a pair of kids' bibs in its catalog and received more than 10,000 requests. The company, according to *Forbes*, was "on the verge of discontinuing the small-fry line, but thought better of doing so when it saw the catalog response." Then President

Charles Hyde decided to see if there was an additional market to be tapped, and, following Kimball's lead, sent direct mail solicitations to children's stores around the country. Among the seven items included in the solicitation were overalls, coveralls, painter's pants, and caps.

The experiment was a success. The line made its big national break in 1971, according to *Working Woman*, when Bloomingdale's in New York asked to pick up the products. The chain's upscale competitors, including Lord and Taylor, Saks Fifth Avenue, and Nordstrom's, soon followed suit. Despite this initial success, however, OshKosh did not readily turn its attention from workwear, even though that market was beginning a steady decline. As the major retail chains came like so many suitors to the company's door, offering to pick up the line and requesting a greater range of styles, Charles Hyde was cautious of what could have been a passing fad. As orders for the children's clothes increased throughout the decade, however, the company realized that workwear was a shrinking market and children's overalls would be the company's new source of growth.

Rapid Growth in the Late 1970s Through Mid-1980s

At the end of the decade, Hyde increased the company's sales force. At the suggestion of then Vice-President Douglas Hyde, the company added a little style into its product by dying the overalls bright primary colors and introducing patterns and stripes. As production rose, Charles Hyde made sure that quality—and the company's good name—did not suffer. Through the 1970s, the garments continued to be cut by hand in Oshkosh, Wisconsin.

The year 1979 was a turning point in several respects. Children's clothing then constituted 16 percent of the company's total clothing sales, or $5 million. To accommodate those sales, the company added two new production plants, paid for entirely out of cash flow. In order to raise its profile, the company also launched a national marketing campaign, enlisting the help of Milwaukee advertising agency Frankenberry, Laughlin & Constable. The agency advised them to adopt the tag, ''The Genuine Article Since 1895,'' on a blue and yellow patch that would adorn all of the company's products. A few years later, the company took that advice a step further by calling its new group of outlet stores—the first of which opened in West Bend, Wisconsin, in 1981—''The Genuine Article'' as well. Through the early to mid-1980s, the company's sales grew exponentially, as the mini-baby boom created a demand for children's products. Whereas children's products accounted for 16 percent of the company's sales in 1979, that percentage better described workwear, the company's former mainstay, by 1988.

In 1981 the company opened a showroom on Seventh Avenue in New York City, the nerve center of the garment business. That same year, OshKosh began to diversify its product offerings, adding infant wear and knit separates. Over the years, the company expanded its line to include newborn to children's size 14 clothing, and added dresses, activewear, and swimwear. In addition, the company signed licensing agreements with producers of accessories and clothing items, including hosiery, shoes, hats, sleepwear, outerwear, and woven and knit accessories. In 1985 the company introduced a line of maternity wear, including but not limited to bib overalls, which, the company learned, pregnant women had been buying for years in men's sizes.

Sales in the United States were increasing, but the company began to devote more resources to sales in the southern and southwestern United States. Prior to that, most of their sales were concentrated in the Midwest and along the two coasts. The company entered the global marketplace in 1985 by incorporating OshKosh B'Gosh International Sales as its first wholly owned subsidiary. Through 1985 and 1986, international sales still accounted for only about 1 percent of the company's total, but the OshKosh name was gaining recognition. In 1986 *U.S. News and World Report* noted that the company was making a splash in London's upscale boutiques. Among the company's satisfied customers were Britain's royal infants, Princes Harry and William, the children of the Prince and Princess of Wales.

Late 1980s and Early 1990s Struggles

In early 1987, Charles Hyde wrote to the company's shareholders that OshKosh was ''monitoring very closely major changes taking place in the retail marketplace, changes which seem to be accelerating. Mergers, acquisitions and leveraged buyouts have changed retailers' sourcing strategies and presented us with challenges that we are positioning our marketing forces to meet. In the confused and competitive retail scene—with no consensus on promoting branded or private label apparel, with retailers doing manufacturing and manufacturers doing retailing—the long-term outlook must remain unclear.'' Hyde's comments were prescient, for in the following year, the company itself became a victim both of this uncertainty and of its own runaway growth: from 1977 to 1987, sales increased almost ninefold, to $226 million.

By the late 1980s, according to *Forbes,* ''the company was sweating as it struggled to keep up with the growing demands of its retailers and customers. New stores such as Kids 'R' Us, started by Toys 'R' Us in 1984, wanted more product to fill their shelves and were looking for OshKosh supplies.'' In late 1987 and early 1988, orders for two consecutive seasons strained the company's production and distribution capacities to the limit, and orders arrived late. According to *Forbes,* retailers reported receiving shipments where the tops of matched separates arrived without bottoms. "We were unable to respond quickly enough to take advantage of stronger than anticipated demand for specific styles," CEO Charles Hyde wrote to his shareholders in April 1988. "External contractors proved harder to line up than usual and the larger design content of our Holiday 1987 and Spring 1988 lines caused hitches in our own production that led to some late deliveries and increased production costs. We encountered these combined difficulties at the very moment that the October stock market decline undermined retailers' confidence and prompted a few of our customers to cut back or cancel their orders." These problems continued through the remainder of 1988 and early 1989, so while the company's overall sales figures continued to grow, unit shipments were sluggish and the company's stock valuation fell by half between 1987 and 1988.

"It was at that point," *Forbes* observed, "that Hyde showed his true mettle. Many businessmen would have shrunk from the problems and cut back their businesses." However, using a strategy the magazine called "investing one's way out of trouble," the company moved quickly to remedy the causes of the distribution problems by upgrading and expanding manufacturing facilities. Four new plants were opened, and in the company's OshKosh plant, woven fabric cutting was computerized. The company also opened a new centralized distribution and finishing center in Tennessee. These expanded facilities cut down the company's dependence on outside contractors—which had caused so much of the trouble—to about 80 percent of total sales in 1990, down from 34 percent in 1988.

In view of all of these new challenges, the company also invested in its future growth by retaining an outside management consultant. Based on the consultant's report, in 1990 the company added three new executive positions: president and chief operating officer, vice-president of human resources, and vice-president of management information systems. Under the change, Harry Krogh, formerly president of Interco Inc., became president, Charles F. Hyde's title changed to chairman and chief executive officer, and Thomas R. Wyman was promoted to vice-chairman. "Both of us have been freed up from the daily operations of the business to concentrate on long-range planning to meet the challenges of a new decade. At the same time a clear and comfortable succession plan is now in place," Hyde wrote of himself and Wyman in March 1990.

Also in 1989, the company began to turn its attention toward diversification, both geographically and in terms of product offerings for both older and younger consumers. Toward the end of the year, the company started a joint venture with Poron S.A., a publicly held company with $130 million in revenues based in Troyes, France. The resulting venture, designed to market both companies' children's wear throughout Europe, was christened OshKosh B'Gosh Europe, with majority ownership going to OshKosh. "The accord," the *Wall Street Journal* observed at the time, "will position OshKosh to take advantage of the breakdown in trade barriers among European countries in 1992." Through the agreement, OshKosh also acquired its second wholly owned subsidiary, the U.S. operations of the company, which made baby and infant clothing under the well-known Absorba label.

In 1990, the company further advanced its diversification campaign. In April, the company acquired its third subsidiary, Essex Outfitters Inc., which held a long-term licensing agreement to use the Boston Trader brand name for children's clothing. The Boston Trader label was known in adult clothing for its classic casual style, and the children's line—fitting kids age six and older—had a similar look and was sold in higher-end retail outlets. A few weeks later, the company reached an agreement to sell some pieces of the OshKosh B'Gosh children's line in J.C. Penney and Sears stores.

The latter agreement constituted more of a change for the company than the former. Throughout the 1980s, the company's children's products were regarded in the same class as Volvos and pricey mineral water: for the consumption of upscale customers. In 1991, *Business Week* noted that when the legendary jeans maker Levi Strauss & Co. began distributing to Sears and Penney's, "R.H. Macy & Co. discontinued its Levi's jeans because it felt their image had been cheapened." Having studied Levi's experience, OshKosh decided to go ahead with the deal for several reasons. First, as Hyde and Krogh told their shareholders in 1991, "the heavy debt loads being carried by some of our major customers [including, according to *Business Week,* the bankruptcy proceedings of Federated Department Stores], as well as Sears' and Penney's repositioning in the retail market" indicated the wisdom of their decision. Second, the company said it would reserve some high-end specialty items for the likes of Saks Fifth Avenue and Bloomingdale's.

In 1992 the company put its succession plan into effect, moving Charles F. Hyde to the position of chairman and his son Douglas W. Hyde, who had been in charge of merchandising for 12 years, to the position of president and chief executive officer. Michael Wachtel became chief operating officer and executive vice-president. In 1992 the company continued its foreign expansion by beginning operations at a manufacturing facility it had purchased in Choloma, Honduras, the year before, its first plant outside of the United States. Foreign business, including sales through OshKosh B'Gosh Europe, export sales to overseas distributors, and sales by foreign licensees totaled approximately $23 million, an 83 percent increase from the previous year. In addition, the company was moving into new markets in Argentina, Brazil, Chile, Mexico, Taiwan, and Thailand. The company's Essex Outfitters also proved a good investment, with its retail stores and sales to other outlets outperforming expectations.

Overall earnings dropped during 1991 because of a number of factors. The largest burden turned out to be the Absorba line, which the company had purchased only the year before. In view of what were seen as weak long-term prospects for the subsidiary, the company decided to take a loss and phase out the label. Both Essex and Absorba, however, added to the company's administrative expenses. Continued trouble for retail stores also gave sales of men's and women's wear rather mixed results.

The company experienced financial loss in 1992 as well. The nationwide recession reduced overall consumer demand, particularly in the company's largest markets, California and the Northeast. The recession, plus the continued expenses of the Absorba phaseout, contributed to a drop in sales figures from the year before. Faced with these problems, the company went to work to improve its main trouble spot, the domestic wholesale business, which continued to be plagued by late deliveries and cost overruns. "Our customers and the marketplace sent a clear message that business as usual could not continue," Douglas Hyde informed shareholders in March 1993. Responding to the challenge, the company began implementing plans to streamline manufacturing and improve flexibility. The company revamped its central children's wear line by adding a new line of coordinated separates with simple styling that met consumer desire for clothing that was easy to mix and match. They also formed a special design team to make the products of the menswear division more appealing.

The bright part of 1992 was that the company increased its penetration into foreign markets. In September 1992, it completed the purchase of Poron, S.A.'s share of OshKosh B'Gosh Europe, making it a wholly owned subsidiary of the company. In addition, the company signed an agreement with Berleca Ltd., a Japanese company that would oversee marketing of OshKosh's products in that country. At the end of the year, the company was in the process of forming a new subsidiary, OshKosh B'Gosh Asia/Pacific Ltd., to provide sales and marketing support in that region.

Mid-1990s and Beyond: Revitalizing Through Global Production and New Initiatives

OshKosh's struggles continued into 1993, when sales dropped another $6 million, to $340.2 million. The company was in the process, however, of improving its productivity and its on-time shipping performance. Having been slow to join the bandwagon of the shifting of clothing production to cheaper overseas venues, OshKosh by late 1994 was operating two plants in Honduras and was contracting with third-party manufacturers in Mexico, Central America, and the Far East. Around this same time, three domestic plants were closed, and 100 workers were laid off from the Oshkosh plant, where the only product being manufactured was men's workwear. By mid-1995, 65 percent of the company's goods were manufactured domestically, 20 percent in Central America, and 15 percent in the Far East.

Also in 1993, the company launched its first catalog, an experiment that lasted only a few years. The following year, OshKosh opened showcase retail stores in New York, Paris, and London. From late 1993 to early 1994, OshKosh also was involved in advanced talks to acquire Rio Sportswear Inc., a major women's clothing maker whose annual revenues were nearly the equal of OshKosh's. The children's clothing maker backed away from the deal, however, after Rio signed an agreement to acquire the jeans business of Calvin Klein Inc. Also in 1994 the Trader Kids business, which included 77 stores, mostly in outlet malls, was replaced with a line called Genuine Kids, which featured girls' and boys' sizes infant through 16 and which had more of a fashion orientation and was more expensive than the OshKosh brand.

Although sales increased to $432.3 million in 1995 and then to $444.8 million in 1996, net income figures in the highly competitive retail environment of the mid-1990s were an anemic $10.9 million and $1.1 million, respectively. Further U.S. plant closings ensued. Whereas the company had 16 U.S. factories in early 1995, just two years later OshKosh owned a mere seven domestic plants. Then in 1997 the company closed its last factory in its namesake city in its continuing move to drive down costs through outsourcing. Only half of all OshKosh products were made in the United States in 1997. That year also saw OshKosh abandon the Genuine Kids line, which never caught on with consumers, and close or convert to the OshKosh format all of the Genuine Kids retail outlets. Replacing the Genuine Kids line were two new lines: Genuine Girls, for girl sizes 7 to 14, and Genuine Blues, for boy sizes 8 to 16, both of which were sold through OshKosh outlets. In a further retrenchment, OshKosh B'Gosh transferred its European operations to a licensee in 1997. The company also changed its domestic distribution strategy, eliminating as carriers of OshKosh products some discount-oriented chains, such as Kohl's and Mervyn's, in favor of higher-end outlets.

Further initiatives aimed at revitalizing the company came in the late 1990s. In 1998 the company began rolling out OshKosh showcase shops within major department stores, garnering large sales increases from the shop-within-a-shop concept. By mid-2000 there were more than 400 such mini-shops operating, with several hundred more in the works. The company also began leveraging the strength of the well-known OshKosh brand by entering into licensing deals with other companies. For example, the company in 1998 reached an agreement to develop a line of OshKosh strollers, high chairs, and car seats. In late 1999 OshKosh began selling its products over the Internet and also began experimenting with retail outlets located in strip malls, the first two of which opened in Denver. The latter initiative was in reaction to market research showing that Americans were beginning to turn away from the regional mall format in favor of the rapid store access offered by strip malls. Revenues for 1999 were $429.8 million, while the net income figure of $32.4 million showed that the company's efforts at improving profitability were beginning to pay off.

OshKosh entered 2000 operating four domestic plants, two each in Tennessee and Kentucky. One of the Tennessee plants was shuttered during 2000, with the other slated for closure during 2001. By the latter year, domestic production had been reduced to just 10 percent of overall production. Overseas, the company had particularly increased its sourcing in Mexico, where the company now owned two manufacturing plants. With its global sourcing strategy beginning to pay dividends, OshKosh B'Gosh sought ways of continuing the revival of a classic American company. The company was, for example, making plans to return its products to the increasingly popular and rapidly expanding Kohl's chain. OshKosh also opened three new strip mall stores in the Seattle area. Finally, sales at the company's web site exceeded projections by 50 percent in 2000, and the company believed that the site could achieve profitability by 2002. OshKosh, in the early years of its second century, seemed to face a bright future given the familiarity of its brand name, its reputation for quality, and the many promising new initiatives that were being undertaken.

Principal Subsidiaries

OBG Sales, Inc.; Manufacturera International Apparel, S.A. (Honduras); OshKosh B'Gosh International Sales, Inc. (Virgin Islands); OshKosh B'Gosh Investments, Inc.; OshKosh B'Gosh Retail, Inc.; OBG Distribution Company, LLC; OBG Manufacturing Company; OshKosh B'Gosh Operations, LLC; Millenia Manufacturing SRL de CV (Mexico).

Principal Competitors

Toys 'R' Us, Inc.; The William Carter Company; The Gap, Inc.; Gerber Childrenswear, Inc.; Garan, Incorporated; Happy Kids Inc.; The Gymboree Corporation; Williamson-Dickie Manufac-

turing Company; VF Corporation; Lands' End, Inc.; Fruit of the Loom, Ltd.; Levi Strauss & Co.

Further Reading

Abelson, Reed, "Investing One's Way Out of Trouble," *Forbes,* June 11, 1990.

Belcove, Julie L., "OshKosh B'Gosh: Not Always Child's Play," *Women's Wear Daily,* August 10, 1992, p. 8.

Byrne, Harlan S., "OshKosh B'Gosh Inc.: It's on the Mend After a Costly Distribution Snarl," *Barron's,* June 19, 1989.

Cedrone, Lisa, "On the Road to Flexibility, OshKosh Takes Many Paths," *Bobbin,* February 1995, p. 26.

Daykin, Tom, "OshKosh B'Gosh Closing Plant: Namesake City Loses Firm's Last Factory There and 75 Jobs," *Milwaukee Journal Sentinel,* January 31, 1997.

DeWitt, John W., "The OshKosh Reinvention," *Apparel Industry Magazine,* December 1994, p. SS2.

Droster, Dianne, "OshKosh B'Gosh Creating New Retail Partnerships," *Northeastern Wisconsin Business Review,* March 3, 1992, p. 23.

Frastaci, Mona, "OshKosh B'Gosh: Innovation Is Key," *Apparel Industry Magazine,* October 1998, p. 32.

Girone, J.A., "OshKosh: Getting Back on Track," *Earnshaw's,* April 1993.

Hajewski, Doris, "No Child's Play: OshKosh B'Gosh Adopts Tough Line," *Milwaukee Journal Sentinel,* January 13, 1997, p. 16.

——, "OshKosh B'Gosh to Offer Outlet on Net," *Milwaukee Journal Sentinel,* May 10, 1999.

Harris, William, "Fashion Is Fickle," *Forbes,* June 22, 1981.

Hill, Suzette, "OshKosh B'Gosh: Growing Market Share Not Exactly Child's Play," *Apparel Industry Magazine,* June 2000, p. 42.

Jakubovics, Jerry, "OshKosh's Upward Climb," *Management Review,* September 1987.

Korman, Richard, "Some Belt-Tightening Revitalizes OshKosh," *New York Times,* September 28, 1997, Sec. 3, p. 6.

Naleid, James C., *Celebrating a Century As the Genuine Article: The Story of OshKosh B'Gosh,* Lyme, Conn.: Greenwich Publishing, 1995.

"OshKosh B'Gosh!: A Rich Heritage," *Children's Business,* May 1995, p. S7.

Patner, Andrew, "At OshKosh B'Gosh, Childhood's Magic Days Are Past: Clothier for Tots Makes Plans for a Future in Which Kids Are Grown," *Wall Street Journal,* March 9, 1989.

Perlick, Gail, "B'Gosh, It's OshKosh: How Humor and Nostalgia Overhauled the Overall," *Working Woman,* August 1987.

Rabon, Lisa C., "A New Era for OshKosh," *Bobbin,* December 1999, pp. 48–52, 54.

Schellhardt, Timothy D., "OshKosh B'Gosh Sets European Venture Through Accord with Poron of France," *Wall Street Journal,* November 8, 1989.

Schmitz, Barbara A., "B'Gosh Poised for Turnaround in 100th Year," *Milwaukee Sentinel,* January 12, 1995, p. 1D.

Siler, Julia Flynn, "OshKosh B'Gosh May Be Risking Its Upscale Image," *Business Week,* July 15, 1991.

—Martha Schoolman
—update: David E. Salamie

Paradise Music & Entertainment, Inc.

53 W. 23rd Street
New York, New York 10010
U.S.A.
Telephone (212) 590-2100
Fax: (212) 590-2121
Web site: http://www.pdse.com

Public Company
Incorporated: 1996
Employees: 48
Sales: $36.4 million (2000)
Stock Exchanges: OTC
Ticker Symbol: PDSE
NAIC: 512290 Other Sound Recording Industries

In its brief history, Paradise Music & Entertainment, Inc. is better known for its connection with notorious characters than for any notable accomplishments. The company has undergone a series of changes in top management and in the course of five years has moved its headquarters from New York to Los Angeles and back again. Its stock, once held by a host of Hollywood celebrities and heavyweights, collapsed within several months, to the point where it traded around 20 cents per share and was delisted by the NASDAQ. Paradise is comprised of three operating groups. The Music Group manages three independent record labels: Push Records for pop and rock, Label M for jazz and indigedisc (African) music, and MVP records for jazz. The Music Group also runs an event production business. The Commercial Group creates television commercials, employing a roster of directors through its Straw Dogs and Shelter Films production subsidiaries. The Film & TV Group creates music videos and through its Picture Vision subsidiary produces televised music concerts. The group's Rave subsidiary provides original music for film and television.

Creation of Paradise: 1996

Paradise was incorporated in July 1996 by cofounders John Loeffler and Jon Small, who then merged their wholly owned companies in October of that year. A musician and composer,

Loeffler created Rave Music in 1979, primarily to provide advertising themes and jingles. He also worked as a composer and producer for Sherman and Cahan, a New York commercial production house, in addition to serving as a consulting music director to Grey Advertising. Small founded Picture Vision in 1984, creating hundreds of music videos for many acclaimed recording artists. In addition, Picture Vision produced a number of television concerts as well as commercials. Loeffler became president, chief executive officer, and chairman of the board of Paradise. Small became an executive vice-president and board member. A music management business, All Access, was also added to the Paradise banner in October 1996, and its co-owners, Brian Doyle and entertainment lawyer Richard Flynn, were named executive vice-presidents and elected to the board. Doyle had managed a number of well-known clients—including Mariah Carey, John Mellencamp, and Daryl Hall and John Oates—while running Horizon Entertainment and Management Group.

The men who created Paradise hoped to bank on their individual successes to create a midsize, multifaceted entertainment company. The plan was to have a wide enough range of different but related businesses so that a downturn in one could be compensated by the cash flow of the others. Paradise, at least in the beginning, was looking to acquire small entertainment companies costing up to $5 million. On January 22, 1997, Paradise made an initial public offering of stock, priced at $6 a share, raising some $6 million, a third of which was intended for acquisitions. The company's first major move was to create the Push record label in February 1997. Although it was intended to feature newcomers, the label's first release, *Marigold Sky,* was from longtime pop songsters Hall & Oates, whose popularity peaked in the 1980s and who had not released an album since 1990. "Marigold Sky" had modest success, but Push would eventually become a drain on Paradise's limited resources.

For fiscal 1997, Paradise lost almost $1 million, in large part as the result of becoming a public company and funding the start-up of Push. The next year, the losses continued to mount, approaching $3 million. Nevertheless, management remained optimistic, buoyed by growth in revenues. In June 1998 Paradise hired attorney and investment banker Philip G. Nappo to

---

Company Perspectives:

As a vertically integrated entertainment company, PDSE is positioned to provide unique content and exclusive access to cutting-edge entertainment.

---

serve as the chief operating officer with the continued intent of growing the company through acquisitions. Although Paradise created a commercial scoring subsidiary for Rave Music called Alchemy, it was not in a position to grow externally. It certainly could use its stock to fund an acquisition, because by the fall of 1998 Paradise was trading below 50 cents a share and the NASDAQ was threatening to delist it. In the company's SEC filing independent auditors expressed reservations about the prospect of the company's ability to stay in business. It had enough trouble paying its New York landlord on time. Clearly, Paradise needed an infusion of new capital, and given the grave state of the young company it would have welcomed help from almost any quarter. In December 1998, not only did help arrive, it came with assets potentially even more important than cash: connections to some of the most talented and influential people in the entertainment industry. Paradise suddenly found itself anointed by Dana Giacchetto, "the money manager of the stars," who began to invest his clients' money in the company and agreed to serve as a consultant.

Giacchetto and the Launch of Cassandra: 1987

Giacchetto, in his mid-30s, was almost as famous as many of his clients. He became a fixture in the gossip columns, well known as a clubbing buddy of movie actor Leonardo DiCaprio, who was enjoying white hot fame after the worldwide popularity of *Titanic*. The press loved to tell the Giacchetto story: how he dropped out of Harvard Business School a couple credits short of earning his M.B.A., then cut his teeth at Shearson American Express in Boston while at night playing keyboards with rock bands, how he bailed out of the stock market before the 1987 crash, then while vacationing in the Caribbean was inspired to become an investment manager for the creative set. These "facts" became the accepted creation myth for his company, The Cassandra Group. He moved to New York in 1991 and approached art galleries, cold calling in an attempt to connect with potential clients. He managed to ingratiate himself with the Pace Gallery and began to represent such artists as George Condo and David Salle. Because Hollywood stars bought his client's artwork, Giacchetto was able to network his way into Hollywood circles. He then played one coast off against the other, in Los Angeles acting like the rising New York financier, and in New York dropping the names of his Hollywood connections.

Perhaps the most significant break for Giacchetto came in the early 1990s when he met Hollywood agent Jay Moloney, again through his connections to the Pace Gallery. Moloney, the quintessential Hollywood wonder boy who achieved a tremendous amount of power at an early age, would eventually figure in with Paradise, but for the moment was Giacchetto's chance to reach an entirely new level in attracting famous and powerful clients. Many of Moloney's friends either belonged to or repre-

sented a young Hollywood set that was just beginning to achieve success and make significant amounts of money. Through Moloney, Giacchetto met talent manager Rick Yorn and Moloney's old boss at Creative Artists Agency, Michael Ovitz, widely considered the most powerful man in Hollywood in the 1980s. Not only would Giacchetto take on both men as clients, he was generally regarded as the matchmaker who brought Yorn and Ovitz together and resulted in the creation of Artists Management Group. It was through Yorn that Giacchetto met and became friends with DiCaprio, whom he began to represent in addition to other Yorn clients, such as Cameron Diaz, Minnie Driver, Jennifer Lopez, and Edward Burns. Thus, Giacchetto became the money manager of the stars, and for many it was now a matter of status to have at least some money invested with Cassandra, which Giacchetto ran out of his trendy SoHo loft. Giacchetto vowed to put clients' money in blue chip companies and other safe investments, maintaining that artists did not need the worry associated with risky ventures. Although the fund was clearly growing, Giacchetto would sometimes tell the press he controlled $300 million, or $400 million, or even $1 billion, but no one seriously questioned a man who was on a first name basis with "Leo" and "Michael."

Giacchetto also caught the eye of Chase Manhattan Bank, especially after he negotiated the $20 million sale of a Seattle independent rock label, Sub Pop Records. In December 1998 they teamed up to create a $100 million fund called Cassandra Chase Entertainment Partners. The Chase partners believed that Giacchetto had his thumb on the pulse of up-and-coming entertainment businesses, but they were quickly concerned about the quality of the projects he presented and his loose management style. It was bad enough that he lost millions of his clients' money on Iradium, a satellite phone venture that went bust, but he then involved Cassandra Chase with new media company Digital Entertainment Network, the stock of which collapsed after allegations surfaced that the company's chairman had sexually molested a 13-year-old boy.

The Giacchetto Connection: 1999

One of the investment opportunities Giacchetto presented to the Chase partners was near-bankrupt Paradise. They refused to get involved. For Giacchetto, Paradise was a ready vessel for grander entertainment ambitions. He turned to Cassandra, investing $2 million of his clients' money in Paradise stock, priced at $1, which attracted a number of other celebrity investors. Cassandra gained three seats on the Paradise board, and Giacchetto became a consultant, compensated by 200,000 shares and warrants to buy 800,000 more. Giacchetto used his influence to install a new chief executive officer, respected television commercial director Jesse Dylan, son of famous musician Bob Dylan. The younger Dylan also agreed to merge his company, Straw Dogs, with Paradise. Paradise agreed to move its headquarters to Los Angeles, to work out of Dylan's building. Giacchetto was then instrumental in the naming of Moloney as the company's president. It was his first job in several years, following a number of rehab stints for cocaine addiction.

Moloney rose quickly in Hollywood and fell even quicker. His father was a Hollywood actor, scriptwriter, and agent. Following the divorce of his parents, Moloney moved to Oregon

<table>
<tr><td colspan="2">Key Dates:</td></tr>
<tr><td>1996:</td><td>Company is incorporated.</td></tr>
<tr><td>1997:</td><td>Push Records is established.</td></tr>
<tr><td>1999:</td><td>Jesse Dylan is named CEO.</td></tr>
<tr><td>2001:</td><td>Kelly Hickel is named CEO following iball Media merger.</td></tr>
</table>

with his mother, then returned to Los Angeles to attend the University of Southern California. In 1983 he became a summer intern at Creative Artists Agency, which was in its ascendancy. He quit school to work at CAA, soon becoming the assistant and protégé of Ovitz. By the age of 21 the extremely personable Moloney was recognized as a rising power broker, fitting neatly into the perennial Hollywood persona of the boy wonder, a role perfected by Irving Thalberg as early as the silent picture era. When Ovitz left to work for Disney, Moloney was one of the ''Young Turks'' that took over the agency in 1995. It was also around this time that he began taking cocaine, which would quickly lead to a debilitating addiction and his leaving CAA in 1996. Over the next few years he would check in and out of rehabilitation centers, and despite a number of interventions by friends, he was unable to overcome his problem. Giacchetto maintained that he brought Moloney to Paradise to help his friend, but some, such as Ovitz, worried about the stress involved in running a cash-strapped start-up.

The price of Paradise stock reflected a changing attitude towards the company, rising to the $5 range. Giacchetto then embarked on a campaign to raise $8 million for Paradise and went back to his Chase partners, who again shied away. Once more, Giacchetto relied on his clients and their friends, but even trading on DiCaprio's name only helped to raise just $4 million by July. A number of Cassandra clients were surprised to find Paradise stock in their portfolios, in some cases against their expressed wishes. Moloney, in the meantime, was simply unable to function. He was forced to take a leave of absence in July, then was fired in September. In November, two days after turning 35, he committed suicide, hanging himself from a shower nozzle with a noose of belts.

Shortly after Moloney's death, Giacchetto lost his partnership with Chase, and his celebrity partners began to leave. Rumors soon circulated that his business was under investigation and the press finally began to look into his background. The *New York Observer* in December 1999 revealed that Giacchetto never attended Harvard Business School; rather, he took some extension courses at the school. It also learned that he failed the only securities test he took, a Series 2 license to make interstate deals. Moreover, it was reported that Cassandra, according to SEC filings, controlled only $100.2 million in funds. In April, while he was out of the country, Giacchetto was charged with securities violations by federal prosecutors in U.S. District Court in Manhattan. Upon his return to the United States, he was arrested and then released on bail. When he tried to tap frozen funds, authorities feared he was trying to run. They tracked him down to the Newark International airport where he had a doctored passport, $44,000 in first class airline coupons, and $4,000 of $5 and $10 bills in a bag. Prosecutors accused

him of using the funds of his clients to support his lavish lifestyle. He was, in effect, running a pyramid scheme, taking the money of new clients to cover the losses of the old clients. In all, he looted accounts of some $10 million. In August 2000 Giacchetto pleaded guilty to fraud charges but it would take several months to sort through his tangled accounting system before he was sentenced. Finally in February 2001 he received 57 months in federal prison.

At one time, people and companies on both coasts wanted to be associated with Giacchetto; now any party close to him was tainted by association. While Chase was certainly embarrassed by its failure to not properly vet Giacchetto, Paradise was all but devastated by its connection to him. An unnamed company official told the *Los Angeles Times,* ''It's like we were hit by a drunk driver and got thrown into jail for it.'' The price of Paradise stock collapsed, as the company continued to post losses: $3.6 million for 1999, and $5.1 million for 2000. In August 2000 the company slashed its workforce by a third, or about 30 employees, while reducing salaries companywide. Despite its difficulties in finding even minimal financing, Paradise continued to try to add new ventures to its mix. It created Paradise Digital Productions to produce and deliver Internet-related content, then created Matter, an Internet design company. Paradise also purchased the Mesa/Bluemoon Recordings label.

In February 2001 Paradise merged with iball Media Inc., whose chairman, Kelly Hickel, was an experienced executive with a record for turning around troubled businesses. In 1989 he became president of MiniScribe and restructured its operations. He was also instrumental in boosting the performance of Maxwell Technologies' Information Systems Group. Hickel became president and chairman of Paradise, instituting changes in management, as well as reorganizing the company into three main groups. The company continued to boast a number of talented directors, musicians, and designers. What remained to be seen was if a seasoned management team would finally be able to transform those assets into a profitable business.

Principal Subsidiaries

All Access Entertainment Management Group, Inc.; John Loeffler Music, Inc.; Picture Vision, Inc.; Push Records, Inc.; PDSE Records, Inc.; PDSE Digital, Inc.; Shelter Films, Inc.; Straw Dogs, Inc.

Principal Operating Units

Music Group; Commercial Group; Film & TV Group.

Principal Competitors

Harmony Holdings; iNTELEFILM; Interscope Music Group.

Further Reading

Brown, Corie, ''The Last Days of Jay Moloney,'' *Newsweek,* November 29, 1999, pp. 80–82.

Eller, Claudia, and James Bates, ''Hollywood Advisor's Shadow Falling Across Former Clients,'' *Los Angeles Times,* April 7, 2000, p. 1.

——, ''Onetime Superagent, Drug Abuser Is Found Hanged,'' *Los Angeles Times,* November 17, 1999, p. A1.

Friedman, Roger D., "The Rise and Fall of Giacchetto," *New York Observer,* December 27, 1999, p. 1.

Goodwin, Christopher, "The Talented Mr. Giacchetto," *Times,* May 13, 2000, p. 22.

Hakim, Danny, "Adviser to Some Hollywood Stars Pleads Guilty to Fraud," *New York Times,* August 3, 2000, p. C2.

Jeffrey, Don, "Entertainment Co. Paradise Eyes Expansion," *Billboard,* November 1, 1997, p. 6.

Orth, Maureen, "Leveraging the Stars," *Vanity Fair,* April 2000, pp. 312–32.

Petrikin, Chris, "Moloney Set for Paradise," *Daily Variety,* April 28, 1999.

Sandler, Adam, "New Paradise Found," *Daily Variety,* August 27, 1997.

—**Ed Dinger**

Pendleton Woolen Mills, Inc.

220 NW Broadway
P.O. Box 3030
Portland, Oregon 97208-3030
U.S.A.
Telephone: (503) 226-4801
Toll Free: (800) 760-4844
Fax: (503) 535-5599
Web site: http://www.pendleton-usa.com

Private Company
Incorporated: 1893 as Pendleton Wool-Scouring and
    Packing Co.
Employees: 1,225
Sales: $150 million (2000 est.)
NAIC: 31321 Broadwoven Fabric Mills; 315999 Other
    Apparel Accessories and Other Apparel
    Manufacturing; 314999 All Other Miscellaneous
    Textile Product Mills; 313221 Narrow Fabric Mills;
    315212 Women's and Girls' Cut and Sew Apparel
    Contractors; 315211 Men's and Boys' Cut and Sew
    Apparel Contractors

A fifth generation family firm, Portland-based Pendleton Woolen Mills, Inc. is one of a handful of family-owned U.S. apparel and textile manufacturing companies still thriving in the early 21st-century's global economy. The company, whose motto is "from fleece to fashion," remains vertically integrated, including operations for scouring, spinning, dyeing, and weaving wool into fabric; manufacturing men's and women's clothing; and retailing its own products, which are also sold in department stores. The company has plants in Washington, Nebraska, and New Hampshire. In the late 1990s, in the wake of NAFTA and GATT, Pendleton moved about half of its sewing operations offshore.

The Early Years: 1893–1909

The Pendleton Wool-Scouring and Packing Co. incorporated on December 20, 1893, in Pendleton, Oregon, the first scouring mill east of the Cascades. Its owners and operators, two Boston wool brokers, wanted to cut rail costs by cleaning the wool before it was shipped to eastern mills. Their enterprise followed the settling of the Pacific Northwest in the mid-1880s, which opened up large tracts of land for ranching sheep. The development of the railroads offered a means of moving the animals and their products to market.

The Pendleton Woolen Mill, which began production in the fall of 1896, was a natural consequence of the scouring mill. Using the clean water of the nearby Umatilla River for washing and dyeing, the mill operated seasonally from May to November. The company wove the traditional designs used by the different Native American tribes of the region into the trade blankets it produced. It sent a factory representative to visit the reservations throughout the West to learn the colors and designs required by each tribe. Pendleton also sold blankets to businessmen who resold them to the miners of the Klondike gold fields.

The mills profited due to increased freight tariffs imposed on shipping scoured wool. In 1895, the company enlarged the scouring plant and converted it to a woolen mill that made bed blankets and robes for Native Americans. Pendleton blankets, renowned for their quality, grew in popularity as far away as the East Coast, and the company capitalized on the Indian lore surrounding its designs. In 1902, it introduced photographs of well-known Indians of various tribes dressed in Pendleton robes as a form of advertising. In 1904, the company launched its famous blue and gold label, which it sewed into the smoking and fancy outing jackets it manufactured as well as its Indian blankets and robes.

By 1905, however, the mill grew idle, due to continued recession and an overabundance of wool. Then in 1909, brothers Clarence, Roy, and Chauncey Bishop purchased the Pendleton scouring and weaving mills, with family and town backing, and constructed a new, more efficient mill with the aid of a local bond issue. The Bishop brothers came from a family of mill owners. In the 1860s, their English grandfather, Thomas Kay, had helped organize Oregon's second woolen mill in Brownsville, whose weaving operation he oversaw. He soon became the company superintendent. In 1889, Kay opened his own mill in Salem, Oregon. Kay's daughter, Fannie, and later, her husband, C.P. Bishop, a Salem, Oregon, boys' and men's wear

---

Company Perspectives:

Pendleton continually strives to maintain its well-deserved reputation by using the best, newest and most innovative state-of-the-art techniques and resources to create a year-round selection of wool and non-wool products that others strive to imitate. By balancing the offering with other non-wool garments that complement the "core competency"—wool. Pendleton provides a full line of merchandise that answers today's consumer request for value, comfort and classic good looks.

---

merchant, took part in mill operation and management. Fannie and C.P. were the parents of the three Bishop brothers.

In September 1909, the Bishop brothers resumed production of Indian blankets using Jacquard looms. Trade rapidly expanded from the Nez Perce nation near Pendleton to the Navajo, Hopi, and Zuni nations. Pendleton blankets became these tribes' basic apparel, ceremonial garb, and a standard of value for trading and credit among nations. So synonymous was the company name with trade blankets, that all trade blankets eventually became known as "Pendletons." In 1910, the brothers opened their first retail store in Seaside, Oregon, and in 1912, expanded production into other areas of woolen manufacturing, adding a second weaving mill in Washougal, Washington. This mill had the capacity for lighter fabrics, including suitings, and for the next 12 years, the plant produced fabric for suits and topcoats. The company moved its headquarters to Portland in 1919 to be closer to its main mill.

The Growth of an American Symbol: 1920s–40s

Then in 1924, the Pendleton virgin wool men's shirt was born, a colorful, plaid variant on the utilitarian men's work shirt of the era, using shirting material woven in Washougal. The shirt's cut was long and roomy and the fabric offered greater comfort, warmth, and durability than had previous work shirts. Ranchers, loggers, and sportsmen quickly adopted the shirt and, by 1929, the company was making a full line of men's wool sportswear.

Throughout the 1930s and 1940s, Pendleton grew under the direction of Clarence (C. M.) Bishop. Chauncey Bishop had died in 1927, and Roy Bishop had left the company in 1918 to manage the Oregon Worsted Company. Pendleton was now in total garment production, from raw wool processing to the manufacture of ready-to-wear clothes, and its products were in steady demand. In 1932, Pendleton was awarded the commission to produce a special blanket for Olympic athletes. During the first half of the 1940s, Pendleton devoted a large share of its operation to producing uniforms, blankets, and sleeping bags for American soldiers serving in World War II. After 1945, as the apparel division thrived, Pendleton expanded the production of non-wool garments to complement its woolen coordinates. In 1949, after market research identified a need and an opportunity for virgin wool classic sportswear, the company entered the women's wear market with its instantly popular 49er jacket.

During the 1950s and 1960s, Pendleton became something of an American symbol. Its finely crafted, long-lasting items,

known as "investment clothing," became a standard of apparel in many well-to-do households. In 1955, along with Pepsi and Carnation, Pendleton opened an old style retail shop in Frontier Town at Walt Disney's newly launched theme park. In 1956, the women's wear division introduced its reversible, plaid pleated skirt, which joined the 49er jacket in furthering the company's branded image. In 1960 Pendleton pioneered washable wool, and the singing group that would later become The Beach Boys took form as the Pendletones, adopting the company's name and shirt as their uniform.

The company acquired several new plants throughout this period to accommodate its increased production needs. In 1941, it purchased the Columbia Wool Scouring Mill, which it had leased since 1923. In 1946, it opened a facility in Omaha, Nebraska. In 1955, it purchased a plant in Portland, Oregon, and then, in 1956, in an interesting twist of events, Pendleton acquired a second Portland facility from the Oregon Worsted Company, the company Roy Bishop had left Pendleton to manage. By 1970, a year after the death of Clarence M. Bishop, the company had two sewing operations in Portland, a plant in St. Helens, Washington, and three plants in Nebraska. It purchased the Dorr Woolen Co. in New Hampshire in 1982, and added facilities in Council Bluffs, Iowa, in 1985.

Decline Within the Industry, Move to Overseas Manufacturing: 1970s–90s

In 1970, Pendleton introduced its own truck fleet for transportation of its goods, and in 1980, the company expanded international distribution with the introduction of Pendleton Country Japan. However, throughout the 1970s and into the 1980s, the apparel industry experienced a steady decline. Pendleton's St. Helens plant closed in 1986. While many other apparel manufacturers moved operations overseas to capitalize on lower labor costs, Pendleton, under the direction of C.M. Bishop II and Broughton Bishop, continued to manufacture its products in the United States and advocated fair rules regulating international trade. In the late 1980s, in response to buyers' return to classic styles and with women's wear making up 65 percent of the company's total sales, it introduced the redesign of its women's 49er shirt. It also began operating its own retail stores as department stores were in decline.

Nonetheless, from 1989 to 1993, when Richard Poth took over as president of the business, sales declined about 36 percent with total units down about 28 percent although the early 1990s' return to casual clothing and the plaid items favored by grunge fashion helped the company somewhat. Pendleton also benefited from increased interest in the culture of the American Southwest. With women's wear still 65 percent of sales, men's wear 30 percent, and blankets and piece goods 5 percent, the company began directing its marketing efforts toward a broader range of men's demographic groups. Pendleton also focused on developing a 12-month business by manufacturing clothes in lighter weight fabrics. In 1992, it decided to test run the production of women's blouses in Mexico as a cost-savings measure.

By 1994, less than 5 percent of Pendleton's total output was being produced offshore, but company officials announced publicly that in order to remain competitive the company would

Key Dates:

1893: Pendleton Wool-Scouring and Packing Co. incorporates.

1896: Pendleton Woolen Mill begins production.

1904: The company launches its famous blue and gold label.

1905: The mill falls idle, due to continued recession and an overabundance of wool.

1909: Clarence, Roy, and Chauncey Bishop purchase the Pendleton scouring and weaving mills.

1910: The company opens its first store in Seaside, Oregon.

1912: The brothers expand production into other areas of woolen manufacturing, adding a second weaving mill in Washougal, Washington.

1918: Roy Bishop leaves the company to manage the Oregon Worsted Company.

1919: Pendleton moves its headquarters to Portland, Oregon.

1924: The first Pendleton virgin wool men's shirts are sold.

1927: Chauncey Bishop dies.

1949: The company enters the women's wear market with its 49er jacket.

1955: Pendleton opens a shop at Walt Disney's newly launched theme park.

1956: Pendleton's women's wear division introduces its reversible, plaid pleated skirt.

1960: Pendleton pioneers washable wool.

1969: Clarence M. Bishop dies; his two sons take over the business.

1970: Pendleton introduces its own truck fleet for transportation of its goods.

1980: The company expands international distribution with the introduction of Pendleton Country Japan.

1992: Pendleton manufactures women's blouses in Mexico.

1993: Richard Poth becomes president of the business.

1996: The company moves the manufacture of men's jackets and shirts to Mexico; begins catalogue and Internet sales.

1999: Pendleton grants Daiwa Seiko, Inc. the right to manufacture shirts and sweaters and sell them under the Pendleton name in Japan; C.M. Bishop III replaces Poth.

continue to make use of low-cost foreign labor to manufacture cotton women's blouses. In 1996, the company moved the manufacture of men's jackets and shirts to Mexico. Management, however, remained opposed to the North American Free Trade Agreement (NAFTA) and the global General Agreement on Tariffs and Trade (GATT) for what it viewed as its corollary reduction of U.S. apparel and textile jobs. It blamed the 1996 shut down of its manufacturing operations in Council Bluffs and the 1998 closings of its Milwaukee, Portland, and Fremont, Nebraska plants on international trade agreements. Together the two closings accounted for layoffs of about 9 percent of Pendleton's nationwide workforce. The company still operated its second Portland plant and the plant in Washougal, Washington.

In 1994, the company also embarked on an effort to re-tailor its corporate image, changing its logo for the first time and consolidating and expanding clothing lines. It also instituted environmentally sensitive manufacturing renovations and computerized ordering and inventory management systems. The new merchandising strategy improved sales, while shifting the company's business away from its classics. In 1996, as part of an effort to explore other market niches, Pendleton introduced its first mail-order catalog, inaugurated its web site, and opened four more company-owned retail outlets. It introduced more casual women's clothes as well as a line of dressier outfits. The company by then employed 1,700 people and enjoyed annual sales estimated at about $150 million, about 60 percent of which comprised department store business. By 1998, women's casual wear accounted for 30 percent of all women's apparel sales—up from 10 percent five years earlier—and all catalogue items were also available online.

In the late 1990s, Pendleton looked increasingly overseas, both for production and sales. By 1997, it manufactured 40 percent of its clothing in Mexico, and in 1999, it granted Daiwa Seiko, Inc. the right to manufacture shirts and sweaters and sell them under the Pendleton name in Japan. The company also opened new shops in Tokyo, Kobe, and Sapporo, bringing its total number of Japanese retail outlets to four. These, combined with the roughly 70 U.S. retail stores, accounted for approximately 25 percent of revenues when C.M. Bishop III took the helm.

As part of its continuing effort to reposition itself, reach a broader audience, and update its image, the company reorganized its four divisions—men's wear, women's wear, retail, and blankets— into one single vertical entity with a focus on brand marketing in 2000. It dedicated about $1 million to its media budget and embarked on a new advertising campaign with the tag line: "Pendleton. Good for Life." The company, which now sold its products in department stores and its own retail stores, via catalogue, and through the Internet, had not grown much in the past several years, yet still enjoyed yearly estimated sales of $120 million to $150 million. Its men's wear now made up about 20 percent of sales, women's wear 50 percent, blankets 15 percent, and textiles 15 percent. Its original blankets had become collector's items. When, in 2001, it became the official men's casual apparel provider for CBS Sports crews, it appeared as much a symbol of Americana as ever.

Principal Subsidiaries

Dorr Woolen Co.; Columbia Wool Scouring Mills.

Principal Competitors

Boucher Boys & the Indian; Pillowtex Corporation; The Talbots, Inc.; WestPoint Stevens Inc.

Further Reading

Berman, Phyllis, "From Sheep to Shirt," *Forbes*, May 22, 1995, p. 162.

Bulman, Robin, "Apparel Workers Stranded As Plant Moves to Mexico," *Journal of Commerce*, September 24, 1996, p. 1A.

Griffin, Linda Gillian, "The Pendleton Label: More Classics to Collect Than Blankets," *Houston Chronicle*, January 11, 2001, p.1.

Hill, Jim, "Forced to Go Foreign: Pendleton Has Some Clothing Made by Contractors," *Oregonian*, December 22, 1994, p. 1A.

Paul, Rick, "The Pendleton Story," *Northwest Living*, April 1987, p. 11.

Senior, Jeanie, "Oregon Icon Bucks Trend, Still Thriving," *Portland Business Tribune*, May 18, 2001, p. 1D.

Waldo, Michael, "Early History: Pendleton Woolen Mills," *Clark County History*, Vancouver, Wash.: Fort Vancouver Historical Society, 1994, pp. 55–59.

Wheeler, Marilynn, "Pendleton's Blankets Still Good As Gold Among American Indians," *Los Angeles Times*, April 1, 1990, p. B5.

—Carrie Rothburd

PREUSSAG

Preussag AG

Karl-Weichert-Allee 4
D-30625
Hannover, Niedersachsen
Germany
Telephone: +49 511 56600
Fax: +49 511 5661901
Web site: http://www.preussag.de

Public Company
Incorporated: 1923 as Preussische Bergwerks-und
   Hütten-Aktiengesellschaft
Employees: 76,956
Sales: EUR 20.40 billion ($17.96 billion) (2000)
Stock Exchanges: Düsseldorf Frankfurt
Ticker Symbol: PRS
NAIC: 561510 Travel Agencies; 561520 Tour Operators;
   541614 Process, Physical Distribution, and Logistics
   Consulting Services

Preussag AG has redefined itself for the 21st century. Once an internationally operating conglomerate with interests in steel and other metals; mining; gas and oil exploration and production; and other industrial activities, Preussag has pulled an about-face at the turn of the century, shedding nearly all of its industrial operations to focus almost exclusively on its new role as the leading travel and tourism group in Europe. An integrated travel group, offering the full range of services, from its own fleets of charter airplanes to travel agencies, packaged tour operations, hotel and resort accommodations, and incoming services, Preussag has also built a strong logistics business around its Hapag Lloyd subsidiary. Having locked up the leading place in Europe's two largest travel markets, Germany and the United Kingdom, Preussag is seeking to lead the further consolidation of Europe's travel industry by building up interests in France—through a strong share in Nouvelles Frontieres—Spain, Italy, and Portugal.

Prussian Steel: 1923–45

Preussag AG was founded in Berlin in December 1923 as Preussische Bergwerks-und Hütten-Aktiengesellschaft (Prussian Mine and Foundry Company) out of a collection of iron, lead, zinc, coal, oil, amber, and potash mining, foundry, and processing works formerly owned by the German state of Prussia. Liberated by the Prussian government from the restrictions imposed by the state budget, the new company's management was charged with building Preussag through the efficiencies and profit opportunities of the free market. Despite antiquated equipment dating to the prewar era and a German economy still reeling from the punitive reparations imposed by the Versaille Treaty of 1919, Preussag's diverse operations began to thrive, and by 1925 it was employing 31,000 workers. Only when the hyperinflation of the Weimar years began to stabilize in the late 1920s, however, was Preussag able to fill its backlog orders, increase production, and enlarge its plant capacity. By continuing to rationalize and mechanize its operations, almost all Preussag's businesses were reporting increased sales by 1928, and by 1929 gross profits stood at 26.6 million reichsmarks (RM).

Nevertheless, in 1929 the Prussian parliament decided to form Vereinigte Elektrizitäts und Bergwerk AG (VEBA AG) out of Preussag, Hibernia, and the Preussischen Elektrizitäts-AG in order to stimulate foreign investment in the three firms. Although Preussag alone claimed a share capital of RM 140 million no foreign investors rose to the Prussian government's invitation. The U.S. stock market crash at the end of the year signaled the beginning of a worldwide depression, and by 1931 Preussag's gross profits had fallen to RM 11 million. When Adolf Hitler was elected chancellor of Germany in 1932 he initiated a military and infrastructural expansion that offered Germany's steel industry some protection from the stagnant world steel market, and by 1933 Preussag's gross profits had bounced back to RM 60.1 million. However, the National Socialists' emphasis on German economic self-sufficiency as well as the general scarcity of foreign currency forced the German iron and steel industry to begin smelting, increasing amounts of low-quality native ore, and by 1934, when Preussag established its petroleum and petroleum products subsidiary

---

Company Perspectives:

The Preussag Group has systematically repositioned itself since 1997. The acquisition of companies in tourism and disposals in the industrial sector have created a new group. Today Preussag is a leading European tourism and services group with strong brands and successful companies. Preussag intends to further streamline its portfolio, focusing on high growth services. Tourism is now the Preussag Group's core activity.

Preussag Handel Gesellschaft mbH, German foreign trade in raw materials and semifinished products had fallen under rigid government control.

With the implementation of Hitler's four-year economic plan in 1936—which effectively placed the German economy on a war footing—the German iron and steel industry had largely subordinated its production and investment decisions to the state's industrial policy. Benefiting from the armaments-led expansion of the economy, however, between 1935 and 1938 Preussag's gross profits rose from RM 78 million to almost RM 100 million, and its workforce climbed to 34,000. On the eve of World War II, Preussag opened the Düsseldorf operation of its Preussag Handel Gesellschaft metal trading subsidiary and at the height of the war in 1942 began developing a major pit coal field in Ibbenbüren in northwestern Germany. Hibernia, one of Preussag's two sister firms in the VEBA Group, had converted some of its operations to armaments manufacture during the prewar buildup but unlike many German armaments firms escaped the wrath of Allied bombing until 1944. During the war, shipbuilder Howaldtswerke-Deutsche Werft AG (HDW) of Kiel, which would become a major Preussag acquisition in 1989, produced 50 U-boats for the German navy. As the war progressed, Allied air raids, the loss of labor personnel to military conscription, and plant relocations hampered the productivity of many German businesses. Following Germany's surrender in 1945, Preussag was placed under the control of the Allied occupation government, all its possessions in eastern and central Germany were lost to the Soviet-controlled government of East Germany, and its operations in West Germany were partly destroyed.

From the Rubble: 1945–59

In the immediate postwar years, the Allied powers pursued a policy of *Entflechtung,* or decartelization, in which many German firms were dismantled and large industry groups were broken up into separate companies with a maximum permitted share capital of RM 100,000 each. As Preussag began reconstructing its shattered operations in 1946–47, the historical alliances between German ore, coal, and steel production were being dismembered, and German steel companies were divested of their raw materials mining operations.

In 1948, however, the institution of the U.S.-sponsored Marshall Plan and the reform of Germany's currency system (in which the reichsmark was replaced with the deutsche mark [DM]) signaled the West's intention to allow the devastated German economy to recover, thereby bolstering the West

against the increasing threat posed by the Soviet Union. In 1951 the dismantling of German plants was halted and bans, controls, and restrictions on German industry were lifted. Preussag immediately began construction of a coal power plant in Ibbenbüren, and as European reconstruction spurred a boom in the demand for steel Preussag's workforce grew to 22,800. In 1952, the lifting of limits on German steel production finally enabled German steel companies to once again become competitive in the world market. Preussag moved its headquarters from Berlin to Hannover and, with the German "economic miracle" now underway, Preussag's Ibbenbüren power station came on line in 1954.

Privatization and Expansion: 1959–89

By the late 1950s Preussag was beginning to reestablish itself as an essential part of the German raw minerals industry, but as a subsidiary of the still state-run company VEBA it faced severe limitations: expansion through acquisition was impossible and, unlike public, stock-selling companies, it could not turn to the financial markets to generate the capital needed for investment or financing. With the government of the Federal Republic of Germany its sole shareholder, Preussag could only raise funds by incurring debt through bank loans. While Preussag's fellow VEBA subsidiary, Hibernia, had managed to recover sufficiently from the war to prosper within the framework of a state-run enterprise, Preussag had not, and in December 1958 the German Bundeskabinett, in an attempt to spread the interest in German companies to a wider portion of the public (specifically, Preussag employees and low-income individuals), decided to initiate a partial privatization of Preussag, with VEBA retaining only 22.4 percent of Preussag's shares. In 1959, Preussag's controversial initial public offering raised DM 75 million, and within a day of the stock sale Preussag shares were worth more than DM 100 million, with roughly 200,000 investors registering purchases of the company's stock.

As world demand for steel began to decline around 1960 and the overproduction of steel of the 1950s created a global glut that lasted until the end of the 1960s, a newly privatized Preussag turned to diversification and acquisition. It founded Elektro-Chemi Ibbenbüren GmbH (ECI), a manufacturer of chloro-alkaline products, with the Dutch firm KNZ in 1960; purchased Europe's largest railroad tank car and transportation services agent, VTG Vereinigte Tanklager and Transportmittel GmbH, of Hamburg, a year later; and acquired its first shares in KIAG of Düsseldorf in 1962. Preussag also founded two offices of its Preussag Stahlhandel iron and steel products/metal services subsidiary in 1962 and then a year later a Stahlhandel operation in Hamburg. In 1963, Preussag's VTG subsidiary purchased the inland waterway shipbuilding operations of the Fanto, Luise, and Comos companies as well as an industrial tank plant in Amsterdam. Its aggressive expansion continued in 1964 with acquisition of container ship construction facilities on the North Sea and the purchase of the remaining shares of KIAG two years later.

In the mid-1960s the collapse of Germany's capital markets and a general recession in the national economy brought the first significant slowdown of Germany's postwar boom. Ironically, the introduction of new steelmaking technologies was enabling German steelmakers like Preussag to lift Germany's total steel

Key Dates:

1923: Preussische Bergwerks-und Hütten-Aktiengesellschaft is formed in Berlin.

1929: Company merges into Vereinigte Elektrizitäts und
Bergwerk AG (VEBA AG).

1945: Allied occupation government takes control of
Preussag.

1952: Company moves headquarters to Hanover.

1958: Preussag, which had been functioning as a subsidiary of state-run VEBA, is partially privatized.

1959: Preussag goes public.

1969: Westdeutsche Landesbank (WLB) buys out German
government share of Preussag.

1989: Preussag is restructured as a holding company.

1997: Company acquires German tourism and logistics
business Hapag Lloyd from WLB.

1998: Company acquires 50.1 percent of Thomas Cook.

1999: Preussag acquires leading German travel agency First
Reiseburo; merges VTG logistics subsidiary with
German freight-forwarding company Lehnkering.

2000: Company begins sell-off of industrial operations;
acquires GTT Holding and Thomson Travel Group
and agrees to sell its Thomas Cook holding.

2001: Preussag acquires minority share of Nouvelles
Frontieres and 10 percent of Alpitours.

production to more than 16 million tons just as worldwide demand for steel was bottoming out. Nevertheless, in the remaining years of the decade Preussag acquired France's largest railroad tank car leasing business through its VTG subsidiary (1966); purchased a three-quarters interest in zincing firm Berliner Grossverzinkerie (1966); expanded into the stationary and mobile fire extinguishing and protection markets with the purchase of Minimax GmbH (1966); established Preussag Energie GmbH to explore for and produce crude oil and natural gas (1968); and expanded its marine and shipbuilding holdings by founding container shipbuilder OSA (1968).

In 1969 Preussag turned to the U.S. market to form a joint venture with Kaiser Aluminum and Chemical Corporation to build an aluminum smelter on the Rhine River near Duisberg. Kaiser provided the technical expertise for the erection and operation of the new Kaiser-Preussag Aluminum GmbH facility, which by 1975 claimed a capacity of 143,000 tons. Ten months later Preussag announced another venture with Kaiser, acquiring a 50 percent interest in its aluminum smelting, fabricating, and sales operations in Germany, Switzerland, Italy, and Belgium under the name Kaiser-Preussag Aluminum. Finally, at the end of 1969, VEBA agreed to sell its remaining interest in Preussag to Westdeutsche Landesbank, making Preussag a wholly public corporation for the first time in its 47-year history.

With share capital now totaling DM 315 million and a workforce of 20,600, in the early 1970s Preussag acquired zincing firm Verzinkerei Bollmeyer of Neumünster; formed Kavernen Bau- und Betriebs-GmbH of Hannover with Salzgitter AG for the planning, construction, and operation of underground storage facilities; established two new subsidiaries, Preussag Anlagenbau

GmbH, a pipeline and plant engineering and construction firm, and Preussag Stahl AG, its steelmaking subsidiary; established a large container tank operation through a joint venture between subsidiary VTG and a Dutch firm; formed a lead industry joint venture, Preussag-Boliden-Blei GmbH, with the Swiss firm Boliden; and acquired the zincing operations of Zinkelektrolyse Nordenham. Several economic trends conspired to make the 1970s a difficult decade for Germany's steel producers, however. Revaluations of the deutsche mark, burdensome wage levels, and government-imposed financial controls squeezed steelmakers' margins, and the onset of the worldwide oil crisis in 1973 drove manufacturing costs higher, further reducing demand. The increased use of thinner gauges of steel and the substitution of other materials for traditional steel-based applications joined with the rise of new, low-priced steelmaking countries and slumps in critical steel-using industries to hand the European steel industry its worst drought since World War II. In its 50th anniversary year, Preussag moved to repair the structural weaknesses exacerbated by the poor economic climate and in 1974 sold off its consumer goods and brand-name product businesses.

By 1975 Preussag had begun testing projects for new technologies in its oil business, dissolved its partnership with Kaiser Aluminum, established a helicopter service business through its VTG subsidiary, and acquired an interest in a French industrial tank firm. It also established a British subsidiary, began constructing an offshore drilling supply base in northwestern Germany, and in a joint venture with the German firms Metalgesellschaft AG and Salzgitter AG founded a study group to explore the offshore extraction of raw materials.

As the second oil crisis of the 1970s began in the latter half of the decade, the West German government began offering Germany's beleaguered steel companies financial inducements to stimulate industry mergers and cooperative arrangements. Preussag turned to new foreign markets to bolster declining revenue in its traditional European base. Between 1976 and 1985, for example, it began a copper exploration operation on the Pacific island of Fiji; participated in the building and operation of two lead mines in Canada; initiated oil drill-boring projects in Egypt and the United Arab Emirates; acquired a crude oil field operation in the Gulf of Mexico, and participated in an offshore drilling platform joint venture in mainland China. Preussag subsidiaries were meanwhile introduced in Brazil, Nigeria, Gabon, Denmark, and Saudi Arabia. Closer to home, the company acquired zincing firm Großverzinkerei Schörg GmbH and a majority interest in the construction firm Bauer Grundbau, founded the zinc producer Preussag-Weser-Zink GmbH with French metals manufacturer Penarroya, and began developing natural gas fields in northern Germany. (A decade later Preussag and Penarroya merged their lead, zinc, and special metals businesses as a France-based Preussag subsidiary named Metaleurop, forming the world's largest lead-processing company.) Preussag's 1977 purchase of Patino N.V., a Dutch metals, mining, and mineral processing company, also positioned it a year later to gain a majority interest in Amalgamated Metal Corporation of the United Kingdom. By 1979 Preussag's sales stood at $1.66 billion, and in 1980 its stock began trading on Germany's eight stock exchanges.

A public relations setback in the mid-1980s, however, inaugurated a string of publicity embarrassments that would dog Preussag for the next ten years. In 1984 the European Community fined Preussag and five other European zinc producers for violating antitrust laws by fixing prices and restraining production. Then in 1988 the U.S. government accused Preussag and four other firms of constructing a poison gas plant in Libya and a chemical arms factory in Iraq, a violation of international trade law. Preussag denied the allegations, claiming it had built a desalinization plant for Libya and nothing more. Within three years, German federal prosecutors officially charged Preussag employees—though not the firm itself—with breaking export laws by selling Iraq $16 million worth of equipment for its chemical weapons program. Finally, in April 1995, 2,000 U.S. veterans of the Gulf War sued Preussag and several other German firms for their alleged Iraqi chemical weapons work, a claim Preussag officials continued to describe as ''substanceless.''

As the world steel industry moved gradually toward the recovery that would finally take hold in the late 1980s, Preussag enjoyed its best postwar year ever in 1981 while adding German container shipbuilding businesses to its stable (1980), initiating crude oil and natural gas projects in the United States (1981), achieving technological advances in its oil machinery production capabilities (1982), jettisoning its freight forwarding holdings (1983), and restructuring its construction engineering and technology operation (1984). With sales topping $4.44 billion in 1985, Preussag continued its ambitious expansion by buying a tin mining business in Indonesia, increasing its holdings in the U.K.-based Amalgamated Metal Corporation and the Swedish firm Boliden, solidifying its presence in the fire protection technology industry, and gaining a majority interest in the German metals trading firm W. & O. Bergmann GmbH. Expansion also necessitated consolidation, however, and in the closing years of the 1980s Preussag sold off coal acid holdings and closed exhausted ore mines; spun off its metal refining businesses to its new Metaleurop subsidiary formed in a joint venture with Penarroya; consolidated its W. &. O. Bergmann holdings; broke its UB Metall operations into four metal industry subsidiaries; and restructured its VTG container shipbuilding operation.

From ''Realignment'' to Transformation in the 1990s

The biggest restructuring of all, however, occurred in 1989, when, under new Chairman Erwin Moeller, Preussag converted itself into a holding company comprised of four legally independent business units centered on its four core businesses: coal, crude oil, natural gas, and plant construction. It then merged with the 50-year-old, state-held steel firm Salzgitter AG, creating a DM 27 billion conglomerate employing 70,000 workers. The two monumental moves enabled Preussag to post sales of $15.3 billion in 1990, and with the formation of two new subsidiaries—Preussag Anthrazit GmbH (coal mining) and Preussag Noell Wassertechnik GmbH (offshore engineering and technology)—as well as the new markets opened up by Germany's reunification, Preussag's announcement that it was ''optimistic about overall developments'' seemed to understate its position.

The readiness with which Preussag expanded and consolidated its businesses in the years since privatization seemed only to increase in the 1990s. It made acquisitions in the limestone, oil drilling, automobile recycling, mining transport, plaster

board, industrial freight forwarding, lead oxide, transport services, engineering, and petroleum industries between 1991 and 1994 and, with the purchase of air-conditioning manufacturer Hagenuk Fahrzeugklima GmbH, began an association with Hagenuk that would soon lead to a short-lived and ill-starred entrée into the telecommunications business. As another recession struck the European steel industry in the mid-1990s, Preussag was forced to admit that it had ''joined the ranks of the other steelmakers, which are all posting large losses.'' Consequently, in 1993 Chairman Michael Frenzel announced Preussag's intention to further expand its international base—which already accounted for 44 percent of total sales—with a special focus on the North American and Asian markets, as part of a new restructuring plan intended to buffer Preussag from the intense competition of the European steel market. In three short years this policy would result in new ventures in Kazakhstan, Russia, China, Croatia, Brazil, and Albania. Moreover, Preussag's submarine-building subsidiary, HDW, landed naval contracts in southeast Asia, and Preussag Energie pursued new projects in Colombia, Ecuador, Tunisia, Australia, Cuba, Argentina, and Syria. In 1995 Preussag launched Preussag North America as a holding company to promote the establishment of new U.S. ventures, such as its acquisition a few months later of an interest in the Indiana-based steel mill operator Steel Dynamics Inc. By 1994–95, Preussag's foreign sales had edged up to 48 percent of total turnover, and its still young North American and Asian markets were accounting for roughly 14 percent of international sales, with plans to double Asian sales to DM 2.4 billion by the turn of the century.

A second thrust of the restructuring program was to streamline Preussag down to its ''core competencies''—now steel, energy, logistics, shipbuilding, and plant and building engineering and technology. Rail-car construction, auto supply, mobile radio, automated transportation systems, telecommunications, and other loss-leading or niche-threatened businesses were therefore discarded in a series of ''strategic disinvestments.'' Free to concentrate on its historical strengths, in the mid-1990s Preussag found a partner for Metaleurop, its long-troubled French subsidiary, and opened two new blast furnaces, an electric steel plant, and an oxygen steel plant in Germany.

Yet Preussag's restructuring soon gave way to a complete transformation of the former industrial giant. Tired of fighting the cycles of its core industries, Frenzel began looking to bring the company into a more stable market. The opportunity came when Frenzel learned that its major shareholder, Westdeutsche Landesbank (WLB), was selling off its stake in major German tourism and logistics business Hapag Lloyd, which included its 30 percent holding of travel group TUI. In 1997, Frenzel and WLB agreed to a transfer of both businesses to Preussag—marking the beginning of Preussag's transformation into one of the world's largest tourism groups. After paying $1.5 billion for Hapag Lloyd, Preussag turned toward building its TUI holding into one of Europe's leading travel businesses.

By the end of 1998, Preussag's new travel division had swelled to include the rest of TUI, the leading German travel agency chain First Reiseburo, and a 25 percent share of Thomas Cook, one of the leaders in the United Kingdom's travel industry. The following year the company boosted its stake in Thomas Cook to 50.1 percent. By the end of 1999, Preussag had successfully recreated itself as a fully integrated travel company—offering the full range of tourism-related services from its own charter airlines operations to tour packages to resort hotels and incoming services. The company then merged its Hapag Lloyd and TUI operations into a single entity, Hapag Touristik Union, which was subsequently renamed TUI Group the following year.

Preussag's travel purchases had left the company saddled with a heavy debt load. Frenzel now moved to enact the second part of the company's turnaround, that of selling off what had once been its core assets in an effort to pay down debt. This began in 1999 with the transfer of much of its plant engineering division and its shipbuilding holdings to the Babcock Borsig company. The company's logistics subsidiary, VTG, then merged with German freight-forwarding company Lehnkering.

By 2000, Preussag's travel and tourism wing had become sufficiently powerful to encourage the company to announce plans to sell off nearly all of its former industrial activities—keeping only its oil and gas subsidiary. The company continued shopping for new add-ons to its travel division, including the February 2000 purchase of Austria's GTT Holding, giving it that group's Gulet Touropa Touristik, the leading tour operator in Austria. Then in May 2000 Preussag jump-started a broader consolidation of Europe's travel industry with the announcement that it had made a takeover offer worth more than £1.8 billion for U.K. tourism leader Thomson Travel Group.

As part of the Thomson deal, Preussag agreed to sell its 50.1 percent holding in Thomas Cook. The company stepped up its sell-off of its newly non-core operations, with plans to complete this operation by 2002. At the same time, the company, which had successfully captured a leading position in the northern European travel industry, turned its sights to the south. In February 2001, the company began acquiring a stake in troubled French travel giant Nouvelles Frontiers, expected to reach more than 30 percent in the early years of the new century. Preussag also targeted Spain, Italy, and Portugal—which represented the primary destination markets for Europe's holiday makers.

In May 2001 the company made a first move into these markets with the indirect acquisition of 10 percent of Italy's Alpitour, the leader of that country's packaged tour and travel market, through a holding in Italian conglomerate Agnelli. This purchase was widely viewed as a possible precursor for Preussag's eventual involvement in another Agnelli holding, the internationally known Club Med. Preussag had successfully negotiated a transition from a relatively minor industrial player into a full-fledged travel and logistics services giant.

Principal Subsidiaries

TOURISM: TUI Group GmbH; First Reisebuero Management GmbH & Co. KG; Hapag-Lloyd Fluggesellschaft mbH; Hapag-Lloyd Geschaftsreise GmbH; Nouvelles Frontières (France); Thomson Travel Group (UK). LOGISTICS: Hapag-Lloyd AG; ALGECO S.A.; (France); Hapag-Lloyd Container Linie GmbH; Pracht Spedition + Logistik GmbH; VTG-Lehnkering AG.

Principal Competitors

Airtours Plc; American Express Company; Carlson Wagonlit Travel; First Choice Holidays PLC; Thomas Cook Holdings Ltd.

Further Reading

Althaus, Sara, "Preussag to Cut 800 Jobs in Shake-up," *Financial Times,* August 20, 1996.

"Bonn Government Sets Salzgitter Sale to Preussag for Reported $1.06 Billion," *Wall Street Journal,* October 2, 1989.

"Bonn Names Four More Firms Linked by U.S. to Libya," *Washington Post,* January 10, 1989, p. A16.

Crimmins, Carmel, "Preussag Enters Italian Tourism with Agnelli," *Reuters,* May 18, 2001.

Dennis, Sylvia, "Germany—Preussag Sells Off Hagenuk Operation," *Newsbytes News Network,* October 5, 1995.

"EC Fines Six Companies for Antitrust Violations," *Wall Street Journal,* August 8, 1984.

Ewing, Jack, "Diversification: Out of the Steel Mill and onto the Beach," *Business Week,* July 26, 1999, p. 118D.

Genillard, Ariane, "Preussag Blames Loss on European Steel Downturn," *Financial Times,* June 22, 1993.

"German Cars to Be Recycled," *New York Times,* November 28, 1994, p. D3.

"Kaiser Aluminum Plans Venture in Germany with Preussag A.G.," *Wall Street Journal,* February 24, 1969.

"Large German Concern Recently Bought 29% of Patino N.V.'s Stock," *Wall Street Journal,* May 31, 1977.

Marquis, Julie, "German Submarines Ready to Dominate Arms Market," *Los Angeles Times,* February 27, 1996, p. D11.

Peel, Quentin, "Preussag Profit Tumbles to DM193m," *Financial Times,* February 10, 1994, p. 18.

Peel, Quentin, and Lionel Barber, "Germany's Private Steelmakers Revolt," *Financial Times,* February 3, 1994.

"Preussag AG Acquires 26% of Patino N.V.," *Wall Street Journal,* March 29, 1977.

"Preussag to Buy Stake in U.S.," *Wall Street Journal,* November 15, 1995, p. A14.

"Reshaping for Preussag," *Financial Times,* November 11, 1988.

Roth, Terence, "Bonn Government Sets Salzgitter Sale to Preussag for Reported $1.06 Billion," *Wall Street Journal,* October 2, 1989, p. A11.

Silber, Steven, "Europe's Travel Merger Race Heightens," *Reuters,* May 16, 2000.

"The Stars of Europe: Turnaround Artists : Michael Frenzel," *Business Week International,* June 12, 2000, p. 107.

"West Germany Holds Seven for Aiding Iraq on Poison Gas Facilities," *Los Angeles Times,* August 18, 1990, p. A27.

"World-Wide: German Prosecutors Charged," *Wall Street Journal,* March 29, 1991, p. A1.

—Paul S. Bodine
—update: M.L. Cohen

Price Communications Corporation

45 Rockefeller Plaza
New York, New York 10020
U.S.A.
Telephone: (212) 757-5600
Fax: (212) 397-3755

Public Company
Incorporated: 1979
Employees: 741
Sales: $270.51 million (2000)
Stock Exchanges: New York
Ticker Symbol: PR
NAIC: 57332 Wireless Telecommunications Carriers
(Except Satellite)

Price Communications Corporation has historically been a nationwide communications company owning and then disposing of a number of television, radio, newspaper, cellular telephone, and other communications and related properties. Its primary holding in 2001 was Price Communications Wireless, Inc., which was engaged in the construction, development, management, and operation of cellular telephone systems serving more than 500,000 subscribers in Alabama, Florida, Georgia, and South Carolina. Price Communications was planning to sell this company to Verizon Wireless, Inc., the largest mobile-phone and paging company in the United States. If approved by the Federal Communications Commission and shareholders of both companies, the sale, valued at about $1.5 billion, would provide ample funds for Price Communications to make new acquisitions.

Highly Leveraged in the 1980s

Born in New York City, Robert Price attended local public schools and universities and became a lawyer. He made his entry into the broadcasting industry in 1963 when, using borrowed money, he took control of Atlantic State Industries Inc., heading a group of four radio stations and improving their financial performance. He sold his interest upon becoming deputy mayor of New York City in 1966. After a brief stint in government service, Price was an investment banker in the Wall Street firms of Dreyfus Corp., where he founded his own mutual fund, Price Capital, and—beginning in 1972—Lazard Freres & Co., where he became a general partner. He founded Price Communications in 1979, but the company was not activated until 1981, when funds were raised from a small group of elite investors, including Citicorp Venture Capital Ltd.; Michel David-Weill, senior partner of Lazard Freres; John Loeb, Sr., formerly of the investment firm of Loeb, Rhoades; and the estate of André Meyer, the Lazard Freres founder who had been his mentor.

The primary goal of Price Communications was to buy broadcast properties with a positive cash flow, improve their performance, reduce expenses, and produce long-term earnings growth. Using borrowed money, it sought to purchase companies, at a discount, that were located in medium-sized markets. After making its initial public offering of stock in 1982, Price's first acquisition, in November 1982 for $6 million, was WOWO-AM, a radio station in Fort Wayne, Indiana. In the fall of 1983 the company purchased for $7 million WIRK-AM/FM of West Palm Beach, Florida, which was subsequently divided into two stations. Price also acquired at this time a San Francisco station, KIOI-FM, for $12.5 million. Its signal was the strongest west of the Mississippi River. Price Communications lost $643,556 on net revenue of $5.16 million in 1983, its first full year of operation.

By the fall of 1984 Price Communications had a roster of six radio stations, including WTIX-AM of New Orleans and KOMA-AM of Oklahoma City. Near the end of the year, the company purchased its first television stations, in East Peoria, Illinois, and Jefferson City, Missouri. For faster and further expansion, Price turned in early 1985 to the junk-bond market, raising about $80 million by issuing ten-year subordinated notes yielding an annual interest rate of 14.75 percent. The company also raised $12.4 million in 1985 through another public offering of its common stock. With the additional funds, Price paid off a $48 million bank loan, reserving the remaining sum for more acquisitions. The company could not yet show any profits, but cash flow from the stations was servicing its debt, and aggressive cost cutting held down expenses. Its Rockefeller Center head-

Key Dates:

1981: Price Communications enters the broadcasting field, seeking undervalued properties.
1985: Price acquires 13 companies at a cost of more than $141 million.
1992: Price Communications enters (and emerges from) bankruptcy.
1995: The company sells the last of its broadcasting properties.
1997: Price acquires Palmer Wireless, Inc., a cellular phone operator.
2000: The company agrees to sell its cellular business to Verizon Wireless, Inc.

quarters, for example, employed a full-time staff of only four. These included two executives who were said to have been given an unusual degree of responsibility for women in the media business—but who were not well-paid by industry standards.

Price Communications held 11 radio and three television stations when it broadened its range in June 1985 by purchasing a daily newspaper, the *New York Law Journal,* and its weekly companion, the *National Law Journal,* for $20.5 million. The purchase also included other operations delegated to Price's son-in-law, including a legal publishing company with about 30 titles, several legal newsletters, a computer information system, and a seminar business. Before the year was out Price Communications had purchased more radio and television stations and two New Jersey publishers, for a total of 13 acquired properties in 1985 at a cost of more than $141 million. Price Communications ended the year with net revenues of $37.19 million but a net loss of $12.34 million because of $15.75 million in interest expenses. Long-term debt plus redeemable preferred stock quadrupled during the year, to $281.58 million. Financing was almost entirely in the form of junk bonds underwritten by Morgan Stanley & Co.

Robert Price managed his empire by working up to 18 hours a day, seven days a week, traveling from city to city, sometimes closing deals in a day or two by paying cash on the spot. Surplus funds at hand were invested in stock market arbitrage deals. His staff—expanded to six—rode herd over 800 employees across the United States, cutting operating expenses and sometimes making changes in broadcasting staff or programming at their boss's direction. Station managers who exceeded their projections for operating profits were rewarded with bonuses. Wall Street analysts generally supported the company, whose bond issues had been oversubscribed and whose stock was more than half-owned by institutions. Its losses were considered paper deficits because they were attributable to depreciation and amortization expenses. "Cash flow should be important in any industry," one analyst told Wendy Diller of *Financial World* in 1986. "People who focus solely on earnings are missing the point." By the end of the year Price Communications was one of the most highly leveraged companies in the communications business, with a net loss of $24.59 million on net revenue of $81.83 million and long-term debt plus redeemable preferred stock of $428.04 million.

Price made no effort to persuade anyone that he was interested in broadcasting properties for any reason other than their cash flow. Interviewed in 1988 by John F. Berry of *Channels,* he said, "My daughter will tell you if I picked records for the radio stations we'd be listening to Winston Churchill speeches all day." One former station employee said he reneged on a pledge to invest money in new equipment and was obviously only interested in readying the station for sale. Price demanded strong performance in covering local news, however, and developed a fearsome reputation for firing people who provoked his displeasure. An unfavorable on-air reference to his Missouri-based billboard company, for example, elicited a volcanic eruption. However, he generally left specific programming decisions to seasoned employees. One company executive told Brady, "I tell the staff, 'If Bob calls, do what he wants. You won't hear from him again for three years.' "

At the end of 1987, Price Communications owned nine radio stations, nine television stations, the legal information enterprises, and the billboard company, which was active in 11 states. Price halved its net loss that year, selling the New Jersey company in one deal and seven radio stations for $120 million in cash and notes in another, retaining a 27 percent interest in the stations. During 1987–88 he sold three television stations for about $100 million (and more than $39 million in profit). When Price Communications offered $50 million in convertible bonds in 1989, however, the prospectus stated that the purchaser of these stations—a start-up company called Fairmont Communications Corp.—was so debt-ridden as to cast "substantial doubt" as to the company's ability to pay its debt to Price. By now a weakening economy was resulting in lower valuation for many of the media properties that Price Communications was counting on selling to service its debts. Fairmont subsequently failed to pay for its purchase and filed for bankruptcy.

The Road to (and from) Bankruptcy: 1990–95

After the brief but severe stock market crash of October 1987, short sellers gravitated to Price Communications like a flock of vultures, whom Price attempted to forestall by repurchases of company stock. Price Communications ended 1989 with a net loss of $40.2 million and, six months later, reported a negative net worth of $184 million. With the U.S. economy in recession, Price in October 1990 proposed a restructuring of its $283 million in outstanding junk-bond debt that would give the holders most of the equity in the company. This proposal and subsequent ones were rejected, and in March 1992 Price Communications filed for Chapter 11 bankruptcy protection. It also sold 75 percent of New York Law Publishing Co. to Apollo Investment Fund, L.P. in return for refinancing its debt to the fund. The company emerged from bankruptcy at the end of 1992, having distributed 94.5 percent of its common stock to holders of its subordinated securities and debentures.

Price Communications still retained three television stations, six radio stations, and the billboard company. Robert Price's interest now, however, was also becoming focused on cellular telephones, stemming from an earlier investment in a Wichita Falls, Texas, franchise, and minority stakes in the operations in several other small cities, including McAllen, Texas, and Biloxi, Mississippi, and in three rural areas in Louisiana, South Dakota, and Texas. ("Rural cellular operators today are characterized as cash cows, recording high cash-flow margins,'' Lynette Luna of *RCR—Radio Communications Report,* observed in 1999.) PriCellular Corp., as this business, incorporated in 1990, was called, established headquarters in White Plains, New York, and was 74 percent owned by Price Communications at the end of 1992. It was 42 percent owned by Robert Price and his son Steven—its chief executive officer—when it went public in 1994.

Cellular Business Only: 1995–2001

Price Communications sold its radio stations in 1994 for a total of $17.5 million in profit and also sold the billboard company that year. In August 1995 Price Communications sold its three prior television stations for a total of $42 million. Two months later the company sold its last broadcasting property, WHTM-TV of Harrisburg, Pennsylvania, for $113 million. (Price had paid only about $45 million for the station in September 1994.) Virtually a shell corporation now, Price Communications recorded net revenues of just $2.96 million in 1996. Meanwhile, PriCellular was growing rapidly, its operating revenues increasing from $3.81 million in 1993 to $179.04 million in 1997, although it registered a net profit only in 1993. Price Communications invested $21.5 million in PriCellular stock and warrants during 1995–96. This business remained primarily a personal investment of Robert Price, however. When the company was sold to American Cellular Corp. in 1998 for a total of about $1.4 billion in cash and the assumption of debt, Price family members owned about 15 percent of the stock.

Price Communications got into the cellular wireless business in a bigger way in 1997, when—through a subsidiary—it acquired Palmer Wireless, Inc., for $486.4 million and the assumption of about $378 million in debt. Palmer, which entered the cellular business in 1987 in the Fort Myers, Florida, area, was providing cellular service under the Cellular One brand name to over 320,000 subscribers in Alabama, Florida, Georgia, and South Carolina in 1996. In that year it had net income of $6.09 million on net revenue of $134.36 million. Price Communications financed the purchase largely from the sale of high-yield bonds, although it sold the Fort Myers operation for $166 million and contributed $44 million of its own equity. The company's long-term debt swelled to $909.43 million at the end of 1998, but it also had $205 million in cash and equivalents in its coffers.

Through its Price Communications Wireless, Inc.—a subsidiary of Price Communications Cellular Holdings, Inc.—Price Communications Corp. was providing cellular telephone service to 528,405 subscribers in 16 markets of the southeastern United States at the end of 2000. The company was selling its service as well as a full line of cellular products and accessories principally through its network of 41 stores, marketing these products through the Cellular One name. Price Communications' revenue rose from $197.33 million in 1998 to $249.12

million in 1999 and $270.51 million in 2000. The net loss of $1.58 million in 1998 turned into net income of $10.22 million in 1999 and $28.38 million in 2000. The long-term debt was $700 million at the end of 2000. Robert Price owned 11 percent of the common stock of Price Communications in March 2000. His grandchildren owned an additional 13 percent.

In November 2000 Price Communications announced that it would sell Price Wireless to Verizon Wireless, Inc., the nation's largest mobile phone and paging company, for about $2.06 billion, consisting of $1.5 billion in stock and assumption of about $550 million in debt. Price Communications would retain other assets valued at about $70 million. This agreement was signed in June 2001. The stock was to be valued at the price for the proposed initial public offering of Verizon Wireless shares, expected in 2002. The transaction was subject to approval by the Federal Communications Commission and company shareholders.

Principal Subsidiaries

Price Communications Cellular, Inc.; Price Communications Cellular Holdings, Inc.; Price Communications Wireless, Inc.

Principal Competitors

BellSouth Mobility Inc.; Contel Cellular Inc.

Further Reading

Anders, George, ''Price Communications Asks Bondholders to Approve a Possible Chapter 11 Filing,'' *Wall Street Journal,* October 15, 1990, p. B6.

''Banking on Broadcasting,'' *Broadcasting,* April 4, 1988, p. 159.

Berry, John F., ''Fighting Wall Street's Shorts,'' *Channels,* October 1988, pp. 30–34.

Diller, Wendy, ''A Question of Cash Flow,'' *Financial World,* August 5, 1986, pp. 102–3.

Gimein, Mark, ''The Price, for Price, Is Right,'' *Mediaweek,* October 23, 1995, p. 8.

Hollie, Pamela G., ''Price Communications in Pact for Law Journals,'' *New York Times,* June 12, 1985, p. D2.

Levy, Theodore, ''Price Communications Corporation,'' *Wall Street Transcript,* August 6, 1984, p. 74,797.

Luna, Lynette, ''Price CEO Is Candid in 3Q Conference Call,'' *RCR—Radio Communications Report,* November 1, 1999, p. 1.

Pouschine, Tatiana, ''Running to Stay in Place,'' *Forbes,* May 4, 1987, pp. 133, 136.

''Price Communications Corporation,'' *Wall Street Transcript,* August 15, 1988, pp. 90,560–90,561.

Taylor, John H., ''Heavy, Heavy Hangs the Debt,'' *Forbes,* October 2, 1989, pp. 52, 56.

Trachtenberg, Jeffrey A., ''It Ain't Heavy, He Says,'' *Forbes,* April 22, 1985, pp. 116–17.

''Verizon Wireless to Buy Price Unit for $2.06b,'' *123Jump,* June 11, 2001.

—Robert Halasz

The Princeton Review, Inc.

2315 Broadway, 2nd Floor
New York, New York 10024
U.S.A.
Telephone: (212) 874-8282
Fax: (212) 874-0775
Web site: http://www.princetonreview.com

Public Company
Founded: 1981
Employees: 1,758
Sales: $40.3 million (1999)
Stock Exchanges: NASDAQ
Ticker Symbol: REVU
NAIC: 611691 Exam Preparation and Tutoring

Originally established to coach high school students taking the Scholastic Aptitude Test (SAT), The Princeton Review, Inc. has grown to provide preparation materials for a wide variety of tests for undergraduate and graduate admissions, as well as professional licensing. The company is known as a maverick in the test preparation industry, a reputation it earned in the early 1980s when it first began to teach students how to outwit the design of the SAT, in contrast to arch-rival Kaplan, which acted more like a traditional tutor. Because it openly derided the SAT and questioned the validity of the test, Princeton Review was viewed by many high school students as their champion. On the other hand, Educational Testing Service (ETS), the producers of the SAT, had virtually nothing positive to say about the company. Close to 100,000 students annually take Princeton Review classes or receive private tutoring at some 500 sites located across the United States and in 12 countries. In addition to test-preparation software, Princeton Review also publishes an extensive list of educational reference books through Random House, which also owns approximately 15 percent of the company. After taking Princeton Review public in 2001, founder John S. Katzman remains the majority shareholder. In recent years the company has diversified beyond test-preparation materials to offer college and career counseling services, relying in large part on Internet delivery. As states have increas-

ingly turned to testing for K-12 students, Princeton Review has also expanded the reach of its business to service that market.

Admissions Testing in the Early 1900s

In 1901 the nonprofit College Entrance Examination Board began conducting essay-based admissions tests for a small number of colleges. It was not until 1926 that the Scholastic Aptitude Test and its multiple choice format was added to the College Boards. By 1942 essays were scrapped completely, a decision the College Board attributed to a labor shortage caused by World War II. Because essays were more difficult to create than multiple choice exams and more expensive to grade, the war was more a pretext than the reason behind the move, which had been under consideration for several years. In 1947 the College Board joined forces with two other nonprofit testing operations, the American Council on Education and the Carnegie Foundation for the Advancement of Teaching, to create a central test-giving organization. The result was ETS, which in 1948 started out by administering the SAT to 75,000 high school students. The organization grew rapidly, doubling its sales every five years from 1948 through the early 1970s. It broadened its scope to include a variety of tests and other educational activities, and grew more powerful than the College Board, which became more of a rubber stamp than a parent of ETS. The organization essentially answered to no one, despite the enormous power it wielded over the fate of countless high school students, who were denied the right to verify that their tests had been accurately scored. In 1979, in spite of intense ETS lobbying efforts, the New York State legislature passed the Educational Testing Act, the so-called "truth in testing" law that went into effect a year later. It not only allowed students to review their tests, it required ETS to be more forthcoming about its methods.

Because ETS was forced to make old SAT tests available, test coaches were given a better opportunity to study the structure of the SAT. For years wealthy students had been receiving private tutoring to prepare for the test. Former high school teacher Stanley Kaplan became the founder of the test-preparation industry when in 1938 he began operating out of a Brooklyn basement. His method to raise SAT scores was heavy on the basics, relying on concerted study of vocabulary, reading comprehension, and math. Kaplan embraced the SAT and in turn was viewed as an ally by ETS, which was far from the reception John Katzman and the Princeton Review received after Katzman began to challenge both ETS and Kaplan in the early 1980s.

Katzman was the product of a self-described entrepreneurial family. His grandfather invented the electric vaporizer and his father ran the manufacturing operation for the device. While raising three children, his mother also worked as a part-time interior decorator. Interested in computers as a youth, he first majored in electrical engineering at Princeton University (after scoring 1,500 out of a possible 1,600 on his SAT exam). He graduated from Princeton with a degree in architecture. To earn extra money at college he worked for an SAT coaching school, Pre-test Review, operated by Bob Scheller, a Wharton Business School graduate. Scheller was able to take old SAT tests made available by New York's Education Testing Act and conduct computer analysis to find ways to outwit the test makers. Upon graduation in 1981, Katzman went to work in the computer department of a Wall Street firm, lasting only six weeks before he quit. With a $3,000 loan from his parents and the use of their Manhattan apartment he started his own SAT coaching school, The Princeton Review, an allusion to his alma mater.

First Princeton Review Classes: 1981

Katzman started out with 19 students in the fall of 1981. Word of mouth would increase the number to 43 for his spring class and lead his mother to evict the blossoming business, which eventually resorted to renting rooms at Hunter College on the Upper East Side of Manhattan. As Katzman's students continued to improve their test scores, his class size grew as well. He laid claim to producing the best results of any SAT course in the city, a boast that came to the attention of an area tutor named Adam Robinson who telephoned Katzman to dispute the matter. Robinson had worked for Scheller before Katzman and had developed some of the techniques that Katzman was using. Rather than remaining rivals, however, they decided to work together. To support the expanding company, they also began the practice of hiring ex-students. Not only were these employees happy to work as part-timers, they were familiar with the techniques and had become true believers in the developing mission of Princeton Review: to expose the SAT as a sham, a test that merely tested a student's ability to take the test.

Essentially Katzman and Robinson taught their students how the SAT was constructed. Questions had to be designed so that the highest-scoring students would know the answers while the lowest-scoring students would not be able to arrive at the right answer by applying the wrong method. The test makers offered

choices that were meant to trap the average test taker. Robinson invented a character he called Joe Bloggs, the average target for these lures. Princeton Review taught its students how to think like Joe Bloggs in order to eliminate deceptive choices. Instructors also helped students to spot experimental sections, which did not count in the final score but were simply included as a way to develop future test questions. In the days before ETS took countermeasures, for instance, the experimental math section was always six pages while the actual math section was four pages. Princeton Review students simply filled in the answers of the experimental section at random. They were also taught the 100 most likely vocabulary words that would appear on the SAT, what Robinson called the "Hit Parade." They learned how to solve geometry questions using the edge of the test booklet as a ruler and protractor. In short, Princeton Review made the SAT a puzzle to crack rather than a wealth of material to master.

Katzman and Robinson were not alone in their contempt for ETS and the SAT. Writer David Owen took on ETS in a 1983 article for *Harper's*. Not only did Owen believe that the SAT measured nothing of value, he was one of the first critics to charge that the test was culturally biased, that the people best suited to score well on the test were those students who shared the same prep school background and mindset as the people who made up the SAT. Owen then authored a book on the subject, *None of the Above: The Truth Behind the SATs*, in which he wrote positively about the Princeton Review. That section of the book was excerpted in *Rolling Stone* in March 1985. According to Katzman, Owen "made me look more political than I was. But the response by ETS was so strong that I sort of became that political."

ETS was not reluctant to express its low opinion of Katzman and Robinson. Princeton Review had gotten into trouble with ETS in 1982 when Robinson was charged with taking an SAT booklet from a test site. The company agreed to refrain from using SAT material, but in 1985 ETS went to court to obtain a restraining order to prevent both Princeton Review and Pre-test Review from using copyrighted material. The matter would not be settled until December 1987 when a U.S. District Court judge ordered Princeton Review to stop violating copyrights on SAT questions and awarded Kaplan $52,000 in damages. The fact that ETS failed to put Princeton Review out of business, however, was viewed as a victory by Katzman. Scheller's Pre-test Review, on the other hand, ceased operations in 1987. Despite its victory, ETS was losing credibility, due in large part to Princeton Review, and was forced to make changes to the SAT, which it soon renamed the Scholastic Assessment Test. No matter how much ETS adjusted the SAT, critics insisted that the underlying nature of the test would remain the same—namely, it measured nothing of value. Princeton Review also received its share of criticism from people who agreed that the SAT was severely flawed. They argued that by teaching affluent students how to beat the SAT, Princeton Review was simply helping the rich to attend the better schools at the expense of the less fortunate. Katzman did, however, make Princeton Review services available to low income and minority students, as well as set up a foundation to serve as an advocate and legal adviser to parents and students on testing issues.

In some ways, drawing the ire of ETS was good for business. In 1985 Princeton Review taught 5,000 students at ten sites. The

Key Dates:

1926: SAT first uses multiple choice test format.
1979: New York passes truth in testing law, making SAT exams publicly available.
1981: Princeton Review is started by John R. Katzman.
1984: *Cracking the SAT* becomes a *New York Times* best-seller.
1993: Princeton Review launches its first Internet web site.
1995: Random House acquires a stake in the company.
1996: Princeton Review Publishing is established.
1999: Princeton Review launches Homeroom.com.
2001: Company makes an initial public offering of stock.

next year it would have 30 sites and revenues of $8 million, according to the company. In 1987 the number of sites increased to 35 and revenues reached $12 million. Katzman grew the business by franchising. In the early years of Princeton Review, he charged between $15,000 and $150,000 for a franchise, depending on the size of the area, plus 8 percent in annual royalties. He also sold test materials to the franchises. Princeton Review expanded so rapidly that in 1988 *Inc.* listed it as the 106th fastest growing company in the United States. It was soon outpacing Kaplan in enrollment, at least in the SAT business. Having already turned down a $1 million offer for the company from publisher Harcourt Brace Jovanovich, Katzman as early as 1987 was reported to be thinking about taking Princeton Review public.

Katzman and Robinson, Parting Ways: 1989

Not only did Katzman and Robinson squabble with ETS and pick fights with Kaplan, they also bickered with each other. At times, according to the *Wall Street Journal,* they refused to speak to one another for weeks at a time. Nevertheless they collaborated with Owen to write a book about the Princeton Review method, *Cracking the SAT.* It became a bestseller, prompting Robinson to envision a line of books as well as tapes and computer software. Afraid they would simply cannibalize their course enrollment, Katzman kept the spinoffs to a minimum. By 1989 Katzman and Robinson decided to finally formalize the nature of their partnership. Katzman offered Robinson a salary of $100,000 per year plus a 3 percent equity stake. Expecting at least 10 percent, Robinson was insulted. Eventually they agreed on 4 percent, then on the advice of his attorney Robinson cashed in his share of the business for $200,000 and severed his relationship with Princeton Review. The two men remained co-authors, however. When Katzman decided to expand that part of the business in 1991, he arranged a royalty deal in order to use Robinson's techniques in future book projects. In 1994, when publisher Random House was looking to acquire a 20 percent stake in Princeton Review, Katzman wanted to gain complete control of his company's backlist of titles. He bought out the rights of Owen and the partners' literary agent, but Robinson refused to consider a $2 million offer until he saw an accounting of Princeton Review's publishing efforts. Nevertheless, Katzman finalized the Random House deal. The unresolved issue with Robinson would result in a court case that would not be settled for several more years.

In the late 1980s Princeton Review began a concerted effort to expand beyond SAT preparation, adding the ACT (the equivalent of the SAT in a number of midwestern states), the LSAT, GMAT, MCAT, and GRE. In 1993 the company began to develop a software product, *Inside the SAT,* which would become a bestseller. It also gained an early presence on the Internet. In 1996 the company launched Princeton Review Publishing, dramatically increasing its number of book titles and the range of subject matter. Kaplan, still the test-preparation industry leader, found itself playing catch-up with its SAT and book business.

In many ways, Princeton Review owed a great deal of its success to Kaplan. In the beginning it could simply play off the Kaplan model, using its rate as a floor in order to establish a premium price, as well as offering smaller class sizes. It positioned itself with its target high school audience as the rebel taking on the SAT, while portraying Kaplan as the establishment toady. Kaplan responded by changing its style and spending considerable advertising dollars on attacking Princeton Review. The two companies became bitter rivals. In 1994 Princeton Review appropriated the Internet address Kaplan.com before Kaplan thought to register it. The supposed joke ended up in court, where Kaplan was eventually awarded the use of the name. The two companies also wrangled over advertising claims, threatening court action. Both regularly sent spies to attend one another's classes. Despite being leading companies, however, neither seemed to be enjoying robust financial health in the late 1990s. Kaplan's financial numbers were difficult to assess because they were included as part of a unit in the balance sheet of The Washington Post Company, its corporate parent. Princeton Review remained a private company, but according to press reports it was losing money in the mid-1990s, showed a profit in 1998, then began posting significant losses as it tried to build up its Internet business. After losing $2 million in 1999, Princeton Review lost an additional $8.2 million on revenues of $43.9 million in 2000.

Both Princeton Review and Kaplan faced stiff competition for new online businesses, which provided electronic college application services and Internet guidance counselor services. In 1999 Princeton Review rolled out Homeroom.com to help K-12 students improve scores on state mandated exams. With the election of George W. Bush as president in 2000, the prospect for increased testing boded well for Princeton Review in this segment. The company already ran Review.com, which targeted college-bound students and college students applying to graduate schools.

In August 2000 Princeton Review announced that it would make a public offering of stock to raise money to pay off debt and fund the growth of its Internet business. It hoped to sell 5.4 million shares of stock at $11 to $13 each. Some analysts questioned the IPO, maintaining that there was no compelling reason to own the stock. Nevertheless, the company arranged a $25 million line of credit in order to buy back franchises in preparation of the offering. Princeton Review, which ran 450 sites itself, also had 16 franchisees operating some 40 sites in the United States and an additional 13 sites in ten other countries. The offering, conducted in June 2001, proved to be somewhat disappointing. Shares sold at the lower end of the $11 to $13 range, resulting in $59.4 million. Trading on the NASDAQ, the stock showed no strength, quickly losing value. Princeton Review, now 20 years old, had established brand recognition, and the nation's increased penchant for testing its youth appeared likely to boost business. Whether the company would be able to prosper going forward, however, remained very much open to question.

Principal Subsidiaries

Apply!; Homeroom.com; Princeton Review Publishing; Review.com.

Principal Competitors

Educational Testing Service; Harcourt General, Inc.; Kaplan, Inc.; Sylvan Learning Systems, Inc.

Further Reading

Bongiorno, Lori, "The Test Tutors Try to Settle a Score," *Business Week,* November 21, 1994, p. 62.

De Lisser, Eleena, "Test Case: Dysfunctional Duo Built SAT Prep Firm," *Wall Street Journal,* October 18, 1999, p. A1.

Hammer, Joshua, "Cram Scam," *New Republic,* April 24, 1989, pp. 15–18.

Kallen, Barbara, " 'This Isn't School,' " *Forbes,* November 16, 1987, p. 246.

Kinsley, Michael, "Viewpoint: SATs Are a) Flawed b) Comical c) Both of the Above," *Wall Street Journal,* September 4, 1986, p. 1.

Murphy, Anne, "Enemies, A Love Story," *Inc.,* April 1995, p. 77.

Owen, David, "Adam and John Say Put Your Pencil Down," *Rolling Stone,* March 28, 1985, pp. 74–80.

——, *None of the Above: The Truth Behind the SATs,* Lanham, Md.: Rowman & Littlefield Publishers, 1999, 325 p.

Robinson, Adam, and John Katzman, *Cracking the SAT & PSAT,* New York: Princeton Review, 2001.

—Ed Dinger

Pulte Homes, Inc.

33 Bloomfield Hills Parkway, Suite 200
Bloomfield Hills, Michigan 48304
U.S.A.
Telephone: (248) 647-2750
Fax: (248) 433-4598
Web site: http://www.pulte.com

Public Company
Incorporated: 1956 as William J. Pulte, Inc.
Employees: 5,200
Sales: $4.15 billion (2000)
Stock Exchanges: New York
Ticker Symbol: PHM
NAIC: 23321 Single Family Housing Construction;
    522292 Real Estate Credit

Pulte Homes, Inc. is the largest homebuilder in the United States. The company also builds and sells homes in Mexico, Argentina, and Puerto Rico. Over the course of its half century in business, it has remained consistently profitable and has completed some 277,000 homes in the form of single-family residences, townhouses, condominiums, and duplexes. Pulte offers a wide variety of home models, and customers can vary the model's style by choosing from a number of facades and interior options. In addition, the company operates Pulte Mortgage, a financial services company that originates loans to buyers of Pulte properties.

Inception and Rapid Growth: 1950s–70s

The company originated when William J. Pulte built his first house in Detroit, Michigan, in 1950. He incorporated his homebuilding activities in 1956 under the name William J. Pulte, Inc. In 1961, the company had one subdivision in Detroit; by 1969 it had 12 active subdivisions in six states. The company recorded $5 million in sales in 1964. That figure nearly tripled by 1967, and sales exceeded $20 million by 1968. Pulte entered the Washington, D.C., market in 1964, the Chicago market in 1966, and the Atlanta market in 1968.

On March 4, 1969, William J. Pulte, Inc. was reincorporated through a merger with American Builders, Inc. of Colorado Springs, Colorado. The newly formed Pulte Home Corporation became a publicly owned company, and 200,000 shares of common stock were issued. The reorganization allowed Pulte entry into the low-cost Federal Home Administration (FHA) and Veterans Administration (VA) housing markets. At the same time, Pulte opened its first subdivision of medium-priced homes and began its first subdivision in the state of Virginia. The company also built high-priced conventionally mortgaged homes, student apartments, and turnkey multifamily housing. To control its construction costs, it implemented a computerized critical path program.

During 1970 Pulte evolved from primarily a supplier of high-priced single family homes to a builder of single family homes across price ranges. For the first time, the company's sales of low- and medium-priced houses exceeded those of high-priced houses in both sales dollars and units. The company completed and delivered 1,000 housing units for the first time, reaching $31.2 million in sales. The company also increased its capital base by selling preferred convertible stock for the first time.

In the early 1970s Pulte architects developed the first Quadrominium project, a single building that resembled large, custom-built, high-priced homes, but contained four separate two-bedroom units with separate entrances and garages. Pulte opened its first Quadrominiums in Chicago in 1971, providing buyers with homes for less than $20,000. To increase quality control and shorten the time period between the first rough carpentry work and the closing in of the exterior against the elements, Pulte started to make extensive use of component parts. It used prebuilt trusses; prefinished cabinets, windows, and doors; and factory-built floor and wall sections.

The company extended its presence into new housing markets and continued to grow during the 1970s and 1980s. Even as national housing starts and deliveries declined, Pulte's sales increased to nearly 5,000 units in 1980. It ranked first among all onsite builders in the United States in revenues and in homes delivered in 1985.

Company Perspectives:

At Pulte, we love the business of building homes and are proud of the houses we deliver. We want to share this passion with our customers and get them actively involved in the process. Buying and building a new home is very different from just about any other product purchase. It provides the unique opportunity of being intimately involved with a work-in-process. Think about it. Unlike buying a car, a dishwasher or a pair of skates, a new homebuyer gets to watch his or her house being built from the foundation right up to the shingles. It's a highly emotional experience that is exciting and, at times, a little stressful.

At Pulte, we encourage customers to be actively involved and to become one of our building partners along with our employees, contractors and suppliers. We have determined that greater involvement is vital for our customers being comfortable with the experience.

Adding Financial Services

One of Pulte's first financial services companies was the Intercontinental Mortgage Company, founded in 1972. Later renamed ICM Mortgage Corporation (ICM), the wholly owned subsidiary provided customers with home mortgage financing and thus made Pulte housing units more attractive to homebuyers. (Over half of all Pulte homebuyers financed through ICM in 1992.) ICM services included originating mortgage loans, placing loans with permanent investors, and servicing loans as an agent for investors. ICM posted its third consecutive year of increasing volume in 1992 as it began to focus on origination of "spot" loans for other than Pulte buyers, development of core business relationships with local real estate brokerage professionals, and refinancing activities.

Other Pulte financial services companies included Pulte Financial Companies, Inc. (PFCI), which was the parent company of several bond issuing subsidiaries, and First Line Insurance Services, Inc. (First Line), which provided customers (principally Pulte homebuyers) with convenient and competitively priced insurance-related services to protect themselves and their new homes. In operation since 1981, PFCI subsidiaries engaged in the acquisition of mortgage loans and mortgage-backed securities principally through the issuance of long-term bonds. First Line was established in 1987.

On September 17, 1987, PHM Corporation was incorporated and became the publicly held parent holding company of the Pulte Home Corporation group of companies, which became the wholly owned subsidiary of Pulte Diversified Companies, Inc. In 1988 home sales were flat and one of Pulte's financing subsidiaries filed for Chapter 11 protection due to foreclosure losses. PHM saw a good opportunity to expand its financial services operations by taking advantage of the federal government's Southwest Plan to purchase five insolvent Texas savings and loan institutions. Under the plan, the government offered excellent purchase terms, assumed the risk for any loans that went bad, and gave tax benefits for any losses generated. The acquisitions included two newly incorporated Federal Savings and Loan Insurance Corporation (FSLIC) insured institutions,

First Heights and Heights of Texas. For $45 million, and with the assistance of the FSLIC, the company acquired substantially all of the five thrifts' assets of $1.3 billion and their business operations and assumed certain of their liabilities. Since Pulte was basically responsible only for loans made after the takeover, it was the Government National Mortgage Association's responsibility when one of the thrifts defaulted on a mortgage servicing contract only a month after the takeover. The $2.4 billion portfolio was Ginnie Mae's largest single default to date.

Heights of Texas merged into First Heights in July 1990 and consolidated operations under the name Heights of Texas. Throughout 1991, the bank sold off home loans and securities not guaranteed against loss by the government, repaid high-priced liabilities, and made other transactions in anticipation of eventually being removed from government backing. The effect was an increase in core capital ratio. By 1992 First Heights had grown to 28 branches that offered a full range of deposit and loan services to retail and small business customers, and it had approximately $2 billion in assets.

The "Pulte Quality Leadership" Initiative

The homebuilding industry is traditionally one of the hardest hit by fluctuations in the economy. Factors that affect the housing market include national and world events that impact consumer confidence and changes in interest rates; property taxes, energy prices, and other costs associated with home ownership; federal income tax laws; and government mortgage financing programs. PHM realized that a conservative financial philosophy, combined with delivery of good products, was not enough to assure that the company's more than 35 years of consecutive profitability would continue; in 1989 the company launched the Pulte Quality Leadership (PQL) proactive initiative. PQL was a process to involve every employee, supplier, and subcontractor in devising ways to continuously improve all aspects of the company's operations and assure its continued success. Since the company was already a decentralized organization, PQL further empowered divisions and subsidiaries to adapt products, services, and business strategies to meet the needs of local markets.

Under the PQL process, Pulte had more than 150 teams in the field working on improvements and innovations that would benefit the corporation's diverse companies. Active councils represented each of Pulte's major disciplines: sales and marketing, land management, construction, and finance. Senior managers from every business unit joined to form the seven task teams of the National Quality Council (NQC) in 1990.

PQL training stressed the concept of "Seven Voices" that must be heard and understood to become integral to decision-making. They were the voices of customers, employees, suppliers, competitors, internal systems, communities, and shareholders. The NQC developed the Customer Satisfaction Measurement System, a communication link with new homebuyers that provided feedback on the expectations of customers nationwide. The system measured quality and satisfaction relative to expectations.

The Construction Council developed performance requirements for nearly 200 distinct processes involved in building a house. The council also implemented a comprehensive "build-

Key Dates:

1950: William Pulte builds his first house in Detroit, Michigan.

1956: Pulte incorporates his business under the name William J. Pulte, Inc.

1969: Company is reincorporated through a merger with American Builders, Inc. and goes public as Pulte Home Corporation.

1972: Pulte forms Intercontinental Mortgage Company to provide its customers with home mortgage financing.

1981: Company establishes Pulte Financial Companies, Inc., which includes several bond-issuing subsidiaries.

1987: Company establishes First Line Insurance Services to provide Pulte buyers with insurance products; incorporates PHM Corporation to serve as the parent company of the Pulte Home Corporation companies.

1993: Company is renamed Pulte Corporation; expands into Mexico.

1994: Pulte reorganizes into geographically based operating units.

1996: Pulte becomes nation's largest homebuilder.

1997: Company again reorganizes to more closely align its operating units with market segments.

2000: Pulte launches national brand development campaign and is renamed Pulte Homes, Inc.

2001: Pulte acquires Del Webb, the nation's largest builder of active adult communities.

---

ing science'' program that was the first in the industry. These initiatives fundamentally changed the way the company viewed the entire construction process. For example, in Charlotte, Pulte decided to complete garage slabs, driveways, walks, stairs, and rough grading far earlier in the construction process so Realtors and brokers could show the houses to prospective customers even in bad weather. The new practice contributed to the company's local success and growth during challenging market conditions. Additionally, the subcontractors liked the ease of entry and cleanliness of the job sites and customers were able to view their homes more conveniently. Pulte's Chesapeake operations converted to a screw system to attach gypsum and subfloors. The new system reduced drywall cracks, nail pops, and floor squeaks—three of the most frequently occurring problems in a new home. It also solved service problems that usually showed up after the customer moved in.

The Land Council changed the procedure Pulte Corporation used to acquire land. Instead of using the traditional industry "price and terms" philosophy, the corporation started to choose land based on an understanding of where targeted customers wanted to live. For instance, Pulte integrated 280 homesites with a large preserve of wetlands, streams, fields, and forests in suburban Baltimore. Boy Scouts, public school groups, and other civic organizations joined in planning and building hiking trails, bird houses, and other enhancements. The community received much praise, including designation by the Urban Wildlife Institute as an ''Urban Wildlife Sanctuary.''

Because of the PQL initiative, ICM Mortgage Corporation switched from issuing traditional mortgage coupon books to a monthly mailing of mortgage statements. The innovation added costs up front, but reduced the number of calls to customer service, improved late charge collections, and decreased delinquencies because the system encouraged customers to communicate problems earlier.

1990s: Thriving in a Changing Market

During the economic downturn of the early 1990s, Pulte continued to enjoy record sales and profits in spite of weakened housing and troubled financial markets, enjoying the highest sales and profit per employee of any firm in the industry. While the country had the lowest number of housing starts since World War II during 1991, PHM Corporation enjoyed a 37 percent increase in earnings. The company was able to compete on the basis of reputation, price, location, design, and quality of its homes. It had more than 150 active subdivisions within 25 markets in the Mid-Atlantic, Central, Southeast, and Southwest geographic areas. Pulte Home Corporation attained its first $1 billion year in 1992, with a unit volume of more than 8,000.

Pulte was ready to respond to changing home design preferences and lifestyles. The typical home design before the 1990s was for a family of four. However, the company was discovering that a demand for a greater variety of styles existed and that, in order for it to remain competitive, it needed to not only ''satisfy'' but ''delight'' its customers, according to an article in *Crain's Detroit Business*. Consequently, the company established four different buyer profiles for which it designed homes: the traditional family; the single person; the empty nester; and the extended family. The last profile included parents with children starting college or with children in their 20s still living at home. To suit the lifestyles and wishes of its customers, Pulte engineered new home designs that decreased formal areas to provide space for larger kitchens with fireplaces, bigger family rooms, and master suites; and ranches gave way to two-story Cape Cods.

PHM Corporation was renamed Pulte Corporation on July 1, 1993, to capitalize on the public's recognition of the Pulte name. PHM Corporation was not widely known outside of financial circles, while Pulte had name recognition and identification throughout the geographic areas in which the company's subsidiaries marketed their products and services. It was thought that the change would decrease confusion, potentially increase awareness of the company and its subsidiaries' products and services, and help attract more investors.

The early 1990s also saw Pulte's expansion into the Mexican market. The company began by building small 850- and 450-square-foot units in Monterrey, which were priced between $7,000 and $13,000. Through an agreement with General Motors and Mexican builder Grupo Condak, Pulte also began building 6,000 homes for GM's Mexican employees in Juarez.

In 1994, the company reorganized into four separate operating divisions, based on geographic territory. The divisions—Pulte Home West, Pulte Home South, Pulte Home Central, and Pulte Home North—were highly autonomous, with each division in charge of making its own asset management decisions. The company also changed the way it evaluated potential land acquisitions. Whereas previously Pulte had used financial criteria to determine land purchase and use in a given market, it began to use a more consumer-driven approach. In a January 1997 edition of *Builder*, Pulte CEO Bob Burgess explained: "Every land purchase must meet the needs of a particular TCG [targeted consumer group]. We normally begin land acquisition and house design addressing the specific needs of two to three TCGs." This approach allowed Pulte to develop standardized homes that met the needs of the consumers it was targeting, and reduced the need for customization of floor plans and features. The reorganization was part of an ambitious growth strategy, dubbed "Plan 2000." Plan 2000 called for Pulte to more than double its size by the year 2000. It also involved the company's focus on new segments of the market, including affordable housing and senior buyers.

Pulte's expansion efforts made it the nation's largest homebuilder in 1996. The company, which was operating in 39 markets, sold 12,456 homes and had revenues of $1.93 billion in 1995 to win the number one spot. Just a few months after being named the biggest, it was also named the best. In November 1996, Pulte received the "America's Best Builder" award from the National Association of Homebuilders and *Builder* magazine.

In 1997, Pulte again reorganized its operations. The reorganization eliminated the geographic divisions established just three years earlier, replacing them with operating units that focused on targeting specific customer groups. One area of focus for the new operating structure was the adult/retirement segment of the market. Pulte jump-started its expansion in this high-growth segment, by partnering with an investment bank to form a new company dedicated to "acquiring and developing major active adult residential communities."

2000 and Beyond

As Pulte left the 1990s behind, it remained poised at the top of its industry. Its activities as it prepared for the new century indicated that it planned to stay there. In late 2000, the company launched a new brand development program designed to make the Pulte name a byword for homebuilding throughout the nation. In a November 7, 2000 press release, Pulte's vice-president of marketing, Jim Lesinski, explained the reason for the initiative: "On a national scale, there is limited brand identity associated with Pulte Homes or with any homebuilder. As companies in other industries and product categories have done, Pulte Homes can distinguish itself by establishing a solid brand identity that resonates strongly with the consumer." Tenets of the marketing plan included changing the company name to Pulte Homes, Inc., redesigning the logo, giving away a Pulte home in a national sweepstakes, and sponsoring a float in the Macy's Thanksgiving Day Parade.

An even more dramatic example of Pulte's commitment to growth, however, was its acquisition of Phoenix-based Del Webb—the nation's leading builder of active adult communities. The July 2001 acquisition, which was valued at $1.8 billion, easily secured Pulte's position as the largest homebuilder in the United States and gave the company a much stronger position in the fast-growing active adult market. In addition, the merger was expected to generate cost savings of up to $50 million annually by leveraging operational efficiencies and eliminating redundancies.

Principal Subsidiaries

Pulte Diversified Companies, Inc.; Pulte Financial Companies, Inc.; Pulte International Corporation; Pulte Home Corporation; Pulte Mortgage Corporation; DiVosta & Company; First Heights Bank; Del Webb Corporation.

Principal Competitors

Centex Corporation; KB Home; Lennar Corporation.

Further Reading

Benoit, Ellen, "PHM: Transactions Speak Louder . . . ," *Financial World,* May 16, 1989, p. 16.

Donohue, Gerry, "Pulte Corp.," Builder, January 1, 1997, p. 302.

Drummond, James, "Sweet Deal," *Forbes,* September 18, 1989, pp. 96, 98.

Halliday, Jean, "No Credit Problem Here: PHM Expected to Add Market Share," *Crain's Detroit Business,* March 16, 1992, p. 2.

King, R.J., "First House Pulte's Base for Success," *Detroit News,* June 11, 2000, p. 01.

——, "Pulte Aims at More Buyers," *Crain's Detroit Business,* March 28, 1992, p. 13.

—Doris Morris Maxfield
—update: Shawna Brynildssen

Quizno's SUBS

The Quizno's Corporation

1415 Larimer Street
Denver, Colorado 80202
U.S.A.
Telephone: (720) 359-3300
Fax: (720) 291-0909
Web site: http://www.quiznos.com

Private Company
Incorporated: 1981 as Quizno's America, Inc.
Employees: 421
Sales: $41.4 million (2000)
NAIC: 533110 Lessors of Nonfinancial Intangible Assets
    (Except Copyrighted Works); 722211 Limited Service
    Restaurants

The Quizno's Corporation is the third largest chain of submarine sandwich shops, with more than 1,150 restaurants open in the United States, Canada, Puerto Rico, United Kingdom, Australia, and Japan. Quizno's Italian-style deli offers Italian submarines and other sandwiches, soups, salads, and pastas. The classic Italian submarines—made from proprietary recipes, such as the fresh-baked soft baguette—are the cornerstone of the Quizno's concept.

An Italian-style Deli Named Quizno's: 1981

Todd Disner and Boyd Bartlett formulated the brand concept and menu for Quizno's America while operating a popular Italian restaurant, Footer's, in the Capital Hill neighborhood of Denver. Using their knowledge of Italian foods, they developed an Italian-style deli, serving submarine sandwiches, soups, salads, and a few pasta dishes. In Footer's kitchen, Disner and Bartlett created recipes for red wine vinegar dressing and a proprietary soft baguette, essential ingredients in the classic Italian submarine that became the cornerstone of the Quizno's concept. They used quality meats, such as honey-cured ham and whole muscle meats, rather than chopped and formed meats; authentic Italian meats included capicola and Genoa salami. Before adding lettuce, tomatoes, and red onions, they oven-toasted the sandwich to melt the cheese and to bring out the flavor of the meat and bread.

Disner and Bartlett sought to attract an upmarket customer with a taste for a healthy alternative to fast-food hamburgers. In contrast to full-service restaurants, Quizno's offered a less expensive option, with an atmosphere more pleasant than typical fast-food restaurants. They invented the faux-Italian name Quizno's, using some of the most remembered letters of the alphabet.

The first Quizno's opened in 1981, a few blocks from Footer's and near city and state offices, attracting a white-collar lunch crowd. Over the next decade 16 more Quizno's franchises opened in the Denver area and along the front range of the Rocky Mountains, and one franchise in Los Angeles. In 1990 each restaurant's sales averaged $27,000 per month. The franchise grew without improvements to individual restaurants, however, and the quality of the product deteriorated at some locations. Disner and Bartlett did not have the capital to continue expanding the chain or to provide managerial or advertising support to existing franchises. They sold the company in 1991 to franchisee Rick Schaden, who owned and operated three units with his father, Dick Schaden, an aviation attorney. Disner maintained an 8 percent interest in the company and acted as consultant, while Bartlett became vice-president of purchasing.

Rick Schaden's idea to own and operate a chain of restaurants began with employment at fast-food chains and a business plan he wrote for a university business class. Rick was prompted to open a Quizno's franchise while patronizing one of the restaurants; he overheard a customer say, "This is the best sandwich I ever ate." With his father, Schaden opened his first Quizno's franchise in Boulder, Colorado, in 1987.

Early 1990s: New Ownership Structure Quizno's for Growth

After purchasing the entire company in January 1991, the Schadens began to develop the infrastructure for future growth. Rick Schaden, as president, organized volume purchasing and standardized procedures for unit operations and new franchisee

---

Company Perspectives:

Quizno's Mission: To be a leader in the sandwich segment by serving the best sandwich in the marketplace: one successful store and one "wowed" customer at a time.

---

training. The Schadens planned for growth, seeking to expand into Florida, California, Kansas City, Chicago, and Detroit. New franchise agreements involved Schaden and Schaden, a franchisee separate from the corporation, for rights to two stores in the Detroit area. Four franchises were sold for the California market; in July Disner agreed to open ten stores in Florida.

To open a franchise required initial capital of approximately $100,000, including the Quizno's franchise fee of $15,000. The franchise company charged an annual royalty of 5 percent of sales as well. The Schadens asserted substantial control over the franchises, influencing choice of location and ingredient vendors and determining training procedures. At 1,800 to 2,000 square feet, each store offered approximately 60 seats. The decor conveyed the look of an Italian deli, with artificial salamis, cheeses, and strings of garlic hung around an open kitchen and with shelves holding olive oil and canned tomatoes. Italian poster art, black and white tile floors, pine wainscoting with oak trim, and carpeting in the dining area completed the atmosphere.

Under the leadership of the Schadens, Quizno's assisted its franchisees with new marketing initiatives. With a budget of $50,000, Quizno's launched an advertising campaign in June, using the tagline "Good food. Good prices." Three television commercials promoted Quizno's as an alternative to fast food, emphasizing the lightness, taste, and healthfulness of a Quizno's meal. In each commercial one character enjoyed a Quizno's meal, while the other suffered the heaviness of eating bricks, the tastelessness of pillow stuffing, or the greasiness of used auto parts. Radio advertising supplemented the television ads. In 1992 Quizno's increased the advertising budget to $250,000, raising $100,000 from franchise owners for cooperative advertising.

Rick Schaden attributed much of the success of the company's low budget advertising to direct contact with customers as a supplement to commercial advertising. Unit managers distributed menus to businesses in their neighborhood, promoting office catering with box lunches and offering frequent buyer discounts. The business lunch crowd, patrons between 25 to 45 years of age, accounted for approximately 80 percent of store revenues, sales which occurred between 11:30 a.m. and 1:30 p.m.

To attract families in the evenings and on weekends, Quizno's offered free kids meals. The kids menu included pizza, spaghetti, and mini-subs, regularly priced at $1.99, including chocolate pudding and fruit punch. The company coordinated a 1992 promotion with the launch of the Colorado Rockies National League baseball team; Denver-area Quizno's restaurants sold baseballs for 99 cents with the purchase of a meal.

By the end of 1992, systemwide store sales increased from $7 million in 1991 to $8.5 million. With average per person

sales at $5, average per unit sales reached $338,000 in 1992. By the end of 1993 Quizno's' company-owned or franchised restaurants operated in Michigan, Illinois, Kansas, Iowa, Missouri, Georgia, Florida, Oregon, California, and Colorado. Average per unit sales increased to $360,000.

In February 1994, the Schadens took Quizno's public with an offering of one million shares of stock at $5 per share. The IPO yielded $4.4 million, which the company used to open new stores and pursue franchise sales, particularly through Area Directors.

Striving for the Number Three Spot: Mid-1990s

The Quizno's program for expansion involved the recruitment of Area Directors. Quizno's sold the rights to certain market territories to Area Directors who agreed to sell and open a specific number of franchises within a predetermined amount of time. The usual schedule involved four new units the first year, six new units the second year, and an additional eight units the third year. Franchise territories followed the location of television markets and general locations were planned ahead so as not to oversaturate a market area, a problem with other chain restaurants. Area Directors paid fees to sell franchises, but earned commissions and royalties from franchise sales and revenues. In 1994 Quizno's found Area Directors for five territories: Dallas-Fort Worth; Seattle; Tucson; Omaha and Lincoln, Nebraska; and Montana, northern Wyoming, and western South Dakota.

In November 1994 Quizno's Franchise Corporation purchased Schaden & Schaden, the Schadens' then separate franchise company, for $2 million. The largest franchisee, Schaden & Schaden owned and operated six restaurants in Denver, three in Chicago, and two in Michigan, and held management contracts for five additional franchisees. The acquisition provided revenue and cash flow for training new franchisees and managers. Also, in order to improve cash flow, Quizno's increased the initial franchise fee to $20,000 for full-size units and $10,000 for new, kiosk-type Express Quizno's units. Additional units that were opened required lower franchise fees.

Quizno's enhanced its Area Director program to promote more rapid development, waiving, for example, the requirement to open a flagship unit. In 1995 the company signed Area Directors for El Paso and Austin, eastern North Dakota, Minneapolis/St. Paul, western Nebraska, Cleveland, and Spokane. Also, BBD Management of Vancouver signed a master franchise agreement, the term for international licensing of franchise rights, to open 30 Quizno's units in Canada over the next six years.

Prompted by higher construction and real estate costs, in 1995 Quizno's changed the store design to reduce start-up costs by 25 percent, from approximately $60,000 to $40,000. The 1,800-square-foot requirement was modified to 1,200 square feet. To accommodate the change, the company altered the kitchen layout from a double production line to a single line. Open counter service allowed for greater customer contact and, hence, fewer mistakes on customer orders. The smaller size of each store was conducive to greater flexibility in finding good store locations.

New store openings in 1995 included Boise; Phoenix; Denver; Raleigh; Indianapolis; Kenosha, Wisconsin; and Loveland,

Key Dates:

1981: Denver restaurateurs open first Quizno's with intent to franchise brand via Quizno's America, Inc.
1987: Father-and-son team Dick and Rick Schaden open their first Quizno's franchise in Boulder, Colorado.
1991: The Schadens buy Quizno's America and rename it The Quizno's Franchise Corporation.
1994: Company goes public.
1995: 100th Quizno's sub shop opens; company changes name to The Quizno's Corporation.
1997: Quizno's becomes the number three submarine sandwich franchise.
1999: First Quizno's restaurant opens in Japan.
2000: Schadens take Quizno's private with tender offer of $8 per share.

Colorado. In December 1995 the 100th Quizno's restaurant opened and, by the end of 1995, 112 Quizno's restaurants were in operation in 19 states with systemwide sales of $26 million.

In 1996 and 1997 Quizno's Corporation's expansion efforts began to culminate in the sale of franchise territories and new restaurant openings. In 1996 the company opened 51 restaurants, including eight company-owned units. Over a dozen Area Directors agreed to sell franchises in Palm Beach County, Florida; Shreveport, Louisiana; Contra Costa County, California; Hartford and New Haven, Connecticut; Philadelphia; Knoxville; Richmond, Virginia; Huntsville, Alabama; and other areas across the United States. In 1997, 140 new restaurants opened. Also, Quizno's acquired Bain's Deli, a chain of 63 restaurants, located primarily in shopping malls along the East Coast for $1.2 million. Quizno's began to convert several stores to the Quizno's brand, and later converted units at shopping mall food courts and airports.

By the end of 1997 Quizno's had become the number three submarine sandwich franchiser, with 278 locations in the United States, Puerto Rico, and Canada. Subway held the number one position with 12,000 units and Blimpie was number two with 1,500 units.

Forging a National and International Identity: Late 1990s

The company launched its first national advertising campaign in 1998 with 15-second television spots on cable stations, including CNN, ESPN, and Discovery. The three television commercials focused on the uniqueness of Quizno's submarine sandwiches being toasted, using the terms "toast" and "toasted" as puns. In "The Wedding," for example, the best man fumbles the toast to the happy couple by forgetting the bride's name. The scene shifts to a view of a Quizno's submarine rolling through the toaster oven; the tagline says, "Nicely toasted." In the Denver area, where the advertisements aired on local stations during new shows, the commercials included a local promotion with the Colorado Lottery. The 30-second spots promoted "The Lucky Combo," by which a customer won a coupon redeemable for a Crazy Eight scratch-and-win

lottery ticket if the combination meal of the day was chosen. Winners had the option of receiving $1 off their meal.

With eight units opened and 50 units planned for 1998, Quizno's Canada obtained master franchise rights to franchise up to 650 restaurants in Canada over the next five to ten years, paying Quizno's $573,000 in fees. In March 1999 Quizno's Canada paid $510,000 for the rights to franchise 100 units in the United Kingdom over ten years. Glenvista Enterprises paid $221,069 for the same number of franchises in Queensland, New South Wales, and Victoria Provinces in Australia.

Quizno's had been looking for someone to open franchises in Japan when Nich Nishigane of KMN USA LLC approached Quizno's to purchase the franchising rights. Nishigane thought that the food fit with Japanese tastes, finding the honey bacon club to be quite popular among KMN employees. He planned to hire a Japanese chef to adjust some of the sauce recipes and to supplement the menu with local dishes. In September 1998 KMN USA signed a Master Franchise Agreement to develop up to 300 Quizno's in Japan over ten years. The agreement involved a percentage of territory and franchise sales as well as royalties on store revenues. The first unit opened in Tokyo in early 1999.

Quizno's did not rely solely on new franchise openings to expand the company's reach. In August 1998 a new subsidiary, Quizno's Kansas LLC, purchased the Stoic Restaurant Group. The 21-year-old company owned and operated 12 Sub & Stuff units, but had filed for bankruptcy. Quizno's Kansas, 70 percent owned by Quizno's Corporation and 30 percent owned by two Area Directors, purchased the company for $500,000. Quizno's planned to convert eight stores in prime locations to Quizno's stores, and either sell or close the remaining four units, bringing the total number of Quizno's units in Wichita to 11. Also, Quizno's sold rights to 49 of the 63 Bain's franchises, converted six of the shops to Quizno's, and retained eight Bain's franchises, hoping that the franchisees might convert to Quizno's.

Quizno's experienced a rise in first time franchisees with adjustments to its fees. The company lowered royalty fees a full percentage point to 7 percent of store revenues and lowered training fees from $15,000 to $10,000. Major areas of new store development included Toronto; Milwaukee; Jacksonville; Detroit; Sacramento; Baltimore; Washington, D.C.; Houston; and Columbus, Ohio. With 167 new restaurant openings in 1998 and 258 openings in 1999, at the end of fiscal 1999, 634 Quizno's sub shops were in operation, including 25 company-owned units and 72 international locations.

With about one unit per day scheduled to open in 2000, Quizno's doubled its advertising budget to $10 million. The company hired a new marketing director, Rob Elliott, formerly with Little Caesar's Pizza. Under Elliot's leadership Quizno's retained a new advertising agency, Cliff Freeman & Partners. Freeman's credits included the Wendy's Hamburgers tagline "Where's the Beef?" and Little Caesar's, "Pizza. Pizza." For Quizno's Freeman developed commercials based on the tagline "It's that good." In "Dog," a man's pet dog nabs the Quizno's sandwich perched on the kitchen counter. The man chases his dog and a tug-of-war for the sandwich ensues. The dog manages to take a bite when the sandwich falls to the floor; the man reassembles the sandwich and takes a big bite himself—"It's that good." In "Trash Can" a professionally dressed woman found the leftovers of a Quizno's sandwich in a trash can. Though her coworker tries to persuade her not to eat it, she does, licking the wrapper in ecstasy.

At the end of fiscal 2000, Quizno's recorded corporate revenues of $41.9 million and garnered a net income of $1.1 million. Same-store sales for units open one year rose 7.9 percent. Of the 380 new sub shops opened in 2000, 52 units were located in foreign markets.

In November 2000 the Schadens restated a proposal to take the company private with a tender offer of $8 per share. The Schadens sought to take Quizno's private in December 1998 with a tender offer of $7.84 to $8.20 per share when the stock value averaged $7.50. They felt that the stock was undervalued on the market, but withdrew an offer of $8 per share in August. When the price decreased to $6.50 per share, they reasserted their desire to take the company private, causing the value to rise to $7.75 per share. The privatization deal finally closed in June 2001, with shareholders receiving $8.50 per share.

Principal Subsidiaries

QUIZ-DIA, Inc.; Quizno's Kansas LLC; The Quizno's Licensing company; The Quizno's Operating Company; The Quizno's Realty Company; S&S, Inc.

Principal Divisions

Franchise Development; Franchise Support Services.

Principal Competitors

Blimpie International, Inc.; Doctors Associates, Inc. (Subway); Miami Subs Corporation; Schlotzsky's, Inc.; Wall Street Deli, Inc.

Further Reading

Bunn, Dina, "Quizno's Bags Juicy Japanese Deal," *Rocky Mountain News*, September 30, 1998, p. 2B.

Cebrzynski, Gregg, "Man Wrestles Dog, Woman Picks Trash in 'Bold' Ads for Quizno's Subs," *Nation's Restaurant News*, June 12, 2000, p. 16.

Chance, Conner, "Quizno's Expands to Florida," *Denver Post*, July 22, 1993, p. C2.

Day, Janet, "Quizno's Hopes Public Will Bite into IPO," *Denver Post*, December 8, 1993, p. 2C.

Draper, Heather, "Quizno's Becomes Private with Shareholder Buyout," *Rocky Mountain News*, June 23, 2001, p. 3C.

Graham, Judith, "Father-Son Team Buys Quizno's Chain," *Denver Post*, February 1, 1991, p. 1C.

Leib, Jeffrey, "Two Quizno's Execs Offer to Buy Company," *Denver Post*, December 30, 1998, p. C1.

Mahoney, Michelle, "Morey/Jones Take Humorous Tack to Position Quizno's," *Denver Post*, June 10, 1991, p. 2C.

Parker, Penny, "Morey Mahoney Campaign Italianizes Quizno's Chain," *Denver Post*, April 7, 1997, p. C2.

——, "Quizno's Bites into Canada Master Franchise Agreement; May Add As Many As 650 Restaurants," *Denver Post*, January 28, 1998, p. C1.

——, "Quizno's Expands Global Reach with Japan Franchises," *Denver Post*, February 1, 1998, p. C1.

——, "Quizno's Takes Cable Route 15-Second Ad to Run Nationally," *Denver Post*, February 23, 1998, p. C2.

"Quizno's Seals Overseas Franchise Pacts," *Nation's Restaurant News*, March 29, 1999, p. 98.

Raabe, Steve, "Quizno's Management Launches a $23 Million Stock Buyback," *Denver Post*, November 14, 2000, p. C5.

"Rolling Carts and Kiosks: Mobile and Modular Foodservice Equipment Represent a Low-Investment Way to Bring the Business to the Customer," *Restaurant Business*, August 10, 1996, p. S50.

Rubinstein, Ed, "Quizno's Sub Chain: On a Roll and in the Black," *Nation's Restaurant News*, July 27, 1998, p. 11.

Rugless, Ron, "A Little Creativity Goes a Long Way for Quizno's," *Nation's Restaurant News*, August 3, 1992, p. 12.

——, "Quizno's Offers GMs Partnership Program," *Nation's Restaurant News*, April 3, 1995, p. 3.

—— "Quizno's Redesign Cuts Costs, Expands Location Options," *Nation's Restaurant News*, July 17, 1995, p. 7.

Walkup, Carolyn, "Quizno's Completes Acquisition of Franchisee, Schaden & Schaden," *Nation's Restaurant News*, November 21 1994, p. 72.

—— "Quizno's: Serving a High-Class Hero," *Nation's Restaurant News*, May 16, 1994, p. 104.

Wood, Christopher, "Quizno's Sub Shops Flourish Under Schaden Ownership," *Denver Business Journal*, April 2, 1993, p. 1.

—Mary Tradii

Radian Group Inc.

1601 Market Street
Philadelphia, Pennsylvania 19103-2337
U.S.A.
Telephone: (215) 564-6600
Toll Free: (800) 523-1988
Fax: (215) 238-5752
Web site: http://radianmi.com

Public Company
Incorporated: 1992 as CMAC Investment Corporation
Employees: 835
Sales: $615.4 million (2000)
Stock Exchanges: New York
Ticker Symbol: RDN
NAIC: 524126 Direct Property and Casualty Insurance
   Carriers; 551112 Offices of Other Holding Companies

Radian Group Inc. is one of the leading mortgage insurance (MI) companies in the United States. Helping consumers buy homes for less money down is the company's mission. Its major subsidiary, Radian Guaranty, offers mortgage insurance to more than 3,500 lenders nationwide. Radian was created following the 1998 merger of CMAC Investment Corporation and Amerin Corporation.

From Subsidiary to Public Company: 1992

Radian Group got its start in 1992 when CMAC Investment Corporation, a wholly owned subsidiary of Reliance Group Holdings, was spun off through an initial public offering in 1992. CMAC Investment's principal subsidiary was named Commonwealth Mortgage Assurance Company and provided private mortgage insurance (PMI) to U.S. mortgage lenders. From 1976 to 1992, the company was a subsidiary of Reliance.

The IPO of 9.1 million shares was priced at $24 per share, but the company went public on the New York Stock Exchange at a reduced $18 per share. Most of the proceeds were directed to the Commonwealth Mortgage Assurance Company subsidiary for expansion and growth. At the time of the public offer-

ing, CMAC was one of the largest U.S. private mortgage insurers and had over 5 percent of the market.

James C. Miller was named president and CEO of CMAC Investment as well as the principal subsidiary, with Frank P. Filipps serving as senior vice-president and chief financial officer. Headquarters for the company were in Philadelphia, Pennsylvania. The company's income grew quickly in 1992, increasing 70 percent over the previous year, to $21.8 million on revenues of $83.5 million.

"Our 1992 business growth resulted from strong refinancing activity and a significant increase in home purchase," said Miller in a corporate press release. "Despite a high level of cancellations due to refinancing, our primary insurance in force has grown by 9 percent to $17.1 billion at Dec. 31, 1992, and our increased level of new insurance written provides a solid renewal base for future years. We are also pleased with the improving trend in our claims department. In addition, our balance sheet has been strengthened substantially and our risk to reserve ratio has been reduced to a conservative 15.8 to 1.''

Years of Growth for CMAC: 1993–99

As a mortgage insurer, CMAC focused in 1993 on how to make home ownership more affordable, and in September it introduced the Monthly Premium Plan to reduce the closing dollars needed by borrowers. The plan was offered in all 50 states and let borrowers take advantage of the low interest rates in the early 1990s even if they lacked a large amount of funds for closing costs.

In 1995, Frank P. Filipps succeeded James Miller as president of the company upon the latter's retirement. One of the first changes Filipps made was to alter the commission structure for the sales team. Before Filipps salespeople had been earning commission for both renewals and new sales. After he became CEO, only new business paid commission. The response among the sales team was quick and predictable, with a rise in sales (as well as the departure of some of the staff). The new aggressiveness of the company came at a good time for the industry.

The MI industry grew in the 1990s as more homeowners chose to purchase their homes with less money used as down payments. In 1992, when CMAC went public, 11 percent of new mortgages were covered by private mortgage insurance, but just three years later in 1995, private mortgage insurers guaranteed 17 percent of new mortgages. CMAC, in particular, gained market share during that same period. At the time of its IPO, CMAC had over 5 percent of the market. By 1995, that number had risen to nearly 10 percent.

In 1996, as part of its ongoing mission to provide mortgage insurance to a greater population, CMAC partnered with the Navajo Nation and Fannie Mae to provide mortgage lending to Navajos living on Native American trust lands in the United States. This program was offered to 250,000 Navajos nationwide. Later that same year, the company announced a partnership with National Credit Counseling Services to provide prepurchase counseling for new homeowners.

Income for 1996 rose 22 percent to $62.2 million, on revenues of $183.6 million. President and CEO Frank Filipps said, "1996 was a tremendous year for CMAC's growth, both in terms of insurance-in-force and earnings, as well as in the range of products and services we offer. We intend to expand such efforts to provide innovative business solutions to our industry partners."

In 1997, the company continued its expansion with the announcement that it would insure loans to those with less than an "A" credit rating in some instances. Also, in August 1997, CMAC partnered with the Kentucky Housing Corporation and Fannie Mae on an affordable housing program in Kentucky that would insure loans with as little as 3 percent down. Earnings also continued to climb in 1997, with income rising 20 percent to $75 million on revenues of $277 million.

CMAC purchased Amerin Corporation of Chicago in November 1998 in a $606 million stock deal. Though announced as a "merger," the combined companies moved to the CMAC headquarters in Philadelphia and Frank Filipps remained as CEO of the company. The newly formed company would serve 3,500 customers and ranked as the second largest mortgage insurer in the country. "The merger is about creativity, breaking the mold, and a commitment to delivering the best of the best," said President and CEO Frank Filipps.

1999 to 2000s: New Company, New Name

When CMAC Investment Corporation announced the purchase of Amerin Corporation in 1998, a new company was formed, which in April 1999 took the name Radian Group Inc.,

with the principal mortgage insurance subsidiary named Radian Guaranty Inc. The company would trade on the New York Stock Exchange under the symbol RDN. Not only was Radian a bigger company than CMAC had been, but the combination of CMAC and Amerin created more efficiency for the company and was expected to save $15 million in 1999 alone.

In 2000, Radian announced that it would begin insuring 100 percent mortgages so that more families could become homeowners even with no downpayment. "This is good news for homebuyers who need zero-down payment options, and for Radian's clients—large and smaller lenders across America," said CEO Frank Filipps. Also in 2000, the company expanded its Internet offerings to provide even more e-commerce options to its customers and lenders. In addition, Radian offered a discount for policies purchased online. The rationale for the discount was that by ordering online, lenders would be saving Radian processing costs.

Radian Group launched a new subsidiary in September 2000. The new business, Radian Reinsurance, planned to offer credit enhancement for home equity loans, second mortgages, and manufactured housing. While Radian Guaranty protected conventional loans, the new subsidiary was designed to protect the unconventional. The new business would also offer protection to subprime borrowers, where Radian Guaranty was applicable for A minus and above borrowers.

Radian announced that it would purchase ExpressClose .com, a Dayton, Ohio Internet company. "ExpressClose.com is an extremely good fit for Radian and our clients in both first and second mortgage markets," said CEO Frank Filipps in a company press release. "Our customers increasingly look to us for end-to-end solutions that lower their origination costs, speed decision-making and get borrowers into homes faster." Soon after the ExpressClose.com deal was finalized, the company announced it would acquire Enhance Financial Services Group Inc. for $558 million in stock.

Early in 2001, the company targeted the European market through a partnership with AGS Financial LLC, a New York mortgage advisory and investment banking firm. The company formed a new subsidiary, Asset Guaranty Insurance Company, to enter the European market. Asset Guaranty, though headquartered in New York, opened a London office in May 2001 and was approved for business in the United Kingdom. Thriving despite competition from rivals MGIC and PMI, Radian Group was clearly focused on remaining a leader in the MI industry as expansions and growth continued in the early 2000s.

Principal Subsidiaries

Expressclose.com; Enhance Financial Services Group Inc.; Amerin Re Corp; Radian Guaranty Inc.; Radian Reinsurance Co.; Asset Guaranty Insurance Company.

Principal Competitors

GE Capital; MGIC Investment; PMI Group; Triad Guaranty, Inc.

Further Reading

Avidon, Eric, "Mortgage Insurers Are Prospering," *National Mortgage News*, May 26, 1997, p. 13.

Bergquist, Erick, "More U.S. Insurers Getting Their Feet Wet in Europe," *American Banker*, February 14, 2001, p. 15.

——, "Mortgage Insurers' Streak Continued in 1Q," *American Banker*, May 1, 2001, p. 10.

——, "Private Mortgage Insurers Possible Takeover Targets," *American Banker*, March 15, 2001, p. 9.

Breskin, Ira, "CMAC Investment Adds Risks, Increases Its Insurance Sales," *Investor's Business Daily*, January 28, 1998, p. A35.

Brickley, Peg, "Home Mortgage Insurer Is on the Rebound," *Philadelphia Business Journal*, October 29, 1999.

——, "When He Became CEO He Did Not Enter Softly," *Philadelphia Business Journal*, February 13, 1998.

Carpenter-Kasprzak, Sheri, "Radian Set to Buy Enhance Financial Will Retain Muni Insurance Firms," *Bond Buyer*, November 15, 2000, p. 1.

DiStefano, Joseph N., "Philadelphia Mortgage Insurer CMAC to Merge with Chicago Company," *Philadelphia Inquirer*, November 24, 1998.

Feder, Barnaby J., "Market Place: Two Insurers of Mortgages May Take Rising Interest Rates in Stride," *New York Times*, June 29, 1994, p. D6.

Fernandez, Bob, "Philadelphia Company Capitalizes on Undercapitalized Home Buyers," *Philadelphia Inquirer*, May 29, 2001.

Finkelstein, Brad, "... As MIs Post Strong Nets ...," *National Mortgage News*, July 23, 2001, p. 1.

——, "Record Month in March for Private Mortgage Insurer Insurance," *National Mortgage News*, May 7, 2001, p. 18.

Garry, Colleen, "Radian Launches New Subsidiary," *Asset Sales Report*, September 25, 2000.

Geiger, Mia, "Mortgage Insurer Sees Strength in Mergers," *Philadelphia Business Journal*, July 9, 1999, p. 17.

Gotlieb, Andy, "Providers Push Upside of Mortgage Insurance," *Philadelphia Business Journal*, August 4, 2000.

Hochstein, Marc, "Insurers Beat 2Q Forecasts, But Stocks Lag the Market," *American Banker*, July 22, 1998, p. 10.

——, "Mortgage Insurer Earnings Show Benefit of Rate Rises," *American Banker*, July 21, 2000, p. 1.

——, "Radian Creates Insurance Unit for Alternative Loans," *American Banker*, September 21, 2000, p. 13.

Julavits, Robert, "GSE Rule Aiding Two Mortgage Insurers?," *American Banker*, July 23, 2001, p. 1.

——, "Insurer Radian Branching into Credit Enhancement," *American Banker*, November 30, 2000, p. 14.

——, "Mortgage Insurers Hot; Radian Profits Surge 40 Percent," *American Banker*, October 24, 2000, p. 2.

La Monica, Paul R., "Four Mortgage Insurers Report Solid Earnings Growth for '96," *American Banker*, January 28, 1997.

——, "Insurer Profits Keep Rising: How Long Can It Last?," *American Banker*, October 1, 1997, p. 10.

——, "Insurers Thriving Despite Sluggish Production," *American Banker*, October 15, 1996, p. 12.

——, "MGIC Leads Gainers As Low Rates Boost Home Loan Insurers," *American Banker*, January 15, 1998, p. 13.

——, "MGIC Rating Cut Drags Down Four Other Insurers," *American Banker*, March 17, 1998, p. 9.

——, "Stopping Short of Subprime, CMAC Investment to Begin Insuring A-Minus Loans," *American Banker*, August 1, 1997, p. 8.

Smith, Aaron T., "Bond Insurers: Fitch Gives High Marks to Two Radian Group Subsidiaries," *Bond Buyer*, July 17, 2001, p. 28.

——, "Bond Insurers: Radian Reports Strong 2Q After Asset Guaranty Purchase," *Bond Buyer*, July 31, 2001, p. 35.

Strachan, Stan, "MIs Continue to Flourish," *National Mortgage News*, December 5, 1994, p. 1.

Talley, Karen, "Mortgage Insurers, Growing in Volume, Catch Analysts' Eyes," *American Banker*, February 14, 1996, p. 10.

—Melissa Rigney Baxter

RECKITT BENCKISER

Reckitt Benckiser plc

103-105 Bath Road
Slough, Berkshire SL1 3UH
United Kingdom
Telephone: (01753) 217800
Fax: (01753) 217899
Web site: http://www.reckittbenckiser.com

Public Company
Incorporated: 1954 as Reckitt & Colman Holdings Ltd.
Employees: 18,900
Sales: £3.2 billion ($4.78 billion) (2000)
Stock Exchanges: London
Ticker Symbol: RB
NAIC: 325320 Pesticide and Other Agricultural Chemical
Manufacturing; 325412 Pharmaceutical Preparation
Manufacturing; 325611 Soap and Other Detergent
Manufacturing; 325612 Polish and Other Sanitation
Good Manufacturing

Reckitt Benckiser plc is one of the world's largest household products companies. Formed in December 1999 from the merger of Reckitt & Colman plc and Benckiser N.V., Reckitt Benckiser owns a wide range of household brands in five main areas. Surface care products, which generated 24 percent of 2000 revenues, include disinfecting, bathroom, general purpose, and specialty cleaning products, as well as polishes and waxes, under such brands as Lysol, Dettox, Harpic, Veja, Easy-Off, Mop & Glo, Lime-A-Way, Poliflor, and Old English. Fabric care, responsible for 26 percent of revenues, includes such areas as fabric treatment (Vanish, Spray'n Wash, Resolve), fine fabric treatment (Woolite), water softeners (Calgon), fabric softeners (Quanto, Flor), and laundry detergent (Dosia). Products used in automatic dishwashers, which generated 13 percent of 2000 revenues, include such brands as Calgonit, Finish, Electrosol, and Jet Dry. About 12 percent of revenues came from the company's home care category, which is comprised of air care products (Air Wick, Wizard, Haze), pest control items (d-Con, Mortein), and shoe care products (Nugget, Cherry Blossom). Finally, health and personal care products generated

another 12 percent of 2000 revenues and encompassed antiseptics (Dettol), depilatories for removing unwanted body hair (Veet, Immac), denture care (Kukident, Steradent), analgesics for pain relief and cold and flu remedies (Disprin, Lemsip, Bonjela), and gastrointestinal products for heartburn and constipation (Gaviscon, Senokot, Fybogel). Reckitt Benckiser also retains a small presence in the food industry through its French's business in the United States, producer of mustards and sauces; this business line is a holdover from Reckitt & Colman, which had a rich legacy in the food industry. Geographically, 2000 revenues broke down as follows: Western Europe, 41 percent; North America, 30 percent; Asia-Pacific region, 11 percent; Latin America, 8 percent; and the rest of the world, 10 percent. Reckitt Benckiser sells its products in 180 countries worldwide.

Forerunners of Reckitt & Colman

Three sets of roots gave rise to Reckitt & Colman. The company's evolution was gradual, marked with repeated attempts to graft the stems together. At a watermill in the English countryside near Norwich, Jeremiah Colman began milling flour and mustard in 1814. The business was named J&J Colman nine years later when the childless founder made his nephew James a partner. When they outgrew their first mill at Stoke Holy Cross, Norwich, in 1854, the Colmans built the first mustard mill in Britain at Carrow, Norwich. They added mills for wheat flour, starch, and laundry bluing at the same location.

The Colman line continued to flourish, and expanded again in 1903 with the purchase of Keen, Robinson and Company, a food company that had been in business since 1742. Keen, Robinson's products included mustard, spices, and foods for infants and invalids such as Robinson's patent barley and groats.

Entry into the starch business had brought the Colmans into rivalry with Isaac Reckitt, a starch manufacturer. Reckitt had started out in business in 1819, milling flour at the Maud Foster Mill in Boston, Lincolnshire. The mill and the flour business were both left behind in 1840 when he bought Middleton's starch works at Dansom Lane, Hull. This business was a success, and he soon made his sons partners and added new products. Washing blue and blacklead for polishing grates were both added in the 1850s, and synthetic ultramarine for bluing was added in 1883.

The Reckitts formed a private company, Reckitt & Sons Ltd., in 1879, and went public in 1888. Reckitt & Sons saw diversification of its product lines as the key to further growth and moved to diversify both through in-house development and through the acquisition of interests in companies with similar products. The introduction of Brasso, a new metal polish, in 1905 led to the acquisition of several polish producers. Reckitt & Sons bought Master Boot Polish Company and the William Berry Company in 1912 and the following year joined Dan and Charles Mason in establishing the Chiswick Polish Company. Reckitt & Sons held equal representation on the board with the Masons as well as a significant share in the company.

Reckitt & Sons continued to add new products related to its original line, even through the difficult years of World War I, and throughout the following decades. In the 1930s, with the addition of a germicide, they began to add pharmaceutical products.

The third branch of Reckitt & Colman began to take shape in 1886, when the Mason family began the Chiswick Soap Company. A producer of soft soap and polishes for metal and furniture, Chiswick received some early complaints about air pollution, but these did not deter the company. Cherry Blossom shoe polish was added in 1906, and a floor polish called Mansion was added about a year later.

Although the Chiswick shoe polish business did well in Britain, the company had a formidable rival for overseas business: the Nugget Polish Company Limited. When Nugget and Chiswick had to compete for allocations of turpentine during World War I, they decided to pool their efforts. In 1929, they merged to form Chiswick Products. The new company was owned jointly by the Nugget Polish Company and the Chiswick Polish Company—in fact, the success of this merger was a model for the merger of Reckitt & Sons and J&J Colman in 1938.

The merger of Reckitt & Sons and J&J Colman was the culmination of efforts begun many years before. In 1913 the two companies had stopped competing with each other for business in South America by forming a joint company, Atlantis Ltd., to penetrate the South American market. Atlantis was so successful that they decided to unite all of their overseas businesses. Finally, Reckitt & Colman Ltd. was formed in 1938 to hold and manage Reckitt & Sons and J&J Colman, although the two companies still kept separate identities and positions on the London stock exchange.

During World War II, the companies struggled to survive supply shortages, manpower problems, and the damage done by bombings. After the war, efforts began anew to bring them together as a single entity. In 1954, a merger of the Reckitt and Colman companies established Reckitt & Colman Holdings Ltd. Later that same year, Chiswick Products became part of the organization.

The newly organized company began to concentrate its efforts on developing new business in Europe and North America while it also continued to expand its markets in other parts of the world. A major concern in the acquisition and development of new companies and products was the preservation of the high quality that had won Colman's Mustard the Legion of Honor Award in Paris in 1878. Another major aim was to continue strengthening brand name recognition.

Reorganizing and Streamlining of Reckitt & Colman: 1960s–80s

As the company grew throughout the 1960s and 1970s, a number of reorganizations were necessary to accommodate the addition of other types of businesses, notably in the leisure industry. But the company maintained its identity as a manufacturer of brand name foods, household products, and pharmaceutical items to the world market. At times the rapid changes gave rise to speculation about the direction the company would take. Comments in the press referred to Reckitt & Colman as a "sprawling" company ready for restructuring because of the weaknesses in leadership brought about by the imminent retirement of both its chairman and vice-chairman. Although the company's overseas business had grown to more than 70 percent of its total trade, only one foreign subsidiary, R.T. French, U.S.A., had a representative on the board.

In the 1970s Reckitt & Colman established new divisions to increase production efficiency and improve communication. This reorganization took two years and was described in the press as a period of "abrasive reform," but it succeeded in focusing the company's efforts on a planned expansion program. During the early 1980s Reckitt & Colman embarked upon a carefully executed program which resulted in the expansion and streamlining of the company. This program included the development of innovative products, such as a dual-purpose toothpaste introduced in 1981 to clean both dentures and teeth.

Reckitt & Colman's position in North America was strengthened greatly by its 1985 acquisition of Airwick Industries, a manufacturer best known for its air fresheners, and the 1986 acquisitions of Durkee Famous Foods, a food producer, and Gold Seal, a manufacturer of laundry aids and bath additives including Mr. Bubble. Reckitt & Colman was widely criticized for overpaying for Airwick (its purchase price was almost 40 times earnings), but within the year, Reckitt & Colman had turned the underperforming Airwick around.

Also in the early 1980s, Reckitt & Colman plowed much of its U.S. profit back into household product development following the successful but very costly launch of Bully bathroom cleaner. But the basic products from which the innovative variations were developed continued to be popular. For example, French's mustard, made by Durkee-French in the North

Key Dates:

1814: Jeremiah Colman begins milling flour and mustard in Norwich, England.

1823: Colman names his business J&J Colman with the addition of a nephew as partner; Johann Adam Benckiser forms an industrial chemicals manufacturing firm in Ludwigshafen, Germany, which will eventually be called Joh. A. Benckiser G.m.b.H.

1840: Isaac Reckitt buys starch works in Hull, England.

1888: Reckitt & Sons goes public.

1938: Reckitt & Sons and J&J Colman merge to form Reckitt & Colman Ltd., although the two firms keep separate identities and positions on the London stock exchange.

1954: The two Reckitt & Colman firms merge, establishing Reckitt & Colman Holdings Ltd.; company acquires Chiswick Products, maker of polishes.

1956: Benckiser diversifies into consumer goods and industrial cleaning products and also launches Calgon water softener.

1964: Benckiser launches Calgonit automatic dishwashing detergent.

1981: Peter Harf joins Benckiser as executive vice-president to implement a new strategy: divest the founding chemicals business and use the proceeds to acquire brand name consumer products.

1985: Reckitt & Colman acquires the Airwick air freshener brand.

1987: Benckiser acquires several household product brands from Ecolab, including Electrosol, Jet-Dry, Scrub Free, and Lime-A-Way.

1990: Reckitt & Colman acquires Boyle-Midway, gaining the Woolite, Wizard, Easy-Off, and Old English brands; Benckiser enters the cosmetics sector with the purchase of the Margaret Astor and Lancaster lines.

1992: Benckiser acquires the Coty fragrance and cosmetics business from Pfizer.

1994: Reckitt & Colman acquires L&F Household from Eastman Kodak Company, adding the Lysol, Mop & Glo, Resolve, and d-Con brands.

1995: Reckitt & Colman sells its U.K. foods business, including Colman's mustard, to Unilever.

1996: Benckiser organizes its cosmetics and fragrances operations into a single holding company called Coty Inc., which is spun off as a separate entity.

1997: Benckiser goes public with the sale of 40 percent of the company.

1999: Reckitt & Colman merges with Benckiser N.V. to form Reckitt Benckiser plc.

American group, continued to be the best-selling mustard in American grocery stores.

Also as a part of the streamlining program, Reckitt & Colman sold its unprofitable U.S. leisure industry businesses and, in 1985, it sold its U.S. potato-processing business. In addition, in 1988 the company sold its North American olive, cherry, and caper business. These sales helped channel the company's resources into lucrative areas more closely related to its brand name products. The one major exception to the company's streamlining strategy was a small group of fine arts, graphics, and pigments companies that were consistently profitable.

In 1989 Reckitt & Colman continued to expand in the personal care field, buying Nenuco, a Spanish babycare company. This acquisition also meshed with another of Reckitt & Colman's goals: preparation for the economic unification of Europe in 1992. In July 1989 the company became one of the first British companies to announce a major restructuring to accommodate the continent's internal market. Under the plan, responsibility for production and marketing of certain products was divided between facilities in the United Kingdom, West Germany, France, and Spain. For instance, all of Reckitt & Colman's metal polishes began to be manufactured in Spain following completion of the rationalization in 1991.

Reckitt & Colman in the 1990s: Emphasizing Household Products

Household products came to the fore for Reckitt & Colman during the 1990s through a series of acquisitions and the divestment of additional peripheral businesses, including most of the food operations. Aiming for global growth, the company was particularly interested in expanding its presence in the huge U.S. market. During 1990 Reckitt & Colman spent $1.3 billion for American Home Products' Boyle-Midway household division. Acquired through this transaction were a number of major brands, including Woolite fabric care products, Wizard air fresheners, Easy-Off oven cleaners, and Old English polishers. Boyle-Midway had 1989 sales of $752 million, with about half coming from the U.S. market, Canada accounting for 9 percent, and France, West Germany, and Spain together accounting for about 20 percent. With the completion of this deal, Reckitt & Colman became the seventh largest household products company in the world and the fifth largest in the United States.

In 1992 Vernon Sankey took over as chief executive of Reckitt & Colman. Under his leadership, the company completed a second key U.S. acquisition in 1994, the $1.55 billion purchase of L&F Household from Eastman Kodak Company. The key brand gained through the acquisition of L&F, which had 75 percent of its $775 million in annual sales in the United States, was the Lysol brand of disinfectants and cleaners, which accounted for about half of L&F's total sales. In addition, Reckitt & Colman also picked up Mop & Glo floor cleaners, d-Con pesticides, and Resolve carpet cleaners. The company was now the fourth largest household products company in both the United States and the world. To help fund this growth initiative, the company announced that it would sell its U.K. foods business, including its flagship Colman's mustard brand. The business was sold to Unilever during 1995 for £250 million in cash. This reduced Reckitt & Colman's involvement in the food business to only its French's unit in the United States, maker of mustard and sauces. Later in 1995 Michael Colman, great-great-great-nephew of Jeremiah Colman, retired as chairman of Reckitt & Colman, ending the more than 180 years of involvement of the Colman family in the business. Alan J. Dalby was named chairman in September 1995.

In addition to Colman's, Reckitt & Colman divested a number of other smaller businesses and brands in the mid-1990s in a continuing effort to focus on core lines, particularly those that held the number one or number two position in their categories. By 1997, 80 percent of revenues were generated by household products, a significant increase from the 50 percent figure of ten years earlier. With the acquisition of four brands from S.C. Johnson & Son, Inc., North America accounted for 36 percent of Reckitt & Colman sales, compared to the 31 percent figure for Europe. Added through this £96 million ($160 million) deal were the following brands: Spray'n Wash laundry stain remover, Glass Plus glass cleaner, Yes laundry detergent, and Vivid color-safe bleach.

By 1998, Reckitt & Colman was suffering from rising costs and the effects of economic turmoil in emerging markets of Latin America and Asia, where about one-third of its sales originated. Pretax profits fell by 25 percent in 1998 and the company's stock began sinking. With shareholder pressure increasing, Sankey resigned as chief executive in February 1999, with Michael Turrell, who had been global operations director, taking over on an acting basis. Restructuring efforts began in March, but Reckitt & Colman soon embarked on a new path to revitalization. The company had an impressive portfolio of household product brands but appeared to suffer from poor management. The company turned to a merger with Benckiser N.V. as its fix, hoping that the strong management at Benckiser could reenergize its strong brand lineup.

History of Benckiser

Johann Adam Benckiser founded Benckiser in 1823 as a manufacturer of industrial chemicals based in Ludwigshafen, near Frankfurt, Germany. For the remainder of the 19th century and more than half of the 20th century, Joh. A. Benckiser G.m.b.H. thrived as a low-key regional producer of a wide range of commodity chemicals, primarily citric acid, phosphates, and citrates. The firm began diversifying into consumer goods and industrial cleaning products in 1956, the same year it launched Calgon water softener. In 1964 Calgonit automatic dishwashing detergent was introduced, followed two years later by Quanto fabric softener.

By the 1970s, Albert Reimann, great-great-grandson of the company founder, had selected Martin Gruber, a loyal company veteran, to head Benckiser. The company had remained an independent family-owned firm, and Gruber told Reimann that he would do his best to see that it remained so. With the chemical industry dominated by huge multinationals, such as Pfizer and Hoffmann-La Roche, however, Benckiser was having difficulty competing and appeared destined to slowly slide downhill. The entrance of Peter Harf into the picture started a dramatic transformation.

Harf was a management consultant with a business degree from Harvard University. Gruber first hired Harf as a consultant, then in 1981 brought him onboard as an executive vice-president to implement a radical, yet simple, new strategy for the $250 million company: divest the founding chemicals business and use the proceeds to acquire brand name consumer products. From the early 1980s through the early 1990s Harf completed 26 acquisitions. Among the first was the St. Marc brand of general household cleaner, based in France, which was purchased in 1985. Two years later Harf undertook his first major acquisition, that of the worldwide branded consumer products division of Ecolab Inc. for $240 million. Benckiser thereby gained Electrosol dishwasher detergent, Jet-Dry dishwasher rinsing aid, and Scrub Free and Lime-A-Way cleaning products, and added $224 million in revenues to its $700 million revenue total of 1986.

Although the Ecolab division had been losing money, Harf was quickly able to turn the brands into profitable ones by adopting a strategy of offering good quality products at low prices, mainly by cutting costs through reduced promotion and packaging. Countering the trend toward brand globalization that was sweeping the industry at the time, Harf also aimed to keep his brands local, building customer loyalty by appealing to local preferences. These same strategies were successfully applied to other brands acquired in the succeeding years. In 1988 Benckiser acquired Mira Lanza and Panigel, two major Italian detergent brands. The following year the company purchased S.A. Camp Group, the largest privately owned detergent firm in Spain, for $282 million. Camp controlled between 20 and 25 percent of the detergent market in Spain, with its main brand called Colon. By this time, Harf was serving as chief executive of Benckiser.

In 1990 Benckiser purchased SmithKline Beecham's household products business in the United States and Canada, which included Cling Free fabric softener. One year later, the firm regained the U.S. rights to the Calgon brand, securing worldwide control of its best-known brand. Benckiser also expanded into the emerging markets of Eastern Europe during the early 1990s and made a push into the cosmetics sector. The latter development began in 1990 when Benckiser purchased SmithKline Beecham's cosmetics business, which included the Margaret Astor and Lancaster lines. The company soon added Jovan, Germaine Monteil (renamed Monteil Paris), Germany's Bogner Cosmetics, and Parfums Joop. Then in 1992 Benckiser paid $440 million to Pfizer for the Coty fragrance and cosmetics business, which encompassed several mass-market fragrances, including Lady Stetson and Exclamation. Coty's $280 million in sales made Benckiser the U.S. leader in mass-market fragrances. By 1994, out of total sales of $3.36 billion, Benckiser's nascent cosmetics business generated $1.53 billion while detergents and household cleaning products accounted for $1.75 billion.

In 1996 Benckiser made a hostile play for Maybelline Inc. in order to further bolster the cosmetics side, but the French cosmetics firm L'Oréal S.A. triumphed in a brief takeover battle. Later in 1996 Benckiser organized its worldwide cosmetics and fragrances operations within a single holding company called Coty Inc., which was spun off from Benckiser. Harf remained chairman of Benckiser but spent most of his time in his role as chairman and chief executive of Coty. Bart Becht, who joined Benckiser from Procter & Gamble in 1988, headed up the detergent side of Benckiser starting in 1995 and then became chief executive of the company following the spinoff of Coty.

By the late 1990s members of the Reimann family, concerned about hefty inheritance taxes that might have to be paid out by their estates, finally decided that the time had come to take the company public. In November 1997, after moving its corporate headquarters to Amsterdam for tax and accounting purposes and adopting the name Benckiser N.V., Benckiser completed a very successful initial public offering, which netted $704 million for the sale of 40 percent of the firm on the Amsterdam and New York exchanges. A little more than two years later, Benckiser merged with Reckitt & Colman to form Reckitt Benckiser plc.

1999 and Beyond: Reckitt Benckiser, Global Household Products Giant

The December 1999 merger of the two companies was engineered via a stock swap valued at about $3.5 billion. Because management wanted the new firm to be based in London and to have a listing on the London Stock Exchange, the deal was essentially structured as a takeover of Benckiser by Reckitt & Colman, which then changed its name to Reckitt Benckiser plc. In addition to the meshing of the strong management of Benckiser with the strong brands of Reckitt & Colman, the merger also made geographic sense in that the Dutch company had had little presence in the Latin American and southeast Asian markets, while the U.K. firm had not penetrated Eastern Europe to any great degree. Reckitt & Colman's Dalby was named chairman of the new firm, while Harf became deputy chairman and Becht was named chief executive. In May 2001, however, Dalby retired and was succeeded by Hakan Mogren, former CEO of pharmaceutical firm Astra AB.

Reckitt Benckiser began its existence as the world's largest maker of household cleaning products, excepting the laundry detergent category. The firm intended to focus on five core areas: surface care, fabric care, dishwashing, and home care products, as well as health and personal care products. In the immediate aftermath of the merger, Reckitt Benckiser concentrated on disposing as many of its brands that fell outside of these areas as possible. By August 2001 this disposal program was completed, with the selling off of numerous brands with aggregate revenues of £110 million. Proceeds from the program were in excess of £140 million. The company, meanwhile, began seeking acquisitions in the Asia-Pacific and Latin American regions to fill in geographic and product line gaps. To this end, the company in March 2001 acquired Oxy Co. Ltd., the number four Korean household products firm, for £87 million. Oxy's leading brands included Oxy Clean fabric treatment, Tinkerbell air care products, and Cherie fabric softener. In August 2001 Reckitt Benckiser announced that profits for the first half of 2001 had jumped 23 percent, indicating that the new company was off to a rousing start.

Principal Subsidiaries

Reckitt & Colman Deutschland AG (Germany; 99.64%); Reckitt & Colman Limitada (Brazil); Reckitt & Colman Products Limited; Reckitt Benckiser (Australia) Pty Limited; Reckitt Benckiser (Canada) Inc.; Reckitt Benckiser (Poland) SA (97%); Reckitt Benckiser España SL (Spain); Reckitt Benckiser France SA; Reckitt Benckiser Inc. USA; Reckitt Benckiser (India) Limited (51%); Reckitt Benckiser Italia SpA (Italy; 99.6%); Reckitt Benckiser (UK) Limited.

Principal Competitors

Unilever; The Procter & Gamble Company; Henkel KgaA; Colgate-Palmolive Company; The Clorox Company; S.C. Johnson & Son, Inc.; The Dial Corporation; Church & Dwight Co., Inc.; The Boots Company PLC; Johnson & Johnson; Pfizer Inc.

Further Reading

Berman, Phyllis, and Michael Schuman, "Globaloney," *Forbes*, November 22, 1993, p. 44.

Day, Julia, "Benckiser Gears Up for Brand Dominance," *Marketing Week*, August 5, 1999, p. 19.

"Flush with Brands," *Economist*, October 1, 1994, p. 84.

Gruner, Stephanie, and Anita Raghavan, "Home-Product Deal Has Powerhouse Potential: Benckiser of Netherlands, U.K.'s Reckitt & Colman in $3.5 Billion Accord," *Wall Street Journal*, July 28, 1999, p. A17.

Hudson, Richard L., and Michael Waldholz, "American Home Products, in Pact to Sell Unit to Reckitt, Narrows Focus to Drugs," *Wall Street Journal*, March 12, 1990, p. A3.

Hunter, David, "Benckiser Cleans Up with Its Niche Strategy," *Chemical Week*, December 10, 1997, p. 37.

Milbank, Dana, and Wendy Bounds, "Reckitt to Buy Kodak Business for $1.55 Billion," *Wall Street Journal*, September 27, 1994, p. A3.

Nayyar, Seema, "With Coty, Benckiser Bucks Its Stingy Image," *Adweek's Marketing Week*, May 11, 1992, p. 9.

Oram, Roderick, "Buying a Spray to Cut the Mustard: Why Reckitt & Colman Is Selling Its Famous Brand," *Financial Times*, October 1, 1994, p. 8.

——, "Cleaning Up Its Act to Fight the Giants," *Financial Times*, September 27, 1994, p. 21.

Reckitt & Colman: A Brief History, London: Reckitt & Colman, 1988.

Reckitt, Basil Norman, *The History of Reckitt and Sons, Limited*, London: A. Brown, 1951, 113 p.

Richards, Amanda, "Reckitt's Reinvents Itself," *Marketing*, May 4, 1995, p. 11.

——, "Will Reckitt's Move Lay Its Global Path?," *Marketing*, January 18, 1996, p. 6.

Rohwedder, Cacilie, "German Firm Seeks U.S. Cosmetics Fix," *Wall Street Journal*, January 16, 1996, p. A6.

Simonian, Haig, "How Benckiser Got Out of a Lather," *Financial Times*, August 31, 1990, p. 10.

Simpson, Michele, "Reckitt Maps Out Its 'Global Vision,'" *Marketing Week*, January 19, 1996, pp. 18–19.

Smith, Alison, "Reckitt Benckiser Aims to Clean Up in Asia," *Financial Times*, March 1, 2001, p. 22.

——, "Reckitt Set to Upgrade Targets," *Financial Times*, July 17, 2001, p. 25.

Tomkins, Richard, "Benckiser Drops Bid for Maybelline," *Financial Times*, January 23, 1996, p. 24.

Valeriano, Lourdes Lee, and Audrey Choi, "Pfizer Will Sell Its Coty Line to Benckiser," *Wall Street Journal*, May 5, 1992, p. A4.

Willman, John, "Reckitt & Colman Hopes Its New Dutch Partner Will Help Buff Up Its Image," *Financial Times*, July 28, 1999, p. 24.

"Will Reckitt Ever Shine?," *Management Today*, April 1997, pp. 38–41.

—update: David E. Salamie

Remington Products Company, L.L.C.

60 Main Street
Bridgeport, Connecticut 06604
U.S.A.
Telephone: (203) 367-4400
Toll Free: (800) 736-4648
Fax: (203) 332-4648
Web site: http://www.remington-products.com

Private Company
Incorporated: 1979
Employees: 830
Sales: $365.1 million (2000)
NAIC: 339999 All Other Miscellaneous Manufacturing

Incorporated in 1979, Remington Products Company, L.L.C. boasts a heritage that links it to legendary gunsmith Eliphalet Remington and Remington Arms Company. Remington Products is best known for its electric shavers, which dramatically increased in visibility and market share after then owner Victor Kiam turned television pitchman. Although the Kiam family retains a majority interest in privately held Remington Products, the board of directors is controlled by Vestar Capital Partners, a New York buyout firm, the result of a refinancing of the company forced upon Kiam in 1996. In addition to shavers for both men and women, Remington Products offers a variety of personal care and grooming products and travel appliances. With its global headquarters located in Bridgeport, Connecticut, the company maintains operations in ten other countries and sells its products throughout the world. It also runs more than 100 retail stores located in the United States, the United Kingdom, and Australia.

Making Guns: Early 1800s

Eliphalet Remington, Jr., was the son of a New York farmer who had his own forge and blacksmith shop that was used to build and repair farm equipment. Remington became so skilled with the forge that when he could not afford a hunting rifle he was able to make a gun barrel out of scrap iron. To have the barrel rifled (scored on the inside with spiral grooves) and stocked, he turned to a gunsmith, who was so impressed by Remington's handiwork that he encouraged the young man to produce more gun barrels. This side work done on the family farm grew to the point that by 1828, when his father died, Remington was producing complete rifles. He built a gunshop near the newly opened Erie Canal, and along with his three sons developed a thriving business, its success fueled in large part by the introduction of the Remington pistol in 1847. Remington was also interested in producing other products, and in 1856 began manufacturing farm equipment. In that same year, the company became known as E. Remington and Sons. With the advent of the Civil War, the company was so inundated with Union Army contracts for firearms that Remington's health was compromised and he died at the age of 68, leaving the business to his sons.

Even after the Civil War ended, the Remington business continued to grow as a major international gunmaker, but it also manufactured a number of other products and earned a reputation as an inventor-friendly company. It ventured into such areas as sewing machines, lathes, burglar alarms, gasoline-powered engines, and pill- and tablet-making machines. One of the inventors who turned to Remington was Christopher Latham Sholes, who developed the first practical typewriter. The machine, which soon became known as the Remington, went on the market in 1874. The Remington company suffered some major financial setbacks in the 1880s and went bankrupt in 1886. It sold its typewriter business, along with the right to use the Remington name, to the Standard Typewriter Manufacturing Company.

In 1902 Standard Typewriter would reorganize and be renamed the Remington Typewriter Company. It would then merge with the Rand Kardex Company in 1927 to become Remington Rand Co. In addition to typewriters, Remington Rand manufactured adding machines, filing cabinets, punch card tabulating machines, as well as other office equipment. In 1936, at the height of the Depression, the company turned in a different direction, establishing the Remington Electric Shaver Division. The electric ''dry'' shaver had been invented by Colonel Jacob Schick, who was so obsessed with it that he sold off a company that produced the Magazine Repeating Razor, his

Company Perspectives:

Remington Products Company, L.L.C. designs, manufactures, markets and distributes men's and ladies' shavers, grooming and personal care products, and travel appliances on a worldwide basis.

invention that anticipated the injector razor, in order to fund his new business. His first electric shaver went on the market in 1929, but it was not until 1931 that he introduced the first successful model. Remington Rand began selling its first electric shaver, the model E Close Shaver, in 1937. The Remington Dual, the company's first two-headed shaver, was brought out in 1940, followed the next year by the Foursome, the first multiheaded shaver with a trimming head.

Remington Rand became involved in the computer business in 1950 when it acquired Eckert-Mauchly Computer Company, founded by the developers of the legendary UNIVAC computer, which Remington Rand would deliver to the U.S. Census Bureau two years later. It was also during this period that retired General Douglas MacArthur, after giving up on his political ambitions in 1952, served as chairman of the company. MacArthur essentially held a ceremonial post, mostly announcing dividends and making banquet speeches to business organizations. In 1955 Remington Rand merged with Sperry Corporation, becoming Sperry Rand Corporation. Originally founded in 1933 to develop aircraft instruments, such as the automatic pilot, Sperry was interested in Remington Rand because of its computer business, not its shavers. Nevertheless, the Remington Shaver Division of Sperry Rand continued on. In 1960 it introduced the first cordless shaver, the Lektronic, which relied on rechargeable nickel cadmium energy cells.

One of the major strengths of Sperry Rand was its emphasis on engineering, which was a mixed blessing for the Remington Electric Shavers Division. Although it developed a product that was considered to be superior to its rivals, the company introduced new models so frequently that its marketing suffered. Retailers, wary that Remington shavers would become obsolete in a short period of time, were reluctant to keep a large inventory. Category leader Norelco, by offering a stable product line, outsold Remington four to one. Furthermore, Remington Shaver models were numbered and preceded by XLR or PM, which may have been considered sexy by the engineers but had proved less than seductive to consumers. By the late 1970s, after losing some $30 million in three years, the division was put on the auction block. A number of suitors stepped forward, but Sperry Rand opted to sell to the least likely of the candidates, a man who did not even have his financing in order. His name was Victor K. Kiam II.

Kiam grew up in New Orleans, where his first exposure to business came at the age of eight when he began selling Coca-Colas for a dime at a streetcar stop, a venture that failed when he gave away too much of the product. Following a stint in the Navy he earned a bachelor's degree from Yale and a certificate of languages at the Sorbonne (University of Paris), followed by an M.B.A. from Harvard. He joined Lever Brothers as a man-

agement trainee in 1951 and drifted into sales when he stepped in for an injured salesman, working his way up to various marketing management positions. He later went to work for Playtex, eventually becoming the president of its Sarong division. In 1968 he bought the Benrus Watch Corp. and became the company's chief executive officer. After leaving Benrus, he was looking for a new venture when he learned that Remington was for sale. After some study he realized that Remington sold a wide variety of products, but he decided to focus on the electric razor business. His wife chided him for even thinking about getting involved with a product that he had never used, prompting him to reply that he had never worn a brassiere but had done pretty well at Playtex. The next day she gave him a Remington shaver, which, as he would later say many times, gave him the best shave he ever had. He bought rival electric shavers and conducted his own comparison tests, eventually satisfying himself that Remington had the best product on the market.

Establishment of Remington Products: 1979

Although Kiam had limited funds, Sperry executives considered him the candidate best suited to run Remington and worked with him to fashion a $25 million leveraged buyout in 1979. Kiam then created Remington Products Incorporated to run the business. Once in charge, he quickly instituted a number of changes. He trimmed staff, mostly at the management level, then assured the workers on the factory floor that their jobs were secure. Furthermore, executive washrooms were closed and everyone now shared the same medical and profit-sharing plans. Kiam cut back on the product line and renamed and repackaged the shavers. He introduced a lower-price shaver and rescinded a price increase on higher-end shavers, planned by prior management, in order to gain a price advantage over rivals. Overseas plants were shut and operations centered in Bridgeport. Kiam also reinstated an old slogan, "Shaves as close as a blade or your money back."

Kiam achieved solid results almost immediately. He was able to pay off bank loans and notes with Sperry well ahead of schedule. After selling one million shavers in 1979, Remington Products would be selling three million by 1983. A large measure of that success could be attributed to the company's legendary television ad campaign that featured Kiam proclaiming that he liked the Remington shaver his wife gave him as a present so much that he decided to buy the company. According to Kiam, he turned company pitchman purely by accident. Shortly after taking over Remington Products he flew to England to discuss possible television commercials for the British market. After he and the advertising agency failed to agree on a concept, Kiam was asked how he came to buy Remington Products. Judging by the interest of his audience as he told how his wife bought his first Remington shaver, Kiam wondered aloud if the British public might be interested as well. While the agency wanted to hire a famous soccer star to tell the story, Kiam announced that because it was his story he was the only man for the job. After a favorable test market, Kiam's first commercial premiered in England on November 1, 1980, resulting in a dramatic surge in sales. A version of the commercial was then released in Australia, France, Norway, Canada, and Hong Kong. It was not until 1981 that the Kiam commercial appeared on television in the United States, and not until the end of the year that the pitch began to take hold. In time, Kiam would tape a multitude of

Key Dates:

1816: Eliphalet Remington, Jr., begins producing gun barrels on farm forge.
1856: E. Remington and Sons is formed; company begins manufacturing farming equipment.
1874: The Remington Typewriter is first introduced.
1886: Typewriter business is sold to Standard Typewriter Manufacturing Company; the gun business survives, reorganized two years later as Remington Arms.
1902: Standard Typewriter changes name to Remington Typewriter.
1927: Remington Typewriter merges with Rand Kardex Company to become Remington Rand Co.
1936: Remington Rand introduces its first electric shaver.
1955: Remington Rand merges with Sperry Corporation to become Sperry Rand Corporation.
1979: Electric shaver business is sold to Victor Kiam, who forms Remington Products Incorporated.
1996: Vestar Capital Partners acquires company, which is reorganized as Remington Products Company, L.L.C.
2001: Victor Kiam dies.

follow-up commercials, shot in his office bathroom to save money. He claimed to be able to knock off 15 commercials in a day, and that he knew 29 seconds worth of 15 different languages. Other chief executives, such as Chrysler's Lee Iacocca, would soon try to emulate Kiam's success.

Not only did the Remington commercials increase shaver sales, as the company doubled its market share within several years, they made Kiam into a national celebrity. With that came a book deal. In 1986 Kiam penned a best-selling business book, *Going For It! How to Succeed As an Entrepreneur,* published by William Morrow. It was followed up by *Live to Win: Achieving Success in Life and Business.* Kiam gained even more prominence in 1988 when, bolstered by money from businessman Fran Murray, he was able to buy the New England Patriots of the National Football League for $85 million. A few years later it was Kiam's celebrity and his football team that led to problems for both Remington Products and its flamboyant owner.

Flourishing in the 1980s, Trouble in the 1990s

Remington Products became a fast-growing consumer products company in the 1980s. While its share of the men's electric razors market continued to grow, Remington Products ventured into electric shavers for women and quickly built a category leader. It also introduced a home hair cutting kit, as well as products that went outside of personal grooming, such as a pool alarm and a Vic Vac carpet cleaner. In 1987 Remington Products acquired the Fransus Co. to expand into the travel appliance and travel accessory business. By the end of the 1980s the company was generating approximately $250 million in annual revenues, although the products outside of electric razors contributed little to the business. Moreover, the market for men's electric razors was becoming stagnant; it appeared that the only men buying new shavers were those replacing old ones.

Kiam had hoped that his Patriots would create synergy with Remington Products, but little came from the use of football pitchmen, such as the team's star quarterback, Tony Eason, or Doug Flutie who had gained national attention at Boston College by winning the Heisman Trophy as the nation's best college quarterback. The Patriots also proved to be a drain on Kiam's own finances, which were especially hampered by a stadium lease that granted him nothing more than ticket sales. Then Kiam's image suffered greatly after he got caught up in a well-publicized incident after several Patriots players taunted a woman sportswriter named Lisa Olson in the team locker room in September 1990. Kiam was quoted as calling Olson a "classic bitch," a remark he denied making, although he did issue a general apology. A few months later, however, Kiam was caught telling an off-color joke involving Olson at a sports banquet. The National Organization for Women had already called for a boycott on Remington Products, so this new remark only made matters worse for both Kiam and Remington. At the same time, the nation of Canada charged the company with airing misleading commercials, making performance claims that could not be substantiated, namely that the Remington shaved closer than other electrics. Because he appeared as a spokesman in the commercials, Kiam was cited along with the company and potentially faced five years in prison under Canada's Competition Act. Eventually the matter was settled when Remington paid a fine of C$75,000.

Sales were falling for Remington, dropping 20 percent between 1989 and 1990, from $250 million to $200 million, prompting Kiam to hire a turnaround expert who began instituting administrative cuts. Kiam faced further difficulties in 1991 when Murray exercised an option in the Patriots deal that allowed him to leave after three years with a guaranteed profit of $13 million on his $25 million stake, forcing Kiam to come up with $38 million in a matter of weeks. Essentially he had to choose between Remington Products and his football team. In the end, Kiam chose Remington Products and sold his interest in the Patriots. Nevertheless, the losses he incurred running the Patriots had an adverse effect on his ability to maintain ownership of Remington Products.

Kiam refinanced Remington in 1992, turning in particular to New York investor Isaac Perlmutter. He also received a $15 million loan from the state of Connecticut, which was anxious to retain jobs. In 1993 Remington Products again looked to diversify its product offerings by acquiring the hair-care appliance business of Bristol-Myers Squibb Co. A former division executive, F. Peter Cuneo, who had gone on to become president at Black & Decker, was hired as the president and chief operating officer of Remington Products. With the Bristol-Myers products, he began to move the company to a younger, more contemporary style. As part of this makeover, Kiam's image was removed from all packaging and advertising. Soon, in fact, he would no longer run the company.

In 1995 attempts by Sunbeam-Oster Co. to purchase Remington Products failed. A year later, however, Vestar Capital Partners acquired a nearly 40 percent stake in the company, equal to Kiam's, but as part of the deal also gained control of the board of directors. Kiam remained as nominal chairman of the board but he no longer ran the company, which was reorganized as Remington Products Company, L.L.C. Vestar was started by seven founding partners in 1988, run by CEO Dan O'Connell. In January 1997 Vestar brought a new management team to Remington Products, headed by a former executive at Clorox, Neil DeFeo, who also had 25 years of experience with Procter & Gamble.

New Leadership for a New Century

Under DeFeo, Remington Products underwent a three-year plan to revitalize the company's fortunes, cutting costs and jobs while unveiling a large number of new products. In January 2000 the company reorganized into two operating divisions: Remington Shaving and Grooming, and Personal Care and Wellness. While the company posted losses of $4.5 million and $15.3 million in 1997 and 1998, revenues grew. In 1999, sales reached $318.8 million and Remington Products returned to the black with a net profit of $6 million. In 2000, revenues grew to $365.1 million and net profits totaled $12.7 million. The company was clearly striding forward. A few months after announcing its 2000 results, however, its longtime chairman, Victor Kiam, died of a heart condition at the age of 74. "He was a wonderful man and he'll be missed by many people," DeFeo commented, according to a *Times Union* obituary. "And he made a difference in American business."

Principal Divisions

Remington Shaving and Grooming; Personal Care and Wellness.

Principal Competitors

Applica; The Gillette Company; Philips Electronics North America Corp.

Further Reading

"Canada Accuses Kiam, Remington Products of a Misleading Ad," *Wall Street Journal,* November 2, 1990.

"Growth Strategies at Remington," *Journal of Business Strategy,* January/February 1989, p. 22.

Kiam, Victor, *Going For It! How to Succeed As an Entrepreneur,* New York: William Morrow, 1986, 260 p.

——, *Live to Win: Achieving Success in Life and Business,* New York: Harper & Row, 1989.

Manchester, William, *American Caesar: Douglas MacArthur 1880–1964,* Boston: Little, Brown and Company, 1978, 793 p.

Much, Marilyn, "Would You Buy a Shaver from This Man?" *Industry Week,* August 24, 1987, pp. 37–38.

Oliver, Joyce Anne, "Kiam Reached for a Star—and Grabbed a Handful," *Marketing News,* February 18, 1991, p. 14.

Oliver, Myrna, "Obituaries: Victor Kiam II," *Los Angeles Times,* May 30, 2001.

Robichaux, Mark, "Victor Kiam Struggles to Save His Troubled Empire," *Wall Street Journal,* November 12, 1991, p. B1.

Smith, Geoffrey, and Lisa Driscoll, "Victor Kiam Needs a Hail Mary Play," *Business Week,* November 11, 1991, p. 72.

——, "Victor Kiam, Self-Sacking Quarterback," *Business Week,* February 25, 1991, p. 46.

"Victor K. Kiam II, Electric Razor Baron," *Times Union,* May 29, 2001, p. B7.

—Ed Dinger

Resource America, Inc.

Resource America, Inc.

1521 Locust Street, Suite 400
Philadelphia, Pennsylvania 19102
U.S.A.
Telephone: (215) 546-5005
Fax: (215) 546-5388
Web site: http://www.resourceamerica.com

Public Company
Incorporated: 1966 as SMTR Corp.
Employees: 199
Sales: $89.2 million (2000)
Stock Exchanges: NASDAQ
Ticker Symbol: REXI
NAIC: 522320 Financial Transactions Processing,
    Reserve and Clearinghouse Activities; 211111 Crude
    Petroleum and Natural Gas Extraction

Based in Philadelphia, Pennsylvania, Resource America, Inc. has been involved in the production of gas and oil throughout its more than 50 years of existence. During the 1990s, however, it evolved into a specialty finance firm that bought up real estate loans. In addition, it established a computer leasing operation. Following a downturn in its stock price, Resource America has since left the leasing business, de-emphasized real estate, and renewed its interest in energy. Through subsidiaries Atlas America and Resource Properties, the company is involved in more than 4,000 gas and oil wells located in the Appalachian Basin. The family of Chairman and CEO Edward E. Cohen owns approximately 5 percent of Resource America.

Forming Original Company As
a Tax Shelter in the 1960s

The company was incorporated originally in 1966 as SMTR Corp., and then in 1970 changed its name to Resource Exploration, Inc. The gas and oil drilling operation, focusing on wells in Ohio and Pennsylvania, was operated out of Shreveport, Louisiana, by longtime oil man J.C. Trahan, who had little more than a high school education but advanced skills as a promoter. He projected an image of careless wealth by flashing gaudy jewelry and handing out large tips to procure choice tables at New York hot spots. Starting in 1968 he began to sell limited partnerships of the corporation and its two operating subsidiaries: Lafayette Funds and Oil & Gas Funds. Trahan was believed to be spending more time selling the over-the-counter shares than actually drilling for gas or oil. Earnings from exploration were a future bonus, but the company was positioned primarily as a tax shelter, promising a 150 percent write-off. Between 1968 and 1976 the company raised more than $34 million but paid out just $2.6 million. The IRS and SEC eventually looked into the activities of Resource Exploration. Trading of its stock was suspended in March 1976, and Trahan resigned. J. Russell Duncan, chairman of the board, replaced Trahan and moved the company's headquarters to Canton, Ohio, which was much closer to its oil and gas fields.

In December 1976 the SEC filed a civil complaint against Resource Exploration alleging material misstatements and omissions connected to the sale of partnerships. A month later, as part of a consent order entered into with the SEC, all of the operating officers of the corporation either resigned or were terminated. A year later the company filed for bankruptcy, and the court named Willard E. White as receiver. It was reorganized three years later but struggled to remain a viable business and continued to court controversy. After fending off a hostile takeover bid by Yankee Oil & Gas in 1983, Resource Exploration suffered through a confusing period in which top management was regularly shuffled. White, in fact, was fired as chief executive officer three times in a single year.

Finally, in 1988 Resource Exploration would come under stable management. Philadelphia businessman Edward E. Cohen and his partners, who included Jack Dorrance, the elderly head of the family that founded Campbell Soups, were looking for the tax shelter benefits of an oil company, but wanted to gain management control to avoid the types of nefarious dealings that so far had marred the existence of Resource Exploration. Cohen also recognized that the company controlled undervalued assets. He was the chairman of the board of Bryn Mawr Resources, Inc., which created a subsidiary it called BMR Newcorp. to hold $600,000 worth of gas and oil properties, in addition to $5 million in cash and no liabilities. It was then sold to Resource Exploration for 2.2 million shares of stock, or roughly a one-third stake in the company. As part of the deal, Bryn Mawr named three directors to the board, including Cohen, who also took over as president and chief executive officer.

Cohen had an unusual background for an executive. In addition to earning a law degree, he received a doctorate from Princeton, where he studied ancient Greek law and economics. He would go on to write three books on ancient Athens. Because of that academic experience, Cohen told a reporter in a 1998 interview with *Investor's Business Daily,* ''I question all kinds of academic theories. I question everything I'm told about business activity, and I tend to be countercyclical.'' Moreover, he said, ''I originally wanted a better understanding of economics to aid my academic research, but I also wanted to be financially independent. It was many years later, after being surrounded by people who in fact wanted to amass all the money there is in the world, that I became infected by a more mercenary system of values. . . . I try to be a winner, but I try to be a winner fairly.'' When he gained control of Resource Exploration at the age of 49, Cohen had 20 years of experience in the banking business. He sat on the board of JeffBanks Inc., founded by his wife Betsy, who served as CEO.

Diversification and Growth Through the 1990s

After changing the name of the company to Resource America in 1989, Cohen began to display his ability to think outside the box. Rather than borrowing heavily to ramp up production in anticipation of rebounding oil prices, he elected to simply pump his existing reserves, earning approximately $10 million in three years. Out of necessity, in 1991 he began to move the company into an entirely new area of business: specialty finance, in particular troubled real estate loans. Because the market was in a downturn, investors were bailing out, enabling Cohen, as usual operating against the grain, to pick up the mortgages at reasonable rates. The loans were typically worth less than $5 million and held by major institutions, which were unwilling to devote the time required to resolve the various issues among their borrowers. The lenders, more interested in obtaining ready cash and ridding themselves of problems, were happy to sell the loans to Resource America at a generous discount to the unpaid principal. Resource America then worked out a payment plan with each of the borrowers, agreeing not to foreclose for a number of years in order to allow the individual properties involved to become profitable. Moreover, the company might even recover its initial investment by selling senior participations in the loans while still retaining an interest. Cohen's willingness to engage in conflict resolution was rewarded with generous profits. By 1994 Resource America would generate $2.5 million in revenues from real estate finance (out of total revenues of $8.2 million). The next year would see

real estate revenues increase by 142 percent, reaching $6.1 million (out of total revenues of $11.4 million).

Resource America continued to move away from the energy business in 1995 by becoming involved in the leasing of business equipment, in particular computers. Again, Cohen targeted a niche: in this case, small ticket contracts worth less than $100,000, as opposed to the $50 million-and-over contracts favored by major leasing operations. Whereas computer leasing appeared on the surface to be entirely different from the company's real estate loan business, it also involved mediation and financial expertise. In essence, Resource America served as the connection between the makers of computers and customers. Resource America, well versed in the tax advantages of business leasing, could simply run the finance operations for computer manufacturers. Resource America's entry into leasing was accomplished through the September 1995 acquisition of the leasing operations of The Fidelity Mutual Life Insurance Co. (Fidelity Leasing Corporation) for approximately $1.5 million in cash and the assumption of $312,000 in liabilities. The company then hired an experienced management team to run the subsidiary. Abraham Bertsein was named its chief executive. He had built up the equipment leasing business of Tokai Bank of Japan, experience that led to Resource America winning the contracts to run the equipment leasing operations at a number of banks, including CoreStates Financial Corp. and Bank of America. Moreover, the Fidelity Leasing acquisition brought with it more than 500 leases that provided a revenue stream of $1.1 million for the subsidiary's first year of operation.

With Resource America's real estate loan business thriving in the mid-1990s, Cohen decided to exploit its dealing even further by establishing a Real Estate Investment Trust (REIT), to be run by his wife. REITs were created by Congress in 1960 as a way for small investors to become involved in real estate in a manner similar to mutual funds. REITs could be taken public and their shares traded like those of any other public company. Unlike other companies, however, REITs were required by law to pay out at least 95 percent of their taxable income to shareholders each year, thus severely limiting the ability of REITs to raise funds internally. During the first 30 years of existence, REITs were hindered in their growth because they were allowed only to own real estate; other parties had to manage the properties. Moreover, the existing tax code made direct real estate investments an attractive tax shelter for many individuals, thereby absorbing funds that might have been invested in REITs. It was the Tax Reform Act of 1986 that began to change the nature of real estate investment. Interest and depreciation deductions were greatly reduced so that taxpayers could not generate paper losses in order to lower their tax liabilities. The act also permitted REITs to provide customary services for property, in effect allowing the trusts to operate and manage the properties they owned. Despite these major changes in law, REITs were still not embraced as an investment option in the late 1980s. It was not until the mid-1990s that REITs finally became an attractive option.

In October 1997 Resource America filed papers regarding its proposed REIT, Resource Asset Investment Trust, indicating that it intended to limit its ownership stake to less than 10 percent. The REIT would concentrate on Philadelphia area office and commercial buildings, as well as multifamily residential properties, rang-

Key Dates:

1966: Company is incorporated originally as SMTR Corp.
1970: Company's name is changed to Resource Exploration, Inc.
1988: Edward E. Cohen gains control of the company.
1989: Company's name is changed to Resource America.
1991: Company becomes involved in buying real estate loans.
1995: Fidelity Leasing is acquired.
1998: Atlas Group is acquired.
2000: Fidelity Leasing is sold to European American Bank for $583 million.

ing in price from $2 million to $20 million. Most of its initial portfolio would be bought from Resource America and JeffBank. In contrast to Resource America's real estate business that focused on real estate loans that were on the verge of default, Resource Asset intended to acquire properties that had progressed to the point at which workout provisions were already in effect. In January 1998 Resource Asset sold approximately 3.3 million shares at $15, raising almost $50 million. Resource America bought 500,000 shares, costing $7.5 million.

Resource America enjoyed robust growth through the 1990s, a situation not lost on investors. Revenues reached $17 million in fiscal 1996, then grew to $31.9 million in 1997, and $83.2 million in 1998 when net income soared to $27.6 million. Between January 1996 and January 1997, the company's stock price increased 167 percent, from $8.50 per share to $21.50. In August 1998 Resource America stock was trading higher than $35. The price started to slide, then all but collapsed when the company became the target of a report by the Off Wall Street Consulting Group of Cambridge, Massachusetts, which questioned the accounting practices of Resource America and maintained that the company was severely overvalued. What was at issue were real estate assets that Resource America listed at appraised values rather than what it actually paid for the loans. Resource America's position, backed up by analysts familiar with the field, was that it followed standard accounting practices and that Off Wall Street simply did not understand the business. Nevertheless, in a matter of days the price of the company's stock plunged to a level below $15.

Resource America was not the first firm to conflict with Off Wall Street. Like Cohen, the latter firm's founder, Mark Roberts, came to business with an uncommon background, having studied French literature as an undergraduate at Swarthmore College and graduate student at the University of California at Berkeley. After working in his family's steel service business, he ran another steel business before becoming an investment analyst in New York. He started Off Wall Street in 1990, gaining early recognition for a report critical of TCBY, whose stock plummeted by 75 percent. His report was distributed to a select group of clients who paid in excess of $30,000 a year. Critics of Off Wall Street contended that its reports were used in nothing less than a cynical ploy to drive down a company's stock price for the benefit of short-sellers. Other Off Wall Street targets included Samsonite, Pillotex Corp., and Miller Indus-

tries. Claiming to be right about 80 percent of the time, Roberts once recommended a short on America Online, advice that he would later retract.

Resource America vehemently questioned Roberts's criticism. Two weeks later, Off Wall Street issued a follow-up report, correcting what it called a technical point. Again, Roberts called into question Resource America's accounting methods, although he refused to release the report to the press or provide any detailed explanation. Resource America insisted that the new report simply confirmed that Roberts failed to understand the company's specialty business. Nevertheless, the stock price dropped further, losing some 80 percent of its value since the first Off Wall Street Report. The company hired an outside auditor, Grant Thornton LLP, which later in September 1998 announced that Resource America's accounting methods were correct. Roberts dismissed the findings, maintaining that even if the company's accounting methods were technically correct they failed to accurately reflect the "quality of earnings."

Adapting to Circumstances, Planning for the Future: 2000s

No matter the reality of the situation, the perception of Resource America created by the Off Wall Street flap would in many ways shape the future of the company. Even a woefully inadequate offer of $15 per share, from an unknown investment firm, to buy the company was given momentary credence. Cohen announced that if a legitimate offer were made and was priced significantly below $30, his family would possibly make a counteroffer. In the meantime, Resource America carried on growing its business, adding to its energy portfolio by acquiring the Atlas Group and its gas and oil drilling operations. Fidelity Leasing also agreed to purchase the U.S. leasing operation of Japan Leasing Corp. for $38 million and the assumption of debt. JLA Credit Corp. and its $367 million in assets increased Fidelity's total assets to $1.4 billion. Nonplussed by the turmoil swirling around Resource America, Cohen told the press, "None of this has much to do with reality. It has to do with calls from lenders and more margin calls that have people dumping stock. Meanwhile, people like us go about our business operating hugely successful companies and wondering what kind of anti-matter universe we've stumbled into."

Revenues exceeded $140 million in 1999, resulting in net income of $18.4 million. The company even changed its accounting methods. Nevertheless, Resource America faced a shareholder lawsuit that, based on Off Wall Street reporting, essentially accused management of fraud. Despite producing solid results, the company received further criticism for management pay hikes and a resetting of stock option prices, measures which Cohen maintained were necessary to retain his top level staff. The company essentially was forced to develop plans to raise cash by spinning off businesses and selling assets.

In January 2000 Resource America made a public offering of 47 percent of the stock in Atlas Pipeline Partners, which combined the 600-mile pipeline business of Atlas with a subsequent acquisition of Viking Resources Corp. and its 150 miles of pipelines. The offering raised $19.5 million. Fidelity Leasing was then sold in August 2000 to European American Bank for $583 million, which included the assumption of $431 million in third party debt. In fiscal 2000 Resource America did not add any new mortgages to its real estate portfolio. Although the company appeared to be reverting to its earlier existence as an energy company, with most of its activity in 2001 involving new drilling and the acquisition of oil and gas rights, it would not be surprising to see Cohen eventually take Resource America in an entirely new direction.

Principal Subsidiaries

Atlas America, Inc.; Resource Properties, Inc.

Principal Competitors

American Residential Investment Trust; Belden & Blake; Ocwen Financial; Transamerica Corporation.

Further Reading

Bailey, Steve, and Steven Syre, "Analyst Aims His Darts at Inflated Stocks," *Boston Globe,* August 26, 1998, p. C1.

Brickley, Peg, "Resources for Sales, at the Right Price," *Philadelphia Business Journal,* October 23, 1998, p. 3.

Cooper, Cord, "Resource America's Ed Cohen," *Investor's Business Daily,* July 22, 1998, p. A1.

Ewing, Terzah, "Resource America Gets More Criticism from Consulting Firm, and Stock Falls," *Wall Street Journal,* September 8, 1998, p. A6.

Hals, Tom, "Resource America's Stock Is Up 167% in One Year," *Philadelphia Business Journal,* January 24, 1997, p. 3.

McClintick, David, "Striking It Poor: More Oil Tax-Shelters Are Encountering Financial Difficulties and IRS Challenges," *Wall Street Journal,* June 9, 1976, p. 38.

Starkman, Dean, "Lending Firm Brands Report As 'Misleading,'" *Wall Street Journal,* August 26, 1998, p. A14.

Timmons, Heather, "Critical Reports Slash 80% from a Lender's Stock Price," *American Banker,* September 10, 1998, p. 20.

—Ed Dinger

RIETER

Rieter Holding AG

Schlosstalstrasse 43
CH-8406 Winterthur
Zurich
Switzerland
Telephone: (+41) 52-208-71-71
Fax: (+41) 52-208-70-60
Web site: http://www.rieter.com

Public Company
Incorporated: 1985 as Rieter Holding Ltd
Employees: 12,232
Sales: CHF 2.93 billion ($1.82 billion) (2000)
Stock Exchanges: Swiss
NAIC: 333292 Textile Machinery Manufacturing

Switzerland's Rieter Holding AG is the world's second largest manufacturer of textile machinery, behind fellow Swiss company Sulzer AG. Rieter Holding has also extended its expertise into the automotive market, manufacturing noise control, interior, and insulation systems for the automobile industry. These two operations make up the company's two primary divisions, Rieter Textile Systems and Rieter Automotive Systems. While textile machinery represents the company's historical base, automotive systems have quickly gained the strongest share of the company's sales, at more than 65 percent of Rieter's 2000 sales of CHF 2.9 billion ($1.8 billion). Under CEO Kurt Feller, the company has expanded aggressively in the late 1990s and early 2000s, helping to lead a consolidation of the worldwide textile machinery manufacturing industry.

Swiss Industrial Pioneer in the 18th Century

Johann Jacob Rieter was 20 years old when he began trading spices in his Winterthur, Switzerland home, joining a partnership in the 1780s. By 1795, Rieter had set up his own full-fledged business, extending his trading activities beyond spices into cotton and other products. Cotton soon became one of Rieter's most important products, and particularly English cotton—which, produced by the new mechanical methods that were to spark the Industrial Revolution—had become coveted throughout the European continent. Toward the turn of the century, Rieter was joined by son Heinrich, who took over as head of the family business in 1810.

In the early decades of the 19th century the cotton supplies were cut short by the political turmoil of the time. Rieter and other Swiss traders turned toward spinning their own cotton, importing English-made machinery and setting up their own spinning mills. Rieter went into the spinning business in 1812, setting up its first mill in Winterthur. By then, Rieter had ended its trading business to concentrate wholly on building and operating spinning mills. The company established its most important mill in 1825, in Niedertöss. That mill also included a mechanical workshop for maintaining the company's English-made machinery. From there, Rieter was to grow into one of the world leaders in textile machinery manufacture.

Typical mills of the day used waterpower to drive the machinery. Rieter was among the first to adapt the new steam engines as a power source. In 1833, the company bought the former convent at Töss and soon transferred its mechanical workshops there. As its various workshops grew, Rieter's mechanical production shifted from the forging of replacement parts to the manufacture of entire mills. Rieter also began to produce spinning mills for other textile factories. Soon Rieter's machinery itself became as well-known as the company's yarns—if not more so. The quality of the Rieter mills had the paradoxical effect of creating rivals from Rieter's customers.

By mid-century, as the next generation of Rieters—in the form of Heinrich Rieter, Jr.—took the helm of the family company, the company decided to transform itself from a textile manufacturer to an industrial machinery manufacturer. Between 1835 and 1925, the Rieter company produced a large variety of goods, ranging from spinning machinery to turbines, machine tools, generators and transmissions, as well as railways, trams, motors, bridges, and even rifles. This diversification was necessary because of extreme fluctuations in demand for the company's spinning machines. The company also developed a broad range of textile-related machinery, such as embroidery machines and doubling and winding machines. As early as 1854, the company was quoted as claiming, "We have equipped ourselves to build steam engines, water wheels,

---

Company Perspectives:

"Comfort thanks to Rieter" is the core statement of Rieter's vision. Rieter aims with its products and services to contribute to people's well-being. Product development therefore focuses on the preferences of the end-users. The yarn produced on Rieter machines is intended to provide clothing, home textiles, sportswear and industrial fabrics with outstanding properties. Car drivers and passengers should feel comfortable, in a pleasant interior and shielded against noise. Rieter also aims to provide comfort for its immediate customers through products which are easy to handle, maintain and install. Rieter believes in development through partnership in order to be able to satisfy these needs. Communication takes high priority.

Rieter's vision is based on three objectives: delight your customers; enjoy your work; fight for joint profits. This means: Rieter can only be successful as a company if it exceeds its customers' expectations, if it creates long-term added value for its shareholders, and if its employees derive satisfaction from their work.

---

drives, etc.; in short, everything coming under the heading of heavy engineering.''

Indeed, the company scored a number of industrial successes, such as the construction of Switzerland's first passenger aerial cableway, completed in Schaffhausen in 1866. Turbines were another important product for the company in the second half of the century, as well as locomotive construction. By the end of the 19th century, Rieter was also building electric power stations. In 1905, the company won the contract to build the Vesuvius Railway. By then, the firm had reorganized as a public limited company and was under the direction of the last Rieter family member to head the company, Benno Rieter, who remained as chairman until 1925.

Focus on Spinning Machines in the 20th Century

Rieter shed its diversified manufacturing operations during a reorganization in 1914. At the same time, the company spun off its profitable spinning mill operations into a new independent company, Spinnerei und Zwirneri Niedertöss AG. From 1915 on Rieter's focus returned to the manufacture of spinning machine systems. The new concentration on a single product line enabled Rieter to invest in developing its designs, introducing better spinning frames, and building the Rieter name as among the most prominent of European spinning machinery manufacturers. Another triumph came in 1931, when the company introduced its first machines capable of spinning from man-made fibers.

At the end of World War II, Rieter and the Swiss spinning machine manufacturing industry as a whole were among the few in Europe left undamaged by the war. The company now engaged in a modernization of its facilities and technologies, taking a leading position in the introduction of new processes and designs. In 1949, the company began producing machinery for the production of continuous man-made fibers and filament processing. Rieter also began to introduce automated systems, beginning in 1947.

Rieter had remained linked to its Switzerland base, expanding in 1947 with the acquisition of Gebrüder Mägerle GmbH. In the 1950s, the company began to expand internationally, buying Famatex in Italy in 1948, and then opening a subsidiary in Arlington, Virginia, in 1951. That subsidiary moved its headquarters to Spartanburg, South Carolina, in 1963. By then, the company had also turned to India, granting a license to that country's Lakshmi to produce Rieter machines in 1962 and helping that company build its works in Coimbatore in 1966.

In 1967, the company entered a joint venture with Geilinger Stahlbau. The company next turned to South America, investing in Buenos Aires' Coghlan SA as a way to get past Argentinean import restrictions. Closer to home, the company acquired Schaltag AG of Effretikon, Switzerland, and in 1973 added Maschinenfabrik Remlingen of Germany.

The acquisition of Ernest Scragg & Sons Ltd. in the United Kingdom marked the beginning of a new phase in Rieter's growth. Renamed Rieter-Scragg Ltd., the subsidiary reinforced Rieter's expertise in the production of machinery for man-made textiles with Scragg's expertise in fine texturing machines for man-made filaments. The Scragg acquisition marked the first of many for Rieter. In 1984, the company acquired fellow Swiss company Unikeller AG, which specialized in noise control and thermal installation systems for the automotive market—marking Rieter's entry into this field. The company brought this acquisition under its newly formed Unikeller division, later to be regrouped as Rieter Automobile Systems.

By 1985, Rieter reorganized its textile operations into its two primary areas—staple and continuous fibers. These divisions were soon replaced by the dual textile divisions of spinning systems (staple fibers) and chemical fibers, a structure that remained in place into the mid-1990s, when the company's textile activities were brought under the Rieter Textile Systems division. In 1985, the company adopted the new name of Rieter Holding Ltd., with a listing on the Zurich stock exchange.

External Expansion in the 1990s

A major acquisition came in 1987 when the company acquired rival Germany-based textile machinery manufacturer Schubert & Salzer GmbH, which had been hard hit by a slump in the staple fiber market during that decade. The company's next major acquisition came in 1992, when it picked up Automatik-Apparate-Maschinenbau, based in Grossostheim, Germany, which was then renamed Rieter-Automatik. This acquisition reinforced the company's synthetic fiber operations.

In 1994, Rieter acquired Firth Furnishing Ltd., based in the United Kingdom, a maker of carpeting for automobiles, which, added to the Unikeller division, formed the basis of the company's Rieter Automotive Systems division, inaugurated in 1995. The company, seeking to even out its textile machine systems' cyclical exposure, stepped up the development of its Automotive Systems division in the second half of the decade, building those sales to equal its textile machinery sales.

In 1995 the company made an important acquisition in the United States, that of Globe Industries, Inc., a company with a complementary array of products located close to the heart of

Key Dates:

1795: Johann Jacob Rieter begins trading business, with an emphasis on cotton.
1815: Company begins production of textile machinery.
1835: Company diversifies into industrial manufacturing.
1915: Rieter returns to a focus on textile machinery.
1931: Company introduces man-made fiber machinery.
1985: Company reorganizes as Rieter Holding Ltd.
1995: U.S.-based Globe Industries, an important supplier to the American automotive industry, is acquired for $160 million.
2001: Rieter acquires the textile machinery operations of Germany's Suessen Group, and thereby becomes the world's leading supplier of spare parts and other components to the textile machinery market.

the American automotive industry. This acquisition, made for $160 million, was boosted with another U.S. expansion two years later, through a joint venture with Pennsylvania's Magee to manufacture car carpets.

Closer to home, Rieter acquired the Czech Republic's Elitex, adding that company's rotor spinning machines, in 1994, then strengthened its European automotive textiles operations with the purchase of Fimit SpA in Italy, in 1996. In South America, the company acquired Brazil's Ello Ltda., leader in Brazil's automotive acoustic, interior trim, and thermal insulation systems markets. A year later, the company entered a joint venture with longtime associate Lakshmi, creating Rieter-LMW Machinery Ltd. in India.

The company pursued further international growth, now with the opening of new manufacturing facilities in Poland, Turkey, and South Africa in 1998. Yet in that year a downturn in worldwide demand for the company's core textile machinery products placed Rieter under pressure. While the company weathered the drop in orders, which picked up only toward the end of 1999, it began to formulate plans to protect itself further from such industrial cycles by extending its textile machinery expertise into the market for spare parts and service and at the same time broadening its range of textile systems to include nonwovens machinery manufacture and glass fiber twisting machinery. This latter goal was partly achieved in 2000 with the acquisition of France's ICBT Group, the leader in its domestic market.

Rieter's move into the spare parts market came in March 2001 when the company announced its agreement to acquire Germany's Suessen Group's textile machinery operations. That purchase, to be made in stages, transformed Rieter into the world's leading supplier of spare parts and other components to the textile machinery market. By then, too, Rieter had boosted itself to the number two position in the global market for textile machinery, behind fellow Swiss firm Sulzer. At the same time, the company had staked out a prime position in its automotive components niche.

Principal Subsidiaries

Magee Rieter Automotive Systems (U.S.A.); Maschinenfabrik Rieter AG; Rieter Asia (Hong Kong) Ltd.; Rieter Asia (Taiwan) Ltd.; Rieter Automatik GmbH (Germany); Rieter Automotive Argentina SA (95%); Rieter Automotive Belgium NV; Rieter Automotive France SA; Rieter Automotive Germany GmbH; Rieter Automotive Great Britain Ltd.; Rieter Automotive Heatshields AG; Rieter Automotive North America, Inc. (U.S.A.); Rieter Automotive Systems AG; Rieter Componentes para Veiculos Lda. (Portugal; 87%); Rieter Corporation; Rieter Elitex a.s. (Czech Republic); Rieter ICBT; (U.S.A.); Rieter India Pvt. Ltd.; Rieter Italiana Srl; Rieter Management AG; Rieter-Ello Artefatos de Fibras Textis Ltda. (Brazil); Saifa-Keller SA (Spain; 49%); Rieter-Scragg Ltd (U.K.).; Rieter Textile Systems; Schaltag AG; Temkom AG; UGN, Inc.

Principal Divisions

Rieter Textile Systems; Rieter Automotive Systems.

Principal Competitors

AGIV-AG für Industrie und Verkehrswesen; Collins & Aikman Corporation; Foamex International Inc.; Johnson Controls, Inc.; Lear Corporation; Saurer AG; Scholler Textil; Somet Weave Tech SpA; Speizman Industries, Inc.; Sulzer Ltd; Textron Inc.

Further Reading

Furrer, Alfred J., *Rieter's 200 Years: 1795–1995*, Meilen: Association for Historical Research in Economics, 1995.
Isaacs, McAllister, III, "Swiss Textile Suppliers Build on Tradition," *Textile World*, August 1, 1994, p. 36.
"Rieter Buys Textile Machinery Activities from Suessen," *Reuters*, March 29, 2001.
"Rieter Sees Tough 2001, Shares Steady," *Reuters*, April 11, 2001.

—M. L. Cohen

Right Management Consultants, Inc.

1818 Market Street
Philadelphia, Pennsylvania 19103-3614
U.S.A.
Telephone: (215) 988-1588
Toll Free: (800) 237-4448
Fax: (215) 988-9112
Web site: http://www.right.com

Public Company
Incorporated: 1980
Employees: 1,702
Sales: $184.25 million (2000)
Stock Exchanges: NASDAQ
Ticker Symbol: RMCI
NAIC: 54161 Management Consulting Services; 541612
    Human Resources & Executive Search Consulting

When a company's workers are "laid off," the rank and file may head for an employment agency (as well as the unemployment office), but the executives very likely are sent to a firm that specializes in "outplacement services." This puts the "dehired" party off premises but presumably focused on a job search rather than a lawsuit or vindictive whistle blowing. Right Management Consultants, Inc. is the largest firm worldwide—and the only publicly traded one—in the outplacement services field, which it prefers to call the "career transition services industry." The company's fees for its services, which typically last six months to a year, are paid exclusively by the employer, and it does not provide its services to employees who are not sponsored by employers. In other words, Right Management Consultants is neither an employment agency nor a "retail" career consulting firm open to all. The company also provides management consulting services in the form of leadership development, organizational performance, and employee management. It is structured into five geographic groups and has more than 200 company-owned and franchised offices worldwide, in every populated continent except Africa.

Starting Out in the 1980s

Frank Louchheim was manager of outplacement for Bernard Haldane Associates, Inc., a Philadelphia-based career-counseling firm when he founded—with three others—Right Management Consultants in 1980 and became its chairman, president, and chief executive officer. The moment was propitious, for the nation was entering one of its most severe recessions. By the spring of 1982 one-third of the 500 biggest U.S. companies, and two-thirds of the biggest 100, in terms of sales, were believed to be using outplacement specialists. The 1982 edition of a directory of outplacement firms found 82 in existence, of which more than two-thirds were formed in the 1970s. Most were charging as their fee 15 percent of the dehired individual's annual salary. Others billed on an hourly basis at $60 to $100 per hour.

Doing business under the name "Right Associates," Right Management Consultants started out on a shoestring, with the four founders operating in different cities and receiving compensation in the form of commissions because there was not enough business volume to pay salaries. The firm developed into a national network by recruiting experienced, entrepreneurial managers with the authority to run local offices as they saw fit. They received a modest base salary for managing the office, another one for time actually spent counseling clients, and a commission based on the office's sales. Each manager was assigned an operating-profit target and given a bonus of 10 percent of the profit for meeting the target, plus an extra percentage point, with a maximum of 20 percent, for every percentage point of profit over the target. The successful office manager also was awarded stock options after a year. Similarly, the skeleton corporate staff at the Philadelphia headquarters received compensation in the form of incentive bonuses as well as salary.

Right Management Consultants operated on a franchised basis as well. Its first office outside Philadelphia, in Houston, was such an "affiliate" until 1984, when it was acquired as a company office. In 1981 Right Management opened company offices in Baltimore and Chicago, as well as three in the New York City metropolitan area. It also opened affiliated offices in Boston, Detroit, Fort Lauderdale, Los Angeles, Miami, Providence, and

Company Perspectives:

Right Management Consultants is an international career management and human resources consulting firm dedicated to helping its clients manage the human side of change.

Founded in 1980, Right Management Consultants quickly became a leader in the outplacement industry. Today, Right provides a full spectrum of services to meet the workforce management needs of client organizations and their employees, ranging from individual coaching to career management assignments to the design and implementation of large-scale organizational change initiatives.

San Francisco in 1982. That year the company earned a nominal $1 in net income on total revenues of $2.25 million.

By the end of 1986 Right Management Consultants had 13 company offices in North America and 23 more operated by 14 affiliates. There was also an affiliate in Paris. Revenues and net income rose each year, reaching $11.92 million and $776,000, respectively, in 1986. That year 75 percent of revenue came from providing outplacement services on a one-on-one basis. These included such job-hunt services as career counseling, resume writing, and preparing and rehearsing for interviews. They also included advice to the employer on conducting the termination interview, terms of severance pay and other termination benefits, and identification of termination-related issues for which the employer might wish to seek legal counsel. Right Management's remaining source of revenue came from outplacement consulting in group contexts for companies making group reductions in their workforce. Group programs had, as their core, seminars for generally up to 12 employees per group, in sessions extending over two to five days. The company made its initial public offering of stock in 1986, garnering net proceeds of $3.68 million. Louchheim remained the largest shareholder, with 17 percent of the common stock.

Between 1987 and 1990 Right Management Consultants paid $7.28 million for ten acquisitions. These included THinc Consulting Group International, Inc., which had offices in five U.S. cities and a British subsidiary; R.S.F. Gestion de Carriere; Compass Inc.; Executive Services Associates, Inc.; Outplacement Resources Group, San Diego Human Resources; and four affiliates, of which two were in the United States and two in Canada. In Europe, the company acquired its Paris affiliate in 1988 and established a French subsidiary. A company-owned London office was established in 1987. Affiliates opened offices in Birmingham, England; Brussels; Frankfurt, Germany; Geneva; Lyons, France; and Oslo.

By 1989 Right Management Consultants was the second largest firm in a field so competitive that a rate war was underway. The standard fee of 15 percent of the annual gross pay of a dehired executive was reported to be likely to apply to base pay only, and even that charge was said to be subject to a volume discount. The two- or three-day group seminar was selling for as low as $1,200 a day or even less, compared with the previous standard of $1,500. But Right Management was doing fine. Revenues rose by about half, to $34.31 million in 1990, and net

income almost doubled, to $2.33 million. The company now had 3,500 corporate customers, served by 74 offices in North America and Western Europe, of which 37 were operated by 19 affiliates.

Looking Beyond Outplacement in the 1990s

The revenues of Right Management Consultants continued to grow each year during the first half of the 1990s, reaching $114 million in 1995. Net income rose each year except 1992, reaching $7.82 million in 1995, when the number of offices came to 126. These were now predominantly company offices (89) rather than franchised ones. Between 1991 and 1995 Right Management Consultants paid $20.69 million for 11 acquisitions. These included Clark & Kevin Associates, Inc.; Green and Herring Job Search Services, Inc.; Jannotta Bray & Associates Inc.; LM&P, a French firm; and Sunbelt Career Development Corp. They also included purchased affiliate offices in Boston; Cupertino, California; and North and South Carolina. Louchheim stepped down as chief executive officer in 1991 and was succeeded by Stanley Tilton, the firm's president and chief operating officer. A year later he was succeeded by Richard Pinola, formerly president and chief operating officer of Penn Mutual Life Insurance Co. Pinola may have been Right Management's biggest success story. After parting company with Penn Mutual—for reasons he refused to discuss—he entered the Right Management outplacement program and within months went to work as the company's chief.

By 1993 Right Management Consultants had expanded its business by offering human resources services in areas other than outplacement. These services were intended to assist employers and their employees in identifying and improving areas of job performance; refining communication skills and improving employee productivity; and assisting companies in encouraging and supporting dual-career families to accept moves by providing spouse employment assistance upon transfer of employment. Other services were designed to enhance the abilities of executives and managers to evaluate employees' performance when making employment and promotion decisions.

Right Management Consultants earned record net income of $9.7 million in 1996 on revenues of $125 million. Revenues were stagnant the following year and, though they continued their march upwards for the rest of the decade, net income declined. With the strong U.S. economy reducing demand for outplacement counseling, the company saw the average length of its contracts decrease from nine to 12 months to three to six months. One response by Right Management was to make organizational consulting a formal sector of its business. The firm entered this field in 1996 with the acquisition of People Tech Consulting Inc., a Toronto-based company. Although companies were not laying off as many of their employees as in the past, they were engaging in mergers and acquisitions and making other changes that required calling in human resources consultants. Consulting activities included assessing whether employees were suited to their jobs and evaluating managerial talent. One of Right Management's assessment tools, Team 360, evaluated employees by querying the people who worked alongside, above, and below them.

In other parts of the world, especially Asia, the economy was not as strong. By focusing on international business, the company raised its share of revenues from outside North America to 28 percent in 1998, compared to only half as much in early 1997. By 1999 Pinola and the company's two other highest officials were spending about 70 percent of their time outside Philadelphia, visiting clients and executives in places as distant as Singapore. Company executives once more began receiving raises and bonuses, which had been suspended following a 78 percent decline in net income in 1997. "The outplacement business is already substantial," President and COO John J. Gavin told Peg Brickley of the *Philadelphia Business Journal.* "But it is only one of the opportunities. All the things driven by pressure on corporate earnings—attention to productivity, merger integration efficiency—present other opportunities."

Right Management Consultants continued to add companies during this period. Between 1996 and 2000 the company made 27 acquisitions at a cost of $68.17 million. Among these were a London-based firm, Cavendish Partners, Inc.; a French firm, Groupe ARJ; two Belgian companies, Jouret Management Center and N.V. Claessens Belgium S.A.; and a controlling interest in Saad Fellipelli/Coaching of Brazil and in Davidson & Associates, Pty., Ltd., with operations in 11 locations throughout Australia, New Zealand, Singapore, and Hong Kong. The company also took a stake in Way Station, Japan's second largest outplacement firm, and raised this stake to 51 percent in 2000. In the United States, acquisitions included Atlanta Consulting Group; Berkshire Consulting Services; Career Development Group Inc.; Career Dynamics, Inc.; Chapel Stowell, Inc.; Corporate Resource Group; Manus; Michael D. McKee & Associates; Nelson, O'Connor & Associates; Teams, Inc.; and Transition Management, Inc. It also purchased its former affiliates in St. Louis; Knoxville, Tennessee; and Richmond, Virginia. By the spring of 2001 the company had bought back all but five of its affiliates.

The pace of acquisitions continued unabated in the first quarter of 2001. Right Management Associates purchased two Norwegian consulting firms and signed a letter of intent to acquire a company in Palo Alto, California. The acquisitions added about $9 million in annual income. Company revenues increased about 28 percent in the first quarter of 2001, as compared to the same period in 2000. Net income rose 34 percent during this period.

Right Management Consultants in 2000

Right Management Consultants enjoyed net revenues of $184.25 million in 2000, of which international operations ac-

counted for 35 percent and human resources consulting comprised about 21 percent, compared to only 9 percent in 1997. Net income amounted to $8.46 million during the year after discounting a loss of $11.41 million reflecting a one-time accounting charge. The company's largest shareholders in March 2001 were FMR Corp., 12 percent; Pinola, 11 percent; and T. Rowe Price Associates, Inc., 9 percent. The long-term debt was $56.97 million at the end of 2000.

Right Management Consultants' career transition, or outplacement, business, accounted for about 79 percent of total revenue in 2000. The company provided these services to about 5,000 companies during the year, including a majority of the *Fortune* 500. Approximately 78 percent of the revenue in this sector came from individual outplacement services. These included advice to the employer on conducting the termination interview, terms of severance pay, and other termination benefits. Services by the company to terminated employees included assistance in handling the initial difficulties of termination; identifying continuing career goals and options and planning an alternative career; aiding in developing skills for the search for a new job, such as resume writing, effective networking, identifying and researching types of potential employers, and preparing and rehearsing for interviews; continuing consulting and motivation throughout the job-search campaign; assessing new-employment offers and methods of accepting such offers; and, where appropriate, consulting with the employee's spouse regarding the stresses of the employment search and the positive role the spouse may play in all aspects of the new job search, as well as assisting with financial planning and health maintenance.

Group outplacement services accounted for about 22 percent of the revenue generated by Right Management Consultants from its career transition services. These one-to-five-day seminars for generally up to 12 employees per group were often preceded or followed by individual counseling. In addition, the company offered to assist corporate clients engaged in a large-scale reduction in force. Career centers typically served groups of 100 or more individuals and were operated for a predetermined time period, usually ranging anywhere from four to 12 months.

The remaining 21 percent of Right Management Consultants' revenue in 2000 came from organizational consulting services to assist organizations and their employees. These services focused on the following: leadership development through executive coaching and feedback-rich customized programs; organizational development—building competencies by identifying the skills, knowledge, and personal characteristics that determine success in a given company, using these competencies to align human-resource systems with strategy; and talent management—growing talent by attracting, motivating, and retaining the best people in a highly competitive talent marketplace.

Principal Subsidiaries

Key Management Strategies, Inc.; Right ARJ Management Consultants, SA (France); Right Associates, Ltd. (U.K.); Right D&A Pty. Ltd. (Australia; 51%); Right Human Resources, Inc. (Canada); Right License Holding, Inc.; Teams International, LLC (51%); Way Station, Inc. (Japan; 51%).

Principal Competitors

Challenger Gray and Christmas Inc.; Drake Beam Morin Inc.; Lee Hecht Harrison Inc.

Further Reading

Amend, Patricia, "Right Associates: 28 Entrepreneurs," *Inc.,* September 1985, p. 74.

Brammer, Rhonda, "The Right Stuff?" *Barron's,* December 29, 1997, p. 18.

Brickley, Peg, "Right Management Execs Advance," *Philadelphia Business Journal,* January 8, 1999, pp. 3+.

Flanagan, William G., "Viva Unemployment," *Forbes,* May 10, 1982, pp. 200–01.

Gotlieb, Andy, "Downturn Suits Right Just Fine," *Philadelphia Business Journal,* May 4, 2001, p. 1.

Hill, Miriam, "Makeover Revitalizing Human-Resources Consulting Company," *Philadelphia Inquirer,* March 30, 1999, p. C5.

Main, Jeremy, "Look Who Needs Outplacement," *Fortune,* October 9, 1989, pp. 85, 88, 92.

—Robert Halasz

RMH Teleservices, Inc.

40 Morris Avenue
Bryn Mawr, Pennsylvania 19010
U.S.A.
Telephone: (610) 520-5300
Toll Free: (800) 367-5733
Fax: (610) 520-5352
Web site: http://www.rmhteleservices.com

Public Company
Incorporated: 1983
Employees: 5,489
Sales: $132.1 million (2000)
Stock Exchanges: NASDAQ
Ticker Symbol: RMHT
NAIC: 561422 Telemarketing Bureaus

RMH Teleservices, Inc. is a telemarketing and customer service company with 21 call centers in the United States and Canada. Its client list includes *Fortune* 500 firms and smaller businesses in many industries but primarily in telecommunications, financial services, and insurance. RMH is a leader in telemarketing and was one of the first firms in the industry to become a publicly traded company. RMH offers inbound, outbound, e-commerce, and technology processing for its clients.

Founding of RMH: Early 1980s

RMH Teleservices, Inc. was founded in 1983 by Raymond J. and MarySue Lucci Hansell. The husband-and-wife team used their collective experience to form the new venture. MarySue Lucci Hansell had the industry background with experience in marketing, training, and customer service for Colonial Penn Insurance Co. Her husband, Raymond, had sales and management experience with his former position in the computer industry. Together, they dispelled myths about couples working together and grew the company into a national corporation.

The real spark behind the company's founding was MarySue Lucci Hansell, who embraced the telemarketing industry when she experienced a telephone sales job while in college. It was Raymond, however, who became the company's CEO, with MarySue filling the COO duties. The couple aggressively grew the company in its home base of the Bryn Mawr suburb of Philadelphia, Pennsylvania. As they expanded, the Hansells selected New Jersey as the next state to target and successfully extended call centers in both states.

Growth Leading to Public Offering in the 1990s

In the 1990s, Raymond and MarySue Hansell focused on further growing their company. They soon found, however, that more capital and a partner would be the tools it would take to bring the company to the next level. In May 1996, the RMH founders sold 8.5 million shares to Advanta Partners, a venture capital subsidiary of Advanta Corporation. In exchange for the shares, the Hansells received $16 million in cash and $8.6 million in other compensation. Part of the agreement with Advanta, as it was now part-owner in RMH, was to take the company public. The Hansells were offered a bonus to do so within six months.

In September 1996, the Hansells kept their part of the agreement, and RMH Teleservices made its initial public offering (IPO). In that same year, two other Philadelphia-area telemarketers became public companies as well. The IPOs were part of a larger trend in telemarketing that was identified as industry maturity by investors. Whereas once telemarketing companies were not prime investment picks, the mid-1990s saw a rise in interest. Another key factor in the increasing appeal of the industry was that telemarketing was one function that a company could easily outsource, and outsourcing in the 1990s was a growing trend.

RMH Teleservices' public offering on the NASDAQ involved 2.8 million shares at $12.50 per share. The stock actually closed at $15 per share, constituting a 20 percent gain on the first day of trading. The company announced plans to use the earnings to pay off bank loans and employ as working capital. After the IPO, the Hansells owned 23 percent of the company and Advanta Partners owned 32 percent, with the remainder publicly held. At the time of the IPO, RMH operated eight call centers in Pennsylvania and New Jersey.

Company Perspectives:

While providing outstanding customer support is a goal of many businesses, at RMH Teleservices, it's our only business. Since 1983, RMH Teleservices has been distinguishing itself as the nation's premier provider of outsourced company relationship management programs. Our program partners not only include industry leaders but also some of the largest multinational corporations. These firms have entrusted us with their names as well as their most important assets, their customers. Through these unique relationships we have developed methodologies which enable us to deliver lower costs, increased operational efficiency, improved customer experience, greater return on investment and significant quality improvements by providing the highest quality outsourced customer relationship management in the teleservices industry.

Once RMH Teleservices became publicly owned, the company wasted no time in moving forward with expansion plans. One month after the IPO, RMH opened its ninth call center, which was planned for a staff of 80 telemarketers, in Harrisburg, Pennsylvania. "The fundamentals of the Company and the industry dynamics remain strong and we continue to be optimistic with regard to the future," said CEO Raymond Hansell about the call center opening.

Call center openings in York, Pennsylvania, and Delran, New Jersey, followed in 1997 and helped make RMH the 16th largest outbound telemarketing firm in the nation. Aside from the growth in actual centers, RMH also was experiencing growth due to new technology tools. Database management, combined with sophisticated dialing equipment, helped put more information in front of telemarketers.

That increase in information, according to CEO Raymond Hansell, helped create more successful calling programs and resulted in growth for the company. "Because of the higher degree of accuracy, there are more campaigns launched, but they're more focused," he stated in an article in the *Philadelphia Business Journal* in 1997. "So much is automated now. You can know who buys what, where they are and who is most likely to buy what you're selling."

Later in 1997, the founding couple repurchased 20,000 shares of stock on the open market; the stock price, at $5.25 per share, had fallen considerably since its $12.50 opening in 1996. In 1998, as both Raymond and MarySue Lucci Hansell stepped down from active duties, the board elected John A. Fellows as the company's new CEO.

RMH and its partial owner Advanta Partners collaborated in 1999 to form a new joint venture, 365biz.com, to help provide Internet services to small and medium-sized businesses with a web presence. For a low price, the company was designed to develop and host e-commerce web sites and market them to Internet search engines.

2000: Change of Ownership for RMH Teleservices

In 2000, RMH Teleservices experienced another changing of the guard. Although the CEO duties were now held by John

A. Fellows, the Hansells, along with Advanta Partners, still owned much of the company. That changed in March when R-T Investors LC purchased 49 percent of the shares of the company—1.41 million shares from the Hansells and 2.6 million shares from Advanta Partners, LP.

R-T Investors, a company owned by the Jensen family of Hurst, Texas, was now the majority stockholder of RMH, and its president, Jeff Jensen, joined RMH's board of directors as part of the purchase agreement. "RT's 49 percent investment in RMH Teleservices speaks clearly of the significant growth potential we see for the Company, and reflects our confidence in the abilities of the management team to capitalize on that potential," said Jensen. "Our family has known John Fellows, CEO of RMH Teleservices, for several years, both professionally and personally, and has the deepest respect for his business acumen and integrity. We also share with John and his team their vision that there are vast opportunities emerging in e-commerce customer service which RMH Teleservices is now targeting."

At the time of the R-T stock purchase, RMH operated 20 facilities in the United States and Canada. RMH CEO John Fellows, who purchased 101,315 shares of stock at the same time, said, "We are very pleased that RT has become a major investor in the Company. Its action demonstrates confidence in RMH Teleservices' future growth and profitability. We anticipate that RT's commitment will be a catalyst for increasing shareholder values."

One of the key strategies for RMH in 2000 was to utilize new technology in the business. One way the company responded to new opportunities was to begin to equip its workstations so that employees could interact with callers on the phone or on the Web. Approximately 500 of the 3,450 workstations were equipped to allow for dual contact in early 2000. The company also continued its investment in 365biz.com, and furthered its presence in the Canadian market.

The company's ownership change and aggressive use of new technology resulted in record-setting third quarter 2000 results. Revenues for the period increased 77 percent and net income increased 104 percent. "Our business continues to achieve record results," said CEO John Fellows. "The strong revenue increase for the quarter was generated from new customers as well as from existing blue-chip customers. We anticipate even greater levels of business in the next few quarters and plan to add a significant amount of capacity in the months ahead. RMH is rapidly gaining scale in the customer relationship management industry."

RMH continued its inclusion of new technology by announcing in 2000 that it would partner with Commerce.TV, a company on the leading edge in the television commerce industry. Commerce.TV, as part of the arrangement, agreed to use RMH exclusively for its inbound customer registration and support of its products.

Growth continued on all fronts for the company in 2000. RMH signed a multiyear agreement with AT&T Corp. and Microsoft Corporation in 2000 to provide inbound customer management for the two companies. The Canadian offices continued to grow with the opening of the company's eighth

Key Dates:

1983: Raymond J. and MarySue Lucci Hansell found RMH Teleservices.
1996: Founders sell 8.5 million shares in company to Advanta Partners, a venture capital subsidiary of Advanta Corporation; company makes initial public offering on NASDAQ exchange.
1998: RMH names John Fellows as CEO.
1999: Company helps create 365biz.com.
2000: Advanta and the Hansells sell their shares, collectively 49 percent of the company, to R-T Investors LC.
2001: R-T Investors increases its RMH stake to 60 percent.

Canadian location on Vancouver Island. "The fourth quarter capped an exciting fiscal 2000 for RMH Teleservices, Inc.," said CEO John Fellows at the end of the year. "We generated record revenues and posted strong earnings performance in the fourth quarter and in the fiscal year. We continued to diversify our revenue base as we experienced growth from clients in all of our principal industry verticals—telecommunications, financial services, and insurance."

New Challenges Ahead in 2001 and Beyond

In April 2001, R-T Investors increased their holdings in RMH Teleservices by purchasing 1.8 million shares of common stock and increasing their ownership to 60 percent. At the time of the purchase, the stock price was $5.50 per share. The company announced that it would use the funds to continue its expansion and develop operations infrastructure. Despite the profit warnings and one-time charges announced in January, the first quarter of 2001 showed a revenue increase of 37 percent.

The company also focused on diversification, adding more technology customers to its client list, which had focused heav-ily on insurance and telecommunications. RMH Teleservices had evolved from its founding in 1983 to a more sophisticated, public company focused on expanding markets and developing technology.

Principal Subsidiaries

Teleservices Management Co.; Teleservices Technology Co.

Principal Competitors

Convergys Corporation; Sitel Corp.; TeleTech Holdings; West Corporation.

Further Reading

Bean, Joanna, "Pennsylvania-Based Firm to Close Colorado Springs, Colo., Call Center," *Gazette* (Colorado Springs), September 23, 1999.

Benjamin, Jeff, "Streetwise: Phone Is Ringing for RMH Centers," *Investment News,* August 21, 2000, p. 21.

Brooke, Bob, "16 Companies Go Public in a Year Like No Other," *Philadelphia Business Journal,* February 21, 1997.

Feiler, Jeremy, "RMH Site Target of Labor Organizing," *Philadelphia Business Journal,* June 29, 2001, p. 3.

Fitzgibbon, John, "IPO Market: Moonshots Are Back!," *IPO Reporter,* September 23, 1996.

Hals, Tom, "Booming Telemarketing Industry Leads Three Local Firms to IPOs," *Philadelphia Business Journal,* August 2, 1996, p. 6.

Kasrel, Deni, "Telemarketing Dials Up Growth," *Philadelphia Business Journal,* August 1, 1997.

Key, Peter, "Add to Vocab: Ecount, for Your Online Gifts," *Philadelphia Business Journal,* December 10, 1999.

——, "Vote Still Out on RMH Teleservices' Moves," *Philadelphia Business Journal,* May 12, 2000.

Knox, Andrea, "Founders of Bryn Mawr, Pa., Telemarketing Firm Reap Rewards of Success," *Philadelphia Inquirer,* June 29, 1997.

"RMH Founders Buy Back Shares," *Philadelphia Business Journal,* December 1, 1997.

—Melissa Rigney Baxter

Roots Canada Ltd.

1162 Caledonia Road
Toronto, Ontario M6A 2W5
Canada
Telephone: (416) 781-3574
Toll Free: (888) 30-ROOTS
Web site: http://www.roots.com

Private Company
Incorporated: 1973
Employees: 2000
Sales: $170 million (1999 est.)
NAIC: 44811 Men's Clothing Stores; 44812 Women's
   Clothing Stores; 44813 Children's and Infants'
   Clothing Stores; 44814 Family Clothing Stores; 44815
   Clothing Accessories Stores; 44819 Other Clothing
   Stores; 44821 Shoe Stores; 44832 Luggage and
   Leather Goods Stores; 481111 Scheduled Passenger
   Air Transportation

Clothing retailer Roots Canada Ltd.—known universally simply as "Roots"—is a lifestyle marketer inspired by the northern summer camp reminiscences of founders Don Green and Michael Budman. Roots remains a family business: Green's wife, Denyse Tremblay, was one of the company's first salespersons; Budman's wife, Diane Bald, designs the company's retail stores. The vertically integrated company is unique in its ability to handle small runs of custom orders. Its leather business and the fact that nearly all of its products are made in Canada also set it apart. Roots has about 175 stores, almost 60 of them in Asia, and its famous clothing has been donned by heads of state, including former President Bill Clinton and Prince Charles, as well as numerous athletes and entertainers.

Earthy Origins

Although they became famous exploiting the essence of Canadian style, both Don Green's and Michael Budman's roots are in Detroit. Both Budman and Green had fallen in love with Canada while camping at Algonquin Park's Camp Tamakwa;

they moved to Toronto in the late 1960s. In addition, both their fathers were successful Detroit entrepreneurs, giving their future business some hereditary grounding.

The two well-off boys, looking for ways to extend their idyllic existence north of the border, decided to get in on the Earth Shoe craze. Anna Kalso, a Dane, had designed the shoe with a heel lower than the toe to mirror the barefoot posture she admired in Brazilian natives. By 1970, the Earth Shoe was a counterculture footwear smash.

After some discussions about acquiring rights to distribute the Earth Shoe in Canada, Budman and Green began to design their own negative heel shoe. Theirs had a milder incline and less radical design. Geoff Pevere, the "pop culture guru" who published a book-length account of the Roots story in 1998, said the homey shoes capitalized on "anti-fashion." Desert Boot, moccasin, city, and sport variations were soon derived from the original shoe.

Bar mitzvah money and $15,000 borrowed from Green's father provided start-up capital for the venture. Methodically searching for manufacturers through the Yellow Pages, Budman and Green were turned down by footwear giant Bata but soon found a winner.

The Boa Shoe Company was run by a Polish family that had once made boots for Czar Nicholas II. Jan Kowalewski and sons Henry, Richard, Stanley, and Karl agreed to make 120 pairs of the new shoes for Budman and Green, despite the fact that the two hipsters had brought a dog to their inaugural meeting.

Budman and Green then rented an 800-square-foot store on Yonge Street in Toronto for $280 a month. They decided on the name "Roots" to emphasize the "Roots Shoe" as a connection to the earth. The trademark logo soon was created, with a beaver borrowed from the Camp Tamakwa crest. The store moved seven pairs of the shoes, priced at $35 each, on opening day, August 15, 1973.

After another few weeks of modest sales, the Roots team suddenly found people cueing up around the block and signing waiting lists to get a pair of the hot shoes. Soon *People* would call it "the Gucci shoe of the crunchy granola set." The firm opened 75 stores between 1973 and 1975.

In the next couple of years, Budman and Green created a firestorm of publicity that made Roots a household word in Canada. They started by sending free pairs to celebrities such as Paul McCartney, Cher, Elton John, and Canadian Prime Minister Pierre Trudeau. Roots garnered immeasurable exposure when these famous feet carried the shoes into the national press. The company founders also appeared in Roots advertising, further stretching their promotional dollars.

According to Pevere, Roots was worth a million dollars within six months. Budman and Green soon signed an exclusive agreement with their supplier that would last at least another 25 years; within a year the Kowalewski family was making 2,000 pairs of Roots footwear a week.

Unlike the Earth Shoe, advertising for the Roots Shoe was low on claims of specific therapeutic benefits regarding its negative heel. Comfort, style, and craftsmanship were its key selling points. Following the advice of an early designer, Robert Burns, the firm also had begun adding conventional heel shoes to its offerings, as well as clothes and other items made of leather. Roots began outfitting sports teams beginning with the Blue Jays in 1977, opening another enduring line of business.

All of these factors helped cushion the company after the floor fell out of the negative heel fad in 1976. Fortunately, European sales were only just beginning to boom. (Twenty years later, Japan would be the only surviving market for the company's negative heel shoes.) A Detroit doctor was credited with issuing the contravening medical opinion that signaled the end of the craze.

In 1979, a New Jersey manufacturing company also named Roots sued Budman and Green for trademark infringement. The suit kept Roots Canada products out of the United States for nine years and ultimately cost the company $1 million.

New Moves for the 1980s

After excitement over the first shoes had died down, Roots moved on to its true business—selling the nostalgia of summer camp to baby boomers. These dreams were embroidered on sweatshirts, hats, and other accessories, adorned with chenille patches touting the virtues of the great Canadian wilderness in the bonding language of athletics. Most important, Roots sold sweatshirts in the 1980s—a decade that emphasized physical fitness as never before. After a forced retreat from the American market, Roots reentered the United States in 1988.

Launched in 1975, the Roots Beaver Athletic sweatshirt—or "RBA" in company lingo—sold modestly until 1985, when it exploded. More than a million RBAs were produced by early 1990. Inspired by the uniforms of collegiate athletes, the sweatshirt appealed not only to baby boomers' health consciousness, but their desire to belong to teams, wrote Pevere. During the late 1980s, "We went from [being] a shoe company to a clothing company to a lifestyle company to a global company," Roots Vice-President Marshall Myles told a textiles industry trade magazine.

A global recession impacted the company in the early 1990s; however, profits continued to rise after 1991. Some of the ventures that did not work out for the company included a Paris-based fashion magazine and an aborted Colorado ski resort. There was still plenty of good news otherwise. Revenues approached $100 million annually in 1992.

Indian Summer *in 1993*

One of Don Green's buddies from Camp Tamakwa, Mike Binder, produced a movie about his reminiscences there for Disney in 1993. The film, called *Indian Summer,* featured Roots gear prominently, and Roots advertising made the most of the connection. As Geoff Pevere noted, the Disney/Roots collaboration was appropriate, for both companies were dedicated to the myth of never growing up.

As the movie and television industry in Toronto grew, Roots took to producing customized clothing for the industry. This ultimately extended to a variety of world-class television shows, movies, and plays produced elsewhere, including *Forrest Gump, Seinfeld, Pulp Fiction,* and *Phantom of the Opera,* as well as rock tours for the likes of Janet Jackson. The large number of Canadian actors, beginning with Dan Aykroyd and Gilda Radner (one of Green's Tamakwa camping buddies) on the cast of *Saturday Night Live,* already had given Roots easy access to numerous celebrities for years. For example, basketball superstar and Nike spokesman Michael Jordan wore a Roots sweatshirt while hosting the show.

By 1997, there were 95 Roots outlets across Canada, six in the United States, and 15 franchises in Asia. The company had 1,000 employees; 225 of them worked at its leather goods factory, still run by the Kowalewski family, which measured 65,000 square feet. In contrast to other lifestyle brands such as Nike and The Gap, 95 percent of the company's wares were made in Canada.

An Olympic Sensation in 1998

Roots outfitted the Canadian teams for the 1998 Winter Olympics in Nagano, Japan. The distinctive jackets they created were wildly popular, as was the poorboy hat, a kind of oversized beret. Roots also signed endorsement deals with Olympic medal athletes including skater Elvis Stojko.

It took two years for Budman and Green to secure the Olympic uniform contract, but the results were enduring. After the Nagano Olympics, a number of famous figures were seen wearing Roots duds, including Prince Charles and President Bill Clinton, singer Sarah McLachlan, and comedian Rosie

Key Dates:

1973: Roots sprouts from Earth Shoe craze and the shared vision of Don Green and Michael Budman.
1975: Roots Beaver Athletic sweatshirt is launched.
1977: Roots begins outfitting sports teams.
1979: Trademark lawsuit knocks Roots Canada out of U.S. retail market for next nine years.
1993: *Indian Summer* film focuses on Camp Tamakwa, a key inspiration of the company founders.
1998: Roots' poorboy cap steals the show at the Nagano Winter Olympics.
2001: Roots Air takes wing.

O'Donnell. Actor Robin Williams even wore a poorboy cap to the Academy Awards. Green and Budman turned down an offer to sell half the company to clothing giant Dylex Limited.

Roots opened a boutique in the SoHo district of Manhattan in June 1998. Later that summer, Ford Motor Company rolled out its Roots Explorer SUV in Canada, which was equipped with a custom storage bag produced by Roots.

Marshall Myles, a Roots veteran of 25 years, was appointed president and CEO in December 2000. Three months earlier, designer Tu Ly had been picked as the company's creative director.

In 2000, the *Wall Street Journal* reported the firm was planning a five-year, $70 million expansion drive in the United States and Europe. In the works were 25 outlets at resorts such as Vail, Colorado. Other stores were planned as part of a joint venture with an as yet unnamed partner. An initial public offering was even being considered to help fund the expansion costs.

Airborne in 2000

Very few would have imagined the co-branding venture unveiled in June 2000. Roots agreed to take a 20 percent equity stake in Skyservice Airlines Inc., a Canadian start-up carrier that aimed to begin taking on national carrier Air Canada in Toronto, Montreal, and Ottawa. The Roots Air fleet was to feature the Roots beaver on the aircrafts' livery.

Roots was about lifestyle—or choice—ostensibly the antithesis of the airline industry. The airline planned to reach the United States (Los Angeles and New York) by the summer of 2001, bolstering Roots's presence south of the border. The new airline was marketed with the same emphasis on rural Canadian splendor as the clothing stores. ''Business travelers will experience an odd feeling on March 26 (the launch date),'' announced one ad. ''It's called relaxation.'' Appropriately, Roots designed the airline's uniforms including—of course—leather bomber jackets for the pilots.

Roots vitamins were introduced in February 2001 in cooperation with pharmaceutical manufacturer Boehringer Ingelheim. Less surprising than the airline or vitamins announcements was the news that Roots was supplying clothes in support of Toronto's (unsuccessful) bid to host the 2008 Olympics.

Principal Subsidiaries

GreenBud Manufacturing Ltd.; Skyservice Airlines Inc. (20%).

Principal Divisions

Roots Air; Roots Athletics; Roots Home; Roots Baby; Roots Custom Products; Roots Kids; Roots Leathers; Roots Men & Women; Roots Passport; Roots Vision; Roots Vitamins.

Principal Competitors

Club Monaco; Banana Republic Inc.; Eddie Bauer, Inc.; The Gap, Inc.

Further Reading

Barrington, Stephen, ''Roots Reaches for the Sky,'' *Advertising Age,* March 26, 2001, p. 16.
Carlisle, Tamsin, ''Canadian Airline, Clothier Set Launch of a New Carrier,'' *Wall Street Journal,* June 9, 2000, p. A8.
Greenberg, Larry M., ''Marketing the Great White North, Eh? How Two Americans Evoked Quintessential Canada and Plan to Sell It Here,'' *Wall Street Journal,* April 21, 2000, p. B1.
Hutchinson, Brian, ''Merchants of Boom,'' *Canadian Business,* May 1997, pp. 38–48.
King, R.J., ''Grunge Trend Makes Pair of Sole Brothers Well-Heeled,'' *Detroit News,* October 29, 1993, p. E3.
Pevere, Geoff, ''The Roots of Roots,'' *Profit,* October 1, 1998, p. 55.
——, *Team Spirit: A Field Guide to Roots Culture,* Toronto: Doubleday Canada, 1998.
Rabon, Lisa C., ''Roots Behind the Brand,'' *Bobbin,* August 1998, pp. 150–62.
''Roots Defined,'' *Bobbin,* August 1998, pp. 152–56.

—Frederick C. Ingram

Saatchi & Saatchi

375 Hudson Street
New York, New York 10014
U.S.A.
Telephone: (212) 463-2000
Toll Free: (888) 322-6010
Fax: (212) 463-9855
Web site: http://www.saatchi-saatchi.com

Wholly Owned Subsidiary of Publicis Groupe S.A.
Incorporated: 1970
Employees: 5,500
Gross Billings: $7 billion (2000 est.)
NAIC: 541810 Advertising Agencies

One of the most prominent names in the world of advertising, Saatchi & Saatchi provides advertising, marketing, and public relations services through its 152 offices worldwide. With clients such as Procter & Gamble and Toyota, the agency is renowned for its innovative ads. Rowland Communications Worldwide handles the company's PR services. Founded by brothers Charles and Maurice Saatchi in 1970, Saatchi & Saatchi has had a tumultuous history, culminating in its purchase in 2000 by French communications giant Publicis Groupe S.A.

Brash Beginnings

Charles and Maurice Saatchi, celebrities of the British advertising industry, were born in Baghdad in 1943 and 1946, respectively. When persecution of Jews intensified in Iraq in the mid-1940s, their family moved to London. Twenty years later, Charles cut his eyeteeth as a copywriter at the London office of Benton & Bowles. There he met Ross Cramer, and after a couple of years of successful collaboration, the two struck out on their own. In 1967, they opened CramerSaatchi, an advertising consultancy. Rather than take on clients directly, the pair offered their services on a project-by-project basis to ad agencies in need of creative input. By 1970, the firm had gained a reputation as a producer of racy and eye-catching ads, including an ad for Britain's Health Education Council (HEC) that featured a distinctly large-bellied man with the caption, "Would you be more careful if it was you that got pregnant?"

Encouraged by their success, Charles wanted to transform the consultancy into a full-fledged ad agency. Cramer wanted out, so Charles brought on his brother Maurice as his partner. They announced the newly named Saatchi & Saatchi agency in a full-page ad in the *Sunday Times*. Setting the tone for the company for the next decade or so, the brash ad claimed that the agency would do away with account executives and revamp the "dying system" of compensation for billings. Within six months, however, the company had hired six account executives. The brothers also leaked to the press that they would be starting the company with £1 million in billings, a gross overstatement. But the early pronouncements had attracted the attention of the London business world, a necessary step to becoming a leading ad agency—and that was the brothers' goal.

In another unorthodox move, Maurice began cold calling potential clients to drum up business. In Britain, agencies waited to be contacted by clients; to move in on another agency's client was not considered ethical. The Saatchi brothers, however, were not going to be hampered by hidebound tradition. Although the cold calling did not immediately gain the agency new clients, it did get them attention. When an account came up for review, they were more likely to be called in to compete for the business.

The agency fared well from the beginning. Another round of popular ads for the HEC, this time comparing Londoners who smoked to lemmings with a death wish jumping off a cliff, garnered the agency publicity. Their client list grew to include Associated Newspapers and the automobile manufacturer British Leyland. By 1972, the company had profits of £90,000; the following year, profits were up to £100,000.

In 1973, Saatchi & Saatchi made its first ad agency acquisitions. It purchased E.G. Dawes and Motley Advertising, doubling the company's size. By 1975, acquisitions and expanded assignments from existing accounts led to profits of £400,000. The company now counted Schweppes and Gillette-Braun among its clients.

That year, Saatchi & Saatchi merged with the much larger Garland-Compton agency. In a complicated reverse takeover, Saatchi & Saatchi sold its company for shares. When the deal was complete, Saatchi & Saatchi would own 36 percent, Compton would own 26 percent, and the public, 48 percent. The deal pleased all the players: Saatchi & Saatchi would gain Compton's long-established international clients, like Procter & Gamble, and the staid Compton would gain from Saatchi & Saatchi's reputation for creativity. The new Saatchi & Saatchi Garland-Compton was now the fifth largest ad agency in the United Kingdom, with a public listing to fuel further acquisitions.

In 1978 Saatchi & Saatchi began work on a campaign for Margaret Thatcher that would enhance their reputation as a hothouse for creative ideas. The first ad agency to be hired by a political party in Britain (heretofore the parties had relied on pro bono work), Saatchi & Saatchi devised a hard-hitting attack on the Labour Party. Their "Labour's Not Working" ad, which depicted a seemingly endless line of people outside an unemployment office, helped propel Thatcher into the prime minister position. The high-profile campaign also brought international attention to Saatchi & Saatchi, especially in the United States.

Saatchi & Saatchi benefited from the boom in ad spending in the early 1980s. The company gained new business from established clients and added several important new ones: Black & Decker, Allied-Lyons, and Campbell Soup. In 1982 the company gained the British Airways account, and their innovative ads would help turn the ailing airway around. The success and popularity of the ads did not hurt Saatchi & Saatchi's reputation, either. The company's streak of record profits continued.

Frantic Growth Through Acquisitions: 1980s

With their eye set on being the number one ad agency in the world, the Saatchi brothers knew their next step was a presence in the United States. In 1982 Saatchi & Saatchi bought Compton Advertising outright for $57 million, $29 million up front and $28 million to be paid over the next ten years. To fund the deal, the Saatchis issued more stock, reducing their stake in the company to 18 percent.

A similar pattern repeated itself over the next several years, with the Saatchis issuing stock to fund a spree of acquisitions. In 1983, Saatchi & Saatchi purchased the ad agency McCaffrey and McCall, who boasted such clients as ABC, Canadian Club, and Mercedes-Benz. They paid $10 million at once, and another $10 million over three years. The Saatchis, as agreed, let the existing executives run the company independently. After all the payments were made, however, most left the company and accounts began to move to other agencies—also a pattern that would repeat itself. The Saatchis allowed the company to founder as they continued their pursuit of number-one status.

To widen their scope for acquisitions, the brothers decided to branch out into public relations, marketing research, and management consulting. In 1984 they purchased two market research companies, McBer & Company and Yankelovich, Skelly & White. They also spent $100 million, plus a $25

million payout over the next few years, to purchase the Hay Group, a management consultancy. With 100 offices in 27 countries, the Hay Group was Saatchi & Saatchi's largest acquisition yet.

The acquisitions continued unabated, with the company buying 13 firms in 1985. The Saatchis were willing to pay top dollar for small and mid-sized companies—ten times earnings or more was not unusual. In addition to ad agencies, the corporate communication consultant firm Siegel & Gale joined the team, as did the merchandising firm Howard Marlboro Group and the public relations firm Rowland Company. By this time, Saatchi & Saatchi had organized itself into two units: communications services, which included advertising and public relations; and consulting services, which included recruitment, management consulting, and market research. That same year, Maurice Saatchi stepped up as chairman of the board.

The size of Saatchi & Saatchi's deals ballooned in 1986. The company purchased the ad agencies Dancer Fitzgerald Sample for $75 million and Backer & Spielvogel for $56 million down and $45 million to be earned out of profits over the next six years. The biggest acquisition that year, however, both raised the company to its coveted number one position and tipped it over the edge into a downward slide. To purchase the ad agency Ted Bates Worldwide, Saatchi and Saatchi issued 57 million new shares, enough to raise the $450 million purchase price.

An Empire Made and Lost: Late 1980s and Early 1990s

Integrating the newly acquired agency into Saatchi & Saatchi proved tortuous. CEO Simmonds-Gooding, in an effort to bring some order to the jumble of acquisitions, decided to merge all the ad agency subsidiaries into one under the Saatchi & Saatchi name. Clients and agency heads, however, were dead set against the plan. Clients feared conflicts of interest, as one agency tried to promote competing brands. Agency heads resented the interference with their authority. In mid-1987, after months of wrangling, Ted Bates Worldwide merged with Backer & Spielvogel to form Backer Spielvogel Bates. In addition, Dancer Fitzgerald Sample merged with Saatchi & Saatchi Compton to form a U.S. subsidiary, Saatchi & Saatchi DFS Compton. Several frustrated executives soon left, including Simonds-Gooding and Donald Zuckert, the chairman and CEO of Bates.

Saatchi & Saatchi posted record profits in 1987, its 17th consecutive year of growth; however, troubles began to accumulate. The brothers felt they were ready to expand in a new direction: financial services. They tried to purchase Midland Bank, Britain's fourth largest bank, but were rejected by the bank's board. When news of the offer leaked to the press, the brothers were ridiculed. Analysts saw no logic in the deal, and the *Financial Times* opined that Saatchi & Saatchi "smacked of a firm which had run out of ideas." Within two days, the company's share price fell 6.2 percent. The stock then fell by another third in the October 19 stock market crash.

Although profits rose again in 1988, the company's financial troubles were coming to a head. Clients dissatisfied with the acquisitions and the management changes had left in droves, creating a $1 billion hole in billings. In addition, ad spending in

Key Dates:

1970: Charles and Maurice Saatchi form the ad agency Saatchi & Saatchi in London.

1975: Company merges with Compton Partners in a reverse takeover, forming the holding company Saatchi & Saatchi Garland-Compton.

1978: Saatchi & Saatchi produces the highly successful ''Labour Isn't Working'' campaign for Margaret Thatcher and the Conservative Party.

1982: Company wins the British Airways account; Saatchi & Saatchi spends $57 million to fully acquire Compton Advertising.

1985: Company adds to its numerous ad agency acquisitions and also purchases merchandising firm Howard Marlboro Group and public relations agency Rowland.

1986: Company purchases rival ad agencies Ted Bates Worldwide, Dancer Fitzgerald Sample, and Backer & Spielvogel.

1989: Profits fall for the first time in 19 years.

1990: Robert Louis-Dreyfus is appointed chief executive officer.

1995: Ccompany board dismisses founder Maurice Saatchi as chairman, Charles Saatchi steps down as president-for-life, and several key executives resign in protest; holding company renames itself Cordiant, although it retains the Saatchi & Saatchi name for its advertising subsidiary.

1997: Cordiant ''demerges'' into Saatchi & Saatchi plc and Cordiant Communications Group.

1999: Ad agency Cliff Freeman & Partners buys itself back from Saatchi & Saatchi.

2000: Publicis Groupe S.A. purchases Saatchi & Saatchi plc for $1.9 billion.

the United States was down and the cost of running the unwieldy holding company was rising. Executives urged a name change for the holding company so Saatchi & Saatchi Advertising, which was doing quite well, would not be tainted by the problems of the holding company. The Saatchi brothers would not hear of it. Efforts to move the company to more modest offices met with the same resistance.

In 1989 profits fell to $37 million, down from $244 million in 1988. Midway through the year the WPP agency became the largest advertising agency in the world, pushing aside Saatchi & Saatchi. In an effort to cut costs, the company began laying off employees. The high note of the year was the creation of Zenith Media, a combination of the media buying units of Saatchi's various agencies. The new subsidiary was immediately successful.

In desperate need of cash, the company decided to sell off its consulting businesses. The unit's revenues as a whole were not up as much as expected in 1989, with the Hay Group posting especially disappointing results. Saatchi & Saatchi was hoping to sell the businesses as a unit for at least $420 million, however, having spent $250 million to acquire them in the first place. In the end, the consulting businesses were sold off piecemeal for a disappointing total of $160 million.

Criticized for the management of the company, Maurice and Charles Saatchi felt it best to step into the background for a while. Robert Louis-Dreyfus was brought on as chief executive late in 1989 with the mission to turn the company around. He continued the cost-cutting strategy, laying off 5,200 employees over the next two years. In 1991 Louis-Dreyfus orchestrated a financial restructuring that included a new stock issuance and extensions on its loans. Although many shareholders were dissatisfied with their diluted holdings, the arrangement bought the company time. The next step was to wait for an economic recovery to raise ad spending.

The next couple of years showed little improvement for Saatchi & Saatchi. Backer Spielvogel Bates was fast losing clients, including Xerox, Prudential Insurance, Fisher-Price, and Miller Lite. Although Saatchi & Saatchi showed a pretax profit in the first half of 1992, by 1993 things were headed back downhill. Saatchi & Saatchi Advertising lost two important clients, first Chrysler, then Helene Curtis, for a total of more than $90 million in billings.

The Mid-1990s: The Founders Ousted

Robert Louis-Dreyfus resigned as CEO that year, leaving an opening for Maurice and Charles Saatchi to take on more prominent roles once again. The shareholders and board had other ideas, however. In December 1993, the board insisted that the brothers leave their lavish offices and join the rest of the company in their more modest space. In addition, they voted Charles Saatchi, who had attended only one board meeting ever, off the board. Battle had been engaged.

As Charles and Maurice searched for ways to regain control of what they considered their company, a group of shareholders, led by money manager David Herro, was looking for ways to rid the company of the brothers entirely. With the opinion that the brothers had mismanaged the company and squandered resources with lavish personal spending, the shareholders called for the board to oust Maurice as chairman of the board. Some encouraging gains in new accounts and stock price left the board unsure if such a change was for the best. After continued wrangling, however, the board voted Maurice off the board in December 1994.

Not wanting to completely lose Maurice's charisma and influence in the outside world, the board offered Maurice the position of chairman of subsidiary Saatchi & Saatchi Advertising. Maurice refused. His brother Charles resigned his honorary position of president-for-life, and the two set out to recreate their agency, regardless of the harm it did to their old company. Three top executives at Saatchi & Saatchi, Bill Muirhead, Jeremy Sinclair, and David Kershaw, resigned and joined forces with the Saatchi brothers. The five became equal partners in what they planned on calling The New Saatchi Agency.

Saatchi & Saatchi sued, claiming conspiracy to injure the company. When the dust settled several months later, the new agency was named M & C Saatchi and had lured some key accounts from Saatchi & Saatchi, including British Airways.

Many on the Saatchi & Saatchi board and in the company had long argued for the need to change the holding company's name to distinguish it from the ad agency subsidiary. With Maurice and Charles no longer around to quash the idea, the board changed the holding company's name to Cordiant in 1995. The subsidiary Saatchi & Saatchi Advertising retained its name.

Cordiant Struggling in the Late 1990s

The first two years after the ouster of the Saatchi brothers were rocky for Cordiant. It posted a pretax loss of $34.5 million in 1995, down from a profit of $21 million in 1994. Saatchi & Saatchi Advertising did make some positive steps forward. It won a $50 million Bell Atlantic account and several others, including Reynolds Wrap and Pepsid AC. The following year, Saatchi & Saatchi was named Agency of the Year at the International Advertising Festival in Cannes. M & C Saatchi continued to lure away executives and accounts from Cordiant, however, including the Hongkong Bank account, which Bates Worldwide had held for 35 years.

In 1997 Cordiant broke the company in two, creating Saatchi & Saatchi plc and Cordiant Communications Group. The two entities each held 50 percent of the successful Zenith Media. Kevin Roberts, an executive from New Zealand, was tapped for the chief executive position of Saatchi & Saatchi plc.

The company's structure shifted yet again in 1999. One of the company's U.S. agencies, Cliff Freeman & Partners, bought itself back from Saatchi & Saatchi, thus regaining its independence. In addition, Saatchi & Saatchi plc combined its PR agency Rowland Worldwide with Saatchi & Saatchi Business Communications. The new Rowland Communications Worldwide was headquartered in New York. Saatchi & Saatchi ended the year with revenues of $732 million.

The circle seemed complete for Saatchi & Saatchi the following year when it was acquired by Publicis Groupe, S.A., for $1.9 billion. The French communications giant was working its way up through the mega-agency chain through a series of acquisitions, much as Saatchi & Saatchi had done in the mid-1980s. With the purchase of Saatchi & Saatchi, Publicis was ranked the fifth largest communications-advertising firm, behind WPP Group, Omnicom Group, Interpublic Group, and Havas Advertising. As part of the transition, Saatchi & Saatchi plc decided to move its headquarters from London to New York.

Publicis kept the Saatchi & Saatchi agency operating independently. Its subsidiaries, Rowland Communications Worldwide and The Facilities Group, were not folded into Publicis divisions. In mid-2001, however, Publicis combined Saatchi & Saatchi's Zenith Media with its own media buying agency, creating one large agency.

Principal Subsidiaries

Rowland Communications Worldwide; The Facilities Group (70%).

Principal Competitors

Interpublic Group of Companies, Inc.; Omnicom Group, Inc.; WPP Group plc; Havas Advertising.

Further Reading

Fallon, Ivan, *Brothers: The Saatchi & Saatchi Story,* New York: Contemporary Books, 1989.

Fendley, Alison, *Saatchi & Saatchi: The Inside Story,* New York: Arcade Publishing, 1996.

Goldman, Kevin, *Conflicting Accounts: The Creation and Crash of the Saatchi & Saatchi Advertising Empire,* New York: Simon & Schuster, 1997.

Hatfield, Stefano, "Saatchi, What Gave Us the Edge," *Campaign,* September 13, 1991.

Healy, Ben, "From Maurice to Maurice (Saatchi to Levy That Is)," *Advertising Age,* June 26, 2000.

Lazarus, George, "French Communications Giant to Acquire British Advertising Firm," *Knight-Ridder,* June 19, 2000.

McMains, Andrew, "Saatchi & Saatchi Is N.Y. Bound," *Adweek,* September 4, 2000.

"Saatchi Brands Its New Entity," *Adweek,* May 24, 1999.

Tomkins, Richard, "Zenith Deal Boosts Publicis' Buying Power," *Financial Times,* July 19, 2001.

—Susan Windisch Brown

Schroders

Schroders plc

31 Gresham St.
London EC2V 7QA
United Kingdom
Telephone: (+44) 20-7658-6000
Fax: (+44) 20-7658-3870
Web site: http://www.schroders.com

Public Company
Incorporated: 1818 as J. Henry Schröder & Co.
Employees: 2,700
Total Assets: £5.95 billion (2000)
Stock Exchanges: London
Ticker Symbol: SDR
NAIC: 523110 Investment Banking and Securities
    Dealing; 522293 International Trade Financing

Schroders plc is one of the world's largest asset management banking groups, offering a range of private banking services to institutions; corporations; charities; local, regional, and national governments; unit trusts and pension funds; and the wealthy. The company's network of more than 40 offices worldwide help it oversee assets of nearly $200 billion. In addition to its investment management operations, the company's Schroder Ventures oversees its venture capital and buyout activities, with investments worth more than $7 billion. Based in London, Schroders generates more than two-thirds of its revenues in Europe, and more than half in the United Kingdom. The U.S. market accounts for 18 percent of sales while the Asian Pacific adds 11 percent of sales. Schroders is quoted on the London Stock Exchange and led by CEO David Salisbury. The founding Schroder family maintains a nearly 50 percent share of the company's stock, enabling it to stick to its independent course against an era of mergers and consolidation resulting in the creation of a smaller field of globally operating mega-banks. Schroders itself was forced to exit the investment banking market, selling off those operations to Salomon Smith Barney, a unit of industry mammoth Citigroup, in 2000. Instead, the company has concentrated fully on asset management, building up its private banking services and extending its range of pension fund offerings.

Merchant Origins in the 19th Century

The Schröder family had already established itself as a prominent merchant family in their Hamburg, Germany base by the beginning of the 19th century. Like many other prominent families active in trade, the Schröders had also branched out into a number of Europe's major cities. In 1804, Johann Heinrich Schröder traveled to London, joining his brother's merchant firm there.

Schröder set out on his own in 1818, founding the firm of J. Henry Schröder & Co. The new company continued the family's traditional trading activities while gradually adding a new dimension, that of merchant banking. The rise of international trade during the 19th century brought a need for more secure payment methods. Merchant banks were created in order to provide trading houses with guaranteed payments. The appearance of merchant banks was to play a central role in encouraging the growth of international trade. Johann Heinrich Schröder was succeeded by son John Henry, who took over the company at the age of 24 in 1849.

The Schröder firm (known as Schröders) profited both from the growth of international trade and the growing demand for its merchant banking services. The firm's trade financing activities were to overtake its trading operations during the century; the company also moved into other financial areas, such as bond issuing and capital investments. In 1863, Schröders became the only source of foreign capital in the United States during the Civil War when it issued £3 million to the Confederates. Back in Europe, the company established a charitable trust, Schröder Stiftung, in 1850, that later was to earn Johann Heinrich Schröder a baronage from the king of Prussia. John Henry Schröder was similarly honored by Queen Victoria at the end of the century, in recognition for the financial assistance he had provided to the British royal family. By then the next generation of Schröders had joined the firm; John Henry's son Bruno became a partner in 1895. Bruno Schröder received a baronage from Kaiser Wilhelm II in 1904.

Schröders had by that point achieved international prominence. The company was the first to bring a foreign loan to the Japanese government, raising £1 million in order to provide funds for building the railroad between Tokyo and Yokohama. While the company continued to rise with the development of international trade through the latter half of the century, it pursued its merchant activities as well. In the 1870s, for example, Schröders acted as one of the major traders for Peruvian guano, then widely used as fertilizer.

At the turn of the century, Schröders had grown to become one of the largest merchant banks in London—and by the outbreak of World War I had claimed the number two spot. The firm was also a leader in the issuing of foreign loans. Among the company's noteworthy transactions of the period was a controversial £15 million loan arranged for the Sao Paulo, Brazil government to help stabilize coffee prices, made in 1909.

Survival in the War Years

Schröders continued to build on its successes in the years leading up to World War I, as London became not only the focus point of a rapidly growing international trade market but also the financial capital of the world. At the same time, Schröders was quick to move into new financial markets and products being developed at the time, such as foreign exchange dealing and commodities futures trading. The company expanded rapidly during this time, with operations covering nearly all of Europe.

The outbreak of World War I inaugurated a long period of struggle for both the Schröders and their company. Despite a long history as one of England's leading merchant banking families, the Schröders had remained German citizens. The outbreak of hostilities between England and Germany opened the Schröder firm to possible seizure by the British government. Bruno Schröder himself was threatened with sequestration for the duration. Yet within days after the declaration of war, Schröder was naturalized as a British citizen.

If Schröder had avoided imprisonment, he could not avoid seeing the family firm suffer as the British and European financial markets collapsed with the war. The U.S. dollar took over from the British sterling as the world's leading currency; the international bonds market meanwhile was shifted to New York. By the end of the war, Schröders, along with England's other merchant banks, struggled to regain their position. Schröders was able to rebuild its position as a leading acceptance house. Yet the United States had emerged from the war as the world's new financial center. In 1923, Schröders opened a new subsidiary in New York, the J. Henry Schröder Banking Corporation, which became known as Schrobanco.

In 1926 the next generation of Schröders, led by Helmut, son of Bruno Schröder, joined the bank in time to face a crisis. At that time, the company branched out into a new business, that of investment management, creating a separate department for this activity. Yet the international financial crisis and, in particular, the collapse of the German economy, nearly forced the company out of business. The ensuing buildup and then outbreak of World War II brought new difficulties for the company, which saw much of its assets frozen for the duration. As the company itself stated, "Survival was J. Henry Schröder & Co.'s foremost achievement in the depression and war years." With its European operations in disarray, the company concentrated on building up its U.S.-based Schrobanco unit. Operated as an independent company, Schrobanco remained largely protected from the misfortunes of its European parent.

When Bruno Schröder died in 1940, son Helmut took over as the firm's senior partner, as well as head of Schrobanco. Following the war, the company refocused its European operations on the slowly recovering London market; the firm's London headquarters concentrated primarily on domestic business, while its U.S. subsidiary became the center of its international finance activity—and the largest part of the Schröder group. At home, however, Schröders focused on developing an investment funds business, which proved the motor for the company's growth in the second half of the decade, as London regained its prominence as one of the top financial centers in the world.

By the end of the 1950s, the company had largely succeeded in redeveloping its fortunes. At the time, the company also anglicized its name, dropping the umlaut to become Schroders. Two years later, in 1959, Schroders converted from a partnership to a private company, then took a listing on the London stock exchange, changing its name to Schroders plc. Despite going public, the Schroder family maintained firm control of the company through a majority shareholder's position. The next generation, in the form of Bruno Schroder, joined one year later, and was named to the board of directors in 1963.

In 1962, the company merged with another merchant bank, Helbert, Wagg & Co. Founded in 1823, that firm had built up a strong specialty with its brokerage operations. The newly enlarged Schroders quickly began expanding worldwide, establishing offices in the major financial markets, launching unit trusts, and broadening its asset management and lending activities. By the end of the 1970s, Schroders was present across Europe, including Switzerland, and in Hong Kong, Singapore, Japan, and Australia.

Asset Management Specialist in the 21st Century

A series of bad loans to the South American market during the 1970s and 1980s brought Schrobanco into difficulty and by 1986 Schroders decided to sell this business to the Industrial Bank of Japan. At the same time, the company temporarily exited its unit trusts operations, selling that business to National Mutual Life. Under terms of that deal, Schroders agreed not to reenter that market before the end of the decade, while continuing to manage some of the unit trusts.

The so-called "Big Bang" deregulation of the British banking industry went into effect in 1986, opening up the country's financial markets. As a result, Schroders began concentrating more closely on its corporate finance and investment business. Boosting this was the company's acquisition of 50 percent of Wertheim & Co. Inc., based in New York. Yet the company's lack of capital prevented it from joining the acquisition fever of

Key Dates:

1818: J. Henry Schröder & Co. is formed.

1863: Company issues £3 million bond during American Civil War.

1870: Company backs first foreign loan to the Japanese government, for Tokyo-Yokohama railroad.

1909: Company arranges £15 million loan for Sao Paulo, Brazil.

1914: Schröder family members are naturalized as British citizens.

1923: J. Henry Schröder Banking Corporation (Schrobanco), based in New York, is formed.

1926: Company launches investment management services.

1957: Schroder name is anglicized.

1959: Schroders converts to private company, then goes public.

1962: Company merges with Helbert, Wagg & Co.

1986: Schroders acquires 50 percent of Wertheim & Co., then gains full control eight years later.

2000: Schroders sells investment banking arm to Salomon Smith Barney; acquires Liberty International Pensions.

2001: Company launches institutional stakeholder pension products.

the period, as banks began acquiring brokerships and other businesses now allowed by the deregulation move. For this reason, Schroders was relatively unaffected by the stock market collapse of 1987.

Schroders returned to unit trusts management at the beginning of the 1990s, focusing especially on the Japanese market. The company's funds management business was also gaining rapidly, building from just £15 billion at the end of the 1980s to more than £50 billion in 1994. In that year, the company acquired full control of Helbert, Wagg & Co., which was then renamed Schroder & Co. Inc. Schroders was also expanding its presence in the Asian markets, notably with the opening of a subsidiary in China, while building up a position in the newly opened Eastern Bloc countries.

Schroders became the target of a takeover attempt by Dutch banking powerhouse ABN/AMRO in 1995. The Schroder family, led by Bruno Schroder, resisted the offer, insisting on remaining independent. By then, however, the world financial community had entered into a new round of consolidation aimed at creating a very few global giants. Schroders began to find it increasingly difficult to compete with this new generation of mega-banks—not only for clients, but also when recruiting top personnel. Schroders itself added to its problems as its investment division struggled to keep up with the industry index. The difficult economic situation in a number of markets in the late 1990s, such as Asia and Russia, also caused the company grief.

Schroders attempted to prop up its investment side by taking on more weight—in 1999, the company entered negotiations to

merge with Beacon Group, founded in 1992 by former Goldman Sachs executive Geoffrey Biosi. The deal would have enabled Schroders to capture a strong position in the international marketplace. When that deal fell through, however, the company, now led by CEO David Salisbury, reviewed its options. By the beginning of 2000, Schroders had adopted a new strategy, announcing that it was selling its investment banking arm to Salomon Smith Barney, part of Citigroup.

Meanwhile, Schroders became a dedicated assets management group. At the end of 2000, Schroders launched a new subsidiary, Schroders & Co., organized around its former Schroders Personal Investment Management Limited subsidiary and incorporating the company's acquisition of Liberty International Pensions Limited, which was renamed Schroders Pensions. Schroders & Co. was also expected to serve as the company's springboard into the wider European private banking market.

Among the moves meant to bolster this effort was the opening of a new branch in Frankfurt, Germany, in August 2001. In that year, also, the company launched a new institutional stakeholder pension product, designed to extend its range of services for corporate clients. At the same time, Schroders renewed its efforts to expand in the Asian markets, as the economies in that region picked up speed again; yet the company's attempt to acquire Taiwan's Masterlink Investment Trust was thwarted when it was outbid by Prudential Insurance Company. This development seemed to highlight the company's vulnerability in an era when it found itself among the last of the remaining independent British merchant banks. Without the deep pockets of its behemoth competitors, observers wondered how long Schroders would resist any future takeover offers. For the moment, however, Schroders seemed to settle in comfortably to its new identity as an assets management specialist for the 21st century.

Principal Subsidiaries

Burnaby Insurance (Guernsey) Limited (Channel Islands); Milk Street Investments (No 5) Limited; Milk Street Investments Limited; PT Schroder Investment Management Indonesia (85%); Schroders & Co.; Schroder & Co. Bank A.G. (Switzerland); Schroder & Co. Limited; Schroder (Deutschland) Holdings GmbH (Germany); Schroder Administration (Guernsey) Limited (Channel Islands); Schroder Cayman Bank and Trust Company Limited (Cayman Islands); Schroder Executor & Trustee Company Limited; Schroder Finance Partners LP (U.S.A.); Schroder Holdings plc; Schroder International Finance B.V. (Netherlands); Schroder International Holdings Limited; Schroder International Limited; Schroder Investment Company Limited; Schroder Investment Management (Guernsey) Limited (Channel Islands); Schroder Investment Management (Hong Kong) Limited; Schroder Investment Management (Italy) S.p.A.; Schroder Investment Management (Japan) Limited; Schroder Investment Management (Luxembourg) S.A.; Schroder Investment Management (Singapore) Limited; Schroder Investment Management Australia Limited; Schroder Investment Management Brasil S.A. (Brazil); Schroder Investment Management Canada Limited; Schroder Investment Management Fondsmæglerselskab A/S (Denmark); Schroder Investment Management International Limited; Schroder Investment Management Limited; Schroder Investment Management North America Inc. (U.S.A.); Schroder Investment Management North America Limited; Schroder Investments (Bermuda) Limited; Schroder Investments (SVIIT) Limited (Bermuda); Schroder Middle East Limited; Schroder Pensions Limited; Schroder Property Investment Management Limited; Schroder Trust Bank (U.S.A.); Schroder U.S. Holdings Incorporated; Schroder Unit Trusts Limited; Schroder Venture Managers Limited (Bermuda); Schroder Ventures (1991) Limited; Schroder Ventures Holdings Limited; Schroder Ventures International Holdings Limited; Schroder Ventures Investment Company Limited; Schroders (Bermuda) Limited; Schroders (C.I.) Limited (Channel Islands); Schroders (Shanghai) Financial Advisory Co. Limited (China; 85%); Schroders Australia Holdings Limited.

Principal Competitors

3i Group Plc.; Abbey National plc; Bank of Ireland; Barclays Plc.; The Charles Schwab Corporation; Close Brothers Group Plc; Goldman Sachs; HSBC Holdings; Jefferies Group; Legg Mason; Lloyds TSB; Merrill Lynch & Co., Inc.; Natexis; The Royal Bank of Scotland Group plc; Singer & Friedlander Group; St. James's Place Capital; UBS Warburg.

Further Reading

Brierley, David, "Schroders: The Great Survivor," *Independent on Sunday*, July 12, 1998, p. 2.

Kaban, Elif, "Schroders Courts German Rich with New Office," *Reuters*, August 1, 2001.

Lalor, Dan, "New Schroders Starts with Cash Pile," *Reuters*, March 3, 2000.

Targett, Simon, "Determined to Steer an Independent Course," *Financial Times*, December 4, 2000.

"The Wisdom of Salomon," *Economist*, January 22, 2000.

—M. L. Cohen

Securitas AB

Lindhagensplan 70
SE-102 28 Stockholm
Sweden
Telephone: (+46) 8-657-74-00
Fax: (+46) 8-657-70-72
Web site: http://www.securitasgroup.com

Public Company
Incorporated: 1934
Employees: 202,794
Sales: SKr 40.86 billion ($4.33 billion) (2000)
Stock Exchanges: Stockholm
Ticker Symbol: SECU-B
NAIC: 561612 Security Guards and Patrol Services;
    561621 Security Systems Services (Except
    Locksmiths)

Sweden's Securitas AB is locking up the world's security services market. Based in Stockholm, Securitas is the world's leading provider of security services, with a 7 percent market share in the highly fragmented industry. Through its acquisitions of Pinkerton's and Burns International, in 1999 and 2000, respectively, Securitas has also become the leading security services firm in the United States, with more than 17 percent of the total market. In 2001, Securitas restructured its operations into five business areas: Security Systems, providing security and alarm systems to corporations and other large-scale customers; Direct, providing alarm systems for small businesses and individual customers; Cash Handling Services, concentrated primarily in Europe and providing 10 percent of the company's sales; Consulting & Investigations, which also provides private security services; and Security Services, the company's single largest market, accounting for nearly 80 percent of sales in 2000. Security Services is further divided in United States (41 percent of total sales) and Europe (39 percent of total sales) components. These sales topped SKr 40 billion in 2000—making the company some 50 times larger than it was just a dozen years earlier. The company trades on the Stockholm stock exchange; Thomas Berglund serves as Securitas's president and CEO.

Securing Scandinavia in the 1930s

Securitas traces its roots back to the turn of the 20th century, when Kjobenhavn Frederiksberg Nattevagt was founded by Philip Sorensen and Marius Hogrefe. The new company offered guard services in Sorensen's and Hogrefe's native Denmark. Sorensen soon became the primary force behind the company's growth. In 1918, Kjobenhavn Frederiksberg Nattevagt merged into De Forenede Vagtselskaber, the predecessor to the future ISS Group.

Sorensen's son Erik Philip-Sorensen joined his father in developing the family business as it began to expand beyond Denmark. In 1934, Erik Philip-Sorensen brought the company into Sweden, buying Hälsingbords Nattvakt, based in Helsingborg. Philip-Sorensen began acquiring other Swedish security companies, building a leading position in that country's security market. While Securitas remained under ISS Group's control, the Philip-Sorensen family was responsible for their company's growth in Sweden and beyond.

After establishing its Swedish position, Securitas began expanding further afield in the 1950s. For this expansion, Philip-Sorensen was aided by his sons Jörgen and Sven. During the 1950s and 1960s, Securitas's expansion helped place it among the leading European security services companies. The company's first international move came with the launch of a subsidiary in the United Kingdom in 1950; at that time, the company combined all of its operations under a single name, Securitas International. Jörgen Philip-Sorensen played an active role in the company's expansion outside of Scandinavia, which targeted especially the United Kingdom and Belgium during this period, while Sven concentrated especially on its Swedish operations, leading a series of acquisitions, including that of Svensk Nattvakt.

In 1963, Securitas formed two new subsidiaries in the United Kingdom, Store Detectives Ltd. and Securitas Alarms Ltd. While Erik Philip-Sorensen remained at the head of the company, son Jörgen was appointed to lead the company's growing U.K. operations in 1965. Three years later, the company restructured its four U.K. businesses under a new subsidiary and brand name, Group 4 (Total Security).

Jorgen and Sven Philip-Sorensen took over the company's leadership only upon Erik Philip-Sorensen's retirement in 1974. In that year, the Philip-Sorensen family bought control of Securitas from the ISS Group. The brothers maintained joint-ownership of the company until 1981, when Securitas was divided equally between them. Sven Philip-Sorensen took over the company's Swedish operations, keeping the Securitas name. Jörgen Philip-Sorensen remained at the head of the company's international activities, now renamed Group 4 Securitas. Group 4 Securitas was later acquired by Falck, of Denmark, creating the world's second largest security services group, Group 4 Falck A/S.

Expansion Drive in the 1980s

Sven Philip-Sorensen did not remain for long at the helm of Securitas. By 1983, he had sold his interest in the company. While parts of Securitas were bought up by Group 4, the largest part was taken over by Swedish investment firm Investment AB Latour in 1985. Latour, led by Gustaf Douglas, who also became vice-chairman of Securitas, led the company on a dramatic expansion drive beginning in 1988.

In the meantime, Securitas's new management, led by Melker Schörling since 1987, had trimmed Securitas's operations, focusing the company entirely on guard and security services. Over its previous decades, Securitas had acquired a number of diversified holdings; these were now sold off, leaving only a core security operation. The newly slimmed down company had sales of less than SKr 1 billion as its acquisition drive began in 1988.

In that year, the company acquired Assa, a Swedish maker of locks. By the following year, Securitas displayed an interest in the international market, acquiring security companies in Norway and Denmark, and then beyond Scandinavia to enter Portugal as well. Not all of the company's expansion came from acquisition: in 1989, the company also launched its own operations in Hungary.

By 1991, the company's sales had topped SKr 3 billion. Yet Securitas's growth had only just begun; fueling the company's further ambitions, Securitas took a listing on the Stockholm stock exchange in that year. Soon after, the company made its first entry into the United States, buying up Arrow and thereby expanding its lock making operations.

The following year, Securitas grew again, now with the purchase of Spain's Esabe, and then Protectas, which gave it operations in France, Austria, Switzerland, and Germany. The company moved into Finland in 1993, acquiring security operations in that country. At the same time, Securitas began focusing more and more on security services—a fast-growing industry in the early 1990s—and merged its Swedish lock-making operations into a joint venture with Finland's Metra, creating Assa-Abloy. The company sold off its part of the joint venture to shareholders in 1994. By then, the company's sales had topped SKr 6 billion.

After taking 1995 off, Securitas rejoined the acquisition trail in 1996, entering new markets, such as Estonia and Poland, and, with the acquisition of DSW Security, Germany. That last acquisition gave Securitas Germany's fourth largest security company, and made Germany one of its largest single markets, accounting for some 20 percent of total sales. The DSW acquisition was topped by a new acquisition in the United Kingdom, of Security Express Armaguard (SEA). The former subsidiary of Australia's Mayne Nickless, SEA had been losing money in the mid-1990s; nonetheless, the purchase boosted Securitas's cash-in-transit operations in the United Kingdom. The SEA acquisition also represented Securitas's first entry into the United Kingdom since the split-up of the company in the early 1980s.

Other acquisitions of 1996 included La Rond de Nuit and Domen Securité in France; Sonasa, in Portugal; Timetech, in Sweden; Krupp Sicherheit, in Germany; and Inkjassaator, in Estonia. In all, the company added more than SKr 2 billion in sales through acquisitions alone that year.

Securitas bundled its consumer-oriented businesses into a new subsidiary, Securitas Direct, overseeing the company's international individual home and small business alarm systems operations, in 1997. Securitas meanwhile continued making acquisitions, particularly in France and Germany through 1997 and 1998. The company's acquisitions in these markets included Raab Karcher Sicherheit of Germany and Proteg and the Kessler Group of France. Both Proteg and Raab Karcher were leaders in their respective countries; the Raab Karcher acquisition also strengthened the company's presence in Austria and Hungary, and introduced it to the Czech Republic. In 1998, also, Securitas launched its first subsidiary operations in Latvia.

By the end of 1998, Securitas's acquisition appetite had boosted its sales to nearly SKr 14 billion. One year later, the company's sales soared past SKr 25.5 billion. In that year, Securitas made its largest acquisition—and one that gave it a position as the world's largest security services company, with a leading share of the United States market.

Securitas's transformation came with its acquisition of famed security services company Pinkerton's Inc. Paying $384 million, Securitas gained control of the 150-year-old U.S. company, founded by Alan Pinkerton in Illinois in 1850. Pinkerton, originally a barrelmaker, became the first private detective in the United States and, with a logo featuring an open eye, spawned the term ''private eye.'' Pinkerton's had been acquired

---

Key Dates:

1901: Kjobenhavn Frederiksberg Nattevagt is founded by Philip Sorensen.

1918: Kjobenhavn Frederiksberg Nattevagt becomes part of future ISS Group.

1934: Company enters Sweden.

1938: Company takes Securitas name.

1950: Company expands into United Kingdom, adopts Securitas International brand name.

1968: Securitas restructures its four U.K. businesses under the name Group 4.

1974: Sven and Jörgen Philip-Sorensen acquire control of Securitas.

1981: Company is divided into Securitas (Sweden) and Group 4 (international); Group 4 is later acquired by Falck and becomes the world's second largest security services group, Group 4 Falck A/S.

1985: Investment firm AB Latour acquires Securitas.

1988: Securitas acquires Swedish lockmaker Assa.

1991: Company is listed on the Stockholm exchange; acquires U.S.-based Arrow.

1992: Company acquires Esabe of Spain and Protectas of Switzerland.

1997: Company forms Securitas Direct.

1999: Securitas acquires Pinkerton's Inc. for $384 million, thus gaining a major share of the U.S. market.

2000: Securitas acquires its second major U.S. firm, Burns International, and sees its revenues surpass SKr 40 billion.

2001: Securitas acquires full control of Loomis Fargo for an estimated $100 million.

---

by tobacco company American Brands in 1983. In 1988, the company was merged into California Plant Protection; the larger company kept the famous Pinkerton's name. The acquisition of Pinkerton's gave Securitas a major share of the U.S. market (the company maintained the Pinkerton's name for its North and South American operations).

In 2000, Securitas swooped again, now picking up another major U.S. security company, Burns International. Burns had its start as part of the former Borg-Warner, when that industrial conglomerate acquired Baker Industries in 1977, giving it entry into the security services market. Baker Industries held the trademarks to two famed names—Wells Fargo and Pony Express, acquired in 1967 from American Express. Borg-Warner proceeded to go on its own acquisition binge, buying up more than 70 companies to build one of the top security services in the United States by the early 1990s. Among its acquisitions was Burns International Security Services, founded in 1909 and acquired by Borg Warner in 1982. Under fire from a hostile takeover, Borg Warner escaped through a leveraged buyout at the end of the 1980s; yet the company's huge debt-load forced it to sell off nearly all of its operations, until in 1993 all that remained of the company was its security services division, including its Wells Fargo armored car subsidiary. That company was merged with Loomis Armored in 1997, giving Borg Warner a 49 percent stake in the newly named Loomis, Fargo &

Co. In 1999, Borg Warner itself changed its name, to Burns International.

The acquisition of Burns International by Securitas boosted the Swedish security giant's revenues past SKr 40 billion and, with a 7 percent share of the global security services market, made it the world leader in its still highly fragmented industry. Burns, folded into the Pinkerton's operation, made Securitas the out-and-out leader of the North American market as well.

Securitas had no intention of ending its drive to consolidate the worldwide security services industry. Announcing a war chest of some SKr 12 billion, the company continued to make acquisitions as the new century began. In 2000, the company acquired B&M Beveiliging & Alermering in Amsterdam; Doyle Protective Service in the United States; Baron Security of Belgium; Micro-route Ltd. of the United Kingdom, and Ausysegur of Spain. At mid-2001, the company announced that it had agreed to pay more than $100 million to acquire full control of the Loomis Fargo Group.

By then, Securitas, which had previously been organized along its geographic operations, now restructured the company into its five key businesses areas of Security Services; Security Systems; Direct; Cash Handling Services; and Consulting & Investigations, which also provided private security services. This reorganization was meant to help the company achieve its future growth goals—by 2005, the company expected its sales to top SKr 69 billion. Given Securitas's strong record of organic and external growth, the company seemed likely to secure its ambitions.

Principal Subsidiaries

Burns International Services Corporation (U.S.A.); Dansikring A/S (Denmark); Pinkerton's, Inc. (U.S.A.); Pinkerton's of Canada Limited; Pinkerton Servicios de Seguridad Privada S.A. de C.V. (Mexico); Protectas S.A. (Switzerland); Securis N.V. (Belgium); Securitas AS (Norway); Securitas C.I.T. Sp. z.o.o. (Poland); Securitas CR s.r.o. (Czech Republic); Securitas Deutschland Holding GmbH (Germany); Securitas Eesti Ltd. (Estonia); Securitas France Holding S.A.; Securitas Holding A/S (Denmark); Securitas Hungary RT; Securitas Oy (Finland); Securitas Polska Sp. z.o.o. (Poland; 95%); Securitas S.A. (Portugal); Securitas Seguridad España S.A. (Spain); Securitas Serviços e Tecnologia de Segurança SA (Portugal); Securitas Sverige AB (Sweden); Securitas Treasury Ireland Limited; Securitas UK Limited; Securitas Werttransporte GmbH (Austria; 98%).

Principal Competitors

AHLS/Argenbright; Allied; Chubb plc; Command Security Corporation; Group 4 Falck A/S; Guardsmark; Home Security International, Inc.; Initial; The Pittston Company; Prosegur, Compañía de Seguridad, S.A; Protection One, Inc.; Rentokil Initial plc; Securicor plc; Transnational Security Group; Tyco International Ltd.; The Wackenhut Corporation.

Further Reading

de Bendern, Paul, ''Securitas Profit Jumps, 2000 EPS Seen up 25 Pct,'' *Reuters*, February 8, 2000.

George, Nicholas, "Securitas Makes Cash Bid for Burns," *Financial Times*, August 4, 2000.

Hardie, Will, "Securitas Sees Windfall from Euro Money Launch," *Reuters*, June 12, 2001.

"Securitas Has 12 Bln SKR for Acquisitions," *Reuters Business Report*, November 4, 1999.

"Securitas Takes Control of the American Loomis Fargo Group," *European Report*, May 30, 2001.

"Sweden's Market Is Smiling on Securitas AB, but Some Wonder If Buying Spree Is a Bit Much," *Wall Street Journal*, August 25, 2000.

"Swedish Firm to Buy Pinkerton," *Dallas Morning News*, February 23, 1999, p. 2D.

—M. L. Cohen

Seibu Department Stores, Ltd.

Seibu Ikebukuro Building
16-15-1-chome Minamiikebukuro
Toshima-ku
Tokyo 171-8530
Japan
Telephone: (03) 3989 0111
Fax: (03) 5396 5285
Web site: http://www.seibu.co.jp

Private Company
Incorporated: 1940 as Musashino Department Store
Employees: 9,451
Sales: ¥5.65 billion (2000)
NAIC: 452110 Department Stores

Seibu Department Stores, Ltd. operates retail businesses such as department stores, specialty stores, shopping centers, and direct marketing, as well as sports clubs and merchandise development. The chain has 25 stores, primarily located in Japan—including the Ikebukuro store in Tokyo, one of the biggest department stores in Japan. Seibu is also one of the major companies that form the Saison Group. The Saison Group participates in various industries, including food, retail, finance, transportation, real estate, and entertainment.

1920–50: A Diverse Range of Businesses

The founder of Seibu Department Stores was Yasujiro Tsutsumi, father of the group's former chairman, Seiji Tsutsumi. Yasujiro was not only an entrepreneur but also a member of the House of Representatives. He achieved success in residential development and the leisure industry between 1920 and 1950. Yasujiro Tsutsumi also launched a private railway business.

In 1935 a small-scale department store, Kikuya Department Store, was opened near Ikebukuro Station, the terminal of a private railway in Tokyo. In 1940 Yasujiro Tsutsumi bought the Kikuya Department Store and changed its name to Musashino Department Store, thereby establishing the department store business. Ikebukuro is now one of Tokyo's large shopping districts. When Musashino Department Store was founded, Ikebukuro was a small town undergoing development. Soon afterward, Japan became involved in World War II. Under the controlled wartime economy, the department store was almost forced to stop doing business, and the store building was destroyed in an air raid. After the war, however, business was resumed in a temporary shelter.

During Japan's postwar rehabilitation, Yasujiro Tsutsumi expanded the business and reopened the department store, under the name of Seibu Department Store (later pluralized), in a two-story building with a selling area of about 1,500 square meters. It sold daily necessities such as food, clothes, and sundry goods. Seibu Department Store expanded, taking advantage of Japan's strong economic growth.

1950s–70s: Expansion

From the 1950s through the 1970s, people in Tokyo and other large Japanese cities increasingly moved to the suburbs. The population in the areas along the railway line from Ikebukuro increased rapidly. Seibu Department Store's profits grew steadily in conjunction with this shift in population. Seiji Tsutsumi began to work for Seibu Department Store in 1954. In 1956 Seibu Department Store extended its selling space for the fourth time, to 43,000 square meters, and ranked top in business performance among department stores based near railway terminals in the Ikebukuro district.

Between the late 1950s and early 1960s, the company opened four small-scale stores and expanded the range of merchandise, introduced credit sales, formed customer clubs, and installed information systems. It also diversified into car sales, petroleum and liquid petroleum gas sales, and helicopter services, and launched leisure and real estate businesses. The car sales, helicopter, and real estate businesses later were separated from the department store operations to become one of the Saison Group's core units. This attempt became the basis for further diversification and paved the way to a mass market business with a wide range of activities.

In 1967 a department store of about 10,000 square meters was opened in Funabashi, a suburb of Tokyo. In 1968 a store of about 24,000 square meters was opened in Shibuya, another large shopping area outside Tokyo. For the next few years until the early 1970s, Seibu Department Stores endeavored to open more stores in Tokyo's satellite cities and towns, and in the Tokai district. The Ikebukuro store continued to occupy an important strategic position as the flagship store.

In 1971 Seibu Department Stores Kansai Co., Ltd. was founded as a stepping-stone for expansion into the Kansai district, another important Japanese economic center. In the same year, a shopping complex called PARCO was opened in Shinsaibashi, Osaka. The company planned to construct a large-scale department store in Takatsuki, Osaka Prefecture, and in Otsu, Shiga Prefecture. These stores were opened in 1974 and 1976, respectively. Between the 1960s and the early 1970s new stores were opened consecutively: Itohan and Darumaya in the Hokuriku district, Matsukiya and Honkin in the Tohoku district, Tabata Department Store in Chiba Prefecture, and Toden Kaikan in the Shikoku district, while other local department stores became affiliates of Seibu Department Stores; all except Matsukiya were bought by Seibu Department Stores.

Late 1970s–80s: Taking a New Approach

After the oil crisis in the autumn of 1973, the Japanese economy's rate of growth slowed. In the late 1970s, consumer consumption decreased and many retailers were faced with stagnant sales. The business results of department stores were poor. In response, Seibu Department Stores adopted an aggressive store improvement strategy.

In 1974 Seibu Takatsuki Shopping Center, with a selling area of about 58,000 square meters, was opened in Takatsukishi, Osaka Prefecture. The center was scheduled to open in 1973, but shortly before opening a fire broke out, postponing the opening for about one year.

In 1975 the Ikebukuro store was extended and refurbished for the ninth time and reappeared as a sophisticated department store, offering a wide range of products. The interior of the store and the accompanying advertising campaign reflected its new focus. A museum and a park were constructed within the store, which was intended to be seen as a cultural and social center rather than an ordinary retail store. This innovative concept was later adopted as other stores were remodeled.

PARCO, at that time a subsidiary of Seibu Department Stores, accelerated the trend of developing retail stores as social and cultural centers. PARCO was formerly the Marubutsu Department Store, which, located in Ikebukuro, was on the verge of bankruptcy. Seibu Department Stores bought out Marubutsu in 1969 and reconstructed it as an urban shopping center. In 1969, PARCO Co., Ltd. was established. In 1973 Shibuya PARCO was opened. Five PARCOs opened in the Hokkaido,

Chiba, and Oita prefectures in the ensuing years. In 1976 Seibu Otsu Shopping Center, with a selling area of about 40,000 square meters, was opened.

In the early 1980s consumption slackened and retail sales were low. In addition, the restrictions of the Large Store Law of 1974 were enforced to prohibit large retailers from opening stores and to protect small retailers.

At this time, Seibu Department Stores developed the second multistore project (the first had occurred in the 1970s), remodeled the existing stores, including those at Ikebukuro and Shibuya, and promoted businesses other than department stores. As a result, Seibu Department Stores ranked top in sales in the Japanese department store industry in 1987.

As part of the multistore project of the 1980s, five department stores opened: Yurakucho Seibu (1984); Tsukuba Store and Tsukashin Store (1985); Tokorozawa Seibu (1986); and Kawasaki Seibu (1988). These stores were innovative in terms of merchandising, layout, and interior design.

Yurakucho Seibu was located in an area adjacent to the Ginza, Tokyo's most popular downtown area. It was constructed on the former site of the Asahi Shimbun newspaper offices and the Nippon Theater. Yurakucho Seibu and Hankyu Department Store completed a twin tower, of which they were co-tenants. Yurakucho Seibu was an up-to-date store providing modern commodities and services, and acted as a showcase for the merchandise and services of the entire Saison Group.

The Tsukuba store was located in the center of the Tsukuba Academic City and incorporated advanced distribution information technology. For this reason the store attracted considerable publicity in the new high-technology city as an experimental store.

The Tsukashin store was a town-like shopping center developed with the support of the entire Saison Group, including Seibu Department Stores. The store was constructed as part of a redevelopment project on the grounds of a spinning factory. In an area of about 66,000 square meters, a mall of specialty shops, an eating and drinking zone including various restaurants and bars, a multipurpose hall, and sporting facilities were constructed, in addition to a department store with a selling area of about 30,000 square meters. Moreover, a park, a river, a sports center, and even a church were added. This big urban development project took 12 years to complete and greatly contributed to the efforts of Seibu Department Stores and the Saison Group to penetrate the Kansai market.

The Tokorozawa Seibu, located in the residential area of a satellite town along a railway line from Ikebukuro, was a suburban-type large-scale department store of about 23,000 square meters. Kawasaki Seibu, covering about 22,000 square meters, was located in Kawasaki, a town next to Tokyo that was changing from an industrial to a more culturally oriented city. Thus Kawasaki Seibu tried to offer not only merchandise but also various services and information, including financial information and information on leisure activities.

While department stores were being created along these new lines, large-scale specialty stores also were established, such as

Key Dates:

1940: Yasujiro Tsutsumi purchases Kikuya Department Store in Kkebukuro, Tokyo and renames the store Musashino Department Store.
1949: Musashino Department Store changes its name to Seibu Department Store.
1969: PARCO Co., Ltd. is established as a subsidiary of Seibu.
1971: Seibu Department Stores Kansai Co., Ltd. is formed to initiate expansion into the important economic center of Kansai.
1989: Seibu Department Stores Co., Ltd. and Seibu Department Stores Kansai Co., Ltd. are merged to form Seibu Department Stores, Ltd.
1990: Seibu opens a store in Hong Kong.
1992: Financially troubled, the company announces restructuring plans and layoffs.
1993: Seibu opens a store in Shenzhen, China.
1996: Seibu sells its Hong Kong and Shenzhen stores to Dickson Concepts.
2000: Itochu purchases a stake in Seibu and forms a business alliance to focus on e-commerce.

WAVE, offering audio-visual goods; THE PRIME, a restaurant complex; SEED, accommodating fashion boutiques; and LOFT, carrying miscellaneous modern goods. Several other businesses were actively promoted, including marketing to corporations, import/export and other trading activities; direct marketing; new media; fitness; and wholesale, handling mainly Japanese and well-known foreign fashion goods brands such as Hermès, Ralph Lauren, Yves Saint Laurent, and Benetton.

In 1989 Seibu Department Stores Co., Ltd. and Seibu Department Stores Kansai Co., Ltd., which had been separate companies, were merged to form Seibu Department Stores, Ltd. At the time, the enterprise ranked fifth among Japanese retail companies, following The Daiei, Ito-Yokado, Seiyu, and Jusco.

The Seibu Department Stores Group consisted of 11 department store companies and 38 miscellaneous companies. Included among the latter were Ikebukuro Shopping Park Co., Ltd.; importers Hermès Japan Co., Ltd., Yves Saint-Laurent-Seibu S.A., and Ellebis, Ltd.; and direct marketing company Saison Direct Marketing Co., Ltd.

The Seibu Department Stores Group and Seibu Saison Group introduced various innovations to their stores, including importing and selling Euro-American high-grade brand goods, offering life and other insurance, participating in financial services, and issuing international credit cards.

1990s: Restructuring

In 1990, Seibu opened its first store outside Japan, in Hong Kong. Three years later, the company opened a store in Shenzhen, China. Despite the expansion, however, the first years of the decade were marked by trouble. Flat sales and losses plagued Seibu—and its parent company, the Saison Group, was likewise burdened by sagging revenues and enormous debt. In

1991, Seiji Tsutsumi, son of Seibu's founder, resigned from several high-level positions within the Saison Group, including that of "representative director" of Seibu Department Stores.

In the middle of 1992, the troubled company announced a restructuring plan that was to include freezing investment in new stores under development in three cities and liquidating or absorbing affiliates that were losing money—which included approximately one-third of 30 affiliated companies. The company also began reducing its workforce substantially, by not replacing workers who retired or left the company and by reassigning workers to affiliated companies.

Turnaround efforts continued into the middle of the decade. In 1994 and early 1995, Seibu sold 25 million shares of three affiliate companies, as well as ¥26.1 billion of its own corporate-owned shares. It also began closing department stores that were losing money. In 1996, the company sold majority ownership of its Hong Kong and China stores to a Hong Kong department store chain, generating approximately ¥1.5 billion.

In 1997, Seibu posted its first revenue increase in seven years. Meanwhile, the company began to make cautious moves toward resuming expansion. In early 1998, Seibu partnered with a Japanese and a U.S. developer to make plans for opening as many as 16 large shopping malls in Japan. In November of the same year, the company teamed up with a Denmark group to develop a chain of Scandinavian-style home furnishings stores in Japan.

Early 2000s: More Problems and New Alliances

In mid-2000, it became apparent that one of the companies under the Saison Group's umbrella—Seiyo Corp.—was in an irretrievably difficult position. Because Seibu was Seiyo's largest stockholder, the department store chain also was affected adversely. To prop up its sagging financial condition, Seibu converted equity in its flagship department store in Ikebukuro into marketable securities. The securitization, which was expected to raise approximately ¥108 billion, was Japan's largest.

The first two years of the new century also saw a number of new partnerships for Seibu. In 2000, Itochu Corporation, a trading house based in Japan, purchased almost 5 percent of Seibu, making it the sixth largest shareholder in the company. Seibu and Itochu planned to work jointly on developing an e-commerce initiative. In early 2001, Seibu took over a struggling department store chain—Sogo Co.—which had filed for court protection from creditors. Under the terms of the purchase, Seibu owned 95 percent of Sogo and installed ten of its own members on Sogo's board of directors.

As Seibu looked to the future, it hoped to leverage technology to reduce its debt and improve efficiency. The company had forged an alliance with NTT Data Corp. and planned to build an information network for use in the distribution sector. The first project for the partnership was expected to be an Internet-based system designed to manage Seibu's sales to corporate clients, from order to fulfillment.

Principal Subsidiaries

The Loft Co., Ltd.; Shell Garden Co., Ltd.; Polo/Ralph Lauren Japan, Co., Ltd.; Liberty Japan Co., Ltd.; Ikebukuro Shopping

Park Co., Ltd.; Millennium Development, Inc.; Yatsugatake Kogen Lodge; The Ellebis, Ltd.; De-Gliffe-Club; Jean-Louis Scherrer Japon Co., Ltd.; F Co., Ltd.; Family Seibu Co., Ltd.; J. Osawa & Co., Ltd.; Asahi Food Processing Co., Ltd.; Asahi Industries Co., Ltd.; PISA Co., Ltd.; Business System Agent Co., Ltd.; Career On Co., Ltd.

Principal Competitors

The Daimaru, Inc.; Mitsukoshi, Ltd.; Takashimaya Company, Limited.

Further Reading

"Itochu Tie-up Key to Seibu's Success," *Yomiuri Shimbun/Daily Yomiuri,* September 9, 2000.

Kamachi, Akihiro, and Toru Takahashi, "Retail Goliaths Undergo Massive Restructuring," *Yomiuri Shimbun/Daily Yomiuri,* May 3, 1998.

"Seibu Plans Biggest Securitisation," *South China Morning Post,* August 17, 2000, p. 16.

Yui, Tsunehiko, *The History of Saison,* Tokyo: Libroport, 1991.

—Yoko Togawa
—update: Shawna Brynildssen

Sevenson Environmental Services, Inc.

2749 Lockport Road, P.O. Box 396
Niagara Falls, New York 14302
U.S.A.
Telephone: (716) 284-0431
Fax: (716) 284-1796
Web site: http://www.sevenson.com

Public Company
Incorporated: 1947 as Albert Elia Building Company, Inc.
Employees: 236
Sales: $126.5 million (2000)
Stock Exchanges: NASDAQ
Ticker Symbol: SEVN
NAIC: 562211 Hazardous Waste Treatment and Disposal

With its headquarters in Niagara Falls, New York, Sevenson Environmental Services, Inc., is a leading environmental cleanup contractor, successfully completing more than 900 projects in the United States, Puerto Rico, and Canada. The company is run by the third generation of the Elia family. Sevenson went public in 1989, but members of the Elia family retain most of the company's stock. Although Sevenson does a good deal of government work, most of its efforts have been devoted to private sector cleanups. The company provides field services for the remediation of land and water contaminated by hazardous materials, offering onsite treatment, containment, or removal. It also decontaminates or disposes of equipment and facilities affected by hazardous waste. Furthermore, Sevenson has become involved in the redevelopment of brownfields, buying contaminated properties, and then cleaning and reselling them at a profit. Overall, it has a sterling reputation for performing quality work in a timely fashion. Sevenson is a tight-knit company with remarkably little turnover, a situation that has contributed to its success.

Construction Roots: 1917

The Elia family became involved in environmental cleanup work through the construction business. The firm's forefather was Albert Elia, a Niagara Falls, New York, architect who started up a general construction business to produce his designs for residential and commercial buildings. His four sons would then become involved in the construction business, taking on outside work in addition to their father's projects. In 1947 the sons incorporated the business as Albert Elia Building Company, Inc., specializing in residential building construction to meet the post-World War II housing shortage. In the 1950s the company also took on industrial, institutional, and heavy civil construction, eventually growing into one of New York's largest general contractors.

In the 1970s a third generation of the Elia family became involved in the construction business and eventually took over. Because the second generation had produced seven sons, the new generation changed the name of the company to Sevenson Construction. In the 1970s, margins were low in the construction industry and competition extremely tight. In 1978 a scandal would erupt in the bedroom community of Love Canal, New York, located just minutes away from Sevenson's offices, providing the company with an opportunity to branch out into a new line of endeavor.

Ever since the end of World War II, the United States had grown increasingly more concerned about the effects of pollution. The first piece of federal law to address the subject was the Water Pollution Control Act of 1948, followed by additional legislation in 1956. It was the publication of Rachel Carson's 1962 book *Silent Spring,* however, that would solidify public opinion and lead to the environmental movement. Carson, in fact, added an entirely new level of meaning to the word "environment," which until *Silent Spring* had been a simple and unassuming term. The book became so controversial that even before its official publication date, public pressure forced President Kennedy to promise an investigation and Congress to establish a score of committees to study the new "environmental problems." The early 1960s saw the passage of clean air and clean water acts. In 1969 the oil spills that fouled the pristine beaches of the affluent community of Santa Barbara, California, created environmental activists out of the rich and politically well connected. In 1970 the first Earth Day was celebrated, the organization of which led to the creation of a permanent Washington lobby. Also in 1970 President Nixon signed the law that created the Environmental Protection Agency (EPA), and for the first time the nation had a single government entity charged with monitoring and enforcing environmental protection laws.

344

During the 1970s, public concern about environmental issues continued to mount. For instance, a 1977 study estimated that 95 percent of the country's river basins were polluted. The situation at Love Canal would soon make Americans painfully aware of the dangers of chemical wastes. The small community was built over an abandoned canal that the Niagara Falls School Board bought from the Hooker Chemical and Plastics Corporation for $1 in 1953. The city allowed homes to be built on the site, but in 1978 state officials discovered that toxic chemicals were seeping into the basements. Further study revealed that the community suffered from an unusually high level of birth defects, miscarriages, cancer, epilepsy, and other diseases. A national scandal then erupted when it was revealed that the abandoned canal had served as a chemical waste dump for almost 22,000 tons of chemical waste from Hooker, the area's largest employer, and that local politicians had withheld the information from the public. The environmental movement now gained an "angry mom" constituency, which politicians simply could not ignore. Just before he left office in 1980, President Carter signed the Comprehensive Environmental Response, Compensation, and Liability Act, what would become commonly known as the Superfund. Funded in part by taxes on petroleum and other chemicals, the $1.6 billion appropriation was earmarked for the cleanup of toxic waste sites and oil spills.

Love Canal and a Shift in Focus for Sevenson: 1978

Aside from its close proximity, Sevenson Construction had direct ties to Love Canal. Members of the second generation of the Elia family built a school that was located above much of the buried contaminants. Before Superfund was created, Love Canal was declared a federal disaster area and Sevenson was awarded the first emergency cleanup contract. As a result of this effort, environmental work quickly became a mainstay of the company. Revenues in the 1980s rose steadily, from $6.1 million in 1984 to $38.9 million in 1988. Net income reached $4.3 million in 1987. Although Sevenson became involved in environmental cleanup work through government contracts, by 1988 more than 60 percent of its business was derived from the private sector. Given the uncertainty of President Reagan's commitment to funding cleanups, Sevenson's focus on private contracts was a prudent strategy.

After the Reagan administration came into power in 1980, the EPA went an entire year before an administrator was named. According to Hal K. Rothman in his book *Saving the Planet*, "The Reagan administration also worked to curtail EPA's reach. . . . Enforcement standards were set so that the $1.6 billion Superfund would not be spent. This meant that the agency generally did not pursue law enforcement, instead resorting to sometimes fruitless negotiation with polluters. . . . Later, in 1986, Reagan signed Executive Order 12580, which gave the Department of Justice the right to disapprove any EPA

enforcement action against a federal facility. The Justice Department held that the executive branch entities could not sue each other, effectively ending EPA's ability to enforce its mandate on federal lands." Congress, some of whose members were outraged, held hearings that revealed that the Pentagon itself recognized 4,611 contaminated sites at 761 military bases, many of which purportedly posed grave threats to local communities. In October 1986 Congress then re-authorized the Superfund cleanup program, allocating $9 billion for the next five years. Hundreds of start-up companies vied for these government contracts. Well established in the business, Sevenson now preferred to work for private companies, rather than bid on government projects that were likely to be low-balled by newcomers eager to land their first contracts. Sevenson had built a reputation for completing work on time at a fixed price, which budget-conscious companies found appealing.

Wall Street soon recognized the potential for growth in the cleanup industry. In 1989 Sevenson went public to take advantage of investor interest and raise money in order to tackle more complex contracts and pay off $2 million of its $5.7 million in long-term debt. The family construction business was spun off, and Sevenson Construction was renamed Sevenson Environmental Services. Shortly after the initial public offering, the company made an important acquisition, purchasing Waste Stream Technology for just under $1 million.

Waste Stream was created in 1984 by Michael J. Barnhart, who had developed a method to clean up contaminated soil using bacteria. While working in the oil industry he became aware of the common problem of wells and piping that became plugged up by bacteria feeding on oil contaminants. Barnhart then sought to take advantage of the phenomena by creating bacterial cultures that could be introduced into contaminated soil. The bacteria ate the contaminants and died off naturally once the food source was exhausted. Barnhart was still working out of his Buffalo apartment in 1988 when he was able to procure laboratory and office space through the nonprofit Western New York Technology Development Center, which was created to assist area high-tech companies. Sevenson recognized the importance of Barnhart's work and bought Waste Stream well before his method became commonly used in remediation efforts.

Impact of Recession: Early 1990s

Sevenson, and the environmental cleanup industry in general, suffered from the economic recession of the early 1990s, when the number of projects decreased and competitive bidding drove down contract prices. After generating almost $75 million in revenues in 1990, Sevenson's business fell off by 35 percent to $48.3 million in 1991. Net earnings of approximately $7.7 million in 1990 also dropped by 36 percent to approximately $5.1 million. The company rebounded nicely in 1992, posting revenues of just under $70 million, although net earnings increased by just 5 percent to $5.4 million.

A trend toward onsite treatment bode well for the company and its Waste Stream technology in the mid-1990s. In 1994 the Securities and Exchange Commission began requiring publicly held companies to disclose potential environment problems at their facilities. Because the listing of those liabilities could hurt stock values, companies were encouraged to fund cleanups.

Key Dates:

1917: Architect Albert Elia establishes general construction business.
1947: Second generation incorporates Albert Elia Building Company.
1978: Love Canal disaster leads to company's entry into waste cleanup business.
1988: Company is renamed Sevenson Environmental Services.
1989: Sevenson Environmental goes public, acquires Waste Stream Technology, Inc.
1995: Company exceeds $100 million in annual revenues.

Moreover, Congress began debating the reauthorization of the Superfund with the possibility of relaxed cleanup standards, which critics contended were simply unworkable. Sevenson hoped that the result would be an even greater incentive for companies to initiate cleanup efforts.

Sevenson grew steadily in the early 1990s. It paid its first dividend in 1994, and followed that with a record year in 1995 when it generated $102.5 million and posted net earnings of $10.1 million, or $1.60 per share. A number of suitors sought to acquire Sevenson, but the Elia family-led management was uninterested in ceding control. The prospects for the company appeared bright, especially because many of its competitors were failing to deliver, a situation that enhanced Sevenson's solid reputation. The company also faced decreasing competition on the contracts it pursued. Budget squabbles in Washington, however, would soon have an adverse effect on Sevenson's fortunes.

In 1996 President Clinton and a Republican-controlled Congress squared off in a budget dispute that resulted in the so-called "government shutdown." Superfund projects were among the many government initiatives affected, as reauthorization of the fund was also delayed by the budget impasse. Although its mix of business had continued to skew towards the private sector, Sevenson was hurt by the lack of federal money because companies that relied on government contracts now sought private contracts, driving down bids to levels that Sevenson found unacceptable. The company's revenues for 1996 would drop 16 percent to $85.7 million, and profits by 38 percent to $6.28 million. The slump would continue into 1997, although the company's poor performance was more the result of two major projects being delayed rather than the lingering effects of the budget stalemate. Revenues in 1997 would fall another 4 percent to just under $82 million, while profits plunged 25 percent, dropping to $4.7 million. Subtracting interest income and the sale of some investments, however, the company actually suffered an operating loss of just $621,000. Management signaled that it would look to cut overhead costs, although it did not expect to eliminate any jobs. The company simply had to adjust to a business environment that offered fewer of the large, highly profitable contracts and more of the smaller, lower-margin contracts.

In an attempt to diversify its business and be less dependent on the uncertainties of government funding, Sevenson became involved in developing brownfields in the late 1990s. It started out by purchasing two properties in Long Beach, California. One, a former Elks Lodge affected by asbestos, was cleaned and sold to a hotel chain for a 25 percent profit. Sevenson then began working with venture capitalists to acquire more brownfield properties. In 2000, Sevenson became involved in another, although uncharacteristic, real estate venture: casino financing. Working with the St. Regis Mohawk Indians and assuming the name of Unity Development Group, Sevenson tried to purchase an option on 60 acres of land in the Catskill area. Northeast Gaming Group of West Springfield, Massachusetts, claimed it had an agreement to sell the land to Sevenson, and filed suit because it said that Sevenson went around them to deal directly with the private owners of the property. Opening up the Catskill Mountains region to gambling was also opposed by many residents. Moreover, real estate and gambling magnate Donald Trump threatened to fight for a casino in Manhattan if Catskill gambling were allowed. At best, the prospect of Sevenson achieving diversification by financing tribal gambling appeared problematic.

Sevenson's cleanup business finally recovered from its swoon of the mid-1990s. In 1998 the company realized revenues of nearly $85 million and earnings of $6.5 million. The next year, revenues would soar, increasing 50 percent to a record $127.2 million, with earnings of $9.7 million. The company enjoyed the best year in its history in attracting new contracts or adding to existing contracts, recording $148 million in business. The year 2000 was another strong one for Sevenson. Although revenues of $126.5 million were flat compared to the previous year, profits surged 25 percent, reaching a record $12.1 million, or $1.15 per share. Even if Sevenson failed to diversify its business mix, given its solid reputation it still appeared to be in good health for the foreseeable future.

Principal Subsidiaries

Waste Stream Technology, Inc.; Sevenson Industrial Services, Inc.; Sevenson Environmental Services of PA, Inc.; Sevenson Resources, Inc.; Senviro Investment Holdings, Inc.

Principal Competitors

Brown and Caldwell; Ecology and Environment, Inc.; IT Group.

Further Reading

Archer, Jules, *To Save the Earth,* New York: Penguin, 1998, 198 p.
Dowie, Mark, *Losing Ground,* Cambridge, Mass.: MIT Press, 1995, 317 p.
Hartley, Tom, "Sevenson to Go Public," *Business First of Buffalo,* March 13, 1989, p. 1.
Odato, James M., "Sevenson Finds 'Gold' in Nation's Brownfields," *Buffalo News,* May 21, 1997, p. B10.
Robinson, David, "Sevenson Environmental Expects Big Drop in Profit," *Buffalo News,* May 22, 1996, p. B7.
Rothman, Hal K., *Saving the Planet,* Chicago: Ivan R. Dee, 2000, 215 p.
Rubin, Debra K., "Family-Run Cleanup Firm Grows up with Superfund Program," *ENR,* November 6, 1995, pp. 44–45.

—Ed Dinger

Société Générale

29, Boulevard Haussmann
75009 Paris
France
Telephone: (+33) 1-42-14-20-00
Fax: (+33) 1-42-14-54-51
Web site: http://www.socgen.com

Public Company
Incorporated: 1864 as Société Générale pour Favoriser le
   Développement du Commerce et de l'Industrie en
   France S.A.
Employees: 71,149
Total Assets: $429.25 billion (2000)
Stock Exchanges: Euronext Paris
*Ticker Symbol*s: GLE; SCGLY (OTC)
NAIC: 522110 Commercial Banking; 522210 Credit Card
   Issuing; 523110 Investment Banking and Securities
   Dealing; 522120 Savings Institutions; 522293
   International Trade Financing

Société Générale is France's second largest banking group, behind rival BNP Paribas, operating more than 2,500 branches in France and another 500 branches internationally and generating more than EUR 2.5 billion from assets of nearly EUR 25 billion. Yet Société Générale remains a small player in what many observers view as a growing climate for cross-border mergers and takeovers as Europe becomes a single-currency market. Société Générale considers itself a marriageable prospect, at least in the long term. Meanwhile, the bank concentrates on retail bank services, asset management and private banking services, and corporate and investment banking operations. Société Générale is actively building a position in Eastern Europe, notably through its EUR 1.2 billion acquisition of majority control of Komercni Banka, the Czech Republic's third largest bank, made in mid-2001. This acquisition adds to Société Générale's holdings in Bulgaria and Romania. Société Générale is also building a position in the United States, especially in the investment market, where it operates through its SG Cowen subsidiary, acquired in 1998, and boosted, in April 2001, by its purchase of 51 percent of Trust Company of the West (TCW), the largest unlisted asset management firm in that market. Société Générale continues to be led by Chairman and CEO Daniel Bouton, who successfully enabled the bank to resist a hostile takeover attempt by BNP in 1999.

Forged in the Industrial Revolution

In 1864, when France was in the midst of its industrial revolution, steel magnate Joseph Schneider along with a group of private Paris bankers formed Société pour Favoriser le Développement du Commerce et de l'Industrie en France S.A. Another Schneider family member, Eugene, was the first president of the bank. At first, Société Générale was both a deposit bank and an investment bank. It grew rapidly by establishing regional banks all over France and by investing in industry, particularly in metals. For several years, this system worked well, yielding large profits.

The bank opened its first branch in 1864, in Bordeaux. The next year it opened nine more in other cities, including Orleans, Lyons, Tours, and Toulouse. The following year several more branches were opened, among them ones in Lille, Marseilles, Nantes, and Rennes. In 1869 and 1870, Société Générale opened branches in two towns important to the metal industries, St. Etienne and Clermont-Ferrand. In 1871, the bank opened its first foreign branch, in London.

Société Générale established itself in Alsace-Lorraine before the Franco-Prussian War in 1870, in Strasbourg and Mulhouse, and a little later in Colmar. After the war, however, the territory belonged to Germany, and in 1880 Germany's assimilation policy forced the bank to either close the branches or divide them with an Alsatian firm. Thus, Société Générale Alsacienne de Banque was founded by an Alsatian venture partly backed by Société Générale. Progress was slow for the next two decades in that region.

By 1875, there were 71 Société Générale branches in all, but during the 1880s and 1890s growth was much more gradual, due largely to losses from risky investments. Because the bank had not accumulated reserves from profits or acquired fresh capital, it suffered heavy losses at the end of the century.

347

After 1900 Société Générale built up its capital again, focused more strictly on deposits, and resumed its growth. In 1914, it had 114 branches covering nearly all commercially or industrially significant towns. The bank had also opened 560 ancillary offices, with limited hours and services, by that time.

World War I slowed Société Générale's progress. The Alsatian bank, however, opened branches within Germany and, despite the conflict between Germany and France, relations between the two banks remained close. Although after the war the Treaty of Versailles returned Alsace-Lorraine to France, Société Générale and the Alsatian bank remained separate entities.

Société Générale continued to grow during the 1920s, when an effective economic stabilization policy was implemented throughout the country. Nonetheless, with the onset of the Great Depression, which hit France in 1930, the Bank of France was not able to soften the blow. Several banks failed, but Société Générale survived. During the 1930s, Société Générale entered into an agreement with Crédit Lyonnais, another large deposit bank, to cut back on expansion.

During World War II, under the Vichy government's plan for a "provisional organization for production," banks were discouraged from opening new branches and forbidden to sell any stock or interests they held in other banks.

Postwar Reconstruction

After the war, the government took on a much greater role in the French banking system. In December 1945, France's four largest deposit banks, including Société Générale, were nationalized. Société Générale's stockholders were duly bought out by the government, and the company became a state-controlled bank. But like all of the nationalized banks, Société Générale retained its essential individuality and autonomy. It also kept its personnel, which helped to quell customers' suspicions of the new structure.

The nationalized banks possessed about half the total assets of all French banks, and as smaller banks were absorbed by larger ones the French financial system became even more concentrated, especially since the government had also passed new laws in 1946 giving the state control over the distribution of credit. As a central part of this system, the nationalized banks experienced three decades of steady growth.

After World War II, there was a trend in banking toward international expansion. Although Société Générale was reluctant to join this movement, by 1955 it had 35 branches spread throughout Algeria and other French colonies and in several foreign countries.

In the 1950s, the National Credit Commission required all banks to reduce the number of their branch offices and to gain its permission before further openings, as part of the government's continued attempt to make the financial industry more efficient.

In the early 1960s prospects for domestic expansion were curtailed even more for banks such as Société Générale when the government imposed sharply restrictive lending ceilings on the financial system in its effort to reduce inflation. This move forced banks to search for avenues of expansion other than those of traditional deposit banking. Many of them entered the eurodollar market; others plunged into merchant banking or extensive overseas banking. Société Générale was one of the first to begin dealing in eurocurrencies.

In the 1960s France enjoyed a period of strong economic growth, as it entered the European Economic Community, and its exports boomed. By 1968, the state was encouraging banks to diversify their roles, especially in the area of housing construction. That year, Société Générale planned to establish a banking concern in the United States called Sogen International Corporation. In addition, the bank continued to expand internationally with a focus on commercial trading and foreign currency.

In 1973 a new law was passed that allowed Société Générale to sell up to 25 percent of its equity to its staff and a limited number of institutional investors. Also, Société Générale was the lead institution behind France's first venture-capital company, Soginnove, which began with FFr 60 million.

In 1974, the bank's involvement in euromarket loans put it in the center of an international crisis. Most of the eurodollar loans were short term and influenced by the flux of world trade. Many companies used the loans only to borrow from the least expensive market, but some were eurodollar borrowers because they could not qualify for loans in their own countries. Also, several borrowers came from underdeveloped countries, where sufficient capital was not always available. These factors and the fact that average loan terms had suddenly lengthened from five to ten years put the euromarket in a precarious situation, especially in the midst of the oil crisis that began in 1973.

Société Générale was also one of the main lenders in a foreign syndicate that lent eurodollars to the failing United States National Bank of San Diego (U.S. National) in 1973. When U.S. National did fail, Société Générale lost $7.5 million.

In 1975, Société Générale introduced Agrifan, a food-products trading company to connect French suppliers with foreign food buyers. The trading company was such a success—handling $70 million in deals within two years—that the bank organized two more trading companies in 1977, one for medical supplies and another for food-industry equipment. The three trading companies were controlled by Sogexport, Société Générale's new subsidiary. The government encouraged the bank's moves because they helped the French export industry. Inspired by Société Générale's success, several other large banks formed their own trading companies.

During the mid-1970s, Société Générale handled almost a quarter of the new French security introductions on the Paris stock market and almost half of the new foreign ones.

Key Dates:

1864: Société Générale pour Favoriser le Développement du Commerce et de l'Industrie en France S.A. is founded.

1945: As one of France's four largest deposit banks, Société Générale is nationalized by the French government.

1974: Firm establishes Soginnove, France's first venture capital company.

1975: Agrifan, a food products trading company, is launched.

1980: Firm acquires controlling share of London-based brokerage Strauss Turnbull and Company.

1983: Firm's name is officially shortened to Société Générale.

1987: Société Générale is privatized, with FFr 21.5 billion in capital.

1998: Firm acquires Japanese bank Yamaichi Capital Management, technology and healthcare investment specialist Cowen & Company, and investment firm Barr Devlin.

1999: Société Générale resists takeover attempt by BNP; finds white knight in Spain's Banco Santander, which acquires a 5 percent share in the company.

Ownership Changes in the 1980s

In 1978, Société Générale began a heavy overseas expansion program. That year the bank opened a branch in New York, and in 1979 it opened branches in Latin America and Asia. In 1979 it also formed a new banking group in a joint effort with the National Bank of Egypt, and continued to look for ways to grow in the Middle East. By that time, the bank had 200 foreign branches in 60 countries.

In 1979, a new law allowed Société Générale to increase its capital without government intervention, although at that time the government still owned 92 percent of the bank's stock. The next year, Société Générale was the first of the nationalized companies to raise a large part of its capital on the stock market, and by 1980 the government's stake had decreased to 87 percent.

In 1980, the bank acquired a controlling interest in the London brokerage Strauss Turnbull and Company, and also acquired its Eurobond operations. In addition, the bank opened branches in Milan, Bucharest, Manila, Taipei, Athens, and Panama City and formed Société Générale Australia Limited Investment Bank and Société Générale North America to issue high-rated commercial paper.

In 1981 France elected a socialist government again, and the state regained full ownership of Société Générale the following year.

In 1982, Jacques Mayoux was appointed chairman of Société Générale. Mayoux was viewed as one of the few leaders of state-owned banks who would keep his position should there be a right-wing victory in the future. He was prominent in financial circles for having served in the French treasury for 11

years and as general manager of France's agricultural bank, Credit Agricole, for 12 years.

Mayoux began to move Société Générale out of commercial banking and into corporate finance and investment banking. He also began to develop the bank's business with small- and medium-sized companies by expanding its work in consumer credit financing and improving its equity base through issues of nonvoting stock and perpetual bonds. In 1983, Société Générale pour Favoriser le Développement du Commerce et de l'Industrie en France officially shortened its name to Société Générale.

Although the bank was very successful within France, its international operations were floundering, a situation some experts blamed on the bank's late arrival to international corporate banking. In 1984, international operations suffered a $2.4 million loss. However, in 1985 the bank began to refocus its international operations by concentrating more on wholesale and financial activities and specialized financing.

In 1985, Mayoux also sought to reduce the bank's number of employees, then at 33,000, in order to cut operational expenses, which had been driven up by what he told American Banker were "atrocious expenses involved in reprogramming software every time the government changes a regulation."

Société Générale, like the other nationalized banks, had long been criticized for its caution, which some said had hindered its progress, but in the mid-1980s it began to strengthen its riskier investment-banking operations. By international standards, the big French banks were undercapitalized, and investment banking was one way to alleviate the condition.

In 1985, the bank organized a new company called Projis, to take stakes in larger companies, and also planned to form its own investment-banking arm with capital of FFr 100 million to complement Projis. Meanwhile Soginnove, its venture-capital company, doubled its capital to FFr 120 million. In general, there was increased activity between entrepreneurs and bankers as commercial banks, including Société Générale, stepped up their investment services. Nonetheless, Société Générale did not shrug off its legacy of caution: one spokesperson told the *Financial Times* in 1985, "we have to fill the investment banking gap. But we will be doing it with prudence, not a flaming torch."

In 1986 the conservatives regained power in the government and soon began an extensive denationalization program, returning the companies nationalized by the Socialist Party in 1981 to the private sector and also beginning to do the same with banks and insurance companies that had been under state control since just after World War II.

In June 1987 Société Générale was officially privatized, with FFr 21.5 billion in capital. To protect the newly private companies from foreign takeover, the Ministry of Finance arranged for a *noyau dur* (hard core) of stable shareholders to invest in them.

Marriage Prospects for the New Century

Société Générale's shares remained at depressed levels following the October 1987 stock market crash. "It was not surprising that the shares seemed attractive to large numbers of buyers,'' said Marc Vienot, the new chairman of Société Générale. Société Générale, anticipating passage of a law that would change the French stock exchanges, also purchased a controlling stake in the Paris brokerage firm of Delahye Ripault.

After the socialists' election in 1988, Société Générale's shares rose sharply, to FFr 550, in late October. About that time, the head of Marceau Investments, George Pébereau, announced that he had a 9.16 percent stake in the bank. But because Pébereau was backed by at least two state-owned companies, there was a conservative outcry, causing a raid on Société Générale. Vienot combated the raid by persuading five private companies to buy a substantial stake in Société Générale. In 1988, Société Générale acquired Touche Remnant Holdings Ltd., a British asset-management firm, and in 1989 it acquired Ingwerson and Company, a Dutch brokerage firm. Earnings in 1988 were very strong, up 28 percent.

During the 1990s, Société Générale concentrated on building up its three core operations: retail banking, asset management and private banking, and corporate and investment banking. These were developed primarily through internal growth, and then, especially later in the decade, in the pursuit of acquisitions. An important acquisition was made in 1997, when the bank took over Crédit de Nord, strengthening its retail banking wing in France.

On the international scene, the bank strengthened its position in Japan with the acquisition of Yamaichi Capital Management in 1998, while launching its Société Générale AM UK subsidiary to bring its assets management activities to London. Société Générale then turned to the United States, buying up technology and healthcare investment specialist Cowen & Company, as well as Barr Devlin, another investment firm. In 2001, Société Générale continued to build on its U.S. holdings with the agreement to acquire Trust Company of the West (TCW), a large privately owned investment firm. That deal gave Société Générale an initial 51 percent of TCW, to be built up to 70 percent by 2006.

The following year, Société Générale believed itself to be on its way to becoming France's leading private bank when it entered friendly takeover talks with fellow French bank Paribas. Yet rival BNP quickly stepped in, bidding not only for Paribas but for Société Générale as well. In a battle that lasted for some weeks, BNP succeeded in gaining control of Paribas—but not of Société Générale, whose stockholders steadfastly resisted the takeover attempt. Société Générale at last found a white knight in Spain's Banco Santander Central Hispano (BSCH), which acquired a 5 percent share. BNP backed down from Société Générale, but kept Paribas, firmly taking the lead as the largest French bank

Société Générale was left to content itself with a number of smaller acquisitions, including acquisitions that brought the bank into Romania, Bulgaria, and Madagascar. The bank built further on its position in Eastern Europe with its acquisition of Komercni Banka, the Czech Republic's third largest bank, made in mid-2001 for a price of EUR 1.2 billion. Meanwhile, Société Générale engaged in a series of strategic partnerships, such as that made with BSCH in 2000 and another, made with

Italy's Societa Assicuratrice Industriale, in which Société Générale acquired 30 percent of Banca SAI.

These moves were emblematic of a wider trend among European banks then gearing up for what many observers viewed as a coming large-scale consolidation of the continent's banking industry. As the conversion to the single euro currency took shape at the end of the century, Europe's many banks— until then largely focused on their domestic markets—had begun to engage in a vast series of cross-border partnerships, while attempting to consolidate their domestic positions, such as BNP had done with its Paribas takeover.

Société Générale remained a small player among such bank industry heavyweights as the Netherlands' ABN AMRO and ING, Spain's BSCH, and Germany's Deutsche Bank. As one observer told *Business Week:* ''It's only a matter of time before there's a crossborder merger between two of the really big banks. And if that happens, it will certainly transform the market.''

Société Générale recognized its own need to search for potential merger partners, even as BNP Paribas continued to woo its smaller rival. With added pressure coming from possible mergers among its other domestic rivals, such as Credit Agricole and Credit Lyonnais, Chairman and CEO Daniel Bouton maintained his resistance against BNP Paribas. Yet the bank acknowledged that it would be forced to gain greater mass in the near future. One executive described the bank's situation to the *Financial Times* as: ''We're not like a bachelor saying we want to remain a bachelor for ever, watching television and drinking coffee on our own.''

Principal Subsidiaries

ALD (Germany); Alorfim; Banca SAI (Italy; 30%); Banco Société Générale SA (Argentina); Banco Sogeral (Brazil); Banque de Polynésie (French Polynesia); Banque Roumaine de Développement (Romania); BFV - SG (Madagascar); Centre d'Affaires Paris-Trocadéro; Compagnie Foncière de la Méditerranée; Crédit du Nord; Eléaparts; Fimat Banque SA; Fimatex; Gefa (Germany); Généfim; Généfimmo; Généfinance (U.S.A.); Généfitec; Génégis I; Géneval; Géninfo; Intersogé (Switzerland); Lyxor Life Ltd. (Ireland); National Société Générale Bank (Egypt); Nofirec; Patriges Gracechurch; PDI Properties Ltd. (Great Britain); Pt Bank SG Indonesia (Indonesia); Réalia (Belgium); SA Théâtre de l'Olympia - SATO; SG Asia Ltd. (Hong Kong); SG Asset Management; SG Énergie; SG Expressbank (Bulgaria); SG Finance Praha (Czech Republic); SG Hambros Ltd. (U.K.); SG Hungaria Bank RT (Hungary); SG Securities Asia Intl Hold Ltd. (Singapore); SG Securities Johannesburg (South Africa); SG Securities Madrid (Spain); SG Vostok (Russia); SG Yugoslav Bk Dd Beograd (Yugoslavia); Socgen Real Estate Company LLC (U.S.A.); Société de la rue Edouard-VII; Société Générale Australia Holding Ltd. (Australia); Société Générale Bank Nederland N.V. (Netherlands); Société Générale Canada (Canada); Société Générale de Banques en Côte-d'Ivoire (Ivory Coast); Société Générale Finance Ltd. (Ireland); Société Générale Investments (UK) Ltd.; Société Générale Marocaine de Banques (Morocco); Société Immobilière 29 Haussmann; Sofital (Argentina); Sogé Colline Sud; Soge Périval I; Soge Périval II; Soge Périval III; Soge Périval IV; Sogéfontenay; Sogen Finanziaria S.P.A. (Italy); Sogen Singapore Merchant Bank; Sogéparts; Sogessur; Soginfo; Super Twin Dragons Ltd. (Hong Kong); Valminvest; Werbrow Holdings (Ireland).

Principal Competitors

ABN AMRO Holding N.V.; Banca Nazionale del Lavoro S.p.A.; BNP Paribas Group; Crédit Commercial de France SA; Crédit Lyonnais; Credit Suisse Group; Caisse Nationale de Crédit Agricole; Deutsche Bank AG; IntesaBci S.p.A.; Natexis Banques Populaires; UniCredito Italiano S.p.A.

Further Reading

Anderson, Robert, and Victor Mallet, "SocGen Outbids Rivals in Czech Bank," *Financial Times*; June 29, 2001.

Clarke, David, "French Banks Show Cross-Holdings a Matter of Taste," *Reuters*, March 30, 2001.

Fairlamb, David, "Europe: The Bankers' Grand Waltz," *Business Week*, September 6, 1999, p. 54.

Mallet, Victor, "SocGen Need for Partner Grows," *Financial Times*, June 8, 2001.

"Trying to Build the Napoleon of Banks," *Business Week*, March 22, 1999, p. 56.

Wallace, Charles P., "The Key to a Closed Door: A Hard-Fought Battle to Combine Three of France's Biggest Banks Sees Market Forces Emerge Victorious," *Time International*, August 30, 1999, p. 36.

Wilson, J.S.G., *French Banking Structure and Credit Policy*, Cambridge: Harvard University Press, 1957.

—update: M.L. Cohen

South Jersey Industries, Inc.

One South Jersey Plaza
Folsom, New Jersey 08037
U.S.A.
Telephone: (609) 561-9000
Toll Free: (888) 754-3100
Fax: (609) 561-8225
Web site: http://www.sjindustries.com

Public Company
Incorporated: 1910 as Atlantic City Gas Company
Employees: 643
Sales: $515.9 million (2000)
Stock Exchanges: New York
Ticker Symbol: SJI
NAIC: 212322 Industrial Sand Mining; 551112 Offices of Other Holding Companies

South Jersey Industries, Inc. provides natural gas to nearly 300,000 customers in southern New Jersey through its main subsidiary, South Jersey Gas. The company is diversified in the energy field and markets both gas and electricity on the East Coast.

The Early Years in Atlantic City: 1873–1910

In 1873 a group of Philadelphia businessmen formed the Atlantic City Gas & Water Company. The new company was located in Atlantic City, New Jersey, on Michigan Avenue and manufactured coal gas for the city. The businessmen had many interests in Atlantic City and, in fact, helped to found and promote the city, incorporated in 1855.

As the city grew, so did the company, and in 1882, electric light service was added to the company's product offerings. Although gas lights were preferred by many, electric lights gained in popularity. The gas services of the company continued to grow and gas mains extended down nearly every street in the city by the end of the 1890s. Hotels, boarding houses, and other businesses hooked up to the gas main, as well as many homes in the area.

Although the company was supplying electric service as well, the board of directors decided to eliminate that portion of the business in 1900 and sold the electric plant to the Electric Company of America for $80,000. The purchase included an agreement that the Electric Company would not compete with Atlantic City Gas in the gas business.

That agreement, however, did not stop another competitor from moving into town—the Consumers Gas & Fuel Company, formed in 1905, with a product offering identical to that of Atlantic City Gas. The two companies were fierce competitors until 1910 when they were purchased by the same investor and merged into a new company.

Clarence Geist and a New Company: 1910s–30s

When Clarence Geist purchased the two competing Atlantic City gas companies, he incorporated the newly formed company as the Atlantic City Gas Company. Geist was a native of LaPorte, Indiana, and owned other utility companies, including the Indianapolis Water Company and the Philadelphia Suburban Water Company. He was a colorful character and a self-made man who began his professional career as a railroad worker. He had no formal education but soon branched out into real estate and then finally to utility ownership.

He and his wife, Florence, owned all of the company's stock except for a small percentage owned by the members of the board of directors. The board members changed often at the whim of Geist. He also was president of the company, although day-to-day operations were handled by his brother Carlton Geist who was named general manager. One of the first changes enacted by the new owners was the construction of new offices at 2001 Atlantic Avenue. Geist purchased the property, razed the hotel that was on it, and constructed the building, which was completed in May 1912.

In 1913, electric lights began to replace the gas lights on the streets of Atlantic City, and in 1917 material costs for oil, coal, and labor increased for the company. The company petitioned the city to raise rates in July. The city failed to respond promptly, however, and soon Atlantic City Gas was in financial trouble. As of November of that year, C.H. Geist's life insurance policies were the only cash assets. He agreed to surrender those as well as reducing the rent of the office building (which he owned and leased back to the company). Dividends were not paid, and Geist took a salary reduction.

Finally, nearly a year after the petition, the city approved new rates on July 1, 1918. Since the company had been unable to pay interest on some mortgage bonds for the previous six months, however, Atlantic City Gas went into receivership later that same month. President C.H. Geist had thought the company had three more months to catch up with the payments. A local court agreed with him, and the company was returned.

In 1920 Atlantic City's transition to electric lights was complete, and it did not renew its contract with Atlantic City Gas. The company continued to provide gas heat as well as water to the area, however, and in 1923 the Public Utility Commission of New Jersey proclaimed the company one of the state's most efficient utilities.

In 1922, C.H. Geist decided to expand his New Jersey utility holdings and purchased New Jersey Gas Company, which provided gas and utilities to the towns of Elmer, Vineland, East Greenwich, Pitman, Swedesboro, Penns Grove, and Bridgeport. He formed a new company, People's Gas Company of New Jersey, and then merged it with the newly acquired company. The company was separate from Atlantic City Gas, however, throughout Geist's ownership of the two companies.

In 1925, a nationwide coal miner's strike caused a coal shortage and resulted in more homeowners switching to gas heat. This helped Atlantic City, especially since the street lighting business was nonexistent by the 1920s. More growth occurred in 1926 when C.H. Geist acquired Pleasantville Gas Company and merged it with Atlantic City Gas. Carlton Geist, general manager and C.H. Geist's brother, resigned from the company in 1925 and was replaced by Chester Grey.

While the 1920s boomed, so did Atlantic City Gas. A total of 80 percent of all hotels were heated by gas, and housing developments were being developed all over the area. Atlantic City was "the place to be" with the resort business in full swing. The Great Depression, however, which began in October 1929, took the wind out of the economy's sails. For Atlantic City Gas, the downturn occurred at a time when C.H. Geist was considering selling the company and his other utility holdings. Despite the economic challenges, Public Service Corporation of New Jersey became the new owners of the company, with the sale completed

in April 1930. Of Geist's holdings, Atlantic City Gas and People's Gas Company both would be owned by Public Service.

1930s and 1940s: A New Era for Atlantic City Gas

In 1930 Atlantic City Gas became a subsidiary of the largest utility in New Jersey, Public Service Corporation of New Jersey. Thomas N. Carter was the president of Public Service, which also was incorporated in 1910. Chester Grey, who had been serving as general manager for Atlantic City, was appointed president of the subsidiary. The worst years of the Depression were still ahead, however, and in 1932, employees' wages were decreased 6 percent. In 1933, another 9 percent reduction was enforced.

In 1933, after only three years as president, Chester Grey resigned due to ill health and was replaced by Robert Wiederwax. Wiederwax was married to the daughter of Atlantic City's mayor. Grey's concerns about his own health were well founded, and he died just two years after leaving the company. In 1934, the company increased its workforce due to the National Recovery Act. The Act required employers to pay time-and-one-half for all hours beyond 40. Most of the employees had been working many extra hours, but the company now hired more workers rather than increase pay to existing workers for overtime.

By 1936, however, the employees had their wages restored to the pre-Depression amounts, and it seemed the worst of the downturn was behind the country and Atlantic City Gas. New appliance sales (and gas hookups) increased in 1937. Wages continued to improve as well, since the Fair Labor Standards Act guaranteed a minimum wage of 40 cents per hour.

With the 1940s came World War II, and the country joined together to support the war effort. Along the East Coast, a "dim out" was ordered in 1942 to conserve energy and black out the vision for the German submarines that were reported to be close to shore. Even motorists traveling along the shore did so without lights. The company and its employees were involved in volunteer efforts for the war, and the blackout finally ended in November 1943.

In December 1944, company President Robert Wiederwax committed suicide in his office. The note he left indicated that poor health and finances were among the reasons why he shot himself at the age of 60. Earl Smith became president in January 1945. The cold winter of 1944–45 combined with a nationwide coal shortage created a record sales year for the company. More and more homeowners wanted to install gas heat in their homes, but the company could not keep up with the high demand.

After World War II ended, Public Service Corporation, in accordance with the Public Utility Holding Company Act of 1935, announced that it would be selling both Atlantic City Gas Company as well as Peoples Gas Company. Public Service Corporation merged Peoples into Atlantic City and then dispersed the stock in the new company to its stockholders. In April 1947, the transaction was complete, and Atlantic City Gas Company became South Jersey Gas Company. The new name better reflected the regional nature of the company.

In 1948, the company reorganized as a publicly owned company. The stock traded on the "over-the-counter" market and

Key Dates:

1873: Philadelphia businessmen form Atlantic City Gas & Water Company.
1910: Clarence Geist purchases Atlantic City Gas & Water and Consumers Gas & Fuel to form Atlantic City Gas Company.
1930: Public Service Corporation acquires Atlantic City Gas Company.
1947: Public Service spins off Atlantic City to shareholders; name of newly independent company changes to South Jersey Gas Company.
1950: Company builds 75 miles of pipeline to connect with the Texas to East Coast span of Transcontinental Gas Pipe Line Corporation (Transco).
1958: Company joins the New York Stock Exchange.
1969: South Jersey Industries, Inc. is created as a holding company.
1971: Company builds new headquarters in Folsom, New Jersey.
1977: Energy & Minerals Inc. becomes a subsidiary.
1996: Non-energy subsidiaries are sold.

opened at $3 on July 1, 1948. Revenues for 1948 were $3.6 million with a net income of $210,000. South Jersey Gas Company, which had always manufactured the gas it sold to the public, was attempting to secure a supplier for natural gas. The Transcontinental Gas Pipe Line Corporation (Transco) was constructing a pipeline to the East Coast from Texas, and South Jersey Gas decided to construct 75 miles of its own pipeline to connect with Transco at the nearest point in Camden, New Jersey.

1950s Through the 1960s: 20 Years of Change

In 1950, the pipeline of natural gas was complete, and the South Jersey Gas contract with Transco was signed for a 20-year period. With the increased capacity, South Jersey branched out to the industrial market and added its first industrial customer, Owens-Illinois Glass Company. Also in 1950 the company acquired Bridgeton Gas Light Company, adding 3,300 customers. Atlantic City Gas continued to grow when, in 1952, it purchased the Cumberland County Gas Company and added 11,000 customers.

In May 1953, Earl Smith stepped down as president, and Theodore H. Kendall was elected president and CEO of the company. Many changes took place in Atlantic City, still the company's headquarters, during the early 1950s. The historic Atlantic City pier was demolished and the city's trolley service was discontinued. Changes were occurring for South Jersey Gas as well, and in 1956, the company listed its stock on the Philadelphia-Baltimore Stock Exchange. Just a few years later, in 1958, the company began trading on the New York Stock Exchange. The initial price was $38 per share.

By the end of the 1950s, 90 percent of residential customers were using natural gas as well as many industrial and commercial customers throughout southern New Jersey. By early 1960, the company was constructing a new commercial office in Millville

as well as modernizing the corporate headquarters at 2001 Atlantic Avenue in Atlantic City. The company attempted in the early 1960s to locate natural gas in New Jersey rather than pipeline it in from Texas. In partnership with New Jersey Natural Gas Company and Anchor Gas Company, South Jersey Gas drilled in three separate, promising locations. The exploratory drilling was unsuccessful, however, and soon was abandoned.

In 1964, Theodore Kendall retired as president, and William Gemmel became the new president after starting with the company in 1947. By 1968, the company had outgrown its Atlantic City headquarters. It was decided by the board of directors that rather than attempt to expand the existing headquarters, it made more sense to construct a new building outside of Atlantic City. A site in Folsom, New Jersey, near the center of the company's territory, was selected.

Because of legal restrictions governing public utilities, the board of South Jersey Gas was forbidden from investing in other types of businesses. In response to this, the company formed a second business as a holding company, South Jersey Industries, Inc., incorporated in 1969. South Jersey Gas effectively became a subsidiary of South Jersey Industries.

Diversification and Growth in the 1970s and 1980s

The new headquarters of South Jersey Industries was completed in 1971 on ten acres in Folsom, New Jersey. Early in the 1970s, the company began diversifying when it purchased Jesse S. Morie & Sons, Inc., a gravel and sand mining company, as well as three small fuel oil distribution companies that became South Jersey Fuel, Inc. In 1972, the company entered the propane business with the purchase of another company, but the venture was not successful and was sold off in 1975.

In 1973, the company opened the Liquefied Natural Gas storage facility at McKee City, New Jersey. As natural gas supplies became further depleted across the nation, the company decided to form South Jersey Energy Company to build and operate a plant to manufacture substitute natural gas and sell it to South Jersey Gas as well as other utilities in neighboring states such as Delaware, Pennsylvania, and New York. The company formed Energy & Minerals, Inc. in 1977 to combine the subsidiaries of Jesse S. Morie & Son, Inc; South Jersey Fuel, Inc.; Delaware Valley Industrial Gases, Inc.; and South Jersey Exploration Company.

Big changes were on the way to southern New Jersey as casino gambling was legalized in 1977. The first casinos opened in 1978, creating more opportunities for South Jersey Industries as well as other area companies; growth in the area from 1980 to 1985 was unprecedented. Although the coastal areas of southern New Jersey had always enjoyed an annual seasonal boom, the economy was now based on a yearlong tourist trade.

In 1981, Bill Gemmel retired, and Bill Ryan became president and CEO of the company. Ryan had been with the company since 1965. The company continued expanding throughout its businesses, purchasing and enlarging different areas.

In 1983, Cape May Division became part of the Gas Company, bringing the total customer count to 157,000 in 112 municipalities. South Jersey Industries lost one of its largest customers in 1983 when Owens-Illinois closed its glass plant in Bridgeton. The softening glass industry also affected South Jersey Industries' Energy & Minerals business, and the company stopped mining for sand to sell to the glass companies.

At the end of the 1980s, the company continued to grow, although two purchases of other companies were attempted but not completed. Record years in 1988 and 1989 yielded $7.9 million in net income. "Gas Company's service area has experienced exceptional growth in the last five years," said President and CEO Bill Ryan. The company acquired five New Jersey utility construction and contracting firms in 1989. The acquired companies focused on utility construction and fit well into the current holdings of South Jersey Industries.

1990s and 2000s: Focusing on Energy

By 1992, South Jersey's gas company operations served 220,000 customers and experienced growth in its operations. Another South Jersey company, however, The Morie Company (sand and mining), was sold to Unimin Corporation in 1996. The sale, for $55 million in cash, was closely followed by the sale of a second subsidiary, R & T Group, Inc., as the company divested itself of all non-energy businesses.

The sales were in response to a 1996 strategic plan that called for a focus of resources on the core energy business of the company. "The plan's second phase focuses on ensuring that SJI's remaining businesses are efficiently coordinated to maintain its competitive edge in the rapidly changing energy industry," said CEO Bill Ryan.

In 1997, "energy" stopped meaning exclusively gas for the company. A new subsidiary, South Jersey Energy, was added to lead the company into electricity trading. The addition was one way the company decided to move toward offering total energy solutions for its customers. In the middle of this new focus, President and CEO Bill Ryan died suddenly in 1997 at the age of 63. Richard Dunham became chairman of the company, and Charles Biscieglia was named president. Both were longtime employees of South Jersey Industries.

South Jersey Industries continued to add business in the late 1990s, including being named as the preferred energy provider by New Jersey chambers of commerce, winning the contract for

Atlantic City's energy and providing gas to more than 269,000 customers.

By the early 2000s, South Jersey Industries was confident in its financial outlook. "We made a statement that we are going to grow our earnings between five and ten percent per year," said CEO Charles Biscieglia in May 2001. "We increased our earnings this year over seven percent, so we're on track moving toward a ten percent growth in earnings."

Principal Subsidiaries

Energy & Minerals Inc.; South Jersey Energy Company; South Jersey Gas Company.

Principal Competitors

Conectiv; New Jersey Resources; NUI.

Further Reading

"Discovering Ways to Improve Its Products and Services," *Business Journal of New Jersey,* February 1992, p. C32.

Gemmel, William A., *From Small Beginnings: A History of South Jersey Industries, Inc. and South Jersey Gas Company 1910–1985,* Philadelphia, Penn.: Consolidated Drake Press, 1987.

Heidorn, Rich, Jr., "Mid-Atlantic Utilities Muddled in Age of Deregulation," *Knight-Ridder/Tribune Business News,* October 14, 1998.

"Jersey Resources Draws New Offer," *New York Times,* November 21, 1983, p. D5.

"Jersey Utility Rejects Suitors," *New York Times,* November 24, 1983, p. D3.

Pittel, Leslie, "Flickers of Excitement?," *Forbes,* February 13, 1984, p. 168.

Pospisil, Ray, "Frustration Peaking on Electricity Deregulation," *Chemical Week New Jersey Supplement,* September 9, 1998, p. S22.

Ravo, Nick, "Shoestring Arbitrage with Discounted Stock," *New York Times,* July 2, 1994, p. 31.

Rubin, Richard, "South Jersey Industries Shops Unit," *Mergers and Acquisitions Report,* April 22, 1996.

Tanaka, Wendy, "Folsom, N.J.-Based Gas Utility Makes Profitable Changes," *Philadelphia Inquirer,* March 7, 2000.

Twyman, Anthony S., "South Jersey Energy Plugging into Electricity Trading," *Star-Ledger,* October 17, 1997.

Wallace, Beatson, "South Jersey Utility the Best Bet As Kansas Power Company Fades," *Boston Globe,* November 25, 1990, p. A38.

—Melissa Rigney Baxter

Stolt-Nielsen S.A.

Aldwych House
71-91 Aldwych
London WC2B 4HN
United Kingdom
Telephone: (+44) 207-611-8963
Fax: (+44) 207-611-8952
Web site: http://www.stoltnielsen.com

Public Company
Incorporated: 1959 as Parcel Tankers Inc.
Employees: 12,000
Sales: $2.27 billion (2000)
Stock Exchanges: Oslo; NASDAQ
Ticker Symbols: SNIB; SNSA
NAIC: 483111 Deep Sea Freight Transportation; 483211
    Inland Water Freight Transportation; 112511 Finfish
    Farming and Fish Hatcheries

Registered in Luxembourg, but headquartered in London, Stolt-Nielsen S.A. is the internationally operating holding company for five primary businesses: Stolt-Nielsen Transportation Group (SNTG); Stolt Sea Farm, Stolt Offshore (formerly Stolt Comex Seaway, in which the company holds a 53 percent controlling share), the Internet-based Optimum Logistics, and SeaSupplier, formed after the May 2001 merger between PrimeSupplier and OneSea.com. SNTG was formed in 1999 by merging the company's sea-based transportation businesses, the company's founding activity, and represents more than 40 percent of Stolt-Nielsen's annual sales. Stolt Offshore is a leading services provider to the offshore oil and gas industry, specializing in offshore and subsea engineering, pipeline laying, diving and related construction, maintenance, and inspection services. Stolt Offshore added 43 percent to the company's annual sales. One of Stolt-Nielsen's fastest-growing and most profitable divisions is its Stolt Sea Farm unit, one of the world's leading ''aquaculturists.'' Stolt Sea Farms produces and markets a variety of fish species in the fresh and prepared fish categories, including Atlantic salmon, salmon trout, turbot, halibut, sturgeon, caviar, tuna, and others. Stolt-Nielsen attempted to take Stolt Sea Farms public

in 2000, but lack of interest, resulting in a low introductory price, led it to withdraw the IPO. Stolt-Nielsen has also set sail on the Internet, launching the e-commerce sites Optimum Logistics, providing Internet-based logistics software, and a controlling share of SeaSupplier, which has adapted the company's logistics software to the marine procurement market. Stolt-Nielsen is led by chairman and founder Jacob Stolt-Nielsen, and his son and CEO Niels Stolt-Nielsen. Another son, Jacob B. Stolt-Nielsen, is behind the start-up of the company's PrimeSupplier subsidiary.

Parcel Tanker Pioneer in the 1960s

Norway's Stolt-Nielsen family had been involved in shipping since the late 19th century when Jacob Stolt-Nielsen began working as a shipbroker in the 1950s. After working in Norway, England, and the United States, Stolt-Nielsen set up his own business in New York, called Parcel Tankers Inc. Stolt-Nielsen had come up with a new idea for the international chemicals shipping trade, that of subdividing a ship's hold into parcels, that is, into several tanks, each outfitted with its own piping and deepwell pumping systems. In this way, a large ship was able to offer more economical transportation to its customers' smaller cargo needs.

Stolt-Nielsen started with just one chartered ship in 1959. By 1963, the company operated a fleet of 18 vessels, and had opened offices in Oslo and Japan. The company continued to expand its fleet throughout the 1960s as it added new shipping routes. By the end of the 1960s, Stolt-Nielsen operated not only transatlantic and transpacific lines, but also provided liquid cargo shipping and handling across the Great Lakes and along the South American coasts.

In 1970, Stolt-Nielsen once again took the lead in the industry it had launched when it ordered seven new vessels. These were to represent a new generation of parcel tanker, featuring double bottoms, double skin and partly stainless steel hulls that provided greater security for the company's cargo. These new ships were later to form the basis of international parcel tanker standards and specifications. By then, the company had been so successful that ''parcel tanker'' had become a generic name. The company then became known as Stolt Parcel Tanker.

The company's fleet expansion was soon joined by growth on land. In 1971, the company acquired a storage terminal, the first of many and the foundation of the company's transition into a full-scale sea-based logistics group. Jacob Stolt-Nielsen was also looking about for new opportunities in the early 1970s.

The discovery of rich hydrocarbon deposits beneath Norway's coastal shelf in 1968 was to transform that small country into one of the world's largest oil producers, giving birth to new numbers of companies providing support and services for the blossoming Norwegian offshore oil industry. Offshore oil exploration and production was still a relatively young business, developed in the comparatively calm waters of the Gulf of Mexico. Norway's coast represented a challenge of an entirely different sort. Stolt-Nielsen quickly recognized the opportunity to get in on the floor of that country's offshore services industry, and joined with another company to develop the so-called "moon-pool" diving support ship—allowing divers to enter the water through a hole in the bottom of the ship's hull, rather than over the side into the rough Norwegian coastal waters. In 1973, Jacob Stolt-Nielsen formed a new company, Stolt-Nielsen Seaway, governing the operations of the vessel *Seaway Falcon* launched the year before.

That year marked the debut of another of Stolt-Nielsen's operations. Norway had long been at the center of the world's fishing industry. By the late 1960s, however, world attention had come to focus on the increasing threat of over-fishing and the resulting worldwide and long-term fish shortages expected to come in the future. Stolt-Nielsen recognized the interest in developing "aquaculture" or fish-farming methods as a means of meeting the demands of the quickly growing world population. In 1972, Jacob Stolt-Nielsen launched a new business, Sea Farm A/S. That company soon became one of the top producers of smolt (young salmon) to the Norwegian market. Sea Farm also began research and breeding programs to develop other farmable fish species, starting with trout and then adding salmon as well.

Both Stolt-Nielsen Seaway and Sea Farm were privately owned by the Stolt-Nielsen family but remained separate from the growing Stolt-Nielsen logistics wing. Nonetheless, the family set up a holding company for their businesses, Stolt-Nielsen SA, registered in Luxembourg, that was eventually to become the vehicle for the formation of the larger Stolt-Nielsen group of companies.

Stolt Parcel Tankers ran into rough seas during the 1970s as the worldwide economy plunged into a deep recession. By 1977, Stolt-Nielsen was losing money and its financial troubles had forced it to seek deeper pockets. In that year, the company reached an agreement giving British Petroleum an option to acquire 50 percent of Stolt-Nielsen. That agreement was never fully completed, however. By 1980, Stolt was once again profitable—posting net earnings of $100 million in that year—and by 1987, BP and Stolt ended their relationship.

By then Stolt had been growing strongly. In 1982, the logistics business acquired United Tank Containers, giving Stolt-Nielsen 400 tank containers and a new subsidiary, Stolt Tank Containers. That year, the company set up another subsidiary, Stolt-Nielsen Inter-Asia Services, entering the small tanker market in Southeast Asia. Another subsidiary, Stolt Tankers Joint Service, was formed in joint partnership with PanOcean-Anco, placing Stolt-Nielsen in charge of marketing that company's 11-vessel fleet.

Conglomerate in the 1990s

By the mid-1980s Stolt-Nielsen had become convinced of the potential for offering door-to-door logistics and transportation services for liquid chemicals. The idea was to bundle all of the various handling points in the typical liquid chemicals move. Stolt-Nielsen would also benefit by being able to market all of its various logistics operations and services from a single office. The company began shopping its new operation, dubbed Stolt Through Transportation Services, in 1987. The company found few early customers for its new service; yet such integrated logistics services were to become an industry norm by the late 1990s.

After ending its shareholder agreement with BP in 1987, Stolt-Nielsen took on a new shareholder, in the form of Japan's NYK Line, which purchased a 10 percent stake in the company. This proved the prelude to a wider opening of the company's shares. In 1988, Stolt-Nielsen went public, taking a listing on the NASDAQ stock exchange. The Stolt-Nielsen family retained majority control of the company. In that same year, the company launched a new subsidiary, Stolt-Nielsen Inter-European Service, adding small tanker service operations to the Northern European market.

The Stolt-Nielsen family's two other ventures, Seaway and Sea Farm, were also progressing during the 1980s. Sea Farm in particular continued to capture Stolt-Nielsen's interest. Fish farming remained a largely marginal industry, and Sea Farm slipped in and out of profitability during the decade. Yet the company was also steadily gaining size. In 1982, Sea Farm acquired a number of turbot, sea bass, and sea bream farming operations located in Spain and France. Two years later, the company acquired salmon farming businesses in the United States and Canada.

The company was also actively exploring new breeding species, such as halibut, the development of which was launched in 1986. By 1993, this research resulted in the launch of the company's Sterling halibut farm stock. The company also entered sturgeon production in California, in 1987, and by the 1990s caviar became one of the company's key products. Both Sea Farm and Seaway remained fairly small operations—neither were capable of generating the revenues needed to pursue a more aggressive expansion program. Nonetheless, both companies were operating in potentially high-growth markets.

Stolt-Nielsen's 1988 public offering gave it the funding to pursue the growth of its logistics operations. But it also encouraged the company to diversify its operations, and to seek further funding through shareholder placements. In 1991, Stolt-Nielsen decided to diversify while remaining close to home, acquiring two Stolt-Nielsen family private holdings. Sea Farm and Seaway both became part of the now larger Stolt-Nielsen SA. The company capped its new sea farming operations with the opening of a sales and marketing office in Norway, as the company began to develop new markets for farm-raised fish products.

In 1992, the company acquired rival offshore services company Comex (UK) Ltd., merging that company with its existing subsidiary to form the new Stolt Comex Seaway company. In that year, parent company Stolt-Nielsen's revenues topped $1 billion for the first time. Stolt-Nielsen then spun off Stolt Comex Seaway in a public offering the following year, nonetheless retaining a 54 percent majority control. At the same time, the parent company made a strategic decision to expand Stolt Comex Seaway beyond its original focus on diving and ROV to become a full-scale subsea engineering and services company. The reorganization began in earnest in 1994, with funding from Stolt-Nielsen, and was boosted in 1997 when Stolt Comex Seaway placed a secondary stock offering.

During this time, Stolt-Nielsen continued to expand its logistics operations, developing three subsidiary businesses, Stolt Parcel Tankers, Stolt Tank Containers, and Stolthaven Terminals, formed to govern its growing terminals activities. The company continued to focus on its specialty, the storage and moving of bulk liquids. From the mid-1980s, Stolt-Nielsen had been steadily expanding the company's capacity, developing a strong interregional business.

The drive toward developing a truly global business continued, however, through the late 1990s. In 1998, the company beefed up its presence in the Asian Pacific with the purchase of a stake in Dovechem Terminals Holdings Ltd. The following year, Stolt-Nielsen moved to simplify its structure and combined its three logistics subsidiaries into a single new entity, Stolt-Nielsen Transportation Group (SNTG). The new subsidiary brought the company still closer to its goal of offering door-to-door services to its customers. One of SNTG's first moves as a new subsidiary was the acquisition of a 50 percent share of the Jeong-II Tank Terminal, in the South Korean port of Ulsan. That year, Stolt-Nielsen celebrated its 40th anniversary with sales of nearly $2 billion.

The SNTG reorganization also sent Stolt Sea Farm out on its own as an independent company. Formerly attached to Stolt Tanker, Stolt Sea Farm was by then one of the fastest growing segments of the Stolt-Nielsen empire. The company had continued growing through the decade, acquiring new turbot plantations in Spain and Portugal in 1992, then acquiring a 12.5 percent stake in a Chilean salmon farming company in 1994. After opening a sales office in Singapore in 1995, Stolt Sea Farm consolidated its Asian presence with the purchase of Cocoon Ltd. Two years later, the company acquired Gaelic Seafoods Scotland Ltd., giving the company a position in another major fish and fish products center. That subsidiary was then renamed Stolt Sea Farm UK.

If aquaculture had remained a minor industry throughout the company's 25-year involvement, its fortunes began to rise dramatically by the end of the 1990s. A number of meat scares—including mad cow disease and foot-and-mouth disease—had shocked consumers into seeking alternative food sources. Continued concern over the depletion of the oceans led a growing number of food producers and distributors to turn to the world's fish farmers. These, in turn, had succeeded in driving down the high cost of farmed fish to within competitive levels of wild fish. Stolt Sea Farm met the rising demand with both internal and external growth. In 1999, the subsidiary purchased U.K.-based International Aqua Foods Ltd. That same year, Stolt Sea Farm opened the world's largest inland fish farm, in Galacia, Spain. Acquisitions continued into 2000, with the purchases of Ocen Horizen, based in Chile, Australian Bluefin Pty, adding tuna operations, and Rokerij La Couronne, of Belgium. By that year, Stolt Sea Farm's revenues reached 14 percent of the company's total sales—but led the other divisions in profitability. Nonetheless, an attempt to float the subsidiary on the Oslo exchange failed when lack of interest left the introductory price too low.

After acquiring 49 percent of NKT Fleibles and all of French offshore construction company ETPM in 2000, the company renamed its subsea engineering subsidiary as Stolt Offshore. That company acquired Paragon Engineering Services Inc. in 2001, becoming the leading player in its market. By then, also, the company had turned to the Internet, launching the e-commerce logistics software sites Optimum Logistics Ltd. and Prime Supplier Ltd. in 2000. The latter agreed to merge with OneSea.com, changing its name to SeaSupplier, in May 2001.

Jacob Stolt-Nielsen stepped down from his CEO position—he remained as chairman—at the end of 2000, naming son Niels as the growing conglomerate's CEO. Another son, Jacob, Jr., was also becoming active in the company, notably in the launch of its Internet subsidiaries. Now led by a second generation, Stolt-Nielsen continued to make growth moves in 2001, acquiring Ingerop Litwin, through Stolt Offshore, in July of that year. At the same time, Stolt Sea Farm grew through its acquisition of full control of France's Ferme Marine de l'Adour, from the Aqualande Group.

Principal Subsidiaries

Stolt Offshore S.A. (53%); Stolt-Nielsen Transportation Group Ltd.; Stolt Sea Farm Holdings Ltd.; Optimum Logistics Ltd.; PrimeSupplier Ltd.

Principal Competitors

A.P. Moller; B + H Ocean Carriers Ltd.; Bouygues Offshore; BT Shipping Limited; Evergreen Marine Corporation (Taiwan) Ltd.; GATX Corporation; Global Industries, Ltd.; Halliburton Company; Hanjin Shipping Co., Ltd.; Horizon Offshore, Inc.; Hyundai Heavy Industries Co., Ltd.; Kawasaki Kisen Kaisha, Ltd.; Matlack Systems, Inc.; McDermott International, Inc.; Neptune Orient Lines Limited; Norsk Hydro ASA; Oceaneering International, Inc.; Odfjell ASA; The Peninsular and Oriental Steam Navigation Company; Royal Vopak NV; Saipem S.p.A.; SEACOR SMIT Inc.; Statia Terminals Group N.V.

Further Reading

Cresswell, Jeremy, "Stolt Heads for US$300 Million in Contracts," *Scotsman*, May 28, 2001.

de Besche, Jan Oscar, "Norway's Fish Farmers Hope to Hook More Customers," *Reuters*, July 13, 2001.

Slovak, Julianne, "Corporate Performance: Companies to Watch," *Fortune*, February 27, 1989, p. 80.

"Stolt Comex Seaway Will Pay up to $248 Million for French Offshore Construction Company," *Petroleum Finance Week*, January 6, 2000.

"Stolt Offshore Acquires Ingerop Litwin (Engineering) from Vinci," *Europe Energy*, July 24, 2001.

—M. L. Cohen

Sumitomo Heavy Industries, Ltd.

◆ SUMITOMO HEAVY INDUSTRIES, LTD.

9-11 Code-Shinagawa 5-chome
Shinagawa-ku, Tokyo 141-8686
Japan
Telephone: (03) 5488-8335
Fax: (03) 5488-8056
Web site: http://www.shi.co.jp

Public Company
Incorporated: 1934 as Sumitomo Machine Manufacturing
    Co., Ltd.
Employees: 12,411
Sales: ¥513.75 billion (2000)
Stock Exchanges: Tokyo OTC
Ticker Symbol: SOHVF
NAIC: 333120 Construction Machinery Manufacturing;
    33329 Other Industrial Machinery Manufacturing;
    333220 Injection Molding Machinery for Plastics
    Manufacturing; 334419 Other Electronic Component
    Manufacturing; 336611 Ship Building and Repairing

Sumitomo Heavy Industries, Ltd., one of the major companies affiliated with the Sumitomo Group of Japan, manufactures industrial machinery and equipment, construction machinery, and environmental systems, in addition to being one of Japan's foremost shipbuilders. It is also a leading maker of mass-production machinery, including injection molding machines, laser processing systems, and electrical equipment.

A Centuries-Old Japanese Business

Sumitomo Group traces its origins to the 17th century when Masatomo Sumitomo opened a medicine and book shop in Kyoto and laid the foundation for the family's business involvement over future generations. Upon Sumitomo's death in 1652, his brother-in-law, Riemon Soga, became head of the Sumitomo family. Soga's earlier experience as an apprentice in a copper refinery influenced the company to shift toward that industry. In 1590 Soga had opened his own shop in Kyoto called the Izumiya and adopted the *igeta*, or well frame, symbol as Izumiya's logo. The *igeta* was registered as the trademark for

the Sumitomo Group in 1885 and later adopted by Sumitomo Heavy Industries and most of the other affiliates.

By 1888, the company's mining operations had expanded sufficiently to warrant the opening of a machinery production and repair shop at Sumitomo's Besshi copper mine. In 1897 Sumitomo established the Uraga Dock Company for shipbuilding. In 1934 the Besshi machine shop was merged with Uraga Dock to form Sumitomo Machine Manufacturing Company, which functioned as a subsidiary of the Sumitomo *zaibatsu,* or conglomerate.

Early 1900s: Name Changes

Over the next 11 years, the company's name was changed several times, from Sumitomo Machine Manufacturing Company to Sumitomo Machinery Company, in 1940, and to Shikoku Machinery Company, in 1945. As one of Japan's leading industrial concerns, the Sumitomo *zaibatsu* was disrupted significantly by military action during World War II. After 1945, the *zaibatsu* was broken up into independent companies, in compliance with the orders of the Supreme Commander of Allied Powers (SCAP). These orders gradually were relaxed over the next decade, allowing the Sumitomo affiliates to reestablish ties with each other and coordinate planning activities.

In 1952, Shikoku Machinery Company again became Sumitomo Machinery Company. In 1957, Sumitomo Machinery opened its first overseas office, in New York City. In 1959, it established its Nagoya manufacturing plant and also incorporated Shin Nippon Machine Manufacturing to produce turbines, pumps, fasteners, blowers, and heat exchangers.

1960s–70s: Diversification and Expansion

Sumitomo Machinery opened Japan Air Filter Company, Ltd. in 1960 to produce air purifying equipment and dust collectors. In 1962, the company formed the Hiratsuka Research Laboratory to develop cryogenic technology. Overseas expansion continued over the next several years, with the opening of a London office in 1964 and the establishment of Sumitomo Machinery Corporation of America in 1966, including a production plant for power transmission equipment in New Jersey. The plant was transferred to a larger facility in Virginia in 1988.

In 1969 Sumitomo Machinery Company merged with Uraga Heavy Industries to form Sumitomo Heavy Industries.

The 1970s was a period of consistent growth and development for Sumitomo. It incorporated Sumitomo Jukikai Environment in 1971 to build water treatment plants and manufacture industrial waste disposal equipment. After completing the world's largest forging press in 1971, the company inaugurated the Oppama Shipyard and Toyo Works in 1972 and incorporated Lightwell Company in 1973 to design and produce data processing equipment and software. Sumitomo established its Systems Research Laboratory in 1975.

Internationally, Sumitomo acquired an interest in Cyclo Getriebebau Lorenz Braren GmbH in West Germany and established Sumitomo Maquinas Pesadas do Brasil in 1974. It opened an office in Singapore in 1979. New products included the first cyclotron (or particle accelerator) medical diagnosis system in 1972. Sumitomo also launched Japan's first supertanker in 1975.

1980s: Shipbuilding Decline, New Focus

In 1980 Sumitomo launched Japan's first gas turbine naval escort ship, and in 1982 completed the *Kinokawa Maru,* the world's first voice-controlled ship. The company also received an order for the *Nippon Maru,* Japan's first original-design schooner, for training merchant mariners. The *Nippon Maru* was launched in 1984.

These developments were bittersweet, however. Stagnation and excessive capacity in the shipbuilding industry forced Sumitomo to deliver its ships at a loss throughout most of the decade, a disappointment when compared with the profits of the previous ten years. Only the continued growth of Sumitomo's machinery divisions, the construction boom in Japan, and internal cost reductions enabled the company to improve profits.

The company focused on technology and software engineering during the 1980s. It entered the business of electron beam accelerators in 1986 by buying Radiation Dynamics. The following year Sumitomo began developing the world's smallest synchrotron for making computer chips. This operation brought together the cryogenic, vacuum, superconducting, and accelerating technologies in which Sumitomo had gained expertise since the establishment of the Hiratsuka Research Laboratory. In 1987, Osaka University ordered a large cyclotron from Sumitomo. In 1989 Sumitomo entered a joint agreement with CGR-MeV, of France, to work on high-energy linear accelerators.

The firm incorporated Sumitomo Heavy Industries Forging in 1980 to manufacture casting and forging equipment and

Sumitomo (S.H.I.) Construction Machinery Company in 1986 to manufacture construction equipment. Several acquisitions during the 1980s strengthened the company's base of operations. These included Nittoku Metal Industries, Ltd., in 1984, which led to the establishment of the precision products group; Radiation Dynamics in 1986; Lumonics Inc. of Canada, the largest laser equipment manufacturer in the world, in 1988; and RPC Industries of San Francisco, California, a manufacturer of low-energy machines, in 1989. Sumitomo also entered the real estate business in 1988 to redevelop idle facilities into more profitable endeavors. The company incorporated SHI Resort Development Company the following year, to turn its old Kawama works site into a seaside resort area.

1990s: Advances and Setbacks

In 1989 Shigeru Gohda was named company chairman and Masataka Kubo was named president. Under the new leadership, the company continued to devote a considerable share of its energies to high-tech businesses. The result was a string of new products introduced during the first two years of the new decade. Mid-1991, the company announced that it had developed a material-scanning device that used neutron rays in place of x-rays. The neutron rays allowed for greater penetration, thereby making it possible to identify materials that x-rays did not detect. The announcement of the scanning device was followed just a few months later by the introduction of a new automatic inspection system for aircraft flaps, which Sumitomo had developed jointly with Japan Airlines. In May 1992, the company unveiled a new molding machine designed to produce parts made from advanced composites. The company also entered partnerships that would expand its technological capabilities. In 1990, it forged an alliance with a U.S.-based company to develop neural networks for use in computer-aided manufacturing and data processing. The company also joined hands with a West German research institute that had developed a technology to rapidly measure the abrasion of automotive engine parts. The agreement allowed Sumitomo to provide measuring services in Japan.

The mid-1990s saw continued efforts to build Sumitomo's technology-related businesses. In December 1994, the company allied with Du Pont to produce thermoplastic sheeting—a material that could serve as a substitute for metal parts. In April 1995, Sumitomo entered into a ten-year partnership with California-based XMR, Inc., a maker of excimer lasers that were used in the manufacture of liquid crystal display panels and semiconductors. The agreement gave Sumitomo exclusive rights to distribute XMR lasers in Japan and also to produce laser systems with the XMR trademark.

Sumitomo's shipbuilding division also made advances during the early part of the 1990s. In 1992, the company unveiled its plans for a new superconducting ship propulsion system, as well as the design for a high-speed container ship driven by an electric propulsion system. The ship was to be more narrow than other ships, which would reduce waves and thereby allow it to navigate at higher speeds. Sumitomo also partnered with Ishikawajima-Harima Heavy Industries (IHI), another Japanese shipbuilder, creating a new company dedicated to designing naval vessels. The new venture, Marine United Inc., was formed to enhance operational efficiencies, share and improve technologies, and reduce building costs.

Key Dates:

1600s: Masatomo Sumitomo opens a medicine and book shop in Kyoto.

1652: Sumitomo dies; his brother-in-law takes over the business, begins copper mining and refining.

1888: The company opens a machinery production and repair shop at its copper mine.

1897: Sumitomo opens Uraga Dock Company to build ships.

1934: Sumitomo's machine shop merges with Uraga Dock Company to form Sumitomo Machine Manufacturing Company.

1957: Company opens its first overseas office in New York City.

1962: Hiratsuka Research Laboratory is established for the development of cryogenic technology.

1969: Sumitomo Machinery Company merges with Uraga Heavy Industries to form Sumitomo Heavy Industries.

1971: Sumitomo Jukikai Environment is established to build water treatment plants and produce waste disposal systems.

1973: The company enters field of data processing and software development.

1980: Sumitomo Heavy Industries Forging is formed to manufacture casting and forging equipment.

1986: The company enters business of electron beam accelerators; Sumitomo (S.H.I.) Construction Machinery Company is formed.

1989: Masataka Kubo is named Sumitomo's president.

1999: The company announces three-year restructuring plan.

Sumitomo's construction machinery division, however, suffered losses in the 1990s. The downturn was due in large part to Japan's depressed economy, which led to reduced construction and a consequent decline in demand for construction equipment. Losses from this division contributed to a ¥12.3 billion net loss for Sumitomo in fiscal 1999. The company remained in the red in 2000, suffering a net loss of ¥6.3 billion.

To turn the company around, Sumitomo's management announced a new three-year restructuring plan. The plan called for strengthening the company's international presence in the markets for plastic processing machines, laser processing systems, and other products for the mass-produced machinery industry. The company took measures to strengthen its positions in the shipbuilding and steel manufacturing industries—both of which were undergoing a wave of consolidation. In 2000, the company expanded its existing shipbuilding partnership with IHI to more completely integrate operations. In 2001, it merged its steel manufacturing and engineering division with two other Japanese manufacturing companies in order to better compete with foreign firms.

Looking Ahead

Judging from Sumitomo's 2000 annual report, the future direction of the company leaned heavily toward the technology sector. The report's letter to shareholders stated, "To expand our business in the future, we are targeting such areas as semiconductors, liquid crystal, information and communication services/IT, and concentrating our management resources on such consolidated businesses as manufacturing equipment, systems, key components and functional components." The company also planned to expand its business in services and software development.

Principal Subsidiaries

Shin Nippon Machinery Co., Ltd.; Sumitomo Heavy Industries Foundry & Forging Co., Ltd.; Sumitomo (S.H.I.) Construction Machinery Co., Ltd.; Sumitomo Machinery Corporation of America (U.S.A.); Link-Belt Construction Equipment Company (U.S.A.); Sumitomo Heavy Industries Construction Crane Co., Ltd.; S.H.I. Examination and Inspection, Ltd.; Ohtsuka Machinery Works, Ltd.; Oshima Shipbuilding Co., Ltd.; Nihon Spindle Mfg. Co., Ltd.; Sumitomo NACCO Material Handling Co., Ltd.; Izumi Food Machinery Co., Ltd.; Lightwell Co., Ltd.; Sumitomo Heavy Industries PTC Sales Co., Ltd.; SHI Plastics Machinery, Ltd.; Sumiju Environmental Engineering, Inc.; Sumitomo Heavy Industries Engineering and Services Co., Ltd.; SHI Control Systems, Ltd.; Marine United, Inc.; Osaka Chain & Machinery, Ltd. Inc.; Sumitomo (SHI) Cyclo Drive Europe, Ltd. (U.K.); Sumitomo (SHI) Cyclo Drive Asia Pacific Pte., Ltd. (Singapore); Sumitomo (SHI) Cyclo Drive Tianjin, Ltd. (China); SHI Plastics Machinery of America; SHI Plastics Machinery (Europe) B.V. (Netherlands); S.H.I. Plastics Machinery (S) Pte., Ltd. (Singapore); SHI Plastics Machinery (TAIWAN) Inc.; SHI Plastics Machinery (Hong Kong) Ltd.; SHI Plastics Machinery (Shanghai) Co., Ltd. (China); SHI Plastics Machinery (Malaysia) Sdn. Bhd.; LBX Company, LLC (U.S.A.); SHI Machinery Service Hong Kong Ltd.; SHI Designing & Manufacturing Inc. (Philippines).

Principal Competitors

The Japan Steel Works, Ltd.; Kubota Corporation; Mitsubishi Heavy Industries, Ltd.

Further Reading

A Brief History of Sumitomo, Tokyo: Sumitomo Corporation, 1990.

"DRAM Synchrotron Called World's Smallest," *Electronic Engineering Times,* January 1, 1990, p. 21.

Henschen, Doug, "Japan Opens the Floodgate," *Boating Industry,* March 1, 1990, p. 38.

"Japan's Sumitomo Heavy to Post First Net Loss in 4 Years," *Asia Pulse,* March 15, 1999.

The Sumitomo Group, Tokyo: Sumitomo Corporation [n.d.].

"Sumitomo Heavy Buys U.S. Laser Equipment Maker," *Japan Economic Newswire,* September 12, 1996.

"Sumitomo Heavy-Du Pont Tieup on New Thermoplastic Materials," *Tokyo Financial Wire,* December 13, 1994.

"Sumitomo Heavy to Cut Debt, Boost Profitability Via Restructuring," *AFX News,* September 29, 2000.

—Sandy Schusteff
—update: Shawna Brynildssen

Swift Transportation Co., Inc.

2200 S. 75th Avenue
Phoenix, Arizona 85043
U.S.A.
Telephone: (602) 269-9700
Toll Free: (800) 800-2200
Fax: (623) 907-7380
Web site: http://www.swifttrans.com

Public Company
Incorporated: 1966
Employees: 13,000
Sales: $1.26 billion (2000)
Stock Exchanges: NASDAQ
Ticker Symbol: SWFT
NAIC: 484121 General Freight Trucking, Long-Distance, Truckload; 48849 Other Support Activities for Road Transportation

Swift Transportation Co., Inc. is the second largest trucking company in the United States, and the largest publicly owned one. The firm operates throughout the United States and in Canada and Mexico, where its 2001 merger with M.S. Carriers, Inc. significantly increased its presence. Swift drivers focus on short- and medium-length routes, averaging 509 miles per run. Major clients of the company include Wal-Mart, Target, Sears, and Volvo. Swift is based in Phoenix, Arizona, but owns or leases more than 35 terminals across the United States.

Beginnings

Swift Transportation got its start in 1966, when brothers Jerry and Ronald Moyes and their father Carl moved to Phoenix, Arizona, from Utah and formed a trucking business, initially with just a single truck. In 1969 they purchased Swift Transportation, a firm that had served the trucking needs of the Swift meat packing company. The firm grew slowly during its first two decades, concentrating on business only in the southwestern United States. Beginning in 1980, deregulation of the trucking industry helped smaller regional operators like Swift

better compete in the marketplace, and the company began to see new opportunities for growth.

In 1984 Jerry Moyes became Swift's president, chairman, and CEO. After his father's death the following year, he bought out the ownership stakes of his brother and another partner, Randy Knight. Jerry Moyes had been more interested than the others in growing the firm, and his new ownership and CEO status gave him a clear path to seek out other trucking companies to acquire. Swift's annual revenues at this time stood at approximately $33 million.

In 1988 the company made its first move outside the Southwest when it bought Cooper Motor Lines of South Carolina. The following year Swift also expanded its fleet by nearly a third. The company now employed 1,700, and its revenues had grown to an estimated $85 million. Swift was offering service to the contiguous 48 states, expanding from its previous regional focus, though a sizable portion of its business remained in Arizona and California.

Initial Public Offering: 1990

In the early summer of 1990 Swift stock debuted on the NASDAQ exchange, with revenue from the 1.65 million shares earmarked for retirement of debt. In the fall of 1991 the company purchased the assets of a bankrupt carrier, Arthur H. Fulton, Inc. of Virginia, for $9 million. Fulton owned several hundred trucks and operated terminals in Richmond, Virginia, and in New York City, all of which were taken over by Swift. Fulton's customer contracts also went to Swift, and these included Anheuser-Busch and Miller Brewing. They were added to Swift's own growing list, which included Michelin Tire, Target, J.C. Penney, K-Mart, Mervyn's, Scott Paper, Kimberly Clark, and James River.

The Fulton purchase was part of Swift's continuing expansion efforts, which also included new terminals in Fontana, California, and Dallas, Texas. This gave the company a total of 11 around the country, with more in the planning stages. In the fall of 1992 Swift issued 1.5 million more shares of stock, 750,000 of which came from Jerry Moyes.

Company Perspectives:

Swift seeks to provide premium service with commensurate rates, rather than compete primarily on the basis of price. The principal elements of Swift's premium service include: regional terminals to facilitate single and multiple pick-ups and deliveries and maintain local contact with customers; well-maintained, late model equipment; a fully-integrated computer system to monitor shipment status and variations from schedule; an onboard communications system that enables the Company to dispatch and monitor traffic; timely deliveries; and extra equipment to respond promptly to customers' varying requirements.

Swift Transportation's established niche was the short- and medium-haul trucking market. The company's drivers were averaging 659 miles each direction of a run, which gave them the opportunity to be home with family more frequently than longer-haul truckers, who sometimes were away from home for a week or more. One of the industry's constant problems was driver turnover—nearly half of new hires typically quit the business within a year—and it was important to treat them well to retain their services. Swift took particular care in this area, emphasizing safety and the comfort of the company's cabs, which were sleeper models complete with air conditioning, television, and other amenities. Trucks were replaced an average of every 36 months, and wages for drivers could more than double after only a few years with the firm.

Swift preferred to train its own drivers from scratch rather than hire seasoned ones, and the company had founded its own driving school in 1987 for this purpose. One reason for the practice was Swift's insistence on a maximum speed of 57 miles per hour, which was sometimes balked at by outside drivers that came to the company. Swift trucks were in fact fitted with engine governors that prevented driving at faster speeds. Part of the company's motivation for this was fuel savings, and part was safety. While the industry average for accident claims stood at about 6 percent of revenues, Swift reported an average of only 2.9 percent.

A Focus on Customer Satisfaction in the Early 1990s

The company also concentrated on offering premium service to its clients, with computerized onboard tracking systems enabling it to locate shipments instantly, and extra equipment maintained on standby to handle last-minute jobs for important customers. Swift located its terminals near its most important clients as well, and often assigned administrative employees to a single account to make sure that these customers had their needs met in full.

Swift's growth was rapid during the early 1990s. By 1992 revenues had jumped to a record $233.4 million, with earnings of $9.8 million. In the winter of 1993 another acquisition took place, that of West's Best Freight System, Inc. of Lewiston, Idaho. The stock trade deal was worth $3.8 million, and gave Swift an additional 105 tractor units and 321 trailers. A terminal facility owned by West's Best was acquired separately for $800,000.

Swift's planned acquisition of Vernon Milling Co. Inc.'s trucking division, based in South Carolina, was scrapped at the same time because of difficulties in integrating the two firms.

During the summer of 1993 Swift was reincorporated in Nevada from Delaware to take advantage of the desert state's more favorable tax laws. The company maintained a headquarters site in Sparks, Nevada, but continued to be run out of Phoenix. The year 1994 saw Swift add two more trucking firms to its stable. The largest of these was Missouri-Nebraska Express (MNX) of St. Joseph, Missouri. The $41 million deal gave Swift more than 530 additional tractor units and 1,800 trailers. The company also purchased East-West Transportation, Inc. of Decatur, Alabama, for $11 million. East-West owned 157 tractors and 250 trailers, and counted International Paper Co. and Georgia-Pacific Co. as customers. Swift was now attracting attention on Wall Street, and its stock price soared to $44 during the fall of the year. *Forbes* magazine named the firm one of the 200 best small companies in the United States for the second year running.

Expansion of Phoenix Headquarters and Further Acquisitions: The Mid-1990s and Beyond

In 1995 Swift started construction of a $16 million, 80-acre terminal and headquarters facility in Phoenix. The site would house Swift's administrative offices, facilities for training and truck maintenance, a convenience store and restaurant, and space for drivers to shower and rest. The following year Swift acquired the dry freight division of Colorado-based Navajo Shippers, Inc. for $7.3 million. The deal brought the company Navajo's terminal in Pueblo, Colorado, and 428 trailer vans. Leases on 258 tractors were also taken over. At the same time Swift won a contract from Volvo Cars of North America, Inc. to transport all of its new vehicles on the West Coast to locations in Florida and New Jersey. Swift also was becoming involved in "intermodal" transport, which consisted of partial shipment by rail. The company ran a train between Los Angeles and Portland, Oregon, once a week, which shipped specialized containers that could be offloaded and then trucked to their final destination.

Late in 1996 Swift announced a secondary stock offering of a total of 3.5 million shares, one million of which came from Jerry Moyes. This followed additional growth in the share price, which had increased nearly 75 percent in value in a year's time. After the sale Moyes would still own some 30 percent of the company's stock, with another 15 percent held by a family trust. Soon after this another acquisition was announced, that of a portion of the assets of the bankrupt Direct Transit, Inc. of South Dakota. Direct had earlier been in line for acquisition by leading U.S. trucker Schneider National, but the latter had backed out of the deal prior to completion. Also during 1997, Jerry Moyes and his brother Ronald provided financing for the management-led buyout of Central Freight Lines, a deal that did not involve Swift itself.

In the summer of 1997 the U.S. Equal Employment Opportunity Commission (EEOC) filed suit against Swift on behalf of a number of women who it claimed had been discriminated against by the company in its training programs. Cited was Swift's practice of using only female instructors to train women

<table>
<tr><td colspan="2">Key Dates:</td></tr>
<tr><td>1966:</td><td>Carl, Jerry, and Ronald Moyes start a trucking company in Phoenix, Arizona.</td></tr>
<tr><td>1969:</td><td>Trucking operations of meat packing firm Swift are acquired.</td></tr>
<tr><td>1985:</td><td>Jerry Moyes buys out his partners.</td></tr>
<tr><td>1988:</td><td>Cooper Motor Lines is acquired.</td></tr>
<tr><td>1990:</td><td>Swift goes public.</td></tr>
<tr><td>1991:</td><td>The company purchases the assets of Arthur H. Fulton, Inc.</td></tr>
<tr><td>1993:</td><td>West's Best Freight System is acquired; company is reincorporated in Nevada.</td></tr>
<tr><td>1994:</td><td>Trucking companies MNX and East-West Transportation are purchased.</td></tr>
<tr><td>1996:</td><td>The dry freight division of Navajo Shippers, Inc. is bought.</td></tr>
<tr><td>1997:</td><td>The assets of Direct Transit, Inc. are acquired.</td></tr>
<tr><td>2000:</td><td>Swift and five other truckers form online logistics firm Transplace.com; company buys a 49 percent stake in Trans-Mex, Inc. of Mexico.</td></tr>
<tr><td>2001:</td><td>A merger with M.S. Carriers, Inc. makes Swift the largest publicly owned trucking firm in the United States.</td></tr>
</table>

drivers. Since there were few of the former, the number of women who could be trained was restricted, and women interested in working for the company allegedly were forced to endure long waits before they could begin the process. Ironically, the Swift same-sex training program had been created in response to concerns that pairing female trainees with male instructors was leaving the company open to sexual harassment complaints. The suit was settled in 1999, with Swift agreeing to pay $530,000 and change its policy to permit coed training. Another EEOC suit regarding six female driver/managers who had been paid less than their male counterparts was settled some time after this for $450,000 in back pay and damages.

Driving for Swift, while hard work, was lucrative, with first-year drivers earning $30,000 and more experienced ones pulling down $45,000 to as much as $95,000. Owner-operators employed by the company could earn even more, though they were also responsible for the maintenance costs of their trucks. Because of Swift's rapid turnover of tractors, used ones were readily available for drivers who wanted to go this route.

In 1998 new $7 million terminals were announced for Atlanta and Salt Lake City, the latter of which would replace a smaller facility. Planned construction of a new terminal in southeastern Idaho was abandoned, however, with an existing site in Ogden, Utah, expanded instead. Swift continued to increase its use of Amtrak's "Roadrailer" service during this time as well. The year 1998 also saw the company raise its mandated speed limit to 60 mph for single drivers, 62 mph for teams, and 65 for owner/operators.

In March 2000 a joint venture involving six of the top public trucking companies was announced. Transplace.com was an online service that facilitated cooperative purchasing of supplies, coordinated shipping among carriers to combine loads, and performed other logistics services. It was expected to create substantial savings through a reduction in costs resulting from the pooling of resources among the firms.

After a three-year abstention from acquisitions, 2000 saw Swift purchase 49 percent of a Mexican carrier, Trans-Mex, Inc. S.A. de C.V. The company planned to acquire the remainder of the firm by the year 2004, when U.S. laws restricting ownership of Mexican companies were to change. Swift also bought the van division of Cardinal Freight Carriers, Inc. and purchased land in Tacoma, Washington, for a new $8.5 million terminal to be located there.

In late 2000 Swift announced plans to merge with M.S. Carriers, Inc. of Memphis. M.S. was only slightly smaller than Swift, and the combined companies, to be headed by Jerry Moyes, would be the largest publicly traded trucking firm in the United States, trailing only the private Schneider National in size. The $383 million stock swap deal was completed the following summer, making Swift a $2 billion-plus company. Swift issued an additional 1.2 million shares to help finance the acquisition. M.S., formed by Michael Starnes in 1978, brought Swift an additional 3,200 tractors and 14,300 trailers, which when combined with Swift's equipment would yield a total of 15,000 tractors and 45,000 trailers. M.S. concentrated on shipping in the eastern United States, Canada, and Mexico, where it owned half of the largest trucking company, Transportes EASO. The two firms, whose CEOs had known one another for ten years, complemented each other well, and both Moyes and Starnes were supporters of Swift's continuing plans for expansion.

After 35 years in business, Swift Transportation had grown from a single truck into the largest public trucking company in the United States. Its network of regional terminals, its contracts with a string of top companies, and its emphasis on quality and service put it in the driver's seat as a premium provider of truckload service, and its prospects looked good for a continued run of success in the field.

Principal Subsidiaries

Swift Transportation Co., Inc.; Swift Leasing Co., Inc.; Common Market Distributing Co., Inc.; Sparks Finance Co., Inc.; Cooper Motor Lines, Inc.; Common Market Equipment Co., Inc.; Swift Transportation Co. of Virginia, Inc.; Swift of Texas Co., Inc.; Swift Logistics Co., Inc.; Swift Transportation Corporation; Swift Receivables Corporation; M.S. Carriers, Inc.

Principal Competitors

Schneider National, Inc.; J.B. Hunt Transport Services, Inc.; Knight Transportation; Covenant Transport, Inc.; U.S. Xpress Enterprises, Inc.; Werner Enterprises, Inc.

Further Reading

Breskin, Ira, "Swift Sticks to Regional Hauls to Become a Leading Trucker," *Investor's Business Daily,* April 24, 1997, p. A29.
Degen, Dorothea, "Six Transportation Firms Merge Logistics Businesses," *Dow Jones News Service,* March 14, 2000.
Foster, Ed, "Swift Transportation in High Gear," *Arizona Republic,* November 12, 1995, p. F1.

Jones, John A., "Swift Transportation Hauls in Profits As Economy Grows," *Investor's Business Daily,* June 1, 1994, p. B12.

Kelly, Lidia, "Truck Companies Hit Bumpy Patch—Swift CEO Steering Through Potholes," *Arizona Republic,* August 7, 2000, p. D1.

Larson, Jane, "EEOC Lawsuit Alleges Sex Bias by Truck Firm," *Arizona Republic,* July 19, 1997, p. E1.

Rhye, Shirley M., "Arizona-Based Swift Transportation Co. Recruits Drivers in Indiana," *Knight-Ridder Tribune Business News,* September 25, 1997.

Schulz, John D., "Safety Pays—Literally," *Traffic World,* November 11, 1996, p. 26.

——, "Swift's One-A-Year Plan," *Traffic World,* September 9, 1996, p. 36.

——, "$2 Billion Truckload Giant," *Traffic World,* July 9, 2001, p. 31.

Thompson, Richard, "M.S. Carriers Accepts Buyout to Form No. 1 Trucking Firm," *Commercial Appeal* (Memphis, Tenn.), December 12, 2000, p. A1.

Wichner, David, "Valley-Based Trucking Giant Makes a . . . Swift Move," *Phoenix Gazette,* November 26, 1992, p. E1.

Wiles, Russ, "Trucker Pulls a Swift One," *Arizona Republic,* April 27, 1997, p. D1.

—Frank Uhle

TATE & LYLE

Tate & Lyle PLC

Sugar Quay
Lower Thames Street
London EC3R 6DQ
United Kingdom
Telephone: (020) 7626-6525
Fax: (020) 7623-5213
Web site: http://www.tateandlyle.com

Public Company
Incorporated: 1921
Employees: 21,500
Sales: £4.09 billion ($6.24 billion) (2000)
Stock Exchanges: London
Ticker Symbol: TATE
NAIC: 311311 Sugarcane Mills; 311312 Cane Sugar
    Refining; 311221 Wet Corn Milling

Formed in 1921 by the merger of two family-run sugar refiners founded in the mid-19th century, Tate & Lyle PLC is one of the world's leading processors of sugar—from both cane and beet—cereal sweeteners (mainly those made from corn, such as high fructose corn syrup), and starches. The company has particularly strong positions in sugar in several countries, including the United Kingdom, Portugal, Canada, and Zimbabwe. Tate & Lyle also produces citric acid, ethanol and potable alcohol, and monosodium glutamate (MSG), as well as various byproducts that arise through the carbohydrate production process, such as molasses, from the production of sugar, and corn oil, from the making of starch. Over the nearly century and a half since its earliest beginnings, Tate & Lyle has successfully adapted to changing conditions, from the threat of government nationalization to the introduction of non-sugar sweetening products. A dramatic company retrenchment in the late 1970s rid the company of unprofitable ventures; Tate & Lyle subsequently completed a number of acquisitions in its core areas of expertise to build its position as a global leader in carbohydrate processing in the early 21st century.

Henry Tate and Abram Lyle: 19th-Century Origins

Henry Tate was born in Liverpool in 1819, the seventh son of a Unitarian clergyman. At age 13, he was apprenticed to his older brother Caleb, a grocer, and at 20 he set out on his own. By age 36, he owned a chain of six grocery shops and began to look for other profitable ventures. In 1859, Tate became the partner of Liverpool sugar refiner John Wright and began to learn about sugar.

Use of sugar at the time was burgeoning in Great Britain, where decreasing prices led to a steady increase in consumption. New uses were being developed for sugars, including jams, condensed milk, and desserts, which made it a staple on British tables.

In 1869, Tate, a man who liked to be his own boss, dissolved his partnership with Wright and, with sons Alfred and Edwin, formed Henry Tate & Sons. He began building his new refinery in Liverpool in 1870. By 1878, the business had grown so much that Tate opened a second refinery on the Thames, which specialized in making sugar cubes using a process developed on the continent. His 250 employees at that refinery worked 60-hour weeks in 12-hour shifts.

If Henry Tate was successful in sugar, that was not true of all sugar producers, most of them family firms like his own. At the end of the 18th century, about 120 sugar refiners in Great Britain had supplied the growing need for sugar. By 1882, that number had been reduced to 26, and there were only 16 by 1900. But the changing business climate for sugar producers did not deter Abram Lyle III.

Lyle, born in 1820, had gone from his father's cooperage into shipping, like Tate setting up a business with his sons. The story goes that he got into the sugar business when he accepted a cargo of sugar in lieu of payment and had to find something to do with it. In 1881, Lyle bought Odam's and Plaistow Wharves on the Thames and began to build his own sugar refinery, which would form the foundation of Abram Lyle & Sons.

Lyle got off to a rocky start. An especially large continental sugar beet crop in 1882 severely depressed the price of sugar. At the same time, the cost of construction for his refinery soared

> ## Company Perspectives:
>
> *The pace of change today in industry is rapid. Companies only survive long term if they are able to adapt and change. Tate & Lyle's history is testament to that. It is one of only five of the original FTSE 100 companies still remaining and has survived by constantly reinventing itself to respond to the needs of its customers and shareholders. As the 21st century begins, Tate & Lyle is a world leader in sugar, cereal sweeteners and starches and citric acid. The Group has unrivaled expertise in processing carbohydrates and is continuing its drive to focus on activities that add value to those carbohydrates.*

well over the estimates. Lyle was forced to adopt severe personal measures, including taking his children out of school, to get his fledgling business off the ground.

Lyle's policy at his Plaistow Wharf refinery was to produce a few types of sugar as cheaply as possible. He specialized in Golden Syrup, a low-price sugar product designed to resemble honey (packaging that highlighted a bee motif enhanced the identification). It was said that the poor of the industrialized cities of England lived on bread and cheap sugar products such as Golden Syrup and treacle.

Although both their refineries were on the Thames, Henry Tate and Abram Lyle never met. But the two firms seem to have had a tacit understanding: Lyle never produced sugar cubes and Tate never produced syrup. When Lyle died in 1891, he left his sons firmly in charge of his business, as Tate did when he died eight years later.

In 1903, Sir William Henry Tate, the founder's oldest son, made a significant change in his father's company by taking it public, perhaps because one of his brother's widows wanted to withdraw her share of the investment. Only 17 shareholders, the majority of them family members, originally invested in the company.

By 1914, both concerns were successful family-run businesses. With the outbreak of World War I, however, they faced a very difficult situation. Between 60 percent and 90 percent of the sugar refined at the two Tate factories and at Lyle's Plaistow Wharf had been raw beet sugar, primarily from Germany and Austria. That supply was quickly cut off, and U-boats threatened cane supplies from regular suppliers in the West Indies, Peru, and Mauritius. In 1914 the government took control of sugar refining, confiscating the Lyles' supplies of raw sugar and portioning out supplies of all incoming sugar to the country's sugar producers. Government wartime policy allowed companies the same profit as they had averaged on granulated sugar for the three preceding years. Since granulated sugar was not the major product of either company, this formula was a blow.

Both companies faced other hardships during the war years, including an inability to replace crucial supplies such as the charcoal used as a filter during sugar manufacture, and overworked staffs of women who replaced the soldiers. But both the Tates and Lyles survived.

Creation of Tate & Lyle in 1921

In 1918, Ernest Tate, the son of Henry Tate's oldest son William, approached second-generation brothers Charles and Robert Lyle about combining the two firms. The products of the two companies were complementary, and there would be advantages in being able to purchase in larger lots and exchange technical expertise.

Tate was probably motivated by two factors: although his company had a greater refining capacity, it also made a lower profit per ton of sugar processed and a lower total profit. Also, the Tates saw a coming dearth of family leadership. Although the two founders were virtually the same age, the second- and third-generation Tates were much older than the Lyles and only one grandson, Vernon, was coming into the firm. The Lyles, on the other hand, had two active second-generation brothers and four family members in the firm from the third generation.

Negotiations began in the autumn of 1918 and dragged on until the spring of 1921, although the actual stumbling blocks in the negotiations were minor. Perhaps the most important deterrent was that the Tates and Lyles had different ideas about management. While the Tates hired people to handle purchasing, sales, and management, the Lyles handled those positions themselves. Philip and Oliver Lyle, grandsons of Abram III, were said to dislike the Tates on principle.

But the advantages of merger finally outweighed the objections, and the two companies became Tate & Lyle in 1921, with Charles Lyle as the first chairman, to be succeeded by Ernest Tate. The actual mechanics of merger were complicated, especially since Tate's was a public company and Lyle's was privately owned. But the merger was designed to form a 50/50 partnership.

Despite agreements between managements and an exchange of personnel between plants, however, fraternization between Tates and Lyles was slow. Even 15 years after the merger, old Tate employees were reluctant to mingle with the Lyle group and vice versa.

Early Challenges for the New Firm: Post-World War I Era

The first challenge the newly amalgamated company faced was to respond to the postwar economy. The end of World War I meant a growing worldwide demand for refined sugar—in West Africa, in fact, sugar cubes were used as currency after the war. Tate & Lyle invested in sugar-cane producing land in Africa (an experiment that was later transferred to local government control after political upheavals), expanded capacity with new refining techniques, and became a leader in the distribution of brand-name goods instead of bulk commodities.

Tate & Lyle also became involved in the effort to develop a homegrown sugar industry so Britain would not have to face the supply crisis precipitated by World War I. The company invested heavily in the Bury Group, which was set up to develop a beet sugar industry in Britain.

But the government also had its eye on beet sugar production. In 1933, national quotas for beet sugar products were established.

Key Dates:

1859: Henry Tate forms partnership with sugar refiner John Wright.

1869: Tate dissolves his partnership and starts his own sugar refining firm, Henry Tate & Sons.

1881: Abram Lyle III buys Odam's and Plaistow Wharves on the Thames and begins building his own sugar refinery, the foundation of Abram Lyle & Sons.

1903: Henry Tate & Sons becomes a publicly traded firm.

1921: Henry Tate & Sons and Abram Lyle & Sons merge to create Tate & Lyle.

1936: The government combines British beet sugar companies into British Sugar Corporation, effectively excluding Tate & Lyle from the domestic beet sugar industry.

1937: Company forms West Indies Sugar Company to buy sugar cane plantations in Jamaica and Trinidad.

1940: World War II sugar rationing begins, cutting back Tate & Lyle's production.

1949: Facing threat of nationalization, Tate & Lyle launches ''Mr. Cube'' campaign, which helps keep the firm independent.

1953: Tate & Lyle buys 50 percent interest in Rhodesian Sugar Refineries.

1959: Canada & Dominion Sugar Company (later renamed Redpath Industries) is acquired.

1964: United Molasses is acquired.

1976: Manbré and Garton, the only other British cane sugar refiner, and Refined Syrups and Sugars, based in the United States, are acquired.

1985: Several U.S. beet sugar factories are acquired, forming basis of the Western Sugar Company.

1988: Staley Continental, major U.S. corn wet milling firm, is acquired in hostile takeover; U.S. sweetener maker Amstar Sugar is acquired and is later renamed Domino Sugar.

1991: Australia-based Bundaberg Sugar is acquired.

1998: Tate & Lyle becomes the leading producer of citric acid in the world by purchasing the citric acid business of Haarmaan & Reimer.

2000: Bundaberg is divested; Tate & Lyle buys out the minority shareholdings in Staley and Amylum.

2001: Company announces that it has reached agreements to sell Western Sugar and Domino Sugar, thereby exiting from the U.S. sugar market.

The government was soon prepared to go even further. In 1936 existing beet sugar companies were combined into the British Sugar Corporation under the supervision of a Sugar Commission. The Bury Group received £1.4 million in British Sugar Corporation shares in exchange for its assets; this money was distributed to its shareholders, including Tate & Lyle.

The company was now effectively excluded from the beet sugar industry at home. But with the money from the transaction, Tate & Lyle looked for new sources of sugar cane to offset the loss. In 1937, Tate & Lyle formed the West Indies Sugar

Company to buy property in Jamaica and Trinidad. The company also built a new central processing center in Frome, Jamaica.

By this time, however, a new crisis was at hand with the opening of hostilities leading to World War II. Sugar rationing began in mid-February 1940 and limited each citizen to ½ pound of sugar a week. That meant a huge reduction in Tate & Lyle production. The directors, still primarily immediate family members, decided to keep both the London and Liverpool refineries open despite the drop in production. Plaistow made Golden Syrup, which was in great demand because of its low price. The Thames facility continued to make sugar cubes, although wartime shortages meant that the quality was lower. Both London factories were hit hard by bombs and required substantial repairs. By 1942 over half of the employees in both refineries were women.

Postwar Era: Fighting to Remain Independent, Expanding Abroad, Diversifying

The end of the war again meant increased demand and an abundant workforce, but it was not long before government intervention in the sugar industry became a direct threat to the company. In 1949, with Socialists in power, it looked as if the government was ready to expand from its base in beet sugar and directly nationalize Tate & Lyle. To avoid becoming a subsidiary of British Sugar, the company enlisted the support of other sugar producers and took its case directly to the people with its ''Mr. Cube'' campaign. The little square cartoon character told homemakers, ''State control will make a hole in your pocket and my packet,'' and ''If they juggle with SUGAR they'll juggle with your SHOPPING BASKET!'' The pressure held off the threat to the company's independence, which was further relieved when the Socialists were defeated in 1951.

Tate & Lyle may have been independent, but in the postwar world the company could not function freely. The U.S. Sugar Act of 1948 set the price of sugar there to protect its own sugar industry. The act also admitted Cuban sugar under a preferential tariff and regulated other imports under a quota system, thus severely limiting Tate & Lyle's expansion in the United States.

Other industry regulations followed. In 1951 the Commonwealth Sugar Agreement, an agreement suggested by the British West Indies Sugar Association (which included Tate & Lyle interests in Jamaica and Trinidad) specified quotas and prices for imported sugar in Great Britain. The agreement was monitored by the Sugar Board to provide fixed quantities of sugar at reasonable prices, and it did provide a stability in the industry that Tate & Lyle welcomed.

The 1950s saw Tate & Lyle begin to branch out into related ventures. In 1951 the company established Tate & Lyle Technical Services to emphasize research and development. That company in turn spawned Tate & Lyle Enterprises, an agricultural planning service to help develop agricultural ventures, especially in the developing world.

The company continued to acquire interests in sugar, buying a 50 percent stake in Rhodesian (later Zimbabwe) Sugar Refineries in 1953. Another major subsidiary, Canada & Dominion Sugar Company (later Redpath Industries), was acquired in 1959, giving Tate & Lyle a new foothold in the beet sugar industry and a better opportunity to serve the large U.S. market (beet sugar imports were not regulated under the same quotas as cane imports). When the United States slashed Fidel Castro's Cuban sugar quotas in the early 1960s for political reasons, Tate & Lyle took advantage of additional quotas for Caribbean cane sugar by buying Belize Sugar Industries. In 1964, the company diversified into a related area when it bought United Molasses. In 1967, as a member of a European consortium, Tate & Lyle expanded its interests in beet sugar outside of Britain by investing in the Say beet sugar factories in France.

Redpath Industries and United Molasses brought with them business areas outside of Tate & Lyle's traditional concerns. Subsidiaries of Redpath manufactured automotive parts and vinyl siding for homes, and United Molasses included shipbuilding capacity.

Tate & Lyle's diversification and expansion abroad proved to be the right course when Britain joined the European Economic Community (EEC) in 1973. One provision of membership that directly affected the company was the EEC's sugar quotas. Traditional suppliers of cane sugar would continue to supply the EEC with specific annual quotas of raw cane sugar, both to assure British producers of an adequate supply and to protect the economies of developing countries dependent on sugar. The EEC Sugar Protocols guaranteed annual quotas of raw sugar from the African, Caribbean, and Pacific producers. These agreements, embodied in 1975 in the Lomé Convention, completely insulated the EEC from the world price of sugar and tightly controlled sugar trading.

Another provision of membership that affected Tate & Lyle was the EEC's subsidization of beet sugar production. Locked out of the beet sugar market at home by government-controlled British Sugar, Tate & Lyle was never satisfied with the EEC's subsidization, as it provided substantial incentives for the beet sugar industry to overproduce and decreased the market for Tate & Lyle's cane products.

Nonetheless, EEC membership had little impact on the company at first. An acute world shortage of sugar in 1975 meant sugar reached all-time high prices. In 1976, Tate & Lyle was able to expand both at home and abroad, purchasing the last remaining independent British sugar refiner, Manbré and Garton (which specialized in starches and glucose), Amylum of Belgium, and Refined Sugars in the United States (which finally gave it a foothold in the U.S. market). But when sugar prices fell dramatically in 1978 at the same time that worldwide sugar production rose 14 percent, Tate & Lyle's earnings plummeted 62 percent in one year.

Restructuring and Revival in the 1980s

That same year Lord Jellicoe became the first non-Tate or Lyle to fill the chairmanship of the company, and Tate & Lyle began a policy of retrenchment because of "a trading climate which [was] unlikely to become easier in the near future," according to Jellicoe. Because of the "crisis of overcapacity" since membership in the EEC, the company closed its Liverpool refinery in 1981 to help reestablish a better balance between

supply and demand. Liverpool had been in operation for more than 100 years, and some workers there were the third generation of their families to work for the company. Tate & Lyle also introduced cost-cutting measures at the Thames refinery and terminated the production of starches and glucose. Finally, the company put a new organizational structure in place, marked by a smaller number of chief executives who had clear lines of responsibility and were held personally accountable for the performance of their divisions.

With unprofitable areas of the business gone and a reinvigorated management team in place, Tate & Lyle worked to regain a position of leadership. In the early 1980s, Tate & Lyle took another step, recognizing that sugar was not the only sweetener consumers wanted. High fructose corn syrup had become an extremely important product early in the 1970s. Corn syrup not only used the bumper corn corps of the United States, but also was easier to use in soft drinks and many types of packaged goods. In 1981 Tate & Lyle's Redpath Industries entered a joint venture with John Labatt to produce high fructose corn syrup for the soft drink industry. Redpath withdrew from the venture, called Zymaize, two years later, but Tate & Lyle was convinced that they would have to compete in the industry to stay on top of sweeteners. In 1985, Tate & Lyle reentered the beet sugar processing business by acquiring several U.S. beet factories; seven midwestern factories began operating as the Western Sugar Company.

As the decade went on, Tate & Lyle bought controlling interests in other foreign sugar producers, including the Alcântara and Sores refineries in Portugal, and developed new sugar technology with a microcrystalline process at the Plaistow plant to provide new types of sugar for packaged foods and industry. It also expanded some of its profitable non-sugar interests with the acquisition of Vigortone, a U.S. producer of animal feed, in 1984 and of Heartland Building Products, a producer of vinyl siding, in 1987. The Heartland acquisition put Tate & Lyle among the top five vinyl siding manufacturers in North America.

At the same time, Tate & Lyle began another strong public relations effort to counteract a trend toward decreased consumption of sugar in developed countries because it has been implicated as a cause of dental cavities, obesity, diabetes, and hyperactivity.

Three major developments in the late 1980s promised to keep the reinvigorated firm at the forefront of the sweetener industry. In June 1988, Tate & Lyle purchased Staley Continental, a major corn wet milling business in the United States. The $1.48 billion hostile takeover gave the company 25 percent of the U.S. high fructose corn syrup market. Tate & Lyle's aggressive new chairman, Neil Shaw (who took over in 1986 after serving as group managing director, beginning in 1980), immediately began restructuring the company to fit with Tate & Lyle by selling Staley's foodservice division. Staley Continental was later renamed A E Staley Manufacturing Company.

In October 1988, after resolving antitrust problems by selling the refining interests of Refined Sugars, Tate & Lyle acquired another major U.S. sweetener business, Amstar Sugar, which produced the Domino brand, for $305 million. Amstar was renamed Domino Sugar in 1991.

Finally, Tate & Lyle announced its development of sucralose, a calorie-free sweetener made from sugar that could compete with aspartame (marketed as Nutrasweet). This discovery was developed in a joint venture with the American company Johnson & Johnson to ensure approval for its use in the United States. The approval process, however, proved slower than anticipated, with final ratification from the U.S. Food and Drug Administration not coming until 1998.

1990s and Beyond: Global Operations, Global Challenges

The early 1990s saw Tate & Lyle expand still further, with the biggest prize being Bundaberg Sugar, which was secured in mid-1991 through another hostile takeover. The addition of the Queensland, Australia-based Bundaberg significantly increased the Asia-Pacific interests of Tate & Lyle. The year 1991 also saw Tate & Lyle make its first venture into the newly emerging markets of eastern Europe through an investment in the Kaba Sugar Factory of Hungary. In April 1991 Stephen Brown was hired by Shaw as group managing director and heir apparent. Formerly with Alcan Aluminum Ltd. of Montreal, Brown was named chief executive in April 1992, with Shaw remaining nonexecutive chairman. "Differences in management style," however, led to Brown's departure in March 1993. Shaw returned to his previous roles of chief executive and executive chairman.

Tate & Lyle extended its global reach in the mid-1990s as the sugar markets in more and more countries were opened to foreign operators. The firm acquired companies or interests in companies in Slovakia, the Czech Republic, Saudi Arabia, Zambia, Namibia, Botswana, China, and Vietnam. In Mexico, Tate & Lyle in 1995 acquired a 49 percent interest in Occidente, the fourth largest sugar group in that nation. Profits suffered during the mid-1990s, however, in part because of difficulties with some of the operations in emerging markets, some of which were initially unprofitable. Ventures into the Ukraine and Bulgaria were abandoned altogether. Another problem was the high fructose corn syrup operation of A E Staley, which was hurt by low prices in the U.S. market caused by sector overcapacity. In 1992 Larry Pillard was hired away from Staley competitor Cargill, Incorporated to run Staley, and Pillard improved the situation by turning Staley into the lowest cost competitor and by finding additional markets for the company's products. Through his efforts at Staley, Pillard emerged as the new heir apparent to Shaw and was named group chief executive in November 1996.

During 1996 Tate & Lyle made its first inroads into the starch and citric acid sectors of India through an investment in Bharat Starch Industries Ltd. and a citric acid joint venture with Bharat. The following year Tate & Lyle became the first foreign firm to enter into a joint sugar venture in India by investing in a new cane sugar plant in Chilwaria being built by Simbhaoli Sugar Mills Ltd. Tate & Lyle became the leading producer of citric acid in the world in 1998 by purchasing the citric acid business of Haarmaan & Reimer, a subsidiary of Bayer AG, for $219 million. This business was renamed Tate & Lyle Citric Acid. In June 1998 Shaw retired from his position as chairman after his long tenure of transformative leadership. David Lees, a former chief executive and current nonexecutive chairman of U.K. industrial giant GKN plc, was named his successor.

Pillard and Lees faced fresh challenges as the 20th century drew to a close. Falling sugar prices around the world put severe pressure on profits. The situation was particularly dire in the United States, where strong beet and cane crops had pushed sugar prices down, forcing Tate & Lyle's U.S. sugar operations into the red. The decline in world sugar prices also turned Bundaberg, the Australian firm acquired in 1991, into a loss-making operation. In starch, Staley's high fructose corn syrup operations suffered from both declining prices of fructose and increasing raw material costs. By March 2000 Tate & Lyle's stock price had fallen to its lowest level since 1989 following a series of warnings about lower than expected profits.

In response to this dire situation, Tate & Lyle began divesting itself of underperforming assets. During the second half of 2000, Bundaberg was sold to Belgium-based Société Financiere des Sucres for $247 million and several other smaller sell-offs were completed. Another important move for the longer term was the purchase in June 2000 of the minority shareholdings in Staley and Amylum. By taking full control of these companies, Tate & Lyle could create global businesses in the areas of cereal sweeteners and starch and achieve significant cost savings in the process. In August 2000 Tate & Lyle entered into a joint agreement with Du Pont to develop bio-based polymers. Further divestments came in 2001, including the sale of the company's interest in Zambia Sugar. Having concluded that the outlook for an improvement in the U.S. sugar market was bleak, Tate & Lyle placed its U.S. sugar operations up for sale. By mid-2001 preliminary agreements had been reached to sell Western Sugar to the Rocky Mountain Sugar Growers Cooperative and to sell Tate & Lyle North American Sugars, which did business as Domino Sugar, to an investment group led by brothers Adolfo and J. Pepe Fanjul. With its exit from the U.S. sugar market, its restructuring of Amylum and Staley, and a goal of being the lowest cost producer in all markets in which it operated, Tate & Lyle hoped for a return to the more robust profitability of earlier years.

Principal Subsidiaries

Amylum UK Limited; Greenwich Distillers Limited; Redpath (UK) Limited; The Molasses Trading Company Limited; Tate & Lyle Holdings Limited; Tate & Lyle Industrial Holdings Limited; Tate & Lyle Industries Limited; Tate & Lyle International Finance PLC; Tate & Lyle Investments Limited; Tate & Lyle Investments (USA) Limited; Tate & Lyle Sugar Quay Investments Limited; Tate & Lyle Ventures Limited; United Molasses (Ireland) Ltd. (50%); Caribbean Antilles Molasses Company Limited (Barbados); Amylum Europe NV (Belgium); Tameco NV (Belgium); Tate & Lyle Management & Finance Limited (Bermuda); Tate & Lyle Reinsurance Limited (Bermuda); Anglo Vietnam Sugar Investments Limited (British Virgin Islands; 60%); Mercocitrico Fermentaçoes S.A. (Brazil); Tate & Lyle North American Sugars Limited (Canada); Orsan Guangzhou Gourmet Powder Company Limited (China; 51%); Nordisk Melasse A/S (Denmark); Amylum France SAS (France); France Melasse SSA (61.6%); Orsan SA (France; 80.4%); Société Européenne des Mélasses SA (France; 66%); Hansa Melasse - Handelsgesellschaft mbH (Germany); Amylum Hellas SA (Greece; 98.6%); Caribbean Molasses Company Inc. (Guyana); Tate & Lyle (Hong Kong) Limited; Tate &

Lyle Investments (India) Pvt Ltd; Melassa Italiana SpA (Italy); East African Storage Company Limited (Kenya); The Mauritius Molasses Company Limited (66.7%); Mexama, SA de CV (Mexico; 65.4%); Tate & Lyle Mexico SA de CV; Amylum Maghreb SA (Morocco); Companhia Exportadora de Melaços (Mozambique); Amylum Nederland BV (Netherlands; 98%); Nederlandsche Melasse Handel Maatschappij BV (Netherlands); Tate & Lyle Holland BV (Netherlands); Tate & Lyle Norge A/S (Norway); Alcântara Empreendimentos SGPS, SA (Portugal); Alcântara Refinarias - Açucares, SA (Portugal); Tate & Lyle (Portugal) Importaçao e Exportaçao Ltda. (Portugal); The Pure Cane Molasses Company (Durban) (Pty) Ltd. (South Africa); Amylum Ibérica SA (Spain; 97.4%); United Molasses (España) SA (Spain); Caribbean Bulk Storage and Trading Company Ltd. (Trinidad); A E Staley Manufacturing Company (U.S.A.); PM Ag Products Inc. (U.S.A.); Staley Grain Inc. (U.S.A.); Staley Holdings Inc. (U.S.A.); Tate & Lyle Citric Acid Inc. (U.S.A.); Tate & Lyle Finance, Inc. (U.S.A.); Tate & Lyle Inc. (U.S.A.); Tate & Lyle North American Finance Company, LLC (U.S.A.); TLI Holding Inc. (U.S.A.); Nighe An Tate & Lyle Sugar Company Limited (Vietnam; 80.9%); ZSR Corporation Ltd. (Zimbabwe; 50.1%).

Principal Competitors

Béghin-Say; Associated British Foods plc; Südzucker AG; Cargill, Incorporated; Corn Products International, Inc.; Archer Daniels Midland Company; Ag Processing Inc.

Further Reading

Chalmin, Philippe, *The Making of a Sugar Giant: Tate and Lyle, 1859–1989,* translated from the French by Erica Long-Michalke, New York: Harwood Academic, 1990, 782 p.

Hugill, Antony, *Sugar and All That . . .: A History of Tate & Lyle,* London: Gentry Books, 1978, 320 p.

Mintz, Sidney W., *Sweetness and Power: The Place of Sugar in Modern History,* New York: Viking Penguin, 1985, 274 p.

Oram, Roderick, "Sweet Success Beckons in Newly Opened Markets," *Financial Times,* November 30, 1995, p. 35.

Perez, Marvin G., "Investment Group to Buy Producer of Domino Sugar," *Wall Street Journal,* July 26, 2001, p. C15.

Urry, Maggie, "A Sweet, Starchy Taste That Soon Turned Sour," *Financial Times,* May 9, 1997, p. 28.

——, "Tate & Lyle Escapes U.S. Sugar Market," *Financial Times,* June 8, 2001, p. 29.

——, "Tate & Lyle Sees Its Hopes Melt Away," *Financial Times,* March 9, 2000, p. 30.

—update: David E. Salamie

THALES

Thales S.A.

173, Boulevard Haussmann
75008 Paris Cedex 08
France
Telephone: (+33) 1-53-77-80-00
Fax: (+33) 1-53-77-86-59
Web site: http://www.thalesgroup.com

Public Company
Incorporated: 1893 as Compagnie Française Thomson-Houston
Employees: 57,312
Sales: EUR 8.58 billion ($8.08 billion) (2000)
Stock Exchanges: Euronext Paris
Ticker Symbol: HO
NAIC: 334511 Aeronautical Systems and Instruments Manufacturing; 336992 Military Armored Vehicle, Tank, and Tank Component Manufacturing; 334220 Communications Equipment Manufacturing

Thales S.A., formerly known as Thomson-CSF, is one of the world's leading providers of advanced electronic systems and equipment for the defense and commercial aerospace and other industries. The company's operations are structured into three main divisions: Aerospace, Defense, and Information Technologies and Services (ITS). Defense is the company's largest segment, representing 58 percent of the company's sales. The company develops radar, missile, and other electronic warfare systems; avionics systems; tactical mobile and defense communication networks; integrated naval combat systems; optronics systems, including detection, guidance, and other optronics warfare systems. Many of the company's defense systems find application in the Aerospace market as well; the company's avionics systems, including flight control and navigation, as well as air traffic management, are developed for both military and civil aviation markets. The company also develops simulation and training systems. Thales's Aerospace division is the European leader and one of the top three worldwide. The company's third division, ITS, generates 24 percent of company revenues. Drawing on its expertise in the Defense and Aerospace markets, Thales develops mobile communications systems, electronic security and payment systems, and other information technology systems. Thales is also the world leader in development of sound and image broadcasting systems. Much of the company's ITS division was acquired through the 1998 acquisitions of certain components of France's Dassault and especially in the 2000 acquisition of the United Kingdom's Racal Electronics. This latter acquisition also has helped transform the company into a truly global—Thales likes the term "multi-domestic"—company, with industrial operations in more than 30 countries and more than half of its 57,000 employees located outside of France. Nonetheless, the company remains firmly wedded to Europe, which accounted for 60 percent of sales in 2000. The difficult-to-enter U.S. market generated only 10 percent of the company's sales. Yet the formation of a joint venture with Raytheon Company in 2001 promised to help build Thales's presence in North America. The company is led by Dennis Ranque and trades on the Euronext Paris stock exchange, with a secondary listing on the London stock exchange. Thales was formerly majority-owned by the French government and by former sister company Thomson Multimedia. The French government was expected to reduce its stake in Thales to below 33 percent by the end of 2001.

Electronics Pioneer at the Turn of the 20th Century

One of the jewels in France's industrial crown, Thales began its operations in 1893 as the Compagnie Française Thomson-Houston. This company was formed to export the patents and processes developed by the Thomson-Houston International Corporation, itself founded in Connecticut in the United States by Edwin Houston and Elihu Thomson in 1879. The French company initially served as a sales and marketing arm for its U.S. parent, which focused especially on the development of tramways and other types of electrical infrastructure systems.

Compagnie Française Thomson-Houston operated as a subsidiary to the Thomson-Houston International Corporation until its parent merged with Edison General Electric to form General Electric (GE) in 1903. At that time, Compagnie Française Thomson-Houston was bought out by a group of French investors, who retained the Thomson-Houston name and an agreement that gave the young French company access to GE's technology, patents, and licenses. Thomson-Houston maintained close ties with GE until after World War II, developing a licensing relationship that ended only when political tensions between France and the United States mounted in the 1950s.

Thomson-Houston began expanding in the 1920s, extending its operations beyond industrial infrastructure to include a variety of diversified applications of electrical technology, including home appliances and radio broadcasting and reception. One of the company's earliest diversification moves came in 1920 when it acquired heating and kitchen equipment manufacturer Usines du Pied-Selle. By then, another prominent French company, which was to play a prominent role in Thomson-Houston's later history, had begun business. Created in 1918, the Compagnie Générale de Télégraphie Sans Fil (CSF—literally, the ''wireless telegraph company'') had started in business. Alongside Thomson-Houston itself, CSF was an important force behind the development of France's own wireless, broadcasting, radio, and other electrical technologies.

Thomson-Houston joined with the Société Alsacienne de Constructions Mécaniques to form Alsthom in 1928. The company's move into radio and the beginnings of the television industry began at the end of the 1920s, when it bought up Etablissements Ducretet in 1929. In the mid-1930s, Thomson-Houston strengthened this activity with a new acquisition, that of Etablissement Kraemer, added in 1936. Increasingly, Thomson-Houston's diversification brought it into competition with GE, which was also establishing itself as one of the world's top home appliance and radio and television companies (GE had joined with AT&T and Westinghouse to form RCA in the 1920s, introducing the first television in 1939).

The years leading up to World War II were lean ones for Thomson-Houston, however, and the company lacked the funds—and a strong government industrial policy—to pursue a vigorous expansion. The outbreak of World War II put a stop altogether to Thomson-Houston's activity. The Nazi invaders maintained in operations only those parts of the company necessary for its own occupational and military needs; the rest of the company was idle. Following the war, however, Thomson was to become one of the main proponents of France's industrial and economic recovery.

French Industrial Jewel in the 1960s

Following the war, the French government turned to Thomson-Houston and others to rebuild the country's shattered infra-structure. Technological developments made during the war years, particularly the use of electrical systems and electronics in aviation and other military applications, placed Thomson-Houston at the center of the French government's desire to establish France's technological independence. Thomson-Houston soon became one of the country's leading defense systems and armaments developers, while also joining in the development of the country's nuclear power industry.

Meanwhile, the recovering economy soon gave way to a vast economic boom, starting what became known to the French as the ''30 glorious years.'' The rising wealth of the country sparked rising consumer interest in a new wave of electrical home appliances. Thomson-Houston began developing its home appliance division as well.

By the early 1950s, Thomson's expansion placed it at the center of new political conflicts between the United States and France, while also setting it more and more in direct competition with GE. As Thomson (the company dropped the second half of its name in the 1950s) took on a growing role as part of France's military and technology effort, while also seeking to expand its role in the consumer products market, the company was forced to end its long licensing relationship with GE in 1953. The now fully independent Thomson was in a better position from which to compete in the booming markets for both consumer electrical appliances and industrial and military applications of its electrical and electronics systems technologies. An agreement with Pathé-Marconi represented a new step in Thomson's involvement in the production of televisions, as that market took off in France at the end of the 1950s.

During this time, the French government, eager to shore up its waning position in its colonial possessions, while also committed to remaining a major player as an international military and diplomatic power, stepped up its funding for military and defense-related spending. With the backing of the French government, Thomson was able to enter a new era of expansion, both in its defense- and aerospace-related operations and its consumer products activities. With a strong balance sheet, Thomson began eyeing larger acquisition targets.

In 1966, the company acquired a leading French consumer appliance manufacturer, Hotchkiss-Brandt. The acquisition, which resulted in a change of the company's name to Thomson-Brandt, also brought Hotchkiss-Brandt's own strengths in the defense and automotive sectors. Yet this name change was to last only two years. In 1968, Thomson-Brandt acquired defense specialist CSF and regrouped its defense operations with those of CSF to form the Thomson-CSF subsidiary. This merger sparked a new period of aggressive growth—and financial problems—for the company.

Nationalization and Reorganization: 1970s–80s

The 1970s saw Thomson's continued expansion and diversification into a variety of new areas, including telephone switching components and systems. Other new areas included medical imaging and even semiconductors. Meanwhile, the company went on a buying spree, picking up a number of new businesses and markets, including operations in Africa, Asia, and the Middle East. The economic difficulties of the era, sparked by the oil embargo of 1973, nonetheless brought some relief to the company, as Middle East countries turned to France—which set itself in contrast to the United States with more pro-Arab government policy—and to Thomson for military and defense orders. At the same time, Thomson could depend on a steady stream of orders from the French government itself to maintain a strong cash flow.

This cash flow was unable to shore up what had become something of a leaky ship by the early 1980s. A number of the company's business areas had long been losing money—only the company's government contracts had given the company liquidity. Thomson-Brandt revealed itself as a bloated, top-heavy company with an extremely inefficient management. Indeed, despite being a subsidiary, Thomson-CSF had continued to operate as an independent company, with its own chief executive, all but ignoring its parents. This situation had been allowed to continue throughout the 1970s because of Thomson-CSF's extreme importance to the French military and defense program.

That importance was underscored at the beginning of the 1980s when the arrival of the new Socialist government, led by François Mitterand, announced its intention to nationalize key French industries. Thomson-Brandt found itself under new ownership in 1982. Named to lead the company was Alain Gomez, who previously had helped restore the financial health of the Saint Gobain industrial conglomerate. The parent company was given a new name, Thomson S.A., while Thomson-CSF remained its more or less autonomous subsidiary.

When Gomez took over, Thomson was bleeding heavily, losing more than $275 million in 1982 alone. Gomez soon forced out the president of Thomson-CSF, placing control of the subsidiary firmly under the parent company's control for the first time. Gomez also led Thomson on a massive restructuring, shrinking the company's bloated management and cutting away a number of diversified operations to return the company to a strong core of defense electronics and consumer electronics. Among the operations shed at this time was Thomson-CSF Téléphone, losing more than $100 million per year, which was traded to Alcatel (then known as CGE) in exchange for that company's own military and consumer electronics businesses. The 1983 deal, described by *Fortune* as "the most important industrial restructuring in postwar France," proved a prime example of the French government's much criticized willingness to assert its influence over the country's industries.

In 1984, Thomson attempted to acquire rival German electronics and consumer appliance maker Grundig. That effort was blocked by Germany's antitrust authority. Instead, Thomson picked up smaller Telefunken, gaining access to the then restrictive German consumer electronics and appliance market. Thomson then undertook a controversial streamlining of Telefunken's operations, maintaining little more than the Telefunken brand name and its marketing network. Despite this episode, Thomson's restructuring had placed it back on the road to health, and by 1985, the company was once again turning a profit.

Growing opposition to France's nationalization policies led the government to rethink its "experiment" and in 1987, Thomson, along with a handful of other companies, was privatized. The French government nonetheless retained majority control of the company. Soon after, Thomson, which had attempted to build up a semiconductor business with the 1984 acquisition of money-losing Mostek, began to disengage from that sector, spinning off the business as ST Microelectronics. The company sold off its semiconductor operations in 1997.

By then, however, the company had made new moves toward becoming one of the world's leading consumer electronics companies. After acquiring the consumer electronics business of Thorn EMI in 1987, Thomson acquired the entire consumer electronics division from GE—including the RCA brand—becoming overnight the largest seller of televisions to the U.S. market and one of the largest in the world. The company sold off its consumer appliance division in 1992, concentrating on its Thomson SA consumer electronics operation and its Thomson-CSF defense group.

Independent Electronics Giant in the 21st Century

Thomson-CSF boosted its defense operations in 1989 with the purchase of MBLE of Belgium and Signaal, based in Denmark but a division of the Dutch firm Philips. The company also picked up fellow French defense electronics firm TRT.

During the 1990s, Thomson-CSF faced a new challenge as the close of the Cold War resulted in a tightening of the worldwide defense market. In response, Thomson-CSF began building up its civil electronics wing—adapting its technologies to the civil aviation and aerospace sectors especially. By the mid-1990s, Gomez recognized a need to place the company closer to its customers in order to secure its place in the global marketplace. As such, the company was reorganized, with management decentralized to concentrate on local markets, forming the basis of what the company called its "multi-domestic" operation. This reorganization was credited with protecting the company's balance sheet during the political turmoil that marked its emancipation at the end of the decade.

In 1996, the French government announced its intention to complete Thomson's privatization. An initial deal, to sell the company to Lagardère Groupe and Matra, which in turn had agreed to transfer the newly named Thomson Multimedia consumer electronics group to Korea's Daewoo, was struck down amid great controversy. Thomson's privatization only came in 1997, when the group accepted Alcatel and Dassault as major shareholders—alongside the government's continued 48 percent holding. The deal involved a transfer of parts of Alcatel and Dassault's defense and aerospace operations to Thomson-CSF. By then, however, Gomez had stepped down from the company's leadership.

The appointment of Dennis Ranque as the company's CEO and chairman in 1998 marked the start of a new era for the company. In 1999, the now independent and publicly listed Thomson-CSF went on a buying spree, enhancing its multidomestic policy by acquiring ADI of Australia, ADS of South Africa, Sextant-in-Flight Systems of the United States, and Avimo, an optronics company with operations in Singapore and the United Kingdom.

The year 2000 marked a turning point for the company. In that year the company acquired Racal Electronics of the United Kingdom, giving it the number two position in that country's defense and aerospace electronics market. The acquisition prompted the company to adopt a new name, Thales, after the Greek philosopher and mathematician, at the end of the year. At that time, the company announced its formation of Thales Raytheon Systems, a joint venture with the U.S.-based Raytheon, to develop air defense systems, which began operations in 2001. At the same time, the French government announced its intention to reduce its holding in the company to below the 33 percent mark, meaning it would no longer have a minority block on company decisions. As it entered the new century, Thales emerged as one of the world's top three defense and aerospace electronics systems companies and expected to remain a force to be reckoned with on a global scale.

Principal Subsidiaries

ADI (Australia); Thales Cryogenics (Netherlands); African Defence Systems (Pty) Ltd (ADS) (South Africa); Thales Atm; Thales Optics; Thales Information Systems (Russia); Thales Optics (Japan); Thales Cryogenics; Thales Optronics (Netherlands); Diehl Avionik Systeme (Germany); Thales Navigation; Eurodisplay; Thales Optronics; Fibre Form (U.K.); Forges De Zeebrugge (Belgium); Thales Identification Systems (U.S.A.); Thales Isr; Thales Technologies & Services; Thales Raytheon Systems; Thales Training & Simulation (U.S.A.); Thales Electron Devices; Thales Electron Devices (Germany); Thales Components (Spain); Thales Air Defence; Thales Atm; Thales Avionics Electrical Systems; Thales Avionics (U.S.A.); Thales Communications; Thales International (Venezuela); Thales Airborne Systems; Thales Systemes Aeroportes; Thales Communications (Italy); Thales Systems & Services (Germany); Thales Communications (Brazil); Thales International (South Africa); Thales International (Switzerland); Thales Idatys; Thales Identification Systems; Thales Industrial Services; Thales International (Chile); Thales International; Thales Optics; Thales Missions & Conseil; Thales Naval (U.K.); Thales Naval France; Thales Information Systems; Trixell; UDS International; UMS; Thales Université; Thales E-Security (U.K.).

Principal Divisions

Aerospace; Defense; Information Technologies and Services.

Principal Competitors

Alliant Techsystems Inc.; BAE SYSTEMS; BellSouth Corporation; The Boeing Company; Bombardier Inc.; Diebold, Incorporated; ECC International Corp.; European Aeronautic Defence and Space Company EADS N.V.; FLIR Systems, Inc.; General Dynamics Corporation; Harris Corporation; Honeywell International Inc.; InteliData Technologies Corporation; ITT Industries, Inc.; LaBarge, Inc.; Litton Industries, Inc.; Lockheed Martin Corporation; Lucent Technologies Inc.; Matsushita Electric Industrial Co., Ltd.; Mitsui Group; Motorola, Inc.; Nokia AS; Nortel Networks Corporation; Northrop Grumman Corporation; Raytheon Company; Reflectone, Inc.; Robotic Vision Systems, Inc.; Rockwell International Corporation; SBC Communications Inc.; Siemens AG; Sony Corporation; Uniden Corporation.

Further Reading

Barkin, Noah, "Thales 2000 Profits Beat Estimates," *Reuters,* March 14, 2001.

Echikson, William, "Why Thomson's Strategy Faltered," *Fortune,* November 29, 1993, p. 34.

Gallard, Philippe, "Thomson revient dans la course," *Expansion,* January 7, 1999.

Gallard, Philippe, and Marc Nexon, "Thomson a résisté à tout, même à une privatisation ratée," *Expansion,* October 9, 1997, p. 76.

Masters, Charles, "Can Jospin Sell Off Without Selling Out?," *European,* July 17, 1997, p. 25.

Nicoll, Alexander, "France to Reduce Thales Stake," *Financial Times,* May 20, 2001.

Tully, Shawn, "The Pentagon's French Connection," *Fortune,* December 9, 1985, p. 137.

—M. L. Cohen

THOMSON MULTI MEDIA

THOMSON multimedia S.A.

46 Quai Alphonse Le Gallo
92648 Boulogne Cedex
France
Telephone: (+33) 1 41 86 50 00
Fax: (+33) 1 41 86 61 00
Web site: http://www.thomson-multimedia.com

Public Company
Incorporated: 1893 as Compagnie Française Thomson
Employees: 61,184
Sales: EUR 9.09 billion (2000)
Stock Exchanges: Euronext Paris New York
Ticker Symbols: TMM; TMS
NAIC: 334310 Audio and Video Equipment
    Manufacturing

THOMSON multimedia S.A. (Thomson multimedia) is one of the world's top four consumer electronics manufacturers, with leading shares in a number of important product categories, including the number one position for televisions sold in the United States, through its RCA brand. Based in France, Thomson multimedia has successfully positioned itself as the leading player in the transition to digital technologies—ranging from DVDs to high-definition-television to high-speed digital networks—and has built up operations spanning five primary divisions: Displays and Components, including a number two worldwide position in very large picture tube production; Digital Media Solutions, with its world-leading share of the media and content services industries through subsidiary Technicolor; Consumer Products, including its TAK interactive television system developed in partnership with Microsoft and its Lyra portable digital music system; New Media and Services; and Patents and Licensing. The company's brands include Thomson, RCA, and Technicolor. Production takes place in 31 sites located worldwide; the company also operates 28 sales and distribution centers, six research and development sites, and 12 patents and licensing facilities. Led by Thierry Breton, formerly of Bull SA, Thomson multimedia is listed on the Paris stock exchange. Primary shareholders include Microsoft, Alcatel,

NEC, and DirectTV (GE); the French government remains Thomson's single largest shareholder.

Consumer Electronics Pioneer in the 20th Century

Thomson was originally founded as the French subsidiary of the Thomson-Houston Electric Corporation, an American tramway-equipment manufacturer with considerable resources in patented machinery for the electric power industry. The company, called Compagnie Française Thomson-Houston, was established in 1893, and operated largely as a sales and administrative office. Ten years later, the parent company was acquired by General Electric Company, and General Electric sold Compagnie Française Thomson-Houston to a group of French investors.

The new owners, who retained the name of the company's American founders, were faced with the difficult task of building a strong group of engineers and project managers. For many years, the company maintained a licensing relationship with General Electric. In search of greater managerial and creative freedom, Thomson-Houston began a diversification program in 1921 which led the company into a variety of new marketing segments, including General Electric's emerging specialty: the consumer market.

Thomson-Houston grew slowly during the 1920s and 1930s. Changes in the government resulted in inconsistent industrial policy, which, on occasion, led to adverse economic conditions. Unwilling to invest heavily in new plants and equipment, Thomson-Houston saw no major growth until the eve of World War II, when the government hastily drew up an industrialization plan which, it hoped, would discourage German military adventurism in Europe. Thomson-Houston scarcely had time to begin planning production schedules before its facilities were overrun by German troops.

During the occupation, Thomson-Houston's facilities were either converted to meet the needs of the German war effort or idled. As in virtually every sector throughout French industry, consumer product manufacturing ceased entirely, leading to a shortage of switches, motors, and lights.

At the end of the war, Thomson-Houston was reorganized to facilitate recovery. At the request of the government, the company first devoted production efforts to rebuilding French infrastructure and industry, but the demand for consumer products remained high for several years as well.

Political discord between France and the United States eventually led many French companies to end associations with American companies. For Thomson, however (the name Houston was dropped during this period), several other factors contributed to the company's decision in 1953 to end its 50-year cooperative agreement with General Electric. Thomson had emerged as an important industrial supplier and strategic military resource. Sensitivity to the security of new French technologies and the French nuclear effort, in addition to Thomson's ability to remain commercially successful on its own, all necessitated independence.

At the same time, Thomson benefited from a government militarization program to support French colonial interests. This provided the company with sufficient capital for a steady and broad internal expansion which continued until 1966. That year, Thomson acquired Hotchkiss-Brandt, a profitable French consumer products company with substantial interests in automotive and military products. The acquisition marked the beginning of a phase of rapid expansion for Thomson.

Reorganization in the 1980s

In 1968 Thomson-Brandt, as the new company was now called, merged its electronics division with the French communications manufacturer Compagnie Generale de Telegraphie Sans Fils. The new subsidiary, Thomson-CSF, became France's primary manufacturer of high-technology professional electronics. Looking beyond its borders, Thomson-Brandt acquired several smaller companies throughout Europe. By the mid-1970s, the company's interests extended to Asia, Africa, and North America.

Thomson-Brandt gradually lost the ability to efficiently manage shortcomings in development, production, and, ultimately, profitability. Overburdened by a bureaucracy which included two autonomous chief executives, Thomson-Brandt had no effective central-planning capability and no real budget control. These problems were exacerbated by a steady diet of government business; because liquidity could be guaranteed through sales volume, Thomson-Brandt continued to sink deeper into financial chaos. The company made numerous attempts to build new markets, including several joint ventures with such companies as Xerox, Contel, and later the Italian electronics company SGS.

During this period, industrial mismanagement became a political issue for French Socialists, who promised nationalization of large industries. In 1981, the year the Socialists came to power, the government took over management of Thomson-Brandt. Alain Gomez, a Harvard-educated manager who had worked several years for Saint Gobain, succeeded Jean Pierre Bouyssonnie as chairman. Administrators appointed by the government found the company in such poor shape that it required a massive reorganization. While production continued unhindered, management's three-year shake-up ended in 1981, when Christian Aubin was appointed to overhaul the company's financial-reporting system. New reporting methods enabled Gomez to identify losing and underperforming assets and recommend divisions for divestiture.

The year-long reorganization began in September 1982 and resulted in the creation of a new holding company called Thomson S.A., which superseded the old Thomson-Brandt organization.

In one of his first moves toward revitalizing Thomson, Gomez participated in a plan led by Industry Minister Laurent Fabius to rationalize French electronics production. Under the agreement, concluded in 1983, Thomson transferred most of its interests in telecommunications equipment and cable manufacturing to French electronics giant Cie Générale d'Electricité (CGE), participating only through a minority interest in a subsidiary managed by CGE. In return, Thomson took over a portion of CGE's interests in consumer electronics, electronic components, and defense electronics. The pact drew much criticism, particularly for Gomez, a visibly frustrated entrepreneur and reluctant government servant. Gomez nevertheless defended the agreement, citing it as an essential step in positioning Thomson for greater competitive innovation.

In a separate move more in keeping with his ambitions, Gomez attempted to acquire the West German electronics company Grundig in 1984. Rebuffed by German antitrust law and the defiance of company founder Max Grundig, Gomez turned his attention to an easier target: the somewhat smaller firm Telefunken. Thomson, while successful in this effort, was widely denounced in West Germany, where the nationalization of French industry was perceived, in Gomez's words, "as something between archaic and obnoxious." Thomson's greatest benefit from the takeover was not Telefunken's product line, but instead the ability to circumvent German import restrictions and use Telefunken's marketing network. The company was later criticized for streamlining Telefunken's operations and laying off workers in Germany.

As Thomson's position in world markets continued to recover, mounting opposition to the nationalization program led the Socialist government to reassess its experiment and declare that several companies would be returned to the private sector. On top of this, in 1986 Socialist President François Mitterand was forced to share power with a conservative element under Jacques Chirac, a strong proponent of privatization. Consequently, during 1987 the French government reduced its ownership in several companies, including Thomson. Gomez, who had become chairman of Thomson as a left-wing functionary, had become a proven turnaround artist, widely admired by conservative industrialists.

Key Dates:

1893: Compagnie Française Thomson-Houston is founded as the French subsidiary of the Thomson-Houston Electric Corporation, an American tramway-equipment manufacturer.

1903: Thomson-Houston Electric is acquired by General Electric Company, which sells Compagnie Française Thomson-Houston to a group of French investors.

1921: Company diversifies into consumer electronics.

1953: Thomson ends cooperation agreement with General Electric (GE).

1966: Company acquires consumer products firm Hotchkiss-Brandt and embarks on a period of rapid expansion.

1982: A new holding company, Thomson S.A., is created.

1984: Telefunken is acquired and the company enters the West German market.

1987: Thomson acquires consumer electronics line from GE.

1995: Company changes its name to Thomson multimedia.

1999: Company goes public on the Paris and New York stock exchanges.

2001: Thomson acquires Technicolor from Carlton Communications and DSL modem division from Alcatel; forms joint-venture with NEC.

Consumer Electronics Leader: 1980s–2000s

In July 1987 Thomson engineered another operations swap. Only one month after acquiring the consumer electronics unit of Thorn-EMI, Thomson took over General Electric Company's entire consumer electronics line—most of which GE had acquired in its 1986 takeover of RCA—in exchange for its Compagnie Generale de Radiologie medical equipment unit and some cash. As with Telefunken, Thomson saw nominal value in the products themselves, but sought to take advantage of an established marketing network.

This strategy of acquiring product lines for their marketing networks was not likely to pay off for several years. Meanwhile, Thomson struggled to revamp its product lines and create a consolidated brand identity. The strategy carried a great risk because of Thomson's increased exposure to the volatile consumer electronics business, which was dominated by companies such as Philips (which succeeded in acquiring Grundig), Matsushita, and Sony. Yet the expansion of its consumer electronics side was seen as a necessary risk if Thomson was to reduce its dependence on profitable but unpredictable military contracts.

Thomson began the 1990s with high hopes. The company celebrated the production of the 50 millionth RCA color television. The following year the company launched a new brand, Proscan, targeting the high-end television market. In 1992, the growing importance of American sales—where RCA remained the leading brand of television—was highlighted by the construction of a new North American headquarters in Indianapolis started in 1992 and completed in 1994. By then the company had already debuted its CinemaScreen television in the United States, with the slogan: "Television Made for the Movies."

The company was also taking an active role in the development of the satellite television market, launching the RCA Digital Satellite System. Thomson's growing commitment to the coming digital television era was further deepened when it joined in the founding of the Digital HDTV Grand Alliance.

In 1995, Thomson Consumer Electronics changed its name to Thomson multimedia to underscore its growing interests in the wider spectrum of interrelated consumer entertainment appliances. But by then the company's own future was coming into doubt. The company had taken a risk at the beginning of the 1990s when it sought to compete at the top levels of the consumer electronics industry. Yet by the middle of the decade, it appeared as if Thomson had not been able to make the risk pay off, and the losses began to mount, topping FFr 25 billion.

A new, conservative-led French government threw a darker cloud over Thomson multimedia. Committed to the wide-scale privatization of France's many government-owned and protected businesses, the French government announced its intention to split Thomson S.A. into its two core components—and then sell them for the grand total of one franc to French arms manufacturer Lagardere. In turn, Lagardere had reached an agreement to give Thomson multimedia to Korea's Daewoo Corp., which would have resulted in making Daewoo the world's number one television manufacturer. Yet public reaction—and union and political criticism—forced the government to back down on the plan. Instead, Thomson CSF was spun off in 1996 (and subsequently renamed Thales), and Thomson S.A. now continued as the government-owned holding company for Thomson multimedia.

In 1997, Thomson multimedia was given a new CEO, Thierry Breton, who joined the company from French computer group Bull. Breton quickly orchestrated a turnaround of the flagging company, restructuring operations while closing down a number of overseas production sites, accepting a cash infusion from the government topping $10 billion, and bringing in a battery of new partners. In 1998, the company opened its shareholding for the first time, selling 7.5 percent stakes in the company to Microsoft, NEC, Alcatel, and GE through its DirectTV subsidiary. With Microsoft, Thomson multimedia began developing a new interactive television system, dubbed TAK. The company also began cooperating with Microsoft as a supplier for the software giant's coming video gaming system, Xbox.

The opening of the company's capital was a prelude to a public offering, made in 1999 on the Paris and New York stock exchanges. The success of the offering, which sold another 17 percent of the company, showed how diligent Breton had been in turning the company around. Indeed, by the beginning of the next century, Thomson multimedia had joined the top four consumer electronics makers—yet led the field in terms of profitability. Part of this success was credited to Thomson's early and strong commitment to building up its digital television and audio interests, giving the company an advance position on its competitors as more and more consumers turned to digital media.

In 2000, the company went further, establishing a new division, Digital Media Solutions, for the creation of digital interactive entertainment and services. That year, the company bought a minority share in Philips Professional Broadcast, and then reached agreement with the U.K.-based Carlton Communications to form an alliance for developing digital interactive television and media content. Thomson also announced its intention to raise another $1 billion on the stock market, with the French government expected to reduce its holding to below the 50 percent mark. At the end of 2000, Thomson launched the first of its TAK interactive televisions, featuring a Windows CE-based browser, and interactive and Internet access features.

Thomson multimedia moved into the new century on a roll, buying up Carlton Communications' media services subsidiary Technicolor in May 2001 and reaching an agreement with shareholder-partner NEC to combine their plasma display operations into a new joint-venture subsidiary. In June, Thomson turned to another shareholder, buying up Alcatel's DSL modem operations. Thomson had placed its bets on the digital entertainment revolution—and this time its bets seemed to paying off, making the company one of the fastest growing and most profitable consumer electronics groups in the world.

Principal Subsidiaries

Atlinks; Deutsche Thomson-Brandt GmbH (Germany); Singingfish.com (U.S.A.); Sofia; Thomson Audio Dongguan (China); Thomson Audio Hong Kong Ltd; Thomson Audio; Thomson Consumer Electronics International SA; Thomson Licensing SA; Thomson Multimedia Digital France; Thomson Multimedia Inc. (U.S.A.); Thomson Multimedia Ltd (Canada); Thomson Tubes & Displays S.A.; Thomson Videoglass SA.

Principal Competitors

Aiwa Co., Ltd.; Daewoo Electronics Co., Ltd.; Harman International Industries, Incorporated; Hitachi, Ltd.; Hughes Electronics Corporation; LG Electronics Inc.; Lucent Technologies Inc; Matsushita Electric Industrial Co., Ltd.; Nokia Corporation; Pace Micro Technology PLC; Koninklijke Philips Electronics N.V.; Pioneer Corporation; Samsung Group; SANYO Electric Co., Ltd.; Sharp Corporation.

Further Reading

Bremer, Catherine, ''Alcatel Sells High-Speed Modems Business to Thomson,'' *Reuters*, June 7, 2001.

Chang, Richard, ''France to Sell Off Thomson in Two Parts,'' *Reuters Business Report*, December 11, 1996.

''France to Sell Thomson for One Franc,'' *European Report*, January 5, 1996.

Michelson, Marcel, ''France Suspends Thomson Privatization Sale,'' *Reuters Business Report*, December 4, 1996.

''The Stars of Europe—Entrepreneurs: Thierry Breton,'' *Business Week International*, June 11, 2001, p. 32.

''Thomson Multimedia: From Rags to Riches,'' *Inside Multimedia*, October 28, 1999.

''Thomson Multimedia Predicts Turnover Growth of 15–30% Up to 2003–04,'' *Tech Europe*, February 15, 2001.

—update: M.L. Cohen

TIMKEN

The Timken Company

1835 Dueber Ave., S.W.
Canton, Ohio 44706-2798
U.S.A.
Telephone: (216) 438-3000
Fax: (216) 471-3810
Web site: http://www.timken.com

Public Company
Incorporated: 1899 as Timken Roller Bearing Axle
   Company
Employees: 20,500
Sales: $2.64 billion (2000)
Stock Exchanges: New York
Ticker Symbol: TKR
NAIC: 332991 Ball and Roller Bearing Manufacturing;
   31111 Iron and Steel Mills

The Timken Company is the world's largest manufacturer of tapered roller bearings. A tapered roller bearing consists of a set of rolling elements between two concentric rings. The design of these bearings, based on Henry Timken's patents from the late 19th century, allows them to virtually eliminate friction created in hauling heavy loads. Timken bearings are used by a wide variety of companies, including those in the automotive, aerospace, and railroad industries. They range in size from the tiny bearings used in disk drives to the nine-ton mother of all bearings custom made for a heavy forge.

Bearings might not seem like the most progressive of industries, yet Timken has maintained a leading 30 percent market share by aggressively investing in R&D and state-of-the-art manufacturing facilities. Timken also produces millions of tons of steel alloy each year through its Latrobe Steel unit. Among the uses of Latrobe's products are components for automobile axles and fasteners for space shuttles. The company's stock is one-third owned by the Timken family and employees.

Steely Origins

Henry Timken founded the earliest form of The Timken Company in St. Louis in 1899. Timken had entered the carriage business as an apprentice 40 years earlier at the age of 16. By the time he was 24, Timken had opened his own carriage shop. In 1877 Timken received the patent for the Timken Buggy Spring, the first of his 13 patents. His spring design became widely used throughout the country, and was produced on a royalty basis by a number of companies. As a result of the spring's success, Timken became well known across the United States, and his carriage business flourished. Around 1895 Timken took an interest in the problems created by friction in wagon design. In 1898 the patent was issued for the Timken tapered roller bearing. The new bearing was a dramatic improvement over the ball bearings and straight roller bearings that had previously been used. The following year, the founder and his two sons, William and Henry (H. H.) Timken, organized the Timken Roller Bearing Axle Company. It produced axles that used the new bearing in their design.

Within the next couple of years, the axle business began to outgrow its allotted space in the St. Louis carriage plant, and in 1902 the company relocated to Canton, Ohio. Canton was seen as an ideal midpoint between Detroit, home of the automotive industry, and Pittsburgh, a major steel-producing city. By that time, the Timkens had recognized the future importance of the automobile, and worked to develop bearings tailored to the needs of that young industry. When Henry Ford introduced the automobile assembly line and the Model T that it produced in 1908, the demand for Timken bearings and axles grew exponentially.

In 1909 the Timken brothers moved the axle division to Detroit, launching the new Timken-Detroit Axle Company with William Timken as its president. The Canton operation continued to manufacture bearings, and its name was changed to The Timken Roller Bearing Company. By 1909, the year Henry Timken died, the company was turning out over 850,000 bearings a year, and it employed about 1,200 people.

Timken began to produce its own steel in 1915 as a way to ensure an adequate supply for its manufacturing in the face of shortages created by World War I. That year, the company added a steel tube mill to its Canton facilities. A year later a melt shop was added. With the inclusion of these steel works, Timken became the first bearing manufacturer to act as its own supplier of steel for its products. The company was soon producing steel in quantities far greater than its own manufacturing

---

Company Perspectives:

We will be the best-performing manufacturing company in the world as seen through the eyes of our customers and shareholders. To grow profitably, maximize shareholder value and sustain industry leadership, our diverse team of associates will capitalize on the relationships between our businesses, emphasize applying advanced technology to products and processes and provide unmatched customer service. We will remain an independent organization with a leadership position in high-quality anti-friction bearing and alloy steel products as well as related services.

---

needs. It therefore began marketing its alloy steel to outside buyers, with such companies as Mack Truck among its early regular customers. In 1919 the Industrial Division was organized, taking the place of the company's Farm Implement and Tractor Division. The mission of the Industrial Division was to develop bearings for a wide variety of industrial uses, including electric motors, elevators, and printing presses.

The market for Timken bearings and steel continued to expand quickly throughout the 1920s. In 1920 the company opened the Columbus Bearing Plant, its first facility outside of Canton. The same year, a waste treatment plant was built at the Canton facility. Timken stock went on sale to the public for the first time in 1922, and the company opened an assembly plant in Canada that year. Timken bearings found their way into the railroad industry in 1923, when bearings specially designed by Timken were tested first on an inter-city streetcar running between Canton and Cleveland, and later that year in a boxcar on the Wheeling and Lake Erie Railroad. By 1926, other railroads recognized that the tapered bearings would allow the speed of their trains to increase. A large order was placed by the Chicago, Milwaukee, St. Paul & Pacific railroad for use in its high-speed trains, such as the Burlington Zephyr and the Santa Fe Super Chief.

Expansion in the 1920s and 1930s

Timken began acquiring smaller companies in the mid-1920s. In 1925 the company purchased the assets of Gilliam Manufacturing Co., a Canton-based roller bearing producer. The Bock Bearing Co. of Toledo, Ohio, was acquired the following year. In 1927 Timken purchased a large interest in British Timken Ltd. from Vickers Ltd., which had been manufacturing Timken bearings and axles under license since 1909. Timken went on to acquire the remainder of the British operation in 1959. The Weldless Steel Company's Wooster, Ohio, piercing mill was purchased in 1928. That year also brought the creation of Société Anonyme Française Timken (SAFT), a French subsidiary of British Timken. In 1929 Timken purchased a 177-acre block of land adjacent to the company's existing facilities in Canton and opened two new plants, the Gambrinus Steel Plant and the Gambrinus Bearing Plant.

In spite of the Depression, Timken continued to grow steadily through the 1930s. During the early 1930s the company developed bearings for propeller drive-shafts, thereby expanding its customer base to include shipbuilders and the U.S. Navy. In 1932 Timken began manufacturing removable rock bits for construction and mining equipment. The production of the rock bits provided a much needed outlet for the company's steel in the face of a badly depressed steel market. By that year, British Timken had stretched to yet another continent, opening a manufacturing subsidiary in South Africa in 1932. In 1934 William Umstattd became president of Timken, succeeding H.H. Timken, who stayed on as chairman of the board. The company's Mt. Vernon Rock Bit Plant opened the following year. When H.H. Timken died in 1940, his son, H.H. Timken, Jr., became the chairman of Timken's board of directors.

The onset of World War II provided the momentum for Timken's continued growth in the 1940s. To meet increasing wartime demand for its products, Timken opened several new facilities in Ohio during this period. In 1941, for example, the Timken Ordnance Company was built in Canton, where about 80,000 gun tubes were manufactured over the next couple of years. The Zanesville Bearing Plant was opened in 1943. Other new locations included Columbus and Newton Falls. During the war, the company's output more than doubled its previous peak. In 1948 Timken began experimenting with automation, beginning a pilot project at a plant in Bucyrus, Ohio. The project was an instant success, and a brand new plant was built in 1950.

Meanwhile, Timken was the subject of an antitrust suit brought by the Justice Department around the same time. After several levels of appeals, the Supreme Court ruled in 1951 that Timken had conspired with its foreign affiliates (British and French Timken) in restraint of trade. The case, initiated in 1947, came about as a result of agreements between the companies regarding sales territories, price coordination, exchange of exclusive information, and other practices. The court's ruling indicated that a company must compete with other companies in which it holds a substantial interest if that company is not a legal subsidiary.

Rolling Through the 1950s and 1960s

In 1954 Timken introduced the "AP" bearing, an innovation that would have a great impact on the railroad industry. The "AP" was a preassembled, prelubricated, self-contained bearing that was inexpensive and easily integrated into nearly any type of railroad car. The new bearing was credited with dramatically reducing the number of freight car set-outs. The "AP" bearing was initially produced at Timken's Columbus plant. So quickly did demand for it grow, however, that by 1958, the new Columbus Railroad Bearing Plant was opened. In 1956 the Bucyrus Distribution Center was opened. The Distribution Center was a huge warehouse, from which bearings were shipped to customers throughout the United States, as well as to the company's foreign plants. In 1958 Australia became the fourth continent on which Timken operations took place, with the opening of a bearing plant at Ballarat, Victoria. That year, SAFT was officially merged into Timken, and its name was changed to Timken France. Timken purchased the remaining shares of British Timken the following year.

Around this time, Timken began its expansion into South America. A sales subsidiary was established in Argentina in 1959. The next year saw the opening of the Sao Paulo Bearing

Plant in Brazil. Also in 1960, W. Robert Timken (another son of H.H. Timken) replaced Umstattd as company president.

Timken's sales continued to grow steadily through the first half of the 1960s, climbing from $240 million in 1961 to $393 million in 1966. In 1963 production began at the company's new Colmar Plant in France. Timken Research, a sprawling research and development center located near the Akron-Canton Airport, was completed in 1966. Railroad companies continued to grow in importance as customers during this period. By 1968, more than 90 percent of the new freight cars being built used tapered roller bearings, and more than 60 percent of those bearings were made by Timken.

During the second half of the 1960s, Timken's sales leveled off, and net income actually shrank, from $49 million in 1966 to $29 million in 1970. The portion of this income that came from foreign sales tripled between 1967 and 1970. In 1968 a continuous casting plant was added to the company's steelmaking facilities. By 1969, the plant had a capacity of 850,000 tons. The company's Ashland Plant was opened in 1969 as well. Timken had a total of 16 plants in operation by 1971, seven of which were in Ohio. Tapered roller bearings and rock bits accounted for about 80 percent of Timken's revenue that year, with specialty steels generating the rest of the company's sales. At that time, about 35 different types of roller bearings were being produced in over 11,000 sizes at its facilities.

Rising Sales in the 1970s

H.H. Timken, Jr., died in 1968, and was succeeded as chairman by his brother W. Robert Timken. The company presidency was assumed by Herbert Markley, who had joined the company as an accountant nearly 30 years earlier. In 1970 the corporation's name was officially shortened to The Timken Company. The following year, the Gaffney Bearing Plant, a highly automated facility in South Carolina, was opened. Timken was hurt in 1970 by strikes at General Motors and in the trucking industry. By 1972, however, sales were once again strong in the automotive

industry, which, as a whole, was the purchaser of nearly half of the bearings sold by Timken. As a result, Timken's sales began to grow once again, reaching a company record of $470 million in 1972. In 1974 a wholly owned sales subsidiary, Nihon Timken K.K., was formed in Japan.

W. Robert Timken stepped down in 1975, and was replaced as chairman of the board by his son, W.R. Timken, Jr. That year Timken acquired Latrobe Steel Company, a Pennsylvania-based producer of specialty steel and alloys. For 1975, Timken was able to post record sales of $804 million, in spite of a terrible year in the automobile industry. In 1978 construction was completed on the company's Canton Water Purification Plant. Timken introduced the UNIPAC bearing in 1979. These pre-lubricated and pre-adjusted bearings made assembly operations much easier for vehicle, industrial machinery, and construction equipment manufacturers. Timken also opened the Lincolnton Bearing Plant that year. The Lincolnton plant, located 50 miles north of Gaffney in North Carolina, featured such advanced automation as driverless trains that transported parts between departments. Markley faced mandatory retirement as company president in 1979. He was succeeded by Joseph F. Toot, Jr., a Timken employee since 1962.

Losses in the 1980s

As the 1980s began, Timken was still the dominant force in the American bearing industry, controlling about 25 percent of the U.S. bearings market, and 75 percent of the market for tapered roller bearings. In 1981 the company earned $101 million on sales of $1.4 billion. The 1980s proved to be a difficult decade for Timken, however. The company reported a loss of $3 million in 1982, its first unprofitable year since the Depression. Part of the problem was the flood of cheap bearings entering the United States from Europe and Japan. Nevertheless, Timken did not stop investing in its facilities during this time. In 1983 an expansion project that doubled the size of Timken Research was completed. The company's $450 million Faircrest Steel Plant went into production in 1985. Upon the opening of the plant, which was situated not far from Canton, Timken's steelmaking capacity increased by 50 percent, to 1.5 million tons.

In 1986 Timken reorganized its corporate structure, cutting costs by consolidating departments and eliminating personnel. The Rock Bit Division was sold off entirely. A new division, the Original Equipment—Bearings group, was formed by combining the Industrial Division with the Automotive and Railroad Divisions. In addition, all Research and Development functions and computer operations were organized into a newly created Technology Center.

After six years of showing little or no profit, Timken rebounded in 1988, earning $65.9 million on net sales of $1.55 billion. During that year offices were opened in Italy, Korea, Singapore, and Venezuela. The following year, a 37-day strike by steelworkers prevented a significant continuation of the rally. Nevertheless, a $1 billion multi-year investment program was launched in 1989 to modernize and expand the company's plants. In 1990 Timken paid $185 million for MPB Corporation, a manufacturer of super-precision bearings (used in sensitive machinery such as aircraft, computer disk drives, and medical equipment) based in Keene, New Hampshire, with annual sales of $120 million.

Retooling: 1990s–2000s

Timken's sales declined slightly in both 1991 and 1992, largely due to reduced demand caused by the global recession. For 1991, the company recorded a net loss of $36 million. Through an active streamlining program, Timken was able to turn a modest profit of $4.45 million in 1992 without making any gains in sales. In April 1993 the company announced the formation of a steel sales unit in Europe, its first such steel operation outside of the United States. Efforts to improve manufacturing efficiency and to reduce costs throughout the corporation continued. In 1993 the company began operations at a steel parts plant in Eaton, Ohio. Latrobe Steel planned to open a new facility in Franklin, Pennsylvania, in 1994.

That same year, Timken's most advanced plant to date opened in Asheboro, North Carolina, at a cost of $120 million. Its automated features allowed the company to produce small batches of custom bearings in a matter of days, rather than weeks, reported *Forbes*. Another new factory was opened in Singapore to produce the minuscule bearings used in computer disk drives. Even as these facilities were being constructed, the company's annual earnings were reaching their highest levels since 1988, though the company had lost money in 1991 and 1993. By 1996, earnings had risen to $138.9 million. Analysts attributed the performance to reducing production costs and finding niches outside the company's traditional, cyclical lines of business.

In late 1997 Toot retired as president and CEO. Chairman William R. Timken, Jr., great grandson of the company founder, took over Toot's duties. After an all-time record first quarter, the Asian financial crisis resulted in reduced orders for farm equipment and less business for Timken in the second half of 1998. For the year, income fell from $171 million to $114 million, on sales of $2.7 billion. Timken's share price also fell during the year, from $41 to $13.

In February 1999, Timken postponed the launch of a new $110 million seamless tube mill, citing weaknesses in the energy, farm, and heavy industrial markets. Most pressing was the lack of suitable agreements with government agencies, suppliers, and unions to get the plant running profitably. Sites in Ohio, Georgia, North Carolina, and Virginia were being considered.

A web site, Timken Direct, debuted in April 1999. It relieved sales reps from routine availability and price questions, and gave Timken's distributor customers more power to find needed information on their own.

The company celebrated its 100th anniversary in style. A detailed company history was commissioned and provided to each of its employees around the world. A small group of Timken employees and retirees restored a rare 1904 St. Louis car, one of the first designs to incorporate Timken's roller bearings.

Timken's 50-year-old plant in Bucyrus, Ohio, continued to spit out small bearings—2.5 million of them a week—from a highly automated, finely tuned mix of vintage and computerized

equipment. Other plants specialized in quick turnarounds of custom orders. In the 1990s, Timken had begun developing "bearings packages," integrating bearings with other components into modular systems.

In March 2000, Timken announced plans to cut 600 jobs worldwide—half of them at the Duston, England plant—while increasing production in Central Europe. The company had already trimmed 1,700 jobs in the previous two years, aiming to reduce costs in the face of excess industry capacity.

Plants in Australia and England were closed. Although sales of excess steel made up a third of Timken's revenues, the company was relying more heavily on outside sources as it expanded production into countries such as China and India. The company also aimed to adopt more efficient processes, opting for hot-forging over metal-cutting in some instances. There was also a trend towards smaller, more specialized factories. Among Timken's most advanced products at the beginning of the millennium were anti-lock bearings for four-wheel-drive vehicles that employed built-in sensors.

In May 2001, Timken was rumored to be in alliance talks with a Japanese rival, NSK Ltd. Timken acknowledged a long-term supplier relationship with NSK but denied any pending joint ventures.

Principal Subsidiaries

Timken Aerospace & Super Precision Bearings; Timken Aerospace & SuperPrecision Bearings-Europa B.V. (Netherlands); Timken Aerospace & Super Precision Bearings-Singapore Pte. Ltd.; Timken Aerospace & Super Precision Bearings-UK, Ltd.; Australian Timken Proprietary, Limited (Australia); Timken do Brasil Comercio e Industria, Ltda. (Brazil); British Timken Limited (U.K.); Canadian Timken, Limited (Canada); Timken Communications Company; Timken Desford Steel Limited (U.K.); EDC, Inc.; Timken Engineering and Research - India Private Limited; Timken España, S.L. (Spain); Timken Europa GmbH (Germany); Timken Europe B.V. (Netherlands); Timken Finance Europe B.V. (Netherlands); Handpiece Headquarters Corp.; Timken India Limited (80%); Timken Italia, S.R.L. (Italy); Timken Latrobe Steel; Timken Latrobe Steel Distribution; Timken Latrobe Steel-Europe Ltd. (U.K.); Timken de Mexico S.A. de C.V.; MPB Export Corporation; Nihon Timken K.K. (Japan); Timken Polska Sp.z.o.o. (Poland); Rail Bearing Service Corporation; Timken Romania S.A. (92%); The Timken Corporation; The Timken Service & Sales Co.; Timken Servicios Administrativos S.A. de C.V. (Mexico); Timken Singapore Pte. Ltd.; Timken South Africa (Pty.) Ltd.; Timken de Venezuela C.A.; Yantai Timken Company Limited (China).

Principal Divisions

Automotive; Industrial; Aerospace and Super Precision; Rail; Alloy Steel; Specialty Steel; Precision Steel Components; Emerging Markets.

Principal Competitors

Aktiebolaget SKF; NSK Ltd.; USX-U.S. Steel Group.

Further Reading

Bottoms, David, "Timken" (Faircrest Steel Plant), *Industry Week,* October 17, 1994, pp. 31+.

Byrne, Harlan S., "Timken Co.: It Spends Big to Compete in Global Bearings Market," *Barron's,* August 6, 1990, pp. 31–32.

Dix, R. Victor, "Steel Industry Still Competitive, Timken Boasts," *Daily Record* (Wooster, Ohio), May 6, 1997, p. B1.

"From a Lost Law Fight, a $4-Million Market," *Business Week,* November 5, 1955, pp. 62–63.

From Missouri to Mars—A Century of Leadership in Manufacturing, Canton: The Timken Company, 1998.

Gerdel, Thomas W., "Timken Abandons Tradition; Outsourcing Steel, Reorganization Aim at Greater Global Efficiency," *Plain Dealer* (Canton, Ohio), May 3, 2001, p. 1C.

——, "Timken Marks First Century," *Plain Dealer* (Canton, Ohio), April 24, 1999, p. 1C.

——, "Timken Says Economic, Labor Conditions to Delay Tube Mill," *Plain Dealer* (Canton, Ohio), February 9, 1999, p. 2C.

——, "Timken to Slash 600 Jobs Worldwide," *Plain Dealer* (Canton, Ohio), March 4, 2000, p. 1C.

"Great-Grandpa Can Smile Again," *Forbes,* May 28, 1990, pp. 226–28.

Hardy, Eric S., "The Soul of an Old Company," *Forbes,* March 13, 1995, p. 70.

History of the Timken Company, Canton: The Timken Company, 1990.

McManus, George J., "Timken Steers Its Own Course—Successfully," *Iron Age,* May 10, 1976, pp. 33–40.

Marsh, Peter, "Making Bearings a Family Affair," *Financial Times,* June 30, 1999, p. 7.

——, "Timken Seeks Bigger Slice of Market," *Financial Times,* May 15, 1997, pp. 29+.

"Must Affiliates Compete?," *Business Week,* April 28, 1951, p. 25.

Pullin, John, "Every Day in Every Way . . . ," *Professional Engineering,* April 14, 1999, pp. 28–29.

Pruitt, Bettye, *Timken,* Harvard Business School, 1999.

"Recession Buying Speeds Timken's Automatic Look," *Business Week,* September 20, 1958, pp. 160–62.

"The Road Points Only Up," *Forbes,* June 1, 1968, p. 66.

Shen Bin, and Xie Liangjun, "Bearing Giants Bolster Business in China," *China Daily,* North American ed., September 29, 1997, p. 5.

Sheridan, John H., "America's Best Plants: Timken," *Industry Week,* October 19, 1992, pp. 53+.

Siuru, Bill, "Timken's 100 Years: From Buggies to Boxsters," *Ward's Auto World,* August 1999, pp. 65–66.

Thomas, Dana L., "Rough to Smooth," *Barron's,* March 6, 1972, p. 3.

"Timken Rolling at Fast Clip," *Financial World,* February 14, 1973, p. 20.

"Timken: Rolling Up Gains," *Financial World,* September 22, 1971, p. 7.

"Timken: Well-Prepared for Future Shocks," *Sales and Marketing Management,* January 17, 1977, pp. 40–42.

Uchitelle, Louis, "Who's Afraid Now That Big Is No Longer Bad?" *Journal Record* (Oklahoma City, Oklahoma), November 10, 2000, pp. 1+.

Vasilash, Gary S., "Timken: Targeted on the 21st Century," *Production,* June 1992, pp. 40+.

Weiss, Gary, "Timken's Folly?," *Barron's,* November 25, 1985, p. 13.

"Why Timken's 'Stability' Will Save Its Bottom Line," *Business Week,* May 17, 1982, pp. 107–08.

Wilder, Clinton, "Timken: A Big Step for an Old-Line Industry," *Informationweek,* September 13, 1999, p. 50.

—update: Frederick C. Ingram

Trigen Energy Corporation

One Water Street
White Plains, New York 10601-1009
U.S.A.
Telephone: (914) 286-6600
Fax: (914) 288-6677
Web site: http://www.trigen.com

Wholly Owned Subsidiary of Suez
Incorporated: 1986
Employees: 846
Sales: $280.4 million (1999)
NAIC: 221330 Steam and Air-Conditioning Supply;
221310 Water Supply and Irrigation Systems; 22111
Electric Power Generation

Owned by a subsidiary of French conglomerate Suez (formerly Suez Lyonnaise des Eaux), Trigen Energy Corporation is a developer, owner, and operator of industrial, commercial, institutional, and district (small, community- or facility-oriented) energy systems in North America. More established electric utilities, however, see it as a threat. Trigen builds and operates smaller power plants, which more effectively convert fuel by taking advantage of the heat given off in the generation of electricity. As much as two-thirds of the fuel consumed by large power plants is lost to the air or water as heat. Trigen facilities capture that exhaust either to drive turbines to generate additional electricity or to create steam. Systems that serve communities can then pipe the steam to customers for hot water and heating. To ensure that steam is not wasted during the summer months, Trigen and other providers of combined heat and power (CHP) systems also use steam to create chilled water for air conditioning. By adding cooling capabilities, the standard practice of cogeneration becomes trigeneration: hence the Trigen corporate name. The White Plains, New York company serves more than 1,500 customers. Urban areas it serves include Baltimore, Boston, Philadelphia, and St. Louis. Individual customers include industrial plants, colleges and universities, office buildings, hospitals, hotels, sports arenas, and convention centers.

District Energy Losing Favor After World War II

From the beginning of the electric age, engineers knew that power plants produced far more heat than electricity. In the first decades of the 20th century, in fact, local power companies practiced cogeneration. They sold steam to area customers for space heating or industrial use. Because steam could not be transported very far without a significant loss of heat, cogeneration was dependent on a district energy strategy; that is, small community plants. The trend after World War II, however, was to build large, centralized power plants that could deliver electricity over a wide region. As a result, steam was no longer a viable commodity. In some urban areas, such as Manhattan, steam continued to be sold, although residents were reminded of the history of cogeneration only when a pipe burst and a street was closed for repair. In addition to district energy, privately maintained power plants that serviced businesses and institutions also were replaced by the cheap energy that could be bought from large centralized utilities. As long as fuel remained inexpensive and utilities had monopoly status, there was no incentive to make use of the heat given off in the production of electricity. The practice of cogeneration continued, but it was generally limited to industries that required a great deal of process steam, such as chemical companies, paper mills, and food processing plants. These businesses combined turbines and generators with their boilers to turn heat exhaust into usable electricity.

In the 1970s the OPEC oil cartel limited the supply of petroleum, causing a dramatic increase in fuel prices. In turn, central power plants lost their competitive edge, as their operating costs now exceeded those plants that were able to take advantage of wasted heat. Talk of cogeneration came back into fashion as an energy-conservation option, especially after President Carter promoted the concept in a 1977 energy speech. A year later Congress passed the Public Utility Regulatory Policies Act, which required that utilities buy electricity produced from cogenerators. By giving cogenerators the opportunity to sell excess electricity, the act spurred commercial interest in developing cogenerating systems.

The founder of Trigen, Thomas R. Casten, became involved in cogeneration in the mid-1970s. In 1964 Casten graduated magna cum laude from the University of Colorado, earning a

B.A. in Economics. He spent four years in the U.S. Marines as an engineering officer, including a one-year tour in Vietnam, and then resumed his education. In 1969 he earned an M.B.A. in finance from Columbia University. He then went to work for Indiana-based Cummins Engine Co., makers of diesel engines.

In 1974 Cummins named Casten director of corporate strategy with the goal of determining what lay in store for the company in light of expert predictions that diesel fuels would be exhausted within 25 years. After several months of study, Casten concluded that fuel would still be available, it would just be more expensive. He also knew that fuel was not being fully exploited in the generation of electricity. In the 1960s Cummins actually had manufactured cogeneration equipment, but dropped out of the business because customers were unable, or unwilling, to properly run and maintain the plants. "A company will spend $5,000 on an office copier and routinely sign a maintenance contract with Xerox," Casten told *Fortune* in 1978. "But they'll spend $250,000 on a total energy plant and let the janitor maintain it." Therefore, he urged Cummins not only to build cogeneration equipment but to become involved in the design, installation, and operation of cogeneration systems. It took him three years to sell his argument to Cummins management. Finally, in 1977 he was named to head Cummins Cogeneration Co., based in New York City, which Casten considered an ideal place to test out his ideas. New York residents were served by Con Edison, which for years had been the source of jokes by Johnny Carson on the *Tonight* show as well as other comics. In addition to its image as being poorly run, Con Edison charged customers twice as much as the average consumer elsewhere in the country, and 50 percent more than residents of Boston, the next most expensive city for electricity.

Con Edison Viewing Cogeneration As a Threat in the 1970s

Cummins sold systems in Westchester, the Bronx, and Queens, but only when it attempted to set up a cogenerating system in midtown Manhattan did Con Edison fight back. In June 1978 Cummins made plans to install a 5,600-kilowatt cogenerating system in a 30-story office building on 11 West 42nd Street. The developers estimated that by producing their own electricity and steam, they could pay off the $2.5 million price tag within six years. It was the prospect of other large customers following suit that alarmed Con Edison, which quickly applied political pressure to stop the installation. Because Con Edison collected approximately 7.5 percent of all city tax revenues through its utility bills, it did not lack the necessary clout. It urged the city to delay approving new cogeneration plants until proper studies on the impact could be conducted. It argued that cogeneration would increase air pollu-

tion, as well as lead to higher Con Edison bills because the fixed costs of its power system would have to be supported by fewer customers. New York already had lost more than 600,000 jobs since 1969, with many businesses leaving because of the high cost of electricity, which resulted in the estimated loss of $200 million a year in tax revenues. Con Edison predicted that cogeneration would deprive the city of even more tax dollars, especially since avoiding utility taxes was a prime inducement for customers to purchase cogeneration systems.

In the end, the midtown office building received its permit to install the Cummins system, but only at the 11th hour and after the developers threatened court action. Cummins's management then showed that it was not as committed to cogeneration as Casten. It was hesitant to fund the division or participate in financing projects. After three years and only six sales, Cummins decided to withdraw from the business. In 1980 Casten and partners bought Cummins Cogeneration and renamed it Cogeneration Development Corp. Casten also deviated from the Cummins strategy: instead of simply selling the equipment, the company would now act as developers of municipal industrial systems that could sell steam to a number of customers. In this vein, Cogeneration Development raised $52 million in December 1982 to build a district heating project in Trenton, New Jersey.

Although media interest in cogeneration fell off in the 1980s, the technology continued to intrigue energy professionals, despite President Reagan's reluctance to fund research or industrial cogeneration projects and the difficulty in sorting out regulatory issues. Utilities also resisted cogenerators' attempts to hook up to their distribution grids. Furthermore, cogenerators were required to provide customers with backup service from utilities, which charged rates that stripped cogenerators of their economic advantage. In order to squeeze even more benefits from fuel, Casten and others began to offer cold water in addition to electricity and steam. Trigeneration either converted excess steam to drive turbines to power air conditioners, or they were fed into chillers, large metal boxes containing tubes that carried a briny solution of water and lithium bromide. The steam heating the lithium bromide created water vapor, which would then undergo a condensation and evaporation process to create chilled water.

Forming Trigen in 1986

In 1986 Cogeneration Development teamed with ELYO, the energy arm of French water company Societé Lyonnaise des Eaux, to create Trigen Energy. Although the French company held a controlling stake in the business, Cogeneration was the managing partner, effectively placing operational control in Casten's hands. Through the French he was able to gain use of ELYO's proprietary technology in building district energy systems. Another subsidiary, Cofreth, ran a number of district heating systems, including one that served Paris. For the French, Trigen was a way to gain a foothold in the United States. After World War II, France nationalized electricity and gas, leaving utility companies such as Lyonnaise des Eaux with only water as a business. French water companies consolidated and with their considerable assets were able to invest heavily in research and development. Water in America, on the other hand, was highly fragmented, with more than 50,000 community water companies. French water companies recognized that

American water systems were aging and that hundreds of billions of dollars would have to be spent to upgrade them. In order to enter this promising market, French water giants forged relationships with U.S. companies in a range of compatible businesses, including Cogeneration Development to create Trigen Energy.

In 1987, its first full year of operation, Trigen generated $1 million in revenues. By 1991 it would reach $25 million, and then begin to grow at an even greater rate. Trigen generated $70.5 million in revenues in 1992, followed by $90.5 million in 1993. Trigen also completed its first major acquisition in 1993, the $65 million purchase of United Thermal Corp., which would more than double the company's revenues. United Thermal delivered steam to customers in Boston, Baltimore, Philadelphia, and St. Louis. As a result of this acquisition, Trigen increased its revenues to $185.6 million in 1994, while posting a net profit of $8.5 million. Moreover, the CEO of United Thermal, Richard E. Kessel, became Trigen's chief operating officer.

To fund its expanding business, Trigen made an initial public offering of stock in August 1994, raising almost $40 million. The company continued its external growth in 1995 with the purchase of a ten-year-old community energy system that served the Province of Prince Edward Island in Canada. Also in 1995 Trigen, holding a 51 percent interest, teamed up with Tucson Electric Power Co. to buy the power plant of the Coors Brewing Co. for approximately $62 million, of which $40 million was earmarked for improvements. Coors also signed a 25-year contract to purchase all of its steam and electricity from the plant, thus taking away some $12 million in annual revenues from the local utility, Public Service Co. of Colorado. As a result, Coors was able to outsource its power operations in order to focus on its core business, Tucson was able to find a way to supplement revenues that would likely be lost because of deregulation, and Trigen gained new business and another calling card as it looked to separate more industrial customers from utilities. At the end of 1995 after generating revenues of almost $200 million, Trigen was the largest commercial owner and operator of community district energy systems in North America.

Trigen continued to make purchases and form alliances in 1996. It acquired Ewing Power Systems, which made specialized compact steam turbine generators. A subsidiary, Trigen-Schuylkill Cogeneration, acquired a one-third interest in Grays Ferry Cogeneration Partnership, which would build and operate a cogeneration facility in Pennsylvania. Trigen also created a joint venture with Mexico's Gentor Industrias to build and operate cogeneration facilities in Mexico. The company further teamed up with Hydro-Quebec to do business throughout New England and upstate New York. Finally, in December 1996, Trigen signed a major deal with Cinergy Corp., one of America's largest utilities, to build and operate cogeneration and trigeneration plants throughout North America, as well as the United Kingdom and Ireland.

At the end of the 1990s, as a number of states moved to deregulate utilities, Trigen was well positioned to enjoy even greater growth. It would do so, however, without Casten. The company's French corporate parent had undergone some changes. In 1997 Lyonnaise des Eaux merged with Compagnie de Suez, the company that had built the Suez Canal in the 1850s. Although the new company, which eventually would rename itself Suez, was extremely large, it remained smaller than its French rival, Vivendia. In 1999 Suez began to aggressively expand its U.S. interests. It purchased Calgon Corp., a water treatment company, for $425 million, then merged it with another acquisition, Nalco Chemical Co., which came with a $4.1 billion price tag. Moreover, Suez began to buy out its American partners. In August 1999, it acquired all the outstanding shares of United Water. The following month its ELYO unit offered to buy the outstanding shares of Trigen for $22 each. After some weeks of negotiating the price with a special committee of Trigen's board of directors, ELYO withdrew the offer, maintaining that the committee had asked for a higher price that was based on what it characterized as unrealistic and aggressive earnings projections. The deal was not dead for long, however. In January 2000, ELYO improved the deal to $23.50 per share and the board accepted. A number of shareholders expressed disappointment in the terms, especially since Trigen's stock recently had been trading in that price range. In the end, ELYO controlled the board and outcome. In conjunction with the announced agreement, Casten resigned as the company's chief executive in order to pursue his own goals. He was immediately replaced by Kessel, who had been with Trigen for seven years and was more than capable of leading the organization.

Under Kessel, Trigen continued to land significant contracts. Teaming with Pepco Energy Service, Inc., it signed a 20-year agreement to provide a trigeneration system for a major new convention center in Washington, D.C. It also was part of a joint venture that signed two separate 15-year contracts with General Motors to build and operate trigeneration systems at facilities in Shreveport, Louisiana, and Oklahoma City, Oklahoma. In 2001, Trigen returned to midtown Manhattan, signing an agreement to provide the high-tech energy needs of the proposed NYCyberCenter. Despite losing Casten, Trigen was clearly well situated to maintain its prominence in the district energy field.

Principal Operating Units

Trigen Boston; Trigen Baltimore; Trigen-People; Trigen Philadelphia; Trigen St. Louis.

Principal Competitors

Sithe Energies; U.S. Energy.

Further Reading

Alexander, Tom, "The Little Engine That Scares Con Ed," *Fortune,* December 31, 1978, pp. 80–84.

"Cogeneration's Heyday May Have Arrived," *Business Week,* March 21, 1983, Industrial Edition, p. 60A.

Feder, Barnaby J., "Cogeneration of Energy," *New York Times,* April 1, 1982, p. D2.

Hennagir, Tim, "CHP's Promise," *Independent Energy,* January/February 1998, pp. 38–40.

Holden, Benjamin A., "Cinergy and Trigen to Help Customers Produce Electricity," *Wall Street Journal,* December 10, 1996, p. B11E.

Marcial, Gene G., "Trigen's Steady Stream of Juice," *Business Week,* May 6, 1996, p. 120.

Parker, Akwela, "Power Firm Sees Steam Cooling As Hot Market," *Philadelphia Inquirer,* April 5, 2001.

Seeley, Robert S., "District Cooling Gets Hot," *Mechanical Engineering,* July 1996, p. 82.

——, "District Energy Growth," *Independent Energy,* November 1995, p. 24.

—Ed Dinger

U.S. Aggregates, Inc.

147 West Election Road
Draper, Utah 84020
U.S.A.
Telephone: (801) 984-2600
Fax: (801) 984-2604
Web site: http://www.usaggregates.com

Public Company
Incorporated: 1994 as USAI Acquisition Corporation
Employees: 1,476
Sales: $291.7 million (2000)
Stock Exchanges: New York
Ticker Symbol: AGA
NAIC: 212321 Construction Sand and Gravel Mining;
212322 Industrial Sand Mining; 212319 Other
Crushed and Broken Stone Mining and Quarrying;
32732 Ready-Mix Concrete Manufacturing

U.S. Aggregates, Inc. is one of the country's major producers of aggregates, defined as crushed stone, sand, and gravel. It serves customers in the southeastern states of Florida, Mississippi, Georgia, Tennessee, and Alabama, and the Mountain states of Arizona, Idaho, Nevada, and Utah. The federal government is the most important ultimate customer for the company's products, since about 50 percent of all aggregates are used to build federal highways and related infrastructure projects. The company ships about half of its products to commercial and residential contractors, so it plays a key role in the construction of homes, office buildings, industrial facilities, and institutional structures. The Golder, Thoma, Cressey, Rauner Fund IV, L.P. owns a majority of the company's common stock.

Origins and Early Operations

On January 13, 1994, USAI Acquisition Corp. was incorporated under Delaware law. Then on February 24, 1994, company President James A. Harris and Treasurer Michael J. Stone certified an amendment to the company's certificate of incorporation that changed the company's name to U.S. Aggregates, Inc.

Harris became the chief executive officer and chairman of the board. Harris previously had served in several executive positions at Koppers Company, Inc., where he oversaw many acquisitions that helped make Koppers the nation's second largest aggregates producer in 1988.

Stone also came to the new company with considerable experience in the aggregates industry. Before 1994 he had been the chief financial officer for Genstar Building Materials and Services Group, a $1 billion division of Genstar Corporation that included Genstar Stone Products, the nation's tenth largest producer of crushed stone.

The third founder was an investment group, Chicago's Golder, Thoma, Cressey, Rauner Fund IV, L.P. (GTCR). Bruce V. Rauner and David A. Donnini, two of its principals, served on the board of directors from the time the new company was started. On January 24, 1994 the fund made its first purchase of the new firm's common stock and thus became its major owner.

The private equity firm of Golder, Thoma, Cressey, Rauner, Inc., the general partner of GTCR IV, was formed in 1980 but then split in 1997, creating GTCR Golder Rauner and Thoma, Cressey Equity Partners. In 1999 GTCR Golder Rauner remained the largest owner of U.S. Aggregates. Limited partners of GTCR Golder Rauner included Bell Atlantic Asset Management Company, Endowment Advisors, The Ford Foundation, Iowa Public Employees Retirement System, Hughes Aircraft Retirement Fund, JP Morgan Private Equity Group, Northwestern University, and Yale University.

Charles Pullin, former chairman of Koppers Company, became a member of U.S. Aggregates' board of directors in 1994. He served until October 30, 2000, when he resigned due to illness; at that time, he was given the title of director emeritus.

U.S. Aggregates from its origin grew by acquisitions. In the summer of 1994 it bought Southern Ready Mix Inc. (SRM) from Finland's Metra Oy. SRM, a producer of rock materials and concrete, had annual revenue of about $49.4 million.

U.S. Aggregates' goal was to help meet the demands of the highway and building construction industries for aggregates.

Key Dates:

1994: USAI Acquisition Corporation is formed; name is changed to U.S. Aggregates, Inc.
1999: U.S. Aggregates completes its IPO in August and in December starts its web site.
2001: Restatement of 2000 finances leads to shareholder lawsuit; Stanford Springel is chosen as the company's new CEO; company announces a definitive agreement to sell its southeastern operations to Florida Rock Industries, Inc.

For example, it took about 85,000 tons of aggregates to build just one mile of a four-lane interstate highway. Aggregates made up about 90 percent of asphaltic concrete and about 80 percent of portland cement concrete by volume. Construction of an average six-room house took 90 tons of aggregates, while an average school or hospital needed 15,000 tons. The U.S. aggregates market in 1998 was about 2.8 billion tons.

Expansion in the Late 1990s

On June 5, 1998, U.S. Aggregates completed its merger with Monroc, Inc. for $57.6 million. Monroc was U.S. Aggregates' largest acquisition at the time. In 1997 Monroc reported net sales of $61.4 million. It operated mainly in Utah, Idaho, and Wyoming. The purchase of Monroc was part of the company's general expansion. It completed 28 acquisitions from January 1994 when it was founded to May 1999. In addition, it began since 1996 eight large greenfield aggregate production sites to serve big cities.

Its growth was fueled by above average demand for aggregates in the nine states it served. While the national compound annual increase in consumption was 5.1 percent, it was 6.7 percent in the nine states from 1993 to 1998, according to the U.S. Geological Survey.

In June 1998 the federal government passed the Transportation Equity Act for the 21st Century (TEA-21), which provided $218 billion for federal highway construction and maintenance for the six years of 1998 through 2003. TEA-21 increased highway spending 44 percent compared to the previous six years. However, spending was expected to increase 61 percent in the nine states served by U.S. Aggregates, thus the significance of what the company called "the largest federal public works spending bill in the history of the United States." At the end of 1998, the corporation recorded net sales of $228.7 million, up from $163.2 million in 1997 and $131.7 million in 1996.

In the 1980s and 1990s the aggregates industry became more consolidated. In 1980 there were about 1,865 independent crushed stone producers. In 1998 that number had declined 22 percent to about 1,450 producers, while the consumption of crushed stone had grown by 71 percent. The number of independent sand and gravel producers decreased 19 percent from 4,512 in 1980 to 3,642 in 1998 at the same time the consumption of sand and gravel increased 47 percent.

In spite of this consolidation, the aggregates industry remained quite fragmented and decentralized. For example, in 1997 the five major aggregates producers together controlled just 25 percent of the total market. The main reason was the local nature of the aggregates business. Since transporting gravel, sand, and other aggregates products was a major expense, local producers had a major competitive advantage.

In some areas, however, no local aggregate sources were available. In the Gulf Coast region that was the case, so large companies like U.S. Aggregates had a significant advantage because of their ability to handle the higher transportation costs.

Developments As a Public Corporation: 1999–2001

In August 1999 U.S. Aggregates, Inc. became a public corporation, with its IPO on the New York Stock Exchange under the ticker symbol of AGA. U.S. Aggregates later in 1999 opened its ninth new greenfield aggregates site through its subsidiary Southern Ready Mix in Pride, Alabama. With operations beginning in October, the site located in northwest Alabama was close to railroad and land transportation facilities, and also water transportation since it was next to the Tennessee River.

The leaders of U.S. Aggregates used high-tech methods to promote their company. For example, in 1999 the company launched its web site at www.usaggregates.com. In May 2000 it participated in the Financial Relations Board/BSMG Worldwide Virtual CEO Summit, a webcast that allowed potential investors and media representatives to learn more about a number of companies. Each CEO took about 30 minutes for a slide presentation and then answered online questions.

The company's financial performance in 2000 proved disappointing. Net sales declined 5.5 percent from $308.6 million in 1999 to $291.7 million in 2000. Compared with 1999 operating profits of $39.6 million, the company lost $5 million from its 2000 operations. The loss came from an $18.2 million decline in the company's asphalt and construction business due to increased fuel costs, the economic downturn, more competition in the Mountain states, and bad weather. U.S. Aggregates also sold its Alabama ready-mix business, resulting in a $9.6 million decline in that segment of the company's operations.

On April 3, 2001, U.S. Aggregates issued a press statement that restated its earnings for its first three quarters of fiscal 2000. In the first quarter, the company's net loss of $2.6 million was changed to $5.1 million. Second quarter net income of $6.8 million was restated as $3.1 million. The third quarter net income of $5.5 million was changed to $1.7 million. This restatement, not surprisingly, led to a 79 percent decrease in the price of U.S. Aggregates' stock.

By early May 2001 a class-action lawsuit was filed against U.S. Aggregates on behalf of those who purchased its common stock between April 25, 2000 through April 2, 2001. Filed in the U.S. District Court for the Northern District of California, the lawsuit alleged that the company released false and misleading financial statements. The company's shareholders were represented by several law firms, including Schiffrin & Barroway, LLP of Bala Cynwyd, Pennsylvania; The Law Offices of Marc S. Henzel of Philadelphia, Pennsylvania; and Cauley Geller Bowman & Coates, LLP of Little Rock, Arkansas.

In response to its legal and financial difficulties, U.S. Aggregates announced on May 11, 2001, that its board had selected Stanford Springel as its new CEO. He replaced James Harris, who remained as the company's board chairman. Springel had spent the previous 14 years helping other companies deal with similar financial challenges, and from 1969 to 1986 he worked for General Electric in financial management positions.

In July 2001 Florida Rock Industries Inc. of Jacksonville, Florida, announced that it planned to acquire certain assets of U.S. Aggregates for about $105 million in cash and debts and equipment leases valued at about $45 million. The deal, expected to close before October of that year, required U.S. Aggregates to sell substantially all assets of its southeastern subsidiaries, including SRM Aggregates, Inc.; Bradley Stone & Sand, Inc.; BHY Ready Mix, Inc.; Mulberry Rock Corporation; Bama Crushed Corporation; Grove Materials Corporation, and DeKalb Stone, Inc. The operations in 2000 produced about 9.1 million tons of aggregates.

In 2000 and 2001 U.S. Aggregates faced some serious challenges as its financial performance declined. It had to borrow more money and sell some of its business assets to reduce debt. The good news was that increased federal government spending on highway and infrastructure projects led to more demand for the company's products. Although the company lost money and its sales declined in the first quarter of 2001, its leaders hoped to return the company to profitability as soon as possible.

Principal Subsidiaries

Western Aggregates Holding Corporation; SRM Holding Corporation; Western Acquisition, Inc.

Principal Competitors

Florida Rock Industries Inc.; Giant Cement Holding, Inc.; Edw. C. Levy Co.

Further Reading

Benjamin, Ericka, "GTCR Golder Rauner, L.L.C.," *Venture Capital Journal*, June 1, 1999, pp. 50–51.

"Metra Oy Sells U.S. Subsidiary," *Wall Street Journal* [European Edition], July 15, 1994.

"Shareholder Class Action Filed Against U.S. Aggregates, Inc. by the Law Firm of Schiffrin & Barroway, LLP," *PR Newswire*, May 1, 2001.

"U.S. Aggregates Announces Resignation of Charles R. Pullin from Board of Directors," *PR Newswire*, November 14, 2000.

"U.S. Aggregates' Board of Directors Names Stanford Springel Chief Executive Officer," *PR Newswire*, May 11, 2001.

—David M. Walden

U.S. Borax, Inc.

26877 Tourney Rd.
Valencia, California 91355-1847
U.S.A.
Telephone: (661) 287-5400
Fax: (661) 287-5495
Web site: http://www.borax.com

Wholly Owned Subsidiary of Rio Tinto plc
Incorporated: 1890 as Pacific Coast Borax Company
Employees: 1,600
Sales: $550 million (2000 est.)
NAIC: 212391 Potash, Soda, and Borate Mineral Mining

U.S. Borax, Inc. is the leading producer of borates in the world. Borates are derived from borax, a mineral salt that the company mines and refines at locations in California and Argentina, then ships throughout the world. Uses for borates include glass and fiberglass production, ceramic glazes, detergents, soaps, agricultural nutrients, and pest control products. The company, famous for its "20 Mule Team" trademark and the long-running "Death Valley Days" radio and television program, is owned by British mining giant Rio Tinto plc.

Early Years

U.S. Borax traces its origins to the year 1872, when a gold prospector named F.M. Smith discovered a borax deposit at Teel's Marsh, Nevada. After establishing a mine there, Smith soon became a leading producer of borax, which was then being used in gold processing, ceramic glazes, detergents, water softening, soaps, and food preservation.

Smith's San Francisco-based sales agent, W.T. Coleman, was also developing his own borax operations, and during the 1880s he acquired a number of borax mines in the California desert, including one at Death Valley. This rich deposit was located 165 hot, arid miles from the nearest train station at Mojave. To bring ore to the railroad, Coleman's employees devised a carefully engineered transport system. This was the famous "20 Mule Team," which actually consisted of 18 mules

and two horses. The animals pulled three wagons, one of which held water, that could haul more than 20 tons of ore from the mine to the railhead. The 185-foot long line of mules, horses, and wagons journeyed for ten days across rough trails that ranged from below sea level to 4,000 feet above, in heat of up to 130 degrees. Use of the large mule teams lasted only from 1884 to 1888, when production at Borate, California, superseded the Death Valley mine's output.

In 1888 Coleman went bankrupt, and his borax holdings were subsequently purchased by F.M. Smith (now known as "Borax" Smith), who established the Pacific Coast Borax Company two years later. The firm used the 20 Mule Team brand name on its products, which it began marketing abroad in 1896 when Smith established a partnership with a British company. Three years later Smith and a group of British investors also formed Borax Consolidated, Ltd., which assumed ownership of Pacific Coast Borax, as well as the mining interests of Desmazures and Groppler and other companies that operated mines in Turkey, Chile, and Peru. Borax Consolidated subsequently acquired additional operations in France and Argentina.

In 1906 Pacific Coast Borax began building a rail line, the Tonapah & Tidewater Railway, to haul ore in California and Nevada. Though the project was never fully completed, what was built did enable the company to more easily transport borax ore to existing railways at Barstow, California, and Beatty, Nevada.

In 1913 "Borax" Smith's financial empire collapsed, and his shares in Borax Consolidated, Ltd. were sold on the London stock exchange. Smith had held controlling interest in the firm and its subsidiary Pacific Coast Borax, and the sale put ownership of both firms completely in British hands.

Pacific Coast Borax continued to prosper following the departure of Smith, however. In 1914 the Death Valley Railroad was built to transport borax to the new Ryan mine that had been developed in the area. The company's production also reached 110,000 tons of borax per year during World War I. In 1923 Pacific Coast Borax consolidated its refining operations with the construction of a new facility in Wilmington, California, near Los Angeles.

Company Perspectives:

Rio Tinto Borax will remain the global borate supplier of choice, with a commitment to excellence in meeting customers' needs.

Discovery of a New Deposit

The company's production capacity grew again in 1925 after a doctor digging a well discovered the world's largest known borax deposit. It was subsequently acquired by Pacific Coast Borax, and a mine and mining town were constructed. The site, appropriately named Boron, California, became operational in 1927, at which time the company shut down most of its other mines. Pacific Coast Borax also diversified around this time into hotel management, opening a luxury resort facility in Death Valley called the Furnace Creek Inn.

In 1930 the company took its marketing efforts to the new medium of radio by sponsoring "Death Valley Days," a dramatic serial that chronicled the exploits of prospectors and cowboys in the Old West. The program caught on with the public and was broadcast for many years, ultimately switching over to television where it lasted until 1968.

By the 1940s, Pacific Coast Borax was primarily mining two sites, at Boron and at neighboring Trona, California. The company's mines operated much like coal mines, with workers taking an elevator to an underground cavern where the ore was extracted from the earth. The ore was then sent to the surface in chunks, where it was crushed and screened to pebble size for shipment to the company's refinery at Wilmington. Working conditions in the desert were hot on the surface, but underground the temperature was a constant 72 degrees, with 25 percent humidity. The company's employees were paid well, with Pacific Coast Borax providing housing and food at a discount rate. The price of borax, which had been $700 a ton during the 20 Mule Team days, was now less than $50 due to the greater efficiency of processing and transport.

Borates, in addition to being used in metal processing, soaps, and water softening, were now utilized for many other purposes. As much as half of the quantity produced went into making glass and enamel glazes, in the latter case as a replacement for the more hazardous lead. Additionally, borates were increasingly used in fertilizers, in leather production, and for washing citrus fruits to help prevent mold and decay. The U.S. government had also reportedly begun employing borates for use in defense projects, in particular as a component of rocket fuel.

In 1956 Pacific Coast Borax was merged with U.S. Potash, another mining concern owned by Borax Consolidated, Ltd., to form U.S. Borax & Chemical Corp. U.S. Potash had been acquired by Borax in 1930 to develop potash deposits in North America. As part of the arrangement, ownership of the reconfigured company would be shared with a New York banking group headed by Lazard Freres & Co., which was investing $7 million for an 8.5 percent interest in the company. A loan of $16 million was also taken out, which would help the firm with new plans to

convert the Boron, California mine into an open-pit operation, enabling greater recovery of ore. Manufacturing facilities were also expanded to handle the higher quantity of mineral being extracted. The U.S. government had reportedly put pressure on the British owners of Pacific Coast to transfer control at least partly to American hands, given the huge deposits held by the company and their importance to national defense.

International Expansion

The early 1960s saw the company building its international business with shipping terminals constructed in Wilmington, California, and Rotterdam, Netherlands. Borax NV was established as a sister company in Europe, along with a joint venture called Deutsche Borax. In Turkey, a major borax source was found in 1960, which was subsequently run by the nationalized Etibank company, U.S. Borax's only major competitor. In 1966 U.S. Borax also sold its Death Valley-based resort to the Fred Harvey Corporation.

U.S. Borax and Chemical was acquired in 1968 by RTZ Corporation (later known as Rio Tinto plc) through a merger with Borax, Ltd., U.S. Borax's principal owner. Rio Tinto was the world's largest mining concern. The Potash operations were subsequently sold to the Canadian government.

In 1980 U.S. Borax spent $80 million to construct a boric acid production plant at its Boron, California mine site. U.S. Borax was the world's leading producer of boric acid, which was largely used in metal refining. The mid-1980s also saw the company acquire Pennsylvania Glass Sand Corp. from ITT for $80 million and the Ottawa Silica Co. of Illinois for $46 million. Both were top producers of silica, used along with borax in the making of glass and fiberglass. They were subsequently merged to form U.S. Silica.

U.S. Borax was also pursuing other mineral interests at this time. The company had acquired a molybdenum deposit site in Alaska during the mid-1970s, and attempted during the 1980s to reach an agreement with the U.S. Forest Service for environmentally acceptable methods of mining it. U.S. Borax was ultimately unable to work the mine, however, and sold it in 1991 after reportedly spending $100 million on the project. More successful was the company's joint venture with Santa Fe Pacific Corporation to operate the Trinity silver mine in Lovelock, Nevada. The short-duration project commenced in early 1988, and depleted the ore in only two years. The company was also looking for gold mining opportunities in Nevada during this time.

Sale of Consumer Products Lines: 1988

In 1988 U.S. Borax sold its consumer products division to Greyhound Corp., owners of soap and cleaning product maker Dial. The new owners continued to use the 20 Mule Team trademark on containers of Borateem bleach, Boraxo powdered hand soap, and Borax cleanser. The company reportedly had been seeing declining revenues for the division, which took in approximately $43 million in annual sales. U.S. Borax would continue to use the 20 Mule Team name when marketing its own industrial products. Also during the year Ian L. White-

Key Dates:

1872: F. M. Smith discovers a borax mine at Teel's Marsh, Nevada.

1884: W. T. Coleman begins using 20 mule teams to haul borax from Death Valley.

1888: Coleman goes bankrupt; Smith acquires his mining operations.

1890: F. M. Smith forms Pacific Coast Borax Company.

1899: Smith and British partners form Borax Consolidated, Ltd. and Pacific Coast Borax becomes a subsidiary company.

1913: Smith, now also bankrupt, sells his majority stake in Borax Consolidated.

1925: Largest known borax deposit is discovered in California and acquired by Pacific Coast Borax.

1930: "Death Valley Days" debuts on radio, sponsored by company for next 38 years.

1956: Pacific Coast Borax merges with U.S. Potash, becomes U.S. Borax & Chemical.

1968: RTZ Corporation (later known as Rio Tinto plc) acquires company.

1977: Potash operations are sold to Canadian government.

1985–86: Company purchases two silica firms and forms U.S. Silica.

1988: Consumer products division is sold to Greyhound Corp.

1993: Company's name is shortened to U.S. Borax, Inc.

1995: U.S. Silica is sold for $120 million.

1999: Restored set of 20 mule team wagons takes their final ride in Rose Bowl Parade.

Thomson was elected president of U.S. Borax. White-Thomson, an Oxford graduate, had begun working for Borax Consolidated, Ltd. in 1960 as an assistant sales director.

In 1991 U.S. Borax announced plans for a new, 125,000-square-foot headquarters and research facility in Valencia, California. The new building would consolidate existing operations in Los Angeles and Anaheim, placing them closer to the Boron, California mine site. Since the early 1980s the company had been improving its efficiency and increasingly using automation at its plant, as well as upgrading equipment.

Consequently, production increased 20 percent while the number of employees dropped, reaching less than half the 1980 total of 2,400 by 1994. The company continued to seek new sources of borax, with its primary mine at Boron projected to have about 40 years of reserves left. Annual sales were now estimated at $500 million, with net profits of more than $100 million a year. U.S. Borax was also actively researching new methods of improving its product, and seeking new uses for borax derivatives. These included environmentally safer methods of manufacturing paper, and a safe-to-humans termite pesticide.

In 1995 U.S. Borax sold its U.S. Silica division to D. George Harris and Associates for $120 million. The move was due in part to the company's desire to shift its focus to the international

borax market, in particular Russia and China. Three regional offices were subsequently opened in the latter country. By this time the company was shipping its products to some 80 countries around the globe.

U.S. Borax celebrated the 125th anniversary of F.M. Smith's first borax mine development in 1997, building a $1 million, 6,000-square-foot visitor's center at its Boron complex that featured educational displays and examples of mining equipment from the past and present. Always aware of its history, U.S. Borax refurbished a set of original 20 mule team wagons the following year. No expense was spared in the restoration, which involved experts from around the country as well as Borax employees. Once completed, the wagons were given their official "last ride" at the January 1, 1999 Rose Bowl Parade in Pasadena, California. Afterwards, they were retired to the visitor's center at Boron, hitched to a train of 20 fiberglass mules—made, in part, from borax.

During 1999 the company acquired the assets of Lake Minerals Corporation, which operated a trona mine at Lone Pine, California. Trona was a mineral salt used in the borate refining process. The year also saw the installation of a new president and CEO, Preston S. Chiaro, with Ian L. White-Thomson assuming the role of chairman. In 2001, the company entered into a joint agreement with Millennium Cell, Inc. to develop a synthesis process for converting sodium borates to sodium borohydride. The latter was used to generate pure hydrogen via a Millennium-developed process.

With a long and storied history behind it, U.S. Borax remained the leading producer of borates on the planet. Its future for the near term looked bright, though when its principal mine in Boron, California, was exhausted new sources of the mineral would be needed. Efforts to locate similarly rich supplies were ongoing, and with Rio Tinto's strong financial backing the company appeared well situated to meet this goal.

Principal Subsidiaries

Borax Argentina S.A.; Borax Asia Pte. Ltd. (Singapore); Borax Benelux (Belgium); Borax España S.A. (Spain); Borax Europe Ltd. (U.K.); Borax Français S.A. (France); Borax Italia S.R.L. (Italy); Borax Japan Ltd.; Borax South America (Brazil); Borax U.K.; Deutsche Borax Gmbh (Germany); Borax Rotterdam NV (Netherlands).

Principal Competitors

Eti Holding, Inc.

Further Reading

Apodaca, Patrice, "U.S. Borax Still Mines 'White Gold,' But Much Has Changed Beneath the Surface for the Company," *Los Angeles Times (Valley Edition)*, April 5, 1994, p. D10.

Benson, Michael, "Borax Says Giddyap! One Last Time to 20 Mule Team," *Wall Street Journal*, September 16, 1998, p. CA1.

"Borax Mule Team Takes Its Final Ride," *Engineering and Mining Journal*, February, 1999, p. 16JJ.

"Borax to Transfer Pacific Coast Borax Ownership to U.S. Firm," *Wall Street Journal*, May 1, 1956, p. 26.

Gooding, Kenneth, ''Borax Steps up Search for New Deposit,'' *Financial Times,* October 16, 1996, p. 41.

——, ''Cleaning Up in the Widening Borax Market,'' *Financial Times,* November 20, 1990.

Marcus, Jerry, ''Rio Tinto Borax and U.S. Borax, Inc.,'' *Engineering and Mining Journal,* October, 1997, p. 24.

''Rio Tinto, Borax Propose a Merger for $127,224,000,'' *Wall Street Journal,* January 8, 1968, p. 6.

Schachter, Jim, ''Dial Hopes to Buy a Bit of History from Borax,'' *Los Angeles Times*, February 25, 1988, p. D1.

Sullivan, Robert J., ''Borax Bonanza—Steaming Mojave Desert Yields Record Output of the Versatile Chemical,'' *Wall Street Journal*, August 6, 1947, p. 1.

—Frank Uhle

U.S. Timberlands Company, L.P.

625 Madison Avenue, Suite 10-B
New York City, New York 10022
U.S.A.
Telephone (212) 755-1100
Fax: (212) 758-4009
Web site: http://www.ustimberlands.com

Public Company
Incorporated: 1996 as U.S. Timberlands Klamath Falls
Employees: 29
Sales: $75.6 million (2000)
Stock Exchanges: NASDAQ
Ticker Symbol: TIMBZ
NAIC: 113110 Timber Tract Operations

U.S. Timberlands Company, L.P. is a publicly traded partnership that owns more than 550,000 acres of timberland in Oregon and Washington; its corporate offices are located in New York City. The company harvests logs that are sold to third parties to be converted into construction products such as doors, millwork, plywood, laminated veneer lumber, particleboard, and hardboard. The timber is also used in paper and other products. To reforest its acreage, U.S. Timberlands also owns and operates a seed orchard, which each year produces five million conifer seedlings, approximately half of which are sold to other forest products companies. U.S. Timberlands has also formed an affiliate, Fiber Resource Services, to develop methods of recovering smaller trees that have been left behind in harvesting efforts. Rather than offering shares like a corporation, U.S. Timberlands elected to sell partnership units in its 1997 initial public offering. Because the company is a master limited partnership it generally pays no taxes. Unitholders are responsible for reporting their portion of income, gains, losses, deductions, and the like. Rather than receiving dividends, unitholders receive quarterly distributions. Unlike most shareholders in a corporation, however, they have no voting rights. Poor economic conditions in the timber industry caused management to suspend distributions in 2001 and to begin efforts to take the company private. Several unitholders filed suit to prevent the move.

Ripe Time for Timber Investments: 1990s

There was only one timberland investment management company in 1981. Five years later there would be six, with assets that amounted to less than $100 million. By 1990 those assets would grow to $600 million, and just two years later would exceed $2 billion. Traditionally institutional investors shied away from timberland because they simply did not understand the business. It was a specialized niche, relegated to the noncore real estate category. The raw numbers, however, now began to attract the big investors. After inflation it was estimated that timberland could produce an 8 percent annual return, with timber prices likely to increase as future demand was expected to outpace supply. Tighter environmental restrictions actually placed a check on supply, resulting in higher prices. Furthermore, the rising standard of living in Japan and other Pacific Rim countries also looked to fuel increasing demand. In 1994 two asset-based timberland performance measures were introduced as much to reassure institutional investors as to provide a tool to assess potential returns on investment. By 1998 institutional timberland investments reached $5.5 billion; yet this was a mere dot on the radar screen when compared to the $5 trillion in total institutional investments. Although timberland was coming into its own with investors, many still questioned whether it would remain competitive in the long-term with other assets.

U.S. Timberlands became an investment choice in 1997 when it made an initial public offering of units, selling more than seven million shares of the limited partnership at $21 each. An additional 1.1 million shares were sold a month later, bringing the total offering to more than 8.5 million shares. In all, the offering raised $225 million. The operations of the company were conducted by a subsidiary, U.S. Timberlands Klamath Falls (USTK), which had been formed a year earlier to buy a large tract of Oregon timberland from Weyerhaeuser Company.

Company Perspectives:

U.S. Timberlands is pursuing a strategy for growth that focuses on increasing cash flow and providing value to Unitholders. At the forefront of this strategy is the objective of maximizing productivity. U.S. Timberlands utilizes various modern forestry practices on its timberlands. In particular, U.S. Timberlands' computerized geographic information system (GIS) enables it to develop optimal harvest plans. U.S. Timberlands' sophisticated forestry practices include the application of selective harvesting and thinning practices, which improve the productivity of the remaining stand while providing merchantable timber for sale, and the development of genetically selected seedlings to grow trees with desirable traits such as smaller branch size and increased volume yield per acre.

After 100 years in business, Weyerhaeuser owned or leased some five million acres of timberland. In 1996 it decided to sell 600,000 acres of forest in the Klamath Falls, Oregon, area as part of a strategy to return to the company's traditional focus: the processing of Douglas Fir trees. The Klamath Falls land consisted mostly of Ponderosa and Lodgepole Pine trees. USTK was actually outbid by another company, Klamath Pacific International Inc., which had also been formed for the sole purpose of acquiring the acreage. Klamath Pacific agreed to pay $304 million, besting USTK's bid of $303 million; but just five days after signing the pact, Weyerhaeuser backed out, concerned over the financing of Klamath Pacific, which planned to take out a loan for $300 million of the total purchase price. Weyerhaeuser then began to negotiate with USTK and several weeks later struck a deal for $309 million. In addition to 600,000 acres of forest, USTK received 3,000 acres from the Weyerhaeuser Foundation, plus three mills, a seed orchard operation, and a nursery. In order to concentrate on managing its lumber holdings, USTK sold the mills to another company, Collins Holdings, with a ten-year agreement to supply logs. The Collins deal was large enough to account for as much as one-quarter of the company's total harvest, but essentially USTK could sell as many trees as it felled; the key was harvesting the timber at the same rate that the forests could be replenished. Klamath Pacific sued Weyerhaeuser over the sale to USTK, alleging that it had been used as a stalking horse to bid up the price. It also contended that Weyerhaeuser agreed to finance $130 million of the USTK deal, an offer that was not made to Klamath Pacific. The breach-of-contract suit would be litigated over the next four years. In June 2000, a jury in the U.S. District Court in Portland, Oregon, awarded Klamath Pacific $12.1 million in damages. Nevertheless, U.S. Timberlands had its acreage.

Purchasing More Acreage: 1997

Before the U.S. Timberlands 1997 public offering, USTK added to its Oregon holdings by acquiring 42,000 acres, plus cutting rights on 3,000 additional acres, from the Ochoco Lumber Company. It considered the Ochoco trees to be a good fit with Klamath Falls, both in terms of species and age classes. So much of the economics of the timber industry is predicated on species and age. The company mostly owned softwood, which

accounts for two-thirds of the world's industrial wood production. Softwood is preferred over hardwood because of its long fibre, strength, and flexibility. Until trees reach a certain age, however, they are not large enough to be considered merchantable timber. Douglas Fir and Hemlock of the Northwest, for instance, is not merchantable until the trees are in the 55- to 70-year range. The smallest merchantable trees, used for pulp, are generally at least ten years of age. Of the land U.S. Timberlands bought from Weyerhaeuser, 180,000 acres were part of a plantation established in the early 1960s. Most of its trees, ranging in age from one to 37 years, were not yet merchantable. The rest of the Klamath Falls acreage were natural stands and represented the immediate source of timber that the company could harvest, estimated to represent 2.2 billion board feet. Over 40 percent of the Ochoco timber was more than 80 years old. Of the company's total merchantable timber, 47 percent was ponderosa pine; 20 percent, white fir; 17 percent, lodgepole pine; 13 percent, Douglas fir; and the remaining 3 percent, other species, including cedar, sugar pine, and western larch.

John M. Rudey was named chairman and chief executive officer to run U.S. Timberlands out of its midtown Manhattan offices. He had experience managing timber holdings, serving since 1992 as CEO of Gerrin Properties Holdings, a private investment firm that concentrated on timber and real estate. After completing U.S. Timberland's IPO he opened a small Seattle, Washington, office to oversee the day-to-day timber operations, naming an experienced Northwest executive, Allen E. Symington, to serve as president and chief financial officer. Symington had held a number of management positions at privately owned Simpson Timber Investment Company, which he joined in 1962.

The company's strategy was simply to sell lumber and grow trees, as well as keep an eye out for undervalued timberland to acquire. Each year it would determine a harvesting plan, targeting tracts where allowing trees to continue to grow would provide diminishing economic returns. Simply put, each species enjoys a growth rate and at a certain age begins to slow down, at which point the additional wood that might be realized falls below the desired rate of return on the investment in the acreage. Once the timber was contracted for, the company would either hire a third party to harvest the acreage and arrange for a trucking company to deliver the logs to the customer, or it would price on a "stumpage" basis to the customer, who would be responsible for harvesting and delivery. Harvested acreage would then be reforested to maintain a consistent level of resources for the company. Moreover, U.S. Timberlands expressed a desire to manage its holding in an environmentally responsible manner. For investors, the company hoped to begin making quarterly distributions on May 15, 1998. The minimum distribution was expected to be 50 cents per unit.

Major Challenges During 1998

U.S. Timberlands would be challenged on two major fronts in 1998. Timber prices that were strong at the beginning of the year would soon weaken because of a number of factors. Demand for wood products in Asia fell dramatically because of a severe economic downturn in the region, thus creating an oversupply in the United States. Fires in Florida blackened almost 3 percent of the state's trees, which had to be harvested

Key Dates:

1996: U.S. Timberlands Klamath Falls (USTK) is formed to acquire acreage from Weyerhaeuser.
1997: U.S. Timberlands Company is incorporated and completes an initial public offering; USTK becomes a subsidiary company.
1999: Seattle office is closed; Washington acreage is purchased from Boise Cascade.
2001: Quarterly distributions are suspended; management-led group of investors makes offer to take company private.

because their bark was now susceptible to attack by disease and insects. Furthermore a U.S. Department of Agriculture program that encouraged farmers to plant pine trees to save land now required farmers to clear 500 trees an acre in order to retain subsidies. After the program had been in effect for more than ten years, conservationists had learned that wildlife had been hurt by a pine canopy that allowed too little sunlight to penetrate. Eliminating the trees would alleviate the problem, but the removal of the trees only added to the glut of lumber and pulp on the market. Even though the United States was enjoying a building boom, usually a good sign for the timber industry, the oversupply of wood resulted in falling prices.

While prices were cyclical and could expect to bounce back, U.S. Timberlands faced a potentially more serious problem in 1998: an Oregon ballot initiative called Measure 64. In essence it would eliminate "clear cutting," a practice in which large areas of forest are completely harvested. Environmentalists backing the measure equated clear cutting with strip mining and maintained that it was a catastrophe for a watershed. Measure 64 would force timber companies to practice selective cutting by protecting all trees more than 30 inches in diameter and requiring a certain number of trees to be left standing. According to the Oregon Department of Forestry the measure would reduce the amount of lumber coming out of the state by 60–65 percent. Because all of U.S. Timberland's acreage was located in the state, the passage of Measure 64 could be devastating. Management announced its willingness to go to court to sue the state for an illegal taking of private property. It joined other timber companies in raising some $5 million for a campaign to fight the ballot question, while proponents scraped together $300,000. In November 1998, Measure 64 was soundly defeated by the voters of Oregon.

U.S. Timberland posted poor results in 1998. Revenues fell to $71.3 million, from $77.3 million the year before, and the company lost $6.4 million. Moreover, because of low prices for timber, the company had logged at an unsustainable rate in order to boost revenues. In the beginning of 1999, Rudey fired Symington and his two lieutenants and closed down the Seattle office. Symington maintained that his team had performed well under adverse business conditions. Nevertheless, Rudey took over as president, and the running of the company was now split between New York and operations headquarters in Klamath Falls.

U.S. Timberlands enjoyed a better year in 1999. The U.S. economy remained strong and Asia showed improvement, resulting in a rebound in the price of logs and timber. In an effort to diversify its holdings, especially important after the scare of Measure 64, the company invested in acreage in Washington. An affiliate, U.S. Timberlands Yakima, bought 56,000 acres of forest for $60 million from paper producer Boise Cascade Corporation. U.S. Timberlands contributed $294,000 in cash for a 49 percent stake in the affiliate. As part of the land deal, U.S. Timberlands Yakima agreed to supply Boise with logs. Just as manufacturers were in recent years selling their factories to outsourcers who would actually produce the goods, paper producers were also selling off their forests. As long as they had access to pulp, there was little need to keep 50 years' worth of trees on the books. Overall in 1999, U.S. Timberlands increased its revenues to just under $77 million, and reported net income of approximately $6.3 million.

The fortunes of U.S. Timberlands again turned sour in 2000. The lumber market experienced another slump and the price of the company's shares fell steadily. By November 2000, units that had originally been sold at $21 had dipped below $5. Management announced that it was investigating the possibility of taking the company private "as a means to enhance shareholder value," according to a company spokesperson. Several class action lawsuits were filed by unitholders against the board of directors, alleging a breach of fiduciary responsibility. For 2000, U.S. Timberlands would report a drop in revenues, from $77 million in 1999 to $75.6 million, as well as a net loss of $4.1 million. Although in January 2001 the company would announce its 12th consecutive quarterly distribution, in May it opted to indefinitely suspend distributions after announcing a loss of $8.8 million in the first quarter of the year. In a comparable period the previous year, the company had lost $1.8 million. Revenues were also down by 20 percent. A group of investors controlled by management then announced that it had made a $100 million buyout offer, comprised of cash and promissory notes. Given this proposal and the pending litigation by unitholders, the future of U.S. Timberlands was, at best, murky.

Principal Subsidiaries

U.S. Timberlands Klamath Falls, L.L.C.; U.S. Timberlands Management Company, L.L.C.

Principal Competitors

Georgia-Pacific Corporation; Hampton Affiliates; Simpson Investment Company.

Further Reading

"Ailing U.S. Timberlands Receives $100 Million Buyout Offer," *Puget Sound Business Journal,* May 11, 2001.
Barnard, Jeff, "Grass-Roots Ballot Measure Seeks to Ax Clear-Cutting in Oregon," *Los Angeles Times,* October 18, 1998, p. 5.
Caulfield, Jon P., "Timberland in Institutional Portfolios and the Question of Persistence," *Forest Products Journal,* April 1998, pp. 23–28.
——, Timberland Return Drivers and Invest Styles for an Asset That Has Come of Age," *Real Estate Finance,* Winter 1998, pp. 65–78.
Erb, George, "A Clearcut Threat," *Puget Sound Business Journal,* September 21, 1998.

——, "Executives Axed at U.S. Timberlands," *Puget Sound Business Journal,* January 22, 1999.

Harwood, Joe, "Executives Consider Privatizing New York-Based Timber Firm," *Register Guard,* November 6, 2000.

Jones, Steven D., "Timber-Cutting Initiative: The Key Is in the Fine Print," *Wall Street Journal/Northwest,* October 7, 1998, p. NW1.

"U.S. Timberlands Unit Buying Boise Cascade Forest Land," *New York Times,* June 10, 1999, p. 4.

"Weyerhaeuser Co.: Oregon Plants and Forest to Be Sold for $309 Million," *Wall Street Journal,* June 24, 1996, p. B4.

Winninghoff, Ellie, "Go Hug a Tree," *Forbes,* September 13, 1993, p. 208.

—Ed Dinger

Unilog SA

97-99 Boulevard Péreire
75017 Paris
France
Telephone: (+33) 1-40-68-40-00
Fax: (+33) 1-40-68-40-05
Web site: http://www.unilog.fr

Public Company
Incorporated: 1968 as Informatique et Entreprise
Employees: 5,531
Sales: EUR 479 million ($450.5 million) (2000)
Stock Exchanges: Euronext Paris
Ticker Symbol: UNG
NAIC: 541511 Custom Computer Programming Services;
    541513 Computer Facilities Management Services;
    541512 Computer Systems Design Services

Fast-growing Unilog SA is a leading information technology (IT) consultant, engineering services, and training services provider. One of the top 10 IT consultants in France, the company also holds top positions in Germany, and in French-speaking Switzerland, and is building up its presence in Austria and the United Kingdom as well. Unilog is organized into three primary divisions: Unilog Management; Unilog IT Services; and Unilog IT Training. Unilog Management groups the company's consulting arm with 500 consultants providing process enhancement and information systems consulting services throughout France and Germany. Unilog Management provided 18 percent of revenues in 2000. Implementing the company's IT systems is its largest unit, Unilog IT Services, providing onsite implementation and upgrading of client IT systems; the company also offers permanent onsite management and maintenance services. IT Services generates 71 percent of Unilog's revenues of EUR 479 million in 2000. Lastly, the company has been building its IT Training division, primarily through its acquisitions in Germany since the late 1990s, providing training services especially to its Management and IT Services clients. IT Training has grown from just 2 percent of sales in 1997 to 11 percent of sales in 2000. Listed on the Paris stock exchange since 1988,

Unilog is led by Chairman, President, and cofounder Gérard Philippot.

An IT Services Pioneer: 1960s

The formation of Unilog dates to 1968 when Gérard Philippot and four partners created the company Informatique et Entreprise. The young Paris-based company quickly began to branch out into a variety of areas of the nascent French computer industry. In 1970, the company formed Investissement Informatique, a holding company that served as an umbrella for a number of new companies, each dedicated to a particular specialty in the computer business. As such, the company was able to gain expertise in a variety of areas in the dawning Information Technology sector, including computer engineering, minicomputers, microprocessing, and office systems.

The company saw steady growth throughout the 1970s and was able to boast repeated profits, despite a long recession. In 1982, the company decided to group its various subsidiaries under a single company name, Unilog. Over the next five years, Unilog continued to develop its expertise, while retaining a focus on the Paris region. Yet the company soon began to prepare to take its operations to a higher level of activity. As part of its new ambitions, the company reorganized its share capital, creating a new holding company, Unilog Associés, owned by the company's founders and management. The creation of this new shareholder structure served to protect the company's independence, guaranteeing that majority control of Unilog was to remain with the company.

In 1987, Unilog made two important expansion moves. The first was to open an office in Lyon, marking its first entry into the French regional market and the first step to offering national coverage. That same year, Unilog launched a new consulting service, which later became known as Unilog Management. The addition of this new unit added support services for its existing systems integration business. The move was a propitious one, as information technology was set to enter a new era of importance—before becoming a critical part of the global corporate landscape. Unilog now sought to step up its growth; in 1988, the company attracted fresh capital by listing on the Paris stock exchange's secondary market.

Unilog expanded steadily into the 1990s, maintaining its record of unbroken profitability while continuously building up its revenues. By 1996, the company was posting the equivalent of EUR 136 million. The company's IT services wing remained the motor for the company's growth, representing more than 80 percent of sales. Until the second half of the decade, Unilog's growth had been wholly internal, as the company won clients among France's largest industrial corporations, banks, and government agencies.

Acquiring Size for the 21st Century

Unilog made its first external growth moves in 1996. In that year, the company acquired two new subsidiaries, Sinorg and Alcatel TITN Answare, both of which had built up agency networks throughout France. The two acquisitions boosted the company's employee total by 400, and also transformed its geographic balance. By the end of that year, the company had reduced the importance of the Paris area to its sales, while its new national coverage boosted regional operations to account for 34 percent of sales. For the time being Unilog remained focused on the French market. In 1997, the company started an acquisition of former public sector IT consulting services provider Cesia. That bid was approved and by December 1998 the company had acquired more than 78 percent of Cesia. Unilog boosted that holding to 100 percent in 2000.

By then, however, Unilog had expanded its focus beyond France. In April 1998, the company acquired 40 percent of Bremen, Germany-based Vulkan Software Systems (VSS), paying the equivalent of more than EUR 4 million. Three months later, Unilog made a new acquisition in Germany, this time of the Integrata Group, based in Tubingen in southern Germany. The company initially acquired a 90 percent stake in Integrata, which was one of the top 15 systems integrators in the German market; by the end of that year, Unilog held 99.9 percent of Integrata, for a cost of EUR 25.4 million.

The Integrata acquisition not only gave Unilog a major stake in the German market, it also gave it a strong new training services operation. Until then, Unilog's own training services operations accounted for little more than 2 percent of its revenues. The acquisition of Integrata was to boost its training sales to 11 percent of revenues by the end of the century. By the end of 1998, its sales had jumped to EUR 285.4 million—the German market now accounted for nearly 20 percent of Unilog's sales. While its acquisitions formed a major part of the company's revenue growth, organic growth remained high as well—as much as 20 percent of the rise in Unilog's revenues were attributed to its own business development, as the company benefited from the rush to secure computer systems

against the Y2K bug, and as French businesses in general stepped up their IT spending.

Not all of Unilog's attempts to expand were successful. In 1998, the company sought to acquire Ploenzke, based in Germany, and Data Science, based in Great Britain, but found itself outgunned by Computer Science Corp. and then IBM. Unilog was more successful in continuing its expansion the following year with the acquisition of fellow French IT specialist New Software Associates for EUR 19 million. That company featured a team of 250 engineering and integration specialists working in offices in seven major French cities. By the end of 1999, Unilog's revenues had grown past EUR 391 million. In that year Unilog, which continued to post its unbroken record of profitability, was also admitted to the Paris bourse's monthly settlement market.

The year 2000 brought renewed impetus to Unilog's expansion. In January, the company acquired 70 percent of GDI, based in Switzerland and active especially in the country's French-speaking region. By the end of the year, Unilog had paid more than EUR 12 million to acquire all of GDI, adding that company's 1,000 employees. The year 2000 also saw the company's participation in the formation of Escan, a European economic interest group, with partners Ibermatica of Spain and Engeneering Ingegneria Informatica of Italy. This alliance was formed in order to create a single-branded range of marketable service projects for the European market countries in an effort to head off foreign competition, particularly from IT heavyweights arriving from the United States.

Rounding out 2000, Unilog completed its acquisition of VSS for EUR 12 million. VSS was then merged into Integrata, with the former company's 250 engineers added to the payroll. In an era when qualified computer engineers and related specialists were in drastically short supply, acquisitions had become a popular means of overcoming recruitment hurdles and securing new personnel.

In September 2000, the company moved to restructure its consulting operations, grouping all consulting activities under a newly created subsidiary, called Unilog Management. This company now represented one-fifth of Unilog's total operations, with revenues split between France at 80 percent and Germany at 20 percent.

The slump in the high-technology sector had as a result a drop in confidence in Unilog's stock as well. As warnings of an economic slowdown began to waft over to Europe from the United States, Unilog nonetheless expressed its confidence in its continued expansion, forecasting continued growth in the 15 to 20 percent range. The company also announced its intention to continue its external expansion moves. In May 2001, the company made two new acquisitions. The first was of Mind France, the Paris-based subsidiary of Sweden's Mind AB, a web creation agency. This acquisition was meant to boost Unilog's growing interest in the e-commerce market. The second acquisition came at the end of May, when the company acquired the technology division of marchFIRST, a company based in the United Kingdom specializing in Internet applications consulting.

This new acquisition coincided with the adoption of a strategy focusing on the three key markets of France, Germany, and

---

Key Dates:

1968: Informatique et Entreprise is created.

1970: Investissement Informatique is formed as a holding company for a number of new companies, each dedicated to a particular specialty in the computer business.

1982: Company and subsidiaries regroup as Unilog.

1987: Company opens first regional office, launches consulting services.

1988: Unilog raises capital by listing on the Paris stock exchange secondary market.

1999: Company acquires French IT specialist New Software Associates, posts revenues of EUR 391 million.

2000: Unilog forms Escan alliance with partners Ibermatica of Spain and Engeneering Ingegneria Informatica of Italy to create a single-branded range of services for the European market.

2001: Company acquires web site developer Mind France, the Paris-based subsidiary of Sweden's Mind AB; purchases the technology division of U.K.-based marchFIRST, a specialist in Internet applications consulting.

---

the United Kingdom, which together accounted for 60 percent of the European IT services market. As Unilog continued to seek new acquisitions in 2001, its ambitions were clearly to become a major IT consulting and services company for the European market.

Principal Subsidiaries

Cesia SA; GDI Gestion et Diffusion (Switzerland); New Software Associates Lille SA; New Software Associates Lyon; New Software Associates SARL; Unilog Integrata AG (Germany); Unilog Integrata UB GmbH (Germany); Unilog Integrata Training AG (Germany); Unilog Integrata Lehrgänge GmbH (Germany); Unilog Integrata AG (Switzerland); Unilog Integrata GmbH (Austria); Unilog Liban (Lebanon; 34.50%); Unilog Régions SA; Win Conseil SA.

Principal Divisions

Unilog Management; Unilog IT Services; Unilog IT Training.

Principal Competitors

Accenture Ltd.; Acer Inc.; Atos Origin; Bull SA; Cap Gemini Ernst & Young; CMG plc; Compaq Computer Corporation; Computer Associates International, Inc.; Computer Sciences Corporation; Dell Computer Corporation; Electronic Data Systems Corporation; Finsiel S.p.A.; Fujitsu Limited; Gateway, Inc.; Getronics NV; GFI Informatique SA; International Business Machines Corporation; International Computers Limited; Logic Plc; NEC Corp.; Sema Group; Siemens AG; Sopra SA; Group Steria SCA; Sun Microsystems Inc.; Toshiba Corp.; Unisys Corp.

Further Reading

Bougeard, Marion, ''Comme la majorité des SSII, Unilog affiche sa confiance pour 2001,'' *La Tribune*, April 6, 2001.

Mazier, Hélène, ''Unilog prevoit une croissance interne de 15 à 20% en 2001,'' *La Tribune*, April 5, 2001.

''Unilog Moves into Great Britain Following Acquisition,'' *European Report*, June 20, 2001.

''Unilog optimiste pour 2001,'' *Les Echos*, April 6, 2001.

—M. L. Cohen

United Biscuits (Holdings) plc

Church Road
West Drayton
Middlesex UB7 7PR
United Kingdom
Telephone: (+44) 1895-432-100
Fax: (+44) 1895-432-201
Web site: http://www.unitedbiscuits.co.uk

Private Company
Incorporated: 1948 as United Biscuits Limited
Employees: 21,000
Sales: £1.3 billion (2000 est.)
NAIC: 311821 Cookie and Cracker Manufacturing;
    311910 Snack Food Manufacturing

United Biscuits (Holdings) plc is the leading biscuit (cookie and cracker) maker in the United Kingdom and one of the leading biscuit makers in Western Europe. Active in seven Western European nations, United Biscuits (UB) owns a number of leading national biscuit brands, including McVitie's (United Kingdom), BN (France), Delacre (France and Belgium), and Verkade (the Netherlands). Other biscuit brands include Oreos, Go-Ahead!, and Chips Ahoy! Out of 2000 sales of £1.3 billion, £1 billion was generated by the European biscuit business; the remaining £300 million came from the company's U.K. snack and nuts businesses, which included KP Snacks, Derwent Valley Foods, and KP Nuts. In May 2000 UB was acquired by Finalrealm Limited, a financial investment consortium connected with both Groupe Danone and Nabisco Holdings Corporation.

History of McVitie & Price

As its name implies, United Biscuits was founded when two biscuit makers—McVitie & Price and Macfarlane Lang & Company—joined forces, in the wake of World War II. Robert McVitie, the son of a prosperous farmer who started a provision store in Edinburgh in the 1830s, was first apprenticed to a baker. He later joined his father in the shop, carrying on the business when his father decided to leave it. By the 1840s, Robert had

left the shop on Rose Street (just a few yards away from the Crawford family's business, which became a part of United Biscuits in 1962) and moved to larger quarters. Robert prospered, opened more shops, and, in 1844, married Catherine Gairns, who brought additional wealth to the family.

Robert and Catherine had four children; sons William and Robert, Jr., were apprenticed in the bakery trade, and were sent to the continent to study French, German, and baking. William became a journalist, but Robert returned to introduce Vienna bread into Scotland and inherited the family business in 1884—the year that McVitie Scotch cakes (shortbread, oatcakes, and biscuits) won the gold medal at an international exhibition in Calcutta. Robert decided to concentrate McVitie's resources on biscuits, which at that time would keep better than bread or cakes—an important point in the expansion of sales territory.

Preparing to leave for the United States in 1887 to study American methods, Robert was behind the counter in the Edinburgh shop when Alexander Grant, 22, came in to seek employment. Told that no job was available, Grant replied, "it's a pity, for I'm a fell fine baker." As he lifted a scone and scrutinized it on his way out he added, "Well, onyway, ye canna make scones in Edinburgh"—and Robert, amused, hired him on the spot. Grant did prove to be a fell fine baker, was promoted, and saved enough money to buy a small bakery of his own. But, undercapitalized, the business failed, and Grant returned to McVitie's employ. He devoted himself to further study and hard work and took on increasing levels of responsibility.

Charles Price, a traveling salesman for Cadbury, joined McVitie in 1888 on the understanding, contingent on his sales volume, that he would become a partner. The company was soon McVitie & Price. Thirteen years after he joined, he departed to become a member of parliament, having transformed the company into a national entity.

Londoners' tastes required something smaller, thinner, and lighter than the traditional Scottish fare, according to George Andrews Brown, another outstanding salesman, who was the first to develop the London market. While the company worked to refine its "Rich Tea" biscuit to suit London tastes, Brown invented a sandwich biscuit with cream filling. Alexander Grant meanwhile developed what he called a digestive biscuit, using a formula he kept secret until the 1930s, when he passed it on to his daughter. Because he was the only one who knew how to supervise the biscuit's mixing at the Edinburgh and London factories, he kept a strenuous schedule, traveling by train between the two.

Queen Victoria's daughter, Princess Mary of Teck, pronounced McVitie and Price's cake the best of those made for her wedding in 1893. Later, as Queen Mary, she named the firm the royal family's official supplier of wedding and christening cakes, a tradition that has continued through all its succeeding generations.

Robert McVitie died in 1910 at age 56, his one-man business now a prominent national enterprise. He had guided it through the mechanization necessary to increase volume—the result, in part, of a fire that destroyed the Edinburgh factory in 1894. The business employed thousands of people, and its products had inspired many tributes. Because McVitie had no heirs, he planned to make the firm a limited liability company and nominated Alexander Grant as managing director. The board of directors agreed.

World War I created pressure to supply ''iron ration'' plain biscuits as government-issued fare. This overtaxed existing factories, so an additional facility was opened in Manchester. Grant, whom the directors had named chairman, wanted to develop the company at a faster pace; consequently, he borrowed the money to buy control of the business in 1916. Grant's son, Robert McVitie Grant, had worked his way up from an entry-level position to managing director, demonstrating his resourcefulness along the way by inventing a product to compete with Scandinavian hardtack: MacVita, which continued to be a popular item.

The hard work Grant demanded from himself and his son was expected of the entire staff. Hector Laing, engaged to Grant's daughter Margaret, began work at McVitie's by stoking ovens when he returned from World War I. Even on the morning of his wedding, in 1922, he had to put in a stint at work.

Grant paid close attention to his sales staff and kept them motivated through special recognition of achievement and through generous commissions. He himself was rewarded in 1924 with a baronetcy. That same year, McVitie & Price received this tribute from the Oxford expedition to the Arctic Circle: ''Every brand which you supplied had its devotees and you can be certain that not one crumb was left uneaten. If any Expedition in the future revisits North Eastland it will find many

of your tins on these icegirt shores—all empty, mute tokens of our appreciation of your biscuits.''

At Sir Alexander's death in 1937, Sir Robert was already in command of a vast business. But World War II brought many changes. The company soon found that, with restrictions on supplies and transportation, cooperation with its competitor, Macfarlane Lang, made good sense. The 370 varieties of biscuits produced in 1939 were reduced to ten by 1945. Robert Grant had begun negotiations for a merger with Macfarlane Lang when, in 1947, he died at the age of 52. He had previously named Peter MacDonald, legal adviser to the company for many years, his successor. Taxation and death duties, together with the need for a reduction in overhead expenses and the promise of economies of scale, made the merger with Macfarlane Lang a natural union.

History of Macfarlane Lang

Macfarlane Lang began with a bakehouse and small shop opened by James Lang in Glasgow in 1817. At Lang's death in 1841, his nephew, John Macfarlane, took over the business, renaming it Macfarlane and using its assets to open a new bakery on another street in Glasgow. When his sons James and John, Jr., joined him in 1878, he had greatly expanded the business and decided to rename it John Macfarlane and Sons. In 1884 his youngest son, George, joined the business. The following year Macfarlane built a new, mechanized bread factory called the Victoria Bread Works. But one of Macfarlane's chief assets was Lang's fine reputation. The name Lang had clung over the years to the bakery's products. Eventually that asset was recognized; in 1885 ''Lang'' was officially restored and the company became known as Macfarlane Lang & Company.

The bakery continued to grow. A depot in London was built in 1894, and soon the demand for Macfarlane Lang products warranted the construction of a new factory on the Thames River—the Imperial Biscuit Works.

John Macfarlane died in 1908, on the day before the date he had set for his retirement. Facing intense competition from other biscuit companies for the bakery business, his sons nonetheless capably carried on their father's expansion programs through the succeeding decades. Despite the supply shortages and transportation problems during World War I, the business continued to expand; between 1914 and 1916 the capacity of the London operations more than doubled. New and larger factories were built in Osterley, Glasgow, and Tallcross, and extensions were built onto these to meet the burgeoning demand for breads and biscuits. Directorship of Macfarlane Lang remained in the family even after the retirements of each of John's sons, until 1973, when John E. Macfarlane, the grandson of the founder, died in his 90th year.

Postwar Era: Formation of UB and Further Acquisitions

The combined trading profits of Macfarlane and McVitie came to £443,000 in 1947, of which Macfarlane had contributed £164,000. When the merger was finalized and United Biscuits incorporated in 1948, Peter MacDonald was named chairman of the new company. MacDonald concentrated on taking advantage of economies of scale, sticking to a shorter list of biscuit

---

Key Dates:

1817: James Lang opens a bakehouse and small shop in Glasgow.

1841: Upon Lang's death, his nephew, John Macfarlane, takes over the business, renaming it Macfarlane.

1884: Robert McVitie inherits the family baking business and begins concentrating on biscuits.

1885: Macfarlane is renamed Macfarlane Lang & Company.

1888: Charles Price joins McVitie; the company is soon renamed McVitie & Price and becomes a national entity.

1948: McVitie & Price and Macfarlane Lang merge to form United Biscuits (UB).

1962: William Crawford and Sons, maker of shortbread, is acquired.

1964: UB acquires William McDonald & Sons, known for its chocolate-covered biscuits.

1967: Company enters the salty snack category with the acquisition of Meredith and Drew, maker of potato chips.

1968: Kenyon Sons and Craven Ltd., Europe's largest nut processor, is acquired.

1974: UB acquires U.S.-based Keebler Company.

Late 1970s: Two U.K. fast-food chains, Wimpy hamburgers and Pizzaland, are acquired.

1988: Ross Young's, a leading U.K. frozen food maker, is acquired.

1989: The fast-food operations are sold off to Grand Metropolitan.

1990: Netherlands-based Verkade is acquired.

1993: The snack food business of Coca-Cola Amatil of Australia is acquired and renamed Smith's Snackfood Company.

1996: Keebler is divested.

1997: UB exchanges its continental European and Australian snack operations for Biscuiterie Nantaise (BN), PepsiCo's French biscuit business.

1998: Delacre, a European biscuit business, is acquired from Campbell Soup Company.

1999: Frozen and chilled food businesses are divested.

2000: Finalrealm consortium acquires United Biscuits for £1.26 billion ($2 billion).

2001: Following series of transactions with Nabisco and Danone, United Biscuits emerges as a leading Western European biscuit maker, with a snack and nuts operation confined to the United Kingdom.

---

varieties. During his 20 years of leadership, UB achieved market dominance in many products, including digestive biscuits, rich tea biscuits, Homewheat, and Jaffa Cakes.

Despite their merger, however, the two companies continued to operate quite independently until the late 1960s. Independence stretched so far, in fact, that the three McVitie factories were not even using identical recipes for the same products. Nonetheless, United Biscuits soon began to grow. In 1962 William Crawford and Sons, best known for its shortbread, joined United Biscuits.

The oldest of the UB bakeries, Crawford and Sons was founded as a family bakery in Leith in 1813. The bakery eventually expanded into restaurants, meat processing, and jam-making under the leadership of successive generations of Crawfords.

In 1964, William McDonald & Sons, best known for its chocolate-covered biscuits, was the next company to join UB. Formed in 1946 by a former salesman with two favorite recipes, Macdonald & Sons went public in 1954 and was acquired by UB in 1964.

Together these four bakeries became the foundation of the UB Brands division of the 1980s. Two acquisitions, in 1967 and 1968, respectively, formed the basis of the KP division: Meredith and Drew, a biscuit and crisp (potato chip) manufacturer since 1830, and Kenyon Sons and Craven Ltd., Europe's largest nut processor, dating back to 1891.

After founding his bakery in 1830, William Meredith quarreled with William Drew, his principal assistant, in 1852 and Drew left to set up a rival business. The sons of these two men reunited the two companies in 1890, deciding by coin toss the order of their names. In 1905 Meredith and Drew merged with Wright and Son, a small company known for a cheddar sandwich biscuit—"a meal for a penny." One of the strengths Meredith and Drew brought to United Biscuits was its experience in concentrating on a single product in each plant; adopting this plan helped UB attain dominance in the biscuit market.

Kenyon Sons and Craven dated back to two British factories that began making sugar confectionery, jams, and pickles in 1853. In 1891 the partners and their families formed a limited liability company. For several decades, the company's facilities and products—as well as profits—increased. But the Depression and then World War II sent the company into a steady decline. In September 1943 the directors resigned, and Simon Heller, of the Hercules Nut Company, became director.

Heller's hard work, ingenuity, and imagination turned the company around. For example, during the war, when there was a glut of vegetables at the local market, the company would fill a van with the low-cost items and rush to the plant to make chutney. In 1953 Heller introduced a twopenny packet of KP Nuts. It became a best-seller and stimulated demand for more nut and mixed nut-and-fruit products. So it was with a strong snack food background that Kenyon Sons and Craven came to United Biscuits in 1968.

Continuing to Grow: 1970s–80s

When United Biscuits formed its Continental businesses division in 1986, it united Westimex (Belgium), Sepa (France), and Productos Ortiz (Spain) under a single management team. Westimex, a crisp manufacturer, had joined United Biscuits in 1970 and had been expanding its line to include lower-fat products; it has been steadily increasing its market share in France and the Netherlands as well as Belgium. Sales of branded crisps and private-label nuts sparked major growth in volume and profits at Sepa. Productos Ortiz, acquired in 1973, profited from increased sales of toasted bread, chocolate granola, and cookies.

The British Carr's of Carlisle, acquired in 1972, was founded in 1831 when Jonathan Dodgson Carr, 25, walked to the town of Carlisle from nearby Kendall to seek his fortune. The bakery he started was so successful that within three years he was able to add a flour mill to the business. In 1841, he became the first biscuit maker to receive a royal warrant from Queen Victoria. At first his biscuits were handmade, but during that decade he designed and installed the first biscuit-cutting machine, based on the hand-operated printing press he had observed at his tin supplier's factory. Described as a giant of a man, Carr was renowned for his work in campaigning for the repeal of the corn tax and for affordable housing. The business expanded until the 1930s, went into a decline, and had recovered to some extent at the time of the United Biscuits purchase.

Kemp's Biscuits Limited was another 1972 acquisition. The business began in 1835 as Watmough and Son Limited, making ship's biscuits—hardtack. During World War I, Watmough made Army biscuits—which were reported on occasion to have been used as money to purchase tram tickets. The market for ship's biscuits was nearly decimated when the Board of Trade passed regulations requiring shipowners to make fresh bread at least three days a week. Ernest Kirman, the founder's grandson, joined the business in 1892. In 1926, the company introduced sweet biscuits for human consumption, and it was producing 300 tons a week at the outbreak of World War II. In 1948, wearied by wartime labor shortages and production schedules for civilian gas masks, Kirman sold Watmough to Scribbans-Kemp Limited, which became Kemps Biscuits.

Reaching across the Atlantic, United Biscuits acquired the Keebler Company in 1974. In many ways, Keebler's development paralleled that of the family-owned bakeries that had come together as United Biscuits.

Godfrey Keebler opened a small Philadelphia bake shop in 1853 and earned a fine reputation for his cookies and crackers. A network of similar bakeries was formed in the United States, coincidentally under the name United Biscuit Company, in 1927 to provide the purchasing economies and transportation that central management made possible. By 1944 United Biscuit had 16 bakeries, from Philadelphia to Salt Lake City, Utah. For the next 22 years, United Biscuit expanded its reach into all but three states, selling products under many brand names. Finally, in 1966 the company adopted Keebler as the single, official corporate and brand name for all these bakeries' products.

Under United Biscuits, Keebler later became a unit of UB Foods U.S., a holding company formed in 1986 that operated companies under the Keebler name. With annual sales in excess of $1 billion, Keebler was the second largest cookie and cracker producer in the United States. The company also produced ice cream cones and salty snacks, and in 1986 opened a product-and-process development center at its headquarters in Elmhurst, Illinois, to develop and test new products.

United Biscuits continued acquiring bakeries and other types of food companies throughout the 1970s and 1980s, including Shaffer Clarke in 1978, Terry's of York in 1982, and Callard and Bowser in 1988. The company also made an early entry into China in the late 1980s, leading to the opening of a joint venture biscuit factory in the south Chinese city of Shenzhen in 1990. In the late 1970s UB ventured into the fast-food business with the acquisition of two U.K. chains, Wimpy hamburgers and Pizzaland. Further diversification came in 1988 with the £335 million acquisition of Ross Young's, a leading U.K. frozen food company. United Biscuits also failed in its efforts to complete two other large acquisitions: tobacco and brewing giant Imperial in 1986 (which was acquired by Hanson PLC) and the European operations of RJR Nabisco in 1989 (which were acquired by BSN, forerunner of Groupe Danone). UB's variety of operations and desire to keep brand names and individual company identities intact necessitated repeated reorganizations. By the late 1980s, the company was divided into five business segments. This was reduced to four during 1989 when the fast-food operations were sold to Grand Metropolitan PLC, one of the forerunners of Diageo plc.

Leading United Biscuits from 1972 through the late 1980s was Hector Laing, the son of Hector Laing and Margaret Grant. The chairman was mindful of the impact of computerization and other technological advances on the business—and particularly on personnel. Reinvestment in expansion and new equipment was set at a minimum of 5 percent of profits. That sometimes left little for raising wages during lean years. To offset that occurrence, UB workers received a rare degree of job security: three years' service guaranteed the job for the next five years, ten years' service guaranteed a job for life. Workforce reductions resulting from technological improvements were accomplished through normal attrition and incentives for early retirement.

International Expansion in the Early 1990s

In May 1990 Laing retired as chairman of United Biscuits, having shepherded the company through a period of astounding growth. Taking over as chairman was Robert Clarke, who had served as chief executive since 1986. Promoted to chief executive in January 1991 was Eric Nicoli, who had headed up the UB Brands division. The new leaders continued to seek acquisitions, aiming on further expansion in the Asian-Pacific region and on bolstering the firm's weak position in continental Europe. In 1990 UB acquired Verkade, a leading biscuit and confectionery firm in the Netherlands. During 1991 UB purchased majority or near-majority stakes in three major European biscuit companies: Fazer Biscuits of Finland; Oxford Biscuits of Denmark, the largest biscuit maker in Scandinavia; and Gyori Keksz, the largest biscuit firm in Hungary. The stakes in Oxford and Gyori Keksz were increased to 100 percent by 1993.

Also in 1993, United Biscuits acquired the snack food business of Coca-Cola Amatil of Australia for $300 million. Renamed Smith's Snackfood Company, the acquired business held 56 percent of the Australian snack food market and also had a leading snack business in Italy. With UB's overseas push, 1993 marked the first year in which more than half of sales were generated outside the United Kingdom. The company was not inactive at home, however. It purchased Derwent Valley Foods, which was based in northern England and produced the Phileas Fogg brand of tortilla chips and other corn-based snack products. To pay down its acquisition-fueled debt load, United Biscuits also made some divestments in 1993, selling the U.S. chocolate maker Terry's to Philip Morris for £220 million ($319 million), and the loss-making Productos Ortiz of Spain to the company's management. Further expansion in Eastern Europe came in early 1994 with the purchase of an 80 percent stake in ZPC San SA. San was one of the two largest biscuit makers in Poland.

Mid-to-Late 1990s: Returning to the Company Core

The mid-1990s were marked by United Biscuits' retreat from the U.S. market. Keebler had long been a distant second to Nabisco in the U.S. cookie and cracker market and suffered from roller coaster-like profit margins. The difficulties at Keebler contributed to UB's poor financial performance in the early 1990s, earnings per share having fallen 15 percent from 1989 to 1994. In mid-1995, then, Keebler was put up for sale. United Biscuits sold the bulk of Keebler to an investment group for $600 million in early 1996. Restructuring costs and costs associated with the exit from the U.S. market led UB into a net loss of £110 million and a reduced dividend for 1995.

United Biscuits retrenched further over the next few years, reducing its international operations to biscuits only by early 1998. In addition to several smaller divestments, UB made a key deal late in 1997 with arch-rival PepsiCo. UB exchanged its continental European and Australian snack operations for Biscuiterie Nantaise (BN), PepsiCo's French biscuit business. UB also received net proceeds from the transaction of £241 million ($410 million). Along with this transaction, Nicoli also spearheaded a restructuring of United Biscuits from regional divisions into two divisions: McVitie's Group, which comprised the international biscuit business, and UK Foods, which included the remaining snack and frozen and chilled food businesses. In April 1998 UB acquired another key European biscuit business by purchasing Delacre from Campbell Soup Company for £125 million. Delacre had operations in the Netherlands, Belgium, Germany, and France and annual revenues of £108 million ($180 million).

In early 1999 Nicoli resigned his position as chief executive in order to take over leadership of EMI Group plc. Leslie Van de Walle, head of McVitie's Group, was promoted to UB chief executive. Around that same time, Colin Short, who had served as nonexecutive chairman since 1995, stepped down from his position and was replaced by Gordon Hourston, a member of the company board who had previously served as chairman of Boots The Chemists Limited, a leading U.K. drugstore chain. The new leaders quickly brought the previous regime's restructuring efforts to what seemed like a logical conclusion by divesting all of the frozen and chilled food businesses through a series of transactions completed by the end of 1999. Despite the slimming down to core operations in international biscuits and U.K. snacks, however, United Biscuits' stock failed to rally and in fact remained at barely half the price it had been at in late 1990 upon Laing's retirement. The much more focused company began gaining the attention of a number of suitors, and the new management team decided the time was right to put the company up for sale.

21st Century: New Era As Private Company

Two main bidders soon emerged, Nabisco Holdings Corporation and Finalrealm, an investment consortium connected to Groupe Danone. After a five-month battle, the two competing groups agreed in late February 2000 to jointly buy United Biscuits for £1.26 billion ($2 billion). The deal involved Nabisco joining the Finalrealm consortium, which took control of UB in April 2000. Malcolm Ritchie, an executive with H.J. Heinz Company, took over as chairman and CEO of UB. Over the next several months, through a whirlwind of activity, a new United Biscuits emerged. UB's operations in China, Hong Kong, and Taiwan were sold to Nabisco. In turn, Nabisco contributed to United Biscuits its biscuits businesses in Europe (primarily in Spain and Portugal), North Africa, and the Middle East, which included the Oreos and Chips Ahoy! brands. UB sold a number of operations to Danone, including businesses in Scandinavia, Malaysia, Singapore, and central and Eastern Europe, as well as its snack food interests in Germany and Italy and certain savory biscuit brands in the United Kingdom.

By mid-2001, then, United Biscuits consisted of a biscuits division that had operations in seven countries in Western Europe and a snack and nuts division operating exclusively within the United Kingdom. The company was also involved in exporting its brands to other nations. Given its ownership by an investment consortium, United Biscuits' future was somewhat cloudy, but there was speculation that Nabisco might eventually take full control of the company.

Principal Competitors

Associated British Foods plc; Northern Foods plc; Bahlsen GmbH & Co. KG; Hibernia Foods plc; Groupe Danone; Kellogg Company; Kraft Foods International, Inc.; Keebler Foods Company; PepsiCo, Inc.

Further Reading

Adam, James S., *A Fell Fine Baker: The Story of United Biscuits, A Jubilee Account of the Men and the Companies Who Pioneered One of Britain's Most Celebrated Industries*, London: Hutchinson Benham, 1974, 164 p.

Ashworth, Jon, "Predators Circle over the Last Crumbs of United Biscuits," *Times* (London), December 15, 1999, p. 27.

Bentley, Stephanie, "UB Boosts Biscuits to Win Global Share," *Marketing Week*, February 19, 1998, pp. 23–24.

Berss, Marcia R., "Biscuit Wars," *Forbes*, April 26, 1993, p. 47.

Clifford, Mark, "A Taste of Asia: Foreign Firms Break into Regional Biscuit Market," *Far Eastern Economic Review*, November 26, 1992.

De Jonquieres, Guy, "Testing Times for a Company with Global Ambitions: United Biscuits' Drive to Internationalise Faces Some Big Challenges," *Financial Times*, February 16, 1993, p. 23.

——, "United Biscuits Snaps Up Snack Maker for £24m," *Financial Times*, February 25, 1993, p. 26.

Elliott, John, "UB Realises a Dream by Biting at Bureaucracy," *Financial Times*, April 9, 1990, p. 13.

Grant, Alexander, *The Business Diaries of Sir Alexander Grant*, edited by James S. Adam, Edinburgh: Donald, 1992, 134 p.

Hoggan, Karen, "Smart Cookie," *Marketing*, October 20, 1988, pp. 23–24.

Jackson, Tony, "How United Biscuits Bit Off More Than It Could Chew," *Financial Times*, October 9, 1999, p. 18.

Johnson, Mike, "Clarke's Bite," *Marketing*, December 7, 1989, p. 27.

Lynn, Matthew, "Profile: Bob Clarke," *Management Today*, April 1992, pp. 55–56.

Murphy, Claire, "When It Comes to the Crunch at UB," *Marketing Week*, February 5, 1993, pp. 14–15.

Oram, Roderick, "Nicoli Shakes Up the Biscuit Barrel—but It Was Long Overdue," *Financial Times,* July 24, 1995, p. 7.

——, "Speaking a Different Language: United Biscuits' Management Continues to Test Shareholders' Patience," *Financial Times,* February 25, 1995, p. 8.

——, "U.S. Hopes Crumble for UB," *Financial Times,* July 18, 1995, p. 20.

——, "When It Comes to the Crunch: The Global Snacks Battle Between UB and PepsiCo Is Highly Instructive," *Financial Times,* February 5, 1996, p. 8.

Parkes, Christopher, "Back to the Basics of Biscuits," *Financial Times,* June 16, 1989, p. 13.

Pitcher, George, "Way UB's Cookie Crumbled," *Marketing Week,* July 28, 1995, p. 25.

——, "Why the UB Empire Has Been Reduced to Crumbling Point," *Marketing Week,* October 14, 1999, p. 23.

Pretzlik, Charles, Richard Rivlin, and Alison Smith, "United Biscuits Set for £1.26bn Crunch: Joint Proposal by Former Bidding Rivals Would Make U.S. Group Nabisco Largest Shareholder," *Financial Times,* February 29, 2000, p. 25.

Rawstorne, Philip, "Nibbling Towards a Bigger Slice," *Financial Times,* August 9, 1990, p. 25.

"When It Comes to the Crunch McVitie's Takes the Biscuit," *Financial Times,* August 16, 1999, p. 18.

Willman, John, "Looking for a Sweet Taste in a Bigger Biscuit Barrel," *Financial Times,* September 10, 1998, p. 33.

Willman, John, Charles Pretzlik, and Andrew Edgcliffe-Johnson, "United Biscuits Is Still a Tasty Snack for Several Vultures Ready to Swoop," *Financial Times,* October 6, 1999, p. 30.

—update: David E. Salamie

USA TRUCK

USA Truck, Inc.

3200 Industrial Park Rd.
Van Buren, Arkansas 72956
U.S.A.
Telephone: (510) 471-2500
Fax: (510) 471-2526
Web site: http://www.usa-truck.com

Public Company
Incorporated: 1988
Employees: 2,155
Sales: $226.6 million (2000)
Stock Exchanges: NASDAQ
Ticker Symbol: USAK
NAIC: 484121 General Freight Trucking, Long Distance
  Truckload

USA Truck, Inc. provides full-load trucking services for medium haul shipping, distances from 700 to 1,000 miles one way, specializing in just-in-time delivery. USA Truck serves the contiguous 48 states, primarily east of the Rocky Mountains; Quebec, and Ontario, Canada; and Mexico through Laredo, Texas. A fleet of more than 1,700 tractors, and 3,400 48-foot and 53-foot trailers carry over 650 truckloads per day. The company transports "dry van" goods, such as paper and paper products, glass, retail merchandise, automotive parts, aluminum, chemicals, and manufacturing materials.

Formation of Company Following Trucking Industry Deregulation: 1983

Arkansas Best Corporation formed CPI, Inc. in 1983 (three years later the subsidiary would be renamed USA Truck), following deregulation of the trucking industry by the Interstate Commerce Commission (ICC). Previously, the ICC required trucking companies to purchase rights to specific travel routes, charging particularly high rates for full "truckload" shipping than for less-than-load (LTL) shipping. Deregulation allowed trucks to travel any route without prior authorization or fee payments. With such restrictions removed, trucking companies had more flexibility in route scheduling and could now deliver fully loaded trailers for the customer to unload, leaving the tractor free to travel to the next destination. Thus trucking companies no longer needed personnel for loading and unloading freight and required fewer truck terminals for storage. Deregulation presented the opportunity for truckload businesses to operate at a lower cost, prompting the formation of many new trucking companies.

USA Truck became an independent company in 1988 when six executives from Arkansas Best subsidiary ABF Freight purchased USA Truck for $20.4 million—$2.4 million in cash and the balance in assumed debt. Assets included the 63 acres of land and facilities in Van Buren, Arkansas. An 84,000-square-foot building housed administrative offices, driver quarters, a driver training facility, and a 12,000-square-foot equipment maintenance shop. Diesel fueling stations with a 40,000 gallon capacity and a 2,500-square-foot dock occupied the site also. The company owned or leased driver support and equipment maintenance facilities in Louisiana, Kentucky, Illinois, and Ohio. USA Truck operated a fleet of 296 tractors and 503 trailers at the time of the acquisition. A mainframe computer utilizing proprietary software allowed for efficient and flexible driver and equipment scheduling.

USA Truck began its independent existence with more than 150 years of high-level management experience among its executives, who included James B. Speed as chairman and Robert M. Powell as president. Having experience with larger shipping operations at ABF and operational capacity for more than twice USA Truck's existing business, management determined from the outset to expand the company's base of business. The group also prepared to take the company public.

With these intentions in mind, USA Truck sought to improve its operations and reduce expenses. The company saved on interest and depreciation by operating with a low tractor-to-trailer ratio, at 1.7 to 1, compared to an industry average of 2.3 to 1. Tractor equipment incorporated fuel efficient Series 60 Detroit Diesel engines, built to specifications determined by USA Truck. Also, a computer tracked and controlled idle speed for fuel efficiency. Not only did the equipment help reduce fuel expense, it also resulted in fuel tax refunds from several states.

Company Perspectives:

USA Truck has adopted the slogan "Running With Pride." This phrase demonstrates our commitment to being on time—all the time—knowing that our jobs depend on conformance with our customers' requirements. USA Truck takes pride in being nothing short of the best that we can be.

Operational improvements involved hiring and retaining quality truck drivers in an industry notorious for high turnover. In choosing to grow with its own drivers, rather than hiring contract drivers, USA Truck sought to improve working conditions for its employees. USA Truck paid top wages in the industry. Moreover, since its drivers were paid by the mile, the company wanted to keep them on-the-road for a steady income, low mileage being one of the prime reasons that drivers quit their jobs. The company also cut road tours from six to two weeks on average. A meeting with senior drivers on comfort and safety led USA Truck to order new equipment with antilock brakes, power steering, air ride suspension, and temperature controlled sleepers. The company expanded its drivers center at its West Memphis, Arkansas, facility. The $1 million project provided sleeping quarters, private showers, a lounge, laundry facilities, and a training classroom.

Though management at USA Truck attempted to maintain a growth rate limited to 15 percent of revenues, the company experienced 25 percent growth in 1990 and 15 percent in 1991. In 1987 USA Truck averaged 99,000 miles per tractor and averaged 113 loads per work day; by 1991 those numbers improved to an average of 122,000 miles per tractor and 201 loads per work day. Efforts to refine processes and control expenses were rewarded with improvement in operating ratios, from 95.8 percent in 1987 to 88.9 percent in 1991. Stated another way, net profit margin increased from 4.2 percent to 11.1 percent. The empty mile factor, the number of non-revenue producing miles traveled, declined from 11.9 percent of total miles traveled to 10.7 percent. With 413 tractors and 750 trailers, USA Truck saw revenues and net income reach $53 million and $2 million, respectively, in 1991.

By March 1992, USA Truck was ready take the company public with an initial offering of 1.2 million shares at $12.50 each. The stock sold well given the size of the company. Experienced management, its excellent operating systems, and a high profit margin made USA Truck an attractive investment. After expenses, the company netted $13 million from the offering. Over 20 percent of USA Truck employees purchased stock during the offering. The share value of the company doubled in 1992, as revenues increased 20 percent to $63 million and net income doubled to $4.1 million.

Much of USA Truck's success stemmed from a careful selection of customers and specialization in high volume and just-in-time delivery. The trucking service concentrated on high volume transportation needs, such as shipping paper and paper products for International Paper, tire fabric for Goodyear, and auto parts for General Motors. For a 3 percent premium over regular shipping rates, USA Truck scheduled pick-up and delivery for a specific day and hour, often scheduling deliveries on short notice. These services were facilitated by placing trailer pools in strategic locations and furnishing high volume customers with extra trailers for convenient loading and unloading. The company utilized 48-foot, "dry van" trailers, with no refrigeration, and only accepted full loads. These types of delivery services tended to experience fewer price fluctuations, providing stable, predictable income. A broad base of customers, with no customer comprising more than 10 percent of revenues, prevented dependence on a single industry and risk of a sudden, severe decline in business.

Internal Growth, Investment in Infrastructure During Mid-1990s

Company management considered driver retention an important aspect of providing quality service on schedule and its efforts to find and retain good drivers produced positive results. In 1993 USA Truck saved $500,000 in retraining costs and driver turnover had declined from 105 percent to 85 percent per year, compared to an industry average of 100 percent turnover per year and an industry high of 200 percent turnover.

To better serve its drivers and to ensure timely delivery, the company initiated a roadside assistance program. Drivers contacted the "breakdown room" when a problem arose, such as a broken fan belt, and received information about the nearest repair shop and instructions on how to get the problem resolved and still deliver the freight on time. The company expressed its motto of driver relations with a sign that said, "Please communicate with our drivers as if one of your family members was sitting in the passenger seat."

USA Truck's revenues rose as the prosperity of the 1990s stimulated trade and shipping. In 1994 USA Truck operated a fleet of 711 tractors and 1,202 trailers with 712 drivers, garnering $92.5 million in revenues and $8.1 million in net income. Average miles per tractor per week peaked at 2,565 miles, but stabilized at approximately 2,400 miles in the years that followed with the conversion to 53-foot trailers, beginning in 1995.

As USA Truck increased the number of trucks and drivers on the road, the company developed new support facilities for drivers. A driver support and maintenance facility opened in Shreveport, Louisiana, in August 1995. The center housed sleeping quarters for 32 drivers, a recruiting office, a driver training center, and a 12,000-square-foot truck maintenance shop. Outdoor facilities involved 15 acres of paved, fenced parking and a two-lane fueling station with a 37,000 gallon capacity. A driver center opened in Vandalia, Ohio, in June 1996. That facility provided 22 sleeping quarters, a 2,400-square-foot maintenance shop, a 10,000 gallon capacity, one-lane fueling station, and eight acres of paved, fenced parking. In addition to a recruiting office, USA Truck installed a sales office at that facility.

Revenues increased to $108.3 million in 1996, a year of slow growth for the company, at 5.8 percent, especially after three consecutive years of 20 percent growth from 1992 to 1994 and 11 percent growth in 1995. By the end of 1996 USA Truck operated 862 tractors and 1,510 trailers, employing 922 drivers. Net income dropped to $3.4 million, however, a 44 percent decrease from the previous year. Factors affecting operating income included high fuel costs, driver shortages resulting in higher recruiting and training expenses, and industry overcapacity resulting in flat trucking rates. The company rebounded as fuel prices decreased and a strong economy fostered a high level of tractor utilization. Revenues increased 10 percent to $129.5 million in 1997, while net income reached $7.9 million.

New developments in 1997 included trailer service to Mexico through Laredo, Texas, whereby USA Truck delivered or received Laredo freight for transfer into Mexico or the United States. The company added 53-foot trailers to its fleet to serve this market, expanding by more than 20 percent to 1,928 trailers, and adding 71 tractors for a total of 1,033 at the end of 1997. In 1997 the company installed onboard communications via two-way satellite mobile messaging and global positioning (GPS). The system allowed the company to provide real-time transit data to its customers and it gave drivers undisturbed rest while waiting for a new assignment.

Driver support facilities were expanded at two sites in Arkansas. Completion of a new 57,000-square-foot headquarters at Van Buren allowed refurbishment to begin on the existing 27,000-square-foot building for use as a training, maintenance, and driver support facility. In 1998 the company augmented the West Memphis, Arkansas facility adding 7,200 square feet to the existing 17,200-square-foot maintenance shop, and four new fueling lanes. The company also opened a driver recruitment and training office there.

In May 1999 the company installed Drop & Swap software to its dispatch technology, giving the company drivers more control over their work schedules. Called the Driver Home Initiative, the software recommended routes that drivers could swap by applying real-time vehicle tracking data to the predispatch assignment planning system. The system enabled enroute changes and relays so that drivers could arrive home in time for that special occasion.

Continuing Growth, Fluctuating Profits During Economic Slowdown of Late 1990s

In November 1999, USA Truck purchased Carco Carrier Corporation, which operated under the name CCC Express and provided medium-haul, truckload shipping. The $37 million acquisition expanded USA Truck's fleet with 498 tractors and 1,103 dry van trailers. The company expected annual revenue to increase approximately $60 million, the amount of CCC Express's 1998 revenues, while consolidation of redundant operations reduced overhead.

The timing of the acquisition was somewhat ill-fated as high interest rates, an unprecedented driver shortage, and a 50 percent increase in diesel fuel costs eroded earnings. Much of CCC Express's fleet did not have drivers, requiring intense driver recruiting and training efforts and doubling those expenses in 1999. In addition to higher training and recruiting costs, the insufficient number of drivers affected the company in two ways. With a high number of unmanned vehicles, peaking at 275 in August 2000, driver turnover reduced overall equipment utilization. The high number of inexperienced drivers resulted in more accidents, causing related increases in insurance claims and costs.

To attract experienced drivers, the company instituted a 16 percent pay increase on October 1, 2000. The cost was offset by elimination of incentive pay, except for drivers providing dedicated services, and decreased incentive pay to managers and executives, such incentives being tied to profitability. The strategy worked as turnover slowed, the number of experienced drivers increased, and the accident rate declined. The equipment utilization rate improved and recruiting and training expenses decreased. Also, the company purchased 267 fewer tractors and 197 fewer trailers than planned for 2000 due to the driver shortage; this led to a net increase of 25 tractors in the fleet, a total of 1,738, and a net decrease of 125 trailers, for a total of 3,400 trailers at year-end. In January 2001, only 93 tractors remained unmanned and by mid-February the company reached 100 percent tractor driver availability.

Working conditions for drivers continued to be a priority. Dispatch personnel received driver relations training to improve interpersonal communication, especially in solving problems. An interactive CD-ROM, called "Daily Dispatch Challenge," simulated several difficult situations that a dispatcher might confront which required skilled interpersonal communication to resolve.

USA Truck applied a number of strategies to handle the increase in fuel prices. A computerized system automatically determined the fuel surcharge billed to customers. Since the surcharge applied only to revenue producing miles, however, empty miles still added $3.1 million to fuel expense, an average per gallon increase of ten cents over 1998. The company worked to minimize empty miles by using a system that determined the shortest routes, resulting in a 9.2 percent empty mile factor. To improve fuel efficiency the company instituted a 63 miles per hour speed policy and, beginning with equipment replacement in November 2000, the company purchased fuel efficient, aerodynamic Freightliner Columbia tractors. The tractors featured monitors that automatically set an "optimized idle." The model also provided greater comfort for drivers with armrests, better visibility, and better on-the-road living quarters.

Another problem caused by the slower economy involved the difficulty of selling used equipment. USA Truck replaced most tractors within 42 months of purchase, allowing the company to maintain a fleet with the latest advances in technology, safety, and comfort, as well as to keep repair costs low. A slowdown in the trucking industry led to a slow market for used tractors and trailers, and dealers reduced their trade-in prices. Also, several dealers closed or went into bankruptcy. USA Truck responded to the situation by initiating direct sales of its used equipment, thus retaining all revenues from such sales.

The combination of all of these factors resulted in a net income of only $94,000 in 2000, despite revenues of $226.6 million. Stability of revenues benefited from repeat customers which accounted for 92 percent of revenues. With the economy stabilizing, USA Truck sustained a fairly even level of fleet availability in 2001. A $41 million equipment contract added 517 replacement tractors to the fleet, for a net decrease of 18 tractors, while the 242 new trailers slightly compensated for the previous year's reductions, for a net increase of 187 trailers. USA Truck anticipated a $52.7 million expenditure in 2002, with the purchase of 647 new tractors, for a net increase of 252 tractors, and purchase and net increase of 360 new trailers.

Principal Subsidiaries

Carco Carrier Corporation.

Principal Divisions

Load Coordinator Group; Fleet Manager Group.

Principal Competitors

J.B. Hunt Transport Services, Inc.; Landair Corporation; Swift Transportation Company, Inc.

Further Reading

"Arkansas Best Confirms Units for Sale," *Arkansas Democrat Gazette*, July 7, 1988, p. C1.

"Denied Grant Has Freight Hauler Examining Options," *Business First-Columbus*, November 24, 2000, p. A16.

Leavitt, Wendy, "Fleets Online," *Fleet Owner*, March 2000, p. 148.

Mehlman, William, "Designer Trucking Sets Tone for Independent USA Truck," *Insiders' Chronicle*, July 6, 1992, p. 1.

Sullivan, R. Lee, " 'It's First Class Here, Man'," *Forbes*, March 14, 1994, p. 102.

USA Truck Chairman J.B. Speed Retiring," *Arkansas Business*, September 4, 2000, p. 31.

"USA Truck Inc.," *Arkansas Business*, June 19, 2000, p. 31.

"USA Truck Is Expanding in W. Memphis," *Memphis Commercial Appeal*, August 19, 1992, p. B4.

"USA Truck Profitable in '91, Struggling to Control Growth," *Arkansas Democrat Gazette*, January 12, 1992, p. G1.

Walters, Dixie, "Building for the Long Haul," *Arkansas Business*, April 12, 1993, p. 13.

Wood, Jeffrey, "USA Truck, P.A.M. Buyouts Expected to Boost Stock," *Arkansas Business*, October 11, 1999, p. 13.

——, "USA Truck Shifts Gears Even Before Acquisition," *Arkansas Business*, November 1, 1999, p. 12.

—Mary Tradii

Usinor SA

11-13, cours Valmy
La Défense 7
92070 Puteaux
La Défense Cedex
France
Telephone: (+33) 1-41-25-9898
Fax: (+33) 1-41-25-9780
Web site: http://www.usinor.com

Public Company
Incorporated: 1986 as Usinor Sacilor
Employees: 60,521
Sales: EUR 15.7 billion ($13.73 billion) (2000)
Stock Exchanges: Euronext Paris
Ticker Symbol: USI
NAIC: 331111 Iron and Steel Mills

Leading French steelmaker Usinor SA is getting set to capture the leading position in the world's steel industry. Usinor's February 2001 proposal to acquire Luxembourg's Arbed and Spain's Aceralia promised to create a steel powerhouse capable of producing more than 46 million tons of steel per year. This would place Usinor—as the largest of the yet unnamed group—ahead of rivals Nippon Steel of Japan and Pohang Iron and Steel of South Korea, as well as its primary European rivals Thyssen Krupp of Germany and Anglo-Dutch concern Corus Group. The new company would see its headquarters transferred to Luxembourg and would be co-chaired, at least at the beginning, by Usinor Chairman Francis Mer and Joseph Kinsch of Arbed. The merger was expected to pass EU monopolies commission scrutiny—which struck down a similar merger attempt among aluminum producers Pechiney, Alcan, and Algroup in 2000—by the end of 2001. The deal, worth more than EUR 3 billion, was expected to create a global giant with sales of more than EUR 30 billion per year and a total workforce of 100,000. The merger was also expected to kick off a new round of steel industry consolidation in the new century.

Steelmakers in the 18th Century

Usinor stemmed from the 1986 merger of the two major French iron and steel groups, Usinor and Sacilor. Usinor had existed for over 150 years in the north of France. Sacilor had been incorporated in 1973, but could trace its history back to 1704, when Jean Martin de Wendel bought the ironworks of Hayange in French Lorraine.

The Sacilor group had deep roots in France's industrial history. It had been associated with the Lorraine region and the de Wendel family since the early 18th century, when Jean Martin de Wendel acquired the ironworks of Hayange in Lorraine. Under de Wendel, the ironworks became one of the largest in France. In 1794, during the French Revolution, the ironworks were able to produce as many as 848 cannonballs, 84 bombshells, and 4,000 bullets per day. In 1822, the de Wendel iron works gained France's first coke blast furnace. The de Wendel factories increased production at a considerable rate during the industrial boom of France's Second Empire: whereas the plants produced about 20,000 tons of cast iron and a little less basic iron in 1850, by 1869 more than 130,000 tons of cast iron and 110,000 tons of iron were obtained from the 15 blast furnaces.

De Wendel, now the foremost ironmaster in France, employed a workforce of 4,000 to fabricate rails, iron bars, iron sheets, tin, and wire. In 1870, however, the Lorraine region was annexed by Germany as a result of its victory over France and the company was split in two until 1918. The factories that were given back after World War I had been run efficiently by the Germans and the company was able to return to 1914's production level by 1924. De Wendel achieved record production levels in 1929, with 1.66 million tons of cast iron and 1.63 million tons of steel. The shock of the 1929 Great Depression, which reached France in 1930–31, followed by World War II, prevented the company from investing capital in modernization during the 1930s and 1940s. In 1948, Sollac (Société Lorraine de Laminage Continu) was formed as a cooperative company by nine different steelmakers, including de Wendel. Sollac was intended to fill the technological gap that had developed during the last 20 years between the French and U.S. steel industries. Sollac began by setting up to produce steel sheets, then added a

Kaldo steel plant using pure oxygen in 1960—the Thomas and Martin processes were still predominant in the profession—and finally introduced cold rolling mills and tin-making units.

The year 1948 also saw the creation of Usinor, through the merger of the two largest steel-producing groups of northern France, Denain-Anzin and Nord-Est. The two groups had complementary product lines, with Denain-Anzin oriented toward steel sheets and Nord-Est favoring shaped products. Both companies originated from small plants dating from the 19th century. The Société des Hauts Fourneaux et Forges de Denain-Anzin had been formed in 1849 from the ironworks of Denain, founded in 1835 by François Dumont with the permission of King Louis Philippe, and a similar plant created the same year by Benoit-Auguste Vasseur and located in Anzin. The Société des Forges et Aciéries du Nord-Est had been founded in 1882. It combined the Mines et Usines du Nord et de l'Est and Steinbach and Company, another iron and steel company. The former, created in 1873, was the result of the merger of the blast furnaces of Jarville; the iron factory of Trith Saint Léger, an old factory founded in 1828; and interests in the Houdemont mines. Nord-Est increased its size considerably after World War I through acquisitions and mergers in the mining and iron and steel industries. In 1919 it took over the Usines de l'Espérance, established in Louvroil in 1858 by Victor Dumont. In 1933 it absorbed the Société des Hauts Fourneaux et Laminoirs de la Sambre, a blast furnaces and rolling mills company that originated from the merger of the Hautmont factory, founded in 1871 by Michel Helson, and the Société des Forges et Fonderies de Montataire, established in 1840.

French Steel Industry Consolidation in the 1960s

Concentration continued to take place in Lorraine's iron and steel industry during the 1950s and 1960s. In 1950, the Grandsons of François de Wendel company merged with the de Wendel company. The year 1950 also saw the creation of Sidélor, a company in which two Sollac partners, the Rombas and the Homécourt groups, took part. In 1963, another merger brought together the UCPMI, another Sollac partner, and the Knutange company to form the company SMS (Société Mosellane de Sidérurgie). Meanwhile, de Wendel and Sidélor decided to form a joint venture, Sacilor, which built a large

modern oxygen steel factory at Gandrange. Finally, in 1967, the de Wendel, Sidélor, and SMS groups decided upon a merger. The new group, de Wendel-Sidélor, thus acquired 65 percent of Sollac's shares and all of Sacilor's shares. In 1968, the group companies produced more than 20 million tons of iron mineral, that is 40 percent of total French production, and 7.8 million tons of rough steel, that is two-thirds of Lorraine's production and one-third of French production. The workforce amounted to more than 60,000.

In 1971 a conversion plan for the new group was issued. It proposed the closing of all the Martin and Thomas steelworks and generally of all the most obsolete factories, the production of which was to be replaced by that of the leading plant at Gandrange. This policy was intended to enable the company to bridge the increasing competitive gap between Lorraine coal and iron mineral supply and that coming from abroad.

In 1973 the group structures were simplified. De Wendel-Sidélor merged with its own subsidiary Sacilor and its two parent companies, de Wendel and Sidélor Mosellane, to form the new company Sacilor. Close industrial cooperation was achieved between Sacilor and its subsidiary Sollac. In 1975, the first year of the steelmaking crisis in France, the de Wendel and Marine-Firminy groups merged. A holding company, Marine-Wendel, united all the steelmaking interests of the two groups, including their shares in Sollac. Lastly, in 1977, the holding company Marine-Wendel gave to Sacilor those of its industrial interests directly linked to steelmaking.

Usinor had been created in order to set up its own wideband train. The train was constructed in Denain, where the existing blast furnaces and steelworks could supply it with raw materials, and went into operation in 1952. Another decision was even more revolutionary: in 1956, Usinor announced its intention to create a new integrated factory oriented exclusively toward steel sheets. This decision was unusual, in that the plant would not be located in the mainlands, near the coal and iron mines, but by the sea, at Dunkirk. For economical reasons, the new factory was intended to receive raw material supplies from abroad. The preparation lasted for years and the factory, one of the most powerful and modern in the world, officially opened only in 1971.

In 1966 Usinor merged with the company Lorraine-Escaut. Lorraine-Escaut had been created in 1953 with the merger of three ancient steelmaking companies: Senelle-Maubeuge, Longwy, and Escaut et Meuse. It was the last of the great postwar mergers. The merger with Usinor led to the creation of a new holding company, Denain-Nord-Est-Longwy, which controlled about 60 companies through Usinor and Vallourec. Usinor combined the mining, steelmaking, and steel-selling activities while Vallourec controlled all the pipe-making activities.

During the early 1970s, the new group carried out several important projects, such as the construction in Mardyck, near Dunkirk, of a large steel sheet cold mill rolling factory. In 1973, benefiting from the financial difficulties encountered by the de Wendel-Sidélor group as a result of the difficult circumstances prevailing in the steel market and the weight of its restructuring plan in Lorraine, Usinor took a stake of 47.5 percent in Solmer, another 47.5 percent of which was retained by Sollac, the

Key Dates:

1948: Usinor is formed through the merger of the two largest steel-producing groups in northern France, Denain-Anzin and Nord-Est.
1950: Sidélor is launched.
1963: Sacilor is created.
1966: Usinor merges with Lorraine-Escaut.
1967: Sidélor, de Wendel, and SMS groups merge to form de Wendel-Sidélor.
1973: De Wendel-Sidélor and Sacilor merge to form Sacilor.
1981: French government takes over control of Sacilor and Usinor.
1986: Usinor and Sacilor merge.
1995: French government, faced with falling steel prices, cashes out of the steel industry and allows Usinor Sacilor to be privatized.
1997: Company changes name to Usinor.
1998: Company acquires 54 percent stake (later raised to 75 percent) in Belgian steel producer Cockerill Sambre; company enters South America with purchase of top Brazilian steel producer CST.
2001: Usinor announces merger agreement with Luxembourg's Arbed and Spain's Aceralia; if approved, the deal would create a new worldwide leader in steel production.

founder of the company. Solmer possessed a large steelmaking unit, in Fos-sur-mer, near Marseilles, that used foreign raw materials.

Privatized Powerhouse in the 1980s

Both Usinor and Sacilor were hit severely by the economic crisis that began in 1975, two years after the first oil shock. While steel prices plummeted because of the diminished demand and the outbreak of the continuous casting, energy and salary costs increased. The two groups kept their workforce intact for the first two years, while their financial results deteriorated considerably, aggravated by the fact that the steelmaking groups were already heavily indebted as a result of the modernization plans launched at the beginning of the 1970s.

At the beginning of 1977, the French steelmaking groups made public a plan that called for reduced steel production, concentration on the leading factories, and the closing of the less modern units. That same year, the steelmaking profession signed a ten-year agreement on job cuts, the Steelmaking Profession Social Protection Covenant, with the government. The agreement allowed the firms to put workers into early retirement from the age of 58 years and eight months and in some cases, 54 years. The cost was shared between the firms and, for the major part, the state.

In 1979, another merger occurred at the government's initiative, between Denain-Nord-Est-Longwy (DNEL-Usinor) and Chiers-Chatillon-Neuves Maisons. The latter was a somewhat smaller group, also the result of multiple mergers between long-

established steelmaking firms—its oldest factory, Chatillon, dated from the 18th century and had belonged to the marshall-duke of Marmont, a Napoleon general. Also in 1979, Usinor took over the Rehon factory from the Cockerill group, while Sacilor became the major shareholder of another old steelmaker, Pompey. Finally, in 1981 the Socialist government decided to make the firms' situation clearer. Sacilor was nationalized by conversion of the state loans while Usinor was controlled up to 90 percent by the state and nationalized companies.

During the 1980s, FFr 100 billion ($16 billion) was poured by the state into the abyss of the steel industry crisis. About 100,000 jobs were lost, even if the redundant workers benefited from the Steelmaking Profession Social Protection Covenant. Production capacities were reduced by 20 percent for flat products and 36 percent for long products, those most affected by the demand slump. Many of the ancient steelworks, such as Trith-Saint-Léger, Pompey, Vireux-Molhain, Decazeville, and Longwy, had to be closed down. Most of the others, such as Les Dunes, Denain, Hautmont, Gandrange, Hagondange, Homécourt, Neuves-Maisons, and Joeuf, saw their activity reduced. A series of state-monitored mergers, intended to accelerate the restructuring of the French steel industry, began in 1982 when Ugine Steels was integrated into the Sacilor group and Sacilor took a majority stake in the Société Metallurgique de Normandie. Another crash, prompted by a decline in demand, occurred on the steel market in 1983, which led to a much more decisive step: the creation in 1984, as part of the Socialist government's restructuring plan for the steel industry, of Unimetal and Ascometal. Both companies combined entire departments from the rival groups Usinor and Sacilor: Unimetal grouped all the current long products and Ascometal all the special long products. Meanwhile, job cuts became effective from 1984, meeting fierce union resistance initially.

Global Leader for the 21st Century

In 1986, the year in which state subsidies for the steel industry were stopped by the European Commission, steel prices broke down again. The merger between the two French giant steelmakers was announced in September 1986 by the Chirac right wing government, with Francis Mer, former number two at Saint-Gobain Pont-à-Mousson, being appointed president of the two companies and then of Usinor Sacilor. In 1986, Usinor achieved sales of FFr 33.7 billion with a workforce of 41,000 and lost FFr 5 billion. Sacilor achieved sales of FFr 42.6 billion with a workforce of 61,000 and lost FFr 7.5 billion. The new president set up a drastic plan aimed at boosting productivity in the group: two years later, in 1988, the group employed 80,000 and had sales of FFr 78.9 billion. Benefiting from this tremendous effort and from the strengthened demand for steel, in particular flat steel, in the world, Usinor Sacilor made a recovery. From that moment on, Francis Mer felt free to conduct an ambitious international strategy that soon led the group to the second position in world steel-production volume, just behind Nippon Steel, with 23 billion tons compared with Nippon Steel's 28 billion.

This external growth strategy was aimed simultaneously at steel producers, so as to gain weight in the steel world market, and steel merchants, in order to come nearer to the group's clients; Usinor Sacilor came to control the distribution of about

30 percent of its output. Mer then led the company on a series of acquisitions that helped spread its operations beyond France and strengthen its international position. Usinor Sacilor bought 70 percent of Germany's Saarstahl. In the United States, the group took over J&L Specialty Products Corporation, a top U.S. stainless steel maker; Techalloy Co., a stainless steel maker; and Alloy & Stainless, Inc., a specialized trade company; and it set up a joint venture with Bethlehem Steel Corporation, and finalized an alliance with major wiremaker Georgetown Steel Corp. The group also invested in Italy, taking a 24 percent stake in Lutrix, a holding company controlling La Magona d'Italia, an important coated steel sheet maker; it also purchased 51 percent of Alessio Tubi. Usinor eventually bought a majority stake in ASD, Britain's second largest steel distributor. Finally, the group invested in France in CMB Acier, formerly Carnaud Basse-Indre, a packaging steel producer, thus becoming the co-world leader, with Nippon Steel in this sector.

Mer was also pushing for release from government control. The company's opportunity came in the mid-1990s, when falling steel prices encouraged the French government to cash out of the steel industry—in this, France was followed by much of the rest of Europe's heavily government-owned and financed steel industry. The dismantling of the European Community's domestic trade borders in 1992 and then the approach of the single European currency, slated to begin its rollout in 1999, added more encouragement to the privatization of Europe's steel industry.

Usinor Sacilor was privatized in 1995, and adopted its simplified name in 1997. The company quickly proved itself a leader in the slowly building wave of steel industry consolidation. In 1998, the company acquired a 54 percent stake in Cockerill Sambre, the former Belgium government-owned steel producer. Usinor's position in Cockerill Sambre climbed to 75 percent in 1999, and gave the French company the European leadership in crude steel production. By then, Usinor had entered South America, acquiring the top Brazilian steel producer, CST. Other acquisitions included boosting its position in J&L Specialty Steel to just under 98 percent, and the acquisition of 40 percent of Italian flat steel manufacturer Arvedi. While making these acquisitions, Usinor also sold off a number of noncore assets, including most of its UGO electrical products unit to Thyssen Krupp and its Unimetal, Trefieurope, and SMR units to Ispat International.

Yet Usinor's competitors had been busy acquiring size as well. At the end of the century, Usinor ranked only fourth among top European steel producers, behind Luxembourg's Arbed, the newly formed Corus—built from the merger of British Steel and Netherlands-based Hoogovens—and Thyssen Krupp. By mid-2000, Usinor and Thyssen Krupp were said to be involved in discussions involving a possible merger between the two companies. These talks went nowhere, however.

At the beginning of 2001, Usinor seemed set to continue on its own—inking a cooperation agreement with Japan's Nippon Steel for the production of automotive grade sheet steel. Then, in February 2001, the steel industry woke up to find a new worldwide leader, when Usinor, Arbed, and Spain's Aceralia—itself already partly controlled by Arbed—announced their decision to merge into a new steel production powerhouse with a total production capacity of 46 million tons and estimated revenues expected to top EUR 30 billion. Although the merger faced review by the European mergers and monopolies commission, it was expected to be finalized by the end of the year, at which time the newly formed group, which was to transfer its headquarters to Luxembourg, was expected to adopt a new name to bring Usinor into the new century.

Principal Subsidiaries

Sollac (99.9%); Forges et Aciéries de Dilling (Germany; 95.1%); GTS Industries; Europipe (Germany; 50%); Unimétal; Ascométal; Saarstahl AG (Germany; 70%); Ugine SA (96%); Ugine-Savoie; Imphy; CLI (Creusot-Loire Industrie); Forcast International (66%); Fortech (66.1%), GPRI (55.4%); Tubeurop Tréfilunion; Techno Saarstahl; Nozal (65.7%); IMS (58.7%); Saarlux Beteiligung (Germany); Valor; Daval; Edgcomb.

Principal Competitors

Acerinox, S.A.; AK Steel Holding Corporation; Allegheny Technologies Incorporated; Shanghai Baosteel Group Corporation; Corus Group plc; Gerdau S.A; Kawasaki Steel Corporation; Nippon Steel Corporation; Outokumpu Oyj; Pohang Iron & Steel Co., Ltd.; Sumitomo Metal Industries, Ltd.; Thyssen Krupp AG; Toyota Tsusho Corporation; USX-U.S. Steel Group.

Further Reading

Marsh, Peter, ''Arbed and Usinor Forge a Global Tie-Up,'' *Financial Times*, February 19, 2001.
——, ''Compelling Logic of a Steel Link-Up,'' *Financial Times*, June 13, 2000.
Ratner, Juliana, ''Usinor Steels Itself for Number-One Slot,'' *Financial Times*, February 17, 2001.
''Usinor Poised to Reveal Revamp,'' *Financial Times*, January 27, 1999.

—update: M.L. Cohen

Varco International, Inc.

743 N. Eckhoff Street
Orange, California 92868
U.S.A.
Telephone: (714) 978-1900
Fax: (714) 937-5029
Web site: http://www.varco.com

Public Company
Incorporated: 1908 as Abegg and Reinhold Company;
     1937 as Pacific Tubular Inspection Company
Employees: 6,660
Sales: $866.6 million (2000)
Stock Exchanges: New York
Ticker Symbol: VRC
NAIC: 213112 Support Activities for Oil and Gas

Varco International, Inc. primarily serves the oil and gas industries, with a presence in every major oilfield of the world. Maintaining dual headquarters in Orange, California, and Houston, Texas, the company has operations in 49 countries spread across six continents. Varco is divided into four business groups. The Drilling Equipment Sales group offers a variety of equipment used in drilling rigs, both offshore and on land, including equipment used in rotating and handling drillpipe, a complete line of standard drilling rig tools, hoisting equipment, and pressure control and motion compensation equipment. The Tubular Services group sells products that coat the inside of pipes and tubes used in drilling and pipelines in order to prevent corrosion and leaks. The group also provides inspection and quality assurance services for tubular goods used in the oil and gas industry. In addition, it inspects tubular products used in steel mills and sells high pressure fiberglass tubular goods. Varco's Drill Services group supports drilling operations by providing advanced equipment that monitors drilling rig instrumentation. The Coiled Tubing & Wireline Products group sells coiled tubing equipment and the supporting equipment that goes with it.

Varco's Origins: 1908

For decades Varco was purely a products company, but in 2000 it joined forces with service company Tuboscope to create a more dynamic business. In the merger of equals it was actually Tuboscope that issued the stock to purchase Varco, but Varco's chief executive, George I. Boyadjieff, took over as chairman and CEO, and Tuboscope subsequently assumed the Varco International name. Originally "Varco" was a trademark of the Abegg and Reinhold Company, founded in Los Angeles in 1908 by two Swiss engineers, Baldwin Reinhold and Walter Abegg. They were lifelong friends who both attended the Polytechnic Institute of Zurich, where they earned degrees in mechanical engineering with an emphasis in metallurgy. At a time when Hollywood was just a sleepy village and most American movies were being filmed in the New York City area, the two men gravitated to southern California. They offered metallurgical and engineering services and also made small hand tools that were primarily used in mining and the nascent automobile industry. In order to strengthen the metal tools, the engineers created their own heat-treating plant in 1909 and were among the first to introduce heat-treated parts to the California oilfields. In fact, Reinhold would be tabbed by many as the father of oilfield metallurgy.

In the early years of the 1900s, drilling techniques were moving away from a reliance on hand tools to the use of far more sophisticated drive tools and derricks. Rotary drilling was introduced and as the technology was refined it gradually replaced cable tool drilling. Abegg and Reinhold already provided rig repair services as early as 1912. In order to fund expansion the founders turned to friend Edgar Vuilleumiere for backing. By 1915 the company's oil industry products began using the "Varco" trademark, which stood for Vuilleumiere, Abegg and Reinhold Company. With the discovery of the major oil field at Signal Hill in southern California in 1921, the company began to focus on manufacturing rotary drill products. Over the ensuing decades the company would sell outside of the Los Angeles area and achieve an international reputation for Varco products. In 1973 the company changed its name to Varco International, Inc. By then, Reinhold had been succeeded by his son, Walter B. Reinhold, as well as Boyadjieff, who joined Abegg and Reinhold in 1969.

In 1975 Varco made an initial public offering of stock with the primary purpose of paying down debt. For the next five years the company enjoyed flush times as the oil industry boomed: revenues grew fourfold to $108.6 million while net income tripled to $11.9 million. In 1981, at the peak of the oil boom, Varco posted even more dramatic gains. It earned $22.3 million on revenues of $193.7 million. In Orange County alone there were five other thriving oil equipment manufacturers, but as oil prices fell and drilling activities dwindled, equipment sales became virtually nonexistent. In 1981 there were approximately 4,000 oil rigs in operation, but in 1987, a year after oil prices collapsed completely, there were little more than 900 in operation. Varco was the only Orange County oil equipment manufacturer left intact.

Varco's survival was the result of Reinhold refusing to cut back on research and development (R&D) at a time when retrenchment was the order of the day and R&D was seen as a ready target for budget cuts. In 1980 a major offshore drilling customer asked Varco to help in developing a better drilling system. With plenty of cash available, Reinhold accepted the challenge. When the oil industry began to stagger two years later, and for the first time in company history Varco saw its customers cancel orders (worth some $60 million), the decision to keep spending on R&D was a much tougher one. Reinhold was convinced, however, that what the company was developing would prove to be revolutionary. It was called the Top Drive drilling system, which placed an electric motor at the top of the drill stem rather than on the floor of the drilling rig, thus allowing far greater flexibility in removing drills and the ability to drill extremely deep or sharp-angled holes. Increased efficiency translated into significant savings, estimated to reduce the cost of drilling by as much as 40 percent, making Top Drive a product especially suited for hard times. Although more R&D spending would be required, Top Drive was introduced in 1982, a year in which Varco would lose $17.2 million and be in danger of defaulting on loans. To support the project and keep the company afloat, Reinhold was forced to take drastic steps, laying off more than 1,000 workers, instituting pay cuts, selling off equipment, and closing down sales offices around the world. Varco actually stepped up its R&D efforts, as it not only developed four new models of the Top Drive offshore drilling systems, it introduced an onshore system that automated pipe handling and drill retrieval.

Returning to Profitability: 1988

Top Drive sales would soon take off. After years of losing money, the company finally returned to profitability in 1988. Revenues totaled $69 million, a far cry from the nearly $200 million generated in 1982, but a significant improvement over 1987 when revenues reached bottom, totaling just $37 million.

Varco also undertook a number of initiatives that significantly lowered its debt. Although Top Drive was vital in Varco's survival, it was important that the company not become overly dependent on the product, which at one point accounted for 75 percent of all sales. To help diversify its business, Varco acquired two units from Baker Hughes International in a $23 million deal: BJ Machinery manufactured drilling equipment, while Technical Drilling Tool provided marketing and sales expertise.

Varco made further acquisitions in the early 1990s that resulted in mounting revenues, which increased from $132 million in 1990 to $341.4 million by 1996. In May 1990 it acquired the Martin-Decker Division from Cooper Industries for $29.3 million. With manufacturing facilities in Houston and Marshall, Texas, Martin Decker produced pipe handling equipment and measuring and monitoring devices. In November 1990, Varco bought the assets of the TOTCO division of Exlog, Inc., in a deal that included stock and $20 million in cash. TOTCO also had roots in southern California. Joseph B. Wood founded the Technical Oil Tool Corporation in 1929 to manufacture a device that would determine if oil drilling was deviating from vertical. In the oil industry, any drift recorder would soon be referred to as a "TOTCO." Over the years, the company developed other recording devices. After purchasing the company, Varco combined it with Martin-Decker to create the M/D TOTCO Instrumentation Division.

Varco continued its external growth in 1992 when it paid $36 million in cash for the Shaffer product line of Baroid Corp. The company was founded in southern California in 1928 by William D. Shaffer as the Shaffer Tool Works. Starting with the flow bean valve to prevent blowouts, Shaffer patented a number of devices for use in drilling operations. The company remained in family hands until 1968 when it was purchased by the Rucker Corporation. Ten years later it was sold to NL Industries, becoming NL Shaffer. It prospered for several years until the oil bust of the 1980s, at which point it dramatically downsized its worldwide operations. NL Industries restructured its operations in 1988 and spun off Shaffer, which then became a subsidiary of Baroid. For Varco the addition of Shaffer's pressure control equipment complemented its other drilling support products.

In 1994 Varco bought Thule Rigtech, a division of Rig Technology Limited, for approximately $9 million. The British acquisition manufactured equipment used in drilling through mud, and further filled out Varco's slate of drilling rig components. Adding to its operations was a strategy that paid off for the company. It prospered and was debt free by the late 1990s. A downturn in oil prices, however, resulted in a decreased demand for its products. Revenues in 1999 fell 32 percent, from $567.7 million in 1998 to $385.5 million, and the company lost $7.2 million after posting net income of $53.1 million and $41.9 million the previous two years. Although extremely healthy, Varco took precautionary measures, including the slashing of its workforce by 25 percent. Then in March 2000 it announced that it had agreed to merge with Tuboscope in a stock deal worth $834 million. Because the two businesses complemented one another, the new entity would offer a broader range of products and become one of the major oilfield service and equipment companies in the world, boasting a market capitalization in the range of $2 billion.

Founding of Tuboscope: 1937

Tuboscope was founded as the Pacific Tubular Inspection Company in 1937 by a German immigrant named Fritz Huntsinger. While running a tool company, he was approached by the Shell Oil Company to help it detect faulty drill pipe. Having fought in World War I, Huntsinger was familiar with Optiscopes, German-made devices used to inspect the interior surface of cannon barrels. He promptly imported a pair and adapted them to a new function. Huntsinger then held an employee contest with a $25 prize for coming up with the best name for the new device. In the end he combined two entries, "tubo instrument" and "scope instrument," to form "tuboscope." It quickly became standard drilling equipment. The company also developed a method for coating the inside of pipes to prevent corrosion and increase working life. Tuboscope's technologies were so important that during World War II its employees were exempt from the draft in order to ensure that the company would be able to help maintain the flow of oil so vital to the war effort. Having expanded to service the Texas oilfields, Huntsinger sold out to area employees, who created the Tuboscope Company of Texas. Pacific Tubular later became Vetco Services and moved its operations to Europe.

In 1963 American Machine and Foundry bought Tuboscope and kept it as a subsidiary until 1985, when AMF was acquired by Minstar Inc., a Minneapolis-based moving and storage business. Although Minstar originally planned to sell off Tuboscope, it held onto it because of the cash flow the unit generated. In 1985 Tuboscope had $176 million in revenues. By 1988, however, Minstar elected to focus on what had become its main business, the manufacture of pleasure boats. It sold Tuboscope to Brentwood Associates, a Los Angeles investor group, in a $142 million leveraged buyout. In March 1990 the company went public to reduce its debt by almost $50 million. A year later it acquired Vetco Services, its parent company (albeit, 50 years removed) for $50 million in cash and stock. The deal increased Tuboscope's presence overseas, where most of the future growth in drilling was expected to take place. Vetco was based in Germany and had operations in more than 30 other countries. In 1992 Tuboscope would change its name to Tuboscope International Corporation.

Saddled with high debt, Tuboscope attempted in 1993 to sell itself to Weatherford International, another drilling-related company, but the deal fell through. With a decline in international drilling, the company was forced to restructure its operations and lay off employees. A year later Tuboscope hired

Goldman, Sachs & Co. to help it maximize shareholder value, with the possibility of selling all or part of the company. In January 1996 the company acquired Drexel Oilfield Services in a stock deal worth over $100 million, but as part of the deal Drexel's largest shareholder, SCF Partners, took control of the combined companies. In turn, Tuboscope received over $30 million in new capital from SCF partners. Under its new management the company initiated an aggressive acquisition strategy. In 1996 it bought seven companies, followed by 11 in 1997 and five in 1998. In 1999 it announced a stock swap to acquire Newpark Resources Inc., a deal that management hoped would allow Tuboscope to offer an array of integrated services to drilling operations. When Tuboscope was unable to arrange suitable financing to support the combined company, it eventually scuttled the deal in November 1999, with only some operational alliances with Newpark to show after months of effort.

A few months after the failed deal with Newpark, Tuboscope would find a new partner in Varco, one with $75 million in the bank and no debt. This time the merger would come to fruition. Varco management took over the new combination of businesses and in March 2001 was adding even more to its portfolio when it bought the oilfield services of ICO for $165 million. Clearly, Varco was broadening its range of services and equipment manufacturing, but it remained very much dependent on drilling activity, which itself was a function of the worldwide price of gas and oil. The cyclical nature of those prices would continue to dictate the fortunes of Varco, no matter how large the company might grow.

Principal Operating Units

Drilling Equipment Sales; Tubular Services; Drill Services; Coiled Tubing & Wireline Products.

Principal Competitors

Cooper Cameron Corporation; Hydril; National-Oilwell; ShawCor; Tesco Corporation; Weatherford International, Inc.

Further Reading

Berkman, Leslie, "1st Profitable Year Since '81; Varco International Finally Turns a Corner," *Los Angeles Times,* March 2, 1989, p. 5.

Brammer, Rhonda, "Blowing in the Wind: The Battered Oil-Service Industry Is Primed for Recovery," *Barron's,* October 28, 1991, p. 10.

David, Michael, "Varco, Tuboscope to Merge in $837 Million Stock Swap," *Houston Chronicle,* March 23, 2000, p. C1.

Haines, Leslie, "Varco-Tuboscope Makes 'Smarter' Company," *Oil & Gas Investor,* July 2000, p. 84.

Schine, Eric, "Comeback Seen for Varco International, Knocked for a Loop by 1982–86 Oil Decline," *Los Angeles Times,* January 24, 1988, p. 5.

——, "Sole Survivor Varco Is Last Oil Equipment Firm in County Where 6 Once Stood," *Los Angeles Times,* October 28, 1988, p. 5.

Selz, Michael, "Fast Track: Taking Long View in Tough Times Pays Off for Varco," *Wall Street Journal,* December 26, 1989, p. 1.

Tejada, Carlos, "Varco, Tuboscope Agree to Merge in All-Stock Deal," *Wall Street Journal,* March 23, 2000, p. C25.

"Varco International, Inc.," *Oil & Gas Investor,* March 1996, p. 32.

—Ed Dinger

Vintage Petroleum, Inc.

110 West Seventh Street
Tulsa, Oklahoma 74119
U.S.A.
Telephone: (918) 592-0101
Fax: (918) 584-5704
Web site: http://www.vintagepetroleum.com

Public Company
Incorporated: 1983
Employees: 764
Sales: $806.18 million (2000)
Stock Exchanges: New York
Ticker Symbol: VPI
NAIC: 211111 Crude Petroleum and Natural Gas
   Extraction

Based in Tulsa, Oklahoma, Vintage Petroleum, Inc. is regarded as an oil and gas exploration and production company. Although it engages in some drilling on undeveloped properties, Vintage primarily buys mature wells at prices below industry averages, then cuts operating costs, lowers overhead, and applies advanced technology to squeeze out any remaining gas and oil, historically resulting in increased reserves, production, and profitability. By carefully choosing its acquisition targets, the company has grown steadily since its foundation in 1983. In North America, Vintage operates in four principal areas: the West Coast, Gulf Coast, east Texas, the mid-continent region of the United States, and Canada. Since 1995 the company has also broadened its activities internationally, acquiring properties or concessions in Argentina, Bolivia, Ecuador, and Yemen. Approximately 60 percent of its total production is generated in North America, with nearly an equal split between gas and oil production.

Cofounders Working Together in the 1970s

The cofounders of Vintage, Charles C. Stephenson, Jr., and Jo Bob Hille, earned degrees in Petroleum Engineering from the University of Oklahoma and the University of Tulsa, respec-
tively. Their first independent oil and gas company was Tulsa's Andover Oil Co., which they built and ran from 1972 to 1982. They sold the business to Santa Fe International for $400 million, out of which $250 million retired outstanding debt. In 1983 the pair launched Vintage, based on some oil and gas properties they retained from their days at Andover. Cash flow from the wells, plus personally guaranteed loans, allowed the new company to gain its feet. Stephenson took over as president, while Hille became executive vice-president as well as treasurer and secretary. In 1987 Stephenson became chief executive officer and Hille became chief operating officer.

Because of a collapse in oil prices in 1986, Vintage's cash flow was hindered, and after servicing debt the company was unable to purchase major new assets. To raise money, the company sold convertible preferred stock, totaling 15 percent of its outstanding shares. Half of the issue was taken by Prudential Capital, which also purchased $20 million worth of ten-year notes. Thus, by 1988 Vintage was able to begin an aggressive acquisition program. Just as they had done with Andover, Stephenson and Hille applied two basic principles when evaluating a possible acquisition: the economics of a purchase had to be sound, and the property had to possess a greater potential than just its current cash flow. As Stephenson explained to *Oil & Gas Investor,* "We look very closely at the economics and if they're not there, we don't buy. We know what we have to do with the banks, so there's not a lot of leeway. A deal that's uneconomic, but which might make sense for other reasons, eats up equity and restricts our ability to make further acquisitions." It was Hille's responsibility to evaluate potential deals, which involved considerable engineering work to determine the hidden worth of a property.

Early in 1988 Vintage spent $19.8 million in cash to acquire oil and gas properties in Oklahoma. In September of that year, the company spent approximately $48 million in cash and agreed to an assumption of liabilities to buy oil and gas properties from Donald Slawson, a Wichita independent. In that same month, a wholly owned subsidiary, Vintage Pipeline, Inc., bought Prairie States Gas Company for $5 million, plus the assumption of $3.25 million in debt. Another responsibility of Hille's was to make the potential of a new property a producing reality. Engineers and operations people would meet regularly to control costs and plan an extraction strategy, using all available means to force mature wells to give up their remaining resources.

Going Public: 1990

By 1989 Vintage participated in 56 wells, generated $44.4 million in revenues, and posted a net income of $3.6 million. Early in 1990, with oil prices down, the company saw a chance to take advantage of a difficult environment, pay down debt, and position itself to acquire additional properties at bargain prices to increase its oil and gas reserves. Vintage decided to make an initial public offering of stock, a move that Stephenson had considered with Andover but opted against when economic conditions were less advantageous. In August 1990 Vintage sold eight million shares on the New York Stock Exchange at $5.25 each, netting $32.8 million. In that same month, the company acquired oil and gas properties in Louisiana from Chevron, paying approximately $14 million. In December 1990 it paid Shell Western $2.4 million for properties in Mississippi. Fueled by its acquisitions, Vintage reported significant gains in 1990, with net earnings of more than $6 million on $51 million in revenues. Those numbers would balloon in 1991. Revenues exceeded $141 million and net income approached $25 million. Despite weak oil prices, company revenues grew to $102 million in 1992.

After acquiring additional oil and gas properties in Texas and Louisiana in 1991, Vintage began a concerted effort to expand into new regions. In April 1992 the company purchased three California oilfields, in the counties of Santa Barbara and Ventura, from Shell Oil. Later in 1992 Vintage completed its largest acquisition to date, adding to its California holdings. Although originally announced as a $90 million deal, the purchase of Atlantic Richfield's 15 oil and gas fields came to $76.4 million. Two of the fields were located in Ventura County and the remainder in Kern County. The purchase increased the oil and gas reserves of Vintage by 60 percent. To help pay off debt incurred by the acquisition, in January 1993 the company sold an additional 7.8 million common shares of stock in a two-for-one adjusted split at $6.75 each, netting almost $45 million. It then bought three more oil and gas properties located in Ventura County, paying $38.1 million to Dupont's Co.'s Conoco Inc. Overall, the company had tripled both its revenues and reserves in just three years.

In 1994 Stephenson, while remaining chairman of the board, gave up the chief executive officer position to Hille. Replacing Hille as the company's chief operating officer was S. Craig George, who had worked for the Andover subsidiary of Santa Fe International before joining Vintage in 1991 to serve as a senior vice-president of the company. Also in 1994 Vintage would become involved in an incident that would remain a concern for the next six years and the subject of frequent reporting by the *Los Angeles Times.*

On August 10, 1994, according to the *Los Angeles Times,* a crew working for contractor Pride Petroleum Services was redrilling a 50-year-old well when a geyser of water shot 15 feet above the wellhead. Three of the men jumped into the work pit to try to contain the leak with a five-gallon bucket, but were unaware that the drill had hit a pocket of hydrogen sulfide gas, a colorless gas that in lower concentrations is recognized by a rotten egg smell. In such concentrations, between 20 and 150 parts per million, the gas can cause eye and upper respiratory irritation. In concentrations of 500 parts per million and 30 minutes of exposure, hydrogen sulfide causes headaches, dizziness, diarrhea, bronchitis, or bronchopneumonia. In extremely high concentrations of 800 to 1,000 parts per million, such as in this case, the nervous system is paralyzed, resulting in suffocation, unless a victim is immediately removed and given artificial respiration. The contracted workers, unaware of any potential danger, were not wearing gas masks. The three men were instantly killed and four others were subsequently injured while attempting a rescue. Several days later, it was learned that just hours before the accident, supervisors disconnected a temporary flow line, a standard safety measure that would have diverted water, oil, or gas from flooding into the well. The victims' families sued Vintage and others. In the drawn-out court case that followed, Vintage maintained that the supervisor as an independent contractor was responsible, not the company. Its position was bolstered by the findings of both California OSHA and the Department of Oil, Gas and Geothermal Resources, which did not cite the company with any violations of safety or workplace rules. A judge in 1998, however, ruled that the well belonged to Vintage and the supervisor represented Vintage, plus the company failed to properly weigh the geologic risks at the site. The judge then awarded more than $6 million in damages to the workers and their families, but the judgments were frozen when Vintage decided to appeal the case. It was not until June 2000 that the appellate court upheld the lower court's ruling. Vintage considered taking its case to the California State Supreme Court, but in the end decided against the move. Almost six years after the Ventura accident, the company announced it would pay the judgments.

Vintage Looks Overseas in the Mid-1990s

While Vintage acquired a number of new oil and gas properties in Louisiana, Texas, and California in 1994 and 1995, spending more than $60 million, the company also began to look overseas, expanding its emphasis on new exploration. The first opportunity came in Argentina. Vintage purchased approximately 72 percent of the common stock of Cadipsa S.A. for $12.4 million in cash. It then bought BG Argentina, S.A. for $37 million in cash. In addition Vintage paid more than $50 million for concessions owned by Astra Compania Argentina de Petroleo S.A. The company's holdings in southern Argentina were greatly enhanced in 1999 when in two separate transactions it acquired an exploitation and exploration concession near Santa Cruz. First the company bought a 70 percent interest from

Key Dates:

1983: Vintage Petroleum is incorporated.
1990: Initial public offering of stock is completed.
1992: First California properties are acquired.
1995: Company makes first acquisitions in Argentina.
1996: Company makes first acquisitions in Bolivia.
1998: Ecuador and Yemen interests are added.
2000: First Canadian property is acquired.

France's Total S.A., followed by a purchase of the remaining 30 percent held by Repsol S.A. In order to help finance the total cost of nearly $122 million, Vintage sold nine million common shares of stock at $9.50 per share. In September 2000 the company expanded into western Argentina by acquiring two concessions held by Perez Companc for $40.1 million in cash.

Vintage entered Bolivia with the 1996 acquisition of Shamrock Ventures for $37 million in cash. The purchase of a three-dimensional seismic survey of its concessions in 1998 led to the identification of a number of potential wells, but the company did little drilling until late 1998, when it increased activity in anticipation of a Bolivia-to-Brazil pipeline that was completed in 1999. Vintage made its first acquisition in Ecuador in 1998, paying $18 million to Brazil's Petroleo Brasileiro S.A. The company then added to its holdings in late 1999. When the Ecuadorian government authorized the building of a new pipeline, Vintage stepped up its activities in the country. Also in 1998, Vintage became involved in another portion of the world, Yemen, when it entered into an agreement with TransGlobe Energy that would give it a 75 percent interest in an exploration concession covering in excess of one million acres, in exchange for an $11 million preliminary exploration commitment. Vintage then looked northward to Canada. In November 2000, it purchased Cometra Energy for $46.3 million, a deal that also brought with it an exploration interest in Trinidad. The 13 producing fields were mostly located in Alberta and British Columbia, with some also in Saskatchewan. Vintage also gained processing and pipeline facilities and 146,000 underdeveloped acres. The company completed a far more significant deal just a few months later when it bought Alberta-based Genesis Exploration Ltd. for $593 million.

By 2001 Vintage was well positioned to pay for Genesis Exploration, although it had a rough patch to endure. When Hille stepped down as CEO in 1997, the company had generated record revenues of $416.6 million and a net profit of almost $55 million. George took over as the chief executive officer but suffered through a difficult 1998, when soft oil and gas prices battered both revenues and profits. Sales fell to $328.9 million and the company posted its only loss since going public, $87.6 million,

although some of that was the one-time result of a change in accounting. In 1999 Vintage began to divest itself of properties that were either marginally economical or no longer fit in with the company's emphasis on core regions. Vintage sold more than 225 leases for approximately $9.5 million. It sold properties in northern California to Calpine Corporation for $70 million. It also sold certain royalty interests in the Los Angeles area for $8.2 million. These sales helped to pay for the $29.6 million purchase of properties from Neuvo Energy in early 2000, adding to the company's presence in the Ventura, California, area. The close proximity to other Vintage properties allowed overhead and operating costs to be lowered considerably.

The company's fortunes rebounded in 1999, helped in large part by divestitures and rising oil prices. Vintage reported $503 million in sales and $73.4 million in net profit. Soaring oil and gas prices in 2000 would lead to even more impressive gains. Vintage saw its revenues exceed $800 million with a net profit of $195.9 million. Although the company could not count on high oil and gas prices to continue, Vintage was taking advantage of the flush times to enter Canada and invest in exploration efforts in South America and Yemen. After many years of exploiting inherited wells, Vintage was clearly looking to enter a new stage in which it was able to risk the costs of drilling for resources in exchange for even greater payoffs should it succeed. The company's reputation for paying attention to detail, and a strong emphasis on engineering, boded well for its future success.

Principal Subsidiaries

Vintage Gas, Inc.; Vintage Marketing, Inc.; Vintage Pipeline, Inc.; Vintage Petroleum International.

Principal Competitors

BPAmoco plc; Chevron Corporation; Texaco Inc.

Further Reading

Haines, Leslie, "Vintage Takes Advantage," *Oil & Gas Investor,* November 1992, p. 52.
Murphy, Barbara, "Vintage Petroleum Buys Ventura Oil, Gas Fields," *Los Angeles Times,* January 11, 2000, p. 6.
Ray, Russell, "Tulsa, Okla.-Based Gas Company to Buy Canadian Firm," *Tulsa World,* March 29, 2001.
Snow, Nick, "Vintage Grows in Argentina with Buy from Total, Repsol," *Oil & Gas Investor,* August 1999, p. 69.
Torres, Craig, "Vintage Petroleum Attracts Some Followers with Its Oil and Gas 'Exploitation' Activities," *Wall Street Journal,* January 25, 1993, p. C2.
Wilson, Tracy, "Firm Agrees to Settlement in Gas Leak," *Los Angeles Times,* July 12, 2000, p. 1.

—Ed Dinger

Waggener Edstrom

3 Centerpointe Drive, Suite 300
Lake Oswego, Oregon 97035
U.S.A.
Telephone: (503) 443-7000
Fax: (503) 443-7001
Web site: http://www.wagged.com

Private Company
Incorporated: 1983 as The Waggener Group
Employees: 454
Sales: $57.2 million (2000)
NAIC: 54182 Public Relations Agencies

Waggener Edstrom is one of the world's leading strategic public relations agencies, specializing in offering high-tech clients public relations services, including brand development, corporate communications, media relations, and consulting. Its interactive services group provides web site design and CD-ROM publishing. The agency, one of the Portland area's first generation of homegrown high-tech public relations firms, has offices in Oregon, Washington, California, and Texas, as well as one in Heidelberg, Germany, and another in London. Its clients have included Amazon.com, Microsoft, GTE Superpages, and SAP—entrepreneurs who create computers and software, and high-growth scientific companies on the cutting edge of computer, medical, and research technology.

Company Origins

Waggener Edstrom's story begins in the mid-1970s at Tektronix Inc. At the time, Regis McKenna handled public relations for most of the high-tech firms in the United States. It was at Tektronix that Melissa Waggener and Pam Edstrom became acquainted while working in the marketing and public relations department. Pam Edstrom was director of public relations at Tektronix for Microsoft. Waggener, then 30, had a reputation for being bright, aggressive, and entrepreneurial; she had worked previously in Regis's Portland office for two years where she headed the Microsoft account.

By 1983, Waggener had developed a business plan for a new public relations firm with an emphasis on teamwork. She approached Pam Edstrom and Tektronix veterans Jody Peake and Julie McHenry with her idea. Julie McHenry also had worked with Waggener at Regis. In 1983, Waggener struck out on her own and founded The Waggener Group. Peake and Edstrom joined her a few months later. The new group shared a top floor office with a view of the Willamette River.

The company's first client was Mindset Corp., a Sunnyvale, California personal computer manufacturer. The Waggener Group's results were notable: in an industry where very little set one firm apart from another, the group achieved outstanding media coverage that included the covers of two industry magazines and big spreads in several others. "We helped them clear the PC noise," Waggener explained to Charles Humble of the *Oregonian,* who opined that "the results were impressive . . . in the wake of the cacophony over the Apple Macintosh." There was a half-day event in the Bay Area at which Bill Gates spoke, promising to write software for Mindset, and where Time Arts, another software firm, demonstrated Mindset's graphic capabilities.

Waggener's efforts were successful, as she explained it, because her group had "been to the opinion leaders with the right message before." Her company operated "on the premise that there are certain key people in the business of high technology that the media trusts as knowledgeable, unbiased sources of information. [T]hese are the people they ask about new trends, products and companies." In lieu of approaching the media on a client's behalf, she explained, her staff approached the people the media approaches. In the early 1980s, a time when computer industry news cycles were primarily product-driven, The Waggener Group began the practice of peppering reporters with product information. They also developed the practice of "overhang," announcing products before they were ready for release in order to slow the adoption of competitors' offerings.

Five months after becoming The Waggener Group, the firm agreed in 1985 to represent then new Microsoft as its client. Almost immediately thereafter, in a winning move that would set the course of its development, the small company was instrumental in getting Gates's photo on the cover of *Time* magazine. By the end of its first year in business, The Waggener Group's client list included high-tech powerhouses Mentor Graphics Corp. and Sequent Computer Systems Inc. in addition to Microsoft Corporation and Mindset "Back then, our challenge was to convince the technical press that our clients were real," recalled Jim Buchanan, who joined the company in 1984 as general manager, in a 1994 *Portland Business Journal* article. In its first year, the new company's projected revenues exceeded estimates by at least 25 percent.

Prominence and Further Growth: Mid-1980s Through the 1990s

Microsoft's success spirited The Waggener Group into the public relations spotlight. As the manufacturing side of the PC industry grew, so did the public relations segment of the business. By the early 1990s, public interest in high-tech had blossomed with the introduction of personal computers. In 1990, with annual revenues of more than $5 million, The Waggener Group changed its name to Waggener Edstrom and founded Waggener Worldwide, a new organization whose mission was to establish a framework for future growth while allowing Waggener Edstrom to focus on technology and science-based account service. Pam Edstrom, who took the lead in representing Microsoft, became senior vice-president of Waggener Edstrom; Melissa Waggener remained president and chief executive officer. Jim Buchanan became chief operating officer, and Vice-President Jody Peake assumed responsibility for a comprehensive agency training program.

Waggener Edstrom kept growing in revenues, client base, and employees throughout the 1990s. When Regis McKenna closed its Portland office in 1991, the firm had only one local competitor—Hastings, Humble, Giardini & Freeman, which later became InSync Communications. In 1992, it added four major clients: Shapeware Corp. of Seattle, McCaw Cellular Communications Inc. of Kirkland, Interactive Home Systems Inc. of Redmond, and Starwave Corp. of Bellevue, which was the new company of Microsoft cofounder Paul Allen. Waggener's 1993 gross billings were $11 million. In 1994, ten years after opening, the firm had three offices, brought in $14 million, and numbered 140 employees. By 1995, it employed 186 and had billings of $27 million.

According to some, Waggener Edstrom mirrored the culture of Microsoft—"combative and intellectually ferocious," as one former employee described it in *PC Week* in 1997. But after more than a dozen years of monopolizing Microsoft's Interactive Media

Group (IMG) account, the firm made the decision to resign it because Microsoft was growing so quickly that Waggener could no longer keep up with the software giant. Waggener Edstrom continued to service more than 30 other Microsoft products, however, including the company's client and server operating systems, Internet platforms and tools, and other products from the company's desktop applications division.

Anticipating Continued Growth into the 21st Century

By 1998, Waggener Edstrom, with 370 employees and billings of $47 million, also represented software giant SAP, Amazon.com, and graphic software firm Visio, although 60 to 65 percent of its total revenues came from Microsoft. It had offices in Washington, California, and Germany, in addition to Portland. In the second half of 1998, it acquired InSync, 75 percent of whose total revenues derived from Microsoft. After a period of turnover in the late 1990s, the firm reorganized its human relations department and, according to Waggener in *Your Company,* it "started to get more creative with benefits packages, recruiting, retention, and the other HR functions." The company also conducted a survey of its employees, which revealed that staff was feeling disconnected from the mission of the company. In response, leadership began a series of small staff meetings to explain Waggener Edstrom's vision and goals and followed up with companywide leadership training.

When Microsoft was investigated by federal antitrust lawyers in 1998 and 1999, Waggener Edstrom came under scrutiny for allegedly destroying documents and e-mail regarding Microsoft's efforts to undercut its competitors. Waggener denied that it had done so, and although Microsoft's public image clearly took a nose dive during and after its trial, Waggener Edstrom appeared not to suffer by virtue of its close association with the software giant.

Meanwhile, Portland was seeing a remarkable boom in its high-tech public relations industry. Four agencies opened their doors in Portland in 1998 alone. Within three years, ten new agencies had opened in Portland, focusing on clients ranging from software companies to dot-coms. A generation of public relations practitioners schooled by Waggener Edstrom, InSync, and rival KVO was striking out on its own. National agencies were opening branch offices in the city as well.

In 1999, high-tech accounts made up more than a quarter of the income generated by the nation's leading public relations agencies. Firms that specialized in serving high-tech clients experienced double-digit growth and had more business than they could handle. Such spectacular growth continued with the development of e-commerce on the business-to-business side. Waggener Edstrom easily topped the high-tech public relations field with almost double the income of its nearest rival. It launched Waggener Edstrom Interactive to extend its core set of public relations and marketing communications services to the Web and formed a strategic relationship with Net Perceptions, Inc. In the wake of this development, Microsoft shifted most of the public relations for its MSN-branded Internet businesses back to Waggener Edstrom.

In anticipation of continued growth, Waggener Edstrom undertook organizational change in 2000, hiring six new

---

Key Dates:

1983: Melissa Waggener founds The Waggener Group; Pam Edstrom, Jim Buchanan, and Jody Peake join the company a few months after its opening.
1985: Waggener takes on Microsoft as its client.
1990: Company changes its name to Waggener Edstrom.
1998: Company acquires InSync Communications.
1999: Waggener Edstrom launches Waggener Edstrom Interactive to further extend its online services.
2000: Company opens a new office in Austin, Texas.
2001: Company acquires pr.com and opens a new office in London.

---

vice-presidents to broaden its senior leadership team. It also moved and expanded its four-person office in Germany and opened a new office in Austin, Texas. The company, which was 15th in billings among worldwide public relations companies in 2000, was ranked by *Working Woman* as among the top 500 women-owned businesses in the United States. It was named repeatedly as one of the best companies to work for in Washington and Oregon by *Washington CEO* and *Oregon Business*.

Early in 2001, Waggener Edstrom acquired pr.com, a Kirkland, Washington-based public relations agency that focused on wireless and wireless Internet communications technology clients, and made it a subsidiary. With high-tech poised for a possible dip in income in coming years, Waggener targeted the telecommunications hardware, biotech, and science and technology sectors to diversify its client base. One of the last independents among the nation's top 20 public relations firms, Waggener Edstrom opened a new office in London and moved to new offices in Washington state.

Principal Subsidiaries

pr.com.

Principal Competitors

atomic PR; BSMG; Brodeur Porter Novelli Convergence Group; Fleishman-Hillard Public Relations (parent of KVO); Omnicom Group; Shandrick; True North Communications Inc.; Weber PR.

Further Reading

Hamm, Steve, "The Gates Keepers," *PC Week,* March 3, 1997, p. A1.
Humble, Charles, "Portland High Tech Public Relations Group Achieves Splashy, Timely Entry," *Oregonian,* April 15, 1984, p. D1.
Marks, Anita, "Waggener Edstrom: Voice of PC Industry," *Business Journal* (Portland), April 8, 1994, p. 15.
McClaran-Saba, Robbie, "Hitched to Microsoft," *Your Company,* June/July 1998, p. 54.
"Pam Edstrom," *Business Journal* (Portland), February 25, 2000, p. 9.
Williams, Elisa, "Microsoft Public Relations Agency Awaits Possible Fallout," *Oregonian,* April 10, 2000, p. A8.
Woodward, Steve, "Tektronix's Marketing Bastion Goes Out, Multiplies," *Oregonian,* June 11, 2001, p. F4.

—Carrie Rothburd

Watson Wyatt Worldwide

Watson Wyatt & Company Holdings
1717 H Street, NW
Washington, D.C. 20817
U.S.A.
Telephone: (202) 715-7000
Fax: (202) 715-7700
Web site: http://www.watsonwyatt.com

Public Company
Incorporated: 1958 as The Wyatt Company
Employees: 4,200
Sales: $700.2 million (2001)
Stock Exchanges: New York
Ticker Symbol: WW
NAIC: 541611 Administrative Management and General
   Management Consulting Services

Watson Wyatt Partners
Watson House, London Road
Reigate, Surrey RH2 9PQ
England
Telephone: +44 1737 241144
Fax: +44 1737 241496
Web site: http://www.watsonwyatt.com

Private Partnership
Founded: 1878 as R. Watson & Sons
Employees: 1,800
NAIC: 541611 Administrative Management and General
   Management Consulting Services

Watson Wyatt Worldwide is an affiliation of two independent entities formed to provide global actuarial, benefits, and human resources consulting services. Watson Wyatt Partners, based in the United Kingdom, is a private partnership with 25 offices in England, Ireland, and Europe. Watson Wyatt & Co., based in the United States, has 62 offices in 18 countries in the Americas and the Asia/Pacific region, and is the principal

subsidiary of Watson Wyatt & Company Holdings, a public company. Watson Wyatt & Co. employees own about two-thirds of the shares. The two affiliates share resources, technologies, processes, and business referrals.

The Wyatt Company: 1946–69

In 1946, Birchard (Byrd) E. Wyatt and seven partners cofounded The Wyatt Company of Consulting Actuaries. B.E. Wyatt was in his 30s, with an M.B.A. from the Wharton School of Business and work experience at the Social Security Administration. Wyatt opened offices in Washington, D.C., and New York, as well as in the midwestern cities of Detroit, Chicago, and Cleveland.

The following year, William Rulon Williamson became president of the company, working in the Washington, D.C. office. Williamson helped set up the Social Security program as chief actuary of what became the Social Security Administration, and it was there that he met B.E. Wyatt. Under Williamson the company established its Executive Compensation Service and initiated an annual survey of the salaries of top managers in companies across the country. Wyatt's first Top Management Survey was released in 1949. Williamson resigned from the company in 1950 to start his own company.

As actuaries, the Wyatt partners evaluated the risks, such as life expectancy and accidental or premature death, on groups of people. In this capacity, they helped clients set up pension plans, determined premium rates, and advised investment managers of the resulting pension funds.

Wyatt expanded as tax and pension laws changed, beginning with the 1957 Federal Welfare and Pension Plans Disclosure Act. In 1958, the partners incorporated the organization as The Wyatt Company. By that time it had eight offices, including one in Canada. By 1962, Wyatt had offices coast to coast.

Pension Concerns: 1970s

In 1971, Wyatt published its first annual Employee Compensation Survey, examining the pay of office workers. With the passage of the 1974 Employee Retirement Income Security Act

(ERISA), more and more businesses turned to pension consultants to help them revise and administer their pension plans. That law resulted in many companies terminating their defined benefit plans and switching to other types of programs. According to a survey reported in a 1977 *Washington Post* article, in 1973, 87 percent of responding companies provided retirement benefits. By 1977, that figure had dropped to 80 percent.

Under defined benefit plans, firms had to pay the promised benefits no matter what happened to their profits or assets. Companies began to explore options such as profit sharing, employee stock ownership plans, and Individual Retirement Funds that defined contributions (how much an employer paid in) rather than how much would be received when someone retired.

During this time, Wyatt grew by opening new offices and buying other actuarial companies. In 1975, it bought Cole & Associates, a Boston-based firm, and in 1979, the company expanded overseas, acquiring U.K.-based Harris Grahman Pattison and opening offices in Hong Kong and Malaysia.

Employee Benefits Consulting: 1980s

By the beginning of the 1980s, Wyatt employed more than 400 actuaries and employee benefits consultants and operated 21 offices in the United States and another 12 in Canada, Europe, and Asia. It soon moved into Latin America, opening an office in Mexico, and in 1985, it conducted the first compensation survey of employees of multinational corporations in the People's Republic of China. In addition to pension planning and plan administration, the company now offered its more than 8,000 clients such consulting services as risk management, international services, and employee communications.

In 1986, Congress passed the Tax Reform Act, adding to employers' demand for consultants. At the same time, many businesses were moving toward offering more diverse and "flexible" kinds of benefits. Recognizing that all employees did not have the same family patterns or saving habits, plans began appearing that let employees choose benefits packages suited to their own needs regarding health and dental insurance, life insurance, annuities, and other retirement options.

By 1988, Wyatt was experiencing growth at a rate of 20 percent a year through aggressive marketing, and Michael H. Davis, operating out of the Boston office, was named chief executive officer. In 1989, the company had 3,500 employees and revenues of $332 million from its benefits consulting, making it the third largest employee benefits consultant in the world, behind William M. Mercer Inc. and TPF&C.

Wyatt created Wyatt Software Services, Inc. to develop software packages to help administer benefits programs and opened its 35th foreign office in Gothenburg, Sweden. The company now had more offices outside the United States than it had in the country.

Uncertain Times: 1990–95

At the beginning of the decade, Wyatt's healthcare consulting business was growing rapidly as employers tried to control health and medical expenses. Its overseas business also grew, with new offices opened in Europe and Indonesia. In 1991, the company had revenues of $440.5 million.

During 1992, the company developed alliances to provide administration and investment management services for 401(k) retirement plans and to offer benefits administration services to its large U.S. clients. It also was appointed to help design healthcare programs for the governments of Costa Rica and New Zealand. But with the recession and uncertainty about federal healthcare proposals, employers began cutting back on using consultants and all major benefits consultants saw revenues slide. Wyatt experienced its first drop in revenue and a loss of more than $10 million. The company indicated that its U.S. operations were making money but losses occurred overseas and in its software operations. Wyatt downsized and created a new regional management structure.

A.W. (Pete) Smith became CEO of Wyatt in 1993. Smith joined Wyatt in 1975 with the acquisition of Cole & Associates and eventually managed the Wyatt office in San Francisco. In that position, he arranged the joint ventures between IBM and Apple Computer that created Taligent and Kaleida. Smith's philosophy, according to an interview with the *Washington Post*'s Jonathan Glater, was that professional service organizations should "provide services that help clients . . . not to have services that need to be sold."

Smith implemented that philosophy through the One Wyatt Vision, which continued the firm's traditions of local independence and professional freedom while urging its offices to use a common approach and make better use of the expertise within the organization. For example, in anticipation of more clients outsourcing the administration of all of their benefits, Smith centralized Wyatt's plan administration services into one profit center. He also announced that Wyatt would be forming a marketing alliance with R. Watson & Sons, a U.K. actuarial firm.

R. Watson & Sons:
Late 19th-Century Company Origins

R. Watson & Sons (Watsons) was a private partnership headquartered in Reigate, outside of London. Started in 1878, it had grown from a family operation to become the leading benefits consultant to major U.K. companies and a strong insurance consulting firm. During the 1980s, the firm began moving into Europe.

In 1982, Watsons combined with two other U.K. actuarial firms, Racon & Woodrow and Duncan C. Fraser, to form European Actuarial Consultancy Services (EURACS). EURACS bought the pension consulting division of Banque Bruxelles

Key Dates:

1878: R. Watson & Sons is founded in England.
1946: B. E. Wyatt and others found The Wyatt Company in the United States.
1958: The Wyatt Company is incorporated.
1995: The Wyatt Company and R. Watson & Sons form a marketing alliance, creating Watson Wyatt Worldwide.
1996: Affiliates change their names to Watson Wyatt & Company and Watson Wyatt Partners.
2000: American unit goes public as Watson Wyatt & Company Holdings.

Lambert, the second largest bank in Belgium. This enabled the firms to expand into continental Europe to better access multinational companies for their employee benefits, insurance, and compensation packages. This was a response to the trend of multinationals to seek pension and related consulting services from one company. In 1989, Watsons formed Watsons Europe, a pan-European financial consulting service.

Changes in legislation and reductions in employee benefits under England's state pension program led Watsons to propose an industrywide pension program for the engineering industry. In 1987, Watsons, working with the Engineering Employers' Federation, appointed Friends Provident, one of Britain's major mutual life insurance companies, to develop and administer the Engineering Industry Pension Scheme (EIPS). Enrollment was voluntary and the new program offered employers an option to the state pension scheme. EIPS was particularly attractive to small and medium-sized companies because it made it possible for them to offer employees diverse packages to meet their specific needs.

Watsons continued to expand internationally, and by 1994 it had 800 employees in 14 offices in the United Kingdom, Ireland, continental Europe, the Caribbean, and Africa.

A Global Alliance: 1995

In April 1995, the alliance between R. Watson & Sons and The Wyatt Company became final. The two firms would operate globally under the name Watson Wyatt Worldwide, sharing resources, technologies, and consulting expertise but maintaining their independent entities. Linkages between a U.S. benefits consulting company and an overseas consulting firm were just beginning to be tried, with several objectives: to help U.S. clients in foreign markets, to gain new customers, and to gain an advantage in a very competitive environment.

Watson Wyatt Worldwide had 4,500 employees in 89 offices and generated more than $500 million in fees. Each firm remained independent—Watsons as a partnership and Wyatt as an employee-owned corporation. Wyatt's actuarial practice was weak on the European continent, while Watsons' was strong. Wyatt had 11 benefits consultant offices, however, and Watsons had only four. Thus the new alliance allowed both companies to combine their expertise into a larger and stronger presence on the continent.

To establish the alliance, Wyatt transferred its U.K. operations to Watsons in exchange for a 10 percent interest in the partnership's defined distribution pool and a seat on Watsons' management committee. Watsons purchased about 2 percent of Wyatt's privately held stock and gained a seat on Wyatt's board. The two firms also consolidated their European operations into Watson Wyatt Holdings (Europe) Limited, with Watsons owning 75 percent of that new entity and Wyatt the remaining share. The alliance resulted in only a few layoffs, with all 200 of Wyatt's employees in its U.K. offices transferring to Watsons' offices. Under the alliance, Wyatt took the lead role in the Americas and the Asia-Pacific region and Watsons had primary responsibility in Europe, Africa, and the British Caribbean.

The alliance formed a four-person management committee to oversee Watson Wyatt's strategy. The committee was chaired by Wyatt's president, "Pete" Smith; its COO, Paul Daoust; Robert Masding, Watsons' incoming senior partner; and Philip Cockbain, head of Watsons' benefits practice. In July 1996, the two firms legally changed their names. Wyatt became Watson Wyatt & Company; Watsons became Watson Wyatt Partners.

In and Out of Outsourcing: 1995–99

The global alliance, the One Wyatt Vision, an improved economy, the movement toward managed healthcare, and employers' interest in streamlining benefits resulted in a nearly 30 percent gain in earnings for Watson Wyatt Worldwide for fiscal 1995. This was the largest increase among the top ten benefits consulting firms, most of which also posted double-digit growth figures.

At the end of December 1995, Watson Wyatt announced a joint venture with State Street Bank and Trust Co. to provide benefits administrative outsourcing. The venture, Wellspring Resources LLC, built on Watson Wyatt's outsourcing centers in Florida and Minnesota, established a few years earlier. Developing an outsourcing practice was a very expensive undertaking, however, costing about $25 million according to Michael Schachner in a December 1995 article in *Business Insurance*.

Over the decade, Watson Wyatt invested heavily in developing proprietary technology to meet clients' human resources needs. Its web-based e-HR systems made it possible for employees to access human resources information and programs very easily. Through these virtual HR departments, employees could go online any time to make changes in their 401(k) plans or add a dependent to a health plan, among other things.

After a comprehensive strategic review of its operations, Watson Wyatt decided to focus on its strengths rather than try to provide every service to a client. Its first move was to get out of the administration outsourcing business. The company wrote off its $58.7 million investment and spent another $60 million to end its relationship with Wellspring Resources. The firm also sold its risk management consulting business to Towers Perrin (1998) and transferred its recordkeeping business for defined contribution plans to First Data Investor Services Group (1999). For 1999, Watson Wyatt had revenues of $761.3 million, with $647.1 million coming from benefits consulting.

The company also got a new president and CEO, John J. Haley. Haley joined Watson Wyatt in 1977 and was global director of the benefits group before becoming president. Later that year, Haley announced plans to sell about 25 percent of Watson Wyatt's stock to the public, the first public stock offering by a major benefits consultant.

Human Capital Consulting: 2000

Watson Wyatt & Company now concentrated on three lines of business: the benefits group, the human capital group, and the e-HR group, each of which contributed to helping clients such as General Electric, IBM, Microsoft, and General Motors attract, retain, and motivate employees.

In October 2000, in conjunction with the IPO, the company merged with a wholly owned subsidiary of Watson Wyatt & Company Holdings, becoming the holding company's primary subsidiary. The holding company was incorporated in January 2000. The stock sale raised $70 million, which Watson Wyatt planned to use to buy other firms.

Also in 2000, Watson Wyatt increased its Canadian benefits consulting services with the acquisition of KPMG Canada and launched the Watson Wyatt Human Capital Index, a research tool that showed a clear connection between human resources strategies and a company's bottom line. Meanwhile, Watson Wyatt Partners added a human capital group to its services, which also included risk and healthcare consulting, insurance and financial services consulting, investment advice, and pension administration.

2001 to the Present

In 2001, a jury awarded the Connecticut Carpenters Pension Fund $32 million in damages in its suit against Watson Wyatt. The suit claimed errors in valuations during the 1990s that resulted in undervalued liabilities. Watson Wyatt's appeal of the amount was denied. In June of that year, the company held a second public offering of stock and in August announced an alliance with Workscape Inc. to develop and deliver Employee.com, an online HR portal that would provide employees with company-sponsored information.

With a fairly tight employment market, the outlook for human resource consultants was rosy. Within the field, however, a major issue continued to be how to provide clients with all of the various services they needed. Watson Wyatt President John Haley explained his philosophy in a 2001 *Consulting Magazine* article: "There are a lot of consulting firms that built their strategy around one-stop shopping. But our view is that these are sophisticated buyers of services. Just because you may have access from providing one service to them, you don't get to sell them other services unless those services are also world-class." Watson Wyatt hoped to develop various partnerships with its competitors to meet specific needs of individual clients. If successful, that strategy would be implemented globally through Watson Wyatt Worldwide. The market, the human resources consulting field, and the clients would decide.

Principal Subsidiaries

Watson Wyatt & Co.; Watson Wyatt Holdings (Europe) Limited.

Principal Competitors

William M. Mercer; Towers Perrin; Hewitt Associates; Accenture; EDS.

Further Reading

"Actuary Who Helped Set Up Social Security," *Washington Post,* August 3, 1980, p. B6.

Barker-Benfield, Simon, "Wellspring Losing Corporate Parent," *Florida Times-Union,* March 10, 1998, p. B4.

Chernoff, Joel, "Wyatt, Watson Join Forces," *Pensions & Investments,* April 3, 1995, p. 37.

Cox, Brian, "U.S. Benefit Consultants Seek Footing Overseas," *National Underwriter, Property & Casualty/Risk & Benefits Management Edition,* June 5, 1995, p. 10.

Cuff, Daniel F., "Next Leader of Wyatt Built Up Boston Office," *New York Times,* December 5, 1988, p. D4.

Elder, Charles, "Actuary Industry Has More Room for Minorities," *Washington Post,* July 31, 1989, p. F5.

"Firm Expands Service," *Pensions & Investment Age,* January 9, 1989, p. 22.

Geisel, Jerry, "Watson Wyatt Plans an IPO," *Business Insurance,* November 29, 1999, p. 1.

Glater, Jonathan D., "Consulting Firm's CEO Bridges Coastal, Culture Shock," *Washington Post,* July 26, 1993, p. F9.

"Industry-Wide Pension Plan for the Engineering Industry," *Universal News Services,* September 16, 1987.

Lippman, Thomas, "Flexible Benefit Plans Getting New Attention by Pension Managers," *Washington Post,* November 8, 1981, p. G4.

"New Name for Wyatt & Watson," *Management Consultant International,* June 1996, p. 7.

"Pension Reform—A 'Boon' That's Backfiring for Many," *U.S. News and World Report,* June 16, 1975, p. 73.

"Public Companies: Consulting/Professional Services," *Washington Post,* April 30, 2001, p. T8.

Ross, Nancy L., "Retirement Concerns Growing," *Washington Post,* November 13, 1977, p. G1.

Schachner, Michael, "Employee Benefits Marketplace," *Business Insurance,* p. 3.

Short, Eric, "Actuaries Launch European Operation," *Financial Times* (London), February 2, 1982, p. 6.

"Watson Wyatt IPO Draws $70 Million," *Washington Post,* October 16, 2000, p. E1.

"Watson Wyatt: The ABCs of Going Public," *Consulting Magazine,* April 2001.

Woolsey, Christine, "Top Consultants Double Revenues in Just Four Years," *Business Insurance,* December 18, 1989, p. 3.

"Wyatt Forms Link with Watsons," *Business Insurance,* June 13, 1994, p. 1.

"Wyatt's Singular Vision," *Management Consultant International,* December 1994, p. 10.

—Ellen D. Wernick and Bill Koerner

The Weitz Company, Inc.

Capital Square
400 Locust Street, Suite 300
Des Moines, Iowa 50309-2331
U.S.A.
Telephone: (515) 698-4260
Fax: (515) 698-4299
Web site: http://www.weitz.com

Private Company
Incorporated: 1929
Employees: 1,450
Sales: $950 million (2001 pro forma est.)
NAIC: 23331 Manufacturing and Industrial Building
    Construction; 23332 Commercial and Institutional
    Building Construction; 233210 Single Family Housing
    Construction

The Weitz Company, Inc. is one of America's top-ranked general building construction companies. Its expertise in building industrial, commercial, and institutional facilities earned it a number of honors as a general contractor, construction manager, and design-build expert. It constructs office buildings, malls, schools, hotels, industrial plants, golf courses and clubhouses, and luxury custom homes. Some of its well-known clients are AT&T, Hyatt Regency, Ritz Carlton, Motorola, TCI, Marriott, Hy-Vee Food Stores, MCI, and Du Pont. The high-rise Fox Building in Los Angeles became one of the company's better known buildings when it was featured in the 1988 movie *Die Hard*. The Weitz Company is the nation's leading builder of senior living communities, assisted living facilities, and continuing care facilities, with 129 projects completed in 25 states, totaling $1.2 billion. Its web site declares it to be "the oldest construction company West of the Mississippi River," based on its 1855 origin. This employee-owned company in April 2001 reported 121 consecutive months, or more than ten years, of profitability, an enviable record, particularly in the construction business.

Origins and Early History

The Weitz Company was started by German immigrant Charles H. Weitz. After living in Columbus, Ohio, for two years, Weitz moved to Des Moines, Iowa, in 1852, just six years after Iowa became a state. He made a strategic decision to settle in Des Moines just as the city was named the state capital. When Charles Weitz Contractors, the original name of the business, was started in 1855, Franklin Pierce was in the White House and slavery controversies were tearing the nation apart.

Charles Weitz's early work included placing windows in the Savery House, building a saloon and saddlery, and erecting fences when other work declined. In 1878 the founder branched out into coal mining for a short while as an adjunct to the construction business. The company continued to win noteworthy commercial and residential projects, such as the Younkers department store in downtown Des Moines, through the end of the 19th century. Many of these buildings still stand and remain an elegant illustration of the company's insistence on quality.

Charles Weitz died in 1906, but his three sons continued under the name Charles Weitz' Sons General Contractors. In 1908 the three brothers built the Des Moines City Hall. In 1910 the company built Des Moines' Lexington Apartments, a six-story building at 18th and Pleasant Street that at the time was "considered the first high-rise building west of the Mississippi River," according to Chris Olson in the July 8, 1996 *Omaha World-Herald*. That was followed by construction of The Hubbell Building in Des Moines in 1913 and Camp Dodge in Johnston, Iowa, in 1917, the year the United States entered World War I. In 1919 the company built Hotel Fort Des Moines.

In 1929 the family business became incorporated under the name The Weitz Company, Inc. While many businesses failed during the Great Depression of the 1930s, The Weitz Company won federal contracts to build post offices in 42 states. With the economy back on its feet during World War II, The Weitz Company grew by building defense facilities, such as the Ankeny Ordnance Plant finished in 1942. The plant later became the John Deere Des Moines Works.

Post-World War II Developments

After the war ended in 1945, The Weitz Company diversified into the construction of different kinds of buildings, such as retail stores, retirement communities, educational buildings, apartments, and mixed-use structures. In 1948 it built the Des Moines Register building. It also built the Des Moines Art Center in 1968.

In 1960 Weitz went international and started building grain storage in Pakistan and other developing nations. Although the specialty need was short-lived, Weitz demonstrated once again a knack for developing expertise in knowledge in a specialized area of construction. That flair for discovering new markets continued to serve Weitz well as it began working in the continuing care and retirement community sector. The company landed its first big project in 1964 with Lakeview Village in Lenexa, Kansas. With an eye for opportunity, Weitz began developing specialized systems and procedures to build these facilities. The company's early entrance into the burgeoning retirement industry gained Weitz recognition as the leading builder of retirement communities and continuing care facilities. In 1971 Weitz complemented its construction expertise with the creation of Life Care Services, a separate company that became one of the first to design, manage, and develop continuing care and retirement homes for senior citizens.

The Weitz Company in 1973 built the Big Creek Dam and then in 1979 completed construction of the Des Moines Civic Center. In the 1980s it finished two other projects in central Iowa: Capital Square in 1983 and the Prairie Meadows horse race track in 1989.

Going National in the 1980s

Beginning in 1981, The Weitz Company began expanding beyond its traditional Iowa market by starting its Florida Division based in West Palm Beach. By 1985 the company had added offices in Phoenix and Boston, although the Boston office later was closed. In 1986 the company almost doubled its business by acquiring Al Cohen Construction based in Denver

and Colorado Springs. In 1987 The Weitz Company won the contract to build the Greenleaf Woods fitness center/office complex in Portsmouth, Massachusetts. It included a 33,000-square-foot sports club and seven office condominium buildings. The company was also the general contractor for Portsmouth's Sheraton Harborside hotel and condominiums. Based on its 1988 dollar volume from constructing institutional, commercial, and industrial buildings, The Weitz Company was ranked as the nation's 36th largest general contractor by *Building Design & Construction* in July 1989.

As Weitz expanded in the Southwest, the company found itself at the middle of a controversy that changed Arizona's bidding laws. In the late 1980s the city of Tempe, Arizona, and the Phoenix Cardinals requested bids to build a new training complex. Although Big D Construction Corporation of Ogden, Utah, had the lower bid, The Weitz Company was selected because of a state law giving local contractors preference if the bid was no more than 5 percent higher than the lowest bid. Although Weitz was based in Iowa, it also had a Phoenix office and had paid state taxes for two consecutive years.

Big D filed its original petition in Maricopa County Superior Court, but that request was denied. The state Court of Appeals also rejected Big D's request. At that point, Big D allowed The Weitz Company to go ahead with construction, but it did appeal to the state supreme court. The Arizona Supreme Court in 1990 ruled that the state law was unconstitutional. It said the law passed to aid local companies during the Depression ''creates an economic burden, not a benefit, for the public entities bound to follow it,'' as reported in the March 31, 1990 *Arizona Republic.*

Meanwhile, The Weitz Company in the late 1980s worked on more projects in eastern Nebraska. ''The company had been working in Omaha out of its Des Moines headquarters for several years before opening an Omaha office,'' said Leonard Martling, president of the company's Omaha Division in the July 8, 1996 *Omaha World-Herald.* ''We opened that office at about the time we were doing the renovation of Westroads Shopping Center and the construction of Two Pacific Place.''

When Bruce Willis starred in the 1988 Hollywood movie *Die Hard,* most viewers did not realize that the high-rise Fox Building in Los Angeles had been built by The Weitz Company. Weitz President Glenn DeStigter cringed when he saw the skyscraper explode into flames as the result of terrorist bombs, even though he knew it was just from special effects. ''You watch it with two eyes, one on the interesting movie and the other on what they're doing to our building,'' said DeStigter in the February 18, 2001 *Des Moines Sunday Register.* ''There's a personal pride in these things we build.''

The Weitz Company in the 1990s and Beyond

In 1995 The Weitz Company and Hy-Vee Food Stores Inc. formed Hy-Vee Weitz Construction to build, remodel, or expand Hy-Vee grocery stores. Before this joint venture, Weitz had built the Hy-Vee corporate headquarters in West Des Moines, Iowa, as well as Hy-Vee stores in Creston and Pella, Iowa. The first project of the joint operation was a new Hy-Vee

Key Dates:

1855: Charles H. Weitz founds the company.
1890: Weitz constructs home for the blind.
1903: Charles Weitz' Sons General Contractors is handed down to three sons.
1929: The business is incorporated as The Weitz Company, Inc.
1930: Weitz wins project to build post offices for the federal government and over the next several years completes projects in 42 states.
1960: Weitz builds grain storage in Pakistan and other developing countries.
1962: Weitz wins contract to build Lakeview Village, a retirement community in Lenexa, Kansas.
1971: Weitz starts Life Care Services, a developer and manager for continuing care retirement communities.
1980: Weitz expands by forming Weitz Southwest in Phoenix, Arizona.
1986: Company acquires Al Cohen Construction with offices in Denver and Colorado Springs and doubles in size.
1995: A management-led employee buyout of the construction company is completed, and Weitz adopts a Federalist style of management with autonomous divi-

sion offices; The Weitz Company, Inc. is incorporated as an "S" corporation, and the Omaha construction office becomes Weitz Nebraska, a full-service division; The Weitz Company and Hy-Vee, Inc. form Hy-Vee Weitz Construction, L.C.
1998: Weitz Golf International LLC is founded in North Palm Beach, Florida, to work with golf course designers including Jack Nicklaus.
1999: Weitz Golf International goes bicoastal with the acquisition of Fairway Construction, a golf course builder in Temecula, California; based on its 1998 revenues, the company is listed for the first time in *Forbes* magazine's list of the nation's largest 500 privately held companies.
2000: Weitz Iowa acquires Abell-Howe Construction Inc. of Cedar Rapids, Iowa, and a new division is launched: Weitz Kansas City in Overland Park, Kansas.
2001: Weitz Colorado purchases Norris & Associates, a Glenwood Springs, Colorado-based builder of commercial buildings and homes; Weitz expands employee ownership opportunities by reorganizing as a limited liability company, effective January 1.

grocery store in Lincoln, Nebraska. The company initially expected to generate annual revenues of between $50 million to $70 million. Weitz and Hy-Vee each owned half of the new firm and shared equally in its profits.

Soon after the Hy-Vee alliance was started, Weitz began another joint venture. It partnered with Impark Limited, a major developer and manager of parking structures, to create Imperial Weitz, which was set up to build and repair parking facilities.

The company in 1995 became an employee-owned firm after four generations of Weitz family ownership. A debt-free buyout resulted in about 150 managers and executives owning the company. According to its web site, in 1995 the "new leadership of Weitz adopted a new management style based on the Federalist model ... by allowing for its diverse operational units to be allied under a common flag with a shared identity." In December 2000 the company's board of directors broadened the opportunities for more employees to own part of the company, so that in 2001 more than 250 employees were Weitz shareholders.

The Weitz Company in 1996 built the Principal Financial Group "Z" Building. In October 1996 officials of Palm Beach Atlantic broke ground on their $5.5 million recreation center to be built by The Weitz Company, the general contractor. The West Palm Beach, Florida complex was designed to include a fitness center, indoor jogging track, courts for handball and racquetball, an 1,800-seat main arena, an auxiliary gym, and four locker rooms.

By summer 1996 the Omaha Division of The Weitz Company had constructed seven projects in Omaha. The Omaha

Division also finished two projects in Blair, Nebraska (Dana College's classroom center and its Trinity Chapel and MidAmerica Computer Corporation's facility) and two in Lincoln, Nebraska (Somerset Apartments and the Gateway Mall's enclosure). At the same time the division was planning or working on the Council Bluffs Holiday Inn Hotel and Suites; the Marble Rose Estates assisted living facility in Bellevue, Nebraska; and the Kellom Heights town homes and St. Vincent de Paul Education Center in Omaha.

In 1998 The Weitz Company seized the opportunity to enter a new arena of business. Weitz Golf International, LLC was founded in December 1998 and immediately teamed with Golden Bear Golf, the design firm of golf great Jack Nicklaus, to work on several projects. The Weitz Company previously had built The Links at Spanish Bay, a Pebble Beach, California golf course; and clubhouses for John's Island Golf Course in Vero Beach, Florida; the Tonto Verde Golf Club in Rio Verde, Arizona; the Ibis Golf and Country Club in Palm Beach Gardens, Florida; Ancala Golf Club in Scottsdale, Arizona; Columbine Country Club in Littleton, Colorado; and Wellington, Florida's Binks Forest Club. In a *Business Wire* dated December 14, 1998, Golden Bear Golf Chairman Jack Nicklaus said, "Golden Bear Golf made a decision to team with a contractor who has a national reputation for quality and integrity. The company's track record speaks for itself."

Building Design & Construction in July 1999 ranked The Weitz Company number 25 out of 70 contractors, based on the 1998 dollar volume of construction of commercial, institutional, and industrial buildings. Commercial buildings accounted for 72 percent of Weitz volume, with 14 percent from industrial buildings, 11 percent from institutional buildings, and the rest from water treatment plants.

In 2000 The Weitz Company acquired Abell-Howe Construction Inc. of Cedar Rapids, Iowa. Founded in 1921 as a Chicago cable and chain company, Abell-Howe became a general contractor in the 1930s and began in Cedar Rapids in 1948. After World War II, it built Iowa City buildings such as the Collins Radio Building, the Square D plant, and structures for the National Biscuit Company and Sheller Globe. It also completed buildings for Iowa Electric, Weyerhaeuser, Alliant, Archer-Daniels-Midland, Cargill, General Mills, Kirkwood Community College, Brenton Banks, and Guaranty Bank & Trust.

Examples of Weitz construction projects included the expansion and renovation of The Breakers Hotel in Palm Beach, Florida; mechanical parts of the central heating and cooling plant in Denver's new airport terminal; and the corporate office building for Hi-Bred International Inc. in Des Moines. Writer William Ryberg reported in February 2001 that The Weitz Company and Kansas City's Turner Construction Company had been selected to construct the $160 million Iowa Events Center in Des Moines.

Experienced leaders played a key role in the company's success in gaining and fulfilling such contracts. For example, its nine division presidents averaged more than 20 years with the company, and all were promoted through the ranks. Its superintendents had more than 25 years' average experience. Weitz President and CEO Glenn DeStigter, a graduate of Iowa State University, began with The Weitz Company in 1968, continuing his own family's tradition in the construction business.

Other factors also were important. Its 35 project web sites strengthened communications among its subcontractors, architects, engineers, and others. In a traditionally male occupation, The Weitz Company hired many women. Such innovations in technical and personnel matters, combined with its heritage of accomplishment and sound leadership, prepared The Weitz Company for future success.

Principal Subsidiaries

Capital Resources Group, Ltd.; Village Distributors, Inc.; Vulcan Construction Company.

Principal Divisions

Weitz Corporate; Weitz National; Weitz Arizona; Weitz Colorado; Weitz Iowa; Weitz Florida; Weitz Nebraska; Weitz Golf International; Hy-Vee Weitz; Imperial Weitz.

Principal Competitors

Sundt Corp.; Turner Corporation; Whiting-Turner; JE Dunn; Kiewit; Taylor Ball.

Further Reading

Bergstrom, Kathy, "Weitz Helps Hy-Vee Build Better Food Stores," *Des Moines Register,* January 31, 2000, p. 3.

"Builder Preference Statute Criticized," *Arizona Business Gazette,* September 29, 1989, p. L9.

"Golden Bear Golf, Weitz Form Construction Venture," *Business Wire,* December 14, 1998.

Olson, Chris, "Weitz Construction Game Still Growing After 141 Years," *Omaha World-Herald,* July 8, 1996, p. 12.

Otterson, Chuck, "PBA's Sports Complex Underway," *Palm Beach Post,* October 25, 1996, p. 8C.

"Portsmouth Contract Awarded," *Boston Globe,* May 10, 1987, p. 22.

Ringo, Kyle, "Century of Construction on Display in VP's Office," *Rocky Mountain News,* June 2, 2001, p. 10C.

Ryberg, William, "Builder's Success Shoots Sky-High," *Des Moines Sunday Register,* February 18, 2001, pp. 1D-2D.

Taylor, John, "Hy-Vee Forms Building Firm," *Omaha World-Herald,* September 28, 1995, p. B19.

Winters, John, "Law Favoring Local Bidders Declared Unconstitutional," *Arizona Republic* (Phoenix), March 31, 1990, p. B4.

—David M. Walden

West Corporation

West Corporation is a major provider of a variety of telephone-based services for large corporations. AT&T, Microsoft, IBM, Nuance, Dell, Compaq, Bank of America, Cisco Systems, MCI Worldcom, Nortel Networks, and Dialogic are some of its customers. West handles live inbound and outbound calls and automated interactive teleservices. It operates 30 call centers and seven automated voice and data processing centers in North America and India. Its approximately 25,000 Information Age employees use the most advanced telephone, voice, and Internet technologies to provide customer service, telemarketing, credit card applications, prepaid phone card service, and a myriad of other specialized phone-based forms of assistance.

Origins and Early Years

Mary West, a teleservices pioneer, in 1973 founded Mardex, described by journalist Ray Tuttle as "one of the first telemarketing service agencies." Mardex grew to become one of the country's major companies handling inbound telemarketing phone calls. In 1978 Mary West founded WATS Marketing of America. Her husband Gary West left his hospital job the following year to become WATS's chairman, president, and CEO, while Mary West served as vice-president of finance. In 1980 they sold WATS to First Data Resources but remained as managers.

By the mid-1980s more such teleservices firms were started, including Sitel in 1985 in Omaha, Nebraska. In 1986 Mary West left WATS to start West TeleServices, her third teleservices firm. It also was founded in Omaha.

The company grew in the early 1990s, so that by 1994 it was handling 55 million operator-assisted calls annually. By December 1996 the company's Texas expansion had resulted in the employment of about 5,000 persons statewide. It was at that time San Antonio's fourth largest private employer and also operated facilities in El Paso and Killeen, Texas. Later several new facilities in Texas and other border states would be built. With clients in cellular services, office products, telecommunications, payroll systems, and financial services, West TeleServices was poised for major growth that required new investments.

IPO, Stock Decline, and Failed Bid to Go Private Again: 1996–98

By the mid-1990s several private companies, including West TeleServices, were succeeding in the relatively new call center business. Then in 1995 and 1996 eight companies in the industry went public. Sitel Corp. led the pack in June 1995, followed by Apac in October. In 1996 the "teleservice floodgates opened," said the *Wall Street Journal*'s Greg Ip on September 15, 1998.

On November 26, 1996 West TeleServices was the last of the eight companies to have its IPO. The first day of the IPO closed with the company's common stock at $21.88 per share, up from the initial price of $18 per share. The company's IPO raised $102.6 million, most of which was planned for repaying debts and notes issued to existing stockholders.

Like that of several competitors, West TeleServices' stock value declined in the next two years. In July 1998 it sold for a little more than $12 a share. This declining stock price was part of an industry trend caused by what Greg Ip called the "collision between flagging demand and expanding capacity." The American bull economy of the 1990s saw so many companies enter the call center business that an oversupply was created. In addition, some large corporations decided to decrease their contracts with teleservice firms. While stock of some of the companies increased from 200 to 600 percent at first, by September 1998 all eight traded below their IPO prices.

In July 1998 the three founders of West TeleServices tried to buy the company's publicly traded common stock and thus return it to a private corporation. Gary L. West, Mary E. West, and Troy L. Eden offered to pay about $126 million for the 14.8 percent of the company's common stock that they did not already own. The company's board formed a special committee to consider the offer, but in August the committee advised against the move. At that point, the three founders gave up their plan.

Company Expansion in the Late 1990s

Although West TeleServices was disappointed in its declining stock value, that did not stop the company from growing rapidly in the late 1990s. In November 1997 the company's Omaha employees were quite crowded, so the firm spent $14 million for the MFS Communications Company building on Miracle Hills Drive. Then it began moving executive and administrative staff to the new headquarters, while its vacated offices at its Maple Street location were quickly filled with employees from other crowded Omaha locations. By early November 1998 West TeleServices occupied most of its new headquarters, while WorldCom Inc., which had acquired MFS Communications, still had some offices in the building. West TeleServices at that time employed 1,850 individuals at 11 Omaha facilities.

The company chose to expand by diversifying its services. According to Ken Winston, vice-president of Boston-based Needham & Company, West TeleServices avoided the overcapacity problem of its competitors by offering three services: outbound calls, inbound calls, and interactive calls using computers.

That company strategy resulted in numerous call centers being opened in the late 1990s. As of May 1, 1997, West TeleServices operated seven call centers in Omaha; Hampton, Virginia; and the five Texas cities of Killeen, San Antonio, Universal City, Waco, and Lubbock. In 1997 the company opened call centers in Tulsa, Oklahoma; Memphis, Tennessee; Mobile, Alabama; and Texarkana, Arkansas. Eight additional call centers were started in 1998: Fayetteville, Arkansas; Reno, Nevada; Rockford, Illinois; Fort Smith, Arkansas; Lafayette, Louisiana; Carbondale, Illinois; and Dothan, Alabama.

West TeleServices' largest call center started in 1998 in Baton Rouge, Louisiana, which initially provided approximately 1,000 new jobs. The new center paid over $12 million annually to its workforce, which in turn created a local economic impact of over $86 million. The Louisiana state government provided a $250,000 grant to the company to train workers at the new center.

The new West TeleServices facility in Baton Rouge helped make that city prominent in the call center industry. By the end of 1999 it employed about 1,600 and planned to add another 2,400 employees in 2000. Other teleservices companies with Baton Rouge operations were Broadwing Communications and Convergys Corporation. In 2000 Baton Rouge led the nation with its addition of 4,500 new call center jobs.

With the advance of teleservices, more people disliked or even hated what they felt were unwanted and irritating telemarketing or phone survey calls. Phone companies began offering caller identification equipment to let people know who was calling before they picked up the phone. According to an Arbitron NewMedia survey reported in the *Omaha World-Herald* on September 26, 1999, 40 percent of Americans used caller identification, up from just 9 percent in 1995. In addition, in 1998 Ameritech began offering its Privacy Manager system to allow customers to block undesired incoming calls. U.S. West likewise provided blocking services, and individuals could write to the Direct Marketing Association to ask for their names to be eliminated from calling lists.

West TeleServices said such efforts would not hurt its business. "I don't see that as a problem," said Carol Padon, vice-president of investor relations, in the September 23, 1998 *Omaha World-Herald*. "We really only want to talk to people who want to talk to us. We certainly don't want to waste their time or ours." Padon added that West TeleServices did not make random calls but phoned only persons who already had some kind of business association with a client.

West TeleServices' expansion reflected the general growth in teleservices. Maureen Pettirossi said in a 1997 industry publication that "the industry has emerged to play a vital and dynamic role in the economy, representing an extremely large and fast-growing market totaling an estimated $81 billion." More companies decided to delegate such duties rather than worry about running an inhouse call center. One of the fastest growing segments of the telecommunications industry, call centers in 1997 brought in $18.3 billion in revenues. By the fall of 1998 over 1,000 companies provided some kind of call center assistance. The leaders of this relatively new industry were Convergys, West TeleServices, APAC Teleservices, and ITI Marketing Services.

West TeleServices used the latest technology to provide its phone services. For example, it began using Unicenter TNG technology provided by Computer Associates. Originally West had used its own software to automatically respond to calls, but it chose Unicenter TNG after one of its bank clients had security problems. Unicenter TNG provided a standardized way for West's UNIX servers to handle the increasing volume of calls for credit card applications, other customer service requests, web applications, and especially prepaid calling card customers. In 1997 *Telemarketing and Call Center Solutions* honored West TeleServices as the top provider of interactive services. In 1997

West handled 935 million minutes of teleservice transactions, and by late 1998 it had in place over 10,000 automated voice response ports, one of the largest capabilities in its industry.

Developments in 2000 and Beyond

In the fall 2000 campaign, Republican Rick Lazio ran against Democrat Hillary Rodham Clinton for the U.S. Senate seat from New York. The state Republican party, not candidate Lazio, sponsored telephone calls that indirectly criticized Mrs. Clinton for her ties to enemies of Israel. The calls made from the Lubbock, Texas facility of West TeleServices lasted only a few days before being discontinued by the GOP, after an article in the *New York Times* alleged that the calls were a form of push-polling that reputable pollsters do not use.

The company continued to increase its capabilities by opening a leased 35,000-square-foot call center in Beaumont, Texas, in early 2001. The new facility hired about 1,000 employees whose annual payroll was between $16 million and $18 million. Other new call centers that were opened in 2001 in Pensacola, Florida, and Harlingen, Texas, employed about 700 and 300, respectively.

In cooperation with eFunds Corporation, West Corporation in January 2001 opened a facility in Mumbai, India, that handled inbound customer service calls 24 hours a day, seven days a week. This call center, which began with 250 positions, was West Corporation's first facility outside North America.

West Corporation and other companies began operating call centers in India for several reasons.

First, many well-educated Indians were available who spoke excellent English, India being a former British colony. They learned American or British accents, depending on the clients they served. They also worked for as much as 70 percent less than what comparable workers would receive in the United States or Canada. Although such information workers earned more money than many in their country, critics said they were being exploited in sweatshop conditions. Others complained about the loss of local culture as a result of such globalized economic activities.

In 2000 West Corporation's total revenue was $724.5 million, an increase of 28.8 percent over 1999 revenue of $562.4 million. The company's net income rose 41.2 percent from $49.8 million in 1999 to $70.3 million in 2000. That excellent financial performance prepared it for the ups and downs ahead in the 21st century.

Principal Subsidiaries

West Telemarketing Corp.; West Interactive Corp.; West Telemarketing Outbound Corp.

Principal Competitors

Convergys Corporation; Sitel Corp.; RMH Teleservices, Inc.; TeleTech Holdings.

Further Reading

Duff-Brown, Beth, "Call-Center Industry Transplanting to India," *Salt Lake Tribune*, June 17, 2001, p. E6.

Ip, Greg, "IPO Profusion: Bull Market Has Sired Lots of New Stocks, But Few Are Stars—Despite Paltry Returns, Capital Chases Latest Fad and Creates Oversupply—The Rush into 'Teleservice,' " *Wall Street Journal* (European edition), September 15, 1998, p. 1.

Jakes, Lara, "GOP to Renew Anti-Clinton Calls," *Times Union* (Albany), October 31, 2000, p. B2.

Jordan, Steve, "West TeleServices Plans to Turn Private Again," *Omaha World-Herald*, July 21, 1998, pp. 14+.

Levy, Clifford J., "Polling Attack Against Clinton Is Reported," *New York Times*, October 28, 2000, p. B1.

Norris, Melinda, "New Headquarters; West to Open House," *Omaha World-Herald*, November 4, 1998, p. 37.

——, "Privacy Manager; Ameritech Sets Up System to Curb Telemarketing Calls," *Omaha World-Herald*, September 23, 1998, p. 22.

——, "Telemarketing Firms Find Good Times Are on Hold," *Omaha World-Herald*, August 9, 1998, p. 1M.

Pettirossi, Maureen, "Funding the Teleservice Growth Wave," *Telemarketing & Call Center Solutions*, February 1997, pp. 56–62.

Redman, Carl, "State Panel Oks Training Grant for Telemarketer," *Advocate* (Baton Rouge), November 21, 1998, p. 2C.

Russo, Ed, "Phone Devices Put Chill on Cold Calls Screening, ID Altering Telemarketing," *Omaha World-Herald*, September 26, 1999, p. 1A.

Tuttle, Ray, "West TeleServices Dialing Up 900 Jobs," *Tulsa World*, March 21, 1997, p. E1.

"West TeleServices Plans Stock Sale," *Omaha World-Herald*, October 15, 1996, p. 18.

"West TeleServices' Shares Rise in IPO," *Omaha World-Herald*, November 27, 1996, p. 14.

"West to Open Center in Waco," *Omaha World-Herald*, December 12, 1996, p. 35.

—David M. Walden

West Pharmaceutical Services, Inc.

101 Gordon Drive
Lionville, Pennsylvania 19341-0645
U.S.A.
Telephone: (610) 594-2900
Toll Free: (800) 345-9800
Fax: (610) 594-3000
Web site: http://www.westpharma.com

Public Company
Incorporated: 1923 as The West Company
Employees: 4,700
Sales: $430.1 million (2000)
Stock Exchanges: New York
Ticker Symbol: WST
NAIC: 326199 All Other Plastics Product Manufacturing
(pt); 33299 All Other Miscellaneous Fabricated Metal
Products Manufacturing; 327215 Glass Product
Manufacturing Made of Purchased Glass

West Pharmaceutical Services, Inc. is a world leading supplier to the pharmaceutical and healthcare industries, offering products to package, deliver, and dispense drugs. It began primarily as a packaging company but has moved, in recent years, into medical testing and medication delivery systems to better serve its customers. Its client list reads like a "who's who" of the medical industry.

1920s–30s: Early Years

Herman West was born in 1893 and raised by his mother in Minnesota after his father deserted the family. After working for two years after high school graduation to earn money to attend college, West traveled to the University of Pennsylvania. After a World War I tour in the Navy, he finished school, got married, and began working in a dental supply house.

It was in that first post-college position that he decided to begin his own dental supply firm. Thus in 1923, he, Frank Mancill, and two former university classmates, Jesse R. Wike

and Norman F. Wiss, founded The West Company. Located at 1117 Shackamaxon Street in Philadelphia, the company manufactured rubber "Burlew" grinding wheels for the dental trade as well as droppers, plungers, and stoppers for pharmaceutical companies. The company grew quickly and soon occupied more of Shackamaxon and nearby Day Streets. Although it was a manufacturing company, The West Company, because of its products, was closely related to the medical industry and innovations throughout that field.

In 1930, Dr. R.B. Waite, the founder of Cook-Waite Laboratories, Inc., acquired a 100-share interest in West and began collaborating on rubber closures that were compatible with medicinal solutions such as Novocain and insulin. Dr. Ralph Grafton was the head of the research and development at the company.

In 1931, The West Company purchased Simonds Abrasive Company. The new division manufactured wheels, measuring up to 20 inches in diameter, as well as a cut-off machine for foundry operations.

1940s: The West Company, Penicillin, and the War

Penicillin, discovered by Dr. Alexander Fleming, became a lifesaving antibiotic that The West Company helped to package. Because of World War II, the U.S. government soon became the largest customer for penicillin, but to deliver it at the speed and in the quantity the government required, new packaging had to be developed. A joint venture between The West Company, Alcoa, and Owens-Illinois created packaging (with The West Company providing the rubber stopper for the bottle). The packaging and collaboration made it possible for the troops and, later, civilians to receive the new "wonder drug." The abrasive division also was affected by the war and provided wheels for use in the production of army tanks, planes, and ships.

After the war was over, The West Company embarked on yet another venture—aluminum closures. The penicillin packaging used in the war had utilized aluminum closures from Alcoa, but after the war, The West Company hired Jim Underwood, an engineer at Alcoa, to work with Frank Andersen and Lee Rohde to develop aluminum caps that would be closely

Company Perspectives:

Our mission is to provide our customers with products and services that continuously improve the safety, comfort and convenience of pharmaceutical, healthcare and consumer products. We will do so by anticipating and creating products and services to meet market needs and challenges; achieving preferred relationships with customers, suppliers and other partners; being good corporate citizens and environmentally responsible; providing the West team with a challenging, rewarding and supportive environment. By serving our customers well, we will be profitable and will provide a reasonable return to our shareholders.

tied with the rubber sealing on the packaging. To achieve this goal, Jim Underwood designed a new piece of machinery, the Westcapper, in 1946. The Westcapper was an automatic capping machine used by the company for many years.

Herman West and one of the first investors in the company, Dr. Waite, had experienced conflict about the direction of the company. In 1945, Herman West, with the assistance of Eli Lilly, purchased all shares held by outside stockholders so that he could control the company.

With this new control, West obtained financing from Fidelity Bank and began construction of a new manufacturing facility. The facility, in Phoenixville, Pennsylvania, was completed in 1948, and the company vacated the Shackamaxon Street location that had been its home since the 1923 founding.

The company's product line had expanded as well. In 1947, the company produced more than 200 million individual rubber items, including penicillin stoppers, dental plungers, insulin stoppers, Burlew wheels, insert plungers for syringes, sleeve stoppers for parenterals (substances for cutaneous or intravenous injection), dropper bulbs, and other pharmaceutical packaging items. The company provided rubber goods to other industries as well, including golf ball centers and rubber bumpers for railroad cars.

1950s–60s: New Equipment and International Ventures

In 1951, a Millville, New Jersey plant was opened featuring larger production presses, designed by Herman West and created by John De Luca. The new presses could machine trim the rubber items, eliminating costly and time-consuming hand-trimming. Production capabilities increased by 300 percent, and in 1962, a third plant in Kearney, Nebraska, was built. By 1965, production increased to two billion rubber items and 560 employees.

Although the company grew in the United States, the international division took root in 1952. The older machinery from the U.S. plants was shipped to Mexico to be used by new subsidiary West Rubber de Mexico. Over the next 15 years, The West Company expanded to Argentina, Brazil, Colombia, Spain, England, Italy, Australia, and India.

In 1965, Herman West's son William S. West was elected president of The West Company. William had worked for the company for 15 years, and the year he became president sales reached $14 million. One of William West's first acts was to create a Corporate Management Committee to lead the company in future development decisions. Founder Herman West died after an illness in July 1965.

1970s: Going Public

In 1970, The West Company became a publicly held corporation through an initial public offering of $15 per share. The investment money was used to grow the company, with development of new products including pour-spouts for alcoholic beverages, intravenous packaging solutions, and dispensers for birth control pills. The H.O. West Foundation was formed in 1971 to provide college scholarships for employees' children. Sales grew from $26 million in 1970 to $43 million in 1973, with much of the growth in the international and pharmaceutical areas.

By 1975, The West Company employed more than 1,900 workers in the United States and 1,200 workers in international divisions. Many new products were introduced, including specimen collection containers, Flip-Off seals, and whiskey closure spouts. Sales in 1975 were $49.3 million.

In 1978, the company acquired Mack-Wayne Plastics. President Bill West wrote in the annual report, ''Mack-Wayne is a leading producer of plastic threaded closures offered in a wide range of designs and sizes. We think there is a very good fit between our companies—by joining forces, we become one of the largest producers, if not the largest, of plastic threaded closures in the U.S. market.''

It was in that same year that sales rose to more than $100 million. Also in 1978, the company was divided into six divisions—International, Mack-Wayne Closures, Medical Plastics, Metals/Glass/Machinery, Rubber, and Citation Plastics.

1980s: Changing with the Times

In 1980, the company became listed on the New York Stock Exchange, under the symbol WST. Two years later, a national scare helped fuel growth for the company. Tampering with Tylenol packaging created explosive growth in tamper-proof packaging, and stocks increased for packaging companies such as The West Company.

The early 1980s were consistently profitable for the company, but a downturn in early 1984 was attributed to reduced medical supply orders and a flood at one of the company's plants. The company responded to the downturn by halting the construction of a new packaging plant in Texas.

In 1985, William (Bill) West stepped down as CEO of The West Company, and for the first time a nonfamily member, Rene L. Guerster, was selected as the new president and CEO. Guerster had 15 years experience with the company, most recently serving as the president of West's Pharma-Packaging Division.

Despite a ten-year contract with Corning Glass and an increase in its plastics division, The West Company struggled to

Key Dates:

1923: The West Company is founded by Herman O. West.
1931: The West Company purchases Simonds Abrasive Company.
1941: The West Company helps to package penicillin.
1945: An Aluminum Closure Division is added to the company.
1948: Operations move to Phoenixville, Pennsylvania.
1952: West International division begins.
1965: William S. West, son of founder Herman, becomes CEO and president.
1970: The West Company goes public.
1980: Company joins the New York Stock Exchange.
1985: Rene Guerster becomes president and CEO.
1991: Guerster steps down; William Little is named as his replacement.
1999: Company name changes to West Pharmaceutical Services, Inc.
2000: Disappointing results cause temporary consideration of sell-off.

meet revenue goals in the middle to late 1980s. In early 1988, the company offered early retirement to its eligible salaried employees. Some 70 percent who were eligible accepted the offer.

At the end of 1988, the company realized an increase in sales to $285 million; in 1989, the trend continued, with sales rising to $308 million.

1990s: Forging Ahead with a New Plan

In 1990, The West Company, affected by an increase in raw materials and a softening European market, saw a decline in sales. In reaction, the company announced in January 1991 that it would be streamlining operations, consolidating glass production facilities, and reducing its salaried workforce further. The West Company's performance had another consequence for its CEO, Rene Guerster, who took early retirement in February 1991 after leading the company for six years.

In May 1991, The West Company selected its next CEO and president from outside the company's ranks. The new leader, William G. Little, had been serving in the healthcare division of The Kendall Company and had experience at Johnson & Johnson. Under Little's leadership, the company restructured its global operations and planned to reduce manufacturing, consolidate plants, and dispose of outdated assets. Sales increased slightly, from $323 million in 1990 to $329 million in 1991, while one-time costs associated with the restructuring netted a loss for the year.

In 1994, The West Company purchased Senetics, Inc., a Boulder, Colorado-based drug delivery company for oral and inhaled drugs. That, combined with other acquisitions, was aimed at adding service and testing businesses to the company.

The company's new strategies began to pay off in the mid-1990s with increases in sales and net income. In 1999, the company completed its shift in emphasis when The West Com-

pany became West Pharmaceutical Services, Inc. "West has transformed itself from a designer and manufacturer of products that support the packaging and delivery of injectable pharmaceutical and consumer healthcare products, to a broad-based supplier of products and services that support our customers' entire product development cycle," said CEO William Little.

2000: Branching Out to the Future

In its new role of testing in addition to manufacturing, West Pharmaceutical Services was involved in Phase I trials in early 2000 for the development of nasal morphine for pain as well as another nasal administered drug for endometriosis. Despite restructuring and development plans, however, the company showed disappointing results in 2000 and a 47 percent decline in profits in the third quarter of the year.

Changes in healthcare, including drug companies conducting in-house packaging and consolidating with other companies, adversely affected the company. West Pharmaceutical Services even considered selling its assets and retained an investment bank, UBS Warburg, to review alternatives for the company.

In late 2000, the company announced a 4 percent workforce reduction as well as the closing of its Cleveland office and two plants in Puerto Rico. William Little said of the year's results that it had been "the Company's most difficult year in recent history." Despite the difficulties, the company decided in 2001 not to offer itself for sale and, instead, to focus on the company's long-term possibilities.

Principal Subsidiaries

West Pharmaceutical Services A/S (Denmark); West Pharmaceutical Services Cornwall Ltd. (U.K.); West Pharmaceutical Services France S.A.; West Pharmaceutical Services Deutschland GmbH & Co. KG (Germany); West Pharmaceutical Services Lewes Limited (U.K.); West Pharmaceutical Services Singapore Pte. Ltd.; West Pharmaceutical Services Brasil Ltda. (Brazil); The West Company Mexico, S.A. de C.V. (49%); Daikyo Seiko, Ltd. (Japan; 25%).

Principal Competitors

Kerr Group; Owens-Illinois Inc.; Tekni-Plex.

Further Reading

Briggs-Gammon, Rosland, "Pennsylvania-Based Packaging Firm Taking a Profitable Direction," *Philadelphia Inquirer,* October 18, 1999.
Brubaker, Harold, "No Sale for Lionville, Pa. Drug Packaging, Services Firm," *Philadelphia Inquirer,* May 2, 2001.
Colyer, Edwin, "Research Groups Have Been Working on Replacing the Dreaded Flu Jab with a Quick Sniff," *Financial Times* (London), September 8, 1999, p. 12.
Gelles, Jeff, "Lionville, Pa.-Based Pharmaceutical Company to Close Plants, Cut Jobs," *Philadelphia Inquirer,* November 17, 2000.
"A History of The West Company: The First Sixty Years," Lionville, Pa.: The West Company, 1983.
Roberts, Ricardo, "West Hires Warburg to Work on Review," *Mergers and Acquisitions Report,* October 23, 2000.

Salmans, Sandra, ''Market Place; Tamper-Proof Packaging,'' *New York Times,* December 30, 1982, p. D6.

Trees, Jim, ''Get a Competitive Edge by Being a Better Customer,'' *Business and Management Practices,* April 1995, pp. 16–17.

Warner, Susan, ''Drug Firms to Develop Nasal-Delivery Flu Vaccine,'' *Philadelphia Inquirer,* July 3, 2001.

——, ''Lionville, Pa.-Based Drug Services Firm Reports Loss, Considers Selling Assets,'' *Philadelphia Inquirer,* October 17, 2000.

West, Franklin H., *Herman O. West—A Man and His Company,* Wynnewood, Pa.: Livingston Publishing Company, 1965.

—Melissa Rigney Baxter

WH Smith PLC

Nations House
103 Wigmore Place
London W1U 1WH
United Kingdom
Telephone: (020) 7409 3222
Fax: (020) 7514 9633
Web site: http://www.whsmithplc.com

Public Company
Incorporated: 1949 as WH Smith & Son (Holdings)
   Limited
Employees: 27,500
Sales: £2.58 billion ($3.77 billion) (2000)
Stock Exchanges: London
Ticker Symbol: SMWH
NAIC: 451211 Book Stores; 451212 News Dealers and
   Newsstands; 511130 Book Publishers; 454110
   Electronic Shopping and Mail-Order Houses; 422920
   Book, Periodical, and Newspaper Wholesalers

WH Smith PLC is one of Britain's oldest and best known retailing companies. The company's activities in book, newspaper, and stationery distribution and retailing over more than two centuries have made it a familiar part of daily commercial activity for British consumers. WH Smith is the United Kingdom's largest retailer of books and magazines through its chain of more than 530 WHSmith high street (main street) stores. These outlets also sell a wide range of other products, including stationery, maps, videos, CDs, DVDs, and electronic products. In addition to its main street stores, the group also runs more than 700 additional stores and newsstands in train stations and airports in Europe, the United States, Hong Kong, Singapore, and Australia. WH Smith is also involved in online retailing through its WHSmith.co.uk web site and in trade and electronic publishing through its ownership of Hodder Headline and Helicon, both of which were acquired in 1999. The group's U.K. market-leading newspaper and magazine distribution arm, WHSmith News, was put up for sale in early 2001.

First 100 Years: From Small "Newswalk" to Chain of Railway Bookstalls

WH Smith had its origins in a small "newswalk," or newspaper agency, in Little Grosvenor Street, London, opened by Henry Walton Smith and his wife, Anna, in 1792. Smith died only a few months later, and Anna ran the business by herself until her death in 1816, when her two sons, Henry Edward and William Henry, began trading as H & W Smith. In 1818 they moved to Duke Street, Mayfair, and by 1820 were in a position to open a second shop in the Strand, London. William Henry became the driving force in the business, and in 1828 the firm became known as WH Smith.

The opening of the business coincided with dramatic economic and social changes in Britain. The industrial revolution and a sharp acceleration in the growth of London changed the way the English lived; among the changes was the increase in importance of newspapers and journals. These catered to a new demand for keeping track of fast-moving economic and political developments and the turbulent international politics of the time, and provided a medium for advertising, which was becoming increasingly important as the English economic structure changed and new kinds of enterprises emerged. Another effect of the economic changes was the construction of an improved network of roads, allowing comparatively swift transport by stronger, safer horse-drawn coaches. William Henry Smith spotted the opportunities offered by these developments and changed the focus of his business from simply retailing publications to distributing them. He built up a fleet of light coaches and fast horses and began carrying papers from London along the new roads to stagecoach stops in the country, allowing rural readers access to metropolitan newspapers more quickly than ever before.

It was another product of the industrial revolution—the railway—that allowed the firm to grow dramatically into the leading newspaper seller in the United Kingdom. The railway network spread quickly across the country during the 1830s and 1840s, and William Henry Smith's son, William Henry Smith II, recognized the potential of the new system for newspaper distribution. The younger Smith had reluctantly abandoned his plans to become a clergyman and agreed to join the business in

Company Perspectives:

WH Smith has a history of innovation and creativity. We were the first to locate shops at points where people gathered to travel. We were also the creator of the "yellow back" book, known today as the paperback. Today we are the UK market leader of books, magazines and, most recently, DVD software.

My vision for WH Smith is to continuously inspire our customers by embracing the fantastic legacy of the WH Smith brand and our tremendous opportunities for the future.

At the heart of the vision lies the WH Smith brand. With its associations of trust and accessibility, it has enormous untapped power and potential.

—Richard Handover, Group Chief Executive

1842, at the age of 17, and soon showed himself to be as perceptive a businessman as his father. After being made a partner in 1846, giving the company the name WH Smith & Son, he took the opportunity offered when the London & North-Western Railway (LNWR) invited tenders for the sole bookstall rights on its lines. WH Smith & Son opened its first railway bookstall at Euston station, London, in 1848, signed a similar deal with the Midland Railway two weeks later, and soon won contracts with other railway companies.

Control of a monopoly retail operation at the heart of the mass transport system gave the company a perfect position from which to benefit from the booming British economy of the late 19th century. The volume of trade was big enough by 1853 for the firm to buy its first news wholesaling warehouse in Birmingham, the first in a large network of warehouses developed over the next few years. In 1849 William Henry Smith II broadened the company's base by creating a book department, and in 1851 he signed the first contract to handle advertising rights at railway stations with the LNWR, beginning an outgrowth of the business that developed swiftly. WH Smith & Son's railway bookstalls and the advertising space they sold made the company a ubiquitous presence in Britain throughout the second half of the 19th century, and created its position as one of Britain's retailing giants.

The success of the firm allowed William Henry Smith II to enter politics. After becoming a member of parliament in 1868, he retired from active partnership in the company and became in turn Parliamentary Secretary to the Treasury, First Lord of the Admiralty, Secretary for War, Irish Secretary, First Lord of the Treasury, and Leader of the House of Commons. His public prominence and attitudes prompted the humorous magazine *Punch* to nickname him "Old Morality." On his death in 1891, his widow was made Viscountess Hambleden and his 23-year-old son, Frederick, who later became the second Viscount Hambleden, became head of the company.

The company continued to develop steadily under Viscount Hambleden—opening a shop in Paris in 1903, followed in 1920 by another in Brussels, Belgium, and a bookbinding works in 1904—until its core business was threatened by a crisis in 1905. When contracts for the 200 bookstalls on the Great Western and LNWR lines ran out at the end of that year, the railway companies demanded higher rents from WH Smith & Son. The company decided that it could not afford the new prices and decided to deal with the loss of the railway bookstall monopoly by opening new shops near the stations, on the station approaches wherever possible. The replacement program succeeded, and the company managed to retain its sales despite the loss of the business upon which it had been founded. The opening of the new shops turned WH Smith & Son's operations into a more conventional newspaper, book, and stationery retail chain, and became the basis of its activities for most of the 20th century.

Viscount Hambleden died in 1928 and was succeeded as head of the company by his son, the third Viscount Hambleden. The need to pay death duties prompted the transformation of the firm into a private limited liability company in 1929. A similar process took place after the death of the third Viscount in 1948; a public holding company, WH Smith & Son (Holdings) Limited, was formed in 1949 to buy up all the share capital, which had been held by Viscount Hambleden, and issue shares publicly.

During the 1950s, the company began to branch out beyond its traditional business under the first chairman of the public company, David Smith, the third viscount's brother. During this decade WH Smith made its first major move into another country, opening several branches in Canada, first in Toronto and later in Ottawa and Montreal. The company also diversified within the United Kingdom by expanding into the specialty book market in 1953 with the acquisition of the Bowes and Bowes group of bookshops, which included City Centre Bookshops, Truslove & Hanson, and Sherratt & Hughes. The company also broadened its activities by adding recorded music to its shelves. The continuing growth in sales prompted the company to reorganize its retail distribution network, transferring the center from Lambeth in south London to a custom-built warehouse in Wiltshire. In the same period, one of the last vestiges of the old railway-based retail network ended when, in 1972, the company decided not to renew its contract for 23 main bookstalls and 63 kiosks in London underground stations after operating there for 70 years.

Diversifying Widely: 1973–89

In 1973, under a new chairman, Charles Troughton, the company launched a radical departure from its core business when it joined in a consortium bidding to take over the travel agency company Thomas Cook. The bid failed, but WH Smith pushed ahead with its plans to enter the travel agency business, opening a chain of agencies operating from within its existing shops in 1973. The company undertook a more ambitious move to diversify under the next chairman, Peter Bennett, when it entered the do-it-yourself hardware market in 1979, paying £12 million for the LCP Homecentres chain, which it renamed Do It

Key Dates:

1792: Henry Walton Smith and his wife, Anna, open a small newspaper agency in Little Grosvenor Street, London; Henry dies only a few months later; Ann continues to run the business.

1816: Ann Smith dies; her two sons, Henry Edward and William Henry, take over the firm, which adopts the name H & W Smith.

1828: After William Henry Smith becomes the driving force in the firm, the company becomes known as WH Smith.

1846: Smith's son, William Henry Smith II, becomes a company partner, prompting a name change to WH Smith & Son.

1848: Company opens its first railway bookstall at Euston station, London.

1905: Shift from railway locations to high street sites begins.

1929: Firm is transformed into a private limited liability company.

1949: Company is changed into a public holding company, WH Smith & Son (Holdings) Limited.

1973: First WH Smith travel agency opens.

1979: Company expands into the do-it-yourself hardware market with the acquisition of LCP Homecentres chain, which is later renamed Do It All.

1983: Company enters the cable and satellite TV industry with the establishment of WH Smith Television.

1985: Elson, a U.S. chain of gift shops in locations catering to the traveling public, is acquired.

1986: Our Price Music, a record shop chain, and Paperchase, a greeting card and stationery chain, are acquired.

1988: Company changes its name to WH Smith Group PLC (later dropping "Group" from its title).

1989: Firm acquires a controlling interest in the Waterstone's bookstore chain; office supplies division, WH Smith Business Supplies, is formed.

1990: The Do It All chain is merged with Boots' Payless chain to form a new Do It All entity, which is 50–50 owned by WH Smith and Boots.

1991: Company divests its travel agency operations and WH Smith Television.

1992: WH Smith acquires a 50 percent interest in Virgin Retail, operator of 14 Virgin Megastores.

1994: Our Price is merged with Virgin Retail to form Virgin Our Price, which is 75 percent owned by WH Smith.

1996: Company sells WH Smith Business Supplies, its stake in Do It All, and Paperchase; WH Smith posts its first loss in company history.

1998: WH Smith exits from the specialty music retailing sector with the sale of its stake in Virgin Our Price to Virgin Retail; the controlling stake in Waterstone's is also divested; 230 retail outlets of newspaper distributor John Menzies are acquired; the Internet Bookshop is acquired.

1999: Company enters the publishing field through the purchases of Helicon, a reference publisher, and Hodder Headline, a leading U.K. trade publisher.

2001: WHSmith News is placed on the auction block; WH Smith acquires Blue Star Consumer Retailing Group, operator of two market-leading bookstore chains, Angus & Robertson in Australia and Whitcoulls in New Zealand.

All, and expanding the chain. This was the first significant step away from the company's traditional businesses and existing shops, and it set the tone for the wave of diversification that was to follow in the 1980s under Simon Hornby, who was appointed chairman in 1982.

Following the move into hardware retailing, WH Smith's next steps to broaden its base took it into the television industry. Aiming to take advantage of the opportunities arising from cable and satellite television in Europe, in 1983 the group established WH Smith Television, a subsidiary designed to supply the industry with programs and related services. The group's involvement in television deepened the following year, when it bought a 15 percent stake in a cable television channel, Screen Sport, and paid £8.5 million for a 29.9 percent slice of Yorkshire Television. In 1985 the company added to these acquisitions by taking a stake in British Cable Programmes, a move that the *Financial Times* said "reinforces the company's emergence as the most significant investor in cable TV programming, after Thorn EMI." Later that year the company launched a satellite-delivered cable television channel marketed mainly toward women.

WH Smith also made a major move into the United States in 1985, paying $65 million for Elson, a chain of gift shops with 189 outlets in hotels, airports, office blocks, and railway stations throughout the country. The purchase was WH Smith's second attempt to break into the U.S. market, following the establishment in 1979 of an operation responsible for publishing and wholesaling English books, which took heavy losses. Hornby assured financial analysts that the earlier effort had been badly managed and that the latest entry would be very different.

In 1985 the company also increased its involvement in the recorded music industry, paying about £5 million for Music Market, a chain of 20 music shops. This move was a precursor to a bigger acquisition in the music market the following year, when the company paid the share equivalent of £46 million for the Our Price Music Ltd. record shop chain, bringing another 130 shops in London and southeast England into the group. A month later WH Smith expanded its stationery retailing activities by buying 75 percent of a greeting card and stationery business, Paperchase. The group also took the next step in its travel industry plans in 1986 by opening 100 freestanding travel agencies. The rash of acquisitions continued in 1987 with the group buying 32 retail outlets in Hawaii, bringing its total number of U.S. outlets to 308. It expanded its travel operations by paying £5.7 million for 32 travel agencies owned by the Ian Allan Group and bought a controlling interest in a television and video production company, Molinaire Visions.

However, as WH Smith diversified swiftly into new businesses, it received a serious blow to its oldest operation. When Rupert Murdoch's News International moved production of its British national newspapers into its new nonunion plant at Wapping in 1986, it appointed the Australian-based transport group TNT Ltd. as its transport contractor, ending WH Smith's 190-year-old role as distributor of the *Times* and the *Sunday Times*. With the papers delivered by road, the company's business delivering them from railway stations to shops and newsstands was redundant. In late 1987, TNT and News International signed an agreement consolidating TNT's move into the wholesale newspaper distribution market. This change cost WH Smith an estimated £40 million in annual sales. The group recovered most of these losses, however, in 1988 when it won wholesale distribution contracts from Express Newspapers, Mail Newspapers, and Mirror Group Newspapers worth an estimated £25 million. In the same year, the company changed its name from WH Smith & Son (Holdings) Ltd. to WH Smith Group PLC.

The problems in newspaper distribution did not stop WH Smith from pushing ahead with new areas of activity during 1988. In addition to its newspaper and book distribution divisions, the company created a third distribution area by moving into the commercial stationery supplies market, buying two stationery suppliers, Pentagon and Satex. It added to its recorded music operations by paying £23 million to Virgin Group for 67 of its smaller music shops and seven sites allotted to new shops. In a deal worth about £40 million, the group also leased two transponders—radio or radar devices which, upon receiving a signal, transmit a signal of their own—from the Luxembourg television satellite, Astra, to transmit a sports channel in which it was the major shareholder, as well as reinforcing its core business by buying a chain of 21 news agencies from Next. At the same time, the group rationalized its book operations by selling its 50 percent share in the U.K.'s largest book club, Book Club Associates, to joint owner Bertelsmann, the West German publishing group, for £60 million.

The breadth of the expansion during the 1980s left the group somewhat unwieldy, and in 1989 management began to dispose of a number of businesses, notably its North American operations. The most prominent of these was the sale of the group's Canadian subsidiary, WH Smith Canada Ltd., which had been operating for nearly 40 years. The trigger for the sale was an order from Canada's government for the group to sell 49 percent of the Canadian subsidiary to domestic investors to ensure a high level of Canadian ownership in the book industry. The company responded by pulling out of Canada completely, selling its entire 86.5 percent stake in the Canadian operation for about C$50 million. The sale included 133 WH Smith bookshops, 82 Classic Bookshops, 91 card shops, and a wholesaler of foreign newspapers and magazines, Gordon & Gotch. As part of a strategy to focus on retailing operations in the United Kingdom and the United States, in 1989 the group also sold its U.S. wholesale news division for $30 million, shortly after selling its U.S. publishing interests to Penguin Books U.S.A., a subsidiary of Pearson PLC. The company reduced its activity in Hawaii by selling a string of 24 shops, and 14 of WH Smith Travel's outlets were also closed.

The company had meanwhile increased its involvement in the U.K. book retailing industry by acquiring a controlling interest in the Waterstone's chain of 31 bookshops, the second largest independent chain in the country. The 1989 deal raised WH Smith's share of the U.K. book market from about 17 percent to 20 percent. The company merged the newly acquired shops with its existing subsidiary of 47 bookshops, Sherratt & Hughes. The commercial stationery arm was enlarged by the purchase of Sandhurst Marketing and Cartwright Brice, while the group also bought the remaining 48.9 percent of Molinaire Visions, which was experiencing problems. These and the previous commercial stationery acquisitions formed the basis of an office supplies division, WH Smith Business Supplies, which was established in 1989.

1990s and Beyond: Refocusing on Bookselling, Entering Book Publishing

WH Smith reorganized its noncore operations in 1990 by merging its Do It All chain of do-it-yourself hardware shops with Payless, a similar chain owned by the pharmaceutical retailing company Boots. WH Smith owned 50 percent of the new operation, which retained the Do It All name, and was expected to have annual sales of £550 million to £575 million. The company also extended its involvement in the U.S. recorded music market when it paid $23 million for a chain of 49 record shops in Pennsylvania, which it integrated with Wee Three, its existing U.S. chain of 36 music shops.

In 1991 the group's new operations in diverse markets began to appear uncertain, partly because of the impact of the recession in the United Kingdom that began toward the end of 1990. In January the company announced that profits in the previous six months had fallen by 7 percent, and as the year progressed, analysts predicted that profits would remain static. After spending an estimated £435 million to fund acquisitions and organic growth over the previous years, the company announced in May a major restructuring of its operations, including the sale of some of its largest noncore businesses and a refocusing on the traditional retail operations. As the U.K. financial journal *Investor's Chronicle* put it, the forays into satellite television, do-it-yourself retailing, and travel had failed. In view of the unexpectedly slow progress of the cable and satellite television market, the company announced the sale of its money-losing satellite television business, WH Smith TV, which had already absorbed £80 million of the group's money and was still believed to be two years away from breaking even. A consortium that included the French television company Canal+; the U.S. communications company Capital Cities/ABC; and the French water company Compagnie Generale des Eaux, paid £65 million for the television subsidiary. Also in 1991 WH Smith sold its travel agency business and launched its first rights share issue, aimed at attracting £147 million to finance a three-year expansion program in its core businesses and help reduce a £170 million debt left over from the company's previous rash of acquisitions.

Following these retrenchments, WH Smith moved forward on the music retailing front with the acquisition in 1992 of a 50 percent interest in Virgin Retail, operator of 14 Virgin Megastores, which sold videos, music CDs, and computer games. That same year, WH Smith acquired 59 stores from Record World and 20 stores from National Record Mart, using these outlets as the base for a new U.S. music retail chain, called The Wall. Two years later, the Our Price music chain was merged with Virgin Retail, forming Virgin Our Price, which was 75 percent owned by WH Smith and 25 percent owned by Virgin Group and which became the largest music retailer in the United Kingdom with annual sales of £350 million.

By the mid-1990s, the core WH Smith chain was suffering from declining sales and profits, with some analysts contending that the company's management had neglected the chain—letting the stores become dull and uninviting—because of the distractions of the remaining diversification ventures. The WH Smith chain was also facing increasing competition from specialty music and book chains and from grocery superstores, the latter of which were being rapidly expanded and included among their vast inventory books, newspapers, magazines, videos, and stationery—the very heart of the WH Smith chain. In response to the chain's travails, a remodeling program was launched, spending on advertising was increased, and the management took a more aggressive approach to promotions.

A turning point for the company as a whole came in 1996, the same year, coincidentally or not, that Philip Smith stepped down from the board, ending the involvement of the founding family in the company management. Early in that year, Bill Cockburn, who had been chief executive of the post office, replaced Malcolm Field as group chief executive. Cockburn immediately set upon a major strategic review of the group's operations. Cockburn quickly proved the wisdom of bringing in an outsider, when he made a number of major changes to the group's composition. In April 1996 WH Smith Business Supplies was sold to Guilbert, a French office supplies company, for £142 million. WH Smith also offloaded its share of the troubled Do It All chain, selling the stake to Boots at a loss of £63.5 million. Also divested was Paperchase, the greeting card and stationery chain. Cockburn made other changes as well, including a workforce reduction of 1,100, the closing of the group's Sloane Square headquarters, and the writing off of a significant amount of stock at the WH Smith chain in an effort to narrow the offerings and free up space for more productive lines. For the fiscal year ending in June 1996, WH Smith posted a pretax loss of £195 million, the first loss in the 204-year history of the company. Much of the loss was attributable to the sell-off of Do It All and to writeoffs taken for the reduction in stock at WH Smith and for the employee cutbacks.

Cockburn's eventful stint as the head of WH Smith ended abruptly in June 1997 when the executive left to take a senior position with British Telecommunications. In September of that year, a 32-year company veteran, Richard Handover, was named chief executive, a move that disappointed many analysts who were hoping for a fresh infusion of new blood from outside the group. Less than one month after taking over, Handover faced a takeover bid from Tim Waterstone, the founder of the Waterstone's chain. Handover and the WH Smith board rejected the bid, deciding instead to refocus the group on three core businesses: WH Smith High Street, the core retail chain; WH Smith Europe and International Travel Retail, consisting of retail stores and newsstands located in train stations and airports in Europe, the United States, and Asia; and WHSmith News, the group's newspaper and magazine distribution arm. To this end, the group exited from the specialty music retailing sector by selling The Wall to Camelot Music Inc. for £28 million ($47 million) in 1997 and by selling its 75 percent stake in Virgin

Our Price to Virgin Retail Group for £145 million the following year. Also in 1998, WH Smith sold its controlling stake in Waterstone's for £300 million to a firm jointly owned by EMI Group plc and Advent International.

While continuing with efforts to enhance the performance of the WH Smith chain, Handover also moved quickly to use the proceeds of the divestments to fund targeted acquisitions. In 1998 WH Smith purchased the retail outlets of newspaper distributor John Menzies for £68 million. Gained thereby were 140 retail units in England and Wales, which were rebranded under the WH Smith name, and about 90 stores in Scotland, which continued to use the John Menzies name under a license arrangement (there having been no WH Smith outlets in Scotland). WH Smith also bought the Internet Bookshop that same year, relaunching it the following year as WHSmith.co.uk, an e-commerce site selling books, CDs, videos, and DVDs. WH Smith also made a surprising move into book publishing during 1999, first acquiring Helicon, the leading U.K. publisher of consumer and educational reference material, then purchasing Hodder Headline, one of the most venerable trade publishing houses in Britain, for £185 million. By becoming a content producer, WH Smith hoped to distinguish its retail chain from its competitors by developing proprietary products that would be available only through the chain. Acquisitions continued in 2000 with the purchase of Hazelwood Enterprises Inc., operator of 71 hotel-based bookstores in the United States, for £12 million ($19 million).

Also during 2000 WH Smith launched an effort to create its own national magazine distribution system. This effort was greeted with loud protests from magazine publishers worried about the death of small-circulation titles and from independent newsagents concerned that the effort would put them out of business. WH Smith finally relented in early 2001, abandoning the effort and taking the further step of putting WHSmith News up for sale. The sale of the newspaper and magazine distribution unit would mean that the group could focus fully on its retailing and publishing operations. In July 2001 WH Smith announced that it had reached an agreement to sell WHSmith News to ABN AMRO Private Equity (UK) Limited for £215 million in cash. The deal was subject to shareholder approval as well as the negotiation of new contracts between WHSmith News and its major customers and suppliers, leaving completion of the sale somewhat in doubt. Proceeds would likely be used by WH Smith to fund further growth of its core retail and publishing units. WH Smith had already showed its desire for more acquisitions in June 2001 when it acquired Blue Star Consumer Retailing Group, the leading bookseller in Australia and New Zealand, for £38 million. Blue Star conducted business primarily under two brands, Angus & Robertson in Australia and Whitcoulls in New Zealand, operating 184 company-owned retail outlets. This acquisition was part of WH Smith's strategy to expand its book retailing presence within the English-speaking world.

Principal Subsidiaries

WH Smith Trading Limited; Hodder Headline Limited; WH Smith UK Limited; Hambleden Estates Limited; WH Smith Group Holdings (USA) Inc.; WH Smith France SA; WH Smith Singapore Pte.; WH Smith Hong Kong Limited; WH Smith

Australia (Pty) Limited; Hodder Moa Becket Publishers Limited (New Zealand); Lexicon Book Company Limited.

Principal Competitors

HMV Media Group plc; Virgin Group Ltd.; John Menzies plc; Dawson Holdings Plc; Lagardère SCA; MTS, Incorporated; Bertelsmann AG; Amazon.com, Inc.

Further Reading

"After 200 Years WH Smith Is Dragging Itself into the Next Century," *Management Today,* October 1998, p. 68.

Bagnall, Sarah, "New WH Smith Chief Plans Strategic Review," *Times* (London), January 25, 1996.

"Battle of the Newsagents," *Economist,* December 2, 2000, p. 7.

Blackwell, David, "Singed by the Heat of the High Street," *Financial Times,* August 26, 1995.

Buckley, Neil, "New Pressures on an Old Name: The City Wants WH Smith to Freshen Up Its Image," *Financial Times,* August 22, 1995, p. 17.

Doran, Amanda-Jane, "WH Smith: A Year of Change Ahead," *Publishers Weekly,* May 14, 2001, p. 22.

Felsted, Andrea, "WH Smith Sells Its Distribution Arm to ABN," *Financial Times,* July 6, 2001.

Hammond, Lawrence, *WH Smith: A Story That Began in 1792,* London: WH Smith Ltd, 1979.

Heller, Robert, "Why Smith's Should Stay Together," *Management Today,* November 1997, p. 25.

Hollinger, Peggy, "Challenge for WH Smith's New Chief: High Street Retailer Is Due for a Shake-Up," *Financial Times,* January 25, 1996, p. 26.

——, "WH Smith with Waterstone's Wood—Would It Be Good?," *Financial Times,* October 15, 1997, p. 21.

Hollinger, Peggy, and Alice Rawsthorn, "WH Smith Books a Place in New Retailing Era: The Group's Acquisition of Hodder Headline May Signal the End of a Mass Market," *Financial Times,* May 25, 1999, p. 12.

Humes, Christopher Brown, "DIY, Disillusionment, and Divorce," *Financial Times,* August 22, 1996, p. 21.

——, "Humbled from Smugness to Streetfighting," *Financial Times,* August 28, 1996, p. 21.

Price, Christopher, "Handover Emphasises Rights to the Title," *Financial Times,* September 20, 1997, p. 20.

——, "Shelves Look Bare at WH Smith," *Financial Times,* June 24, 1997, p. 27.

Rees, Jon, "Can WH Smith Get Its Act Together?," *Marketing Week,* June 2, 1995, pp. 22–23.

Robinson, Elizabeth, "WH Smith in Agreed Bid for Hodder," *Financial Times,* May 25, 1999, p. 21.

Smith, Alison, "WH Smith to End Distribution Fight," *Financial Times,* January 3, 2001, p. 22.

Snoddy, Julia, "WH Smith 'Electrical' to Challenge Dixons," *Financial Times,* August 12, 2001.

"WH Smith's Designs on the High Street," *Director,* November 1987, pp. 40+.

"WH Smith's Leisure Principle," *Management Today,* August 1988, pp. 50+.

Wilson, Charles, *First with the News: The History of WH Smith, 1792–1972,* London: Jonathan Cape, 1985.

Wright, Robert, "WH Smith Backs Retail Specialist to Get the Story Right," *Financial Times,* November 29, 1997, p. 16.

——, "WH Smith Buys John Menzies' Retail Side," *Financial Times,* March 10, 1998, p. 26.

——, "WH Smith Plans to Shed Books Subsidiary and Sell Music Chains," *Financial Times,* October 17, 1997, p. 21.

——, "Why Tim Wants to Show He Really Cares," *Financial Times,* October 4, 1997, p. 21.

—Richard Brass
—update: David E. Salamie

ZURICH
FINANCIAL SERVICES
Zurich Financial Services

Mythenquai 2
8022 Zurich
Switzerland
Telephone: (01) 625 25 25
Fax: (01) 625 35 35
Web site: http://www.zurich.com

Public Company
Incorporated: 1872 as Versicherungs-Verein
Employees: 70,000
Total Assets: $231.36 billion (2000)
Stock Exchanges: Swiss London
Ticker Symbol: ZURN
NAIC: 524126 Direct Property and Casualty Insurance
Carriers; 524113 Direct Life Insurance Carriers;
523920 Portfolio Management; 525910 Open-End
Investment Funds; 551112 Offices of Other Holding
Companies

Zurich Financial Services is one of the largest Europe-based insurance firms. The group has strong positions in the property and casualty insurance markets of Switzerland, the United Kingdom, and the United States. In life insurance, Zurich focuses on the same three nations, with particularly strong positions in the United Kingdom and Switzerland. The group's key insurance brands include Zurich Insurance (in Europe), Allied Dunbar and Eagle Star (both in the United Kingdom), and Farmers Group and Universal Underwriters (both in the United States). Zurich Financial Services was formed in 1998 from the merger of Swiss-based Zurich Insurance Company and the financial services operations of U.K.-based B.A.T. Industries PLC, the latter of which included Allied Dunbar, Eagle Star, and Farmers. In addition to its main insurance operations, Zurich was also involved in other sectors of the financial services industry as of mid-2001, including reinsurance and asset management, but the group's reinsurance unit, Zurich Re, was in the process of being spun off into a separate, independent firm, and Zurich Scudder Investments, the group's main asset management business, was on the verge of being sold off in whole or in part.

Early Years: Focusing on Reinsurance and Marine Insurance

The insurance business developed relatively late in Switzerland but has gone on to achieve great importance. Initially the basic concepts of the business were taken from neighboring countries and adapted to Swiss conditions. Swiss insurance practice, legislation, and expertise reached such a high level, however, that they spread abroad. The forerunners of Zurich Financial Services—including Zürich Versicherungs-Gesellschaft (Zürich Insurance Company)—played a decisive part in the international activities of the Swiss insurance business from the start.

The original phase of growth in the Swiss insurance business took place in the middle of the 19th century. Its development was sustained by the beginning of industrialization, the building of the railway network, the creation of more efficient credit banks, and the enterprising spirit of the time. Switzerland was emerging then as a leading financial center and was set to become one of the most important countries in the insurance industry. Statesman and entrepreneur Alfred Escher made a considerable contribution to the insurance business, and with the founding in 1856 of the Schweizerische Kreditanstalt (Swiss Credit Bank) he paved the way for Zürich's international influence as a financial center.

Initially insurance business was carried out by specialist companies in the individual insurance classes. Two insurance companies in Basel and in St. Gall were already working in marine insurance. As exports were growing, it was felt by Swiss economists and other financial experts that it was necessary to create another marine insurance company in Zürich. Seventeen leading manufacturers and traders became members of the founding committee, formed in June 1869 on the initiative of the board of the Swiss Credit Bank. On October 9, 1869, the statutes of the Schweiz Transport-Versicherungs-Gesellschaft (Switzerland Transport Insurance Company) were approved by the ruling council of the canton of Zürich and on January 15, 1870, the company began trading. The first president of the

Company Perspectives:

Connecting here. To there. This is how we are striving to do business at Zurich. Connecting people to ideas and to solutions that best respond to their needs and aspirations. Connecting capital to promising investment opportunities. Connecting our worldwide resources—people, knowledge and technology—so we can continue to discover new possibilities.

board was John Syz-Landis and the first managing director Wilhelm Berend Witt. It was intended from the outset that the company should be international in its activities.

It soon became apparent to the young company that it required the support of considerable reinsurance, which could not be covered by existing companies. Schweiz therefore took the decision to found its own reinsurance company. The shareholders in Schweiz were invited to take a share in the proposed company through a circular letter, dated October 23, 1872, from a ten-man founding committee under the leadership of John Syz-Landis. The members of the committee already had collaborated in the founding of Schweiz and belonged to the board of the company. The new company was to be run by the firm Versicherungs-Verein (Insurance Association) and was to take on a part of Schweiz's risks in the manner of a surplus reinsurance. By November 16, 1872, the statutes had already been approved by the ruling council of the canton of Zürich. The licensing document carried the signature of the poet Gottfried Keller, who was first state clerk in Zürich from 1861 to 1876, and in that capacity signed the documents for the ruling council.

Close ties existed between the two companies thanks to the unified personnel in all their divisions, operating from one office. Together with reinsurance, the Versicherungs-Verein from its inception also dealt with direct marine insurance both at home and abroad. Substantial damage claims and fierce competition in the insurance markets caused considerable problems for the young company. The direct marine and reinsurance businesses on their own proved insufficiently profitable to sustain the young company, which consequently looked towards new fields of activity.

Late 19th Century: Switching to Accident and Liability Insurance

On a proposal put forward by the board, it was therefore decided at the Versicherungs-Verein general meeting in April 1874 to extend the company's activities to accident insurance. This class of insurance had grown rapidly in importance as industrialization spread. At first, however, this type of insurance had been limited, covering travel insurance and workers' insurance. Accident insurance first became available in England, where from 1849 the Railway Passengers Assurance Company was the first to provide insurance cover against railway accidents. Later it was to extend cover to other types of transportation. In Germany a law was first passed on June 7, 1871, which took into consideration the greater risks for employees caused by the increasing mechanization of factories. This law forced

manufacturers to pay compensation for any personal injury to their workers. The increased liability made it necessary for companies to insure their workforce against accidents in the factory and the requirement brought about the creation of collective workers' insurance (*Arbeiterkollektivversicherung*).

In view of the high level of industrialization occurring in the Swiss economy, it was evident that similar developments would take place in the confederation. The board of Versicherungs-Verein recognized the sign of the times and broke new ground in Switzerland with its introduction of accident insurance, which occurred in 1875. The significance of this step was underlined by the change in the company's name to the Transport- und Unfall-Versicherungs-Aktiengesellschaft Zürich (Transport and Accident Insurance plc Zürich). The importance that Swiss industry attached to this branch of insurance is shown by the fact that a further accident insurance company was also created in Winterthur in 1875.

Zurich's growth as a separate company only began with the introduction of accident insurance. Transport insurance was discontinued "for the foreseeable future" at the end of 1880, and the company stopped taking on more reinsurance business. For a while the name of the company stayed as it had been, although from 1886 it added an explanatory sentence to clarify its activities, declaring that "the company deals exclusively in accident insurance." When liability insurance began to be developed in Germany as a new branch of insurance alongside accident insurance, with the two branches becoming independent of one another, Zurich also started offering liability insurance. The company was able from then on to offer insurance coverage not only against accidents but also against employers' liabilities for assessment of damages. The expansion of business into these areas led to the company's change of name to the Zürich Allgemeine Unfall- und Haftpflicht-Versicherungs Aktiengesell-schaft (Zurich General Accident and Liability Insurance plc) on December 14, 1894. The company kept this name until 1955. These changes finally brought about the complete separation of Zurich from Schweiz, although friendly relations and business contacts were preserved. Zurich now began to develop into a worldwide company.

The company first had to build up its own independent workforce. Until 1875 Schweiz's staff had also taken care of Zurich's business. The development of accident insurance required a specialized staff, both for internal running of the company and for customer services, since this insurance sector catered to a different clientele and operated within a completely different structure. This was particularly the case for liability insurance, with its complex legal aspects. In 1880 the company had 27 employees. By the turn of the century the number had grown to 140. Business in this branch of insurance was stimulated in Switzerland by laws passed between 1875 and 1881 establishing liability for railway and steamer companies as well as for factories.

Together with its activities in Switzerland, company business was extended to other areas at an early stage. The first step was taken as early as 1875 in Germany, where agencies were opened in Berlin, Hamburg, Stuttgart, and Reutlingen. Further areas of business to be developed were the Rhineland, Westphalia, Saxony, and Alsace-Lorraine, the latter at that time part

Key Dates:

1872: Versicherungs-Verein (Insurance Association) is formed to provide reinsurance for Switzerland Transport Insurance Company.

1875: Company expands into accident insurance and changes its name to Transport- und Unfall-Versicherungs-Aktiengesellschaft Zürich (Transport and Accident Insurance plc Zürich); expansion outside of Switzerland begins as well.

1894: Expansion into liability insurance prompts another name change, to: Zürich Allgemeine Unfall- und Haftpflicht-Versicherungs Aktiengesellschaft (Zurich General Accident and Liability Insurance plc).

1912: U.S. expansion begins with the formation of an accident and liability insurance firm in New York.

1955: Company name is simplified to Zurich Versicherungs-Gesellschaft (Zurich Insurance Company).

1965: Alpina Versicherungs-Aktiengesellschaft of Switzerland is acquired.

1969: Agrippina Versicherungs AG, based in Germany, is acquired.

1989: Baltimore-based Maryland Casualty Group is acquired.

1996: Zurich acquires an 80 percent interest in Kemper Corporation, a U.S. life insurance firm, and a 97 percent interest in Kemper Financial Services, which is renamed Zurich Kemper Investments.

1997: Zurich gains majority control of Scudder, Stevens & Clark, which is merged into Zurich Kemper to form Scudder Kemper Investments (later renamed Zurich Scudder Investments).

1998: Zurich merges with British American Financial Services (BAFS) to form Zurich Financial Services, which is set up with a dual Swiss-U.K. holding company structure.

2000: Group is unified under a single Swiss holding company, Zurich Financial Services, which is listed on the Swiss and London exchanges.

2001: Zurich announces that it will spin off its reinsurance division into a separate, independent firm, and that it is exploring the sale of all or part of Zurich Scudder.

of the German empire. In the same year representative offices were opened in Austria-Hungary and in Denmark. Dealings in France followed in 1878. The Berlin branch which was opened in 1880 came to take on a particularly important role in the company's further development, since it was from here that business in Denmark, Norway, Sweden, Finland, and Russia was coordinated.

Early 20th Century: Entering U.S. and Other Markets

At the end of 1880, with the resignation of W. Witt, Zurich was for the first time given its own chief executive, Heinrich Müller. He was devoted to the business and set the company on a firm footing without neglecting the continued development of its activities abroad. His successor, Fritz Meyer, came from the treasury for the town of Zürich and made sure he consolidated the company's technical reserves. During his time in office, from 1900 to 1918, the company erected its own administrative office building on the Mythenquai in Zürich, where the company headquarters are still to be found. Above all, it also developed its workers' accident insurance business in France and considerably expanded its business in offering insurance against liability in Germany, where the introduction of the Civil Code on January 1, 1900, extended the need for such insurance into numerous new areas. The company's premium income in 1900 was SFr 15.4 million. Business in Switzerland accounted for SFr 3.7 million of this total, while France represented the largest premium income with SFr 5.5 million, followed by Germany with SFr 5 million.

A decisive move for Zurich was engaging in new business in the United States, although Zurich already ran its U.S. subsidiary in Chicago in collaboration with a German fire insurance company. Zurich received the authorization to trade in the state of New York in 1912. The New York insurance commissioner had great influence on other states in the union. The U.S. accident and liability insurance company grew unexpectedly strong and brought in considerable premium income, but was also a heavy burden in terms of provisions and costs. To cover reserves, a large amount of capital was invested in U.S. dollars in the United States; after World War I this capital formed the basis for the further expansion of the U.S. company. Since then it occupied a particularly important central role in the Zurich insurance group's activities. At the same time Zurich gained a foothold in England, Canada, Italy, and Spain. In 1925 an agreement was made with Ford, the largest car manufacturer of that time, whereby preferential insurance terms were offered on Ford cars.

While establishing branches and founding subsidiaries under its own name in foreign countries according to national law, Zurich also acquired domestic insurance companies. This policy, like the starting of activities in the United States and the creation of a life assurance company for the group, dated from the time of August Leonhard Tobler, who first served as vice-director of the company and then became the head of Zurich from 1918 to 1927. It was under his leadership that the company developed into an internationally active insurance group, a status that continued to grow with the acquisition of substantial insurance companies. The continuity in the management of the company contributed to this achievement.

During the first 50 years of its existence, Zurich's activities were limited to damage and accident insurance. As a result of the decline of the German currency because of inflation after World War I, the German life assurance companies that held a strong position in the Swiss insurance markets were no longer able to fulfill their commitments in Swiss francs. They were therefore forced to withdraw from Switzerland. Swiss companies filled the gaps created in the market, with the result that numerous new life assurance companies were founded there. In the course of these developments the Vita Lebensversicherungs-Gesellschaft was created as a subsidiary of Zurich. It soon undertook business abroad, where it grew rapidly. It showed pioneering spirit when in 1926 it introduced a health service which offered regular checkups with a doctor and published medical leaflets giving advice on healthy living.

Numerous Acquisitions in Postwar Era

World War II caused the loss for Zurich of important areas of business in central and Eastern Europe. The rebuilding of Zurich in Germany began in Düsseldorf and Frankfurt. The Frankfurt tower block next to the old opera house became the administrative center for the German Zurich network in 1961. A string of further insurance companies was tied to the German branch of the company. The Deutsche Allgemeine Versicherungs-Aktiengesellschaft (German General Accident Insurance Ltd.), founded in 1923, concentrated particularly on offering motor insurance through direct sales. Zurich resumed its policy of international expansion, which had been halted by the war, in numerous other countries. The company opened many new offices as well as its own life assurance companies, in particular in the United States, Canada, the United Kingdom, and Australia.

The period after World War II was marked for Zurich by its development into a company dealing in all branches of insurance. Because of the systematic extension of the classes covered by the company, the branch-related balancing-out of risks was put alongside the international one. Until the beginning of the 1950s, the emphasis of activities had lain in the field of accident and liability insurance, whose dominant position was expressed in Zurich's slogan "The world's largest purely accident and liability insurer." The company was innovative in its introduction of these branches of insurance in major countries. The company's expansion into further sectors was reflected in its change of name to Zürich Versicherungs-Gesellschaft (Zurich Insurance Company) in 1955. In 1970 fire insurance was also offered by the company for the first time in Switzerland.

The acquisition of large insurance companies and groups in various foreign countries had a crucial bearing on the scope of the company's business and was a policy carried out under the management of Fritz Gerber, the chairman and for many years director general of the company. Three important examples illustrated this policy. In 1965 Zurich bought the Alpina Versicherungs-Aktiengesellschaft in Switzerland, which had established its own network abroad. In 1969 Agrippina Versicherungs AG was acquired from a private bank. Agrippina had been created in Cologne in 1844 as a marine insurance company and was therefore well established in the German insurance market, with a number of subsidiaries of its own. The acquisition in 1989 of the Maryland Casualty Group, with its headquarters in Baltimore, Maryland, greatly strengthened Zurich's business with private customers as well as doubling premium income in the United States.

1990s and Beyond: Becoming a Global Insurance Power

From 1972, Zurich's centenary year, to 1990, the parent company's gross premiums rose from SFr 2.3 billion to SFr 6.1 billion, and those of the Zurich insurance group from SFr 4 billion to SFr 17.1 billion. By 1990, Zurich did business worldwide in some 80 countries, with a particularly strong presence in its traditional markets in Switzerland, the United States, and Germany. Its successful international development could be attributed largely to the use the company had made of the respected name of the financial center of Zürich together with

its historical role in the expansion of accident and personal liability insurance. With a view to future business in the European Common Market, Zurich International companies were established in Belgium, Germany, the United Kingdom, France, Italy, and the Netherlands and offered special Euro-policies for industrial insurance. This type of insurance was supported by computer system Zurinet, ensuring international communication of information.

In 1991 Rolf Hüppi took over as president and CEO of Zürich, with Gerber remaining chairman. Under the leadership of Hüppi, a 28-year veteran of the firm, Zurich in the early 1990s placed an emphasis on targeting specific sectors of the insurance market within the countries in which it operated. Faced with the heightened—and increasingly globalized—competitive landscape of the 1990s, Hüppi believed that his company needed to rein in its sprawling international operations to successfully compete. Peripheral and underperforming businesses were jettisoned in favor of such core niches as the Swiss life insurance market. Hüppi bolstered the latter through the 1991 acquisition of Geneva Insurance and through a 1992 deal with Swiss Bank Corp. (SBC), through which Zurich began selling life insurance at SBC branches. U.S. operations were expanded in 1993 with the establishment of Zurich Reinsurance Center, which quickly became one of the largest reinsurers in the United States.

In the mid- to late 1990s, with the global consolidation of the financial services sector progressing at a rapid clip, Hüppi (who became chairman in 1995) thoroughly transformed Zurich through a series of major transactions. In early 1996 Zurich, through a $2 billion transaction, acquired an 80 percent interest in Kemper Corporation, which was headquartered in Long Grove, Illinois, and a 97 percent interest in Kemper Financial Services, the latter being the asset management unit of the former. By gaining control of Kemper and its two life insurance subsidiaries, Zurich gained its first significant presence in the U.S. life insurance market and increased its overall presence in the life insurance sector, a company goal. The addition of Kemper Financial Services greatly advanced Zurich's position in asset management and gave it a foothold in the U.S. money management business. The group had first entered this sector in 1990 with the establishment of Zurich Investment Management. Kemper, which was renamed Zurich Kemper Investments Inc., managed $42 billion in mutual fund assets at the time of the takeover.

Zurich Kemper was soon greatly expanded with the acquisition of majority control of Scudder, Stevens & Clark Inc., a New York mutual fund firm with about $120 billion in assets under management. In a complicated transaction, Zurich paid about $2 billion to take control of Scudder and merge it into Zurich Kemper to form Scudder Kemper Investments, which initially was 69.5 percent owned by Zurich and 30.5 percent owned by Scudder's senior management. Scudder Kemper (which was later renamed Zurich Scudder Investments) was based in New York.

Further growth occurred in 1998 when Zürich merged with British American Financial Services (BAFS), the financial services unit of U.K.-based B.A.T. Industries PLC, in a $38 billion transaction. The merger created a "new" Zurich, which began operating under the name Zurich Financial Services. A dual holding company structure was set up whereby Zurich was 55 percent owned by Zurich Allied AG, which had a listing on the Swiss Exchange, and 45 percent owned by Allied Zurich p.l.c., which had a listing on the London Stock Exchange. The addition of BAFS increased Zurich's gross premiums written from $23.7 billion to $40 billion and made Zurich the fifth largest insurance group in the world. Among the insurance holdings of BAFS was Los Angeles-based Farmers Group, Inc., one of the largest property-casualty insurance firms in the United States. BAFS also brought to Zurich substantial U.K. insurance operations, including Allied Dunbar Assurance, one of the largest life insurance and pension firms in the United Kingdom, and Eagle Star Holdings, a leading U.K. multiline insurer with strong commercial lines. The enlarged U.K. operations of Zurich led the group to begin speaking of having three "home" markets: the United States, the United Kingdom, and Switzerland. Zurich also gained an additional asset management business, that of London-based Threadneedle Asset Management, which increased the group's assets under management from $262 billion to $341.8 billion. This made Zurich one of the top ten asset managers in the world. Overall the newly formed Zurich intended to focus on four core businesses: non-life insurance, life insurance, reinsurance, and asset management.

In October 2000 the complicated structure of Zurich Financial was simplified with the unification of the group under a single Swiss holding company, also called Zurich Financial Services. The new Zurich had a primary stock listing on the Swiss Exchange and a secondary listing in London. Unfortunately, by this time, Zurich was being hurt by poor performance at the Zurich Scudder unit, which was suffering from difficulties integrating the varied corporate cultures that had existed at Scudder and Kemper, as well as from the volatile equity markets of 2000 and 2001.

Disappointing groupwide earnings led to the announcement in early 2001 that Zurich planned to exit from the reinsurance market in order to focus on non-life insurance, life insurance, and asset management. With completion planned by the end of 2001, the reinsurance division, Zurich Re, would be spun off into an independent, separately traded public firm, under a new name. Other underperforming units were slated to be divested as well. Zurich also planned to restructure its head office with the aim of achieving annual savings of $200 million by 2002. Soon after the announcement of the spinoff of Zurich Re, Zurich announced that it was exploring strategic options for its troubled Zurich Scudder unit, options that reportedly ranged from a joint venture to an outright sale of the unit. The most likely scenario appeared to be that Zurich would sell a significant stake in Zurich Scudder to another financial services firm, merge Zurich Scudder into that firm, and retain an ownership stake in the merged entity. Zurich launched further restructuring efforts in July 2001 with the consolidation of its global operations into five divisions, four of which were geographically oriented: Continental Europe, North America Corporate, North America Consumer/Latin America, and United Kingdom, Ireland, Southern Africa, and Asia/Pacific. The other division, Global Asset, included Zurich Scudder and other asset management businesses, such as Zurich Capital Markets, Centre, and Capital Z Partners. Clearly, Zurich Financial Services was working on many fronts in its attempt to accomplish an early 21st-century turnaround.

Principal Subsidiaries

Zurich Argentina; Zurich Iguazú Comp. de Seg. (Argentina); Zurich Australian Insurance; Zurich Australia Ltd.; Zurich Financial Services Australia; Zürich Kosmos (Austria; 99.98%); Micoba Holdings (Bahamas); D.B.V. Algemene Verzekerings-maatschappij (Belgium); Zurich International (Belgique) (Belgium); Zurich Universal (Belgium; 66.94%); BG Investments (Bermuda); Centre Group Holdings (Bermuda); Centre Life Reinsurance (Bermuda); Centre Reinsurance (Bermuda); Centre Reinsurance (U.S.) (Bermuda); CentreLine Reinsurance (Bermuda); Centre Solutions (Bermuda); Centre Solutions (U.S.) (Bermuda); Coral Shield Insurance (Bermuda); ZCM Holdings (Bermuda); Zurich Asia Holdings (Bermuda; 90%); Zurich Centre Group Holdings (Bermuda); Zurich International (Bermuda); Berfin Ltd. (Bermuda); Capital Z Investments, L.P. (Bermuda; 99.5%); ZG Investments II Ltd. (Bermuda); ZG Investments III Ltd. (Bermuda); ZG Investments Ltd. (Bermuda); Zurich Global Energy Ltd. (Bermuda); La Boliviana Ciacruz de Seguros (Bolivia; 51%); Zurich-Brasil Seguros (Brazil); Zurich Participaçoes e Representaçoes (Brazil); Peopleplus Insurance Company (Canada); World Travel Protection Canada; Zurich Canadian Holdings; Zurich Life Insurance Company of Canada; Zurich Life of Canada Holdings; Chilena Consolidada (Chile; 78.46%); Chilena Consolidada Vida (Chile; 98.94%); Inversiones Suizo Chilena (Chile); Zurich Investments Chile S.A. (99.96%); Rimswell Investments (Cyprus); Zürich Kindlustuse Eest Aktiaselts (Estonia); Eagle Star Vie (France); Zurich Epargne (France); Zurich International (France; 99.98%); ZURITEL (France; 99.99%); DA Deutsche Allgemeine (Germany); DA Deutsche Allgemeine Leben (Germany); Patria Versicherung (Germany; 99.2%); Zürich-Agrippina Beteiligungs-AG (Germany); Zürich-Agrippina Krankenversicherung (Germany); Zürich Investmentgesellschaft mbH (Germany); Zürich Rückversicherung (Köln) (Germany; 98%); Zürich Agrippina Versicherung Aktiegesellschaft (Germany; 99.6%); Zürich Agrippina Lebensversicherungs AG (Germany; 99.2%); Zurich Insurance (Guam; 90%); Paofoong Insurance Company (Hong Kong); Zurich Insurance (Asia), Ltd. (Hong Kong); Centre Representative (Asia) Limited (Hong Kong); Rimswell Hungary Consulting (Hungary); Zürich Biztosító Rt. (Hungary); Zurich Asset Management (India) Ltd. (75%); P.T. Zurich Insurance (Indonesia; 80%); P.T. Zurich PSP Life Insurance (Indonesia; 77.5%); Centre Insurance International (Ireland); Centre Reinsurance International (Ireland); Eagle Star Insurance (Ireland); Eagle Star Life Assurance of Ireland; Orange Stone Holdings (Ireland); Orange Stone Reinsurance (Ireland); Orange Stone Reinsurance Dublin (Ireland); Centre Finance Dublin International (Ireland); Erbasei (Italy); SIAR (Italy); La Sicurtà 1879 (Italy); Zurich International (Italia) (Italy; 99.99%); Zurich Investments Life (Italy); Zurich Investments SGR (Italy); Zurich Investments Sim (Italy); Zurich Investments Gest. SIM (Italy); ZurigoSim S.p.A. (Italy); AAS Zurich Latvia; UADB Zurich Draudimas (Lithuania); Zurich Eurolife (Luxembourg); Zurich Insurance (Malaysia; 90%); Eagle Star Malta; Zurich Finance (Mauritius); Zurich Compañia de Seguros (Mexico; 98.8%); Zurich Vida (Mexico; 99.99%); Zurich Afore (Mexico; 90.9%); Zurich Compagnie Marocaine d'Assurances (Morocco; 96.73%); Zurich International (Nederland) (Netherlands); Zurich Leven (Netherlands); Zurich Atrium B.V. (Netherlands); Z.I.C. International N.V. (Netherlands Antilles); Cursud N.V. (Netherlands Antilles); Zurich Holding Norge (Norway); Zurich Protector Forsikring (Norway); Zurich Pacific Insurance (Papua New Guinea); Zurich General Insurance (Philippines); Zurich Life Insurance (Philippines); Zurich Insurance Company (Poland); Zurich Life Insurance Company (Poland); Zurich Polska Sp.z.o.o. (Poland); Zurich Powszechne (Poland); Zurich Sp.z.o.o. (Poland); Zurich Companhia de Seguros (Portugal); Companhia de Seguros Eagle Star Vida (Portugal); Zurich Insurance (Singapore); Zurich Poistovna (Slovakia); South African Eagle Insurance (83.6%); Zurich España (Spain; 99.78%); Zurich Vida SA (Spain); Eagle Insurance Company (Sri Lanka; 51%); Eagle NDB Fund Management Co. Ltd. (Sri Lanka; 51%); Zurich NDB Fin. Lanka (Private) Ltd. (Sri Lanka; 58.44%); Alpina; Assuricum; Centre Solutions; INZIC; La Genevoise Générale; La Genevoise Vie; Orion (56%); Rüd, Blass & Cie AG; Turegum Versicherungsgesellschaft; Zurich Insurance Company; Zurich Group Holding; Zürich Invest Bank; Zürich Leben; Zurich Insurance (Taiwan; 83.1%); Zurich Securities Inv. Trust (Taiwan); Allied Dunbar Assurance (U.K.); Eagle Star Group Services (U.K.); Eagle Star Holdings (U.K.); Eagle Star Insurance (U.K.); Eagle Star (International Life) (U.K.); Eagle Star Life Assurance (U.K.); Gresham Investment Trust (U.K.); Sterling Assurance (U.K.); Turegum Insurance Company (U.K.); Zurich Financial Services (UKISA) (U.K.); Zurich Financial Services (Jersey) (U.K.); Zurich GSG (U.K.); Zurich Holdings (UK); Zurich Insurance (Jersey) (U.K.); Zurich International (UK); Zurich Life (U.K.); Zurich Specialties London (U.K.); Allied Dunbar International (U.K.); Allied Zurich Holdings Limited (U.K.); Centre Re Representative Ltd. (U.K.); Allied Zurich p.l.c. (U.K.); Zurich Scudder Inv. Holdings (U.K.); ZFS UK IFA Group Limited; Cedar Hill Holdings (U.S.A.; 93.75%); Centre Holdings (Delaware) (U.S.A.); Centre Insurance Company (U.S.A.); Centre Life Insurance Company (U.S.A.); Empire Fire and Marine (U.S.A.); Empire Indemnity (U.S.A.); Farmers Group, Inc. (U.S.A.); Farmers New World Life Insurance (U.S.A.); Farmers Reinsurance (U.S.A.); Federal Kemper Life Assurance (U.S.A.); Kemper Corp. (U.S.A.); Kemper Investors Life Insurance (U.S.A.); Orange Stone Delaware Holdings (U.S.A.); REM (U.S.A.); Zurich Scudder Investments (U.S.A.; 80%); Universal Underwriters (U.S.A.); Universal Underwriters Life (U.S.A.); Universal Underwriters of Texas (U.S.A.); ZC Specialty Insurance (U.S.A.); ZC Sterling Corporation (U.S.A.); Zurich American Insurance Company (U.S.A.); Zurich Finance (USA); Zurich Holding Company of America; Zurich Life Insurance Company of America (U.S.A.); Zurich Reinsurance Centre Holdings (U.S.A.); Zurich Reinsurance (North America) (U.S.A.); Centre Group Holdings (U.S.) Ltd.; ZC Resource LLC (U.S.A.); Zurich Centre Group LLC (U.S.A.); Zurich Payroll Solutions Ltd. (U.S.A.); Seguros Sud America (Venezuela; 68.09%); Zurich International de Venezuela.

Principal Divisions

Continental Europe Business Division; Global Asset Business Division; North American Consumer and Latin America Business Division; North American Corporate Business Division; United Kingdom, Ireland, Southern Africa and Asia/Pacific Business Division.

Principal Competitors

AXA; Allianz AG; American International Group, Inc.; ING Groep N.V.; Citigroup Inc.; Assicurazioni Generali S.p.A.; The Allstate Corporation; State Farm Insurance Companies.

Further Reading

Banks, Howard, "A Zurich in Your Future?," *Forbes,* April 20, 1998, pp. 85–86.

Deogun, Nikhil, and Tom Lauricella, "Zurich Financial Seeks a Merger to Reinvigorate Its Scudder Unit," *Wall Street Journal,* April 23, 2001, p. C1.

Evans, Richard, "Premium Insurer: Zurich Financial Stresses Service over Price, but Sells at a Discount," *Barron's,* January 31, 2000, pp. 22, 24.

Fleming, Charles, "Zurich Insurance Group Is Looking for a New Focus: Multinational Seeks to Distinguish Itself by Targeting Specific Markets," *Wall Street Journal,* June 26, 1992, p. B3.

Hall, William, "Zurich Chief Survives Vote," *Financial Times,* May 17, 2001.

Howard, Lisa S., "Zurich Financial Services to Exit Reinsurance Market," *National Underwriter Property and Casualty-Risk and Benefits Management,* March 26, 2001, p. 2.

Hundert Jahre "Schweiz" Allgemeine Versicherungs-Aktien-Gesellschaft Zürich, 1869–1969, Zürich: Art Institut Orell Füssli Zürich AG, [1969].

Koch, Peter, "Der schweizerische Beitrag zur Entwicklung des Versicherungs-wesens," *Versicherungswirtschaft,* 1985.

——, "Versicherer aus aller Welt in Deutschland," *Versicherungskaufmann,* July 1987.

Lipin, Steven, "Kemper Agrees to Be Acquired by Group Headed by Zurich Insurance for $2 Billion," *Wall Street Journal,* April 11, 1995, p. A3.

Lucchetti, Aaron, and Nikhil Deogun, "Zurich Scudder Pares Potential Partners," *Wall Street Journal,* July 2, 2001, p. C27.

Steinmetz, Greg, "Kemper Purchase to Make Zurich Insurance a Tougher Competitor in the U.S. Market," *Wall Street Journal Europe,* June 7, 1995, p. 9.

Steinmetz, Greg, and Margaret Studer, "B.A.T. Seals Its Union with Zurich Insurance," *Wall Street Journal,* October 17, 1997, p. B14.

Studer, Margaret, "Hüppi Isn't Done with Makeover of Swiss Insurance: Big Year Is on the Horizon for an Empire Builder Who's Eager to Please," *Wall Street Journal Europe,* December 29, 1998, p. 9.

——, "Weak Dollar Aids Zurich Insurance's Shopping Spree: Bidder for Kemper Seeks Stronger Life Operations and Global Expansion," *Wall Street Journal,* April 12, 1995, p. B4.

25 Jahre "Vita," 1922–1947, Zürich: "Vita" Lebensversicherungs-Aktiengesellschaft, [1948].

Unsworth, Edwin, "Deal Strengthens Zurich: Merger with B.A.T. Unit to Create Financial Services Giant," *Business Insurance,* October 20, 1997, pp. 1+.

Woodruff, David, Richard A. Melcher, and Paula Dwyer, "Who Says Insurers Are Dull?: A Buying Binge by Rolf Hüppi Has Zurich Insurance Hopping," *Business Week,* June 23, 1997, p. 54.

Zürich Allgemeine Unfall und Haftpflicht-Versicherungs-Aktiengesellschaft, *75 Jahre "Zürich," Werden und Wachsen der Gesellschaft, 1872–1947,* Zürich: Art Institut Orell Füssli AG, 1948.

"Zurich" Allgemeine Unfall- und Haftpflicht-Versicherungs-Aktien gesellschaft in Zürich, Die Gesellschaft in den ersten fünfzig Jahren ihres Bestehens, 1872–1922, Zürich: Zürich Allgemeine in Zürich, 1923.

—Peter Koch (translated from the German by Philippe A. Barbour)
—update: David E. Salamie

zygo®

Zygo Corporation

Laurel Brook Rd.
Middlefield, Connecticut 06455
U.S.A.
Telephone: (860) 347-8506
Toll Free: (800) 994-6669
Fax: (860) 347-8372
Web site: http://www.zygo.com

Public Company
Incorporated: 1970
Employees: 486
Sales: $87.2 million (2000)
Stock Exchanges: NASDAQ
Ticker Symbol: ZIGO
NAIC: 333314 Optical Instrument and Lens
Manufacturing; 334513 Instruments and Related
Products Manufacturing for Measuring, Displaying,
and Controlling Industrial Process Variables

With its headquarters located in the small town of Middlefield, Connecticut, Zygo Corporation has been a world leader in its manufacturing niche since the company was created in 1970. As a result of its work in the physics of light, Zygo has evolved from a company intended to make prisms to one with three lines of business that take advantage of its optical technology. Zygo's Industrial/Optical division provides instrumentation that allows manufacturers to measure the roughness of surfaces without touching them or requiring a sample. In conjunction with this process, Zygo offers automated parts handling systems so that precise measurements can be taken. The optical side of this division offers an array of components, ranging from eight millimeters to more than a meter in size. Zygo's Semiconductor division provides semiconductor and data storage manufacturers with light-based measuring devices. Because computer chips have become minuscule and the range for their uses has grown exponentially, Zygo's measuring devices have become increasingly more important. Rather than simply spot checking components in the lab, chip makers now use Zygo instrumentation to maintain quality control on the production floor. The result has been the sale of more Zygo instruments and the division producing the lion's share of corporate revenues. The third Zygo division, Telecom, looks to leverage the company's expertise with light to become a major player in fiber optics, which is expected to take the Internet to an entirely new level in terms of speed and capability. Fiber Optics holds the most promise for Zygo's continuing growth.

Creation of Zygo: 1970

The three men who founded Zygo in 1970 were Paul Forman, Carl Zanoni, and Sol Laufer. Forman had originally recruited the other men while working at Parkin-Elmer in Norwalk, Connecticut. Among the optical devices the men worked on at Parkin-Elmer were prisms that were taken to the moon to perform measurement studies. The three men brought together a complementary set of abilities. Forman was the businessman, adept at marketing and administration, Zanoni an engineer, and Laufer a manufacturing specialist. For Laufer, Zygo represented a testament to one man's remarkable persistence. As a German Jew forced to serve five years as a slave laborer during World War II, Laufer was simply fortunate to survive. When the war ended he was 17 and alone, his entire family having been exterminated in the concentration camps of Auschwitz and Bergen-Belsen. Laufer immigrated to the newly formed state of Israel, where he started a family and began his career in optics. He moved to the United States in 1960.

With funding from Canon Inc., which would become a major customer and 20 percent owner, and Wesleyan University (located in Middletown, Connecticut), Laufer, Forman, and Zanoni created Zygo to produce optics with the highest precision surfaces and angles in the world. That goal would require a highly accurate interferometer to provide precise measurements of glass surfaces. The team found that the commercially available interferometers were simply inadequate for Zygo's purposes. The first order of business, therefore, became the creation of an interferometer for the company's own use. It soon became apparent, however, that Zygo was not alone in needing such advanced instrumentation. As a result, the in-house interferometer became Zygo's first product offering, the Model GH, first introduced in 1972 at the Optical Society of America's annual

Company Perspectives:

Zygo continues to develop new hardware and software to address specialized measurement problems and improve the capability of their instruments.

In less than 20 years, the interferometer became a commodity item used in an increasing number of applications to measure and assure that precision parts are made and are performing correctly. Although Zygo pioneered much of the technology which forms the basis of instruments in use today and originally held almost the entire market share, Zygo is no longer the sole supplier of such instruments. The increasing variety of measurements that customers desire has encouraged the development of a number of different instruments, a growing market, and, as a result, a number of competitors making interferometric instrumentation. Such competition is good, inasmuch as it accelerates the implementation of new ideas and techniques into new instruments, keeps prices competitive, and provides customers with a steady flow of measurement tools of ever greater utility. We at Zygo are proud of our past and present role in developing such measurement instruments and look forward to the challenge of maintaining our leadership position.

meeting. It was so much more superior than competing products that Zygo quickly became the world's leading supplier of interferometers, a position it would hold for the next decade. The sale of optics, the company's original emphasis, became a secondary source of income.

In 1973 Zygo moved its 16 employees into a new 10,000-square-foot facility in Middlefield, where it would eventually become the town's largest employer and taxpayer. The company earned a reputation as a good corporate citizen. Executive offices were described by the local press as being little more than cubicles. Zygo became very much a tight-knit company, enjoying an extremely low turnover of staff. All the while, it continued to make advances on the interferometer. In 1978 Zygo introduced the Mark II, the first interferometer suitable for industrial use. Not only did it incorporate a closed circuit television system, it was durable and could be mounted in any orientation required. The company also introduced the Zygo Automatic Pattern Processor (ZAPP), which scanned the video output of the interferometer to calculate the best fitting plane. In 1980 Zygo then introduced the Mark III, which increased accuracy by employing phase measuring instead of the old system that relied on the variance between two wavefronts. The Mark III was thus able to measure more complex shapes.

Going Public: 1983

To keep up with growth, Zygo expanded to a 100,000-square-foot facility in 1981. It also incurred a lot of debt and had difficulty obtaining financing. In order to raise money to continue growth and pay down debt, in 1983 Zygo went public at $14 a share and began trading on the NASDAQ. Revenues stood at $17.5 million by 1984, then reached $21.6 million in 1985, as the company continued to make advances in its line of interferometers. In 1984 Zygo introduced the Production Test

Interferometer, a smaller and less expensive device that could be used for online production testing. A year later it introduced the Mark IV, the first programmable interferometer that was suitable for a large number of applications. In 1987 Zygo challenged Hewlett-Packard in the distance-measuring segment of the interferometer business by offering the Axiom 2/20, which would form the basis of the company's ZMI product line. Also in 1987 Zygo introduced the Mark IVxp interferometer and the Maxim 3D interference microscope. Both of these products helped to continue the transformation of the interferometer from being simply a laboratory measuring device to serving an integral function in a manufacturing process, thereby providing quality assurance and process control.

Despite the company's considerable technical achievements, Zygo was not enjoying comparable financial progress. After suffering through a sluggish stock price and some poor quarters, Zygo hired Richard T. Fedor to serve as president and chief operating officer. For a while the company appeared to make progress under Fedor's guidance; its revenues reached $30.4 million in 1991, with a net income of $1.26 million, but the numbers could not paper over some serious deficiencies at Zygo. After years of reigning supreme in the interferometer business, it was losing market share, manufacturing was inefficient, and the new products were not being developed fast enough. Moreover, a worldwide recession was stunting orders for equipment and its stock fell well below its initial offering price. Fedor resigned in June 1991, replaced by Forman who had been serving as chairman of the company. He instituted cost-cutting measures, including the layoff of about 10 percent of the workforce. In 1992 revenues would slide to $26.7 million and net income to $600,000. The company's numbers would bottom out in 1993 when revenues sank to $22.7 million and net income to $500,000. As part of the effort to restructure the company, Forman hired Gary K. Willis to replace Fodor in February 1992. Willis had been the CEO of the Foxboro Company and was quite familiar with Zygo after serving as an independent consultant at Zygo for the previous 16 months. A year later, as part of a planned transition, he was named chief executive officer. Both Forman and Laufer, who had become vice-president of the optics group, announced they would retire from Zygo on June 30, 1994. Moreover, Zygo terminated an arrangement that had placed appointments to the board in the hands of the three founders, plus Canon and Wesleyan. The change was intended to make Zygo more of a public company and stimulate its market value. The price of Zygo stock had fallen so low that it almost reached the penny stock category.

Zygo began to turn around in fiscal 1994, with revenues rebounding to $24.1 million and net earnings approaching $1 million. By 1995 the company was entering a growth phase; investors recognized this and began to bid up the price of Zygo stock to the point that management authorized a three-for-two split. For fiscal 1995, the company would generate $32.3 million in revenues and post $2.7 million in net income. Zygo was benefiting from the increasing need of the data storage and semiconductor industries to test throughout the production process. Furthermore, as components continued to shrink, there was less tolerance for error. In essence, the market was catching up with the kind of precise measuring instruments that had always been Zygo's strong suit. The company also developed new products to service the computer industry. Its small Simi

Valley division introduced an instrument capable of testing the microscopic space between a spinning hard drive disk and a magnetic stylus. In addition to opening a small office in Singapore to gain a presence in Asia, Zygo began to earnestly look for companies with complementary businesses to acquire. In order to have sufficient capital available, the company made an additional offering of 1.3 million shares, of which 845,000 were provided by the company itself, at a price of $29 per share.

Developing External Channels of Growth: 1996

Zygo's first effort to grow externally came in 1996 when it made two acquisitions. In April it announced the purchase of NexStar Automation, a Canadian company with an operating business located in Boulder, Colorado. NexStar made automation and parts handling equipment for use in the data storage and semiconductor markets, providing expertise to help Zygo automate testing and measurement in the production process. The deal was a stock swap worth approximately $7.5 million. Zygo's second acquisition of 1996 was the $14.7 million cash and stock deal for the manufacturing operation of Technical Instrument Co. (TIC), located in Sunnyvale, California. TIC designed and manufactured precision microscopes and systems used in testing in the semiconductor, data storage, and other high technology industries. Again, the acquisition complemented a core business. In 1997 Zygo completed a pair of smaller deals, purchasing Sight Systems Inc., involved in improving the yield of data storage devices, and the remaining 50 percent of Synotec Neue Technologien und Instrumente GmbH Co., in which TIC had gained a stake before merging with Zygo. In July 1997 Zygo announced its most ambitious deal by far, the $220.5 million stock purchase of Digital Instruments, a Santa Barbara, California, maker of measurement products and systems used in the data storage and semiconductor industries. The parties, however, failed to finalize the details of the deal and ultimately in October 1997 the merger talks ceased.

Zygo grew rapidly through fiscal 1998. Revenues reached $53.5 million in 1996, then $87.2 million in 1997, and topped out at $97.9 million in 1998. Although profits were affected in 1997 because of acquisitions, Zygo was posting solid earnings and its stock was doing well enough to permit the company to institute a two-for-one split in February 1997. A severe downturn in the Asian economy, especially in the high-tech industries, would cripple Zygo in 1999. Moreover, the economics of data storage made the company's instrumentation superfluous. The price of

computer hard drives fell so rapidly that manufacturers simply could not afford to purchase instrumentation to test individual units. Hard drives became all but disposable items.

Once again Zygo was forced to restructure its management and business focus. As early as July 1998, just after reporting record results, the company initiated cost containment measures. Staff was cut, salaries frozen, and discretionary spending slashed. The hope was that the company could save as much as $3 million in fiscal 1999. Nevertheless, Zygo posted a loss of $4 million for the year, unable to compensate for revenues that fell some 40 percent in 1999 to $60.8 million. In January 1999 the company hired Canadian J. Bruce Robinson as president with the intention of grooming him to replace Willis, who had suffered a heart attack in the fall of 1997. Like Willis, Robinson had served as president of The Foxboro Company before joining Zygo. By November 1999 he also become chief executive officer while Willis remained as chairman of the board.

In March 2000 Zygo turned in a new direction that offered solid prospects for the future when it purchased Firefly Technologies for approximately $60 million in cash and stock. Through Firefly, Zygo would be able to apply its expertise to fiber optics used in the telecommunications and optical storage markets. The company renamed the operation Zygo TeraOptix. As far as Wall Street was concerned, the timing could not have been better, since fiber optics IPOs typically found eager buyers. Investors clearly saw fiber optics as the way to bridge the electronic world with the optical world and make possible the next step in the communications revolution, in particular broadband Internet access. Zygo was caught up in investor enthusiasm, as the price of its stock soared to unprecedented heights, peaking just below $100, at one point transforming Zygo into a company with a market value in excess of $1 billion.

Zygo stock returned to more realistic levels later in 2000. The company reported fiscal 2000 revenues of $87.2 million, a significant improvement over the previous year, but it lost $16 million as it changed the emphasis of its business. In November 2000, Willis retired and Robinson became chairman as well as CEO. In 2001 Zygo issued more shares of stock, an offering that netted $51.8 million that was intended to upgrade manufacturing facilities for its micro-optics business. Management was optimistic about Zygo's future, convinced that the company was uniquely situated to provide what it called the three pieces to solve the Internet Infrastructure manufacturing puzzle: optics, metrology (measurement), and automation. With the U.S. economy suffering through a sluggish patch, the upgrading of the Internet infrastructure was not occurring at the pace that many had hoped for during the bid-up of fiber optics stocks in 2000. The long-term outlook, however, still favored the prospects of established and respected support companies such as Zygo.

Principal Subsidiaries

Technical Instrument Corporation; NexStar Corporation; Sight Systems, Inc.; Zygo TeraOptix.

Principal Divisions

Industrial/Optical; Semiconductor; Telecom.

Principal Competitors

ADE; CyberOptics; Jenoptik AG; Robotic Vision Systems, Inc.; Veeco Instruments Inc.; Yokogawa Electric Works, Limited.

Further Reading

Haar, Dan, "By Any Measure, Zygo Flying High at 25," *Hartford Courant,* June 3, 1995.

Lubanko, Matthew, "Zygo's Future in Fiber Optics Looks Bright," *Hartford Courant,* July 29, 2000.

Moran, John M., "Zygo Seeks $100 Million for Expansion," *Hartford Courant,* January 6, 2001.

Weiss, Eric M., "By Any Measure, Zygo's Growth Impressive," *Hartford Courant,* June 9, 1997.

"Zygo Restructures Operations," *Electronic News,* March 22, 1999.

—Ed Dinger

INDEX TO COMPANIES

Index to Companies

Listings in this index are arranged in alphabetical order under the company name. Company names beginning with a letter or proper name such as Eli Lilly & Co. will be found under the first letter of the company name. Definite articles (The, Le, La) are ignored for alphabetical purposes as are forms of incorporation that precede the company name (AB, NV). Company names printed in bold type have full, historical essays on the page numbers appearing in bold. Updates to entries that appeared in earlier volumes are signified by the notation **(upd.)**. Company names in light type are references within an essay to that company, not full historical essays. This index is cumulative with volume numbers printed in bold type.

461

Borman's, Inc., **II** 638; **16** 249
Borneo Airways. *See* Malaysian Airlines System BHD.
Borneo Co., **III** 523
Borregaard Osterreich AG, **18** 395
Borror Corporation. *See* Dominion Homes, Inc.
Borsheim's, **III** 215; **18** 60
Borun Bros., **12** 477
Bosanquet, Salt and Co., **II** 306
Bosch. *See* Robert Bosch GmbH.
Boschert, **III** 434
Boscov's Department Store, Inc., 31 68–70
Bose Corporation, 13 108–10; **36** 98–101 (upd.)
Bosendorfer, L., Klavierfabrik, A.G., **12** 297
Bosert Industrial Supply, Inc., **V** 215
Boso Condensed Milk, **II** 538
Bostich, **III** 628
Boston Acoustics, Inc., 22 97–99
Boston and Maine Corporation, **16** 350
Boston Beer Company, 18 70–73; **22** 422; **31** 383
Boston Brewing Company, **18** 502
Boston Casualty Co., **III** 203
Boston Celtics Limited Partnership, 14 67–69
Boston Chicken, Inc., 12 42–44; **23** 266; **29** 170, 172
Boston Co., **II** 451–52
Boston Consulting Group, **I** 532; **9** 343; **18** 70; **22** 193
Boston Corp., **25** 66
Boston Distributors, **9** 453
Boston Edison Company, 12 45–47
Boston Educational Research, **27** 373
Boston Fruit Co., **II** 595
Boston Garden Arena Corporation, **14** 67
Boston Gas Company, **6** 486–88
Boston Globe, **7** 13–16
Boston Herald, **7** 15
Boston Industries Corp., **III** 735
Boston Marine Insurance Co., **III** 242
Boston National Bank, **13** 465
Boston News Bureau, **IV** 601
Boston Overseas Financial Corp., **II** 208
Boston Popcorn Co., **27** 197–98
Boston Professional Hockey Association Inc., 39 61–63
Boston Properties, Inc., 22 100–02
Boston Scientific Corporation, 37 37–40
Boston Ventures Limited Partnership, **17** 444; **27** 41, 393
Boston Whaler, Inc., **V** 376–77; **10** 215–16; **26** 398
Bostrom Seating, Inc., **23** 306
BOTAS, **IV** 563
Botsford Ketchum, Inc., **6** 40
Botswana General Insurance Company, **22** 495
Botto, Rossner, Horne & Messinger, **6** 40
Bottu, **II** 475
BOTWEB, Inc., **39** 95
Bougainville Copper Pty., **IV** 60–61
Boulanger, **37** 22
Boulder Creek Steaks & Saloon, **16** 447
Boulder Natural Gas Company, **19** 411
Boulet Dru DuPuy Petit Group. *See* Wells Rich Greene BDDP.
Boulevard Bancorp, **12** 165
Boulton & Paul Ltd., **31** 398–400
Boundary Gas, **6** 457

Boundary Healthcare, **12** 327
Bouquet, **V** 114
Bourdon, **19** 49
Bourjois, **12** 57
Boussois Souchon Neuvesel, **II** 474; **III** 677; **16** 121–22
Bouygues S.A., I 562–64; **13** 206; **23** 475–76; **24** 77–80 (upd.); **31** 126, 128
Bouzan Mines Ltd., **IV** 164
Bovaird Seyfang Manufacturing Co., **III** 471
Bovis Construction, **38** 344–45
Bovis Ltd., **I** 588
Bow Bangles, **17** 101, 103
Bowater PLC, III 501–02; **IV** 257–59; **7** 208; **8** 483–84; **25** 13; **30** 229
Bower Roller Bearing Company. *See* Federal-Mogul Corporation.
Bowery and East River National Bank, **II** 226
Bowery Savings Bank, **II** 182; **9** 173
Bowes Co., **II** 631
Bowman Gum, Inc., **13** 520
Bowmar Instruments, **II** 113; **11** 506
Bowne & Co., Inc., 18 331–32; **23** 61–64
Bowthorpe plc, 33 70–72
Box Innards Inc., **13** 442
Box Office Attraction Co., **II** 169
BoxCrow Cement Company, **8** 259
The Boy Scouts of America, 34 66–69
Boyd Bros. Transportation Inc., 39 64–66
The Boyds Collection, Ltd., 29 71–73
Boyer Brothers, Inc., **14** 17–18
Boyer's International, Inc., **20** 83
Boykin Enterprises, **IV** 136
Boyles Bros. Drilling Company. *See* Christensen Boyles Corporation.
Boys Market, **17** 558–59
Boz, **IV** 697–98
Bozel Électrométallurgie, **IV** 174
Bozell, Jacobs, Kenyon, and Eckhardt Inc. *See* True North Communications Inc.
Bozell Worldwide Inc., 25 89–91
Bozkurt, **27** 188
Bozzuto's, Inc., 13 111–12
BP. *See* British Petroleum Company PLC.
BP Amoco plc, **31** 31, 34; **40** 358
BPB, **III** 736
BPD, **13** 356
BPI Communications, Inc., **7** 15; **19** 285; **27** 500
BR. *See* British Rail.
Braas, **III** 734, 736
Brabant, **III** 199, 201
Brabazon, **III** 555
Brach and Brock Confections, Inc., 15 63–65; **29** 47
Brad Foote Gear Works, **18** 453
Bradbury Agnew and Co., **IV** 686
Braden Manufacturing, **23** 299–301
Bradford District Bank, **II** 333
Bradford Exchange Ltd. Inc., **21** 269
Bradford Insulation Group, **III** 687
Bradford Pennine, **III** 373
Bradlees Discount Department Store Company, II 666–67; **12** 48–50; **24** 461
Bradley Lumber Company, **8** 430
Bradley Producing Corp., **IV** 459
Bradstreet Co., **IV** 604–05; **19** 133
Braegen Corp., **13** 127
Bragussa, **IV** 71

BRAINS. *See* Belgian Rapid Access to Information Network Services.
Bramalea Ltd., 9 83–85; **10** 530–31
Brambles Industries Limited, III 494–95; **24** 400; **42** 47–50
Bramco, **III** 600
Bramwell Gates, **II** 586
Bran & Lübbe, **III** 420
Brand Companies, Inc., **9** 110; **11** 436
Branded Restaurant Group, Inc., **12** 372
Brandeis & Sons, **19** 511
Brandenburgische Motorenwerke, **I** 138
Brandywine Asset Management, Inc., **33** 261
Brandywine Insurance Agency, Inc., **25** 540
Brandywine Iron Works and Nail Factory, **14** 323
Brandywine Valley Railroad Co., **14** 324
Braniff Airlines, **I** 97, 489, 548; **II** 445; **6** 50, 119–20; **16** 274; **17** 504; **21** 142; **22** 406; **36** 231
Branigar Organization, Inc., **IV** 345
Brascade Resources, **IV** 308
Brascan Ltd., **II** 456; **IV** 165, 330; **25** 281
Braspetro, **IV** 454, 501–02
Brass Craft Manufacturing Co., **III** 570; **20** 361
Brass Eagle Inc., 34 70–72
Brasseries Kronenbourg, **II** 474–75
Braswell Motor Freight, **14** 567
Braud & Faucheux. *See* Manitou BF S.A.
Brauerei Beck & Co., 9 86–87; **33** 73–76 (upd.)
Braun, **III** 29; **17** 214–15; **26** 335
Braunkohlenwerk Golpa-Jessnitz AG, **IV** 230
Brauns Fashions Corporation. *See* Christopher & Banks Corporation.
Brazilian Central Bank, **IV** 56
Brazos Gas Compressing, **7** 345
Brazos Sportswear, Inc., 23 65–67
Breakstone Bros., Inc., **II** 533
Breakthrough Software, **10** 507
Breckenridge-Remy, **18** 216
Breco Holding Company, **17** 558, 561
Bredel Exploitatie B.V., **8** 546
Bredell Paint Co., **III** 745
Bredero's Bouwbedrijf of Utrecht, **IV** 707–08, 724
BREED Technologies, Inc., **22** 31
Breedband NV, **IV** 133
Brega Petroleum Marketing Co., **IV** 453, 455
Breguet Aviation, **I** 44; **24** 86
Breitenburger Cementfabrik, **III** 701
Bremner Biscuit Co., **II** 562; **13** 426
Brenco Inc., **16** 514
Brenda Mines Ltd., **7** 399
Brennan College Services, **12** 173
Brenntag AG, 8 68–69, 496; **23** 68–70 (upd.), **23** 453–54
Bresler's Industries, Inc., **35** 121
Breslube Enterprises, **8** 464
Bresser Optik, **41** 264
Brewster Lines, **6** 410
Breyers Ice Cream Co. *See* Good Humor-Breyers.
BRI Bar Review Institute, Inc., **IV** 623; **12** 224
BRI International, **21** 425
Brian Mills, **V** 118
Briarpatch, Inc., **12** 109
Brickwood Breweries, **I** 294

Harris Microwave Semiconductors, **14** 417
Harris Oil Company, **17** 170
Harris Pharmaceuticals Ltd., **11** 208
Harris Publications, **13** 179
Harris Publishing. *See* Bernard C. Harris
  Publishing Company, Inc.
Harris Queensway, **24** 269
Harris Teeter Inc., 23 260–62
Harris Transducer Corporation, **10** 319
Harrisburg National Bank and Trust Co., **II**
  315–16
Harrison & Sons (Hanley) Ltd., **III** 681
Harrisons & Crosfield plc, III 696–700.
  See also Elementis plc.
Harrods, **21** 353
Harrow Stores Ltd., **II** 677
Harry and David. *See* Bear Creek
  Corporation.
Harry F. Allsman Co., **III** 558
Harry Ferguson Co., **III** 651
Harry N. Abrams, Inc., **IV** 677; **17** 486
Harry's Farmers Market Inc., 23 263–66
Harry's Premium Snacks, **27** 197
Harsah Ceramics, **25** 267
Harsco Corporation, 8 245–47; 11 135;
  30 471
Harshaw Chemical Company, **9** 154; **17**
  363
Harshaw/Filtrol Partnership, **IV** 80
Hart Glass Manufacturing, **III** 423
Hart Press, **12** 25
Hart Schaffner & Marx. *See* Hartmarx
  Corporation.
Hart Son and Co., **I** 592
Harte & Co., **IV** 409; **7** 308
Harte-Hanks Communications, Inc., 17
  220–22
Harter Bank & Trust, **9** 474–75
Hartford Container Company, **8** 359
Hartford Electric Light Co., **13** 183
Hartford Financial Services Group, **41** 64
Hartford Fire Insurance, **11** 198
Hartford Insurance Group, **I** 463–64; **22**
  428
Hartford Machine Screw Co., **12** 344
Hartford National Bank and Trust Co., **13**
  396
Hartford National Corporation, **13** 464,
  466–67
Hartford Trust Co., **II** 213
Hartley's, **II** 477
Hartmann & Braun, **III** 566; **38** 299
Hartmann Fibre, **12** 377
Hartmann Luggage, **12** 313
Hartmarx Corporation, 8 248–50; 25
  258; **32 246–50 (upd.)**
The Hartstone Group plc, 14 224–26
The Hartz Mountain Corporation, 12
  230–32
Harvard Private Capital Group Inc., **26**
  500, 502
Harvard Sports, Inc., **19** 144
Harvard Table Tennis, Inc., **19** 143–44
Harvard Ventures, **25** 358
Harvest Day, **27** 291
Harvest International, **III** 201
Harvest Partners, Inc., **40** 300
Harvestore, **11** 5
Harvey Aluminum Inc., **I** 68; **22** 188
Harvey Benjamin Fuller, **8** 237–38
Harvey Group, **19** 312
Harvey Hotel Corporation, **23** 71, 73
Harvey Lumber and Supply Co., **III** 559
Harveys Casino Resorts, 27 199–201

Harwood Homes, **31** 386
Harza Engineering Company, 14 227–28
Hasbro, Inc., III 504–06; IV 676; 7 305,
  529; **12** 168–69, 495; **13** 561; **16**
  264–68 (upd.); **17** 243; **18** 520–21; **21**
  375; **25** 313, 380–81, 487–89; **28** 159;
  34 369
Haslemere Estates, **26** 420
Hasler Holding AG, **9** 32
Hassenfeld Brothers Inc., **III** 504
Hasten Bancorp, **11** 371
Hastings Entertainment, Inc., 29 229–31
Hastings Filters, Inc., **17** 104
Hastings Manufacturing Company, **17** 106
Hatch Grinding, **29** 86, 88
Hatersley & Davidson, **16** 80
Hatfield Jewelers, **30** 408
Hathaway Manfacturing Co., **III** 213
Hathaway Shirt Co., **I** 25–26
Hattori Seiko Co., Ltd. *See* Seiko
  Corporation.
Hausted, Inc., **29** 451
Havas, SA, IV 616; 10 195–96, 345–48;
  13 203–04; **33 178–82 (upd.)**; **34** 83.
  See also Vivendi Universal Publishing
Haven Automation International, **III** 420
Haverty Furniture Companies, Inc., 31
  246–49
Havertys, **39** 174
Haviland Candy Co., **15** 325
Hawaii National Bank, **11** 114
Hawaiian Airlines Inc., 9 271–73; 22
  251–53 (upd.); **24** 20–22; **26** 339. *See
  also* HAL Inc.
Hawaiian Dredging & Construction Co., **I**
  565–66
Hawaiian Electric Industries, Inc., 9
  274–77
Hawaiian Fertilizer Co., **II** 490
Hawaiian Pineapple Co., **II** 491
Hawaiian Tug & Barge, **9** 276
Hawaiian Tuna Packers, **II** 491
Hawker Siddeley Group Public Limited
  Company, I 41–42, 50, 71, 470; **III**
  507–10; **8** 51; **12** 190; **20** 311; **24**
  85–86
Hawkeye Cablevision, **II** 161
Hawkins Chemical, Inc., 16 269–72
Hawley & Hazel Chemical Co., **III** 25
Hawley Group Limited, **12** 10
Hawley Products, **16** 20
Haworth Inc., 8 251–52; 27 434; 39
  205–08 (upd.)
Hawthorn Company, **8** 287
Hawthorn-Mellody, **I** 446; **11** 25
Hawthorne Appliance and Electronics, **10**
  9–11
Haxton Foods Inc., **21** 155
Hay Group, **I** 33; **42** 329–30
Hayakawa Electrical Industries, **II** 95–96
Hayakawa Metal Industrial Laboratory, **II**
  95; **12** 447
Hayaku Zenjiro, **III** 408
Hayama Oil, **IV** 542
Hayashi Kane Shoten, **II** 578
Hayashikane Shoten K.K., **II** 578
Hayden Clinton National Bank, **11** 180
Hayden Publications, **27** 499
Hayden Stone, **II** 450; **9** 468
Hayes Conyngham & Robinson, **24** 75
Hayes Corporation, 24 210–14
Hayes Industries Inc., **16** 7
Hayes Lemmerz International, Inc., 27
  202–04

Hayes Microcomputer Products, **9** 515
Hayes Wheel Company, **7** 258
Hayne, Miller & Swearingen, Inc., **22** 202
Hays Petroleum Services, **IV** 451
Hays Plc, 27 205–07
Hazard, **I** 328
HAZCO International, Inc., **9** 110
Hazel-Atlas Glass Co., **I** 599; **15** 128
Hazel Bishop, **III** 55
Hazelden Foundation, 28 176–79
Hazell Sun Ltd., **IV** 642; **7** 312
Hazeltine, Inc., **II** 20
Hazlenut Growers of Oregon, **7** 496–97
Hazleton Laboratories Corp., **30** 151
Hazlewood Foods plc, 32 251–53
Hazzard and Associates, **34** 248
HBO. *See* Home Box Office Inc.
HCA - The Healthcare Company, 35
  215–18 (upd.)
HCI Holdings, **I** 264
HCL America, **10** 505
HCL Sybase, **10** 505
HCR Manor Care, **25** 306, 310
HCS Technology, **26** 496–97
HDM Worldwide Direct, **13** 204; **16** 168
HDR Inc., **I** 563
HDS. *See* Heartland Express, Inc.
Head Sportswear International, **15** 368; **16**
  296–97
Headrick Outdoor, **27** 280
Heads and Threads, **10** 43
Headway Corporate Resources, Inc., 40
  236–38
Heal's, **13** 307
Heald Machine Co., **12** 67
Healey & Baker, **IV** 705
Healing Arts Publishing, Inc., **41** 177
Health & Tennis Corp., **III** 431; **25** 40
Health and Diet Group, **29** 212
Health Care & Retirement Corporation,
  III 79; **22 254–56**; **25** 306, 310
Health Care International, **13** 328
Health Maintenance Organization of
  Pennsylvania. *See* U.S. Healthcare, Inc.
Health Maintenance Organizations, **I** 545
Health Management Center West, **17** 559
Health-Mor Inc. *See* HMI Industries.
Health O Meter Products Inc., 14
  229–31; **15** 307
Health Plan of America, **11** 379
Health Plan of Virginia, **III** 389
Health Products Inc., **I** 387
Health Risk Management, Inc., 24
  215–17
Health Services, Inc., **10** 160
Health Systems International, Inc., 11
  174–76; **25** 527
Health Way, Inc., **II** 538
HealthAmerica Corp., **III** 84
Healthcare, L.L.C., **29** 412
HealthCare USA, **III** 84, 86
HealthCo International, Inc., **19** 290
Healthdyne, Inc., **17** 306–09; **25** 82
Healthmagic, Inc., **29** 412
HealthRider Corporation, **38** 238
Healthshares L.L.C., **18** 370
Healthsource Inc., **22** 143
HealthSouth Corporation, 33 183–86
  (upd.)
HealthSouth Rehabilitation Corporation,
  14 232–34; **25** 111
Healthtex, Inc., 17 223–25, 513
HealthTrust, **III** 80; **15** 112; **35** 215, 217
Healthy Choice, **12** 531

Manischewitz Company. *See* B. Manischewitz Company.

Manistique Papers Inc., **17** 282

Manistique Pulp and Paper Co., **IV** 311; **19** 266

Manitoba Bridge and Engineering Works Ltd., **8** 544

Manitoba Paper Co., **IV** 245–46; **25** 10

Manitoba Rolling Mill Ltd., **8** 544

Manitou BF S.A., **27 294–96**

Manitowoc Company, Inc., **18 318–21**

Mann Egerton & Co., **III** 523

Mann Theatres Chain, **I** 245; **25** 177

Mann's Wine Company, Ltd., **14** 288

Mannatech Inc., **33 282–85**

Manne Tossbergs Eftr., **II** 639

Mannesmann AG, **I** 411; **III 564–67**; **IV** 222, 469; **14 326–29** (upd.); **34** 319; **38 296–301** (upd.). *See also* Vodafone Group PLC.

Mannheimer Bank, **IV** 558

Manning, Selvage & Lee, **6** 22

Mannstaedt, **IV** 128

Manor Care, Inc., **6 187–90**; **14 105–07**; **15** 522; **25 306–10** (upd.)

Manor Healthcare Corporation, **26** 459

Manorfield Investments, **II** 158

Manos Enterprises, **14** 87

Manpower, Inc., **6** 10, 140; **9 326–27**; **16** 48; **25** 432; **30 299–302** (upd.); **40** 236, 238

Mantrec S.A., **27** 296

Mantua Metal Products. *See* Tyco Toys, Inc.

Manufactured Home Communities, Inc., **22 339–41**

Manufacturers & Merchants Indemnity Co., **III** 191

Manufacturers and Traders Trust Company, **11** 108–09

Manufacturers Casualty Insurance Co., **26** 486

Manufacturers Fire Insurance Co., **26** 486

Manufacturers Hanover Corporation, **II** 230, 254, **312–14**, 403; **III** 194; **9** 124; **11** 16, 54, 415; **13** 536; **14** 103; **16** 207; **17** 559; **22** 406; **26** 453; **38** 253

Manufacturers National Bank of Brooklyn, **II** 312

Manufacturers National Bank of Detroit, **I** 165; **11** 137; **40** 116

Manufacturers Railway, **I** 219; **34** 36

Manufacturing Management Inc., **19** 381

Manus Nu-Pulse, **III** 420

Manville Corporation, **III 706–09**, 721; **7 291–95** (upd.); **10** 43, 45; **11** 420–22

Manweb plc, **19** 389–90

MAPCO Inc., **IV 458–59**; **26** 234; **31** 469, 471

Mapelli Brothers Food Distribution Co., **13** 350

Maple Grove Farms of Vermont, Inc., **40** 51–52

Maple Leaf Foods Inc., **41 249–53**

Maple Leaf Mills, **II** 513–14; **41** 252

MAPP. *See* Mid-Continent Area Power Planner.

Mapra Industria e Comercio Ltda., **32** 40

Mar-O-Bar Company, **7** 299

A.B. Marabou, **II** 511

Marantha! Music, **14** 499

Marantz Co., **14** 118

Marathon Insurance Co., **26** 486

Marathon Oil Co., **IV** 365, 454, 487, 572, 574; **7** 549, 551; **13** 458

Marathon Paper Products, **I** 612, 614

Marauder Company, **26** 433

Maraven, **IV** 508

Marblehead Communications, Inc., **23** 101

Marbodal, **12** 464

Marboro Books, Inc., **10** 136

Marbro Lamp Co., **III** 571; **20** 362

Marc's Big Boy. *See* The Marcus Corporation.

Marcade Group. *See* Aris Industries, Inc.

Marceau Investments, **II** 356

March-Davis Bicycle Company, **19** 383

March of Dimes, **31 322–25**

Marchand, **13** 27

Marchesi Antinori SRL, **42 245–48**

marchFIRST, Inc., **34 261–64**

Marchland Holdings Ltd., **II** 649

Marchon Eyewear, **22** 123

Marciano Investments, Inc., **24** 157

Marcillat, **19** 49

Marcon Coating, Inc., **22** 347

Marconi plc, **33 286–90** (upd.)

Marconi Wireless Telegraph Co. of America, **II** 25, 88

Marconiphone, **I** 531

The Marcus Corporation, **21 359–63**

Marcus Samuel & Co., **IV** 530

Marcy Fitness Products, Inc., **19** 142, 144

Mardon Packaging International, **I** 426–27

Mardorf, Peach and Co., **II** 466

Maremont Corporation, **8** 39–40

Margarete Steiff GmbH, **23 334–37**

Margarine Unie N.V. *See* Unilever PLC (Unilever N.V.).

Marge Carson, Inc., **III** 571; **20** 362

Margo's La Mode, **10** 281–82

Marico Acquisition Corporation, **8** 448, 450

Marie Brizard & Roger International S.A., **22 342–44**

Marie Callender's Restaurant & Bakery, Inc., **13** 66; **28 257–59**

Marie-Claire Album, **III** 47

Marigold Foods Inc., **II** 528

Marinduque Mining & Industrial Corp., **IV** 146

Marine Bank and Trust Co., **11** 105

Marine Bank of Erie, **II** 342

Marine Computer Systems, **6** 242

Marine Diamond Corp., **IV** 66; **7** 123

Marine-Firminy, **IV** 227

Marine Group, **III** 444; **22** 116

Marine Harvest International, **13** 103

Marine Midland Corp., **I** 548; **II** 298; **9** 475–76; **11** 108; **17** 325

Marine Office of America, **III** 220, 241–42

Marine United Inc., **42** 361

Marinela, **19** 192–93

Marineland Amusements Corp., **IV** 623

MarineMax, Inc., **30 303–05**; **37** 396

Marion Brick, **14** 249

Marion Foods, Inc., **17** 434

Marion Freight Lines, **6** 370

Marion Laboratories Inc., **I 648–49**; **8** 149; **9** 328–29; **16** 438

Marion Manufacturing, **9** 72

Marion Merrell Dow, Inc., **9 328–29** (upd.)

Marionet Corp., **IV** 680–81

Marisa Christina, Inc., **15 290–92**; **25** 245

Maritime Electric Company, Limited, **15** 182

Maritz Inc., **38 302–05**

Mark Controls Corporation, **30** 157

Mark Cross, Inc., **17** 4–5

Mark Goldston, **8** 305

Mark Hopkins, **12** 316

Mark IV Industries, Inc., **7 296–98**; **21** 418; **28 260–64** (upd.)

Mark Travel Corporation, **30** 448

Mark Trouser, Inc., **17** 338

Markborough Properties, **II** 222; **V** 81; **8** 525; **25** 221

Market Growth Resources, **23** 480

Market Horizons, **6** 27

Market National Bank, **13** 465

Marketime, **V** 55

Marketing Data Systems, Inc., **18** 24

Marketing Equities International, **26** 136

Marketing Information Services, **6** 24

MarketSpan Corp. *See* KeySpan Energy Co.

Markham & Co., **I** 573–74

Marks and Spencer p.l.c., **I** 588; **II** 513, 678; **V 124–26**; **10** 442; **17** 42, 124; **22** 109, 111; **24** 268, 270; **313–17** (upd.), 474; **28** 96; **35** 308, 310; **41** 114; **42** 231

Marks-Baer Inc., **11** 64

Marks Brothers Jewelers, Inc., **24 318–20**

Marland Refining Co., **IV** 399–400

Marlene Industries Corp., **16** 36–37

MarLennan Corp., **III** 283

Marley Co., **19** 360

Marley Holdings, L.P., **19** 246

Marley Tile, **III** 735

Marlin-Rockwell Corp., **I** 539; **14** 510

Marlow Foods, **II** 565

Marman Products Company, **16** 8

The Marmon Group, **III** 97; **IV 135–38**; **16 354–57** (upd.)

Marmon-Perry Light Company, **6** 508

Marolf Dakota Farms, Inc., **18** 14–15

Marotte, **21** 438

Marquam Commercial Brokerage Company, **21** 257

Marquardt Aircraft, **I** 380; **13** 379

Marquette Electronics, Inc., **13 326–28**

Marquette Paper Corporation, **III** 766; **22** 545

Marquis Who's Who, **17** 398

Marriage Mailers, **6** 12

Marriner Group, **13** 175

Marriot Inc., **29** 442

Marriot Management Services, **29** 444

Marriott Corporation, **II** 173, 608; **III** 92, 94, 99–100, **102–03**, 248; **7** 474–75; **9** 95, 426; **15** 87; **17** 238; **18** 216; **19** 433–34; **21** 91, 364; **22** 131; **23** 436–38; **27** 334; **38** 386; **41** 82

Marriott International, Inc., **21** 182, **364–67** (upd.); **29** 403, 406; **41** 156–58

Mars, Incorporated, **II** 510–11; **III** 114; **7 299–301**; **22** 298, 528; **40 302–05** (upd.)

Marschke Manufacturing Co., **III** 435

Marsene Corp., **III** 440

Marsh & McLennan Companies, Inc., **III** 280, **282–84**; **10** 39; **14** 279; **22** 318

Marsh Supermarkets, Inc., **17 300–02**

Marshalk Company, **I** 16; **22** 294

Marshall Die Casting, **13** 225

MCT Dairies, Inc., **18** 14–16
McTeigue & Co., **14** 502
McVitie & Price, **II** 592–93
McWhorter Inc., **8** 553; **27** 280
MD Distribution Inc., **15** 139
MD Pharmaceuticals, **III** 10
MDC. *See* Mead Data Central, Inc.
MDI Co., Ltd., **IV** 327
MDS/Bankmark, **10** 247
**MDU Resources Group, Inc., 7 322–25;
42 249–53 (upd.)**
The Mead Corporation, IV 310–13, 327,
329, 342–43; **8** 267; **9** 261; **10** 406; **11**
421–22; **17** 399; **19 265–69 (upd.); 20**
18; **33** 263, 265
Mead Cycle Co., **IV** 660
Mead Data Central, Inc., IV 312; **7** 581;
10 406–08; 19 268. *See also* LEXIS-
NEXIS Group.
Mead John & Co., **19** 103
Mead Johnson, **III** 17
Mead Packaging, **12** 151
Meade County Rural Electric Cooperative
Corporation, **11** 37
**Meade Instruments Corporation, 41
261–64**
Meadow Gold Dairies, Inc., **II** 473
Meadowcraft, Inc., 29 313–15
Means Services, Inc., **II** 607
Mears & Phillips, **II** 237
Measurex Corporation, **8** 243; **14** 56; **38**
227
Mebetoys, **25** 312
MEC - Hawaii, UK & USA, **IV** 714
MECA Software, Inc., **18** 363
Mecair, S.p.A., **17** 147
Mecca Leisure PLC, **I** 248; **12** 229; **32** 243
Mechanics Exchange Savings Bank, **9** 173
Mechanics Machine Co., **III** 438; **14** 63
**Mecklermedia Corporation, 24 328–30;
26** 441; **27** 360, 362
Medal Distributing Co., **9** 542
Medallion Pictures Corp., **9** 320
Medar, Inc., **17** 310–11
**Medco Containment Services Inc., 9
346–48; 11** 291; **12** 333
Medcom Inc., **I** 628
Medeco Security Locks, Inc., **10** 350
Medfield Corp., **III** 87
Medford, Inc., **19** 467–68
Medi Mart Drug Store Company. *See* The
Stop & Shop Companies, Inc.
Media Arts Group, Inc., 42 254–57
Media Exchange International, **25** 509
Media General, Inc., III 214; **7 326–28;
18** 61; **23** 225; **38 306–09 (upd.)**
Media Groep West B.V., **23** 271
Media News Corporation, **25** 507
Media Play. *See* Musicland Stores
Corporation.
MediaBay, **41** 61
Mediacom Inc., **25** 373
Mediamark Research, **28** 501, 504
Mediamatics, Inc., **26** 329
MediaOne Group Inc. *See* U S West, Inc.
MEDIC Computer Systems, **16** 94
Medical Care America, Inc., **15** 112, 114;
35 215–17
Medical Development Corp. *See* Cordis
Corp.
Medical Development Services, Inc., **25**
307
Medical Economics Data, **23** 211
Medical Expense Fund, **III** 245

Medical Indemnity of America, **10** 160
Medical Innovations Corporation, **21** 46
Medical Marketing Group Inc., **9** 348
Medical Service Assoc. of Pennsylvania,
III 325–26
Medical Tribune Group, **IV** 591; **20** 53
Medicare-Glaser, **17** 167
Medicine Bow Coal Company, **7** 33–34
Medicine Shoppe International. *See*
Cardinal Health, Inc.
Medicor, Inc., **36** 496
Medicus Intercon International, **6** 22
Medifinancial Solutions, Inc., **18** 370
MedImmune, Inc., 35 286–89
Medinol Ltd., **37** 39
Mediobanca Banca di Credito Finanziario
SpA, **II** 191, 271; **III** 208–09; **11** 205
The Mediplex Group, Inc., **III** 16; **11** 282
Medis Health and Pharmaceuticals Services
Inc., **II** 653
Medite Corporation, **19** 467–68
Meditrust, 11 281–83
Medlabs Inc., **III** 73
MedPartners, **36** 367
Medtech, Ltd., **13** 60–62
Medtronic, Inc., 8 351–54; 11 459; **18**
421; **19** 103; **22** 359–61; **26** 132; **30
313–17 (upd.); 37** 39
Medusa Corporation, 8 135; **24 331–33;
30** 156
Mees & Hope, **II** 184
The MEGA Life and Health Insurance Co.,
33 418–20
MEGA Natural Gas Company, **11** 28
MegaBingo, Inc., **41** 273, 275
Megafoods Stores Inc., 13 335–37; 17
560
Megasource, Inc., **16** 94
Meggitt PLC, 34 273–76
MEI Diversified Inc., **18** 455
Mei Foo Investments Ltd., **IV** 718; **38** 319
Meier & Frank Co., 23 345–47
Meijer Incorporated, 7 329–31; 15 449;
17 302; **27 312–15 (upd.)**
Meiji Commerce Bank, **II** 291
Meiji Fire Insurance Co., **III** 384–85
**Meiji Milk Products Company, Limited,
II 538–39**
**Meiji Mutual Life Insurance Company,
II** 323; **III 288–89**
Meiji Seika Kaisha, Ltd., I 676; **II
540–41**
Meikosha Co., **II** 72
Meinecke Muffler Company, **III** 495; **10**
415
Meineke Discount Muffler Shops, **38** 208
Meis of Illiana, **10** 282
Meisei Electric, **III** 742
Meisel. *See* Samuel Meisel & Co.
Meisenzahl Auto Parts, Inc., **24** 205
Meissner, Ackermann & Co., **IV** 463; **7**
351
Meister, Lucious and Company, **13** 262
Meiwa Manufacturing Co., **III** 758
N.V. Mekog, **IV** 531
Mel Farr Automotive Group, 20 368–70
Mel Klein and Partners, **III** 74
Melaleuca Inc., 31 326–28
Melamine Chemicals, Inc., 27 316–18
Melbourne Engineering Co., **23** 83
Melbur China Clay Co., **III** 690
Melco, **II** 58
Meldisco. *See* Footstar, Incorporated.
Melkunie-Holland, **II** 575

Mellbank Security Co., **II** 316
Mello Smello. *See* The Miner Group
International.
Mellon Bank Corporation, I 67–68, 584;
II 315–17, 342, 402; **III** 275; **9** 470; **13**
410–11; **18** 112
Mellon Financial Corporation, **42** 76
Mellon Indemnity Corp., **III** 258–59; **24**
177
Mellon-Stuart Co., I 584–85; 14 334
Melmarkets, **24** 462
Mélotte, **III** 418
Meloy Laboratories, Inc., **11** 333
Melroe Company, **8** 115–16; **34** 46
Melville Corporation, V 136–38; 9 192;
13 82, 329–30; **14** 426; **15 252–53;, 16**
390; **19** 449; **21** 526; **23** 176; **24** 167,
290; **35** 253
**Melvin Simon and Associates, Inc., 8
355–57; 26** 262
Melwire Group, **III** 673
MEM, **37** 270–71
Memco, **12** 48
Memorex Corp., **III** 110, 166; **6** 282–83
**The Men's Wearhouse, Inc., 17 312–15;
21** 311
Menasco Manufacturing Co., **I** 435; **III**
415
Menasha Corporation, 8 358–61
Menck, **8** 544
Mendelssohn & Co., **II** 241
Meneven, **IV** 508
Menka Gesellschaft, **IV** 150; **24** 357
The Mennen Company, **I** 19; **6** 26; **14** 122;
18 69; **35** 113
Mental Health Programs Inc., **15** 122
The Mentholatum Company Inc., IV
722; **32 331–33**
Mentor Corporation, 26 286–88
Mentor Graphics Corporation, III 143; **8**
519; **11** 46–47, **284–86,** 490; **13** 128
MEPC plc, IV 710–12
Mepco/Electra Inc., **13** 398
MeraBank, **6** 546
MERBCO, Inc., **33** 456
Mercantile Agency, **IV** 604
Mercantile and General Reinsurance Co.,
III 335, 377
Mercantile Bancorporation Inc., **33** 155
Mercantile Bank, **II** 298
Mercantile Bankshares Corp., 11 287–88
Mercantile Credit Co., **16** 13
Mercantile Estate and Property Corp. Ltd.,
IV 710
Mercantile Fire Insurance, **III** 234
Mercantile Mutual, **III** 310
Mercantile Property Corp. Ltd., **IV** 710
Mercantile Security Life, **III** 136
**Mercantile Stores Company, Inc., V 139;
19 270–73 (upd.)**
Mercantile Trust Co., **II** 229, 247
Mercator & Noordstar N.V., **40** 61
Mercedes Benz. *See* Daimler-Benz A.G.
Mercedes Benz of North America, **22** 52
Merchant Bank Services, **18** 516, 518
Merchant Co., **III** 104
Merchant Distributors, Inc., **20** 306
Merchants & Farmers Bank of Ecru, **14** 40
Merchants Bank, **II** 213
Merchants Bank & Trust Co., **21** 524
Merchants Bank of Canada, **II** 210
Merchants Bank of Halifax, **II** 344
Merchants Dispatch, **II** 395–96; **10** 60

INDEX TO INDUSTRIES

Index to Industries

CONSTRUCTION

CONTAINERS

FINANCIAL SERVICES: BANKS

FINANCIAL SERVICES: NON-BANKS

FOOD PRODUCTS

FOOD SERVICES & RETAILERS

HOTELS

INFORMATION TECHNOLOGY

LEGAL SERVICES

MANUFACTURING

MATERIALS

Quanex Corporation, 13
RAG AG, 35
Reliance Steel & Aluminum Co., 19
Republic Engineered Steels, Inc., 7; 26 (upd.)
Reynolds Metals Company, IV
Rio Tinto plc, 19 (upd.)
RMC Group p.l.c., 34 (upd.)
Rouge Steel Company, 8
The RTZ Corporation PLC, IV
Ruhrkohle AG, IV
Ryerson Tull, Inc., 40 (upd.)
Saarberg-Konzern, IV
Salzgitter AG, IV
Sandvik AB, IV
Schnitzer Steel Industries, Inc., 19
Southern Peru Copper Corporation, 40
Southwire Company, Inc., 8; 23 (upd.)
Steel Authority of India Ltd., IV
Stelco Inc., IV
Sumitomo Metal Industries, Ltd., IV
Sumitomo Metal Mining Co., Ltd., IV
Tata Iron and Steel Company Ltd., IV
Teck Corporation, 27
Texas Industries, Inc., 8
Thyssen AG, IV
The Timken Company, 8; 42 (upd.)
Titanium Metals Corporation, 21
Tomen Corporation, IV
U.S. Borax, Inc., 42
Ugine S.A., 20
Usinor SA, 42 (upd.)
Usinor Sacilor, IV
VIAG Aktiengesellschaft, IV
Voest-Alpine Stahl AG, IV
Walter Industries, Inc., 22 (upd.)
Weirton Steel Corporation, IV; 26 (upd.)
Westmoreland Coal Company, 7
Wheeling-Pittsburgh Corp., 7
Worthington Industries, Inc., 7; 21 (upd.)
Zambia Industrial and Mining Corporation Ltd., IV

PAPER & FORESTRY

Abitibi-Consolidated, Inc., 25 (upd.)
Abitibi-Price Inc., IV
Amcor Limited, IV; 19 (upd.)
American Pad & Paper Company, 20
Arjo Wiggins Appleton p.l.c., 34
Asplundh Tree Expert Co., 20
Avery Dennison Corporation, IV
Badger Paper Mills, Inc., 15
Beckett Papers, 23
Bemis Company, Inc., 8
Bohemia, Inc., 13
Boise Cascade Corporation, IV; 8 (upd.); 32 (upd.)
Bowater PLC, IV
Bunzl plc, IV
Canfor Corporation, 42
Caraustar Industries, Inc., 19
Champion International Corporation, IV; 20 (upd.)
Chesapeake Corporation, 8; 30 (upd.)
Consolidated Papers, Inc., 8; 36 (upd.)
Crane & Co., Inc., 26
Crown Vantage Inc., 29
CSS Industries, Inc., 35
Daio Paper Corporation, IV
Daishowa Paper Manufacturing Co., Ltd., IV
Dillard Paper Company, 11
Domtar Inc., IV
Enso-Gutzeit Oy, IV
Esselte Pendaflex Corporation, 11
Federal Paper Board Company, Inc., 8
FiberMark, Inc., 37

Fletcher Challenge Ltd., IV
Fort Howard Corporation, 8
Fort James Corporation, 22 (upd.)
Georgia-Pacific Corporation, IV; 9 (upd.)
Groupe Rougier SA, 21
Guilbert S.A., 42
Honshu Paper Co., Ltd., IV
International Paper Company, IV; 15 (upd.)
James River Corporation of Virginia, IV
Japan Pulp and Paper Company Limited, IV
Jefferson Smurfit Group plc, IV
Jujo Paper Co., Ltd., IV
Kimberly-Clark Corporation, 16 (upd.)
Kruger Inc., 17
Kymmene Corporation, IV
Longview Fibre Company, 8; 37 (upd.)
Louisiana-Pacific Corporation, IV; 31 (upd.)
MacMillan Bloedel Limited, IV
The Mead Corporation, IV; 19 (upd.)
Metsa-Serla Oy, IV
Mo och Domsjö AB, IV
Monadnock Paper Mills, Inc., 21
Mosinee Paper Corporation, 15
Nashua Corporation, 8
National Envelope Corporation, 32
NCH Corporation, 8
Oji Paper Co., Ltd., IV
P.H. Glatfelter Company, 8; 30 (upd.)
Packaging Corporation of America, 12
Papeteries de Lancey, 23
Pope and Talbot, Inc., 12
Potlatch Corporation, 8; 34 (upd.)
PWA Group, IV
Rayonier Inc., 24
Rengo Co., Ltd., IV
Reno de Medici S.p.A., 41
Rexam PLC, 32 (upd.)
Riverwood International Corporation, 11
Rock-Tenn Company, 13
St. Joe Paper Company, 8
Sanyo-Kokusaku Pulp Co., Ltd., IV
Scott Paper Company, IV; 31 (upd.)
Sealed Air Corporation, 14
Sierra Pacific Industries, 22
Simpson Investment Company, 17
Specialty Coatings Inc., 8
Stone Container Corporation, IV
Stora Enso Oyj, 36 (upd.)
Stora Kopparbergs Bergslags AB, IV
Svenska Cellulosa Aktiebolaget SCA, IV; 28 (upd.)
Temple-Inland Inc., IV; 31 (upd.)
TJ International, Inc., 19
U.S. Timberlands Company, L.P., 42
Union Camp Corporation, IV
United Paper Mills Ltd. (Yhtyneet Paperitehtaat Oy), IV
Universal Forest Products Inc., 10
UPM-Kymmene Corporation, 19
West Fraser Timber Co. Ltd., 17
Westvaco Corporation, IV; 19 (upd.)
Weyerhaeuser Company, IV; 9 (upd.); 28 (upd.)
Wickes Inc., 25 (upd.)
Willamette Industries, Inc., IV; 31 (upd.)
WTD Industries, Inc., 20

PERSONAL SERVICES

AARP, 27
ADT Security Systems, Inc., 12
American Retirement Corporation, 42
Arthur Murray International, Inc., 32
Berlitz International, Inc., 39 (upd.)
Carriage Services, Inc., 37
Childtime Learning Centers, Inc., 34

Corinthian Colleges, Inc., 39
Correctional Services Corporation, 30
CUC International Inc., 16
DeVry Incorporated, 29
Educational Testing Service, 12
The Ford Foundation, 34
Franklin Quest Co., 11
Goodwill Industries International, Inc., 16
The John D. and Catherine T. MacArthur Foundation, 34
Kaplan, Inc., 42
KinderCare Learning Centers, Inc., 13
The Loewen Group Inc., 16; 40 (upd.)
Management and Training Corporation, 28
Manpower, Inc., 9
Regis Corporation, 18
The Rockefeller Foundation, 34
Rollins, Inc., 11
Rosenbluth International Inc., 14
Rotary International, 31
The Salvation Army USA, 32
Service Corporation International, 6
SOS Staffing Services, 25
Stewart Enterprises, Inc., 20
Supercuts Inc., 26
Weight Watchers International Inc., 12; 33 (upd.)
Youth Services International, Inc., 21

PETROLEUM

Abu Dhabi National Oil Company, IV
Agway, Inc., 21 (upd.)
Alberta Energy Company Ltd., 16
Amerada Hess Corporation, IV; 21 (upd.)
Amoco Corporation, IV; 14 (upd.)
Anadarko Petroleum Corporation, 10
ANR Pipeline Co., 17
Anschutz Corp., 12
Apache Corporation, 10; 32 (upd.)
Arctic Slope Regional Corporation, 38
Ashland Inc., 19
Ashland Oil, Inc., IV
Atlantic Richfield Company, IV; 31 (upd.)
Baker Hughes Incorporated, 22 (upd.)
Belco Oil & Gas Corp., 40
BJ Services Company, 25
The British Petroleum Company plc, IV; 7 (upd.); 21 (upd.)
British-Borneo Oil & Gas PLC, 34
Broken Hill Proprietary Company Ltd., 22 (upd.)
Burlington Resources Inc., 10
Burmah Castrol PLC, IV; 30 (upd.)
Caltex Petroleum Corporation, 19
Chevron Corporation, IV; 19 (upd.)
Chiles Offshore Corporation, 9
Chinese Petroleum Corporation, IV; 31 (upd.)
CITGO Petroleum Corporation, IV; 31 (upd.)
The Coastal Corporation, IV; 31 (upd.)
Compañia Española de Petróleos S.A., IV
Conoco Inc., IV; 16 (upd.)
Cooper Cameron Corporation, 20 (upd.)
Cosmo Oil Co., Ltd., IV
Crown Central Petroleum Corporation, 7
DeepTech International Inc., 21
Den Norse Stats Oljeselskap AS, IV
Deutsche BP Aktiengesellschaft, 7
Diamond Shamrock, Inc., IV
Egyptian General Petroleum Corporation, IV
Elf Aquitaine SA, 21 (upd.)
Empresa Colombiana de Petróleos, IV
Energen Corporation, 21
Enron Corporation, 19
Ente Nazionale Idrocarburi, IV

PUBLISHING & PRINTING

TEXTILES & APPAREL

TOBACCO

TRANSPORT SERVICES

UTILITIES

WASTE SERVICES

GEOGRAPHIC INDEX

Geographic Index

NOTES ON CONTRIBUTORS

Notes on Contributors

BAXTER, Melissa Rigney. Indiana-based freelance writer.

BROWN, Susan Windisch. Freelance writer and editor.

BRYNILDSSEN, Shawna. Freelance writer and editor based in Bloomington, Indiana.

COHEN, M. L. Novelist and freelance writer living in Paris.

COVELL, Jeffrey L. Freelance writer and corporate history contractor.

CULLIGAN, Susan B. Minnesota-based freelance writer.

DINGER, Ed. Freelance writer and editor based in Brooklyn, New York.

HALASZ, Robert. Former editor in chief of *World Progress* and *Funk & Wagnalls New Encyclopedia Yearbook*; author, *The U.S. Marines* (Millbrook Press, 1993).

HEER-FORSBERG, Mary. Freelance writer in the Minneapolis area.

INGRAM, Frederick C. South Carolina-based business writer who has contributed to *GSA Business, Appalachian Trailway News,* the *Encyclopedia of Business,* the *Encyclo-*

pedia of Global Industries, the *Encyclopedia of Consumer Brands,* and other regional and trade publications.

KOERNER, Bill. Freelance editor in Washington, D.C.

LORENZ, Sarah Ruth. Minnesota-based freelance writer.

ROTHBURD, Carrie. Freelance writer and editor specializing in corporate profiles, academic texts, and academic journal articles.

SALAMIE, David E. Part-owner of InfoWorks Development Group, a reference publication development and editorial services company.

TRADII, Mary. Freelance writer based in Denver, Colorado.

UHLE, Frank. Ann Arbor-based freelance writer; movie projectionist, disc jockey, and staff member of *Psychotronic Video* magazine.

WALDEN, David M. Freelance writer and historian in Salt Lake City; adjunct history instructor at Salt Lake City Community College.

WERNICK, Ellen. Freelance writer and editor.

WOODWARD, A. Freelance writer.